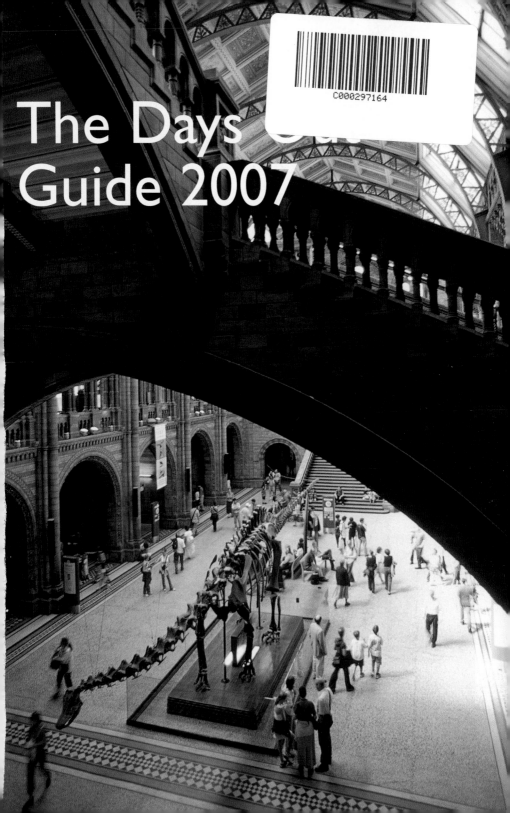

The Days Out Guide 2007

Produced by AA Publishing
© Automobile Association Developments Limited 2006 All rights reserved.

Advertisement Sales: advertisingsales@theAA.com

Editorial: lifestyleguides@theAA.com

Cover pictures: Group of teenagers on rollercoaster – Purestock/Alamy

Typeset/Repro by Servis Filmsetting Ltd Manchester, England.

Printed in Italy by Printer Trento SRL, Trento

Published by AA Publishing, which is a trading name of Automobile Association Developments Limited whose registered office is Fanum House, Basingstoke, Hampshire, RG21 4EA

CIP catalogue record for this book is available from the British Library Registered number 1878835.

ISBN-10: 0-7495-4923-7
ISBN-13: 978-0-7495-4923-7

A02828

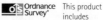 This product includes mapping data licensed from Ordnance Survey® with the permission of the Controller of Her Majesty's Stationery Office. © Crown copyright 2006. All rights reserved. Licence number 399221.

 This product includes mapping based upon data licensed from Ordnance Survey of Northern Ireland® reproduced by permission of the Chief Executive, acting on behalf of the Controller of Her Majesty's Stationery Office. © Crown copyright 2006. Permit number 60017

Republic of Ireland mapping based on Ordnance Survey Ireland Permit number MP000106. © Ordnance Survey Ireland and Government of Ireland.

Maps prepared by the Cartography Department of The Automobile Association.
Maps © Automobile Association Developments Limited 2006

Contents

How to use the Guide

The AA Days Out Guide provides useful information about a large number of museums, art galleries, theme parks, national parks, visitor centres and stately homes across Britain and Ireland. Entries include contact details for each attraction, along with a short description and details of opening times, prices and special facilities. We hope this guide will help you and your family get the most out of your visit.

The Directory

The directory is arranged in countries, counties, and in alphabetical location order within each county. Each county has an introductory page that gives general information on the area.

❶ Map References and Atlas Map references for attractions are based on the National Grid, and can be used with the Atlas at the back of this book. First comes the map page number, followed by the National Grid reference. To find the location, read the first figure horizontally and the second figure vertically within the lettered square.

❷ Directions may be given after the address of each attraction and where shown have been provided by the attractions themselves.

❸ Telephone Numbers have the STD code shown before the telephone number. (If dialling Northern Ireland from England use the STD code, but for the Republic you need to prefix the number with 00353, and drop the first zero from the Irish area code).

❹ 2-FOR-1 Voucher Scheme 2 for 1
This symbol indicates which attractions have chosen to participate in our 2-for-1 voucher scheme. Visitors using one of the vouchers from the back of this guide will be able to buy 2 tickets for the price of one, with certain restrictions that are detailed on the voucher itself. Some attractions also have individual restrictions, which are detailed in their entries.

❺ Opening Times quoted in the guide are inclusive - for instance, where you see Apr-Oct, that place will be open from the beginning of April to the end of October.

❻ Fees quoted for the majority of entries are current. If no price is quoted, you should

---

BEDFORD ❶-MAP 04 TL04

Bedford Museum 2 for 1
Castle Ln MK40 3XD
❷ ⮑ *(close to town bridge and Embankment)*
❸ ☎ 01234 353323
e-mail: bmuseum@bedford.gov.uk
web: www.bedfordmuseum.org

Embark on a fascinating journey through the human and natural history of north Bedfordshire, pausing briefly to glimpse at wonders from more distant lands. Go back in time and visit the delightful rural room sets and the Old School Museum, where Blackbeard's Sword, 'Old Billy' the record breaking longest-living horse, and numerous other treasures and curiosities can be found. Housed in the former Higgins and Sons Brewery, Bedford Museum is situated within the gardens of what was once Bedford Castle, beside the Great Ouse embankment. The courtyard and galleries provide an excellent setting for the varied collections.

❺ **Times** Open all year, Tue–Sat 11–5, Sun 2–5 (Closed Mon ex BH Mon afternoon, Good Fri & Xmas) **Fee ✱** Return ticket £6 (ch 2–15 £3, pen £5 & ❻ ch under 2 free) **Facilities** ⓟ (50mtrs) ♨ & (lift available on request, subject to staff availability) toilets for disabled shop ⊗ (ex guide dogs) ▬

---

check with the attraction concerned before you visit. Places which are open 'at all reasonable times' are usually free, and many places which do not charge admission at all may ask for a voluntary donation. Remember that prices can go up, and those provided to us by the attractions are provisional.

✱ Admission prices followed by an asterisk relate to 2006. It should be noted that in some entries the opening dates and times may also have been supplied as 2006. Please check with the establishment before making your journey.

Free Entry FREE
These attractions do not charge a fee for entry, although they may charge for use of audio equipment, for example. We have not included attractions that expect a donation in this category.

es Theme Parks Statery
or centres Theme Parks
s Visitor centres Theme
Galleries Visitor centres
rks Art Galleries Visitor
onal Parks Art Galleries
ms National Parks Art
mesMuseums National
ely Homes Museums

Key to Symbols

Key to Symbols Legend

☎ Telephone number

& Suitable for visitors in wheelchairs

❷ Parking at Establishment

℗ Parking nearby

☕ Refreshment

▥ Worksheets

🍽 Restaurant

⊗ No Dogs

🚌 No Coaches

✳ Admission prices relate to 2006

⊕ Cadw (Welsh Mouments)

⊞ English Heritage

❧ National Trust

�　National Trust for Scotland

⋀ Historic Scotland

Abbreviations

BH Bank Holidays

PH Public Holidays

Etr Easter

ex except

Free Admission free

ch Children

Pen Senior Citizens

Conc Concessions (Students, unemployed etc)

❼ **Facilities** This section includes parking, dogs allowed, refreshments, worksheets etc. See this page for a key to Symbols and Abbreviations used in this guide.

❽ **Visitors with Mobility Disabilities** should look for the wheelchair symbol showing where all or most of the establishment is accessible to the wheelchair-bound visitor. We strongly recommend that you telephone in advance of your visit to check the exact details, particularly regarding access to toilets and refreshment facilities. Assistance dogs are usually accepted where the attractions show the 'No Dogs' symbol ⊗ unless stated otherwise. For the hard of hearing induction loops are indicated by a symbol at the attraction itself.

❾ **Credit & Charge cards** are taken by a number of attractions for admission charges. To indicate which accept credit cards we have used this symbol at the end of the entry. ▬

Photography is restricted in some places and there are many where it is only allowed in specific areas. Visitors are advised to check with places of interest on the rules for taking photographs and the use of video cameras.

Special events are held at many of these attractions, and although we have listed a few in individual entries, we cannot hope to give details of them all, so please ring the attractions for

details of exhibitions, themed days, talks, guided walks and more.

Attractions with Italic headings These are entries that were unable to provide the relevant information in time for publication.

...and finally Opening times and admission prices can be subject to change. Please check with the attraction before making your journey.

Public Holidays

Date	Holiday	Date	Holiday
I January	New Year's Day	12 July	Battle of the Boyne (Orangemen's Day) (N.I)
3 January	New Year's Holiday (Scotland only)	6 August	Summer Bank Holiday (Scotland & R.O.I only)
19 March	St Patrick's Day (N.I & R.O.I)	27 August	Summer Bank Holiday (excluding R.O.I)
6 April	Good Friday	25 October	Bank Holiday (R.O.I)
9 April	Easter Monday	25 December	Christmas Day
7 May	May Day Bank Holiday	26 December	Boxing Day (St Stephen's Day in R.O.I)
28 May	Spring Bank Holiday (excluding R.O.I)		

NEW!

Real-time, online booking at

www.theAA.com

Take the hassle out of booking accommodation online

We are delighted to announce that it is now possible
to book many AA establishments on the website

Bedfordshire

Whipsnade Wild Animal Park,
Whipsnade

Bedfordshire may be one of England's smallest counties, but it contains some
delightfully varied scenery and a wide range of places to visit. Throughout the
county are unspoilt villages of thatched houses, much the same today as they
were in the 17th century when John Bunyan preached on village greens. From
historic aircraft at Biggleswade to wild animals at Whipsnade there is plenty to
do and see throughout the year.

England

Houghton House   FREE

➲ *(1m NE off A421)*
web: www.english-heritage.org.uk

Now a ruin, the mansion was built for Mary Countess of Pembroke, the sister of Sir Philip Sidney. Inigo Jones is thought to have been involved in work on the house, which may have been the original 'House Beautiful' in Bunyan's *Pilgrim's Progress*.

Times: Open at all reasonable times. **Facilities:** ❷ ৬ ✿

Bedford Museum   FREE

Castle Ln MK40 3XD
➲ *(close to town bridge and Embankment)*
☎ 01234 353323
e-mail: bmuseum@bedford.gov.uk
web: www.bedfordmuseum.org

Embark on a fascinating journey through the human and natural history of north Bedfordshire, pausing briefly to glimpse at wonders from more distant lands. Go back in time and visit the delightful rural room sets and the Old School Museum, where Blackbeard's Sword, 'Old Billy' the record breaking longest-living horse, and numerous other treasures and curiosities can be found. Housed in the former Higgins and Sons Brewery, Bedford Museum is situated within the gardens of what was once Bedford Castle, beside the Great Ouse embankment. The courtyard and galleries provide an excellent setting for the varied collections.

Times: Open all year, Tue-Sat 11-5, Sun 2-5. (Closed Mon ex BH Mon afternoon, Good Fri & Xmas). **Facilities:** ℗ (50mtrs) ꟼ ৬ (lift available on request, subject to staff availability) toilets for disabled shop ⊗ (ex guide dogs) ◀

Cecil Higgins Art Gallery & Museum   FREE

Castle Ln MK40 3RP
➲ *(in town centre close to Embankment)*
☎ 01234 211222
e-mail: chag@bedford.gov.uk
web: www.cecilhigginsartgallery.org

A recreated Victorian mansion, with the rooms arranged as though the house is still lived in. Includes a bedroom with furniture designed by Victorian architect William Burges, and the adjoining gallery has an outstanding collection of ceramics, glass and changing exhibition of prints, drawings and watercolours. Also includes the Thomas Lester lace collection.

Times: Open all year, Tue-Sat 11-5, Sun & BH Mon 2-5. (Closed Mon, Good Fri, 25-26 Dec & 1 Jan). **Facilities:** ℗ (100yds) (pay & display) (free on Sun) ꟼ ৬ (wheelchair available) toilets for disabled shop ⊗ (ex guide dogs) ◀

Leighton Buzzard Railway   2 for 1

Pages Park Station, Billington Rd LU7 4TN
➲ *(0.75m SE on A4146 signposted in and around Leighton Buzzard, near rdbt junct with A505)*
☎ 01525 373888
e-mail: info@buzzrail.co.uk
web: www.buzzrail.co.uk

The Leighton Buzzard Railway offers a 70 minute journey into the vanished world of the English light railway, with its sharp curves, steep gradients, level crossings and unique roadside running. Built in 1919 to serve the local sand industry, the railway has carried a steam passenger service, operated by volunteers, since 1968.

Times: Open 11 Mar-28 Oct, Sun; 9 Apr, 7 & 28 May & 27 Aug, Mon; 31 Jul-21 Aug, Tue; 4 & 11 Apr, 30 May-22 Aug & 24 Oct, Wed; 2-23 Aug, Thu; 6 Apr, Fri; 7 Apr, 5 & 26 May, 4 Aug-15 Sep & 6 Oct, Sat. **Fee:** Return ticket £6 (ch 2-15 £3, ch under 2 free, concessions £5). Party 10+. **Facilities:** ❷ ꟼ ◪ ৬ (platform & train access for wheelchairs) toilets for disabled shop ◀

John Dony Field Centre   FREE

Hancock Dr, Bushmead LU2 7SF
➲ *(signposted from rdbt on A6, at Barnfield College on New Bedford Rd)*
☎ 01582 486983
e-mail: donyj@luton.gov.uk
web: www.luton.gov.uk/museums

This is a purpose built study centre for exploring the landscapes, plants and animals of the Luton area. Featuring permanent displays on local archaeology, natural history and the management of the local nature reserve, it explains how ancient grasslands and hedgerows are conserved and follows 4000 years of history from Bronze Age to modern times.

Times: ✱ Open all year, Mon-Fri 9.30-4.45. Closed BHs. **Facilities:** ❷ ৬ toilets for disabled ⊗ (ex assist dogs)

Stockwood Craft Museum & Gardens   FREE

Stockwood Country Park, Farley Hill LU1 4BH
➲ *(signposted from M1 junct 10 and from Hitchin, Dunstable, Bedford and from Luton town centre)*
☎ 01582 738714 & 546739
e-mail: museum.gallery@luton.gov.uk
web: www.luton.gov.uk/museums

The Museum is set in period gardens which incorporate the Ian Hamilton Finlay Sculpture Gardens. The Mossman collection of horse-drawn vehicles traces the history of transport from Roman times to the 1940s. Craft demonstrations are held at weekends in the summer. Please telephone for details of special events.

Times: ✱ Open all year; Mar-Oct, Tue-Sun 10-5; Nov-Mar, wknds 10-4. (closed Xmas & 1 Jan) **Facilities:** ❷ ꟼ ◪ ৬ (stair lift, parking, induction loop, automatic door) toilets for disabled shop ⊗ (ex guide & hearing dogs)

England

Wardown Park Museum `FREE`
Wardown Park, Old Bedford Rd LU2 7HA
➲ *(Follow brown signs from the town centre north. Turn off A6 towards Bedford)*
☎ 01582 546722 & 546739
e-mail: museum.gallery@luton.gov.uk
web: www.luton.gov.uk/museums
A Victorian mansion, with displays illustrating the natural and cultural history, archaeology and industries of the area, including the development of Luton's hat industry, and the Bedfordshire and Hertfordshire Regimental Collections. New 'Luton Life' displays tell the story of the town and its residents over the past 200 years. Exhibitions and events throughout the year.

Times: ✱ Open all year, Tue-Sat 10-5, Sun 1-5 (Closed Xmas, 1 Jan & Mon ex BH Mons). **Facilities:** ❷ ❤ ▣ ⓺ (parking adjacent to entrance, lift to 1st floor) toilets for disabled shop ⊗ (ex guide & hearing dogs)

OLD WARDEN   MAP 04 TL14

The Shuttleworth Collection
Old Warden Park SG18 9EA
➲ *(2m W from rdbt on A1, Biggleswade by-pass)*
☎ 01767 627927
web: www.shuttleworth.org

Housed in eight hangars on a classic grass aerodrome, 40 working historic aeroplanes span the progress of aviation with exhibits ranging from a 1909 Bleriot to a 1941 Spitfire. A garage of roadworthy motor vehicles explores the eras of the 1898 Panhard Levassor to the Railton sports car of 1937. The 19th-century coach house displays horse-drawn vehicles from 1880 to 1914.

Times: Open Apr-Oct 10-5 (last admission 4), Nov-Mar 10-4 (last admission 3). Closed Xmas-New Year. **Fee:** ✱ £8 (pen £7). Most flying displays £16. **Facilities:** ❷ ❤ ⑩ licensed ▣ ⓺ (wheelchairs) toilets for disabled shop ⊗ (ex on leads/guide dogs) ◀

SANDY   MAP 04 TL14

RSPB Nature Reserve
The Lodge Shop SG19 2DL
➲ *(1m E, on B1042 Potton road)*
☎ 01767 680541
e-mail: claire.wallace@rspb.org.uk
web: www.rspb.org.uk
The headquarters of the Royal Society for the Protection of Birds. The house and buildings are not open to the public, but there are waymarked paths and formal gardens, and two species of woodpecker, nuthatches and woodland birds may be seen, as may muntjac deer. Another feature is the specialist wildlife garden created in conjunction with the Henry Doubleday Association.

Times: ✱ Open all year, Mon-Fri 9-5, Sat, Sun & BHs 10-5. Closed 25-26 Dec. **Facilities:** ❷ ▣ ⓺ (partial access) toilets for disabled shop ⊗ (ex in restricted areas) ◀

SILSOE   MAP 04 TL03

Wrest Park Gardens
MK45 4HS
➲ *(0.75m E off A6)*
☎ 01525 860152
web: www.english-heritage.org.uk
Audio tour through a century and a half of gardening styles as you explore the 90 acres of formal gardens that make up Wrest Park.

Times: Open Apr-Sep, Sat, Sun & BH 10-6; Oct, Sat, Sun 10-5. **Fee:** £4.50 (ch £2.30, concessions £3.40) Family £11.30. Prices and opening times are subject to change in Spring 2007. Please check web site or call 0870 333 1181 for the most up to date prices and opening times when planning your visit. **Facilities:** ❷ ⊗ (ex on lead in certain areas) ▤

WHIPSNADE   MAP 04 TL01

Whipsnade Wild Animal Park
LU6 2LF
➲ *(signposted from M1 junct 9 & 12)*
☎ 01582 872171
e-mail: marketing@zsl.org
web: www.whipsnade.co.uk
Located in beautiful Bedfordshire countryside, Whipsnade is home to more than 2,500 rare and exotic animals and is one of the largest conservation centres in Europe. Hop aboard the Jumbo Express, a fantastic steam train experience, and see elephants, rhino, yaks, camels and deer, along with wild horses, and learn about their lives in the wilds of Asia and Africa. Other highlights include the Lions of the Serengeti, the sealion pool, and Birds of the World. The Discover Centre is home to tamarins, turtles, big snakes and sea horses among others. Visitors can also enjoy the picnic areas, keeper talks and animal shows.

Times: Open all year, daily. (Closed 25 Dec). Closing times vary.
Fee: Seasonal pricing. Telephone or see website for up to date pricing.
Facilities: ❷ (charged) ❤ ▣ ⓺ (1 carer free per registered disabled visitor) toilets for disabled shop ⊗ ◀

England

WILDEN
MAP 04 TL05

Bedford Butterfly Park NEW
2 for 1
Renhold Rd MK44 2PX
➲ (Signed from Gt Barford, E of Bedford)
☎ 01234 772770
e-mail: enquiries@bedford-butterflies.co.uk
web: www.bedford-butterflies.co.uk

Wildflower meadows, wildlife garden and bird hide are just a few of the countryside pleasures to be enjoyed at the park. A tropical house features exotic flowers, butterflies, waterfalls and ponds. Childrens activities are a regular event at weekends and during the holidays.

Times: Open 4 Jan-4 Feb & 8 Nov-23 Dec, Thu-Sun 10-4. Daily 8 Feb-4 Nov, 10-5. **Fee:** Jan-mid Feb & Nov-Dec £4.25 (ch under 16yrs £3.50, under 3yrs free, concessions £3.50). Mid Feb-Oct £4.75 (ch under 16yrs £3.90, under 3yrs free, concessions £4.25).
Facilities: ⊘ ⬛ & toilets for disabled shop ⊗ (ex guide dogs) ⬛

WOBURN
MAP 04 SP93

Woburn Abbey
2 for 1
MK17 9WA
➲ (Just off M1 junct 12/13)
☎ 01525 290333
e-mail: admissions@woburnabbey.co.uk
web: www.discoverwoburn.co.uk

Set in a beautiful 3,000 acre deer park, Woburn Abbey has been the home of the Russell family for nearly 400 years, and is now occupied by the 15th Duke of Bedford. Built on a Cistercian Monastery founded in 1145, the Abbey was given to the 1st Earl in the will of Henry VIII. It houses one of the most important private art collections in the world, including paintings by Gainsborough, Reynolds, Van Dyck and Cuyp. Wooburn Abbey is where the concept of afternoon tea was introduced by Anna Maria, wife of the 7th Duke, back in the 19th century. There are extensive formal gardens and a fine antiques centre.

Times: 8 Apr-1 Oct **Fee:** ✱ Deer Park & Abbey Grounds £2. House £10.50 (ch 5-15yrs £6, under 5's free, concessions £9.50) **Facilities:** ⊘ ⬛ ⦿ licensed ⬛ & (wheelchairs accommodated by prior arrangement) toilets for disabled shop ⊗ ⬛

Woburn Safari Park
2 for 1
Woburn Park MK17 9QN
➲ (Signposted from M1 junct 13)
☎ 01525 290407
e-mail: info@woburnsafari.co.uk
web: www.discoverwoburn.co.uk

Set in the 3,000 acres of parkland belonging to Woburn Abbey, Woburn Safari Park has an extensive collection of many species. Visitors can tour the reserves from the safety of their own car, and experience the thrill of being alongside white rhino, buffalo, giraffes, or Siberian tigers. Walkthrough areas are home to wallabies, squirrel monkeys, and lemurs, and feature a full programme of keeper talks and demonstrations. All attractions are included in the entry price, including the Great Woburn Railway and the Swanboats.

Times: 11 Mar-29 Oct 10-5. 30 Oct-9 Mar wknds only 11-3. (Closed 23-24 Dec) **Fee:** ✱ Please phone for details **Facilities:** ⊘ ⬛ ⦿ licensed & toilets for disabled shop ⊗ ⬛

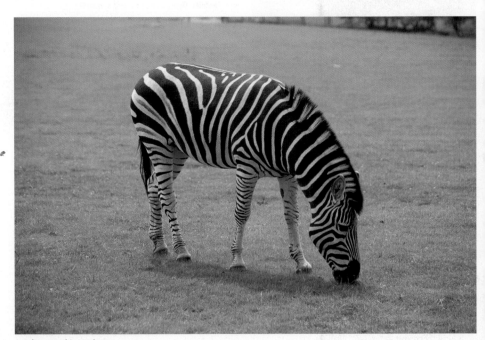

A zebra at Whipsnade Zoo

Berkshire

1st Battalion Scots Guards at Windsor Castle, Windsor

Berkshire is a narrow county reaching from the suburban edge of London to the expanse of rolling countryside that is Lambourn Downs in the West. Home to Windsor Castle, iron age forts and Legoland there is something to suit every one including boating. Immortalised by Kenneth Grahame in *The Wind in the Willows*, the River Thames as well as the rivers Pang and Bourne and the Kennet and Avon Canal offer watery highways that are ideal for 'messing about in boats'.

BRACKNELL MAP 04 SU86

The Look Out Discovery Centre
Nine Mile Ride RG12 7QW
➲ *(3m S of town centre. From M3 junct 3, take A322 to Bracknell and from M4 junct 10, take A329M to Bracknell. Follow brown tourist signs)*
☎ 01344 354400
e-mail: thelookout@bracknell-forest.gov.uk
web: www.bracknell-forest.gov.uk/lookout

A hands-on, interactive science and nature exhibition where budding scientists can spend many hours exploring and discovering over 70 fun filled exhibits within five themed zones, linked to the National Curriculum. Zones include Light and Colour, Forces and Movement and the Body and Perception. A new exciting zone, Woodland and Water; has a vortex, stream, ant colony and many more interactive exhibits. Climb the 88 steps to the Look Out tower and look towards Bracknell and beyond or enjoy a nature walk in the surrounding 2,600 acres of Crown Estate woodland. Interactive shows for the public and schools running throughout the year. Please note the tower is closed when wet.

Times: Open all year (Closed 24-26 Dec, 8-12 Jan) **Fee:** £5.20 (ch & concessions £3.45). Family (2 ad + 2 ch or 1 ad + 3 ch) £13.85.
Facilities: ♥ ▆ ⬛ ♿ (lift to 1st floor) toilets for disabled shop (Open 10-5) ✖ (ex guide dogs) ◼

ETON MAP 04 SU97

Dorney Court `2 for 1`
Dorney SL4 6QP
➲ *(signposted from M4 junct 7, via B3026)*
☎ 01628 604638
e-mail: palmer@dorneycourt.co.uk
web: www.dorneycourt.co.uk

An enchanting brick and timber manor house (c1440) in a tranquil setting. With tall Tudor chimneys and a splendid great hall, it has been the home of the present family since 1510.

Times: Open BH Sun & Mon in May 1.30-4.30. Aug every afternoon ex Sat 1.30-4.30. **Fee:** ✱ £6 (ch £4, under 10's free). **Facilities:** ♥ ▆ ⬛ ♿ (ramps) toilets for disabled garden centre ✖ (ex guide dogs)

HAMPSTEAD NORREYS MAP 04 SU57

The Living Rainforest
RG18 0TN
➲ *(follow brown tourist signs from M4/A34)*
☎ 01635 202444
e-mail: enquiries@livingrainforest.org
web: www.livingrainforest.org

By providing education and supporting research into the relationship between humanity and the rainforests, this wonderful attraction hopes to promote a more sustainable future. Visitors to the Living Rainforest will see plants and wildlife that are under threat in their natural habitat, and be encouraged to take part in a large variety of activities, workshops and exhibitions.

Times: ✱ Open all year daily 10-5.15. (Closed from 1pm 24 Dec & 25-26 Dec) **Facilities:** ♥ ▆ ⬛ toilets for disabled shop ✖ (ex guide dogs) ◼

LOWER BASILDON MAP 04 SU67

Basildon Park
RG8 9NR
➲ *(7m NW of Reading on W side of A329 between Reading & Wallingford)*
☎ 0118 984 3040
e-mail: basildonpark@nationaltrust.org.uk
web: www.nationaltrust.org.uk/basildonpark

This 18th-century house, built of Bath stone, fell into decay in the 20th century, but has been beautifully restored by Lord and Lady Iliffe. The classical front has a splendid central portico and pavilions, and inside there are delicate plasterwork decorations on the walls and ceilings. The Octagon drawing room has fine pictures and furniture, and there is a small formal garden. The house more recently featured in the 2005 film adaptation of Jane Austens *Pride & Prejudice*.

Times: House open Apr-end Oct, Wed-Sun & BH Mon 12-5. Park & garden Apr-end Oct, Wed-Sun & BH Mon 11-5. **Fee:** House & grounds £5.50 (ch £2.75), family ticket £13.75; Please phone for Grounds only prices.
Facilities: ♥ ⦿ licensed ⬛ ♿ (driven buggy, ltd access to main show rooms) toilets for disabled shop ✖ ◼

Beale Park
Lower Basildon RG8 9NH
➲ *(M4 junct 12, follow brown tourist signs to Pangbourne, A329 towards Oxford)*
☎ 0870 777 7160
web: www.bealepark.co.uk

Beale Park is home to an extraordinary collection of birds and animals including peacocks, swans, owls and parrots. It also offers a steam railway, rare breeds of farm animals, a great pet corner, meerkats, wallabies, ring-tailed lemurs, a deer park, three splash pools, a huge adventure playground, acres of gardens, and sculptures in a traditional, family park beside the Thames. There are summer riverboat trips and excellent lake and river fishing.

Times: Open Mar-Oct. **Fee:** £6.50 (ch £4.50, under 2 free, pen £5.50). Family (2 ad & 2 ch) £20 **Facilities:** ♥ ▆ ⦿ licensed ⬛ ♿ (wheelchair available, parking) toilets for disabled shop ✖ (ex guide dogs)

NEWBURY MAP 04 SU46

West Berkshire Museum `FREE`
The Wharf RG14 5AS
➲ *(from London take M4 junct 13, then southbound on A34, follow signs for town centre)*
☎ 01635 30511
e-mail: museum@westberks.gov.uk
web: westberkshiremuseum.org.uk

Occupying two adjoining buildings in the centre of Newbury; the Cloth Hall built in 1627 and the Granary built in 1720. The museum includes displays of fine and decorative art, costume, local history and archaeology.

Times: Open all year Tue-Sat 10-5. Open BH Feb-Nov .
Facilities: ℗ (15yds) ⬛ ♿ shop ✖ (ex guide dogs)

OLD WINDSOR
MAP 04 SU97

Runnymede

North Lodge, Windsor Rd SL4 2JL

➲ *(From M25 junct 13. On the Thames, 2m W of Runnymede Bridge on S side of A308. 6m E of Windsor)*

☎ 01784 432891

e-mail: runnymede@nationaltrust.org.uk

web: www.nationaltrust.org.uk/runnymede

Partly designated as a Site of Special Scientific Interest, Runnymede is an area of meadows, grassland, and woodland that sits alongside the Thames. Best known as the site where King John signed the Magna Carta in 1215, this momentous event was commemorated by the American Bar Association, who built a monument here in 1957. There is also a memorial to American President, John F Kennedy. Also the Fairhaven Lodges, designed by Edward Lutyens.

Times: Car parks; Oct-Mar 9-5, Apr-Sep 9-7 **Fee:** ✱ Car parking £1-5
Facilities: ♿ (charged) 💼 ⦿ ♿ (Braille guide) toilets for disabled shop

---

READING
MAP 04 SU77

Museum of English Rural Life `FREE`

University of Reading, Redlands Rd RG1 5EX

➲ *(close to the Royal Berkshire Hospital)*

☎ 0118 378 8660

e-mail: merl@reading.ac.uk

web: www.merl.org.uk

Recently moved to larger premises, this museum houses a national collection of agricultural, domestic and crafts exhibits, including wagons, tools and a wide range of other equipment used in the English countryside over the last 150 years. Special facilities are available for school parties. The museum also contains extensive documentary and photographic archives, which can be studied by appointment. There is a regular programme of events and activities, please see website for details.

Times: Open all year, Tue-Fri, 10-4.30, Sat & Sun 2-4.30 (Closed BH's & Xmas-New Year). **Facilities:** ♿ ♿ (Chair lifts, hearing loop) toilets for disabled shop ⦿ (ex guide dogs)

RISELEY
MAP 04 SU76

Wellington Country Park `2 for 1`

RG7 1SP

➲ *(signposted off A33, between Reading & Basingstoke)*

☎ 0118 932 6444

e-mail: info@wellington-country-park.co.uk

web: www.wellington-country-park.co.uk

350 acres of woodland walks and parkland provided for a family outing. Attractions appealing to younger and older children include; miniature railway, variety of childrens play areas, crazy golf and 'in season' rowing boat hire.

Times: Open Mar-Oct, daily 10-5.30. **Fee:** ✱ £6 (ch £4, under 3's free, concessions £5) **Facilities:** ♿ 💼 ♿ (fishing platform & nature trail) toilets for disabled shop ⦿

England

Frogmore House

Home Park SL4 1NJ

⮑ *(entrance via the long walk, from B3021 between Datchet & Old Windsor)*

☎ 020 7766 7305

e-mail: bookinginfo@royalcollection.org.uk

web: www.royalcollection.org.uk

Frogmore House has been a royal retreat since the 18th century, and is today used by the Royal Family for private entertaining. It is especially linked with Queen Charlotte, the wife of George III, and her daughters, whose love of botany and art is reflected throughout the house. Queen Victoria loved Frogmore so much that she broke with royal tradition and chose to build a mausoleum for herself and Prince Albert there.

Times: Open 16-18 May, 10-5.30 (last admission 4). Aug BH wknd, 10-5.30 (last admission 4). Prebooked group guided tours Aug-28 Sep Tue-Thu. **Fee:** Contact Ticket Sales and Information Office (020 7766 7305) for details of admission prices. **Facilities:** ♿ (charged) shop ⊗ (ex assist dogs) ◀

Household Cavalry Museum

Combermere Barracks, St Leonards Rd SL4 3DN

⮑ *(on St Leonards Rd opposite King Edward VII Hospital)*

☎ 01753 755112

One of the finest military museums in Britain, with comprehensive displays of the uniforms, weapons, horse furniture (tack, regalia, etc) and armour used by the Household Cavalry from 1600 to the present day.

Times: ✱ Open all year Mon-Fri (ex BH) 9-12.30 & 2-4.30. Museum undergoing refurbishmnent due to re-open Spring 2007 **Facilities:** ♿ shop ⊗

Legoland Windsor

Winkfield Rd SL4 4AY

⮑ *(on B3022 Windsor to Ascot road signposted from M3 junct 3 & M4 junct 6)*

e-mail: customer.services@legoland.co.uk

web: www.legoland.co.uk

With over 50 interactive rides, live shows, building workshops, driving schools and attractions. Set in 150 acres of beautiful parkland, LEGOLAND Windsor is a different sort of family theme park. An atmospheric and unique experience for the whole family, a visit to LEGOLAND Windsor is more than a day out, it's a lifetime of memories. 2006 was LEGOLAND'S 10th anniversary.

Times: ✱ Open daily 12 Mar-5 Nov **Facilities:** ♿ (charged) 💺 ⦿ 🎫 ♿ (signing staff, wheelchair hire, parking) toilets for disabled shop ⊗ (ex guide dogs) ◀

See advert on page 13

England

St George's Chapel

SL4 1NJ

➲ *(M4 junct 6 & M3 junct 3)*

☎ 01753 865538

St George's Chapel, within the precincts of Windsor Castle, is one of the most beautiful ecclesiastical buildings in England. Founded by Edward IV in 1475, it is the burial place of ten monarchs, including Henry VIII and his favourite wife Jane Seymour. The Chapel is the spiritual home of the Order of the Garter, the oldest and most senior order of British Chivalry.

Times: Open Mar-Oct (9.45-5.15) Nov-Feb (9.45-4.15). May close at short notice - 24hr info line - 01753 831118. (Closed Sun, worshippers very welcome) **Fee:** ✱ Free entry to the Chapel is included in the price of entry to Windsor Castle. **Facilities:** ℗ 400 yds & shop ⊗ (ex guide dogs)

Savill Garden (Windsor Great Park) 2 for 1

Wick Ln, Englefield Green TW20 0UU

➲ *(M25 junct 13, signposted off A30 between Egham & Virginia Water)*

☎ 01753 847518

e-mail: savillgarden@thecrownestate.co.uk

web: www.theroyallandscape.co.uk

The work of master landscape gardener, Sir Eric Savill, this is one of the greatest woodland gardens in England. It was created in the 1930s

and offers year-round interest with colourful displays of interesting and rare plants. The Savill Building, opened in June 2006, is a visitor centre built to a unique and innovative gridshell design, made with timber harvested from Windsor Great Park. The Royal Landscape is an area of a thousand acres of gardens and parkland accessible to the public, at the southern end of Windsor Great Park. It includes the Savill Garden, the Valley Gardens and Virginia Water, and was shaped and planted over a period of 400 years.

Times: Open all year, daily 10-6 (10-4 Nov-Feb). (Closed 25-26 Dec). **Fee:** Mar-Oct: £5.50 (ch 6-16 £2.75, concessions £4.95); Nov-Mar: £4 (ch £2, concessions £3.60). Group rates available. Prices valid until 31 Mar 2007. **Facilities:** ❷ ➌ ⅋ licensed ⊞ & (wheelchairs available) toilets for disabled shop garden centre ⊗ (ex guide dogs)

Windsor Castle

SL4 1NJ

➲ *(M4 junct 6 & M3 junct 3)*

☎ 020 7766 7304

e-mail: bookinginfo@royalcollection.org.uk

web: www.royalcollection.org.uk

Covering 13 acres, this is the official residence of HM The Queen, and the largest inhabited castle in the world. Begun as a wooden fort by William the Conqueror, it has been added to by almost every monarch since. A visit takes in the magnificent state apartments, St Georges chapel, Queen Marys dolls house, the drawings gallery, and between October and March, the semi-state rooms created by George IV. An exhibition of photography celebrating the Queens 80th birthday is on display until March 2007.

Times: Open all year, daily except Good Fri, 19 Jun & 25-26 Dec. Nov-Feb, 9.45-4.15 (last admission 3), Mar-Oct 9.45-5.15 (last admission 4). As Windsor Castle is a royal residence the opening arrangements may be subject to change at short notice - 24hr info line - 01753 831118 **Fee:** ✱ £13.50 (ch under 17 £7.50, under 5's free, concessions £12) Family ticket £34.50 (2ad+3ch) **Facilities:** ℗ (400yds) & (contact 020 7766 7324) toilets for disabled shop ⊗ (ex guide dogs)

We endeavour to be as accurate as possible, but changes to times and other information can occur after the guide has gone to press.

Bristol

Brunel's Clifton Suspension Bridge,
Bristol

Once one of England's major ports, this is an ancient city with lots of
history and a very modern outlook. Historic attractions include Isambard
Kingdom Brunel's Clifton Suspension Bridge and the marvellously restored
iron-built ship *SS Great Britain*. The heart of the city is reflected in the lively
quayside, full of bars, restaurants and galleries and the place to be
entertained by musicians, performers and street artists.

England

BRISTOL
MAP 03 ST57

Arnolfini NEW
FREE
16 Narrow Quay BS1 4QA
➲ *(From M32 follow brown signs)*
☎ 0117 917 2300 & 0117 917 2301
e-mail: boxoffice@arnolfini.org.uk
web: www.arnolfini.org.uk

Located in a 19th-century warehouse in Bristol's harbourside, Arnolfini is one of Europe's leading centres for contemporary arts. The internationally acclaimed programme includes; visual arts exhibitions, live art, performance, dance, cinema and talks and lectures.

Times: Open all year, daily 10-8. (Thu, galleries close at 6).
Facilities: ℗ (100mtrs) (Disabled parking on site) 💷 🍴 licensed 🗄 🚻 toilets for disabled shop ⊗ (ex guide dogs) ◀

At-Bristol
Anchor Rd, Harbourside BS1 5DB
➲ *(from city centre, A4 to Anchor Rd. Located on left opposite Cathedral)*
☎ 0845 345 1235
e-mail: information@at-bristol.org.uk
web: www.at-bristol.org.uk

For the interactive adventure of a lifetime head for At-Bristol's three attractions on the city's habourside. A clever fusion of sci-fi architecture and historic buildings are home to 'Wildwalk', a breathtaking journey through the plant and animal kingdoms; Explore, the UK's most exciting hands-on science centre; and the IMAX theatre, the largest cinema screen in the West of England.

Times: Open all year, term-time wkdays 10-5, wknds & school hols 10-6. (Closed 25 Dec). **Fee:** Ticket for 3 attractions £20 (ch £15, concessions £15). Family ticket £62. **Facilities:** ℗ (charged) 💷 🍴 licensed 🗄 🚻 (induction loop & mini com 0117 914 3475) toilets for disabled shop ⊗ (ex guide dogs) ◀

Blaise Castle House Museum
FREE
Henbury Rd, Henbury BS10 7QS
➲ *(4m NW of city, off B4057)*
☎ 0117 903 9818
e-mail: general_museum@bristol-city.gov.uk
web: www.bristol-city.gov.uk/museums

Built in the 18th century for a Quaker banker, this mansion is now Bristol's Museum of Social History. Nearby Blaise Hamlet is a picturesque estate village, designed by John Nash.

Times: Open all year, Sat-Wed 10-5. (Closed 25-26 Dec).
Facilities: ℗ 🚻 shop ⊗ (ex guide dogs)

Bristol's City Museum & Art Gallery
FREE
Queen's Rd, Clifton BS8 1RL
➲ *(follow signs to city centre, then follow tourist board signs to City Museum & Art Gallery)*
☎ 0117 922 3571
e-mail: general_museum@bristol-city.gov.uk
web: www.bristol-city.gov.uk/museums

Regional and international collections representing ancient history, natural sciences, and fine and applied arts. Displays include dinosaurs, Bristol ceramics, silver, Chinese and Japanese ceramics. A full programme of Special Exhibitions take place throughout the year. Ring for details.

Times: Open all year, daily 10-5. (Closed 25-26 Dec).
Facilities: ℗ (400yds) 💷 🚻 (lift) toilets for disabled shop ⊗ (ex guide dogs)

Bristol's Georgian House
FREE
7 Great George St, off Park St BS1 5RR
➲ *(5 mins walk from city centre)*
☎ 0117 921 1362
e-mail: general_museum@bristol-city.gov.uk
web: www.bristol-city.gov.uk/museums

A carefully preserved example of a late 18th-century merchant's town house, with many original features and furnished to illustrate life both above and below stairs. A bedroom is now open, featuring a four-poster bed plus a small display recounting Bristol's involvement in the slave trade.

Times: Open all year Sat-Wed, 10-5. (Closed 25-26 Dec).
Facilities: ℗ (pay & display street parking) ⊗ (ex guide dogs)

Bristol's Red Lodge
FREE
Park Row BS1 5LJ
➲ *(5 mins walk from city centre)*
☎ 0117 921 1360
e-mail: general_museum@bristol-city.gov.uk
web: www.bristol-city.gov.uk/museums

The house was built in 1590 and then altered in 1730. It has fine oak panelling and carved stone chimney pieces and is furnished in the style of both periods. The garden has now been laid out in the Elizabethan style.

Times: Open all year Sat-Wed 10-5. (Closed 25-26 Dec).
Facilities: ℗ (Adjacent) ⊗ (ex guide dogs)

Are there any excellent Days Out that we have missed? Use the Readers' Report form at the back of the book to tell us about them.

Bristol Zoo Gardens

Clifton BS8 3HA

➲ *(M5 junct 17, take A4018 then follow brown elephant signs. Also signed from city centre)*

☎ 0117 974 7399

e-mail: information@bristolzoo.org.uk

web: www.bristolzoo.org.uk

From the smallest and rarest tortoise in the world to the largest ape, there are 300 exotic and endangered species to explore. The Zoo is dedicated to conservation and involved in international breeding programmes. In Zona Brazil, visitors can experience first hand, the stunning and diverse species found in the threatened coastal rainforests of Brazil. A winding wooden walkway will lead you past stunning birds, dainty agouti, grazing tapirs, and the world's largest living rodent - the capybara. Award-winning Seal & Penguin Coasts enable visitors to come face-to-face with penguins and seals in their natural element - beneath the waves - through transparent underwater walkways. Other favourites include Bug World, Twilight World, and the Reptile House. New for 2006: Monkey Jungle, featuring Meet the Lemurs.

Times: Open all year, daily (ex 25 Dec). 9-5.30 (British summer time), 9-4.30 (standard hrs) **Fee:** £11 (ch £7, concessions £9.70). Family ticket (2ad+2 ch) £33. **Facilities:** ❷ (charged) 🍽️ licensed 🍴 ♿ (wheelchairs/electric scooters for use in zoo grounds) toilets for disabled shop ⊗ (kennels for service dogs) 🛥️

British Empire & Commonwealth Museum

2 for 1

Station Approach, Temple Meads BS1 6QH

➲ *(in city centre, near Temple Meads station)*

☎ 0117 925 4980

e-mail: admin@empiremuseum.co.uk

web: www.empiremuseum.co.uk

Exploring the dramatic 500-year history of the rise and fall of the British Empire and the emergence of the modern Commonwealth, this internationally acclaimed museum uses video stations, interactive exhibits, and computer games, as well as more traditional techniques. Visitors have the opportunity to dress in period costume, learn Morse code or sample exotic spices. The museum is divided into three sections: Britain's first empire 1500-1790, the British Empire at its height 1790-1914, and Independence and Beyond, and is housed in a restored railway terminus built by Brunel. A visit to the museum includes entry to the hands on exhibition Pow Wow.

Times: Open all year, daily 10-5. (Closed 25-26 Dec) **Fee:** ✱ £6.95 (ch 5-15yrs £3.95, concessions £5.95). Family of 4 £16. **Facilities:** ❷ (charged) 🍽️ ♿ (all but one conference room accessible, lifts) toilets for disabled shop ⊗ (ex guide dogs) 🛥️

Brunel's SS Great Britain

Great Western Dock, Gas Ferry Rd BS1 6TY

➲ *(off Cumberland Rd)*

☎ 0117 926 0680

e-mail: admin@ssgreatbritain.org

web: www.ssgreatbritain.org

Built and launched in Bristol in 1843, Isambard Kingdom Brunel's maritime masterpiece was the first ocean-going, propeller-driven, iron ship. After a life as a passenger liner, troop transport, cargo carrier and floating warehouse, she was abandoned in the Falkland Islands in 1937. In 1970 she was towed back to Bristol, restored to her former glory, and is now conserved in the Great Western Dock where she was built.

Times: Open all year daily 10-5.30, 4.30 in winter. (Closed 18, 24-25 Dec). **Fee:** ✱ £8.95 (ch £4.95, under 3yrs free, concessions £6.95). Family ticket (2 ad + 3 ch) £24.95. Annual ticket allows free return visits. Last ticket sale 1hr before closing. **Facilities:** ❷ (charged) 🍽️ ♿ toilets for disabled shop ⊗ (ex guide dogs) 🛥️

HorseWorld

Staunton Manor Farm, Staunton Ln, Whitchurch BS14 0QJ

➲ *(A37 Bristol to Wells road, follow brown signs from Maes Knoll traffic lights)*

☎ 01275 540173

e-mail: visitor.centre@horseworld.org.uk

web: www.horseworld.org.uk

One of the largest horse rescue centres in Britain, set in Mendip-stone

continued

farm buildings on the edge of Bristol. Meet the friendly horses, ponies and donkeys. Enjoy the miniature farm, 'touch and groom' areas, pony rides, daily presentations, nature trail, educational displays, video theatre and adventure playground.

Times: ✱ Open all year daily 10-5 (Winter; closed Mon) **Facilities:** ℗ ➍ ⏺ ▥ ♿ toilets for disabled shop ⬛

John Wesley's Chapel (The New Room)

36 The Horsefair, Broadmead BS1 3JE
↪ *(M32 in Broadmead Shopping Centre)*
☎ 0117 926 4740
e-mail: wesleynewroom@surefish.co.uk
web: www.newroombristol.org.uk

The oldest Methodist chapel in the world, built in 1739 and extended in 1748. Above the chapel are the preacher's rooms where John Wesley, Charles Wesley and the early Methodist preachers stayed.

Times: Open all year, Mon-Sat 10-4. **Fee:** ✱ Donation requested. £4 per person for pre-arranged group tours **Facilities:** ℗ (250yds) (main entrance in pedestrian precinct) ➍ ▥ ♿ shop ⊗ (ex guide dogs) ⬛

Maritime Heritage Centre

Gas Ferry Rd BS1 6UN
↪ *(M5 junct 18, follow brown signs 'Anchor')*
☎ 0117 926 0680
e-mail: commerical@ss-great-britain.com
web: www.ss-great-britain.com

Exploring 200 years of Bristol shipbuilding, with special reference to Charles Hill & Son, and their predecessor, James Hillhouse. At the Great Western Dock the museum forms part of the *SS Great Britain* and John Cabot's *Matthew* experience.

Times: ✱ Open all year, daily 10-5.30, 4.30 in winter. (Closed 24 & 25 Dec). **Facilities:** ℗ (charged) ➍ ♿ toilets for disabled shop ⊗ (ex guide dogs) ⬛

Bristol Docks, view from Prince's Wharf with Canon's Quay in background

Buckinghamshire

West Wycombe House,
West Wycombe

Visitors to Buckinghamshire can only be enchanted by the majestic sweep of the Chiltern Hills, and fascinated by the history and heritage of the county's many attractive towns and villages – the pretty market towns of Marlow, Amersham and Buckingham are well worth exploring. There are many stately homes and country houses in Buckinghamshire including Chequers Court, the official country residence of the British Prime Minister and West Wycombe Park, a National Trust property set in 300 acres of beautiful parkland.

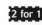

England

AYLESBURY   MAP 04 SP81

Boarstall Duck Decoy
Boarstall HP18 9UX
➲ *(A41/B4011, towards Long Crendon. Turn right to Boarstall & follow brown sign - decoy 200yds on right, through Manor Farm)*
☎ 01280 822850
e-mail: stowegarden@nationaltrust.org.uk
web: www.nationaltrust.org.uk

A rare survival of a 17th century decoy in working order. Working decoy demonstration on Saturday and Sunday, please phone for more details.

Times: Open Wed 3.30-6.30, Sat-Sun 10-4, mid Mar-Aug **Fee:** ✱ £2.40 (ch £1.20) Family £6 **Facilities:** ❷ 🍴 ♿ ⊗ (ex assist dogs) ♨

King's Head
King's Head Passage, Market Square HP20 2RW
➲ *(A41 follow signs for town centre, located at top of Market Sq)*
☎ 01296 381501
e-mail: kingshead@nationaltrust.org.uk
web: www.nationaltrust.org.uk

This historic coaching inn was established in 1455 and is still trading today. It has many notable architectural features, including a medieval stained glass window, extensive timber framing and an ancient cobbled courtyard. Once a base for Oliver Cromwell it now houses among other features a history centre.

Times: Open all year NT office 9-6. (Inn Mon-Sat 11-11 & Sun 11-10.30) **Fee:** £2 (ch £1). **Facilities:** ❷ (2-10min walk) 🍽 🍴 (Hearing loop) ⊗ (ex assist dogs) ♨

Tiggywinkles Visitor Centre & Hedgehog World Museum NEW   ▌2 for 1▐
Aston Rd HP17 8AF
➲ *(Turn off A418 towards Haddenham then follow signs to 'Wildlife Hospital')*
☎ 01844 292511
e-mail: mail@sttiggywinkles.org.uk
web: www.tiggywinkles.com

Look through the glass into our bird and mammal nursery wards in the hospital. Find out all about the hospital, our patients and their treatment on our education boards dotted around the gardens. See some of the other hospital wards on our CCTV monitor. Wander round the worlds first Hedgehog Memorabilia Museum or watch the foxes in their permanent enclosure. Try to catch a glimpse of one of our permanent badgers or see the deer in the recovery paddocks. The animals live as natural a life as possible, so dont be surprised if they do not come out to visit.

Times: Open Etr-Sep, daily 10-4 **Fee:** ✱ £4.20 (ch & concessions £3). Family ticket £12.20. **Facilities:** ❷ ♿ shop ⊗

BEACONSFIELD   MAP 04 SU99

Bekonscot Model Village and Railway   ▌2 for 1▐
Warwick Rd HP9 2PL
➲ *(M40 junct 2, 4m M25 junct 16, take A355 and follow signs to Model Village)*
☎ 01494 672919
e-mail: info@bekonscot.co.uk
web: www.bekonscot.com

A miniature world, depicting rural England in the 1930s. A Gauge 1 model railway meanders through six little villages, each with their own tiny population. Rides on the sit-on miniature railway take place weekends and school holidays.

Times: Open mid Feb-Oct, 10-5. **Fee:** Telephone for prices **Facilities:** ❷ 🍽 🍴 ♿ (wheelchair loan by prior booking) toilets for disabled shop ⊗ (ex guide dogs) 🍴

BLETCHLEY   MAP 04 SP93

Bletchley Park
The Mansion, Bletchley Park MK3 6EB
➲ *(Approach Bletchley from V7 Saxon St. At rdbt, southern end of Saxon St go under railway bridge towards Buckingham & follow signs to Bletchley Park)*
☎ 01908 640404
e-mail: info@bletchleypark.org.uk
web: www.bletchleypark.org.uk

Known as 'Station X' during World War II, this was the home of the secret scientific team that worked to decipher German military messages sent using the Enigma code machine. Visitors can find out more about the Enigma machine; the 'bombes', computers used to crack the code; Alan Turing, one of the leading mathematicians of his day, who worked on the project; as well as see a number of other

continued

21

England

displays including the use of pigeons during the war, wartime vehicles, and a Churchill collection.

Bletchley Park

Times: ✳ Open daily 9.30-5.30 (Tours at 11 & 2). Wknds open 10.30-5. Closed 25 & 26 Dec. **Facilities:** ❷ (charged) 💺🍽 licensed ♿ toilets for disabled shop ◾

CHALFONT ST GILES   MAP 04 SU99

Chiltern Open Air Museum
Newland Park, Gorelands Ln HP8 4AB
➲ *(M25 junct 17, M40 junct 2. Follow brown signs)*
☎ 01494 871117
e-mail: coamuseum@netscape.net
web: www.coam.org.uk

Saved from demolition and moved brick by brick to Newland Park, this collection of old buildings includes barns, granaries and even a tin chapel. Step back in time and get a feel of the 1940s in a fully furnished Prefab, or experience 50AD at the Iron Age House. Demonstrations including brick making, rug making, black smithing and storytelling. Regular living history re-enactments.

Times: ✳ Open 31 Mar-Oct, daily 10-5. **Facilities:** ❷ 💺 🗐 ♿ (Braille guide books & taped guides available, wheelchairs) toilets for disabled shop ⊗ (ex on lead) ◾

Milton's Cottage
Dean Way HP8 4JH
➲ *(0.5m W of A413. 3m N of M40 junct 2)*
☎ 01494 872313
e-mail: info@miltonscottage.org
web: www.miltonscottage.org

A timber-framed, 16th-century cottage, with a charming garden, the only surviving home in which John Milton lived and worked. He completed *Paradise Lost* and started *Paradise Regained* here. First editions of these works are among the many rare books and artefacts on display.

Times: Open Mar-Oct, Tue-Sun 10-1 & 2-6. Also open Spring & Summer BH. **Fee:** ✳ £3 (ch 15 £1.50). Party 20+ £2 each. **Facilities:** ❷ 🍽 licensed 🗐 ♿ (special parking area closer to cottage) shop ⊗ (ex guide dogs)

CLIVEDEN   MAP 04 SU98

Cliveden
SL6 0JA
➲ *(2m N of Taplow, follow brown signs on A4)*
☎ 01628 605069
e-mail: cliveden@nationaltrust.org.uk
web: www.nationaltrust.org.uk

The 375 acres of garden and woodland overlook the River Thames, and include a magnificent parterre, topiary, lawns with box hedges, and water gardens. The palatial house, former home of the Astors, is now a hotel - The Great Hall and French Dining Room can be visited on certain afternoons.

Times: Open Grounds 15 Mar-Oct daily 11-6, Nov-22 Dec daily 11-4 (Woodlands open all year). House Apr-Oct, Thu & Sun 3-5.30 by timed ticket. **Fee:** ✳ Grounds: £7.50 (ch £3.70). House: £1 extra (ch 50p extra). Family ticket £18.70. Group £6 each. Woodlands £3 (ch £1.50) Family £7.50 **Facilities:** ❷ 🍽 licensed ♿ (powered vehicle & wheelchairs available, parking) toilets for disabled shop ⊗ (woodland only, ex guide dogs) 💷 ◾

GREAT MISSENDEN   MAP 06 SP80

The Roald Dahl Museum & Story Centre
81-83 High St HP16 0AL
➲ *(from London/Amersham turn left off A413 into Great Missenden link road)*
☎ 01494 892192
e-mail: info@roalddahlmuseum.org
web: www.roalddahlmuseum.org

Roald Dahl's life and displays from his unique archive in the village where he lived for over 70 years. Discover more of the world famous writer and some of his contemporaries. Unearth secrets about the people and places which inspired Dahl's tales and in interactive galleries, discover how he wrote. Use the touch-screens to read his hand written notes and visit a replica of his writing hut. Check out top tips from today's leading authors - use your own Ideas Book just as Dahl did and you too could be a writer! Rolling programme of workshops and events.

Times: Open all year, Tue-Fri & BH Mon 10-5. Closed 25-26 Dec **Facilities:** ℗ (3 mins walk) 💺♿ (audio loops, tactile maps) toilets for disabled shop ⊗ (ex assist dogs) 🚐 ◾

HIGH WYCOMBE

MAP 04 SU89

Hughenden Manor

HP14 4LA

➲ *(1.5m N of High Wycombe, on W side of A4128)*

☎ 01494 755573

e-mail: hughenden@nationaltrust.org.uk

web: www.nationaltrust.org.uk

Fascinating Victorian Manor, home of Prime Minister Benjamin Disraeli from 1847-1881. Many of his possessions are still on display, along with beautiful gardens designed by his wife Mary-Anne. Other facilities include circular woodland walks, family tracker packs, I-spy sheets in the Manor and an exhibition revealing Hughenden's role in WWII.

Times: House open Mar-Oct, Wed-Sun & BH Mon 1-5. Last admission 4.30. Gardens same dates as house 11-5. Park open all year. Also open Good Fri. **Fee:** ✱ £6 (ch £3). Family ticket £15. Garden only £2.50 (ch £1.80). Park free. **Facilities:** ❷ ⏺️ licensed 🏛 (Braille leaflet, wheelchairs, ramp to house) shop ⊗ (ex guide dogs) 🐾 ◀

West Wycombe Park

HP14 3AJ

➲ *(S of A40, at W end of West Wycombe)*

☎ 01494 513569

e-mail: hughenden@nationaltrust.org.uk

web: www.nationaltrust.org.uk

Set in 300 acres of beautiful parkland, the house was rebuilt in the Palladian style, between 1745 and 1771, for Sir Francis Dashwood. Of particular note are the painted ceilings by Borgnis. The park was laid out in the 18th century and given an artificial lake and classical temples.

Times: Open, House & grounds Jun-Aug, Sun-Thu 2-6. Grounds only Apr-May, Sun-Thu 2-6 & Etr, May Day & Spring BH Sun & Mon 2-6. (Last admission 5.15). Entry by timed tickets. Parties must book in advance. **Fee:** ✱ House & grounds £5.70 (ch £2.80) Family £14.50. Group £4.50. Grounds only £3 (ch £1.50). **Facilities:** ❷ ⚹ (partial access to ground floor & gardens) ⊗ (ex guide dogs) 🐾

Wycombe Local History & Chair Museum

FREE

Castle Hill House, Priory Av HP13 6PX

➲ *(signposted by brown tourism sign from A404 (Amersham Hill) N of High Wycombe town centre just past railway station)*

☎ 01494 421895

e-mail: museum@wycombe.gov.uk

web: www.wycombe.gov.uk/museum

High Wycombe is famous for chair making and the museum has an extensive collection of chairs and artefacts from the furniture industry. There is also a gallery featuring local scenes and artists. Other aspects of Wycombe's history are also represented along with changing exhibitions.

Times: Open all year, Mon-Sat 10-5, Sun 2-5. Closed on BHs except special events - ring for details. **Facilities:** ❷ ⏺️ 🏛 ⚹ (portable induction loop, special parking & drop off point) toilets for disabled shop ⊗ (ex guide dogs) ◀

LONG CRENDON

MAP 04 SP60

Courthouse

HP18 9AN

➲ *(2m N of Thame, via B4011 when entering village turn right into the High St. Courthouse on left at end of High St next to parish church)*

☎ 01280 822850

e-mail: stowegardens@nationaltrust.org.uk

web: www.nationaltrust.org.uk

One of the finest examples of early timber framed building in the area. Probably built as a wool store in the early 1400s, but also used as a manorial courthouse until the late 19th century, this timber-framed building stands out, even in this picturesque village. Although the windows and doors have been altered and the chimney stack is Tudor, the magnificent timber roof is original.

Times: Open, Upper storey Apr-Sep, Wed 2-6, Sat, Sun & BH Mons 11-6. **Fee:** ✱ £1.10 **Facilities:** ℗ (street) (not suitable for large vehicles) ⊗ 🐾

MIDDLE CLAYDON

MAP 04 SP72

Claydon House

MK18 2EY

➲ *(M40 junct 9 off A413 in Padbury, follow National Trust signs. Entrance by north drive only)*

☎ 01296 730349

e-mail: claydon@nationaltrust.org.uk

web: www.nationaltrust.org.uk

The rather sober exterior of this 18th-century house gives no clue to the extravagances that lie inside, in the form of fantastic rococo carvings. Ceilings, cornices, walls and overmantels are adorned with delicately carved fruits, birds, beasts and flowers by Luke Lightfoot. The Chinese room is particularly splendid. There is also a spectacular parquetry staircase.

Times: House open 25 Mar-29 Oct, Sat-Wed 1-5. Last admission 4.30. (Closed Good Fri). **Fee:** ✱ £5.50 (ch £2.70). Family ticket £13. Grounds £4.50. Private Gardens £2.50 **Facilities:** ❷ ⏺️ ⏺️ licensed 🏛 ⚹ (Braille guide, photograph albums) toilets for disabled ⊗ (ex guide dogs or in park) 🐾

QUAINTON　　　　　　MAP 04 SP72

Buckinghamshire Railway Centre
Quainton Rd Station HP22 4BY
➲ (Signed off A41 Aylesbury-Bicester road at
Waddesdon, 7m NW of Aylesbury)
☎ 01296 655720
e-mail: bucksrailcentre@btopenworld.com
web: www.bucksrailcentre.org

Housed in a former Grade II listed building, the Centre features an
interesting and varied collection of about 20 locomotives with 40
carriages and wagons from places as far afield as South Africa, Egypt
and America. Items date from the 1800s up to the 1960s. Visitors can
take a ride on full-size and miniature steam trains, and stroll around
the 20-acre site to see locomotives and rolling stock. The Centre runs
locomotive driving courses for visitors. Regular 'Days out with Thomas'
events take place throughout the year.

Times: Open with engines in steam Apr-Oct, Sun & BH Mon; School hol
Wed; 10.30-5.30. Dec Sat & Sun Santa's Magical Steamings-advanced
booking essential. Also open for static viewing Wed-Sat. **Facilities:** ● �
& (ramped bridge with wheelchair lift) toilets for disabled shop ■

STOWE　　　　　　MAP 04 SP63

Stowe House
MK18 5EH
➲ (3m NW Buckingham)
☎ 01280 818229
e-mail: amcevoy@stowe.co.uk
web: www.stowe.co.uk

Set in the National Trust's landscaped gardens, Stowe is a splendid
18th-century mansion. The leading designers of the day were called in
to lay out the gardens, and leading architects - Vanbrugh, Gibbs, Kent
and Leoni - commissioned to decorate them with garden temples. The
house is now a major public school.

Times: Open various dates & times. Call information line 01280 818166 or
check website. **Fee:** £3 (ch £1.50). Guided tours £4 (ch £2.50).
Facilities: ● ▨ ▦ & toilets for disabled shop ⊗ (ex guide dogs)

Stowe Landscape Gardens
MK18 5EH
➲ (3m NW of Buckingham via Stoke Ave, off A422)
☎ 01280 822850
e-mail: stowegarden@nationaltrust.org.uk
web: www.nationaltrust.org.uk

Stowe is a breathtaking 18th century creation, an idealised version of
nature and is one of the first and foremost of the great English
landscape gardens. Hidden amongst spectacular views and vast open
spaces there are over 40 monuments, temples and secret corners to
be discovered.

Times: Open all year early Mar-Oct, Wed-Sun, 10.30-5.30, (last admission
4); Nov-Feb, Sat-Sun 10.30-4. Open BHs. **Fee:** ✱ £6 (ch £3). Family ticket
£15 **Facilities:** ● ▧ licensed ▦ & (manual wheelchairs unsuitable,
powered batricars) toilets for disabled shop garden centre ⧓ ■

WADDESDON　　　　　　MAP 04 SP71

Waddesdon Manor
HP18 0JH
➲ (entrance off A41, 6m NW of Aylesbury)
☎ 01296 653211, 653226 & 653203
e-mail: waddesdonmanor@nationaltrust.org.uk
web: www.waddesdon.org.uk

Built in the 19th century by Baron Ferdinand de Rothschild, this
French-style chateau was created as a showcase for his fine collection
of French decorative arts. Its Victorian gardens are known for its
parterre, seasonal displays, walks, views, fountains and statues. The
aviary is stocked with species that were once part of Baron Ferdinand's
collection and the wine cellar contains Rothschild wines dating back to
1868. Special Events: Please telephone 01296 653226 for details of
events running throughout the year.

Times: Gardens: 29 Mar-23 Dec, Wed-Sun & BH Mons 10-5. Open
18-19 Dec. 7 Jan-26 Mar wknds only. House: 29 Mar-29 Oct, Wed-Sun & BH
Mons 11-4. (East Wing for Xmas 15 Nov-23 Dec Wed-Sun & 18-19 Dec
12-4). **Fee:** ✱ House & Gardens £12 (ch £8.50), pre-Xmas £9 (ch £4.50).
Gardens £5 (ch £2.50). Bachelors Wing £3. (Under 5's free.)
Facilities: ● ▧ licensed & (wheelchairs, Braille guide, parking, scented
plants) toilets for disabled shop ⊗ (ex guide dogs) ⧓ ■

WEST WYCOMBE　　　　　　MAP 04 SU89

The Hell-Fire Caves　　［2 for 1］
HP14 3AJ
➲ (on A40 in West Wycombe)
☎ 01494 524411 (office) & 533739 (caves)
e-mail: mary@west-wycombe-estate.co.uk
web: www.hellfirecaves.co.uk

The entrance to West Wycombe caves is halfway up the hill that
dominates the village. On the summit stands the parish church and
the mausoleum of the Dashwood family. The caves are not natural but
were dug on the orders of Sir Francis Dashwood between 1748 and
1752. Sir Francis, the Chancellor of the Exchequer, was also the
founder of the Hell Fire Club, whose members were reputed to have
held outrageous and blasphemous parties in the caves, which extend
approximately half a mile underground. The entrance, from a large
forecourt, is a brick tunnel that leads into the caves, where tableaux
and curiosities are exhibited.

Times: Open all year, Apr-Oct, daily 11-6; Nov-Mar, Sat & Sun 1-5.
Fee: ✱ £4 (ch, concessions £3). Family ticket £12 (max 3 ch)
Facilities: ● ▧ ▦ & toilets for disabled shop ⊗ (ex guide dogs) ■

WING　　　　　　MAP 04 SP82

Ascott
LU7 0PS
➲ (0.5m E of Wing, 3m SW of Leighton Buzzard on S
side of A418)
☎ 01296 688242
e-mail: info@ascottestate.co.uk
web: www.ascottestate.com

A National Trust property since 1949, Ascott holds an exceptional
collection of paintings, Chinese porcelain and English and French
furniture. The 30-acre garden is a fine example of Victorian gardening
and the grounds are stunning at any time of year.

Times: House & Gardens: 27 Mar-30 Apr daily (ex Mon), May-26 Jul Tue-
Thu, 31Jul-14 Sep daily (ex Mon). Open BH Mons. **Fee:** House & Garden
£8 (ch £4). Gardens only: £4 (ch £2). **Facilities:** ● & (w/chairs avail,
assistance required, large print guide) toilets for disabled ⊗ ⧓

Cambridgeshire

Knot Gardens at Elton Hall,
Elton

Many visitors concentrate solely on the City of Cambridge, with its ancient colleges and rich history,
miss out on all that the county has to offer. There are many country houses with beautiful gardens,
the Gog Magog hills, miles of canal, the Rivers Nene and Ouse, and thousands of miles of public
paths, not to mention around a thousand acres of reclaimed fenland that is now a nature reserve.

England

CAMBRIDGE MAP 05 TL45

Cambridge & County Folk Museum

2/3 Castle St CB3 0AQ

⮑ (off A14 onto A3019, museum NW of town)

☎ 01223 355159

e-mail: info@folkmuseum.org.uk

web: www.folkmuseum.org.uk

This timber-framed inn houses items covering the everyday life of the people of Cambridgeshire from the early times to the present day. There are also temporary exhibitions. Special exhibitions and children's activity days take place throughout the year. Please telephone for details.

Times: Open all year, Apr-Sep, Mon-Sat 10.30-5, Sun 2-5. Oct-Mar, Tue-Sat 10.30-5, Sun 2-5. (Last admissions 30 mins before closing). Closed 1 Jan, Good Fri, 24-31 Dec **Fee:** ✱ £3 (ch 5-12 £1, concessions £2) one free ch with every full paying adult. **Facilities:** ℗ (300yds) (pay and display on street parking) ▦ ⅋ (Braille touch tables, tape guides & large print guides) toilets for disabled shop ⊗ (ex guide dogs)

Cambridge University Botanic Garden

Cory Lodge, Bateman St CB2 1JF

⮑ (1m S of city centre)

☎ 01223 336265

e-mail: enquiries@botanic.cam.ac.uk

web: www.botanic.cam.ac.uk

The Cambridge University Botanic Garden is a 40-acre oasis of beautifully landscaped gardens and glasshouses close to the heart of the historic city. Opened on its present site in 1846, the garden showcases a collection of some 8000 plant species. This Grade II heritage landscape features the Rock Garden, displaying alpine plants, the Winter and Autumn Gardens, tropical rainforest and seasonal displays in the Glasshouses, the historic Systematic Beds, the Scented Garden, Herbaceous Beds and the finest collection of trees in the east of England.

Times: Open all year daily Apr-Sep 10-6; Feb-Mar, Oct 10-5; Nov-Jan 10-4. Glasshouses close 30mins before garden. Please call to check Christmas closure. Entry by Bateman St & Station Rd gates on wkdays & by Bateman St gate only at wknds & BH. **Fee:** £3 (concessions £2.50). **Facilities:** ℗ (on street parking or park & ride) ➽ ⅋ (guiding service, manual & motorised wheelchairs-prebooked) toilets for disabled shop (open Mar-Oct) ⊗ (ex guide dogs)

Fitzwilliam Museum `FREE`

Trumpington St CB2 1RB

⮑ (M11 junct 11, 12 or 13. Near city centre)

☎ 01223 332900

e-mail: fitzmuseum-enquiries@lists.cam.ac.uk

web: www.fitzmuseum.cam.ac.uk

The Fitzwilliam is the art museum of the University of Cambridge and one of the oldest public museums in Britain. It contains magnificent collections spanning centuries and civilisations including antiquities from Ancient Egypt, Greece and Rome; sculpture, furniture, armour, ceramics; manuscripts, coins and medals, paintings, drawings and prints.

Times: Open all year Tue-Sat 10-5, Sun 12-5. (Closed Mon ex BH, & 24-26, 31 Dec & 1 Jan). **Facilities:** ℗ (400yds) (2hr max, metered) ➽ ⅋ (induction loop) toilets for disabled shop ⊗ (ex assist dogs)

Scott Polar Research Institute Museum

Lensfield Rd CB2 1ER

⮑ (1km S of City Centre)

☎ 01223 336540

e-mail: enquiries@spri.cam.ac.uk

web: www.spri.cam.ac.uk

An international centre for polar studies, including a museum featuring displays of Arctic and Antarctic expeditions, with special emphasis on those of Captain Scott and the exploration of the Northwest Passage. Other exhibits include Eskimo work and other arts of the polar regions, as well as displays on current scientific exploration. Public lectures run from October to December and February to April.

Times: Open all year, Tue-Sat 2.30-4. Closed some BHs wknds, public & university hols. **Facilities:** ℗ (400mtrs) ⅋ shop ⊗ (ex guide dogs)

University Museum of Archaeology & Anthropology `FREE`

Downing St CB2 3DZ

⮑ (located opposite Crowne Plaza Hotel in city centre)

☎ 01223 333516

e-mail: cumaa@hermes.cam.ac.uk

web: http://museum.archanth.cam.ac.uk

The museum is part of the Faculty of Archaeology and Anthropology of the University of Cambridge. It was established in 1884 and is still housed in its 1916 building on the Downing Site in the city centre. Some of the highlights are Pacific material collected on Captain Cook's voyages of exploration and a 46-foot high totem pole from Canada. Find out about local, national and world archaeology in the Archaeology Galleries, including painted pottery from Peru, giled Anglo-Saxon brooches, and Roman altar stones.

Times: Open all year Tue-Sat 2-4.30. (Closed 1wk Etr & 1wk Xmas). Telephone for extended summer hours. **Facilities:** ℗ (100yds) ▦ ⅋ (lift available) shop ⊗ (ex guide dogs)

DUXFORD MAP 05 TL44

Imperial War Museum Duxford

CB2 4QR

⮑ (off M11 junct 10, on A505)

☎ 01223 835000

e-mail: duxford@iwm.org.uk

web: www.iwm.org.uk

Duxford is one of the world's most spectacular aviation heritage complexes with a collection of nearly 200 aircraft, the American Air Museum and a fine collection of military vehicles plus special exhibitions including The Battle of Britain, Normandy Experience and Monty. The Museum holds four Air Shows throughout the summer plus other special events such as the Military Vehicle Show and Flying Proms.

Times: Open all year, mid Mar-mid Oct daily 10-6; mid Oct-mid Mar daily 10-4. (Closed 24-26 Dec) **Fee:** ✱ £13 (pen £11 & concessions £8). (Ch under 16yrs free) Different rates apply for air shows. **Facilities:** ❷ ➽ ⅋⊙⅋ licensed ▦ ⅋ (w/chair available-phone in advance, ramps) toilets for disabled shop ⊗ (ex guide dogs)

England

ELY
MAP 05 TL58

Ely Cathedral

CB7 4DL

➲ (A10 or A142, 15m from Cambridge)

☎ 01353 667735

e-mail: receptionist@cathedral.ely.anglican.org

web: www.cathedral.ely.anglican.org

The Octagon Tower of Ely Cathedral can be seen for miles as it rises above the surrounding flat fenland. A monastery was founded on the site by St Etheldreda in 673, but the present cathedral church dates from 1083 and is a magnificent example of Romanesque architecture.

Times: Open daily, Summer 7-7, Winter 7.30-6 (5pm Sun). **Fee:** £5.20 (ch free in family group) (concessions £4.50). Group reductions (15+)
Facilities: ℗ (walking distance) 💷 🍴 licensed 🏛 ♿ (touch tour for blind/partially sighted) toilets for disabled shop ⊗ (ex assist dogs) ➟

Ely Museum NEW
The Old Gaol, Market St CB7 4LS

➲ (On corner of Market St and Lynn Rd. In centre of Ely, 250mtrs from west door of Ely Cathedral)

☎ 01353 666655

e-mail: admin@elymuseum.org.uk

web: www.elymuseum.org.uk

Centre of history for the Isle of Ely and the Fens, telling the story of the area from prehistoric times to the twentieth century. The museum is within a building dating from the 13th century that has been a private house, a tavern, a registry office and most famously the Bishop's Gaol. Sensitively renovated in 1997 much of the building's history can still be seen, including prisoner's graffiti, hidden doorways and original planking on the walls.

Times: Open during summer, Mon-Sat 10.30-5 & Sun 1-5. **Fee:** ✱ £3 (concessions £2.50) **Facilities:** ℗ ♿ toilets for disabled shop

Oliver Cromwell's House
2 for 1
29 St Mary's St CB7 4HF

➲ (follow brown tourist signs from main roads. Adjacent to Saint Mary's Church)

☎ 01353 662062

e-mail: tic@eastcambs.gov.uk

web: www.eastcambs.gov.uk/tourism

Cromwell inherited the house and local estates from a maternal uncle and moved here in 1636, along with his mother, sisters, wife and eight children. There are displays and period rooms dealing with Cromwell's life, the Civil War and domestic life in the 17th century, as well as the history of The Fens and the house itself, from its medieval origins to its role as an inn in the 19th century.

Times: Open all year: Apr-Oct, daily 10-5.30; Nov-Mar, Mon-Fri 11-4, Sat 10-5. Sun, 11.15-4. **Fee:** ✱ £3.95 (ch £2.70, concessions £3.45). Family ticket £11. **Facilities:** ℗ (100yds) ♿ shop ⊗ (ex guide dogs) ➟

The Stained Glass Museum
2 for 1
The South Triforium, Ely Catherdral CB7 4DL

➲ (15m N of Cambridge via A10, located inside Ely Cathedral)

☎ 01353 660347

e-mail: curator@stainedglassmuseum.com

web: www.stainedglassmuseum.com

Nine hundred years of stained glass history are illustrated in this unique museum inside Ely Cathedral. Over 100 panels of original stained glass windows rescued from the UK and abroad are on display. The medieval section includes important loans from the Victoria and Albert Museum in London. There are also exhibits from Buckingham Palace and Windsor Castle and work by William Morris and John Piper.

Times: Open all year, Etr-Oct daily Mon-Fri 10.30-5, Sat 10.30-5.30, Sun 12-6. Nov-Etr daily Mon-Fri 10.30-5, Sat 10.30-5, Sun 12-4.30 **Fee:** £3.50 (ch under 16yrs, concessions £2.50). Family ticket (up to 4 with 1 under 16yrs) £7 **Facilities:** ℗ (400yds) 💷 🍴 🏛 ♿ (Interactive video visit) toilets for disabled shop ⊗ (ex guide dogs) ➟

HAMERTON
MAP 04 TL17

Hamerton Zoo Park
PE28 5RE

➲ (off A1 junct 15, signed Sawtry)

☎ 01832 293362

e-mail: office@hamertonzoopark.com

web: www.hamertonzoopark.com

A wildlife breeding centre, dedicated to the practical conservation of endangered species including gibbons, marmosets, lemurs, wildcats, meerkats, sloths and many more. There is also a large and varied bird collection, with several species unique to Hamerton. Over 120 species in all. Other attractions include a children's play area, and new "creature contact" sessions.

Times: ✱ Open Summer daily 10.30-6; Winter daily 10.30-4. Closed 25 Dec
Facilities: ℗ 💷 ♿ toilets for disabled shop ⊗ ➟

LINTON
MAP 05 TL54

Chilford Hall Vineyard
Chilford Hall, Balsham Rd CB1 6LE

➲ (signposted from A1307 and A11)

☎ 01223 895600

e-mail: annette@chilfordhall.co.uk

web: www.chilfordhall.co.uk

Taste and buy award-winning wines from the largest vineyard in Cambridgeshire. See the grapes growing in the 18-acre vineyard and take a winery tour to learn how English wine is made and appreciate the subtle difference between each of the Chilford quality wines. Telephone for details of special events.

Times: Open Mar-Oct , Fri-Sun & BHs **Fee:** Guided tours £6.50 (ch free). Party 15+. Includes wine to taste & tour of the vineyards. **Facilities:** ℗ 💷 ♿ (ramps, lift, all areas are ground floor) toilets for disabled shop (11-4.30) ➟

England

Linton Zoological Gardens
Hadstock Rd CB1 6NT
➲ *(M11 junct 9/10, on B1052 off A1307 between Cambridge & Haverhill, signposted)*
☎ 01223 891308
web: www.lintonzoo.co.uk

Linton Zoo places emphasis on conservation and education where visitors can see a combination of beautiful gardens and a wealth of wildlife from all over the world. There are many rare and exotic creatures to see including tapirs, snow leopards, tigers, lions, zebra, tamarin monkeys, lemurs, owls, parrots, giant tortoises, snakes, tarantula spiders and many others. The zoo is set in 16-acres of gardens with plenty of picnic areas, children's play area and bouncy castle.

Times: Open all year, daily 10.30-4 (last admission 3). Hours extended during summer. Closed 25-26 Dec. **Fee:** ✱ £7 (ch 2-13 £4.50, concessions £6.50) **Facilities:** ❷ 💻 & toilets for disabled shop ⊗ ◼

LODE   MAP 05 TL56

Anglesey Abbey
CB5 9EJ
➲ *(6m NE of Cambridge on B1102, signposted from A14)*
☎ 01223 810080
e-mail: angleseyabbey@ntrust.org.uk
web: www.nationaltrust.org.uk/angleseyabbey

A medieval undercroft has survived from the priory founded here in 1135, but the house dates mainly from 1600. Thomas Hobson of *Hobson's Choice* was one of the owners. A later owner was Lord Fairhaven, who amassed the huge collection of pictures, and laid out the beautiful gardens.

Times: Open House & Mill: 22 Mar-29-Oct, Wed-Sun & BH Mon's, 1-5. Gardens open 10.30-5.30 and winter 11 Nov-18 Mar, Wed-Sun, 10.30-4.30. (Closed 23-30 Dec). **Fee:** ✱ House and garden £8. Garden only £4.50 (£4 in winter). Family & party discounts available. **Facilities:** ❷ ⵏ licensed 🍴 & (electric buggy, wheelchairs, large print & braille guides) toilets for disabled shop garden centre ⊗ (ex guide dogs) ⵧ◼

PETERBOROUGH   MAP 04 TL19

Flag Fen Bronze Age Centre
The Droveway, Northey Rd PE6 7QJ
➲ *(Join A1139, exit at Boongate junct. At rdbt 3rd exit, through lights and turn right. At t-junct turn right, Flag Fen is signed)*
☎ 01733 313414
e-mail: office@flagfen.freeserve.co.uk
web: www.flagfen.com

Although visitors enter this site through a 21st-century roundhouse, the rest of their day will be spent in the Bronze Age, some 3,000 years ago. Flag Fens Museum contains artefacts found over the last 20 years of excavating on site, and includes among them the oldest wheel in Britain. In the Park there is a reconstructed Bronze Age settlement and Iron Age roundhouse, while in the Preservation Hall visitors can see the excavated Bronze Age processional way that spanned over one mile. The Hall also contains a 60-ft mural depicting the fens in ancient times.

Times: Open daily Oct-Mar 10-4 (last admission 3), Apr-Sep 10-5 (last admission 4). Closed 24 Dec-2 Jan **Fee:** ✱ £4.75 (pen £4.25, ch & students £3.50). Family £13. **Facilities:** ❷ 💻 🍴 & toilets for disabled shop ⊗ (ex guide dogs) ◼

Longthorpe Tower
Thorpe Rd, Longthorpe PE1 1HA
☎ 01733 268482
web: www.english-heritage.org.uk

See the finest domestic wall paintings in northern Europe hidden in the tower for centuries until revealed by a World War II bomb.

Times: Open May-Aug, pre-booked guided tours only tel: 01799 522842. **Fee:** £2.40 (ch £1.20, concessions £1.80). Prices and opening times are subject to change in Spring 2007. Please check web site or call 0870 333 1181 for the most up to date prices and opening times when planning your visit. **Facilities:** ❷ ⊗ ♿

Peterborough Cathedral
PE1 1XS
➲ *(access from A1 junct with A605 or A47, follow signs for city centre)*
☎ 01733 343342 & 355300
e-mail: a.watson@peterborough-cathedral.org.uk
web: www.peterborough-cathedral.org.uk

With one of the most dramatic West fronts in the country, its three arches an extraordinary creation of medieval architecture, it would be easy for the interior to be an anticlimax, but it is not. The dramatic Romanesque interior is little altered since its completion 800 years ago. Particular highlights of a visit include the unique painted nave ceiling, the elaborate fan vaulting of the 'new' building, Saxon carvings from an earlier church and the burial place of two Queens. An exhibition in the North aisle tells the story of the cathedral. A range of tours can be booked in advance: please contact the Chapter office for details.

Times: Open all year, Mon-Fri 9-6.30 (ltd access from 5.30), Sat 9-5, Sun services from 7.30 visitors from 12. (Closed 25-26 Dec). **Fee:** ✱ No fixed charge, donations towards the cost of upkeep are requested but £3.50 charge for group tours (£2.50 for concessions). **Facilities:** ❷ (300yds) (no parking within cathedral precincts) 💻 ⵏ licensed 🍴 & (touch & hearing centre, Braille guide, ramps) toilets for disabled shop ⊗ (ex guide dogs or in grounds)

Railworld   2 for 1
Oundle Rd PE2 9NR
➲ *(from A1(M) Peterborough, turn onto A1139 then off at junct 5 to city centre. At 1st rdbt, follow "Little Puffer" tourist signs. Entrance for Railworld is off Oundle Rd at city end through car park)*
☎ 01733 344240 & 319362
e-mail: railworld@aol.com
web: www.railworld.net

An exhibition centre and museum dedicated to all things rail related, especially the environment. Attractions include model railways, hands on exhibits, a rail industry showcase, hover-trains, local rail history gallery and a car.

Times: Mar-Oct daily 11-4, Nov-Feb Mon-Fri 11-4 **Fee:** £5 (ch £2.50, concessions £4). Family £13 (up to 4 ch). **Facilities:** ❷ 💻 🍴 & (reasonable access) toilets for disabled shop ⊗ (ex guide dogs & outside) ◼

England

RAMSEY   MAP 04 TL28

Ramsey Abbey Gatehouse   FREE
Abbey School PE17 1DH
➲ *(SE edge of Ramsey, where Chatteris Road joins B1096)*
☎ 0870 609 5388
web: www.nationaltrust.org.uk/regions/eastanglia
The ruins of this 15th-century gatehouse, together with the 13th-century Lady Chapel, are all that remain of the abbey. Half of the gatehouse was taken away after the Dissolution. Built in ornate late-Gothic style, it has panelled buttresses and friezes.
Times: Open Apr-Oct, daily 10-5. **Facilities:** ⊛ ❧

THORNHAUGH   MAP 04 TL00

Sacrewell Farm & Country Centre NEW
PE8 6HJ
➲ *(E of A1/A47 intersection. Brown tourist signs from both directions)*
☎ 01780 782254
e-mail: info@sacrewell.fsnet.co.uk
web: www.sacrewell.org.uk
Treasures of farming and the country await discovery at this farm and 18th century watermill. All aspects of agriculture and country life through the ages are here, listed buildings, working watermill, mill house and farm bygones. Farm animals, tractor rides, mini maze and pedal tractors are just a few of the activities to be experienced.
Times: Open all year daily Mar-Sep, 9.30-5; Oct-Feb 10-4. (Closed 24 Dec-2 Jan). **Fee:** ✱ £5.25 (ch £3.75, concessions £4.25) Family ticket £15. **Facilities:** ❾ ☞ ⅍ (upstairs in watermill not accessible) shop ◼

WANSFORD   MAP 04 TL09

Nene Valley Railway
Wansford Station, Stibbington PE8 6LR
➲ *(A1 at Stibbington, W of Peterborough, 1m south of the A47 junct)*
☎ 01780 784444
e-mail: nvrorg@aol.com
web: www.nvr.org.uk
Originally opened as a working railway in 1845, closed in 1966, then re-opened in 1977 as a tourist railway, Nene Valley Railway has steam and diesel engines, carriages and wagons from Europe including the UK. All the sights and sounds of the golden age of steam come alive here. Travelling between Yarwell Junction, Wansford and Peterborough the 7.5 miles of track pass through the heart of the 500-acre Ferry Meadows Country Park. Nene Valley Railway is also the home of 'Thomas'- children's favourite engine.
Times: ✱ Train services operate on Sun from Jan; wknds from Apr-Oct; Wed from May, plus other mid-week services in summer. **Fee:** £10.50 (ch 3-15 £5.50, concessions £8). Family ticket £26. **Facilities:** ❾ ☞ ⅍ (disabled access to trains) toilets for disabled shop ◼

WATERBEACH   MAP 05 TL46

The Farmland Museum and   2 for 1
Denny Abbey
Ely Rd CB5 9PQ
➲ *(on A10 between Cambridge and Ely)*
☎ 01223 860988
e-mail: f.m.denny@tesco.net
web: www.dennyfarmlandmuseum.org.uk
Explore two areas of rural life at this fascinating museum. The Abbey tells the story of those who have lived there, including Benedictine monks, Franciscan nuns, and the mysterious Knights Templar. The farm museum features the craft workshops of a wheelwright, a basketmaker, and a blacksmith. There is also a 1940s farmworker's cottage and a village shop. Special events on Easter, May and August Bank Holidays.
Times: Open daily Apr-Oct, noon-5 **Fee:** £3.90 (ch £1.70, concessions £3) **Facilities:** ❾ ☞ 𝄞 ⅍ (wheelchairs) toilets for disabled shop ◼

WIMPOLE   MAP 05 TL35

Wimpole Hall
SG8 0BW
➲ *(M11 junct 12, 8m SW of Cambridge off A603)*
☎ 01223 206000
e-mail: wimpolehall@nationaltrust.org.uk
web: www.wimpole.org
Wimpole Hall is one of the grandest mansions in East Anglia, and has 360 acres of parkland devised and planted by no less than four celebrated landscape designers, Charles Bridgeman, 'Capability' Brown, Sanderson Miller and Humphrey Repton. The house dates back to 1640, but was altered into a large 18th-century mansion with a Georgian façade. The chapel has a trompe l'oeil ceiling.
Times: Open Mar-Oct, Sat-Wed, BH Mon & Good Fri, 1-5; Aug Sat-Thu, BH Mon 11-5; Nov, Sun only 1-4. **Fee:** £7.50 (ch £4). **Facilities:** ❾ ☞ ❍ licensed 𝄞 ⅍ (Braille & large print guide, buggies, stairlift, w/chair) toilets for disabled shop ⊗ (ex in park) ❧ ◼

Wimpole Home Farm
SG8 0BW
➲ *(M11 junct 12 8m SW of Cambridge off A603)*
☎ 01223 206000
e-mail: wimpolehall@nationaltrust.org.uk
web: www.wimpole.org
When built in 1794, the Home Farm was one of the most advanced agricultural enterprises in the country. The Great Barn, now restored, holds a display of farm machinery and implements of the kind used at Wimpole over the past two centuries. On the farm there are rare breeds of domestic animals, and visitors can see the new lambs in spring, and sheep shearing in June. Please ring for details of special events.
Times: Open Mar-Oct, Sat-Wed, Good Fri & BH Mon's 10.30-5; Aug, Sat-Thu 10.30-5; Nov-Mar, Sat & Sun 11-4. (Open daily Cambridge Etr hols & Oct/Feb half terms) **Fee:** ✱ £6 (ch £4). NT members £3 (ch £2). **Facilities:** ❾ ☞ ❍ licensed 𝄞 ⅍ (Large print guide, wheelchairs, electric buggies) toilets for disabled shop ⊗ (ex guide dogs) ❧ ◼

England

WISBECH   MAP 09 TF40

Peckover House & Garden   2 for 1
North Brink PE13 1JR

➲ *(Leave A47 & take town centre signs, then follow brown signs)*

☎ 01945 583463

e-mail: peckover@nationaltrust.org.uk

web: www.peckoverhouse.co.uk

Dating from 1722, Peckover House is a beautiful Georgian brick townhouse with a two-acre walled town garden, one of the finest such gardens in Britain and home to over 70 types of rose. The Victorian glasshouses include a fern house, and an orangery with 300-year-old trees that still bear fruit. Visitors can borrow a croquet set and play on the lawn. Lots of special events each year, ring for details.

Times: Open, mid Mar-mid Nov, Sat-Sun & Tue-Wed, noon-5 **Fee:** ✱ £5 (ch £2.50), family ticket £12.50 **Facilities:** Ⓟ (400yds) 💭 🍽 licensed 🔥 (Batricar, induction loops, large print & Braille guides) toilets for disabled shop 🚫 (ex guide dogs) 🍴🥃

WOODHURST   MAP 05 TL37

The Raptor Foundation   2 for 1
The Heath, St Ives Rd PE28 3BT

➲ *(B1040 to Somersham, follow brown signs)*

☎ 01487 741140

e-mail: heleowl@aol.com

web: www.raptorfoundation.org.uk

Permanent home to over 250 birds of which there are 40 different varieties. This is a unique opportunity to meet and learn about birds of prey. Depending on weather and time of year flying demonstrations are held, usually three times a day and audiences have the chance to participate in displays. There are nearly 60 birds in the flying team, so each display has a different set of birds. Educational trail linking to new education room. 2006 was the tenth anniversary of The Raptor Foundation.

Times: Open all year, daily 10-5. Closed 25-26 Dec & 1 Jan. **Fee:** ✱ £4 (ch £2.50 ages 2-5 £1, concessions £3) **Facilities:** Ⓟ 💭 🍽 🔥 (ramped areas) toilets for disabled shop 🚫 🥃

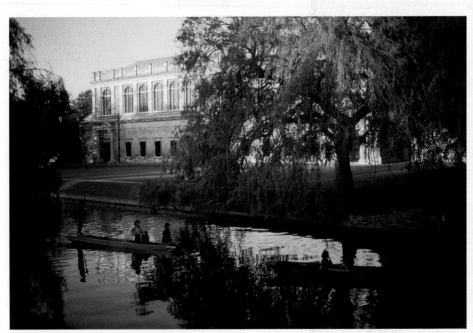

Boats punting past the Wren Library, Trinity College, Cambridge

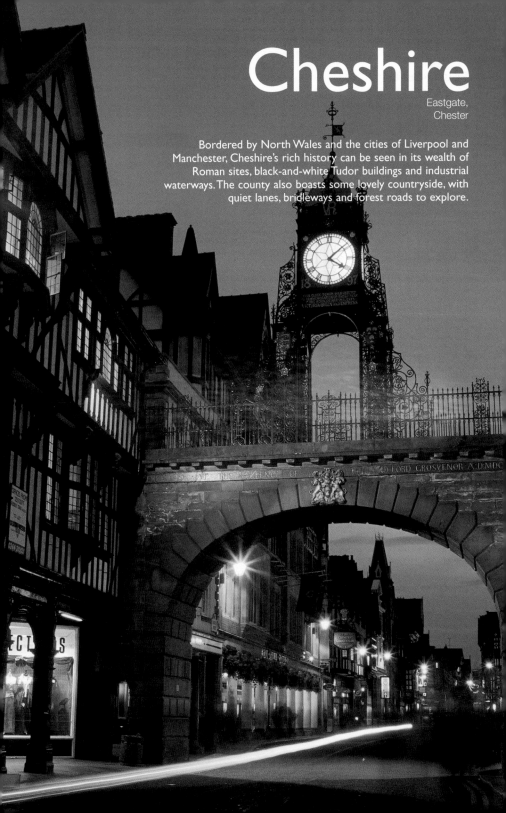

Cheshire

Eastgate,
Chester

Bordered by North Wales and the cities of Liverpool and
Manchester, Cheshire's rich history can be seen in its wealth of
Roman sites, black-and-white Tudor buildings and industrial
waterways. The county also boasts some lovely countryside, with
quiet lanes, bridleways and forest roads to explore.

England

BEESTON

MAP 07 SJ55

Beeston Castle

Tarporley CW6 9TX
➲ (on minor road off A49 or A41)
☎ 01829 260464
web: www.english-heritage.org.uk

Legend tells of a vast treasure hidden here by Richard II, but the real treasure at Beeston lies in its 4,000 years of history waiting to be discovered. Breathtaking views extend from the Pennines to the mountains of Wales.

Times: Open all year, Apr-Sep, daily 10-6; Oct-Mar, Thu-Mon 10-4. Closed 24-26 Dec & 1 Jan. **Fee:** £4 (ch £2, concessions £3). Prices and opening times are subject to change in Spring 2007. Please check web site or call 0870 333 1181 for the most up to date prices and opening times when planning your visit. **Facilities:** ℗ shop ⊗ (in certain areas) ♯

CAPESTHORNE

MAP 07 SJ87

Capesthorne Hall

SK11 9JY
➲ (On A34 between Congleton and Wilmslow)
☎ 01625 861221
e-mail: info@capesthorne.com
web: www.capesthorne.com

Capesthorne has been the home of the Bromley-Davenport family and their ancestors since Domesday times. The present house dates from 1719 and was designed by the Smiths of Warwick. It was subsequently altered by Edward Blore in 1837 and after a disastrous fire in 1861 the whole of the centre portion was rebuilt by Anthony Salvin. Capesthorne contains a great variety of sculptures, paintings and other items including a collection of boxes, from a Victorian oak letterbox to hat and cigar boxes.

Times: Open Apr-Oct, Sun & Mon (inc BH) Closed Xmas & New Year. Park & Garden 12-5.30, Hall 1.30-3.30 **Fee:** Park, Garden & Chapel £4 (ch £2). Park, Gardens, Chapel & Hall £6.50 (ch £3 & concessions £5.50). Family ticket £15. Special deal on Mon's £10 per car (up to 4 persons). Coach £50, Mini-bus £25 **Facilities:** ℗ ♨ †◯† licensed ▥ ♿ (ramp access to ground floor of hall & gardens) toilets for disabled ⊗ (ex guide dogs & in gardens)

CHESTER

MAP 07 SJ46

Cheshire Military Museum

The Castle CH1 2DN
➲ (follow signs to Military Museum from town centre)
☎ 01244 327617
web: www.chester.ac.uk/militarymuseum

This military museum boasts exhibits from the history of the Cheshire Regiment, Cheshire Yeomanry, 5th Royal Inniskilling Dragoon Guards, and 3rd Carabiniers. Display of the work of George Jones, Victorian battle artist, and an exhibition of life in barracks in the 1950s. Research available by written appointment and donation. There are special events throughtout the year, please phone for details.

Times: Open all year, daily 10-5 (last entry 4). (Closed 22 Dec-3 Jan). **Fee:** £2 (concessions £1). **Facilities:** ℗ (400yds) ▥ ♿ (wheelchair accessible) toilets for disabled shop ⊗ (ex guide dogs)

Chester Cathedral

Saint Werburgh St CH1 2HU
➲ (opposite the town hall)
☎ 01244 324756
e-mail: office@chestercathedral.com
web: www.chestercathedral.com

Founded as a Benedictine monastery in 1092 on the sites of earlier churches, in 1541 it became the cathedral of the newly created Diocese of Chester and is a good example of a medieval monastic complex. Restored in the 19th century, the building contains work by Gilbert Scott, Clayton, Pugin and Kempe. There are daily services and visitors are welcome to join in. A summer music festival is held in July.

Times: Open Mon-Sat, 9-5, Sun 1-5, Please telephone to check. **Fee:** ✱ £4 (concessions & groups 10+ £3, ch 5-16 £1.50). Family ticket £10 **Facilities:** ℗ (200yds) (multi-storey) ♨ †◯† licensed ♿ (induction loop, tactile model, wide doors) toilets for disabled shop ⊗ (ex guide dogs) ◼

Chester Visitor Centre

FREE

Vicars Ln CH1 1QX
➲ (opposite St Johns Church Roman Amphitheatre on Vicars Lane.)
☎ 01244 351609
e-mail: tis@chestercc.gov.uk
web: www.chestertourism.com

Among the attractions at this large visitor information centre are guided walks of Chester; World of Names, which explores the history of family and first names; displays on the history of Chester; a café and a gift shop. Chester is the most complete walled city in Britain, and was originally settled by the Romans in the first century AD. The city also played its part in battles with the Vikings, the Norman invasion, and the Civil War.

Times: Open all year, Mon-Sat 10-5, Sun 10-4 **Facilities:** ℗ (200mtrs) (short stay) ♨ ♿ (ramped access from Vicars Lane) toilets for disabled shop

Chester Zoo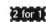

Upton-by-Chester CH2 1LH

➲ *(2m N of city centre off A41& M53 junct 10 southbound, junct 12 all other directions)*

☎ 01244 380280

e-mail: marketing@chesterzoo.co.uk

web: www.chesterzoo.org

The largest zoological gardens in the UK, with more than 7000 animals of more than 500 species. Catch feeding time on Sealion Beach, visit Islands in Danger with the Komodo Dragons, feel the Spirit of the Jaguar and the awesome Tsavo-the Black Rhino Experience. Take to the treetops in the Zoofari overhead railway.

Times: Open all year, daily from 10. Last admission varies with season from 5.30pm high summer to 3.30pm winter. (Closed 25-26 Dec). **Fee:** ✱ £14.50 (ch £10.50). Family ticket £47.50 **Facilities:** ❷ ☛ ⁰ licensed ▦ & (electric scooters, audio guide, induction loop, Braille) toilets for disabled shop ⊗ (ex guide & sensory dogs) ◄

Dewa Roman Experience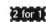

Pierpoint Ln, (off Bridge St) CH1 1NL

➲ *(city centre)*

☎ 01244 343407

e-mail: info@dewaromanexperience.co.uk

web: www.dewaromanexperience.co.uk

Stroll along reconstructed streets experiencing the sights, sounds and smells of Roman Chester. From the streets of Dewa (the Roman name for Chester) you return to the present day on an extensive archaeological 'dig', where you can discover the substantial Roman, Saxon and medieval remains beneath modern Chester. Roman soldier patrols available.

Times: Open all year, daily Feb-Nov 9-5, Dec-Jan 10-4 . (Closed 25-26 Dec & 1st Jan). **Fee:** ✱ £4.25 (ch £2.50, under 5's free, concessions £3.75). Family ticket £12. Party £3.25 (10 or more) **Facilities:** Ⓟ (200yds) ▦ & shop ⊗ (ex guide dogs)

CHOLMONDELEY   MAP 07 SJ55

Cholmondeley Castle Gardens

SY14 8AH

➲ *(off A49 Tarporley to Whitchurch road)*

☎ 01829 720383

e-mail: penny@cholmondeleycastle.co.uk

Dominated by a romantic Gothic Castle built in 1801 of local sandstone, the gardens are laid out with fine trees and water gardens, and have been replanted with rhododendrons, azaleas, cornus, and acer. There is also a rose and lavender garden, lakeside and woodland walks, and rare breeds of farm animals. The Duckery, a derelict 19th-century lakeside pleasure ground has recently been developed and restored. The castle is not open to the public.

Times: ✱ Open Apr-Sep, Wed-Thu, Sun & BHs 11.30-5. **Fee:** ✱ £4 (ch £1.50). **Facilities:** ❷ ☛ ▦ & (disabled car park, part of garden accessible) toilets for disabled shop garden centre

CONGLETON   MAP 07 SJ86

Little Moreton Hall

CW12 4SD

➲ *(4m SW of Congleton, on E side of A34)*

☎ 01260 272018

e-mail: littlemoretonhall@nationaltrust.org.uk

web: www.nationaltrust.org.uk

One of the best-known examples of moated, half-timbered architecture in England. By 1580 the house was much as it is today, and the long gallery, chapel and the great hall are very impressive. The garden has a knot garden, orchard and herbaceous borders. Wall paintings are also of some significant interest, and the manor house had a starring role in the recent movie adaptation of *Moll Flanders*. Ring for details of special events.

Times: Open 3-11 Mar, Sat & Sun 11.30-4; 17 Mar-4 Nov, Wed-Sun 11.30-5 (dusk if earlier); 10 Nov-16 Dec, Sat & Sun 11.30-4; BH 11.30-5 **Fee:** £5.80 (ch £3) Family ticket £13.50, Groups £5, Special Openings £10.50 **Facilities:** ❷ (charged) ⁰ licensed & (wheelchair, electric vehicle, Braille & large print guides) toilets for disabled shop ⊗ (ex guide & assistance dogs) ⁑ ◄

DISLEY   MAP 07 SJ98

Lyme Park

SK12 2NX

➲ *(off A6, 6.5m SE of Stockport. 12m NW of Buxton. House & car park 1m from entrance)*

☎ 01663 762023

e-mail: lymepark@nationaltrust.org.uk

web: www.nationaltrust.org.uk

Home of the Legh family for 600 years and the largest house in Cheshire, Lyme Park featured as Pemberley in the BBC's production of *Pride and Prejudice*. It also featured in Granada's production of *Forsyte Saga*. Parts of the original Elizabethan house remain, with 18th and 19th century additions. Set in extensive historic gardens with a lake and also a 1,400 acre park, home to red and fallow deer.

Times: ✱ Open daily Park: Apr-Oct, 8am-8.30pm; Nov-30 Mar, 8-6. Gardens: 31 Mar-30 Oct, Fri-Tue 11-5, Wed-Thu 1-5; 6 Nov-18 Dec, wknds 12-3. House: 21 Mar-30 Oct, Fri-Tue 1-5 (last admission 4.30), BH Mon 11-5. Cage: Apr-Oct, 2nd & 4th wknd of each month 12-4. Paddock Cottage Apr-Oct, 1st & 3rd wknd of each month, 1-4. **Facilities:** ❷ (charged) ☛ ⁰ licensed ▦ & (Braille guide, courtesy minibus from parking) toilets for disabled shop ⊗ (ex in park on lead) ⁑ ◄

England

England

Blue Planet Aquarium
Cheshire Oaks CH65 9LF
➲ (off M53 junct 10 at Cheshire Oaks. Follow signs for aquarium).
☎ 0151 357 8804
e-mail: info@blueplanetaquarium.co.uk
web: www.blueplanetaquarium.com

A voyage of discovery on the longest moving walkway in the world. Beneath the waters of the Carribean Reef, see giant rays and menacing sharks pass inches from your face, stroke some favourite fish in the special rock pools, or pay a visit to the incredible world of poisonous frogs. Divers hand feed the fish and sharks throughout the day and can answer questions via state of the art communication systems.

Times: Open all year, daily from 10. (Closed Xmas). Seasonal variations in closing times, please call to confirm. **Fee:** ✱ £9.95 (ch (3-15) £7.50, under 3's free, concessions £7.50). Family ticket from £34.
Facilities: ❷ ❢❢❢ licensed 🍴 ♿ (wheelchair hire, lifts, hearing loop) toilets for disabled shop ⊗ (ex guide dogs) ◀

Boat Museum   **2 for 1**
South Pier Rd CH65 4FW
➲ (M53 junct 9)
☎ 0151 355 5017
e-mail: bookings@thewaterwaystrust.org
web: www.boatmuseum.org.uk

Occupying a historic dock complex at the junction of the Shropshire Union and Manchester Ship Canals, this museum has the world's largest collection of floating canal craft, from a small weedcutter to a 300-ton coaster. Boat trips are also available. There are indoor exhibitions on canal life and local history, together with period worker's cottages, a blacksmith's forge and working engines.

Times: Open Summer daily 10-5. Winter daily 10-4. (Closed 25 & 26 Dec). **Fee:** ✱ £6.45 (ch £4.75, concessions £5.25). Family ticket £18.50, senior family ticket £17.75. **Facilities:** ❷ 🍴 ♿ (tactile map for blind, free wheelchair use) toilets for disabled shop ⊗ ex guide dogs ◀

Gawsworth Hall
SK11 9RN
➲ (2.5m S of Macclesfield on A536)
☎ 01260 223456
e-mail: enquiries@gawsworthhall.com
web: www.gawsworthhall.com

This fine Tudor black-and-white manor house was the birthplace of Mary Fitton, thought by some to be the 'Dark Lady' of Shakespeare's sonnets. Pictures and armour can be seen in the house, which also has a tilting ground - now thought to be a rare example of an Elizabethan pleasure garden. Watch out for open air theatre in July and August, and craft fairs in spring and autumn.

Times: Telephone for details. Flower Festival in Dec **Fee:** ✱ £6 (ch £3). Party 20+ £5 each. **Facilities:** ❷ 🍴 (disabled parking in front of house) shop ⊗ (guide dogs in garden only) ◀

Jodrell Bank Visitor Centre & Arboretum
SK11 9DL
➲ (M6 junct 18, A535 Holmes Chapel to Chelford road)
☎ 01477 571339
web: www.manchester.ac.uk/jodrellbank

At Jodrell Bank, a scientific and engineering wonder awaits you - the magnificent Lovell telescope, one of the largest radio telescopes in the world. A pathway leads you 180 degrees around the telescope as it towers above you surveying and exploring the Universe. Then, the visitor can wander along pathways amongst the trees of the extensive arboretum. The Centre is currently under a redevelopment, which will take 2-3 years to complete.

Times: Open daily Nov-mid Mar 10.30-3, wknds 11-4; mid Mar-end Oct 10.30-5.30 **Fee:** ✱ £1.50 (ch 4-16yrs £1) 3D theatre £1 **Facilities:** ❷ 🍴 🍴 ♿ (wheelchair loan) toilets for disabled shop ⊗ (ex guide dogs) ◀

Tabley House
WA16 0HB
➲ (leave M6 junct 19 onto A556 S towards Chester. Entrance for cars off A5033, 2m W of Knutsford)
☎ 01565 750151
e-mail: enquiries@tableyhouse.co.uk
web: www.tableyhouse.co.uk

This finest Palladian House in the North West, holds the first great collection of English pictures ever made, including works by Turner, Lawrence, Fuseli and Reynolds. This is also furniture by Chippendale, Gillow and Bullock, and fascinating Leicester family memorabilia. Friendly stewards are available to talk about the Leicesters' 700 years at Tabley.

Times: Open Apr-end Oct, Thu-Sun & BHs, 2-5 (last entry 4.30). **Fee:** £4 (ch & students £1.50). **Facilities:** ❷ 🍴❢❢ ♿ (phone administrator in advance for help) toilets for disabled shop ⊗ (ex guide dogs)

Tatton Park
WA16 6QN
➲ (5m from M6 junct 19, or M56 junct 7. Signed on A556, 4m S of Altrincham. Entrance to Tatton Park on Ashley Rd, 1.5m NE of junct A5034 with A50)
☎ 01625 534400
e-mail: tatton@cheshire.gov.uk
web: www.tattonpark.org.uk

Tatton is one of England's most complete historic estates, with gardens and a 1000-acre country park. The centrepiece is the Georgian mansion, with gardens laid out by Humphry Repton and Sir Joseph Paxton. More recently, a Japanese garden with a Shinto temple was created. The Tudor Old Hall is the original manor house, where a guided tour is available. There is also a working 1930s farm and a childrens adventure playground. Special events most weekends include the RHS flower show and open air concerts.

continued

England

Tatton Park

Times: Open mid Mar-early Oct, Tue-Sun & BH 1-5; Gardens & parkland all year Tue-Sun & BH. **Fee:** ✱ Mansion, £3.50 (ch £2), family £9, groups 12+ £2.80 (ch £1.60) Saver tickets available **Facilities:** ❷ (charged) 💺 🍽 licensed 📶 ♿ (old hall & areas of farm not accessible, Braille guides) toilets for disabled shop garden centre ❽ (ex in parkland) 🌿 ⛴

MACCLESFIELD   MAP 07 SJ97

Hare Hill
Over Alderley SK10 4QB
➲ *(Between Alderley Edge and Macclesfield(B5087). Turn off onto Prestbury Road, continue 0.75m. Hare Hill entrance on left.)*
☎ 01625 584412
web: www.nationaltrust.org.uk

The beautiful parkland at Hare Hill also features a pretty walled garden and pergola. There are woodland paths and ponds, and, in late spring, a brilliant display of rhododendrons and azaleas. The grounds were originally developed as the setting for a Georgian mansion.

Times: ✱ Open Apr-8 May, Wed-Thu, Sat-Sun 10-5. Daily 9-29 May, 10-5. Jun-30 Oct, Wed-Thur, Sat-Sun 10-5. (Last admission 1 hr before closing). **Fee:** *Prices not confirmed for 2007* **Facilities:** ❷ (charged) ♿ (Braille guides) ❽ (ex guide dogs) 🌿

Macclesfield Silk Museum
Heritage Centre, Roe St SK11 6UT
➲ *(Turn off A523 & follow brown signs. Museum in town centre)*
☎ 01625 613210
e-mail: info@macclesfield.silk.museum
web: www.macclesfield.silk.museum

The story of silk in Macclesfield, told through a colourful audio-visual programme, exhibitions, textiles, garments, models and room settings. The Silk Museum is part of the Heritage centre, a restored Georgian Sunday school, which runs a full programme of musical and artistic events throughout the year.

Times: Open all year, Mon-Sat 11-5, Sun & BH Mon 1-5. Closed 25-26 Dec, 1 Jan & Good Fri. Please ring for winter opening times. **Fee:** ✱ £3.60 (concessions £2.95). Joint ticket with Paradise Mill £7.25 (concessions £5.95). Accompanied ch free **Facilities:** ℗ (50mtrs) 💺 🍽 licensed 📶 ♿ (ramps, chairlift, audio guides, induction loop) toilets for disabled shop ❽ (ex guide dogs) ⛴

Paradise Mill & Silk Industry Museum
Park Ln SK11 6TJ
➲ *(turn off A523 'The Silk Rd' & follow brown signs)*
☎ 01625 612045
e-mail: info@macclesfield.silk.museum
web: www.macclesfield.silk.museum

A working silk mill until 1981, with restored jacquard hand looms in their original location. Knowledgeable guides, many of them former silk mill workers, illustrate the silk production process with the help of demonstrations from weavers. Exhibitions and room settings give an impression of working conditions at the mill during the 1930s. Adjacent Silk Industry Museum opened in 2001 and focuses on design and manufacturing processes.

Times: Open all year, BH Mon & Mon-Sat from 11-5 (Closed Sun, 25-26 Dec & 1 Jan, Good Fri). Closed Oct 2006 to Easter 2007 **Fee:** ✱ £4.10 (concessions £3.45), family £10.80, joint ticket with Silk Museum £7.25 (concessions £5.95) **Facilities:** ℗ (100yds) 📶 ♿ (care needed on uneven floors in Paradise Mill) toilets for disabled shop ❽ (ex guide dogs) ⛴

MOULDSWORTH   MAP 07 SJ57

Mouldsworth Motor Museum
Smithy Ln CH3 8AR
➲ *(6m E of Chester, off B5393, close to Delamere Forest & Oulton Park Racing Circuit, signposted. Or M56 junct 12 into Frodsham then B5393 into Mouldsworth, follow brown heritage signs in village)*
☎ 01928 731781
web: www.mouldsworthmotormuseum.com

Housed in a 1937 Art Deco building close to Delamere Forest, this is a superb collection of over 60 motor cars, motorcycles and bicycles. There is a massive collection of automobilia - old signs, pumps, tools, mascots and badges, as well as old motoring toys, Dinky cars and pedal cars all complemented by a motoring art gallery, that has posters and advertising material. School parties are encouraged for a guided tour and structured talk. Motoring clubs visit on Sundays. There is also a Harry Potter car for children to sit in. Also holds a collection of early teapots, many from 1920s and 30s.

Times: Open Feb-Nov (Sun only), Etr wknd, early May BH Mon, Spring BH Sun-Mon & Aug BH wknd; Sun, Feb-Nov; also Wed, Jul-Aug, noon-5. **Fee:** £4 (ch £2, including free quiz with prizes) **Facilities:** ❷ 📶 ♿ (hands on items) shop

NANTWICH   MAP 07 SJ65

Hack Green Secret Nuclear Bunker
French Ln, Hack Green CW5 8AP
➲ *(from Nantwich take A530 towards Whitchurch, follow brown signs)*
☎ 01270 629219
e-mail: coldwar@hackgreen.co.uk
web: www.hackgreen.co.uk

One of the nation's most secret defence sites. Declassified in 1993, this underground bunker would have been the centre of regional government had nuclear war broken out. Observe the preparations the government made for nuclear war and step into the lives of people who worked here. View the Minister of State's office, life support, communication centre, decontamination facilities, telephone exchange and much more.

Times: Open 20 Apr-30 Oct, daily 10.30-5.30; Nov, Jan, Feb wknds, 11-4. Closed Dec. **Fee:** £6.30 (ch £4.50, concessions £5.90), family £19 **Facilities:** ❷ 💺 🍽 📶 ♿ (facilities for blind & hard of hearing) toilets for disabled shop ❽ (ex guide dogs) ⛴

Stapeley Water Gardens

London Rd, Stapeley CW5 7LH

➲ *(off M6 junct 16, 1m S of Nantwich on A51)*

☎ 01270 623868 & 628628

e-mail: info@stapeleywg.com

web: www.stapeleywg.com

Stapeley Water Gardens consists of three main areas. The Palms Tropical Oasis is a glass pavilion which is home to sharks, piranhas, parrots, skunks and exotic flowers. The two-acre Water Garden Centre houses the national collection of water-lilies, as well as Koi carp and other water features. There is also a garden centre with a children's play area.

Times: Open Summer: Mon-Sat 9-6, BHs 10-6, Sun 10-4, Wed 9-8; Winter: Mon-Sat 9-5, BHs 10-5, Sun 10-4, (Wed 9-8 Angling dept only). The Palms Tropical Oasis open from 10. **Fee:** The Palms Tropical Oasis £4.45 (ch £2.60, concessions £3.95). Family ticket (2 ad & 2 ch) £12.10 (2 ad & 3 ch) £14.30. **Facilities:** ❷ 💺 🍴 licensed 🏬 ㅊ (free wheelchair loan service) toilets for disabled shop garden centre ❽ (ex guide dogs) ◀

NESTON   MAP 07 SJ27

Liverpool University Botanic Gardens (Ness Gardens)

Ness Gardens CH64 4AY

➲ *(off A540 near Ness-on-Wirral, follow signs)*

☎ 0151 353 0123

e-mail: nessgdns@liv.ac.uk

web: www.nessgardens.org.uk

A long association with plant collectors ensures a wide range of plants, providing interest for academics, horticulturists and amateurs alike. There are tree and shrub collections, water and rock gardens, herbaceous borders and glasshouses. A regular programme of lectures, courses and special events take place throughout the year for which tickets must be obtained in advance. A new visitor centre offers meeting and conference facilities, and weekly exhibitions by local artists.

Times: Open all year, Nov-Feb, daily 9.30-4; Mar-Oct, daily 9.30-5. (Closed 25 Dec). **Fee:** ✱ £4.70 (ch free admission when accompanied with an adult, concessions £4.30) **Facilities:** ❷ 💺 ㅊ (wheelchair route, induction loop in lecture theatre) toilets for disabled shop garden centre ❽ (ex guide dogs) ◀

NETHER ALDERLEY   MAP 07 SJ87

Nether Alderley Mill

Congleton Rd SK10 4TW

➲ *(1.5m S of Alderley Edge on E side of A34)*

☎ 01625 527468

e-mail: barry.cook@nationaltrust.org.uk

web: www.nationaltrust.org.uk

Built in the 15th century, this water-mill is much larger inside than it looks. Inside there are tandem overshot water-wheels, original Elizabethan timber work, and Victorian machinery which was restored to full working order in the 1960s after being derelict for 30 years. Mill wheels are turned on once a fortnight.

Times: Open Apr-Oct, Thu, Sun & BH Mon 1-5. Parties by arrangement. **Fee:** £2.50 (ch £1.20) family ticket £8 **Facilities:** ❷ ❽ 📷

NORTHWICH   MAP 07 SJ67

Arley Hall & Gardens   `2 for 1`

CW9 6NA

➲ *(5m N of Northwich on B5075. 5m NW of Knutsford A556)*

☎ 01565 777353 & 777284

e-mail: enquiries@arleyhallandgardens.com

web: www.arleyhallandgardens.com

Owned by the same family since medieval times, the present Arley Hall is a good example of the early Victorian Jacobean style and contains fine furniture, plasterwork, panelling and family portraits. The gardens include a walled garden, unique clipped Ilex avenue, herb garden, scented garden and a woodland garden with rhododendrons, azaleas and exotic trees as well as the double herbaceous borders, one of the earliest to be established in England (1846). Special events: Country Fair 26-27 May 2007, Garden Festival 23-24 June 2007, Outdoor concerts and plays, ring for details.

Times: Gardens, grounds & chapel: Open Etr-end Sep, Tue-Sun & BH 11-5. Hall dates TBC **Fee:** ✱ Gardens, Grounds & Chapel £4.70 (ch 6-16 £2, concessions £4.20) Family ticket £11.80 Hall £2.50 (ch 6-16 £1, concessions £2). Party 15+. **Facilities:** ❷ 💺 🍴 licensed 🏬 ㅊ (ramps, parking by entrance) toilets for disabled shop garden centre ❽ (ex in gardens on lead) ◀

Salt Museum   `2 for 1`

162 London Rd CW9 8AB

➲ *(on A533 0.5m S of town centre and 0.5m N of A556. Well signposted from A556)*

☎ 01606 41331

e-mail: cheshiremuseums@cheshire.gov.uk

web: www.saltmuseum.org.uk

Britain's only Salt Museum tells the fascinating story of Cheshire's oldest industry. Models, reconstructions, original artefacts and audio-visual programmes throw new light on something we all take for granted.

Times: Open Tue-Fri 10-5, wknds 2-5 (Sun 12-5 in Aug). Open BH & Mons in Aug 10-5. **Fee:** ✱ £2.50 (ch £1.20, concessions £2) Family ticket (2 ad + 2 ch) £6 **Facilities:** ❷ 💺 🏬 ㅊ (introductory video with induction loop facilities) toilets for disabled shop ❽ (ex guide dogs) ◀

England

RUNCORN MAP 07 SJ58

Norton Priory Museum & Gardens `2 for 1`
Tudor Rd, Manor Park WA7 1SX

➲ *(from M56 junct 11 in direction of Warrington, follow brown signs)*

☎ 01928 569895

e-mail: info@nortonpriory.org

web: www.nortonpriory.org

Thirty-eight acres of peaceful woodland gardens are the setting for the medieval priory remains, museum and Walled Garden. Displays tell the story of the transformation of the priory into a Tudor manor house and then into an elegant Georgian mansion. Please telephone for details of special events.

Times: Open all year, Apr-Oct, Mon-Fri 12-5; Sat, Sun & BHs 12-6; Nov-Mar daily 12-4. Closed 24-26 Dec & 1 Jan. Walled Garden open Apr-Oct, daily 1.30-4.30 **Fee:** £4.75 (ch 5-16, concessions £3.45). Family ticket £12.50.(2ad & 3ch) **Facilities:** ❷ ➽ 🍴 ♿ (wheelchairs, large print & audio guides, induction loop) toilets for disabled shop garden centre ⊗ (ex in wall garden) ➽

STYAL MAP 07 SJ88

Quarry Bank Mill & Styal Estate
SK9 4LA

➲ *(1.5m N of Wilmslow off B5166, 2.5m from M56 junct 5, 10m S of Manchester. Heritage signs from A34 and M56)*

☎ 01625 527468

e-mail: quarrybankmill@nationaltrust.org.uk

web: www.quarrybankhill.org.uk

Founded in 1784, Quarry Bank Mill is one of the finest surviving cotton mills of the period. Inside the water and steam-powered mill

continued

there are hands-on exhibits and demonstrations that show how traditional spinning and weaving was transformed through the ingenuity of early textile engineers. Using the most powerful working waterwheel in Europe, two mill engineers bring the past to life. At the Apprentice House you can discover what home life was like for the pauper children who worked in the mill in the 1830s. After all this history take a walk through surrounding wood and farmland along the River Bollin.

Times: Apr-Sep daily 11-5 (last admission 4); Oct-Mar, Wed-Sun 11-4. Last admission 3. Apprentice House & Garden, Tue-Sun, Oct-Mar Wed-Sun: Timed tours **Fee:** Mill & Apprentice House £9 (ch £4.70). Family ticket £20. Mill only £6 (ch £3.70). Family ticket £16. **Facilities:** ❷ (charged) ➽ 🍴 licensed 🍴 ♿ (wheelchairs, chairlift, ramps, Braille & large print guide) toilets for disabled shop ⊗ (ex in park) ➽ ➽

WIDNES MAP 07 SJ58

Catalyst Science Discovery Centre
Mersey Rd WA8 0DF

➲ *(signed from M62 junct 7 and M56 junct 12)*

☎ 0151 420 1121

e-mail: info@catalyst.org.uk

web: www.catalyst.org.uk

Enter a colourful world of science and technology in interactive galleries, and experience an amazing journey of discovery in the interactive theatre. Take a trip in an all-glass external lift to the Observatory, 100 feet above the River Mersey. A range of special events is planned throughout the year. Please ring for details.

Times: Open all year, Tue-Fri daily & BH Mon 10-5, wknds 11-5. (Closed Mon ex BH's, 24-26 & 31 Dec & 1 Jan). **Fee:** ✱ £4.95 (ch 5-16 & concessions £3.95). Family ticket (2+2, 1+3) £15.95, (2+3) £17.95. **Facilities:** ❷ ➽ 🍴 ♿ toilets for disabled shop ⊗ (ex guide dogs) ➽

Cornwall & The Isles of Scilly

St Michael's Mount

Cornwall is striking in the contrast of its countryside, from the rolling hills in the south to the majestic cliff tops and fabulous beaches of the northern coast. Local legend has it that Cornwall was once the home of King Arthur, and that St Michael's Mount was part of the lost kingdom of Lyonesse where the Knights of the Round Table once rode. But it's not all landscape and legend. Many of the pretty coastal towns remain largely untouched by time and modern development, while Newquay is a leader in the European surfing scene, and The Eden Project near St Austell is at the cutting edge of

BODMIN
MAP 02 SX06

Military Museum

The Keep PL31 1EG

➲ (on B3268, Lostwithiel Rd, beside steam railway station)

☎ 01208 269516

e-mail: dclimus@talk21.com

The history of a famous County Regiment with fascinating displays of uniforms, weapons, medals, badges and much more. Please telephone for details of events planned throughout the year. Special Event: 150th Anniversary of 'Seige of Lucknow' in 2007.

Times: Open all year Mon-Fri 9-5, Sun during Jul & Aug 10-5. (Closed Xmas). **Fee:** ✱ £2.50 (ch 50p). Parties 10+ £2 each. **Facilities:** ❷ 🗐 ♿ (presentation of inaccessible areas) shop

Pencarrow
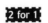

Washaway PL30 3AG

➲ (4m NW of Bodmin, signposted off A389 & B3266)

☎ 01208 841369

e-mail: pencarrow@aol.com

web: www.pencarrow.co.uk

Still a family home, this Georgian house has a superb collection of pictures, furniture and porcelain. The 50 acres of formal and woodland gardens include a Victorian rockery, a lake, 700 different rhododendrons and an acclaimed conifer collection. There is also a craft centre and a children's play area. Special events throughout the year. Ring for details.

Times: House: Apr-25 Oct, Sun-Thu 11-5 (last house tour 4). Gardens: Daily Mar-Oct 9.30-5.30. **Fee:** House & Garden £8. Gardens only £4 (ch £1). Family ticket £22. Party 20-30 £7 each, Party 31+ £6 each. **Facilities:** ❷ ➖ 🗐 ♿ (1 wheelchair, disabled parking at house) toilets for disabled shop garden centre ⊗ (ex in grounds) ◀

CALSTOCK
MAP 02 SX46

Cotehele
St Dominick PL12 6TA

➲ (between Tavistock & Callington. Turn off A390 at St. Anne's Chapel, signed 2.5m S of junct)

☎ 01579 351346 & 352739 (info)

e-mail: cotehele@ntrust.org.uk

web: www.nationaltrust.org.uk

A 15th-century house that contains tapestries, embroideries, furniture and armour; and outside, a beautiful garden on different levels, including a formal Italian-style garden, medieval stewpond, dovecote, and an 18th-century tower with lovely views. There is a restored water mill in the valley below, and at the Victorian riverside quay a Maritime Museum.

Times: Open 17 Mar-Oct daily ex Fri (open Good Fri), 11-4. Garden open all year, daily 10.30-dusk. Limited opening from 1 Nov to 23 Dec. **Fee:** House, Garden & Mill £8.40. Garden & Mill £5.40 (ch 1/2 price, under 5's & NT members free). Family tickets available. **Facilities:** ❷ ➖ ❍ licensed 🗐 ♿ (garden limited access, Braille guide, audio loop, wheelchairs) toilets for disabled shop garden centre ⊗ (except guide dogs) ✖ ◀

CAMELFORD
MAP 02 SX18

British Cycling Museum

The Old Station PL32 9TZ

➲ (1m N of Camelford on B3266 at junct with B3314)

☎ 01840 212811

web: www.chycor.co.uk/britishcyclingmuseum

This is the nation's foremost museum of cycling history from 1818 to the present day, with over 400 cycles; more than 1000 cycling medals, fobs and badges; an extensive library; displays of gas, candle, battery and oil lighting; and many advertising posters and enamel signs.

Times: Open all year, Sun-Thu 10-5. **Fee:** ✱ £3.25 (ch 5-17 £1.90). **Facilities:** ❷ 🗐 shop ⊗ (ex guide dogs)

CHYSAUSTER ANCIENT VILLAGE
MAP 02 SW43

Chysauster Ancient Village
TR20 8XA

➲ (2.5m NW of Gulval, off B3311)

☎ 07831 757934

web: www.english-heritage.org.uk

This unique Celtic settlement includes probably the oldest known 'Village Street' in the country. Explore the remains of 2,000-year-old stone houses.

Times: Open Apr-Jun & Sep, daily 10-5; Jul-Aug, daily 10-6; Oct, daily 10-4. **Fee:** £2.40 (ch £1.20, concessions £1.80). Prices and opening times are subject to change in Spring 2007. Please check web site or call 0870 333 1181 for the most up to date prices and opening times when planning your visit. **Facilities:** ❷ ⊗ ♿

DOBWALLS
MAP 02 SX26

Dobwalls Family Adventure Park
PL14 6HB

➲ (turn off A38 in centre of Dobwalls and follow the brown signs for approx 0.5m)

☎ 01579 320325 & 321129

e-mail: dobwallsadventurepark@hotmail.com

web: www.dobwallsadventurepark.co.uk

Plenty to do here, with stretches of miniature American railroads to ride -there are steam and diesel locos, and visitors can take the Rio Grande ride through the forests or the Union Pacific route over the prairies. Also Adventureland - action-packed areas filled with both indoor and outdoor adventure play equipment.

Times: ✱ Open Etr to Oct, daily 10.30-5 (10-5.30 high season). Closed some days in Apr, May & Oct **Facilities:** ❷ ➖ ♿ (manual wheelchairs subject to availability) toilets for disabled shop ◀

FALMOUTH
MAP 02 SW83

National Maritime Museum Cornwall
Discovery Quay TR11 3QY

➲ (follow signs from A39 for park/float ride and museum)

☎ 01326 313388

e-mail: enquiries@nmmc.co.uk

web: www.nmmc.co.uk

Among the reasons to visit this important museum, include breathtaking views from its 29 metre tower, one of only three natural

continued

England

underwater viewing locations in the world, hands-on interactives, audio-visual immersive experiences, talks, special exhibitions and the opportunity to get out onto the water and discover marine life around the coastline. Use the Park & Float and sail to the museum in a classic ferry.

National Maritime Museum Cornwall

Times: Open daily 10-5. Closed 25 & 26 Dec **Fee:** £7 (ch & concessions £4.80). Family ticket (2ad&3ch) £18.50. **Facilities:** ● (charged) ➍ ➎ licensed ➍ ⅁ (wheelchairs provided on arrival) toilets for disabled shop ⊗ (ex guide dogs) ➎

Pendennis Castle

TR11 4LP
➲ *(1m SE)*
☎ 01326 316594
web: www.english-heritage.org.uk

Together with St Mawes Castle, Pendennis forms the end of a chain of castles built by Henry VIII along the south coast as protection from attack from France. Journey through 450 years of history and discover the castle's wartime secrets.

Times: Open all year, Apr-Jun & Sep, daily 10-5 (Sat 10-4); Jul-Aug, daily 10-6 (Sat 10-4); Oct-Mar, daily 10-4. Closed 24-26 Dec & 1 Jan). **Fee:** £4.80 (ch £2.40, concessions £3.60). Family £12. Prices and opening times are subject to change in Spring 2007. Please check web site or call 0870 333 1181 for the most up to date prices and opening times when planning your visit. **Facilities:** ● ➍ ⅁ shop ⊗ (ex on lead in certain areas) ⌗

St Catherine's Castle   FREE

➲ *(0.75m SW of Fowey along footpath off A3082)*
web: www.english-heritage.org.uk

A small sixteenth-century fort built by Henry VIII to defend Fowey Harbour. It has two storeys with gun ports at ground level.

Times: Open at any reasonable time. **Facilities:** ⓟ (0.5m) ⊗ (ex on leads) ⌗

Godolphin House

TR13 9RE
➲ *(situated on a minor road from Godolphin Cross to Townsend)*
☎ 01736 763194
e-mail: godo@euphony.net
web: www.godolphinhouse.com

A romantic Tudor and Stuart mansion, begun in 1475 and considerably extended over the centuries. The Godolphin family's taste is evident throughout the mansion, and of particular note are examples of 16th and 17th-century English oak furniture and Wootton's 1731 painting, *Godolphin Arabian*, one of the three Arab stallion ancestors of all British bloodstock. The gardens are Tudor, with some areas even earlier. Major repair programme on the mansion funded by English Heritage.

Times: ✱ National Trust Estate open all year. House open May-Sep, Thu & Fri 11-5 & Sun 2-5 (also Tue 11-5 in Jul & Aug). Open BH Mon 11-5. Phone for Etr opening details. **Facilities:** ● ➍ ➎ ➍ ⅁ (telephone prior to visit, lift to first floor) toilets for disabled shop garden centre ⊗ (ex guide dogs) ➎

World in Miniature

Bodmin Rd TR4 9QE
➲ *(turn off A30 at Boxheater junct onto B3285)*
☎ 0870 458 4433
e-mail: info@worldinminiature.co.uk
web: www.worldinminiature.co.uk

There are six major attractions for the price of one at this theme park. Visitors can stroll amongst famous landmarks such as the Taj Mahal and the Statue of Liberty, all in miniature scale, set in spectacular gardens. Then there is Tombstone, a wild-west town complete with saloon, bank, shops, livery stable and jail. The Adventure Dome is the original super cinema 180 direct from the USA, which shows two exciting films. The 12-acre gardens are beautifully landscaped with over 70,000 plants and shrubs. See Jurassic Adventure World, Super X Simulator and children's fairground rides.

Times: ✱ Open Etr-Oct, daily from 10. **Facilities:** ● ➍ ⅁ toilets for disabled shop garden centre ➎

Caerhays Castle Gardens   2 for 1

PL26 6LY
➲ *(off A390 onto B3287. Right at T-junct, left at next T-junct, next left and continue to Porthluney Beach car park)*
☎ 01872 501144 & 501310
e-mail: estateoffice@caerhays.co.uk
web: www.caerhays.co.uk

For centuries this magnolia filled garden was a deer park, and it was not until the late 19th century that John Charles Williams ("JCW") inherited Caerhays and not until the early 20th that new and exotic plants were introduced here. Now the gardens are a blaze of plants from Chile, China, New Zealand, the Himalayas, and many other distant lands. Magnolias, Rhododendrons, Camellia, and Japonicas can all be seen on marked walks, and the house can be visited in small groups during the spring.

continued

Times: Gardens open mid Feb-Jun 10-5.30. House open mid Mar-Jun. **Fee:** ✱ £5.50 house or garden; £9.50 combined ticket **Facilities:** 🅿 💺 🗐 ⚬ toilets for disabled garden centre ⊗ (ex on lead) 🍴

GWEEK   MAP 02 SW72

National Seal Sanctuary   2 for 1

TR12 6UG

➲ *(pass RNAS Culdrose & take A3293 & then B3291 to Gweek, the sanctuary is signed from village)*

☎ 01326 221361 & 221874

e-mail: slcgweek@merlin-entertainments.com

web: www.sealsanctuary.co.uk

Britain's largest seal rescue facility - offering a unique opportunity to learn more about these beautiful creatures. Every year it rescues, rehabilitates and releases around 30 sick or abandoned seal pups. Newest residents are Chaff and Mika, South African Cape fur seals.

Times: Open all year, daily from 10. Closed 25 Dec. **Fee:** ✱ Please call for admission prices. **Facilities:** 🅿 💺 🗐 ⚬ toilets for disabled shop 🍴

HELSTON   MAP 02 SW62

The Flambards Experience   2 for 1

Culdrose Manor TR13 0QA

➲ *(0.5m SE of Helston on A3083, Lizard road)*

☎ 01326 573404

e-mail: info@flambards.co.uk

web: www.flambards.co.uk

Three award-winning, all-weather attractions can be visited on one site here. Flambards Victorian Village is a recreation of streets, shops and houses from 1830-1910. Britain in the Blitz is a life-size wartime street featuring shops, a pub and a living room with Morrison shelter. The Science Centre is a science playground that brings physics alive for the whole family. Along with the Thunderbolt and Extreme Force, we also offer the Hornet Rollercoaster, the Family Log Flume, Go-Kart circuit, and rides and play areas for the very young. The Wildlife Experience show features lizards, snakes, large spiders and birds of prey.

Times: Open winter Feb-early Apr 11-4. Open summer early Apr. **Fee:** ✱ £12.50 (ch 5-14 £9.55 over 55's £6.95). Family of 3 £31.50, of 4 £41, of 5 £50, of 6 £58.50. **Facilities:** 🅿 💺 🗐 ⚬ (95% accessible, free loan of wheelchairs, route guides) toilets for disabled shop garden centre ⊗ (ex guide dogs) 🍴

Goonhilly Satellite Earth Station Experience   2 for 1

Goonhilly Downs TR12 6LQ

➲ *(7m from Helston on B3293, Helston to St Keverne road)*

☎ 0800 679593

e-mail: goonhilly.visitorscentre@bt.com

web: www.goonhilly.bt.com

Making a dramatic impression on the Lizard Peninsula landscape, this is the largest earth station in the world, with over 60 dishes. Opened in 1962 with only one dish, Goonhilly now handles millions of e-mails, phone calls, and TV broadcasts. In the fully interactive visitors centre, explore the world of communications, experience tomorrow's technology today, and see your own animated 3D virtual head.

Times: Mid Feb-Mar, 11-4, closed Mon, Apr-May, 10-5 daily, Jun-Sep, 10-6 daily, Oct, 10-5 daily, Nov-Dec, 11-4, closed Mon. Closed 5 Jan-9 Feb. **Fee:** ✱ £6.50 (ch5-16 £4.50, under 4's free; concessions £5) **Facilities:** 🅿 💺 🍴 licensed 🗐 ⚬ induction loop, wheelchair height terminals toilets for disabled shop ⊗ (ex guide dogs) 🍴

Trevarno Estate Garden & Museum of Gardening   2 for 1

Trevarno Manor, Crowntown TR13 0RU

➲ *(E of Crowntown. Leave Helston on the Penzance road signed B3302)*

☎ 01326 574274

e-mail: enquiry@trevarno.co.uk

web: www.trevarno.co.uk

Victorian gardens with the splendid fountain garden conservatory, unique range of crafts and the National Museum of Gardening. In the tranquil gardens and grounds, follow the progress of restoration projects, visit craft areas including handmade soap workshop, explore Britain's largest and most comprehensive collection of antique tools, implements, memorabilia and ephemera, creatively displayed to illustrate how gardens and gardening influences most peoples lives. Adventure play area for the youngsters, extended estate walk and viewing platform.

Times: Open daily 10.30-5. Closed 25-26 Dec **Fee:** £5.15 (ch 5-14 £1.95, concessions £4.45, disabled £2.75). Group 12+ **Facilities:** 🅿 💺 ⚬ parking, disabled route toilets for disabled shop garden centre 🍴

LANHYDROCK — MAP 02 SX06

Lanhydrock

PL30 5AD

➲ *(2.5m SE of Bodmin, signed from A30, A38 & B3268)*

☎ 01208 265950

e-mail: lanhydrock@nationaltrust.org.uk

web: www.nationaltrust.org.uk

Part-Jacobean, part-Victorian building that gives a vivid picture of life in Victorian times. The 'below stairs' sections have a huge kitchen, larders, dairy, bakehouse, cellars, and servants' quarters. The long gallery has a moulded ceiling showing Old Testament scenes, and overlooks the formal gardens with their clipped yews and bronze urns. The higher garden, famed for its magnolias and rhododendrons, climbs the hillside behind the house.

Times: Open mid Mar-Oct: House daily (ex Mon), 11-5.30 (11-5 in Oct), open BH Mon. Gardens daily from mid Feb, (last admission half hour before closing). Winter: Gardens, Nov-Feb during daylight hours. **Fee:** House & Grounds £9.40 (ch £4.70). Grounds £5.30 (ch £2.65). Family ticket £23.50 one adult £14.10. Pre-booked group £8 each (ch £4 each) **Facilities:** ❷ ➡ ⑩ licensed ⑪ & (lift, self drive buggy (pre-book), wheelchairs) toilets for disabled shop garden centre ⊗ (ex on lead in park) ❷ ➡

LAUNCESTON — MAP 02 SX38

Launceston Castle

Castle Lodge PL15 7DR

☎ 01566 772365

web: www.english-heritage.org.uk

Commanding the town and surrounding countryside, this castle controlled the route onto Cornwall.

Times: Open Apr-Jun & Sep, daily 10-5; Jul-Aug, daily 10-6; Oct, daily 10-4. Closed Nov-Mar. **Fee:** £2.30 (ch £1.20, concessions £1.70). Prices and opening times are subject to change in Spring 2007. Please check web site or call 0870 333 1181 for the most up to date prices and opening times when planning your visit. **Facilities:** & (outer bailey only) shop ⊗ ❣

Launceston Steam Railway

St Thomas Rd PL15 8DA

➲ *(turn off A30 Launceston, well signed)*

☎ 01566 775665

The Launceston Steam Railway links the historic town of Launceston with the hamlet of New Mills. Tickets are valid for unlimited travel on the day of issue and you can break your journey at various points along the track. Launceston Station houses railway workshops, a transport museum, gift shop and book shop.

Times: Open Whitsun to mid Sep, daily ex Sat. **Fee:** ✱ £6.75 (ch £4.40, concessions £5). Family ticket £20 (2 ad & up to 4 ch). Dogs 50p. **Facilities:** ❷ ➡ ⑪ & shop

The Tamar Otter Sanctuary

North Petherwin PL15 8GW

➲ *(5m NW off B3254 Bude road)*

☎ 01566 785646

web: www.ottertrust.org.uk/Tamar_Home.html

The Tamar Otter Sanctuary has a breeding programme for the British otter and has to date bred and released over 100 otters into the wild. Visitors to the sanctuary can see otters in large natural enclosures, as well as fallow and muntjac deer, waterfowl, and wallabies.

continued

Times: ✱ Open Apr-Oct, daily 10.30-6 **Facilities:** ❷ ➡ & shop ⊗ (ex guide dogs)

LOOE — MAP 02 SX25

The Monkey Sanctuary Trust

St Martins PL13 1NZ

➲ *(signposted on B3253 at No Man's Land between East Looe & Hessenford)*

☎ 01503 262532

e-mail: info@monkeysanctuary.org

web: www.monkeysanctuary.org

Visitors can see a colony of Amazonian woolly monkeys in extensive indoor and outdoor territory. There are also conservation gardens, children's play area, activity room, a display room and vegetarian cafe. In addition a bat cave is on site where visitors can watch a colony of rare 'horseshoe' bats.

Times: Open Sun-Thu from the Sun before Etr-end Sep. Also open Autumn Half Term. **Fee:** ✱ £6 (under 5's free, ch £3.50 & concession £4.50). Family ticket (2ad+2ch) £16. **Facilities:** ❷ ➡ & toilets for disabled shop ⊗ ➡

MARAZION — MAP 02 SW53

St Michael's Mount

TR17 0HT

➲ *(access is by Causeway on foot at low tide. 0.5m S of A394 at Marazion)*

☎ 01736 719476 & 710507

e-mail: godolphin@manor-office.co.uk

web: www.nationaltrust.org.uk

Reached on foot by causeway at low tide, or by ferry at high tide in the summer only, St Michael's Mount rises dramatically from the sea, a medieval castle to which a magnificent east wing was added in the 1870s. It is home to Lord St Leven, whose ancestor John St Aubyn acquired it in the 17th century.

Times: Open Apr-Oct, Mon-Fri 10.30-5.30. Last admission 4.45 on the island; Nov-Mar, telephone for details. **Fee:** £6.40 (ch £3.20) Family ticket £16. Party 20+ £5.60 each. **Facilities:** ℗ (on mainland) ➡ ⑩ licensed ⑪ (Braille guide, sandchair available) shop ⊗ (ex guide dogs) ❷ ➡

MAWNAN SMITH — MAP 02 SW72

Glendurgan

TR11 5JZ

➲ *(4m SW of Falmouth. 0.5m SW of Mawnan Smith on road to Helford Passage)*

☎ 01872 862090

e-mail: glendurgan@nationaltrust.org.uk

web: www.nationaltrust.org.uk

This delightful garden, set in a valley above the River Helford, was started by Alfred Fox in 1820. The informal landscape contains trees and shrubs from all over the world, including the Japanese loquat and tree ferns from New Zealand. There is a laurel maze, and a Giant's Stride which is popular with children. The house is not open.

Times: Open mid Feb-Oct, Tue-Sat & BH Mon. Last admission 4.30 (Closed Good Fri). **Fee:** £5.20 (ch £2.60). Family ticket £13, family 1 ad £7.80 **Facilities:** ❷ ➡ ⑪ & (Braille guide, limited access to gardens/ground floor) toilets for disabled shop garden centre ⊗ (ex guide dogs) ❷ ➡

England

Trebah Garden

TR11 5JZ

➲ (signed at Treliever Cross rdbt at junct of A39/A394 & follow brown tourist signs)

☎ 01326 250448

e-mail: mail@trebah-garden.co.uk

web: www.trebah-garden.co.uk

A 25-acre wooded valley garden, descending 200 feet from the 18th-century house down to a private cove on the Helford River. The cascading Water Garden has pools of giant koi and exotic water plants, winding through two acres of blue and white hydrangeas to the beach. There are glades of sub-tropical tree ferns and palms, as well as rhododendrons and many other trees and shrubs from all over the world. The beach is open to visitors and there are children's trails and activities all year.

Times: Open daily 10.30-5 (last admission). In winter 10.30 til dusk.
Fee: ✱ Mar-Oct £5.80 (ch & disabled £2, pen £5.30, ch under 5 free); Nov-Feb 1/2 price **Facilities:** ❶ ☕ ⛉ licensed ▣ ♿ (3 powered wheelchairs & wheelchair route) toilets for disabled shop garden centre plant sales ◣

NEWQUAY   MAP 02 SW86

Blue Reef Aquarium   `2 for 1`

Towan Promenade TR7 1DU

➲ (from A30 follow signs to Newquay, follow Blue Reef Aquarium signs to car park in town centre)

☎ 01637 878134

e-mail: newquay@bluereefaquarium.co.uk

web: www.bluereefaquarium.co.uk

Take the ultimate undersea safari at the Blue Reef Aquarium. Discover Cornish marine life from native sharks and rays to the incredibly intelligent and playful octopus. From here journey through warmer waters to watch the magical seahorses, unusual shape shifting, jet-propelled cuttlefish and the vibrant, swaying tentacles of living sponges and anemones. Continue your safari through the underwater tunnel below a tropical sea. Here you will encounter the activities of a coral reef alive with shoals of brightly coloured fish and the graceful, black tip reef sharks which glide silently overhead. Daily talks and regular feeding demonstrations bring the experience to life.

Times: Open all year, daily 10-5. (Closed 25 Dec). Open until 6 during summer holidays. **Fee:** ✱ £6.99 (ch £4.99, concessions £5.99).
Facilities: ℗ (5mins walk) (prior contact for disabled parking) ☕ ▣ ♿ (lifts, wheelchair, ramps) toilets for disabled shop ⊗ (ex guide & service dogs) ◣

Dairy Land Farm World

Summercourt TR8 5AA

➲ (Signed from A30 at exit for Mitchell/Summercourt)

☎ 01872 510246

e-mail: info@dairylandfarmworld.co.uk

web: www.dairylandfarmworld.com

Visitors can watch while the cows are milked to music on a spectacular merry-go-round milking machine. The life of a Victorian farmer and his neighbours is explored in the Heritage Centre, and a Farm Nature Trail features informative displays along pleasant walks. Children will have fun getting to know the farm animals in the Farm Park. They will also enjoy the playground, assault course and indoor play areas.

Times: Open daily, late Mar-Oct 10-5. (Bull pen additional winter openings Thu-Sun & school hols, please telephone for more information)
Facilities: ❶ ☕ ▣ ♿ (wheelchairs for loan; disabled viewing gallery - milking) toilets for disabled shop ⊗ ◣

Newquay Zoo

Trenance Gardens TR7 2LZ

➲ (off A3075 and follow signs to Zoo)

☎ 01637 873342

e-mail: info@newquayzoo.org.uk

web: www.newquayzoo.org.uk

There's always something new at Newquay Zoo. Explore the rainforest exhibit in the tropical house where you'll discover a world of exotic animals. Water cascades down the ancient temple walls to pools filled with tropical fish. Spot the iguanas, sloths and flying foxbats, and explore the mini-beasts room complete with Arrow Poison Frog enclosure. Among the sub-tropical lakeside gardens live hundreds of animals from around the world ranging from small monkeys to shy red pandas. Look out for meerkats on sentry duty, penguins splashing in their pool, or glimpse the endangered lemurs and fossa. The zoo gardens feature a Tarzan trail, children's play area, dragon maze, as well as picnic areas, snack bar and gift shop.

Times: Open Apr-Sep, daily 9.30-6; Oct-Mar 10-dusk. (Closed 25 Dec)
Fee: Check website for admission charges. **Facilities:** ❶ (charged) ☕ ⛉ licensed ▣ ♿ (80% access, wheelchairs, guided tours, sensory sculpture) toilets for disabled shop ⊗ (ex guide dogs) ◣

PADSTOW   MAP 02 SW97

Prideaux Place

PL28 8RP

➲ (off B3276 Padstow to Newquay road. Follow brown heritage signs)

☎ 01841 532411

e-mail: office@prideauxplace.co.uk

web: www.prideauxplace.co.uk

Built by Sir Nicholas Prideaux in 1592, this impressive country house has been inhabited by his family for fourteen generations, and is still in use by them today. Visitors can see relics of the English Civil War, including a pardon from Charles II and a double-sided brooch of Cromwell and the King, as well as fascinating rooms filled with antique furniture, paintings and a 16th-century ceiling depicting the biblical story of Susannah. The house was used as a location for Trevor Nunn's film version of *Twelfth Night* and has been used in the making of many *Rosamunde Pilcher* films and television productions.

Times: Open early May-early Oct, Sun-Thu 1.30-4 (house tours). Grounds 12.30-5. Open all year to pre-booked groups (15+) **Fee:** ✱ House & grounds £6.50 (ch £2), Grounds only £2 (ch £1) **Facilities:** ❶ ☕ ▣ ♿ (ramps to main entrance and tea room) toilets for disabled shop ⊗ (ex on leads in grounds) ◣

PENDEEN   MAP 02 SW33

Geevor Tin Mine

TR19 7EW

➲ (beside the B3306 Lands End to St Ives coast road. From Penzance take A3071 towards St Just, then the B3318 towards Pendeen. From St Ives follow B3306 to Pendeen)

☎ 01736 788662

e-mail: bookings@geevor.com

web: www.geevor.com

A preserved tin mine and museum provide an insight into the methods and equipment used in the industry that was once so important in the area. The Geevor Tin Mine only actually stopped operation in 1990. Guided tours let visitors see the tin treatment plant,

continued

43

and a video illustrates the techniques employed. The underground tour is well worth the trip.

Times: Open daily except Sat 9-5, closes at 4pm Nov-Mar. Closed 21-26, 31 Dec & 1 Jan. **Fee:** ✱ £7.50 (ch & students £4.30, pen £7) Family £21
Facilities: ❷ ☗ ⶮ 🍴 & (lift, ramps) toilets for disabled shop ⊗ ➤

PENTEWAN   MAP 02 SX04

The Lost Gardens of Heligan
PL26 6EN
➲ (signposted from A390 & B3273)
☎ 01726 845100
e-mail: info@heligan.com
web: www.heligan.com

Heligan, seat of the Tremayne family for more than 400 years, is one of the most mysterious estates in England. At the end of the 19th-century its thousand acres were at their zenith, but only a few years after the Great War, bramble and ivy were already drawing a green veil over this sleeping beauty. Today the garden offers 200 acres for exploration, which include productive gardens, pleasure grounds, sustainably-managed farmland, wetlands, and ancient woodlands. Please telephone for details of spring-time and harvest-time events and for summer evening theatre.

Times: ✱ Open daily 10-6 (last admission 4.30): winter 10-dusk. Closed 24-25 Dec. **Facilities:** ❷ ☗ ⶮ licensed 🍴 & (free loan of wheelchairs and trained access advisors) toilets for disabled shop garden centre ➤

PENZANCE   MAP 02 SW43

Trengwainton Garden
TR20 8RZ
➲ (2m NW Penzance, 0.5m W of Heamoor off Penzance - Morvah road (B3312), 0.5m off St Just road, A3071)
☎ 01736 363148
e-mail: trengwainton@nationaltrust.org.uk
web: www.nationaltrust.org.uk

Trengwainton has one of the best collections of tender plants on the British mainland. Thanks to the Gulf Stream and its sheltered position, plants grow here all year round. The garden is long and thin, flanking a drive that winds uphill beside a tranquil stream. Unusual plants from four continents fill a range of walled gardens, and from the top are breathtaking views over Mounts Bay and the Lizard Peninsula.

Times: Open 12 Feb-Oct, daily 10-5.30 (closed Fri-Sat) but open Good Fri 10-5.30 (Feb, Mar & Oct 10-5). Last admission 30mins before closing.
Fee: ✱ £5. Family ticket £12.50 (2 adults), £7.50 (1 adult). Party £4.10 each.
Facilities: ❷ ☗ 🍴 & (special route, 2 wheelchairs) toilets for disabled shop garden centre ⶮ ➤

POOL   MAP 02 SW64

Cornish Mines & Engines
TR15 3NP
➲ (2m W of Redruth on A3047, signposted from A30, Pool exit)
☎ 01209 315027 & 210900
e-mail: jane.affleck@nationaltrust.org.uk

Impressive relics of the tin mining industry, these great beam engines were used for pumping water from 2000ft down and for lifting men and ore from the workings below ground. The mine at East Pool has been converted into the Cornwall Industrial Heritage Centre which

continued

includes audio visual theatre giving background to all aspects of Cornwall's industrial heritage.

Times: Open Apr-Oct, Sun-Fri 11-5. **Fee:** ✱ £5 (ch £2.50, under 5's free, £2 adult family £12.50, 1 adult family £7.50) Groups 15+ £4.30 each.
Facilities: ❷ 🍴 & (lift to all levels) toilets for disabled shop ⊗ (ex guide dogs) ⶮ ➤

PROBUS   MAP 02 SW84

Trewithen Gardens
Grampound Rd TR2 4DD
➲ (on A390 between Truro & St Austell)
☎ 01726 883647
e-mail: gardens@trewithen-estate.demon.co.uk
web: www.trewithengardens.co.uk

The Hawkins family has lived in this charming, intimate country house since it was built in 1720. The internationally renowned landscaped garden covers some 30 acres and grows camellias, magnolias and rhododendrons as well as many rare trees and shrubs seldom seen elsewhere. The nurseries are open all year.

Times: Open Mar-Sep, Mon-Sat 10-4.30; daily Feb-May. **Fee:** Feb-Jun: £5 (group 20+ £4.75); Jul-Sep: £4.75 (group 20+ £4.25) **Facilities:** ❷ ☗ 🍴 & toilets for disabled garden centre ➤

RESTORMEL   MAP 02 SX16

Restormel Castle
PL22 0BD
➲ (1.5m N of Lostwithiel off A390)
☎ 01208 872687
web: www.english-heritage.org.uk

High on a moated mound, this splendid Norman stronghold offers spectacular views across the Cornish countryside.

Times: Open Apr-Jun & Sep, daily 10-5; Jul-Aug, daily 10-6; Oct, daily 10-4. **Fee:** £2.40 (ch £1.20, concessions £1.80). Prices and opening times are subject to change in Spring 2007. Please check web site or call 0870 333 1181 for the most up to date prices and opening times when planning your visit. **Facilities:** ❷ & shop ⊗ (ex dogs on leads) ⶮ

ST AUSTELL   MAP 02 SX05

Charlestown Shipwreck & Heritage Centre
Quay Rd, Charlestown PL25 3NJ
➲ (signed off A390 from St. Austell close to Eden Project)
☎ 01726 69897
e-mail: admin@shipwreckcharlestown.com
web: www.shipwreckcharlestown.com

Charlestown is a small and unspoilt village with a unique sea-lock, china-clay port, purpose built in the 18th century. The Shipwreck and Heritage Centre was originally a dry house for china clay built on underground tunnels. Now it houses the largest display of shipwreck artefacts in the UK, along with local heritage, diving exhibits, and a Titanic display. A recent addition is a Nelson display to commemorate the Battle of Trafalgar.

Times: Open Mar-Oct, daily 10-5 (later in high season). (Last admission 1 hour before closing) **Fee:** £5.95 (ch under 10 free if accompanied by paying adult, ch under 16 £2.50, concessions £3.95) group prices on request. **Facilities:** ❷ (charged) ☗ 🍴 licensed 🍴 & (ramps in place) toilets for disabled shop ➤

The China Clay Museum - Wheal Martyn

Carthew PL26 8XG

➲ *(2m N on B3274, follow brown signs 'China Clay Museum')*

☎ 01726 850362

e-mail: info@chinaclaycountry.co.uk

web: www.chinaclaycountry.co.uk

This museum tells the story of Cornwall's most important present-day industry: china clay production. The open-air site includes a complete 19th-century clayworks, with huge granite-walled settling tanks, working water-wheels and a wooden slurry pump. There is a fully interactive gallery, nature trails and a children's adventure trail. New exhibition halls and interactive displays depict the life of claypit workers from 1800 to the present.

Times: Open all year 10-6, last admission 3 Easter-Oct. Telephone for winter times. **Fee:** ✱ £7.50 (ch £3.50, concessions £6.) **Facilities:** ⊕ ⚑ ⛭ (interactive museum gallery) toilets for disabled shop ➡

Eden Project

Bodelva PL24 2SG

➲ *(overlooking St Austell Bay signposted from A390/A30/A391)*

☎ 01726 811911

e-mail: information@edenproject.com

web: www.edenproject.com

An unforgettable experience in a breathtaking location, the Eden Project is a gateway into the fascinating world of plants and human society. Space age technology meets the lost world in the biggest greenhouse ever built. Located in a 50 metre deep crater the size of 30 football pitches are two gigantic geodesic conservatories: the Humid Tropics Biome and the Warm Temperate Biome. This is a startling and unique day out.

Times: Open daily Mar-Oct 10-6 (last admission 4.30), Nov-Mar 10-4.30 (last admission 3). **Fee:** ✱ £13.80 (ch 5-15 £5, student £7 concessions £10). Family ticket £34. Annual membership available. **Facilities:** ⊕ ⚑ ⛐ licensed ⛭ ⛭ (wheelchairs, car shuttle to visitor centre/biomes) toilets for disabled shop garden centre ⊗ (ex guide dogs) ➡

ST IVES · MAP 02 SW54

(Park your car at Lelant Station and take advantage of the park and ride service. The fee includes parking and journeys on the train between Lelant and St Ives during the day).

Barbara Hepworth Museum & Sculpture Garden

Barnoon Hill TR26 1AD

➲ *(M5 to Exeter, A30 onto Penzance & St Ives, in town centre)*

☎ 01736 796226

e-mail: tatestivesinfo@tate.org.uk

web: www.tate.org.uk/stives

Visiting the museum and garden is a unique experience, which offers a remarkable insight into the work and outlook of one of Britain's most important twentieth-century artists, Dame Barbara Hepworth.

Times: Open Mar-Oct, daily 10-5.30 (last admission 5); Nov-Feb, Tue-Sun 10-4.30 (last admission 4). Closed 25 Dec **Facilities:** ⓟ (880yds) ⛭ ⛭ (accessible with assistance, please call) toilets for disabled ⊗ (ex guide dogs)

Tate St Ives

Porthmeor Beach TR26 1TG

➲ *(M5 to Exeter, then A30 onto Penzance & St Ives. Located on Porthmeor Beach)*

☎ 01736 796226

e-mail: tatestivesinfo@tate.org.uk

web: www.tate.org.uk/stives

Home of post-war British Modernism, St Ives provides the artistic foundations for Tate St Ives. Built in 1993, the gallery celebrates the surroundings and atmosphere that inspired the Modernists, and its unique architecture recalls the 'White Relief' work of Ben Nicholson as well as the unexpected twists and turns of the town itself. The gallery presents a varied programme of both Cornish and international artists, from the past and present, including displays on loan from Tate Modern.

Times: ✱ Open Mar-Oct, daily 10-5.30; Nov-Feb, Tue-Sun 10-4.30. Closed 24-26 Dec **Facilities:** ⓟ (800yds) ⛭ ⛐ licensed ⛭ ⛭ (access ramp, lift, wheelchairs) toilets for disabled shop ⊗ (ex guide dogs) ➡

ST MARY'S · MAP 02

Isles of Scilly Museum

Church St, Hugh Town TR21 0LP

➲ *(Located in the centre of Hugh Town)*

☎ 01720 422337

e-mail: info@iosmuseum.org

web: www.iosmuseum.org

A small, independent museum, which seeks to safeguard and promote the islands' history and traditions, and reflect every aspect of island life.

Times: Etr-Sep, Mon-Sat 10-4.30. Oct-Etr, Mon-Sat 10-12 **Facilities:** ⛭ ⛭

ST MAWES · · · · · · · · · · · · · · · · · · · MAP 02 SW83

St Mawes Castle

TR2 3AA

➲ *(on A3078)*

☎ 01326 270526

web: www.english-heritage.org.uk

Wonderful location alongside the pretty fishing village of St Mawes, this castle is Henry VIII's most picturesque fort.

Times: Open all year Apr-Jun & Sep, Sun-Fri 10-5; Jul-Aug, Sun-Fri 10-6; Oct, daily 10-4; Nov-Mar, Fri-Mon 10-4. Closed between 24-26 Dec & 1 Jan. May close 4pm on Sun & Fri for private events. Closed between 1-2pm in winter. Closed 24-26 Dec and 1 Jan **Fee:** £3.60 (ch £1.80, concessions £2.70). Prices and opening times are subject to change in Spring 2007. Please check web site or call 0870 333 1181 for the most up to date prices and opening times when planning your visit. **Facilities:** ⊕ ⛭ shop ⊗ (ex dogs on leads in grounds) ⛭

SANCREED · · · · · · · · · · · · · · · · · · · MAP 02 SW42

Carn Euny Ancient Village

➲ *(1.25m SW of Sancreed, off A30)*

web: www.english-heritage.org.uk

The remains of an Iron-Age settlement. Surviving features include the foundations of stone huts and an intriguing curved underground passage or 'fogou'.

Times: Open at any reasonable time. **Facilities:** ⓟ (600mtrs) ⛭

45

TINTAGEL   MAP 02 SX08

Tintagel Castle
PL34 0HE

➲ *(on Tintagel Head, 0.5m along uneven track from Tintagel, no vehicles)*

☎ 01840 770328

web: www.english-heritage.org.uk

Overlooking the wild Cornish coast, Tintagel is one of the most spectacular spots in the country associated with King Arthur and Merlin. Recent excavations revealed Dark Age connections between Spain and Cornwall, alongside the discovery of 'Arthnou' stone suggesting that this was a royal place for the Dark Age rulers of Cornwall.

Times: Open all year, Apr-Sep, daily 10-6; Oct, daily 10-5; Nov-Mar, daily 10-4. Closed 24-26 Dec & 1 Jan. **Fee:** ✱ £4.30 (ch £2.20, concessions £3.20). Prices and opening times are subject to change in Spring 2007. Please check website or call 0870 333 1181 for the most up to date prices and opening times when planning your visit. **Facilities:** ℗ (in village) shop ⊗ (ex dogs on leads) ♯

TORPOINT   MAP 02 SX45

Antony House
PL11 2QA

➲ *(2m NW, off A374 from Trerulefoot rdbt, 2m from Torpoint Ferry)*

☎ 01752 812191

e-mail: philip.brunsdon@nationaltrust.org.uk

web: www.nationaltrust.org.uk/antony

A fine, largely unaltered mansion, built in brick and Pentewan stone for Sir William Carew between 1711 and 1721. The stable block and outhouses remain from an earlier 17th-century building. The house contains contemporary furniture and family portraits. The grounds include a dovecote and the Bath Pond House.

Times: Open Apr-Oct, Tue-Thu & BH Mon 1.30-5.30 (last admission 4.45). Also open Sun in Jun-Sep. **Fee:** ✱ House & Garden £5.50. Woodland garden £4. Combined Gardens only £4.60. Party rates available. **Facilities:** ❶ ℗ ⓧ ⓓ (Braille guide, recommended route in garden) toilets for disabled shop ⊗ (ex guide dogs) ♨ ▄

Mount Edgcumbe House & Country Park   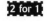
Cremyll PL10 1HZ

➲ *(from Plymouth via Cremyll Foot Ferry, Torpoint ferry or Saltash Bridge. Via Liskeard to A374, B3247 follow brown heritage signs)*

☎ 01752 822236

e-mail: mt.edgcumbe@plymouth.gov.uk

web: www.mountedgcumbe.gov.uk

Covering some 800 acres, the country park surrounding Mount Edgcumbe contains a deer park, an amphitheatre, formal gardens, sculpture, the 18th-century Earl's Garden, and woodlands containing California redwoods. The coastal footpath runs along the shores of the Park from Cremyll to Whitsand Bay. Sir Richard Edgcumbe of Cotehele built Mount Edgcumbe between 1547 and 1553. It survived a direct hit by bombs in 1941, and was restored in the 1950s. It now contains antique paintings and furniture, 16th-century tapestries, and 18th-century porcelain. Events and exhibitions held each year.

Times: Open: House & Earl's Garden Apr-Sep, Sun-Thu & BH Mon, 11-4.30. (Closed Fri & Sat). Country Park open all year. **Fee:** House & Earl's Garden

continued

£4.50 (ch 5-15 £2.25, concessions £3.50) Family ticket (2ad +2ch or 1ad+3 ch) £10. Country Park free. **Facilities:** ❶ (charged) ▄ ⑩ licensed ⓓ toilets for disabled shop ⊗ (ex guide dogs & in park) ▄

TREDINNICK   MAP 02 SW97

Cornwall's Crealy Great Adventure Park
Trelow Farm PL27 7RA

➲ *(signposted off A39)*

☎ 01841 541215

e-mail: shirespark@tiscali.co.uk

Cornwall's best kept Park is once again even more fun this year with 'The Haunted Castle', full of demons, skeletons and ghosts. Enter the 'Dragon Kingdom', the Country's largest indoor adventure zone consisting of two floors of slides, climbs, ropes, balls and towers. Take a walk through the Enchanted Forest to Greengate Meadow and meet fully animated moles, Mr Badger and their woodland friends. New attractions include Thunder Falls, double log flume ride, plus Raging River Watercoaster and Viking Warrior Pirate Ship. Acres of outdoor adventure play with the highest aerial bridges and the longest, steepest slides in Cornwall. Plus train rides around the lakes and the majestic Shire Houses including new born foals with farmyard friends.

Times: ✱ Open Good Fri-end Oct, daily 10-5. **Facilities:** ❶ ▄ ⑩ licensed ⓓ (most areas are ramped) toilets for disabled shop

See advert on opposite page

TRELISSICK GARDEN   MAP 02 SW83

Trelissick Garden
TR3 6QL

➲ *(Trelissick is located 4m S of Truro on both sides of B3289, King Harry Ferry Road)*

☎ 01872 862090

e-mail: trelissick@nationaltrust.org.uk

web: www.nationaltrust.org.uk

Set amidst more than 500 acres of park and farmland, with panoramic views down the Carrick Roads to Falmouth and the sea. The garden is well known for its large collection of hydrangeas, camellias, rhododendrons and exotic and tender plants. The Cornish Apple Orchard contains the definitive collection of Cornish apple varieties and is particularly lovely in the spring. Two galleries on the property display Cornish Arts and Crafts.

Times: Open mid Feb-Oct, daily 10.30-5.30. Phone for winter opening hours. Park & woodland walks open all year. **Fee:** £5.80 (ch £2.90). Family

continued

£14.50, family 1ad £8.70, group rate £5.20. **Facilities:** ℗ (charged) 🍽 ⓘ licensed 📷 ♿ (audio guide, wheelchairs, batricar, induction loops) toilets for disabled shop garden centre ⊗ assist dogs 🐾 ☎

TRERICE   MAP 02 SW85

Trerice
TR8 4PG
⮡ *(3m SE of Newquay off A3058 at Kestle Mill)*
☎ 01637 875404
e-mail: trerice@nationaltrust.org.uk
web: www.nationaltrust.org.uk

The Trerice you see today was built in 1571 by Sir John Arundell IV and, having suffered no major changes since then due to a succession of absentee landlords, it is still somehow caught in the spirit of its age. The plaster ceilings in the Great Hall and Great Chamber are of particular merit and the façade of the building is now thought to be the oldest such example of Dutch influenced architecture still extant in the country. The house contains many fine pieces of furniture and a large collection of clocks. A barn houses a fascinating display of lawnmowers. The garden is planted so as to provide colour and interest throughout the year and features an orchard containing many varieties of Cornish apple trees.

Times: Open end Mar-Oct, daily (ex Sat) 11-4.30. Garden open 10.30-5.30, last admission 4.30. **Fee:** ✱ House: £6 Family ticket (2 ad & 3 ch) 2 adult family ticket £15, 1 adult family ticket £9. Groups £5.10 each.
Facilities: ℗ 🍽 📷 ♿ (Braille/large print guide, tape tour, 2 wheelchairs) toilets for disabled shop ⊗ (ex guide dogs) 🐾 ☎

TRURO   MAP 02 SW84

Royal Cornwall Museum   [FREE]
River St TR1 2SJ
⮡ *(follow A390 towards town centre)*
☎ 01872 272205
e-mail: enquiries@royalcornwallmuseum.org.uk
web: www.royalcornwallmuseum.org.uk

Cornwall's oldest and most prestigious museum, famed for its internationally important collections. Visitors can see large collections of minerals, a unwrapped mummy, and many aspects of Cornwall's unique culture. The art gallery has a fine collection of Newlyn School paintings, while the museum has a range of exhibitions throughout the year together with an extensive programme for all the family. Contact the museum for details of events and activities.

Times: Open all year, Mon-Sat 10-5. Library closes 1-2, 10-1 Sat. (Closed BHs & Sun). **Facilities:** ℗ (200yds) (disabled parking on street) 🍽 ⓘ licensed 📷 ♿ (lift, ramps to main entrances) toilets for disabled shop ⊗ (ex guide dogs) ☎

WENDRON   MAP 02 SW63

Poldark Mine and Heritage Complex
TR13 0ER
⮡ *(3m from Helston on B3297 Redruth road, follow brown signs)*
☎ 01326 573173
e-mail: info@poldark-mine.com
web: www.poldark-mine.com

The centre of this attraction is the 18th-century tin mine where visitors can join a guided tour of workings which retain much of their original character. The site's Museum explains the history of tin production in

continued

Cornwall from 1800BC through to the 19th century and the fascinating story of the Cornish overseas. In addition to the Museum, the audio-visual presentation gives more insight into Cornwall's mining heritage.

Times: ✱ Open Etr-1st wk Nov, 10-5.30 (last tour 4). **Facilities:** ℗ 🍽 📷 ♿ (newly refurbished museum allowing disabled access) shop ☎

ZENNOR   MAP 02 SW43

Wayside Folk Museum
TR26 3DA
⮡ *(4m W of St Ives, on B3306)*
☎ 01736 796945

Founded in 1937, this museum covers every aspect of life in Zennor and surrounding district from 3000BC to the 1930s. Over 5000 items are displayed in 12 workshops and rooms covering wheelwrights, blacksmiths, agriculture, fishing, wrecks, mining, domestic and archaeological artefacts. A photographic exhibition entitled People of the Past tells the story of the village. The museum also contains a watermill to which visitors have access.

Times: Open Etr-end Oct, daily 10.30-5.30. **Fee:** ✱ £3 (ch £1.85). Party rates 10+. **Facilities:** ℗ (50yds) 📷 ♿ (not suitable for wheelchair users) shop ☎

England

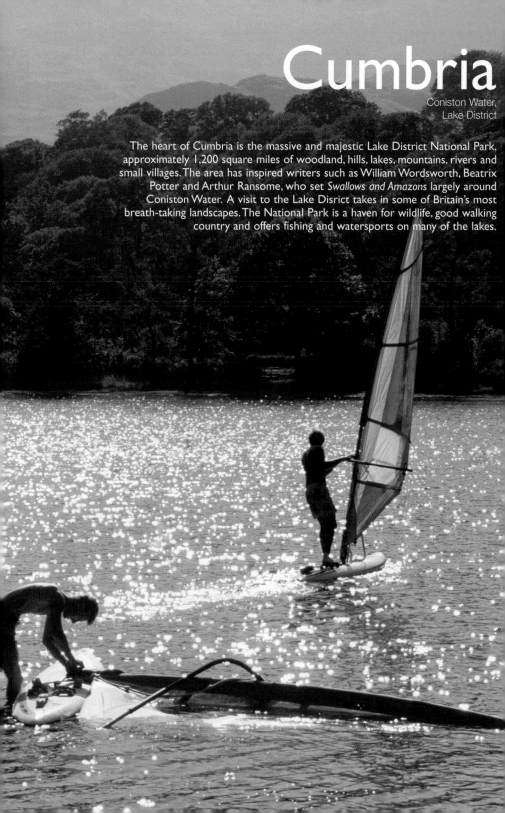

Cumbria

Coniston Water,
Lake District

The heart of Cumbria is the massive and majestic Lake District National Park, approximately 1,200 square miles of woodland, hills, lakes, mountains, rivers and small villages. The area has inspired writers such as William Wordsworth, Beatrix Potter and Arthur Ransome, who set *Swallows and Amazons* largely around Coniston Water. A visit to the Lake District takes in some of Britain's most breath-taking landscapes. The National Park is a haven for wildlife, good walking country and offers fishing and watersports on many of the lakes.

ALSTON   MAP 12 NY74

Nent Valley

Nenthead Mines Heritage Centre, Nenthead CA9 3PD

➲ *(5m E of Alston, on A689)*

☎ 01434 382726

e-mail: info@npht.com

web: www.npht.com

Set in 200 acres in the North Pennines, this hands-on heritage centre contains exhibitions and displays on geology, local wildlife, and social history. Visitors can operate three enormous water wheels, gaze down a 328ft deep brewery shaft, and take an underground trip through the Nenthead mines, last worked for lead in 1915. Special events take place throughout the year.

Times: Open Etr-Oct, daily during school hols & BH's 10.30-5 (last entry to mine 3.30). Closed Mon & Tue in term time. **Fee:** £4-£6.50 (ch site free, mine £2, concessions £3.25-5.50). Family ticket £15.50 **Facilities:** ❷ ☕ ▥ ♿ (ramps & motorised scooter) toilets for disabled shop ◀

South Tynedale Railway   `2 for 1`

The Railway Station, Hexham Rd CA9 3JB

➲ *(0.25m N, on A686)*

☎ 01434 381696

web: www.strps.org.uk

Running along the beautiful South Tyne valley, this narrow-gauge railway follows the route of the former Alston to Haltwhistle branch. At present the line runs between Alston and Kirkhaugh.

Times: Open Apr-Oct & Dec, wknds and BHs; 15 Jul-Aug, daily. Also open school hols & some wknds in Dec. Please enquire for times of trains. **Fee:** ✱ Return £5 (ch 3-15 £2.50). Single £3 (ch 3-15 £1.50). All day £8 (ch 3-15 £4). Family ticket £14. **Facilities:** ❷ ☕ ▥ ♿ (railway carriage for wheelchairs, pre-booking required) toilets for disabled shop ◀

AMBLESIDE   MAP 07 NY30

The Armitt

Rydal Rd LA22 9BL

➲ *(On the main Kendal-Keswick A591 road, opposite Rydal Rd car park in Ambleside. Next to St Martins College)*

☎ 015394 31212

e-mail: info@armitt.com

web: www.armitt.com

A fascinating and entertaining place that celebrates over 2000 years of Lake District history, from the time of Ambleside's Roman occupation to the 20th century. Facts, artefacts, historic photographs and renowned works of art by not only the area's better known former inhabitants such as Beatrix Potter, Kurt Schwitters and John Ruskin, but also displays about the daily lives of its hard-working townspeople in past times. Over 11,000 books are contained within a reference library and a changing programme of exhibitions.

Times: ✱ Open all year, daily 10-5 (last entrance 4.30). Closed 25-26 Dec. **Facilities:** ℗ (50yds) ▥ ♿ (chairlift to upstairs library, parking at establishment) toilets for disabled shop ⊗ (ex guide dogs) ◀

BARROW-IN-FURNESS   MAP 07 SD26

The Dock Museum   `FREE`

North Rd LA14 2PW

➲ *(A590 to Barrow-in-Furness. Follow brown tourist signs)*

☎ 01229 894444

e-mail: dockmuseum@barrowbc.gov.uk

web: www.dockmuseum.org.uk

Explore this museum and relive the fascinating history of Barrow-in-Furness. Discover how the industrial revolution prompted the growth of the town from a small hamlet into a major industrial power through models, graphics and computer kiosks.

Times: Open mid Apr-Nov (Tue-Fri 10-5, Sat-Sun 11-5); Nov-Mar (Wed-Fri 10.30-4, Sat-Sun 11-4.30) **Facilities:** ❷ ☕ ▥ ♿ (hearing & induction loops, 2 w/chairs for loan) toilets for disabled shop ⊗ (ex assist dogs) ◀

Furness Abbey

LH13 0TJ

➲ *(1.5m NE on unclass road)*

☎ 01229 823420

web: www.english-heritage.org.uk

Located in a peaceful valley, the majestic red sandstone remains of this beautiful abbey once housed a wealthy monastic order. View the fine stone carvings and visit the exhibition to find out more about the powerful religious community that was once based here.

Times: Open all year, Apr-Sep, daily 10-6; Oct-Mar, Thu-Mon 10-4. Closed 24-26 Dec & 1 Jan. **Fee:** £3.40 (ch £1.70, concessions £2.60). Prices and opening times are subject to change in Spring 2007. Please check web site or call 0870 333 1181 for the most up to date prices and opening times when planning your visit. **Facilities:** ❷ ♿ shop ⊗ (ex on lead in certain areas) ⌗

England

BASSENTHWAITE
MAP 11 NY23

Trotters World of Animals
2 for 1

Coalbeck Farm CA12 4RD

➲ *(follow brown signs on A591/A66 from Bassenthwaite Lake)*

☎ 017687 76239
e-mail: info@trottersworld.com
web: www.trottersworld.com

Home to hundreds of friendly creatures including lemurs, wallabies, zebras, red pandas, otters and other exotic animals along with reptiles and birds of prey and a family of gibbons which will keep families amused for hours. Informative, amusing demonstrations daily bring visitors closer to the animals. "Clown About" is an indoor play centre with soft play area and ballpools for toddlers upwards.

Times: Open all year, except 25 Dec & 1 Jan, 10-5.30 or dusk if earlier.
Fee: ✱ £5.95 (ch £4.50, under 3 free) **Facilities:** ❷ ☐ ⑩ licensed ☐ ♿ toilets for disabled shop ⊗ (ex guide dogs) ☐

BIRDOSWALD
MAP 12 NY66

Birdoswald Roman Fort
CA8 7DD

➲ *(signposted off A69 between Brampton & Hexham)*

☎ 016977 47602
e-mail: birdoswald@dial.pipex.com
web: www.birdoswaldromanfort.org

A visitor centre introduces you to Hadrian's Wall and the Roman Fort. This unique section of Hadrian's Wall overlooks the Irthing Gorge, and is the only point along the Wall where all the components of the Roman frontier system can be found together. Birdoswald isn't just about the Romans, though, it's also about border raids in the Middle Ages, and recent archaeological discoveries.

Times: Open Mar-9 Nov, daily 10-5.30. Winter season exterior only
Facilities: ❷ ☐ ⑩ ♿ (ramp outside, disabled parking, lift) toilets for disabled shop ☐

BORROWDALE
MAP 11 NY21

Honister Slate Mine
Honister Pass CA12 5XN

➲ *(from Keswick take B5289 through Borrowdale & Rosthwaite, follow road to top of pass. From Cockermouth take B5292 towards Keswick for 4m, turn right onto B5289 to Low Larton & Buttermere. Follow road to top of pass)*

☎ 01768 777230
e-mail: info@honister.com
web: www.honister.com

The last working slate mine in England. Fully guided tours allow you to explore the caverns hacked out by Victorian miners. Learn the history of the famous Honister green slate, see local skills in action, and how to rive slates.

Times: ✱ Open Mon-Fri 9-5; wknds 10-5. Closed 23 Dec-11 Jan. Telephone for details as may be open during Xmas hols. **Facilities:** ❷ ☐ ⑩ licensed ☐ ♿ toilets for disabled shop garden centre

BOWNESS-ON-WINDERMERE
MAP 07 SD49

Blackwell The Arts & Crafts House
LA23 3JR

➲ *(M6 junct 36. 1.5m S of Bowness on B5360, off A5074)*

☎ 015394 46139
e-mail: info@blackwell.org.uk
web: www.blackwell.org.uk

Blackwell was designed by architect M H Baillie Scott (1865-1945) and completed in 1900. Part of the late 19th-century Arts and Crafts Movement it houses changing exhibitions of high quality applied arts and crafts, as well as original design features including stained glass, stonework, carved oak panelling, and plasterwork.

Times: Open Feb-Xmas daily 10.30-5, other times close 4 **Fee:** ✱ £5.45 (ch & students £3) Family ticket £15, groups £5 per person.
Facilities: ❷ ☐ ♿ (lift to upper floor, photos for inaccessible rooms) toilets for disabled shop ⊗ (ex assist dogs) ☐

BRAMPTON
MAP 12 NY56

Lanercost Priory
CA8 2HQ

➲ *(2.5m NE)*

☎ 01697 73030
web: www.english-heritage.org.uk

Close to Hadrian's Wall are the atmospheric ruins of this Augustinian priory founded in the 12th-century.

Times: Open Apr-Sep, daily 10-5; Oct, Thu-Mon, 10-4. **Fee:** ✱ £2.70 (ch £1.40, concessions £2). Prices and opening times are subject to change in Spring 2007. Please check website or call 0870 333 1181 for the most up to date prices and opening times when planning your visit.
Facilities: ❷ shop ♿

BROUGH
MAP 12 NY71

Brough Castle

CA17 4EJ

➲ *(8m SE of Appleby, S of A66)*

☎ 0191 261 1585
web: www.english-heritage.org.uk

Dating from Roman times the twelfth-century keep at this site replaced an earlier stronghold destroyed by the Scots in 1174. It was restored by Lady Anne Clifford in the seventeenth century. You can still see the outline of her kitchen gardens.

Times: Open at any reasonable time. **Facilities:** ❷ ⊗ (ex dogs on leads) ♿

BROUGHAM
MAP 12 NY52

Brougham Castle
CA10 2AA

➲ *(1.5m SE of Penrith on minor road off A66)*

☎ 01768 862488
web: www.english-heritage.org.uk

Explore the maze of stairs and passages in the ruins of this once glorious 11th-century castle on the banks of the River Eamont. Enjoy the lively exhibition where you'll see relics from the nearby Roman Fort.

Times: Open all year, Apr-Sep, daily 10-5; Oct, Thu-Mon, 10-4. **Fee:** £2.70 (ch £1.40, concessions £2).Prices and opening times are subject to change

continued

in Spring 2007. Please check web site or call 0870 333 1181 for the most up to date prices and opening times when planning your visit.
Facilities: 🅿 ♿ (ex keep) shop ⚑

CARLISLE   MAP 11 NY35

Carlisle Castle
CA3 8UR
➲ *(north side of city centre, close to station)*
☎ 01228 591992
web: www.english-heritage.org.uk

Discover a thrilling and bloody past and enjoy panoramic views over the city and hills of the Lake District and Southern Scotland. Uncover an exciting history through lively exhibitions, which tell of William Rufus, Mary Queen of Scots and Bonnie Prince Charlie.

Times: Open all year, Apr-Sep, daily 9.30-5; Oct-Mar, daily 10-4. Closed 24-26 Dec & 1 Jan. **Fee:** £4.10 (ch £2.10, concessions £3.10). Prices and opening times are subject to change in Spring 2007. Please check web site or call 0870 333 1181 for the most up to date prices and opening times when planning your visit. **Facilities:** 🅿 (400yds) ♿ (parking for disabled at Castle) shop ✖ (ex on lead in certain areas) ⚑

Carlisle Cathedral
Castle St CA3 8TZ
➲ *(M6 junct 42,43 or 44, located in city centre)*
☎ 01228 535169 & 548151
e-mail: office@carlislecathedral.org.uk
web: www.carlislecathedral.org.uk

The Cathedral, founded in 1122 as a Norman Priory for Augustinian canons has had services conducted for nearly 900 years. Items of special interest include the East Window, with its tracery containing some very fine 14th-century stained glass and the Brougham Triptych, a magnificent 16th-century carved Flemish altarpiece in St. Wilfrid's Chapel. There is an interesting 14th-century barrel vaulted painted ceiling in the Choir and in the north and south aisles medieval paintings depict the Life of St. Cuthbert and St. Anthony and the figures of the 12 Apostles.

Times: Open daily throughout the year, Mon-Sat 7.30-6.15, Sun 7.30-5, summer BHs 9.45-6.15, winter BHs, Xmas & New Year 9.45-4.
Fee: Suggested donation of £4 per adult. Treasury £1 charge.
Facilities: 🅿 (5 mins walk) (2 disabled spaces only) 🍴 licensed 🍽 ♿ (parking, ramps, loop system, large print books, chairlifts) toilets for disabled shop ✖ (ex guide dogs)

Guildhall Museum
Green Market CA3 8JE
➲ *(town centre, opposite The Crown & Mitre Hotel)*
☎ 01228 534781
e-mail: enquiries@tulliehouse.co.uk
web: www.tulliehouse.co.uk

One of Carlisle's oldest buildings, c.1405 and Grade I listed. The Guildhall was once the meeting place of Carlisle's eight trade guilds, few of which still meet today. Experience the cabin-like atmosphere of the shoemaker's room and the 'modernised' butcher's room with its Victorian features. There are amazing objects such as the medieval town chest, dating from around 1400, two small silver balls (one dated 1599)- reputed to be the earliest surviving horse racing prizes in the country.

Times: Open Apr-Oct, 12-4.30 **Facilities:** 🅿 (500yds) (disc parking on street, 1 hr limit) 🍽 shop ✖ (ex guide dogs)

Tullie House Museum & Art Gallery
Castle St CA3 8TP
➲ *(M6 junct 42, 43 or 44 follow signs to city centre. Car park in Devonshire Walk)*
☎ 01228 534781
e-mail: enquiries@tulliehouse.co.uk
web: www.tulliehouse.co.uk

Dramatic audio-visual displays, striking recreations of long vanished scenes and imaginative hands-on displays. There is something for everyone, no matter what age - the stunning underground millennium gallery or Border River pathway linking to Carlisle Castle. This unique project combines the museum's own collections with the cutting edge of contemporary art. The new multi-media room features touch sensitive computer screens and a short film.

Times: Open: Nov-Mar, Mon-Sat 10-4, Sun 12-4; Apr-Jun & Sep-Oct, Mon-Sat 10-5, Sun 12-5; Jul-Aug, Mon-Sat 10-5, Sun 11-5. Closed 25-26 Dec & 1 Jan. **Fee:** ✱ Ground floor (including Art Gallery & Old Tullie House) - Free. Upper floors & New Millennium Gallery - £5.20 (ch £2.60 concessions £3.60) Family ticket (2ad+3ch) £14.50 **Facilities:** 🅿 (5mins walk) (disabled parking on site by request) 🍴 licensed 🍽 ♿ (chair lift, ramped access, lifts to all floors) toilets for disabled shop ✖ (ex guide dogs) ◼

COCKERMOUTH   MAP 11 NY13

Jennings Brewery Tour and Shop
The Castle Brewery CA13 9NE
➲ *(A66 to Cockermouth, follow tourist signs to brewery)*
☎ 0845 129 7190
e-mail: tourandshop@jenningsbrewery.co.uk
web: www.jenningsbrewery.co.uk

Jennings Brewery was originally established as a family business in 1828 and moved to its current location in 1874. It is a traditional brewer, using Lakeland water drawn from the Brewery's own well, malt made from Maris Otter barley and hops from Kent and Herefordshire.

Times: Tours: Jan-Feb & Nov- Dec, Mon-Sat at 2; Mar-Jun & Sep-Oct, Mon-Sat, at 11 & 2; Jul-Aug, daily, at 11 & 2. **Fee:** ✱ £4.95 (ch over 12 £2). **Facilities:** 🅿 (250mtrs) 🍽 ♿ toilets for disabled shop ✖ (ex assist dogs) ◼

Lakeland Sheep & Wool Centre

Egremont Rd CA13 0QX

➲ *(M6 junct 40, W on A66 to rdbt at Cockermouth on A66/A586 junct)*

☎ 01900 822673

e-mail: sheepshow@btconnect.com

web: www.sheep-woolcentre.co.uk

Come face to face with 19 different breeds of live sheep. Stage show with 'One Man and his Dog' demonstration and our Jersey cow. Shows four times daily, March-end Oct (Sun-Thu only). All indoors.

Times: Open all year, daily 9.30-5.30 (Closed 25 Dec & 5-19 Jan). **Fee:** £4.50 (ch £3.50) for sheep shows **Facilities:** ❷ ▣ ⏻ licensed ⏳ (hearing loop system) toilets for disabled shop ⊗ (ex assist dogs) ▰

Wordsworth House

Main St CA13 9RX

➲ *(W end of Main Street)*

☎ 01900 820882

e-mail: wordsworthhouse@nationaltrust.org.uk

web: www.wordsworthhouse.org.uk

William Wordsworth was born here on 7th April 1770, and happy memories of the house had a great effect on his work. The house is imaginatively presented for the first time as the home of the Wordsworth family in the 1770s. It offers a lively and interactive visit with hands-on activities and costumed living history.

Times: Open 27 Mar-28 Oct, 11-4.30. Jul, Aug & BHs Mon-Sat, other times Tues-Sat. **Fee:** £4.70 (ch £2.60). Family ticket £13.50. Groups 15+ £3.70 (ch£1.60). **Facilities:** ❷ (300yds) ⏳ (Braille guide, touch list, computer) toilets for disabled shop ⊗ (ex assist dogs) ▰

CONISTON   MAP 07 SD39

Brantwood

LA21 8AD

➲ *(2.5m SE off B5285, unclass road. Regular ferry services from Coniston Pier)*

☎ 015394 41396

e-mail: enquiries@brantwood.org.uk

web: www.brantwood.org.uk

Brantwood, home of John Ruskin, is a beautifully situated house with fine views across Coniston Water. Inside, there is a large collection of Ruskin paintings and memorabilia, and visitors can enjoy delightful nature walks through the Brantwood Estate.

Times: Open mid Mar-mid Nov, daily 11-5.30. Winter, Wed-Sun 11-4.30. (Closed 25-26 Dec). **Fee:** ✱ House & Estate £5.50 (ch £1, student £4). Family ticket £11.50. Estate only £3.75 **Facilities:** ❷ ▣ ⏻ licensed ▣ ⏳ (wheelchairs, photos of inaccessible areas, Braille guides) toilets for disabled shop ⊗ (ex guide dogs & in grounds) ▰

Ruskin Museum   `2 for 1`

The Institute, Yewdale Rd LA21 8DU

➲ *(In village centre opposite fire station, accessed from Mines Rd between Black Bull and Co-op)*

☎ 015394 41164

e-mail: vmj@ruskinmuseum.com

web: www.ruskinmuseum.com

John Ruskin (1819-1900) was one of Britain's most versatile and important political thinkers and artists. The museum contains many of his watercolours, drawings, letters, sketchbooks and other relics. The

continued

---

geology, mines and quarries of the area, Arthur Ransome's *Swallows and Amazons* country, and Donald Campbell's *Bluebird* are also explored in the Museum.

Times: Open mid Mar-mid Nov, daily 10-5.30; Winter opening, mid Nov-mid Mar, Wed-Sun 10.30-3.30. **Fee:** ✱ £4.25 (ch £2). Family ticket £11. Ticket gives 50p discount for cruise on S.Y. Gondola/Coniston Launch). **Facilities:** ❷ ▣ ⏳ (audio guide, handling specimens, guided walks) toilets for disabled shop ⊗ (ex guide dogs) ▰

Steam Yacht Gondola

Coniston Pier LA21 8AJ

➲ *(A593 to Coniston, follow signs near garage 'to boats' & S Y Gondola. Coniston Pier is at end of Lake Road.)*

☎ 015394 41288

e-mail: gondola@nationaltrust.org.uk

web: www.nationaltrust.org.uk/gondola

Originally launched in 1859, the graceful Gondola worked on Coniston Water until 1936. Beautifully rebuilt, she came back into service in 1980, and visitors can once again enjoy her silent progress and old-fashioned comfort.

Times: Open Apr-Oct to scheduled daily timetable. Trips commence from 11 at Coniston Pier. Piers at Coniston & Brantwood. **Fee:** ✱ Round trip £5.90 (ch £2.90). Family ticket (2 ad + 2 ch) £14.50 **Facilities:** ❷ (charged) shop ⊗ (ex outside salloons) ▱ ▰

DALEMAIN   MAP 12 NY42

Dalemain

CA11 0HB

➲ *(M6 junct 40, between Penrith & Ullswater on A592)*

☎ 017684 86450

e-mail: admin@dalemain.com

web: www.dalemain.com

Originally a mediaeval pele tower, Dalemain was added to in Tudor times, and the imposing Georgian façade was completed in 1745. It has oak panelling, Chinese wallpaper, Tudor plasterwork and fine period furniture. The tower contains the Westmorland and Cumberland Yeomanry Museum, and there is a countryside collection in the 16th-century Great Barn. The gardens include a collection of old fashioned roses, and in early summer a magnificent display of blue Himalayan poppies.

Times: Open Gardens, Mediaeval Hall and agricultural & countryside collections: 26 Mar-29 Oct , Sun-Thu 10.30-5. House open 11-4. **Fee:** ✱ House & Garden £6.50, Garden only £4. (ch 16 free when accompanied). **Facilities:** ❷ ▣ ⏻ licensed ⏳ (ramp access at entrance, electric scooter) toilets for disabled shop garden centre ⊗ (ex guide dogs) ▰

DALTON-IN-FURNESS   MAP 07 SD27

South Lakes Wild Animal Park

Crossgates LA15 8JR

➲ *(M6 junct 36, A590 to Dalton-in-Furness, follow tourist signs)*

☎ 01229 466086

e-mail: office@wildanimalpark.co.uk

web: www.wildanimalpark.co.uk

The North's leading zoo park is a unique safari on foot with many animals wandering free. Visitors can walk with kangaroos and emus in the bush, and watch parrots fly free in the trees. Hand feed (supervised at 2pm) families of nine different species of lemur,

continued

wonder at the amazing skills of gibbons, macaques and spider monkeys, and see the lions and tigers climb high into trees to catch their food. See both Amur and Sumatran tigers, and spectacled bears. An African plain is approximated by keeping four rhino, six giraffes and a family of baboons in the same field. Also see cheetah, red panda, and over 100 other species. There is a new Indonesian village-themed shopping area, and a new restaurant that overlooks the savannah.

Times: Open all year, daily 10-5 (last admission 4.15); Nov-Feb 10-4.30 (last admission 3.45). (Closed 25 Dec). **Fee:** £10.50 (ch, pen, wheelchair users & registered blind £7). Reduced prices Nov-Mar. **Facilities:** ❷ 🖳 🍴 ⬡ (wheelchair users may need help) toilets for disabled shop ⊗ 🚌

EGREMONT   MAP 11 NY01

Florence Mine Heritage Centre

Florence Mine CA22 2NR

⮕ *(on A595 Egremont by-pass. Turn off at Wilton/Haile, follow signs)*

☎ 01946 825830

e-mail: info@florencemine.co.uk
web: www.florencemine.co.uk

Based in the last deep working, iron ore mine in Western Europe, the centre offers a mining museum, geology and mineral room, a reconstructed drift (or tunnel) and a research facility. Underground tours are also available all year, including weekdays, by prior arrangement. Please phone the mine for details. Suitable footwear and old clothes are advised for underground tours.

Times: Open Apr-Oct, daily, 10-4. Nov-Mar, Mon-Fri 9.30-3.30
Fee: ✱ Centre: £2 (ch £1); Mine Tour: £6.50 (ch £4.50) **Facilities:** ❷ 🖳 ⬡ (hands-on display) toilets for disabled shop ⊗ (ex guide dogs)

GRASMERE   MAP 11 NY30

Dove Cottage & The Wordsworth Museum

LA22 9SH

⮕ *(S, off A591, immediately before Grasmere village)*

☎ 015394 35544

e-mail: enquiries@wordsworth.org.uk
web: www.wordsworth.org.uk

Dove Cottage was the inspirational home of William Wordsworth for over eight years (1799-1808), and it was here that he wrote some of his best-known poetry. The cottage has been open to the public since 1891, and is kept in its original condition. The museum displays manuscripts, works of art and items that belonged to the poet.

Times: ✱ Open daily 9.30-5.30, last admission 5. (Closed early Jan-early Feb & 24-26 Dec). **Facilities:** ❷ 🖳 🍴 licensed 📖 ⬡ (ramps, induction loop, virtual tour) toilets for disabled shop ⊗ (ex guide dogs) 🚌

HARDKNOTT CASTLE   MAP 07 NY20
ROMAN FORT

Hardknott Castle Roman Fort   FREE

⮕ *(9m NE of Ravenglass, at W end of Hardknott Pass)*

One of the most dramatic Roman sites in Britain, with stunning views of the Lakeland fells. The fort built between AD120 and AD138, controlled the road from Ravenglass to Ambleside. The remains include the headquarters building and Commandant's house, with a bath house and parade ground outside the fort.

Times: Open any reasonable time. Access may be hazardous in winter.
Facilities: ❷ ⊗ (ex dogs on leads) 🚐 🚌

HAWKSHEAD   MAP 07 SD39

Beatrix Potter Gallery

Main St LA22 0NS

⮕ *(situated on main street in village centre)*

☎ 015394 36355

e-mail: beatrixpottergallery@nationaltrust.org.uk
web: www.nationaltrust.org.uk

An annually changing exhibition of Beatrix Potter's original illustrations from her children's storybooks, housed in the former office of her husband, solicitor William Heelis.

Times: Open Apr- 29 Oct & Good Fri, Sat-Wed 10.30-4.30 (last admission 4). Also open Thu in Jul/Aug. Admission is by timed ticket including NT members. **Fee:** £3.80 (ch £1.90) Family ticket £9.50 (2ad+3ch)
Facilities: ℗ (300mtrs) (Braille guide) shop ⊗ (ex guide dogs) 🚌 🚌

HOLKER   MAP 07 SD37

Holker Hall & Gardens

Cark in Cartmel, Grange over Sands LA11 7PL

⮕ *(from M6 junct 36, follow A590, signposted)*

☎ 015395 58328

e-mail: publicopening@holker.co.uk
web: www.holker-hall.co.uk

Dating from the 16th century, the new wing of the Hall was rebuilt in 1871, after a fire. It has a notable woodcarving and many fine pieces of furniture which mix happily with family photographs from the present day. There are magnificent gardens, both formal and woodland and the Lakeland Motor Museum, exhibitions, deer park and adventure playground are further attractions.

Times: Open 26 Mar-29 Oct, Sun-Fri 10.30-5.30. Hall open 11-4.
Fee: ✱ Gardens & Grounds £5.70 (ch 6-15 £3) Family ticket £15.50. All 3 attractions £10.50 (ch £6) Family ticket £29. **Facilities:** ❷ 🖳 🍴 licensed 📖 ⬡ (ramps, wheelchairs & scooters available for hire) toilets for disabled shop 🚌

KENDAL   MAP 07 SD59

Abbot Hall Art Gallery

LA9 5AL

⮕ *(M6 junct 36, follow signs to Kendal. Located at south end of town centre beside parish church)*

☎ 01539 722464

e-mail: info@abbothall.org.uk
web: www.abbothall.org.uk

The ground floor rooms of this splendid house have been restored to their former glory, with original carvings and fine panelling. The walls are hung with paintings by Romney, Gardner, Turner and Ruskin. The gallery has notable temporary exhibitions and a fine permanent collection of 18th- and 19th-century watercolours of the Lake District, and 20th-century British art, including works by Hepworth, Frink, Nicholson, Sutherland, Riley and Freud.

Times: Open Jan-Xmas, Mon-Sat 10.30-5 (4pm Jan-Mar, Nov-Dec)
Fee: ✱ £5 (ch & students £4). Family ticket £14. Groups £4.50 per person.
Facilities: ❷ 🖳 ⬡ (chair lifts in split level galleries, large print labels) toilets for disabled shop ⊗ (ex assist dogs) 🚌

England

Kendal Museum

2 for 1

Station Rd LA9 6BT

➲ *(opposite railway station)*

☎ 01539 721374

e-mail: info@kendalmuseum.org.uk

web: www.kendalmuseum.org.uk

The archaeology and natural history of the Lakes is explored in this popular museum which also features a world wildlife exhibition and a display devoted to author Alfred Wainwright, who was honorary clerk to the museum.

Times: Open 17 Feb-22 Dec 10.30-5 (4pm Feb-Mar & Nov-Dec)
Fee: £2.70 (ch & full time students free, pen £2.10). Groups 10+ £2.10
Facilities: ☻ 🍴 ⓓ toilets for disabled shop ⊗ (ex guide dogs) ⌷

Museum of Lakeland Life

Abbot Hall LA9 5AL

➲ *(M6 junct 36, follow signs to Kendal. Located at south end of Kendal beside Abbot Hall Art Gallery)*

☎ 01539 722464

e-mail: info@lakelandmuseum.org.uk

web: www.lakelandmuseum.org.uk

The life and history of the Lake District is captured by the displays in this museum, housed in Abbot Hall's stable block. The working and social life of the area are well illustrated by a variety of exhibits including period rooms, a Victorian Cumbrian street scene and a farming display. Two of the rooms are devoted to the memory of Arthur Ransome.

Times: Open 12 Jan-9 Dec, Mon-Sat 10.30-5. (Closing at 4pm Jan-Mar & Nov-Dec) **Fee:** ✱ £3.76 (ch & students £2.75). Family ticket £11. Combined ticket with Abbot Hall & Lakeland Life (same day), £5 **Facilities:** ☻ 🍴 ⓓ (listening posts, large print labels) toilets for disabled shop ⊗ (ex service dogs) ⌷

KESWICK   MAP 11 NY22

Cars of the Stars Motor Museum NEW

Standish St CA12 5LS

➲ *(M6 junct 40, A66 to Keswick, continue to town centre, close to Bell Close car park)*

☎ 017687 73757

e-mail: cotsmm@aol.com

web: www.carsofthestars.com

This unusual museum features celebrity TV and film vehicles. Some notable exhibits to look out for are *Chitty Chitty Bang Bang*, James Bond's DB5 Aston Martin, Harry Potter's Ford Anglia, Del Boy's Robin Reliant, A-Team van and Batmobiles. Each vehicle is displayed in its individual film set.

Times: Open Feb half term. Daily Etr-Nov (wknds Dec) 10-5 **Fee:** ✱ £4 (ch 3-14yrs £3) **Facilities:** ☻ (100yds) ⓓ shop

Cumberland Pencil Museum

2 for 1

Southey Works, Greta Bridge CA12 5NG

➲ *(M6 N onto A66 at Penrith. Left at 2nd Keswick exit, left at T-Junct, left over Greta Bridge)*

☎ 017687 73626

e-mail: museum@acco-uk.co.uk

web: www.pencils.co.uk

Investigating the history and technology of an object most of us take utterly for granted, this interesting museum includes a replica of the

continued

Borrowdale mine where graphite was first discovered, the world's longest pencil, childrens activity area, and various artistic techniques that use pencils.

Times: Open daily 9.30-4 (hours may be extended during peak season). (Closed 25-26 Dec & 1 Jan) **Fee:** £3 (ch & pen £1.50, students £2). Family ticket (3ad + 3ch) £7.50, group 10+ £2, ch & pen £1 **Facilities:** ☻ 🍴 ⓓ toilets for disabled shop ⌷

See advert on opposite page

Keswick Museum & Gallery

Fitz Park, Station Rd CA12 4NF

➲ *(M6 junct 40, A66 to Keswick, then follow tourist signs for Museum & Art Gallery)*

☎ 017687 73263

e-mail: keswick.museum@allerdale.gov.uk

web: www.allerdale.gov.uk/keswick-museum

Keswick's surprising past, from industrial mining centre to peaceful tourist town, is revealed in this fine example of a late Victorian museum. Set in the beautiful Fitz Park, the collections cover local and natural history, famous inhabitants and visitors, including the Lake Poets, and houses the work of many artists who have been captivated by the local landscape and history. The art gallery hosts a variety of special exhibitions, which change monthly.

Times: Open Good Fri-Oct, Tue-Sat 10-4 **Facilities:** ℗ (on road outside) (2 hour limit) 🍴 ⓓ (ramp at front entrance, with handrails) shop ⊗ (ex guide & hearing dogs)

Mirehouse

CA12 4QE

➲ *(3m N of Keswick on A591)*

☎ 017687 72287

e-mail: info@mirehouse.com

web: www.mirehouse.com

Visitors return to Mirehouse for many reasons: close links to Tennyson and Wordsworth, the spectacular setting of mountain and lake, the varied gardens, changing displays on the Poetry Walk, free children's nature notes, four woodland playgrounds, live classical piano music in the house, generous Cumbrian cooking in the tearoom, and a relaxed, friendly welcome.

Times: Open Apr-Oct. Grounds: daily 10.30-5.30 House: Wed, Sun, (also Fri in Aug) 2-last entry 4.30. Parties by arrangement. **Fee:** ✱ House & grounds £4.60 (ch £2.30). Grounds only £2.20 (ch £1.10). Family ticket £13.80 (2 ad & up to 4 ch). **Facilities:** ☻ 🍴 ⓓ toilets for disabled ⊗ (ex on leads & guide dogs)

LAKESIDE   MAP 07 SD38

Aquarium of the Lakes

LA12 8AS

➲ *(M6, junct 36, take A590 to Newby Bridge. Turn right over bridge, follow Hawkshead Rd to Lakeside. Well signed)*

☎ 015395 30153

e-mail: aquariumofthelakes@reallive.co.uk

web: www.aquariumofthelakes.co.uk

Explore the secret world of the Lakes at Britain's unique freshwater aquarium. See menacing pike, eels, perch, charr and many more in over thirty naturally themed displays. Kids can get close to small mammals including harvest mice and brown rats. See diving ducks

continued

and carp in the incredible underwater tunnel, then find out more about British sharks and rays at the Morecombe Bay display. Regular lectures and events. See website for details.

Times: Open all year, daily from 9. Closed 25 Dec. **Fee:** ✱ £7 (ch £4.50, pen £6). Family ticket (2ad+2ch £21, 2ad+3ch £25, 2ad+4ch £29).
Facilities: ❸ (charged) 💻 📶 ♿ (lift to first floor, wheelchair) toilets for disabled shop ⊗ (ex guide dogs) 🍴

LEVENS   MAP 07 SD48

Levens Hall
LA8 0PD
➲ (M6 junct 36. 5m S of Kendal, on A6)
☎ 015395 60321
e-mail: houseopening@levenshall.co.uk
web: www.levenshall.co.uk

An Elizabethan mansion, built onto a 13th-century pele tower, with fine plasterwork and panelling. The topiary garden, laid out in 1694, has been little changed.

Times: ✱ Open: House & gardens mid Apr-mid Oct, Sun-Thu. Gardens 10-5. House 12-5. Last admission 4.30. **Fee:** ✱ House & garden £9 (ch £4), garden only £6 (ch £3). **Facilities:** ❸ 💻 📶 ♿ (ramps within garden) toilets for disabled shop garden centre ⊗ (ex guide dogs) 🍴

NEAR SAWREY   MAP 07 SD39

Hill Top
LA22 0LF
➲ (2m S of Hawkshead. Behind The Tower Bank Arms)
☎ 015394 36269
e-mail: hilltop@nationaltrust.org.uk
web: www.nationaltrust.org.uk

This small 17th-century house is where Beatrix Potter wrote many of her famous children's stories. It remains as she left it, and in each room can be found something that appears in one of her books.

Times: Open 31 Mar-28 Oct Sat-Wed & Good Fri, 10.30-4.30 (Last admission 4) Also open Thu Jun-Aug **Fee:** £5.40 (ch £2.70) Family ticket £13.50 (2ad+3ch) **Facilities:** ℗ (200mtrs) (no parking for coaches) ♿ (Braille guide, handling items, accessibility by arrangement) shop ⊗ (ex guide dogs) 🍴🍴

PENRITH   MAP 12 NY53

Rheged - Enter into the Spirit of Cumbria
Redhills CA11 0DQ
➲ (M6 junct 40, on A66 near Penrith)
☎ 01768 868000
e-mail: enquiries@rheged.com
web: www.rheged.com

A cinema screen as big as six double decker buses shows giant family

continued

movies daily. Rheged is also home to the National Mountaineering Exhibition, twelve shops, restaurants and a childrens' play area. There are year-round daytime and evening events, including food and drink festivals, films, lectures, childrens fun days and live music. Call for details.

Rheged

Times: Open daily 10-5.30. (Closed 25 Dec) **Fee:** Each attraction £5.95 (ch £4 & pen £4.95). Family ticket £17 **Facilities:** ❸ 💻 🍴 licensed ♿ (Wheelchairs and motorised scooters) toilets for disabled shop ⊗ (ex guide dogs) 🍴

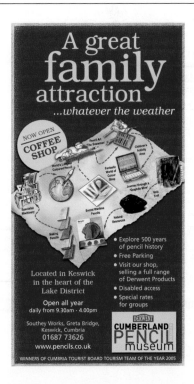

Wetheriggs Country Pottery   `FREE`

Clifton Dykes CA10 2DH

➥ *(approx 2m off A6, S from Penrith, signed)*

☎ 01768 892733

e-mail: info@wetheriggs-pottery.co.uk

web: www.wetheriggs-pottery.co.uk

The only steam-powered pottery in Britain, with 7.5 acres of things to do, including the Pots of Fun Studio, where you can throw or paint a pot, Designer-Makers at work, Café and shops. Newt pond, play areas and pottery museum.

Times: ✱ Open daily, Etr-Oct 10-5.30; Nov-Etr 10-4.30 **Facilities:** ❷ ▣
🍽 licensed ♿ toilets for disabled shop ⊗ (ex guide dogs) ⬛

RAVENGLASS   MAP 06 SD09

Ravenglass & Eskdale Railway

CA18 1SW

➥ *(close to A595, Barrow to Carlisle road)*

☎ 01229 717171

e-mail: steam@ravenglass-railway.co.uk

web: www.ravenglass-railway.co.uk

From the Lake District National Park's only coastal village of Ravenglass, small steam engines haul trains through 7 miles of outstanding, unspoilt beauty to the foot of England's highest mountains in Eskdale. Enjoy the freedom of open or cosy covered carriages. Children learn about steam with 'La'al Ratty', the Water-vole Stationmaster. Thomas the Tank Engine days in May and October. A new station should be opening at Dalegarth, some time in 2007, but the date is not confirmed yet.

Times: Open: trains operate daily mid Mar-early Nov. Most winter wknds, plus daily in Feb Half term. **Fee:** ✱ Return fare £9 (ch 5-15 £4.50). Family tickets available **Facilities:** ❷ (charged) ▣🍽♿ (special coaches - prior notice advisable) toilets for disabled shop ⬛

RYDAL   MAP 11 NY30

Rydal Mount and Gardens

LA22 9LU

➥ *(1.5m from Ambleside on A591 to Grasmere)*

☎ 015394 33002

e-mail: rydalmount@aol.com

web: www.rydalmount.co.uk

The family home of William Wordsworth from 1813 until his death in 1850. The house contains important family portraits, furniture, and many of the poet's personal possessions, together with first editions of his work. In a lovely setting overlooking Windermere and Rydal Water, the gardens were designed by Wordsworth himself. Evening visits for groups can be organised.

Times: Open Mar-Oct daily 9.30-5; Nov & Feb daily (ex Tue) 10-4 **Fee:** £5 (ch £2, pen £4 & student £3.75). Garden only £2.50. Party 10+ (pre booked groups £3.75). Reciprocal discount ticket with Dove Cottage and Wordsworth House. **Facilities:** ❷ ▤ ♿ shop ⊗ (ex guide dogs & garden) ⬛

SHAP   MAP 12 NY51

Shap Abbey   `FREE`

CA10 3NB

➥ *(1.5m W of Shap on bank of River Lowther)*

Dedicated to St Mary Magdalene, the abbey was founded by the Premonstratensian order in 1199, but most of the ruins are of 13th-

continued

century date. The most impressive feature is the 16th-century west tower of the church.

Times: Open at any reasonable time. **Facilities:** ❷ ♿ ⊗ (ex dogs on leads)

SIZERGH   MAP 07 SD48

Sizergh Castle & Garden

LA8 8AE

➥ *(3.5m S of Kendal, signed from A590)*

☎ 015395 60951

e-mail: sizergh@nationaltrust.org.uk

web: www.nationaltrust.org.uk

The castle has a 60-foot high tower, built in the 14th century, but most of the castle dates from the 15th to the 18th centuries. There are panelled rooms with fine carved overmantles and adze-hewn floors, and the gardens, laid out in the 18th century, contain the National Trust's largest limestone rock garden.

Times: ✱ Open Apr-Oct, Sun-Thu 1.30-5.30; Garden open Apr-Oct, from 12.30. (Last admission 5). **Facilities:** ❷ ▣♿ (ramps, Braille guide, wheelchair, powered buggy) toilets for disabled shop ⊗ (ex guide & hearing dogs) ⬛⬛

SKELTON   MAP 12 NY43

Hutton-in-the-Forest

CA11 9TH

➥ *(6m NW of Penrith on B5305 to Wigton, 2.5m from M6 junct 41)*

☎ 017684 84449

e-mail: info@hutton-in-the-forest.co.uk

web: www.hutton-in-the-forest.co.uk

A beautiful house, set in woods which were once part of the medieval forest of Inglewood, belonging to the Inglewood family since 1605. The house consists of a 14th-century pele tower with later additions, and contains a fine collection of furniture, portraits, tapestries and china, a 17th-century gallery and cupid staircase. The walled garden has a large collection of herbaceous plants, and there are 19th-century topiary terraces, a 17th-century dovecote and a woodland walk with impressive specimen trees.

Times: Open: Gardens Apr-Oct daily (ex Sat) 11-5; House 4-15 Apr & 2 May-30 Sep 12.30-4 **Fee:** Prices not confirmed for 2007
Facilities: ❷ ▣♿ shop Giftstall in tearoom ⊗ (ex in grounds on leads)

TEMPLE SOWERBY   MAP 12 NY62

Acorn Bank Garden and Watermill

CA10 1SP

➲ *(6m E of Penrith on A66)*

☎ 017683 61893

e-mail: acornbank@nationaltrust.org.uk

web: www.nationaltrust.org.uk

A delightful garden of some two and a half acres, where an extensive collection of over 180 varieties of medicinal and culinary herbs is grown. Scented plants are grown in the small greenhouse, and a circular walk runs beside the Crowdundle Beck to the partially restored watermill. Please ring for details of special events.

Times: Open late Mar-Oct, daily (ex Mon & Tue) 10-5 (last admission 4.30).
Fee: ✱ £3.20 (ch £1.60). Family ticket £8. Party 15+ £2.70.
Facilities: ♿ ✉ ♿ (Braille/large print guide, wheelchairs available) toilets for disabled shop ⊗ (ex on lead on woodland walk) ♨ ▰

TROUTBECK   MAP 07 NY40

Townend

LA23 1LB

➲ *(3m SE of Ambleside at S end of village)*

☎ 015394 32628

e-mail: townend@nationaltrust.org.uk

web: www.nationaltrust.org.uk

The house is one of the finest examples of a 'statesman' (wealthy yeoman) farmer's house in Cumbria, built in 1626 for George Browne, whose descendents lived here until 1943. Inside is the original home-made carved furniture, with domestic utensils, letters and papers of the farm.

Times: Open Apr-Oct, Tue-Fri, Sun & BH Mon 1-5 or dusk if earlier. Last admission 4.30. **Fee:** ✱ £3.60 (ch £1.80). Family ticket £9
Facilities: ♿ (Braille guide and sensory guide) ⊗ (except assistance dogs) ♨

WHITEHAVEN   MAP 11 NX91

The Beacon   `2 for 1`

West Strand CA28 7LY

➲ *(A595, after Parton right onto New Rd. Follow one way system & town museum tourist signs to The Beacon on harbourside)*

☎ 01946 592302

e-mail: thebeacon@copelandbc.gov.uk

web: www.thebeacon-whitehaven.co.uk

Home to the town's museum collection, The Beacon traces the social, industrial and maritime heritage of the area using local characters, audio-visual displays and museum pieces. Enjoy panoramic views of the town and coast from the Met Office Weather Gallery. Regular art exhibitions in Habour gallery. Maritime Festival June 2007.

Times: ✱ Open Tue-Sun, Etr-Oct 10-5.30, Nov-Mar 10-4.30. Open school & BH Mons. Closed 25 Dec. **Fee:** *Prices not confirmed for 2007*
Facilities: ♿ (charged) ✉ ♿ (chair/stair lift, Braille signs) toilets for disabled shop ⊗ (except assistance dogs) ▰

The Rum Story   `2 for 1`

27 Lowther St CA28 7DN

➲ *(A595, follow town centre signs)*

☎ 01946 592933

e-mail: dutymanagers@rumstory.co.uk

web: www.rumstory.co.uk

Set in the original shop, courtyards, cellars and bonded warehouses of the Jefferson family, - the oldest rum trading family in the UK - this fascinating story takes the visitor back in time to the days of the rum trade, its links with the slave trade, sugar plantations, the Royal Navy, barrel-making and more. Set pieces include a tropical rainforest, an African village, a slave ship, and a coopers workshop.

Times: Open daily, Apr-Sep 10-4.30, Oct-Mar 10-4. Closed 25 Dec & 1 Jan.
Fee: £4.95 (ch £2.95, concessions £3.95) Family £14.95. Groups 15+ £3
Facilities: Ⓟ 50 to 200 metres ✉ ┃◯┃ licensed ▦ ♿ (wheelchairs, wide doors, lifts) toilets for disabled shop ▰

WINDERMERE   MAP 07 SD49

Lake District Visitor Centre at Brockhole

LA23 1LJ

➲ *(on A591, between Windermere and Ambleside, follow brown tourist signs)*

☎ 015394 46601

e-mail: infodesk@lake-district.gov.uk

web: www.lake-district.gov.uk

Set in 32 acres of landscaped gardens and grounds, on the shore of Lake Windermere, this house became England's first National Park Visitor Centre in 1969. It offers exhibitions, audio-visual programmes, lake cruises, an adventure playground and an extensive events programme. Contact the Centre for a copy of their free Out and About guide.

Times: Open Apr-Oct daily, 10-5. Grounds & gardens open all year.
Fee: Free admission but pay & display parking. **Facilities:** ♿ (charged) ✉ ┃◯┃ licensed ▦ ♿ (manual & electric wheelchairs, lifts, induction loops) toilets for disabled shop ▰

Windermere Steamboat Centre

Rayrigg Rd LA23 1BN

➲ *(0.5m N of Bowness-on-Windermere on A592)*

☎ 015394 45565

e-mail: steamboat@ecosse.net

web: www.steamboat.co.uk

A unique collection of Victorian and Edwardian steamboats and vintage motorboats, including the oldest steamboat in the world - the S L Dolly of 1850. Displays tell the social and commercial history of England's largest lake, and there are steamboat trips daily, weather permitting.

Times: ✱ Open 17 Mar-7 Nov daily, 10-5. Steamboat trips subject to availability & weather. **Facilities:** Ⓟ ✉ ▦ ♿ toilets for disabled shop ▰

Derbyshire

River Dove,
Peak District

The natural features of this central English county range from the
heights of the Peak District National Park, where Kinder Scout stands
at 636m (2,088ft), to the depths of its remarkable underground
caverns, floodlit to reveal the exquisite Blue John stone. The caverns
are extensive, but those who prefer to stay above ground can explore
the landscape on the High Peak Trail; walk through the Dove valley;
visit one of the many fine old manor houses; a Norman church or
spend some time in the Tramway Museum at Crich.

BOLSOVER   MAP 08 SK47

Bolsover Castle
Castle St S44 6PR
➲ *(on A632)*
☎ 01246 822844
web: www.english-heritage.org.uk

This award winning property has the air of a romantic storybook castle, with its turrets and battlements rising from a wooded hilltop. See the stunning Venus garden with its beautiful statuary and fountain. State of the art audio tours are available.

Times: Open all year, Apr, Oct, Thu-Mon 10-5 (4 on Sat); May-Sep, daily 10-6 (4 on Sat); Aug, daily 10-7; Nov-Mar, Thu-Mon 10-4. Closed 24-26 Dec & 1 Jan. May also close early for evening events **Fee:** £6.60 (ch £3.30, concessions £5). Family £16.50. Prices and opening times are subject to change in Spring 2007. Please check web site or call 0870 333 1181 for the most up to date prices and opening times when planning your visit.
Facilities: ❷ ➟ ᴜ (keep not accessible) shop ⊗ ⌗

BUXTON   MAP 07 SK07

Poole's Cavern (Buxton Country Park)
Green Ln SK17 9DH
➲ *(1m from Buxton town centre, off A6 and A515)*
☎ 01298 26978
e-mail: info@poolescavern.co.uk
web: www.poolescavern.co.uk

Limestone rock, water, and millions of years created this natural cavern containing thousands of crystal formations. A 45-minute guided tour leads the visitor through chambers used as a shelter by Bronze-Age cave dwellers, Roman metal workers and as a hideout by the infamous robber Poole. Attractions include the underground source of the River Wye, the 'Poached Egg Chamber', Mary, Queen of Scots' Pillar, the Grand Cascade and underground sculpture formations.

Times: ✱ Open Mar-Oct, daily 10-5. (Open in winter for groups only). **Fee:** ✱ £6.20 (ch £3.50) **Facilities:** ❷ ⌗ ᴜ (audio loops, wheelchair ramps, controllable underground cameras) toilets for disabled shop ⊗ (ex guide dogs or in park) ➟

See advert on page 60

CALKE   MAP 08 SK32

Calke Abbey
DE73 1LE
➲ *(10m S of Derby, on A514 between Swadlincote and Melbourne)*
☎ 01332 863822
e-mail: calkeabbey@nationaltrust.org.uk
web: www.nationaltrust.org.uk

This fine baroque mansion was completed in 1704, and built for Sir John Harpur. Among its treasures are an extensive natural history collection, a magnificent Chinese silk state bed, and a spectacular red and white drawing room. The house stands in 600 acres of wooded parkland and also has walled flower gardens. Lots of special events all year round. Contact for details.

Times: Open 18 Mar-29 Oct, Sat-Wed & BH Mon; House 12.30-5; Gardens & Church 11-5; Restaurant & Shop 10.30-5 **Fee:** ✱ £6.80 (ch £3.40). Family ticket £17 **Facilities:** ❷ ⍟ licensed ᴜ (Braille guide, hearing system, buggy/wheelchair available) toilets for disabled shop ⊗ (ex guide dogs) ➠

CASTLETON   MAP 07 SK18

Blue-John Cavern & Mine
Buxton Rd S33 8WP
➲ *(follow brown "Blue-John Cavern" signs from Castleton)*
☎ 01433 620638 & 620642
e-mail: lesley@bluejohn.gemsoft.co.uk
web: www.bluejohn.gemsoft.co.uk

A remarkable example of a water-worn cave, over a third of a mile long, with chambers 200ft high. It contains 8 of the 14 veins of Blue John stone, and has been the major source of this unique form of fluorspar for nearly 300 years.

Times: Open all year, daily, 9.30-5 (or dusk). Guided tours of approx 1hr every 10 mins tour. **Fee:** ✱ £7 (ch £3.50, pen & student £5) Family ticket £19. Party rates on request. **Facilities:** ❷ ➟ ⌗ (not suitable for disabled visitors) shop ➟

Peak Cavern   `2 for 1`
S33 8WS
➲ *(on A6187, in centre of Castleton)*
☎ 01433 620285
e-mail: info@peakcavern.co.uk
web: www.devilsarse.com

One of the most spectacular natural limestone caves in the Peak District, with an electrically-lit underground walk of about half a mile. Ropes have been made for over 500 years in the 'Grand Entrance

continued

Hall', and traces of a row of cottages can be seen. Rope-making demonstrations are included on every tour.

Peak Cavern

Times: Open all year, daily 10-5. Closed 25 Dec **Fee:** ✱ £6.25 (ch £4.25, other concessions £5.25). Family ticket £18.50. **Facilities:** ❷ (charged) 🍴 shop ◀

Peveril Castle

Market Place S33 8WQ

➲ *(on S side of Castleton)*

☎ 01433 620613

web: www.english-heritage.org.uk

The romantic ruins of this Norman fortress are situated high on a rocky crag and the views from the great square tower of the surrounding Peak District are breathtaking. Sir Walter Scott glamourised the castle in his novel, *Peveril of the Peak*.

Times: Open Apr, daily 10-5; May-Aug, daily 10-6. Sep-Oct: 10-5 daily; Nov-Mar: 10-4, Thu-Mon. Closed 24-26 Dec & 1 Jan. **Fee:** £3.50 (ch £1.80, concessions £2.60). Family £8.80. Prices and opening times are subject to change in Spring 2007. Please check web site or call 0870 333 1181 for the most up to date prices and opening times when planning your visit. **Facilities:** shop ⚙

Speedwell Cavern

2 for 1

Winnats Pass S33 8WA

➲ *(A625 becomes A6187 at Hathersage. 0.5m W of Castleton)*

☎ 01433 620512

e-mail: info@speedwellcavern.co.uk

web: www.speedwellcavern.co.uk

Descend 105 steps to a boat that takes you on a one-mile underground exploration of floodlit caverns part of which was once a lead mine. The hand-carved tunnels open out into a network of natural caverns and underground rivers. See the Bottomless Pit, a huge subterranean lake in a huge, cathedral-like cavern.

Times: Open all year, daily 10-5.30 (Closed 25 Dec). Phone to check Winter opening times due to weather. Last boat 4 **Fee:** ✱ £6.75 (ch £4.75). **Facilities:** ❷ (charged) 🍴 shop ⊗ (ex assist dogs) ◀

Treak Cliff Cavern

2 for 1

S33 8WP

➲ (0.75m W of Castleton on A6187)

☎ 01433 620571

e-mail: treakcliff@bluejohnstone.com

web: www.bluejohnstone.com

An underground world of stalactites, stalagmites, flowstone, rock and cave formations, minerals and fossils. There are rich deposits of the rare and beautiful Blue John Stone, including The Pillar, the largest piece ever found. Show caves include the Witch's Cave, Aladdin's Cave, Dream Cave and Fairyland Grotto. These caves contain some of the most impressive stalactites in the Peak District. Visitors can also polish their own Blue John Stone, and purchase Blue John Stone jewellery and ornaments in the Castleton Gift Shop.

Times: Open all year, Mar-Oct, daily 10-last tour 4.20, Nov-Feb daily 10-last tour at 3.20. All tours are guided & last about 40 mins. Enquire for last tour of day & possible closures. Closed 24-26 & 31 Dec & 1 Jan **Fee:** ✱ £6.50 (ch 5-15 £3.50). Family ticket (2 ad & 2 ch) £18. **Facilities:** ♿ ☕ 🅿 (establishment can only cater for walking disabled) shop ◪

CHATSWORTH   MAP 08 SK27

Chatsworth

DE45 1PP

➲ (8m N of Matlock off B6012. 16m from M1 junct 29, signposted via Chesterfield, follow brown signs)

☎ 01246 582204

e-mail: visit@chatsworth.org

web: www.chatsworth.org

Home of the Duke and Duchess of Devonshire, Chatsworth contains a massive private collection of fine and decorative arts. There is a splendid painted hall, and a great staircase leads to the chapel, decorated with statues and paintings. There are pictures, furniture and porcelain, and a trompe l'oeil painting of a violin on the music room door. The park was laid out by 'Capability' Brown, but is most famous as the work of Joseph Paxton, head gardener in the 19th century. The park is also home to the Duke and Duchess personal collection of contemporary sculpture.

Times: Open 15 Mar-23 Dec, House & Garden 11-5.30, Farmyard 10.30-5.30. **Fee:** House & Garden: £9.75 (ch £3.50, concessions £7.75). Family ticket £23. Pre-booked group discounts available. Garden only: £6 (ch £2.75, concessions £4). Family ticket £14.50. Farmyard & Adventure Playground: £4.50 (ch under 3 free, pen £3). Groups 5+ £3.90. Family pass to all attractions £42. **Facilities:** ♿ (charged) ☕ 🍽 licensed 🅿 ♿ (3 electric wheelchairs available for garden) toilets for disabled shop garden centre ⊗ (ex park & gardens on lead) ◪

CRESWELL   MAP 08 SK57

Creswell Crags Museum and Education Centre

Crags Rd, Welbeck S80 3LH

➲ (off the B6042, Crags Road, between A616 and A60, 1m E of Creswell village)

☎ 01909 720378

e-mail: info@creswell-crags.org.uk

web: www.creswell-crags.org.uk

Creswell Crags, a picturesque limestone gorge with lakes and caves, is one of Britain's most important archaeological sites. The many caves on the site have yielded Ice Age remains, including bones of woolly mammoth, reindeer, hyena and bison, stone tools of Ice Age hunters from over 10,000 years ago and new research has revealed the only Ice Age rock art in Britain (about 13,000 years old). Visit the Museum and Education Centre to learn more about your Ice Age ancestors through an exhibition, touch-screen computers and video. Join a 'Virtually the Ice Age' cave tour, picnic in Crags Meadow, or try the new activity trail. Plenty of special events year round, contact for details.

Times: Open all year, Feb-Oct, daily, 10.30-4.30; Nov-Jan, Sun only 10.30-4.30. **Fee:** ✱ Museum & site free. Ice Age tour £3.90, (£2.50 ch); Rock Art tour £6 adults, (£3 ch) no under 5's on tours. £2 parking donation requested. **Facilities:** ♿ 🅿 ♿ (mobility scooter, tour may be unsuitable due to steps) toilets for disabled shop ⊗ (only assist dogs in museum) ◪

CRICH   MAP 08 SK35

Crich Tramway Village

2 for 1

DE4 5DP

➲ (off B5035, 8m from M1 junct 28)

☎ 01773 854321

e-mail: enquiry@tramway.co.uk

web: www.tramway.co.uk

A mile-long scenic journey through a period street to open countryside with panoramic views. You can enjoy unlimited vintage tram rides, and the exhibition hall houses the largest collection of vintage electric trams in Britain. The village street contains a bar and restaurant, tearooms, a sweet shop, ice cream shop, and Police sentry box, among others. Ring for details of special events.

Times: Open Apr-Oct, daily 10-5.30 (6.30 wknds Jun-Aug & BH wknds). Nov-Dec wknds 10.30-4 **Fee:** ✱ £9 (ch 3-15 £4.50, pen £8). Family ticket (2ad+3ch) £24 **Facilities:** ♿ ☕ 🍽 licensed 🅿 ♿ (Braille guidebooks, converted tram, talktype facility) toilets for disabled shop ◪

CROMFORD   MAP 08 SK25

Arkwright's Cromford Mill

Mill Ln DE4 3RQ
➲ *(off A6, 3m S of Matlock)*
☎ 01629 823256
e-mail: info@cromfordmill.co.uk
web: www.cromfordmill.co.uk

Sir Richard Arkwright established the world's first successful water-powered cotton spinning mill at Cromford in 1771. The Arkwright Society are involved in a major restoration to create a lasting monument to an extraordinary genius. Guided tours are available, and there is a programme of lectures and visits - ring for details. The Mill site is part of the Derwent Valley Mill World Heritage site.

Times: Open all year, daily 9-5 (Closed 25 Dec). **Fee:** ✱ Guided tour & exhibitions £2 (ch & pen £1.50). Mill site free. **Facilities:** ❽ ⬛️ & (ramps) toilets for disabled shop ▰

DENBY   MAP 08 SK34

Denby Pottery Visitor Centre   2 for 1

Derby Rd DE5 8NX
➲ *(8m N of Derby off A38, on B6179, 2m S of Ripley)*
☎ 01773 740799
e-mail: visitor.centre@denby.co.uk
web: www.denbyvisitorcentre.co.uk

Situated around a cobbled courtyard with shops and a restaurant. Pottery tours are available daily including hands on activities such as paint-a-plate and make a clay souvenir. Extensive cookshop with free half hour demonstrations daily. There are lots of bargains on Denby seconds in the factory shop, hand-made blown glass from the Glass Studio, Dartington Crystal Shop, gift shop, gallery, garden shop and hand painted Denby. (2-for-1 Voucher applies to factory tour only.)

Times: Open all year. Factory tours, Mon-Thu 10.30 & 1. Craftroom tour, daily 11-3. Visitor Centre Mon-Sat 9.30-5, Sun 10-5. Closed 25-26 Dec. **Fee:** Free. Factory tour £4.95 (ch £3.95). Craftroom tour £3.50 (ch £2.50) **Facilities:** ❽ ⬛️ ⬛️ licensed & (lift) toilets for disabled shop garden centre ❽ (outside only, ex guide dogs) ▰

DERBY   MAP 08 SK33

Derby Museum & Art Gallery   FREE

The Strand DE1 1BS
➲ *(follow directions to city centre)*
☎ 01332 716659
e-mail: david.fraser@derby.gov.uk
web: www.derby.gov.uk/museums

The museum has a wide range of displays, notably of Derby porcelain, and paintings by the local artist Joseph Wright (1734-97). Also antiquities, natural history and militaria, as well as many temporary exhibitions.

Times: Open all year, Mon 11-5, Tue-Sat 10-5, Sun & BHs 1-4. Closed Xmas & New Year, telephone for details. **Facilities:** ❽ (50yds) & (lift to all floors, portable mini-loop, large print labels) toilets for disabled shop ❽ (ex guide dogs)

Pickford's House Museum of   FREE
Georgian Life & Costume

41 Friar Gate DE1 1DA
➲ *(from A38 into Derby, follow signs to city centre)*
☎ 01332 255363
e-mail: elizabeth.spencer@derby.gov.uk
web: www.derby.gov.uk/museums

The house was built in 1770 by the architect Joseph Pickford as a combined workplace and family home. It now shows domestic life at different periods, with Georgian reception rooms and service areas and a 1930s bathroom. Other galleries are devoted to temporary exhibitions. There is also a display on the growth of Georgian Derby, and on Pickford's contribution to Midlands architecture.

Times: Open all year, Mon 11-5, Tue-Sat 10-5, Sun & BHs 1-4. (Closed Xmas & New Year, telephone for details). **Facilities:** ❽ & (tape guides, video with sign language subtitles) shop ❽ (ex guide dogs)

Royal Crown Derby Visitor Centre   2 for 1

194 Osmaston Rd DE23 8JZ
➲ *(on A514, opposite Derby Royal Infirmary)*
☎ 01332 712800
e-mail: enquiries@royal-crown-derby.co.uk
web: www.royal-crown-derby.co.uk

This museum traces the history of the company from 1750 to the present day, while the factory tour demonstrates the making of Royal Crown Derby in detail from clay through to the finished product. A demonstration studio gives you the opportunity to watch craftspeople at close quarters and try out a variety of different skills.

Times: Open all year, daily, Mon-Sat 9-5 & Sun 10-4 (shop, Sun 10.30-4.30). **Fee:** ✱ Visitor centre £2.95 (concessions £2.75). Factory tour £4.95 (concessions £4.75). **Facilities:** ❽ ⬛️ ⬛️ licensed & (ramps) toilets for disabled shop ❽ (ex assist dogs) ▰

The Silk Mill, Derby's Museum   FREE
of Industry and History

Silk Mill Ln, off Full St DE1 3AR
➲ *(From Derby inner ring road, head for Cathedral & Assembly Rooms car park. 5 mins walk)*
☎ 01332 255308
e-mail: roger.shelley@derby.gov.uk
web: www.derby.gov.uk/museums

The museum is set in an early 18th-century silk mill and adjacent flour

continued

mill on the site of the world's first modern factory. Displays cover local mining, quarrying and industries, and include a major collection of Rolls Royce aero-engines from 1915 to the present. There is also a section covering the history of railway engineering in Derby. The building is now part of the Derwent Valley Mills World Heritage Site.

Times: Open all year, Mon 11-5, Tue-Sat 10-5, Sun & BHs 1-4. (Closed Xmas & New Year, telephone for details). **Facilities:** Ⓟ 5 min walk (museum parking restricted to disabled) ㊃ (lift to all floors) toilets for disabled shop ⊗ (ex guide dogs)

EYAM — MAP 08 SK27

Eyam Hall — 2 for 1
S32 5QW

➲ *(Turn off A623 just after Calver Crossroads & village of Stoney Middleton. Turn left at the top of the hill. Eyam Hall in centre of village opposite the stocks).*
☎ 01433 631976
e-mail: nicola@eyamhall.com
web: www.eyamhall.com

An intimate 17th-century manor house in the heart of the famous "plague village". Home to the Wright family since 1671, the Hall offers a glimpse of domestic history through the eyes of one family, in portraits, furniture, tapestries, costumes and memorabilia. Converted farm buildings house the Eyam Hall Craft Centre. Please telephone for details of musical and theatrical events throughout the season.

Times: Open House & Garden: Etr Sun & Mon, Spring Bank Hol Sun & Mon, Jul & Aug: Wed, Thu, Sun, BH Mon 12-4. Craft Centre year round Tue-Sun 11-5 **Fee:** House £6.25 (ch £4, concessions £5.75). Family ticket £19. Craft centre free admission. **Facilities:** Ⓟ ▉ ❑ licensed ㊃ (disabled entrance via special gate, ramps) toilets for disabled shop ⊗ (ex guide & dogs in grounds) ◣

HADDON HALL — MAP 08 SK26

Haddon Hall
DE45 1LA

➲ *(1.5m S of Bakewell off A6)*
☎ 01629 812855
e-mail: info@haddonhall.co.uk
web: www.haddonhall.co.uk

Originally held by the illegitimate son of William the Conqueror, Haddon has been owned by the Manners family since the 16th century. Little has been added since the reign of Henry VIII, and, despite its time-worn steps, few medieval houses have so successfully withstood the ravages of time.

Times: Open Apr-Sep, Sat-Sun only; Etr Good Fri-Tue; May-Sep daily (closed 1-2 Jul): 12-5 **Fee:** ✱ £7.75 (ch £4 & pen £6.75). Party 15+. **Facilities:** Ⓟ (charged) ❑ licensed ▣ ㊃ (access is impossible for those in wheelchairs) toilets for disabled shop ⊗ (ex guide dogs) ◣

HARDWICK HALL — MAP 08 SK46

Hardwick Hall
Doe Lea S44 5QJ

➲ *(2m S M1 junct 29 via A6175. Access by Stainsby Mill entrance only)*
☎ 01246 850430
e-mail: hardwickhall@nationaltrust.org.uk
web: www.nationaltrust.org.uk

An outstanding example of Elizabethan architecture, described as
continued

more glass than wall, Hardwick Hall was built by Bess of Hardwick between 1590 and 1597, and is surrounded by 300 acres of historic parkland. Other attractions on the estate include Stainsby Mill, a fully functioning water-powered mill with 17-foot waterwheel; the Stone Centre where visitors can learn about the art of stonemasonry; and the Park Centre which details local wildlife. Lots of talks and special events. Contact for details.

Times: Open 25 Mar-29 Oct, Wed-Thu, Sat-Sun, BH Mon, 12-4. (Last admission 30mins before closing). Garden Wed-Sun, 11-5. Old Hall Wed, Thur, Sat & Sun 10-6. Parkland gates all year 8-6 (5.30 in winter). **Fee:** ✱ House & Garden £7.80 (ch £3.90). Family ticket £19.50. Garden only £4 (ch £2). Family £10. **Facilities:** ❽ ❑ licensed ㊃ (large print & Braille guide, wheelchair (pre-book)) toilets for disabled shop ⊗ (ex in park on leads) ◥

ILKESTON — MAP 08 SK44

American Adventure Theme Park
DE7 5SX

➲ *(off M1 junct 26, signed, take A610 to A608 then A6007)*
☎ 0845 330 2929
e-mail: sales@americanadventure.co.uk
web: www.americanadventure.co.uk

This is one of Britain's few fully themed parks, based on the legend of a whole continent. Take a cruise on the Harleys Angels bikes or take the wheel of a New York Dodger. Pick up the pace on the Mini Mine Rush coaster or enjoy a unique 4D cinema experience in the Motion Master. All this as well as favourites like the Buffalo Stampede, Digger Depot, Yankee Clipper and The Runaway Train. Live shootout with Sheriff Rocky Raccoon at weekends, and keep an eye out for Miss Hugsy Bear.

Times: Open 8 Apr-5 Sep & 21-29 Oct, daily from 10.30; 9 Sep-15 Oct wknds only from 10.30 **Fee:** ✱ £12.50 ad and ch 1.05metres and above, below 1.04metres £4.99 **Facilities:** ❽ ▉ ❑ ㊃ (free wheelchair hire, must pre book, call 0845 330 2929) toilets for disabled shop ⊗ (ex guide dogs) ◣

KEDLESTON HALL — MAP 08 SK34

Kedleston Hall
DE22 5JH

➲ *(5m NW of Derby, entrance off Kedleston Rd, signed from Rdbt where A38 crosses A52, close to Markeaton Pk)*
☎ 01332 844059
e-mail: kedlestonhall@nationaltrust.org.uk
web: www.nationaltrust.org.uk

Kedleston has been the Derbyshire home of the Curzon family for over eight centuries. The original house was demolished at the end of the 17th century. In 1760 Robert Adam built the south front and designed most of the interior including the marble hall. There are pictures, furniture and china displayed in the house together with an Indian Museum containing the collection accumulated by Lord Curzon, Viceroy of India.

Times: Open all year: House; 11 Mar-29 Oct, Sat-Wed 12-4.30. Last admission 4. Garden; same as house but open 10-6. Park open daily, 30 Oct-9 Mar 2007 10-4 rest of year 10-6 **Fee:** £6.90 (ch £3.30). Family ticket £17; Park and garden only: £3.10 (ch £1.55) Family ticket £7.70 (refundable against tickets for house) **Facilities:** ❽ ❑ licensed ▣ ㊃ (Braille guide, w/chair, self-drive vehicle) toilets for disabled shop ⊗ (ex in park, must be on leads) ◥

MATLOCK BATH   MAP 08 SK25

The Heights of Abraham Cable Cars, Caverns & Hilltop Park
DE4 3PD

⮑ *(on A6, signposted from M1 junct 28 & A6. Base station next to Matlock Bath railway station)*
☎ 01629 582365
e-mail: enquiries@h-of-a.co.uk
web: www.heights-of-abraham.co.uk

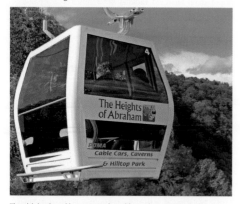

The visit begins with a spectacular cable car journey across the Derwent Valley to the summit of the hill top country park. The most famous aspects of the Heights of Abraham are the two spectacular show caverns, which provide exciting tours to the underground world within the hillside. There's the 'miners tale', in the Great Rutland Cavern-Nestus Mine and the 'story of the rock' at the Masson Cavern Pavilion. There is also an Explorer's Challenge, woodland walks and the Victoria Prospect Tower.

Times: ✱ Open daily 14-22 Feb & Etr-Oct 10-5 (later in high season), 28 Feb-26 Mar wknds only, for Autumn & Winter opening telephone for details. **Facilities:** Ⓟ (300mtrs) 🍴 licensed 🛏 & (please ring for details) toilets for disabled shop ⊗ (ex in grounds & cable car) 🧺

Peak District Mining Museum   2 for 1
The Pavilion DE4 3NR

⮑ *(On A6 alongside River Derwent)*
☎ 01629 583834
e-mail: mail@peakmines.co.uk
web: www.peakmines.co.uk

A large display explains the history of the Derbyshire lead industry from Roman times to the present day. The geology of the area, mining and smelting processes, the quarrying and the people who worked in the industry, are illustrated by a series of static and moving exhibits. The museum also features an early 19th-century water pressure pumping engine. There is a recycling display in the Pump Room.

Times: Open all year, daily Apr-end Sep 10-5, Oct-end Mar 11-3. Closed 25 Dec. **Fee:** Museum & Mine: £5 (ch £3, concessions £4.50). Family £11.50. Museum only or mine only £3 (ch £2, concessions £2.50). Family £8.50. Party rates. **Facilities:** Ⓟ (charged) 🍴& (chair lift to mezzanine) shop ⊗ (ex guide dogs)

Temple Mine   2 for 1
Temple Rd DE4 3NR

⮑ *(off A6. Telephone for directions.)*
☎ 01629 583834
e-mail: mail@peakmines.co.uk
web: www.peakmines.co.uk

A typical Derbyshire mine which was worked from the early 1920s until the mid 1950s for fluorspar and associated minerals and shows examples of mining methods which give an insight into working conditions underground.

Times: Apr-end Sep timed visits 12 noon and 2 daily, Oct-end Mar timed visits 12noon & 2 weekends only **Fee:** Museum & Mine: £5 (concessions £4.50, ch £3), Family ticket £11.50. Museum only or mine only: £3 (concessions £2.50, ch £2), Family £8.50. **Facilities:** Ⓟ Pay & Display 🛏 ⊗ (ex guide dogs)

MELBOURNE   MAP 08 SK32

Melbourne Hall & Gardens
DE73 8EN

⮑ *(9m S of Derby on A514, in Melbourne take turn by bus shelter in the Market Place, follow road to Church Sq)*
☎ 01332 862502
e-mail: melbhall@globalnet.co.uk
web: www.melbournehall.com

Sir John Coke (Charles I's Secretary of State) bought the lease of Melbourne Hall in 1628 and the house has been home to two Prime Ministers: Lord Melbourne and Lord Palmerston. The glorious formal gardens are among the finest in Britain.

Times: Open, house daily throughout Aug only (ex first three Mons) 2-5 (last admission 4.15). Prebooked parties by appointment in Aug. Gardens Apr-Sep, Wed, Sat, Sun & BH Mon 1.30-5.30. Upstairs rooms available by appointment. **Fee:** ✱ House Tue-Sat (guided tour) £3.50 (ch £2, pen £3), Sun & BH Mon (no guided tour) £3 (ch £1.50, pen £2.50). House & Garden (Aug only) £5.50 (ch £3.50, pen £4.50). Garden only £3.50 (pen £2.50). Family £9.50. **Facilities:** Ⓟ (200yds) (no parking in visitor centre courtyard) 🍴🛏& (ramp at garden entrance) shop ⊗ (ex guide dogs)

MIDDLETON BY   MAP 08 SK25
WIRKSWORTH

Middleton Top Engine House
Middleton Top Visitor Centre DE4 4LS

⮑ *(Signed off A6 in Cromford then, 0.5m S from B5036 Cromford/Wirksworth road)*
☎ 01629 823204
e-mail: middletontop@derbyshire.gov.uk
web: www.derbyshire.gov.uk/countryside

A beam engine built in 1829 for the Cromford and High Peak Railway, and its octagonal engine house. The engine's job was to haul wagons up the Middleton Incline, and its last trip was in 1963 after 134 years' work. The visitor centre tells the story of this historic railway.

Times: ✱ Open: Information Centre, daily, wknds only winter. Engine House Etr-Oct 1st wknd in month (engine in motion). **Fee:** ✱ Static engine 70p (ch 40p). Working engine £1.30 (ch 70p). **Facilities:** Ⓟ (charged) & toilets for disabled shop

OLD WHITTINGTON — MAP 08 SK37

Revolution House — FREE

High St S41 9JZ

➲ *(3m N of Chesterfield town centre, on B6052 off A61, signposted)*

☎ 01246 345727

e-mail: tourism@chesterfield.gov.uk

web: www.visitchesterfield.info

Originally the Cock and Pynot alehouse, this 17th-century cottage was the scene of a meeting between local noblemen to plan their part in the Revolution of 1688, a series of events that led to the overthrow of James II in favour of William and Mary of Orange. The house is now furnished in 17th-century style. A video relates the story of the Revolution and there is a small exhibition room.

Times: Open daily (ex Tue) 8 Apr-Sep, 11-4. Xmas: 16-24, 27-31 Dec from 11-4 **Facilities:** ℗ (100yds) & (signing available by prior arrangement) shop ⊗ (ex guide dogs)

RIPLEY — MAP 08 SK35

Midland Railway Butterley — 2 for 1

Butterley Station DE5 3QZ

➲ *(M1 junct 28, A38 towards Derby, then signposted)*

☎ 01773 747674 & 749788

e-mail: mrc@rapidial.co.uk

web: www.midlandrailwaycentre.co.uk

A regular steam-train passenger service runs here, to the centre where the aim is to depict every aspect of the golden days of the Midland Railway and its successors. Exhibits range from the steam locomotives of 1866 to an electric locomotive, with a large section of rolling stock spanning the last 100 years. Also a farm and country park, along with narrow gauge, miniature and model railways. Regular rail-related special events throughout the year. Contact for details.

Times: Open all year, trains run wknds Feb-Dec & most school holidays **Fee:** ✻ £9.95 (ch 5-16 £5.50, pen £8.95) children under 5 free. Party 15+. **Facilities:** ❷ ☕ ▦ & (special accommodation on trains) toilets for disabled shop ◄

SUDBURY — MAP 07 SK13

Sudbury Hall

DE6 5HT

➲ *(6m E of Uttoxeter at junct of A50 Derby-Stoke and A515 Ashbourne)*

☎ 01283 585305

e-mail: sudburyhall@nationaltrust.org.uk

web: www.nationaltrust.org.uk

This country house was started in 1664 by Lord George Vernon. It has unusual diapered brickwork, a carved two-storey stone frontispiece, a cupola and tall chimneys. The interior features work by craftsmen including Edward Pierce and Grinling Gibbons. Parts of the interior featured as Mr Darcy's rooms in the BBC adaptation of *Pride and Prejudice*. The Museum of Childhood contains a Victorian schoolroom, collections of toys, and displays.

Times: Open House & Museum 11 Mar-29 Oct, Wed-Sun 1-5 (open BH Mons). Last admissions 30 mins before closing. Gardens open 11-6. **Fee:** ✻ House £5.50 (ch £2.50). Family ticket £13. Museum of Childhood £6 (ch £4). Family ticket £16. Joint ticket £10 (ch £5.50). Joint Family ticket £25. (All costs higher in summer holidays) Garden only £1 (ch 50p). Joint family ticket £2.50. **Facilities:** ❷ ☕ & (w/chair available, large print/Braille guide & touch list) toilets for disabled shop ⊗ (ex in grounds) ⚘

WIRKSWORTH — MAP 08 SK25

Wirksworth Heritage Centre — 2 for 1

Crown Yard DE4 4ET

➲ *(on B5023 off A6 in centre of Wirksworth)*

☎ 01629 825225

e-mail: heritage@heritagecentre.wanadoo.co.uk

web: www.storyofwirksworth.co.uk

The Centre has been created in an old silk and velvet mill. The three floors of the mill have interpretative displays of the town's past history as a prosperous lead-mining centre. Each floor offers many features of interest including a computer game called 'Rescue the injured lead-miner', a mock-up of a natural cavern, and a Quarryman's House. During the Spring Bank Holiday you can also see the famous Well Dressings. Newly renovated exhibits on the top floor include one on quarrying, information about local girl round-the-world yachtswoman Ellen MacArthur, and local memories from the Second World War. Theres also a small art gallery carrying local works.

Times: Open Etr-Sep, Wed-Sun & BHs 10.30-4.30 **Fee:** ✻ £3 (ch £1, pen £2). Party 20+ 10% discount. **Facilities:** ℗ (80yds) (pay & display) ☕ ⑩ licensed shop ⊗ (ex guide dogs)

Devon

Clovelly

One of England's most attractive counties, Devon has rolling farmland, moorland, pretty villages and lovely beaches. Dartmoor is the largest of the moorland areas at 953km² (368 sq miles) and has National Park status. To the east of Dartmoor, the coastal area is known as the 'English Riviera' thanks to its favourable micro-climate where palm trees and other semi-tropical plants flourish quite happily

ARLINGTON
MAP 02 SS64

Arlington Court
EX31 4LP

➲ *(7m NE of Barnstaple, on A39)*

☎ 01271 850296

e-mail: arlingtoncourt@nationaltrust.org.uk

web: www.nationaltrust.org.uk

Arlington Court was built in 1822 and is situated in the thickly wooded Yeo Valley. The centrepiece is the Victorian mansion, surrounded by formal and informal gardens. Also open to visitors is the working stable yard, housing a collection of carriages and horse-drawn vehicles. The extensive parkland around the house is grazed by Jacob sheep and Red Devon cattle. Please telephone for details of events running throughout the year.

Times: Open 26 Mar-29 Oct, daily (ex Sat) 10.30-5. Last admission 4. Grounds open Nov-Mar during daylight hours. **Fee:** ✱ House & grounds £7 (ch £3.50), Family £17.50. Grounds & carriage collection £5 (ch £2.50). Parties 15+ pre-booked 15% discount. **Facilities:** ● ● 🕮 ⚫ (wheelchairs, ramps at house, batricar, Braille guide) toilets for disabled shop garden centre ⊗ (ex in grounds on lead) ⭐ ◄

BARNSTAPLE
MAP 02 SS53

Marwood Hill Gardens
Marwood EX31 4EB

➲ *(signed off A361 Barnstaple to Braunton road, follow brown tourist signs)*

☎ 01271 342528

web: www.marwoodhillgarden.co.uk

The 18-acre gardens with their three small lakes contain many rare trees and shrubs. There is a large bog garden and a walled garden, collections of clematis, camellias and eucalyptus. Alpine plants are also a feature, and there are plants for sale.

Times: ✱ Open daily (ex 25 Dec), dawn to dusk. **Facilities:** ● ● ⚫ garden centre ◄

BEER
MAP 03 SY28

Pecorama Pleasure Gardens
Underleys EX12 3NA

➲ *(from A3052 take B3174, Beer road, signed)*

☎ 01297 21542

e-mail: pecorama@btconnect.com

web: www.peco-uk.com

The gardens are high on a hillside, overlooking Beer. A miniature steam and diesel passenger line offers visitors a stunning view of Lyme Bay as it runs through the Pleasure Gardens. Attractions include an aviary, crazy golf, children's activity area and the Peco Millennium Garden. The main building houses an exhibition of railway modelling in various small gauges. There are souvenir and railway model shops,

continued

plus full catering facilities. Please telephone for details of events running throughout the year.

Pecorama Pleasure Gardens

Times: Open Etr-Oct , Mon-Fri 10-5.30, Sat 10-1. Open Sun Etr & 27 May-early Sep. **Fee:** ✱ £5.75 (ch 4-14 £3.80, pen £5.25, over 80 & under 4 free) **Facilities:** ● ● 🍽 licensed ⚫ (access with helper, wheelchair. Garden steep in places) toilets for disabled shop ⊗ (ex guide dogs) ◄

BICTON
MAP 03 SY08

Bicton Park Botanical Gardens
East Budleigh EX9 7BJ

➲ *(2m N of Budleigh Salterton on B3178, leave M5 at junct 30 & follow brown tourist signs)*

☎ 01395 568465

e-mail: info@bictongardens.co.uk

web: www.bictongardens.co.uk

Unique Grade 1-listed 18th-century historic gardens with palm house, orangery, plant collections, extensive countryside museum, indoor and outdoor activity play areas, pinetum, arboretum, nature trail, woodland railway garden centre and restaurant. All this set in 63 acres of beautiful parkland that has been cherished for 300 years.

Times: Open Winter 10-5, Summer 10-6. Closed 25 & 26 Dec. **Fee:** ✱ £5.95 (ch & concessions £4.95). Family ticket (2 ad, 2 ch) £19.95. **Facilities:** ● ● 🍽 licensed 🕮 ⚫ (adapted carriage on woodland railway, wheelchairs) toilets for disabled shop garden centre ◄

BLACKMOOR GATE MAP 03 SS64

Exmoor Zoological Park 2 for 1
South Stowford, Bratton Fleming EX31 4SG
➲ (off A361 link road onto A399, follow brown tourist signs)
☎ 01598 763352
e-mail: exmoorzoo@fsbdial.co.uk
web: www.exmoorzoo.co.uk

Exmoor Zoo is both personal and friendly. Open since 1982 it is an ideal family venue, catering particularly for the younger generation. The zoo specialises in smaller animals, many endangered, such as the golden headed lion tamarins. Over 14 species of this type of primate are exhibited. Contact pens are provided throughout and children are encouraged to participate. Twice daily guided tours at feeding times along with handling sessions.

Times: Open daily, Apr-Oct 10-6; Nov-Mar 10-4. **Fee:** ✱ £7.50 (ch £5.50, concessions £6.50). **Facilities:** ❷ ♨ ♿ toilets for disabled shop ⊗ (ex guide dogs) ◗

BUCKFASTLEIGH MAP 03 SX76

Buckfast Abbey FREE
TQ11 0EE
➲ (0.5m from A38, midway between Exeter and Plymouth. Turn off at 'Dart Bridge' junct and follow brown tourist signs)
☎ 01364 645500
e-mail: enquiries@buckfast.org.uk
web: www.buckfast.org

The Abbey, founded in 1018, was dissolved by Henry VIII in the 16th century. Restoration began in 1907, when four monks with little building experience began the work. The church was built on the old foundations, using local blue limestone and Ham Hill stone. The precinct contains several medieval monastic buildings, including the 14th-century guest hall which contains an exhibition of the history of the Abbey.

Times: Open all year daily. Closed Good Fri, 24-26 Dec. **Facilities:** ❷ ♨ ♿ (Braille & audio information) toilets for disabled shop ⊗ (ex guide dogs) ◗

Buckfast Butterfly Farm & Dartmoor Otter Sanctuary
TQ11 0DZ
➲ (off A38, at Dart Bridge junct, follow tourist signs)
☎ 01364 642916
e-mail: contact@ottersandbutterflies.co.uk
web: www.ottersandbutterflies.co.uk

Visitors can wander around a specially designed, undercover tropical garden, where free-flying butterflies and moths from around the world can be seen. The otter sanctuary has large enclosures with underwater viewing areas. Three types of otters can be seen - the native British otter along with Asian and North American otters.

Times: Open Good Fri-end Oct, daily 10-5.30 or dusk (if earlier). **Fee:** ✱ £5.95 (ch £4.50, pen £5.50). Family ticket £16.95. **Facilities:** ❷ ♨ ♿ (wheelchair ramps) shop ⊗ (ex guide dogs) ◗

BUCKLAND ABBEY MAP 02 SX46

Buckland Abbey
PL20 6EY
➲ (off A386 0.25m S of Yelverton, signed)
☎ 01822 853607
e-mail: bucklandabbey@nationaltrust.org.uk
web: www.nationaltrust.org.uk

Originally a prosperous 13th-century Cistercian Abbey, and then home of the Grenville family, Buckland Abbey was sold to Sir Francis Drake in 1581, who lived there until his death in 1596. Several restored buildings house a fascinating exhibition about the abbey's history. Among the exhibits is Drake's drum, which is said to give warning of danger to England. A recently created Elizabethan garden is also open.

Times: Open end Mar-Nov, daily (ex Thu) 10.30-5.30. Nov-end Mar, Sat - Sun. Closed Xmas to mid-Feb. (Last admissions 45mins before closing). **Fee:** Abbey & grounds £7. Grounds only £3.70. Party 15+ £5.20 each. **Facilities:** ❷ ❢⊙❢ licensed ♨ ♿ (wheelchairs & motorised buggy available) toilets for disabled shop ⊗ (ex assist dogs) ◖

CHITTLEHAMPTON MAP 03 SS62

Cobbaton Combat Collection 2 for 1
Cobbaton EX37 9RZ
➲ (signed from A361 & A377)
☎ 01769 540740
e-mail: info@cobbatoncombat.co.uk
web: www.cobbatoncombat.co.uk

World War II British and Canadian military vehicles, war documents and military equipment can be seen in this private collection. There are over 50 vehicles including tanks, one a Gulf War Centurian, and a recently added Warsaw Pact section. There is also a section on 'Mum's War' and the Home Front. The Home Front section is now in a new purpose-built building.

Times: Open Apr-Oct, daily (ex Sat) 10-5; Jul-Aug daily. Winter most wkdays, phone for details. **Fee:** ✱ £5.25 (ch £3.75, pen £4.75). **Facilities:** ❷ ♨ ♨ ♿ (most areas accessible) toilets for disabled shop ⊗ (ex guide dogs, outside) ◗

CHUDLEIGH MAP 03 SX87

Canonteign Falls 2 for 1
EX6 7NT
➲ (off A38 at Chudleigh/Teign Valley junct onto B3193 and follow tourist signs for 3m)
☎ 01647 252434
e-mail: info@canonteignfalls.com
web: www.canonteignfalls.com

A magical combination of waterfalls, woodlands and lakes.

Times: Open all year, summer 10-6, winter 10-dusk. Last admission 1 hour before closing **Fee:** ✱ £5.75 (ch £3.50, pen £4.75). Family ticket £16.50. **Facilities:** ❷ ♨ ❢⊙❢ licensed ♨ ♿ (grounds partly accessible) toilets for disabled shop ◗

England

CHURSTON FERRERS   MAP 03 SX95

Greenway Garden

TQ5 0ES

➲ *(off A3022 into Galmpton. Follow Manor Vale Rd into village then brown signs for Greenway Garden, establishment signed)*

☎ 01803 842382

e-mail: greenway@nationaltrust.org.uk

web: www.nationaltrust.org.uk/devoncornwall

Greenway is a beautiful woodland garden set on the banks of the River Dart which time seems to have passed by. A garden held on the edge of wilderness, renowned for rare half-hardy trees and shrubs, underplanted by native wild flowers, Devon's best kept secret. The surrounding estate has many walks which give stunning views over the estuary. Travel by river to enjoy this peaceful haven. Greenway is not easily accessible, having some steep and slippery paths and all visitors are asked to wear walking shoes and to follow routes and directions according to their fitness on the day.

Times: Open Mar-7 Oct, Wed-Sat, 10.30-5. **Fee:** ✱ £5 (ch £2.50) Groups £4.25. Green visitors (not by car) £4.25 (ch £2). **Facilities:** ❷ ☕ 🍴 ♿ (part access to garden, Braille guide, large print, T Loop) toilets for disabled shop ⊗ (ex guide dogs & in parkland) 🐾 ⛴

Crealy Adventure Park

Times: ✱ Open all year, Jan-mid July & 6 Sep-Dec, daily 10-5. Closed winter term time Mon-Tue; mid Jul-5 Sep, daily 10-6. **Fee:** ✱ £8.95-£9.95 (ch under 92cm free, pen £6.20-£7.20). Party 4+ £8.65-£9.65. Lower rates during winter months. **Facilities:** ❷ ☕ 🍴 licensed 🍴 ♿ (carers admitted free, rollercoaster has disabled facility) toilets for disabled shop ⛴

See advert below

CLOVELLY   MAP 02 SS32

The Milky Way Adventure Park

EX39 5RY

➲ *(on A39, 2m from Clovelly)*

☎ 01237 431255

e-mail: info@themilkyway.co.uk

web: www.themilkyway.co.uk

One of the West Country's leading attractions for the biggest rides and the best shows. Attractions include Clone Zone - Europe's first interactive adventure ride featuring a suspended roller coaster; Time Warp - indoor adventure play area; daily displays from the North Devon Bird of Prey Centre; archery centre; golf driving nets; railway; pets corner and more. 'Droid Destroyer Dodgems' invites pilots to save the Earth from the Vega Asteroid. Rest for a drink, snack or meal at the Thatched Café or the Galactic Café.

Times: Open Apr-Oct, daily 10.30-6. **Fee:** ✱ £8 (ch under 1m £6, pen £6, under 3's free). **Facilities:** ❷ ☕ ♿ (ramps) toilets for disabled shop ⛴

CLYST ST MARY   MAP 03 SX99

Crealy Adventure Park

Sidmouth Rd EX5 1DR

➲ *(M5 junct 30 onto A3052 Exeter to Sidmouth road)*

☎ 01395 233200

e-mail: fun@crealy.co.uk

web: www.crealy.co.uk

Crealy Adventure Park offers an unforgettable day for all the family with Tidal Wave log flume, El Pastil Loco Coaster, Queen Bess Pirate Ship, Techno Race Karts, Bumper Boats, Victorian Carousel, Funosaurus show and all weather play area. Visit the Animal Realm to ride, feed, milk, groom or cuddle the animals. Relax on the Prairie Train tour around the worlds 1st Sunflower Maze.

continued

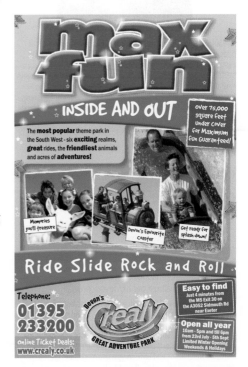

COMBE MARTIN — MAP 02 SS54

Combe Martin Wildlife Park & Dinosaur Park

EX34 0NG

➲ (M5 junct 27 then A361 towards Barnstaple, turn right onto A399)

☎ 01271 882486

e-mail: info@dinosaur-park.com

web: www.dinosaur-park.com

The land that time forgot. A subtropical paradise with hundreds of birds and animals and animatronic dinosaurs, so real they're alive! Fantastic sealion shows, falconry displays and animal handling sessions. Snow leopards, meerkats, timber wolves, apes and monkeys. Host to the UK's only Wolf Education and Research Centre. Also featuring 'Tomb of the Pharaohs' exhibition. A spectacular lightshow, Destination Mars, and Earthquake Canyon, the most unique train ride in the UK.

Times: Open 18 Mar-29 Oct, daily 10-5.30 (last admission 3). **Fee:** ✱ £12 (ch 3-15 £7, ch under 3 free, pen £8). Family (2ad+2ch) £34. **Facilities:** 🅿 ♨ 📷 shop ⊗ 🍴

COMPTON — MAP 03 SX86

Compton Castle

TQ3 1TA

➲ (off A381 Newton Abbot to Totnes road at Ipplepen. Or, off A380 Torquay, Pakinton ring road at Marldon (no coaches on this road)

☎ 01803 842382

e-mail: greenway@nationaltrust.org.uk

web: www.nationaltrust.org.uk/devoncornwall

Within an eight metre high curtain wall, which was built after French raids in the area, lies this impressive house built and extended during the 14th to 16th centuries. Compton has been the home of the Gilbert family for 600 years, and visitors can find out about their part in the exploration of the New World. The Great Kitchen still has its spiral staircase, bread ovens and knife-sharpening marks, and the withdrawing room has squints through which occupants could watch services in the chapel.

Times: Open Apr-Oct, Mon, Wed & Thu 10-1, 2-5. **Fee:** ✱ Castle & garden £3.70 (ch £1.85) Party 15+ £3.20 (ch £1.60) **Facilities:** 🅿 📷 ⊗ (ex guide dogs) 🐕

CULLOMPTON — MAP 03 ST00

Diggerland

Verbeer Manor EX15 2PE

➲ (M5 junct 27. E on A38 & at rdbt turn right onto A3181. Diggerland is 3m on left)

☎ 08700 344437

e-mail: mail@diggerland

web: www.diggerland.com

An adventure park with a difference, where kids of all ages can experience the thrills of driving real earth moving equipment. Choose from various types of diggers and dumpers ranging from 1 ton to 8 and a half tons. Supervised by an instructor complete the Dumper Truck Challenge or dig for buried treasure. New rides include JCB Robots, the Supertrack, Landrover Safari and Spin Dizzy. Even under 5's can join in, with mum or dad's help. Please telephone for details of events during school and Bank Holidays.

Times: ✱ Open mid Feb-Nov, BHs & school hols. **Facilities:** 🅿 ♨ ♿ shop ⊗ (ex guide dogs) 🍴

DARTMOUTH — MAP 03 SX85

Bayard's Cove Fort — FREE

TQ6 9AT

➲ (in Dartmouth on riverfront)

web: www.english-heritage.org.uk

Built by the townspeople to protect the harbour, the remains of the circular stronghold still stand at the southern end of the harbour.

Times: Open at any reasonable times. **Facilities:** ⊗ ⊞

Dartmouth Castle

Castle Rd TQ6 0JN

➲ (1m SE off B3205, narrow approach road)

☎ 01803 833588

web: www.english-heritage.org.uk

Built at the water's edge in a superb scenic setting, the castle's military history spans well over 500 years.

Times: Open all year, 24 Mar-Jun & Sep, daily 10-5; Jul-Aug, daily 10-6; Oct, daily 10-4; Nov-Mar, Sat-Sun, 10-4. Closed 24-26 Dec & 1 Jan. **Facilities:** 🅿 (charged) shop ⊗ ⊞

Woodlands Leisure Park

Blackawton TQ9 7DQ

➲ (W, off A3122)

☎ 01803 712598

e-mail: fun@woodlandspark.com

web: www.woodlandspark.com

An all weather park, with 60 acres of attractions for all ages. The park features; 15 palyzones, 3 Watercoasters, 500m Toboggan Run, Arctic Gliders, centres for pre-schoolers and the new Avalanche Ride. The large indoor fun houses contain action challenges and interactive play, including; 2 rides, a train, Trauma Tower with 50ft sheer drop and Master Blaster game. The Falconry Centre and Animal Funtime host a vast selection of animals and birds.

continued

Woodlands Leisure Park

Times: Open daily 10 Mar-4 Nov, 5 Nov-Mar wknds and school holidays only. **Fee:** ✱ £8.75. Family ticket £33.20 (2ad+2ch). **Facilities:** ◎ 💻 🗑 ৬ (ramps) toilets for disabled shop ⊗ (ex guide dogs) 📧

See advert on this page

DREWSTEIGNTON   MAP 03 SX79

Castle Drogo
EX6 6PB
➲ *(5m S of A30 Exeter-Okehampton. Coaches turn off A382 at Sandy Park)*
☎ 01647 433306
e-mail: castledrogo@nationaltrust.org.uk
web: www.nationaltrust.org.uk

India tea baron Julius Drewe's dream house. This granite castle, built between 1910 and 1930, is one of the most remarkable works of Sir Edward Lutyens, and combines the grandeur of a medieval castle with the comfort of the 20th century. A great country house with terraced formal garden, woodland spring garden, huge circular croquet lawn and colourful herbaceous borders. Standing at more than 900ft overlooking the wooded gorge of the River Teign with stunning views of Dartmoor, and delightful walks.

Times: Castle open 17 Mar-4 Nov, daily (ex Tue) 11-5. Garden, tearooms & shop open 17 Mar-4 Nov daily. **Fee:** ✱ House & garden £6.80 (ch £3.30). Family £16.50. Garden only £4.50 (ch £2.50) **Facilities:** ◎ 💻 ৬ (Braille & large print guide, touch list) toilets for disabled shop garden centre ⊗ (ex guide/hearing dogs) 🦮 📧

EXETER   MAP 03 SX99

Exeter Cathedral
1 The Cloisters EX1 1HS
☎ 01392 285983
e-mail: visitors@exeter-cathedral.org.uk
web: www.exeter-cathedral.org.uk

A fine example of a medieval cathedral, famous for its two Norman towers, impressive West Front carvings and the longest unbroken stretch of Gothic vaulting in the world. It has been the seat of the bishops of Exeter for over one thousand years and remains a vibrant worshipping community. The Cathedral has an on-going programme of concerts and recitals throughout the year.

Times: Open all year, Mon-Fri 9.30-6.30, Sat 9.30-5, Sun 7.30-6. Times may vary according to special services. **Fee:** £3.50 (students £2)
Facilities: ◎ 💻 🗑 ৬ toilets for disabled shop ⊗ (ex assist dogs)

Guildhall   `FREE`
High St EX4 3EB
➲ *(city centre)*
☎ 01392 665500
e-mail: guildhall@exeter.gov.uk
web: www.exeter.gov.uk/visiting

This is one of the oldest municipal buildings still in use. It was built in 1330 and then altered in 1446, and the arches and façade were added in 1592-5. The roof timbers rest on bosses of bears holding staves, and there are portraits of Exeter dignitaries, guild crests, civic silver and regalia.

Times: Open when there are no mayoral functions. Times are posted outside weekly. Special opening by arrangement. **Facilities:** ◎ (200yds) ৬ toilets for disabled ⊗ (ex guide dogs)

Killerton House & Garden
EX5 3LE
☎ 01392 881345
(For full entry see Killerton House & Garden page 73)

Quay House Visitor Centre   `FREE`
46 The Quay EX2 4AN
☎ 01392 271611
e-mail: quayhouse@exeter.gov.uk
web: www.exeter.gov.uk/visiting

Two thousand years of Exeter history in an audio-visual presentation of the city from Roman times to present day. Learn about the cities quayside history from the small museum.

Times: Open all year, Apr-Oct, daily 10-5; Nov-Mar, Sat-Sun 11-4.
Facilities: ◎ (no parking on quayside) 🗑 shop ⊗ (ex guide dogs)

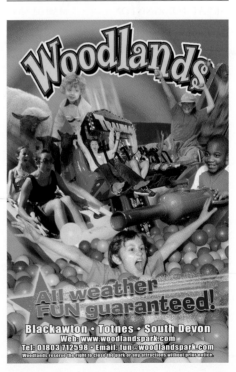

Royal Albert Memorial Museum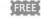

Queen St EX4 3RX
➲ *(in city centre)*
☎ 01392 665858
e-mail: ramm@exeter.gov.uk
web: www.exeter.gov.uk/museums

Situated in the heart of Exeter and home to 16 galleries of displays and a lively programme of events and exhibitions. Travel in time from pre-history to the present day and take a voyage of discovery from Exeter all around the world. Also home to the city's largest gallery and exhibition space.

Times: Open Mon-Sat 10-5 until spring 2007 then closed for redevelopment. **Facilities:** ℗ (200yds) 🍽 🛍 ♿ (parking, ramp, entrance lift) toilets for disabled shop ⊗ (ex guide dogs)

EXMOUTH   MAP 03 SY08

The World of Country Life

Sandy Bay EX8 5BU
➲ *(M5 junct 30, take A376 to Exmouth. Follow signs to Sandy Bay)*
☎ 01395 274533

All-weather family attraction including owl displays, and a safari train that rides through a forty acre deer park. Kids will enjoy the friendly farm animals, pets centre and animal nursery. There are also a Victorian street, working models and thousands of exhibits from a bygone age, including steam and vintage vehicles.

Times: Open Etr-Oct, daily 10-5. **Fee:** ✱ £8 (ch 3-17 & pen £7). Family ticket (2 ad & 2 ch) £28. **Facilities:** ❷ 🍽 ⊮🍽 ♿ (all parts accessible ex 'safari train') toilets for disabled shop ⊗ (ex guide dogs) 🍽

GREAT TORRINGTON   MAP 02 SS41

Dartington Crystal   2 for 1

EX38 7AN
➲ *(Turn off A386 in centre of Great Torrington down School Lane (opposite church). Dartington Crystal is 200mtrs on left)*
☎ 01805 626242
e-mail: sfrench@dartington.co.uk
web: www.dartington.co.uk

Dartington Crystal has won many international design awards in recognition of its excellence. The factory tour allows visitors to watch the glassware being crafted, from the safety of elevated viewing galleries. All age groups are encouraged to have fun in the glass activity area and to discover the fascinating story of glass and the history of Dartington in the Visitor Centre.

Times: Open all year. Visitor centre, Factory tour, Pavilion Cafe and Shops Mon-Fri 9-5 (last tour 3.15), Sat 10-5, Sun 10-4 (tours closed wknds). For Xmas, New Year and BH opening please telephone for details. **Fee:** ✱ £5 (ch under 16 free, pen £4.50). Max 5 ch with every full paying adult. **Facilities:** ❷ 🍽 ⊮🍽 licensed 🛍 ♿ (wheelchairs available) toilets for disabled shop ⊗ (ex guide dogs) 🍽

RHS Garden Rosemoor

EX38 8PH
➲ *(1m SE of Great Torrington on A3124)*
☎ 01805 624067
e-mail: rosemooradmin@rhs.org.uk
web: www.rhs.org.uk/rosemoor

RHS Garden Rosemoor is situated in the beautiful Torridge Valley, set within extensive woodlands. Rich in variety, the Formal Garden includes 200 varieties of roses, and there is a herb garden, potager, cottage garden, winter garden, alpine terrace and extensive herbaceous borders. Please telephone for details of events running throughout the year.

Times: Open: Gardens all year; Apr-Sep 10-6, Oct-Mar 10-5. Closed 25 Dec; Visitor Centre as for Gardens but closed 24-26 Dec. **Fee:** ✱ £5.50 (ch 6-16 £1.50, under 6 free). Party 10+ £4.50. RHS members 1 guest free. **Facilities:** ❷ 🍽 ⊮🍽 licensed 🛍 ♿ (herb garden for disabled, wheelchairs) toilets for disabled shop garden centre ⊗ (ex guide dogs) 🍽

HONITON   MAP 03 ST10

Allhallows Museum

High St EX14 1PG
➲ *(next to parish church of St Paul in High Street)*
☎ 01404 44966 & 42996
e-mail: info@honitonmuseum.co.uk
web: www.honitonmuseum.co.uk

The museum, housed in a chapel dating back to around 1200, has a wonderful display of Honiton lace, and there are lace demonstrations from June to August. The town's history is also illustrated.

Times: Open Mon before Etr-Sep; Mon-Fri 9.30-4.30 & Sat 9.30-1; Oct, Mon-Fri 9.30-3.30, Sat 9.30-12.30. **Fee:** ✱ £2 (accompanied ch free, pen £1.50). **Facilities:** ℗ (400yds) 🛍 ♿ (stair lift, wheelchair, hearing loop) shop ⊗ (ex guide dogs)

England

ILFRACOMBE MAP 02 SS54

Ilfracombe Museum `2 for 1`

Runnymede Gardens, Wilder Rd EX34 8AF
➲ *(next to Landmark Theatre & TIC on seafront)*
☎ 01271 863541
e-mail: ilfracombe@devonmuseums.net
web: www.devonmuseums.net

Ilfracombe was an important trading port from the 14th to the 16th centuries and during the Napoleonic Wars became a popular resort. The history, archaeology, geology, natural history and maritime traditions of the area are illustrated here, along with Victoriana, costumes, photographs and china.

Times: Open all year, Easter-Oct, daily 10-5; Nov-Mar, Mon-Fri 10-1. **Fee:** £2 (accompanied ch free, concessions £1.50). Booked disabled and school groups free. **Facilities:** ℗ (10yds) ▤ ♿ (ramp to front door, wide aisles) shop ⊗ (ex guide dogs)

Watermouth Castle & Family Theme Park

EX34 9SL
➲ *(3m NE off A399, midway between Ilfracombe & Combe Martin)*
☎ 01271 863879
web: www.watermouthcastle.com

A popular family attraction including mechanical music demonstrations, musical water show, dungeon labyrinths, Victorian displays, bygone pier machines, animated fairy tale scenes, tube slide, mini golf, children's carousel, swingboats, aeroplane ride, water fountains, river ride, gardens and a maze.

Times: Open Apr-end Oct, closed Sat. (Also closed some Mon & Fri off season). Ring for further details. **Fee:** ✱ £10 (ch 3-13 £8.50 & pen £7) **Facilities:** ❷ ⬛ ♿ (special wheelchair route) toilets for disabled shop ⊗ (ex guide dogs) ◼

KILLERTON HOUSE & GARDEN MAP 03 SS90

Killerton House & Garden

EX5 3LE
➲ *(off B3181 Exeter to Cullompton road)*
☎ 01392 881345

Elegant 18th-century house set in an 18-acre garden with sloping lawns and herbaceous borders. A majestic avenue of beech trees runs
continued

up the hillside, past an arboretum of rhododendrons and conifers. The garden has an ice house and rustic summer house where the family's pet bear was once kept. Inside the house are displays from the Killerton Dress Collection, and a Victorian kitchen. Please telephone for details of annual events.

Times: Open: House, daily (ex Tue), Mar & Oct, Wed-Sun, Aug daily 11-5. Gardens open all year, daily from 10.30. **Fee:** ✱ House & grounds £7. Grounds only £5.30. **Facilities:** ❷ ⬛ ▯◯▯ licensed ▤ ♿ (wheelchairs & motorised buggy available) toilets for disabled shop garden centre ⊗ (ex in park & guide dogs) ◥◣ ◼

KINGSBRIDGE MAP 03 SX74

Cookworthy Museum of Rural Life

The Old Grammar School, 108 Fore St TQ7 1AW
➲ *(A38 onto A384, then A381 to Kingsbridge, museum at top of town)*
☎ 01548 853235
e-mail: wcookworthy@talk21.com
web: www.devonmuseums.net

The 17th-century schoolrooms of this former grammar school are now the setting for another kind of education. Reconstructed room-sets of a Victorian kitchen, an Edwardian pharmacy, a costume room and extensive collection of local historical items are gathered to illustrate South Devon life. A walled garden and farm gallery are also features of this museum, founded to commemorate William Cookworthy, 'father' of the English china clay industry. The Local Heritage Resource Centre with public access databases, microfilm of local newspapers since 1855 and Devon record service point are available to visitors. Please ring for details of special events. All in a Days Work explores and celebrates the long tradition of skilled craftsmen and women.

Times: Open all year, 26 Mar-Sep, Mon-Sat 10.30-5; Oct 10.30-4. Nov-Mar groups by arrangement. Local Heritage Resource Centre open all year, Mon-Thu 10-12 & Wed also 2-4, other times by appointment. **Fee:** £2 (ch £1, concessions £1.50). Family ticket £5 (2ad+4ch). **Facilities:** ℗ (100mtrs) (max 3hrs) ▤ ♿ (Braille labels on selected exhibits, viewing gallery) toilets for disabled shop ⊗ (ex guide dogs)

KINGSWEAR MAP 03 SX85

Coleton Fishacre House & Garden

Brownstone Rd TQ6 0EQ
➲ *(3m from Kingswear. Take Ferry Rd and turn off at Toll House, follow brown tourist signs)*
☎ 01803 752466
e-mail: coletonfishacre@nationaltrust.org.uk
web: www.nationaltrust.org.uk

The house, set in a stream-fed valley on a beautiful stretch of south Devon coastline, was designed in the 1920s for Rupert and Lady D'Oyly Carte (of Gilbert & Sullivan fame) reflecting the Arts & Crafts tradition, but with art deco-influenced interiors. A luxuriant garden was created around it, and has year-round interest with a wide variety of rare and exotic plants. Please telephone for details of music events throughout the year.

Times: Garden open 1-30 Mar, Sat & Sun only 11-5; 31 Mar-29 Oct, Wed-Sun & BH Mon 10.30-5. House open 29 Mar-29 Oct, Wed-Sun & BH Mon 11-4.30. **Fee:** ✱ House & garden £6 (ch £3). Family ticket £15. 1 ad family ticket £9 Party £5.60 (ch £2.80). Garden only £5.40 (ch £2.70) Party £4.75. **Facilities:** ❷ ⬛ ▤ ♿ (wheelchairs available, Braille guides, mobile T loop) toilets for disabled shop garden centre ⊗ (ex assist dogs) ◥◣ ◼

England

KNIGHTSHAYES COURT MAP 03 SS91

Knightshayes Court
EX16 7RQ
➲ (M5 junct 27, 2m N of Tiverton off A396)
☎ 01884 254665 & 257381
e-mail: knightshayes@nationaltrust.org.uk
web: www.nationaltrust.org.uk

This fine Victorian mansion, a rare example of William Burges' work, offers much of interest to all ages. The garden is one of the most beautiful in Devon, with formal terraces, amusing topiary, a pool garden and woodland walks.

Times: House & garden open 25 Mar-31 Oct, daily (House closed Fri) 11-4.30 (11-4 in Oct). **Fee:** ✳ House & garden £7 (ch £3.50). Party rates available. **Facilities:** ☻ ⚟ �🍴 licensed 🗐 ൧ (wheelchairs available, lift, Braille & audio guide) toilets for disabled shop garden centre ⊗ (ex guide dogs in house) 🐾 ◀

LYDFORD MAP 02 SX58

Lydford Castle and Saxon Town `FREE`
EX20 4BH
➲ (in Lydford off A386)

Standing above the gorge of the River Lyd, this tower, dating back to the twelfth century, was notorious as a prison. The earthworks of the original Norman fort lie to the south.

Times: Open at any reasonable times. **Facilities:** ☻ ✿

Lydford Gorge
EX20 4BH
➲ (off A386, between Okehampton & Tavistock)
☎ 01822 820320 & 820441
e-mail: lydfordgorge@nationaltrust.org.uk
web: www.nationaltrust.org.uk

The spectacular gorge has been formed by the River Lyd, which has cut into the rock and caused swirling boulders to scoop out potholes in the stream bed. This has created some dramatic features, notably the Devil's Cauldron close to Lydford Bridge. At the end of the gorge is the 90ft-high White Lady Waterfall.

Times: Open Mar-Sep, daily 10-5; Oct, daily 10-4. (Winter opening Nov-Mar, please ring for details). **Fee:** ✳ £5 (ch 5-16 £2.50, under 5 free). Family ticket (2ad & 3ch) £12.50. **Facilities:** ☻ ⚟ (easy access path, audio tapes, braille guide) shop garden centre 🐾 ◀

MORWELLHAM MAP 02 SX47

Morwellham Quay
PL19 8JL
➲ (4m W of Tavistock, off A390. Midway between Gunnislake & Tavistock. Signed)
☎ 01822 832766 & 833808
e-mail: enquiries@morwellham-quay.co.uk
web: www.morwellham-quay.co.uk

A unique, open-air museum based around the ancient port and copper mine workings in the heart of the Tamar Valley. Journey back into another time as costumed interpreters help you re-live the daily life of a 19th-century mining village and shipping quay. A tramway takes you deep into the workings of the George and Charlotte mine.

continued

Special events include music festivals, classic car shows, and a Victorian food festival.

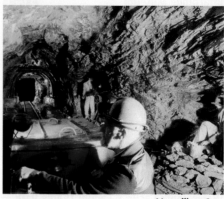

Morwellham Quay

Times: ✳ Open all year (ex Xmas wk) 10-6 (4.30 Nov-Etr). Last admission 3.30 (2.30 Nov-Etr). **Facilities:** ☻ ⚟ 🍴 licensed 🗐 ൧ (smooth paths, but difficult areas in Victorian village) toilets for disabled shop ◀

NEWTON ABBOT MAP 03 SX87

Bradley Manor
TQ12 6BN
➲ (SW of Newton Abbot on A381 Totnes road. 1m from town centre)
☎ 01626 354513
e-mail: greenway@nationaltrust.org
web: www.nationaltrust.org.uk/devoncornwall

A National Trust property of 70 acres, the 15th-century house and chapel are surrounded by woodland. The River Lemon and a millstream flow through the estate.

Times: Open Apr-Sep, 2-5; Oct by appointment **Fee:** ✳ £3.70 (ch £1.85) **Facilities:** ☻ 🗐 ൧ T loop, large print guide ⊗ 🚐 🐾

Hedgehog Hospital at Prickly Ball Farm
Denbury Rd, East Ogwell TQ12 6BZ
➲ (1.5m from Newton Abbot on A381 towards Totnes, follow brown heritage signs)
☎ 01626 362319 & 330685
e-mail: enquiries@pricklyballfarm.co.uk
web: www.pricklyballfarm.co.uk

See, touch and learn about this wild animal. In mid-season see baby hogs bottle feeding. Find out how to encourage hedgehogs into your garden and how they are put back into the wild. Talks on hedgehogs throughout the day, with a big screen presentation. There are also pony and cart rides, goat walking, pony grooming, lamb feeding (in season), and a petting zoo.

Times: Open Etr-end Oct, 10-5. (Recommended last admission 3.30) **Fee:** ✳ £5.75 (ch 4-14 £4.75, ch under 3 free, concessions £5). Family ticket £18.95. **Facilities:** ☻ ⚟ 🗐 ൧ (large print menu, use of wheelchair, Braille menu) toilets for disabled shop ⊗ (ex guide dogs) ◀

Tuckers Maltings

Teign Rd TQ12 4AA

➲ (follow brown tourist signs from Newton Abbot railway station)

☎ 01626 334734

e-mail: info@tuckersmaltings.com
web: www.tuckersmaltings.com

The only working Malthouse in England open to the public, producing malt from barley for over 30 West Country breweries. Learn all about the process of malting - and taste the end product at the in-house brewery. Guided tours last an hour.

Times: Open Good Fri-end Oct, Mon-Sat (Closed Sun). Speciality bottled beer shop open throughout the year. Phone to check winter opening.
Fee: ✱ £5.45 (ch 5-15 £3.45, 16-17 £3.95, pen £4.95). Family ticket £15.45.
Facilities: Ⓟ (100yds) (pay & display car park) ♿ toilets for disabled shop 🛍

OKEHAMPTON — MAP 02 SX59

Museum of Dartmoor Life — 2 for 1

3 West St EX20 1HQ

➲ (follow brown signs off all major roads into Okehampton. Museum on main road next to White Hart Hotel)

☎ 01837 52295

e-mail: dartmoormuseum@eclipse.co.uk
web: museumofdartmoorlife.eclipse.co.uk

Housed on three floors in an early 19th-century mill, the museum tells the story of how people have lived, worked and played on and around Dartmoor through the centuries. It shows how the moorland has shaped their lives just as their work has shaped the moorland. In the Cranmere Gallery, temporary exhibitions feature local history, art and crafts.

Times: Open Etr-Nov, Mon-Sat 10.15-4.30. Winter opening times, telephone for details. **Fee:** ✱ £2.50 (students £1). Family ticket £6.25. Party 10+.
Facilities: Ⓟ 🖥 🗄 ♿ (Braille, desk loop, lift) toilets for disabled shop

Okehampton Castle

Castle Lodge EX20 1JB

➲ (1m SW of town centre)

☎ 01837 52844

web: www.english-heritage.org.uk

Once the largest castle in Devon set amongst the stunning Dartmoor foothills. A free audio tour brings this romantic ruin to life.

Times: Open Apr-Jun & Sep, daily 10-5; Jul-Aug, daily 10-6. Closed Oct-Mar.
Fee: £3 (ch £1.50, concessions £2.30). Prices and opening times are subject to change in Spring 2007. Please check web site or call 0870 333 1181 for the most up to date prices and opening times when planning your visit.
Facilities: Ⓟ shop ♿

An asterisk ✱ indicates that opening times or prices are for 2006. Please contact the attraction for more up-to-date information.

OTTERTON — MAP 03 SY08

Otterton Mill Centre — FREE

EX9 7HG

➲ (on the B3178 between Budleigh Salterton and Newton Poppleford)

☎ 01392 568521

e-mail: escape@ottertonmill.com
web: www.ottertonmill.com

Set beside the River Otter in one of Devon's loveliest valleys, Otterton Mill is a centuries-old working watermill, a famous bakery and shop full of local produce, a restaurant, and a gallery of arts and crafts from local artists. Please see website for details of music nights and art events

Times: Open daily, 10-5. **Facilities:** Ⓟ 🖥 🍴 licensed 🗄 ♿ (free entry to ground floor) toilets for disabled shop 🛍

PAIGNTON — MAP 03 SX86

Paignton & Dartmouth Steam Railway

Queens Park Station, Torbay Rd TQ4 6AF

➲ (from Paignton follow brown tourist signs)

☎ 01803 555872

e-mail: mail@pdsr.eclipse.co.uk
web: www.paignton-steamrailway.co.uk

Steam trains run for seven miles from Paignton to Kingswear on the former Great Western line, stopping at Goodrington Sands, Churston, and Kingswear, connecting with the ferry crossing to Dartmouth. Combined river excursions available. Ring for details of special events.

Times: Open Jun-Sep, daily 9-5.30 & selected days Oct & Apr-May.
Fee: ✱ Paignton to Kingswear £7.40 (ch £5.10, pen £6.80). Family £23. Paignton to Dartmouth (including ferry) £9 (ch £6, pen £8.50). Family £28.
Facilities: Ⓟ (5mins walk) 🖥 ♿ (wheelchair ramp for boarding train) toilets for disabled shop 🛍

Paignton Zoo Environmental Park

Totnes Rd TQ4 7EU

➲ (1m from Paignton town centre on A3022 Totnes road. Follow brown signs)

☎ 01803 697500

e-mail: info@paigntonzoo.org.uk
web: www.paigntonzoo.org.uk

Paignton is one of Britain's biggest zoos, set in a beautiful and secluded woodland valley, where new enclosures are spacious and
continued

England

naturalistic. A tour will take you through some of the world's threatened habitats - Forest, Savannah, Wetland and Desert, with hundreds of species, many of them endangered and part of conservation breeding programmes. There are regular keeper talks, a children's play area, and special events throughout the year.

Times: Open all year, daily 10-6 (5 in winter). Last admission 5 (4 in winter). Closed 25 Dec. **Fee:** £11.35 (ch 3-15 £7.60, concessions £9.35). Family ticket (2ad & 2ch) £34.10. Joint family saver ticket with Living Coasts £49.15. **Facilities:** ℗ ⬛ �🅾 licensed ♿ (some steep hills, wheelchair loan-booking essential) toilets for disabled shop ⊗ (ex guide dogs) ◀

PLYMOUTH   MAP 02 SX45

The Elizabethan House NEW
32 New St, The Barbican PL1 7FW
➲ (A38/A374 follow signs to city centre, house located just behind Southside St)
☎ 01752 304774
e-mail: enquiry@plymouthmuseum.gov.uk
web: www.plymouthmuseum.gov.uk

On Plymouth's historic Barbican, find an ancient doorway and go back in time to Drake's Plymouth. Home of an Elizabethan merchant or sea captain, the house is an opportunity to see how an Elizabethan mariner might have lived. A rare Tudor time-capsule with furniture and fabrics dating back to the 1600s.

Times: Open Apr-Sep, Tue-Sat & BH Mon, 10-5 (last entry 4.30)
Fee: ✱ £1.30 (ch 80p). Family tickets & other concessions available
Facilities: ℗ (200yds) ♿ shop garden centre

The Green House Visitor Centre
The Ride PL9 7JA
➲ (2 miles E of Plymouth city centre on A379 Kingsbridge road. Follow signs for Chelson Meadow)
☎ 01752 482392
e-mail: nowaste@the greenhouseplymouth.org.uk
web: www.thegreenhouseplymouth.org.uk

The UK's first leisure-based, sustainable waste, education exhibition. A responsible attitude to waste is promoted via informal, yet informative, interactive exhibitions. These include a giant energy-generating hamster wheel; underground caves where the whole family can learn about waste separation and the machinery used to do it, helped along by Colin the Can and Betty the Bottle; waste disposal challenges, and more.

Times: ✱ Open Tue-Sat 10-5. (Last entry at 4) **Facilities:** ℗ ⬛ 🅾 ♿ toilets for disabled shop ⊗ (ex guide dogs)

National Marine Aquarium
Rope Walk, Coxside PL4 0LF
➲ (A38 to Marsh Mills (Sainsbury's) then head for city centre & follow brown signs for Barbican & Coxside car park)
☎ 01752 600301
e-mail: enquiries@national-aquarium.co.uk
web: www.national-aquarium.co.uk

Britains biggest aquarium is now even bigger, thanks to a brand-new, three-floor, multi-million pound interactive centre. Explorocean is a new attraction within the aquarium, which showcases the very latest in ocean technology, and includes underwater obstacle courses and Remote Operated Vehicle games, along with virtual sonar tours, satellite images from space, and 3D deep-sea journeys. This is all on

continued

top of over 3,000 fish in more than 50 tanks, including one that is the height of a three-storey building.

Times: Open all year daily, mid Mar-Oct 10-6; Nov-mid Mar 10-5
Fee: £9.50 (ch £5.75, concessions £8). Family £27 (2+2)
Facilities: ℗ 200yds ⬛ 🅾 ♿ toilets for disabled shop ⊗ (ex guide dogs) ◀

Plymouth City Museum & Art Gallery [FREE]
Drake Circus PL4 8AJ
➲ (off A38 onto A374, museum on NW of city centre, opposite university)
☎ 01752 304774
e-mail: enquiry@plymouthmuseum.gov.uk
web: www.plymouthmuseum.gov.uk

The City Museum and Art Gallery is home to a Fine and Decorative Art Collection of paintings, prints and Reynolds family portraits, silver and Plymouth China, and the Cottonian Collection of drawings, sculpture and books. There is a lively programme of art exhibitions, as well as archaeology, local and natural history displays, and the Discovery Centre with a 'hands-on' section for children.

Times: Open all year, Tue-Fri 10-5.30, Sat & BH Mon 10-5. Closed Good Fri & 25-26 Dec. **Facilities:** ℗ (200yds) (time restricted on-street parking) ♿ (wheelchair available) toilets for disabled shop ⊗ (ex guide dogs)

Royal Citadel
PL1 2PD
➲ (at the end of Plymouth Hoe)
☎ 01752 775841
e-mail: plymouthbbg@hotmail.com
web: www.english-heritage.org.uk

A dramatic 17th-century fortress built to defend the coastline from the Dutch. It is still in use today.

Times: Open May-Sep, Tue-Thu 2.30 by guided tour only **Fee:** £3.50 (EH Members £3.) Prices and opening times are subject to change in Spring 2007. Please check web site or call 0870 333 1181 for the most up to date prices and opening times when planning your visit. **Facilities:** ⊗ ⊞

PLYMPTON   MAP 02 SX55

Saltram
PL7 1UH
➲ (3.5m E of Plymouth, between A38 & A379. Take Plympton turn at Marsh Mill rdbt, turn right at 4th traffic lights to Cot Hill. At t-junct right into Merafield Rd, Saltram 0.25m on right)
☎ 01752 333500 & 333503
e-mail: saltram@nationaltrust.org.uk
web: www.nationaltrust.org.uk

This magnificent George II house still has its original contents. The collection of paintings was begun at the suggestion of Reynolds and includes many of his portraits. The saloon and dining room were designed by Robert Adam and have superb decorative plasterwork and period furniture. The extensive gardens include a working Orangery and several follies, and part of their 500 acres is alongside the River Plym.

Times: Open House: Apr-Oct, 12-4.30 (ex Fri). Garden open all year, 11-4.30. Park open all year, dawn to dusk. **Fee:** ✱ House and garden £7. Garden only £3.50. NT members free. **Facilities:** ℗ 🅾 licensed ⊞ ♿ (wheelchairs available, lift, Braille & audio guides) toilets for disabled shop ⊗ (ex in park on leads) ⬛ ◀

POWDERHAM

MAP 03 SX98

Powderham Castle

EX6 8JQ

⮎ *(signed off A379 Exeter/Dawlish road)*

☎ 01626 890243

e-mail: castle@powderham.co.uk

web: www.powderham.co.uk

Built between 1390 and 1420, this ancestral home of the Earls of Devon was damaged in the Civil War. The house was restored and altered in later times and is set in beautiful rose gardens with views over the deer park to the Exe Estuary. Please telephone for details of special events.

Times: ✱ Open Etr-end Oct, 10-5.30 (last admission 5). Closed Sat. **Facilities:** ♿ 🖵 �🅞�`licensed & (ramps) toilets for disabled shop garden centre ▄

SALCOMBE

MAP 03 SX73

Overbeck's

Sharpitor TQ8 8LW

⮎ *(1.5m SW of Salcombe, signed from Malborough & Salcombe, narrow approach road)*

☎ 01548 842893

e-mail: overbecks@nationaltrust.org.uk

web: www.nationaltrust.org.uk

The garden is on the most southerly tip of Devon, and allows many exotic plants to flourish. The Edwardian house displays toys, dolls and a natural history collection, and there is a secret room for children where they can search for 'Fred' the friendly ghost.

Times: Open Apr-Jul, Sun-Fri 11-5.30; Aug, daily 11-5.30; Sep, Sun-Fri 11-5.30; Oct, Sun-Thu 11-5. Gardens open all year, 10-6 (or sunset if earlier). **Fee:** Gardens & house £5.80 (ch £2.90). Family ticket £14.50. **Facilities:** ♿ 🖵 📶 (ramp from garden, Braille guide, hearing loop) shop ⊗ (ex assist dogs) 🚍(by arrangement only) 🐾 ▄

SOUTH MOLTON

MAP 03 SS72

Quince Honey Farm

`2 for 1`

EX36 3AZ

⮎ *(3.5m W of A361, on N edge of South Molton)*

☎ 01769 572401

e-mail: info@quincehoney.co.uk

web: www.quincehoney.com

Follow the story of honey and beeswax from flower to table. The exhibition allows you to see the world of bees close up in complete safety; hives open at the press of a button revealing the honeybees' secret life. After viewing the bees at work, sample the fruits of their labour in the café or shop.

Times: Open daily, Apr-Sep 9-6; Oct 9-5; Shop only Nov-Etr 9-5, closed Sun. Closed 25 Dec-4 Jan. **Fee:** ✱ £3.95 (ch 5-16 £2.75, pen £3.25) **Facilities:** ♿ 🖵 📶 & toilets for disabled shop ⊗ (ex guide dogs) ▄

STICKLEPATH

MAP 03 SX69

Finch Foundry

EX20 2NW

⮎ *(off A30 at Okehampton junct, follow brown signs to Finch Foundry. Located in main street of village)*

☎ 01837 840046

Finch Foundry was, in the 19th century, a water-powered factory for making sickles, scythes, shovels and other hand tools. Although no longer in production, three waterwheels can still be seen driving huge hammers, shears, grindstone and other machinery, with daily working demonstrations. These demonstrations explain the key role the foundry played in the local community. Special Event: St. Clements Day (St Clements is the patron saint of blacksmiths) 3rd Sat in Nov.

Times: Open Apr-Nov, daily (ex Tue), 11-5.30 (Last entry 5). **Fee:** ✱ £3.70 (ch £1.85). **Facilities:** ♿ 🖵 📶 & (access to shop/tea room, view main foundry via shop) shop 🐾 ▄

TIVERTON

MAP 03 SS91

Tiverton Castle

`2 for 1`

EX16 6RP

⮎ *(M5 junct 27, then 7m on A361 towards Tiverton to rdbt where Castle is signposted)*

☎ 01884 253200 & 255200

e-mail: tiverton.castle@ukf.net

web: www.tivertoncastle.com

The original castle, built in 1106 by order of Henry I, was rebuilt in the late 13th-14th centuries. It resisted General Fairfax during the Civil War but fell to him when a lucky shot hit the drawbridge chain. Now a private house, the gardens are lovely and there's a fine Civil War armoury. 2006 was the 900th anniversary of original castle building.

Times: Open Etr Sun-end Oct, Sun,Thu & BH Mon only 2.30-5.30. Last admission 5. **Fee:** ✱ £4 (ch 7-16 £2, under 7 free). Disabled half price if accessing ground floor only. **Facilities:** ♿ shop ⊗ (ex guide dogs)

Tiverton Museum of Mid Devon Life

Beck's Square EX16 6PJ

⮎ *(in centre of town next to Beck's Square car park)*

☎ 01884 256295

e-mail: curator04@tivertonmuseum.org.uk

web: www.tivertonmuseum.org.uk

This large and comprehensive museum now with 15 galleries, re-opened after extensive rebuilding and redisplayed throughout. It is housed in a 19th-century school and the exhibits include a Heathcote Lace Gallery featuring items from the local lace-making industry. There is also an agricultural section with a collection of farm wagons and implements. Other large exhibits include two waterwheels and a railway locomotive with many GWR items. The railway gallery has recently re-opened after an 18 month redesign.

Times: Open Feb-mid Dec, Mon-Fri 10.30-4.30, Sat 10-1. Open BHs. **Fee:** ✱ £4 (ch £1, pen £3). Family (2+4) £9. **Facilities:** Ⓟ (100yds) & (lift, induction loop) toilets for disabled shop ⊗ (ex guide dogs)

TORQUAY   MAP 03 SX96

Babbacombe Model Village

Hampton Av, Babbacombe TQ1 3LA

➲ *(follow brown tourist signs from outskirts of town)*

☎ 01803 328669 & 315315

e-mail: ss@babbacombemodelvillage.co.uk

web: www.babbacombemodelvillage.co.uk

Set in four acres of beautifully maintained, miniature landscaped garden, the village contains over 400 models and 1200ft of model railway. City Lights, an evening illuminations feature, depicts Piccadilly Circus in miniature. At the end of your visit, enjoy a new facility that offers breathtaking views over the model village. Vintage model railway layout; the Aquaviva, an evening water, light and sound spectacular and the new 'Silvers Model Circus'.

Times: May-Sep, 10-9.30 (10-5 Sat), winter 10-3.30 (ex 18 Nov-Dec, 10-7).
Fee: ✱ £6.90 (ch £4.50, pen £5.90). Family ticket £20.
Facilities: ❷ (charged) 💻 🍴 🗐 ⓓ (push button audio information) toilets for disabled shop garden centre ◀

'Bygones'   2 for 1

Fore St, St Marychurch TQ1 4PR

➲ *(follow tourist signs into Torquay and St Marychurch)*

☎ 01803 326108

web: www.bygones.co.uk

Step back in time in this life-size Victorian exhibition street of over 20 shops including a forge, pub and period display rooms, housed in a former cinema. Exhibits include a large model railway layout, illuminated fantasyland, railwayana and military exhibits including a walk-through World War I trench. At Christmas the street is turned into a winter wonderland. A new set piece features Babbacombe's John Lee ('the man they couldn't hang') in his cell. There is something here for all the family.

Times: Open all year, Summer 10-6, (Wed & Thur 10-9.30, Jul-Aug); Spring & Autumn 10-6; Winter 10-4, wknds & school hols 10-5. (Last entry 1hr before closing). **Fee:** ✱ £5.50 (ch 4-14 £3.50, pen £4.95). Family ticket (2ad & 2ch) £16. Prices may change, contact in advance.
Facilities: ❷ (50yds) 💻 🗐 (ramp) shop ⊗ (ex guide dogs)

Kents Cavern

Cavern House, 91 Ilsham Rd, Wellswood TQ1 2JF

➲ *(1.25m NE off B3199, follow brown tourist signs. 1m from Torquay Harbour)*

☎ 01803 215136

e-mail: caves@kents-cavern.co.uk

web: www.kents-cavern.co.uk

Probably the most important Palaeolithic site in Britain and recognised as one of the most significant archaeological areas. This is not only a world of spectacular natural beauty, but also a priceless record of past times, where a multitude of secrets of mankind, animals and nature have become trapped and preserved over the last 500,000 years. 170 years after the first excavations and with over 80,000 remains already unearthed, modern research is still discovering new clues to our past. Please visit website for details of special events.

Times: Open all year daily from 10, last tour 3.30 Nov-Feb, 4 Mar-Jun & Sep-Oct, 4.30 Jul-Aug. For up to date info visit website. **Fee:** ✱ Daytime: £6.50 (ch 4-15 £5) Family £21. Ghost evening tour: £5.50. For up to date info visit website. **Facilities:** ❷ 💻 🍴 licensed ⓓ toilets for disabled shop ⊗ (ex guide dogs) ◀

Living Coasts

Beacon Quay TQ1 2BG

➲ *(once in Torquay follow A379 and brown tourist signs to Torquay harbour)*

☎ 01803 202470

e-mail: info@livingcoasts.org.uk

web: www.livingcoasts.org.uk

Living Coasts is an unusual and ambitious attraction that allows visitors to take a trip around the coastlines of the world without leaving Torquay. Specially designed environments are home to fur seals, puffins, penguins, ducks, rats, and waders among others. All the animals can be seen above and below the water, while the huge meshed aviary allows the birds to fly free over your head. Visitors can obtain special joint tickets which will allow them to visit nearby Paignton Zoo.

Times: Open daily from 10. Closed 25 Dec. **Fee:** £6.75 (ch over 3 £4.70, concessions £5.25). Family ticket (2ad+2ch) £20.50 **Facilities:** ❷ 💻 🍴 licensed 🗐 ⓓ (pre-booked wheelchair hire) toilets for disabled shop ⊗ (ex assist dogs) ◀

TOTNES   MAP 03 SX86

Guildhall

Ramparts Walk, off High St TQ9 5QH

➲ *(behind St Mary's Church on the main street)*

☎ 01803 862147

e-mail: office@totnestowncouncil.gov.uk

web: www.totnestowncouncil.gov.uk

Originally the refectory, kitchens, brewery and bakery for the Benedictine Priory of Totnes (1088-1536), the building was established as the Guildhall in 1553 during the reign of Edward VI. A magistrates' court and a prison opened in 1624, and the council chamber is still used today.

Times: Open Apr-Sep, Mon-Wed 10-3; Other times by appointment.
Fee: £1 (ch 25p). **Facilities:** ❷ (50yds) 🗐

Totnes Castle

TQ9 5NU

⊃ (on hill overlooking town)

☎ 01803 864406

web: www.english-heritage.org.uk

One of the best surviving examples of a Norman motte and bailey castle with spectacular views. The once great ditch that surrounded the keep is today filled with the cottages and gardens of the town.

Times: Open Apr-Jun & Sep, daily 10-5; Jul-Aug, daily 10-6; Oct, daily 10-4. **Fee:** £2.40 (ch £1.20, concessions £1.80). Prices and opening times are subject to change in Spring 2007. Please check web site or call 0870 333 1181 for the most up to date prices and opening times when planning your visit. **Facilities:** Ⓟ (70yds) (payment required) shop ⊞

Totnes Museum

2 for 1

70 Fore St TQ9 5RU

⊃ (from bottom of Totnes Town, turn into Fore St, museum on left of main street, just before East Gate Arch Clock Tower)

☎ 01803 863821

e-mail: totnesmuseum@btconnect.com

web: www.devonmuseums.net/totnes

An Elizabethan merchant's house, dating from 1575, said to have been built for Sir Walter Kelland, a wealthy merchant. The building houses archaeological and social history collection and a room dedicated to Charles Babbage, inventor of the first computer. Study centre archives located at the rear of the museum.

Times: Open 13 Mar-27 Oct, Mon-Fri 10.30-5 (last entry 4.30) **Fee:** ✱ £1.50 (ch 5-16 50p, concessions £1). **Facilities:** Ⓟ (440yds) (restricted parking on main street) ▥ (personal guided tours available) shop

Coldharbour Mill Working Wool Museum

Coldharbour Mill EX15 3EE

⊃ (2m from M5 junct 27, off B3181. Follow signs to Willand, then brown signs to museum)

☎ 01884 840960

e-mail: info@coldharbourmill.org.uk

web: www.coldharbourmill.org.uk

The Picturesque Coldharbour Mill is set in idyllic Devon countryside. It has been producing textiles since 1799 and is now a working museum, still making knitting wools and fabrics on period machinery. The Fox Gallery exhibits a variety of temporary exhibitions including textiles, photography, mixed media and craft. With machine demonstrations, a water wheel and steam engines, Coldharbour Mill is a wonderful and very different family day out.

Times: Mar-Sep 10.30-5, Oct-Feb 11-4 **Fee:** ✱ £6.25 (ch 5-16 £2.95, pen £5.75). Family ticket £17. **Facilities:** Ⓟ ▣ ⑪ licensed ▥ & (helpful guides & lift, indoor restaurant not accessible) toilets for disabled shop ⊗ (ex guide dogs or in grounds) ◀

Yelverton Paperweight Centre

FREE

4 Buckland Ter, Leg O'Mutton Corner PL20 6AD

⊃ (at Yelverton off A386, Plymouth to Tavistock road)

☎ 01822 854250

e-mail: paperweightcentre@btinternet.com

web: www.paperweightcentre.co.uk

This unusual centre is the home of the Broughton Collection - a glittering permanent collection of glass paperweights of all sizes and designs. The centre also has an extensive range of modern glass paperweights for sale. Prices range from a few pounds to over £1000. There is also a series of oil and watercolour paintings by talented local artists.

Times: Open Apr-Oct, daily 10.30-5; 10-24 Dec, daily; Nov & Jan-Mar by appointment. **Facilities:** Ⓟ (100yds) & (ramp on request) shop ◀

Torquay Harbour

Dorset

Durdle Door
Lulworth Cove

Rural Dorset has retained much of the charm and tranquillity of an earlier age.
Shaftesbury is the site of an abbey founded by Alfred the Great, and the view
from the top of Gold Hill and the abbey gardens are breath-taking. The area
around Dorchester is known as 'Hardy country' – the setting for most of the
novels by 19th-century novelist Thomas Hardy – and designated as an Area of
Outstanding Natural Beauty. On the coast, the major resorts of Weymouth,
Poole and Bournemouth offer plenty of family entertainment, while Lulworth
Cove, Lyme Regis and the Jurassic Coast brings out the naturalist in all of us.

ABBOTSBURY — MAP 03 SY58

Abbotsbury Swannery

New Barn Rd DT3 4JG

⮕ *(turn off A35 at Winterborne Abbas near Dorchester. Abbotsbury on B3157 coastal road, between Weymouth and Bridport)*

☎ 01305 871858
e-mail: info@abbotsbury-tourism.co.uk
web: www.abbotsbury-tourism.co.uk

Abbotsbury is the breeding ground of the only managed colony of mute swans. The swans can be seen safely at close quarters, and the site is also home or stopping point for many wild birds. The highlight of the year is the cygnet season, end of May to the end of June, when there may be over 100 nests on site. Visitors can often take pictures of cygnets emerging from eggs at close quarters. There is an audio-visual show, as well as mass feeding at noon and 4pm daily, and an ugly duckling trail. Childrens play area available.

Times: Open 18 Mar-29 Oct, daily 10-6 (last admission 5). **Fee:** ✱ £7.50 (ch £4.50 & pen £7). **Facilities:** ♿ 🅿 ⚌ 🅸🅾🅸 licensed 🍴 ♿ (free wheelchair loan, herb garden for blind) toilets for disabled shop ⊗ ◀

ATHELHAMPTON — MAP 03 SY79

Athelhampton House & Gardens `2 for 1`

DT2 7LG

⮕ *(off A35 Northbrook junct, follow brown tourist signs towards Puddletown. Left at traffic lights, attraction approx 1m on left)*

☎ 01305 848363
e-mail: enquiry@athelhampton.co.uk
web: www.athelhampton.co.uk

Athelhampton, one of the finest 15th-century houses in England, contains magnificently furnished rooms including The Great Hall of 1485 and the library, which contains 3,000 books and an original 1915 Riley Imperial billiard table. The glorious Grade I gardens contain the world-famous topiary pyramids, fountains, and collections of tulips, magnolias, roses, clematis and lilies in season. The West Wing Gallery features paintings by Marevna (1892-1984), a Russian painter who lived and painted at Athelhampton.

Times: Open Mar-Oct, daily 10.30-5. Also Sun in Winter (ex Xmas). (Closed Fri & Sat, open Good Fri). **Fee:** ✱ House & garden £8 (ch free, pen £7.25, student & disabled £5.75). Garden only £5.75 (ch free). **Facilities:** ♿ ⚌ 🅸🅾🅸 licensed ♿ (wheelchairs available) toilets for disabled shop ⊗ (ex assistance dogs) ◀

BEAMINSTER — MAP 03 ST40

Mapperton

DT8 3NR

⮕ *(2m SE off A356 & B3163)*

☎ 01308 862645
e-mail: office@mapperton.com
web: www.mapperton.com

Several acres of terraced valley gardens with specimen trees and shrubs, and formal borders surround a manor house that dates back to the 16th century. There are also fountains, grottoes, stone sculpture fishponds and an orangery, and the garden offers good views and walks. A plant fair is held annually, usually in April.

Times: Open Gardens: Mar-Oct, daily (ex Sat) 11-5. House open 25 Jun-3 Aug, 28 May, 27 Aug, wkdays only, 2-4.30 (last admission 4).

Fee: Gardens £4 (ch 5-18 £2, under 5 free). House £4. Groups 20+ £7.50 (house & garden) £3.50 (house or garden). **Facilities:** 🅿 ⚌ 🍴 ♿ (ramp from parking area to garden) toilets for disabled shop ⊗ (ex guide dogs)

BLANDFORD FORUM — MAP 03 ST80

Royal Signals Museum `2 for 1`

Blandford Camp DT11 8RH

⮕ *(signposted off the B3082 Blandford/Wimborne road & A354 Salisbury road. Follow brown signs for the Royal Signals Museum.)*

☎ 01258 482248
e-mail: info@royalsignalsmuseum.com
web: www.royalsignalsmuseum.com

The Royal Signals Museum depicts the history of military communications, science and technology from the Crimea to current day. As well as displays on all major conflicts involving British forces, there are the stories of the ATS, the Long Range Desert Group, Air Support, Airborne, Para and SAS Signals. D-Day and Dorset explores the Royal Signals involvement in Operation Overlord. For children there are trails and interactive exhibits.

Times: Open Mar-Oct Mon-Fri 10-5, Sat-Sun 10-4. Closed 10 days over Xmas & New Year **Fee:** ✱ £6 (ch £4, pen £5). Family £17.50

Facilities: 🅿 ⚌ 🍴 ♿ (ramps & lifts) toilets for disabled shop ⊗ (ex guide dogs) ◀

BOURNEMOUTH — MAP 04 SZ09

Oceanarium `2 for 1`

Pier Approach, West Beach BH2 5AA

⮕ *(from A338 Wessex Way, follow Oceanarium tourist signs)*

☎ 01202 311993
e-mail: oceanarium@reallive.co.uk
web: www.oceanarium.co.uk

Explore the secrets of the ocean in an adventure that will take you to some of the world's most amazing waters. The Oceanarium Bournemouth brings you face to face with a vast array of creatures from piranhas and clownfish to tiny freshwater turtles. Take a walk through our amazing underwater tunnel to get even closer to sharks, sea turtles, stingrays and eels.

Times: Open all year, daily from 10. Late night opening during school summer hols. Closed 25 Dec. **Fee:** Telephone for admission charges
Facilities: 🅿 (100mtrs) ⚌ 🍴 ♿ toilets for disabled shop ⊗ (ex guide dogs) ◀

BOVINGTON CAMP — MAP 03 SY88

Clouds Hill

BH20 7NQ

⮕ *(1m N of Bovington Camp & Tank Museum)*

☎ 01929 405616
web: www.nationaltrust.org.uk

T E Lawrence ('Lawrence of Arabia') bought this cottage in 1925 when he was a private in the Tank Corps at Bovington. He would escape here to play records and entertain friends to feasts of baked beans and China tea. The furniture and contents were Lawrence's own and a new display tells the story of Lawrence's life.

Times: Open 23 Mar-Oct, Thu-Sun. 12-5 **Fee:** ✱ £3.50.
Facilities: ♿ (Braille guide) shop ⊗ 🚌 ♨

continued

England

The Tank Museum

BH20 6JG

➲ *(off A352 or A35, follow brown tank signs from Bere Regis & Wool)*

☎ 01929 405096

e-mail: info@tankmuseum.org

web: www.tankmuseum.org

The Tank Museum houses the world's finest international collection of Armoured Fighting Vehicles. Tanks in Action displays are held every Thursday at noon during July-September, every Tuesday from end July to August Bank Holiday, and every Sunday in August. Armoured vehicle rides are available throughout the summer, and various special events take place - please telephone for details.

Times: Open all year, daily 10-5. Closed 21-27 Dec 2006. **Fee:** ✽ £10 (ch £7, pen £9). Family saver £28 (2ad+2ch); £26 (1ad+3ch). Group rates available. **Facilities:** ♿ 🅿 ⬛ 🍽 licensed 🛒 ⬛ (wheelchairs available & audio tours) toilets for disabled shop ⊗ (ex in grounds) ⬛

BROWNSEA ISLAND   MAP 03 SZ08

Brownsea Island

BH13 7EE

➲ *(located in Poole Harbour)*

☎ 01202 707744

e-mail: brownseaisland@nationaltrust.org.uk

web: www.nationaltrust.org.uk

This is a 250-acre nature reserve partly managed by the Dorset Trust for Nature Conservation. The island is most famous as the site of the first scout camp, held by Lord Baden-Powell in 1907. Scouts and Guides are still the only people allowed to stay here overnight. It is a haven for red squirrels and seabirds.

Times: Open daily 25 Mar -21 Jul, 10-5; 22 Jul -3 Sep, 10-6; 4-30 Sep 10-5; 1-29 Oct, 10-4 **Fee:** ✽ £4.40 (ch £2.20). Family ticket £11. Group £3.80 (ch £1.90) **Facilities:** ⬛ 🍽 ⬛ (Braille/Audio guide, 2 selfdrive vehicles-booking advised) toilets for disabled shop ⊗ 🌿

CANFORD CLIFFS   MAP 04 SZ08

Compton Acres Gardens   `2 for 1`

Canford Cliffs Rd BH13 7ES

➲ *(on B3065, follow brown tourist signs)*

☎ 01202 700778

e-mail: sales@comptonacres.co.uk

web: www.comptonacres.co.uk

The ten acres of Compton Acres incorporate Japanese and Italian gardens, rock and water gardens, and heather gardens. There are fine views over Poole Harbour and the Purbeck Hills. The beautiful wooded valley is an amazing place to explore the wide range of plants. The Italian garden was used as a location in Stanley Kubrick's 1975 movie, *Barry Lyndon*.

Times: Open Apr-Oct 9-6, Nov-Mar 9-4 (last entry 1hr before close). Closed 25 & 26 Dec. **Fee:** ✽ £5.95 (ch £3.95, pen £5.45). Party 15+ £5.45 (ch £3.95, pen £4.95). **Facilities:** ♿ 🅿 ⬛ 🍽 licensed 🛒 ⬛ (level paths and ramps into shops and cafe) toilets for disabled shop garden centre ⊗ (ex guide & hearing dogs) ⬛

CHRISTCHURCH   MAP 04 SZ19

Christchurch Castle & Norman House `FREE`

➲ *(near Christchurch Priory)*

web: www.english-heritage.org.uk

Set on the river bank, the ruins of this Norman keep and constable's house date back to the twelfth century.

Times: Open at any reasonable time. **Facilities:** ⬛

Red House Museum & Gardens `FREE`

Quay Rd BH23 1BU

➲ *(follow brown tourist signs from Christchurch, Red House is on corner of Quay Rd)*

☎ 01202 482860

web: www.hants.gov.uk/museum/redhouse

A museum with plenty of variety, featuring local history, archaeology, and natural history, displayed in a beautiful Georgian house. There's an excellent costume collection, some Arthur Romney-Green furniture and gardens with a woodland walk and herb garden. Regularly changing temporary exhibitions include contemporary art and crafts, plus historical displays.

Times: Open Tues-Sat 10-5, Sun 2-5 (last admission 4.30). Open BHs (spring & summer) Closed 25 Dec-1 Jan & Good Fri.

Facilities: 🅿 (200yds) ⬛ 🛒 ⬛ (hearing aid and loop in reception only) toilets for disabled shop ⊗ (ex guide & hearing dogs)

CORFE CASTLE   MAP 03 SY98

Corfe Castle

BH20 5EZ

➲ *(follow A351 from Wareham to Swanage. Corfe Castle approx 5m along this road)*

☎ 01929 481294

e-mail: corfecastle@nationaltrust.org.uk

web: www.nationaltrust.org.uk

Built in Norman times, the castle was added to by King John. It was defended during the Civil War by Lady Bankes, who surrendered after a stout resistance. Parliament ordered the demolition of the castle, and today it is one of the most impressive ruins in England. Ring for details of special events.

continued

Times: Shop & Castle open daily, Mar 10-5; Apr-end Sep 10-6; Oct 10-5; Nov-Feb 10-4. (Last admission 30 mins before closing). Closed 25-26 Dec. Tearoom open daily Mar 10-5, Apr-Sep 10-5.30, Oct 10-5, Nov-Feb 10-4. **Fee:** ✱ £5 (ch £2.50). Family ticket (2ad+3ch) £12.50 or (1ad+3ch) £7.50. NT members free. Groups £4.30 (ch £2.15) **Facilities:** ⊕ 🅿️ 🍴 licensed (Braille/large print guide & menu) shop ♿ ⊟

DORCHESTER   MAP 03 SY69

Dinosaur Museum

Icen Way DT1 1EW

↪ *(off A35 into Dorchester, museum in town centre just off High East St)*

☎ 01305 269880

e-mail: info@thedinosaurmuseum.com

web: www.thedinosaurmuseum.com

Britain's award-winning museum devoted to dinosaurs has an appealing mixture of fossils, skeletons, life-size reconstructions and interactive displays such as the 'feelies'. There are audio-visual presentations and computer displays providing an all-round family attraction with new displays each year. It is part of the Jurassic Coast experience.

Times: Open all year, daily 9.30-5.30 (10-4.30 Nov-Mar). Closed 24-26 Dec. **Fee:** £6.50 (ch £4.75, concessions £5.50, under 4's free). Family ticket £19.95 **Facilities:** ℗ (50yds) 🍴 ♿ (many low level displays) shop ⊟

Dorset County Museum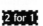

High West St DT1 1XA

↪ *(off A354 signed Dorchester, attraction on right half way up main street)*

☎ 01305 262735

e-mail: dorsetcountymuseum@dor-mus.demon.co.uk

web: www.dorsetcountymuseum.org

Displays cover prehistoric and Roman times, including sites such as Maiden Castle, and there's a gallery on Dorset writers with sections on the poet William Barnes, Thomas Hardy (with a reconstruction of his study), and 20th-century writers. Also geology, local wildlife and social history are explored in the museum. New Jurassic Coast geology gallery opening at the time of going to press.

Times: Open all year, Mon-Sat, 10-5. Also open Sun, Jul-Sep. Closed 24-26 Dec **Fee:** ✱ £6 (up to 2 accompanied ch free, additional ch £1, concessions £5) **Facilities:** ℗ (600yds) (nearby parking charged) ♿ (free entry for disabled visitors, ramp, audio commentary) shop ⊗ (ex guide dogs) ⊟

Dorset Teddy Bear Museum

Eastgate, High East St & Salisbury St DT1 1JU

↪ *(off A35, museum in town centre near Dinosaur Museum)*

☎ 01305 266040

e-mail: info@teddybearmuseum.co.uk

web: www.teddybearmuseum.co.uk

Enter the enchanting world of the teddy bear in this wonderful family museum. There are teddies from the very earliest, over 100 years ago, to today's TV favourites. They are all displayed in period settings with human-sized teddy bears.

Times: Open daily, 10-5.30, (4.30 in winter). Closed 24-26 Dec. **Fee:** £5.50 (ch £3.75, under 4's free, pen & concessions £4.50). Family £17 **Facilities:** ℗ (150mtrs) 🍴 shop ⊗ (ex guide dogs) ⊟

Hardy's Cottage

Higher Bockhampton DT2 8QJ

↪ *(3m NE of Dorchester, 0.5m S of A35. Turn off A35 at Kingston Maurward rdbt towards Stinsford and Bockhampton. Left onto Bockhampton Ln, signed to Hardy's Cottage)*

☎ 01305 262366

web: www.nationaltrust.org.uk

The small cob and thatch cottage where novelist and poet Thomas Hardy was born in 1840 and from where he would walk 6 miles to school in Dorchester every day. It was built by his great-grandfather and is little altered since. The interior has been furnished by the Trust. It was here that he wrote his early novels *Under the Greenwood Tree* and *Far from the Madding Crowds*. It has a charming cottage garden.

Times: Open 2 Apr-Oct, Thurs-Mon, 11-5 **Fee:** ✱ £3 (ch £1.50) **Facilities:** ℗ (10 min walk) (no coach parking) ♿ (parking by arrangement, large print/Braille guide) ⊗ ♿

Maiden Castle

DT1 9PR

↪ *(2m S of Dorchester, access off A354, N of bypass)*

web: www.english-heritage.org.uk

The Iron Age fort ranks among the finest in Britain. It covers 47 acres, and has daunting earthworks, with a complicated defensive system around the entrances. One of its main purposes may well have been to protect grain from marauding bands. The first single-rampart fort dates from around 700BC, and by 100BC the earthworks covered the whole plateau. It was finally overrun by Roman troops in AD43.

Times: Open at any reasonable time. **Facilities:** ⊕ ⊞

The Military Museum of Devon & Dorset

The Keep, Bridport Rd DT1 1RN

↪ *(situated near the top of High West St leading out of town towards Bridport)*

☎ 01305 264066

e-mail: keep.museum@talk21.com

web: www.keepmilitarymuseum.org

Three hundred years of military history, with displays on the Devon Regiment, Dorset Regiment, Dorset Militia and Volunteers, the Queen's Own Dorset Yeomanry, and Devonshire and Dorset Regiment (from 1958). The Museum uses modern technology, interactive and creative displays to tell the stories of the Infantry, Cavalry and

continued

Artillerymen. From June 2006 to February 2007, there will be an exhibition to commemorate the 90th anniversary of Battle of Somme.

Times: Open Apr-Sep, Mon-Sat 9-5; Oct-Mar, Tue-Sat 9-5; Closed Xmas & New Year. **Fee:** £4 (ch, concessions £3). Family ticket £12
Facilities: ❷ ᵭ (lift availble to 3 floors) toilets for disabled shop ⊗ (ex guide dogs) ◀

Tutankhamun Exhibition

High West St DT1 1UW

⮡ *(off A35 into Dorchester town centre)*

☎ 01305 269571

e-mail: info@tutankhamun-exhibition.co.uk
web: www.tutankhamun-exhibition.co.uk

The exhibition recreates the excitement of one of the world's greatest discoveries of ancient treasure. A reconstruction of the tomb and recreations of its treasures are displayed. The superbly preserved mummified body of the boy king can be seen, wonderfully recreated in every detail. Facsimiles of some of the most famous treasures, including the golden funerary mask and the harpooner can be seen in the final gallery.

Times: Open all year daily, Apr-Oct, 9.30-5.30; Nov-Mar wkdays 9.30-5, wknds 10-4.30. Closed 24-26 Dec. **Fee:** £6.50 (ch £4.75, concessions £5.50, under 5's free). Family ticket £19.95 **Facilities:** ℗ (200yds) ᵭ shop ⊗ (ex guide dogs) ◀

MINTERNE MAGNA   MAP 03 ST60

Minterne Gardens   `2 for 1`

DT2 7AU

⮡ *(2m N of Cerne Abbas on A352 Dorchester-Sherborne road)*

☎ 01300 341370

e-mail: enquiries@minterne.co.uk
web: www.minterne.co.uk

Wander through 20 acres of wild woodland, where magnolias, rhododendrons, eucryphias, hydrangeas, water plants and water lillies provide a new vista at each turn. This has been the home of the Churchill and Digby families for 350 years, and contains small lakes and cascades landscaped in the 18th century.

Times: Open Mar-Oct, daily 10-6. **Fee:** £4 (accompanied ch free)
Facilities: ❷

ORGANFORD   MAP 03 SY99

Farmer Palmer's Farm Park NEW

BH16 6EU

⮡ *(From Poole, just off A35 straight over rdbt past Bakers Arms, signed on left, take 2nd turning, 0.5m after rdbt)*

☎ 01202 622022

e-mail: info@farmerpalmers.co.uk
web: www.farmerpalmer.co.uk

Family owned and run Farmer Palmers has been specially designed for families with children 8 years and under. Many activities include meeting and learning about the animals, climbing the straw mountain, going for a tractor trailer ride and exercising in the soft play area. A fun and busy day for the family.

Times: Open 11-19 Feb, daily 10-4; 20 Feb-24 Mar & 30 Oct-17 Dec Fri & wknds 10-4, 25 Mar-29 Oct, daily 10-5.30. **Fee:** ✱ £4.95 (ch 4.75,

continued

under 2yrs free, concessions £4.50). Family (2 ad, 2ch) £18.50. Disabled & carer £4.50 each. **Facilities:** ❷ ❌ licensed (ramps & wide doorways) shop ⊗ (ex guide dogs) ◀

POOLE   MAP 03 SZ09

Waterfront Museum   `FREE`

4 High St BH15 1BW

⮡ *(off Poole Quay)*

☎ 01202 262600

e-mail: museums@poole.gov.uk
web: www.boroughofpoole.com/museums

The Waterfront Museum tells the story of Poole's history, including the Studland Bay wreck and trade with Newfoundland with displays and hands-on activities. The museum will be closed for major refurbishment from October 2006 to early 2007. Please contact the Poole Museums Service for further information. The local history centre with research facilities on local and family history will remain open during the refurbishment.

Times: Local History Centre only: Tue-Sat 10-3 (closed on Tue following a BH). **Facilities:** ℗ (250mtrs) ▥ ᵭ (Scaplen's Court not accessible) toilets for disabled shop ⊗ (ex guide dogs) ◀

PORTLAND   MAP 03 SY67

Portland Castle

Castleton DT5 1AZ

⮡ *(overlooking Portland harbour)*

☎ 01305 820539

web: www.english-heritage.org.uk

Visit one of Henry VIII's finest coastal forts in use right up to the Second World War. Home to the Wrens and scene of the US troops' embarkation for the D-Day invasion in 1944. Explore the Captain's House and Gardens.

Times: Open Apr-Jun & Sep, daily 10-5; Jul-Aug, daily 10-6; Oct, daily 10-4. Closed Nov-Mar. **Fee:** £3.70 (ch £1.90, concessions £2.80). Prices and opening times are subject to change in Spring 2007. Please check web site or call 0870 333 1181 for the most up to date prices and opening times when planning your visit. **Facilities:** ❷ ᵭ shop ⊗ ✿

Portland Museum   `2 for 1`

217 Wakeham DT5 1HS

⮡ *(A354, through Fortuneswell to Portland Heights Hotel, then English Heritage signs)*

☎ 01305 821804

e-mail: tourism@weymouth.gov.uk
web: www.weymouth.gov.uk

Avice's cottage in Thomas Hardy's book *The Well-Beloved*, this building is now a museum of local and historical interest, with varied displays. Regular temporary exhibitions are held. The adjoining Marie Stopes cottage houses the shop and a display of maritime history. Exhibitions and events throughout the year. Contact for details.

Times: ✱ Open Good Fri-Oct, Fri-Tue (ex school hols open daily), 10.30-5 (Closed 1-1.30 daily) **Fee:** ✱ £2.10 (accompanied ch free, pen £1.05) **Facilities:** ❷ ᵭ shop ⊗ (ex guide dogs)

SHAFTESBURY MAP 03 ST82

Shaftesbury Abbey Museum & Garden

Park Walk SP7 8JR

➲ *(follow signs to town centre. Shaftesbury Abbey is signed from opposite Wharf's Restaurant)*

☎ 01747 852910

e-mail: user@shaftesburyabbey.fsnet.co.uk

web: www.shaftesburyabbey.co.uk

The Abbey at Shaftesbury was part of a nunnery founded by King Alfred in 888. Patronage and pilgrims to the shrine of St Edward helped to make the abbey both rich and famous. It became one of the wealthiest in the country but was destroyed during the Dissolution in 1539. The excavated ruins show the foundations of the abbey church. The story is told through the use of carved stone and medieval floor tiles and illustrations from ancient manuscripts.

Times: Open Apr-Oct, daily, 10-5. **Fee:** ✱ £2.50 (ch £1, concessions £2). **Facilities:** ℗ (250yds) (2hr restriction on nearest car park) ⛴ ♿ (large print guides, audio tour, interactive display) toilets for disabled shop

SHERBORNE MAP 03 ST61

Sherborne Castle

New Rd DT9 5NR

➲ *(off A30/A352, 0.5m SE of Sherborne)*

☎ 01935 813182 & 812072 (castle)

e-mail: enquiries@sherbornecastle.com

web: www.sherbornecastle.com

Built by Sir Walter Raleigh in 1594, Sherborne Castle has been the home of the Digby family since 1617. Prince William of Orange was entertained here in 1688, and George III visited in 1789. Splendid collections of art, furniture and porcelain are on show in the Castle. Lancelot 'Capability' Brown created the lake in 1753 and 30 acres of beautiful gardens and grounds surround it. Special events include flower weekends, classic car shows, outdoor theatre, and fireworks. Contact for details.

Times: Open Apr-Oct, Tue-Thu, Sat-Sun & BH Mon 11-4.30. (Last admission 4.30). Castle open from 2.30 on Sat. **Fee:** ✱ £8 (ch £4). Gardens only £4 (ch under 15 free, max 4 ch per adult). Party 15+ £7 **Facilities:** ℗ ♨ ♿ (Braille guide book) toilets for disabled shop ⛴

Sherborne Museum

Abbey Gate House, Church Ln DT9 3BP

➲ *(From the bottom of Cheap St, walk through Church Ln towards the Abbey, museum on left)*

☎ 01935 812252

e-mail: info@sherbornemuseum.co.uk

web: www.sherbornemuseum.co.uk

The museum features a model of Sherborne's original Norman castle, as well as a fine Victorian doll's house and other domestic and agricultural bygones. There are also items of local geological, natural history and archaeological interest, including Roman material. The Sherborne Missal, one of the greatest medieval manuscripts can be seen using the latest digital technology which enables the visitor to 'turn the pages' of the manuscript with the sweep of a hand - with touch, zoom and audio facilities.

Times: Open Apr-Oct, Tue-Sat 10.30-4.30, & Sun & BH Mon 2.30-4.30
Fee: £1 (ch & concessions free) **Facilities:** ℗ (200yds) ♿ (video of upper floor displays) toilets for disabled shop ✲ (ex guide dogs)

Sherborne Old Castle

Castleton D19 3SA

➲ *(0.5m E off B3145)*

☎ 01935 812730

web: www.english-heritage.org.uk

The ruins of this early 12th-century castle are a testament to the 16 days Oliver Cromwell's army took to capture it during the Civil War.

Times: Open Apr-Jun & Sep, daily 10-5; Jul-Aug, daily 10-6; Oct, daily 10-4. Closed Nov-Mar. **Fee:** £2.40 (ch £1.20, concessions £1.80). Prices and opening times are subject to change in Spring 2007. Please check web site or call 0870 333 1181 for the most up to date prices and opening times when planning your visit. **Facilities:** ℗ ♿ shop ✲ ♨

SWANAGE MAP 03 SZ07

Swanage Railway

Station House BH19 1HB

➲ *(signed from A351)*

☎ 01929 425800

e-mail: general@swanrail.freeserve.co.uk

web: www.swanagerailway.co.uk

The railway from Swanage to Wareham was closed in 1972, and in 1976 the Swanage Railway took possession and have gradually restored the line, which now runs for 6 miles, passing the ruins of Corfe Castle. On train meals are offered on the Wessex Belle, the Travelling Tavern and the Dorsetman. Ring for details of special events.

Times: Open every wknd ex Jan, daily Apr-Oct. **Fee:** ✱ Swanage-Corfe/Norden £7.50 return (ch & concessions £5.50 return). Family ticket £21. Day Rover £8.50 (ch & concessions £6.50) **Facilities:** ℗ ☕ ♨ ⅼ⦿⅟ licensed ♨ ♿ (disabled persons coach) shop ⛴

TOLPUDDLE MAP 03 SY79

Tolpuddle Martyrs Museum

DT2 7EH

➲ *(off A35 from Dorchester, Tolpuddle is signed at Troytown turn off. Continue on old A35, Museum has brown heritage sign giving clear directions)*

☎ 01305 848237

e-mail: jpickering@tuc.org.uk

web: www.tolpuddlemartyrs.org.uk

One dawn, in the bitter February of 1834, six Tolpuddle farm labourers were arrested after forming a trade union. A frightened squire's trumped up charge triggered one of the most celebrated stories in the history of human rights. That dawn arrest created the Tolpuddle Martyrs, who were punished with transportation as convicts to Australia. Packed with illustrative displays, this new state-of-the-art, interactive exhibition tells the Tolpuddle Martyrs story. Every summer the weekend of the third Sunday in July, the museum holds the Tolpuddle Martyrs Festival. The weekend combines celebration with tradition offering traditional and contemporary music as well as many other attractions.

Times: Open all year, Apr-Oct, Tue-Sat 10-5, Sun 11-5; Nov-Mar, Thu-Sat 10-4, Sun 11-4, closed Mon-Wed. Closed 17 Dec-3 Jan. Open other BHs. **Facilities:** ℗ (outside museum) ♨ ♿ (parking, interactive computers at wheelchair height) toilets for disabled shop ✲ (ex guide dogs) ⛴

England

WEST LULWORTH   MAP 03 SY88

Lulworth Castle & Park

BH20 5QS

➲ *(from Wareham, W on A352 for 1m, left onto B3070 to E Lulworth, follow tourist signs)*

☎ 0845 450 1054

e-mail: estate.office@lulworth.com

web: www.lulworth.com

Glimpse life below stairs in the restored kitchen, and enjoy glorious views from the top of the tower of this historic castle set in beautiful parkland. The 18th-century chapel is the first Catholic chapel built in England after the Reformation. Children will enjoy the animal farm, play area, indoor activity room and pitch and putt.

Times: Open 25 Mar-Sep, Sun-Fri 10.30-6; 2 Oct-Dec, Sun-Fri 10.30-4; 2-7 Jan, Sun-Fri 10.30-4; 23-24 Mar, Sun-Fri 10.30-4. Closed 24-25 Dec & 7-21 Jan. **Facilities:** ♿ 💺 🎑 ♿ (limited in castle due to grade one listing) toilets for disabled shop ◼

WEYMOUTH   MAP 03 SY67

Deep Sea Adventure & Sharky's Play & Party

9 Custom House Quay, Old Harbour North DT4 8BG

➲ *(A35 to Weymouth, then Old Harbour North. Attraction between pavillion & town bridge. Follow brown tourist signs.)*

☎ 0871 222 5760

e-mail: enquiries@deepsea-adventure.co.uk

web: www.deepsea-adventure.co.uk

A fascinating attraction telling the story of underwater exploration and marine exploits. Discover the history of Weymouth's Old Harbour, compelling tales of shipwreck survival, explore the Black Hole and search for Ollie the Oyster. Also a unique display telling the gripping tale of the Titanic disaster. Sharky's Play Area is four floors of fun-packed adventure. Separate toddler area for the under fives. 'Paint your own Pottery' studio can also be found on site. Laser shoot out evenings now available.

Times: ✱ Open all year, daily from 9.30. Closed 25-26 Dec & 1 Jan. **Fee:** ✱ Starky's Play Zone: Adults free (ch £3.50). Dee Sea Adventure £3.95 (ch 5-15 £2.95, concessions £3.50). **Facilities:** Ⓟ (100yds) 🍴 licensed 🎑 ♿ (lift & sign language for deaf) toilets for disabled shop ◈ (ex guide dogs) ◼

RSPB Nature Reserve Radipole Lake

The Swannery Car Park DT4 7TZ

➲ *(close to seafront & railway station)*

☎ 01305 778313

web: www.rspb.org.uk

Covering 222 acres, the Reserve offers firm paths, hide and a visitor centre. Several types of warblers, mute swans, gadwalls, teals and great crested grebes may be seen, and the visitor centre has viewing windows overlooking the lake. Phone for details of special events.

Times: ✱ Open daily 9-5 **Facilities:** ♿ (charged) 🎑 ♿ toilets for disabled shop ◼

Sea Life Park & Marine Sanctuary

Lodmoor Country Park DT4 7SX

➲ *(on A353)*

☎ 01305 788255

e-mail: slcweymouth@merlinentertainments.biz

web: www.sealifeeurope.com

A unique mix of indoor and outdoor attractions set in 7 acres. The park offers a day of fun, bringing you face to face with penguins, otters, seals and much more.

Times: Open all year, daily from 10. (Closed 25 Dec). **Facilities:** ♿ (charged) 💺 🍴 ♿ toilets for disabled shop ◈ (ex guide dogs) ◼

WIMBORNE   MAP 03 SZ09

Kingston Lacy House, Garden & Park

BH21 4EA

➲ *(1.5m W of Wimborne, B3082)*

☎ 01202 883402 (Mon-Fri) & 880413 (infoline)

e-mail: kingstonlacy@nationaltrust.org.uk

web: www.nationaltrust.org.uk

Kingston Lacy House was the home of the Bankes family for over 300 years. The original house is 17th century, but in the 1830s was given a stone façade. The Italian marble staircase, Venetian ceiling, treasures from Spain and an Egyptian obelisk were also added. There are outstanding pictures by Titian, Rubens, Velasquez, Reynolds and Van Dyck. No photography is allowed in the house.

Times: Open: House 18 Mar-29 Oct, 11-5, Wed-Sun. Garden & Park 10.30-6, daily 3 Nov-17 Dec, 10.30-4, Fri-Sun 3 Feb-20 Mar, 10.30-4, Sat-Sun. **Fee:** ✱ House, Garden & Park £9 (ch £4.50) Family £22. Park & Gardens only £4.50 (ch £2.30) Family £11. **Facilities:** ♿ 💺 🍴 licensed ♿ (wheelchairs, large print & Braille guides, parking) toilets for disabled shop ◈ (ex on leads in park & wood) 🦮

Knoll Gardens

Stapehill Rd, Hampreston BH21 7ND

➲ *(3m E between Wimborne and Ferndown off A31, at Canford Bottom rdbt, into B3073 signed Ham Lane. Follow brown signs)*

☎ 01202 873931

e-mail: enquiries@knollgardens.co.uk

web: www.knollgardens.co.uk

Over 5000 plant species from all over the world thrive here, within a six-acre site. There are water gardens with waterfalls, pools and a stream, herbaceous borders, and many other features. There is also a 'Dragon' formal garden and a Mediterranean-style gravel garden. The nursery offers a wide range of plants; best known for its range of Ornamental Grasses and 'plants for the modern lifestyle'.

Times: Open all year, Wed-Sun, 10-5 (or dusk if earlier). Closed 18 Dec-1 Feb. **Fee:** ✱ £4.25 (ch 5-15 £2.50, concessions £3.75). Family £9.50 Party 15+ £3. **Facilities:** ♿ 💺 ♿ (wheelchairs available) toilets for disabled garden centre ◈ (ex guide dogs) ◼

Priest's House Museum and Garden

23-27 High St BH21 1HR

➲ *(located on High Street, opposite The Minster)*

☎ 01202 882533

e-mail: priestshouse@eastdorset.gov.uk

An award-winning local history museum, set in an historic house. The 17th-century hall, Georgian parlour and working Victorian kitchen reveal the history of the building and its inhabitants. The museum houses exhibitions on East Dorset from prehistoric to modern times. There are regular special exhibitions and a walled garden to explore.

Times: Open Apr-Oct, Mon-Sat, 10-4.30. **Facilities:** ℗ (200yds) 💻 📖 ᕼ (hands on archaeology gallery) shop ⊗ (ex guide dogs)

Stapehill Abbey

Wimborne Rd West BH21 2EB

➲ *(2.5m E off A31 at Canford Bottom rdbt)*

☎ 01202 861686

This early 19th-century abbey, home for nearly 200 years to Cistercian nuns, is now a busy working crafts centre with many attractions under cover. There are award-winning landscaped gardens, parkland and picnic spots, and the Power to the Land exhibition. Telephone for details of special events.

Times: Open Etr-Sep, daily 10-5; Oct-Etr, Wed-Sun 10-4. Closed 22 Dec-Feb. **Facilities:** ℗ 💻 ᕼ toilets for disabled shop garden centre ⊗ (ex guide dogs) 🍴

Directions are provided by the attractions.

WOOL   MAP 03 SY88

Monkey World

Longthorns BH20 6HH

➲ *(1m N of Wool on Bere Regis road)*

☎ 01929 462537 & 0800 456600

e-mail: apes@monkeyworld.org

web: www.monkeyworld.org

Set up in order to rescue monkeys and apes from abuse and illegal smuggling, Monkey World houses over 160 primates in 65 acres of Dorset woodland. There are 58 chimps, the largest grouping outside Africa, as well as orang-utans, gibbons, woolly monkeys, lemurs, macaques and marmosets. Those wishing to help the centre continue in its quest to rescue primates from lives of misery may like to take part in the adoption scheme which includes free admission to the park for one year. There are keeper talks every half hour, and a Great Ape Play Area for the kids. 2007 is the 20th anniversary of Monkey World.

Times: Open daily 10-5 (Jul-Aug 10-6). (Last admission 1 hour before closing) **Fee:** ✱ £9 (ch & concessions £6.50). Family ticket (1 ad + 2 ch) £20, (2 ad + 2 ch) £27. Group 15+ £8 (£5.50) **Facilities:** ℗ 💻 🍴 📖 ᕼ toilets for disabled shop ⊗ (ex guide dogs) 🍴

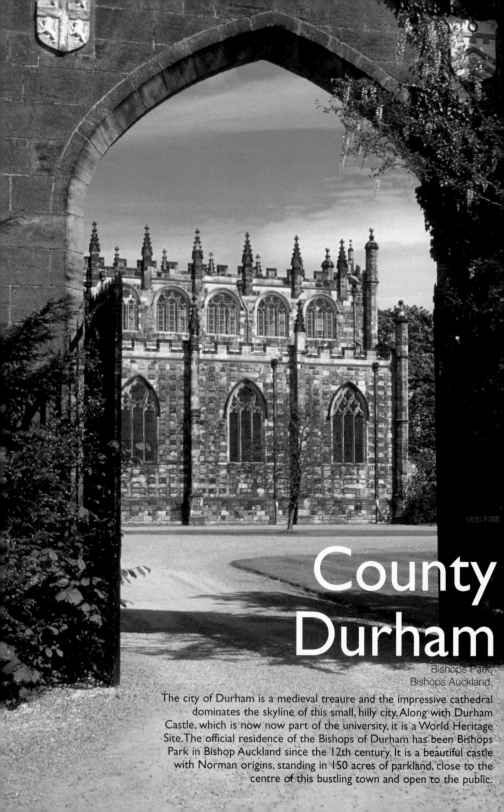

County Durham

Bishops Park,
Bishops Auckland.

The city of Durham is a medieval treasure and the impressive cathedral dominates the skyline of this small, hilly city. Along with Durham Castle, which is now now part of the university, it is a World Heritage Site. The official residence of the Bishops of Durham has been Bishops Park in Bishop Auckland since the 12th century. It is a beautiful castle with Norman origins, standing in 150 acres of parkland, close to the centre of this bustling town and open to the public.

BARNARD CASTLE   MAP 12 NZ01

Barnard Castle
DL12 9AT
☎ 01833 638212
web: www.english-heritage.org.uk

Imposing remains of one of England's largest medieval castles perched high on a rugged escarpment above the banks of the River Tees.

Times: Open all year, Apr-Sep, daily 10-6; Oct, daily 10-4; Nov-Mar, Thu-Mon 10-4. Closed 24-26 Dec & 1 Jan. **Fee:** £3.40 (ch £1.70, concessions £2.60). Prices and opening times are subject to change in Spring 2007. Please check web site or call 0870 333 1181 for the most up to date prices and opening times when planning your visit. **Facilities:** & shop ♿

The Bowes Museum   2 for 1
DL12 8NP
➲ (located in Barnard Castle, just off A66)
☎ 01833 690606
e-mail: info@thebowesmuseum.org.uk
web: www.thebowesmuseum.org.uk

John and Joséphine Bowes founded the Bowes Museum over 100 years ago. The magnificent building houses a collection of treasures from fine and decorative art to major temporary exhibitions of international quality and interest. The icon of the collection is The Silver Swan, a unique life-size, musical automaton which plays every day. There are also works by El Greco, Goya and Canaletto. A continuous, rolling programme of major exhibitions is also in place.

Times: Open all year daily 11-5. Closed 25-26 Dec & 1 Jan. **Fee:** £7 (ch under 16 free, concessions £6) **Facilities:** ❂ ❣ ▥ & (lift, ramped entrance, reserved parking, audio guide/loop) toilets for disabled shop ❂ (ex guide dogs & in park) ◄

Egglestone Abbey   FREE
DL12 8QN
➲ (1m S of Barnard Castle on minor road off B6277)
web: www.english-heritage.org.uk

The scant, but charming remains of a small medieval monastery. The picturesque ruins of Egglestone are located above a bend in the River Tees. A large part of the church can be seen, as can remnants of monastic buildings.

Times: Open daily, 10-6. **Facilities:** ❂ & ♿

BEAMISH   MAP 12 NZ25

Beamish, The North of England Open-Air Museum
DH9 0RG
➲ (off A693 & A6076. Signed from A1M junct 63.)
☎ 0191 370 4000
e-mail: museum@beamish.org.uk
web: www.beamish.org.uk

Set in 200 acres of countryside, award winning Beamish recreates life in the early 1800s and 1900s. Costumed staff welcome visitors to a 1913 town street, colliery village, farm and railway station; a re-creation of how people lived and worked. Ride on early electric tramcars, take a ride on a replica of an 1825 steam railway and visit Pockerley Manor where a yeoman farmer and his family would have lived.

Times: Open Apr-29 Oct daily, 10-5; Oct-Mar 10-4, closed Mon & Fri & 11 Dec-1 Jan. (Last admission 3) **Fee:** ✱ Summer £16 (ch £10, pen £12.50). Winter £6 (ch & pen £6). Winter visit is centered on town & tramway only, other areas are closed. **Facilities:** ❂ ❣ ▥ & (not ideal for wheelchairs, assistance recommended) shop ❂ (ex in grounds & assist dogs) ◄

BISHOP AUCKLAND   MAP 08 NZ22

Auckland Castle
DL14 7NR
➲ (follow signs to Market Place then brown tourist sign for Castle)
☎ 01388 601627
e-mail: auckland.castle@zetnet.co.uk
web: www.auckland-castle.co.uk

Serving as the principal county residence of the Prince Bishops since the 12th century, Auckland Castle is the home of the Bishop of Durham. Built on a promontory overlooking the River Wear and the Roman Fort of Binchester, the Castle has been added to and adapted over the centuries. St Peter's Chapel houses many of the treasures of past Bishops.

Times: ✱ Open Etr Mon-Sep, Sun & Mon 2-5; Aug also Wed. **Facilities:** ❂ ❣ ▥ & (chair walker available by prior arrangement) toilets for disabled shop ❂ (ex guide dogs) ◄

BOWES
MAP 12 NY91

Bowes Castle
FREE

DL12 9LD

⤳ *(in Bowes village, just off A66)*

web: www.english-heritage.org.uk

Massive ruins of Henry II's tower keep, three storeys high, set within the earthworks of a Roman fort and overlooking the valley of the River Greta.

Times: Open at any reasonable time. **Facilities:** ☾ 🚐 ♨

The Otter Trust's North Pennines Reserve

Vale House Farm DL12 9RH

⤳ *(S side of A66 Scotch Corner to Penrith Rd, 2m W of Bowes)*

☎ 01833 628339

web: www.ottertrust.org.uk/Pennines_Home.html

Set in 230 acres of upland farmland, the Otter Trust reserve isn't just about otters, although there is an ongoing release programme that aims to protect the otter from extinction. Visitors can also see red and fallow deer, mouflon sheep, and a wide range of birds including curlew, oystercatchers, snipe, and black grouse. The visitor centre contains exhibits on some of the animals as well as local history, and overlooks the charming River Greta.

Times: ✱ Open Apr-Oct, daily 10.30-6 **Facilities:** ❷ 🅿 🗊 ♿ toilets for disabled shop ⊗ (ex guide dogs)

COWSHILL
MAP 12 NY84

Killhope The North of England Lead Mining Museum
2 for 1

DL13 1AR

⤳ *(beside A689 midway between Stanhope & Alston)*

☎ 01388 537505

e-mail: killhope@durham.gov.uk

web: www.durham.gov.uk/killhope

Equipped with hard hats and lamps, you can explore the working conditions of lead miners. The lead mine and 19th-century crushing mill have been restored to look as they would have done in the 1870s, and the 34ft water wheel has been restored to working order. There is also a visitor centre and mineral exhibition, a woodland walk, children's play area and a red squirrel and bird hide.

Times: Open Apr-Oct, daily 10.30-5 (BHs & summer school hols open until 5.30) **Fee:** ✱ Mine & Site: £6 (ch £3, concessions £5.50). Family £17. Site: £4.50 (ch £1.70, concessions £4). Family £11 **Facilities:** ❷ 🅿 🗊 ♿ (2 electric scooters, sympathetic hearing scheme) toilets for disabled shop 🖃

DARLINGTON
MAP 08 NZ21

Darlington Railway Centre & Museum
2 for 1

North Rd Station DL3 6ST

⤳ *(0.75m N, off A167)*

☎ 01325 460532

e-mail: museum@darlington.gov.uk

web: www.drcm.org.uk

Housed in the carefully restored North Road Station, this museum's prize exhibit is *Locomotion*, which pulled the first passenger train on the Stockton to Darlington railway and was built by Robert

continued

Stephenson & Co in 1825. Several other steam locomotives are also shown, together with models and other exhibits relating to the Stockton and Darlington and the North Eastern Railway companies. Recently arrived at the museum for a two year period is an A2 Pacific No60532 'Blue Peter'. Refreshments are available.

Times: Open daily 10-5. Closed 25-26 Dec & 1 Jan. **Fee:** ✱ £2.50 (ch £1.50, pen £1.50). **Facilities:** ❷ 🅿 🗊 ♿ toilets for disabled shop ⊗ (ex guide dogs) 🖃

DURHAM
MAP 12 NZ24

Crooks Hall & Gardens NEW
2 for 1

Sidegate DH1 5SZ

⤳ *(In city centre)*

☎ 0191 384 8028

e-mail: info@crookhall.co.uk

web: www.crookhallgardens.co.uk

Grade I listed medieval manor house with attractive gardens. A few minutes walk from the city centre and close to the River Wear.

Times: Open late May-early Sep, Wed-Sun 11-5 **Fee:** ✱ £4.50 (concessions £4). Family ticket £14 **Facilities:** ❷ 🅿 ♿ ⊗

Durham Cathedral

DH1 3EH

⤳ *(A690 into city, follow signs to car parks)*

☎ 0191 386 4266

e-mail: enquiries@durhamcathedral.co.uk

web: www.durhamcathedral.co.uk

Founded in 1093 as a shrine to St Cuthbert, the cathedral is a remarkable example of Norman architecture, set in an impressive position high above the River Wear. A full programme of concerts throughout the year. St Cuthbert's Day Procession (phone for details).

Times: Open all year, daily 9.30-6.15; 12 Jun-8 Sep 9.30-8. (Sun 12.30-5). Cathedral is closed to visitors during evening recitals & concerts. **Fee:** ✱ £4 donation requested **Facilities:** 🅿 (in city centre) 🅿 🍴 licensed 🗊 ♿ (large print guide, touch/hearing centre, stairclimber) toilets for disabled shop ⊗ (ex assist dogs)

Durham Light Infantry Museum & Durham Art Gallery

Aykley Heads DH1 5TU

⤳ *(0.5m NW, turn right off A691)*

☎ 0191 384 2214

e-mail: dli@durham.gov.uk

web: www.durham.gov.uk/dli

The history of the Regiment is told in displays of artefacts, medals, uniforms and vehicles. The Art Gallery has a continuous programme of temporary exhibitions, and holds regular lectures and concerts.

Times: Open all year, Apr-Oct, daily 10-5; Nov-Mar, daily 10-4. Closed 25 Dec. **Fee:** £3 (£1.25 ch, £2 concessions). Family ticket £7.
Facilities: ❷ 🅿 🗊 ♿ (wheelchair available, lift, ramps) toilets for disabled shop ⊗ (ex guide dogs) 🖃

Finchale Priory

Brasside, Newton Hall DH1 5SH

⊃ *(3m NE)*

☎ 0191 386 3828

web: www.english-heritage.org.uk

Dating from the 13th-century, these beautiful priory ruins are in a wooded setting besides the River Wear.

Times: Please call keykeeper on 0191 386 6528 **Facilities:** ❷ (charged) 💻 shop ✜

Oriental Museum

University of Durham, Elvet Hill DH1 3TH

⊃ *(signed from A167 & A177)*

☎ 0191 334 5694

e-mail: oriental.museum@durham.ac.uk

web: www.dur.ac.uk/oriental.museum

The Marvels of China gallery opened in 2000 and introduces the visitor to contemporary China, its history and decorative arts. Other displays cover the Islamic World, Buddhism, Chinese archaeology, the story of writing, a Javanese Gamelan Orchestra and an Egyptian Gallery containing everything from mummies to magic amulets.

Times: Open Mon-Fri 10-5, wknds 12-5. Closed Xmas-New Year.
Fee: ✱ £1.50 (concessions 75p). Family ticket £3.50. **Facilities:** ❷ 💻 🔟 ♿ (lifts to all floors) toilets for disabled shop ⊗ 🔊

HARTLEPOOL   **MAP 08 NZ53**

Hartlepool's Maritime Experience

Maritime Av TS24 0XZ

⊃ *(from A19 take A179 and follow signs for marina then historic quay)*

☎ 01429 860077

e-mail: info@hartlepoolsmaritimeexperience.com

web: www.hartlepoolsmaritimeexperience.com

Britain's maritime heritage is brought to life, with the sights, sounds and smells of an 1800s quayside. Learn about the birth of the Royal Navy, and visit the Quayside shops, the admiral's house, the oldest warship afloat HMS Trincomalee or the naval prison. Other features include children's maritime adventure centre, regular demonstrations of sword fighting, and canon firing. There's a full programme of events, for further details see website.

Times: ✱ Open all year daily 10-5. Closed 25-26 Dec & 1 Jan.
Facilities: ❷ 💻 🍽 licensed ♿ (all areas ramped or lift access, auto doors) toilets for disabled shop ⊗ (ex assist dogs) 🔊

HMS Trincomalee

Jackson Dock TS24 0SQ

⊃ *(From A19 take A689 or A179, follow signs for Hartlepool Historic Quay)*

☎ 01429 223193

e-mail: office@hms-trincomalee.co.uk

web: www.hms-trincomalee.co.uk

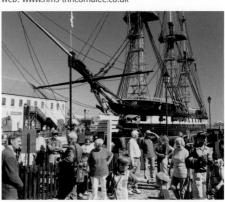

HMS Trincomalee, is the oldest ship afloat in the UK and the last of the commissioned frigates of the Nelson era. Now fully restored in an award-winning maritime heritage project. Come aboard for a unique experience of navy life two centuries ago.

Times: ✱ Open all year, Summer: 10-5, Winter: 10.30-4. Closed Xmas & New Year. **Facilities:** ❷ ♿ (3 out of the 4 decks are accessible by lift) shop ⊗ (ex guide dogs) 🔊

LANGLEY PARK   **MAP 12 NZ24**

Diggerland

DH7 9TT

⊃ *(A1(M) junct 62. Head W following signs to Consett. After 6m left at rdbt, signed Langley Park, then right into Riverside Ind Est)*

☎ 08700 344437

e-mail: mail@diggerland.com

web: www.diggerland.com

An adventure park with a difference, where kids of all ages can experience the thrills of driving real earth moving equipment. Choose from various types of diggers and dumpers ranging from 1 ton to 8 and a half tons. Supervised by an instructor complete the Dumper Truck Challenge or dig for buried treasure. New rides include JCB Robots, the Supertrack, Landrover Safari and Spin Dizzy. Even under 5s can join in, with mum or dad's help.

Times: ✱ Open mid Feb-Nov, 10-5, wknds BHs & school hols only
Facilities: ❷ 💻 ♿ toilets for disabled shop ⊗ (ex guide dogs) 🔊

We endeavour to be as accurate as possible, but changes to times and other information can occur after the guide has gone to press.

England

SHILDON MAP 08 NZ22

Locomotion: The National Railway Museum at Shildon `FREE`

DL4 1PQ

➲ *(A1(M) junct 68, take A68 & A6072 to Shildon, attraction is 0.25m SE of town centre)*

☎ 01388 777999

e-mail: gill@hamer-loco.fsnet.co.uk

web: www.locomotion.uk.com

Timothy Hackwood (1786-1850) was an important figure in the development of steam travel. He constructed *Puffing Billy* for William Hedley, ran Stephenson's Newcastle Works, and also became the first superintendent of the Stockton & Darlington Railway. The museum and house detail Hackwood's life and the steam transport revolution, as well as displaying working models and locomotives from various periods. Steam train rides are available throughout the year, on event days. The Collections building contains 60 vehicles from the National Collection.

Times: ✱ Telephone for details **Facilities:** ♥ ⬛ 🎞 ♿ (bus available to transport guests, please contact) toilets for disabled shop ⊗ (ex guide dogs) ◀

STAINDROP MAP 12 NZ12

Raby Castle

DL2 3AH

➲ *(on A688, Barnard Castle to Bishop Auckland road, 1m N of Staindrop)*

☎ 01833 660202

e-mail: admin@rabycastle.com

web: www.rabycastle.com

This dramatic 14th-century castle, built by the Nevills has been home to Lord Barnard's family since 1626. It has an impressive gateway, nine

continued

towers, a vast hall and an octagonal Victorian drawing room that has re-emerged as one of the most striking interiors from the 19th century. Rooms contain fine furniture, impressive artworks and elaborate architecture. In the grounds are a deer park, large walled gardens, coach and carriage collections, a woodland adventure playground, a picnic area and gift shop.

Times: Open May, Jun & Sep, Wed & Sun only. Jul & Aug, Sun-Fri. Castle 1-5. Park & Gardens open daily (ex Sat) 11-5, open BH wk ends.

Fee: Castle, Park & Gardens £9 (ch £4 & pen £8). Family ticket £25 (2ad+3ch). Park & Gardens £4 (ch £2.50 & pen £3.50). Family ticket £12.50 (2ad+3ch). Party 12+ **Facilities:** ♥ ⬛ (most of ground floor accessible, DVD interpretation) shop ⊗ (ex guide dogs & on lead) ◀

TANFIELD MAP 12 NZ15

Tanfield Railway

Old Marley Hill NE16 5ET

➲ *(on A6076 1m S of Sunniside)*

☎ 0191 388 7545

e-mail: tanfield@ingsoc.demon.co.uk

web: www.tanfield_railway.co.uk

A 3-mile working steam railway and the oldest existing railway in the world. The Causey Arch, the first large railway bridge of its era, is the centrepiece of a deep wooded valley, with picturesque walks. You can ride in carriages that first saw use in Victorian times, and visit Marley Hill shed, the home of 35 engines; inside the shed you can see the stationary steam engine at work driving some of the vintage machine tools. The blacksmith is also often at work forging new parts for the restoration work. Special events are held throughout the year, please telephone for details.

Times: ✱ Open all year, Summer daily 10-5; Winter daily 10-4. Trains: Sun & Summer BHs wknds; also Thu & Sat mid Jul-Aug. Santa's Specials Sat & Sun in Dec (booking essential). Mince pie specials Boxing Day.

Facilities: ♥ ⬛ ♿ (all trains carry ramps for wheelchair access) toilets for disabled shop

Barnard Castle

Essex

Windmill in Thaxted

The many different faces of Essex show a changing landscape offering a variety of pursuits and plenty of open spaces. Epping Forest has nearly 6,000 acres of beautiful woodland, the coastal areas of marshland, reclaimed by 17th century Dutch engineers, are a haven for wildfowl and small boats. The Rodings, centred on the town of Saffron Walden, is an idyllic region of timber-framed cottages and handsome houses in pretty villages and small towns. Notable examples are Great Dunmow, Thaxted and Finchingfield.

England

AUDLEY END   MAP 05 TL53

Audley End House & Gardens
CB11 4JF
- *(1m W of Saffron Walden on B1383)*
☎ 01799 522399
web: www.english-heritage.org.uk

One of the most significant Jacobean houses in England with 31 opulent rooms on view. Set in 'Capability' Brown landscaped park, with walled Victorian kitchen garden.

Times: Open House; 4-26 Mar & 7-29 Oct, Sat-Sun, 10-4 (Tours Only); Apr-Jun, Wed-Sun, 11-5, closed 3pm Sat (Tours only); Jul-Aug, Wed-Sun, 11-5, closed 3pm Sat; Sep-1 Oct, 11-5, closed 3pm Sat (Tours only). Last entry 1 hour before closing. Garden: 4-26 Mar Sat-Sun, 10-5; Apr-1 Oct, Wed-Sun & BHs, 10-6; 3-31 Mar & 7-29 Oct, Sat-Sun 10-5. **Fee:** House & Gardens: £8.95 (ch £4.50, concessions £6.70), family £22.40. Grounds only £4.80 (ch £2.40, concessions £3.60), family £12. Prices & opening times are subject to change in Spring 2007. Please check web site or call 0870 333 1181 for the most up to date prices and opening times.
Facilities: ❷ (charged) 💺 ♿ shop 🎪

BRENTWOOD   MAP 05 TQ69

Kelvedon Hatch Secret Nuclear Bunker   `2 for 1`
CM14 5TL
- *(on A128 Brentwood to Chipping Ongar road at Kelvedon Hotel)*
☎ 01277 364883
e-mail: bunker@japer.demon.co.uk
web: www.secretnuclearbunker.co.uk

Witness the three phases of the bunker's life. From its role with the RAF where the overall tactical controller would react to a nuclear attack from Britain's enemies, through to its role as Regional Government HQ. When there could have been up too 600 personnel, possibly including the Prime Minister, organising the survival of the civilian population in the aftermath of nuclear war. See for yourself the equipment and rooms needed to support the plotting of nuclear fall-out patterns.

Times: Mar-Oct, wkdays 10-4 wknds 10-5; Nov-Feb, Thu-Sun 10-4. **Fee:** ✱ £6 (ch £4). Family ticket (2ad+2ch) £15. **Facilities:** ❷ 💺 🍴 licensed ♿ (stairlift, ramps) toilets for disabled shop ⊗ (ex guide dogs)

CASTLE HEDINGHAM   MAP 05 TL73

Colne Valley Railway & Museum
Castle Hedingham Station CO9 3DZ
- *(4m NW of Halstead on A1017)*
☎ 01787 461174
web: www.colnevalleyrailway.co.uk

Many former Colne Valley and Halstead railway buildings have been rebuilt here. Stock includes seven steam locomotives plus 80 other engines, carriages and wagons. Visitors can dine in style in restored Pullman carriages while travelling along the line. Please telephone for a free timetable and details of the many special events.

Times: ✱ Open all year, daily 10-dusk. Steam days, rides from 12-4. Closed 23 Dec-1 Feb. Steam days every Sun and BH from Mothering Sunday to end Oct, Wed of school summer hols & special events. Railway Farm Park open May-Sep. Phone 01787 461174 for timetable information or visit website for details. **Facilities:** ❷ 💺 🍴 licensed 🍽 ♿ (ramps for

continued

---

wheelchairs to get onto carriages) toilets for disabled shop ⊗ (ex guide dogs) 🛥

Hedingham Castle
CO9 3DJ
- *(on B1508, 1m off A1017 Colchester/Cambridge. Follow brown heritage signs to Hedingham Castle)*
☎ 01787 460261
e-mail: hedinghamcastle@aspects.net
web: www.hedinghamcastle.co.uk

This impressive Norman castle was built in 1140. It was besieged by King John, visited by Henry VII, Henry VIII and Elizabeth I, and was home to the de Veres, Earls of Oxford, for over 500 years. During the summer months Hedingham's colourful heritage comes to life with a full programme of special events. There are medieval jousts and sieges with authentic living history displays and encampments. Please telephone for details.

Times: ✱ Open Etr-Oct, Thu, Fri & Sun, 11-4. **Facilities:** ❷ 💺 🍽 shop ⊗ (ex in grounds) 🛥

CHELMSFORD   MAP 05 TL70

RHS Garden Hyde Hall
Buckhatch Ln, Rettendon CM3 8ET
- *(from M25 junct 28 (signed A12) or 29 (signed A127). SE of Chelmsford signed from A130. Exit Rettendon Turnpike, N through Rettendon Village, follow brown tourist signs)*
☎ 01245 400256
e-mail: hydehall@rhs.org.uk
web: www.rhs.org.uk

Calling itself "A garden of inspirational beauty", RHS Garden Hyde Hall is a great day out for plant-lovers, and includes highlights such as the Dry Garden, a modern rose garden designed by Robin Williams, colour themed herbaceous borders, a farmhouse garden, and the NCCPG National Collection(tm)of Viburnum. New areas include The Queen Mother's Garden and a model Garden for Wildlife.

Times: Open all year (ex 25 Dec) from 10, closing times vary with season - contact garden for details. **Fee:** ✱ £5 (ch 6-16 £1, ch under 6 free). Member & guest free. **Facilities:** ❷ 🍴 licensed ♿ (ramps and easy access to visitor centre) toilets for disabled shop garden centre ⊗ (ex guide dogs)

COGGESHALL   MAP 05 TL82

Paycocke's
West St CO6 1NS
- *(Signposted from A120, on S side of West Street)*
☎ 01376 561305

This timber-framed house is a fine example of a medieval merchant's home. It was completed in about 1505 and has interesting carvings on the outside timbers, including the Paycocke trade sign. Inside there are further elaborate carvings and linenfold panelling. Behind the house is a pretty garden.

Times: Open 2 Apr-8 Oct Tue, Thu, Sun & BH Mon 2-5. **Fee:** ✱ £3 (ch £1.50), joint ticket with Coggleshall Grange Barn £4 (ch £2). **Facilities:** ❷ (400yds) ♿ (Large print & Braille guide, photo album) ⊗ (ex guide dogs) 🛥

COLCHESTER — MAP 05 TL92

Beth Chatto Gardens
Elmstead Market CO7 7DB
➲ *(5m E of Colchester on A133)*
☎ 01206 822007
e-mail: info@bethchatto.fsnet.co.uk
web: www.bethchatto.co.uk

Begun almost 40 years ago, when Beth Chatto and her late husband began working on acres of wasteland. Now an area of landscaped gardens with many unusual plants grown in a variety of conditions.

Times: Open all year, Mar-Oct, Mon-Sat 9-5; Nov-Feb, Mon-Fri 9-4. **Fee:** £4.50 (accompanied ch under 14 free) **Facilities:** ♿ 🖼 & (parts of garden may be awkward, parking, large print guide) toilets for disabled garden centre ⊗ (ex guide dogs) ◀

Colchester Castle Museum
Castle Park, High St CO1 1TJ
➲ *(at E end of High St)*
☎ 01206 282939
web: www.colchestermuseums.org.uk

The largest Norman castle keep in Europe - built over the remains of the magnificent Roman Temple of Claudius which was destroyed by Boudicca in AD60. Colchester was the first capital of Roman Britain, and the archaeological collections are among the finest in the country. Please telephone for details of a range of events held throughout the year.

Times: ✻ Open all year, Mon-Sat 10-5, Sun 11-5. Closed Xmas/New Year **Facilities:** ℗ (town centre) 🖼 & (all parts accessible except vaults/roof tour) toilets for disabled shop ⊗ (ex guide dogs) ◀

Colchester Zoo
Stanway, Maldon Rd CO3 0SL
➲ *(turn off A12 onto A1124 and follow elephant signs)*
☎ 01206 331292
e-mail: enquiries@colchester-zoo.co.uk
web: www.colchester-zoo.co.uk

One of England's finest zoos, Colchester Zoo has over 250 species of animal. Visitors can meet the elephants, handle a snake, and see parrots, seals, penguins and birds of prey all appearing in informative daily displays. Enclosures include Spirit of Africa with baby elephants Kito and Jambo, Playa Patagonia where sea lions swim above your head in a 24m underwater tunnel, Penguin Shores, the Wilds of Asia for orang-utans, Chimp World, and the Kingdom of the Wild, with giraffes, zebras and rhinos. There is also an undercover soft play complex, road train, four adventure play areas, eating places and gift shops, all set in 60 acres of gardens.

Times: Open all year, daily from 9.30. Last admission 5.30 (1hr before dusk out of season). Closed 25 Dec. **Fee:** ✻ £13.50 (ch 3-14 £7.50). **Facilities:** ♿ 🖼 🍴 licensed 🖼 & (easy route developed, but zoo has hills, electric scooters) toilets for disabled shop ⊗ (ex guide dogs) ◀

HADLEIGH — MAP 05 TQ88

Hadleigh Castle `FREE`
➲ *(0.75m S of A13)*
☎ 01760 755161
web: www.english-heritage.org.uk

The subject of several of Constable's paintings, the castle has fine views of the Thames estuary. It is defended by ditches on three sides, and the north-east and south-east towers are still impressive.

Times: Open at any reasonable time. **Facilities:** (limited access due to hilly surroundings) ⚏

HARWICH — MAP 05 TM23

Harwich Redoubt Fort `2 for 1`
CO12 3TE
➲ *(behind 29 Main Rd)*
☎ 01255 503429
e-mail: theharwichsociety@quista.net
web: www.harwich-society.com

The 180ft-diameter circular fort was built in 1808 in case of invasion by Napoleon. It has a dry moat and 8ft-thick walls, with 18 rooms for stores, ammunition and quarters for 300 men. The Redoubt is being restored by the Harwich Society, and contains three small museums. Ten guns can be seen on the battlements.

Times: Open May-Aug, daily 10-4; Sep-Apr, Sun only 10-4. **Fee:** £2 (accompanied ch free). **Facilities:** ℗ (200yds) 🖼 shop

HEDINGHAM
See **Castle Hedingham**

LAYER MARNEY — MAP 05 TL91

Layer Marney Tower
CO5 9US
➲ *(off B1022 Colchester to Maldon road, signposted)*
☎ 01206 330784
e-mail: info@layermarneytower.co.uk
web: www.layermarneytower.co.uk

The tallest Tudor gatehouse in the country, intended to be the entrance to a courtyard which would have rivalled Hampton Court Palace. The death of Henry, 1st Lord Marney in 1523, and of his son in 1525, meant that the building work ceased before completion. The beautiful parish church lies within the grounds and a wildlife walk offers the chance to see a range of livestock.

Times: Open Apr-Sep, Sun-Thu 12-5, & BHs (Sun & Mon) 11-5. **Fee:** ✻ £4 (ch £2.50). Family ticket (2ad + 2ch) £12. Guided tour £5. **Facilities:** ♿ 🖼 🍴 licensed & (ramps in garden and farm) toilets for disabled shop ⊗ (ex guide dogs & dogs on lead) ◀

England

MISTLEY   MAP 05 TM13

Mistley Towers   FREE
CO11 1NJ
⮕ *(on B1352, 1.5m E of A137 at Lawford)*
☎ 01206 393884
web: www.english-heritage.org.uk

All that remains of the grand hall and church, designed by Robert Adam, are the lodges built in 1782 for the hall, and two square towers, topped with drums and domes which came from an earlier church.

Times: Open all reasonable times. Key available from Mistley Quay Workshops 01206 393884 **Facilities:** &

NEWPORT   MAP 05 TL53

Mole Hall Wildlife Park
Widdington CB11 3SS
⮕ *(M11 junct 8 between Stansted & Saffron Walden, off B1383)*
☎ 01799 540400 & 541359
e-mail: enquiries@molehall.co.uk
web: www.molehall.co.uk

The Park covers 20 acres and has been lovingly developed by the Johnstone family for over 40 years. The wide variety of animals range from South American Lama Guanaco to Red squirrels, Leopard-like Serval Cat and the Formosan Sika Deer, which is extinct in the wild. Mole Hall is also home to 2 species of otter, being the first regular breeders in the UK of the North American Otter. Other residents include chimpanzees, capuchins, lemurs and much more. In the tropical butterfly pavilion, see butterflies on the wing and free flying small birds. Tarantulas, snakes, pools of aquatic life, small monkeys, tortoises and lovebirds. Small children will also be entertained by the straw castle, water maze, sand pit and play area.

Times: Open all year, daily 10-5.30 (or dusk). Closed 25 Dec. Butterfly House and Water Maze open mid Mar-Oct. **Fee:** ✷ £6.30 (ch £4.30 under 3's free, pen, student & disabled £3). **Facilities:** ❷ 💺 📶 & (Difficult in wet weather for wheelchairs) toilets for disabled shop garden centre ⊗ (ex guide dogs) 🍴

SAFFRON WALDEN   MAP 05 TL53

Saffron Walden Museum   2 for 1
Museum St CB10 1JL
⮕ *(Close to M11, take B184/B1052 & follow signs to Saffron Walden)*
☎ 01799 510333
e-mail: museum@uttesford.gov.uk
web: www.saffronwaldenmuseum.org

Opened in 1835, this friendly, family-size museum lies near the castle ruins in the centre of town. Its collections include local history and archaeology, natural history, ceramics, glass, costume, furniture, toys, an ancient Egyptian room, a natural history gallery, Discovery Centre and important ethnography collections. This museum has won the Museum of the Year award for being the best museum of social history, and awards for disabled access. There is a regular programme of special exhibitions, events and family holiday activities.

Times: Open all year, Mar-Oct, Mon-Sat 10-5, Sun & BHs 2-5; Nov-Feb, Mon-Sat, 10-4.30, Sun & BHs 2-4.30. Closed 24 & 25 Dec. **Fee:** £1 (concessions 50p, ch 18 & under free) **Facilities:** ❷ & (ramps, wheelchairs available, stairlifts, hearing loop) toilets for disabled shop ⊗ (ex guide & hearing dogs)

SOUTHEND-ON-SEA   MAP 05 TQ88

Southend Museum, Planetarium
& Discovery Centre
Victoria Av SS2 6ES
⮕ *(take A127 or A13 towards town centre. Museum is adjacent to Southend Victoria Railway Station)*
☎ 01702 434449
e-mail: southendmuseum@hotmail.com
web: www.southendmuseums.co.uk

A fine Edwardian building housing displays of archaeology, natural history and local history, telling the story of man in the south-east Essex area. Also the only planetarium in the South East. Ring for details of special events, or see website.

Times: Open Central Museum: Tue-Sat 10-5 (Closed Sun-Mon & BH); Planetarium: Wed-Sat, shows at 11, 2 & 4. **Fee:** Central Museum free. Planetarium £2.60 (ch & pen £1.90). Family tickets £8. Party rates on request. **Facilities:** ❷ (50mtrs) (disabled only behind museum) & (planetarium not accessible, disabled access to centre) shop ⊗ (ex guide dogs)

Southend Pier Museum
Western Esplanade SS1 2EL
⮕ *(A127 follow signs to seafront and pier, attraction is at shore end of pier, access from shore train station)*
☎ 01702 611214 & 614553
web: www.southendpiermuseum.com

Southend Pier is one and a third miles long and was built in 1830. This living museum portrays the history of the pier, its railway, its disasters, and the people who have lived and worked there. Exhibits include ex-pier rolling stock, a reconstructed signal box with working levers, and antique slot machines.

Times: Open May-Oct. Tue, Wed, Sat, Sun & BHs 11-5 (during school hols 5.30) **Fee:** ✷ £1 (accompanied ch under 12 free). Subject to change. **Facilities:** ❷ (50yds) 📶 & (Access to museum through fire door at Adventure Island) shop ⊗ (ex guide dogs)

STANSTED   MAP 05 TL52

House on the Hill Museum Adventure
CM24 8SP
⮕ *(off B1383 in the centre of Stansted Mountfitchet)*
☎ 01279 813567
e-mail: office@mountfitchetcastle.com
web: www.mountfitchetcastle.com

A large, privately-owned toy museum, housed on two floors covering 7,000 sq. ft. A huge variety of toys, books and games from the late Victorian period up to the 1970s. There is a space display, Teddy Bears' picnic, Action Man, Sindy, Barbie, military displays and much more. Additional displays of film, theatre, rock n roll and television memorabilia are on show, plus end of the pier slot machines.

Times: Open all year daily, 10-5; (closed for a few days over the Xmas period & Mon in Jan & Feb) **Fee:** ✷ £4 (ch under 14 £3.30, pen £3.50). Party 15+. **Facilities:** ❷ (charged) shop ⊗ (ex guide dogs) 🍴

Mountfitchet Castle & Norman Village
CM24 8SP
➲ *(off B1383, in village centre. 5 min from M11 junct 8)*
☎ 01279 813237
e-mail: office@mountfitchetcastle.com
web: www.mountfitchetcastle.com

Norman motte and bailey castle and village reconstructed as it was in Norman England of 1066, on its original historic site. A vivid illustration of village life in Domesday England, complete with houses, church, seige tower, seige weapons, and many types of animals roaming freely. Animated wax figures in all the buildings give historical information to visitors.

Times: Open daily, mid Mar-mid Nov, 10-5. **Fee:** ✱ £6.50 (ch under 2 free, ch 3-13 £5, pen £5.50). **Facilities:** ♥ (charged) 🍴 🅿 ♿ (laser commentaries) toilets for disabled shop ⊗ (ex guide dogs) ◀

TILBURY   MAP 05 TQ67

Tilbury Fort
No 2 Office Block, The Fort RM18 7NR
➲ *(0.5 mile E off A126)*
☎ 01375 858489
web: www.english-heritage.org.uk

View the finest example of 17th-century military engineering, a spectacular sight on the River Thames. View the World War I and II gun emplacements and even fire a real anti-aircraft gun.

Times: Open all year, Apr-Oct, daily 10-5; Nov-Mar, Thu-Mon 10-4. **Fee:** £3.40 (ch £1.70, concessions £2.60). £1.30 to fire anti-aircraft gun. Prices and opening times are subject to change in Spring 2007. Please check web site or call 0870 333 1181 for the most up to date prices and opening times when planning your visit. **Facilities:** ♿ shop ⊗ (ex on lead in certain areas) ▦

WALTHAM ABBEY   MAP 05 TL30

Lee Valley Park Farms
Stubbins Hall Ln, Crooked Mile EN9 2EG
➲ *(M25 junct 26, follow to Waltham Abbey. 2m from Waltham Abbey on B914)*
☎ 01992 892781 & 702200
e-mail: hayeshill@leevalleypark.org.uk
web: www.leevalleypark.org.uk

Set in the heart of Lee Valley Country Park, Hayes Hill Farm offers young and old the chance to view many types of farm animals. Meet a variety of rare breeds in the traditional-style farmyard. In the pet centre, see many creatures from meerkats to chipmunks. During summer, there are tractor and trailor rides to Holyfield Hall, a 700-acre working dairy and arable farm.

Times: ✱ Open all year, Mon-Fri 10-4.30, wknds & BHs 10-5.30. **Facilities:** ♥ 🍴 🅿 ♿ (graded concrete paths, signed routes) toilets for disabled shop ◀

Royal Gunpowder Mills
Beaulieu Dr EN9 1JY
➲ *(M25 junct 26. Follow signs for A121 to Waltham Abbey at rdbt, entrance in Beaulieu Drive)*
☎ 01992 707370
e-mail: info@royalgunpowdermills.com
web: www.royalgunpowdermills.com

Set in 175 acres of parkland, this amazing scientific complex has 21 buildings of historical importance. Before it closed in 1991 this was a site of major scientific research and development, including work on Congreve's Rocket in the early 19th century, up to more recent work on ejector seats and fuel for rocket motors. Explosives were made in many of the buildings on the site which are connected by five miles of navigational canals.

Times: ✱ Open 30 Apr-25 Sep, 11-5, last entry at 3.30. (Wknds and BHs only) **Facilities:** ♥ 🍴 🅿 ♿ (ramps, lift, tactile with audio tour) toilets for disabled shop ⊗ (ex guide dogs) ◀

Waltham Abbey Gatehouse, Bridge & Entrance to Cloisters
➲ *(in Waltham Abbey off A112)*
☎ 01992 702200
web: www.english-heritage.org.uk

Beside the great Norman church at Waltham are the slight remains of the abbey buildings - bridge, gatehouse and part of the north cloister. The bridge is named after King Harold, founder of the abbey.

Times: Open at any reasonable time. **Facilities:** ♿ (sensory trail guide)

Gloucestershire

Tewkesbury Abbey Nave

Most of the Cotswolds lie in this picturesque county of limestone hills with charming villages built from local stone, varying in hue from honey gold to silver grey. The substantial churches and large manor houses are a legacy of the medieval wool trade. To the Southwest and bordering Wales, is the Wye Valley and the Forest of Dean. The forest was utilised by the Romans for iron ore and charcoal; by Tudor shipbuilders for timber, including that which built the Mary Rose; and during the 19th century for its coal deposits. Despite this industrial history, the forest still covers 27,000 acres with broad leaved trees and is a walker's paradise.

ALDSWORTH
MAP 04 SP11

Lodge Park & Sherborne Estate
GL54 3PP
➲ *(approach from A40 only, between Northleach & Burford rdbts)*
☎ 01451 844130 & 844257
e-mail: lodgepark@nationaltrust.org.uk
web: www.nationaltrust.org.uk

Situated on the picturesque Sherborne Estate in the Cotswolds, Lodge Park was created in 1634 by John 'Crump' Dutton. Inspired by his passion for gambling and banqueting it is a unique survival of what would have been called a Grandstand, with its deer course and park.

Times: Open Grandstand: 24 Mar-29 Oct, Mon, Fri & Sun 11-4, Sat 11-3; Estate: daily all year. **Fee:** ✱ grandstand: £4.50 (ch £2.50). Family £11. Estate: free. **Facilities:** ℗ 🍴 ⓰ (Braille guide, manual wheelchair, drop off point) toilets for disabled ⓖ

BERKELEY
MAP 03 ST69

Berkeley Castle
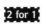
GL13 9BQ
➲ *(just off A38 midway between Bristol & Gloucester. From M5 take junct 14 or 13)*
☎ 01453 810332
e-mail: info@berkeley-castle.com
web: www.berkeley-castle.com

Berkeley Castle is the amazing fortress home of the Berkeley family, who have lived in the building since the Keep was completed in 1153. The castle is still intact, from dungeon to elegant drawing rooms, and reflects nearly a thousand years of English history: a king's murder, the American Colonies, London's Berkeley Square. Rose-clad terraces surround this most romantic castle.

Times: Open Apr-2 Oct, Tue-Sat & BH Mon 11-4, Sun 2-5; Oct, Sun only 2-5. **Fee:** ✱ Castle & Gardens & Butterfly House: £7.50 (ch 5-15 £4.50, pen £6). Family ticket (2ad+2ch) £21. **Facilities:** ℗ 🍴 ⓰ ⓖ (Special tours can be arranged) shop garden centre ⓧ (ex guide dogs) ◀

Jenner Museum
2 for 1
Church Ln, High St GL13 9BN
➲ *(follow tourist signs from A38 to town centre, turn left into High Street & left again into Church Lane)*
☎ 01453 810631
e-mail: manager@jennermuseum.com
web: www.jennermuseum.com

This beautiful Georgian house was the home of Edward Jenner, the discoverer of vaccination against smallpox. The house and the garden, with its Temple of Vaccinia, are much as they were in Jenner's day. The displays record Jenner's life as an 18th-century country doctor, his work on vaccination and his interest in natural history.

Times: Open Apr-Sep, Tue-Sat 12.30-5.30, Sun 1-5.30. Oct, Sun 1-5.30. (Closed Mon, ex BH Mon 12.30-5.30). **Fee:** ✱ £4.25 (ch £2.50, concessions £3.50). Family ticket £10.75. Party 20+. **Facilities:** ℗ 🍴 ⓖ toilets for disabled shop ⓧ (ex guide dogs) ◀

BOURTON-ON-THE-HILL
MAP 04 SP13

Bourton House Garden
GL56 9AE
➲ *(1.75m W of Moreton-in-Marsh on A44)*
☎ 01386 700754
e-mail: cd@bourtonhouse.com
web: www.bourtonhouse.com

Since 1983 a dedicated team has been working to restore this 18th-century house and its large gardens. The result is an impressive landscape full of hedges, water features, paths and plants.

Times: Open end May-Aug, Wed-Fri, end Sep-Oct Thu-Fri, 10-5 **Fee:** ✱ £5 (ch free) **Facilities:** ℗ 🍴 ⓖ (garden is 70% accessible) toilets for disabled shop garden centre ⓧ

BOURTON-ON-THE-WATER
MAP 04 SP12

Birdland
2 for 1
Rissington Rd GL54 2BN
➲ *(on A429)*
☎ 01451 820480
e-mail: simonb@birdland.co.uk
web: www.birdland.co.uk

Birdland is a natural setting of woodland, river and gardens, which is inhabited by over 500 birds; flamingos, pelicans, penguins, cranes, storks, cassowary and waterfowl can be seen on various aspects of the water habitat. Over 50 aviaries of parrots, falcons, pheasants, hornbills, touracos, pigeons, ibis and many more. Tropical, Toucan and Desert Houses are home to the more delicate species.

Times: Open all year, Apr-Oct, daily 10-6; Nov-Mar, daily 10-4. (Last admission 1hr before closing). Closed 25 Dec. **Fee:** £5.20 (pen £4.20). Family ticket (2ad+2ch) £15. **Facilities:** ℗ (adjacent) 🍴 ⓰ ⓖ toilets for disabled shop ◀

Model Village
Old New Inn GL54 2AF
☎ 01451 820467
e-mail: reception@theoldnewinn.co.uk
web: www.theoldnewinn.co.uk

The model is built of Cotswold stone to a scale of one-ninth, and is a perfect replica of the village. It includes a miniature River Windrush, a working model waterwheel, churches and shops, with tiny trees, shrubs and alpine plants.

Times: Open all year 10-5.45 (summer), 10-dusk (winter). Closed 25 Dec. **Fee:** £3 (ch £2.50, pen £2.75). **Facilities:** ℗ (500yds) 🍴 🍽 licensed shop ⓧ (ex guide dogs) ◀

CHEDWORTH
MAP 04 SP01

Chedworth Roman Villa
Yanworth GL54 3LJ
➲ *(3m NW of Fossebridge on A429)*
☎ 01242 890256
e-mail: chedworth@nationaltrust.org.uk
web: www.nationaltrust.org.uk

The remains of a Romano-British villa, excavated 1864-66 and known as 'Britains oldest county house'. Set in a beautiful wooded combe, there are fine 4th-century mosaics, two bath houses, and a temple

continued

with spring. The museum houses the smaller finds and there is a 9-minute video programme. Telephone for further details of special events.

Times: Open 1-25 Mar, daily 11-4; 26 Mar-28 Oct, daily 10-5; 26 Oct-12 Nov, daily 11-4. (Closed Mons ex BH Mon). **Fee:** ✱ £5.50 (ch £3). Family ticket £14. **Facilities:** ℗ ♿ (audio tour, induction loop, Braille guide) toilets for disabled shop ⊗ ♨ ◥

CHELTENHAM   MAP 03 SO92

Cheltenham Art Gallery & Museum
Clarence St GL50 3JT

➲ *(close to town centre and bus station, 2 min walk from promenade)*

☎ 01242 237431
e-mail: artgallery@cheltenham.gov.uk
web: www.cheltenham.artgallery.museum

The museum has an outstanding collection relating to the Arts and Crafts Movement, including fine furniture and exquisite metalwork. The Art Gallery contains Dutch and British paintings from the 17th century to the present day. The Oriental Gallery features pottery, costumes and treasures from the Ming Dynasty to the reign of the last Chinese Emperor. There is also a display about Edward Wilson who journeyed with Captain Scott in 1911-12, together with the history of Britain's most complete Regency town and archaeological treasures from the neighbouring Cotswolds. Special exhibitions are held throughout the year.

Times: Open all year, Mon-Sat 10-5.20 (first Thu in month, 11-5.20). Closed BHs. **Fee:** Free, donations welcome. **Facilities:** ℗ (500 mtrs) (disabled parking on site) ⬛ ▥ ♿ (handling tables; speech reinforcement system) toilets for disabled shop ⊗ (ex guide dogs) ◥

Holst Birthplace Museum
4 Clarence Rd GL52 2AY

➲ *(opposite gateway of Pittville Park. 10 min walk from town centre)*

☎ 01242 524846
e-mail: holstmuseum@btconnect.com
web: www.holstmuseum.org.uk

Gustav Holst, composer of *The Planets* was born at this Regency house in 1874. The museum contains unique displays on Holst's life, including his original piano. The rooms of the house have been carefully restored, each area evoking a different period in the history of the house from Regency to Edwardian times.

Times: Open Tue-Sat 10-4 (Closed Mon & Dec-Jan, ex pre-booked groups). **Fee:** £3.50 (ch & concessions £3). Family ticket (2ad+3ch) £8. **Facilities:** ℗ (250yds) (large print & Braille guide, special hands-on tours) shop ⊗ (ex guide dogs)

CIRENCESTER   MAP 04 SP00

Corinium Museum
Park St GL7 2BX

➲ *(in town centre)*

☎ 01285 655611
e-mail: museums@cotswold.gov.uk
web: www.cotswold.gov.uk

Discover the treasures of the Cotswolds at the new Corinium Museum. Two years and over £5 million in the making, it has been transformed into a must-see attraction. Featuring archaeological and

historical material from Cirencester and the Cotswolds, from prehistoric times to the 19th century. The museum is known for its Roman mosaic sculpture and other material from one of Britain's largest Roman towns. New on display are Anglo-Saxon treasures from Lechlade bringing to life this little known period. The museum also houses Medieval, Tudor, Civil War and 18th-19th century displays.

Times: Open Mon-Sat 10-5, Sun 2-5. Closed 25-26 Dec & 1 Jan. **Fee:** £3.90 (ch & students £2.00, pen £2.90). Family ticket £9. **Facilities:** ℗ (2mins walk) ⬛ ⎰◯⎱ ♿ Large print & Braille guides toilets for disabled shop ⊗ assist dogs ◥

CLEARWELL   MAP 03 SO50

Clearwell Caves Ancient Iron Mines   2 for 1
GL16 8JR

➲ *(1.5m S of Coleford town centre, off B4228 follow brown tourist signs)*

☎ 01594 832535
e-mail: jw@clearwellcaves.com
web: www.clearwellcaves.com

These impressive natural caves have also been mined since the earliest times for paint pigment and iron ore. Today visitors explore nine large caverns with displays of local mining and geology. Colour room where ochre pigments are still produced and blacksmith shop. Deep level excursions available for more adventurous visitors, must be pre booked. Christmas fantasy event when the caverns are transformed into a world of light and sound.

Times: Open Mar-Oct daily 10-5; Jan-Feb Sat-Sun 10-5; Christmas Fantasy 1-24 Dec, daily 10-5. **Fee:** £5 (ch £3, concessions £4.50) Family ticket £14. **Facilities:** ℗ ⬛ ▥ ♿ (hands-on exhibits, Braille guide book, contact in advance) toilets for disabled shop ⊗ (ex guide & hearing dogs) ◥

CRANHAM   MAP 03 SO81

Prinknash Abbey and Pottery
GL4 8EX

➲ *(on A46 between Cheltenham & Stroud)*

☎ 01452 812066
e-mail: prinknashshop@waitrose.com
web: www.prinknashabbey.org.uk

Set in a large park, the old priory building is a 12th to 16th-century house, used by Benedictine monks and guests of Gloucester Abbey until 1539. It became an abbey for Benedictine monks from Caldey in

continued

continued

1928. Home to the reconstruction of the Great Orpheus Pavement. It is the largest mosaic in Britain, as mentioned in the Guinness Book of Records. Also visit the bird and deer park.

Times: Open all year. Abbey Church: April-end Oct 9-5.30, Nov-end Mar 10-4.30. Closed Good Fri, 25-26 Dec. **Fee:** ✱ Admission free to grounds. Orpheus Pavement £3.25 (ch 1.75). Family ticket £7. **Facilities:** ❷ ♥ ⑤ (Radar approved) toilets for disabled shop ◼

Prinknash Bird & Deer Park

GL4 8EU

➲ *(A46 Stroud. Follow brown tourist signs)*

☎ 01452 812727

web: www.prinknash-bird-and-deerpark.com

Nine acres of parkland and lakes make a beautiful home for black swans, geese and other water birds. There are also exotic birds such as white and Indian blue peacocks and crown cranes, as well as tame fallow deer and pygmy goats. The Golden Wood is stocked with ornamental pheasants, and leads to the reputedly haunted monks' fishpond, which contains trout. An 80-year old, free-standing, 16ft tall Wendy House in the style of a Tudor house has recently been erected near the picnic area.

Times: Open all year, daily 10-5 (4 in winter). Closed 26 Dec & Good Fri. **Fee:** ✱ £5 (ch £3.50, pen £4.50). Party 10+ £4 (ch £3, pen £4). **Facilities:** ❷ ♥ ⑤ shop ⊗

DEERHURST   MAP 03 SO82

Odda's Chapel   FREE

➲ *(off B4213 near River Severn at Abbots Court SW of parish church)*

This rare Saxon chapel was built by Earl Odda and dedicated in 1056. When it was discovered, it had been incorporated into a farmhouse. It has now been carefully restored.

Times: Open Apr-Oct, daily 10-6; Nov-Mar, daily 10-4. Closed 24-26 Dec & 1 Jan. **Facilities:** ❷ (charged) ⊗

DYRHAM   MAP 03 ST77

Dyrham Park

SN14 8ER

➲ *(8m N of Bath, 2m from M4 junct 18)*

☎ 0117 937 2501

e-mail: dyrhampark@nationaltrust.org.uk

web: www.nationaltrust.org.uk

Dyrham Park is a splendid Baroque Country house, with interiors that have hardly altered since the late 17th century. It has contemporary Dutch-style furnishings, Dutch pictures and blue-and-white Delft ware. Around the house is an ancient park with fallow deer, where Dyrham derives its name. In the beautiful gardens, famous for the tulip festival in April, is a medieval Church.

Times: House 24 Mar-29 Oct, 12-4.45, Fri-Tue. Garden 24 Mar-29 Oct, 11-5, Fri-Tue. Park all year, 11-5, all week. Shop 24 Mar-29 Oct, 11-5, Fri-Tue. Tea room, 24 Mar-29 Oct, 11-5, Fri-Tue. **Fee:** ✱ House £9 (ch £4.50). Family £22.50 Ground only £3.50 (ch £1.80). Family £8). Park only £2.30 (ch £1.10). Family £5.20 **Facilities:** ❷ ♥ ⑩ licensed ⑤ ♿ (Braille/audio guides, stairclimber, free bus from car park) toilets for disabled shop ⊗ (ex in dog walk area) 🐾

GLOUCESTER   MAP 03 SO81

Gloucester City Museum & Art Gallery   FREE

Brunswick Rd GL1 1HP

➲ *(centre of Gloucester)*

☎ 01452 396131

e-mail: city.museum@gloucester.gov.uk

web: www.gloucester.gov.uk

An impressive range of Roman artefacts including the Rufus Sita tombstone; the amazing Iron Age Birdlip Mirror; one of the earliest backgammon sets in the world; dinosaur fossils; and paintings by famous artists such as Turner and Gainsborough. There is something for everyone, full-sized dinosaurs; wildlife from the City and the Gloucestershire countryside; beautiful antique furniture, glass, ceramics and silver; hands-on displays, computer quizzes and activity workstations throughout the galleries. There is an exciting range of temporary exhibitions from contemporary art and textiles to dinosaurs and local history; children's holiday activities and regular special events.

Times: Open all year, Tue-Sat 10-5. **Facilities:** ℗ (500yds) ⑤ ♿ (lift to 1st floor galleries, induction loops) toilets for disabled shop ⊗ (ex guide dogs) ◼

Gloucester Folk Museum   FREE

99-103 Westgate St GL1 2PG

➲ *(from W - A40 & A48; from N - A38 & M5, from E - A40 & B4073; from S - A4173 & A38)*

☎ 01452 396868 & 396869

e-mail: folk.museum@gloucester.gov.uk

web: www.gloucester.gov.uk

Three floors of splendid Tudor and Jacobean timber-framed buildings dating from the 16th and 17th centuries along with new buildings housing the Dairy, Ironmonger's shop and Wheelwright and Carpenter workshops. Local history, domestic life, crafts, trades and industries from 1500 to the present, including Toys and Childhood gallery with hands-on toys and a puppet theatre, the Siege of Gloucester, a Victorian Class Room, Victorian Kitchen and laundry equipment. A wide range of exhibitions, hands-on activities, events, demonstrations and role play sessions are held throughout the year. There is an

continued

attractive cottage garden and courtyard for events, often with live animals, and outside games.

Gloucester Folk Museum

Times: Open all year, Tue-Sat, 10-5 **Facilities:** Ⓟ (500yds) ☐ ♿ (virtual tour in Protal gallery, induction loops) shop ⊗ (ex guide dogs) ◼

The National Waterways Museum `2 for 1`

Llanthony Warehouse, The Docks GL1 2EH

➲ (From M5, A40 and within the city follow brown signs for historic docks)

☎ 01452 318200

e-mail: bookingsnwm@thewaterwaystrust.org

web: www.nwm.org.uk

Based in Gloucester Docks, this museum takes up three floors of a seven-storey Victorian warehouse, and documents the 200-year history of Britain's water-based transport. The emphasis is on hands-on experience, including working models and engines, interactive displays, actual craft, computer interactions and the national collection of inland waterways. Boat trips are also available between Easter and October.

Times: Open all year, daily 10-5. (Last admission 4). Closed 25 Dec. **Fee:** £5.95 (under 5's free, concessions £4.95). Family ticket £17.50 **Facilities:** Ⓟ (charged) ▆ ◉ ☐ ♿ (wheelchair, lifts, limited access to floating exhibits) toilets for disabled shop ⊗ (ex guide dogs) ◼

Nature in Art `2 for 1`

Wallsworth Hall, Tewkesbury Rd, Twigworth GL2 9PA

➲ (0.5m off main A38 between Gloucester and Tewkesbury, 2m N of Gloucester. Follow brown tourist signs)

☎ 01452 731422 & 0845 450 0233

e-mail: enquiries@nature-in-art.org.uk

web: www.nature-in-art.org.uk

Nature is the theme at this museum and art gallery set in a Georgian Mansion, where there are many outstanding exhibits including sculpture, tapestries and ceramics. There is an 'artist in residence' programme Feb-Nov, and events include regular monthly talks, film showings and a full programme of temporary exhibitions and art courses. See website for full details. Work from over 60 countries spanning 1500 years is included in the collection, which has been specially commended twice in the National Heritage Museum of the Year Awards. From Picasso to David Shepherd, Flemish masters to

ethnic art, contemporary sculpture to Japanese prints - there is something for everyone.

Nature in Art

Times: Open all year, Tue-Sun & BHs 10-5. Closed 24-26 Dec. **Fee:** ✱ £4.50 (ch, concessions £4, ch under 8 free). Family ticket £13. Party 15+. **Facilities:** Ⓟ ▆ ◉ licensed ♿ (lift & ramps at entrance) toilets for disabled shop ⊗ (ex guide dogs)

continued

GUITING POWER MAP 04 SP02

Cotswold Farm Park `2 for 1`

GL54 5UG

➲ (signed off B4077 from M5 junct 9)

☎ 01451 850307

e-mail: info@cotswoldfarmpark.co.uk

web: www.cotswoldfarmpark.co.uk

At the Cotswold Farm Park there are nearly 50 breeding herds and flocks of the rarest British breeds of sheep, cattle, pigs, goats, horses, and poultry. Lots of activities for children including rabbits and guinea pigs to cuddle, lambs and calves to bottle feed, tractor and trailer rides, battery powered tractors and safe rustic-themed play areas indoors and outdoors. Lambing occurs in early May, followed by shearing and then milking demonstrations later in the season.

Times: Open mid Mar-mid Sep, daily (then open wknds only until end Oct & Autumn half term 10.30-5). **Fee:** ✱ £5.50 (ch £4.50 pen £5). Family ticket £18. **Facilities:** Ⓟ ▆ ☐ ♿ (ramps) toilets for disabled shop ⊗ (ex guide dogs) ◼

HAILES   MAP 04 SP02

Hailes Abbey

GL54 5PB

➲ *(2m NE of Winchcombe off B4632)*

☎ 01242 602398

web: www.english-heritage.org.uk

Explore the atmospheric ruins of this great medieval pilgrimage abbey, in the midst of the Cotswolds. Built in the 13th-century Hailes became famous when presented with a phial that was said to contain the blood of Christ.

Times: Open Apr-Jun & Sep, daily 10-5; Jul-Aug, daily 10-6; Oct, daily 10-4. **Fee:** £3.30 (ch £1.70, concessions £2.50). Prices and opening times are subject to change in Spring 2007. Please check web site or call 0870 333 1181 for the most up to date prices and opening times when planning your visit. **Facilities:** ❷ ᵹ shop ♯

LYDNEY   MAP 03 SO60

Dean Forest Railway

Norchard Railway Centre, New Mills, Forest Rd GL15 4ET

➲ *(At Lydney, turn off the Gloucester to Chepstow (A48) road and follow brown tourist signs to Norchard Railway Centre, on B4234 Lydney-Parkend road)*

☎ 01594 843423 (info) & 845840

e-mail: commercial@deanforestrailway.co.uk

web: www.deanforestrailway.co.uk

Travel on a heritage steam railway through the beautiful and historic Forest of Dean. A relaxing round trip of over 8 miles to the recently opened Parkend Station. Theres free car parking at Norchard Station (near Lydney) with a well-stocked gift shop, museum and café. Regular family events include Thomas the Tank Engine and Santa Specials.

Times: Open Apr-Oct, Sun; Jun-Sep, Wed, Sat, Sun; also Tue & Thu in Aug and BH's; Dec wknds (Santa Specials) & New Year. **Fee:** ✱ £8 (under 5's free, ch £5, pen £7). Family ticket (2ad+2ch) £24. Different charges may apply to events. **Facilities:** ❷ ᵹ ⑩ᴵ ᵹ (specially adapted coach for wheelchairs, phone for details) toilets for disabled shop ◀

MICKLETON   MAP 04 SP14

Hidcote Manor Garden

Chipping Campden GL55 6LR

➲ *(1m E of B4632, near village of Mickleton)*

☎ 01386 438333

e-mail: hidcote@nationaltrust.org.uk

web: www.nationaltrust.org.uk/hidcote

One of the most delightful arts and crafts gardens in England, created by the horticulturist Major Laurence Johnston and comprising a series of small gardens within the whole, separated by walls and hedges of different species. It is famous for its rare shrubs and trees, outstanding herbaceous borders and unusual worldwide plant species.

Times: Garden: 25 Mar-1 Oct, 10.30-6, Sat-Wed, 2-29 Oct 10.30-5 Sat-Wed. **Fee:** ✱ £7 (ch £3.50). Family £17. Groups £6.20 (ch £3.10) **Facilities:** ❷ ᵹ ⑩ᴵ licensed ᵹ (partial access, ltd due to stone paths, w/chair available) toilets for disabled shop garden centre ⊗ (ex guide dogs) ▨

Kiftsgate Court Garden

Mickleton GL55 6LN

➲ *(0.5m S off A46, adjacent Hidcote NT garden)*

☎ 01386 438777

e-mail: info@kiftsgate.co.uk

web: www.kiftsgate.co.uk

Kiftsgate Garden is spectacularly set on the edge of the Cotswold Escarpment, with views over the Vale of Evesham. It contains many rare plants collected by three generations of women gardeners, including the largest rose in England, the R. Filipes Kiftsgate.

Times: Open Apr, Aug & Sep; Sun, Mon & Wed, 2-6. May-Jul, open daily (ex Thu & Fri), 12-6. **Fee:** ✱ £5.50 (ch £1.50). **Facilities:** ❷ ᵹ ⑩ shop garden centre ⊗ (ex guide dogs) ◀

MORETON-IN-MARSH   MAP 04 SP23

Cotswold Falconry Centre   `2 for 1`

Batsford Park GL56 9QB

➲ *(1m W of Moreton-in-Marsh on A44)*

☎ 01386 701043

e-mail: geoffdalton@yahoo.co.uk

web: www.cotswold-falconry.co.uk

Conveniently located by the Batsford Park Arboretum, the Cotswold Falconry gives daily demonstrations in the art of falconry. The emphasis here is on breeding and conservation, and eagles, hawks, owls and falcons can be seen.

Times: Open mid Feb-mid Nov, 10.30-5.30. (Last admission 5). **Fee:** ✱ £6 (ch 4-15 £2.50, concessions £5). Joint ticket with Batsford Arboretum £10 (ch 4-15 £4, concessions £9.50). **Facilities:** ❷ ᵹ ᵹ (no steps, wide doorways) toilets for disabled shop garden centre ⊗ (ex on leads in arboretum) ◀

Sezincote

GL56 9AW

➲ *(1.5m out of Moreton-in-Marsh on A44, Evesham road)*

☎ 01386 700444

e-mail: edwardpeake64@hotmail.com

web: www.sezincote.co.uk

The Indian-style house at Sezincote was the inspiration for Brighton Pavilion; its charming water garden adds to its exotic aura and features trees of unusual size.

continued

Times: Open: House, May-Jul & Sep, Thu & Fri 2.30-6. Garden only, all year (ex Dec) Thu, Fri & BH Mon 2-6 or dusk if earlier. **Fee:** ✻ House & garden £6 Garden only £4 (ch £1.50 under 5 free). Children not allowed in the House. Groups by appointment only. **Facilities:** ❷ & toilets for disabled ⊗ (ex guide dogs)

NEWENT   MAP 03 SO72

The National Birds of Prey Centre
GL18 1JJ

➲ *(follow A40, right onto B4219 towards Newent. Follow brown tourist signs from Newent town)*
☎ 0870 9901992
e-mail: katherine@nbpc.co.uk
web: www.nbpc.co.uk

Trained birds can be seen at close quarters in the Hawk Walk and the Owl Courtyard and there are also breeding aviaries, a gift shop, bookshop, picnic areas, coffee shop and children's play area. Birds are flown three times daily in summer and winter, giving an exciting and educational display. There are over 80 aviaries on view with 40 species.

Times: ✻ Open Feb-Oct, daily 10.30-5.30. **Facilities:** ❷ ☕ 🍴 & (special tours available, pre-booking required) toilets for disabled shop ⊗ ◀

The Shambles
Church St GL18 1PP

➲ *(close to town centre near church)*
☎ 01531 822144
web: www.shamblesnewent.co.uk

Cobbled streets, alleyways, cottages and houses set in over an acre with display shops and trades, even a tin chapel and cottage garden all helping to recreate the feel and atmosphere of a small Victorian town.

Times: Open mid Mar-end Oct, Tue-Sun & BHs 10-5 (or dusk); Nov-Dec wknds only. **Fee:** ✻ £4.35 (ch £2.75, pen £3.75). **Facilities:** ℗ (100yds) ☕ 🍴 & toilets for disabled shop ◀

NORTHLEACH   MAP 04 SP11

Keith Harding's World of Mechanical Music   `2 for 1`
The Oak House, High St GL54 3ET

➲ *(at crossroads of A40 & A429)*
☎ 01451 860181
e-mail: keith@mechanicalmusic.co.uk
web: www.mechanicalmusic.co.uk

A fascinating collection of antique clocks, musical boxes, automata and mechanical musical instruments, restored and maintained in the world-famous workshops, displayed in a period setting, and played

continued

---

during regular tours. There is an exhibition of coin operated instruments which visitors can play.

Keith Harding's World of Mechanical Music

Times: Open all year, daily 10-6. Last tour 5. Closed 25-26 Dec. **Fee:** ✻ £6 (ch £3, concessions £5). Discounts for families & groups.
Facilities: ❷ & (Safety rails, non-slip floor) toilets for disabled shop ⊗ (ex guide dogs) ◀

OWLPEN   MAP 03 ST79

Owlpen Manor   `2 for 1`
GL11 5BZ

➲ *(3m E of Dursley, signed at village green in Uley off B4066)*
☎ 01453 860261
e-mail: sales@owlpen.com
web: www.owlpen.com

A romantic Tudor manor house, with unique 17th-century painted cloth wallhangings, furniture, pictures and textiles. The house is set in formal terraced gardens, and is part of a picturesque Cotswold manorial group including a Jacobean Court House, a Victorian church and medieval tithe barn.

Times: Open May-Sep, Tue, Thur & Sun 2-5 **Fee:** ✻ £5.25 (ch £2.25).
Facilities: ❷ 🍴 licensed 🍽 ⊗ ◀

PAINSWICK   MAP 03 SO80

Painswick Rococo Garden
GL6 6TH

➲ *(on B4073 0.5m NW of Painswick)*
☎ 01452 813204
e-mail: info@rococogarden.co.uk
web: www.rococogarden.co.uk

This beautiful Rococo garden (a compromise between formality and informality) is the only one of its period to survive complete. There are ponds, woodland walks, a maze, kitchen garden and herbacious borders, all set in a Cotswold valley famous for snowdrops in the early spring. Ring for details of special events.

Times: Open 10 Jan-Oct, daily 11-5. **Fee:** £5 (ch £2.50, pen £4)
Facilities: ❷ ☕ 🍴 licensed 🍽 shop garden centre ◀

SLIMBRIDGE · MAP 03 SO70

WWT Slimbridge · 2 for 1

GL2 7BT

➲ *(off A38, signed from M5 junct 13 & 14)*

☎ 0870 33 44 000

e-mail: slimbridge@wwt.org.uk

web: www.wwt.org.uk

Slimbridge is home to the world's largest collection of exotic wildfowl - and the only place in Europe where all six types of flamingo can be seen. Up to 8,000 wild birds winter on the 800-acre reserve of flat fields, marsh and mudflats on the River Severn. Facilities include a tropical house, discovery centre, shop and restaurant.

Times: Open all year, daily from 9.30-5 (winter 4). Closed 25 Dec. **Fee:** ✱ £6.75 (ch £4, pen £5.50). Family ticket £18.50. **Facilities:** ❷ ♨ ¶○¶ licensed ♿ (wheelchair loan, tapes for blind, hearing pads & loops) toilets for disabled shop ⊗ (ex guide & hearing dogs) ◣

SNOWSHILL · MAP 04 SP03

Snowshill Manor

WR12 7JU

➲ *(3m SW of Broadway, off A44)*

☎ 01386 852410

e-mail: snowshillmanor@nationaltrust.org.uk

web: www.nationaltrust.org.uk

Arts and crafts garden designed by its owner Charles Paget Wade in collaboration with M.H. Baillie Scott, as a series of outdoor rooms to compliment his traditional Cotswold manor house filled with his unique collection of craftsmanship including musical instruments, clocks, toys, bicycles and Japanese armour. This was the first National Trust garden to be managed following organic principles. It is a lively mix of cottage flowers, bright colours and delightful scents with stunning views across Cotswold countryside.

Times: House: 25 Mar-29 Oct, 12-5, Wed-Sun; Garden: 25 Mar-29 May, 11-5.30, Thu-Sun, 4 May-30 Oct, 11-5.30, Wed-Sun; Shop: As garden, also 4 Nov-10 Dec, 12-4, Sat & Sun; Restaurant: As shop **Fee:** ✱ House & Garden: £7.30, (ch £3.65). Family £18.50, groups £6.20. Garden, Restaurant & Shop: £4, (ch £2). Family £10 **Facilities:** ❷ ¶○¶ licensed ♿ (Braille guides, audio tapes, 2 manual wheelchairs) toilets for disabled shop ⊗ (ex guide dogs) ♨ ◣

SOUDLEY · MAP 03 SO61

Dean Heritage Centre

Camp Mill GL14 2UB

➲ *(on B4227, in Forest of Dean)*

☎ 01594 822170

e-mail: deanmuse@btconnect.com

web: www.deanheritagemuseum.com

The Centre tells the story of this unique area, and its people, from pre-historic times to present day. Displays include a reconstructed cottage, a working beam engine from Lightmore Colliery, charcoal burners camp and art gallery. There are also nature trails with animals. There is an adventure playground that includes a maze and swing bridge. Library and research facilities are available by appointment. Annual events include the Sheep Fair in April and a Herb Day in July.

continued

Times: Open all year, daily, Winter 10-4, Summer 10-5.30. Closed 24-26 Dec & 1 Jan. **Fee:** ✱ £4.50 (ch £2.50, under 5's free, pen & concessions £3.50). Family ticket £13. **Facilities:** ❷ (charged) ♨ ♿ (lift, ramps, help from establishment staff) toilets for disabled shop ⊗ (ex guide dogs) ◣

TETBURY · MAP 03 ST89

Chavenage House · 2 for 1

Chavenage GL8 8XP

➲ *(2m NW of Tetbury signed off B4014. 7m SE of Stroud, signed off A46)*

☎ 01666 502329

e-mail: info@chavenage.com

web: www.chavenage.com

Built in 1576, this unspoilt Elizabethan house contains stained glass from the 16th-century and earlier with some good furniture and tapestries. The owner during the Civil War was a Parliamentarian, and the house contains Cromwellian relics. In more recent years, the house has been the location for *Grace and Favour*, *Poirot*, *The House of Elliot*, *Berkeley Square*, *Casualty* and *Cider with Rosie*. Tours of the house are enlivened by ghost stories.

Times: Open May-Sep, Thu, Sun & BHs 2-5. Also Etr Sun & Mon. Other days by appointment only. **Fee:** £6 (ch £3). **Facilities:** ❷ ♿ ⊗ (ex guide dogs)

TODDINGTON · MAP 04 SP03

Gloucestershire Warwickshire Steam Railway PLC NEW

The Railway Station GL54 5DT

➲ *(10m E of M5 junct 9 near junct of B4077 and B4632 between Winchcombe and Broadway)*

☎ 01242 621405

e-mail: enquiries@gwsr.com

web: www.gwsr.com

The railway runs along a part of the former Great Western Railways mainline from Birmingham to Cheltenham, via Stratford-upon-Avon. The line commands wonderful views of the sleepy hamlets and villages, as it runs though the beautiful Cotswold countryside. The line was primarily built (1900-1906) to improve through services from Birmingham to Bristol and the West Country.

Times: Open Mar-Dec, selected days & times. Call 01242 621405 for details. **Fee:** ✱ £9.50 (ch 5-15 £6, under 5 free, concessions £8). Family (2 ad+3 ch) £26. **Facilities:** ❷ ♨ ♿ (specially converted carriage) toilets for disabled shop ◣

ULEY · MAP 03 ST79

Uley Long Barrow (Hetty Pegler's Tump) · FREE

➲ *(3.5m NE of Dursley on B4066)*

web: www.english-heritage.org.uk

This 180ft Neolithic long barrow is popularly known as Hetty Pegler's Tump. The mound, surrounded by a wall, is about 85ft wide. It contains a stone central passage, and three burial chambers.

Times: Open at any reasonable time. **Facilities:** ⊞

England

WESTBURY ON SEVERN   MAP 03 SO71

Westbury Court Garden

GL14 1PD

➲ *(9m SW of Gloucester on A48)*

☎ 01452 760461

e-mail: westburycourt@nationaltrust.org.uk

web: www.nationaltrust.org.uk

This formal water garden with canals and yew hedges was laid out between 1696 and 1705. It is the earliest of its kind remaining in England and was restored in 1971 and planted with species dated pre-1700, including apple, pear and plum trees.

Times: Open 8 Mar-Jun Wed-Sun 10-5, Jul-Aug daily, Sep-Oct Wed-Sun 10-5. Nov-Feb by appointment. Open BHs. **Fee:** ✱ £4 (ch £2). Family £10. **Facilities:** ❷ ♿ (Braille guide, w/chair available) toilets for disabled ⊗ (ex guide dogs) ⌘

WESTONBIRT   MAP 03 ST88

Westonbirt The National Arboretum

GL8 8QS

➲ *(3m S Tetbury on A433)*

☎ 01666 880220

web: www.westonbirtarboretum.com

Begun in 1829, this arboretum contains one of the finest and most important collections of trees and shrubs in the world. There are

continued

18,000 specimens, planted from 1829 to the present day, covering 600 acres of landscaped Cotswold countryside. Magnificent displays of Rhododendrons, Azaleas, Magnolias and wild flowers, and ablaze with colour in the autumn from the national collection of Japanese Maples.

Times: Open all year, daily 10-8 or sunset. Visitor centre & shop all year. Closed Xmas & New Year. **Fee:** ✱ Mar-Nov £6.50 Family ticket £13. Nov-Mar £5 (pen £4) Family ticket £11. **Facilities:** ❷ ◧ ⦿ licensed ♿ (electric & manual wheelchair for loan, telephone to book) toilets for disabled shop garden centre ⌘

WINCHCOMBE   MAP 04 SP02

Sudeley Castle, Gardens & Exhibitions

GL54 5JD

➲ *(B4632 to Winchcombe, Castle is signed from town)*

☎ 01242 602308

e-mail: enquiries@sudeley.org.uk

web: www.sudeleycastle.co.uk

Sudeley Castle was home to Katherine Parr, who is buried in the Chapel. Henry VIII, Anne Boleyn, Lady Jane Grey and Elizabeth I all stayed or visited here; and it was the headquarters of Prince Rupert during the Civil War. The Queen's Garden is famous for its rose collection. There are exhibitions, a full and varied special events programme and plant centre.

Times: Please phone for opening times. **Fee:** Please phone for admission rates. **Facilities:** ❷ ⦿ licensed ▤ ♿ (limited access to gardens only, parking) shop garden centre ⊗ ⌘

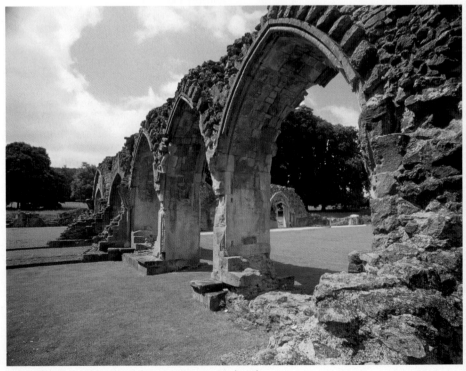

Hailes Abbey, founded in 1246 and now in ruins, near Winchcombe

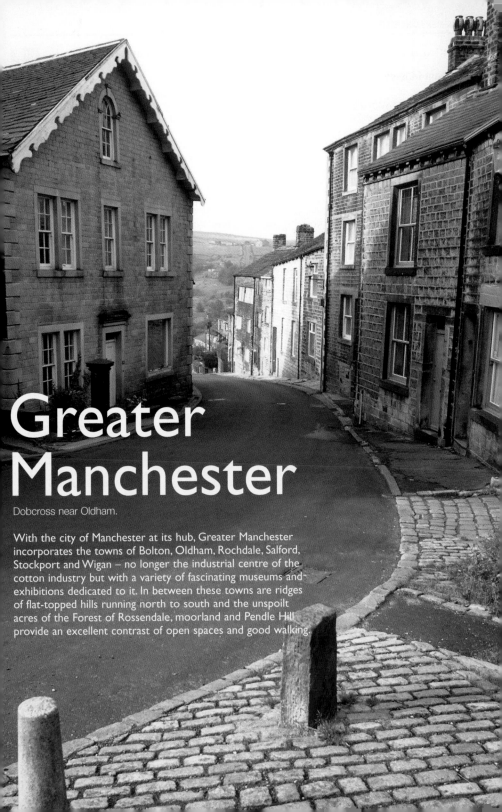

Greater Manchester

Dobcross near Oldham.

With the city of Manchester at its hub, Greater Manchester incorporates the towns of Bolton, Oldham, Rochdale, Salford, Stockport and Wigan – no longer the industrial centre of the cotton industry but with a variety of fascinating museums and exhibitions dedicated to it. In between these towns are ridges of flat-topped hills running north to south and the unspoilt acres of the Forest of Rossendale, moorland and Pendle Hill provide an excellent contrast of open spaces and good walking.

England

ALTRINCHAM
MAP 07 SJ78

Dunham Massey
WA14 4SJ

➲ *(3m SW of Altrincham (off A56), off M6 junct 19 or off M56 junct 7, then follow brown signs)*

☎ 0161 941 1025

e-mail: dunhammassey@nationaltrust.org.uk

web: www.nationaltrust.org.uk

A fine 18th-century house, garden and park, home of the Earls of Stamford until 1976. The house contains fine furniture and silverware, and some thirty rooms, including the library, billiard room, fully-equipped kitchen, butler's pantry and laundry. The garden is on an ancient site with waterside plantings, mixed borders and fine lawns. There is also a 300 acre deer park. Telephone for details of special events.

Times: Open: Park, restaurant & shop open all year. House open 17 Mar-28 Oct, 12-5 (11 Sun & BH Mon). Garden, 11-5.30. Last entry 30mins before closing time. **Fee:** House & Garden £7.50 (ch £3.75). House only £5 (ch £2.50). Group rate (pre-booked only) House & Garden £6. Family ticket £18.75. Reduced rate when arriving on public transport.
Facilities: ❷ (charged) ⑭ licensed ♿ (wheelchairs, lift, Braille & large print guide, parking) toilets for disabled shop ⊗ (ex on lead in park) 🐾 ◀

ASHTON-UNDER-LYNE
MAP 07 SJ99

Central Art Gallery

Central Library Building, Old St OL6 7SG

➲ *(near centre of town, off A635)*

☎ 0161 342 2650

e-mail: central.artgallery@tameside.gov.uk

web: www.tameside.gov.uk

Set in a fine Victorian Gothic building, the Central Art Gallery has three areas, each of which offers a varied programme of temporary exhibitions. A range of tastes and styles are covered, with group and solo shows of work by artists from the region including paintings, sculpture, installation and textiles. Holiday activities available for families.

Times: ✱ Open all year, Tue, Wed & Fri 10-12.30 & 1-5; Thu 1-7.30 & Sat 9-12.30 & 1-4. **Facilities:** ℗ (100mtrs) (pay and display) 🍴 ♿ (induction loop) toilets for disabled shop ⊗ (ex guide dogs)

Museum of The Manchester Regiment

The Town Hall, Market Place OL6 6DL

➲ *(in town centre, on market square, follow signs for museum)*

☎ 0161 342 2812 & 3710

e-mail: portland.basin@tameside.gov.uk

web: www.tameside.gov.uk

The social and regimental history of the Manchesters is explored at this museum, tracing the story back to its origins in the 18th century. Children can try on military headwear, experience a First World War trench, and try out the interactive A Soldiers Life.

Times: ✱ Open all year, Mon-Sat, 10-4. (Closed Sun).
Facilities: ℗ (50yds) (pay & display) ♿ Lift toilets for disabled ⊗ (ex guide dogs)

Portland Basin Museum

Portland Place OL7 0QA

➲ *(M60 junct 23 into Ashton town centre. Museum is near Cross Hill Street & car park)*

☎ 0161 343 2878

e-mail: portland.basin@tameside.gov.uk

web: www.tameside.gov.uk

Exploring the social and industrial history of Tameside, this museum is part of the recently rebuilt Ashton Canal Warehouse, built in 1834. Visitors can walk around a 1920s street, dress up in old hats and gloves, steer a virtual canal boat, and see the original canal powered waterwheel that once drove the warehouse machinery. Portland Basin Museum also features changing exhibitions and event programme- so there's always something new to see!

Times: ✱ Open all year, Tue-Sun 10-5. (Closed Mon, ex BHs)
Facilities: ❷ ⑭ 🍴 ♿ (wheelchair, lift, loop system) toilets for disabled shop ⊗ (ex guide dogs) ◀

BRAMHALL
MAP 07 SJ88

Bramall Hall & Park

SK7 3NX

➲ *(from A6 right at Blossoms public house through Davenport village then right - signed)*

☎ 0845 833 0974

e-mail: bramall.hall@stockport.gov.uk

web: www.bramallhall.org.uk

This large timber-framed hall dates from the 14th century, and is one of the finest black-and-white houses in the North West. It has rare 16th-century wall paintings and period furniture, and was the home of the Davenport family for 500 years. Much of the house is open to the public and available for hire. Open air concerts and plays are a feature in summer.

Times: Open all year, Apr-Sep Sun-Thu 1-5, Fri & Sat 1-4, BH 11-5; Oct-1 Jan Tue-Sun 1-4, BH 11-4; 2 Jan-Good Fri Sat & Sun 12-4. Closed 25-26 Dec. **Fee:** ✱ £3.95 (concessions £3). Family ticket £11.
Facilities: ❷ (charged) �P 🍴 ♿ (access for wheelchair users) toilets for disabled shop ⊗ (ex guide dogs) ◀

MANCHESTER
MAP 07 SJ89

Gallery of Costume

Platt Hall, Rusholme M14 5LL

➲ *(situated in Platt Fields Park, Rusholme, access from Wilmslow Rd. 2m S of city centre)*

☎ 0161 224 5217

e-mail: a.jarvis@notes.manchester.gov.uk

With one of the most comprehensive costume collections in Great Britain, this gallery makes captivating viewing. Housed in a fine Georgian mansion, the displays focus on the changing styles of everyday fashion and accessories over the last 400 years. Contemporary fashion is also illustrated. Because of the vast amount of material in the collection, no one period is permanently illustrated.

Times: ✱ Open to public on last Sat of month. Mon-Fri by appointment, please ring 0161 224 5217 **Facilities:** ❷ ♿ shop ⊗ (ex guide dogs)

Imperial War Museum North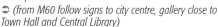

The Quays, Trafford Wharf Rd, Trafford Park
M17 1TZ

➲ *(M60 junct 9, join Parkway (A5081) towards Trafford Park. At 1st island take 3rd exit onto Village Way. At next island take 2nd exit onto Warren Bruce Rd. Right at T-junct onto Trafford Wharf Rd. Alternatively, leave M602 junct 2 and follow signs)*

☎ 0161 836 4000
e-mail: info@iwmnorth.org.uk
web: www.iwm.org.uk

This recently-opened war museum is built to resemble three shards of a shattered globe, representing conflict on land, sea, and in the air. Inside are thousands of exhibits, interactive sessions, performances, and recreations that explore the way that 20th and 21st century conflict has shaped our lives.

Times: Open daily Mar-Oct 10-6, Nov-Feb 10-5. Closed 24-26 Dec.
Facilities: ♿ (charged) 💺 ♿ (lifts, parking, wheelchairs, Braille sign in lift) toilets for disabled shop ⊗ (ex guide dogs)

John Rylands Library   FREE

150 Deansgate M3 3EH

➲ *(on Deansgate, a main thoroughfare in city centre, A56. Situated next to the Manchester Evening News Building)*

☎ 0161 834 5343
e-mail: jrul.special-collechais@manchester.ac.uk
web: http://rylibweb.man.ac.uk/spcoll/

Founded as a memorial to Manchester cotton-magnate and millionaire John Rylands, this is a public library, and also the Special Collections Division of the John Rylands University Library of Manchester. Internationally renowned, it extends to two million books, manuscripts and archival items representing some fifty cultures and ranging in date from the third millennium BC to the present day. The library will be closed until late 2006. A new entrance wing is being built along with improved visitor facilities and a new range of exhibitions.

Times: Closed until late 2006 **Facilities:** ℗ (400yds) (pay and display) 💺 shop ⊗ (ex guide dogs by arrangement)

Manchester Art Gallery   FREE

Mosley St M2 3JL

➲ *(from M60 follow signs to city centre, gallery close to Town Hall and Central Library)*

☎ 0161 235 8888
web: www.manchestergalleries.org

Manchester Art Gallery houses the city's magnificent art collection in stunning Victorian and contemporary surroundings. Highlights of the collection include outstanding Pre-Raphaelite works, crafts and design, and early 20th-century British art. The Clore Interactive Gallery has lively exhibits and multimedia facilities. There are also a wide range of events, from talks and tours to hands-on activities for children and adults. Contact for details of events and changing exhibitions.

Times: Open Tue-Sun, 10-5 (closed Mon except BH). Closed Good Fri, 24-26 & 31 Dec & 1 Jan. **Facilities:** ℗ (NCP-5 mins walk) 💺 🍴 licensed 📷 ♿ (wheelchairs, induction loops, audio guides) toilets for disabled shop ⊗ (ex assist dogs)

Manchester Museum   FREE

The University, Oxford Rd M13 9PL

➲ *(S of city centre on B5117)*

☎ 0161 275 2634 & 2643
e-mail: anna.j.davey@man.ac.uk
web: www.museum.man.ac.uk

The Manchester Museum has leading research facilities and collections in archaeology, botany, Egyptology, ethnology, mineralogy, numismatics, and zoology, among others. There are large galleries devoted to most of these departments, but the Egyptology collection is particularly impressive, and includes mummies excavated by Sir William Flinders Petrie.

Times: ✱ Open all year, Mon-Sat 10-5, Sun & BHs 11-4.
Facilities: ⊖ (charged) 💺 📷 ♿ (lift access, hearing loop, accessible parking) toilets for disabled shop ⊗ (ex guide dogs) 🥪

England

Manchester United Museum & Tour Centre

Sir Matt Busby Way, Old Trafford M16 0RA

➲ *(2m from city centre, off A56)*

☎ 0870 442 1994

e-mail: tours@manutd.co.uk

web: www.manutd.com

This museum was opened in 1986 and is the first purpose-built British football museum. It covers the history of Manchester United in words, pictures, sound and vision, from its inception in 1878 to the present day.

Times: Open daily 9.30-5 (open until 30mins before kick off on match days). Closed some days over Xmas & New Year. **Facilities:** ☻ ⍾ licensed 🍴 ⓱ (w/chair, audio visual scripts) toilets for disabled shop ⊗ (ex guide dogs) ◀

The Museum of Science and Industry in Manchester

FREE

Liverpool Rd, Castlefield M3 4FP

➲ *(follow brown tourist signs from city centre)*

☎ 0161 832 2244 & 832 1830

e-mail: marketing@msim.org.uk

web: www.msim.org.uk

This museum is on the site of the world's oldest passenger railway station. Colourful galleries packed full of fascinating facts and amazing artefacts bring the past to life. Walk away from your own shadow in Xperiment! The mind bending science centre, see wheels of industry turning in the Power Hall, and the planes that made flying history in the Air and Space Hall. A programme of changing exhibitions.

Times: Open all year, daily 10-5. Last admission 4.30. Closed 24-26 Dec & 1 Jan. (Extended hrs for some special events) **Facilities:** ☻ (charged) 🍴 ⍾ licensed ⓱ (lifts, wheelchair loan service) toilets for disabled shop ⊗ (ex guide dogs) ◀

Museum of Transport

Boyle St, Cheetham M8 8UW

➲ *(museum adjacent to Queens Rd bus depot. 1.25m N of city centre on Boyle St)*

☎ 0161 205 2122

e-mail: e-mail@gmts.co.uk

web: www.gmts.co.uk

This museum is a must-see for fans of public transport! Among the many interesting exhibits are more than 80 beautifully restored buses and coaches from the region - the biggest collection in the UK. Displays of old photographs, tickets and other memorabilia complement the vehicles, some of which date back to 1890. Please telephone for details of special events, most of which, unsurprisingly, relate to transport in some way.

Times: Open all year Mar-Oct, 10-5; Nov-Feb, 10-4; Wed, Sat, Sun & BH are Xmas **Fee:** £4 (ch under 5 free, ch 5-15 & concessions £2, registered disabled, unemp free). Family ticket £10 (2ad+3ch). **Facilities:** ☻ 🍴 ⓱ ⍾ toilets for disabled shop ⊗ (ex assist dogs) ◀

See advert on opposite page

Urbis

FREE

Cathedral Gardens M4 3BG

➲ *(opposite to Victoria Railway Station)*

☎ 0161 605 8200

e-mail: info@urbis.org.uk

web: www.urbis.org.uk

Urbis explores the dynamic culture of the modern city. The top three floors of interactive exhibits explore cities around the world from Tokyo to Paris, revealing how different cities work, how they change and how they affect others.

Times: Open daily, Sun-Wed, 10-6; Thu-Sat, 10-8. **Facilities:** ℗ (200yds) 🍴 🍴 ⍾ toilets for disabled shop ⊗ (ex guide dogs) ◀

The Whitworth Art Gallery

The University of Manchester, Oxford Rd
M15 6ER

⊃ *(follow brown tourist signs, on Oxford Rd (B5117) to S of city centre. Gallery in Whitworth Park, opp Manchester Royal Infirmary)*

☎ 0161 275 7450
e-mail: whitworth@manchester.ac.uk
web: www.manchester.ac.uk/whitworth

The gallery houses an impressive range of modern and historic drawings, prints, paintings and sculpture, as well as the largest collection of textiles and wallpapers outside London and an internationally famous collection of British watercolours. The gallery hosts an innovative programme of touring exhibitions. A selection of tour lectures, workshops and concerts complement the exhibition programme.

Times: Open Mon-Sat 10-5, Sun 2-5. Closed Good Fri & Xmas-New Year. **Facilities:** ♿ 💺 ♿ (wheelchair available, induction loop, Braille lift buttons) toilets for disabled shop ⊗ (ex guide dogs)

PRESTWICH　　　　　　　　　**MAP 07 SD80**

Heaton Park

Heaton Park M25 2SW

⊃ *(4m N of Manchester city centre. M60 Junct 19, S on A576, then onto A6044 and A665, then into St Margaret's Road. Park 100yds on R)*

☎ 0161 773 1085
e-mail: heatonpark@manchester.gov.uk
web: www.manchester.gov.uk/leisure/parks

600 acres of rolling parkland on the edge of Manchester; a traditional park for the whole family. Facilities include a Tram Museum, sports pitches, stables, farm and animals centres, and a horticultural centre. The hall was designed by James Wyatt for Sir Thomas Egerton in 1772, the house has magnificent period interiors decorated with fine plasterwork, paintings and furniture. Other attractions include a unique circular room with Pompeian-style paintings, and the original Samuel Green organ still in working order.

Times: Park: Open all year daily; Hall: Open early Apr-early Oct, Wed-Sun & BH 11-5.30 **Facilities:** ♿ (charged) 💺 shop ⊗ (ex guide dogs)

SALFORD　　　　　　　　　**MAP 07 SJ89**

The Lowry

Pier Eight, Salford Quays M50 3AZ

⊃ *(M60 junct 12 for M602. Salford Quays is 0.25m from junct 3 of M602, follow brown Lowry signs)*

☎ 0870 787 5774
e-mail: info@thelowry.com
web: www.thelowry.com

The Lowry is an award-winning building housing galleries, shops, cafés and a restaurant, plus two theatres showing everything from West End plays and musicals, comedians, ballet and live bands. With regular family activity too, you can make a whole day of your visit.

Times: ✱ Open daily from 10. Galleries, Sun-Fri from 11, Sat from 10. Closed 25 Dec. **Facilities:** ♿ (charged) 💺 🍴 licensed 🏠 ♿ (Sennheiser System) toilets for disabled shop ⊗ (ex guide dogs)

Salford Museum & Art Gallery

Peel Park, Crescent M5 4WU

⊃ *(from N leave M60 junct 13, A666. From S follow signs from end of M602. Museum on A6)*

☎ 0161 736 2649
e-mail: salford.museum@salford.gov.uk
web: www.salfordmuseum.org

The museum features a reconstruction of a 19th-20th century northern street with original shop fronts. Upstairs in the galleries there are temporary exhibitions and a gallery displaying paintings, sculptures and ceramics. Recent additions include the lifetimes gallery, featuring audio, IT zones, temporary exhibitions, a spectacular Pilkington's display and lots of hands-on activities and dressing up areas.

Times: Open all year Mon-Fri 10-4.45, Sat & Sun 1-5. Closed Good Fri, Etr Sat, 25 & 26 Dec, 1 Jan. **Facilities:** ♿ 💺 🏠 ♿ (Braille & large print labels & visitor packs, hearing loop) toilets for disabled shop ⊗ (ex guide dogs) ◀

England

STALYBRIDGE
MAP 07 SJ99

Astley Cheetham Art Gallery
FREE

Trinity St GK15 2BN

➲ (N of town centre)

☎ 0161 338 6767

e-mail: astley.cheetham@tameside.gov.uk

web: www.tameside.gov.uk

Built as a gift to the town in 1901 by mill owner John Frederick Cheetham, this one-time lecture hall has been an art gallery since 1932 when Cheetham left his collection to the town. Among the works are Italian paintings from the Renaissance, British masters such as Cox and Burne-Jones, and more recent gifts such as works by Turner and local artist Harry Rutherford. The gallery hosts a programme of temporary exhibitions of the collection and regional artists, and a variety of workshops are run for families throughout the year.

Times: Open all year, Mon-Wed & Fri 10-12.30, 1-5; Sat 9-12.30, 1-4. **Facilities:** ℗ (2hrs on street parking) ▥ ♿ (induction loop) ⊗ (ex guide dogs)

STOCKPORT
MAP 07 SJ89

Hat Works Museum
FREE

Wellington Mill, Wellington Rd South SK3 0EU

➲ (M60 junct 1, follow signs for town centre. Museum opp bus station)

☎ 0845 833 0975

e-mail: bookings.hatworks@stockport.gov.uk

web: www.hatworks.org.uk

Hat Works is the UK's only museum of the hatting industry, hats and headwear, offering an insight into a once flourishing industry. See how hats are made with a unique working collection of Victorian millinery machinery and take a tour with expert guides who will give visitors an insight into the Hatter's World. Browse an extensive collection of hats before relaxing in the Level 2 café. Exhibitions and events throughout the year, contact for details.

Times: ✱ Open daily Mon-Fri 10-5, Sat, Sun & BHs 1-5. (Telephone for Xmas opening times) **Facilities:** ℗ (5min walk) (limited pay & display parking) ▣ ▥ ♿ (hearing loops) toilets for disabled shop ⊗ (ex guide dogs) ◀

UPPERMILL
MAP 07 SD90

Saddleworth Museum & Art Gallery
2 for 1

High St OL3 6HS

➲ (M62 E junct 22 or M62 W junct 21. On A670)

☎ 01457 874093

e-mail: curator@saddleworthmuseum.co.uk

web: www.saddleworthmuseum.co.uk

Based in an old mill building next to the Huddersfield canal, the museum explores the history of the Saddleworth area. Wool weaving is the traditional industry, displayed in the 18th-century Weaver's Cottage and the Victoria Mill Gallery. The textile machinery is run regularly by arrangement. The Art Gallery has regular exhibitions.

Times: Open all year: Apr-Oct, Mon-Sat 10-4.30; Sun 12-4; Nov-Mar, Mon-Sun 1-4; closed 24-25 Dec & 1 Jan **Fee:** ✱ Museum - £2 (concessions £1) Family ticket £4. Art gallery - free **Facilities:** ❷ ▥ ♿ (stairlift, ramps, Braille & large print guides, wheelchair) toilets for disabled shop ⊗ (ex guide dogs)

WIGAN
MAP 07 SD50

Wigan Pier

Wallgate WN3 4EU

➲ (follow brown tourist signs from M6 junct 25-27/M61 junct 6-8)

☎ 01942 323666

e-mail: wiganpier@wlct.org

web: www.wiganpier.net

Wigan Pier is a journey never to be forgotten. Part museum, part theatre, Wigan Pier is a mixture of entertainment and education. Step back in time at 'The Way We Were' heritage centre, visit the world's largest original mill steam engine, or enjoy trips along the Leeds-Liverpool canal, walks in the grounds, or events from a regular programme.

Times: Open all year, Mon-Thu 10-5; Sun 11-5. Closed every Fri & Sat, 25-26 Dec & 1 Jan. **Facilities:** ❷ ▥ ♿ (Braille guide, audio tape, large text leaflet, minicom) toilets for disabled shop ⊗ (ex guide dogs) ◀

Hampshire

HMS Victory,
Portsmouth

The most diverse of the southern counties, Hampshire has rolling chalk
downs; pretty river valleys; vast open areas such as the New Forest National
Park, covering some 300 square kilometres, and a sharply contrasting coastline.
Portsmouth, traditionally the home of the British fleet, has a very large natural
harbour which still accommodates the navy base and additionally offers a wide
variety of maritime attractions, most notably HMS *Victory*, Lord Nelson's
flagship of the battle of Trafalgar and now wonderfully preserved.

England

ALDERSHOT — MAP 04 SU85

Airborne Forces Museum

Browning Barracks, Queens Av GU11 2BU

➲ *(M3 take A325 to Aldershot then next left)*

☎ 01252 349619

The museum traces the history of the Parachute Regiment and British Airborne Forces since 1940. Using weapons, equipment, dioramas and briefing models it depicts the story of airborne actions such as the early raids, D-Day, Arnhem, the Rhine Crossing, and post-war campaigns such as Suez, the Falklands and Kosovo.

Times: Open all year, Mon-Fri 10-4.30 (last admission 3.45), Sat-Sun & BH 10-4. Closed Xmas. **Facilities:** ❷ ⅋ (wheelchair ramps) shop ⊗ (ex guide dogs)

Aldershot Military Museum   `2 for 1`

Evelyn Woods Rd, Queens Av GU11 2LG

➲ *(A331 exit for 'Aldershot Military Town (North)', attraction near to North Camp)*

☎ 01252 314598

e-mail: sally.1.day@hants.gov.uk

web: www.hants.gov.uk/museum/aldershot

Follow the development of the 'Home of the British army' and the 'Birthplace of British aviation' through brand new displays. Also discover the fascinating local history of Aldershot and Farnborough including the first British powered flight.

Times: Open daily 10-5. **Fee:** £2 (ch & unemployed £1, pen £1.50) **Facilities:** ❷ ▥ ⅋ shop ⊗ (ex guide dogs)

AMPFIELD — MAP 04 SU42

The Sir Harold Hillier Gardens   `2 for 1`

Jermyns Ln SO51 0QA

➲ *(3m NE of Romsey, signed off A3090 & A3057)*

☎ 01794 368787

e-mail: info@hilliergardens.org.uk

web: www.hilliergardens.org.uk

Established in 1953, this 180-acre public garden comprises the greatest collection of hardy trees and shrubs in the world. A garden for all seasons with stunning range of seasonal colour and interest and featuring eleven national plant collections. Champion trees, the Gurkha Memorial Garden and the largest Winter Garden in Europe. Events take place all year round, contact for details.

Times: Open all year, daily, 10-6 (or dusk if earlier). Closed 25-26 Dec. **Fee:** £7.50 (ch under 16 free, concessions £6.50). Group bookings £6 **Facilities:** ❷ ▥ ⅋⍩ licensed ⅋ (all ability path) toilets for disabled shop garden centre ⊗ (ex guide dogs)

ANDOVER — MAP 04 SU34

Finkley Down Farm Park

SP11 6NF

➲ *(signed from A303 & A343, 1.5m N of A303 & 2m E of Andover)*

☎ 01264 352195

e-mail: admin@finkleydownfarm.co.uk

web: www.finkleydownfarm.co.uk

This fun family farm park is jam packed with things to do. You can join in with feeding time, groom a pony, cuddle a rabbit, or collect duck

eggs. Lots of activities are scheduled throughout the day, or kids can just let off steam in the playground or on the trampolines. From chipmunks to chinchillas, pygmy goats to peacocks, and lambs to llamas, Finkley Down Farm has something for everyone!

Times: ✱ Open mid Mar-Oct, daily 10-6. Last admission 5. **Fee:** ✱ £5.75 (ch £4.75, pen £5.25). Family ticket £20 (2ad+2ch). **Facilities:** ❷ ▥ ⅋ toilets for disabled shop ⊗ (ex guide dogs)

ASHURST — MAP 04 SU31

Longdown Activity Farm   `2 for 1`

Longdown SO40 7EH

➲ *(off A35 between Lyndhurst & Southampton)*

☎ 023 8029 3326

e-mail: enquiries@longdownfarm.co.uk

web: www.longdownfarm.co.uk

Fun for all the family with a variety of hands-on activities every day, including small animal handling and bottle feeding calves and goat kids. Indoor and outdoor play areas, with trampolines and ball pools. Tearoom, picnic area and excellent gift shop.

Times: Open Feb-Dec, daily 10-5. **Fee:** ✱ £6 (ch 3-14 & pen £5). Saver ticket £21 (2ad+2ch). **Facilities:** ❷ ▥ ⅋ (concrete path for wheelchairs) toilets for disabled shop ⊗ (kennels provided)

AVINGTON — MAP 04 SU53

Avington Park   `2 for 1`

SO21 1DB

➲ *(off B3047 at Itchen Abbas between Winchester and Alresford. 4m from both on River Itchen)*

☎ 01962 779260

e-mail: enquiries@avingtonpark.co.uk

web: www.avingtonpark.co.uk

Avington Park is a privately-owned house, which was once described by William Cobbett as one of the prettiest places in the county, and has played host to Charles II and George IV. The state rooms consist of the beautifully painted main hall, the library overlooking the south lawns, adjoining and leading onto a unique pair of conservatories, the old dining room and the ballroom upstairs with a magnificent gold plasterwork ceiling and painted panels.

Times: Open May-Sep, Sun, BHs 2.30-5.30 & Mon in Aug **Fee:** ✱ £4 **Facilities:** ❷ ▥ ⅋ toilets for disabled ⊗ (ex on leads)

BASINGSTOKE — MAP 04 SU65

Milestones - Hampshire's Living History Museum   `2 for 1`

Basingstoke Leisure Park, Churchill Way West RG21 6YR

➲ *(M3 junct 6, take ringway road (West) and follow brown signs for Leisure Park)*

☎ 01256 477766

e-mail: jane.holmes@hants.gov.uk

web: www.milestones-museum.com

Milestones brings Hampshire's recent past to life through stunning period street scenes and exciting interactive areas, all under one roof. Nationally important collections of transport, technology and everyday life are presented in an entertaining way. Staff in period costumes, mannequins and sounds all bring the streets to life.

continued

Milestones - Hampshire's Living History Museum

Times: Open Tue-Fri & BHs 10-5, Sat-Sun 11-5. Closed 25-26 Dec & 1 Jan. **Fee:** ✱ £7.25 (ch £4.25, under 5s free, concessions £6.50). Family ticket (2ad+2ch) £21. **Facilities:** ❷ ☕ 🗑 ♿ (induction loops, subtitles screens, scooters, wheelchairs) toilets for disabled shop ⊗ (ex guide dogs) 🍴

BEAULIEU   MAP 04 SU30

Beaulieu : National Motor Museum

SO42 7ZN

➲ *(M27 junct 2, A326, B3054, then follow tourist signs)*
☎ 01590 612345
e-mail: info@beaulieu.co.uk
web: www.beaulieu.co.uk

Set in the heart of William the Conqueror's New Forest, on the banks of the Beaulieu River, stands this 16th-century house. It has become most famous as the home of the National Motor Museum. The site also contains the picturesque abbey building ruins, which have an exhibition on life in the middle ages, and various family treasures and memorabilia. The Secret Army Exhibition tells the story of the secret agents trained at the Beaulieu 'Finishing School' during WWII.

Times: ✱ Open all year - Palace House & Gardens, National Motor Museum, Beaulieu Abbey & Exhibition of Monastic Life, May-Sep 10-6; Oct-Apr 10-5. Closed 25 Dec. **Fee:** ✱ Please contact for current prices **Facilities:** ❷ ☕ 🗑 ♿ (ramp access, lift to upper level, induction loop) toilets for disabled shop 🍴

BISHOP'S WALTHAM   MAP 04 SU51

Bishop's Waltham Palace

SO32 1DH

➲ *(on A333)*
☎ 01489 892460
web: www.english-heritage.org.uk

Discover the medieval seat of the Bishops of Winchester. Enjoy the wonderful moated grounds and an exhibition about the powerful Winchester Bishops.

Times: Grounds only: May-Sep, 10-5, Sun-Fri. Farmhouse and Grounds, May-Sep, 10-5, Sun & BHs **Fee:** £2.80 (ch £1.40, concessions £2.10). Prices and opening times are subject to change in Spring 2007. Please check web site or call 0870 333 1181 for the most up to date prices and opening times when planning your visit. **Facilities:** ❷ ♿ shop ⊗ (ex on lead in certain areas) ⚏

BOLDRE   MAP 04 SZ39

Spinners Garden and Nursery

School Ln SO41 5QE

➲ *(off A337, between Brockenhurst & Lymington)*
☎ 01590 673347

The garden has been entirely created by the owners since 1960. It has azaleas, rhododendrons, camellias, magnolias and Japanese Maples interspersed with a huge range of woodland and bog plants. The nursery is well known for its rare trees, shrubs and plants.

Times: Open Apr-mid Sep, daily 10-5. Other times on application. Mid Sep-Mar Nursery & part of garden open **Fee:** £2.50 (ch under 6 free). Nursery & part of garden, free (mid Sep-Mar) **Facilities:** ❷ ♿ (help provided where possible) garden centre ⊗ (ex guide dogs)

BREAMORE   MAP 04 SU11

Breamore House & Countryside Museum

SP6 2DF

➲ *(turn off A338, between Salisbury & Fordingbridge and follow signs for 1m)*
☎ 01725 512468
e-mail: breamore@ukonline.co.uk
web: www.breamorehouse.com

The handsome manor house was completed in around 1583 and has a fine collection of paintings, china and tapestries. The museum has good examples of steam engines, and uses reconstructed workshops and other displays to show how people lived and worked a century or so ago. There is also a children's playground.

Times: Open Apr, Tue, Sun & Etr, May-Sep, Tue-Thu & Sat, Sun & all BH; daily 2-5.30 (Countryside Museum 1pm). **Fee:** ✱ £7 (ch £5). Party £6 each. **Facilities:** ❷ ☕ 🗑 ♿ (ramps, parking, recorded message & book about 1st floor) toilets for disabled shop ⊗ (ex guide dogs)

BUCKLER'S HARD   MAP 04 SU40

Buckler's Hard Village & Maritime Museum

SO42 7XB

➲ *(M27 junct 2, A326, B3054 then follow tourist signs to Beaulieu & Buckler's Hard)*
☎ 01590 616203
e-mail: info@bucklershard.co.uk
web: www.bucklershard.co.uk

An enticing port of call, the historic and picturesque shipbuilding village of Buckler's Hard is where ships from Nelson's fleet were built. After setting a course for the Buckler's Hard Story and authentically reconstructed 18th-century Historic Cottages savour the sights and sounds of the countryside on a ramble along the Riverside Walk or enjoy a cruise on the Beaulieu River on 'Swiftsure' during the summer months.

Times: ✱ Open all year, Etr-Sep 10.30-5, winter 11-4. Closed 25 Dec. **Fee:** Please contact for current prices **Facilities:** ❷ ☕ 🍴 licensed 🗑 ♿ toilets for disabled shop 🍴

BURGHCLERE   MAP 04 SU46

Sandham Memorial Chapel

Harts Ln RG20 9JT

➲ *(4m S Newbury, 0.5m E of A34. Follow signs to Highclere/Burghclere, then brown signs or white NT signs to Sandham Memorial Chapel)*

☎ 01635 278394

e-mail: sandham@nationaltrust.org.uk

web: www.nationaltrust.org.uk/sandham

This red brick chapel was built in the 1920s for the artist Stanley Spencer to fill with paintings inspired by his experiences in WWI. Influenced by Giotto's Arena Chapel in Padua, Spencer took 5 years to complete what is arguably his finest achievement. The chapel is set amongst lawns and orchards with views over Watership Down. The chapel has no internal lighting, so its best to visit on a bright day. 2007 is the 80th anniversary of the consecration of the chapel, and a special thanksgiving service will be held. Contact NT for details.

Times: ✱ Open 23 Mar-Oct, Wed-Sun, 11-5 & BH Mon. Wknds in early Mar & Nov open 11-4, Dec-Feb by arrangement. **Fee:** ✱ £3 (ch £1.50) **Facilities:** ℗ (20yds) 🍴 ♿ (Braille guide, large print guide, hearing loop, ramps) ⊗ (ex assist dogs) 🐾

CHAWTON   MAP 04 SU73

Jane Austen's House

GU34 1SD

➲ *(1m SW of Alton, in centre of village)*

☎ 01420 83262

e-mail: enquiries@jane-austens-house-museum.org.uk

web: www.jane-austens-house-museum.org.uk

Jane Austen lived and wrote here from 1809 to 1817. Restored to look as it would have done in the early 1800s, with items such as the author's donkey cart and writing table to be seen.

Times: Open daily Mar-Dec; Jan-Feb wknds only. Also open 27 Dec-1 Jan & Feb half term. **Facilities:** ℗ (100yds) 🍴 ♿ (wheelchair ramp) toilets for disabled shop ⊗ (ex guide dogs & assist dogs) ◀

EXBURY   MAP 04 SU40

Exbury Gardens & Railway   `2 for 1`

Exbury Estate Office SO45 1AZ

➲ *(from M27 W junct 2, 3m from Beaulieu, off B3054)*

☎ 023 8089 1203

e-mail: nigel.philpott@exbury.co.uk

web: www.exbury.co.uk

A 200-acre landscaped woodland garden on the east bank of the Beaulieu River, with one of the finest collections of rhododendrons, azaleas, camellias and magnolias in the world - as well as many rare and beautiful shrubs and trees. A labyrinth of tracks and paths enable you to explore the beautiful gardens and walks. Year round interest is ensured in various parts of the gardens and a steam railway has several features. 2-for-1 voucher does not apply during April and May.

Times: Open Mar-5 Nov, daily 10-5.30; Santa Steam Specials in Dec **Fee:** ✱ £5-£7.50 (ch under 3 free, ch 3-15 £1-£1.50, pen £4.50-£6.50, £6 Mon-Fri). Railway £2.50-£3. **Facilities:** ℗ 🍴 licensed ♿ (free wheelchair loans & access maps, buggy tours £3.50) toilets for disabled shop garden centre ◀

FAREHAM   MAP 04 SU50

Royal Armouries Fort Nelson   `FREE`

Portsdown Hill Rd PO17 6AN

➲ *(from M27 junct 11, follow brown tourist signs for Royal Armouries).*

☎ 01329 233734

e-mail: fnenquiries@armouries.org.uk

web: www.royalarmouries.org

Home to the Royal Armouries' collection of over 350 big guns and cannon, this superbly restored Victorian fort overlooks Portsmouth Harbour. Built in the 1860s to deter a threatened French invasion, there are secret tunnels, underground chambers and grass ramparts to explore with daily guided tours. Events throughout the year include re-enactments of American Civil War, WWI and Napoleonic battles, and the Royal Armouries Military Tattoo. Contact Fort Nelson for details.

Times: Open Apr-Oct, daily 10-5 (Tue 11-5); Nov-Mar, daily 10.30-4 (Tue 11.30-4) **Facilities:** ℗ 🍴 ♿ (access & audio guide, ramps, induction loop, wheelchair) toilets for disabled shop ⊗ (ex guide & hearing dogs) ◀

GOSPORT   MAP 04 SZ69

Explosion! Museum of Naval Firepower   `2 for 1`

Priddy's Hard PO12 4LE

➲ *(M27 junct 11, A32 and follow signs)*

☎ 023 9250 5600

e-mail: info@explosion.org.uk

web: www.explosion.org.uk

Explosion! The Museum of Naval Firepower is set in the green Heritage Area of Priddy's Hard in Gosport on the shores of Portsmouth Harbour, telling the story of naval firepower from the days of gunpowder to modern missiles. Come face to face with the atom bomb, the Exocet missile and the Gatling Gun and take a trip into the fascinating story of the men and women who supplied the Royal Navy. Walk around the buildings that were a state secret for 200 years and discover the Grand Magazine, an amazing vault once packed full with gunpowder, now a stunning multimedia film show.

Times: Open all year, Apr-Oct & all school hols, daily 10-5.30; Nov-Mar, Thu, Sat & Sun 10-4.30. Closed 24-26 Dec. **Fee:** £5 (ch £3.50, pen £4.50). Family ticket £15 **Facilities:** ℗ 🍴 ⦿ licensed 🍴 ♿ toilets for disabled shop ⊗ (ex guide dogs) ◀

Royal Navy Submarine Museum

Haslar Jetty Rd PO12 2AS

➲ *(M27 junct 11, follow signs)*

☎ 023 9252 9217 & 9251 0354

e-mail: rnsubs@rnsubmus.co.uk

web: www.rnsubmus.co.uk

The great attraction of this museum is the chance to see inside a submarine, and there are guided tours of *HMS Alliance*, as well as displays exploring the development of submarines. Two periscopes from *HMS Conqueror* can be seen in the reconstruction of a nuclear submarine control room, giving panoramic views of Portsmouth Harbour. A new gallery shows the development of submarine weapons from the tiny torpedo to the huge polaris nuclear missile.

continued

England

The Navy's first submarine is back on display in a new gallery and exhibition space.

Royal Navy Submarine Museum

Times: ✱ Open all year, Apr-Oct 10-5.30; Nov-Mar 10-4.30. Closed 24 Dec-1 Jan. (Allow 3 hrs for visit. Last tour 1 hour before closing).
Facilities: ♿ ♨ ♿ (information in Braille, lift to upper gallery) toilets for disabled shop ⊗ (ex guide dogs) 🔊

HARTLEY WINTNEY   MAP 04 SU75

West Green House Gardens   `2 for 1`
West Green RG27 8JB
⊃ *(off A30, at Phoenix Green take sign to West Green, along Thackhams Lane. House last left)*
☎ 01252 844611
e-mail: marylynabbott.westgreenhouse@btinternet.com
web: www.westgreenhouse.co.uk

The gardens are considered to be one of the top 50 gardens in England and were the subject of a whole edition of the BBC's *Gardeners' World*. Today the Queen Anne house is surrounded by four walled gardens, lakes, follies, the green theatre, nymphaeum, mixed border and potager. The owner is a noted garden writer and lecturer. Music and opera performances are a regular feature.

Times: Open Etr-Sep, Wed-Sun 11-4.30 **Fee:** £5 (ch £2.50)
Facilities: ♿ ⦿ ♿ (most areas accessible) shop garden centre ⊗ (ex guide dogs) 🔊

HAVANT   MAP 04 SU70

Staunton Country Park   `2 for 1`
Middle Park Way PO9 5HB
⊃ *(off B2149, between Havant & Horndean)*
☎ 023 9245 3405
e-mail: amanda.fallbrown@hants.gov.uk
web: www.hants.gov.uk/staunton

Set in the Regency pleasure grounds of Sir George Staunton, 19th-century traveller, Orientalist and patron of horticulture, Staunton boasts an ornamental farm, the largest ornamental glasshouses on the South Coast, 1,000 acres of parkland, with ancient woodland and intriguing follies and much, much more. Children can feed farm animals, or visit the play area while the grown-ups stroll through the walled gardens.

Times: Open 10-5 (4 winter). **Fee:** ✱ £5 (ch £3.60, pen £4.10).
Facilities: ♿ ⦿ ⦿ ♿ (wheelchair for visitors, most areas accessible) toilets for disabled shop ⊗ (ex in parkland) 🔊

HIGHCLERE   MAP 04 SU45

Highclere Castle & Gardens   `2 for 1`
RG20 9RN
⊃ *(4.5m S of Newbury, off A34)*
☎ 01635 253210
e-mail: theoffice@highclerecastle.co.uk
web: www.highclerecastle.co.uk

This splendid early Victorian mansion stands in beautiful parkland on the site of a previous house, which in turn was built on the site of an even earlier house owned by the Bishops of Winchester. It has sumptuous interiors and numerous Old Master pictures. Also shown are early finds by the 5th Earl of Carnarvon, one of the discoverers of Tutankhamun's tomb. During WWI it was a hospital, and during WWII it was a home for evacuee children.

Times: Open Jun-Aug, Mon-Fri; 2 BHs wknds in May, Aug BH Mon 11-4 (last entry 3). Telephone 01635 253210 before travelling as Highclere Castle reserves the right to close at other times. **Fee:** ✱ £7.50 (ch 4-15 £4, concessions £6). Family ticket (2 ad + 2 ch or 1 ad + 3 ch) £18 Grounds & gardens only free. **Facilities:** ♿ ⦿ ♿ (wheelchair available) toilets for disabled shop open 12-5 ⊗ (ex guide dogs) 🔊

HINTON AMPNER   MAP 04 SU62

Hinton Ampner Garden
SO24 0LA
⊃ *(off A272, 1m W of Bramdean)*
☎ 01962 771305
e-mail: hintonampner@nationaltrust.org.uk
web: www.nationaltrust.org.uk

A masterpiece of design by Ralph Dutton, 8th and last Lord Sherborne, the 12 acre garden unites a formal layout with varied and informal plantings in pastel shades. There are magnificent vistas over 80 acres of parkland and rolling Hampshire countryside. The house, which is tenanted, contains Ralph Dutton's fine collection of Regency furniture, Italian paintings and hardstone items.

Times: ✱ Open Garden: Apr-Sep, Sat-Wed 12-5. House: Apr-Sep, Tue & Wed 1.30-5 (also Aug, Sat & Sun 1.30-5). **Fee:** ✱ House and Garden £6.50 (ch £3.75). Group £5.75 each. Garden only £5.50 (ch £2.75)
Facilities: ♿ ⦿ ♨ ♿ (Braille guides, special parking, wheelchair loan) toilets for disabled ⊗ (ex guide dogs) 🐾

HURST CASTLE   MAP 04 SZ38

Hurst Castle
SO4 0FF
⊃ *(on Pebble Spit S of Keyhaven)*
☎ 01590 642344
web: www.english-heritage.org.uk

Built by Henry VIII, Hurst Castle was the pride of Tudor England's coastal defences. Crouched menacingly on a shingle spit, the castle has a fascinating history, including involvement in the smuggling trade in the 17th and 18th centuries.

Times: Open Apr-Oct, daily 10.30-5.30 **Fee:** £3 (ch £1.80, concessions £2.80). Prices and opening times are subject to change in Spring 2007. Please check web site or call 0870 333 1181 for the most up to date prices and opening times when planning your visit. **Facilities:** ♨ ⊗ (ex on lead in certain areas) ⧉

England

LIPHOOK   MAP 04 SU83

Hollycombe Steam Collection

Iron Hill, Midhurst Rd GU30 7LP

➲ *(1m SE Liphook on Midhurst road, follow brown tourist signs)*

☎ 01428 724900

e-mail: info@hollycombe.co.uk

web: www.hollycombe.co.uk

A comprehensive collection of working steam-power, including a large Edwardian fairground, three railways, one with spectacular views of the South Downs, traction engine hauled rides, steam agricultural machinery, pets corner, sawmill and even a paddle steamer engine.

Times: Open 2 Apr-8 Oct Sun & BHs, 30 Jul-28 Aug, daily 12-5
Facilities: ❷ ❤ & toilets for disabled shop ⊗ (ex assist dogs) ◼

LYNDHURST   MAP 04 SU30

New Forest Museum & Visitor Centre

Main Car Park, High St SO43 7NY

➲ *(leave M27 at Cadnam & follow A337 to Lyndhurst. Museum signed)*

☎ 023 8028 3444

e-mail: office@newforestmuseum.org.uk

web: www.newforestmuseum.org.uk

The story of the New Forest - history, traditions, character and wildlife, told through an audio-visual show and exhibition displays. With life-size models of Forest characters, and the famous New Forest embroidery. Events and exhibitions throughout the year, contact for details.

Times: Open all year daily, from 10. Closed 25 & 26 Dec. **Fee:** £3 (concessions £2.50). Family ticket (2ad+4ch) £9 , under 8yrs free.
Facilities: ❷ (charged) ▥ & (lift to 1st floor) toilets for disabled shop ◼

MARWELL   MAP 04 SU52

Marwell Zoological Park

Colden Common SO21 1JH

➲ *(M3 junct 11 or M27 junct 5. Zoo located on B2177, follow brown tourist signs)*

☎ 01962 777407

e-mail: marwell@marwell.org.uk

web: www.marwell.org.uk

Marwell has over 200 species of rare and wonderful animals including tigers, snow leopards, rhino, meerkats, hippo and zebra. Highlights include The World of Lemurs, Encounter Village with unusual domesticated animals, Tropical World with its rainforest environment, Into Africa for giraffes and monkeys, Penguin World and Desert Carnivores. Recent additions include an exciting new snow leopard enclosure and a walkway that enables visitors to come face to face with the giraffes. Marwell is dedicated to saving endangered species and every visit helps conservation work. With road and rail trains, holiday activities, restaurant, gift shops and adventure playgrounds Marwell provides fun and interest for all ages.

Times: Open all year, daily 10-6 (summer), 10-4 (winter). (Last admission 90 min before closing). Closed 25 Dec. **Fee:** ✱ £13.50 (ch £10, pen £11.50). Family ticket (2ad+2ch) £45. Prices include a 10% donation **Facilities:** ❷ ❤ ꙮ & (wheelchairs & tours for visually impaired/disabled groups) toilets for disabled shop ⊗ ◼

MIDDLE WALLOP   MAP 04 SU23

Museum of Army Flying

SO20 8DY

➲ *(on A343, between Andover & Salisbury)*

☎ 01264 784421

e-mail: enquiries@flying-museum.org.uk

web: www.flying-museum.org.uk

One of the country's finest historical collections of military kites, gliders, aeroplanes and helicopters. Imaginative dioramas and displays trace the development of Army flying from before the First World War to more recent conflicts in Ireland, the Falklands and the Gulf. Sit at the controls of a real Scout helicopter and test your skills on the flight simulator, plus children's education centre and 1940s house.

Times: ✱ Open all year, daily 10-4.30. Closed week prior to Xmas. Evening visits by special arrangement. **Fee:** ✱ £6 (ch £3.50, concessions £4) Family £18. Party 10+. **Facilities:** ❷ ❤ ꙮ licensed ▥ & (lifts to upper levels) toilets for disabled shop ⊗ (ex assist dogs) ◼

MINSTEAD   MAP 04 SU21

Furzey Gardens

SO43 7GL

➲ *(1m S of junct A31/M3 Cadnam off A31 or A337 near Lyndhurst)*

☎ 023 8081 2464 & 8081 2297

e-mail: info@furzey-gardens.org

web: www.furzey-gardens.org

A large thatched gallery is the venue for refreshments and displays of local arts and crafts, and the eight acres of peaceful glades which surround it include winter and summer heathers, rare flowering trees and shrubs and a mass of spring bulbs. There is a 16th-century

continued

cottage, lake, and the nursery, run by the Minstead Training Project for Young People with Learning Disabilities, sells a wide range of produce.

Times: Gardens open daily, 10-5 (or dusk if earlier). Gallery open: Mar-Oct, 10-5 & wknds unitl mid Dec. Closed Xmas. **Fee:** ✱ Mar-Oct: £4.50 (ch £1.50, pen £3.50) Family £10 **Facilities:** 🅿 ⬛ 📷 ⬛ ♿ (garden access for wheelchair visitors with assistance) toilets for disabled shop garden centre ⊗ (ex guide dogs) 🔊

MOTTISFONT   MAP 04 SU32

Mottisfont Abbey Garden

SO51 0LP

⮕ *(4.5m NW Romsey, 1m W of A3057)*

☎ 01794 340757

e-mail: mottisfontabbey@nationaltrust.org.uk

web: www.nationaltrust.org.uk/mottisfontabbey

In a picturesque setting by the River Test, Mottisfont Abbey is an 18th-century house adapted from a 12th-century priory. The north front shows its medieval church origins quite clearly, and the garden has splendid old trees and a walled garden planted with the national collection of old-fashioned roses. The estate includes Mottisfont village and surrounding farmland and woods.

Times: Garden & House: 27 Feb-2 Jun, Sat-Wed 11-5; 3-30 Jun daily from 11-5 (garden to 8.30); 1 Jul-3 Sep, Sat-Thu 11-5; 4 Sep-29 Oct, Sat-Wed 11-5. Garden only 4 Feb-26 Mar 11-4, 30 Oct-17 Dec Sat-Sun 11-4. (Last admission to grounds 1hr before closing). **Fee:** ✱ £7 (ch £3.50) Family ticket £17.50 **Facilities:** 🅿 ⬛ 📷 licensed 📷 ♿ (Braille guide, wheelchair available, driven buggy) toilets for disabled shop closed 5 Feb-20 Mar garden centre ⊗ (ex assist dogs) 🥗 🔊

NETLEY   MAP 04 SU40

Netley Abbey   `FREE`

SO31 5FB

⮕ *(4m SE of Southampton, facing Southampton Water)*

☎ 02392 581059

web: www.english-heritage.org.uk

A romantic ruin, set among green lawns and trees, this 13th-century Cistercian abbey was founded by Peter des Roches, tutor to Henry III. Nearby is the 19th-century Gothic Netley Castle.

Times: Open all year, Apr-Sep, daily 10-6; Oct-Mar, daily 10-4

Facilities: 🅿 ♿ ⊗ ⌗

NEW ALRESFORD   MAP 04 SU53

Watercress Line   `2 for 1`

The Railway Station SO24 9JG

⮕ *(stations at Alton & Alresford signed off A31, follow brown tourist signs)*

☎ 01962 733810

e-mail: info@watercressline.co.uk

web: www.watercressline.co.uk

The Watercress Line runs through ten miles of rolling scenic countryside between Alton and Alresford. All four stations are 'dressed' in period style, and there's a locomotive yard and picnic area at Ropley. Special events throughout the year including Thomas the Tank Engine and Santa Specials. 2007 is the 30th anniversary of the lines re-opening in 1977.

Times: Open May-Sep, Tue-Thu & wknds; Jan-Apr & Oct, wknds only. **Fee:** ✱ Unlimited travel for the day, £10 (ch £5, pen £9). Family ticket £25. Charge for dogs. **Facilities:** 🅿 (charged) ⬛ 📷 licensed ♿ (ramp access to trains) toilets for disabled shop (at Alresford, Alton & Ropley stations) 🔊

NEW MILTON   MAP 04 SZ29

Sammy Miller Motorcycle Museum

Bashley Cross Rd BH25 5SZ

⮕ *(signed off A35, 15m W of Southampton, 10m E of Bournemouth, N of New Milton town centre)*

☎ 01425 620777

e-mail: info@sammymiller.co.uk

web: www.sammymiller.co.uk

The museum houses over 300 rare and classic bikes and with machines dating back to 1900, some are the only surviving examples of their type. The Racing collection features World Record breaking bikes and their history, including the first bike to lap a Grand Prix Course at over 100 miles per hour. Special events include marque days.

Times: Open daily 10-4.30. (Closed 2 Jan-mid-Feb) **Fee:** £4.90 (ch £2.50). **Facilities:** 🅿 ⬛ 📷 licensed ♿ (special rates for disabled people) toilets for disabled shop ⊗ (ex guide dogs) 🔊

England

OLD BASING MAP 04 SU65

Basing House
Redbridge Ln RG24 7HB
➲ *(signed from Basingstoke Ring Road)*
☎ 01256 467294

The largest house of Tudor England, almost entirely destroyed by Parliamentary forces during a two-year siege ending in 1645. Built on the site of a Norman castle in 1530, the ruins include a 300ft long tunnel. There is a re-creation of a garden of 1600 and exhibitions showing the history of the house. A fine 16th-century barn stands nearby.

Times: ✱ Open Apr-Sep, Wed-Sun & BH 2-6. **Facilities:** ♿ 🏛
♿ (disabled parking by prior arangement) toilets for disabled shop

OWER MAP 04 SU31

Paultons Park
SO51 6AL
➲ *(exit M27 junct 2, near junct A31 & A36)*
☎ 023 8081 4442
e-mail: info@paultons.co.uk
web: www.paultonspark.co.uk

Paultons Park offers a great day out for all the family with over 50 different attractions. Many fun activities include new Cobra ride, drop rides, roller coaster, 6-lane astroglide, teacup ride, log flume, pirate ship swingboat, dragon roundabout, and wave-runner coaster. Attractions for younger children include Kid's Kingdom, Tiny Tots Town, Rabbit Ride, the Magic Forest where nursery rhymes come to life, Wonderful World of Wind in the Willows and the Ladybird ride. In beautiful parkland setting with extensive 'Capability' Brown gardens landscaped with ponds and aviaries for exotic birds; lake and hedge maze. There is also the Romany Experience Museum with unique collection of gypsy wagons and the Village Life Museum. Something for everyone.

Times: ✱ Open mid Mar-Oct, daily 10-6; Nov & Dec, wknds only until Xmas. **Fee:** ✱ £13.50 (ch under 14). Children under 1m tall enter for free. Range of family supersavers. **Facilities:** ♿ 💺 🍴 licensed ♿ (pre-booked wheelchair hire, some rides unsuitable) toilets for disabled shop ⊗ (ex guide dogs) ▬

PORTCHESTER MAP 04 SU60

Portchester Castle
Castle St PO16 9QW
➲ *(off A27)*
☎ 023 9237 8291
web: www.english-heritage.org.uk

Discover 2,000 years of history from its Roman beginnings to the years of medieval splendour. Stand where Henry V rallied his troops before setting out to the battle of Agincourt in 1415.

Times: Open all year, Apr-Sep, daily 10-6; Oct-Mar, daily 10-4. Closed 24-26 Dec & 1 Jan. **Fee:** £3.90 (ch £2, concessions £2.90). Prices and opening times are subject to change in Spring 2007. Please check web site or call 0870 333 1181 for the most up to date prices and opening times when planning your visit. **Facilities:** ♿ ♿ shop ⊗ (ex on lead in certain areas) ⊞

PORTSMOUTH MAP 04 SU60

Blue Reef Aquarium `2 for 1`
Clarence Esplanade PO5 3PB
➲ *(on approach to city follow brown tourist signs to seafront or Aquarium. Located on Southsea seafront between D-Day Museum and The Hoverport)*
☎ 023 9287 5222
e-mail: portsmouth@bluereefaquarium.co.uk
web: www.bluereefaquarium.co.uk

Spectacular underwater walkthrough tunnels offer amazing sights of exotic coral reefs - home to sharks and shimmering shoals of brightly-coloured fish. Mediterranean and tropical waters are recreated in giant ocean tanks, home to a stunning array of undersea life including seahorses, puffer fish, coral, piranhas, and incredible crustaceans. Visit the website for current special events.

Times: ✱ Open daily from 10. Closing times vary with season, please telephone for details. **Fee:** £7.50 (pen £6.50, ch 3-16 £4.99)
Facilities: ℗ (under 50mtrs) 💺 🏛 ♿ (all on 1 level) toilets for disabled shop ⊗ (ex assist dogs) ▬

Charles Dickens' Birthplace Museum
393 Old Commercial Rd PO1 4QL
➲ *(accessible from M27, 1st left at 1st rdbt)*
☎ 023 9282 7261
e-mail: mvs@portsmouthcc.gov.uk
web: www.charlesdickensbirthplace.co.uk

A small terraced house built in 1805 which became the birthplace and early home of the famous novelist, born in 1812. On display are items pertaining to Dickens' work, portraits of the Dickens' family, and the couch on which he died. Dickens readings are given in the exhibition room on the first Sunday of each month at 3pm.

Times: ✱ Open Apr-Sep, daily 10-5.30; Oct, daily 10-5. (Last admission 5).
Fee: £3 (ch & student £1.80, accompanied ch 13 free, pen £2.25). Family ticket £7.80. **Facilities:** ℗ (150mtrs) shop ⊗ (ex guide & assist dogs) ▬

City Museum & Records Office `FREE`
Museum Rd PO1 2LJ
➲ *(M27/M275 into Portsmouth, follow museum symbol signs)*
☎ 023 9282 7261
e-mail: mvs@portsmouthcc.gov.uk
web: www.portsmouthcitymuseums.co.uk/

Dedicated to local history, fine and decorative art, 'The Story of Portsmouth' displays room settings showing life here from the 17th century to the 1950s. The 'Portsmouth at Play' exhibition features leisure pursuits from the Victorian period to the 1970s. The museum has a fine and decorative art gallery, plus a temporary exhibition gallery with regular changing exhibitions. The Record Office contains the official records of the City of Portsmouth from the 14th century.

Times: ✱ Open all year, Apr-Oct daily 10-5.30; Nov-Mar daily 10-5. Closed 24-26 Dec and Record Office closed on public hols. **Facilities:** ♿ 💺 ♿ (induction loops, lift & wheelchairs, parking) toilets for disabled shop ⊗ (ex guide & assist dogs)

D-Day Museum & Overlord Embroidery

Clarence Esplanade PO5 3NT

⮑ *(M27/M275 into Portsmouth, follow D-Day Museum & seafront signs)*

☎ 023 9282 7261

e-mail: mvs@portsmouthcc.gov.uk

web: www.ddaymuseum.co.uk

Portsmouth's D-Day Museum tells the dramatic story of the Allied landings in Normandy in 1944. Centrepiece is the magnificent 'Overlord Embroidery', 34 individual panels and 83 metres in length. Experience the world's largest ever seaborne invasion, and step back in time to scenes of wartime Britain. Military equipment, vehicles, landing craft and personal memories complete this special story.

Times: Open all year, Apr-Sep daily 10-5.30. Oct-Mar, 10-5. Closed 24-26 Dec **Fee:** £6 (ch £3.60, pen £4.50). Family ticket £15.60 **Facilities:** ❷ (charged) 🖵 ♿ (induction loops, sound aids, w/chairs available) toilets for disabled shop ⊗ (ex guide & assist dogs) ◨

Eastney Beam Engine House `FREE`

Henderson Rd, Eastney PO4 9JF

⮑ *(accessible from A3(M), A27 & A2030, turn left at Bransbury Park traffic lights)*

☎ 023 9282 7261

e-mail: mvs@portsmouthcc.gov.uk

web: www.portsmouthmuseums.co.uk

The main attraction here is a magnificent pair of James Watt Beam Engines still housed in their original High-Victorian engine house opened in 1887. One of these engines is in steam when the museum is open. A variety of other pumping engines, many in running order are also on display.

Times: ✱ Open last wknd of month, 1-5 (last admission 30 minutes before closing). (Closed Aug & Dec). **Facilities:** ℗ (300mtrs) shop ⊗ (ex guide & assist dogs)

Natural History Museum & Butterfly House `FREE`

Cumberland House, Eastern Pde PO4 9RF

⮑ *(accessed via A3(M), A27 or A2030, follow signs to seafront)*

☎ 023 9282 7261

e-mail: mvc@portsmouthcc.gov.uk

web: www.portsmouthnaturalhistory.co.uk

Focusing on the natural history and geology of the area, with wildlife dioramas including a riverbank scene with fresh water aquarium. During the summer British and European butterflies fly free in the Butterfly House.

Times: ✱ Open all year daily, Apr-Oct 10-5.30; Nov-Mar 10-5. **Facilities:** ℗ (200mtrs) shop ⊗ (ex guide & assist dogs) ◨

Portsmouth Historic Dockyard

HM Naval Base PO1 3LJ

⮑ *(M27/M275 & follow brown historic waterfront and dockyard signs)*

☎ 023 9283 9766

e-mail: enquiries@historicdockyard.co.uk

web: www.historicdockyard.co.uk

Portsmouth Historic Dockyard is home to the world's greatest historic ships: *Mary Rose* - King Henry VIII's favourite ship, *HMS Victory* - Lord Nelson's flagship at the Battle of Trafalgar and *HMS Warrior* - the first iron-hulled warship. In addition, the Royal Naval Museum has the most significant, permanent collections relating to Nelson and the Battle of Trafalgar, and Action Stations gives an interactive insight into the modern day Royal Navy.

Times: Open Apr-Oct, daily 10-6; Nov-Mar, daily 10-5.30. Last entry, 30 minutes before closing **Fee:** All inclusive ticket: £16 (ch & pen £13, under 5's free). Family £46 **Facilities:** ❷ (charged) 🖵 ⦁◎⦁ licensed ♿ (wheelchairs, facilities for visually & hearing impaired) toilets for disabled shop ⊗ (ex assist dogs) ◨

The Royal Marines Museum `2 for 1`

Southsea PO4 9PX

⮑ *(signed from seafront)*

☎ 023 9281 9385

e-mail: info@royalmarinesmuseum.co.uk

web: www.royalmarinesmuseum.co.uk

Telling the story of the 340-year history of the Marines through dramatic displays, exciting films and videos, state of the art interactives and even a live snake and scorpion. Also a world famous medal collection, portraits and silverware.

Times: Open all year, Jun-Aug, daily 10-5; Sep-May, daily 10-4.30. Closed 24-26 Dec. **Fee:** ✱ £4.75 (ch under 16 free, students £2.25, disabled £1.50, pen £3.50). **Facilities:** ❷ 🖵 ♿ (wheelchairs, hearing loops, special tours-prior notice) toilets for disabled shop ⊗ (ex guide dogs or in grounds) ◨

Southsea Castle

Clarence Esplanade PO5 3PA

⮑ *(accessible from M27, A27, A3M, A2030, follow castle signposts)*

☎ 023 9282 7261

e-mail: mvs@portsmouthcc.gov.uk

web: www.southseacastle.co.uk

Part of Henry VIII's national coastal defences, this fort was built in 1544. In the 'Time Tunnel' experience, the ghost of the castle's first master gunner guides you through the dramatic scenes from the castle's eventful history. Audio-visual presentation, underground passages, Tudor military history displays, artillery, and panoramic views of the Solent and Isle of Wight.

Times: ✱ Open all year, Apr-Sep, daily 10-5.30; Oct-Mar, daily 10-5. **Fee:** £3 (ch & students £1.80, ch accompanied under 13 free, pen £2.25). Family ticket £7.80. **Facilities:** ❷ ♿ (wheelchair available) shop ⊗ (ex guide & assist dogs) 🍴

Spinnaker Tower

Gunwharf Quays PO1 3TT

⮑ *(from M275 follow tourist signs for Tower)*

☎ 023 9285 7520

e-mail: info@spinnakertower.co.uk

web: www.spinnakertower.co.uk

Elegant, sculptural and inspired by Portsmouth's maritime heritage, the Spinnaker Tower is a new national icon - a 'must-see' landmark for visitors worldwide. Soaring 170 metres above Portsmouth Harbour, with three viewing decks, the Spinnaker Tower is now open to view. Glide to the top in style in the panoramic lift or take the high speed internal lift and step right out into the best view in the country. Dare you 'walk on air' on the glass floor, the largest in Europe? Watch history unfold through our unique 'Time Telescopes'. Back down to earth and shop for souvenirs or talk about your travels over a snack in the waterfront Tower Café bar.

Times: Apr-26 May, Sun-Thu 10-5, Fri-Sat 10-10; 27 May-3 Sep daily 10-10; 4 Sep-29 Oct Sun-Thu 10-5, Fri-Sat 10-10; 30 Oct-Mar, Sun-Fri 10-5, Sat 10-10 **Fee:** ✱ £5.95 (ch 5-15 £4.80, ch under 5 free, concessions £5.40). Family ticket (2ad+2ch) £19. **Facilities:** ❷ (charged) 🍴♿ (hearing loop) toilets for disabled shop ⊗ (ex assist dogs) 🍴

Spitbank Fort

Town Quay House, 99 Gosport Rd PO16 0PY

⮑ *(Ferries depart from HM Naval Base Portsmouth, Portsmouth Hard, Gosport Ferry Pontoon, by the side of Portsmouth Harbour Railway Stn and Gunwarf Quays shopping centre)*

☎ 01329 242077

e-mail: info@spitbankfort.co.uk

web: www.spitbankfort.co.uk

Built in the 1860s as part of the coastal defences against the French, this massive granite and iron fortress stands a mile out to sea, with magnificent views across the Solent. The interior is a maze of passages connecting over 50 rooms on two levels.

Times: Open all year **Fee:** ✱ Boat ride takes approx 20mins. Pub nights: (Wed/Thu) £17.50 (ch £10). Parties: (Fri/Sat) £25 (adult only). Sun lunch: £17.50 (ch £10). **Facilities:** ❷ 🍴 🍴 licensed ♿ (many steps) ⊗ (ex guide dogs) 🍴

RINGWOOD　　　　　　　　　　　MAP 04 SU10

Moors Valley Country Park

Horton Rd, Ashley Heath BH24 2ET

⮑ *(1.5m from Ashley Heath rdbt on A31 near Three Legged Cross)*

☎ 01425 470721

e-mail: moorsvalley@eastdorsetdc.gov.uk

web: www.moors-valley.co.uk

Fifteen hundred acres of forest, woodland, heathland, lakes, river and meadows provide a home for a wide variety of plants and animals, and there's a Visitor Centre, Adventure Playground, picnic area, Moors Valley Railway, Tree Top Trail and the 'Go Ape'- high ropes course (book on 0870 444 5562). Cycle hire is also available.

Times: Open all year, 8-dusk (8pm at latest). Visitor centre open 9.30-4.30 (later in summer). Closed 25 Dec. **Fee:** No admission charge but parking up to £7 per day. **Facilities:** ❷ (charged) 🍴 🍴 licensed ♿ (scooter & wheelchairs) toilets for disabled shop 🍴

ROCKBOURNE　　　　　　　　　　MAP 04 SU11

Rockbourne Roman Villa　　　　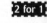

SP6 3PG

⮑ *(from Salisbury exit A338 at Fordingbridge, take B3078 westwards through Sandleheath & follow signs. Or turn off A354 Salisbury to Blandford road, W of Coombe Bissett)*

☎ 01725 518541

web: www.hants.gov.uk/museum/rockbourne

Discovered in 1942, the site features the remains of a 40-room Roman villa and is the largest in the area. Displays include mosaics and a very rare hypocaust system. The museum displays the many artefacts found on the site during excavations. Roman re-enactments are performed - please ring for details.

Times: ✱ Open Apr-Sep, daily 10.30-6. (Last admission 5.30) **Fee:** ✱ £2.25 (concessions £1.25). **Facilities:** ❷ 📷 ♿ (ramps in & out of museum) toilets for disabled shop ⊗ (ex guide/hearing dogs)

England

ROMSEY   MAP 04 SU32

Broadlands

SO51 9ZD

➲ *(main entrance on A3090 Romsey by-pass)*

☎ 01794 505010

e-mail: admin@broadlands.net

web: www.broadlands.net

Famous as the home of the late Lord Mountbatten, Broadlands is now home to his grandson Lord Brabourne. An elegant Palladian mansion in a beautiful landscaped setting on the banks of the River Test, Broadlands was also the country residence of Lord Palmerston, the great Victorian statesman.

Times: Open wkdays, 28 Jun-1 Sep, 1-5.30. Last admission 4. Open BHs.
Fee: ✱ £8 (ch 12-16 £4, concessions £7). Party 15+.
Facilities: ♿ & toilets for disabled ⊗ (ex guide dogs)

ROWLAND'S CASTLE   MAP 04 SU71

Stansted Park

PO9 6DX

➲ *(follow brown heritage signs "Stansted House" from A3 or A27)*

☎ 023 9241 2265

e-mail: enquiry@stanstedpark.co.uk

web: www.stanstedpark.co.uk

Stansted Park is set in 1750 acres of park and woodland. The mansion rooms house the Beesborough family collection of furniture and paintings, and below stairs the restored servants quarters can be found, with an extensive collection of household artefacts giving an insight into the running of the house. The ancient Chapel of St Paul was an inspiration to the poet John Keats and is open in conjunction with the house.

Times: Open Etr Sun-end Sep, Sun & Mon 1-5; Jul & Aug, Sun-Wed (last admission 4) **Fee:** ✱ £5.50 (ch £3.50, pen £4.50). Family £14.50 (2 ad + 2 ch). **Facilities:** ♿ †◯¶ licensed & (wheelchair lift to house) toilets for disabled garden centre ⊗ (ex guide dogs)

SELBORNE   MAP 04 SU73

Gilbert White's House & The Oates Museum

High St GU34 3JH

➲ *(on village High St)*

☎ 01420 511275

e-mail: info@gilbertwhitehouse.org.uk

web: www.gilbertwhitehouse.org.uk

Charming 18th-century house, home of famous naturalist, the Rev. Gilbert White, author of *The Natural History and Antiquities of Selborne*. Over 20 acres of garden and parkland, shop and tea parlour serving some 18th-century fare. There is also an exhibition on Captain Lawrence Oates and his ill-fated expedition to the South Pole in 1911. Special events include an unusual plants fair and concert evening in June, Gilbert White day in July and mulled wine day in December.

continued

Gilbert White's House & The Oates Museum

Times: Open Tue-Sun & BH, Jan-24 Dec, 11-5. Last admissions 4.30
Fee: ✱ £6 (ch free, concessions £5). **Facilities:** ℗ (100mtrs) 🍴
†◯¶ licensed & toilets for disabled shop garden centre ⊗ (ex guide dogs) 🍴

SHERBORNE ST JOHN   MAP 04 SU65

The Vyne

RG24 9HL

➲ *(4m N of Basingstoke, off A340, signed from A33, A339 & A340)*

☎ 01256 883858

e-mail: thevyne@nationaltrust.org.uk

web: www.nationaltrust.org.uk

Built in the early 16th-century for Lord Sandys, Henry VIII's Lord Chamberlain, the house acquired a classical portico in the mid-17th century (the first of its kind in England) and contains a fascinating Tudor chapel with renaissance glass, a palladian staircase and a wealth of old panelling and fine furniture. The attractive grounds feature herbaceous borders and a wild garden, with lawns, lakes and woodland walks.

Times: ✱ Open House & Gardens 20 Mar-Oct daily (ex Thu & Fri) 1-5, wknds 11-5. Gardens also open wknds in Feb & Mar, 11-5. (Gardens 11-5 Mon-Wed). **Fee:** ✱ House & Grounds £7.50 (ch £3.75). Family £18.75, Group £6.30. Grounds & Gardens only £4.50 (ch £2.25) **Facilities:** ♿ 🍴
†◯¶ licensed & (Braille guides, hearing loop & touch tours) toilets for disabled shop ⊗ (ex guide & hearing dogs) ♨ 🍴

England

SOUTHAMPTON — MAP 04 SU41

Museum of Archaeology — FREE

God's House Tower, Winkle St SO14 2NY

⮑ *(near the waterfront close to Queen's Park and the Town Quay)*

☎ 023 8063 5904 & 8083 2768

e-mail: museums@southampton.gov.uk

web: www.southampton.gov.uk/leisure

The museum housed in an early fortified building, dating from the 1400s and taking its name from the nearby medieval hospital. Exhibits on the Roman, Saxon and medieval towns of Southampton are displayed.

Times: Open Tue-Fri 10-4, Sat 10-12, 1-4, Sun 1-4 **Facilities:** ℗ (400 yds) (designated areas only, parking charges) 🍴 shop ⊗ (ex guide dogs)

Southampton City Art Gallery — FREE

Civic Centre, Commercial Rd SO14 7LP

⮑ *(situated on the Watts Park side of the Civic Centre, a short walk from the station, on Commercial Rd)*

☎ 023 8083 2277

e-mail: art.gallery@southampton.gov.uk

web: www.southampton.gov.uk/art

The largest gallery in the south of England, with the finest collection of contemporary art in the country outside London. Varied displays of landscapes, portrait paintings or recent British art are always available, as well as a special display, selected by members of the public.

Times: Open all year, Tue-Sat 10-5, Sun 1-4. Closed 25-27 & 31 Dec. **Facilities:** ℗ (50yds) (nearby street parking is 1hr only) ⬛🍴🍴 & (free BSL signed tours by arrangement, 'touch tour') toilets for disabled shop ⊗ (ex guide dogs)

Southampton Maritime Museum — FREE

The Wool House, Town Quay SO14 2AR

⮑ *(on the waterfront, near to the Town Quay)*

☎ 023 8022 3941 & 8063 5904

e-mail: museums@southampton.gov.uk

web: www.southampton.gov.uk/leisure

The Wool House was built in the 14th century as a warehouse for wool, and now houses a maritime museum, with models and displays telling the history of the Victorian and modern port of Southampton. There are exhibitions of the *Titanic*, *The Queen Mary* and an interactive area for children.

Times: Open Tue-Fri 10-4; Sat 10-1 & 2-4; Sun 1-4 **Facilities:** ℗ (400yds) (metered parking adjacent) 🍴 & (hearing loop on Titanic presentation) shop ⊗ (ex guide dogs)

TITCHFIELD — MAP 04 SU50

Titchfield Abbey — FREE

Place House Studio, Mill Ln PO15 5RA

⮑ *(0.5m N off Titchfield, off A27)*

☎ 01329 842133

Also known as 'Place House', in Tudor times this was the seat of the Earl of Southampton, built on the site of the abbey founded in 1232. He incorporated the gatehouse and the nave of the church into his house.

Times: Open Apr-Sep, daily 10-6; Oct, daily 10-5; Nov-Mar, daily 10-4. Closed 25 Dec. **Facilities:** ℗ &

WEYHILL — MAP 04 SU34

The Hawk Conservancy and Country Park

SP11 8DY

⮑ *(3m W of Andover, signed from A303)*

☎ 01264 773850

e-mail: info@hawk-conservancy.org

web: www.hawk-conservancy.org

This is the largest centre in the south for birds of prey from all over the world including eagles, hawks, falcons, owls, vultures and kites. Exciting birds of prey demonstrations are held daily at noon, 2pm, and 3.30pm, including the 'Valley of the Eagles' at 2pm. Different birds are flown at these times and visitors may have the opportunity to hold a bird and adults can fly a Harris hawk.

Times: Open Feb half term-Oct half term, daily from 10.30-5.30 (last admission 4). **Fee:** ✱ £8.75 (ch £5, concessions £8). Family ticket £27.50 **Facilities:** ℗ ⬛🍴 🍴 & (wheelchair area in grounds, viewing areas in hides, ramps) toilets for disabled shop ⊗ ◼

WHITCHURCH — MAP 04 SU44

Whitchurch Silk Mill — 2 for 1

28 Winchester St RG28 7AL

⮑ *(halfway between Winchester & Newbury signposted clearly on the A34. Located in centre of the town)*

☎ 01256 892065

e-mail: silkmill@btinternet.com

web: www.whitchurchsilkmill.org.uk

The mill is idyllically located on the River Test. Whitchurch Silk Mill is the oldest surviving textile mill in Southern England. Fine silks and ribbons are still woven for interiors and fashion. See the 19th-century waterwheel pounding and learn about winding, warping and weaving. There is a programme of exhibitions, workshops and children's activities.

Times: ✱ Open Tue-Sun & BH Mon 10.30-5 (last admission 4.15). Closed 24 Dec-1 Jan. **Fee:** ✱ £3.50 (ch £1.75, pen & students £3). Family ticket (2 ad & 3 ch) £8.75. **Facilities:** ℗ ⬛ & (disabled parking adjacent site) toilets for disabled shop ⊗ (ex guide dogs) ◼

Gurkha Museum

Peninsula Barracks, Romsey Rd SO23 8TS

⮕ *(M3 junct 9 to Winchester, follow round traffic circuit into High St, 1st left after Westgate)*

☎ 01962 842832

e-mail: curator@thegurkhamuseum.co.uk
web: www.thegurkhamuseum.co.uk

This museum tells the fascinating story of the Gurkha's involvement with the British Army. Travel from Nepal to the North-West Frontier and beyond, with the help of life-sized dioramas, interactive exhibits and sound displays.

Times: Open all year, Mon-Sat 10-5, Sun 12-4. Closed 25-26 Dec & 1 Jan
Facilities: ♿ 🏪 ⛄ (lift & chair lift) toilets for disabled shop ⊗ (ex guide dogs)

Horsepower, The King's Royal Hussars Regimental Museum

Peninsula Barracks, Romsey Rd SO23 8TS

⮕ *(M3 junct 9/10 follow signs for city centre, then hospital A&E red signs to Romsey road. Vehicle access is from Romsey road.*

☎ 01962 828539 & 828541

e-mail: beresford@krhmuseum.freeserve.co.uk
web: www.krh.org.uk

The Royal Hussars were formed by the amalgamation of two regiments raised at the time of the Jacobite Rebellion in 1715, the 10th Royal Hussars and the 11th Hussars. This museum tells their story. The Museum reopened in 2006 after a major refurbishment.

Times: Open 2006: mid-June-18 Dec, Tue-Fri 10-4, wknds, BH's & half term Mon, 12-4. (Closed daily between 12.45-1.15) 2007: 3 Jan-20 Dec Tue-Fri 10-4 **Facilities:** ♿ 🍴 ⛄ (lift to first floor) toilets for disabled shop ⊗ (ex guide dogs)

Hospital of St Cross

St Cross SO23 9SD

⮕ *(on B3335, 0.5m from M3 junct 11)*

☎ 01962 851375

e-mail: administrator@stcrosshospital.co.uk
web: www.stcrosshospital.co.uk

A beautiful group of Grade I listed medieval and Tudor buildings, in a tranquil setting by the water meadows, St. Cross is home to 25 elderly brothers. In keeping with tradition, they wear gowns and trencher hats and act as visitor guides. The hospital is world-famous for its ancient and unique tradition of the Wayfarers Dole - a beaker of beer and a morsel of bread is given by the porter to all visitors who request it. Visitors can admire the medieval and Tudor architecture, explore the medieval hall, the Georgian kitchen and the Tudor cloister as well as the walled garden with many plants of American origin.

Times: Open all year, Apr-Oct, 9.30-5; Nov-Mar 10.30-3.30. (Closed Good Fri, 25 Dec, Sun mornings (summer) and Sun (winter)) **Fee:** £2.50 (ch 50p, pen £2). **Facilities:** ♿ 💺 🍴 ⛄ toilets for disabled shop ⊗ (ex guide dogs) ◀

INTECH - Family Science Centre

Telegraph Way, Morn Hill SO21 1HX

⮕ *(M3 junct 10 (S) or junct 9 (N) onto A31 then B3404 Alresford road)*

☎ 01962 863791

e-mail: htct@intech-uk.com
web: www.intech-uk.com

This purpose-built, 3500 square metre family attraction houses 100 interactive exhibits, which demonstrate the science and technology of the world around us in an engaging and exciting way. The philosophy is most definitely 'hands-on', and the motto of the centre is 'Doing is Believing'. Exhibits deal with things like viscosity, tornados, and Newton's Cradle among others. Activities and science shows take place during school holidays.

Times: Open all year, daily 10-4. Closed Xmas. **Fee:** ✱ £6.50 (ch £4, pen £5) Family ticket (2ad + 2ch) £18.90 **Facilities:** ♿ 💺 🍴 ⛄ toilets for disabled shop ⊗ (ex guide dogs) ◀

Royal Hampshire Regiment Museum & Memorial Garden

Serle's House, Southgate St SO23 9EG

⮕ *(Museum near city centre, 150mtrs from traffic lights in High St)*

☎ 01962 863658

e-mail: serleshouse@aol.com
web: www.royalhampshireregimentmuseum.co.uk

Regimental Museum of the Royal Hampshire Regiment 1702-1992, set in an 18th-century house by the regiment's Memorial Garden. The museum tells the history of the regiment, its regulars, militia, volunteers and Territorials.

Times: ✱ Normally open all year (ex 2 wks Xmas & New Year), Mon-Fri 10-4; Apr-Oct wknds & BH 12-4. **Facilities:** Ⓟ (1000mtrs) ⛄ shop ⊗ (ex guide dogs)

If an attraction name appears in *italics*, details have not been confirmed for 2007

England

The Great Hall

Castle Av SO23 8PJ

⮑ *(situated at top of High St. Park & Ride recommended)*

☎ 01962 846476

e-mail: the.great.hall@hants.gov.uk

web: www.hants.gov.uk/discover/places/great-hall.html

The only surviving part of Winchester Castle, once home to the Domesday Book, this 13th-century hall was the centre of court and government life. Built between 1222-1235 during the reign of Henry III, it is one of the largest and finest five bay halls in England to have survived to the present day. The Round Table based on the Arthurian Legend and built between 1230-1280 hangs in the hall. Queen Eleanor's Garden, a re-creation of a late 13th century ornamental garden, was opened in 1986 by the Queen Mother.

Times: Open all year, Mar-Oct daily 10-5; Nov-Feb, daily 10-5, wknds 10-4. Closed 25-26 Dec. **Facilities:** Ⓟ (200yds) 🍴 & toilets for disabled shop ⊗ (ex guide/hearing dogs) 🔴

Winchester Cathedral

1 The Close SO23 9LS

⮑ *(in city centre - follow city heritage signs)*

☎ 01962 857200 & 866854

e-mail: cathedral.office@winchester-cathedral.org.uk

web: www.winchester-cathedral.org.uk

The longest medieval church in Europe, founded in 1079 on a site where Christian worship had already been offered for over 400 years. Among its treasures are the 12th-century illuminated Winchester Bible, the font, medieval wall paintings and Triforium Gallery Museum. Items of interest include Jane Austen's tomb and the statue of the Winchester diver, William Walker, who in 1905 saved the cathedral by underpinning its foundations, working up to six hours a day over a period of six years, often in 20 feet of water. Visitors can also descend into the crypt to see a sculpture by Anthony Gormley, best known as creator of The Angel of The North, or ascend to the tower and bell chamber.

Times: ✳ Open all year, daily 8.30-5.30. (Subject to services and special events.) **Facilities:** Ⓟ (500mtrs) 🍴🍴 licensed 🍴 & (chair lift to east end of Cathedral, touch & hearing model) toilets for disabled shop ⊗ (ex guide dogs) 🔴

Winchester City Mill

Bridge St SO23 8EJ

⮑ *(by the city bridge between King Alfred's statue & Chesil St)*

☎ 01962 870057

e-mail: winchestercitymill@nationaltrust.org.uk

web: www.nationaltrust.org.uk

Built over the fastflowing River Itchen in 1744, the mill has a delightful small island garden and an impressive millrace. There are regular milling demonstrations and guided wildlife walks.

Times: ✳ Open: Mill & Shop, 5-27 Mar, Sat-Sun 11-5, 28 Mar-10 Apr & 4 Jul-23 Dec, daily 11-5, 13 Apr-3 Jul, Wed-Sun 11-5. Last admission to Mill 4.30 **Facilities:** Ⓟ (200yds) 🍴 & (hearing loop, large print guide, photo album) shop ⊗ (ex guide dogs) 🦮🔴

Winchester College

College St SO23 9NA

⮑ *(in Winchester City Centre S of Cathedral Close, beyond Kingsgate arch. Limited vehicle access along College St)*

☎ 01962 621209

e-mail: enterprises@wincoll.ac.uk

web: www.winchestercollege.org

Founded in 1382, Winchester College is believed to be the oldest continuously running school in England. The College has greatly expanded over the years but the original buildings remain intact. Visitors can follow in the footsteps of John Keats, and see the College's many historic buildings, including a schoolhouse thought to have been designed by Christopher Wren. Also the 14th-century gothic chapel with one of the earliest examples of a fan-vaulted roof constructed from wood rather than stone, the original scholars dining room and the cloister containing memorials to former members of the college including one to Mallory the Mountaineer.

Times: Open all year. Closed 24 Dec-1 Jan. Guided tours available Mon, Wed, Fri & Sat; 10.45, 12, 2.15 & 3.30. Tue & Thu 10.45 & 12. Sun 2.15 & 3.30. Groups of 10+ at times to suit by arrangement only. **Fee:** £3.50 (ch, concessions £3). **Facilities:** Ⓟ (250yds) (street parking max stay 1hr) & (access ramps) toilets for disabled shop ⊗ (ex guide dogs) 🔴

Herefordshire

River Wye,
Ross-on-Wye

Herefordshire is split in two by the River Wye, which meanders through the county on its way to the Severn and the sea. The Wye itself is largely free from pollution, and one of the best rivers for salmon fishing. The area around Hereford is famous for its orchards, producing apples and pears for cider and perry. The county is still largely rural, with the city of Hereford and the towns of Leominster and Ross-on-Wye the only places of any size. Shadowed by the Welsh mountains, the border country, known as the Welsh Marches, has several castles built to defend the now peaceful villages from raiding parties. Perfect for walking or a scenic drive, the Wye valley in particular has some spectacular views.

England

ASHTON
MAP 03 SO56

Berrington Hall

Berrington HR6 0DW

⮑ *(3m N of Leominster, on A49)*

☎ 01568 615721

e-mail: berrington@nationaltrust.org.uk

web: www.nationaltrust.org.uk

An elegant neo-classical house of the late 18th century, designed by Henry Holland and set in a park landscape by 'Capability' Brown. There is a restored bedroom suite, a nursery, a Victorian laundry and a tiled Georgian dairy.

Times: Open 3-18 Mar Sat-Sun, 19 Mar-end Oct & Good Fri 1-4.30. (Last admission 30mins before closing). Garden open 12-5 (4.30 in Oct). Park walk open Jul-Oct, 12-5. Open Good Fri. **Fee:** £5.30 (ch £2.65) Family ticket £13.25. Garden only £3.70. Joint ticket with Croft Castle £7.50. **Facilities:** ❷ ⬛ licensed 📖 ♿ (by arrangement, wheelchairs/batricar, steps to entrance) toilets for disabled shop ⊗ (ex guide dogs) 🐾 ⬛

BROCKHAMPTON
MAP 03 SO65

Brockhampton Estate

WR6 5TB

⮑ *(2m E of Bromyard on A44)*

☎ 01885 482077 & 488099

e-mail: brockhampton@nationaltrust.org.uk

web: www.nationaltrust.org.uk

This traditionally formed 1700 acre estate has extensive areas of wood and parkland, with a rich variety of wildlife and over 5 miles of walks. At the heart of the estate lies Lower Brockhampton House, a late 14th-century moated manor house with a beautiful timber-framed gatehouse and ruined chapel.

Times: Open Apr-Oct daily (ex Mon & Tue) but open BH Mons Apr-Oct 12-5 (12-4 in Oct). Mar weekends only, 12-4. Woodland walks open to dusk throughout the year. **Fee:** ✱ Lower Brockhampton £4 (ch £2) Family £10. **Facilities:** ❷ ⬛ 📖 ♿ (special parking, ramps, Braille guide) toilets for disabled shop ⊗ (no dogs in house ex assist) 🐾

CROFT
MAP 03 SO46

Croft Castle

HR6 9PW

⮑ *(off B4362)*

☎ 01568 780246

e-mail: croft@nationaltrust.org.uk

web: www.nationaltrust.org.uk

Home of the Croft family since Domesday (with a break of 170 years from 1750); walls and towers date from the 14th and 15th centuries; the interior is mainly 18th century. There is a splendid avenue of 350-year-old Spanish chestnuts, and an Iron Age Fort (Croft Ambrey) may be reached by footpath.

Times: Park open all year, daily, dawn-dusk. House open Mar, Sat-Sun, 1-5; Apr-Sep Wed-Sun, 1-5; Oct, Sat-Sun, 1-4.30. Gardens & tea-room open 1hr before house. **Fee:** ✱ Garden only £3.50. Castle & Garden £5 (ch £2.50). Family ticket £12.50. Joint ticket with Berrington £7.50. Car park £3. **Facilities:** ❷ (charged) ⬛ 📖 ♿ (parking available, Braille guide, wheelchair buggy) toilets for disabled ⊗ (ex guide dogs & in park) 🐾 ⬛

GOODRICH
MAP 03 SO51

Goodrich Castle

HR9 6HY

⮑ *(5m S of Ross-on-Wye, off A40)*

☎ 01600 890538

web: www.english-heritage.org.uk

A magnificent red sandstone fortress rising out of a rocky outcrop above the Wye Valley. Climb the huge towers for exhilarating views and explore a maze of small rooms and passageways. Hear about the doomed civil war lovers on our audio tour.

Times: Open all year, Mar-May, Sep-Oct, daily, 10-5; Jun-Aug, daily, 10-6; Nov-Feb, Thu-Mon, 10-4. Closed 24-26 Dec & 1 Jan. **Fee:** £4.50 (ch £2.30, concessions £3.40, family £11.30). Prices and opening times are subject to change in Spring 2007. Please check web site or call 0870 333 1181 for the most up to date prices and opening times when planning your visit. **Facilities:** ❷ shop ⊗ ♯

HEREFORD
MAP 03 SO53

Cider Museum & King Offa Distillery

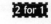

21 Ryelands St HR4 0LW

⮑ *(off A438 Hereford to Brecon road)*

☎ 01432 354207

e-mail: enquiries@cidermuseum.co.uk

web: www.cidermuseum.co.uk

Explore the fascinating history of cider making - old cidermaking equipment, the cooper's workshop and vat house with hydraulic presses and bottling machinery. An annual International cider competition is held and cidermaking festival weekends take place.

Times: Open all year, Apr-Oct 10-5; Nov-Mar 11-3, closed Sun-Mon. **Fee:** ✱ £3 (ch & students £2, pen £2.50). Party 15+, 50p reduction per person. **Facilities:** ❷ ⬛ ♿ (audiotapes, large print guide sheets) toilets for disabled shop ⊗ (ex guide dogs)

Hereford Cathedral

HR1 2NG

⮑ *(A49 signed from city inner ring roads)*

☎ 01432 374200

e-mail: office@herefordcathedral.org

web: www.herefordcathedral.org

Built on the site of a place of worship that dated back to Saxon times, Hereford Cathedral contains some of the finest examples of architecture from the Norman era to the present day, including the 13th-century Shrine of St Thomas of Hereford, the recently restored 14th-century Lady Chapel, and the award-winning new library building. The Mappa Mundi and Chained Library exhibition tells the stories of these famous national treasures through models, artefacts and changing exhibitions.

Times: Cathedral open daily 7.30-Evensong; Mappa Mundi & Chained Library Exhibition Summer: Mon-Sat 10-4.30, Sun 11-3.30. Winter: Mon-Sat 11-3.30 (closed Sun). **Fee:** ✱ Cathedral admission free (donation invited). Mappa Mundi & Chained Library Exhibition £4.50 (concessions £3.50). Family ticket £6-£10. Party 10+. **Facilities:** ℗ (0.25m) ⬛ 📖 ♿ (touch facility for blind, Braille & large print info) toilets for disabled shop ⊗ (ex guide dogs) ⬛

Old House

FREE

High Town HR1 2AA

➲ *(located in the centre of the High Town)*

☎ 01432 260694

e-mail: herefordmuseums@herefordshire.gov.uk

web: www.herefordshire.gov.uk

The Old House is a fine Jacobean building dating from around 1621, and was once in a row of similar houses. Its rooms are furnished in 17th-century style and give visitors the chance to learn what life was like in Cromwell's time.

Times: Open all year, 10-5. Apr-Sep, Tue-Sat 10-5, Sun & BH Mon 10-4.
Facilities: ℗ (400mtrs) 📖 & (virtual tour, Braille guide, tactile images) shop ⊗ (ex guide dogs)

KINGTON   MAP 03 SO25

Hergest Croft Gardens

2 for 1

HR5 3EG

➲ *(off A44 W of Kington and follow signs)*

☎ 01544 230160

e-mail: gardens@hergest.co.uk

web: www.hergest.co.uk

From spring bulbs to autumn colour, this is a garden for all seasons. A fine collection of trees and shrubs surrounds the Edwardian house. There's an old fashioned kitchen garden with spring and summer borders, and Park Wood, a hidden valley with splendid rhododendrons.

Times: Open Apr-end Oct, 12.30-5.30; May-Jun, noon-6. Open wknds in Mar 12.30-5.30 **Fee:** ✱ £5 (ch under 16 free). Party 20+ £4 (£6 with tour). **Facilities:** ❷ 🍴 & (portable ramp & wheelchair available) toilets for disabled shop garden centre 🍴

The National Trust: For over a hundred years, the NT has been acquiring and protecting threatened coastline, countryside and buildings. To find out more about this organisation, its sites, and policies, visit their website: **www.nationaltrust.org.uk**

LEDBURY   MAP 03 SO73

Eastnor Castle

2 for 1

Eastnor HR8 1RL

➲ *(the castle is 2.5m E of Ledbury on the A438 Tewkesbury road)*

☎ 01531 633160

e-mail: enquiries@eastnorcastle.com

web: www.eastnorcastle.com

A magnificent Georgian castle in a lovely setting, with a deer park, arboretum and lake. Inside are tapestries, fine art and armour, and the Italianate and Gothic interiors have been beautifully restored. There's an adventure playground, nature trails and lakeside walks. Events take place throughout the year.

Times: Open 5-9 Apr, every Sun & BH from 15 Apr-Sep, daily 16 Jul-Aug (ex Sat) 11-4.30 (last admission 4). **Fee:** Castle & grounds £7.50 (ch £4.50, pen £6.50) Family £19.50. Grounds only £3.50 (ch £1.50, pen £2.50). Family £8.50. **Facilities:** ❷ 🍴 📖 & (wheelchair climber, lift) shop 🍴

SWAINSHILL   MAP 03 SO44

The Weir Gardens

HR4 7QF

➲ *(5m W of Hereford, on A438)*

☎ 01981 590509

e-mail: theweir@nationaltrust.org.uk

web: www.nationaltrust.org.uk

A delightful riverside garden, with lovely displays of naturalised bulbs set in woodland and grassland walks. Garden walks can be taken here, with fine views of the River Wye and the Black Mountains. The tranquil garden, planted largely with trees and shrubs, stretches over 9 acres.

Times: Open Mar-Apr daily, 11-5; May-Sep, Wed-Sun, 11-5; Oct & Jan, Sat-Sun 11-4; Feb, Wed-Sun, 11-4. **Fee:** ✱ £3.80 (ch £1.90) Family £9.
Facilities: ❷ & (access limited) toilets for disabled ⊗ (ex guide dogs) 🐾

England

Hertfordshire

The Knot Garden of Jacobean,
Hatfield House

Situated to the north of London, Hertfordshire is home to an exceptional number of
Elizabethan and Jacobean houses, including Hatfield House which is surrounded by
42 acres of attractive gardens that reflect their Jacobean origins. Other historical
attractions include: Hertford Museum; Walter Rothschild Zoological Museum, which
holds one of the finest collections of stuffed mammals, reptiles, birds and insects in
the UK; and the Roman Theatre of Verulamium in St. Michaels. To the west, the
Chilterns provide a charming, unspoilt landscape for any keen walker.

England

AYOT ST LAWRENCE   MAP 04 TL11

Shaw's Corner

AL6 9BX

➲ *(A1(M) junct 4 or M1 junct 10. Follow B653 signed Wheathampstead & follow National Trust signs to Shaw's Corner)*

☎ 01438 820307

e-mail: shawscorner@nationaltrust.org.uk

web: www.nationaltrust.org.uk/shawscorner

An Edwardian arts and crafts influenced house, the home of George Bernard Shaw from 1906 until his death in 1950. The rooms remain much as he left them, with many literary and personal effects evoking the individuality and genius of this great dramatist. The kitchen and outbuildings are evocative of early 20th-century domestic life. Shaw's writing hut is hidden at the bottom of the garden, which has richly planted borders and views over the Hertfordshire countryside. A selection of plants in addition to a small collection of George Bernard Shaw plays are available to buy. 2006 marks the 150th anniversary of George Bernard Shaw's birth and 100 years since he took up residence at the house.

Times: Open 18 Mar-29 Oct, Wed-Sun (also open BH Mons), Gardens 12-5.30, House 1-5 (last admission 4.30). **Facilities:** ♿ ▦ ♿ (Braille/large print guides, scented plants, items to touch) ⊗ (ex on lead in car park) ⚑

BERKHAMSTED   MAP 04 SP90

Ashridge Estate Visitor Centre

Moneybury Hill, Ringshall HP4 1LX

➲ *(between Northchurch & Ringshall, just off B4506)*

☎ 01442 851227 & 755557

e-mail: ashridge@nationaltrust.org.uk

web: www.nationaltrust.org.uk

Miles of paths through woodland and open country with spring bluebells, ancient trees, fungi and breath-taking views. Discover more about the wildlife in the visitor centre next to the Bridgewater monument, with an interactive exhibition room. A wide range of activities and events for all the family take place through out the year.

Times: Open; Estate all year. Visitor Centre; 17 Mar-16 Dec, 12-5, (or dusk if earlier) Tea Room; 17 Mar-16, 10-5 (or dusk if earlier). Bridgewater Monument; 17 Mar-16 Dec, Sat, Sun, BH Mon 12-5 (last entry 4.30) **Fee:** Visitor centre & estate free, Monument £1.30 (ch 60p) **Facilities:** ♿ ☕ ♿ (Disabled parking next to visitor centre) toilets for disabled shop ⚑

Berkhamsted Castle   [FREE]

HP4 1HF

➲ *(by Berkhamsted station)*

web: www.english-heritage.org.uk

Roads and a railway have cut into the castle site, but its huge banks and ditches remain impressive. The original motte-and-bailey was built after the Norman Conquest, and there is a later stone keep, owned by the Black Prince, eldest son of King Edward III, where King John of France was imprisoned.

Times: Open all year, Summer, daily 10-6; Winter, daily 10-4. Closed 25 Dec & 1 Jan. **Facilities:** ⊞

HATFIELD   MAP 04 TL20

Hatfield House, Park and Gardens

AL9 5NQ

➲ *(2m from junct 4 A1(M) on A1000, 7m from M25 junct 23. House is opposite Hatfield railway station)*

☎ 01707 287010

e-mail: visitors@hatfield-house.co.uk

web: www.hatfield-house.co.uk

The house, built by Robert Cecil in 1611, is the home of the 7th Marquess of Salisbury and is full of exquisite tapestries, furniture and famous paintings. The 42 acres of gardens include formal, knot, scented and wilderness areas, and reflect their Jacobean history. Includes the national collection of model soldiers and children's play area. The Tudor Palace of Hatfield, close by the house, is the childhood home of Elizabeth I and where she held her first Council of State when she became Queen in 1558. Events take place throughout the year see website for details.

Times: Open Etr Sat-Sep. House: Wed-Sun & BH's 12-4; Park & West Garden: daily 11-5.30. East Garden, Thu. **Fee:** House, park & West Garden: £9 (ch £4.50, pen £8.50). Park only £2.50 (ch £1.50, pen £2.50), Park & West Garden £5 (ch £4, pen £5). Park & Gardens on Thu: £7.50 (ch £7, pen £6). House tour £5. **Facilities:** ♿ ☕ ▥ licensed ▦ ♿ (lift to 1st floor, wheelchairs) toilets for disabled shop ⊗ (ex in park) ◀

An asterisk ✱ indicates that opening times or prices are for 2006. Please contact the attraction for more up-to-date information.

England

Knebworth House, Gardens & Country Park

SG3 6PY

➲ *(direct access from A1(M) junct 7 Stevenage South)*

☎ 01438 812661

e-mail: info@knebworthhouse.com

web: www.knebworthhouse.com

Home of the Lytton family since 1490, the original Tudor Manor was transformed in 1843 by the spectacular high Gothic decoration of Victorian novelist Sir Edward Bulwer Lytton. The formal gardens, laid out by Edwin Lutyens in 1908, include a Gertrude Jekyll herb garden, a maze, recently restored walled garden and the dinosaur trail in the wilderness garden. The 250-acre park includes a miniature railway, an adventure playground and a deer park.

Times: Open daily 31 Mar-15 Apr, 26 May-3 Jun, 30 Jun-5 Sep; wknds & BHs 24-25 March, 21 Apr-20 May, 9-24 Jun, 8-30 Sep. Park, playground & gardens 11-5.30; House 12-5 (last admission 4.15) **Fee:** House & grounds £9 (ch & pen £8.50) Family ticket £31. Grounds £7, family ticket £24. **Facilities:** ❷ 💺 📷 ♿ (transport to door, wheelchair available) toilets for disabled shop garden centre ⊗ (ex guide dogs & in park) 🛏

See advert on opposite page

Museum & Art Gallery

FREE

Broadway SG6 3PF

➲ *(situated next door to Public Library, in town centre, near Broadway Cinema)*

☎ 01462 685647

e-mail: letchworth.museum@north-herts.gov.uk

web: www.north-herts.gov.uk

Opened in 1914 to house the collections of the Letchworth Naturalists' Society, this friendly town-centre museum has exhibits on local wildlife, geology, arts and crafts, and archaeology. There is also a museum shop and a regular programme of art exhibitions and workshops.

Times: Open all year Mon-Tue, Thu-Sat (Closed BHs), 10-5. **Facilities:** ℗ (100yds) 📷 ♿ (ramp, touch screeen computer) shop ⊗ (ex guide dogs)

de Havilland Aircraft Heritage Centre

2 for 1

Salisbury Hall AL2 1EX

➲ *(M25 junct 22. Follow signs for 'Mosquito Aircraft Museum' onto B556)*

☎ 01727 826400 & 822051(info)

e-mail: w4050.dhamt@fsmail.net

web: www.dehavillandmuseum.co.uk

The oldest aircraft museum in Britain, opened in 1959 to preserve and display the de Havilland Mosquito prototype on the site of its conception. A working museum with displays of 20 de Havilland aircraft and sections together with a comprehensive collection of de Havilland engines and memorabilia. Selective cockpits are open to enter. Education storyboard 'maze style' now open.

Times: Open first Sun Mar-last Sun Oct, Sun & BHs 10.30-5.30, Tue, Thu & Sat 2-5.30. **Fee:** ✱ £5 (ch under 5 free, ch 5-16 £3, pen £4) Family ticket £13 (2ad+2ch) **Facilities:** ❷ 💺 📷 ♿ (w/chairs available) toilets for disabled shop ⊗ (ex assist dogs) 🛏

Clock Tower

Market Place AL3 3DR

➲ *(city centre, junct of High St (A1081) & Market Place)*

☎ 01727 819340

e-mail: museum@stalbans.gov.uk

web: www.stalbansmuseums.org.uk

This early 15th-century curfew tower, which faces the High Street, provides fine views over the city (especially of the abbey) and the surrounding countryside. It is the only medieval curfew tower in the country. It has a bell, older than the tower itself, which strikes on the hour.

Times: Open Etr-Oct, Sat, Sun & BH 10.30-5. **Fee:** ✱ 50p (ch 5-11 20p, accompanied ch under 5 free) **Facilities:** ℗ (400yds) ♿ (wheelchair access not possible) shop ⊗

England

Gorhambury

AL3 6AH

⮕ *(entry via lodge gates on A414)*

☎ 01727 855000

This house was built by Sir Robert Taylor between 1774 and 1784 to house an extensive picture collection of 17th-century portraits of the Grimston and Bacon families and their contemporaries. Also of note is the 16th-century enamelled glass collection and an early English pile carpet.

Times: Open May-Sep, Thu 2-5. **Fee:** ✻ £6 (ch £3, pen £4). **Facilities:** ❷ ⓧ

Museum of St Albans

FREE

9A Hatfield Rd AL1 3RR

⮕ *(city centre on A1057 Hatfield road)*

☎ 01727 819340

e-mail: history@stalbans.gov.uk

web: www.stalbansmuseums.org.uk

Exhibits include the Salaman collection of craft tools, and reconstructed workshops. The history of St Albans is traced from the departure of the Romans up to the present day. There is a special exhibition gallery with a surprising variety of exhibitions and a wildlife garden with picnic area.

Times: Open all year, daily 10-5, Sun 2-5. Closed 25-26 Dec. **Facilities:** ❷ � toilets for disabled shop ⓧ (ex guide dogs) ◀

Roman Theatre of Verulamium

St Michaels AL3 6AH

⮕ *(Gorhambury Drive off Bluehouse Hill A4147)*

☎ 01727 835035

The theatre was first found in 1847, was fully excavated by 1935. It is semicircular in shape with a stage area. The seating would have accommodated over 2000 spectators.

Times: Open all year, daily 10-5 (4 in winter). Closed 25-26 Dec. 1 Jan by appointment only. **Fee:** ✻ £2 (ch £1, concessions £1.50, school parties 50p). **Facilities:** ❷ ⓕ (limited access to viewing path) shop

St Albans Cathedral

Sumpter Yard AL1 1BY

⮕ *(M25 junct 22a, in the centre of St Albans)*

☎ 01727 860780

e-mail: mail@stalbanscathedral.org.uk

web: www.stalbanscathedral.org.uk

An imposing Norman abbey church built on the site of the execution of St Alban, Britain's first martyr (c250AD). The cathedral is constructed from recycled Roman brick taken from nearby Verulamium.

Times: Open daily, 9-5.45. Closed 25 Dec from 1. **Fee:** Admission free. Suggested donation £2.50 per adult. **Facilities:** ℗ (200mtrs) 🍴 ⦿ licensed ⓕ ⓕ (touch & hearing centre, Braille guides) toilets for disabled shop

Verulamium Museum

2 for 1

St Michaels AL3 4SW

⮕ *(follow signs for St Albans, museum signed)*

☎ 01727 751810

e-mail: museum@stalbans.gov.uk

web: www.stalbansmuseums.org.uk

Verulamium was one of the largest and most important Roman towns in Britain - by the 1st century AD it was declared a 'municipium', giving its inhabitants the rights of Roman citizenship, the only British city granted this honour. A mosaic and underfloor heating system can be seen, and the museum has wall paintings, jewellery, pottery and other domestic items. On the second weekend of every month legionaries occupy the galleries and describe the tactics and equipment of the Roman Imperial Army and the life of a legionary.

Times: Open all year wkdys 10-5.30, Sun 2-5.30. Closed 25-26 Dec. **Fee:** ✻ £3.30 (ch, concessions £2). Family ticket £8. Subject to change. **Facilities:** ❷ (charged) ⓕ ⓕ (ramp access to main entrance) toilets for disabled shop ⓧ (ex guide dogs) ◀

TRING · MAP 04 SP91

The Walter Rothschild Zoological Museum
Akeman St HP23 6AP
➲ (signed from A41)
☎ 020 7942 6171
e-mail: tring-enquiries@nhm.ac.uk
web: www.nhm.ac.uk/museum/tring

FREE

An unusual museum, founded in the 1890s by Lionel Walter, 2nd Baron Rothschild, scientist, eccentric and natural history enthusiast.

continued

Now part of the Natural History Museum, it houses more than 4000 specimens from whales to fleas, and humming birds to tigers.

Times: Open all year, Mon-Sat 10-5, Sun 2-5. Closed 24-26 Dec.
Facilities: 🅿 🍴 📖 ♿ (ramps, virtual tour, disabled parking space) toilets for disabled shop ⊗ (ex guide dogs) 🚌

WARE · MAP 05 TL31

Scott's Grotto
Scott's Rd SG12 9JQ
➲ (off A119)
☎ 01920 464131
e-mail: jg@ware-herts.org.uk
web: www.scotts-grotto.org

Scott's Grotto, built in the 1760s by the Quaker poet John Scott, has been described by English Heritage as 'one of the finest in England'. Recently restored by the Ware Society, it consists of underground passages and chambers decorated with flints, shells, minerals and stones, and extends 67ft into the side of the hill. Please wear flat shoes and bring a torch, the grotto is not lit.

Times: Open Apr-Sep, Sat & BH Mon 2-4.30. Other times by appointment only. **Fee:** Donations welcome **Facilities:** 🅿 (on street restricted at times) ♿ (web link virtual tour) ⊗ 🚐

Knebworth House and gardens

Kent

St Margaret's Bay near Dover.

Known as the 'garden of England', reflecting its production of fruit, vegetables and hops, Kent is a place of striking contrasts, from the seaside fun of coastal towns like Margate, Broadstairs and Ramsgate, ever popular with holiday-making Londoners, to the World Heritage Site that includes Canterbury's cathedral. The county is also the gateway to Europe, with the Channel Tunnel, and the ports of Dover and Folkestone providing access to the Continent. Ships have been built here too. Chatham Docks retains its historic naval shipyards as a heritage site.

England

AYLESFORD
MAP 05 TQ75

Aylesford Priory
The Friars ME20 7BX

⮞ *(M20 junct 6 onto A229, M2 junct 3 onto A229, signposted)*

☎ 01622 717272
e-mail: friarspa@hotmail.com
web: www.thefriars.org.uk

Built in the 13th and 14th centuries, the Priory has been restored and is now a house of prayer, guesthouse, conference centre and a place of pilgrimage and retreat. It has fine cloisters, and displays sculpture and ceramics by modern artists.

Times: ✱ Open all year, daily 9-dusk. Gift, book shop & tea rooms May-Sep, 10-5; Oct-Apr, 10-4 (Sun 11). Guided tours of the priory by arrangement. **Fee:** ✱ Free, donations welcome **Facilities:** ♿ 🍽️ ♿ (wheelchairs available, ramps) toilets for disabled shop 🐾 (ex guide & hearing dogs)

BEKESBOURNE
MAP 05 TR15

Howletts Wild Animal Park
`2 for 1`

CT4 5EL

⮞ *(off A2, 3m S of Canterbury, follow brown tourist signs)*

☎ 0870 750 4647
e-mail: info@totallywild.net
web: www.totallywild.net

Set in 90 acres of parkland, Howletts is home to some of the world's most rare and endangered animals. Howletts boasts the UK's largest group of African elephants, Indian and Siberian tigers, many small cats and rare monkeys and the world's largest group of Western Lowland gorillas. Glass fronted tiger enclosures, children's adventure playground and the new Jurassic Mine with ice and gem cave are not to be missed. Visit the new Natureworks Arts and Craft Studio for painting, pottery, arts and crafts and the new opentopped Javan Langur enclosure where the endangered monkeys can be seen in a natural environment.

Times: Open all year, daily 10-6 during summer (last admission 4.30), 10-dusk during winter (last admission 3). Closed 25 Dec. **Fee:** £13.95 (ch 4-14 £10.95, pen £8.95). Family ticket (2 ad & 2 ch) £42, (2 ad & 3 ch) £49. **Facilities:** ♿ 🍽️ ⑩ licensed ♿ (wheelchairs for hire, book in advance) toilets for disabled shop garden centre 🐾 🍴

BELTRING
MAP 05 TQ64

Hop Farm & Country Park
TN12 6PY

⮞ *(on A228 at Paddock Wood)*

☎ 01622 872068
e-mail: enquiry@thehopfarm.co.uk
web: www.thehopfarm.co.uk

The Hop Farm is a popular South East family visitor attraction and event location. Set among the largest collection of Victorian Oast houses, attractions include museums and exhibitions, indoor and outdoor play areas, animal farm and shire horses, and restaurant and gift shop. Special events throughout the year include craft shows, motor shows, food and drink festivals and themed holiday weeks.

Times: ✱ Open from 10. Closed 24-26 Dec, 23 May & 20 June **Facilities:** ♿ 🍽️ ⑩ licensed ⑩ ♿ toilets for disabled shop 🍴

BIDDENDEN
MAP 05 TQ83

Biddenden Vineyards & Cider Works
Little Whatmans, Gribble Bridge Ln TN27 8DF

⮞ *(0.5m S off A262, 0.5m from Biddenden Village. Bear right at Woolpack Corner)*

☎ 01580 291726
e-mail: info@biddendenvineyards.co.uk
web: www.biddendenvineyards.com

The present vineyard was established in 1969 and now covers 20 acres. Visitors are welcome to stroll around the vineyard and to taste wines, ciders and apple juice available at the shop. English wine week is held here at the end of May.

Times: ✱ Open all year, Shop: Mon-Fri 10-5, Sat 10-5, Sun & BH 11-5. Closed noon 24 Dec-2 Jan & Sun in Jan & Feb. **Fee:** ✱ Non-guided groups and individuals free. Pre-booked guided tours (min 15 ad) £3.75 (ch 10-17 £1.50, ch under 10 free) Evening guided tour max 35 people £5.75. **Facilities:** ♿ 🍽️ ♿ shop 🍴

BIRCHINGTON
MAP 05 TR36

Powell-Cotton Museum, Quex House & Gardens
`2 for 1`

Quex Park CT7 0BH

⮞ *(W of Margate on A28. In Birchington right into Park Lane before rdbt in town centre. Entrance 600yds on left)*

☎ 01843 842168
e-mail: powell-cotton.museum@virgin.net
web: www.powell-cottonmuseum.co.uk

Major Powell-Cotton spent much of his life on the study of African animals and many different cultures. This museum, founded in 1895, is his legacy, consisting of animal dioramas, photographs, extensive notes, and artefacts from around the world. Also on display in Quex House, the family home, are collections of Eastern and Asian furniture, Kashmir walnut wall carvings, Chinese silk embroidery, and English period furniture. All set within 15 acres of mature gardens, including a Victorian walled garden. Various events throughout the summer.

Times: ✱ Open Apr-Oct, Tue-Thu, Sun & BH 11-5, Quex House 2-4.30; Mar, Sun 11-4, Quex House closed Nov-Feb. **Fee:** ✱ Summer £5 (ch & pen £4, under 5's free). Family ticket (2 ad + 3 ch) £14. Winter £4 (ch & pen £3). Family ticket (2 ad + 3 ch) £10. Garden only £1.50 (ch & pen £1). **Facilities:** ♿ 🍽️ ⑩ licensed ⑩ ♿ (two wheelchairs available) toilets for disabled shop 🐾 (ex assistance dogs) 🍴

BOROUGH GREEN
MAP 05 TQ65

Great Comp Garden
TN15 8QS

⮞ *(2m E off B2016)*

☎ 01732 882669 & 886154
e-mail: greatcompgarden@aol.com
web: www.greatcomp.co.uk

A beautiful seven-acre garden created since 1957 by Mr and Mrs R Cameron for low maintenance and year-round interest. There is a plantsmans' collection of trees, shrubs, heathers and herbaceous plants in a setting of fine lawns and grass paths. The 17th-century house is not open. Chamber music, classical concerts and other events are organised by the Great Comp Society, details from the Secretary, Great Comp Society at the above address.

Times: ✱ Open Apr-Oct, daily 11-5.30. **Facilities:** ♿ 🍽️ ⑩ ⑩ ♿ (wheelchair for hire) toilets for disabled garden centre 🐾 (ex guide dogs)

England

BRASTED
MAP 05 TQ45

Emmetts Garden

Ide Hill TN14 6AY

➲ *(1m S of A25, Sundridge-Ide Hill road)*

☎ 01732 750367

e-mail: emmetts@nationaltrust.org.uk

web: www.nationaltrust.org.uk/emmettsgarden

Emmetts is a charming hillside shrub garden, with bluebells, azaleas and rhododendrons in spring and fine autumn colours. It has magnificent views over Bough Beech Reservoir and the Weald.

Times: Open 25 Mar-May, Tue-Sun; Jun-2 Jul Wed-Sun; 5 Jul-29 Oct Wed, Sat & Sun & BHs 11-5 (Last admission 4.15) **Fee:** ✱ £5 (ch £1). Family ticket £9. Pre-booked group 15+ £4. Joint adult ticket with Quebec House £7 **Facilities:** ♿ 💺 🍴 ♿ (wheelchairs, buggy service, Braille/large print guide) toilets for disabled shop ♿ ☎

BROADSTAIRS
MAP 05 TR36

Dickens House Museum

2 Victoria Pde CT10 1QS

➲ *(on the seafront)*

☎ 01843 863453

e-mail: leeault@tiscali.co.uk

web: www.dickenshouse.co.uk

The house was immortalised by Charles Dickens in *David Copperfield* as the home of the hero's aunt, Betsy Trotwood, whom Dickens based on owner Miss Mary Pearson Strong. Dickens' letters and possessions are shown, with local and Dickensian prints, costumes and general Victoriana. In 2007 the museum will be holding special events to mark the 170th anniversary of Dickens first visit to Broadstairs.

Times: Open Etr-Oct, daily 2-5, also Sat-Sun mid Jun-Aug 10.30-5. **Fee:** £2 (ch & student £1). Family ticket (2 ad & 2 ch) £5. **Facilities:** ♿ (400yds) (pay & display) 🍴 shop ♿ (ex guide dogs)

CANTERBURY
MAP 05 TR15

Canterbury Roman Museum

Butchery Ln, Longmarket CT1 2JR

➲ *(in centre close to cathedral and city centre car parks)*

☎ 01227 785575

e-mail: museums@canterbury.gov.uk

web: www.canterbury-museum.co.uk

Step below today's Canterbury to discover an exciting part of the Roman town including the real remains of a house with fine mosaics. Experience everyday life in the reconstructed market place and see exquisite silver and glass. Try your skills on the touch screen computer, and in the hands-on area with actual finds. Use the computer animation of Roman Canterbury to join the search for the lost temple.

Times: ✱ Open all year, Mon-Sat 10-5 & Sun (Jun-Oct) 1.30-5. (Last admission 4). Closed Good Fri & Xmas period. **Fee:** £3 (ch 5-18, disabled, pen & students £1.85). Family ticket £7.60 **Facilities:** ♿ (walking distance) ♿ (lift) toilets for disabled shop ♿ (ex guide dogs) ☎

The Canterbury Tales
2 for 1

St. Margaret's St CT1 2TG

➲ *(In heart of city centre, located in St Margaret's St)*

☎ 01227 479227

e-mail: info@canterburytales.org.uk

web: www.canterburytales.org.uk

Step back in time to experience the sights sounds and smells of the Middle Ages in this reconstruction of 14th century England. Travel from the Tabard Inn in London, to St. Thomas Becket's Shrine in Canterbury with Chaucer's colourful pilgrims. Their tales of chivalry, romance and intrigue are brought vividly to life for you to enjoy along your journey.

Times: Open all year, Mar-Jun 10-5, Jul-Aug 9.30-5, Sep-Oct 10-5 & Nov-Feb 10-4.30. Closed 25 & 26 Dec, 1 Jan **Fee:** ✱ £7.25 (ch £5.25, concessions £6.25) Family ticket (2 ad & 2 ch) £22.50

Facilities: ♿ (200mtrs) 💺 🍴 ♿ (notice required for wheelchairs, hearing loop facility) toilets for disabled shop ♿ (ex guide dogs) ☎

Canterbury West Gate Towers

St. Peter's St CT1 2RA

➲ *(at end of main street beside river. Entrance under main arch)*

☎ 01227 789576

e-mail: museums@canterbury.gov.uk

web: www.canterbury-museum.co.uk

The last of the city's fortified gatehouses sits astride the London road with the river as a moat. Rebuilt in around 1380 by Archbishop Sudbury, it was used as a prison for many years. The battlements give a splendid panoramic view of the city and are a good vantage point for photographs. Arms and armour can be seen in the guardroom, and there are cells in the towers. Brass rubbings can be made and children can try on replica armour.

Times: ✱ Open all year (ex Good Fri & Xmas period), Mon-Sat; 11-12.30 & 1.30-3.30. Last admission 15 mins before closure. **Fee:** £1.20 (ch & concessions 70p). Family ticket £2.80. **Facilities:** ♿ (100yds) shop ♿ (ex guide dogs)

England

Druidstone Park

Honey Hill, Blean CT2 9JR

➲ *(3m NW on A290 from Canterbury)*

☎ 01227 765168

web: www.druidstone.net

Idyllic garden setting with enchanted woodland walks where dwells the sleeping dragon. See the mystical Oak circle with the old man of the oaks. Children's farmyard, play areas, gift shop and cafeteria.

Times: ✱ Open Etr-Nov, daily, 10-5.30. **Fee:** ✱ £5.10 (ch £3.80 & pen £4.30). Family ticket £15 **Facilities:** ❷ 🍽 & toilets for disabled shop ⊗ (ex guide dogs) ◀

Museum of Canterbury

Stour St CT1 2RA

➲ *(in the Medieval Poor Priests' Hospital, just off St Margaret's St or High St)*

☎ 01227 475202

e-mail: museums@canterbury.gov.uk

web: www.canterbury-museum.co.uk

Discover the story of Canterbury in new interactive displays for all the family. See the city's treasures including the famous Canterbury Cross. Try the fun activities in the Medieval Discovery Gallery, find out about the mysteries surrounding Christopher Marlowe's life and death and spot friend or foe planes in the WW2 Blitz gallery. Meet favourite children's TV character Bagpuss and friends, and enjoy the Rupert Bear Museum - full of adventure and surprises.

Times: ✱ Open all year, Mon-Sat 10.30-5 & Sun (Jun-Sep) 1.30-5 (last admission 4). (Closed Good Fri & Xmas period). **Fee:** £3.30 (concessions £2.20). Family ticket £8.70 (2 ad + 3 ch) **Facilities:** ℗ (walking) & toilets for disabled shop ⊗ (ex guide dogs)

Royal Museum & Art Gallery with Buffs Museum

High St CT1 2RA

➲ *(in Beaney Institute (1st floor) in High St)*

☎ 01227 452747

e-mail: museums@canterbury.gov.uk

web: www.canterbury-artgallery.co.uk

A splendid Victorian building, houses decorative arts and the city's picture collections- including a gallery for T.S. Cooper, England finest cattle painter. The art gallery is the major space in the area for the visual arts with a varied exhibition programme. Here too is the Buffs Museum, which tells the story of one of England's oldest infantry regiments and its worldwide service.

Times: ✱ Open all year, Mon-Sat 10-5. Closed Good Fri, BH and Xmas period. (Last admission 4.45) **Facilities:** ℗ (500mtrs) shop ⊗ (ex guide dogs)

St Augustine's Abbey

CT1 1TF

➲ *(off A28)*

☎ 01227 767345

web: www.english-heritage.org.uk

Part of the Canterbury World Heritage site, this is considered by many as the birthplace of Christianity in England. Visit the fascinating museum and take the free interactive audio tour.

Times: Open all year, Apr-Sep, daily, 10-6; Oct-Mar, Wed-Sun, 10-4. Closed 24-26 Dec & 1 Jan. **Fee:** £3.90 (ch £2, concessions £2.90). Prices and

continued

opening times are subject to change in Spring 2007. Please check web site or call 0870 333 1181 for the most up to date prices and opening times when planning your visit. **Facilities:** ℗ & shop ✚

CHARTWELL MAP 05 TQ45

Chartwell

TN16 1PS

➲ *(off A25 onto B2026 at Westerham, Chartwell 2m S of village)*

☎ 01732 866368 (info line) & 868381

e-mail: chartwell@nationaltrust.org.uk

web: www.nationaltrust.org.uk/chartwell

The former home of Sir Winston Churchill is filled with reminders of the great statesman, from his hats and uniforms to gifts presented by Stalin, Roosevelt, de Gaulle and many other State leaders. There are portraits of Churchill and other works by notable artists, and also many paintings by Churchill himself. The gardens command breathtaking views over the Weald of Kent.

Times: Open House, Garden & Studio 25 Mar-29 Oct, Wed-Sun 11-5. Open BH Mon & Tue in Jul & Aug. (Last admission 4.15) **Fee:** ✱ House, Garden & Studio £10 (ch £5). Garden & Studio £5 (ch £2.50). Family ticket £25 **Facilities:** ❷ 🍽 licensed 🎫 & (2 steps to lift, parking, guides, sensory facilities) shop 🎈 ◀

CHATHAM MAP 05 TQ76

Fort Amherst

Dock Rd ME4 4UB

➲ *(adjacent to A231 dock road, 0.5m from Chatham Dockyard)*

☎ 01634 847747

e-mail: info@fortamherst.com

web: www.fortamherst.com

A fine Georgian fortress set in over 15 acres of attractive parkland. A fascinating collection of caves, tunnels, gun-batteries and barracks gives visitors an insight into the life of the Napoleonic soldier. Please telephone for details of special events, including historic re-enactments.

Times: ✱ Open Mar-Sep Sat-Sun and every day during school holidays. 10.30-4 **Facilities:** ❷ 🍽 & (road access up to fort) toilets for disabled shop ⊗ (ex guide dogs) ◀

The Historic Dockyard Chatham

ME4 4TZ

➲ *(M20 & M2 junct 3, follow signs for Chatham on A229. Then A230 and A231, following brown tourist signs. Brown anchor signs lead to visitors entrance)*

☎ 01634 823807

e-mail: info@chdt.org.uk

web: www.thedockyard.co.uk

The Historic Dockyard celebrates over 400 years of naval history in one 80-acre site. Exhibits include Battle Ships with WWII destroyer *HMS Cavalier* and the spy sub *Ocelot*. Lifeboat with a display of 15 full size boats, archive film and artefacts; and Wooden Walls which looks at the life of a carpenter's apprentice in the 18th century. The naval architecture is spectacular.

Times: ✱ Open mid Feb-early Nov, daily 10-6. Last entry 4. **Facilities:** ❷ 🍽 🍴 licensed 🎫 & (wheelchair available, virtual tours) toilets for disabled shop ◀

CHIDDINGSTONE   MAP 05 TQ54

Chiddingstone Castle

TN8 7AD

➲ *(off B2027, at Bough Beech)*

☎ 01892 870347

The 'castle' is a 17th-century house, almost completely rebuilt in the castle style c1800 by William Atkinson. It contains Stewart and Jacobite paintings and other relics, Egyptian and Oriental antiquities, and a fine collection of Japanese lacquer and swords. The interior has recently been refurbished with extra rooms open to visitors.

Times: ✱ Open Apr-May, Oct, Etr & Public Hols, Jun-Sep, Wed-Fri & Sun. Wkdays 2-5.30; Sun & BH 11.30-5.30. **Facilities:** ❷ 🍽 🗐 ♿ shop ⊗ (ex guide dogs on lead)

DEAL   MAP 05 TR35

Deal Castle

Victoria Rd CT14 7BA

➲ *(SW of Deal town centre)*

☎ 01304 372762

web: www.english-heritage.org.uk

Discover the history of this formidable fortress as you explore the long, dark passages that once linked a garrison of 119 guns.

Times: Open Apr-Sep, daily 10-6. Open for events during Oct half-term. Please call for details **Fee:** £3.90 (ch £2, concessions £2.90). Prices and opening times are subject to change in Spring 2007. Please check web site or call 0870 333 1181 for the most up to date prices and opening times when planning your visit. **Facilities:** ♿ (parking available) shop ⊗ ⚭

Walmer Castle

Kingsdown Rd CT14 7LJ

➲ *(1m S on coast, off A258)*

☎ 01304 364288

web: www.english-heritage.org.uk

Originally built by Henry VIII as a formidable and austere fortress, the castle has since been transformed into an elegant stately home, formerly used by HM The Queen Mother. Many of her rooms are open to view, but the special highlight is the magnificent gardens.

Times: Open Apr-Sep, daily 10-6 (closes 4pm Sat); Oct, Wed-Sun 10-4; Mar, daily, 10-4. Closed when Lord Warden in residence. **Fee:** £6.20 (ch £3.10, concessions £4.70). Family ticket £15.50. Prices and opening times are subject to change in Spring 2007. Please check web site or call 0870 333 1181 for the most up to date prices and opening times when planning your visit. **Facilities:** ❷ 🍽 ♿ (parking available) shop ⊗ ⚭

DOVER   MAP 05 TR34

Crabble Corn Mill

Lower Rd, River CT17 0UY

➲ *(A2 to Whitfield rdbt then 2nd turning down Whitfield Hill, left. At traffic lights right into River Crabble, under railway bridge and 1st right. Mill 500mtrs on left)*

☎ 01304 823292

e-mail: miller@ccmt.org.uk

web: www.ccmt.org.uk

Visit this beautifully restored working Kentish water mill dating from 1812. Regular demonstrations of waterwheel working and making stoneground wholemeal flour from Kentish organic wheat. Flour for sale, also home-baked produce in café. Exhibition space displays work of local artists and craftspeople.

Times: ✱ Open all year, Mar-Sep, daily 11-5; Winter, Sun only (except by appointment). Open all year for groups by arrangement. Closed Xmas & Jan. **Facilities:** ❷ 🍽 🗐 ♿ shop ⊗ (ex guide dogs)

Dover Castle & Secret Wartime Tunnels

CT16 1HU

☎ 01304 211067

web: www.english-heritage.org.uk

Various exhibitions demonstrate how Dover Castle has served as a vital strategic centre for the Iron Age onwards. In May 1940 the tunnels under the castle became the nerve centre for 'Operation Dynamo' - the evacuation of Dunkirk. These wartime secrets are now revealed for all to see.

Times: Open Apr-Jul, 10-6, daily; Aug, 9.30-6, daily. Sep, 10-6, daily. Oct, 10-5, daily. Nov-Jan, 10-4, Thu-Mon. Feb-Mar, 10-4 daily. Closed 24-26 Dec & 1 Jan. Note : Keep closes at 5pm on Sat if hospitality event booked **Fee:** £9.50 (ch £4.80, concessions £7.10). Family £23.80. Prices and opening times are subject to change in Spring 2007. Please check web site or call 0870 333 1181 for the most up to date prices and opening times when planning your visit. **Facilities:** ❷ 🍽 ♿ shop ⊗ (ex on lead in certain areas) ⚭

Roman Painted House

New St CT17 9AJ

➲ *(follow A20 to York St bypass, located in town centre)*

☎ 01304 203279

Visit five rooms of a Roman hotel built 1800 years ago, famous for its unique, well-preserved Bacchic frescos. The Roman underfloor heating system and part of a late-Roman defensive wall are also on view. There are extensive displays on Roman Dover.

Times: Open Apr-Sep, Tue-Sun 10-5, also BH Mon & Mon Jul & Aug. **Fee:** £2 (ch & pen 80p) **Facilities:** ❷ 🗐 ♿ (touch table, glass panels on gallery for wheelchairs) toilets for disabled shop ⊗ (ex assist dogs)

DYMCHURCH   MAP 05 TR12

Dymchurch Martello Tower

High St CT16 1HU

➲ *(access from High St not seafront)*

☎ 01304 211067

web: www.english-heritage.org.uk

This artillery tower formed part of a chain of strongholds intended to resist invasion by Napoleon.

Times: Open Aug BH and Heritage Open Days **Fee:** £2.50 (ch £1.30, concessions £1.90). Prices and opening times are subject to change in Spring 2007. Please check website or call 0870 333 1181 for the most up to date prices and opening times when planning your visit. **Facilities:** ⊗ ⚭

continued

We endeavour to be as accurate as possible, but changes to times and other information can occur after the guide has gone to press.

EDENBRIDGE

See **Hever**

EYNSFORD
MAP 05 TQ56

Eagle Heights
2 for 1

Lullingstone Ln DA4 0JB

➲ *(M25 junct 3/A20 towards West Kingsdown. Right after 2 rdbts onto A225. Follow brown signs)*

☎ 01322 866466

e-mail: office@eagleheights.co.uk

web: www.eagleheights.co.uk

Eagle Heights is an impressive display of birds of prey from all over the world. Many are flown out across the Darenth valley twice daily. Meet the owls, pygmy goat and rabbits in the paddock.

Times: Open Mar-Nov daily 10.30-5. Nov, Jan-Feb wknd only 11-4. Dec closed. **Fee:** ✳ £6.95 (ch £4.95 4-14yrs, concessions £5.95) **Facilities:** ❷ ➍ ⓱ toilets for disabled shop ⊗ ➟

Eynsford Castle
FREE

➲ *(in Eynsford, off A225)*

web: www.english-heritage.org.uk

One of the first stone castles to be built by the Normans. The moat and remains of the curtain wall and hall can still be seen.

Times: Open Apr-mid Jul & early Aug-Sep, daily 10-6; Oct-Nov, daily, 10-4; Dec-Jan, Wed-Sun, 10-4; Feb-Mar, daily, 10-4. Closed 24-26 Dec and 1 Jan. mid Jul-early Aug property may be closed for live events tickets to be booked. **Facilities:** ❷ ⓱ ✤

Lullingstone Castle

DA4 0JA

➲ *(1m SW of Eynsford via A225 & Lullingstone Roman Villa)*

☎ 01322 862114

The house was altered extensively in Queen Anne's time, and has fine state rooms and beautiful grounds. The 15th-century gate tower was one of the first gatehouses in England to be made entirely of bricks, and there is a church with family monuments. The two-acre walled garden is currently being turned into a World Garden of Plants, which will contain 10,000 different plant species. Please telephone for details of special events.

Times: Open House & Garden Apr-Oct, Fri-Sat 12-5, Sun & BH 2-6. Closed Good Fri. Parties by arrangement. **Fee:** ✳ House & Gardens £5.50 (ch £2.50 & pen £5) Family £12.50. **Facilities:** ❷ ⓱ ⓱ shop ⊗ (ex guide dogs)

Lullingstone Roman Villa

Lullingstone Ln DA4 0JA

➲ *(0.5m SW off A225)*

☎ 01322 863467

web: www.english-heritage.org.uk

One of the most exciting finds with wonderful mosaic floors, wall paintings and skeletal remains. Audio tours offer a fascinating insight into the life of a well-to-do Roman family.

Times: Open Apr-Sep, daily 10-6; Oct-Nov, daily, 10-4; Dec-Jan, Wed-Sun, 10-4; Feb-Mar, daily 10-4. Closed 24-26 Dec & 1 Jan **Fee:** £3.90 (ch £2, concessions £2.90) Prices and opening times are subject to change in Spring 2007. Please check web site or call 0870 333 1181 for the most up to date prices and opening times when planning your visit. **Facilities:** ❷ ⊗ ✤

FAVERSHAM
MAP 05 TR06

Fleur de Lis Heritage Centre
2 for 1

10-13 Preston St ME13 8NS

➲ *(3 minutes drive from M2 junct 6)*

☎ 01795 534542

e-mail: ticfaversham@btconnect.com

web: www.faversham.org/society

Recently expanded and updated, and housed in 16th-century premises, the Centre features colourful displays and room settings that vividly evoke the 2000 year history of Faversham. Special features include the 'Gunpowder Experience' and a working old-style village telephone exchange, one of only two remaining in Britain. In July, during the Faversham Open House Scheme, over 20 historic properties in the town are opened to the public.

Times: ✳ Open all year, Mon-Sat, 10-4; Sun 10-1. **Fee:** £2 (ch & pen £1) **Facilities:** ℗ (200yds) ⓱ (DVD show of parts that are inaccessible) toilets for disabled shop ➟

GILLINGHAM
MAP 05 TQ76

Royal Engineers Museum & Library
2 for 1

Prince Arthur Rd ME4 4UG

➲ *(follow brown signs from Gillingham & Chatham town centres)*

☎ 01634 822839

e-mail: mail@re-museum.co.uk

web: www.remuseum.org.uk

The museum covers the diverse and sometimes surprising work of the Royal Engineers. Learn about the first military divers, photographers, aviators and surveyors; see memorabilia relating to General Gordon and Field Marshal Lord Kitchener, Wellington's battle map from Waterloo and a Harrier jump-jet. The superb medal displays include 26 Victoria Crosses, among 6,000 medals. There are 25 galleries that cover numerous campaigns over the last 300 years. Among the exhibits are locomotives, tanks, the first wire guided torpedo, bridges, and models. Special events sometimes take place in conjunction with Chatham Historic Shipyard and Fort Amherst.

Times: Open all year, Tue-Fri 9-5, Sat-Sun & BH Mon 11.30-5. Closed Good Fri, Xmas week & 1 Jan. Library open same times (ex wknds) but by appointment. **Fee:** ✳ £5.75 (concessions £3). **Facilities:** ❷ ⓱ ⓱ (help available if required, chair lift to upper level) toilets for disabled shop ⊗ (ex guide dogs) ➟

GOUDHURST
MAP 05 TQ73

Finchcocks

TN17 1HH

➲ *(off A262)*

☎ 01580 211702

e-mail: katrina@finchcocks.co.uk

web: www.finchcocks.co.uk

This fine early Georgian house stands in a spacious park with a beautiful garden, and contains an outstanding collection of keyboard instruments from the 17th century onwards. They have been restored to playing condition, and there are musical tours on all open days and private visits. Visually handicapped visitors may touch the instruments as well as hear them.

Times: Open Etr-Sep, Sun & BH Mon 2-6; Aug, Wed, Thu & Sun only 2-6. Private groups on other days by appointment Apr-Oct & Dec. **Fee:** £8 **Facilities:** ❷ ➍ ⓞ licensed ⓱ (wheelchair available, Braille signs) toilets for disabled shop garden centre ⊗ (ex guide dogs)

GROOMBRIDGE PLACE   MAP 05 TQ53

Groombridge Place Gardens & Enchanted Forest

TN3 9QG

➲ *(M25 junct 5, follow A21 S, exit at A26 (signed Tunbridge Wells), then take A264 - follow signs to Groombridge village and Groombridge Place Gardens)*

☎ 01892 861444

e-mail: office@groombridge.co.uk

web: www.groombridge.co.uk

This award-winning attraction, set in 200 acres, features a series of magnificent walled gardens set against the backdrop of a romantic 17th-

continued

century moated manor. Explore the herbaceous border, the white rose garden, the 'Drunken Topiary', the 'Secret Garden' and the peacock walk. By way of contrast in the ancient woodland of the 'Enchanted Forest', the imagination is stimulated by mysterious features such as the 'Dark Walk', 'Dinosaur and Dragon Valley' and 'Groms' Village'. Groombridge was used as a major location in the recent movie adaptation of Jane Austens *Pride and Prejudice*. There are also bird of prey flying displays, canal boat cruises, and a full programme of special events.

Times: Open Apr-Nov, daily 10-5.30 **Fee:** ✱ £8.70 (ch 3-12 & pen £7.20). Family ticket (2 ad + 2 ch) £29.50. Groups 20+ available on request.
Facilities: ❷ ⑩ 🎒 ♿ toilets for disabled shop ⊗ (ex guide/hearing dogs) ◀

See advert on this page

HAWKINGE   MAP 05 TR23

Kent Battle of Britain Museum

Aerodrome Rd CT18 7AG

➲ *(off A260, 1m along Aerodrome road)*

☎ 01303 893140

e-mail: kentbattleofbritainmuseum@btinternet.com

web: www.kbobm.org

Once a Battle of Britain Station, today it houses the largest collection of relics and related memorabilia of British and German aircraft involved in the fighting. Also shown, full-size replicas of the Hurricane, Spitfire and Me109 used in Battle of Britain films. The year 2000 was the 60th anniversary of the Battle of Britain and a new memorial was dedicated. Artefacts on show, recovered from over 600 battle of Britain aircraft, all form a lasting memorial to all those involved in the conflict.

Times: ✱ Open Etr-Sep, daily 10-5; Oct, daily 11-4. (Last admission 1 hour before closing). **Facilities:** ❷ 🍴 ♿ shop ⊗ (ex guide dogs)

HEVER   MAP 05 TQ44

Hever Castle & Gardens

TN8 7NG

⮑ *(M25 junct 5 or 6, 3m SE of Edenbridge, off B2026)*
☎ 01732 865224
e-mail: mail@hevercastle.co.uk
web: www.hevercastle.co.uk

This enchanting, double-moated, 13th-century castle was the childhood home of Anne Boleyn. Restored by the American millionaire William Waldorf Astor at the beginning of the 20th century, it shows superb Edwardian craftsmanship. Astor also transformed the grounds, creating topiary, a yew maze, 35 acre lake and Italian gardens filled with antique sculptures. There is also a 100 metre herbaceous border, 'splashing' water maze' on the Sixteen Acre Island, as well as a woodland walk known as Sunday Walk. Adventure play area with the Henry VIII Tower Maze.

Times: ✱ Open Mar-Nov, daily. Castle 12-6, Gardens 11-6. (Last admission 5). (Closes 4pm Mar & Nov). **Fee:** ✱ Castle & Gardens £9.80 (ch 5-14 £5.30, pen £8.20). Family ticket £24.90. Gardens only £7.80 (ch 5-14 £5, pen £6.70). Family ticket £20.60 **Facilities:** ℗ ⬛ ⏐⊙⏐ licensed ♿ (wheelchairs available, book in advance) toilets for disabled shop garden centre ◀

HYTHE   MAP 05 TR13

Romney, Hythe & Dymchurch Railway

TN28 8PL

⮑ *(M20 junct 11, off A259 signed New Romney)*
☎ 01797 362353 & 363256
e-mail: info@rhdr.org.uk
web: www.rhdr.org.uk

The world's smallest public railway has its headquarters here. The concept of two enthusiasts coincided with Southern Railway's plans for expansion, and so the thirteen-and-a-half mile stretch of 15 inch gauge

continued

railway came into being, running from Hythe through New Romney and Dymchurch to Dungeness Lighthouse.

Romney, Hythe & Dymchurch Railway

Times: ✱ Open daily Etr-Sep, also wknds in Mar & Oct. For times apply to: The Manager, RH & DR, New Romney, Kent. **Facilities:** ℗ (charged) ⬛ ⏐⊙⏐ ♿ (stairlift to Toy & Model Museum) toilets for disabled shop (Dymchurch & Dungeness high season only) ◀

IGHTHAM   MAP 05 TQ55

Ightham Mote

TN15 0NT

⮑ *(2.5m S off A227, 6m E of Sevenoaks)*
☎ 01732 810378 & 811145 (info line)
e-mail: igthammote@nationaltrust.org.uk
web: www.nationaltrust.org.uk

This moated manor house, nestling in a sunken valley, dates from 1330. The main features of the house span many centuries and include the Great Hall, old chapel and crypt, Tudor chapel with painted ceiling, drawing room with Jacobean fireplace, frieze and 18th-century handpainted Chinese wallpaper and the billiards room. There is an extensive garden as well as interesting walks in the surrounding woodland. Following completion of all conservation work visitors can enjoy the most extensive visitor route to date, including the bedroom of Charles Henry Robinson who bequeathed Ightham Mote to the National Trust.

Times: Open 12 Mar-29 Oct, daily ex Tue & Sat, 10-5.30. Open Good Fri. (Last admission 5). **Fee:** ✱ £8.50 (ch £4). Family ticket £21. **Facilities:** ℗ ⬛ ⏐⊙⏐ licensed ⏐⏐ ♿ (wheelchairs, special parking ask at office, virtual tour) shop garden centre ⊗ (ex hearing & guide dogs) ✖ ◀

LAMBERHURST   MAP 05 TQ63

Bayham Abbey

TN3 8DE

⮑ *(off B2169, 2m W in East Sussex)*
☎ 01892 890381
web: www.english-heritage.org.uk

Explore the romantic ruins of this 13th-century abbey built by French monks in an 18th-century landscaped setting.

Times: Open Apr-Sep, daily 11-5. **Fee:** £3.50 (ch £1.80, concessions £2.60). Prices and opening times are subject to change in Spring 2007. Please check web site or call 0870 333 1181 for the most up to date prices and opening times when planning your visit. **Facilities:** ℗ ♿ ✿

Scotney Castle Garden

TN3 8JN

⮕ *(1m S, of Lamberhurst on A21)*

☎ 01892 893898

e-mail: scotneycastle@nationaltrust.org.uk

web: www.nationaltrust.org.uk

The beautiful gardens at Scotney were planned in the 19th century around the remains of the old, moated Scotney Castle. There is something to see at every time of year, with spring flowers followed by rhododendrons, azaleas and a mass of roses, and then superb autumn colours. Estate walks all year through 770 acres of woodlands and meadows, estate explorer map available.

Times: Open Garden: Apr-end Oct. Old Castle: May-mid Sep, Wed-Sun & 4 Nov-17 Dec wknds only 11-6 or sunset if earlier. BH Mon 11-6. Closed Good Fri. (Last admission 1hr before closing). **Fee:** ✱ £5.20 (ch £2.60) Family £13 **Facilities:** ℗ 🗍 ᕆ (wheelchair hire, Braille/large print guidebook, audio tape) toilets for disabled shop garden centre ⊗ (ex guide & hearing dogs) ♨ ⛴

LYDD   MAP 05 TR02

RSPB Nature Reserve

Boulderwall Farm, Dungeness Rd TN29 9PN

⮕ *(off Lydd to Dungeness road, 1m SE of Lydd, follow tourist signs)*

☎ 01797 320588

e-mail: dungeness@rspb.org.uk

web: www.rspb.org.uk

This coastal reserve comprises 2106 acres of shingle beach and flooded pits. An excellent place to watch breeding terns, gulls and other water birds. Wheatears, great crested and little grebes also nest here, and outside the breeding season there are large flocks of teals, shovelers, and goldeneyes, goosanders, smews and both Slavonian and red-necked grebes.

Times: Open: Visitor Centre all year, daily 10-5 (10-4 Nov-Feb). Reserve open all year, daily 9am-9pm (or sunset if earlier). Closed 25-26 Dec. **Facilities:** ℗ 🗍 ᕆ (access by car to some hides) toilets for disabled shop ⊗ (ex guide dogs) ⛴

LYMPNE   MAP 05 TR13

Port Lympne Wild Animal Park, Mansion & Garden

CT21 4PD

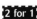

⮕ *(M20 junct 11, follow brown tourist signs)*

☎ 0870 750 4647

e-mail: info@totallywild.net

web: www.totallywild.net

A 400-acre wild animal park that houses hundreds of rare animals: Indian elephants, rhinos, wolves, bison, snow leopards, Siberian and Indian tigers, gorillas and monkeys. New features include a glass-fronted lion enclosure and an open-topped woodland home for the Colobus monkeys. The mansion designed by Sir Herbert Baker is surrounded by 15 acres of spectacular gardens. Inside, notable features include the restored Rex Whistler Tent Room, a Moroccan patio, and the hexagonal library where the Treaty of Paris was signed after World War I. Visit the Spencer Roberts mural room and the Martin Jordan animal mural room.

Times: Open all year, daily 10-6 (closes at dusk in summer). (Last admission 4.30 summer, 3 winter. Closed 25 Dec. **Fee:** ✱ £13.95 (ch 4-14

continued

& pen £10.95). Family ticket £42 (2ad+2ch) £49 (2ad+3ch).

Facilities: ℗ 💺 ❌ licensed ᕆ (very limited access for disabled, special route available) toilets for disabled shop garden centre ⊗ ⛴

MAIDSTONE   MAP 05 TQ75

Leeds Castle

ME17 1PL

⮕ *(7m E of Maidstone at junct 8 of M20/A20, clearly signed)*

☎ 01622 765400

e-mail: enquiries@leeds-castle.co.uk

web: www.leeds-castle.com

Set on two islands in the centre of a lake, Leeds Castle has been called the 'loveliest castle in the world', and was home to six medieval Queens of England, as well as being Henry VIII's Royal Palace. Among the treasures inside are many paintings, tapestries and furnishings. Attractions in the grounds include formal gardens, exotic aviary, dog collar museum, vineyard, woodland walks, toddlers play area, yew maze with secret underground grotto and daily falconry displays. Plenty of special events, contact for details.

Times: Open daily, Apr-Sep 10-7 (Castle 10.30-7) Last admission 5. Oct-Mar 10-5 (Castle 10.30-5) Last admission 3. Last entry to the castle is 30min after the last admission time. **Fee:** ✱ Fully incl ticket £13.50 (ch £8, concessions £11). **Facilities:** ℗ ❌ licensed 🗍 ᕆ (Braille information, induction loops & wheelchair, lift) toilets for disabled shop ⊗ (ex assist dogs) ⛴

Maidstone Museum & Bentlif Art Gallery

St Faith's St ME14 1LH

⮕ *(close to County Hall & Maidstone E train stn, opp Fremlin's Walk)*

☎ 01622 602838

e-mail: museum@maidstone.gov.uk

web: www.museum.maidstone.gov.uk

Set in an Elizabethan manor house which has been much extended over the years, this museum houses an outstanding collection of fine and applied arts, including watercolours, furniture, ceramics, and a collection of Japanese art and artefacts. The museum of the Queen's Own Royal West Kent Regiment is also housed here. Please apply for details of temporary exhibitions, workshops etc.

Times: Open all year, Mon-Sat 10-5.15, Sun & BH Mon 11-4. Closed 25-26 Dec & 1 Jan **Facilities:** ℗ (150 mtrs) 💺 🗍 ᕆ (Lifts) shop ⊗ (ex guide dogs) ⛴

Museum of Kent Life

Lock Ln, Sandling ME14 3AU

⮕ *(from M20 junct 6 onto A229 Maidstone road, follow signs for Aylesford)*

☎ 01622 763936

e-mail: enquiries@museum-kentlife.co.uk

web: www.museum-kentlife.co.uk

Kent's award-winning open air museum is home to an outstanding collection of historic buildings which house exhibitions on life in Kent over the last 100 years. An early 20th-century village hall and reconstruction of cottages from the 17th & 20th-centuries are more recent buildings to be viewed.

Times: ✱ Open Feb-Nov, daily 10-5, in winter open every wknd 10-3. **Facilities:** ℗ 💺 ❌ 🗍 ᕆ (wheelchairs available, ramps, transport available) toilets for disabled shop ⛴

Tyrwhitt Drake Museum of Carriages `FREE`
The Archbishop's Stables, Mill St ME15 6YE
➲ *(close to River Medway & Archbishops Palace, just off A229 in town centre)*
☎ 01622 602838
e-mail: museuminfo@maidstone.gov.uk
web: www.museum.maidstone.gov.uk

The museum is home to a unique collection of horse-drawn vehicles and transport curiosities. More than 60 vehicles are on display, from grand carriages and ornate sleighs to antique sedan chairs and Victorian cabs, there is even an original ice-cream cart.

Times: Open May-mid Sep, 10.30-4.30 **Facilities:** ℗ (50yds) 🍴 ♿ shop 10.30-4 ⊗ (ex guide dogs)

PENSHURST　　　　　　　　MAP 05 TQ54

Penshurst Place & Gardens
TN11 8DG
➲ *(M25 junct 5 take A21 Hastings road then exit at Hildenborough & follow signs)*
☎ 01892 870307
e-mail: enquiries@penshurstplace.com
web: www.penshurstplace.com

Built between 1340 and 1345, the original house is perfectly preserved. Enlarged by successive owners during the 15th, 16th and 17th centuries, the great variety of architectural styles creates a dramatic backdrop for the extensive collections of English, French and Italian furniture, tapestries and paintings. The chestnut-beamed Baron's Hall is the oldest and finest in the country, and the house is set in magnificent formal gardens. There is a toy museum, venture playground, woodland trail and 10 acres of walled formal gardens.

Times: Open: wknds from early Mar, daily from late Mar-late Oct. Grounds open 10.30-6. House open noon-4. **Fee:** ✱ House & Grounds £7.50 (ch 5-16 £5, concessions £7). Family £21. Grounds only £6 (ch 5-16 £5, concessions £5.50) Family £18. Party 20+. Garden season ticket £35. **Facilities:** ℗ 🍴 licensed ♿ (ramp into Barons Hall, Braille & large print guides) toilets for disabled shop ⊗ (ex guide dogs) 🔲

RAMSGATE　　　　　　　　MAP 05 TR36

Ramsgate Maritime Museum `2 for 1`
Clock House, Pier Yard, Royal Harbour CT11 8LS
➲ *(follow Harbour signs)*
☎ 01843 570622
e-mail: museum@ekmt.fsnet.co.uk
web: www.ekmt.fsnet.co.uk

The Maritime Museum Ramsgate is housed in the early 19th-century Clock House, and contains four galleries depicting various aspects of the maritime heritage of the East Kent area. A temporary gallery/conservation room features a 17th century naval gun. The 'Dunkirk Little Ship' motor yacht *Sundower* may also be visited by prior arrangement.

Times: Open Etr-Sep, Tue-Sun 10-5. Oct-Etr Thu-Sun 11-4.30.
Fee: ✱ Combined ticket for museum £1.50. (ch & pen 75p). Family £4.
Facilities: ℗ (charged) 🍴 ♿ (restricted) shop ⊗ (ex assist dogs)

RECULVER　　　　　　　　MAP 05 TR26

Reculver Towers & Roman Fort `FREE`
CT6 6SU
➲ *(3m E of Herne Bay)*
☎ 01227 740676
web: www.english-heritage.org.uk

An imposing 12th-century landmark: twin towers and the walls of a Roman fort.

Times: Open any reasonable time, external viewing only.
Facilities: ℗ ♿ (long slope from car park to fort) ⧓

RICHBOROUGH　　　　　　MAP 05 TR36

Richborough Castle
CT13 9JW
➲ *(1.5m N of Sandwich off A257)*
☎ 01304 612013
web: www.english-heritage.org.uk

Explore the site of the first Roman landing in Britain and visit the museum with its collection of artefacts uncovered on site. See the remains of the huge triumphal arch, once 25 metres high.

Times: Open Apr-Sep, daily 10-6. **Fee:** £3.90 (ch £2, concessions £2.90). Prices and opening times are subject to change in Spring 2007. Please check web site or call 0870 333 1181 for the most up to date prices and opening times when planning your visit. **Facilities:** ℗ ♿ shop ⧓

ROCHESTER　　　　　　　MAP 05 TQ76

Guildhall Museum `FREE`
High St ME1 1PY
➲ *(follow signs from A2 to Rochester city centre, museum is at N end of High St)*
☎ 01634 848717
e-mail: guildhall.museum@medway.gov.uk
web: www.medway.gov.uk

Housed in two adjacent buildings, one dating from 1687 and the other from 1909. The collections are arranged chronologically from Prehistory to the Victorian and Edwardian periods. They cover local history and archaeology, fine and decorative art. There is a gallery devoted to the prison hulks of the River Medway, and a new room

continued

detailing the links between Charles Dickens and the Medway Towns. The museum stages a regular programme of temporary exhibitions. Fashion & Identity from Dec 2006 to Sep 2007.

Times: ✱ Open all year, daily 10-4.30. (Last admission 4). Closed Xmas & New Year. **Facilities:** ℗ (250 yds) ♿ shop ⊗ (ex guide & hearing dogs)

Rochester Castle

ME1 1SX

⮑ *(M2 junct 1 & M25 junct 2, A2, by Rochester Bridge)*

☎ 01634 402276

web: www.english-heritage.org.uk

Built on the Roman City Wall, this Norman bishop's castle was a vital royal stronghold.

Times: Open all year, Apr-Sep, daily 10-6; Oct-Mar, daily 10-4. Closed 24-26 Dec & 1 Jan. **Fee:** £4 (ch & concessions £3). Family £11. Prices and opening times are subject to change in Spring 2007. Please check web site or call 0870 333 1181 for the most up to date prices and opening times when planning your visit. **Facilities:** shop ⊗

ROLVENDEN   **MAP 05 TQ83**

C M Booth Collection of Historic Vehicles

 2 for 1

Falstaff Antiques, 63 High St TN17 4LP

⮑ *(on A28, 3m from Tenterden)*

☎ 01580 241234

e-mail: info@morganmuseum.co.uk

web: www.morganmuseum.co.uk

Not just vehicles, but various other items of interest connected with transport. There is a unique collection of three-wheel Morgan cars, dating from 1913, and the only known Humber tri-car of 1904, as well as a 1929 Morris van, a 1936 Bampton caravan, motorcycles and bicycles. There is also a toy and model car display.

Times: Open all year, Mon-Sat 10-5.30. Closed 25-26 Dec. **Fee:** £2 (ch £1) **Facilities:** ℗ (roadside) shop 🍴

SEVENOAKS   **MAP 05 TQ55**

Knole

TN15 0RP

⮑ *(From town centre, off A225 Tonbridge road)*

☎ 01732 462100 & 450608 (info line)

e-mail: knole@nationaltrust.org.uk

web: www.nationaltrust.org.uk/knole

Knole's historic links with kings, queens and the nobility, as well as literary connections with Vita Sackville-West and Virginia Woolf, make this one of the most intriguing houses in England. Thirteen staterooms are laid out much the same as they were in the 17th century, to impress visitors with the wealth and standing of those who lived there. The house includes rare furniture, paintings by Gainsborough, Van

continued

If an attraction name appears in *italics*, details have not been confirmed for 2007

Dyck and Reynolds, as well as many 17th-century tapestries. Knole is set at the heart of the only remaining medieval deer park in Kent.

Knole

Times: House open end 17 Mar-28 Oct, Wed-Sun & BH Mon 12-4 (last entry 3.30). Garden Wed only 11-4, last entry 3.30 £2; ch £1 **Fee:** ✱ £8.50 (ch £4.25). Family ticket £21.25. Parking £2.50 per car. Groups 15+ £6.50. **Facilities:** ℗ (charged) 💺 ♿ (audio loop, Braille guide, virtual tour) toilets for disabled shop ⊗ (ex assist dogs & in park) 🐾 🍴

SISSINGHURST   **MAP 05 TQ73**

Sissinghurst Castle Garden

TN17 2AB

⮑ *(1m E of Sissinghurst village on A262)*

☎ 01580 710700

e-mail: sissinghurst@nationaltrust.org.uk

web: www.nationaltrust.org.uk

Created in the ruins of a large Elizabethan house and set in unspoilt countryside, Sissinghurst Castle Garden is one of the most celebrated gardens made by Vita Sackville-West and her husband Sir Harold Nicolson. Phone for details of special events and info on the bus link.

Times: Open: Gardens mid Mar-end Oct, Fri-Tue 11-5.30. (Peace & Tranquillity after 3.30) **Fee:** ✱ £7.50 (ch £3.50) Family £18.50. **Facilities:** ℗ (charged) 🍽 licensed ♿ (admission restricted to 4 wheelchairs at any one time) shop ⊗ (ex guide dogs) 🐾 🍴

SMALLHYTHE   **MAP 05 TQ83**

Smallhythe Place

TN30 7NG

⮑ *(2m S of Tenterden, on E side of the Rye Road on B2082)*

☎ 01580 762334

e-mail: smallhytheplace@nationaltrust.org.uk

web: www.nationaltrust.org.uk

Once a Tudor harbour master's house, this half-timbered, 16th-century building was Dame Ellen Terry's last home, and is now a museum of Ellen Terry memorabilia. The Barn Theatre houses a display and the cottage garden contains roses, an orchard and spring garden.

Times: Open 3-18 Mar, Sat & Sun only; 24 Mar-28 Oct, Sat-Wed 11-5 (last admission 4.30) **Fee:** ✱ £4.50 (ch £2.25). Family £11 **Facilities:** ℗ 💺 📖 ♿ (album of descriptions & photos of upstairs, Braille guide) ⊗ (ex guide dogs) 🐾

England

STROOD **MAP 05 TQ76**

Diggerland

Medway Valley Leisure Park, Roman Way ME2 2NU

➲ *(M2 junct 2, follow A228 towards Rochester. At rdbt turn right. Diggerland on right)*

☎ 08700 344437

e-mail: mail@diggerland.com

web: www.diggerland.com

An adventure park with a difference. Experience the thrills of driving real earth moving equipment. Choose from various types of diggers and dumpers ranging from 1 ton to 8.5 tons. Complete the Dumper Truck Challenge or dig for buried treasure supervised by an instructor. New rides include JCB Robots, the Supertrack, Landrover Safari, Spin Dizzy and the Diggerland Tractors.

Times: ✳ Open all year, 10-5, wknds, BHs & school hols only
Facilities: ♥ ♨ ♿ toilets for disabled shop ⊗ (ex guide dogs) ⬛

SWINGFIELD MINNIS **MAP 05 TR24**

The Butterfly Centre

MacFarlanes Garden Centre CT15 7HX

➲ *(on A260 by junction with Elham-Lydden road)*

☎ 01303 844244

e-mail: macfarlanes@gardensandtress.fsnet.co.uk

A tropical greenhouse garden with scores of colourful free-flying butterflies from all over the world among exotic plants such as bougainvillea, oleander and banana. The temperate section houses British butterflies, with many favourite species and some rarer varieties.

Times: Open Apr-1 Oct, daily 10-5. Closed Etr Sun. **Facilities:** ♥ ♨
🍴 ⏹ ♿ toilets for disabled shop garden centre ⊗ (ex guide dogs) ⬛

TENTERDEN **MAP 05 TQ83**

Kent & East Sussex Railway

Tenterden Town Station, Station Rd TN30 6HE

➲ *(A28 turn into Station Rd beside The Vine Public House, station 200yds on right)*

☎ 087 060 060 74

e-mail: enquiries@kesr.org.uk

web: www.kesr.org.uk

Less than an hour from the M25 lies an area of hills, woods and marshland. The railway line joins together the Weald, Tenterden Town and Bodiam Castle, brushing past the Sussex village of Northiam on the way. The railway has featured many times in both films and television.

Times: ✳ Open Etr-Sep wkdays & wknds. Other times of the year wknds & school hols. See web site for details. Five trains per day **Fee:** ✳ £10.50 (ch £5.50, pen £9.50) Family £27 **Facilities:** ♥ ♨ 🍴 licensed ♿ (Converted coach for w/chairs, induction loop) toilets for disabled shop ⬛

TUNBRIDGE WELLS (ROYAL) **MAP 05 TQ53**

Tunbridge Wells Museum and Art Gallery

FREE

Civic Centre, Mount Pleasant TN1 1JN

➲ *(adjacent to Town Hall, off A264)*

☎ 01892 554171 & 526121

e-mail: museum@tunbridgewells.gov.uk

web: www.tunbridgewellsmuseum.org

This combined museum and art gallery tells the story of the borough of Tunbridge Wells. There are collections of costume, art, dolls and toys along with natural and local history from dinosaur bones to the original Pantiles. There is also a large collection of Tunbridge ware, the intricate wooden souvenirs made for visitors to the Wells. The art gallery features a changing programme of contemporary and historic art, touring exhibitions, and local art and craft.

Times: Open all year, daily 9.30-5. Sun 10-4. Closed BHs & Etr Sat.
Facilities: ℗ (200 yds) ⏹ ♿ (parking adjacent to building) shop ⊗ (ex guide dogs)

UPNOR **MAP 05 TQ77**

Upnor Castle

2 for 1

ME2 4XG

➲ *(on unclass road off A228)*

☎ 01634 718742 & 338110

web: www.english-heritage.org.uk

16th-century gun fort built to protect Elizabeth I's warships. It saw action in 1667, when the Dutch navy sailed up the Medway to attack the dockyard at Chatham.

Times: Open Apr-Sep, daily 10-6; Oct, daily 10-4. **Fee:** £4 (ch & concessions £3). Family ticket £11. Prices and opening times are subject to change in Spring 2007. Please check web site or call 0870 333 1181 for the most up to date prices and opening times when planning your visit.
Facilities: ℗ ♿ ⚙

WESTERHAM **MAP 05 TQ45**

Quebec House

TN16 1TD

➲ *(at E end of village on N side of A25 facing junct with B2026 Edenbridge Road)*

☎ 01732 868381

e-mail: chartwell@nationaltrust.org.uk

web: www.nationaltrust.org.uk

A house of architectural and historical interest situated near the village green in Westerham. For some years the childhood home of General James Wolfe, it contains family and military memorabilia and an exhibition on the Battle of Quebec.

Times: Open Apr-29 Oct, Wed-Sun (& BH) 1-4.30, last entry 4
Fee: ✳ £3.50 (ch £1.50). Family ticket £8.50. Booked groups £3. Adult joint ticket with Emmetts Garden £7 **Facilities:** ℗ (150m) (Pay & Display) ⏹ ♿ (tactile items) shop ⊗ (ex guide dogs) 🐾

Squerryes Court

TN16 1SJ

⮑ *(0.5m W of town centre, signed off A25)*

☎ 01959 562345 & 563118

e-mail: squerryes.court@squerryes.co.uk

web: www.squerryes.co.uk

This beautiful manor house, built in 1681 by Sir Nicholas Crisp, has been the home of the Wardes since 1731. It contains a fine collection of pictures, furniture, porcelain and tapestries. The lovely garden was landscaped in the 18th century and has a lake, restored formal garden, and woodland walks.

Times: Open Apr-Sep, Wed, Thu, Sun & BH Mon. Garden open 11.30-5, House 1-5 (last entry 4.30) **Fee:** ✱ House & grounds £6 (ch 16 £3 & pen £5.50). Family ticket £13.50. Grounds £4 (ch 16 £2 & pen £3.50)

Facilities: ♿ 🍴 📖 ♿ (telephone in advance, part of grounds accessible) shop ⊗ (ex on leads in grounds)

WEST MALLING
MAP 05 TQ65

St Leonard's Tower

FREE

ME19 6PE

⮑ *(on unclass road W of A228)*

☎ 01732 870872

web: www.english-heritage.org.uk

Early example of a Norman tower keep, built c.1080 by Gundulf, Bishop of Rochester. The tower stands almost to its original height and takes its name from a chapel dedicated to St Leonard that once stood nearby.

Times: Open any reasonable time for exterior viewing. Contact West Malling Parish Council for interior viewing - 01732 870872. **Facilities:** ♿ ♿

YALDING
MAP 05 TQ75

Garden Organic Yalding

Benover Rd ME18 6EX

⮑ *(on B2162, 0.5m S of Yalding.)*

☎ 01622 814650

e-mail: enquiry@gardenorganic.org.uk

web: www.gardenorganic.org.uk

Eighteen gardens tell the history of gardening in an imaginatively landscaped setting. Travel through representations of ancient woodlands, medieval physic, knot and paradise gardens and a 19th-century artisan's plot, borders inspired by Gertrude Jekyll's ideas before reaching a 1950s 'Dig for Victory' allotment. The remainder of the garden is devoted to the vision of the 'organic' future of horticulture, growing flowers, fruit and vegetables without added chemicals. The garden was founded and is still owned by, Garden Organic, the national charity for organic growing, almost fifty years ago.

Times: Open Apr-Oct Wed-Sun (inc BH) 10-5 **Fee:** ✱ £4 (ch £1, concessions £3.50) **Facilities:** ♿ 🍴 ♿ shop garden centre ⊗ (ex guide dogs)

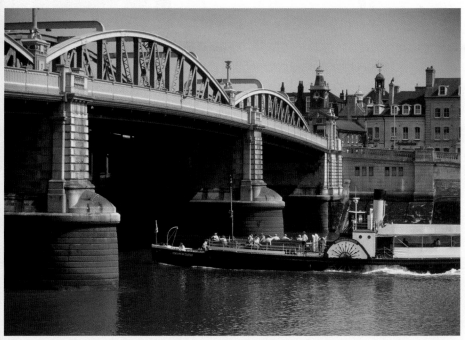

Pleasure craft on the River Medway, beneath the bridge linking Stroud with Rochester

Lancashire

Blackpool

For seekers of 'sun and fun', Blackpool is perfect as a popular
coastal resort with lively piers and sea-side entertainments.
Inland from the lights of Blackpool are the Pennines, a series
of hills stretching from the Peak District National Park to
Scotland and known as 'the backbone of England'. Some of
the most inspiring and exhilarating landscapes in Britain can
be found here, and the surrounding area offers great
opportunities for bird-watching, walking and climbing.

BLACKPOOL
MAP 07 SD33

Blackpool Zoo & Dinosaur Safari
East Park Dr FY3 8PP

➲ (M55 junct 4, follow brown tourist signs)

☎ 01253 830830

e-mail: info@blackpoolzoo.org.uk

web: www.blackpoolzoo.org.uk

This modern zoo, built in 1972, houses over 1500 animals within its 32 acres of landscaped gardens. There is a miniature railway, lots of close encounters and animals in action, a children's play area, animal feeding times and keeper talks throughout the day. The Dinosaur Safari takes you on a walking trail with 32 lifesize dinosaurs in Jurassic gardens. Special events include plays and music.

Times: Open all year daily, summer 10-6; winter 10-dusk. Jul-Aug, Wed 10-9. Closed 25 Dec. **Fee:** ✱ £10 (ch £7, pen £8.50, disabled & carers £5, concessions for groups). Family (2 ad+2 ch) £30, (2 ad+3 ch) £36. Pen £8.50, disabled & carers £5, concessions for groups **Facilities:** ♿ 🖳 🍴 licensed 🔗 ♿ (wheelchair loan, talking & signing tours) toilets for disabled shop ⊗ 📼

CHARNOCK RICHARD
MAP 07 SD51

Camelot Theme Park

PR7 5LP

➲ (from M6 junct 27/28, or M61 junct 8 follow brown tourist signs)

☎ 01257 452100

e-mail: kingarthur@camelotthemepark.co.uk

web: www.camelotthemepark.co.uk

Join Merlin, King Arthur and the Knights of the Round Table at the magical kingdom of Camelot. Explore five magic lands filled with thrilling rides, spectacular shows, and many more attractions. From white-knuckle thrills on The Whirlwind spinning rollercoaster, to wet-knuckle thrills on Pendragon's Plunge, there's something for everyone.

Times: Open 31 Mar-28 Oct. Telephone for further details. **Fee:** ✱ £16.50 (ch under 1mtr, free). Family ticket £56. **Facilities:** ♿ 🖳 🔗 ♿ (disabled car parking) toilets for disabled shop ⊗ (ex assist dogs) 📼

CHORLEY
MAP 07 SD51

Astley Hall Museum & Art Gallery   FREE
Astley Park PR7 1NP

➲ (M61 junct 8, signed Botany Bay. Follow brown signs)

☎ 01257 515555

e-mail: astley.hall@chorley.gov.uk

web: www.astleyhall.co.uk

A charming Tudor/Stuart building set in beautiful parkland, this lovely Hall retains a comfortable 'lived-in' atmosphere. There are pictures and pottery to see, as well as fine furniture and rare plasterwork ceilings. Special events throughout the year.

Times: Open Apr (or Etr)-Oct, Sat-Sun & BH Mon 12-5; By appointment only during the week **Facilities:** ♿ 🔗 ♿ (video of upper floors, print/Braille guide, CD audio guide) shop ⊗ (ex guide dogs) 📼

CLITHEROE
MAP 07 SD74

Clitheroe Castle Museum
Castle House, Castle Gate, Castle St BB7 1BA

➲ (follow Clitheroe signs from A59 Preston-Skipton by-pass. Museum located in castle grounds near town centre)

☎ 01200 424635

e-mail: museum@ribblevalley.gov.uk

web: www.ribblevalley.gov.uk/castlemuseum

The museum has a good collection of carboniferous fossils, and items of local interest. Displays include local history and the industrial archaeology of the Ribble Valley, while special features include the restored Hacking ferry boat believed to be the inspiration for 'Buckleberry Ferry' featured in JRR Tolkien's *Fellowship of the Ring*, printer's and clogger's shops and Edwardian kitchen. The area is renowned for its early 17th-century witches, and the museum has a small display on witchcraft.

Times: Open late Feb-Etr, Mon-Sat 11.15-4.30, Sun 1-4.30; Etr-Oct, daily inc BH; Nov, Dec & Feb, wknds & school half terms. Closed Jan **Facilities:** ℗ (500yds) (disabled only parking at establishment) 🖳 ♿ shop ⊗ (ex guide dogs)

LANCASTER
MAP 07 SD46

City Museum (also 15 Castle Hill)
Market Sq LA1 1HT

➲ (in city centre just off A6)

☎ 01524 64637

e-mail: paul.thompson@mus.lancscc.gov.uk

web: www.lancsmuseums.gov.uk

The fine Georgian town hall is the setting for the museum, which explores the history and archaeology of the city from prehistoric and Roman times onwards. Also housed here is the museum of the King's Own Royal Lancaster Regiment. The Cottage Museum, furnished in the style of an artisan's house of around 1820, faces Lancaster Castle.

Times: Open all year, Mon-Sat, 10-5. Closed 25 Dec-1 Jan. 15 Castle Hill, Apr-Sep, daily 2-5. **Fee:** ✱ City Museum free. 15 Castle Hill £1 (accompanied ch free, concessions 75p). **Facilities:** ℗ (5 mins walk) ♿ (ramp to entrance/ground floor, 2 stairlifts) shop ⊗ (ex guide dogs)

England

Lancaster Maritime Museum

St George's Quay LA1 1RB

➲ (close to M6, junct 33 & 34. From A6 follow signs to town centre)

☎ 01524 382264

e-mail: paul.thompson@mus.lancscc.gov.uk

web: www.lancsmuseums.gov.uk

Graceful Ionic columns adorn the front of the Custom House, built in 1764. Inside, the histories of the 18th-century transatlantic maritime trade of Lancaster, the Lancaster Canal and the fishing industry of Morecambe Bay are well illustrated.

Times: Open all year, daily, Etr-Oct 11-5; Nov-Etr 12.30-4. **Fee:** ✱ £3 (concessions £2). Free to accompanied children and residents of Lancaster district **Facilities:** ❷ ● 🍴 ⚅ (ramped access, lift to all floors, ground floor entry) toilets for disabled shop ❽ (ex guide dogs)

Shire Hall

Lancaster Castle, Castle Pde LA1 1YJ

➲ (follow brown tourist signs from M6 junct 33/34)

☎ 01524 64998

e-mail: christine.goodier@mus.lancscc.gov.uk

web: www.lancastercastle.com

Founded on the site of three Roman forts, Lancaster Castle dominates Castle Hill, above the River Lune. The Norman keep was built in about 1170 and King John added a curtain wall and Hadrian's Tower. The Shire Hall, noted for its Gothic revival design, contains a splendid display of heraldry. The Crown Court was notorious as having handed out the greatest number of death sentences of any court in the land. Various events through the year.

Times: Open daily 10.30 (1st tour)-4 (last tour). Court sittings permitting - it is advisable to telephone before visiting. Closed Xmas & New Year. **Fee:** ✱ £5 (concessions £4). Family ticket £14. **Facilities:** ❷ ⚅ shop ❽ (ex guide dogs) ◀

Leighton Hall

LA5 9ST

➲ (M6 junct 35 onto A6 & follow signs)

☎ 01524 734474

e-mail: info@leightonhall.co.uk

web: www.leightonhall.co.uk

Early Gillow furniture is displayed among other treasures in the fine interior of this neo-Gothic mansion. Outside, a large collection of birds of prey can be seen, and flying displays are given each afternoon. There are also fine gardens, a maze and a woodland walk. A programme of events takes place throughout the year, including craft fairs.

Times: Open May-Sep, Tue-Fri & BH Sun/Mon; Aug, Tue-Fri, Sun & BH Mon 12.30-5. Groups all year by arrangement **Fee:** ✱ £5.50 (ch 5-12 £4, pen & concessions £5). Family ticket £17. **Facilities:** ❷ ● 🍴 ⚅ shop garden centre ❽ (ex guide dogs & in park)

British Commercial Vehicle Museum

King St PR25 2LE

➲ (0.75m from M6 junct 28 in town centre)

☎ 01772 451011

e-mail: enquiries@bcvm.co.uk

web: www.commercialvehiclemuseum.co.uk

A unique line-up of historic commercial vehicles and buses spanning a century of truck and bus building. There are more than 50 exhibits on permanent display.

Times: Open Apr-Sep, Sun, Tue-Thu & BH Mon (Oct open Sun only). **Fee:** £4 (ch & pen £2). Family ticket (2ad+3ch) £10. **Facilities:** ❷ ● ⚅ (ramps to decked viewing area) toilets for disabled shop ❽ (ex guide dogs)

WWT Martin Mere

L40 0TA

➲ (signed from M61, M58 & M6, 6m from Ormskirk, off A59)

☎ 01704 895181

e-mail: info@martinmere.co.uk

web: www.martinmere.co.uk

One of Britain's most important wetland sites, where you can get really close to a variety of ducks, geese and swans from all over the world as well as two flocks of flamingos. Thousands of wildfowl, including pink-footed geese, Bewick's and Whooper swans, winter here. Other features include a children's adventure playground, exhibition gallery, craft area and an educational centre. The Annual North West Bird Fair takes place during November and wild swans by floodlight from 1st November to 31st January.

Times: Open all year, daily 9.30-5.30 (5 in winter). Closed 25 Dec. **Fee:** ✱ £6 (ch £3.80, concessions £4.80). Family ticket £15.55. **Facilities:** ❷ ● ⚅ (wheelchair loan, Braille trail, heated hide, audio tours) toilets for disabled shop ❽ (ex guide dogs) ◀

Gawthorpe Hall

BB12 8UA

➲ (on E outskirts of Padiham, 0.75m on A671)

☎ 01282 771004

e-mail: gawthorpehall@nationaltrust.org.uk

web: www.nationaltrust.org.uk

An early 17th-century manor house, built around Britain's most southerly pele tower, restored in 1850. A collection of portraits from the National Portrait Gallery and the Kay Shuttleworth Collections of costume, embroidery and lace are on show in the expanded exhibition areas.

Times: Open Apr-29 Oct, Garden: daily 10-6. Hall: Tue-Thu, Sat & Sun 1-5. Also open BH Mon & Good Fri. (Last admission 4.30). **Fee:** ✱ House: £4 (ch & concessions £3). Children free if accompanied by adult. Garden free. **Facilities:** ❷ ● ⚅ (Braille & large print guide, photo album) toilets for disabled ❽ (ex in grounds) ♨

PRESTON   MAP 07 SD52

Harris Museum & Art Gallery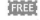

Market Square PR1 2PP

➲ *(M6 junct 31, follow signs for city centre, park at bus stn car park)*

☎ 01772 258248

e-mail: harris.museum@preston.gov.uk

web: www.harrismuseum.org.uk

An impressive grade I listed Greek Revival building containing extensive collections of fine and decorative art including a gallery of Clothes and Fashion. The Story of Preston covers the city's history and the lively exhibition programmes of contemporary art and social history are accompanied by events and activities throughout the year.

Times: Open all year, Mon & Wed-Sat 10-5, Tues 11-5, Sun 11-4.
Facilities: Ⓟ (5 mins walk) (blue badge disabled parking only) 🖥 🗊 ♿ (wheelchair available, chair lift to mezzanine galleries) toilets for disabled shop ⊗ (ex guide & assist dogs) ◀

The National Football Museum

Sir Tom Finney Way, Deepdale PR1 6RY

➲ *(2m from M6 juncts 31, 31A or 32. Follow brown tourist signs)*

☎ 01772 908442

e-mail: enquiries@nationalfootballmuseum.com

web: www.nationalfootballmuseum.com

What location could be more fitting for a National Football Museum than Deepdale Stadium, the home of Preston North End, first winners of the professional football league in 1888-9? This fascinating trip through football past and present includes the FIFA Museum Collection, a fine display of memorabilia and artefacts; interactive displays that allow visitors to commentate on matches, and take virtual trips to every League ground in the country. There's also an art gallery dedicated to the Beautiful Game.

Times: Open all year Tue-Sat 10-5, Sun 11-5. Closed Mon ex BHs and school hols. Contact for opening times on match days. **Facilities:** Ⓟ 🖥 🗊 ♿ (lifts, multi-sensory exhibitions) toilets for disabled shop ⊗ (ex guide dogs) ◀

ROSSENDALE   MAP 07 SD72

Whitaker Park & Rossendale Museum

Whitaker Park, Haslingden Rd, Rawtenstall BB4 6RE

➲ *(off A681, 0.25m W of Rawtenstall centre)*

☎ 01706 244682

e-mail: rossendalemuseum@btconnect.com

Former mill owner's house, built in 1840 and set in the delightful Whitaker Park. Displays include fine and decorative arts, a Victorian drawing room, natural history, costume, local and social history and regular temporary exhibitions.

Times: Open Apr-Oct, Tue-Thu, Sat-Sun & BHs, 1-4.30; Nov-Mar, 1-4.
Facilities: Ⓟ ♿ (large print, audio guides, induction loop, lift) toilets for disabled shop ⊗ (ex guide dogs)

RUFFORD   MAP 07 SD41

Rufford Old Hall

L40 1SG

➲ *(M6 junct 27 & follow signs to Rufford. Hall on E side of A59)*

☎ 01704 821254

e-mail: ruffordoldhall@nationaltrust.org.uk

web: www.nationaltrust.org.uk

There is a story that William Shakespeare performed here for the owner Sir Thomas Hesketh in the magnificent Great Hall. Built in 1530, Rufford remained in the Hesketh family for over 400 years. The Carolean Wing, altered in 1821, features fine collections of 16th and 17th century oak furniture, arms, armour and tapestries.

Times: Open mid Mar-Oct, Sat-Wed. Hall 1-5 (last admission 4.30). Garden, restaurant & shop 11-5. Nov-Dec, Garden, restaurant & shop, Wed-Sun, 12-4. **Fee:** ✱ House and garden: £4.90 (ch £2.50). Family ticket £12. Groups £3.10 each (ch £1.30). Garden only £2.80 (ch £1.30). No groups Sun and BH Mon. **Facilities:** Ⓟ 🍴 licensed ♿ (Braille guide, wheelchairs, large print guide) toilets for disabled shop ⊗ (ex assist dogs) 🐾

SAMLESBURY   MAP 07 SD53

Samlesbury Hall

Preston New Rd PR5 0UP

➲ *(M6 junct 31/A677 for 3m, as indicated by brown tourist signs)*

☎ 01254 812010 & 812229

e-mail: enquiries@samlesburyhall.co.uk

web: www.samlesburyhall.co.uk

A well restored half-timbered manor house, built during the 14th and 15th centuries, and set in 5 acres of beautiful grounds. Sales of antiques and collector's items, craft shows and temporary exhibitions are held all year round. Live theatre productions and seasonal events throughout the year.

Times: Open all year, Sun-Fri 11-4.30. Closed 25-26 Dec & 1 Jan and Sat for weddings **Fee:** £3 (ch 4-16 £1). **Facilities:** Ⓟ 🖥 🍴 licensed 🗊 ♿ toilets for disabled shop garden centre ⊗ (ex guide dogs)

SILVERDALE
MAP 07 SD47

RSPB Leighton Moss Nature Reserve
 2 for 1

Myers Farm LA5 0SW

➲ *(M6 junct 35, west on A501(M) for 0.5m. Turn right and head N on A6. Follow brown tourist signs)*

☎ 01524 701601
e-mail: leighton.moss@rspb.org.uk
web: www.rspb.org.uk

The largest remaining reedbed in north-west England, this reserve covers 321 acres, and is home to a large concentration of bitterns, together with bearded tits, reed, sedge and grasshopper warblers, shovelers, pochards, tufted ducks and marsh harriers. Black terns and ospreys regularly pass through in spring and greenshanks and various sandpipers in the autumn. Wintering wildfowl include large flocks of mallards, teals, wigeons, and shovelers.

Times: Reserve: open daily 9-dusk . Visitor Centre daily 9.30-5. Feb-Oct 9.30-4.30 Nov-Jan. Closed 25 Dec. **Fee:** £4.50 (ch £1, concessions £3) Family £9. RSPB members Free **Facilities:** ❷ ♨ ❖ ▥ ♿ (stairlift available to tea room) toilets for disabled shop ❽ (ex guide dogs) ◧

Waterslack Farm Shop, Café & Garden Centre
FREE

Ford Ln LA5 0UH

➲ *(M6 junct 35, follow A6 towards Milnthorpe. Turn off A6 at Nineteen Acre Lane & follow signs for Leighton Moss Nature Reserve. Pass Reserve, turn right at T-junct & follow signs)*

☎ 01524 701255
e-mail: info@waterslack.com
web: www.waterslack.com

With a beautiful plant section, unique Vesage arts and crafts collection, freshly made foods and stunning surroundings, Waterslack offers everything for your perfect day out. Come and see the pygmy goats and pigs, geese, chickens, ducks and many other animals or enjoy a walk through one of the nature reserves around Waterslack.

Times: Open Mar-Oct, Mon-Sat 9-6 & Sun 10-5; Nov-Feb, Mon-Sat 9-5 **Facilities:** ❷ ♨ ▥ ♿ toilets for disabled shop garden centre ◧

TURTON BOTTOMS
MAP 07 SD71

Turton Tower

BL7 0HG

➲ *(on B6391, off A666 or A676)*

☎ 01204 852203
e-mail: turton.tower@mus.lanscc.gov.uk

A historic house incorporating a 15th-century tower house and Elizabethan half-timbered buildings, and displaying a major collection of carved wood furniture. During the 19th century, the house became associated with the Gothic revival and later typified the idealism of the Arts and Crafts movement. The gardens are being restored in late-Victorian style.

Times: Open May-Sep, Mon-Thu 11-5, wknds 1-5; Mar-Oct, Mon-Wed 1-5, wknds 1-4; Apr Sat-Wed 1-5; Nov & Feb, Sun 1-4. Other times by prior arrangement. **Facilities:** ❷ ♨ ♿ toilets for disabled shop ❽ (ex in grounds) ◧

WHALLEY
MAP 07 SD73

Whalley Abbey

BB7 9SS

➲ *(off A59 4m S of Clitheroe)*

☎ 01254 828400
e-mail: office@whalleyabbey.org
web: www.whalleyabbey.co.uk

The ruins of a 14th-century Cistercian abbey, set in the delightful gardens of the Blackburn Diocesan Retreat and Conference House, a 17th-century manor house with gardens reaching down to the River Calder. The remains include two gateways, a chapter house and the abbot's lodgings and kitchen.

Times: Open 4 Jan daily, 10-5. Closed Xmas & New Year. **Fee:** £2 (ch 50p, pen £1.25) Family (2ad+ch) £4.50 **Facilities:** ❷ ♨ ▥ ♿ (chair lifts, ramps) toilets for disabled shop ❽ (ex guide dogs)

Leicestershire

Ashby-de-la-Zouche

A surprisingly diverse county, with many large country estates and famous stately homes amid the traditionally rural countryside of its eastern side, Leicestershire also has some of the most beautiful stretches of waterways in the country. There are many interesting places to visit, including the impressive ruins of a late-medieval castle at Ashby-de-la-Zouche, and the notable towns of Melton Mowbray, home of the pork pie, and Market Bosworth, where Richard III was killed at the Battle of Bosworth Field in 1485.

England

ASHBY-DE-LA-ZOUCH　　　MAP 08 SK31

Ashby-de-la-Zouch Castle
South St LE65 1BR
☎ 01530 413343
web: www.english-heritage.org.uk

Impressive ruins of a late medieval castle. The magnificent 24 metre Hastings Tower offers panoramic views of the surrounding countryside. Ashby was the setting for the famous jousting scene in Sir Walter Scott's classic romance *Ivanhoe*.

Times: Open Apr-Jun & Sep-Oct, Thu-Mon 10-5; Jul-Aug, daily 10-6; Nov-Mar, Thu-Mon 10-4. Closed 24-26 Dec & 1 Jan. **Fee:** £3.40 (ch £1.70, concessions £2.60, Family £8.50). Prices and opening times are subject to change in Spring 2007. Please check web site or call 0870 333 1181 for the most up to date prices and opening times when planning your visit. **Facilities:** ❂ & shop ♯

BELVOIR　　　MAP 08 SK83

Belvoir Castle　　　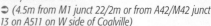2 for 1
NG32 1PD
➲ *(between A52 & A607, follow the brown heritage signs from A1, A52, A607 & A46)*
☎ 01476 871002
e-mail: info@belvoircastle.com
web: www.belvoircastle.com

Although Belvoir Castle has been the home of the Dukes of Rutland for many centuries, the turrets, battlements, towers and pinnacles of the house are a 19th-century fantasy. Amongst the many treasures to be seen inside are paintings by Murillo, Holbein and other famous artists. Also here is the museum of the Queens Royal Lancers. Lovingly restored gardens are also open to visitors. Special events planned every weekend throughout the season, phone for details.

Times: Open Apr-Sep, closed Mon & Fri **Fee:** ✱ £10 (ch £5, pen £9). **Facilities:** ❂ 💄 🍴 licensed 🎫 & (permitted to be driven/drive right up to castle entrance) toilets for disabled shop ⊗ (ex guide dogs) 🍴

Are there any excellent Days Out that we have missed? Use the Readers' Report form at the back of the book to tell us about them.

COALVILLE　　　MAP 08 SK41

Snibston Discovery Park　　　2 for 1
Ashby Rd LE67 3LN
➲ *(4.5m from M1 junct 22/2m or from A42/M42 junct 13 on A511 on W side of Coalville)*
☎ 01530 278444
e-mail: snibston@leics.gov.uk
web: www.snibston.com

Snibston has recently had a major makeover, making it an even more up-to-date science centre. In the Extra Ordinary hands-on gallery visitors can see how technology has affected everyday life, by lifting up a Mini Cooper. The Fashion Gallery has a wide selection of historic and modern costumes, while the underground life of a miner can be explored in the colliery tour. There are also rides on a diesel locomotive, or fun in the adventure play area.

Times: Open daily, Apr-Oct 10-5; Nov-Mar 10-3. School hols & wknds 10-5. Closed 2 weeks in Jan for maintainence. **Fee:** £6 (ch £4, concessions £4.20). Family ticket £18 **Facilities:** ❂ 💄 & (Braille labels, touch tables, parking available) toilets for disabled shop ⊗ (ex guide dogs) 🍴

DONINGTON-LE-HEATH　　　MAP 05 SK41

Donington-le-Heath Manor House　　　FREE
Manor Rd LE67 2FW
➲ *(S of Coalville)*
☎ 01530 831259
e-mail: museum@leics.gov.uk
web: www.leics.gov.uk/museums

This is a rare example of a medieval manor house, tracing its history back to about 1280. It has now been restored as a period house, with fine oak furnishings. The surrounding grounds include period gardens, and the adjoining stone barn houses a restaurant.

Times: Open Mar-Nov 11-4 daily, Dec-Feb Sat-Sun 11-4 **Facilities:** ❂ 💄 🍴 licensed & toilets for disabled shop ⊗ (ex guide dogs)

LEICESTER   MAP 04 SK50

Abbey Pumping Station

Corporation Rd, Abbey Ln LE4 5PX

⊃ *(off A6, 1m N from city centre)*

☎ 0116 299 5111

web: www.leicester.gov.uk/museums

Built as a sewage pumping station in 1891, this fascinating museum features some of the largest steam beam engines in the country, and an exhibition on the history and technology of toilets, water and hygiene. There are also a steam shovel and a passenger-carrying narrow gauge railway.

Times: ✱ Open Apr-Sep, Mon-Sat 10-5, Sun 1-5; Oct-Mar, Mon-Sat 10-4, Sun 1-4. Closed 24-26 & 31 Dec-1 Jan. **Facilities:** Ⓟ 🗐 ♿ (loan of wheelchairs, wheelchair lift) toilets for disabled shop ⊗ (ex guide dogs) ◀

Belgrave Hall & Gardens   FREE

Church Rd, off Thurcaston Rd, Belgrave LE4 5PE

⊃ *(off Belgrave/Loughborough road, 1m from city centre)*

☎ 0116 266 6590

web: www.leicester.gov.uk/museums

A delightful three-storey Queen Anne house dating from 1709 with beautiful period and botanic gardens. Authentic room settings contrast Georgian elegance with Victorian cosiness and include the kitchen, drawing room, music room and nursery.

Times: ✱ Open all year, Apr-Sep, Mon-Sat 10-5, Sun 1-5; Oct-Mar, Mon-Sat 10-4, Sun 1-4. Closed 24-26 Dec & 31 Dec-1 Jan. **Facilities:** Ⓟ 🗐 ♿ (loan of wheelchair) toilets for disabled shop ⊗ (ex guide dogs)

The Guildhall

Guildhall Ln LE1 5FQ

⊃ *(next to Leicester Cathedral)*

☎ 0116 253 2569

web: www.leicester.gov.uk/museums

A preserved medieval building dating back to the 14th century, the Guildhall is the city's oldest building still in use. Over the centuries it has served as the Hall of the Guild of Corpus Christi, the Civic Centre and Town Hall, a judicial centre for court sessions and home to Leicester's first police force. The Guildhall now houses one of the oldest libraries in the country, as well as hosting events, activities and performances.

Times: ✱ Open all year: Apr-Sep, Mon-Sat 10-5, Sun 1-5; Oct-Mar, Mon-Sat 10-4, Sun 1-4. Closed 24-26 Dec & 1 Jan. **Facilities:** Ⓟ (100yds) 🖳 🗐 ♿ (wheelchair loan, induction loop, voice minicom) toilets for disabled shop ⊗ (ex guide dogs) ◀

Jewry Wall Museum & Site

St Nicholas Circle LE1 4LB

⊃ *(opposite The Holiday Inn)*

☎ 0116 225 4971

web: www.leicester.gov.uk/museums

Behind the massive fragment of the Roman Jewry wall and a Roman Baths site of the 2nd century AD is the Museum of Leicestershire Archaeology, which covers finds from the earliest times to the Middle Ages.

Times: ✱ Open Apr-Sep, Mon-Sat 10-5, Sun 1-5; Oct-Mar, Mon-Sat 10-4, Sun 1-4. Closed 24-26 & 31 Dec & 1 Jan. **Facilities:** Ⓟ (300yds) (limited on-street parking) 🗐 ♿ toilets for disabled shop ⊗ (ex guide dogs)

Leicestershire Museum & Art Gallery

53 New Walk LE1 7EA

⊃ *(situated on New Walk. Access by car from A6 onto Waterloo Way at Railway Stn. Right into Regent Rd, right onto West St, right onto Princess Rd which leads to car park)*

☎ 0116 225 4900

web: www.leicester.gov.uk/museums

This major regional venue houses local and national collections. There's an internationally famous collection of German Expressionism and other displays include the Rutland Dinosaur and the Egyptian Gallery. An Extensive Natural History collection augmented by art from the renaissance to contemporary.

Times: ✱ Open all year, Apr-Sep, Mon-Sat 10-5, Sun 1-5. Oct-Mar, Mon-Sat 10-4, Sun 1-4. Closed 24-26 & 31 Dec & 1 Jan) **Facilities:** Ⓟ 🖳 🗐 ♿ (wheelchairs for loan, minicom, induction loop) toilets for disabled shop ⊗ (ex guide dogs) ◀

National Space Centre

Exploration Dr LE4 5NS

⊃ *(off A6, 2m N of city centre midway between Leicester's central & outer ring roads. Follow brown rocket signs from M1 (junct 21, 21a or 22) & all arterial routes around Leicester)*

☎ 0870 607 7223

e-mail: info@spacecentre.co.uk

web: www.spacecentre.co.uk

The award-winning National Space Centre offers a great family day out, with six interactive galleries, a full-domed Space Theatre, a 42-metre high Rocket Tower, and the new Human Spaceflight Experience with 3D SIM ride. Explore the universe, orbit Earth, join the crew on the lunar base, and take the astronaut fitness tests, all without leaving Leicester!

Times: Open during school term: Tue-Sun, 10-5 (last entry 3.30). During school hols: daily, 10-5 (last entry 3.30) **Fee:** £11 (ch 4-16yrs & concessions £9). Family of 4 £34, of 5 £42 **Facilities:** Ⓟ (charged) 🖳 ⚏ licensed 🗐 ♿ (induction loop, large text, wheelchairs, lifts) toilets for disabled shop ⊗ (ex guide dogs) ◀

Newarke Houses

The Newarke LE2 7BY

⊃ *(opposite De Montfort University)*

☎ 0116 225 4980

web: www.leicester.gov.uk/museums

This museum follows Leicestershire's social history from the 15th century to the present, showing everyday life and social change throughout the county. Clocks, toys, domestic objects, greetings cards and Asian arts are among the many collections. A reconstructed street scene gives a glimpse of Victorian life and the fascinating story of Daniel Lambert, the famous 52-stone gaoler of the 18th century, is also told.

Times: ✱ Open Apr-Sep, Mon-Sat 10-5, Sun 1-5; Oct-Mar, Mon-Sat 10-4, Sun 1-4. Closed 24-26 & 31 Dec & 1 Jan. **Facilities:** Ⓟ (200yds) 🗐 ♿ (car parking can be arranged) shop ⊗ (ex guide dogs)

England

The Record Office for Leicestershire & Rutland

Long St, Wigston Magna LE18 2AH

➲ *(old A50, S of Leicester City)*

☎ 0116 257 1080

e-mail: recordoffice@leics.gov.uk

web: www.leics.gov.uk/museums

Housed in a converted 19th-century school in Wigston, the Record Office holds photographs, electoral registers and archive film, files of local newspapers, history tapes and sound recordings, all of which can be studied.

Times: Open all year, Mon, Tue & Thu 9.15-5, Wed 9.15-7.30, Fri 9.15-4.45, Sat 9.15-12.15. Closed Sun & BH wknds Sat-Tue. **Facilities: ❷** & toilets for disabled ⊗ (ex guide dogs) 🚌

University of Leicester Harold Martin Botanic Garden

Beaumont Hall, Stoughton Dr South, Oadby LE2 2NA

➲ *(3m SE A6, entrance at 'The Knoll', Glebe Rd, Oadby)*

☎ 0116 271 7725 & 2933 (tours)

e-mail: bufi@le.ac.uk

web: www.le.ac.uk/biology/botanicgarden/

The grounds of four houses, now used as student residences and not open to the public, make up this 16-acre garden. A great variety of plants in different settings provide a delightful place to walk, including rock, water and sunken gardens, trees, borders, glasshouses and national collections of hardy fuchsias, aubrieta, skimmia and Lawson cypress.

Times: Open Mon-Fri 10-4, Sat & Sun 10-4 (from 3rd wknd in Mar to 2nd wknd in Nov inclusive). Closed 25-26 Dec & 1 Jan. **Fee:** ✱ Free except charity 'Open Days'. **Facilities: ℗** (adjacent) & toilets for disabled ⊗ (ex guide dogs)

LOUGHBOROUGH   MAP 08 SK51

Great Central Railway

Great Central Rd LE11 1RW

➲ *(signed from A6)*

☎ 01509 230726

e-mail: booking_office@gcrailway.co.uk

web: www.gcrailway.co.uk

This private steam railway runs over eight miles from Loughborough Central to Leicester North, with all trains calling at Quorn & Woodhouse and Rothley. The locomotive depot and museum are at Loughborough Central. A buffet car runs on most trains.

Times: Open all year daily, trains run daily Jun-Aug & school hols; Sep-May, Sat, Sun & BHs **Facilities: ❷** 🍴 ⓘ licensed & (disabled coach available on most trains, check beforehand) toilets for disabled shop 🛍

MARKET BOSWORTH   MAP 04 SK40

Bosworth Battlefield Visitor Centre & Country Park

Ambion Hill, Sutton Cheney CV13 0AD

➲ *(follow brown tourist signs from A447, A444 & A5)*

☎ 01455 290429

e-mail: bosworth@leics.gov.uk

web: www.leics.gov.uk

The Battle of Bosworth Field was fought in 1485 between the armies of Richard III and the future Henry VII. The visitor centre offers a comprehensive interpretation of the battle, with exhibitions, models and a film theatre. Special medieval attractions are held in the summer months.

Times: Open: Country Park and Battle Trails all year. Visitor Centre open Apr-Oct, daily, 11-5; Nov-Dec, Sun 11-4; Mar, wknds 11-5. Parties all year by arrangement. **Facilities: ❷** (charged) 🍴 ⓘ licensed 🏛 & (wheelchair & electric scooter hire, tactile exhibits) toilets for disabled shop 🛍

MOIRA   MAP 08 SK31

Conkers

Millennium Av, Rawdon Rd DE12 6GA

➲ *(on B5003 in Moira, signed from A444 and M42)*

☎ 01283 216633

e-mail: info@visitconkers.com

web: www.visitconkers.com

Explore over one hundred indoor interactive exhibits, together with 120 acres that contain lakeside walks and trails, habitats, an assault course, adventure play areas, a miniature train, and bike hire facilities. There are also events in the covered amphitheatre, and many other opportunities for you and your family to be entertained and educated.

Times: Open daily, summer 10-6, winter 10-5. Closed 25 Dec. **Fee:** ✱ £6.50 (ch 3-15yrs £4.50, ch under 3 free, concessions £5.50). Family ticket (2ad+2ch) £18.95 **Facilities: ❷** 🍴 ⓘ licensed & (multi access walks & trails accessible to wheelchairs) toilets for disabled shop ⊗ (ex guide dogs) 🛍

SHACKERSTONE   MAP 04 SK30

Battlefield Line Railway

Shackerstone Station CV13 6NW

➲ *(follow brown signs from A444 & A447 trunk roads)*

☎ 01827 880754

web: www.battlefield-line-railway.co.uk

The Battlefield Line is the last remaining part of the former Ashby and Nuneaton Joint Railway which was opened in 1873. It runs from Shackerstone via Market Bosworth to Shenton in Leicestershire and is operated by the Shackerstone Railway Society.

Times: Open all year Sat, 12-5, Sun & BH Mon 10.30-5.30. Closed Xmas **Facilities: ❷** 🍴 & toilets for disabled shop 🛍

SWINFORD
MAP 04 SP57

Stanford Hall
LE17 6DH

➲ *(7.5m NE of Rugby, 1.5m from Swinford. 2m from the M1, M6, A14 junct)*

☎ 01788 860250
e-mail: enquiries@stanfordhall.co.uk
web: www.stanfordhall.co.uk

A beautiful William and Mary house, built in 1697 by Sir Roger Cave, ancestor of the present owner. The house contains antique furniture, paintings (including the Stuart Collection) and family costumes. Special events include car and motorcycle owners' club rallies.

Times: ✱ Open Etr Sun-end Sep, Sun & BH Mon 1.30-5; grounds open noon on BH & earlier on Event Days. Open any day or evening (ex Sat) during season for pre-booked parties of 20+. **Fee:** ✱ House & Grounds £5 (ch £2); Grounds only £3 (ch £1); Party 20+ £4.75 each. **Facilities:** ♿ 🍽️ & (please contact for details) toilets for disabled shop ⊗ (ex guide dogs & in park)

TWYCROSS
MAP 04 SK30

Twycross Zoo Park
CV9 3PX

➲ *(on A444 Burton to Nuneaton road, directly off M42 junct 11)*

☎ 01827 880250
web: www.twycrosszoo.com

Set in 50 acres of parkland, the zoo is home to around 1000 animals, most of which are endangered species. Twycross is the only zoo in Britain to house Bonobos - humans' 'closest living relative'. There are also various other animals such as lions, elephants and giraffes, and a pets' corner for younger children. Other attractions include a Penguin Pool with underwater viewing and a Children's Adventure Playground.

Times: Open all year, daily 10-5.30 (4 in winter). Closed 25 Dec. **Fee:** ✱ £8.50 (ch £5) pen £6. **Facilities:** ♿ 🍽️ 📷 & toilets for disabled shop ⊗ (ex guide dogs) 🍴

Market Harborough

Lincolnshire

Tattershall Castle

Lincolnshire is an east coast county with attractive seaside resorts, some lovely countryside, and quintessentially English market towns. Tattershall Castle, a large fortified house built in 1400, is one of the most splendid examples of medieval brick building, complete with a 110 foot tall red-brick keep tower. The sandy beaches, in towns like Skegness, Cleethorpes or Ingoldmells, are ideal for a seaside holiday. Inland, the chalky margin of the Lincolnshire Wolds offers an undulating landscape of hills and valleys, designated as an Area of Outstanding Natural Beauty.

England

BELTON   MAP 08 SK93

Belton House Park & Gardens

NG32 2LS

(3m NE Grantham on A607)

☎ 01476 566116

e-mail: belton@nationaltrust.org.uk

web: www.nationaltrust.org.uk

The ground floor of the house has a succession of state rooms, with the Marble Hall as its centrepiece. Splendid furnishings and decorations throughout the house include tapestries and hangings, family portraits, porcelain and fine furniture.

Times: Open 25 Mar-29 Oct, daily except Mon-Tue (open BH) 12.30-5. Grounds and adventure playground open daily Aug; Shop, Restaurant/Garden 3 Nov-17 Dec, Fri-Sun 12-4 **Fee:** ✱ House & garden £8 (ch £4.50). Family ticket £20.50. Grounds only £6 (ch £3.50) Family ticket £15.50 **Facilities:** ♿ ⦿ licensed ⮴ (Braille guide, hearing scheme, audio guide) toilets for disabled shop ⊗ (ex in grounds) ♨

CLEETHORPES   MAP 08 TA30

Pleasure Island Family Theme Park

Kings Rd DN35 0PL

(Follow signs from A180)

☎ 01472 211511

e-mail: reception@pleasure-island.co.uk

web: www.pleasure-island.co.uk

Pleasure Island is packed with over seventy rides and attractions. Hold on tight as the colossal wheel of steel rockets you into the sky at a G-force of 2.5, then hurtles you around 360 degrees, sending riders into orbit and giving the sensation of complete weightlessness. It's not just grown ups and thrill seekers who are catered for at Pleasure Island. For youngsters there's hours of fun in Tinkaboo Town, an indoor themed area full of rides and attractions. New attractions include the Booster, and the Masai Warrior Show.

Times: Open Apr-3 Sep, daily from 10. Plus wknds during Sep-Oct & daily during half term (23 Oct-29 Oct). **Fee:** ✱ £14 (ch under 4 free, pen £8.50). **Facilities:** ♿ ⦿ ⊗ licensed ⮴ toilets for disabled shop ⊨

CONINGSBY   MAP 08 TF25

Battle of Britain Memorial Flight Visitor Centre

LN4 4SY

(on A153 in Coningsby village - follow heritage signs)

☎ 01526 344041

e-mail: bbmf@lincolnshire.gov.uk

web: www.lincolnshire.gov.uk/bbmf

View the aircraft of the Battle of Britain Memorial Flight, comprising the only flying Lancaster in Europe, five Spitfires, two Hurricanes, a Dakota and two Chipmunks. Because of operational commitments, specific aircraft may not be available. Ring for information before planning a visit.

Times: Open Mon-Fri, conducted tours 10.30-3.30; (winter 10.30-3) (Closed 2 wks Xmas). **Fee:** ✱ £3.80 (concessions £2.50) Family £9.90 **Facilities:** ♿ ⦿ ⊞ ⮴ (electric wheelchairs not allowed in hangar) toilets for disabled shop ⊗ (ex guide dogs) ⊨

EAST KIRKBY   MAP 08 TF36

Lincolnshire Aviation Heritage Centre NEW

The Old Airfield PE23 4DE

(off A16 onto A155, museum on east side of village)

☎ 01790 763207

e-mail: enquiries@lincsaviation.co.uk

web: www.lincsaviation.co.uk

Relive a World War Two bomber airfield here at East Kirkby. Experience the sights and sounds, smells and atmosphere. The only place in the country to see a Lancaster bomber on its original airfield.

Times: Open 2 Jan-Etr, 10-4; Etr-Nov, 10-5. Closed Sun. **Fee:** ✱ £6.75 (ch 6-15 £2.50, concessions £5.75) **Facilities:** ♿ ⦿ ⊗ ⮴ (Hand rails) toilets for disabled shop ⊨

EPWORTH   MAP 08 SE70

Old Rectory

1 Rectory St DN9 1HX

(on A161, 3m S of M180 junct 2. Follow brown signs)

☎ 01427 872268

e-mail: curator@epwortholdrectory.org.uk

web: www.epwortholdrectory.org.uk

John and Charles Wesley were brought up in this handsome rectory, built in 1709. Maintained by the World Methodist Council as 'The Home of the Wesleys', the house displays items which belonged to John and Charles Wesley and their parents Samuel and Susanna. The house is a registered museum.

Times: ✱ Open daily Mar-Oct, Mon-Sat, 10-12 & 2-4, Sun 2-4 (only in Mar, Apr & Oct); May-Sep Mon-Sat 10-4.30, Sun 2-4.30. Other times by prior arrangement. **Facilities:** ♿ ⮴ toilets for disabled shop ⊗ (ex guide dogs) ⊨

GAINSBOROUGH   MAP 08 SK88

Gainsborough Old Hall

Parnell St DN21 2NB

(turn off A1 onto A57 to Gainsborough. Follow brown heritage signs in city centre. Old Hall is adjacent to town centre.)

☎ 01427 612669

e-mail: gainsboroughholdhall@lincolnshire.gov.uk

web: www.english-heritage.org.uk

A complete medieval manor house dating back to 1460-80 and containing a remarkable Great Hall and original kitchen with a variety of room settings. Richard III, Henry VIII, the Mayflower Pilgrims and John Wesley all visited the Old Hall.

Times: Open early Apr-end Oct, Mon-Sat 10-5 (ex Sun 1-4.30); end Oct-Mar, Mon-Sat 10-5 Closed 24-26, 31 Dec & 1 Jan **Fee:** £3.70 (ch & concessions £2.50). Family ticket £9.99. Prices and opening times are subject to change in Spring 2007. Please check web site or call 0870 333 1181 for the most up to date prices and opening times when planning your visit. **Facilities:** ♿ (100yds) (unrestricted parking 100yds from Hall) ⊞ ⊞ ⮴ (audio tour, induction loop, wheelchair for visitors use) toilets for disabled shop ⊗ (ex guide dogs)

England

GRIMSBY   MAP 08 TA20

National Fishing Heritage Centre

Alexandra Dock DN31 1UZ

➲ *(follow signs off M180)*

☎ 01472 323345

web: www.nelincs.gov.uk

Sign on as a crew member for a journey of discovery, and experience the harsh reality of life on board a deep sea trawler built inside the Centre. Through interactive games and displays, your challenge is to navigate the icy waters of the Arctic in search of the catch.

Times: Open Etr-Oct, Mon-Fri 10-5, Wknds & BHs 10.30-5.30
Facilities: ❷ (charged) ⬛ & toilets for disabled shop ⊗ (ex guide dogs)

GRIMSTHORPE   MAP 08 TF02

Grimsthorpe Castle

PE10 0LY

➲ *(on A151, 8m E of Colsterworth rbt on A1)*

☎ 01778 591205

e-mail: ray@grimsthorpe.co.uk

web: www.grimsthorpe.co.uk

Seat of the Willoughby de Eresby family since 1516, the castle has a medieval tower and a Tudor quadrangular house with a Baroque north front by Vanbrugh. There are eight state rooms and two picture galleries, and an important collection of furniture, pictures and tapestries.

Times: Open early Apr-late Sep, Sun, Thu & BH Mon. Daily in Aug ex Fri & Sat. Park & Gardens also open daily Jun-Aug ex Fri & Sat; 12-6. Castle 1-5 (last admission 4.30). **Facilities:** ❷ ⬛ ⦿⬩ licensed & (virtual castle tour via laptop) toilets for disabled shop ◀

LINCOLN   MAP 08 SK97

The Collection: Art & Archaeology in Lincolnshire

Danes Ter LN2 1LP

➲ *(located on the lower part of Lincoln, between Central Library and St Swithins close to the Waterside Shopping Centre)*

☎ 01522 550990

e-mail: thecollection@lincolnshire.gov.uk

web: www.thecollection.lincoln.museum

The county's main archaeology museum, housed in a magnificent medieval building, forms part of Greyfriars.

Times: Open all year, daily, 10-5 **Facilities:** ℗ 300mtrs (Broadgate multi storey car park) ⬛ ⦿⬩ licensed ⬛ & (Parking for disabled) toilets for disabled shop ⊗ (ex guide dogs) ◀

Lincoln Castle

Castle Hill LN1 3AA

➲ *(off A46 Lincoln Ring Road in heart of historic city)*

☎ 01522 511068

e-mail: lincoln_castle@lincolnshire.gov.uk

web: www.lincolnshire.gov.uk/lincolncastle

Situated in the centre of Lincoln, the Castle, built in 1068 by William the Conqueror, dominates the Bailgate area alongside the great Cathedral. In addition to its many medieval features, Lincoln Castle has strong 19th-century connections and the unique Victorian prison chapel is perhaps the most awe-inspiring. The beautiful surroundings are ideal for historical adventures, picnics and special events that include jousting, Roman re-enactments, and Vintage vehicle rallies. The Castle is the home of the Magna Carta and there is an exhibition interpreting and displaying this important document.

Times: Open: Summer, Mon-Sat 9.30-5.30, Sun 11-5.30. Winter, Mon-Sat 9.30-4, Sun 11-4. Closed 24-26 & 31 Dec & 1 Jan. **Fee:** £3.80 (ch £2.50) Family ticket (2ad+3ch) £9.90 **Facilities:** ℗ (100yds) ⬛ ⬛ & (hearing loop, audio visual tour) toilets for disabled shop ⊗ (ex guide dogs) ◀

Museum of Lincolnshire Life

Burton Rd LN1 3LY

➲ *(100mtr walk from Lincoln Castle)*

☎ 01522 528448

e-mail: lincolnshirelife.museum@lincolnshire.gov.uk

web: www.lincolnshire.gov.uk/museumoflincolnshirelife

A large and varied social history museum, where two centuries of Lincolnshire life are illustrated by enthralling displays of domestic implements, industrial machinery, agricultural tools and a collection of horse-drawn vehicles. The exciting and interactive Royal Lincolnshire Regiment Museum contains videos, an audio tour, and touch screen computers.

Times: ✱ Open all year, May-Sep, daily 10-5; Oct-Mar, Mon-Sat 10-5 (last admission 4). Closed 24-26 & 31 Dec, 1 Jan. **Facilities:** ❷ ⬛ & (wheelchair available, parking space) toilets for disabled shop ⊗ (ex assist dogs)

Usher Gallery   **FREE**

Lindum Rd LN2 1NN

➲ *(in city centre, signed)*

☎ 01522 527980

e-mail: usher.gallery@lincolnshire.gov.uk

web: www.lincolnshire.gov.uk/usher

Built as the result of a bequest by Lincoln jeweller James Ward Usher, the Gallery houses his magnificent collection of watches, porcelain and miniatures, as well as topographical works, watercolours by Peter de Wint, Tennyson memorabilia and coins. The gallery has a popular and changing display of contemporary visual arts and crafts. There is a lively lecture programme and children's activity diary.

Times: ✱ Open all year, Tue-Sat 10-5 (last entry 4.30), Sun 1-5 (last entry 4.30), from 1 Jun daily 10-5. Open BHs. Closed 24-26 Dec & 1 Jan.
Facilities: ❷ ⬛ ⬛ & (large print guides, induction loop, parking) toilets for disabled shop ⊗ (ex guide dogs) ◀

SCUNTHORPE — MAP 08 SE81

Normanby Hall Country Park   **2 for 1**
Normanby DN15 9HU
➲ *(4m N of Scunthorpe off B1430)*
☎ 01724 720588
e-mail: normanby.hall@northlincs.gov.uk
web: www.northlincs.gov.uk

A whole host of activities and attractions are offered in the 300 acres of grounds that surround Normanby Hall, including riding, nature trails and a farming museum. Inside the Regency mansion the fine rooms are decorated and furnished in period style. Fully restored and working Victorian kitchen garden. There is also a Victorian walled garden selling a wide range of Victorian and other unusual plants from barrows located at the gift shop and Farming Museum.

Times: ✱ Open: Park all year, daily, 9-dusk. Walled garden, daily 10.30-5 (4 in winter). Hall & Farming Museum, Apr-Sep, daily 1-5. **Fee:** ✱ Mar-Sep £4.40 (ch £2.20, under 5s free, concessions £4). Family season ticket £17. **Facilities:** ❷ (charged) ⬛ ⑪ licensed 📷 ♿ (audio tour, wheelchair/scooter) shop garden centre ⊗ (ex guide dogs, & on leads) ◀

SKEGNESS — MAP 09 TF56

Church Farm Museum
Church Rd South PE25 2HF
➲ *(follow brown museum signs on entering Skegness)*
☎ 01754 766658
e-mail: churchfarmmuseum@lincolnshire.gov.uk

A farmhouse and outbuildings, restored to show the way of life on a Lincolnshire farm at the end of the 19th century, with farm implements and machinery plus household equipment on display. Temporary exhibitions are held in the barn with special events throughout the season. A timber framed mud and stud cottage is restored on site.

Times: Open Apr-Oct, daily 10-5 (last entry 4.30) **Facilities:** ❷ ⬛ 📷 ♿ (wheelchair available, grounds accessible with care) toilets for disabled shop ⊗ (ex guide dogs)

Skegness Natureland Seal Sanctuary
North Pde PE25 1DB
➲ *(N end of seafront)*
☎ 01754 764345
e-mail: natureland@fsbdial.co.uk
web: www.skegnessnatureland.co.uk

Natureland houses seals, penguins, tropical birds, aquarium, reptiles, pets' corner etc. Also free-flight tropical butterflies (May-Oct). Natureland is well known for its rescue of abandoned seal pups, and has successfully reared and returned to the wild a large number of them. The hospital unit incorporates a public viewing area, and a large seascape seal pool (with underwater viewing).

Times: Open all year, daily at 10. Closing times vary according to season. Closed 25-26 Dec & 1 Jan. **Fee:** ✱ £5.50 (ch under 3 free, ch £3.60, pen £4.15). Family ticket £16.40 **Facilities:** ℗ (100yds) ⬛ ⑪ ♿ (low windows on seal pools) toilets for disabled shop ◀

SPALDING — MAP 08 TF22

Butterfly & Wildlife Park   **2 for 1**
Long Sutton PE12 9LE
➲ *(off A17 at Long Sutton)*
☎ 01406 363833 & 363209
e-mail: butterflypark@hotmail.com
web: www.butterflyandwildlifepark.co.uk

The Park contains one of Britain's largest walk-through tropical houses, in which hundreds of butterflies and birds from all over the world fly freely. Outside are 15 acres of butterfly and bee gardens, wildflower meadows, nature trail, farm animals, a pets' corner and a large adventure playground. At The Lincolnshire Birds of Prey Centre, there are daily birds of prey displays. See an ant room where visitors can observe leaf-cutting ants in their natural working habitat, and Reptile Land, home to crocodiles and snakes.

Times: ✱ Open 20 Mar-end Oct, daily 10-5. (Sep & Oct 10-4). **Fee:** ✱ £5.70 (ch 3-16 £4.20, pen £5.20). Family ticket £17-£20. Party rates on application. **Facilities:** ❷ ♿ (wheelchairs available) toilets for disabled shop ⊗ (ex guide dogs) ◀

STAMFORD — MAP 04 TF00

Burghley House
PE9 3JY
➲ *(1.5m off A1 at Stamford)*
☎ 01780 752451
e-mail: burghley@burghley.co.uk
web: www.burghley.co.uk

This great Elizabethan palace, built by William Cecil, has all the hallmarks of that ostentatious period. The vast house is three storeys high and the roof is a riot of pinnacles, cupolas and paired chimneys in classic Tudor style. However, the interior was restyled in the 17th century, and the state rooms are now Baroque, with silver fireplaces, elaborate plasterwork and painted ceilings. These were painted by Antonio Verrio, whose Heaven Room is quite awe-inspiring. The Sculpture Garden is dedicated to exhibiting the best in contemporary sculpture, in pleasant surroundings.

Times: Open end Mar-Oct, daily (ex Fri). Please telephone for details. **Fee:** ✱ £9 (ch 5-15 £4, pen £8) Family £22 **Facilities:** ❷ ⬛ ⑪ licensed ♿ (chairlift access, some mobility required) toilets for disabled shop garden centre ⊗ (ex in park & on lead) ◀

Stamford Museum   FREE
Broad St PE9 1PJ
➲ *(from A1 follow town centre signs from any Stamford exit)*
☎ 01780 766317
e-mail: stamford_museum@lincolnshire.gov.uk
web: www.lincolnshire.gov.uk/stamfordmuseum

Displays illustrate the history of this fine stone town and include Stamford Ware pottery, the visit of Daniel Lambert and the Town's more recent industrial past. The new Stamford Tapestry depicts the history of the town in wool.

Times: Open all year, Apr-Sep, Mon-Sat 10-5, Sun 1-4; Oct-Mar Mon-Sat 10-5. Closed 24-26 & 31 Dec & 1 Jan. **Facilities:** ℗ (200yds) (on street parking is limited waiting) 📷 ♿ (audio loop at reception, Braille leaflets) shop ⊗ (ex guide dogs)

England

TATTERSHALL

MAP 08 TF25

Tattershall Castle

LN4 4LR

⮑ *(S of A153, 15m NE of Sleaford)*

☎ 01526 342543

e-mail: tattershallcastle@nationaltrust.org.uk

web: www.nationaltrust.org.uk

This large fortified house was built in 1440 by Ralph Cromwell, Treasurer of England, and has a keep 100ft high. Restored in 1911-14, it contains four great chambers with large Gothic fireplaces, tapestries and brick vaulting. Spectacular views from battlements and museum room in guardhouse.

Times: Open 4-19 Mar, Sat & Sun, 12-4; 25 Mar-1 Nov, daily Sat-Wed, 11-5.30 (11-4 in Oct); 4 Nov-10 Dec, Sat & Sun 12-4 **Fee:** ✱ £4 (ch £2). Family ticket £10 **Facilities:** ❷ ৬ (Braille guide) toilets for disabled shop ⊗ (ex guide dogs) ⛳

THORNTON

MAP 08 TA11

Thornton Abbey and Gatehouse `FREE`

DN39 6TU

⮑ *(7m SE of Humber Bridge, on road E of A1077)*

This abbey, founded in 1139 for a community of Augustinian canons, was reconstructed from the 1260s as its prestige and riches grew. The

continued

remains of a beautiful octagonal chapter-house are notably fine. Most impressive is the 14th-century gatehouse, recognised as one of the grandest in England.

Times: Open Abbey Grounds: Apr-Sep, daily, 10-6; Oct-Mar, daily, 10-4. Gatehouse: Apr-Sep, 1st & 3rd Sun of month, 12-6; Oct-Mar, 3rd Sun of month 12-4. **Facilities:** ❷ ৬ (mostly accessible apart from gatehouse) ⛗

WOOLSTHORPE

MAP 08 SK92

Woolsthorpe Manor

23 Newton Way NG33 5NR

⮑ *(7m S of Grantham, 1m W of A1)*

☎ 01476 862826

e-mail: woolsthorpemanor@nationaltrust.org.uk

web: www.nationaltrust.org.uk

A fine stone-built, 17th-century farmhouse which was the birthplace of the scientist and philosopher Sir Isaac Newton. He also lived at the house from 1665-67 during the Plague. An early edition of his Principia Mathematica (1687) is in the house. Science Discovery Centre and exhibition.

Times: Open 4-26 Mar, Sat & Sun 1-5; 29 Mar-1 Oct, Wed-Sun (open BHs) 1-5; 7-29 Oct, Sat & Sun 1-5 **Fee:** ✱ £4.50 (ch £2.20). Family ticket £11.20 **Facilities:** ❷ ৬ (Braille & large print guide, wheelchair available) toilets for disabled ⊗ (ex guide dogs) ⛳

The Humber Bridge

London

Piccadilly Circus,
Greater London

Amongst the bright lights of London, one of the most visited capital cities on Earth, there are four World Heritage Sites, the Royal Botanic Gardens at Kew; Westminster Palace; the Tower of London and Maritime Greenwich. Much of the period architecture dates from the late 17th century, including Britain's only domed cathedral, St Paul's. London has a vast range of museums including the British Museum, the nations' largest museum, a multitude of royal residences, famous art galleries, theatres, street markets and, of course, fantastic shopping. There is plenty of greenery, too, from the many royal parks to the 105 acres of the London Wetland Centre.

E2

Geffrye Museum   FREE

136 Kingsland Rd, Shoreditch E2 8EA
➲ (S end of Kingsland Rd A10 in Shoreditch between Cremer St & Pearson St)
☎ 020 7739 9893
e-mail: info@geffrye-museum.org.uk
web: www.geffrye-museum.org.uk

The only museum in the UK to specialise in the domestic interiors and furniture of the urban middle classes. Displays span the 400 years from 1600 to the present day, forming a sequence of period rooms which capture the nature of English interior style. The museum is set in elegant, 18th-century buildings, surrounded by delightful gardens including an award-winning walled herb garden and a series of historical gardens which highlight changes in urban middle-class gardens from the 17th to 20th centuries. One of the museum's historic almshouses has recently been fully restored to its original condition and is open on selected days (ring for details).

Times: Open all year, Tue-Sat 10-5, Sun & BH Mon 12-5. Closed Mon, Good Fri, 24-26 Dec & New Year. **Facilities:** ℗ (150yds) (meter parking, very restricted) ⦿ licensed 🍴 ৬ (ramps, lift, wheelchair available, induction loop) toilets for disabled shop ⊗ (ex guide dogs)

V & A Museum of Childhood   FREE

Cambridge Heath Rd E2 9PA
➲ (Underground - Bethnal Green)
☎ 020 8980 2415
e-mail: moc@vam.ac.uk
web: www.museumofchildhood.org.uk

The V&A Museum of Childhood has re-opened following a £4.7 million transformation. There is a stunning new entrance, fully updated galleries and displays, a brand new gallery and expanded public spaces. Galleries include Creativity, Moving Toys, World in the East End, Design in Focus, and Children in Trouble. There is also a full programme of activities. The museum is 150 in 2007. Exhibitions include a birthday celebration of Dick Bruna's Miffy the rabbit, Picasso's natural history, and Lost in Space.

Times: Open all year, daily 10-5.50, closed 25-26 Dec, 1 Jan. **Facilities:** ℗ (metered parking) ⦿ 🍴 ৬ (disabled parking by arrangement) toilets for disabled shop ⊗

E9

Sutton House

2 & 4 Homerton High St E9 6JQ
➲ (10 min walk from Hackney Central train station)
☎ 020 8986 2264
e-mail: suttonhouse@nationaltrust.org.uk
web: www.nationaltrust.org.uk

In London's East End, the building is a rare example of a Tudor red-brick house. Built in 1535 by Sir Ralph Sadleir, Principal Secretary of State for Henry VIII, the house has 18th-century alterations and later additions.

Times: Open Feb-23 Dec, Thu-Sun & BH Mon, 12.30-4.30, closed Good Fri. **Fee:** ✱ £2.50 (ch 50p) Family ticket £5.50. Group £2 each **Facilities:** ℗ (on street parking) (meters) ⦿ ⦿ licensed 🍴 ৬ (induction loop, Braille/large print/audio guide) toilets for disabled shop ⊗ (ex assist dogs) 🐾

E14

Museum in Docklands   2 for 1

West India Quay E14 4AL
➲ (Signposted from West India Quay DLR)
☎ 0870 444 3855 & 3856
e-mail: info@museumindocklands.org.uk
web: www.museumindocklands.org.uk

Housed in a converted 18th-century warehouse the museum explores the 2000 year history of London's river, port and people. Four floors of interactive displays and a unique collection that journeys through the history of the Thames, from the first Roman settlements to the massive regeneration that brought the Docklands into the 21st century. A changing programme of activities for all ages, includes character re-enactments, talks by history experts, films and guided walks through Docklands. A soft play gallery, Mudlarks is for children under eleven, and offers an opportunity to learn how to winch and weigh cargo or to take a diver's eye view of work under water. Discover archaeological finds on the foreshore, or even reconstruct a simple model of Canary Wharf.

Times: Open all year, daily 10-6 (last admission 5.30) **Fee:** ✱ £5 (ch 16 free, concessions £3) **Facilities:** ℗ (opp rear museum) (Disabled parking on quayside) ⦿ ⦿ licensed 🍴 ৬ (w/chairs, power scooters & various aids) shop ⊗ (ex guide dogs)

E17

William Morris Gallery

Lloyd Park, Forest Rd E17 4PP

⮱ *(Underground - Blackhorse Rd, take bus no. 123 along Forest Rd, get off at the Lloyd Park stop)*

☎ 020 8527 3782

e-mail: wmg.enquiries@walthamforest.gov.uk

web: www.walthamforest.gov.uk/wmg

Victorian artist, craftsman, poet and free thinker William Morris lived here from 1848 to 1856, and the gallery houses displays illustrating his life and work. Exhibits include fabrics, stained glass, wallpaper and furniture, as well as Pre-Raphaelite paintings, ceramics and a collection of pictures by Frank Brangwyn, who worked briefly for Morris.

Times: Open all year, Tue-Sat and 1st Sun in each month 10-1 & 2-5. Closed Mon & BHs. Telephone for Xmas/New Year opening times.
Fee: Free admission, guided tours charged for. **Facilities:** ℗ 🛗 ♿ shop ⊗ (ex guide dogs) ◀

EC1

Museum of The Order of St John

St John's Gate, St John's Ln, Clerkenwell EC1M 4DA

⮱ *(Underground - Farringdon, Barbican)*

☎ 020 7324 4070

e-mail: museum@nhq.sja.org.uk

web: www.sja.org.uk/museum

The Priory of Clerkenwell was built in the 1140s by the Crusading Hospitallers and it is their remarkable story which lies behind the modern work of St John Ambulance. The Knights' surprising tale is revealed in the ground floor galleries housed in the Tudor gatehouse and includes furniture, paintings, silver, armour, stained glass and an interactive, multimedia gallery 'Time to Care' which explores the work of St John Ambulance from 1877 to the present day.

Times: Open all year, Mon-Sat 10-5, Sat 10-4. Closed Etr, Xmas wk & BH wknds. Guided tours 11 & 2.30 Tue, Fri & Sat. **Fee:** ✱ Museum free. For tours of St John's Gate & Grand Priory Church a donation of £5 (concessions £4). **Facilities:** ℗ (meters/NCP 300yds) 🛗 ♿ toilets for disabled shop ⊗ (ex guide dogs) ◀

Wesley's Chapel, House & Museum Of Methodism **FREE**

49 City Rd EC1Y 1AU

⮱ *(Underground - Old Street - exit number 4)*

☎ 020 7253 2262

e-mail: museum@wesleyschapel.org.uk

web: www.wesleyschapel.org.uk

Wesley's Chapel has been the Mother Church of World Methodism since its construction in 1778. The crypt houses a museum which traces the development of Methodism from the 18th century to the present day. Wesley's house - built by him in 1779 - was his home when not touring and preaching. Special events are held on May 24th (the anniversary of Wesley's conversion), and November 1st (the anniversary of the Chapel's opening).

Times: Open all year, Mon-Sat , 10-4, Sun 12-2. Closed Thu 12.45-1.30, Xmas-New Year, BHs. (Last entry 30mins before closing).
Facilities: ℗ (5min) (NCP at Finsbury Square) 🛗 ♿ (lift to the crypt of the chapel) toilets for disabled shop ⊗ (ex guide dogs) ◀

EC2

Bank of England Museum **FREE**

Bartholomew Ln EC2R 8AH

⮱ *(museum housed in Bank of London, entrance in Bartholomew Lane. Bank underground, exit 2)*

☎ 020 7601 5545

e-mail: museum@bankofengland.co.uk

web: www.bankofengland.co.uk/museum

The museum tells the story of the Bank of England from its foundation in 1694 to its role in today's economy. Interactive programmes with graphics and video help explain its many and varied roles. Popular exhibits include a unique collection of banknotes and a genuine gold bar, which may be handled.

Times: Open all year, Mon-Fri 10-5. Closed wknds & BHs. Open on day of Lord Mayor's Show. **Facilities:** ℗ (10 mins walk) 🛗 ♿ (special need presentation, advance notice helpful) toilets for disabled shop ⊗ (ex assist dogs)

The Guildhall **FREE**

Gresham St EC2V 5AE

⮱ *(Underground - Bank, St Paul's)*

☎ 020 7606 3030

e-mail: pro@corpoflondon.gov.uk

web: www.cityoflondon.gov.uk

The Court of Common Council (presided over by the Lord Mayor) administers the City of London and meets in the Guildhall. Dating from 1411, the building was badly damaged in the Great Fire and again in the Blitz. The great hall, traditionally used for the Lord Mayor's Banquet and other important civic functions, is impressively decorated with the banners and shields of the livery companies, of which there are more than 90. The Clock Museum, which has a collection of 700 exhibits, charts the history of 500 years of time-keeping.

Times: ✱ Open all year, May-Sep, daily 10-5; Oct-Apr, Mon-Sat 10-5. Closed Xmas, New Year, Good Fri, Etr Mon & infrequently for Civic occasions. Please contact 020 7606 3030 ext 1463 before visit to be certain of access. **Facilities:** ℗ (NCP parking nearby) 🛗 ♿ (lift for east and west crypts) toilets for disabled shop ⊗

Museum of London **FREE**

150 London Wall EC2Y 5HN

⮱ *(Underground - St Paul's, Barbican. N of St Paul's Cathedral at the end of St Martins le Grand and S of the Barbican. S of Aldersgate St)*

☎ 0870 444 3851

e-mail: info@museumoflondon.org.uk

web: www.museumoflondon.org.uk

Dedicated to the story of London and its people, the Museum of London exists to inspire a passion for London in all who visit it. As well as the permanent collection, the Museum has a varied exhibition programme with major temporary exhibitions and topical displays each year. There are also smaller exhibitions in the foyer gallery. A

continued

England

wide programme of lectures and events explore London's history and its evolution to the city we know today.

Museum of London

Times: ✱ Open all year, Mon-Sat 10-5.50, Sun 12-5.50. Last admission 5.30. **Facilities:** ℗ 🚻 📷 ♿ (w/chairs & power scooters, lifts & induction loops) toilets for disabled shop ⊗ (ex guide dogs) ◀

EC3

Tower of London

Tower Hill EC3N 4AB

➲ *(Underground - Tower Hill)*

☎ 0870 756 6060

web: www.hrp.org.uk

Perhaps the most famous castle in the world, the Tower of London has played a central part in British history. The White Tower, built by William the Conqueror as a show of strength to the people of London, remains one of the most outstanding examples of Norman military architecture in Europe. For hundreds of years the Tower was used, among other things, as the State Prison. It was here that Henry VIII had two of his wives executed, here that Lady Jane Grey died and here that Sir Walter Raleigh was imprisoned. The Yeoman Warders, or 'Beefeaters' play an important role in the protection of the Tower - home of the Crown Jewels - and are informative and entertaining. Look out for the ravens, whose continued residence is said to ensure that the Kingdom does not fall. The Crowns and Diamonds exhibition features a number of crowns never displayed to the public before and more than 12,000 rough and polished diamonds. Also open to the public are the Royal Armouries, which received their first recorded visitor as long ago as 1489. The displays include an extensive range of arms and armour dating from the Norman ages, a collection of Spanish arms and the Line of Kings.

Times: ✱ Open all year, Mar-Oct, Mon-Sat 9-6, Sun 10-6 (last admission 5); Nov-Feb, Tue-Sat 9-5, Sun 10-5 (last admission 4). Closed 24-26 Dec & 1 Jan. **Facilities:** ℗ (100yds) (NCP Lower Thames St) 🍽 🍴 licensed 📷 ♿ (access guide can be obtained in advance call 020 7488 5694) toilets for disabled shop ⊗ (ex guide dogs) ◀

EC4

Dr Johnson's House

17 Gough Square EC4A 3DE

➲ *(Underground - Temple, Blackfriars, Chancery Lane)*

☎ 020 7353 3745

e-mail: curator@drjohnsonshouse.org

web: www.drjohnsonshouse.org

The celebrated literary figure, Dr Samuel Johnson, lived here between 1748 and 1759. He wrote his English Dictionary here, and a facsimile third edition is on display at the house. The dictionary took nine and a half years to complete and contained 40,000 words. Johnson then undertook the formidable task of editing the complete works of Shakespeare. The house is a handsome example of early 18th-century architecture, and includes a collection of prints, letters and other Johnson memorabilia.

Times: ✱ Open all year, May-Sep, daily 11-5.30; Oct-Apr 11-5. Closed Sun, BHs, Good Fri & 24 Dec. **Facilities:** ℗ (500yds) (limited meters) ♿ (large print info sheets, handrails, seating) shop ⊗ (ex guide dogs)

Middle Temple Hall FREE

The Temple EC4Y 9AT

➲ *(Underground - Temple, Blackfriars. Turn left at the embankment & left into Middle Temple Lane. Hall half way up on left)*

☎ 020 7427 4800 & 4820

e-mail: banqueting@middletemple.org.uk

web: www.middletemple.org.uk

Between Fleet Street and the Thames are the Middle and Inner Temples, separate Inns of Court, so named after the Knights Templar who occupied the site from about 1160. Middle Temple Hall is a fine example of Tudor architecture and was completed in about 1570. The hall has a double hammerbeam roof and beautiful stained glass. The 29ft-long high table was made from a single oak tree from Windsor Forest. Sir Francis Drake was a visitor to and friend of the Middle Temple, and a table made from timbers from the *Golden Hind* - the ship in which he sailed around the world - is shown.

Times: Open all year, Mon-Fri 10-12 & 3-4. Closed BH & legal vacations. **Facilities:** ℗ (meters) 🍴 licensed ♿ toilets for disabled shop ⊗ (ex assist dogs) 🚌

St Paul's Cathedral

St Pauls Courtyard EC4M 8AD

☎ 020 7246 8348

e-mail: chapterhouse@stpaulscathedral.org.uk

web: www.stpauls.co.uk

Completed in 1710, Sir Christopher Wren's architectural masterpiece is the cathedral church of the Bishop of London, and arose, like so much of this area of London, from the ashes of the Great Fire of London in 1666. Among the worthies buried here are Nelson and the Duke of Wellington, while Holman Hunt's masterpiece, *Light of the World* hangs in the nave. St Pauls also hosted the weddings of Charles and Diana, and the funeral of Sir Winston Churchill. Impressive views of London can be seen from the Golden Gallery.

Times: Open Cathedral, Crypt, Ambulatory, Mon-Sat 8.30. Galleries 9.30. (Last admission 4). Cathedral may close for special services. **Fee:** £9 (ch £3.50, concessions £8) Family £21.50 (2ad+2ch). **Facilities:** ℗ (400mtrs) (meter parking in area) 🍽 🍴 licensed 📷 ♿ toilets for disabled shop ⊗ (ex guide dogs) ◀

N1

The London Canal Museum

12/13 New Wharf Rd N1 9RT

➲ (Underground - Kings Cross. Follow York Way along East side of King's Cross Stn, turn right at Wharfdale Rd, then left into New Wharf Rd).

☎ 020 7713 0836

e-mail: info@canalmuseum.org.uk

web: www.canalmuseum.org.uk

The museum covers the development of London's canals (particularly Regent's Canal), canal vessels and trade, and the way of life of the canal people. Housed in a former ice warehouse and stables, it also illustrates horse transport and the unusual trade of importing ice from Norway; there are two large ice wells under the floor. Facilities include temporary moorings, so you can arrive by boat if you want. There are regular special exhibitions.

Times: Open all year, Tue-Sun & BH Mon 10-4.30 (last admission 3.45). Closed 24-26 & 31 Dec. **Fee:** £3 (ch £1.50, students, pen & UB40s £2, under 8's free). Groups 10+ **Facilities:** ⓟ (0.25m) (parking Mon-Fri before 6.30pm, Sat 1.30) 🍴 ♿ (large print guides, induction loop, Braille signs) toilets for disabled shop ⊗ (ex guide dogs) 🔗

N3   MAP 03 TQ29

The Jewish Museum

The Sternberg Centre, 80 East End Rd, Finchley N3 2SY

➲ (Underground - Finchley Central, 10 mins walk via Station Rd & Manor View)

☎ 020 8349 1143

e-mail: enquiries@jewishmuseum.org.uk

web: www.jewishmuseum.org.uk

The Jewish Museum traces the story of Jewish immigration and settlement in London, including a reconstruction of an East End tailoring workshop. It also has a Holocaust Education Gallery with an exhibition on Leon Greenman - British Citizen and Auschwitz survivor. There is a regular programme of changing exhibitions and events.

Times: Open all year, Sun 10.30-4.30, Mon-Thu 10.30-5. Closed Jewish festivals, public hols & 24 Dec-4 Jan. Also closed Sun in Aug & BH wknds. **Fee:** £2 (ch free, concessions £1) **Facilities:** ⓟ (50mtrs) (on street parking) 🔗 🍴 ♿ toilets for disabled shop ⊗

N6

Highgate Cemetery

Swains Ln N6 6PJ

➲ (Underground - Archway, see directions posted at exit)

☎ 020 8340 1834

web: www.highgate-cemetery.org.uk

Highgate Cemetery is the most impressive of a series of large, formally arranged and landscaped cemeteries which were established around the perimeter of London in the mid-19th century. There's a wealth of fine sculpture and architecture amongst the tombstones, monuments and mausoleums as well as the graves of such notables as the Rossetti family, George Eliot, Michael Faraday and Karl Marx. It is also a Grade II listed park.

Times: Open all year. Eastern Cemetery: daily 10 (11 wknds)-5 (4 in winter). Western Cemetery by guided tour only: Sat & Sun 11-4 (3 in winter); midweek tours at 2, advisable to book. Closed 25-26 Dec & during funerals. **Fee:** ✱ East cemetery £2. Tour of West cemetery £3 (ch 8-16 £1, no ch under 8 on tours). Donations encouraged to assist restoration.

continued

Camera permits for private use £1 on each side (no video or flash). **Facilities:** 🍴 ⊗ (ex guide dogs)

N7

Freightliners City Farm   FREE

Sheringham Rd, Islington N7 8PF

➲ (off Liverpool Rd)

☎ 020 7609 0467

e-mail: robert@freightlinersfarm.org.uk

web: www.freightlinersfarm.org.uk

A city farm bringing rural life into an urban setting. A variety of animals can be seen at the farm, including cows, pigs, goats, sheep and poultry. Some interesting building projects are taking place at the farm, including a strawbale building, solar dome, an outside bread oven and a continental beehive. A Saturday market offers organic produce, arts and crafts and much more.

Times: Open Winter: 10-4. Summer: 10-4.45 **Facilities:** ⓟ (charged) 🍴 🍴 ♿ toilets for disabled shop garden centre ⊗ (ex guide dogs)

NW1

The Jewish Museum   2 for 1

Raymond Burton House, 129-131 Albert St, Camden Town NW1 7NB

➲ (Underground - Camden Town, 3 mins walk from station)

☎ 020 7284 1997

e-mail: marketing@jewishmuseum.org.uk

web: www.jewishmuseum.org.uk

Attractive galleries illustrating Jewish history and religious life in Britain and beyond. One of the world's finest collections of Jewish ceremonial art. There are constantly-changing temporary exhibitions, events and workshops. 2006/7 sees an exhibition on Polish educator, Janusz Korczak, who went to the Nazi death camps with children from his orphanage. In May 2007 there will be an exhibition on Jewish boxers. The site will be closing for re-development in autumn 2007. 2007 is also the 75th anniversary of the Jewish Museum.

Times: Open Mon-Thu, 10-4, Sun 10-5. Closed Jewish Festivals. **Fee:** £3.50 (ch, students, disabled & UB40 £1.50, pen £2.50) Family ticket £8. **Facilities:** ⓟ (outside museum) (pay & display parking) 🍴 ♿ (induction loop in lecture room linked to audio-visual unit) toilets for disabled shop ⊗ (ex guide dogs) 🔗

London Zoo

Regents Park NW1 4RY

➲ (Underground - Camden Town or Regents Park)

☎ 020 7449 6235

e-mail: marketing@zsl.org

web: www.londonzoo.co.uk

London Zoo is home to over 12,000 animals, insects, reptiles and fish. First opened in 1828, the Zoo can claim the world's first aquarium, insect and reptile house. Theres lots to do, plenty to see and so much to learn. Get closer to your favourite animals, learn about them at the keeper talks and watch them show off their skills at special events. By visiting London Zoo, visitors help protect endangered species, conserve natural habitats and bring learning to life for all ages.

Times: Open all year, daily from 10, (closing time dependant on time of year). Closed 25 Dec. **Fee:** ✱ £14.50 (ch 3-15 £11.50, concessions £12.70). **Facilities:** ⓟ (charged) 🍴 🍴 licensed ♿ (wheelchairs & booster scooter available) toilets for disabled shop ⊗ 🔗

England

Madame Tussauds and Stardome

Marylebone Rd NW1 5LR

⮌ (Underground - Baker Street)

☎ 0870 400 3000

e-mail: csc@madame-tussauds.com

web: www.madame-tussauds.com

Madame Tussaud's world-famous waxwork collection was founded in Paris in 1770. It moved to England in 1802 and found a permanent home in London's Marylebone Road in 1884. The 21st century has brought new innovations and new levels of interactivity. Listen to Kylie Minogue whisper in your ear, become an A-list celeb in the 'Blush' nightclub, and take your chances in a high security prison populated by dangerous serial killers. Madame Tussaud's has recently been combined with the equally memorable London Planetarium, where visitors can interact with characters from Disney's *Treasure Planet*.

Times: Open all year 9.30-5.30 (9-6 wknds/summer) **Fee:** ✱ £17.99 (ch under 16 £13.99. (Includes entry into Stardome & The Wonderful World of Stars). **Facilities:** ℗ (200mtrs) 🍴 licensed ৬ (all parts accessible except Spirit of London ride) toilets for disabled shop ⊗ (ex guide dogs) ◥

NW3

Fenton House

Windmill Hill NW3 6RT

⮌ (Underground - Hampstead, right out of station. Cross Heath St, up Holly Hill. Take right fork at top of hill into Hampstead Grove. Entrance on left)

☎ 020 7435 3471

e-mail: fentonhouse@nationaltrust.org.uk

web: www.nationaltrust.org.uk

A William and Mary merchants house built about 1686 and set in a walled garden, Fenton House is now owned by the National Trust. It contains outstanding displays of Oriental and European porcelain, 17th-century needlework pictures and Georgian furniture as well as the Benton Fletcher collection of early keyboard instruments.

Times: Open Mar, Sat & Sun 2-5; Apr-Oct, Sat-Sun & BH Mon 11-5, Wed-Fri 2-5. (Last admission 4.30). **Fee:** ✱ £4.90 (ch £2.45). Family ticket £12. Group 15+ £4.10. Garden only £2 (ch £1). **Facilities:** 🗐 ৬ (photographs of areas which are not accessible) ⊗ (ex assist dogs) ☘

Freud Museum

20 Maresfield Gardens, Hampstead NW3 5SX

⮌ (Underground - Finchley Road, follow blue signs to museum)

☎ 020 7435 2002 & 5167

e-mail: info@freud.org.uk

web: www.freud.org.uk

In 1938, Sigmund Freud left Vienna as a refugee from the Nazi occupation and chose exile in England, transferring his entire domestic and working environment to this house. He worked here until his death a year later. His extraordinary collection of Egyptian, Greek, Roman and Oriental antiquities, his working library and papers, and his fine furniture including the famous desk and couch are all here.

Times: Open all year, Wed-Sun 12-5. Closed BHs, telephone for Xmas Holiday times. **Fee:** ✱ £5 (ch 12-18, students, UB40 & pen £3, ch under 12 free). **Facilities:** ℗ (100yds) (metered parking) 🗐 ৬ (personal tours can be arranged if booked in advance) shop ⊗ (ex guide dogs) ◥

Keats House

Keats Grove, Hampstead NW3 2RR

⮌ (Underground - Hampstead, about 15 mins walk from station)

☎ 020 7435 2062

e-mail: keatshouse@corpoflondon.gov.uk

web: www.cityoflondon.gov.uk

The poet John Keats lived in this house from 1818-1820 and wrote some of his most famous poems, including *Ode to a Nightingale* here. His fiancee, Fanny Brawne, lived next door, and they often walked together on nearby Hampstead Heath. The house contains many of his personal items including inkstand, engagement ring, paintings, jewellery and manuscripts.

Times: Open 23 Apr-10 Dec, Tue-Sun 1-5. Tue-Sat between 10-12 guided tours, schools & visits by appointment take place. **Fee:** ✱ £3.50 (under 16's free, concessions £1.75). Party 10+. Garden free. **Facilities:** ℗ (500yds) (residents parking in operation) 🗐 ৬ toilets for disabled shop ⊗ (ex assist dogs) ◥

Kenwood House

:FREE:

Hampstead Ln NW3 7JR

⮌ (Underground - Hampstead)

☎ 020 8348 1286

web: www.english-heritage.org.uk

In splendid grounds beside Hampstead Heath, this outstanding neo-classical house contains one of the most important collections of paintings ever given to the nation. Works by Rembrandt, Vermeer, Turner, Gainsborough and Reynolds are all set against a backdrop of sumptuous rooms. Scenes from *Notting Hill* and *Mansfield Park* were filmed here.

Times: Open all year, Apr-Oct, daily 11-5; Nov-Mar, daily 11-4. Closed 24-26 Dec & 1 Jan. **Facilities:** ℗ ◨ 🍴 licensed ৬ toilets for disabled shop ⌗

2 Willow Road

2 Willow Rd, Hampstead NW3 1TH

⮌ (Hampstead tube (Northern Line), along High Street, left Flask Walk, right at end into Willow Rd)

☎ 020 7435 6166

e-mail: 2willowroad@nationaltrust.org.uk

web: www.nationaltrust.org.uk

Discover the 1939 home built by the architect Erno Goldfinger for himself and his family. On display is his modern art collection including works by Henry Moore, Bridget Riley, Max Ernst and Marcel Duchamp as well as an extensive collection of original furniture designed by the architect.

Times: Open Mar & Nov, Sat only (open Good Fri). Apr-end Oct, Thu, Fri & Sat: guided tours 12,1 & 2; 3-5 except 1st Thu of each month open 5-9, tours at 5 & 6; Free flow 7-9. **Fee:** ✱ £4.70 (ch £2.35). Joint admission with Fenton House £6.70. **Facilities:** ℗ (100mtrs) (very limited, car park closes often) 🗐 ৬ (video tour of house in cinema) ⊗ (ex assist dogs) ☘

NW8

Ben Uri Gallery, London Jewish Museum of Art

108A Boundary Rd, St John's Wood NW8 0RH

⮑ *(straight on West End Lane (B510), left onto Abbey Rd (B507), pass Beatle landmark, left onto Boundary Rd)*

☎ 020 7604 3991

e-mail: info@benuri.org.uk

web: www.benuri.org.uk

Ben Uri Gallery, The London Jewish Museum of Art, is Britain's oldest Jewish cultural organisation. The Ben Uri Art Society was established in 1915 in London's East End to provide support for the many Jewish artists and craftspeople who were flourishing there in the face of poverty, anti-semitism and isolation from mainstream culture. It was founded by Lazar Berson, a Lithuanian-born designer-maker.

Times: Open Summer: Mon-Fri, 10-5.30, Sun 12-4. Winter: Mon-Thu, 10-5.30, Fri 10-3, Sun 12-4. **Fee:** ✱ £3 (£2 concessions) **Facilities:** Ⓟ (£1.20/hr) ⅙ ⊗

Lord's Tour & M.C.C. Museum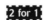

Lord's Ground NW8 8QN

⮑ *(Underground - St John's Wood)*

☎ 020 7616 8595 & 8596

e-mail: tours@mcc.org.uk

web: www.lords.org

Established in 1787, Lord's is the home of the MCC and cricket. Guided tours take you behind the scenes, and highlights include the Long Room and the MCC Museum, where the Ashes and a large collection of paintings and memorabilia are displayed. The Museum is open on match days for spectators. 2-for-1 Voucher applies to public guided tours only, not match day admission to museum.

Times: Open all year, Oct-Mar tours at 12 & 2. Apr-Sep 10, 12 & 2 (restrictions on some match days). Telephone for details & bookings. **Fee:** ✱ Guided tour £8 (ch £5, concessions £6). Family ticket (2ad+2ch) £22. Party 25+. Museum only £3 (concessions £1) plus ground admission (match days only). **Facilities:** Ⓟ ⅐⊙⅟ licensed ⅙ (by arrangement) toilets for disabled shop ⊗ (ex guide dogs) ⊷

NW9

Royal Air Force Museum [FREE]

Grahame Park Way, Hendon NW9 5LL

⮑ *(within easy reach of the A5, A41, M1 and North Circular A406 roads. Tube on Northern Line to Colindale. Rail to Mill Hill Broadway station. Bus route 303 passes the door)*

☎ 020 8205 2266

e-mail: groups@rafmuseum.org

web: www.rafmuseum.org

Take off to the Royal Air Force Museum and soar through the history of aviation from the earliest balloon flights to the latest Eurofighter. Gaze at a world-class collection of over 100 aircraft, aviation/wartime memorabilia and artefacts together with a sound and light show that takes you back in time to the Battle of Britain. The Aeronauts Interactive Centre offers hands-on entertainment and education for all ages and includes cockpit controls, co-ordination tests, engine lifting, air speed, drop zone and pilot testing.

Times: Open daily 10-6. (Last admission 5.30). Closed 24-26 Dec & 1 Jan. Closed 8-12 Jan 2007. **Facilities:** Ⓟ ⅐⊙⅟ licensed ⅙ (lifts, ramps & wheelchairs available) toilets for disabled shop ⊗ (ex guide dogs) ⊷

SE1

Bankside Gallery [FREE]

48 Hopton St SE1 9JH

⮑ *(E of Blackfriars Bridge, South Bank of the Thames, adjacent to Tate Modern and the Millennium Bridge)*

☎ 020 7928 7521

e-mail: info@banksidegallery.com

web: www.banksidegallery.com

Bankside Gallery is the home of the Royal Watercolour Society (RWS) and the Royal Society of Painter-Printmakers (RE). A series of regularly changing exhibitions throughout the year displays the work of both societies.

Times: Open daily during exhibitions, 11-6. **Facilities:** Ⓟ ⅐ ⅙ shop ⊗ (ex assist dogs) ⊷

British Airways London Eye

Riverside Building, County Hall, Westminster Bridge Rd SE1 7PB

⮑ *(Underground - Waterloo/Westminster)*

☎ 0870 500 0600

e-mail: customer.services@ba-londoneye.com

web: www.ba-londoneye.com

British Airways London Eye is one of the most inspiring and visually dramatic additions to the London skyline. At 135m/443ft high, it is the world's tallest observation wheel, allowing you to see one of the world's most exciting cities from a completely new perspective. The London Eye takes you on a gradual, 30 minute, 360 degree rotation, revealing parts of the city, which are simply not visible from the ground. For Londoners and visitors alike, it is the best way to see London and its many celebrated landmarks. The London Eye provides the perfect location for private parties and entertaining and offers a wide variety of in-flight hospitality packages, like champagne and canapés, which are available to enjoy from the privacy of a private capsule.

Times: Open daily, Oct-May, 10-8; Jun-Sep, 10-9. Closed 25 Dec & annual maintenance. **Fee:** ✱ £13 (ch under 5 free, ch £6.50, disabled visitors £10). Fast track entry £25. **Facilities:** Ⓟ (500yds) ⅌ ⅙ (Braille guidebooks, w/chair hire, T-loop, carer ticket) toilets for disabled shop ⊗ (ex guide & hearing dogs) ⊷

Dali Universe

County Hall Gallery, Riverside Building, South Bank SE1 7PB

⮑ *(Waterloo Station - follow signs to South Bank and County Hall, attraction next to London Eye. Westminster Underground - cross Westminster Bridge, County Hall on left).*

☎ 0870 744 7485

e-mail: info@countyhallgallery.com

web: www.countyhallgallery.com

Set in County Hall Gallery, the Dali Universe is host to the world's largest exhibit of surreal and anthropomorphic sculpture by Salvador Dali, including the *Profile of Time* and *Alice in Wonderland*. The exhibition also features a multiplicity of gold ornaments and works in crystal, an unrivalled collection of rare graphics and surreal furniture - including the *Mae West Lips Sofa* - and the monumental *Spellbound* canvas commissioned for the 1945 Hitchcock film of the same name.

Times: ✱ Open daily 10-6.30 (last entry 5.30). Closed 25 Dec. Check website for late summer openings. **Facilities:** Ⓟ (5 mins) ⅐ ⅙ (elevator, ramp access) toilets for disabled shop ⊗ (ex guide dogs) ⊷

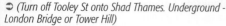

England

Design Museum

2 for 1

Shad Thames SE1 2YD

➲ *(Turn off Tooley St onto Shad Thames. Underground - London Bridge or Tower Hill)*

☎ 0870 909 9009
e-mail: info@designmuseum.org
web: www.designmuseum.org

The Design Museum is the first museum in the world to be dedicated to 20th and 21st century design. Since opening in 1989, it has become one of London's most inspiring attractions and has won international acclaim for its ground-breaking exhibition and education programmes. As one of the leading museums of design, fashion and architecture, the Design Museum has a changing programme of exhibitions, combining compelling insights into design history with innovative contemporary design.

Times: Open all year, daily 10-5.45 (last entry 5.15). Late opening on Fri, during summer months only 9 (last entry 8.30). Closed 25 Dec. **Fee:** £7 (ch under 12 free, concessions £4) **Facilities:** Ⓟ (3 mins) (Gainsford St car park is chargeable) 🅿 🍴 ♿ (ramped entrance, wheelchair & lift) toilets for disabled shop ⊗ (ex guide dogs) 🔳

The Fashion & Textile Museum

83 Bermondsey St SE1 3XF

☎ 020 7403 0222
e-mail: info@ftmlondon.org
web: www.ftmlondon.org

Set on the South Bank, and opened in 2002, the FTM is the first exhibition space in London to dedicate itself to the global fashion industry. The Museum will hold two or three major exhibitions a year, manage an education and outreach programme, and host an extensive digital fashion and textile archive.

Times: ✳ Open all year Tue-Sun 11-5.45 (last admission 5.15)
Facilities: Ⓟ ♿ toilets for disabled shop ⊗ 🔳

Florence Nightingale Museum

2 for 1

St Thomas' Hospital, Gassiot House, 2 Lambeth Palace Rd SE1 7EW

➲ *(Underground - Westminster, Waterloo. On the site of St Thomas' Hospital)*

☎ 020 7620 0374
e-mail: info@florence-nightingale.co.uk
web: www.florence-nightingale.co.uk

Florence Nightingale needs no introduction, but this museum shows clearly that she was more than 'The Lady with the Lamp'. Beautifully designed, the museum creates a personal setting in which a large collection of Florence's personal items including childhood souvenirs, her dress, furniture from her houses and honours awarded to her in old age are displayed. There is a small military history collection of souvenirs from the Crimean War, including military medals and a military nursing uniform.

Times: Open Mon-Fri 10-5; wknds & BHs 10-4.30. (Last admission 1hr before closing). Closed Good Fri, Etr Sat & Sun & 22 Dec-2 Jan. **Fee:** £5.80 (ch & concessions £4.80). Family ticket (2ad+ up to 5ch) £16. Discounted rates for pre-booked groups of 15+. **Facilities:** Ⓞ (charged) 🍴 ♿ toilets for disabled shop ⊗ (ex guide dogs) 🔳

Golden Hinde Educational Trust

2 for 1

6A Horseshoe Wharf, Clink St SE1 9FE

➲ *(On the Thames path between Southwark Cathedral and the new Globe Theatre)*

☎ 020 7403 0123
e-mail: info@goldenhinde.co.uk
web: www.goldenhinde.co.uk

A full size replica of Sir Francis Drake's famous 16th-century galleon. Just like the original, this *Golden Hinde* has circumnavigated the globe. You can explore the five decks, and replica furnishings add to the atmosphere. Special events include Living History re-enactments. There are holiday workshops for children and the ship is also available for private hire.

Times: Open all year, 10-6. Visitors are advised to check opening times as they may vary due to closures for functions. **Fee:** ✳ £5.50 (ch & concessions £5). Family (2ad+3ch) £18 **Facilities:** Ⓟ (on street parking) 🍴 shop ⊗ (ex guide dogs) 🔳

HMS Belfast

Morgans Ln, Tooley St SE1 2JH

➲ *(Underground - London Bridge/Tower Hill/Monument. Rail: London Bridge)*

☎ 020 7940 6300
e-mail: hmsbelfast@iwm.org.uk
web: www.iwm.org.uk/hmsbelfast

Europe's last surviving big gun armoured warship from the Second World War, *HMS Belfast* was launched in 1938 and served in the North Atlantic and Arctic with the Home Fleet. She led the Allied naval bombardment of German positions on D-Day, and was saved for the nation in 1971. A tour of the ship will take you from the Captain's Bridge through nine decks to the massive Boiler and Engine Rooms. You can visit the cramped Mess decks, Officers' Cabins, Galley, Sick Bay, Dentist and Laundry.

Times: Open all year, daily. Mar-Oct 10-6 (last admission 5.15); Nov-Feb 10-5 (last admission 4.15). Closed 24-26 Dec. **Fee:** ✳ £8.50 (ch under 16 free, concessions £5.25). Party £6.50 per person. **Facilities:** 🅿 🍴 ♿ (wheelchair lift for access on board) toilets for disabled shop ⊗ (ex guide dogs) 🔳

Imperial War Museum

Lambeth Rd SE1 6HZ

➲ *(Underground - Lambeth North, Elephant & Castle or Waterloo)*

☎ 020 7416 5320 & 5321
e-mail: mail@iwm.org.uk
web: www.iwm.org.uk

Founded in 1917, this museum illustrates and records all aspects of the two World Wars and other military operations involving Britain and the Commonwealth since 1914. There are always special exhibitions and the programme of special and family events include film shows and lectures. The museum also has a wealth of military reference material, although some reference departments are open to the public by appointment only.

Times: Open all year, daily 10-6. Closed 24-26 Dec. **Fee:** Free admission (charges apply for some temporary exhibitions) **Facilities:** Ⓟ (on street, 100mtrs) (metered Mon-Fri) 🅿 🍴 ♿ (parking & w/chair hire book in advance, study room, T-Loop) toilets for disabled shop ⊗ (ex guide dogs) 🔳

London Aquarium

County Hall, Riverside Building, Westminster Bridge Rd SE1 7PB

➲ (Underground-Waterloo & Westminster. On south bank next to Westminster Bridge, nr Big Ben & London Eye)

☎ 020 7967 8000
e-mail: info@londonaquarium.co.uk
web: www.londonaquarium.co.uk

The London Aquarium is one of Europe's largest displays of global aquatic life with over 350 species in over 50 displays, ranging from the mystical seahorse to the deadly stonefish. The huge Pacific display is home to a variety of jacks, stingrays and seven sharks. Come and witness the spectacular Atlantic feed where our team of divers hand feed rays and native British sharks. The rainforest feed incorporates a frenzied piranha attack with the amazing marksmanship of the archerfish. There is also a range of education tours and literature to enhance any visit.

Times: ✱ Open all year, daily 10-6. (Last admission 1hr before closing). Closed 25 Dec. Late opening over summer months see website for details.
Facilities: Ⓟ (300mtrs) ♿ 🍴 ⓰ (wheelchairs available) toilets for disabled shop ⓧ (ex guide & hearing dogs) 🍴

London Dungeon

28-34 Tooley St SE1 2SZ

➲ (Next to London Bridge Station)

☎ 020 7403 7221
e-mail: london.dungeon@merlinentertainments.biz
web: www.thedungeons.com

Blood and guts, torture and terror, in re-enactments of some of the most gruesome events in British history. Brave the Great Fire of London, sail down the Thames towards Traitor's Gate, or visit Executioners corner. You can also meet some especially Wicked Women. Step back to the 1660s to dodge the rats inhabiting 'The Great Plague', then dodge the flames at The Great Fire before examining the facts concerning The Ripper known as Jack.

Times: Open all year, daily, Apr-Sep 10-5.30; Oct-Mar 10.30-5. Late night opening in the Summer. Telephone for exact times. **Fee:** £16.95 (ch £11.95, concessions £13.95). **Facilities:** Ⓟ (NCP 200yds) ♿ 🍴 ⓰ (cards for deaf visitors) toilets for disabled shop ⓧ (ex guide dogs) 🍴

Museum of Garden History

Lambeth Palace Rd SE1 7LB

➲ (Underground - Waterloo, Westminster, Vauxhall. Next to Lambeth Palace, near Lambeth Bridge)

☎ 020 7401 8865
e-mail: info@museumgardenhistory.org
web: www.museumgardenhistory.org

Situated in the restored church of St. Mary-At-Lambeth, adjacent to Lambeth Palace, the Museum of Garden History provides an insight into the history and development of gardens and gardening in the UK. It houses a fine public display of tools and artefacts. In addition, there is a replica 17th-century knot garden filled with flowers and shrubs of the period, created around the tombs of the famous plant hunters, the John Tradescants, father and son, and Captain William Bligh of the 'Bounty'.

Times: Daily, 10.30-5. Closed 23 Dec-2 Jan **Fee:** ✱ Donations appreciated. Suggested donations: £3 (concessions £2.50) **Facilities:** Ⓟ (100yds) (metered) ♿ 🍴 ⓰ toilets for disabled shop ⓧ (ex guide dogs)

Shakespeare's Globe Exhibition and Theatre Tour

21 New Globe Walk, Bankside SE1 9DT

➲ (Underground - London Bridge, walk along Bankside. Mansion House, walk across Southwark Bridge. St Pauls, walk across Millennium Bridge)

☎ 020 7902 1500
e-mail: info@shakespearesglobe.com
web: www.shakespeares-globe.org

Guides help to bring England's theatrical heritage to life at the 'unparalleled and astonishing' recreation of this famous theatre. Discover what an Elizabethan audience would have been like, find out about the rivalry between the Bankside theatres, the bear baiting and the stews, hear about the penny stinkards and find out what a bodger is.

Times: ✱ Open all year, May-Sep, daily 9-12 (12-5 Rose Theatre tour); Oct-Apr 10-5. **Facilities:** Ⓟ (0.5m) (very limited on-street parking) ♿ 🍴 licensed ⓰ (parking spaces, 'touch tours' available by appointment) toilets for disabled shop ⓧ (ex guide & hearing dogs) 🍴

Southwark Cathedral

London Bridge SE1 9DA

➲ (adjacent to London Bridge (Rd & Station), off Borough High St)

☎ 020 7367 6700
e-mail: cathedral@southwark.anglican.org
web: www.southwark.anglican.org/cathedral

Originally an Augustinian priory, this is London's oldest gothic church building, and has been a place of worship for more than 1,000 years. It became a cathedral for the Diocese of Southwark in 1905, and has links with Chaucer, Dickens and Shakespeare. John Gower and Shakespeare's brother Edmund are buried here. John Harvard of US university fame was baptised here in 1607, and there is a chapel to his memory. Visitors can view part of a Roman road, 14th-century cloister work, and kilns used for Southwark delftware in the 17th/18th centuries.

Times: Open daily: Cathedral 9-6. No tourism permitted on Good Fri & 25 Dec. **Fee:** ✱ Free, suggested donation £4. Mandatory charge for groups, which should pre-book on 020 7367 6734 **Facilities:** Ⓟ (10min walk) 🍴 licensed ⓰ (induction loop, wheelchair available) toilets for disabled shop ⓧ (ex service dogs)

Tate Modern

Bankside SE1 9TG

➲ (Underground - Southwark, Blackfriars)

☎ 020 7887 8008 (info) & 8888
e-mail: information@tate.org.uk
web: www.tate.org.uk

This is the UK's largest museum of modern art and is housed in the impressive Bankside power station. Entrance to the permanent collection, which includes works from artists like Picasso, Warhol and Dalí, is free. Tate Modern also holds world-acclaimed temporary exhibitions as well as education programmes, events and activities.

Times: Open all year, Sun-Thu 10-6 (last admission 5.15), Fri & Sat 10am-10pm (last admission 9.15). Closed 24-26 Dec. **Fee:** Free. A charge is made for special exhibitions. **Facilities:** Ⓟ (reserved for mobility impaired) ♿ 🍴 licensed ⓰ (parking & wheelchairs available call 020 7887 8888) toilets for disabled shop ⓧ (ex guide dogs) 🍴

England

The Tower Bridge Exhibition

Tower Bridge Rd SE1 2UP

➲ *(Underground - Tower Hill or London Bridge)*

☎ 020 7940 3985

e-mail: enquiries@towerbridge.org.uk

web: www.towerbridge.co.uk

One of the capital's most famous landmarks, its glass-covered walkways stand 142ft above the Thames, affording panoramic views of the river. Much of the original machinery for working the bridge can be seen in the engine rooms. The Tower Bridge Exhibition uses state-of-the-art effects to present the story of the bridge in a dramatic and exciting fashion.

Times: Open all year, Apr-Sep 10-6.30 (last ticket 5.30); Oct-Mar 9.30-6 (last ticket 5) **Fee:** ✱ £5.50 (ch £3, concessions £4.25) Family tickets from £14. **Facilities:** ℗ (100yds) ⊞ & toilets for disabled shop ⊗ (ex guide dogs) ◀

Vinopolis, City of Wine

1 Bank End SE1 9BU

➲ *(Underground-London Bridge. Borough High St West exit, right into Stoney St, then left into Park St & follow road round to Vinopolis main entrance)*

☎ 0870 241 4040

e-mail: sales@vinopolis.co.uk

web: www.vinopolis.co.uk

Vinopolis is London's premiere wine attraction, situated on a 2.5 acre site on the vibrant Bankside. It offers an imaginative, interactive tour around the world of wine as well as great tastings. The setting is delightful, with Victorian vaulted ceilings and intricate, almost rustic red brickwork.

Times: Open all year, Mon, Fri & Sat 12-9, Tue-Thu & Sun 12-6, (last admission 2 hrs before closing). Please call for opening hours in Dec and BHs. **Fee:** ✱ Prices start from £15. **Facilities:** ℗ (5-10 min walk) (NCP parking) ▦ ⏺ licensed & (lifts & ramps) toilets for disabled shop ⊗ (ex guide dogs) ◀

Winston Churchill's Britain at War Experience

2 for 1

64/66 Tooley St SE1 2TF

➲ *(mid way down Tooley St, between London Bridge & Tower Bridge. 2min walk from London Bridge Stn)*

☎ 020 7403 3171

e-mail: info@britainatwar.org.uk

web: www.britainatwar.co.uk

A realistic adventure back to the home front to experience life in war-torn Britain during World War II. Take the lift to the underground, where many spent sleepless nights. Explore evacuation, weddings, rationing, air-raids, gas masks, the blackout and walk through the London blitz.

continued

Winston Churchill's
Britain at War Experience

Times: Open all year, Apr-Sep 10-6; Oct-Mar 10-5 (last entry 1hr before closing). Closed 24-26 Dec. **Fee:** ✱ £9.50 (ch 5-16 £4.85, concessions £5.75). Family ticket (2ad+2ch) £25. **Facilities:** ℗ (400mtrs) ⊞ & toilets for disabled shop ⊗ (ex guide dogs) ◀

SE5

South London Gallery

FREE

65 Peckham Rd SE5 8UH

➲ *(from Vauxhall take A202 to Camberwell Green. Gallery halfway between Camberwell Green and Peckham).*

☎ 020 7703 6120 & 9799 (info)

e-mail: mail@southlondongallery.org

web: www.southlondongallery.org

The gallery presents a programme of up to eight exhibitions a year of cutting-edge contemporary art, and has established itself as South East London's premier venue for contemporary visual arts. The Gallery also aims to bring contemporary art of the highest standards to audiences in South London and to assist in the regeneration of the area by attracting audiences from across Britain and abroad.

Times: Open Tue-Sun, 12-6. Closed Mon **Facilities:** ℗ (on-street parking) ▦ ⊞ & (disabled access, induction loop) toilets for disabled ⊗ (ex guide dogs)

SE9

Eltham Palace House & Gardens

Court Yard SE9 5QE

☎ 020 8294 2548

web: www.english-heritage.org.uk

Stephen and Virginia Courtauld's stunning country house shows the glamour and allure of 1930s Art Deco style and is a feast of luxurious design ideas. The house incorporates the medieval Great Hall and stunning moated gardens.

Times: Open Apr-Oct, Sun-Wed 10-5; Nov-20 Dec & 4 Feb-Mar, Sun-Wed 10-4. Closed 21 Dec-3 Feb. **Fee:** House & Gardens: £7.60 (ch £3.80, concessions £5.70). Gardens only: £4.80 (ch £2.40, concessions £3.60). Family £19. Prices and opening times are subject to change in Spring 2007. Please check web site or call 0870 333 1181 for the most up to date prices and opening times when planning your visit. **Facilities:** ℗ & shop ⊗ 🚌 ⊞

SE10

Cutty Sark Clipper Ship

King William Walk, Greenwich SE10 9HT

➲ *(situated in dry dock beside Greenwich Pier)*

☎ 020 8858 2698

e-mail: enquiries@cuttysark.org.uk

web: www.cuttysark.org.uk

The fastest tea clipper ever, built in 1869, she once sailed 363 miles in a single day. Preserved in dry dock since 1957, her graceful lines dominate the riverside at Greenwich. The world's only surviving tea clipper with an amazing history is the highpoint of the age of sail. Cutty Sark contains the largest collection of merchant figureheads in the world and fascinating and historic crew quarters.

Times: Open daily 10-4.30. Currently undergoing restoration. It is planned to keep the ship open as much as possible during the conservation programme, to allow members of the public to experience the science of ship preservation and maintain its heritage. **Facilities:** Ⓟ (50mtrs) 🍴 ♿ shop ⊗ (ex guide dogs) ◀

The Fan Museum NEW

12 Crooms Hill SE10 8ER

➲ *(approached via DLR)*

☎ 020 8305 1441

e-mail: admin@fan-museum.org

Two elegant Georgian houses have been beautifully restored as the setting for the first museum in the world devoted entirely to all aspects of the ancient art and craft of fan making. It exhibits the Helene Alexander collection of fans which has been gifted to the nation.

Times: Open all year Tue-Sat, 11-5 & Sun noon-5. Closed Mon. **Fee:** ✱ £4 (ch under 7 free, concessions £3). Free for OAP's & disabled on Tue after 2pm (ex groups). **Facilities:** Ⓟ 500mtrs ♿ (lift, ramp) toilets for disabled shop garden centre ⊗ (ex assist dogs)

National Maritime Museum

Romney Rd SE10 9NF

➲ *(central Greenwich)*

☎ 020 8312 6565

e-mail: bookings@nmm.ac.uk

web: www.nmm.ac.uk

Britain's seafaring history displayed in an impressive modern museum. Themes include exploration and discovery, Nelson, trade and empire, passenger shipping and luxury liners, maritime London, costume, art

continued

and the sea, and the future of the sea. There are interactive displays for children.

Times: Open all year, daily 10-5 (10-6 Jul-Aug). Closed 24-26 Dec. **Facilities:** Ⓟ (50 yds) (parking in Greenwich limited) 🍺 🍴 licensed 🍴 ♿ (wheelchairs, advisory service for hearing/sight impaired) toilets for disabled shop ⊗ (assist dogs) ◀

See advert on this page

Old Royal Naval College

2 Cutty Sark Gardens, Greenwich SE10 9LW

➲ *(In centre of Greenwich, off the one way system, (college approach), located on the Thames next to the Cutty Sark and Greenwich Pier)*

☎ 020 8269 4799

e-mail: info@greenwichfoundation.org.uk

web: www.greenwichfoundation.org.uk

The old Royal Naval College is one of Londons most famous riverside landmarks. The grade one listed Old Royal Naval College buildings occupy the site of the Tudor palace where Henry VIII and Elizabeth I were born, and were originally designed by Sir Christopher Wren as Greenwich Hospital. The buildings incorporate the magnificent Painted Hall by Thornhill and a Chapel by James Stuart. Also open to the public are the beautiful grounds of the estate, and a visitor centre featuring an exhibition on the World Heritage Site of maritime Greenwich and the history of the site.

Times: Open all year (Painted Hall, Chapel and Visitor Centre), daily 10-5 (last admission 4.15). Chapel open to visitors from 12.30 on Sun, public worship from 11. Closed 24-26 Dec. **Fee:** ✱ Admission free, guided tours £4 (ch under 16 free). **Facilities:** Ⓟ (200mtrs) (all local streets, yellow line roads) 🍺 🍴 licensed 🍴 ♿ (parking, wheelchair, staircrawler, access, all with notice) toilets for disabled shop ⊗ (ex guide dogs) ◀

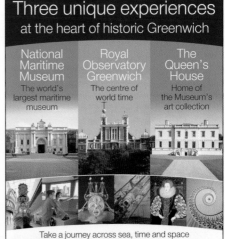

The Queens House

Romney Rd, Greenwich SE10 9NF

➲ (central Greenwich)

☎ 020 8312 6565

e-mail: bookings@nmm.ac.uk

web: www.nmm.ac.uk

The first Palladian-style villa in England, designed by Inigo Jones for Anne of Denmark and completed for Queen Henrietta Maria, wife of Charles I. The Great Hall, the State Rooms and a Loggia overlooking Greenwich Park are notable features. Also displays the extensive art collection of the National Maritime Museum including Tudor and Stuart royalty.

Times: Open daily 10-5. Please telephone for closed dates. Closed 24-26 Dec. **Fee:** Free, except special exhibitions **Facilities:** ❷ (charged) ⚑ licensed ♿ (blind kit/lift/wheelchairs) toilets for disabled shop ⊗ (ex assist dogs) ◀

Royal Observatory Greenwich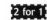

Greenwich Park, Greenwich SE10 9NF

➲ (off A2, Greenwich Park, enter from Blackheath Gate only)

☎ 020 8312 6565

e-mail: bookings@nmm.ac.uk

web: www.nmm.ac.uk

Charles II founded the Royal Observatory in 1675 'for perfecting navigation and astronomy'. It stands at zero meridian longitude and is the original home of Greenwich Mean Time. It houses an extensive collection of historic timekeeping, astronomical and navigational instruments. New astronomy galleries and the Peter Harrison Planetarium will open in June 2007.

Times: Open all year, daily 10-5 (10-6 Jul-Aug). Partial closures 31 Dec, 1 Jan and Marathon day. **Facilities:** ❷ (charged) ♿ (assistance on request) toilets for disabled shop ⊗ ◀

The Wernher Collection at Ranger's House

Chesterfield Walk, Blackheath SE10 8QY

☎ 020 8853 0035

web: www.english-heritage.org.uk

Handsome 18th-century house with lovely views over London, Greenwich Park, Blackheath and the Thames. View the 'Wernher Collection' of self-made millionaire Julius Wernher, who made his fortune in the diamond mines of South Africa.

Times: Open Apr-Sep, Sun-Wed 10-5; Oct-Mar, by appointment only. Closed 23 Dec-28 Feb **Fee:** £5.50 (ch £2.80, concessions £4.10). Prices and opening times are subject to change in Spring 2007. Please check web site or call 0870 333 1181 for the most up to date prices and opening times when planning your visit. **Facilities:** ❷ ♿ toilets for disabled shop ♯

SE18

Firepower

Royal Arsenal, Woolwich SE18 6ST

➲ (A205, right at Woolwich ferry onto A206, attraction signed)

☎ 020 8855 7755

e-mail: info@firepower.org.uk

web: www.firepower.org.uk

Firepower is the Royal Artillery Museum in the historic Royal Arsenal. It spans 2000 years of artillery and shows the development from Roman

continued

catapult to guided missile to self-propelled gun. Put science into action with touchscreen displays and be awed by the big guns.

Times: ✱ Open Wed-Sun & BHs 11-5.30. Phone for winter opening times. **Facilities:** ❷ (charged) ⚑ ♿ (wheelchairs available) toilets for disabled shop ⊗ (ex guide dogs) ◀

Thames Barrier Information & Learning Centre

1 Unity Way SE18 5NJ

➲ (Turn off A102(M) onto A206, turn onto Eastmoor St and follow signs)

☎ 020 8305 4188

e-mail: learningcentre@environment-agency.gov.uk

web: www.environment-agency.gov.uk

Spanning a third of a mile, the Thames Barrier is the world's largest movable flood barrier. The visitors' centre and exhibition on the South Bank explains the flood threat and the construction of this £535 million project, now valued at £1 billion. Each month a test closure of all ten gates, lasting over 2 hours, is carried out and the annual full day closure of all ten gates takes place in the autumn.

Times: Open Apr-Sep, 10.30-4.30. Oct-Mar 11-3.30. Closed 25 Dec-3 Jan **Fee:** £2 (ch £1, pen & students £1.50). **Facilities:** ❷ (charged) ⚑ ♿ (lift from river pier approach) toilets for disabled shop ⊗ (ex guide dogs) ◀

SE21

Dulwich Picture Gallery `2 for 1`

Gallery Rd, Dulwich SE21 7AD

➲ (off South Circular A205, follow signs to Dulwich village)

☎ 020 8693 5254

e-mail: info@dulwichpicturegallery.org.uk

web: www.dulwichpicturegallery.org.uk

This is the oldest public picture gallery in England, housing a magnificent collection of Old Masters, including works by Poussin, Claude, Rubens, Murillo, Van Dyck, Rembrandt, Watteau and Gainsborough. The gallery was designed by Sir John Soane in 1811. The collection, the building and the critically acclaimed loan exhibitions make the gallery a must see for art lovers.

Times: Open all year Tue-Fri 10-5, wknds & BH Mon 11-5. Closed 24-26 Dec, 1 Jan & Good Fri. **Fee:** ✱ £4 (pen £3, ch, students, unemployed & disabled free). £3 for special exhibitions. **Facilities:** ❷ ⚑ licensed ⚑ ♿ (wheelchairs available, hearing loop) toilets for disabled shop ⊗ (ex guide dogs) ◀

SE23

The Horniman Museum & Gardens `FREE`

London Rd, Forest Hill SE23 3PQ

➲ *(situated on A205)*

☎ 020 8699 1872

e-mail: enquiry@horniman.ac.uk

web: www.horniman.ac.uk

Founder Frederick Horniman, a tea merchant, gave the museum to the people of London in 1901. The collection covers the natural and cultural world including Natural History with displays on Vanishing Birds and African Worlds, The Music Gallery, which displays Britain's largest collection of musical instruments and the Centenary Gallery which showcases world cultures. There are 16 acres of gardens, and the museum hosts a variety of workshops and activities for all ages.

Times: Open all year, daily 10.30-5.30. Closed 24-26 Dec. Gardens close at sunset. **Facilities:** ℗ (opposite museum) ☕ 🍴 ♿ (large print leaflets, induction loop) toilets for disabled shop ⊗ (ex guide dogs or in gardens)

SW1

The Banqueting House, Whitehall

Whitehall SW1A 2ER

➲ *(Underground - Westminster, Charing Cross or Embankment)*

☎ 0870 751 5178

web: www.hrp.org.uk

Designed by Inigo Jones, this is the only surviving building of the vast Whitehall Palace, destroyed by fire 300 years ago. The Palace has seen many significant royal events, including the execution of Charles I in 1649. The Banqueting House's Rubens ceiling paintings are stunning examples of the larger works of the Flemish Master and its classical Palladian style set the fashion for much of London's later architecture.

Times: Open all year, Mon-Sat 10-5. Closed Sun, BHs, 24 Dec-1 Jan. Subject to closure at short notice. **Fee:** ✱ £4.50 (ch 5-16 £3, concessions £3.50). **Facilities:** ℗ (5 mins) (no parking in Whitehall) ♿ toilets for disabled shop ⊗ (ex guide/hearing dogs) 🚐

Buckingham Palace

Buckingham Palace Rd SW1 1AA

➲ *(Underground - Victoria, Green Park, St James' Park)*

☎ 020 7766 7300

e-mail: bookinginfo@royalcollection.org.uk

web: www.royalcollection.org.uk

Buckingham Palace has been the official London residence of Britain's sovereigns since 1837. Today it serves as both the home and office of Her Majesty the Queen. Its nineteen State Rooms, which open for eight weeks a year, form the heart of the working palace and more than 50,000 people visit each year as guests at State, ceremonial and official occasions and garden parties. After visiting the State Rooms, visitors can enjoy a walk along the south side of the garden, which offers superb views of the west front of the Palace and the 19th-century lake.

Times: Open Aug-Sep 9.45-6 (last admission 3.45). Entry by timed-ticket. **Fee:** ✱ £14 (ch under 17 £8, ch under 5 free, concessions £12.50) Family ticket (2ad+3ch) £36. **Facilities:** ℗ (200yds) (very limited, driving not recommended) ♿ (ex gardens, pre-booking essential - 020 7766 7324) toilets for disabled shop ⊗ (ex guide dogs) 🚐

Churchill Museum & Cabinet War Rooms

Clive Steps, King Charles St SW1A 2AQ

➲ *(Underground - Westminster (exit 6) or St James Park)*

☎ 020 7930 6961

e-mail: cwr@iwm.org.uk

web: www.iwm.org.uk

Learn more about the man who inspired Britain's finest hour at the interactive and innovative Churchill Museum, the world's first major museum dedicated to the life of the 'Greatest Briton'. Step back in tome and discover the secret underground headquarters that were the nerve centre of Britain's war effort. Located in the heart of Westminster, visitors can view this complex of historic rooms left as they were in 1945, while at the same time taking in the new Churchill Museum.

Times: Open all year, daily 9.30-6. (last admission 5). Closed 24-26 Dec. **Facilities:** ℗ (2 mins walk) (meter parking) ☕ 🍴 ♿ (education service, object handling session, induction loop) toilets for disabled shop ⊗ (ex guide dogs) 🚐

Houses of Parliament

Westminster SW1A 0AA

➲ *(Underground - Westminster)*

☎ 020 7219 4272

web: www.parliament.uk

The Houses of Parliament occupy the Palace of Westminster, a royal palace for nearly 1000 years. Visitors will see the Queen's Robing Room, the Royal Gallery, the Chambers of both the House of Lords and House of Commons, the voting lobbies, historic Westminster Hall (c.1097) where Charles I and Guy Fawkes were put on trial, plus other areas normally hidden from public view.

Times: ✱ Open 24 Jul-4 Sep, Mon, Tue, Fri & Sat, 9.15-4.30, Wed & Thu, 1.15-4.30; 18 Sep-2 Oct, Mon, Fri & Sat, 9.15-4.30, Tue, Wed & Thu 1.15-4.30. Times are for 1st and last tours of the day. **Facilities:** ℗ (50mtrs) (limited parking, metered) ☕ ♿ (touch & sound model for visually impaired) toilets for disabled shop ⊗ (ex guide dogs) 🚌 🚐

Mall Galleries

The Mall SW1Y 5BD

➲ *(Underground - Charing Cross, situated on the Mall, near Trafalgar Square and Admiralty Arch)*

☎ 020 7930 6844

e-mail: info@mallgalleries.com

web: www.mallgalleries.org.uk

The venue for the annual open exhibitions of nine national art societies. There is also a wide range of individual and group shows. The galleries display work which is both traditional and contemporary by a large number of prominent international artists. A variety of subjects are displayed in a number of mediums, including oil, watercolour, drawings and sculpture. Phone for details of special events.

Times: Open all year, daily 10-5. Closed between exhibitions and at Xmas. Some late night opening, please phone for details **Fee:** £2.50 (ch & concessions £1.50). Groups 10+ £1.50 each (Special exhibitions may have different prices - phone for details) **Facilities:** ℗ (50 yds) (no parking on the Mall) ☕ 🍴 ♿ (chairlift to galleries) toilets for disabled ⊗ (ex assist dogs) 🚐

England

The Queen's Gallery

Buckingham Palace, Buckingham Palace Rd SW1A 1AA

⮕ *(Underground - Victoria, Green Park & St. James' Park)*

☎ 020 7766 7301

e-mail: bookinginfo@royalcollection.org.uk

web: www.royalcollection.org.uk

Some of the greatest works of art acquired by kings and queens over 500 years are brought together at the Queens Gallery from royal residences across the UK. The exhibition includes world-famous paintings, some of the finest furniture ever made, spectacular jewels, dazzling works by Fabergé, and historic pieces of silver and gold that are still used for ceremonial occasions today. Exhibitions for 2006/7 include watercolours from the collection of Queen Elizabeth The Queen Mother, and a collection of fans.

Times: Open all year, daily, 10-5.30 (last admission 4.30). 25 Jul-24 Sep, 9.30-5 (last admission 4). Closed 25-26 Dec. **Fee:** ✱ £7.50 (ch under 5 free, ch under 17 £4, pen £6.50). Family Ticket (2ad+3ch) £19.
Facilities: Ⓟ (200yds) (driving not advisable, limited parking) ▥ ♿ (contact 020 7766 7324) toilets for disabled shop ⊗ (ex guide dogs) ◀

The Royal Mews

Buckingham Palace, Buckingham Palace Rd SW1W 0QH

⮕ *(Underground - Victoria, Green Park, St. James Park)*

☎ 020 7766 7302

e-mail: bookinginfo@royalcollection.org.uk

web: www.royalcollection.org.uk

Designed by John Nash and completed in 1825, the Royal Mews houses the State Coaches, horse drawn carriages and motor cars used for coronations, state visits, royal weddings and the State Opening of Parliament. These include the Gold State Coach, made in 1762, with panels painted by the Florentine artist Cipriani. As one of the finest working stables in existence, the Royal Mews provides a unique opportunity for you to see a working department of the Royal Household.

Times: Open Mar-Oct (closed Fri), 11-4; Aug-Sep, daily, 10-5. (Last admission 3.15; Aug-Sep 4.15). Closed Fri. **Fee:** ✱ £6.50 (ch under 5 free, ch 5-16 £4, concessions £5.50) Family ticket (2ad+3ch) £17.50.
Facilities: Ⓟ (200yds) (driving not advisable, parking limited) ▥ ♿ (telephone 020 7766 7324 for access information) toilets for disabled shop ⊗ (ex guide dogs) ◀

Tate Britain

Millbank SW1P 4RG

⮕ *(Underground - Pimlico)*

☎ 020 7887 8888 & rec info 8008

e-mail: information@tate.org.uk

web: www.tate.org.uk

Tate Britain is the national gallery of British art from 1500 to the present day, from Tudors to the Turner Prize. Tate holds the greatest collection of British art in the world, including works by Blake, Constable, Epstein, Gainsborough, Gilbert and George, Hatoum, Hirst, Hockney, Hodgkin, Hogarth, Moore, Rossetti, Sickert, Spencer, Stubbs and Turner. The gallery is the world centre for the understanding and enjoyment of British art. Tate Britain also has regular special exhibitions that reflect the history of British art, and numerous public events. See website for details.

Times: Open daily 10-5.50. Closed 24-26 Dec. **Fee:** ✱ Free. Donations welcomed. Prices vary for special exhibitions. **Facilities:** Ⓟ (100mtrs) (metered parking) ▣ �🍽 licensed ▥ ♿ (wheelchairs on request, parking by prior arrangement) toilets for disabled shop ⊗ (ex guide & hearing dogs) ◀

Westminster Abbey

Broad Sanctuary SW1P 3PA

⮕ *(Underground - Westminster, St James's Park. Next to Parliament Square and opposite the Houses of Parliament)*

☎ 020 7222 5152 & 7654 4900

e-mail: press@westminster-abbey.org

web: www.westminster-abbey.org

Westminster Abbey was originally a Benedictine monastery. In the 11th century, it was re-founded by St. Edward the Confessor. The great Romanesque abbey Edward built next to his royal palace became his burial place shortly after it was completed. Over the centuries that followed, many more kings and queens have been buried, and many great figures commemorated, in the abbey. The abbey has been the setting for nearly every coronation since that of William the Conqueror in 1066, and for numerous other royal occasions. The present building, begun by Henry III in 1245, is one of the most visited churches in the world.

Times: ✱ Open Abbey: Mon-Fri 9.30-3.45, Sat 9-1.45. Wed late night til 7. (Last admission 1hr before closing). No tourist visiting on Sun, however visitors are welcome at services. The Abbey may at short notice be closed for special services & other events. **Facilities:** ▣ ♿ (areas accessible induction loop) shop ⊗ (ex guide dogs) ◀

Westminster Cathedral   FREE

Victoria St SW1P 1QW

⮕ *(300 yds from Victoria Station)*

☎ 020 7798 9055

e-mail: barrypalmer@rcdow.org.uk

web: www.westminstercathedral.org.uk

Westminster Cathedral is a fascinating example of Victorian architecture. Designed in the Early Christian Byzantine style by John Francis Bentley, its strongly oriental appearance makes it very distinctive. The foundation stone was laid in 1895 but the interior decorations are not fully completed. The Campanile Bell Tower is 273ft high and has a four-sided viewing gallery with magnificent views over London. The lift is open daily 9am-5pm Mar-Nov but shut Mon-Wed from Dec-Feb.

Times: Open all year, daily 7am-7pm. **Facilities:** Ⓟ (0.25m) (2hr metered parking) ▣ ▥ ♿ (all parts accessible except side chapels, loop system) shop ⊗ (ex guide dogs)

Westminster Hall

Houses of Parliament, Westminster SW1A 0AA

⮑ *(Underground - Westminster Tube)*

☎ 020 7219 4272

web: www.parliament.uk

Visitors to the home of the British Parliament are guided by a qualified Blue Badge Guide. They follow the route taken by the Queen when she performs the State Opening of Parliament, which includes the Queen's Robing Room, the Royal Gallery, and the Prince's Chamber. The route goes from the House of Lords, through the various lobbies and into the chamber of the House of Commons.

Times: Summer opening: Aug-Sep, open to all. At other times by application to MP. (UK constituents only) **Fee:** ✱ £7 (concessions £5, tours in English), (concessions £7, foreign language tours £9). Tours via MP free. **Facilities:** ℗ (limited 50yds) ♿ toilets for disabled shop ⊗ (ex guide dogs) ➡

SW3

Carlyle's House

24 Cheyne Row SW3 5HL

⮑ *(Underground - Sloane Square. Off Cheyne Walk between Battersea & Albert Bridges)*

☎ 020 7352 7087

e-mail: carlyleshouse@nationaltrust.org.uk

web: www.nationaltrust.org.uk/carlyleshouse

'The Sage of Chelsea' - distinguished essayist and writer of historical works, Thomas Carlyle - lived here, with his wife Jane, from 1834 until his death in 1881. Such literary notables as Tennyson, Thackeray, Browning, George Eliot and Dickens were frequent visitors.

Times: Open Apr-Oct, Wed-Fri 2-5, Sat-Sun & BH Mon, 11-5. (Last admission 4.30). Closed Mon-Tue. Open late Mar-Oct. **Fee:** ✱ £4.20 (ch 5-16, £2.10). Family ticket £10.50. **Facilities:** ℗ (street metered) (residents parking Mon-Sat) ♿ (not suitable for wheelchair users) ⊗ (ex guide & hearing dogs) ➡ ⚏

Chelsea Physic Garden

66 Royal Hospital Rd, SW3 4HS (entrance in Swan Walk)

⮑ *(Underground - Sloane Square)*

☎ 020 7352 5646

e-mail: enquiries@chelseaphysicgarden.co.uk

web: www.chelseaphysicgarden.co.uk

Begun in 1673 for the study of plants used by the Society of Apothecaries, this garden is one of Europe's oldest botanic gardens and is the only one to retain the title 'Physic' after the old name for the healing arts. The garden is still used for botanical and medicinal research, and offers displays of many fascinating plants in lovely surroundings.

Times: Open Apr-Oct, Wed 12-5, Sun 12-6. Additional opening during Chelsea Flower Show week, late May & Chelsea Festival week late Jun. Groups at other times by appointment. **Fee:** ✱ £6 (ch 5-15, students & UB40 £3.50, ch under 5 free) **Facilities:** ℗ (0.5m) (west end of Battersea Park) ➡ 🍴 ♿ (disabled parking, wheelchair access) toilets for disabled shop ⊗ (ex guide dogs)

National Army Museum

FREE

Royal Hospital Rd, Chelsea SW3 4HT

⮑ *(Underground - Sloane Square)*

☎ 020 7730 0717

e-mail: info@national-army-museum.ac.uk

web: www.national-army-museum.ac.uk

The museum offers a unique insight into the lives of Britain's soldiers, with displays including weapons, paintings, equipment, models, medals, and uniforms.

Times: Open all year, daily 10-5.30. Closed Good Fri, May Day, 24-26 Dec & 1 Jan. **Facilities:** ⊙ ➡ 🍴 ♿ (wheelchair lift to access lower ground floor) toilets for disabled shop ⊗ (ex guide dogs)

Royal Hospital Chelsea

FREE

Royal Hospital Rd SW3 4SR

⮑ *(near Sloane Square, off A3216 & A3031)*

☎ 020 7881 5204

e-mail: info@chelsea-pensioners.org.uk

web: www.chelsea-pensioners.org.uk

Founded in 1682 by Charles II as a retreat for army veterans who had become unfit for duty, through injury or long service. The Royal Hospital Chelsea was built on the site of a theological college founded by James I in 1610. The buildings were designed and built by Sir Christopher Wren, and then added to by Robert Adam and Sir John Soane. The hospital houses some 300 'In-Pensioners', some of whom do voluntary work as tour guides, clerical assistants and ground staff. Visitors can stroll around the grounds, gain admission to the Chapel, Great Hall and visit the Museum.

Times: Open daily Mon-Sat, 10-12 & 2-4, Sun 2-4. (Museum closed Oct-Mar) **Facilities:** ℗ (limited) ♿ (induction loop in post office) shop ⊗ (ex staff & guide dogs) ➡

SW7

The Natural History Museum

Cromwell Rd SW7 5BD

⮑ *(Underground - South Kensington)*

☎ 020 7942 5000

e-mail: feedback@nhm.ac.uk

web: www.nhm.ac.uk

This vast and elaborate Romanesque-style building, with its terracotta facing showing relief mouldings of animals, birds and fishes, covers an area of four acres. Holding over 70 million specimens from all over the globe, from dinosaurs to diamonds and earthquakes to ants, the museum provides a journey into Earth's past, present and future. Discover more about the work of the museum through a daily programme of talks from museum scientists or go behind the scenes of the Darwin Centre, the museums scientific research centre.

Times: Open daily 10-5.50 (last admission 5.30). Closed 24-26 Dec. **Fee:** ✱ Free. Charge made for some special exhibitions. **Facilities:** ℗ (180yds) (limited parking, use public transport) ➡ 🍴 licensed 🍴 ♿ (top floor/one gallery not accessible, wheelchair hire) toilets for disabled shop ⊗ (ex guide dogs) ➡

England

Science Museum

Exhibition Rd, South Kensington SW7 2DD

⮑ *(Underground - South Kensington, signed from tube stn)*

☎ 0870 870 4868

e-mail: sciencemuseum@nmsi.ac.uk

web: www.sciencemuseum.org.uk

See iconic objects from the history of science, from Stephenson's Rocket to the Apollo 10 command module; be amazed by a 3D IMAX movie; take a ride in a simulator; visit an exhibition; and encounter the past, present and future of technology in seven floors of free galleries, including the famous hands-on section where children can have fun investigating science with the Museum's dedicated Explainers. The Museum is free, but charges apply to the IMAX cinema, special exhibitions and simulators.

Times: Open all year, daily 10-6. Closed 24-26 Dec. **Fee:** Admission free. Charges apply for IMAX 3D cinema, simulators & some special exhibitions. **Facilities:** ℗ (metered 0.5m away) 🖤 🍴 licensed 🛍 ♿ (personal 2hr tour of museum, hearing loop) toilets for disabled shop ⊗ (ex guide dogs) ◀

Victoria and Albert Museum

Cromwell Rd, South Kensington SW7 2RL

⮑ *(Underground - South Kensington, Museum situated on A4, Buses C1, 14, 74, 414 stop outside the Cromwell Road entrance)*

☎ 020 7942 2000

e-mail: vanda@vam.ac.uk

web: www.vam.ac.uk

The world's finest museum of art and design, with collections spanning 3000 years, and comprising sculpture, furniture, fashion and textiles, paintings, silver, glass, ceramics, jewellery, books, prints, and photographs from Britain and all over the world. Highlights include the national collection of paintings by John Constable, the Dress Court showing fashion from 1500 to the present day, a superb Asian collection, the Jewellery Gallery including the Russian Crown Jewels, and the 20th Century Gallery, devoted to contemporary art and design. The stunning British Galleries 1500-1900 tell the story of British design from the Tudor age to the Victorian era.

Times: Open all year, Mon-Sun 10-5.45. Wed & last Fri of month open late, 10am-10pm. Closed 24-26 Dec. **Fee:** ✱ Free admission but some exhibitions may carry an extra charge. **Facilities:** ℗ (500yds) (limited, charged parking) 🖤 🍴 licensed ♿ (Facilities available. Call for details 020 7942 2211) toilets for disabled shop ⊗ (ex guide dogs) ◀

London Wetland Centre

2 for 1

Queen Elizabeth Walk SW13 9WT

⮑ *(underground - Hammersmith).*

☎ 020 8409 4400

e-mail: info@wetlandcentre.org.uk

web: www.wwt.org.uk

An inspiring wetland landscape that stretches over 105 acres, almost in the heart of London, in Barnes SW13. 30 wild wetland habitats have been created from reservoir lagoon to ponds, lakes and reedbeds and all are home to a wealth of wildlife.

Times: Winter 9.30-4, Summer 9.30-5. **Fee:** ✱ £7.25 (ch £4.50 & concessions £6). Family ticket £18.50. Groups 10+. Car park £2 charge on Sun & BH's per vehicle. **Facilities:** ℗ (charged) 🖤 🍴 licensed ♿ (ramps, lifts) toilets for disabled shop ⊗ (ex guide dogs)

Wimbledon Lawn Tennis Museum

Museum Building, The All England Club, Church Rd SW19 5AE

⮑ *(Underground - Southfields, 15mins walk)*

☎ 020 8946 6131

e-mail: museum@aeltc.com

web: www.wimbledon.org/museum

Visitors to the Wimbledon Lawn Tennis Museum are invited to explore the games evolution from a garden party pastime to a multi-million dollar professional sport played worldwide. Highlights include the Championship Trophies, a cinema that captures the Science of Tennis using Matrix-style special effects, film and video footage of some of the most memorable matches, and an extensive collection of memorabilia dating back to 1555.

Times: Open daily all year, 10.30-5. Closed middle Sun of Championships, Mon immediately following the Championships, 24-26 Dec & 1 Jan. **Fee:** ✱ £7.50 (ch £4.75, ch under 5 free, concessions £6.25). Party 15+. **Facilities:** ❷ 🖤 ♿ (lift, stairlift to cafe) toilets for disabled shop ⊗ (ex guide dogs) ◀

Apsley House, The Wellington Museum

149 Piccadilly, Hyde Park Corner W1J 7NT

⮑ *(Underground - Hyde Park Corner, exit 1 overlooking rdbt)*

☎ 020 7499 5676

web: www.english-heritage.org.uk

Number One, London, is the popular name for one of the Capital's finest private residences, 19th-century home of the first Duke of Wellington. Built in the 1770s, its rich interiors have been returned to their former glory, and house the Duke's magnificent collection of paintings, silver, porcelain, sculpture and furniture.

Times: Open all year Apr-Oct, Tue-Sun & BHs 10-5; Nov-Mar, Tue-Sun 10-4. Closed 24-26 Dec & 1 Jan. **Fee:** £5.10 (ch £2.60, concessions £3.80). Joint ticket to House & Wellington Arch: £6.50 (ch £3.50, concessions £4.90. Family £16.30). Prices & opening times are subject to change in Spring 2007. Please check web site or call 0870 333 1181 for the most up to date prices and opening times. **Facilities:** ℗ (NCP 10mins walk) 🛍 ♿ (lift) shop ⊗ (ex guide dogs) ⧗ ◀

Handel House Museum

25 Brook St W1K 4HB

⮑ *(off Park Lane into Brook Gate, then Upper Brook Street. Pass Claridge's Hotel on right. The entrance is in Lancashire Court)*

☎ 020 7495 1685

e-mail: mail@handelhouse.org

web: www.handelhouse.org

Home to George Frideric Handel from 1723 until his death in 1759, the Handel House Museum celebrates Handel's career and times. It was here that Handel composed his *Messiah*, *Zadok the Priest* and *Music for the Royal Fireworks*. Over 200 years later, live music, educational projects and public events still bring Handel's former home to life.

Times: Open all year Tue, Wed, Fri & Sat 10-6, Thu 10-8, Sun 12-6. Closed Mon & BHs, 25-26 Dec & 1-2 Jan. **Fee:** ✱ £5 (ch £2, concessions £4.50). Free for children on Sat. **Facilities:** ℗ (10-20mtrs) (congestion charge during week) 🛍 ♿ (lift) toilets for disabled shop ⊗ (ex guide dogs) ◀

Pollock's Toy Museum

1 Scala St W1T 2HL

⮑ *(Underground - Goodge St)*

☎ 020 7636 3452

e-mail: pollocks@btconnect.com

web: www.pollockstoymuseum.com

Teddy bears, wax and china dolls, dolls' houses, board games, toy theatres, tin toys, mechanical and optical toys, folk toys and nursery furniture, are among the attractions to be seen in this appealing museum. Items from all over the world and from all periods are displayed in two small, interconnecting houses with winding staircases and charming little rooms.

Times: Open all year, Mon-Sat 10-5. Closed BH, Sun & Xmas. **Fee:** ✱ £3 (ch 3-18 £1.50) **Facilities:** ℗ (100yds) (Central London restrictions) ♿ shop ◥

Royal Academy Of Arts

Burlington House, Piccadilly W1J 0BD

⮑ *(Underground - Piccadilly Circus, head towards Green Park)*

☎ 020 7300 8000 & 5760

e-mail: traveltrade@royalacademy.org.uk

web: www.royalacademy.org.uk

Known principally for its exhibitions, the Royal Academy of Arts was founded in 1768 and is Britain's oldest Fine Arts institution. Two of its founding principles were to provide a free school and to mount 'an annual exhibition open to all artists of distinguished merit', now known as the Summer Exhibition. Both continue today. The Royal Academy's most prized possession, Michelangelo's Tondo, *The Virgin and Child with the Infant St John*, one of only four marble sculptures by the artist outside Italy, is on permanent display in the Sackler Wing. The recently opened John Madejski Fine Rooms are a suite of six rooms displaying the highlights from the RA collection.

Times: Open daily 10-6. Late night opening Fri 10am-10pm. **Fee:** £7-£11 (ch, students, pen & group visitors reduced price). Prices vary for each exhibition. Free entry to permanent collection. **Facilities:** ℗ (400yds) (disabled parking call in advance) ▆ ⑩ licensed ▥ ♿ (large-print guides/labels, sign language) toilets for disabled shop ⊗ (ex guide dogs) ◥

Wallace Collection FREE

Hertford House, Manchester Square W1U 3BN

⮑ *(Underground - Bond St, Baker St, Oxford Circus)*

☎ 020 7563 9500

e-mail: enquiries@wallacecollection.org

web: www.wallacecollection.org

An elegant 18th-century town house is an appropriate gallery for this outstanding collection of art. Founded by the 1st Marquis of Hertford, it was bequeathed to the nation in 1897 and came on public display three years later. As well as an unrivalled representation of 18th-century French art with paintings by Boucher, Watteau and Fragonard, Hertford House is the home of Frans Hals' *Laughing Cavalier* and of paintings by Gainsborough, Rubens, Delacroix and Titian. It also houses the largest collection of arms and armour outside the Tower of London.

Times: ✱ Open all year, Mon-Sat 10-5, Sun 12-5. Closed Good Fri, May BH, 24-26 Dec & 1 Jan. **Facilities:** ℗ (NCP & meters) (meters free on Sun) ▆ ⑩ licensed ▥ ♿ (lift, ramp, wheelchair available upon request) toilets for disabled shop ⊗ (ex guide dogs) ◥

W2

Serpentine Gallery FREE

Kensington Gardens W2 3XA

⮑ *(Underground - Knightsbridge, Lancaster Gate, South Kensington. Bus 9, 10, 12, 52, 94)*

☎ 020 7402 6075

e-mail: varind@serpentinegallery.org

web: www.serpentinegallery.org

The Serpentine Gallery, named after the lake in Hyde Park, is situated in the heart of Kensington Gardens in a 1934 tea pavilion, and was founded in 1970 by the Arts Council of Great Britain. Today the Gallery attracts over 400,000 visitors a year and is one the best places in London for modern and contemporary art and architecture.

Times: ✱ Open daily 10-6. **Facilities:** ℗ (charged) ▥ ♿ toilets for disabled shop ⊗ (ex guide dogs) ◥

W4

Chiswick House

Burlington Ln, Chiswick W4 2RD

⮑ *(Underground - Gunnersbury)*

☎ 020 8995 0508

web: www.english-heritage.org.uk

Discover the story of this celebrated Palladian villa, a fine example of 18th-century English architecture with lavish interiors and classical landscaping.

Times: Open Apr-Oct, Wed-Sun & BHs 10-5 (closes 2 Sat). Closed Nov-Mar but pre-booked are available, please telephone for details. **Fee:** £4 (ch £2, concessions £3). Family £10. Prices and opening times are subject to change in Spring 2007. Please check web site or call 0870 333 1181 for the most up to date prices and opening times when planning your visit. **Facilities:** ℗ ▆ ♿ (telephone in advance for wheelchair facilities) shop ⌗

Hogarth House FREE

Hogarth Ln, Great West Rd W4 2QN

⮑ *(50yds W of Hogarth rdbt on Great West Road A4)*

☎ 020 8994 6757

e-mail: info@cip.org.uk

web: www.hounslow.info

This 18th-century house was the country home of artist William Hogarth (1697-1764) during the last 15 years of his life. The house contains displays on the artist's life, and many of his satirical engravings. The gardens contain Hogarth's famous mulberry tree.

Times: Open Apr-Oct, Tue-Fri 1-5, Sat-Sun 1-6; Nov-Mar, Tue-Fri 1-4, Sat-Sun 1-5. Closed Mon (ex BHs), Jan, Good Fri & 25-26 Dec. **Facilities:** ℗ (25 & 50yds) (spaces marked in Axis Centre car park) ♿ (telephone in advance to confirm) toilets for disabled shop ⊗ (ex guide dogs)

Directions are provided by the attractions.

England

W8

Kensington Palace State Apartments & Royal Ceremonial Dress Collection

Kensington Gardens W8 4PX

➲ *(Underground - High Street Kensington or Notting Hill Gate)*

☎ 0870 751 5170

web: www.hrp.org.uk

Highlights of a visit to Kensington include the Kings and Queens Apartments with a fine collection of Old Masters; Tintoretto and Van Dyke amongst them. The rooms used by Princess Victoria are also shown, including her bedroom, where she was woken to be told she was Queen. The Royal Ceremonial Dress Collection includes representations of tailor's and dressmaker's workshops, and a display of dresses that belonged to Diana, Princess of Wales.

Times: Open Mar-Oct 10-6 (last admission 5); Nov-Feb 10-5 (last admission 4). Closed 24-26 Dec. **Fee:** £11.50 (ch £7.50, concessions £9). Family ticket (2ad+3ch) £34. **Facilities:** ℗ (500yds) ♥ ﴾ (cafeteria has wheelchair access ramp) toilets for disabled shop ⊗ (ex guide dogs) ◄

Linley Sambourne House

18 Stafford Ter W8 7BH

➲ *(Underground - High Street Kensington)*

☎ 020 7602 3316 ext 305

e-mail: museums@rbkc.gov.uk

web: www.rbkc.gov.uk/linleysambournehouse

The home of Linley Sambourne (1844-1910), chief political cartoonist at *Punch* magazine, has had its magnificent artistic interior preserved, almost unchanged, since the late 19th century. Also displayed are many of Sambourne's own drawings and photographs. Tours are lead by costumed actors with scripts developed from the Sambourne family archive.

Times: ✱ all access by guided tour. 5 Mar-11 Dec. Sat & Sun tours 10, 11.15, 1, 2.15, 3.30. Wkdays book in advance **Facilities:** ℗ (2 min walk) (metered parking) shop ⊗ ◄

W12

BBC Television Centre Tours

BBC Television Centre, Wood Ln W12 7RJ

➲ *(Underground - Central Line/White City)*

☎ 0870 603 0304

e-mail: bbctours@bbc.co.uk

web: www.bbc.co.uk/tours

Take a look behind the scenes at the world's most famous TV centre. As the BBC TV Centre is a working building, no guarantees can be made as to what visitors will see, although dressing rooms, the News Centre, the Weather Centre, and various studios are all possible. The uncertain nature of the visit means that no two are the same, and that only pre-booked guided tours are available. For children 7 years and over find out what goes on behind the scenes of CBBC's television programmes.

Times: Open Mon-Sat. Tours at 10, 10.20, 10.40, 1.15, 1.30, 1.45, 3.30, 3.45 & 4. Closed Xmas & BH's. All tours must be pre-booked. **Fee:** ✱ £8.95 (concessions £7.95, student £6.50). Family ticket £25 **Facilities:** ℗ (10min walk) (no site disabled parking only) ﴾ (wheelchair & sign language available) toilets for disabled shop ⊗ (ex assist dogs) ◄

W14

Leighton House Museum & Art Gallery

12 Holland Park Rd W14 8LZ

➲ *(Underground - High St Kensington. Museum is N of Kensington High St, off Melbury Rd)*

☎ 020 7602 3316

e-mail: museums@rbkc.gov.uk

web: www.rbkc.gov.uk/leightonhousemuseum

An opulent and exotic example of high Victorian taste, Leighton House was built for the President of the Royal Academy, Frederic Lord Leighton. The main body of the house was built in 1866 but the fabulous Arab Hall, an arresting 'Arabian Nights' creation, was not completed until 13 years later.

Times: ✱ Open all year, daily 11-5.30. Closed Tue. **Facilities:** ℗ (100mtrs) (metered) ▥ shop ⊗ ◄

WC1

British Museum `FREE`

Great Russell St WC1B 3DG

➲ *(Underground - Russell Sq, Tottenham Court Rd, Holborn)*

☎ 020 7323 8000

e-mail: information@thebritishmuseum.ac.uk

web: www.thebritishmuseum.ac.uk

Of the world and for the world, the British Museum brings together astounding examples of universal heritage, for free. Enter through the largest covered square in Europe. Pick up your audio guide, children's pack or What's On programme. Then discover the world through objects like the Aztec mosaics, the Rosetta Stone, El Anatsui's African textiles or the colossal Ramesses II. And if you want a more intimate look, a fantastic evening meal or some world cinema, come late - every Thursday and Friday.

Times: ✱ Open all year, Gallery: Sat-Wed 10-5.30 & Thu-Fri 10-8.30. Great Court: Sun-Wed 9-6, Thu-Sat 9am-11pm. Closed Good Fri, 24-26 Dec & 1 Jan. **Facilities:** ℗ (5 mins walk) ♥ ♨ licensed ▥ ﴾ (parking by arrangement) toilets for disabled shop ⊗ (ex guide/companion dogs) ◄

The Cartoon Museum NEW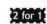

35 Little Russell St WC1A 2HH

➲ *(left off New Oxford St into Museum St, then left into Little Russell St)*

☎ 020 7580 8155

e-mail: info@cartoonmuseum.org

web: www.cartoonmuseum.org

The main galleries display over 200 original cartoons, comics, cartoon strips and caricatures by many of the greatest and funniest of British cartoonists past and present. There is also a programme of temporary exhibitions which change regularly.

Times: Open all year Tue-Sat 10.30-5.30, Sun 12-5.30. **Fee:** £3 (ch under 18 free, concessions £2) **Facilities:** ℗ (charged) ﴾ (hearing loop, large print labels) toilets for disabled shop ⊗ (ex assist dogs) ◄

The Charles Dickens Museum

48 Doughty St WC1N 2LX

➲ *(Underground - Russell Square or Chancery Lane)*

☎ 020 7405 2127

e-mail: info@dickensmuseum.com

web: www.dickensmuseum.com

Charles Dickens lived in Doughty Street in his twenties and it was here he worked on his first full-length novel, *The Pickwick Papers*, and later *Oliver Twist* and *Nicholas Nickleby*. Pages of the original manuscripts are on display, together with valuable first editions, his marriage licence and many other personal mementoes.

Times: ✱ Open all year, Mon-Sat 10-5, Sun 11-5. **Facilities:** ℗ (in street) (metered, 2 hrs max) 🍴 ᕼ shop ✖ ◼

Petrie Museum of Egyptian Archaeology   `FREE`

Malet Place, Univerity College London WC1E 6BT

➲ *(on 1st floor of the D M S Watson building, in Malet Place, off Torrington Place)*

☎ 020 7679 2884

e-mail: petrie.museum@ucl.ac.uk

web: www.petrie.ucl.ac.uk

One of the largest and most inspiring collections of Egyptian archaeology anywhere in the world. The displays illustrate life in the Nile Valley from prehistory, through the era of the Pharoahs to Roman and Islamic times. Especially noted for its collection of the personal items that illustrate life and death in Ancient Egypt, including the world's earliest surviving dress (c 2800BC).

Times: ✱ Open all year, Tue-Fri 1-5, Sat 10-1. Closed for 1 wk at Xmas/Etr. **Facilities:** 🍴 ᕼ (wheelchair lift) toilets for disabled shop ✖ (ex guide dogs)

WC2

Courtauld Gallery

Somerset House, Strand WC2R 0RN

➲ *(Underground - Temple, Embankment, & Covent Garden)*

☎ 020 7848 2526

e-mail: galleryinfo@courtauld.ac.uk

web: www.courtauld.ac.uk

The Galleries contain the superb collection of paintings begun by Samuel Courtauld in the 1920s and 1930s and presented to the University of London in memory of his wife. This is the most important collection of Impressionist and post-Impressionist works in Britain and includes major works by Cezanne, Renoir, Degas, van Gogh, Monet, Manet, Seurat and others. A programme of temporary exhibitions regularly includes works from the prints and drawings collection, while the long-term loan of early 20th-century paintings have added to the depth and range of the displays. Contact the gallery for current exhibition schedule.

Times: Open daily 10-6. (Last admission 5.15). **Fee:** £5 (concessions £4). **Facilities:** ℗ (NCP Drury Lane) 🍽 🍴 ᕼ (parking by arrangement only, call 020 7836 8686, lift) toilets for disabled shop ✖ (ex guide dogs) ◼

Gilbert Collection

Somerset House, Strand WC2R 1LA

➲ *(Underground - Temple, Covent Garden)*

☎ 020 7420 9400

e-mail: info@gilbert-collection.org.uk

web: www.gilbert-collection.org.uk

An outstanding collection of decorative arts and an important bequest to the nation. The Gilbert Collection is the gift of Sir Arthur Gilbert and is on permanent display at Somerset House. The museum includes European silver, gold snuff boxes and Italian mosaics, the displays also include furniture, clocks and portrait miniatures. Temporary exhibitions run throughout the year.

Times: Open daily 10-6, last admission 5.15. **Facilities:** ℗ (400mtrs) 🍽 🍴 licensed 🍴 ᕼ (lifts, hearing loop, wheelchair hire, disabled parking) toilets for disabled shop ✖ (ex guide dogs) ◼

Hunterian Museum   `FREE`

The Royal College of Surgeons, 35-43 Lincoln's Inn Fields WC2A 3PE

➲ *(Underground - Holborn)*

☎ 020 7869 6560

e-mail: museums@rcseng.ac.uk

web: www.rcseng.ac.uk

The Hunterian Museum at the Royal College of Surgeons houses over 3000 anatomical and pathological preparations collected by the surgeon John Hunter (1728-1793). New interpretive displays explore Hunter's life and work, the history of the Hunterian Museum and the College, and the development of surgery from the 18th century to the present. The MacRae Gallery provides a dedicated space for learning based on the museum's reserve collections. The museum also stages a changing programme of temporary exhibitions, lectures and other public events on themes related to the history and current practice of surgery.

Times: Open all year Tue-Sat 10-5. Closed 21 Dec-3 Jan, Good Fri & Etr Sat. **Facilities:** ℗ (15mtrs) (pay & display 8.30-6.30pm) 🍴 ᕼ (Descriptive tours by arrangement) toilets for disabled shop ✖ (ex guide dogs)

England

National Gallery

Trafalgar Square WC2N 5DN

➲ (Underground - Charing Cross, Leicester Square, Embankment & Piccadilly Circus. Rail: Charing Cross. Located on N side of Trafalgar Sq)

☎ 020 7747 2885

e-mail: information@ng-london.org.uk

web: www.nationalgallery.org.uk

All the great periods of Western European painting from 1260-1900 are represented here. The Gallery's particular treasures include Velázquez's *Toilet of Venus*, Leonardo da Vinci's Cartoon (*The Virgin and Child with Saints Anne and John the Baptist*), Rembrandt's *Belshazzar's Feast*, Van Gogh's *Sunflowers*, and Titian's *Bacchus and Ariadne*. The British paintings include Gainsborough's *Mr and Mrs Andrews* and Constable's *Haywain*. Free guided tours everyday.

Times: Open all year, daily 10-6, (Wed until 9). Special major charging exhibitions open normal gallery times. Closed 24-26 Dec & 1 Jan. **Fee:** Free. Admission charged for some major exhibitions. **Facilities:** Ⓟ (100yds) 🍽 licensed 🛗 ♿ (wheelchair, induction loop, lift, deaf/blind visitor tours) toilets for disabled shop ⊗ (ex guide & hearing dogs) 🅿

National Portrait Gallery

St Martin's Place WC2H 0HE

➲ (Underground - Charing Cross, Leicester Square. Buses to Trafalgar Square)

☎ 020 7306 0055

web: www.npg.org.uk

The National Portrait Gallery is home to the largest collection of portraiture in the world featuring famous British men and woman who have created history from the Middle Ages until the present day. Over 1000 portraits are on display across three floors from Henry VIII and Florence Nightingale to The Beatles and HM The Queen. And, if you want to rest those weary feet, visit the fabulous Portrait Restaurant on the top floor with roof-top views across London. Special events take place throughout the year, see website for details.

Times: Open all year, Mon-Wed & Sat-Sun 10-6, Thu-Fri 10-9. Closed Good Fri, 24-26 Dec & 1 Jan. (Gallery closure commences 10mins prior to stated time). **Fee:** ✱ Free (ex special exhibitions) **Facilities:** Ⓟ (200yds) 🍽 licensed 🛗 ♿ (stair climber, touch tours, audio guide, large print captions) toilets for disabled shop ⊗ (ex guide dogs) 🅿

Sir John Soane's Museum

13 Lincoln's Inn Fields WC2A 3BP

➲ (Underground - Holborn)

☎ 020 7405 2107

e-mail: jbrock@soane.org.uk

web: www.soane.org

Sir John Soane was responsible for some of the most splendid architecture in London, and his house, built in 1812, contains his collections of antiquities, sculpture, paintings, drawings and books. Amongst his treasures are the *Rake's Progess* and *Election* series of paintings by Hogarth.

Times: Open all year, Tue-Sat 10-5. Also first Tue of month 6-9pm. (Closed BH, Good Fri & 24 Dec). Lecture tour Sat 2.30 (limited no of tickets sold from 2pm) **Fee:** Donations welcome. **Facilities:** Ⓟ (200yds) (metered parking) 🛗 ♿ (wheelchair available, phone for details of accessibility) shop ⊗ (ex guide dogs) 🅿

Theatre Museum

Russell St, Covent Garden WC2E 7PR

➲ (Underground - Covent Garden, Leicester Sq)

☎ 020 7943 4700

e-mail: tmenquiries@vam.ac.uk

web: www.theatremuseum.org

Major developments, events and personalities from the performing arts, including stage models, costumes, prints, drawings, posters, puppets, props and a variety of other theatre memorabilia. There are guided tours, demonstrations on the art of stage make-up, and you can dress up in costumes from National Theatre companies. Groups are advised to book in advance. Theatre and walking tours 2pm Saturdays.

Times: Open all year, Tue-Sun 10-6. Closed 24-26 Dec & 1 Jan. **Fee:** ✱ Free (ex pre-booked groups which are charged for) **Facilities:** Ⓟ (meters, NCP 250yds) 🛗 ♿ (Braille guides, audio tours, workshops) toilets for disabled shop ⊗ (ex guide dogs) 🅿

We endeavour to be as accurate as possible, but changes to times and other information can occur after the guide has gone to press.

BARNET MAP 04 TQ29

Museum of Domestic Design & Architecture

Middlesex University, Cat Hill EN4 8HT

➲ *(from M25, junct 24 signed A111 Cockfosters to Cat Hill rdbt, straight over onto Chase side. Entrance 1st right opposite Chicken Shed Theatre on Cat Hill Campus)*

☎ 020 8411 5244

e-mail: moda@mdx.ac.uk

web: www.moda.mdx.ac.uk

MoDA is a museum of the history of the home. It holds one of the world's most comprehensive collections of decorative design for the period 1870 to 1960, and is a rich source of information on how people decorated and lived in their homes. MoDA has two galleries, a lecture theatre for study days, a seminar room with practical workshops for both adults and children, and a study room which gives visitors access to the collections.

Times: Open Tue-Sat 10-5, Sun 2-5. Closed Mon, Etr, Xmas & New Year.
Facilities: ❷ 🔊 & (induction loop fitted in lecture theatre) toilets for disabled shop ⊗ (ex guide dogs)

BEXLEY MAP 05 TQ47

Hall Place   `FREE`

Bourne Rd DA5 1PQ

➲ *(near junct of A2 & A233)*

☎ 01322 526574

web: www.hallplace.com

Hall Place is an attractive Grade I listed mansion of chequered flint and brick, with wonderful gardens. There is topiary in the form of the 'Queen's Beasts'; rose, rock, peat and water gardens; and a herb garden with a fascinating range of plants (labelled in Braille) for medicine and cooking. There is also a conservatory, a local studies centre and museum. Please telephone for details of the programme of temporary exhibitions, lectures and concerts in the museum and Great Hall.

Times: ✱ Open all year, House: Mon-Sat 10-5, Sun & BHs 11-5 (Apr-Oct); Tue-Sat 10-4.15 (Nov-Mar). Gardens: Mon-Fri 7.30-dusk, Sat & Sun 9-dusk.
Facilities: ❷ 🔊 �🍴 licensed 🔊 & toilets for disabled shop garden centre ⊗ (ex guide/hearing dogs)

BEXLEYHEATH MAP 05 TQ47

Red House

Red House Ln DA6 8JF

➲ *(off A221 Bexleyheath. At 1st rdbt take 2nd exit then 3rd exit at next rdbt, then 1st left into Danson Rd)*

☎ 020 8304 9878

web: www.nationaltrust.org.uk/redhouse

Commissioned by William Morris in 1859 and designed by Philip Webb, Red House is of enormous international significance in the history of domestic architecture and garden design. The building is constructed of warm red brick, under a steep red-tiled roof, with an emphasis on natural materials and a strong gothic influence. The garden was designed to 'clothe' the house with a series of subdivided areas which still exist. Inside, the house retains many of the original features and fixed items of furniture designed by Morris and Webb.

Times: ✱ 16-27 Feb & Oct-Dec, 11-4.15; 2 Mar-Sep, 11-5. Open BH Mons. Closed 25-26 Dec & Jan-14 Feb. **Fee:** ✱ £6 (ch £3). Family ticket £15. NT members free. **Facilities:** ℗ 20 min walk 🔊& shop ⊗ (ex assist dogs) 🐾🍴

BRENTFORD MAP 04 TQ17

Kew Bridge Steam Museum

Green Dragon Ln TW8 0EN

➲ *(Underground - Kew Gardens, District line then 391 bus. Museum 100yds from N side of Kew Bridge)*

☎ 020 8568 4757

e-mail: info@kbsm.org

web: www.kbsm.org

This Victorian pumping station has steam engines and six beam engines, five of which are working and one of which is the largest in the world. The Grand Junction 90 inch engine is over 40 feet high, and weighs around 250 tons. A diesel house and waterwheel can also be seen along with London's only steam narrow-gauge railway, which operates every Sunday (Mar-Nov). The Water for Life Gallery tells the story of London's water supply from Pre-Roman times.

Times: Open all year (ex Mon) daily 11-5. Engines in steam, wknds & BHs.
Fee: ✱ Wkdays £4.25, wknds £5.75 (ch free, concessions available)
Facilities: ❷ 🔊 ⓓ & (wheelchairs, large print guide) toilets for disabled shop 🍴

Musical Museum

399 High St TW8 0DU

➲ *(Underground - Gunnersbury, nr Kew Bridge)*

☎ 020 8560 8108

web: www.musicalmuseum.co.uk

This museum will take you back to a bygone age to hear and see a marvellous working collection of automatic musical instruments from small music boxes to a mighty Wurlitzer theatre organ. Working demonstrations. The museum is closed throughout 2006 for relocation to new purpose-built premises, which will open towards the end of Jan 2007.

Times: Closed 2006 for relocation. Will re-open at the end of Jan 2007.
Facilities: ❷ 🔊 ⓓ & toilets for disabled shop ⊗ (guide dogs)

CHESSINGTON MAP 04 TQ16

Chessington World of Adventures

Leatherhead Rd KT9 2NE

➲ *(M25 junct 9/10, on A243)*

☎ 0870 444 7777

web: www.chessington.com

With over 90% of its rides suitable for under-12s, this is the ideal place for an action-packed family day out. Very small children are entertained in Animal Land, Land of the Dragons, and on the Toytown fun-rides. Among the multitude of fun-packed areas are Beanoland, the Mystic East, the Forbidden Kingdom, Mexicana, Transylvania, and the Market Square. 2006 saw the introduction of the bubbletastic Bubbleworks water ride, where riders float in bubble tubs over chutes, fountains and foam. The Monkey & Bird Garden is a new animal attraction, as is Creature Features with skunks, porcupines and meerkats. Plenty of special events and shows including Halloween fun and TV characters.

Times: Open 27 Mar-Oct (excluding some off peak days in Sep) either 10-5 or 10-6 (telephone for details). Zoo opens 9.30 **Fee:** ✱ £29 (ch £19.50) 1 ch under 12 free with each full paying adult. Family ticket (2 ad & 2 ch) £58 **Facilities:** ❷ 🔊 ⓓ🍴 licensed 🔊 & (some rides not accessible, disabled guide available) toilets for disabled shop ⊗ (ex assist dogs) 🍴

England

CHISLEHURST MAP 05 TQ47

Chislehurst Caves
2 for 1

Old Hill BR7 5NB

➲ *(off A222 near Chislehurst railway stn. Turn into station approach, then right & right again into Caveside Close)*

☎ 020 8467 3264

e-mail: enquiries@chislehurstcaves.co.uk

web: www.chislehurstcaves.co.uk

Miles of mystery and history beneath your feet. Grab a lantern and get ready for an amazing adventure! Visit the caves and your whole family can travel back in time as you explore the maze of passageways dug through the chalk deep beneath Chislehurst. Accompanied by an experienced guide on a 45 minute tour you'll see the tunnels made famous as a shelter during the Second World War, visit the cave's church, druid altar, the haunted pool and much more!

Times: Open all year, Wed-Sun, 10-4. Daily during local school hols (incl half terms). Closed Xmas. **Fee:** £5 (ch & pen £3). **Facilities:** ♿ 💺 🍽 licensed 🛍 shop ⊗ (ex guide dogs) 🔊

DOWNE MAP 05 TQ46

Down House - Home of Charles Darwin

BR6 7JT

➲ *(off A233, signed)*

☎ 01689 859119

web: www.english-heritage.org.uk

Charles Darwin, perhaps the most influential scientist of the 19th-century, lived at Down House for over 40 years. He wrote the revolutionary book, *On the Origin of Species* here. Explore the exhibition on the first floor and visit the ground floor study, which was the centre of his life.

Times: Open Early Feb-Mar, Wed-Sun, 10-4; Apr-mid Jul & Sep, Wed-Sun & BHs 10-6; mid Jul-Aug, daily (House 11-5); Oct, Wed-Sun 10-5; Nov-mid Dec, Wed-Sun 10-4.Closed 18 Dec-6 Feb. **Fee:** £6.90 (ch £3.50, concessions £5.20). Family £17.30. Prices and opening times are subject to change in Spring 2007. Please check web site or call 0870 333 1181 for the most up to date prices and opening times when planning your visit. **Facilities:** ♿ 🚻 shop ⊗ ⚞

ESHER MAP 04 TQ16

Claremont Landscape Garden

Portsmouth Rd KT10 9JG

➲ *(1m S of Esher on A307)*

☎ 01372 467806

e-mail: claremont@nationaltrust.org.uk

web: www.nationaltrust.org.uk/claremont

Laid out by Vanbrugh and Bridgeman before 1720, extended and naturalised by Kent, this is one of the earliest surviving example of an English landscaped garden. Its 50 acres include a lake with an island pavilion, a grotto and a turf amphitheatre.

Times: Open all year Apr-Oct daily, Mon-Fri 10-6, Sat-Sun & BH Mon 10-7, Nov-Mar daily (ex Mon) 10-5 or sunset if earlier. (Closed all day 19-22 & 26 Jul, closed 2pm 23-24 Jul). Closed 25 Dec & 1 Jan. House not National Trust. **Fee:** £5 (ch £2.50). Family ticket £12.50 **Facilities:** ♿ 💺 🍽 ♿ (wheelchairs available, Braille guide) toilets for disabled shop ⊗ (ex on leads, Nov-Mar only) 🐾 🔊

HAM MAP 04 TQ17

Ham House

Ham St TW10 7RS

➲ *(W of A307, between Kingston & Richmond)*

☎ 020 8439 8241

e-mail: hamhouse@nationaltrust.org.uk

web: www.nationaltrust.org.uk/hamhouse

Ham House is a fine example of 17th-century fashion and power. Built in 1610, the house was enlarged in the 1670s when it was at the heart of Restoration court life and intrigue. It was then occupied by the same family until 1948. The formal garden is significant for its survival in an area known as the cradle of the English Landscape Movement. The outbuildings include an orangery, an ice house, a still house, and a dairy. Open-air theatre and ghost tours, contact for details.

Times: Open Gardens: all year, Sat-Wed 11-6 or dusk if earlier. Closed 25-26 Dec & 1 Jan. House: 25 Mar-29 Oct, Sat-Wed 1-5. (Last admission 4.30). **Fee:** ✱ House & Garden £8 (ch £4). Family ticket £19. Garden only £4 (ch £2). Family ticket £9. **Facilities:** ♿ 💺 🛍 ♿ (Braille guide, wheelchairs, induction loop, lift, parking) toilets for disabled shop ⊗ (ex assist dogs) 🐾 🔊

HAMPTON COURT MAP 04 TQ16

Hampton Court Palace

KT8 9AU

➲ *(A3 to Hook underpass then A309. Train from Waterloo - Hampton Court, 2mins walk from station)*

☎ 0870 752 7777

e-mail: hamptoncourt@hrp.org.uk

web: www.hrp.org.uk

With over 500 years of royal history Hampton Court Palace has something to offer everyone, from the magnificent State Apartments to the domestic reality of the Tudor Kitchens. Costumed guides and audio tours bring the palace to life and provide an insight into how the palace would have been in the time of Henry VIII and William III. There is also an exhibition that explores community life after the departure of the monarchy from the Palace, along with an audio installation in the world famous maze. The newest addition is a multi-sensory experience involving the Tudor kitchens.

Times: Open all year from 10, closes 6 mid Mar-mid Oct, 4.30 mid Oct-mid Mar. Closed 24-26 Dec. **Fee:** £12.30 (ch £8, concessions £10). Family £36.40 **Facilities:** ♿ (charged) 💺 🍽 licensed ♿ (lifts, buggies for gardens, wheelchairs, wardens to assist) toilets for disabled shop ⊗ (ex guide/hearing dogs) 🔊

ISLEWORTH MAP 04 TQ17

Syon House

TW8 8JF

⮑ *(A310 Twickenham road into Park Rd)*

☎ 020 8560 0882 & 0883

e-mail: info@syonpark.co.uk

web: www.syonpark.co.uk

Set in 200 acres of parkland, Syon House is the London home of the Duke of Northumberland, whose family have lived here since the late 16th century. During the second half of the 18th century the first Duke of Northumberland engaged Robert Adam to remodel the interior and 'Capability' Brown to landscape the grounds. Adam was also responsible for the furniture and decorations, and the result is particularly spectacular in the superbly coloured Ante-Room and Long Gallery.

Times: ✱ Open 28 Mar-Oct, Wed-Thu, Sun & BH 11-5 (last ticket 4). **Fee:** House & Garden £7.50 (ch/concessions £6.50). Family ticket £17. **Facilities:** ℗ ♨ ⅃ (stairclimer available) toilets for disabled shop garden centre ⊗ ⧢

Syon Park

TW8 8JF

⮑ *(A310 Twickenham road into Park Rd)*

☎ 020 8560 0882

e-mail: info@syonpark.co.uk

web: www.syonpark.co.uk

Contained within the 40 acres that make up Syon Park Gardens is one of the inspirations for the Crystal Palace at the Great Exhibition of 1851: a vast crescent of metal and glass, the first construction of its kind in the world and known as the Great Conservatory. Although the horticultural reputation of Syon Park goes back to the 16th century, its beauty today is thanks to the master of landscape design, 'Capability' Brown.

Times: ✱ Open all year, Apr-Oct daily, 10.30-5.30; (4pm Nov-Mar) **Fee:** £3.75 (ch/concessions £2.50). Family ticket £6. **Facilities:** ℗ ♨ ⅃ toilets for disabled shop garden centre ⊗ (ex guide dogs) ⧢

KEW MAP 04 TQ17

Kew Gardens (Royal Botanic Gardens)

TW9 3AB

⮑ *(Underground - Kew Gdns)*

☎ 020 8332 5655

e-mail: info@kew.org

web: www.kew.org

Kew Gardens is a paradise throughout the seasons. Lose yourself in the magnificent glasshouses and discover plants from the world's deserts, mountains and oceans. Wide-open spaces, stunning vistas, listed buildings and wildlife contribute to the Gardens unique atmosphere. As well as being famous for its beautiful gardens, Kew is world renowned for its contribution to botanical and horticultural science.

Times: Open all year, Gardens daily 9.30. Closing times vary (seasonal, visit website or phone to verify). Closed 24&25 Dec. **Fee:** £9.50 (ch under 17 free, concessions £6.50). **Facilities:** ℗ (charged) ♨ ⅌ licensed ⌸ ⅃ (16 seat bus tour: enquiries ring 020 8332 5643) toilets for disabled shop garden centre ⊗ (ex guide dogs) ⧢

Kew Palace

Royal Botanic Gardens TW9 3AB

⮑ *(Underground - Kew Bridge)*

☎ 0870 751 5179

web: www.hrp.org.uk

A fairly modest red-brick building, built in the Dutch style with gables, Kew Palace was built in 1631 and used until 1818 when Queen Charlotte died. A major renovation project was completed in April 2006, and the palace was reopened to the public after ten years of closure. Visitors can see artefacts that belonged to George III and his family, and gain access to the second floor, which has never before been open to the public. There are also rooms on the second floor, faithfully recreated with décor and furnishings as George III and his family would have known them in the early 1800s.

Times: Open Apr-Sep, Tue-Sun 10-6 (last admission 5) **Fee:** £5 (ch £3 concessions 34) Admission ticket to Kew Gardens must be purchased in order to access Kew Palace **Facilities:** ℗ (charged) ⅃ toilets for disabled ⊗

The National Archives `FREE`

Ruskin Av TW9 4DU

⮑ *(Underground - Kew Gardens)*

☎ 020 8392 5202 & 020 8487 9202

e-mail: events@pro.gov.uk

web: www.pro.gov.uk/

The National Archives houses one of the finest, most complete archives in Europe, comprising the records of the central government and law courts from the Norman Conquest to the present century. It is a mine of information and some of the most interesting material including Domesday Book.

Times: ✱ Open Mon, Wed & Fri, 9-4.45; Tue, 10-7; Thu, 9-7. Closed 1st wk in Dec, Sun & public holiday wknds. **Facilities:** ℗ ♨ ⅃ (hearing loops & large print text in museum) toilets for disabled shop ⊗ (ex guide dogs)

Queen Charlotte's Cottage

Royal Botanic Gardens TW9 3AB

⮑ *(Underground - Kew Gardens)*

☎ 0870 751 5179

web: www.hrp.org.uk

Typical of the fashionable rustic style popular with the gentry in the 18th century, the cottage was built for George III and Queen Charlotte as a home for their menagerie of exotic pets, as well as a picnic spot and summer house.

Times: Open wknds Jul & Aug. **Fee:** Free with entry to Kew Gardens **Facilities:** ℗ ⊗

The National Trust: For over a hundred years, the NT has been acquiring and protecting threatened coastline, countryside and buildings. To find out more about this organisation, its sites, and policies, visit their website: **www.nationaltrust.org.uk**

England

MORDEN

MAP 05 TQ26

Morden Hall Park

FREE

Morden Hall Rd SM4 5JD

➲ (A298 (Bushey Rd), right at 2nd lights into Martin Way. Morden Hall signed)

☎ 020 8417 8091

e-mail: mordenhallpark@nationaltrust.org.uk

web: www.nationaltrust.org.uk

A green oasis in the heart of South West London. A former deer park, with a network of waterways including meadow, wetland and woodland habitats. Also discover the picturesque rose garden with over 2000 roses, fragrant from May to September.

Times: Open daily, 8-6. **Facilities:** 🅿 💻 🍴 🛗 ♿ (wheelchair, Braille guides, large handled cutlery) toilets for disabled shop (open 10-5) garden centre 🐾 🍴

OSTERLEY

MAP 04 TQ17

Osterley Park and House

Jersey Rd TW7 4RB

➲ *(signed from A4. Underground - Osterley)*

☎ 020 8232 5050

e-mail: osterley@nationaltrust.org.uk

web: www.nationaltrust.org.uk/osterley

In 1761, the founders of Child's Bank commissioned Robert Adam to transform a Tudor mansion into an elegant, neo-classical villa. This was their house in the country, created to entertain and impress friends and business associates. Today the spectacular interiors contain one of Britain's most complete examples of Adam's work. The house is set in over 350 acres of park and farm land, complete with Pleasure Grounds, ornamental lakes and garden buildings.

Times: ✱ Open all year: Park & pleasure grounds, daily 9-7.30 or sunset if earlier. House: Mar Sat & Sun 1-4.30, Apr-Oct, Wed-Sun 1-4.30, BH Sun & Mon 1-4.30. Closed 25-26 Dec. **Facilities:** 🅿 (charged) 💻 🍴 ♿ (Braille guide, wheelchairs, electric carts, stair climber) toilets for disabled shop ⊗ (ex assist dogs in house) 🐾 🍴

TWICKENHAM

MAP 04 TQ17

Marble Hill House

Richmond Rd TW1 2NL

☎ 020 8892 5115

web: www.english-heritage.org.uk

A magnificent Thames-side Palladian villa built for Henrietta Howard, mistress of King George II, set in 66 acres of riverside parklands.

Times: Open Apr-Oct, Sat 10-2, Sun & BHs 10-5. Tours on Tue & Wed 12 & 3. Closed Nov-Mar but pre-booked groups by arrangement. Closed 22 Dec-7 Feb. **Fee:** £4 (ch £2, concessions £3). Family ticket £10. Closed 22 Dec-7 Feb. Closed 22 Dec-7 Feb. Prices and opening times are subject to change in Spring 2007. Please check web site or call 0870 333 1181 for the most up to date prices and opening times when planning your visit. **Facilities:** 🅿 💻 🍴 licensed ♿ toilets for disabled shop ⊗ (ex on lead in certain areas) 🚻

Museum of Rugby & Twickenham Stadium Tours

Rugby Football Union, Rugby Rd TW1 1DZ

➲ *(A316, follow signs to museum)*

☎ 0870 405 2021

e-mail: museum@rfu.com

web: www.rfu.com/microsites/museum/

Combine a behind the scenes guided tour of the world's most famous rugby stadium with a visit to The Museum of Rugby. The tour includes breathtaking views from the top of the North Stand, a visit to the England dressing room and ends by walking through the players tunnel to pitch side. The multi-media museum appeals to enthusiasts of all ages and charts the history and world-wide growth of rugby. You can also test your skills on the scrum machine.

Times: Open, Tue-Sat 10-5 (last museum admission 4.30), Sun 11-5 (last admission 4.30). Closed post Twickenham match days, Etr Sun, 24-26 Dec & 1 Jan. On match days museum only available to match ticket holders. **Fee:** ✱ Museum & Tour £9 (concessions £6). Family £30. **Facilities:** 🅿 ♿ toilets for disabled shop ⊗ (ex guide dogs) 🍴

Orleans House Gallery

FREE

Riverside TW1 3DJ

➲ *(Richmond road (A305), Orleans Rd is on right just past Orleans Park School)*

☎ 020 8831 6000

e-mail: m.denovellis@richmond.gov.uk

web: www.richmond.gov.uk

Stroll beside the Thames and through the woodland gardens of Orleans House, where you will find stunning 18th-century interior design and an excellent public art gallery. Visitors of all ages can try out their own artistic talents in pre-booked workshops, and wide-ranging temporary exhibitions are held throughout the year - please telephone for details.

Times: ✱ Open Oct-Mar, Tue-Sat 1-4.30, Sun & BH 2-4.30; Apr-Sep Tue-Sat 1-5.30, Sun & BH 2-5.30. **Facilities:** 🅿 🍴 ♿ (handling objects & large print labels for some exhibitions) toilets for disabled shop ⊗ (ex guide dogs)

Merseyside

Metropolitan Cathedral of Christ the King,
Liverpool

Europe's City of Culture 2008 has plenty to offer the visitor. There are more listed
buildings here than anywhere outside London, and the docks and city centre are a
World Heritage Site. The Roman Catholic Cathedral ia a gem of modern architecture
and home to one of the finest choirs in the UK. Britain's largest and busiest port for
centuries, Liverpool's maritime past has had a huge impact on the identity of the city. In
recent years it has seen a massive investment and huge regeneration in the waterfront
areas, especially Albert Dock, home of Tate Liverpool.

England

BIRKENHEAD
MAP 07 SJ38

Historic Warships
East Float, Dock Rd CH41 1DJ

➲ *(end of M53 all docks turn off follow tourist signs. From Liverpool Wallasey tunnel 1st exit after toll & follow brown heritage signs)*

☎ 0151 650 1573
e-mail: manager@historicwarships.org
web: www.historicwarships.org

HMS *Onyx* served in the Falklands and is the only submarine afloat in the UK that visitors can explore. HMS *Plymouth*, an anti-submarine frigate also served in the Falklands. The U534 is the only WWII German U-Boat to be raised from the sea bed. Pre-booking required, only adults and children over 12 years (2 per adult) admitted to U-Boat.

Times: ✱ Open all year, Sep-Mar daily 10-4, Apr-Aug daily 10-5. Closed 24-26 Dec, only open wknds for first 6 wks of year. **Facilities:** ℗ ▪ 🖬 ⬛ Ġ (museum, ltd access to HMS Plymouth, multimedia tour of U534) toilets for disabled shop ⊗ (ex guide dogs) ◀

LIVERPOOL
MAP 07 SJ39

The Beatles Story
`2 for 1`
Britannia Pavilion, Albert Dock L3 4AD

➲ *(follow signs to Albert Dock. Located outside Britannia Pavilion, next to Premier Travel Inn)*

☎ 0151 709 1963
e-mail: info@beatlesstory.com
web: www.beatlesstory.com

Relive the story of the four lads from Liverpool who took the world by storm and changed the face of popular music for ever. Features include a replica of the Cavern, George Harrison's first guitar, and exhibitions on John Lennon's post-Beatles career, the Quarrymen and the Yellow Submarine. The audio guide is narrated by John Lennon's sister, Julia, and other contributions come from the likes of George Martin, Pete Best and Gerry Marsden.

Times: Open all year 10-6 (last admission 5). Closed 25-26 Dec. **Fee:** £8.99 (ch 5-16yrs £4.99 & concessions £5.99). Family ticket (2ad+3ch) £25. **Facilities:** ℗ (charged) ⬛ Ġ (hearing loop, large print guide) shop ⊗ (ex guide dogs) ◀

Central Library
`FREE`
William Brown St L3 8EW

➲ *(located between museum and art gallery)*

☎ 0151 233 5858
e-mail: refhum.central.library@liverpool.gov.uk
web: www.liverpool.gov.uk

The Picton, Hornby and Brown buildings, situated in the Victorian grandeur of William Brown Street, house Liverpool's collection of over one million books, forming one of Britain's largest and oldest public libraries. The Liverpool Record Office is one of the country's largest and most significant County Record offices. Regular exhibitions of treasures from the collections are held, please telephone for details.

Times: ✱ Open all year, Mon-Fri 9-6, Sat 10-4 & Sun 12-4. Closed BHs. **Facilities:** ℗ (50 yds) (pay & display parking only) Ġ (lift, text magnification, reading machine) toilets for disabled ⊗ (ex guide dogs)

Conservation Centre
`FREE`
White Chapel L1 6HZ

➲ *(follow brown tourist signs to Whitechapel)*

☎ 0151 478 4999
web: www.nmgm.org.uk

Award winning centre, the only one of its kind, gives the public an insight into the world of museum and gallery conservation.

Times: ✱ Mon-Sat 10-5, Sun 12-5. Closed 23-26 Dec & 1 Jan. **Facilities:** ℗ (charged) ⬛ 🖬 Ġ toilets for disabled shop ⊗ (ex guide dogs) ◀

The Grand National Experience
Aintree Racecourse, Ormskirk Rd L9 5AS

➲ *(Aintree Racecourse on A59 (Liverpool to Preston road), clearly signed)*

☎ 0151 522 2921
e-mail: aintree@rht.net
web: www.aintree.co.uk

A fascinating look at Britain's most famous horserace, the Grand National. Visitors can sit in the jockeys' weighing-in chair, walk around the dressing rooms, watch video presentations, and view a gallery of paintings and photography depicting the race.

Times: Please telephone for details. **Facilities:** ℗ ⦿ licensed Ġ toilets for disabled ⊗ (ex guide dogs) ◀

HM Customs & Excise National Museum
`FREE`
Merseyside Maritime Museum, Albert Dock L3 4AQ

➲ *(Albert Dock - follow brown signs)*

☎ 0151 478 4999
web: www.nmgm.org.uk

Enter the exciting world of smuggle busting where everyday items reveal their hidden secrets. Find a fake, rummage for hidden goods and spot a suspect traveller. Look into the illustrious history of HM Customs & Excise, it's the longest battle in history and it's still going on today!

Times: ✱ Open daily 10-5. Closed 23-26 Dec & 1 Jan. **Facilities:** ℗ ⬛ ⦿ licensed 🖬 Ġ (restricted wheelchair access, no access to basement) toilets for disabled shop ⊗ (ex guide dogs) ◀

Liverpool Cathedral
St James' Mount L1 7AZ

➲ *(follow city centre signs 'Cathedrals'. St James' Mount is off Upper Duke St in S side of city centre, adjacent to 'Chinatown')*

☎ 0151 709 6271
e-mail: eryl.parry@liverpoolcathedral.org.uk
web: www.liverpoolcathedral.org.uk

Although it appears at first sight to be as old as any other monumental cathedral in Britain, Liverpool Cathedral is in fact a 20th-century structure that was only completed in 1978. Its foundation stone was laid in 1904, and through two World Wars the building continued. It is the largest Anglican Cathedral in Europe, and has the largest pipe organ and the heaviest ringing peal of bells in the world. 2007 sees the launch of a new visitor centre with a film, audio tours

continued

and interactive stations. There will also be a full programme of family activities throughout the year, contact for details.

Times: Open daily 8-6, 26 Dec 8-3. **Fee:** Free. £3 donation per person recommended. Tower £4.25 (concessions £2.50) Family ticket (2ad+3ch) £10. **Facilities:** ❷ (charged) ⬛ ⭐ licensed 🍴 ♿ (Braille leaflets, handrails, lift) toilets for disabled shop ⊗ (ex assist dogs) ◀

Liverpool Football Club Visitors Centre Tour

Anfield Rd L4 0TH

☎ 0151 260 6677

e-mail: Museum1@liverpoolfc.tv

web: www.liverpoolfc.tv

Touch the famous "This is Anfield" sign as you walk down the tunnel to the sound of the crowd at the LFC museum and tour centre. Celebrate all things Liverpool, past and present. Bright displays and videos chart the history of one of England's most successful football clubs and more recent glories are recalled, as the 2001 "Treble" is on display, as well as the "Fab Four" European cups.

Times: ✱ Open all year: Museum daily 10-5 last admission 4. Closed 25-26 Dec. Match days 9 until last admission - 1hr before kick off. Museum & Tour - tours are run subject to daily demand. Advance booking is essential to avoid disappointment. **Facilities:** ❷ ⬛ ⭐ licensed ♿ (lifts, ramps to all areas for wheelchairs) toilets for disabled shop ⊗ (ex guide dogs) ◀

Liverpool Museum

William Brown St L3 8EN

➲ (in city centre next to St George's Hall and Lime St, follow brown signs)

☎ 0151 478 4393

e-mail: themuseum@liverpoolmuseums.org.uk

web: www.liverpoolmuseums.org.uk

One of Britain's most interesting museums, the Liverpool Museum has diverse collections ranging from the Amazonian rain forests to the mysteries of outer space. Special attractions include the award-winning hands-on Natural History Centre and the Planetarium.

Times: ✱ Open Mon-Sat 10-5, Sun noon-5. Closed 23-26 Dec & 1 Jan. **Facilities:** ❷ ⬛ 🍴 ♿ toilets for disabled shop ⊗ (ex guide dogs)

Merseyside Maritime Museum

Albert Dock L3 4AQ

➲ (entry into Dock from The Strand)

☎ 0151 478 4499

web: www.liverpoolmuseums.org.uk

Set in the heart of Liverpool's magnificent waterfront, the Merseyside Maritime Museum offers a unique insight into the history of the great port of Liverpool, its ships and its people.

Times: ✱ Open daily 10-5. Closed 23-26 Dec & 1 Jan. **Facilities:** ❷ ⭐ licensed 🍴 ♿ (lifts, wheelchairs, ramps, ex pilot boat & basement) toilets for disabled shop ⊗ (ex guide dogs) ◀

Metropolitan Cathedral of Christ the King

Mount Pleasant L3 5TQ

➲ (10 mins walk from either Liverpool Lime St or Liverpool Central Railway Station. 'Smart' buses stop outside. Cathedral well signed from city centre)

☎ 0151 709 9222

e-mail: info@metcathedral.org.uk

web: www.liverpoolmetrocathedral.org.uk

A modern Roman Catholic cathedral which provides a focal point on the Liverpool skyline. The imposing structure of curving concrete ribs and stained glass was designed by Sir Frederick Gibberd and consecrated in 1967. Monumental crypt of brick and granite by Sir Edwin Lutyens 1933. Numerous modern works of art.

Times: Open daily 8-6 (Sun 5 in winter). **Fee:** Free admission, although donation of £3 requested **Facilities:** ❷ (charged) ⬛ ⭐ licensed 🍴 ♿ (lift, loop system, no access to Crypt) toilets for disabled shop ⊗ (ex guide dogs) ◀

National Wildflower Centre

Court Hey Park, Roby Rd L16 3NA

➲ (M62 junct 5, take A5080 to rdbt. Exit into Roby Rd, entrance 0.5m on left)

☎ 0151 738 1913

e-mail: info@nwc.org.uk

web: www.nwc.org.uk

Set in a public park on the outskirts of Liverpool, the National Wildflower Centre promotes the creation of wildflower habitats around the country and provides educational materials, wildflower seeds and interactive facilities. The Centre has demonstration areas, children's activities, a working nursery, compost display and rooftop walk. The centre has a comprehensive programme of events through the summer. Special Events: Green Fayre June 2007, Knowsley Flower Show August 2007, Winter celebration December 2007.

Times: Open Mar-Aug, daily 10-5. **Fee:** ✱ £3 (ch 5-16, pen, students & unemployed £1.50). Family ticket (2 ad + 2 ch) £7.50. Season ticket & group discount tickets available. **Facilities:** ❷ ⬛ 🍴 ♿ (electric buggy & wheelchair available) toilets for disabled shop garden centre ⊗ (ex guide dogs & in park) ◀

England

Sudley House `FREE`

Mossley Hill Rd L18 8BX

➲ *(near Aigburth Station and Mossley Hill Station)*

☎ 0151 724 3245

e-mail: sudley@liverpoolmuseums.org.uk

web: www.sudleyhouse.org.uk

The former family home of the Liverpool merchant George Holt in the Liverpool suburb of Mossley Hill. Works on show are drawn mainly from his collection of British paintings including Landseer, Turner, Gainsborough, Reynolds and Romney as well as major pre-Raphaelite painters. Many of the original Victorian features of the building survive, including tiles, ceramics, stained glass and wallpaper.

Times: ✱ Open Mon-Sat 10-5, Sun noon-5. Closed 23-26 Dec & 1 Jan.
Facilities: ❷ ♨ ⬛ ♿ ⊗ (ex guide dogs)

Tate Liverpool

Albert Dock L3 4BB

➲ *(within walking distance of Liverpool Lime Street train station)*

☎ 0151 702 7400 & 7402

e-mail: visiting.liverpool@tate.org.uk

web: www.tate.org.uk/liverpool/

Tate Liverpool is one of the largest galleries of modern and contemporary art outside London and is housed in a converted warehouse in the historic Albert Dock. The gallery is home to the National Collection of Modern Art in the North, and has four floors displaying work selected from the Tate Collection, as well as special exhibitions which bring together artwork loaned from around the world. Upcoming shows include Jake & Dinos Chapman; Liverpool and the Avant-garde; Peter Blake, and Contemporary Chinese Art.

Times: ✱ Open Tue-Sun, BH Mon & all Mons in Jun-Aug, 10-5.50. Closed 24-26 Dec, 1 Jan & Good Fri **Fee:** Admission free. £5 (concessions £4) for special exhibitions, phone for details. **Facilities:** ℗ (5 min walk Pay & Display) ♨ ♿ (wheelchairs available, leaflets in Braille, hearing loop) toilets for disabled shop ⊗ (ex assist dogs) ◀

Walker Art Gallery `FREE`

William Brown St L3 8EL

➲ *(follow brown and white signs)*

☎ 0151 478 4199

web: www.nmgm.org.uk

For over 120 years, visitors have been surprised, charmed & moved by The Walker's world-famous collection including masterpieces by Rembrandt, Poussin, Rubens and Murillo. Newly refurbished galleries will display an exciting and varied programme of must see exhibitions.

Times: ✱ Open Mon-Sat 10-5, Sun 12-5. Closed 23-26 Dec & 1 Jan.
Facilities: ❷ (charged) ♨ ♨ ⬛ ♿ (prior notice appreciated, wheelchair on request) toilets for disabled shop ⊗ (ex guide dogs)

PORT SUNLIGHT   MAP 07 SJ38

Lady Lever Art Gallery `FREE`

CH62 5EQ

➲ *(Follow brown heritage signs)*

☎ 0151 478 4136

e-mail: ladyleverartgallery@nmgm.org

web: www.nmgm.org.uk

The Lady Lever Art Gallery houses many world famous works of art, including Pre-Raphaelite masterpieces by Millais, Burne-Jones and Rossetti. Dramatic landscapes by the great British painters, Turner and Constable are also displayed alongside portraits by Gainsborough, Romney and Reynolds.

Times: ✱ Open all year, Mon-Sat 10-5, Sun 12-5. Closed 23-26 Dec & 1 Jan. **Facilities:** ❷ (charged) ♨ ⬛ ♿ (prior notice appreciated, wheelchair on request) toilets for disabled ⊗ (ex guide dogs)

PRESCOT   MAP 07 SJ49

Knowsley Safari Park

L34 4AN

➲ *(M57 junct 2. Follow 'safari park' signs)*

☎ 0151 430 9009

e-mail: safari.park@knowsley.com

web: www.knowsley.com

A five-mile drive through the reserves enables visitors to see lions, tigers, elephants, rhinos, monkeys and many other animals in spacious, natural surroundings. Also a children's amusement park, reptile house, pets' corner plus sealion shows. Other attractions include an amusement park and a miniature railway.

Times: Open all year, Mar-Oct, daily 10-4. Winter Nov-Feb, 11-3.
Fee: ✱ £10 (ch & pen £7). **Facilities:** ❷ ♨ ♿ toilets for disabled shop ⊗ (kennels provided) ◀

Prescot Museum `FREE`

34 Church St L34 3LA

➲ *(situated on corner of High St (A57) & Church St. Follow brown heritage signs)*

☎ 0151 430 7787

e-mail: prescot.museum.dlcs@knowsley.gov.uk

web: www.knowsley.gov.uk/leisure

Permanent exhibitions reflecting the local history of the area, including its important clock and watch making heritage. There is a programme of special exhibitions, events and holiday activities, telephone for details.

Times: Open all year, Tue-Sat 10-5 (closed 1-2), Sun 2-5. Closed BHs. Mon by appointment **Facilities:** ℗ (100 yds) ⬛ ♿ (ramp to ground floor) shop ⊗ (ex guide dogs)

ST HELENS MAP 07 SJ59

World of Glass

Chalon Way East WA10 1BX

⮑ (5mins from M62 junct 7)

☎ 08700 114466

e-mail: info@worldofglass.com

web: www.worldofglass.com

Ideal for all the family, this fascinating attraction is in the heart of St Helens, a town shaped by glass-making. Features include the world's first continuous glass-making furnace, and two museum galleries that show glass in the ancient world and Victorian life in St Helens. There is also a Mirror Maze where Wizard Filigrano works, a café and a gift shop.

Times: ✱ Open Tue-Sun & BH, 10-5. Closed 25-26 Dec & 1 Jan. **Fee:** £5.30 (ch £3.80, pen £3.80) Family & group discounts. **Facilities:** ❷ 💺 🍴 ᴋ (Induction loop) toilets for disabled shop ⊗ (ex guide dogs) ◀

SOUTHPORT MAP 07 SD31

Atkinson Art Gallery FREE

Lord St PR8 1DH

⮑ (located in centre of Lord St, next to Town Hall)

☎ 01704 533133 ext 2110

e-mail: atkinson.gallery@leisure.sefton.gov.uk

web: www.atkinson-gallery.co.uk

The gallery specialises in 19th-and 20th-century oil paintings, watercolours, drawings and prints, as well as 20th-century sculpture. Temporary exhibitions are shown regularly at the art gallery.

Times: Open all year, Tue-Thu 10-5, Fri 12-5, Sat 10-5, Sun 2-5. Closed Mon **Facilities:** ⓟ (next street) (pay & display) 🍴 licensed ᴋ shop ⊗ (ex guide dogs)

The British Lawnmower Museum 2 for 1

106-114 Shakespeare St PR8 5AJ

⮑ (From M6, M58 or M57 follow signs towards town centre, then brown heritage signs to museum)

☎ 01704 501336

e-mail: info@lawnmowerworld.com

web: www.lawnmowerworld.com

This award-winning museum houses a private collection of over 250 rare exhibits of garden machinery of special interest dating from 1799. There is also the largest collection of vintage toy lawnmowers and games in the world. See the water-cooled Egg Boiler, a genuine 2" lawnmower, the first electric lawnmower, and the Lawnmowers of the Rich and Famous, including machines that belonged to Nicholas Parsons, Princess Diana and Brian May.

Times: Open daily, 9-5.30, ex Sun & BH Mon. **Fee:** £1 (ch 50p). Guided tour or Audio tour £4. **Facilities:** ❷ 🍴 shop ⊗ (ex guide dogs) ◀

Pleasureland 2 for 1

Marine Dr PR8 1RX

⮑ (signed from town centre)

☎ 0870 220 0204

e-mail: mail@pleasurelandltd.freeserve.co.uk

web: www.pleasureland.uk.com

Pleasureland is home to over 100 rides and attractions, including the TRAUMAtizer suspended rollercoaster, the Lucozade Space Shot, the Cyclone rollercoaster, Ghost Train and Lost Dinosaurs of the Sahara.

Times: Open Mar-Nov opening times vary please call for information. **Fee:** ✱ £18 all day (ch £12). Entry for 4 (adults and/or children) £60. **Facilities:** ❷ (charged) 💺 🍴 licensed 🛍 ᴋ (access on some rides) toilets for disabled shop ⊗ (ex guide dogs) ◀

SPEKE MAP 07 SJ48

Speke Hall

The Walk L24 1XD

⮑ (on N bank of Mersey, 1m off A561 on W side of Liverpool Airport. Follow brown signs)

☎ 0151 427 7231

e-mail: spekehall@nationaltrust.org.uk

web: www.nationaltrust.org.uk

A remarkable timber-framed manor house set in tranquil gardens and grounds. The house has a Tudor Great Hall, Stuart plasterwork, and William Morris wallpapers. Outside are varied grounds, including a rose garden, bluebell woods and woodland walks. Also, live interpretation by costumed guides, childrens quiz-trail and adventure playground. Lots of events throughout the year, contact for details.

Times: House open: 17 Mar-28 Oct, Wed-Sun (open BH Mon) 1-5.30; 3 Nov-2 Dec, Sat & Sun 1-4.30. Garden open daily 11-5.30 or dusk. Closed Mon (ex BH), 24-26 & 31 Dec, 1 Jan & Good Fri. **Fee:** Hall & Gardens: £6.70 (ch £3.70). Family ticket £20.50. Gardens only: £4 (ch £1.90). Gardens Family ticket £11. Reduced rate when arriving by public transport, cycle or on foot. **Facilities:** ❷ 💺 🍴 ᴋ (wheelchairs, electric car, Braille guide, induction loop) toilets for disabled shop grounds 🐾 ◀

Norfolk

Great Yarmouth

Norfolk is sparsely populated, with big skies and open spaces, not to mention dozens of unspoilt villages and plenty of wildlife. The Broads are a series of waterways through marshy fenland dotted with the occasional windmill, and best explored by boat in a leisurely fashion. The coastline encompasses fenland around the Wash and has a variety of seaside towns including Cromer and Great Yarmouth. Two of the country's most important nature reserves are at Blakeney Point and the Cley marshes.

BACONSTHORPE   MAP 09 TG13

Baconsthorpe Castle   FREE

NR25 6LN

➲ *(0.75m N of Baconsthorpe off unclass road, 3m E of Holt)*

☎ 01799 322399

web: www.english-heritage.org.uk

The remains of a fifteenth-century castle, built by Sir John Heydon during the Wars of the Roses. The exact date when the building was started is not known, since Sir John did not apply for the statutory royal licence necessary to construct a fortified house. In the 1560s, Sir John's grandson added the outer gatehouse, which was inhabited until the 1920s, when one of the turrets fell down. The remains of red brick and knapped flint are reflected in the lake, which partly embraces the castle as a moat.

Times: Open at any reasonable time. **Facilities:** ❷ ♿

BANHAM   MAP 05 TM08

Banham Zoo

The Grove NR16 2HE

➲ *(on B1113, signed off A11 and A140. Follow brown tourist signs)*

☎ 01953 887771 & 887773

e-mail: info@banhamzoo.co.uk

web: www.banhamzoo.co.uk

Set in 35 acres of magnificent parkland, see hundreds of animals ranging from big cats to birds of prey and siamangs to shire horses. Tiger Territory is a purpose-built enclosure for Siberian tigers, including a rock pool and woodland setting. See also Lemur Island and Tamarin and Marmoset Islands. The Heritage Farm Stables & Falconry displays Norfolk's rural heritage with majestic shire horses and birds of prey. Other attractions include Children's Farmyard Barn and Adventure Play Area.

Times: ✱ Open all year, daily from 10. (Last admission 1 hour before closing). Closed 25 & 26 Dec. **Facilities:** ❷ 💻 🍽 licensed ♿ (3 wheelchairs for hire, parking) toilets for disabled shop ⊗ 🎫

BLICKLING   MAP 09 TG12

Blickling Hall

NR11 6NF

➲ *(on B1354, 1.5m NW of Aylsham, signposted off A140 Norwich to Cromer road)*

☎ 01263 738030

e-mail: blickling@nationaltrust.org.uk

web: www.nationaltrust.org.uk/blickling

Flanked by dark yew hedges and topped by pinnacles, the warm red brick front of Blickling is a memorable sight. Fifty five acres of grounds include woodland and a lake, a formal parterre, topiary yew hedges, a Secret Garden, an orangery, and a dry moat filled with roses, camellias and other plants. Inside there are fine collections of furniture, paintings and tapestries, along with a spectacular Jacobean plaster ceiling, and a library of some 12,000 books.

Times: Hall open 25 Mar-29 Oct, Wed-Sun & BH, 1-4.30 (1-3.30 Oct). Garden, shop & restaurant same days as hall 10.15-5.15 **Fee:** ✱ £8 (ch £4). **Facilities:** ❷ 💻 🍽 licensed 🅿 ♿ (wheelchairs & batricars, Braille guide, lift, parking) toilets for disabled shop garden centre ⊗ (ex guide dogs) 🐾 🎫

BRESSINGHAM   MAP 05 TM08

Bressingham Steam Museum   2 for 1
& Gardens

IP22 2AB

➲ *(on A1066 2.5m W of Diss, between Thetford & Diss)*

☎ 01379 686900 & 687386

e-mail: info@bressingham.co.uk

web: www.bressingham.co.uk

Alan Bloom is an internationally recognised nurseryman and a steam enthusiast, and has combined his interests to great effect at Bressingham. There are three miniature steam-hauled trains, including a 15in gauge running through two and a half miles of the wooded Waveney Valley. The Dell Garden has 5000 species of perennials and alpines; Foggy Bottom has wide vistas, pathways, trees, shrubs, conifers and winter colour (restricted opening). A steam roundabout is another attraction, and the Norfolk fire museum is housed here. Various events are held, including Dad's Army Day, and Friends of Thomas the Tank Engine, please telephone for details.

Times: Open: Steam Museum, Dad's Army collection, Foggy Bottom & Dell Garden Apr-Sep, daily 10.30-5.30 (Mar & Oct 10.30-4.30). (Last admission 1 hour before closing time). **Fee:** £7-£12 (ch 3-16 £5-£8, pen £7-£10). Family £22-£35. Season tickets available. **Facilities:** ❷ 💻 🍽 licensed ♿ (wheelchairs can be taken onto Nursery & Waveney lines) toilets for disabled shop garden centre ⊗ (ex guide dogs) 🎫

BURGH CASTLE   MAP 05 TG40

Berney Arms Windmill

NR30 1SB

☎ 01493 700605

web: www.english-heritage.org.uk

One of the largest and best-preserved Victorian windmills in Norfolk, with seven floors to explore. Built to grind cement, its superb machinery is still fully operational.

Times: Open May-Aug; pre-booked guided tours only. Please telephone 01799 522842 **Fee:** £2.40 (ch £1.20, concessions £1.80). Prices and opening times are subject to change in Spring 2007. Please check web site or call 0870 333 1181 for the most up to date prices and opening times when planning your visit. **Facilities:** shop ⊗ ♿

England

England

Burgh Castle

FREE

NR31 9PZ

⮕ *(at far W end of Breydon Water on unclass road, 3m W of Great Yarmouth)*

web: www.english-heritage.org.uk

Burgh Castle was built in the third century AD by the Romans, as one of a chain of forts along the Saxon Shore - the coast where Saxon invaders landed. Sections of the massive walls still stand.

Times: Open at any reasonable time. **Facilities:** ⊗

CAISTER-ON-SEA MAP 09 TG51

Caister Roman Site

FREE

⮕ *(3m N of Great Yarmouth)*

web: www.english-heritage.org.uk

The name Caister has Roman origins, and this was in fact a Roman naval base. The remains include the south gateway, a town wall built of flint with brick courses and part of what may have been a seamen's hostel.

Times: Open at any reasonable time. **Facilities:** ⊗

CASTLE ACRE MAP 09 TF81

Castle Acre Priory and Castle

Stocks Green PE32 2XD

☎ 01760 755394

web: www.english-heritage.org.uk

Britain's best-preserved Cluniac priory with walled herb garden where visitors can find out about the medieval uses of herbs. Nearby Castle Acre Castle is also well worth a visit.

Times: Priory: Open all year Apr-Sep, daily 10-6; Oct-Mar, Thu-Mon 10-4. Closed 24-26 Dec & 1 Jan. Castle open at any reasonble time. **Fee:** Castle; Free entry; Priory; £4.50 (ch £2.30, concessions £3.40) Family £11.30. Prices and opening times are subject to change in Spring 2007. Please check web site or call 0870 333 1181 for the most up to date prices and opening times when planning your visit. **Facilities:** ❷ ♿ shop ⌗

CASTLE RISING MAP 09 TF62

Castle Rising Castle

PE31 6AH

⮕ *(off A149)*

☎ 01553 631330

web: www.english-heritage.org.uk

A fine twelfth-century domestic keep, set amid huge defensive earthworks, once the palace and home to Isabella, the 'She Wolf' of France, dowager Queen of England. The keep walls stand to their original height.

Times: Open all year, Apr-Nov, daily 10-6 (closes at dusk if earlier in Oct); 2 Nov-Mar, Wed-Sun 10-4. Closed 24-26 Dec. **Fee:** £3.85 (ch £2.20, concessions £3.10) Family £11.50. Prices and opening times are subject to change in Spring 2007. Please check web site or call 0870 333 1181 for the most up to date prices and opening times when planning your visit. **Facilities:** ❷ ♿ (exterior only) toilets for disabled shop ⌗

CROMER MAP 09 TG2◄

Cromer Museum

East Cottages, Tucker St NR27 9HB

⮕ *(On Church St next to Cromer Church)*

☎ 01263 513543

e-mail: cromer.museum@norfolk.gov.uk

web: www.norfolk.gov.uk/tourism/museums

The museum is housed in five 19th-century fishermen's cottages, one of which has period furnishings. There are pictures and exhibits from Victorian Cromer, with collections illustrating local natural history, archaeology, social history and geology. Items to discover include the scandal of mixed bathing, the daring rescues of Henry Blogg and the Cromer Lifeboatmen, and the incredible story of the West Runton elephant, Britain's oldest and most complete elephant fossil. Contact for details of special events.

Times: Apr-Oct Mon-Sat 10-5, Sun 2-5 (closed Sun in Oct); Nov-Feb Mon-Sat 10-4 Closed Good Fri, 24-26 Dec & 1 Jan **Fee:** £2.50 (ch £1.25, under 4's free, concessions £1.90) **Facilities:** ❷ (100mtrs) �🅿 ♿ (lift and ramps) toilets for disabled shop ⊗ (ex guide dogs) ◢

Henry Blogg Museum

Rockethouse Building, The Promenade NR27 9HE

⮕ *(located at the bottom of East Gangway)*

☎ 01263 511294

e-mail: rnlicromermuseum@rnli.org.uk

A lifeboat has been stationed at Cromer since 1804, and the museum at the bottom of The Gangway covers local lifeboat history and the RNLI in general. The main exhibit is the WWII Watson Class lifeboat H F Bailey, the boat Henry Blogg coxed. In ten years he helped to save over 500 lives, and is still the RNLI's most decorated crew member. The new building opened in April 2006 hosts a number of new features including; interactive displays and radio/navigation instruction

Times: Tue-Sat 10-5 **Fee:** Donations welcome. **Facilities:** ❷ (under 1m) �🅿 ♿ (full disabled access) toilets for disabled shop

---

ERPINGHAM MAP 09 TG1

Wolterton Park

NR11 7LY

⮕ *(signed from A140 Norwich to Cromer)*

☎ 01263 584175

web: www.manningtongardens.co.uk

Covering some 800 hectares this estate contains managed conservation areas, 18th-century landscaped gardens, and Wolterton Hall, built in the 1720s for Horatio Walpole, younger brother of Britain's first Prime Minister, Sir Robert Walpole. Special events include gardening demonstrations, concerts, plays, opera, craft fairs, guided walks and history lectures.

Times: ✱ Open: Park daily; Hall, late Apr-end Oct, Fri 2-5 (last entry 4). **Fee:** Hall £5. Car park £2 (free for hall visitors) **Facilities:** ❷ (charged) ♿ (partly accessible) toilets for disabled shop ⊗ (ex guide dogs) ◢

FAKENHAM
MAP 09 TF93
See also Thursford Green

Pensthorpe Waterfowl Park & Nature Reserve
Pensthorpe NR21 0LN
➲ *(1m from Fakenham on the A1067 to Norwich)*
☎ 01328 851465
e-mail: info@pensthorpe.com
web: www.pensthorpe.co.uk

Covering 500 acres of beautiful Wensum Valley countryside, with five lakes which are home to one of the largest collections of waterfowl and waders in Europe. Spacious walk-through enclosures and a network of hardsurfaced pathways ensures close contact with birds at the water's edge. Gardens by acclaimed designers Piet Dudolf and Julie Toll.

Times: ✱ Open Jan-Mar, daily 10-4. Apr-Dec, 10-5 **Fee:** ✱ £7 (ch £3.50, pen £5.50) **Facilities:** ❷ 💷 ₺ (network of hard surfaced pathways ensures access) toilets for disabled shop ⊗ (ex guide dogs) ◀

FELBRIGG
MAP 09 TG23

Felbrigg Hall
NR11 8PR
➲ *(off B1436 betweeen A148 Cromer to Kings Lynn & A140 Cromer to Norwich)*
☎ 01263 837444
e-mail: felbrigg@nationaltrust.org.uk
web: www.nationaltrust.org.uk

Felbrigg is a 17th-century house built on the site of an existing medieval hall. It contains a superb collection of 18th-century furniture and pictures and an outstanding library. A 550-acre wood shelters the house from the North Sea and contains waymarked walks and a working dovecot.

Times: ✱ Open House and Garden: 19 Mar-30 Oct, Sat-Wed, House 1-5, Garden 11-5. Park walks available daily dawn-dusk. **Fee:** ✱ House & Garden £7 (ch £3.50). Garden only £3 (ch £1.50) **Facilities:** ❷ 💷 ◉licensed ₺ (electric wheelchair for garden, Braille guide) toilets for disabled shop ⊗ (ex guide dogs) ⚌ ◀

FILBY
MAP 09 TG41

Thrigby Hall Wildlife Gardens
NR29 3DR
➲ *(on unclass road off A1064, between Acle & Caister-on-Sea)*
☎ 01493 369477
web: www.thrigbyhall.co.uk

The 250-year-old park of Thrigby Hall is now the home of animals and birds from Asia, and the lake has ornamental wildfowl. There are tropical bird houses, a unique blue willow pattern garden and tree walk, and a summer house as old as the park. The enormous jungled swamp hall has special features such as underwater viewing of large crocodiles.

Times: Open all year, daily from 10. **Fee:** ✱ £7.90 (ch 4-14 £5.90, pen £6.90) **Facilities:** ❷ 💷 🗐 ₺ (wheelchairs available, ramps, parking) toilets for disabled shop ⊗ (ex guide dogs) ◀

GREAT BIRCHAM
MAP 09 TF73

Bircham Windmill
`2 for 1`
PE31 6SJ
➲ *(0.5m W off unclassified Snettisham road).*
☎ 01485 578393
e-mail: birchamwindmill@btinternet.com
web: www.birchamwindmill.co.uk

This windmill is one of the last remaining in Norfolk. Sails turn on windy days, and the adjacent tea room serves home-made cakes, light lunches and cream teas. There is also a bakery shop and cycle hire. In addition, crafts people feature on a number of weekends throughout the year.

Times: Open Etr-Sep, 10-5. **Fee:** ✱ £3.25 (ch £2, pen £3) **Facilities:** ❷ 💷 🗐 ₺ toilets for disabled shop ◀

GREAT YARMOUTH
MAP 05 TG50

Elizabethan House Museum
4 South Quay NR30 2QH
➲ *(from A12 & A47 follow town centre signs, then Historic South Quay signs, leading onto South Quay)*
☎ 01493 855746
e-mail: yarmouth.museums@norfolk.gov.uk
web: www.museums.norfolk.gov.uk

Experience the lives of families who lived in this splendid quayside house from Tudor to Victorian times. Decide for yourself if the death of Charles I was plotted in the Conspiracy Room. Dress the family in Tudor costumes. Discover Victorian life, upstairs and downstairs, and what it was like to work in the kitchen and scullery. Children can play in the toy room, while parents relax in the small but delightful walled garden.

Times: Open 2 Apr-28 Oct, Mon-Fri 10-5; Sat & Sun 1.15-5. **Fee:** ✱ £3 (ch £1.60, concessions £2.50). Adult in a family group £2.40 **Facilities:** ℗ (250yds) 🗐 (Braille guide) shop ⊗ (ex guide dogs)

Merrivale Model Village
`2 for 1`
Marine Pde NR30 3JG
➲ *(Marine parade seafront, next to Wellington Pier)*
☎ 01493 842097
web: www.merrivalemodelvillage.co.uk

Set in more than an acre of attractive landscaped gardens, this comprehensive miniature village is built on a scale of 1:12, and features streams, a lake and waterfalls. Among the models are a working fairground, a stone quarry, houses, shops, and a garden railway. There are even illuminations at dusk! The Penny Arcade gives you the chance to play old amusements.

Times: Open daily Etr-end Oct **Fee:** Please telephone for details, or visit website **Facilities:** ℗ (opposite) 💷 🗐 ₺ toilets for disabled shop ◀

England

Row Houses/Old Merchant's House and Greyfriars Cloisters

South Quay NR30 2RQ

⮎ *(follow signs to dock and south quay)*

☎ 01493 857900

web: www.english-heritage.org.uk

Visit these 17th-century houses unique to Great Yarmouth, and the remains of a Franciscan friary with rare early wall paintings. Guided tours explain how the rich and poor lived in these properties over various time periods.

Times: Apr-Sep, daily 12-5. Free guided tour of Greyfriars' Cloisters at 10.30 on the first Wed of every month. Please call site for details **Fee:** £3.40 (ch £1.70, concessions £2.60). Prices and opening times are subject to change in Spring 2007. Please check web site or call 0870 333 1181 for the most up to date prices and opening times when planning your visit. **Facilities:** shop ⊗ ⚌

Time and Tide Museum of Great Yarmouth Life

Tower Curing Works, Blackfriar's Rd NR30 3BX

⮎ *(from A12 & A47 follow brown signs)*

☎ 01493 743930

e-mail: yarmouth.museums@norfolk.gov.uk

web: www.museums.norfolk.gov.uk

Set in one of the UK's best preserved Victorian herring curing works, Time and Tide tells the story of Great Yarmouth from its Ice Age origins to the present day. Visitors can learn about the colourful characters who have made their living from the sea over the years.

Times: Open 30 Oct-Apr Mon-Fri 10-4, Sat & Sun 12-4; 2 Apr-28 Oct 10-5. Closed: 21-26 & 31 Dec & 1 Jan **Fee:** ✱ £5.80 (ch £3.70, concessions £5.20. Adult in family group £5.10) **Facilities:** ℗ 💻 📖 ᕫ (lift) toilets for disabled shop ⊗ (ex guide dogs) ◼

Tolhouse Museum

Tolhouse St NR30 2SH

⮎ *(from A12 & A47 follow AA signs to town centre, then signs to South Quay. Museum attached to Central Library.)*

☎ 01493 858900

e-mail: yarmouth.museums@norfolk.gov.uk

web: www.museums.norfolk.gov.uk

Visit one of the oldest prisons in the country and explore Great Yarmouth's story of crime and punishment. With the free audio guide you can hear the gaoler and his prisoners describe their experiences. Discover the fate of the thieves, smugglers, witches, pirates and murderers at a time when punishments included transportation or execution. Other exhibits detail the history of this 12th-century former merchant's house that went on to become one of the town's most important civic buildings.

Times: Open 2 Apr-28 Oct, Mon-Fri 10-5; Sat & Sun 1.15-5. **Fee:** ✱ £2.90 (ch £1.50, concessions £2.40). Adult in family group £2.30 **Facilities:** ℗ (500yds) 📖 ᕫ (lift to ground & 2nd floor, notice preferable) shop ⊗ (ex guide dogs)

Gressenhall Farm and Workhouse

NR20 4DR

⮎ *(on B1146 3m NW of Dereham, follow brown signs)*

☎ 01362 860563

e-mail: gressenhall.museum@norfolk.gov.uk

web: www.museums.norfolk.gov.uk

This fascinating journey through the history of rural Norfolk includes an historic workhouse, a traditional farm, extensive collections, and a brand new adventure playground. The farm has lambs and piglets as well as horses working the fields. Visitors can explore the grounds, gardens and country trails, then take a break in the Café.

Times: Open 12-19 Feb, 11-4. 26 Mar-29 Oct, 10-5. **Fee:** ✱ £7 (£4.65, under 4's free, concessions £5.95) **Facilities:** ℗ 💻 📖 ᕫ (sound guide, wheelchair loan) toilets for disabled shop ⊗ (ex assist dogs) ◼

Grimes Graves

IP26 5DE

⮎ *(7m NW of Thetford off A134)*

☎ 01842 810656

web: www.english-heritage.org.uk

These unique and remarkable Neolithic flint mines are the earliest major industrial site in Europe.

Times: Open 3-31 Mar; Thu-Mon, 10-5; Apr-Sep, daily 10-6; Oct, Thu-Mon 10-5. **Fee:** £2.70 (ch £1.40, concessions £2) Family £6.80. Prices and opening times are subject to change in Spring 2007. Please check web site or call 0870 333 1181 for the most up to date prices and opening times when planning your visit. **Facilities:** ℗ ᕫ (exhibition area, grounds only, access track rough) shop ⚌

Norfolk Lavender

Caley Mill PE31 7JE

⮎ *(follow signs on A149 & A148. Car park entrance on B1454, 100yds E of junct with A149)*

☎ 01485 570384

e-mail: admin@norfolk-lavender.co.uk

web: www.norfolk-lavender.co.uk

This is the largest lavender-growing and distilling operation in Britain. Different coloured lavenders are grown in strips and harvested in July and August. There are also herb gardens and a fragrant Plant Centre, as well as guided tours of the distillery and gardens.

Times: Open all year, daily, Apr-Oct 9.30-5; Nov-Mar 9.30-4. (Closed 25-26 Dec & 1 Jan). **Fee:** ✱ Admission to grounds free. Guided tours £3 (May-Sep). Trip to Lavender Field £5, mid Jul-mid Aug. **Facilities:** ℗ 💻 �🍴 licensed ᕫ (2 wheelchairs for loan) toilets for disabled shop garden centre ◼

HOLKHAM   MAP 09 TF84

Holkham Hall & Bygones Museum
NR23 1AB

➲ *(off A149, 2m W of Wells-next-the-Sea, coaches should use B1105 at New Holkham, signed "Holkham Coaches")*

☎ 01328 710227
e-mail: enquiries@holkham.co.uk
web: www.holkham.co.uk

This classic Palladian mansion was built between 1734 and 1764 by Thomas Coke, 1st Earl of Leicester, and is home to his descendants. It has a magnificent alabaster entrance hall and the sumptuous state rooms house Roman statuary, fine furniture and paintings by Rubens, Van Dyck, Gainsborough and others. The Bygones Museum, housed in the stable block, has over 5,000 items of domestic and agricultural display - from gramophones to fire engines. The adjacent free History of Farming exhibition illustrates how a great agricultural estate such as Holkham works and has evolved.

Times: Open 25 May-Sep, Sun-Thu 12-5; also Sat-Mon & all BHs, 12-5 **Fee:** Hall £7 (ch £3.50). Bygones £5 (ch £2.50). Combined ticket Hall & Bygones: £10 (ch £5). Family ticket £25. **Facilities:** ❷ 💻 🗒 ♿ (wheelchair ramps, stairclimbing equipment) toilets for disabled shop ⊗ (ex guide dogs) ◀

HORSEY   MAP 09 TG42

Horsey Windpump
NR29 4EF

➲ *(15m N of Great Yarmouth, on the B1159 4m NE of Martham)*

☎ 01493 393904
web: www.nationaltrust.co.uk

Set in a remote part of the Norfolk Broads, the windpump mill was built 200 years ago to drain the area, and then rebuilt in 1912 by Dan England, a noted Norfolk millwright. It has been restored since being struck by lightning in 1943, and overlooks Horsey Mere and marshes, noted for their wild birds and insects, as a site of International Importance for Nature Conservation.

Times: Open Mar; Sat-Sun 10-4.30, Apr-Oct; Wed-Sun 10-4.30, BH Mon 10.30-4. **Fee:** ✱ £2 (ch £1). NT members free entry & parking. Mooring fees payable to the Horsey Estate (inc NT members) **Facilities:** ❷ (charged) 💻 ♿ (parking, ramps to ground floor) shop 🍴 ◀

HORSHAM ST FAITH   MAP 09 TG21

City of Norwich Aviation Museum
Old Norwich Rd NR10 3JF

➲ *(follow brown tourist signs from A140 Norwich to Cromer road)*

☎ 01603 893080
e-mail: norwichairmuseum@hotmail.com
web: www.cnam.co.uk

A massive Avro Vulcan bomber, veteran of the Falklands War, dominates the collection of military and civilian aircraft at this museum. There are several displays relating to the aeronautical history of Norfolk, including some on the role played by Norfolk-based RAF and USAAF planes during World War II, and a section dedicated to the operations of RAF Bomber Command's 100 group.

continued

Times: Open all year, Apr-Oct Tue-Sat, 10-5. Sun & BH Mons 12-5 (Mons during school hols). Nov-Mar, Wed & Sat 10-4. Sun 12-4. **Fee:** £3.25 (ch & concessions £1.50, pen £2.75) Family ticket £9. **Facilities:** ❷ 💻 ♿ (assistance available) shop ⊗ (ex guide dogs) ◀

HOUGHTON   MAP 09 TF72

Houghton Hall   2 for 1
PE31 6UE

➲ *(1.25m off A148. 13m E of King's Lynn & 10m W of Fakenham on A148)*

☎ 01485 528569
e-mail: administrator@houghtonhall.com
web: www.houghtonhall.com

Houghton Hall built in the 1720s by Sir Robert Walpole, Britain's first Prime Minister, is one of the grandest surviving Palladian Houses in England. Now owned by the 7th Marquess of Cholmondeley. The spectacular 5-acre walled garden, restored by Lord Cholmondeley, has been divided into areas for fruit and vegetables, spacious herbaceous borders, and formal rose gardens with over 150 varieties. A collection of Model Soldiers contains over 20,000 models laid out in various battle formations. There are musical events in the summer, and the Houghton horse trials in August.

Times: House open 1.30-5 (last entry 4.30). Grounds and Soldier Museum open 11-5.30. **Fee:** ✱ £7 (ch £3). Family ticket £15. Grounds only £4.50 (ch £2). **Facilities:** ❷ 🍴 licensed 🗒 ♿ (lift, motorised buggies) toilets for disabled shop ⊗ (ex guide dogs) ◀

HUNSTANTON   MAP 09 TF64

Hunstanton Sea Life Sanctuary   2 for 1
Southern Promenade PE36 5BH

➲ *(A149 King's Lynn to Hunstanton, then follow brown sealife signs)*

☎ 01485 533576
web: www.sealsanctuary.co.uk

With over 30 fascinating displays of marine life, this fascinating aquarium offers close encounters with starfish, sharks, octopus, eels and many other underwater wonders. Feeding demonstrations, talks and special presentations. Latest addition: Claws. Six displays featuring strange clawed creatures from around the world.

Times: Open all year, daily from 10. (Closed 25 Dec) **Fee:** ✱ £9.95 (ch £7.25 & concessions £7.95) **Facilities:** ❷ (charged) 💻 ♿ toilets for disabled shop ⊗ (ex guide dogs) ◀

England

KING'S LYNN
MAP 09 TF62

African Violet Centre
FREE

Terrington St Clement PE34 4PL

➲ *(situated beside A17 5m from King's Lynn and 3m from A47/A17 junct)*

☎ 01553 828374

e-mail: info@africanvioletcentre.ltd.uk

web: www.africanvioletcentre.ltd.uk

A warm and friendly welcome awaits you at the African Violet Centre. As a major plant specialist the centre offers a wide variety of plants for any enthusiast. Best known for their vast selection and display of African violets. The African Violet Centre is a winner of many Chelsea Gold Medals.

Times: ✱ Open all year Mon-Sat 9-5, Sun 10-5. Closed Xmas & New Year. **Facilities:** ⓟ ⬤ 占 (ramps & wide doors) toilets for disabled shop garden centre ⊗ (ex guide dogs) ◀

King's Lynn Arts Centre
FREE

St George's Guildhall, 29 King St PE30 1HA

➲ *(located just off Tuesday Market Place in King Street, next to Globe Hotel)*

☎ 01553 765565

e-mail: entertainment_admin@west-norfolk.gov.uk

web: www.kingslynnarts.co.uk

Although it has been used for many purposes, the theatrical associations of this 15th-century Guildhall are strongest: Shakespeare himself is said to have performed here. A year round programme of film, performing and visual arts takes place. Contact box office on 01553 764864 for details.

Times: Open Mon-Sat, 10-2. Closed show days, Sun, BHs, Good Fri & 24 Dec-1st Mon in Jan. **Facilities:** ⓟ (50yds) (pay & display) ⬤ ✱◀ licensed 🍴 占 (hearing loop, ramp) ⊗ ☙

Town House Museum

46 Queen St PE30 5DQ

➲ *(in town centre close to historic South Quay)*

☎ 01553 773450

e-mail: lynn.museum@norfolk.gov.uk

web: www.museums.norfolk.gov.uk

A charming museum set in a 19th-century town house. Explore everyday life in King's Lynn through the ages in a series of carefully re-constructed rooms, from medieval times to the 1950s. Enjoy collections of historic toys and costumes, and take the air in the delightful garden. Dotted around the displays are colourful games and activities that will keep the children amused.

Times: ✱ Open May-Sep, Mon-Sat 10-5. Oct-Apr, Mon-Sat 10-4. **Fee:** ✱ £2.60 (ch £1.50, concessions £2.20) **Facilities:** ⓟ (100yds) 占 shop ⊗ ◀

LENWADE
MAP 09 TG01

Dinosaur Adventure Park

Weston Park NR9 5JW

➲ *(From A47 or A1067 follow brown signs to Park)*

☎ 01603 876310

e-mail: info@dinosaurpark.co.uk

web: www.dinosaurpark.co.uk

Visitors can help the Ranger Track: T-Rex on the Dinosaur Trail and meet giants from the past including the new spinosaurus. They can also make friends with animals from hedgehogs to wallabies, or bugs and snakes in the secret animal garden. There are also a new adventure play area including a Climb-o-saurus, Raptor Racers, Jurassic Putt Crazy Golf, and the Lost World Amazing Adventure.

Times: Open daily until 10 Sep & Oct half term; 11 Sep-22 Oct, Fri-Sun. **Fee:** ✱ £7.95 (ch & pen £6.95, under 3's free) **Facilities:** ⓟ ⬤ 🍴 占 (Swing) toilets for disabled shop ⊗ (ex guide dogs) ◀

LITTLE WALSINGHAM
MAP 09 TF93

Walsingham Abbey Grounds & Shirehall Museum

NR22 6BP

➲ *(follow B1105 from Fakenham. Entrance to museum through tourist info centre in village)*

☎ 01328 820510 & 820259

e-mail: walsingham.museum@farmline.com

In the grounds of the Abbey are the ruins of the original Augustinian priory built in the 1100s. The priory was built over the shrine of Our Lady of Walsingham which had been established in 1061. Shirehall Museum consists of an original Georgian Courthouse, displays on the history of Walsingham and local artefacts. The museum is situated in 20 acres of tranquil and picturesque gardens with access to woodland and river walks across the historic parkland.

Times: Open Feb daily 10-4. 19 Mar-28 Oct, daily 10-4.30; Nov-Dec, wknds only 10-4; **Fee:** ✱ £3 (concessions £2) **Facilities:** ⓟ (100yds) 🍴 占 toilets for disabled shop garden centre ◀

NORTH CREAKE
MAP 09 TF83

Creake Abbey
FREE

NR21 9LF

➲ *(off B1355)*

web: www.english-heritage.org.uk

The ruins of the church of an Augustinian almshouse, later converted to an abbey.

Times: Open at any reasonable time. **Facilities:** ⊗ (ex dogs on leads) ⊞

NORWICH
MAP 05 TG20

Air Defence Radar Museum
2 for 1

RAF Neatishead NR12 8YB

➲ *(follow brown signs from A1062 at Horning)*

☎ 01692 631485

e-mail: curator@radarmuseum.co.uk

web: www.radarmuseum.co.uk

This multi-award winning Museum, housed in the original 1942 Radar Operations building, features the Battle of Britain Room, 1942 Ground Controlled Interception Room, Radar Engineering, Military

continued

Communications Systems, Cold War Operations Room, Royal Observer Corps, Space Defence, Bloodhound Missiles and Original Mobile Radar Vehicles.

Times: Open year round 2nd Sat each month; Apr-Oct Tue & Thu & BH Mons 10-5 **Fee:** £4 (ch £3, under 13 free, concessions £3.50) **Facilities:** ℗ ➹ 🍴 ♿ (video tour for inaccessible areas) shop ⊗ (ex guide dogs)

The Bridewell

Bridewell Alley NR2 1AQ

⮑ *(in city centre, Lanes area, 5 min from Norwich Market Place)*

☎ 01603 629127

e-mail: museums@norfolk.gov.uk

web: www.museums.norfolk.gov.uk

Built in the late 14th century, this flint-faced merchant's house was used as a prison from 1583 to 1828. It now houses displays illustrating the trades and industries of Norwich during the past 200 years, including a large collection of locally made boots and shoes. There are also a reconstructed 1930s pharmacy, pawnbrokers shop and a blacksmith's smithy. Fans of Norwich City FC will enjoy the exhibition on the team's history.

Times: Open Apr-28 Oct, Tue-Fri 10-4.30; Sat 10-5. School hols, Mon-Sat 10-5. **Fee:** £3 (ch £1.60, concessions £2.50) Family ticket £6.90. **Facilities:** ℗ (5 min walk) 🍴 shop ⊗ (ex guide dogs) ⊠

Norwich Castle Museum

Castle Meadow NR1 3JU

⮑ *(in city centre)*

☎ 01603 493625

e-mail: museums@norfolk.gov.uk

web: www.museums.norfolk.gov.uk

The Castle keep was built in the 12th century, and the museum houses displays of art, archaeology, natural history, Lowestoft porcelain, Norwich silver, a large collection of paintings (with special emphasis on the Norwich School of Painters) and British ceramic teapots. There are also guided tours of the dungeons and battlements. A programme of exhibitions, children's events, gallery and evening talks takes place throughout the year. Please ring for details.

Times: Open all year, Mon-Fri 10-4.30, Sat 10-5, Sun 1-5; School hols, Mon-Sat 10-5.30, Sun 1-5. **Fee:** ✱ All zones £5.95 (ch 4-16 £4.45, concessions £4.95). Castle & History Zone £3.95 (ch £2.95, concessions £3.35). Art & Exhibitions Zone £3.45 (ch £2.60, concessions £2.95)

Facilities: ℗ (200mtrs) ➹ 🍴 ♿ (lift to first floor, disabled parking, virtual tour) toilets for disabled shop ⊗ (ex guide dogs) ⊠

Norwich Cathedral

The Close NR1 4DH

⮑ *(A47, A11 to city centre, inner ring road to Barrack St rdbt, take road towards city centre to Tombland)*

☎ 01603 218300

e-mail: vis-profficer@cathedral.org.uk

web: http://www.cathedral.org.uk

The splendour and tranquillity of Norwich Cathedral have attracted visitors and pilgrims for nearly 1000 years. Norwich has the second highest spire, and the largest monastic cloister in England, and the 1,000 carved medieval roof bosses are amazing. The building remains a place of quiet reflection and prayer as well as for participation in daily worship or the rich pageantry of the Church's festivals.

continued

Times: Open daily, 7.30-7 (6 mid Sep-mid May). **Fee:** Donations welcomed £4 (ch £1). Guided tours £4 (ch £1). **Facilities:** ℗ (440yds) ➹ 🍴 licensed 🍴 ♿ (lift, touch & hearing centre, audio-induction loop) toilets for disabled shop ⊠

Royal Norfolk Regimental Museum

Shirehall, Market Av NR1 3JQ

⮑ *(adjacent to Norwich Castle Museum)*

☎ 01603 493649

e-mail: regimental.museum@norfolk.gov.uk

web: www.norfolk.gov.uk

Museum displays deal with the social as well as military history of the county regiment from 1685, including the daily life of a soldier. Audio-visual displays and graphics complement the collection and there's a programme of temporary exhibitions.

Times: Open School term-time & Xmas hols: Tue-Fri 10-4.30, Sat 10-5; School half-terms, Easter & Summer hols: Mon-Sat 10-5 **Fee:** £3 (ch £1.60, concessions £2.50). Family £6.90 **Facilities:** ℗ (400yds) ♿ (stair lift available, ring for details) shop ⊗ (ex guide dogs) ⊠

Sainsbury Centre for Visual Arts ⬛FREE⬛

University of East Anglia NR4 7TJ

⮑ *(A47 bypass W towards Swaffham. 1st exit onto B1108, follow brown signsd)*

☎ 01603 593199

e-mail: scva@uea.ac.uk

web: www.scva.ac.uk

The collection of Sir Robert and Lady Sainsbury was given to the University in 1973. This outstanding collection is housed in two buildings designed by Norman Foster and combines modern Western art with fine and applied arts from Africa, the Pacific, the Americas, Asia, Egypt, Medieval Europe and the ancient Mediterranean.

Times: Open Tue-Sun 10-5, Wed 10-8 **Facilities:** ℗ (charged) ➹ 🍴 licensed 🍴 ♿ (parking at main entrance, wheelchair available on loan) toilets for disabled shop ⊗ (guide dogs by arrangement) ⊠

OXBOROUGH   MAP 05 TF70

Oxburgh Hall

PE33 9PS

⮑ *(Signed from A134 at Stoke ferry & Swaffham)*

☎ 01366 328258

e-mail: oxburghhall@nationaltrust.org.uk

web: www.nationaltrust.org.uk

The outstanding feature of this 15th-century moated building is the 80ft high Tudor gatehouse which has remained unaltered throughout the centuries. Henry VII lodged in the King's Room in 1487. A parterre garden of French design stands outside the moat. Rare needlework by Mary Queen of Scots and Bess of Hardwick is on display. A particular attraction is a genuine 16th-century priests hole, which is accessible to members of the public.

Times: Open House: 25 Mar-29 Oct, daily (ex Thu & Fri) 1-5, BH Mon 11-5, (last admission 4.30). Garden: 1-19 Mar, wknds, 11-4; 25 Mar-29 Oct daily (ex Thu & Fri) 11-5.30 (4.30 Oct); Aug daily 11-5.30. **Fee:** ✱ House & Gardens £6.50 (ch £3.25), Family ticket £17. Gardens only £3.25 (ch £1.65). Party 15+ £5.50. **Facilities:** ℗ ➹ 🍴 licensed 🍴 ♿ (DVD tour of first floor, wheelchairs available, touch tour) toilets for disabled shop ⊗ (ex guide dogs) 🐾 ⊠

REEDHAM — MAP 05 TG40

Pettitts Animal Adventure Park

NR13 3UA

➲ *(off A47 at Acle then follow brown signs)*

☎ 01493 700094 & 701403

e-mail: pettittsreedham@aol.com

web: www.pettittsadventurepark.co.uk

Three parks in one, aimed at the younger child. Rides include a railway and roller coaster; the adventure play area has a golf course, ball pond and tearoom; and entertainment is provided by clowns, puppets and live musicians. Among the animals that can be seen are small horses, wallabies, birds of prey, goats, chickens and ducks.

Times: ✱ Open daily 19 Mar-30 Oct, 10-5/5.30. **Fee:** ✱ £7.95 (ch £7.95, under 3's free, concessions £5.85). **Facilities:** ❷ ⬛ ♿ (ramps to all areas) toilets for disabled shop ⊗ (ex assist dogs) ◀

ST OLAVES — MAP 05 TM49

St Olave's Priory   FREE

➲ *(5.5m SW of Great Yarmouth on A143)*

web: www.english-heritage.org.uk

Remains of an Augustinian priory founded nearly 200 years after the death in 1030 of the patron saint of Norway, after whom it was named.

Times: Open at any reasonable time. **Facilities:** ♯

SANDRINGHAM — MAP 09 TF62

Sandringham House, Grounds, Museum & Country

PE35 6EN

➲ *(off A148)*

☎ 01553 612908

e-mail: visits@sandringhamestate.co.uk

web: www.sandringhamestate.co.uk

The private country retreat of Her Majesty The Queen, this neo-Jacobean house was built in 1870 for King Edward VII. The main rooms used by the Royal Family when in residence are all open to the public. Sixty acres of glorious grounds surround the House and offer beauty and colour throughout the season. Sandringham Museum contains fascinating displays of Royal memorabilia. A new exhibition, *Behind the Lines*, features cartoons and caricatures from the Duke of Edinburgh's private collection.

Times: Open Etr Sat-mid Jul & early Aug-Oct. House open 11-4.45, Museum 11-5 & Grounds 10.30-5. **Fee:** ✱ House, Museum & Grounds: £8 (ch £5, pen £6.50). Family ticket £21. **Facilities:** ❷ ⬛ ℸ◯ℸ licensed ⬚ ♿ (wheelchair loan, free transport in grounds, Braille guide) toilets for disabled shop garden centre ⊗ (ex guide dogs) ◀

SAXTHORPE — MAP 09 TG13

Mannington Gardens & Countryside

Mannington Hall NR11 7BB

➲ *(signed from Corpusty/Saxthorpe on B1149 Norwich-Holt road. Follow signs)*

☎ 01263 584175

e-mail: laurelwalpole@manningtongardens.co.uk

web: www.manningtongardens.co.uk

The moated manor house, built in 1460 and still a family home, forms a centre-piece for the pretty gardens which surround it. Visitors can
continued

take in the Heritage rose garden, lakes, a scented garden, a ruined church, and horse graves. Music and theatre events are a regular feature. Contact for more details.

Times: ✱ Open: Gardens Jun-Aug, Wed-Fri 11-5; also Sun noon-5; Apr-1 Oct. Walks open every day from 9. Hall open by prior appointment only. **Fee:** Garden £4 (accompanied ch 16 free, concessions £3). Walks free (car park for walkers £2). **Facilities:** ❷ ⬛ ⬚ ♿ (boardwalk across meadow, wheelchair entrance) toilets for disabled shop ⊗ (ex guide dogs) ◀

SHERINGHAM — MAP 09 TG14

North Norfolk Railway (The Poppy Line)

Sheringham Station NR26 8RA

➲ *(from A148 take A1082. Next to large car park by rdbt in town centre)*

☎ 01263 820800

e-mail: enquiries@nnrailway.co.uk

web: www.nnr.co.uk

A full size heritage railway running between Sheringham and Holt, with an intermediate station at Weybourne. The route runs for 5.5m along the coast, through the heathland and features genuine Victorian stations. The William Marriott Railway Museum at Holt, is due to open in 2006.

Times: Open mid Feb-Oct and wknds in Dec; daily steam trains mid Mar-end Oct, Santa specials. Please telephone or see website for details **Fee:** ✱ £9 (ch £5.50, pen £8). Family ticket £27, cycles & dogs £1. **Facilities:** ❷ (charged) ⬛ ⬚ ♿ (ramps to trains, carriage converted for wheelchair access) toilets for disabled shop ◀

See advert on opposite page

SOUTH WALSHAM — MAP 09 TG31

Fairhaven Woodland & Water Garden   2 for 1

School Rd NR13 6DZ

➲ *(follow brown heritage signs from A47 onto B1140 to South Walsham. Through village towards Gt Yarmouth. Left into School Rd, 100yds past South Walsham Hall)*

☎ 01603 270449

web: www.fairhavengarden.co.uk

These delightful woodland and water gardens offer a combination of cultivated and wild flowers. In spring there are masses of primroses and bluebells, with azaleas and rhododendrons in several areas.

continued

Candelabra primulas and some unusual plants grow near the waterways, and in summer the wild flowers provide food for butterflies, bees and dragonflies. Summer flowers include Day Lilies, Ligularia, Hostas, Hydrangeas and flowering shrubs, including *Viburnum Mariesii* (Wedding Cake Viburnum), *Cornus Kousa Chinensis* and *Cornus Florida Rubra*.

Fairhaven Woodland & Water Garden

Times: Open daily 10-5, May-Aug extended opening Wed & Thu 10-9. Closed 25 Dec. **Fee:** ✱ £4.50 (ch £2, under 5 free, pen & concessions £4). Single membership tickets £15. Family membership ticket £35. Dog membership £2.50. **Facilities:** ℗ 🅿 📷 ♿ (ramp, grab rail) toilets for disabled shop garden centre 🍴

THETFORD   MAP 05 TL88

Ancient House Museum

White Hart St IP24 1AA
➲ *(in town centre)*
☎ 01842 752599
e-mail: ancient.house.museum@norfolk.gov.uk
web: www.norfolk.gov.uk/tourism/museums

An early Tudor timber-framed house with beautifully carved beamed ceilings, it now houses an exhibition on Thetford and Breckland life. This has been traced back to very early times, and there are examples from local Neolithic settlements. Brass rubbing facilities are available and there is a small period garden recreated in the rear courtyard.

Times: ✱ Open all year, Mon-Sat, 10-5 (Closed Mon 12.30-1); Jun-Aug also Sun 2-5. Closed Good Fri, Xmas period & New Year's Day.
Facilities: ℗ (20yds) shop garden centre ♿

Thetford Priory   FREE

➲ *(on W side of Thetford near station)*
web: www.english-heritage.org.uk

A glimpse of medieval religious life before the dissolution of the monasteries. The Priory of Our Lady of Thetford belonged to the Order of Cluny, and was founded in 1103 by Roger Bigod, an old soldier and friend of William the Conqueror.

Times: Open all year at any reasonable time. **Facilities:** ♿

Thetford Warren Lodge   FREE

➲ *(2m W of Thetford, off B1107)*
web: www.english-heritage.org.uk

The remains of a two-storey hunting lodge, built in the 15th century of flint with stone dressings.

Times: Open at any reasonable time. **Facilities:** ♿

THURSFORD GREEN   MAP 09 TF93

Thursford Collection   2 for 1

NR21 0AS
➲ *(1m off A148. Halfway between Fakenham and Holt)*
☎ 01328 878477
e-mail: admin@thursfordcollection.co.uk
web: www.thursford.com

This exciting collection specialises in organs, with a Wurlitzer cinema organ, fairground organs, barrel organs and street organs among its treasures. There are live musical shows every day. The collection also includes showmen's engines, ploughing engines and farm machinery. There is a children's play area and a breathtaking 'Venetian gondola' switchback ride.

Times: Open Good Fri-last Sun in Sep, daily, 12-5. Closed Sat.
Fee: ✱ £5.75 (ch under 4 free, ch 4-14 £3.25, students £5 pen £5.45). Party 15+ £5 each. **Facilities:** ℗ 🅿 🍴 licensed ♿ toilets for disabled shop ♿ (ex guide dogs) 🍴

England

TITCHWELL
MAP 09 TF74

RSPB Nature Reserve
FREE

PE31 8BB

➲ (6m E of Hunstanton on A149, signed entrance)

☎ 01485 210779

e-mail: titchwell@rspb.org.uk

web: rspb@org.uk

On the Norfolk coast, Titchwell Marsh is the RSPB's most visited reserve. Hundreds and thousands of migrating birds pass through in spring and autumn and many stay during winter, providing an opportunity to see many species of ducks, waders, seabirds and geese and also the RSPB emblem bird, the Avocet.

Times: Open at all times. Visitor Centre daily 9.30-5 (4 Nov-Mar).
Facilities: ✪ (charged) ♨ ◨ ♿ (ramps to hides, wheelchair bays in hides) toilets for disabled shop ◪

WEETING
MAP 05 TL78

Weeting Castle
FREE

IP27 0RQ

➲ (2m N of Brandon off B1106)

web: www.english-heritage.org.uk

This ruined 11th-century fortified manor house stands in a moated enclosure. There are interesting but slight remains of a three-storey cross-wing.

Times: Open at any reasonable time. **Facilities:** ✜

WELLS-NEXT-THE-SEA
MAP 09 TF94

Wells & Walsingham Light Railway

NR23 1QB

➲ (A149 Cromer road)

☎ 01328 711630

The railway covers the four miles between Wells and Walsingham, and is the longest ten and a quarter inch gauge track in the world. The line passes through some very attractive countryside, particularly noted for its wild flowers and butterflies. This is the home of the unique Garratt Steam Locomotive specially built for this line.

Times: ✱ Open daily Good Fri-end Oct. **Fee:** £7 return (ch £5.50 return).
Facilities: ✪ ♨ ♿ shop

English Heritage: Find out more
about English Heritage sites, their policies
and the work they do, at their website:
www.english-heritage.org.uk

WELNEY
MAP 05 TL59

WWT Welney
2 for 1

Hundred Foot Bank PE14 9TN

➲ (off A1101, N of Ely)

☎ 01353 860711

e-mail: welney@wwt.org.uk

web: www.wwt.org.uk

This important wetland site on the beautiful Ouse Washes is famed for the breathtaking spectacle of wild ducks, geese and swans which spend the winter here. Impressive observation facilities, including hides, towers and an observatory, offer outstanding views of the huge numbers of wildfowl which include Bewicks and whooper swans, wigeon, teal and shoveler. Floodlit evening swan feeds take place between November and February. There are two hides for wheelchair users.

Times: ✱ Open all year, daily 10-5. Closed 25 Dec. **Fee:** ✱ £4.50 (ch £2.70, pen £3.70). Family ticket £12 **Facilities:** ✪ ♨ ♿ toilets for disabled shop ⊗ (ex guide/hearing dogs) ◪

WEST RUNTON
MAP 09 TG14

Norfolk Shire Horse Centre

West Runton Stables NR27 9QH

➲ (off A149 in village of West Ranton half-way between Cromer & Sheringham, follow brown signs)

☎ 01263 837339

e-mail: bakewell@norfolkshirehorse.fsnet.co.uk

web: www.norfolk-shirehorse-centre.co.uk

The Shire Horse Centre has a collection of draught horses and some breeds of mountain and moorland ponies. There are also exhibits of horse-drawn machinery, waggons and carts, and harnessing and working demonstrations are given twice every day. Other attractions include a children's farm, a photographic display of draught horses past and present, talks and a video show. There is a riding school on the premises as well. Please telephone for details of special events.

Times: Open Apr-25 Oct daily (last admission 3.45); Apr & May after Etr Closed Fri & Sat; Jun-Aug closed Sat; Sep-Oct closed Fri & Sat **Fee:** £4.50 (ch £5.50, pen £6.50). **Facilities:** ✪ ♨ ♿ (video room, concrete yards all ramped) toilets for disabled shop ◪

WEYBOURNE
MAP 09 TG14

The Muckleburgh Collection

Weybourne Military Camp NR25 7EG

➲ (on A149, coast road, 3m W of Sheringham)

☎ 01263 588210 & 588608

e-mail: info@muckleburgh.co.uk

web: www.muckleburgh.co.uk

The largest privately-owned military collection of its kind in the country, which incorporates the Museum of the Suffolk and Norfolk Yeomanry. Exhibits include restored and working tanks, armoured cars, trucks and artillery of WWII, and equipment and weapons from the Falklands and the Gulf War. Live tank demonstrations are run daily (except Sat) during school holidays.

Times: Open 11-18 Feb, 28 Feb-28 Mar (Sat only), Apr-28 Oct, daily ex Sat after 16 Oct. Open 10-5 **Fee:** £6 (ch £3.50 & pen £5). Family ticket £14.50.
Facilities: ✪ ♨ ℈ ♿ (ramped access, wheelchairs available) toilets for disabled shop ⊗ (ex guide, kennels provided) ◪

Northamptonshire

The Rushton Triangular Lodge,
Rushton

This is a mainly rural county of gentle beauty, with farmland, forest and great country estates. Rivers, canals and watermeadows are all part of the tranquil scene, providing a real haven for wildlife. The ruined remains of Fotheringhay Castle and Rushton Triangular Lodge are both worthwhile visits. Traditionally, Northampton was the centre of shoe manufacture and Northampton Museum has the world's largest collections of shoes.

ALTHORP   MAP 04 SP66

Althorp

NN7 4HQ

➲ *(from S, exit M1 junct 16, & N junct 18, follow signs towards Northampton until directed by brown signs)*

☎ 01604 770107 & 0870 167 9000

e-mail: mail@althorp.com

web: www.althorp.com

Althorp House has been the home of the Spencer family since 1508. The house was built in the 16th century, but has been changed since, most notably by Henry Holland in the 18th century. Recently restored by the present Earl, the house is carefully maintained and in immaculate condition. The award-winning exhibition 'Diana, A Celebration' is located in six rooms and depicts the life and work of Diana, Princess of Wales. There is in addition, a room which depicts the work of the Diana, Princess of Wales Memorial Fund.

Times: ✱ Open Jul-Sep, daily 11-5. Closed 31 Aug. **Facilities:** ♿ 🍽 ⛔ (disabled parking, wheelchairs, audio tour, shuttle) toilets for disabled shop ⊗ (ex guide dogs) 🍴

CANONS ASHBY   MAP 04 SP55

Canons Ashby House

NN11 3SD

➲ *(easy access from either M40, junct 11 or M1, junct 16)*

☎ 01327 861900

e-mail: canonsashby@nationaltrust.org.uk

web: www.nationaltrust.org.uk

Home of the Dryden family since the 16th century, this is an exceptional small manor house, with Elizabethan wall paintings and Jacobean plasterwork. It has restored gardens, a small park and a church - part of the original 13th-century Augustinian priory.

Times: Open 25 Mar-5 Nov: daily except Thurs and Fri. House, 1-5.30 (1-4.30 Oct-5 Nov). Gardens, 11-5.30 (11-4.30 Oct-5 Nov). Park and Church, 11-5.30 (11-4.30 Oct-5 Nov). Garden, shop, tea-room, park and church, 11 Nov-17 Dec, Sat and Sun only 12-4. **Fee:** ✱ £6.10 (ch £3.10) Family £15.20. Garden only £2.20. Donation box for church. **Facilities:** ♿ 🍽 ⛔ (Braille/large print guide, taped guide, w/chair available) toilets for disabled shop 🐾

DEENE   MAP 04 SP99

Deene Park

NN17 3EW

➲ *(0.5m off A43, between Kettering & Stamford)*

☎ 01780 450278 & 450223

e-mail: admin@deenepark.com

web: www.deenepark.com

A mainly 16th-century house of great architectural importance, and home of the Brudenell family since 1514 (including the 7th Earl of Cardigan who led the Charge of the Light Brigade). There's a large lake and park, and extensive gardens with old-fashioned roses, rare

continued

trees and shrubs. Phone for details of garden openings and any other special events.

Times: Open Etr, May, Spring & Aug; 2-5 BHs (Sun & Mon) Jun-Aug, Sun. Party 20+ by prior arrangement with House Keeper. **Fee:** ✱ House & Gardens: £6.50 (ch 10-14 £2.50, concessions £5.50). Gardens only: £4 (ch £1.50). Children under 10 free admission with accompanying adult. **Facilities:** ♿ 🍽 ⛔ (ramps to cafeteria and gardens) toilets for disabled shop ⊗ (ex guide dogs in garden only)

Kirby Hall

NN17 5EN

➲ *(on unclass road off A43, 4m NE of Corby)*

☎ 01536 203230

web: www.english-heritage.org.uk

An outstanding Elizabethan mansion with unusually strict symmetry and amazing Renaissance detail. The beautiful formal gardens gained a reputation in the 17th-century as being the finest in England.

Times: Open all year, Apr-Jun & Sep-Oct, Thu-Mon 10-5; Jul-Aug, daily 10-6; Nov-Mar, Thu-Mon 10-4. Closed 24-26 Dec & 1 Jan. **Fee:** £4.50 (ch £2.30, concessions £3.40) Family £11.30. Prices and opening times are subject to change in Spring 2007. Please check web site or call 0870 333 1181 for the most up to date prices and opening times when planning your visit. **Facilities:** ♿ ⛔ shop

KETTERING   MAP 04 SP87

Alfred East Gallery   🟥 FREE

Sheep St NN16 OAN

➲ *(A43/A6, located in town centre, next to library)*

☎ 01536 534274

e-mail: museum@kettering.gov.uk

web: www.kettering.gov.uk

The Gallery has a permanent exhibition space showing work by Sir Alfred East, Thomas Cooper Gotch and other local artists, as well as selections from the Gallery's contemporary collection. Two further display spaces are dedicated to monthly changing exhibitions of art, craft and photography by local artists. There is also a monthly lunchtime talks programme.

Times: Open all year, Tue-Sat 9.30-5 (closed BHs) **Facilities:** ♿ (300yds) 📖 ⛔ shop ⊗ (ex guide dogs)

LYVEDEN NEW BIELD   MAP 04 SP98

Lyveden New Bield

PE8 5AT

➲ *(4m SW Oundle via A427)*

☎ 01832 205358

e-mail: lyvedennewbield@nationaltrust.org.uk

web: www.nationaltrust.org.uk

An incomplete Elizabethan garden house and moated garden. Building began in 1595 by Sir Thomas Tresham, to symbolise his Catholic faith, and Lyveden remains virtually unaltered since work stopped when he died in 1605. The house has fascinating Elizabethan detail and in the grounds is one of the oldest garden layouts in Britain.

Times: 24 Mar- 29 Oct, daily ex Mon and Tues, 10.30-5 (31 Jul-Aug daily, 10.30-5) 4-26 Nov and 3 Feb-25 Mar 2007 Sat and Sun, 10.30-4 **Fee:** ✱ £3.50 (ch free) **Facilities:** ♿ (0.5 m along track) 🐾

NASSINGTON
MAP 04 TL09

Prebendal Manor House
2 for 1

PE8 6QG

➲ (off A605 Warmington rdbt and follow brown heritage signs, manor is opposite church)

☎ 01780 782575

e-mail: info@prebendal-manor.co.uk

web: www.prebendal-manor.co.uk

Dating from the early 13th-century, this is the oldest manor in Northamptonshire. There's a 15th-century dovecote and tithe barn museum, and the largest re-created medieval garden in Europe, boasting fishponds, herbers, arbours, turf seats, trellised herbers, medieval vegetable garden and vineyard. The gardens and the manor have been featured in BBC2's *Royal Gardeners* and Channel 4's *Time Team* respectively. Special events every month throughout the summer.

Times: Open Etr Mon-Sep, Wed & Sun & BH Mon 1-5.30. **Fee:** ✱ House & garden £5.50 (ch £2.50, pen £5). Garden only £4. **Facilities:** Ⓟ 💻 🎮 ♿ (ramps, video of house and garden) shop ⊗ (ex guide dogs)

NORTHAMPTON
MAP 04 SP76

Northampton Museum & Art Gallery
FREE

Guildhall Rd NN1 1DP

➲ (situated in town centre, in Guildhall Rd)

☎ 01604 838111

e-mail: museums@northampton.gov.uk

web: www.northampton.gov.uk/museums

Home to the worlds largest collection of shoes, Northampton Museum and Art Gallery displays shoes that have been in fashion through the ages, from Ferragamo to Vivienne Westwood. Life and Sole tells the history of footwear, and other displays detail the history of Northampton, and British and Oriental ceramics and glass. There is also a gallery of Italian paintings depicting scenes from the Bible and ancient mythology.

Times: Open all year, Mon-Sat 10-5, Sun 2-5. (closed 25-26 Dec & 1 Jan) **Facilities:** Ⓟ (200 yds) (Carparks at bottom of Guildhall Rd). 🎮 ♿ (wheelchairs available, large print catalogues) toilets for disabled shop ⊗ (ex guide/assistance dogs) 📠

If an attraction name appears in *italics*, details have not been confirmed for 2007

ROCKINGHAM
MAP 04 SP89

Rockingham Castle
2 for 1

LE16 8TH

➲ (2m N of Corby, off A6003)

☎ 01536 770240

e-mail: a.norman@rockinghamcastle.com

web: www.rockinghamcastle.com

Set on a hill overlooking five counties, the castle was built by William the Conqueror. The site of the original keep is now a rose garden, but the outline of the curtain wall remains as do the foundations of the Norman hall, and the twin towers of the gatehouse. A royal residence for 450 years, the castle was granted to Edward Watson in the 16th century, and the Watson family have lived there ever since.

Times: Open May: Sun and BH Mon, Jun-Sep: Sun, BH, Mon and Tues. Grounds open from 12. Castle open from 1. **Fee:** ✱ £7.50 (ch 5-16yrs £4.50 & pen £6.50). Family ticket (2ad+2ch) £19.50. **Facilities:** Ⓟ 💻 🎮 ♿ (ramps, audio tour, parking adjacent to Castle) toilets for disabled shop 📠

RUSHTON
MAP 04 SP88

Triangular Lodge

NN14 1RP

☎ 01536 710761

web: www.english-heritage.org.uk

A delightful Elizabethan folly designed to symbolise the Holy Trinity, with its three sides, three floors, trefoil windows and three triangular gables on each side. Designed and built by Sir Thomas Gresham.

Times: Open Apr-Oct, Thu-Mon 10-5 **Fee:** £2.40 (ch £1.20, concessions £1.80) Prices and opening times are subject to change in Spring 2007. Please check web site or call 0870 333 1181 for the most up to date prices and opening times when planning your visit. **Facilities:** Ⓟ shop ⊞

SULGRAVE
MAP 04 SP54

Sulgrave Manor
2 for 1

Manor Rd OX17 2SD

➲ (off B4525 Banbury to Northampton road.)

☎ 01295 760205

e-mail: enquiries@sulgravemanor.org.uk

web: http://www.sulgravemanor.org.uk

Home to George Washington's ancestors until 1656 when his great grandfather, John, emigrated to Virginia. Inside the house there are many relics of George Washington. Though much of the house is a 20th-century restoration, original parts include the porch (with a carving of the original American flag), a screens passage, the great hall and the great Chamber.

Times: Open Apr-Oct. Closed Mon & Fri ex BHs. Other times by appointment. Wknds: 12-5.30, Tue, Wed and Thu: 2-5.30. (Last entry 4). **Fee:** ✱ £5.75 (ch £2.50). Party 20+. £5 (ch £2.50) Special event days £7.50 (ch £3.50). Family ticket £20. **Facilities:** Ⓟ 💻 🎮 ♿ toilets for disabled shop 📠

England

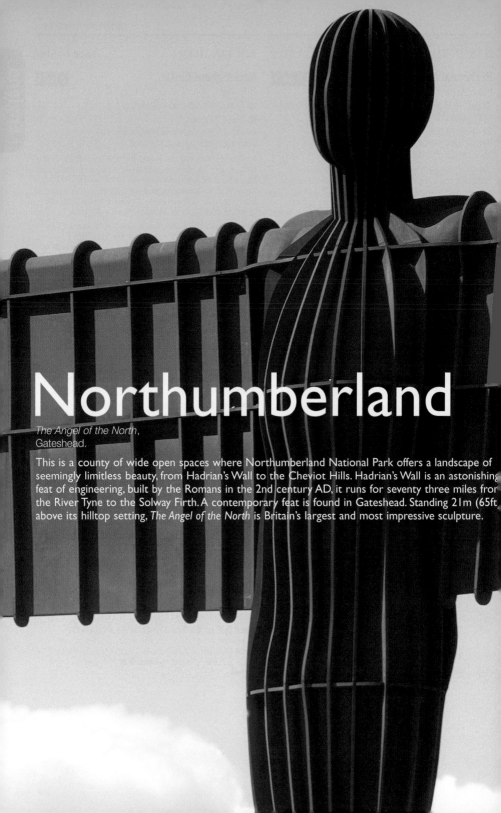

Northumberland

The Angel of the North,
Gateshead.

This is a county of wide open spaces where Northumberland National Park offers a landscape of seemingly limitless beauty, from Hadrian's Wall to the Cheviot Hills. Hadrian's Wall is an astonishing feat of engineering, built by the Romans in the 2nd century AD, it runs for seventy three miles from the River Tyne to the Solway Firth. A contemporary feat is found in Gateshead. Standing 21m (65ft above its hilltop setting, *The Angel of the North* is Britain's largest and most impressive sculpture.

England

ALNWICK MAP 12 NU11

Alnwick Castle `2 for 1`

NE66 1NQ

➲ *(off A1 on outskirts of town signed)*

☎ 01665 510777

e-mail: enquiries@alnwickcastle.com

web: www.alnwickcastle.com

Set in a stunning landscape, Alnwick Castle overlooks the historic market town of Alnwick. Although it was originally built for the Percy family, who have lived here since 1309, -the current Duke and Duchess of Northumberland being the current tenants- the castle is best known as one of the locations that served as Hogwarts School in the Harry Potter movies. The castle is full of art and treasures and there are plenty of activities for all the family.

Times: Open 5 Apr-29 Oct, daily 10-6 (last admission 4.30). **Fee:** ✱ £8.50 (ch £3.50, concessions £7.50). Family ticket £22.00. Party 14+.

Facilities: ❷ 💺 🍴 licensed � (Castle lift for those able to walk a little) toilets for disabled shop ⊗ (ex assist dogs) ◀

The Alnwick Garden NEW

Denwick Ln NE66 1YU

➲ *(in centre of Alnwick)*

☎ 01665 511350

e-mail: info@alnwickgarden.com

web: www.alnwickgarden.com

A vision of the Duchess of Northumberland and is leading garden visitor attraction in North East England. The 12-acre garden is the creation of Belgian designers and British architect Sir Michael Hopkins designed the Pavilion and Visitor Centre. This unique project in a deprived rural area has transformed a derelict and forgotten plot into a stimulating landscape. Now in its second phase of development, the garden includes one of the largest wooden tree houses in the world, a Poison Garden, Labyrinth and Serpent Garden.

Times: Open all year Apr, May & Oct, daily 10-6; Jun-Sep daily, 10-7; Nov-Mar daily 10-4 (last admission 45 mins before closing) **Fee:** ✱ £8 (ch £2.50 in educational group otherwise free, concessions £7.50). Groups £6.25 **Facilities:** ❷ 💺 🍴 licensed ⅟ (ramps, w/chairs & scooters for hire) toilets for disabled shop garden centre ⊗ (ex assist dogs) ◀

BAMBURGH MAP 12 NU13

Bamburgh Castle

NE69 7DF

➲ *(A1 Belford by-pass, E on B1342 to Bamburgh)*

☎ 01668 214515 & 214208

e-mail: bamburghcastle@aol.com

web: www.bamburghcastle.com

Rising dramatically from a rocky outcrop, Bamburgh Castle is a huge, square Norman castle. Last restored in the 19th century, it has an impressive hall and an armoury with a large collection of armour from the Tower of London. Guide services are available.

Times: Open 11 Mar-Oct, daily 11-5 (last admission 4.30).
Facilities: ❷ (charged) 💺 🍴 ⅟ toilets for disabled shop ⊗ (ex guide dogs)

Grace Darling Museum

Radcliffe Rd NE69 7AE

➲ *(follow A1, turn off at Bamburgh & follow signposts to Northumbria Coastal route, museum on right)*

☎ 01668 214465

Pictures, documents and other reminders of the heroine are on display, including the boat in which Grace Darling and her father, keeper of Longstone Lighthouse, Farne Islands, rescued nine survivors from the wrecked SS Forfarshire in 1838.

Times: ✱ Open Etr-Oct, daily 10-5 (Sun 12-5). **Facilities:** ❷ (400yds) 🍴 ⅟ (ramps) shop ⊗ (ex guide dogs)

BARDON MILL MAP 12 NY76

Vindolanda (Chesterholm)

Vindolanda Trust NE47 7JN

➲ *(signed from A69 or B6318)*

☎ 01434 344277

e-mail: info@vindolanda.com

web: www.vindolanda.com

Vindolanda was a Roman fort and frontier town. It was started well before Hadrian's Wall, and became a base for 500 soldiers. The civilian settlement lay just west of the fort and has been excavated. The excellent museum in the country house of Chesterholm nearby has displays and reconstructions. There are also formal gardens and an open-air museum with Roman Temple, shop, house and Northumbrian croft.

Times: Open Feb-Mar, daily 10-5. Apr-Sep 10-6, Oct & Nov 10-5.
Facilities: ❷ 💺 🍴 ⅟ (please contact for further info) toilets for disabled shop ⊗ (ex guide dogs) ◀

BELSAY MAP 12 NZ07

Belsay Hall, Castle and Gardens

NE20 0DX

➲ *(on A696)*

☎ 01661 881636

web: www.english-heritage.org.uk

Beautiful neo-classical hall, built from its own quarries with a spectacular garden deservedly listed Grade I in the Register of Gardens. It is slightly unclear who built the 'Grecian-style hall', however it was designed by Sir Charles in 1807, in Greek Revival style. The magnificent 30 acres of grounds contain the ruins of a 14th-century castle.

continued

England

Times: Open all year, Apr-Sep, daily 10-5; Oct, daily 10-4; Nov-Mar, Thu-Mon 10-4. Closed 24-26 Dec & 1 Jan. **Fee:** £5.50 (ch £2.80, concessions £4.10) Family £13.80. Prices and opening times are subject to change in Spring 2007. Please check web site or call 0870 333 1181 for the most up to date prices and opening times when planning your visit. **Facilities:** ℗ 🖳 ⅚ toilets for disabled shop ⚏

BERWICK-UPON-TWEED   MAP 12 NT95

Berwick-Upon-Tweed Barracks

TD15 1DF

➲ *(on the Parade, off Church St, in town centre)*

☎ 01289 304493

web: www.english-heritage.org.uk

Take an informative journey into our military past at the famous border town's barracks.

Times: Open Apr-Sep, daily 10-5; Oct daily 10-4; Nov-Mar, call site for details. Closed 24-26 Dec & 1 Jan and during Tattoo events. **Fee:** £3.30 (ch £1.70, concessions £2.50). Prices and opening times are subject to change in Spring 2007. Please check web site or call 0870 333 1181 for the most up to date prices and opening times when planning your visit. **Facilities:** ℗ (town centre) shop ⚏

Paxton House   2 for 1

TD15 1SZ

➲ *(3m from A1 Berwick-upon-Tweed bypass on B6461 Kelso road)*

☎ 01289 386291

e-mail: info@paxtonhouse.com

web: www.paxtonhouse.com

Built in 1758 for the Laird of Wedderburn, the house is a fine example of neo-Palladian architecture. Much of the house is furnished by Chippendale and there is a large picture gallery. The house is set in 80 acres beside the River Tweed, and the grounds include an adventure playground.

Times: Open daily from Apr-Oct, House & gallery 11-5 (last tour of house 4.15). Grounds 10-sunset. **Fee:** House & Grounds: £6 (ch £3) Family ticket £16. Grounds only: £3 (ch £1.50) Family ticket £8. **Facilities:** ℗ 🖳 🍴 licensed 🞔 ⅚ (lifts to main areas of house, parking close to reception) toilets for disabled shop ⊗ (ex in grounds & assist dogs) 🛥

CAMBO   MAP 12 NZ08

Wallington House Walled Garden & Grounds

NE61 4AR

➲ *(6m NW of Belsay)*

☎ 01670 773600

e-mail: wallington@nationaltrust.org.uk

web: www.nationaltrust.org.uk

Wallington is the largest country estate protected by the National Trust. With 13,000 acres that include the entire village of Cambo, the main attraction is the country house set among woods and gardens. There is a Pre-Raphaelite central hall, and a Cabinet of Curiosities that includes dolls houses. There are plenty of walks exploring the historic landscape, and a walled garden created by the Trevelyan family in the 1920s. Contact the estate for details of open-air theatre and rock and classical music concerts.

Times: Open: House daily (ex Tue) Apr-Aug 1-5.30; Sep & Oct 1-4.30. Walled garden open daily Apr-Sep 10-7; Oct 10-6; Nov-Mar 10-4. Grounds

continued

open all year (except Christmas day) dawn-dusk. **Fee:** ✱ House, walled garden & grounds: £8 (ch £4). Family £20; Garden & grounds only £5.50 (ch £2.75). Family £14. **Facilities:** ℗ 🖳 🍴 ⅚ (Wheelchairs available) toilets for disabled shop garden centre 🐾 🛥

CARRAWBROUGH   MAP 12 NY87

Temple of Mithras (Hadrian's Wall)

➲ *(3.75m W of Chollerford on B6318)*

web: www.english-heritage.org.uk

This fascinating Mithraic temple was uncovered by a farmer in 1949. Its three altars to the war god Mithras, date from the third century AD, and are now in the Museum of Antiquities in Newcastle, but there are copies on site.

Times: Open at any reasonable time. **Facilities:** ℗ ⚏

CHILLINGHAM   MAP 12 NU02

Chillingham Castle   2 for 1

NE66 5NJ

➲ *(signed from A1 & A697)*

☎ 01668 215359

e-mail: enquiries@chillingham.castle.com

web: www.chillingham-castle.com

This remarkable castle with its alarming dungeons and torture chamber is now undergoing restoration. Romantic grounds laid out by Sir Jeffry Wyatville command views over the Cheviots and include topiary gardens and woodland walks. Weddings, private functions and meals can be arranged, and fishing is available. Please ring for details of special events.

Times: Open Etr wknd & May-Sep, Sun-Fri (last admission 4.30). Other times by prior arrangement. Castle 1-5, grounds & tearoom 12-5. **Fee:** ✱ £6.75 (ch £3, pen £5.50). Party 10+ £5.30 **Facilities:** ℗ 🖳 🞔 ⅚ shop ⊗ (ex guide dogs) 🛥

Chillingham Wild Cattle Park

NE66 5NP

➲ *(off B6348, follow brown tourist signs off A1 and A697)*

☎ 01668 215250

web: www.chillingham-wildcattle.org.uk

The park, a registered charity, at Chillingham boasts an extraordinary survival: a herd of wild white cattle descended from animals trapped

continued

in the park when the wall was built in the 13th century; they are the sole surviving pure-bred examples of their breed in the world. Binoculars are recommended for a close view. Visitors are accompanied into the park by the Warden.

Times: Open Apr-Oct, daily 10-12 & 2-5, Sun 2-5. (Closed Tue).
Fee: ✱ £4.50 (ch £1.50 & pen £3). Family ticket £10 (2ad + 2ch)
Facilities: ❷ 🏮 shop ⊗

CORBRIDGE   MAP 12 NY96

Corbridge Roman Site and Museum

NE45 5NT

➲ (0.5m NW of Corbridge on minor road - signed)
☎ 01434 632349
web: www.english-heritage.org.uk

Originally a fort, which evolved into a prosperous town during the Roman era. An excellent starting point to explore Hadrian's Wall. The museum houses a fascinating collection of finds.

Times: Open all year, Apr-Sep, daily 10-5.30 (last admission 5); Oct, daily 10-4; Nov-Mar, Sat-Sun 10-4. Closed 24-26 Dec & 1 Jan. **Fee:** £3.80 (ch £1.90, concessions £2.90). Prices and opening times are subject to change in Spring 2007. Please check web site or call 0870 333 1181 for the most up to date prices and opening times when planning your visit.
Facilities: ❷ ᵹ toilets for disabled ⚏

EMBLETON   MAP 12 NU22

Dunstanburgh Castle

Craster NE66 2RD

➲ (1.5m E on footpaths from Craster or Embleton)
☎ 01665 576231
web: www.english-heritage.org.uk

An easy 12 mile coastal walk leads to the eerie skeleton of this wonderful 14th-century castle situated on a basalt crag more than 30 metres high with breathtaking views. The castle was built by Thomas Earl of Lancaster, nephew to King Edward II.

Times: Open all year, Apr-Sep, daily 10-5; Oct, daily 10-4; Nov-Mar, Thu-Mon 10-4. **Fee:** £2.70 (ch £1.40, concessions £2). Prices and opening times are subject to change in Spring 2007. Please check web site or call 0870 333 1181 for the most up to date prices and opening times when planning your visit. **Facilities:** ❷ (charged) ⚏

GREENHEAD   MAP 12 NY66

Roman Army Museum

Carvoran CA8 7JB

➲ (follow brown tourist signs from A69 or B6318)
☎ 016977 47485
e-mail: info@vindolanda.com
web: www.vindolanda.com

Situated alongside the Walltown Crags Section of Hadrian's Wall, the museum is a great introduction to the Roman Army. Find out about Roman weapons, training, pay, off-duty activities and much more. See if you can be persuaded to join up by watching the recruitment film, or view the Eagle's Eye film and soar with the eagle over Hadrian's Wall.

Times: Open Feb-Mar & Oct-Nov, 10-5; Apr-Sep 10-6 **Facilities:** ❷ ▦ 🏮 ᵹ (ramps, subtitles on main film) toilets for disabled shop ⊗ (ex guide dogs) ◀

HOLY ISLAND   MAP 12 NU14
(LINDISFARNE)

Lindisfarne Castle

TD15 2SH

➲ (8m S Berwick from A1 on Holy Island via 3m tidal causeway)
☎ 01289 389244
e-mail: lindisfarne@nationaltrust.org.uk
web: www.nationaltrust.org.uk

This 16th-century fort was restored by Sir Edwin Lutyens in 1903. The austere outside walls belie the Edwardian comfort within, which includes antique Flemish and English furniture, porcelain and polished brass. A small walled garden designed by Gertrude Jekyll is set on the southward facing slope, some 500 metres to the north of the castle. Spectacular views from the ramparts to the Farne Islands, Bamburgh Castle and beyond.

Times: Open mid Mar-Oct, daily (closed Mon ex BHs). As Lindisfarne is a tidal island, the Castle opening times will vary. Garden open all year (10-dusk). **Fee:** ✱ Castle & garden £5.20 (ch £2.60) Family ticket £13. Garden only £1 (ch free) **Facilities:** ℗ (1m in village) ᵹ (Braille guide) shop ⊗ ♨ 🏮

Lindisfarne Priory

TD15 2RX

➲ (can only be reached at low tide across a causeway. Tide tables posted at each end of the causeway)
☎ 01289 389200
web: www.english-heritage.org.uk

One of the holiest Anglo-Saxon sites in England, renowned for the original burial place of St Cuthbert whose corpse was discovered 11 years after his burial and found to be mysteriously undecayed. An award-winning museum.

Times: Open all year, Feb-Mar, daily 10-4; Apr-Sep, daily 9.30-5; Oct, daily 9.30-4; Nov-Jan, Sat-Mon 10-2. Closed 24-26 Dec & 1 Jan. **Fee:** £3.70 (ch £1.90, concessions £2.80). Prices and opening times are subject to change in Spring 2007. Please check web site or call 0870 333 1181 for the most up to date prices and opening times when planning your visit.
Facilities: shop ⚏

HOUSESTEADS   MAP 12 NY76

Housesteads Roman Fort

Haydon Bridge NE47 6NN

➲ (2.5m NE of Bardon Mill on B6318)
☎ 01434 344363
web: www.english-heritage.org.uk

The jewel in the crown of Hadrian's Wall and the most complete Roman fort in Britain. These superb remains offer a fascinating glimpse into the past glories of one of the world's greatest empires.

Times: Open all year, Apr-Sep, daily 10-6; Oct-Mar, daily 10-4. Closed 24-26 Dec & 1 Jan. **Fee:** £3.80 (ch £1.90, concessions £2.90) Family £9.50. Prices and opening times are subject to change in Spring 2007. Please check web site or call 0870 333 1181 for the most up to date prices and opening times when planning your visit. **Facilities:** ℗ (0.25m from fort) (charge payable) ᵹ (disabled parking) shop

England

LONGFRAMLINGTON   MAP 12 NU10

Brinkburn Priory

NE65 8AF

➲ *(off B6344)*

☎ 01665 570628

web: www.english-heritage.org.uk

This late 12th-century church is a fine example of early gothic architecture set in beautiful riverside surroundings. Look out for some unusual modern sculptures.

Times: Open Apr-Sep, Thu-Mon, 10-5. **Fee:** £2.70 (ch £1.40, concessions £2). Prices and opening times are subject to change in Spring 2007. Please check web site or call 0870 333 1181 for the most up to date prices and opening times when planning your visit. **Facilities:** ❷ shop ♿

MORPETH   MAP 12 NZ28

Morpeth Chantry Bagpipe Museum   `FREE`

Bridge St NE61 1PD

➲ *(off A1in Morpeth town centre)*

☎ 01670 500717

e-mail: anne.moore@castlemorpeth.gov.uk

This unusual museum specialises in the history and development of Northumbrian small pipes and their music. They are set in the context of bagpipes from around the world, from India to Inverness.

Times: Open all year, Mon-Sat, 10-5, open Sun in Aug & Dec. Closed 25-26 Dec, 1 Jan & Etr Mon. **Facilities:** ℗ (100mtrs) 📷 ♿ (induction loop, large print text, DVD guide to museum) shop

NORHAM   MAP 12 NT94

Norham Castle   `FREE`

TD15 2JY

☎ 01289 382329

web: www.english-heritage.org.uk

A mighty border fortress built in 1160, was one of the strongest of the border castles. Take an audio tour conjuring up four centuries of sieges and war with the Scots.

Times: Admission Limited. Please call 01289 304493 for details. **Facilities:** ❷ ♿ ⊗ ♿

PRUDHOE   MAP 12 NZ06

Prudhoe Castle

NE42 6NA

➲ *(on minor road off A695)*

☎ 01661 833459

web: www.english-heritage.org.uk

Explore the romantic remains of this 13th-century fortress perched on a steep wooded spur rising above the Tyne and set in lovely grounds.

Times: Open Apr-Sep, Thu-Mon 10-5. **Fee:** £3.40 (ch £1.70, concessions £2.60). Prices and opening times are subject to change in Spring 2007. Please check web site or call 0870 333 1181 for the most up to date prices and opening times when planning your visit. **Facilities:** ❷ shop ♿

ROTHBURY   MAP 12 NU00

Cragside

NE65 7PX

➲ *(15m NW of Morpeth on A697, left onto B6341, entrance 1m N of Rothbury)*

☎ 01669 620333 & 620150

e-mail: cragside@nationaltrust.org.uk

web: www.nationaltrust.org.uk

The aptly named Cragside was the home of Victorian inventor and landscape genius, Lord Armstrong, and sits on a rocky crag high above the Debden Burn. Crammed with ingenious gadgets it was the first house in the world to be lit by water-powered electricity. In the 1880s it also had hot and cold running water, central heating, fire alarms, telephones, and a passenger lift. The house has recently be re-wired, and will re-open in April 2007. In the estate there are forty miles of footpaths to explore, including a stroll through some of the best Victorian gardens in the country.

Times: Open, Estate & Gardens: Apr-Oct, Tue-Sun & BH Mons 10.30-7; Nov-mid Dec Wed-Sun 11-4 (or dusk if earlier); House closed until April 2007. (Last admission 1hr before closing). **Fee:** ✱ Estate & Gardens £6.50 (ch £3) Family £16. Winter opening £3 (ch £1.50) Family £7.50. **Facilities:** ❷ 🍴 licensed ♿ (ltd access, Braille guide, wheelchair path, lift) toilets for disabled shop ♿

WALWICK   MAP 12 NY97

Chesters Roman Fort & Museum

Chollerford NE46 4EP

➲ *(0.5m W of Chollerford on B6318)*

☎ 01434 681379

web: www.english-heritage.org.uk

The best-preserved Roman cavalry fort in Britain. The museum holds displays of carved stones, altars and sculptures from all along Hadrian's Wall.

Times: Open all year, Apr-Sep, daily 9.30-6; Oct-Mar, daily 10-4. Closed 24-26 Dec & 1 Jan **Fee:** £3.80 (ch £1.90, concessions £2.90). Prices and opening times are subject to change in Spring 2007. Please check web site or call 0870 333 1181 for the most up to date prices and opening times when planning your visit. **Facilities:** ❷ 🍴 ♿ (wheelchair access limited) shop ♿

WARKWORTH   MAP 12 NU20

Warkworth Castle & Hermitage

NE66 0UJ

☎ 01665 711423

web: www.english-heritage.org.uk

The magnificent eight-towered keep of Warkworth Castle stands on a hill high above the River Coquet, dominating all around it. A complex stronghold, it was home to the Percy family, which at times wielded more power in the North than the King himself.

Times: Open all year. Castle; Apr-Sep, daily 10-5; Oct, daily 10-4; Nov-Mar, Sat-Mon 10-4. Hermitage; Apr-Sep, Wed, Sun & Bank Hols 11-5. Closed 24-26 Dec & 1 Jan. **Fee:** Castle; £3.40 (ch £1.70, concessions £2.60) Family £8.50. Hermitage; £2.40 (ch £1.20, concessions £1.80). Prices and opening times are subject to change in Spring 2007. Please check web site or call 0870 333 1181 for the most up to date prices and opening times when planning your visit. **Facilities:** ❷ ♿ (limited access) shop ♿

Nottinghamshire

Robin Hood,
Nottingham

The land-locked county of Nottinghamshire has long been associated with the legend of Robin Hood, and although there is much controversy over the existence of the outlaw, Sherwood Forest is very much in evidence. Covering some 450 acres, it contains an oak tree thought to be around 800 years old with a circumference of 10m (33ft). Nottingham, the regional capital, has many historical attractions, such as The Lace Centre, full of exquisite Nottingham lace, 17th-century Nottingham Castle, and the 750-year-old Caves of Nottingham.

EASTWOOD
MAP 08 SK44

D. H. Lawrence Heritage
2 for 1

Durban House Heritage Centre, Mansfield Rd
NG16 3DZ

➲ *(A610 or A608 follow brown tourist signs)*

☎ 01773 717353

e-mail: culture@broxtowe.gov.uk

web: www.broxtowe.gov.uk

D H Lawrence Heritage, in the writer's home town of Eastwood, brings together the D H Lawrence Birthplace Museum and the Durban House Heritage Centre, along with two quality gift shops, a contemporary art gallery and a bistro. Discover more about the son of a miner who went on to become one of the 20th century's most influential writers.

Times: Open all year, Apr-Oct, daily 10-5; Nov-Mar, daily 10-4. Closed over Xmas, telephone for details. **Fee:** Free Mon-Fri. Single site £2 (concessions £1.20). Both sites £3.50 (concessions £1.80). Family Ticket (2ad+2ch) Joint Site £8; Single Site £5.80 **Facilities:** ♥ ♨ ⦿ licensed (lift to exhibition, wheelchair available) shop ⊗ (ex guide dogs) ◄

EDWINSTOWE
MAP 08 SK66

Sherwood Forest Country Park & Visitor Centre
FREE

NG21 9HN

➲ *(on B6034 N of Edwinstowe between A6075 and A616)*

☎ 01623 823202 & 824490

e-mail: sherwood.forest@nottscc.gov.uk

web: www.nottinghamshire.gov.uk/countryparks

At the heart of the Robin Hood legend is Sherwood Forest. Today it is a country park and visitor centre with 450 acres of ancient oaks and shimmering silver birches. Waymarked pathways guide you through the forest. A year round programme of events includes the spectacular Robin Hood Festival.

Times: Open all year. Country Park: open daily dawn to dusk. Visitor Centre: open daily 10-5 (4.30 Nov-Mar) **Facilities:** ♥ (charged) ♨ ⦿ licensed ⬛ ⅙ (wheelchair and electric buggy loan) toilets for disabled shop ◄

An asterisk ✳ indicates that opening times or prices are for 2006. Please contact the attraction for more up-to-date information.

FARNSFIELD
MAP 08 SK65

White Post Farm Centre

NG22 8HL

➲ *(12m N of Nottingham on A614)*

☎ 01623 882977 & 882026

e-mail: admin@whitepostfarmcentre.co.uk

web: www.whitepostfarmcentre.co.uk

With over 25 acres theres lots to see and do at the White Post Farm Centre. There are more than 3000 animals including pigs, goats and sheep, along with more exotic animals like bats, reptiles and meerkats. The new indoor play area is ideal for small children, and there's also a sledge run, trampolines and pedal go-karts.

Times: Open daily from 10 **Fee:** ✳ £7.30 (ch 2-16 £6.60, under 2's free) **Facilities:** ♥ ♨ ⅙ (free hire wheelchairs, book if more than 6) toilets for disabled shop ⊗ (ex guide dogs) ◄

NEWARK-ON-TRENT
MAP 08 SK75

Millgate Museum
FREE

48 Millgate NG24 4TS

➲ *(easy access from A1 & A46)*

☎ 01636 655730

e-mail: museums@nsdc.info

web: www.newark-sherwooddc.gov.uk

The museum is home to diverse social collections and features fascinating exhibitions - recreated streets, shops and houses in period settings. There are also children's activities. The mezzanine gallery, home to a number of temporary exhibitions shows the work of local artists, designers and photographers.

Times: Open Apr-Sep Tue-Sun, 10.30-4.30, Oct-Mar: Tue-Sun, 10.30-4. Open spring and summer BH Mon, 10.30-4. **Facilities:** ℗ (250yds) ♨ ⬛ shop ⊗ (ex assistance dogs)

Newark Air Museum

The Airfield, Winthorpe NG24 2NY

➲ *(easy access from A1, A46, A17 & Newark relief road, follow tourist signs, next to county showground.)*

☎ 01636 707170

e-mail: newarkair@onetel.com

web: www.newarkairmuseum.co.uk

A diverse collection of transport, training and reconnaissance aircraft, jet fighters, bombers and helicopters, now numbering more than seventy. Two Undercover Aircraft Display Halls and an Engine Hall make the museum an all-weather attraction. Everything is displayed around a WWII airfield.

Times: Open all year, Mar-Sep daily 10-5; Oct-Feb, daily 10-4. Closed 24-26 Dec & 1 Jan. Other times by appointment. **Fee:** ✱ £6 (ch £3.50, pen £5.50). Family ticket (2ad+2ch) £16.50. Party 15+. **Facilities:** ℗ 🍽 🗒 🕭 toilets for disabled shop ◄

Vina Cooke Museum of Dolls & Bygone Childhood

The Old Rectory, Cromwell NG23 6JE

➲ *(5m N of Newark off A1)*

☎ 01636 821364

e-mail: info@vinasdolls.co.uk

web: www.vinasdolls.co.uk

All kinds of childhood memorabilia are displayed in this 17th-century house: prams, toys, dolls' houses, costumes and a large collection of Victorian and Edwardian dolls including Vina Cooke hand-made character dolls.

Times: Open Apr-Sep, Tue, Thu, Sat-Sun & BH 10.30-4.30. Mon, Wed, Fri and Oct-Mar by appointment, please telephone. **Fee:** £3 (ch £1.50, pen £2.50). **Facilities:** ℗ shop ◯

NEWSTEAD   MAP 09 SK55

Newstead Abbey

Newstead Abbey Park NG15 8NA

➲ *(off A60, between Nottingham & Mansfield, at Ravenshead)*

☎ 01623 455900

e-mail: sallyl@newsteadabbey.org.uk

web: www.newsteadabbey.org.uk

This beautiful house is best known as the home of poet Lord Byron. Visitors can see Byron's own rooms, mementoes of the poet and other splendidly decorated rooms. The grounds of over 300 acres include waterfalls, ponds, water gardens and Japanese gardens. Special events include outdoor theatre and opera, Christmas events and Ghost Tours. Special Events: Please telephone for details of events running throughout the year.

Times: Open: Grounds all year, daily 9-dusk or 6 whichever is earliest (ex last Fri in Nov & 25 Dec); House Apr-Sep, daily 12-5. (Last admission 4). **Fee:** ✱ House & Grounds £6 (ch £1.50, concessions £2.50) Family ticket £16. Grounds only £3 (concessions £2.50) Family ticket £8.50. Subject to change. **Facilities:** ℗ 🍽 🗒 🕭 (audio tour & wheelchair for loan Apr-Sep) toilets for disabled shop ◯ (ex guide dogs) ◄

NOTTINGHAM   MAP 08 SK53

Galleries of Justice

The Shire Hall, High Pavement, Lace Market NG1 1HN

➲ *(follow signs to city centre, brown heritage signs to Lace Market & Galleries of Justice)*

☎ 0115 952 0555

e-mail: info@nccl.org.uk

web: www.nccl.org.uk

The Galleries of Justice are located on the site of an original Court and County Gaol. New developments include the arrival of the HM Prison Service Collection, which will now be permanently housed in the 1833 wing. Never before seen artefacts from prisons across the country offer visitors the chance to experience some of Britain's most gruesome, yet often touching, reminders of what prison life would have been for inmates and prison staff over the last three centuries. 2007 is the 100th anniversary of the Probation Service.

Times: Open all year, Tue-Sun & BH Mon 10-5 (also open Mon in school hols). (Last admission one hour before closing). Contact for Xmas opening times. **Fee:** ✱ £7.95 (concessions £5.95). Family ticket £22.95 (2ad+2ch). **Facilities:** ℗ (5 mins walk) 🍽 🕭 (Braille control lifts, induction loop, large print lables) toilets for disabled shop ◯ (ex guide dogs) ◄

Green's Windmill

Windmill Ln, Sneinton NG2 4QB

➲ *(off B686, 500yds from Ice Centre)*

☎ 0115 915 6878

e-mail: info@greensmill.org.uk

web: www.greensmill.org.uk

Restored to working order, take a look around the mill and see how grain is turned into flour by harnessing the power of the wind. Find out about the "mathematician miller" George Green and his theories, and test your mind with hands on puzzles and experiments. There's also a guinea pig piggery. 2007 is the bicentenary of the mill.

Times: Open all year Wed-Sun, 10-4, also BHs. Phone for Xmas & New Year closing. **Facilities:** ℗ 🗒 🕭 (parking in Millyard) toilets for disabled shop ◯ (ex assist dogs) ◄

The Lace Centre

Severns Building, Castle Rd NG1 6AA

➲ *(follow signs for Castle, situated opposite Robin Hood statue)*

☎ 0115 941 3539

Exquisite Nottingham lace fills this small 14th-century building to capacity, with panels also hanging from the beamed ceiling. There are weekly demonstrations of lace-making on Thursday afternoons from Easter to October. Telephone for details.

Times: Open all year. Jan-Mar, daily 10-4; Apr-Nov, 10-5. Every Sun 11-4. Closed Xmas & New Year **Facilities:** ℗ (100yds) (metered street parking) shop ◄

England

The Museum of Nottingham Life

Brewhouse Yard, Castle Boulevard NG7 1FB

⮑ *(follow signs to city centre, the museum is a 5 min walk from city centre with easy access from train, tram and bus.)*

☎ 0115 915 3640

e-mail: anni@ncmg.org.uk

web: www.nottinghamcity.gov.uk

Nestled in the rock below Nottingham Castle and housed in a row of 17th-century cottages, the museum presents a realistic glimpse of life in Nottingham over the last 300 years. Discover the caves behind the museum and peer through 1920s shop windows.

Times: Open daily, 10-4.30. Last admission 4. Closed 24-26 Dec, 1-2 Jan.
Fee: Joint ticket with castle £3 (concessions £1.50) Family ticket £7.
Facilities: Ⓟ (100yds) ⬛ ♿ (call 0115 915 3600 for info on access) toilets for disabled shop ⊗ (ex guide dogs)

Nottingham Castle

NG1 6EL

⮑ *(follow signs to city centre, then signs to castle)*

☎ 0115 915 3700

web: www.nottinghamcity.gov.uk

This 17th-century building is both museum and art gallery, with major temporary exhibitions, by historical and contemporary artists, as well as the permanent collections. There is a 'Story of Nottingham' exhibition and a gallery designed especially to entertain young children. Guided tours of the underground passages take place on most days.

Times: Open all year, daily 10-5. Grounds 8-dusk. Closed 24-26 Dec.
Fee: Joint ticket with Brenhouse Yard. £3 (ch and concessions £1.50, under 5's free) Family £7 (2 ad up to 3 ch) Group ticket: 1 free ticket for every 10. **Facilities:** Ⓟ (400yds) (ltd disabled spaces, can book in advance) ⬛ ⬛ ♿ (parking at castle, for more info call 0115 915 3676) toilets for disabled shop ⊗ (ex guide dogs) ◀

Nottingham Industrial Museum

Courtyard Buildings, Wollaton Park NG8 2AE

⮑ *(4m from city centre off A6514)*

☎ 0115 915 3900

e-mail: carol@ncmg.demon.co.uk

web: www.nottinghamcity.gov.uk

Nottingham's industrial history is on display in this 18th-century stable block. Lace, hosiery, pharmaceuticals (Nottingham was the home of the founder of Boots the Chemists), tobacco and much else are among the exhibits. There is a beam engine and other steam engines, regularly in steam.

Times: Open all year daily 11-5 **Facilities:** Ⓞ (charged) ⬛ ♿ (hand & powered wheelchairs available) toilets for disabled shop ⊗ (ex guide dogs)

Tales of Robin Hood

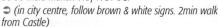

30-38 Maid Marian Way NG1 6GF

⮑ *(in city centre, follow brown & white signs. 2min walk from Castle)*

☎ 0115 948 3284

e-mail: robinhoodcentre@mail.com

web: www.robinhood.uk.com

Explore the intriguing and mysterious story of the legendary tales of Robin Hood in medieval England. Enjoy film shows, live performances, an adventure ride, falconry and even try your hand at archery. Banquets and live entertainment in the evening.

Times: Open all year, daily 10-5.30. Last admission 4. Closed 25-26 Dec.
Fee: ✱ £8.95 (ch £6.95, concessions £7.95) Family £26.95
Facilities: Ⓟ (NCP 200 yds) ⬛ ⬛ ♿ (specially adapted 'car', lift) toilets for disabled shop ⊗ (ex guide dogs) ◀

Wollaton Hall & Park

Wollaton NG8 2AE

⮑ *(M1 junct 25 signed from A52, A609, A6514, A60 and city centre).*

☎ 0115 915 3900

e-mail: info@wollatonhall.org.uk

web: www.wollatonhall.org.uk

Built in the late 16th century, and extended in the 19th, Wollaton Hall and Park holds Nottingham's Natural History Museum, Nottingham's Industrial Museum, the Wollaton Park Visitor Centre, and the Yard Gallery, which has changing exhibitions exploring art and the environment. The Hall itself is set in 500 acres of deer park, with herds of red and fallow deer roaming wild. There are also formal gardens, a lake, nature trails, adventure playgrounds and a sensory garden. The many events throughout the year include pop concerts, and twilight bat walks.

Times: Due to ongoing refurbishment please ring 0115 915 3900 for details, will reopen summer 2007. **Fee:** ✱ Free wkdays. Ticket for both Hall & Museum £1.50 (ch & concessions £1). Family ticket £4. Charge made at wknds & BHs only. Group rate 1 free for every 10 tickets.
Facilities: Ⓞ (charged) ⬛ ⬛ ♿ (call 0115 915 3700 for info on access) shop ⊗ (ex guide dogs) ◀

OLLERTON   MAP 08 SK66

Rufford Abbey and Country Park   FREE

NG22 9DF

⮑ *(2m S of Ollerton, adjacent to A614)*

☎ 01623 822944

e-mail: rufford.park@nottscc.gov.uk

web: www.nottinghamshire.gov.uk/countryparks

At the heart of the wooded country park stand the remains of a 12th-century Cistercian Abbey, housing an exhibition on the life of a Cistercian Monk at Rufford. Many species of wildlife can be seen on the lake, and there are lovely formal gardens, with sculptures and Britain's first centre for studio ceramics.

Times: Open all year 10.30-5 (craft centre closes 3pm Jan & Feb). For further details of opening times telephone establishment. Closed 25 Dec.
Facilities: Ⓞ (charged) ⬛ ⅋◎ licensed ⬛ ♿ (lift to craft centre, w/chair and electric buggy loan) toilets for disabled shop garden centre ◀

SOUTHWELL   MAP 08 SK65

The Workhouse

Upton Rd NG25 0PT

➲ *(13m from Nottingham on A612)*

☎ 01636 817250

e-mail: theworkhouse@nationaltrust.org.uk

web: www.nationaltrust.org.uk

Enter this 19th-century brick institution and discover the thought-provoking story of the 'welfare' system of the New Poor Law. The least altered workhouse in existence today, it survives from hundreds that once covered the country. Explore the segregated stairs and rooms, use the audio guide, based on archive records, to bring the 19th-century inhabitants to life in the empty rooms, then try the interactive displays exploring poverty through the years and across the country.

Times: Open 25 Mar-9 Apr, 30 Sept-29 Oct: Sat and Sun 12-5. 10 Apr-1 Sep: open daily except Tue 12-5. 27 Apr- 30 Jul and 2-29 Sep: Thu, Fri, Sat and Sun 12-5. **Fee:** ✱ £4.90 (ch £2.40). Family ticket £12.20 (2 ad and 3 ch) **Facilities:** ❷ ♿ (virtual tour, photo album, wheelchairs available) toilets for disabled (ex guide dogs) ♨

SUTTON-CUM-LOUND   MAP 08 SK68

Wetlands Waterfowl Reserve & Exotic Bird Park

Off Loundlow Rd DN22 8SB

➲ *(signed on A638)*

☎ 01777 818099

The Reserve is a 32-acre site for both wild and exotic waterfowl. Visitors can see a collection of birds of prey, parrots, geese, ducks, and

continued

wigeon among others. There are also many small mammals and farm and wild animals, including llamas, wallabies, emus, monkeys, red squirrels, deer and goats.

Times: ✱ Open all year, daily 10-5.30 (or dusk - whichever is earlier). Closed 25 Dec. **Facilities:** ❷ 🍴 ♿ (wheelchair available) shop ⊗ (ex guide dogs)

WORKSOP   MAP 08 SK57

Clumber Park

The Estate Office, Clumber Park S80 3AZ

➲ *(4.5m SE of Worksop, 6.5m SW of Retford, 1m from A1/A57)*

☎ 01909 476592

e-mail: clumberpark@nationaltrust.org.uk

web: www.nationaltrust.org.uk

An impressive, landscaped park, laid out by 'Capability Brown'. An outstanding feature is the lake running through the park, a haven for wildfowl, covering an area of 80 acres. The park is a mixture of woodland, open grass and heathland.

Times: Open: park daily except 19 Aug and 25 Dec. Kitchen Garden, Chapel and Plant sales open: Apr-1 Oct, Mon-Fri 10-5, Sat-Sun and BH Mon, 10-6. Shop and restaurant: open all year at same times as Kitchen Garden. **Fee:** ✱ Pedestrians, cyclists and coaches free; cars and motorbikes £4.30. Kitchen Garden £2 (ch free) National trust members free. **Facilities:** ❷ (charged) 🍴 🍴 licensed ♿ (powered self-drive vehicle available if booked) toilets for disabled shop garden centre ♨

Elizabeth Wollaton Hall, home of Nottingham's Natural History Museum

Oxfordshire

The Radcliffe Camera,
Bodleian Library
Oxford

The City of Oxford, situated on the River Thames, is home to Britain's oldest university, established during the 12th century and famous for its ancient buildings; the 'dreaming spires' of literature. Henley-on-Thames is well known for its annual Royal Regatta, a rowing competition of world renown and a highlight of the social calendar. The county also boasts ranges of hills, the Cotswolds and Chilterns, both of which make excellent walking country.

BANBURY   MAP 04 SP44

Banbury Museum   **FREE**

Spiceball Park Rd OX16 2PQ

➲ *(M40 junct 11 straight across at first rdbt into Hennef Way, left at next rdbt into Concord Ave, right at next rdbt & left at next rdbt, Castle Quay Shopping Centre & Museum on right)*

☎ 01295 259855

e-mail: banburymuseum@cherwell-dc.gov.uk

web: www.cherwell-dc.gov.uk/banburymuseum

Banbury's stunning new museum is situated in an attractive canal-side location in the centre of Banbury. Exciting modern displays tell of Banbury's origins and historic past. The Civil War; the plush manufacturing industry; the Victorian market town; costume from the 17th century to the present day; Tooley's Boatyard and the Oxford Canal, are just some of the subjects illustrated in the new museum.

Times: Open all year, Mon-Sat, 10-5, Sun 10.30-4.30.
Facilities: Ⓟ (500yds) �🍴 licensed 🅹 ♿ toilets for disabled shop ⊗ (ex guide dogs) ⬛

BROUGHTON   MAP 04 SP43

Broughton Castle   **2 for 1**

OX15 5EB

➲ *(2m W of Banbury Cross on B4035 Shipston-on-Stour in Broughton village, turn off B4035 by Saye & Sele Arms)*

☎ 01295 276070

e-mail: admin@broughtoncastle.demon.co.uk

web: www.broughtoncastle.com

Built by Sir John de Broughton, then owned by William of Wykeham, and later by the first Lord Saye and Sele, the castle is an early 14th- and mid 16th-century house with a moat and gatehouse. Period furniture, paintings and Civil War relics are displayed. There are fine borders in the walled garden, and against the castle walls.

Times: Open Etr Sun & Mon, May-14 Sep, Wed, Sun & BH Mon, 2-5 (also open Thu in Jul & Aug). **Fee:** £6.50 (ch 5-15 £2.50, concessions & group rate £5.50). Family ticket (2ad & up to 3ch) £15. **Facilities:** ❷ ⬛ 🅹 ♿ toilets for disabled shop ⊗ (ex guide dogs)

See advert on this page

BROUGHTON CASTLE
Banbury, Oxfordshire

Broughton Castle, Banbury, Oxfordshire – home of Lord and Lady Saye & Sele and the Fiennes family ... and Shakespeare in Love!
"about the most beautiful castle in all England ... for sheer loveliness of the combination of water, woods, and picturesque buildings of the later and more decorative age of military architecture" Sir Charles Oman, historian, 1860–1946

The Castle is open at the following times: 1400–1700 hours on these days in 2007
• Bank Holiday Sundays and Mondays (Easter, MayDay, Whit/Spring, & August)
• Wednesdays and Sundays between 1st May and 14th September, also Thursdays in July and August

Individual admission prices:
Adults £6.00, Children (5–15) £2.50, Students & Seniors £5.00. Garden only £2.50
Guided Groups (over 16 people): Adults & Seniors £5.50, Schools £2.50, Students £5.00. Garden only £2.50

For further information or to make a booking please telephone or fax
00 44 1295 276070 from outside the UK or
01295 276070 from the UK

www.broughtoncastle.com
e-mail: admin@broughtoncastle.demon.co.uk

BURFORD   MAP 04 SP21

Cotswold Wildlife Park

OX18 4JW

➲ *(on A361 2m S of A40 at Burford)*

☎ 01993 823006

web: www.cotswoldwildlifepark.co.uk

This 160-acre landscaped zoological park, surrounds a listed Gothic-style manor house. There is a varied collection of animals from all over the world, many of which are endangered species such as Asiatic lions, leopards, white rhinos and red pandas. There's an adventure

continued

England

playground, a children's farmyard, and train rides during the summer. The park has also become one of the Cotswold's leading attractions for garden enthusiasts, with its exotic summer displays and varied plantings offering interest all year.

Times: Open all year, daily from 10, (last admission 4.30 Mar-Sep, 3.30 Oct-Feb). Closed 25 Dec. **Fee:** £9.50 (ch 3-16 & pen £7). **Facilities:** ❷ 🖵 🍴 licensed & (parking, free hire of wheelchairs) toilets for disabled shop 🔳

See advert on opposite page

BUSCOT
MAP 04 SU29

Buscot Park
SN7 8BU

➲ *(on A417 between Faringdon & Lechlade)*
☎ 01367 240786
e-mail: estbuscot@aol.com
web: www.buscot-park.com

An 18th-century Palladian house with park and water garden. Home of the Faringdon collection of paintings and furniture. The park is landscaped with extensive water gardens designed by Harold Peto with parkland walks and a walled garden boasting seasonal herbaceous borders.

Times: Open Grounds only 2 Apr-28 Sep, Mon & Tue 2-6. House & Grounds open 4 Apr-28 Sep, Wed-Fri 2-6 (last entry 5) also open BHs & Sat-Sun: 7-9, 14-15 Apr, 5-7, 12-13, 26-27 May, 9-10, 23-24 Jun, 7-8, 21-22 Jul, 11-12, 25-27 Aug, 8-9, 22-23 Sep. **Fee:** ✱ House & Grounds £7 (ch £3.50); Grounds only £5 (ch £2.50). NT members free. **Facilities:** ❷ 🖵 & (2 motorised mobility vehicles-must pre-book) toilets for disabled ⊗ assist dogs 🐾 🔳

CHASTLETON
MAP 04 SP22

Chastleton House
GL56 0SU

➲ *(6m from Stow-on-the-Wold. Approach from A436 between A44)*
☎ 01608 674355
e-mail: chastleton@nationaltrust.org.uk
web: www.nationaltrust.org.uk

One of England's finest and most complete Jacobean houses, Chastleton House is filled with a mixture of rare and everyday objects, furniture and textiles maintaining the atmosphere of this 400-year-old home. The gardens have a typical Elizabethan and Jacobean layout

continued

with a ring of topiary. The National Trust has focussed on conserving rather than restoring the house.

Times: Open 28 Mar-29 Sep, 1-5, 3-27 Oct, 1-4. **Fee:** ✱ £6 (ch £3) Family £15. Group £5 each **Facilities:** ❷ 🖵 & toilets for disabled ⊗ 🐾

DEDDINGTON
MAP 04 SP43

Deddington Castle
🎫 FREE

OX5 4TE

➲ *(S of B4031 on E side of Deddington)*
web: www.english-heritage.org.uk

The large earthworks of the outer and inner baileys can be seen; the remains of 12th-century castle buildings have been excavated, but they are not now visible.

Times: Open any reasonable time. **Facilities:** ✿

DIDCOT
MAP 04 SU58

Didcot Railway Centre
🎫 2 for 1

OX11 7NJ

➲ *(on A4130 at Didcot Parkway Station)*
☎ 01235 817200
e-mail: didrlyc@globalnet.co.uk
web: www.didcotrailwaycentre.org.uk

Based around the original GWR engine shed, the Centre is home to the biggest collection anywhere of Great Western Railway steam locomotives, carriages and wagons. A typical GWR station has been re-created and a section of Brunel's original broad gauge track relaid, with reconstruction of 'Fire Fly' locomotive of 1840.

Times: Open all year, Sat & Sun. Daily 31 Mar-16 Apr, 26 May-3 Jun, 23 Jun-2 Sep. Steamdays, Easter 6-9 Apr, 28 Apr-2 Sep (Sat & Sun), Wed 11 Jul-29 Aug. Day out with Thomas 9-11 Mar, 5-7 Oct. Thomas Santa Special 7-24 Dec, Fri-Sun. **Fee:** £4-£9.50 depending on event (ch £3-£8, pen £3.50-£8). **Facilities:** ℗ (100yds) 🖵 🍴 🗄 & (advance notice recommended, awkward steps at entrance) toilets for disabled shop 🔳

GREAT COXWELL
MAP 04 SU29

Great Coxwell Barn

➲ *(2m SW of Faringdon between A420 & B4019)*
☎ 01793 762209
e-mail: greatcoxwellbarn@nationaltrust.org.uk
web: www.nationaltrust.org.uk

William Morris said that the barn was 'as noble as a cathedral'. It is a 13th-century stone-built tithe barn, 152ft long and 44ft wide, with a beautifully crafted framework of timbers supporting the lofty stone roof. The barn was built for the Cistercians.

We endeavour to be as accurate as possible, but changes to times and other information can occur after the guide has gone to press.

Times: Open all reasonable times. For details please contact Estate Office. **Fee:** ✱ £1 **Facilities:** ❷ ♨

HENLEY-ON-THAMES   MAP 04 SU78

Greys Court

Rotherfield Greys RG9 4PG

➲ (A4130 take B481. Property signed 3m on left. From town centre follow signs to Peppard/Greys for 3m)

☎ 01491 628529

e-mail: greyscourt@nationaltrust.org.uk

web: www.nationaltrust.org.uk

A picturesque house, originating from the 14th century but with later additions. There is a beautiful courtyard and the surviving tower which dates from 1347. The outbuildings include a Tudor wheelhouse - one supplying water to the house, walled gardens and an ornamental vegetable garden.

Times: Open: House: Apr-29 Sep Wed-Fri 2-5. Garden & Tearoom: Apr-29 Sep, Tue-Sat 11-5. **Fee:** House & Garden £5.50 (ch £2.80). Garden only £4 (ch £2). **Facilities:** ❷ 🍴 ⅄ (ground floor & gardens partly accessible) shop ⊗ (ex assist dogs) ♨

River & Rowing Museum

Mill Meadows RG9 1BF

➲ (off A4130, signed to Mill Meadows)

☎ 01491 415600

e-mail: museum@rrm.co.uk

web: www.rrm.co.uk

The award-winning River and Rowing Museum is the only museum in the world with galleries dedicated to rowing and the 'Quest for Speed', from the Greek Trireme to modern Olympic rowing boats; the River Thames from source to sea with its rich history and varied wildlife. See the boats that won gold in Sydney and the riverside town of Henley featuring the Royal Regatta. The permanent *Wind in the Willows* exhibition recreates the drawings of E. H. Shepard in a walk through attraction using models, lighting and sound to bring the classic book to life.

Times: Open May-Aug 10-5.30. Sep-Apr 10-5. Closed 24-25 & 31 Dec & 1 Jan. **Fee:** £7 (concessions £6). Family ticket from £20. Party 10+. **Facilities:** ❷ 🍴 🍽 licensed ⅄ (lift access to upstairs galleries, ramps at entrance) toilets for disabled shop ⊗ (ex guide dogs) ◀

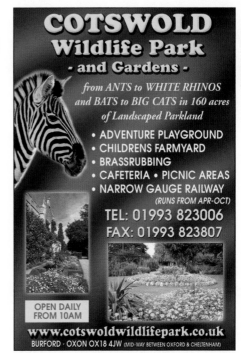

LONG WITTENHAM   MAP 04 SU59

Pendon Museum   `2 for 1`

OX14 4QD

➲ (follow brown signs from A4130 Didcot-Wallingford or A415 Abingdon-Wallingford road)

☎ 01865 407365

web: www.pendonmuseum.com

This charming exhibition shows highly detailed and historically accurate model railway and village scenes transporting the visitor back into 1930s country landscapes. Skilled modellers can often be seen at work on the exhibits.

Times: Open Sat & Sun 2-5.30 (last admission 4.45), BH wknds from 11 also Wed in school hols. Closed Dec. **Fee:** £5 (ch £3, under 6's free, pen £4). Family ticket (2ad+3ch) £16. **Facilities:** ❷ 🍴 📷 ⅄ (phone in advance, special seating with handrails, lift) toilets for disabled shop ⊗ (ex guide dogs) ◀

MAPLEDURHAM   MAP 04 SU67

Mapledurham House

RG4 7TR

➲ (off A4074, follow brown heritage signs from Reading)

☎ 0118 972 3350

e-mail: mtrust1997@aol.com

web: www.mapledurham.co.uk

The small community at Mapledurham includes the house, a watermill and a church. The fine Elizabethan mansion, surrounded by quiet

continued

parkland that runs down to the River Thames, was built by the Blount family in the 16th century. The estate has literary connections with the poet Alexander Pope, with Galsworthy's *Forsyte Saga* and Kenneth Graham's *Wind in the Willows*, and was a location for the film *The Eagle has Landed*.

Times: Open Etr-Sep, Sat, Sun & BHs 2-5.30 Picnic area 2-5.30. (Last admission 5). Group visits midweek by arrangement. **Fee:** ✱ Combined house, watermill & grounds £6.50 (ch £3). House & grounds £4 (ch £2). Watermill & grounds £3 (ch £1.50). **Facilities:** ℗ ⬛ & shop ⊗ (ex in grounds) ◀

Mapledurham Watermill

RG4 7TR

➲ *(off A4074, follow brown heritage signs from Reading)*

☎ 0118 972 3350

e-mail: mtrust1997@aol.com

web: www.mapledurham.co.uk

Close to Mapledurham House stands the last working corn and grist mill on the Thames, still using traditional wooden machinery and producing flour for local bakers and shops. The watermill's products can be purchased in the shop. When Mapledurham House is open the mill can be reached by river launch.

Times: ✱ Open Etr-Sep, Sat, Sun & BHs 2-5.30. Picnic area 2-5.30. (Last admission 5). Groups midweek by arrangement. **Fee:** ✱ Watermill & grounds £3 (ch £1.50) **Facilities:** ℗ ⬛ 🗐 & shop ◀

MINSTER LOVELL   MAP 04 SP31

Minster Lovell Hall & Dovecot   FREE

OX8 5RN

➲ *(adjacent to Minster Lovell Church, 3m W of Witney off A40)*

web: www.english-heritage.org.uk

Home of the ill-fated Lovell family, the ruins of the 15th-century house are steeped in history and legend. One of the main features of the estate is the medieval dovecote.

Times: Open any reasonable time. Dovecote-exterior only **Facilities:** ⏣

NORTH LEIGH   MAP 04 SP31

North Leigh Roman Villa   FREE

OX8 6QB

➲ *(2m N of North Leigh)*

web: www.english-heritage.org.uk

This is the remains of a large and well-built Roman courtyard villa. The most important feature is an almost complete mosaic tile floor, which is intricately patterned in reds and browns.

Times: Open, grounds all year. Viewing window for mosaic tile floor. Pedestrian access only from the main road - 600 yds. **Facilities:** ℗ ⏣

OXFORD   MAP 04 SP50

Ashmolean Museum of Art & Archaeology

Beaumont St OX1 2PH

➲ *(city centre, opposite The Randolph Hotel)*

☎ 01865 278000

web: www.ashmol.ox.ac.uk

The oldest museum in the country, opened in 1683, the Ashmolean contains Oxford University's priceless collections. Many important historical art pieces and artefacts are on display, including work from Ancient Greece through to the twentieth century.

Times: Open all year, Tue-Sat 10-5, Sun 12-5 BH Mons 10-5. Closed Etr & during St.Giles Fair in early Sep, Xmas & 1 Jan. **Fee:** Free. Guided tours by arrangement. **Facilities:** ℗ (100-200mtrs) (pay & display) ⬛ ⦿ licensed 🗐 & (entry ramp from Beaumont St. Tel. before visit) toilets for disabled shop ⊗ ◀

Harcourt Arboretum

Nuneham Courtenay OX44 9PX

➲ *(400yds S of Nuneham Courtenay on A4074)*

☎ 01865 343501

e-mail: piers.newth@obg.ox.ac.uk

web: www.botanic-garden.ox.ac.uk

The gardens consist of 75 acres of mixed woodland, meadow, pond, rhododendron walks and fine specimen trees.

Times: Open Apr-Nov, daily 10-5, Dec-Mar, Mon-Fri 10-4.30. Closed 22 Dec-4 Jan. **Fee:** £2 pay & display for car park or £5 for 1yr season ticket. **Facilities:** ℗ (charged) 🗐 & toilets for disabled ⊗ (ex guide dogs)

Museum of Oxford   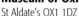 2 for 1

St Aldate's OX1 1DZ

☎ 01865 252761

e-mail: museum@oxford.gov.uk

web: www.oxford.gov.uk/museum

Permanent displays depict the archaeology and history of the city through the ages. There are temporary exhibitions, facilities for school parties and groups, and an audio tour.

Times: Open all year, Tue-Fri 10-5, Sat 12-5 & Sun 12-5. Closed 25-26 Dec. **Fee:** £2 (ch under 17 50p, concessions £1.50). Family ticket £4. **Facilities:** 🗐 & (virtual tour online) shop ⊗ (ex guide dogs) ◀

Museum of the History of Science   FREE

Old Ashmolean Building, Broad St OX1 3AZ

➲ *(next to Sheldonian Theatre in city centre, on Broad St)*

☎ 01865 277280

e-mail: museum@mhs.ox.ac.uk

web: www.mhs.ox.ac.uk

The first purpose built museum in Britain, containing the world's finest collection of early scientific instruments used in astronomy, navigation, surveying, physics and chemistry.

Times: Open Tue-Sat 12-4, Sun 2-5. Closed Xmas and Etr hols. **Facilities:** ℗ (300mtrs) (limited street parking, meters) 🗐 & (lift) shop ⊗ (ex guide dogs)

Oxford University Museum of Natural History

Parks Rd OX1 3PW

➲ *(opposite Keble College)*

☎ 01865 272950

e-mail: info@oum.ox.ac.uk

web: www.oum.ox.ac.uk

Built between 1855 and 1860, this museum of "the natural sciences" was intended to satisfy a growing interest in biology, botany, archaeology, zoology, entomology and so on. The museum reflects Oxford University's position as a 19th-century centre of learning, with displays of early dinosaur discoveries, Darwinian evolution and Elias Ashmole's collection of preserved animals. Although visitors to the Pitt-Rivers Museum must pass through the University Museum, the two should not be confused.

Times: Open daily 12-5. Times vary at Xmas & Etr. **Facilities:** ℗ (200mtrs) (meter parking) 🍴 ♿ (lift access to gallery) toilets for disabled shop ⊗

Pitt Rivers Museum

South Parks Rd OX1 3PP

➲ *(10 min walk from city centre, visitors entrance on Parks Rd through the Oxford Univiersity Museum of Natural History)*

☎ 01865 270927

e-mail: prm@prm.ox.ac.uk

web: www.prm.ox.ac.uk

The museum is one of the city's most popular attractions. It is part of the University of Oxford and was founded in 1884. The collections held at the museum are internationally acclaimed, and contain many objects from different cultures of the world and from various periods, all grouped by type, or purpose.

Times: Open all year. Mon-Sun 12-4.30. Closed Xmas & Etr, open BHs. **Facilities:** 🍴 ♿ (audio guide, wheelchair trail) toilets for disabled shop ⊗ (ex guide dogs)

St Edmund Hall FREE

College of Oxford University OX1 4AR

➲ *(Queen's Lane Oxford at end of High St)*

☎ 01865 279000

e-mail: bursary@seh.ox.ac.uk

web: www.seh.ox.ac.uk

This is the only surviving medieval academic hall and has a Norman crypt, 17th-century dining hall, chapel and quadrangle. Other buildings are of the 18th and 20th centuries.

Times: Open all year. Closed 24 Dec-4 Jan, 9-18 Apr & 28-31 Aug. **Facilities:** 🍴 ♿ toilets for disabled ⊗ (ex guide dogs)

University of Oxford Botanic Garden

Rose Ln OX1 4AZ

➲ *(E end of High St on banks of River Cherwell)*

☎ 01865 286690

e-mail: postmaster@obg.ox.ac.uk

web: www.botanic-garden.ox.ac.uk

Founded in 1621, this botanic garden is the oldest in the country. There is a collection of over 7000 species of plants from all over the world. Consisting of 3 sections: the Glasshouses contain plants that need protection from the British weather. The area outside the Walled Garden contains a water garden and rock garden as well as the spring border and autumn border. Within the Walled Garden plants are grouped by country of origin, botanic family or economic use.

Times: Open all year daily: Jan-Feb & Nov-Dec 9-4.30 (last admission 4.15). Mar-Apr, Sep-Oct 9-5 (last admission 4.15) May-Aug 9-6. **Fee:** £2.70 (ch free, disabled with 1 carer free, concessions £2). **Facilities:** ℗ (0.5m) (park and ride system) 🍴 ♿ toilets for disabled shop ⊗ (ex guide dogs) 🍴

Unlocked - Oxford Castle NEW

44-46 Oxford Castle OX1 1AY

➲ *(in city centre off New Rd)*

☎ 01865 260666

e-mail: info@oxfordcastleunlocked.co.uk

web: www.oxfordcastleunlocked.co.uk

For the first time in 1000 years, the secrets of Oxford Castle will be Unlocked, revealing episodes of violence, executions, great escapes, betrayal and even romance. Walk through these ancient buildings and experience the stories that connect the real people to these extraordinary events.

Times: Open daily 10-5.30 (last tour 4.30). Closed 25 Dec. **Fee:** ✱ £6.95 (ch £5.25, concessions £5.95) **Facilities:** ℗ 🍴 (lift & ramp) shop ⊗ (ex assist dogs) 🍴

ROUSHAM — MAP 04 SP42

Rousham House

OX25 4QX

➲ *(1m E of A4260. 0.5m S of B4030)*

☎ 01869 347110

web: www.rousham.org

This attractive mansion was built by Sir Robert Dormer in 1635. During the Civil War it was a Royalist garrison. The house contains over 150 portraits and other pictures, and also much fine contemporary furniture. The gardens are a masterpiece by William Kent, and are his only work to survive unspoiled.

Times: Open all year, garden only, daily 10-4.30. House, Jun-Aug, Sun & BH Mon 2-4.30 (last entry). Groups by arrangement on other days.
Fee: House £3, Garden £4. Groups by arrangement. No children under 15.
Facilities: ❷ ⊗ (ex guide dogs)

RYCOTE — MAP 04 SP60

Rycote Chapel

OX9 2PE

➲ *(off B4013)*

web: www.english-heritage.org.uk

This small private chapel was founded in 1449 by Richard Quatremayne. It has its original font, and a particularly fine 17th-century interior. The chapel has been visited by both Elizabeth I and Charles I.

Times: Open Apr-Sep, Fri-Sun, 2-6. May close at short notice for services or functions. **Fee:** £3.50 (ch £1.50, concessions £2.50) Prices and opening times are subject to change in Spring 2007. Please check web site or call 0870 333 1181 for the most up to date prices and opening times when planning your visit. **Facilities:** ❷ ⓵ (if assisted) shop ⊗ ♯♯

STONOR — MAP 04 SU78

Stonor House & Park

RG9 6HF

☎ 01491 638587

e-mail: jweaver@stonor.com

web: www.stonor.com

The house dates back to 1190 but features a Tudor façade. It has a medieval Catholic chapel which is still in use today, and shows some of the earliest domestic architecture in Oxfordshire. Its treasures include rare furniture, paintings, sculptures and tapestries from Britain, Europe and America. The house is set in beautiful gardens commanding views of the surrounding deer park.

Times: Open Apr-Sep, Sun 2-5.30; Jul & Aug, also Wed 2-5.30; BH Mons. Parties by appointment Tue-Thu, Apr-Sep. **Fee:** ✱ £6 (ch 14 accompanied free). Gardens only £3.50. Private guided tours £7 each. **Facilities:** ❷ 💺 ⓵ shop

UFFINGTON — MAP 04 SU38

Uffington Castle, White Horse & Dragon Hill

➲ *(S of B4507)*

☎ 01793 762209

The 'castle' is an Iron Age fort on the ancient Ridgeway Path. It covers about eight acres and has only one gateway. On the hill below the fort is the White Horse, a 375ft prehistoric figure carved in the chalk hillside and thought to be about 3000 years old.

Times: Open at any reasonable time. **Facilities:** ❷ (charged) ⓵ ⓵ (disabled car park) 🐾

WATERPERRY — MAP 04 SP60

Waterperry Gardens

OX33 1JZ

➲ *(2.5m from A40, turn off at Wheatley)*

☎ 01844 339226 & 339254

e-mail: office@waterperrygardens.co.uk

web: www.waterperrygardens.co.uk

The manor of Waterperry is mentioned in the Domesday Book. The present house (not open) was rebuilt by Sir John Curson in 1713. The peaceful gardens and nurseries which surround the house were the home of a celebrated horticultural school between 1932 and 1971, and have fine herbaceous borders, a rock garden, riverside walk, shrub borders, lawns and trees. Please phone for details of special events.

Times: Open all year, Gardens, Apr-Oct 9-5.30, Nov-Mar 9-5 daily. Closed Xmas, New Year & during "Art in Action" 13-16 Jul. **Fee:** £4.50 (ch 10-16 £3, ch under 10 free, pen £3.75). Nov-Mar £3 Party 20+ £3.50.
Facilities: ❷ 💺 🍴 licensed ⓵ ⓵ (grounds mostly accessible) toilets for disabled shop garden centre ⊗ (ex guide dogs) 📧

WITNEY — MAP 04 SP31

Cogges Manor Farm Museum

Church Ln, Cogges OX28 3LA

➲ *(0.5m SE off A4022)*

☎ 01993 772602

web: www.cogges.org

The museum includes the Manor, dairy and walled garden, and has breeds of animals typical of the Victorian period. The first floor of the manor contains period rooms. Special events take place through the season.

Times: Open Apr-Oct, Tue-Fri 10.30-5.30, Sat, Sun & BH Mon, 12-5.30. Early closing Oct. Closed Good Fri. **Fee:** ✱ £5.40 (ch £2.30, concessions £3.85). Family ticket £13.90 (2ad+2ch). **Facilities:** ❷ 💺 (wheelchair available, audio tour) shop 📧

WOODSTOCK

MAP 04 SP41

Blenheim Palace

2 for 1

OX20 1PX

➲ *(M40 junct 9, follow signs to Blenheim, on A44 8m N of Oxford)*

☎ 08700 602080

e-mail: admin@blenheimpalace.com

web: www.blenheimpalace.com

Home of the 11th Duke of Marlborough and birthplace of Sir Winston Churchill, Blenheim Palace is an English Baroque masterpiece. Fine furniture, sculpture, paintings and tapestries are set in magnificent gilded staterooms that overlook sweeping lawns and formal gardens. 'Capability' Brown landscaped the 2100-acre park, which is open to visitors for pleasant walks and beautiful views. Please telephone for details of events running throughout the year.

Times: Open Palace & Gardens mid Feb-mid Dec (ex Mon & Tue in Nov & Dec) daily 10.30-5.30 (last admission 4.45). Park daily all year 9-4.45. Closed 25 Dec. **Fee:** Palace, Park & Gardens £12-£14 (ch £6.50-£8.50, concessions £9.50-£11.50). Park & Gardens £7-£9 (ch £2.50-£4.50, concessions £5-£7) **Facilities:** ℗ ☕ 🍴 licensed ⅃ (lift, ramps, disabled parking, buggies, wheelchairs) toilets for disabled shop ⊗ assist dogs ⊠

Oxfordshire Museum

FREE

Fletcher's House, Park St OX20 1SN

➲ *(A44 Evesham-Oxford, follow signs for Blenheim Palace. Museum opposite church)*

☎ 01993 811456

e-mail: oxon.museum@oxfordshire.go.uk

web: www.oxfordshire.gov.uk/the_oxfordshire_museum

Situated in the heart of the historic town of Woodstock, the award-winning redevelopment of Fletcher's House provides a home for the new county museum. Set in attractive gardens, the new museum celebrates Oxfordshire in all its diversity and features collections of local history, art, archaeology, landscape and wildlife as well as a gallery exploring the Country's innovative industries from nuclear power to nanotechnology. Interactive exhibits offer new learning experiences for visitors of all ages. The museum's purpose built Garden Gallery houses a variety of touring exhibitions of regional and national interest.

Times: Open all year, Tue-Sat 10-5, Sun 2-5. Closed Good Fri, 25-26 Dec & 1 Jan. Galleries closed on Mon, but open BH Mons, 2-5.

Facilities: ℗ (outside entrance) (free parking) ☕ 🍴 licensed ⅃ ⅃ (chair lifts to all galleries) toilets for disabled ⊗ (ex guide dogs)

The Uffington White Horse

Rutland

Normanton Church,
Rutland Water

Rutland is a mere twenty miles across and a significant part of this is taken up with Rutland Water, 5,000 acres of man-made reservoir, a haven for wildlife and aquatic sports. The reservoir lends itself to several interests and pursuits, including 25 miles of cycle track, sailing, trout fishing, a bird-watching hide and the opportunity to see Osprey fish eagles. Rutland county has two market towns, Oakham and Uppingham, undulating green hills, pretty villages and an air of peace and tranquility.

LYDDINGTON
MAP 04 SP89

Lyddington Bede House
Blue Coat Ln LE15 9LZ
☎ 01572 822438
web: www.english-heritage.org.uk

Once a prominent medieval palace later converted into an almshouse for the poor. Its history is bought to life in an evocative audio tour.

Times: Open Apr-Oct, Thu-Mon 10-5. **Fee:** £3.30 (ch £1.70, concessions £2.50, Family £8.30). Prices and opening times are subject to change in Spring 2007. Please check web site or call 0870 333 1181 for the most up to date prices and opening times when planning your visit.
Facilities: & ⊗ ⛿

OAKHAM
MAP 04 SK80

Oakham Castle
FREE
Catmos St LE15 6HW
➲ (off Market Place)
☎ 01572 758440
e-mail: museum@rutland.gov.uk
web: www.rutland.gov.uk/castle

An exceptionally fine Norman Great Hall of a 12th-century fortified manor house. Earthworks, walls and remains of an earlier motte can be seen along with medieval sculptures and unique presentation horseshoes forfeited by peers of the realm and royalty to the Lord of the Manor. Licensed for Civil Marriages. Please enquire for details of the Oakham Festival.

Times: Open all year, Mon-Sat 10.30-5 (closed 1-1.30), Sun 2-4. Closed Good Fri & Xmas. **Facilities:** ℗ (400yds) (disabled parking only by notification) ▨ & toilets for disabled shop ⊗ (ex guide dogs)

Rutland County Museum
FREE
Catmos St LE15 6HW
➲ (on A6003, S of town centre)
☎ 01572 758440
e-mail: museum@rutland.gov.uk
web: www.rutland.gov.uk/museum

Rutland County Museum is the perfect introduction to England's smallest county. The 'Welcome to Rutland' gallery is a guide to its history. The museum includes a shop and study area. On show in the 18th-century Riding School are displays of archaeology, history and an extensive rural life collection.

Times: Open all year, Mon-Sat 10.30-5, Sun 2-4. Closed Good Fri, Xmas & 1 Jan. **Facilities:** ℗ (charged) ▨ & (induction loop in meeting room) toilets for disabled shop ⊗ (ex guide dogs)

An asterisk ✳ indicates that opening times or prices are for 2006. Please contact the attraction for more up-to-date information.

Cyclists on the path by Rutland Water

Shropshire

Colemere Country Park

England's least populated county, it has rural views that are among the most beautiful in Britain, in sharp contrast to the new town of Telford. Developed in the 1960s to accommodate the then-new computer industries, and named after Thomas Telford, an 18th-19th century civil engineer. In Ironbridge, Shropshire can lay claim to the birthplace of the Industrial Revolution. By the end of the 18th century the iron and ceramic industries were the most technically advanced in the world. This pretty little river gorge is now a World Heritage site and is home to a series of quite remarkable museums.

ACTON BURNELL · MAP 07 SJ50

Acton Burnell Castle · `FREE`

SY5 7PE

⮑ *(in Acton Burnell on unclass road 8m S of Shrewsbury)*

web: www.english-heritage.org.uk

The warm red sandstone shell of a fortified thirteenth-century manor house. The site of the first parliament at which the commons were fully represented.

Times: Open at all reasonable times. **Facilities:** ♿ ⚏

ATCHAM · MAP 07 SJ50

Attingham Park

SY4 4TP

⮑ *(4m SE of Shrewsbury on B4380)*

☎ 01743 708123

e-mail: attingham.park@nationaltrust.org.uk

Attingham Park is centred on one of Britain's finest regency mansions, set in a landscaped deer park designed by Humphry Repton. Also on the estate visitors can visit Home Farm, one of Britain's only organic open farms, and sample their homemade ice cream. Please contact the park for details of the events programme.

Times: House open wknds only 3-31 Mar. House open Fri-Tues 26 Mar-30 Oct 1-5. Costume guided tours available from 12. Open BH Mons 11-5. Deer park and Grounds open daily except 25 Dec. Mar-Oct 10-8 and Nov-Feb 10-5. **Fee:** Please call 01743 708 162 for details. National Trust members free. **Facilities:** ⓟ ⬛ 🪑 ♿ (2 electric self drive buggies, 1 staff driven 8-seater) toilets for disabled shop (ex guide & hearing dogs) 🅿 ⬛

BENTHALL · MAP 07 SJ60

Benthall Hall

TF12 5RX

⮑ *(on B4375)*

☎ 01952 882159

e-mail: benthall@nationaltrust.org.uk

The main part of the house was built around 1585. A wing at the back, which has been altered at various times, dates originally from about 1520. It is an attractive sandstone building with mullioned windows, fine oak panelling and a splendid carved staircase.

Times: Open Apr-Sep, Tue, Wed, BH Mon & Sun before BH Mon; Jul-Sep open every Sun. House 2-5.30, Garden 1.30-5.30. **Fee:** ✱ House and garden £4.20 (ch £2.10). Garden only £2.75 (ch £1.35) **Facilities:** ⓟ 🪑 ♿ (Braille, large print guides) toilets for disabled ⊗ (ex guide dogs) 🅿

BOSCOBEL · MAP 07 SJ80

Boscobel House and The Royal Oak

Brewood ST19 9AR

⮑ *(on unclass road between A41 and A5)*

☎ 01902 850244

web: www.english-heritage.org.uk

This fully restored and refurbished lodge and famous Royal Oak tree is where King Charles II sought refuge from Cromwell's troops in 1651. The house was built around 1632.

Times: Open Apr-May & Sep-Oct, Thu-Mon, 10-5; Jun-Aug, daily, 10-6. Last entry one hour before closing. **Fee:** £4.80 (ch £2.40, concessions £3.60) Family £12. Grounds only; £1.60 (ch 80p, concessions £1.20). Prices and opening times are subject to change in Spring 2007. Please check web site or call 0870 333 1181 for the most up to date prices and opening times when planning your visit. **Facilities:** ⓟ ⬛ shop ⊗ ⚏

Whiteladies Priory · `FREE`

⮑ *(1m SW of Boscobel House, off an unclass road between A41 and A5)*

web: www.english-heritage.org.uk

Only the ruins are left of this Augustinian nunnery, which dates from 1158 and was destroyed in the Civil War. After the Battle of Worcester Charles II hid here and in the nearby woods before going on to Boscobel House.

Times: Open Apr-Oct, daily 10-5. Closed Nov-Mar. **Facilities:** ⚏

BUILDWAS · MAP 07 SJ60

Buildwas Abbey

Iron Bridge TF8 7BW

⮑ *(on S bank of River Severn on B4378)*

☎ 01952 433274

web: www.english-heritage.org.uk

Set beside the River Severn, against a backdrop of wooded grounds, are the extensive remains of this Cistercian abbey founded in 1135.

Times: Open Apr-May & Sep, Thu-Mon, 10-5; Jun-Aug, daily, 10-6. **Fee:** £2.70 (ch £1.40, concessions £2). Prices and opening times are subject to change in Spring 2007. Please check web site or call 0870 333 1181 for the most up to date prices and opening times when planning your visit. **Facilities:** ⓟ ♿ shop ⊗ ⚏

BURFORD · MAP 03 SO56

Burford House Gardens ·

WR15 8HQ

⮑ *(off A456, 1m W of Tenbury Wells, 8m from Ludlow)*

☎ 01584 810777

e-mail: info@burford.co.uk

web: www.burford.co.uk

Burford House and Garden Centre set within 15 acres, incorporates a Georgian mansion, which houses a shop and riverside gardens housing the National Clematis Collection.

Times: Open all year 9-6 or dusk if earlier. **Fee:** ✱ Gardens: £3.95 (ch £1). Party 20+ £3 each. All other attractions free. **Facilities:** ⓟ ⬛ 🍴 licensed 🪑 ♿ (ramp into gardens, sloping paths, wheelchairs available) toilets for disabled shop garden centre ⊗ (ex guide dogs) 🅿

If an attraction name appears in italics, details have not been confirmed for 2007

COSFORD
MAP 07 SJ70

Royal Air Force Museum

TF11 8UP

⮑ *(on A41, 1m S of M54 junct 3)*

☎ 01902 376200

e-mail: cosford@rafmuseum.org

web: www.rafmuseum.org

This is one of the largest aviation collections in the UK. Exhibits include the Victor and Vulcan bombers, the Hastings, York and British Airways airliners, the Belfast freighter and the last airworthy Britannia. The research and development collection includes the notable TSR2, Fairey Delta, Bristol 188 and many more important aircraft.

Times: Open all year daily, 10-6 (last admission 4). Closed 24-26 Dec & 1 Jan **Fee:** ✱ Charges made for special events only.
Facilities: ❷ ❀ licensed 🍴 ❤ (free loan of 3 manual w/chairs and 3 motor scooters) toilets for disabled shop ⊗ (ex guide dogs)

CRAVEN ARMS
MAP 07 SO48

The Shropshire Hills Discovery Centre
`2 for 1`

School Rd SY7 9RS

⮑ *(on A49, on S edge of Craven Arms)*

☎ 01588 676000

e-mail: zoe.griffin@shropshire-cc.gov.uk

web: www.shropshirehillsdiscoverycentre.co.uk

This attraction explores the history, nature and geography of the Shropshire Hills, through a series of interactive displays and simulations. These include Landscape of Contrasts, Ancient Landscape, a simulated Balloon Flight, and Land of Inspiration. The Centre has 23 acres of meadow lands sloping down to the River Onny for all visitors to explore. There is a network of cycle routes and walks and during the summer a shuttle bus service operates from the centre, at weekends, which allows visitors to explore the local landscape, hills, villages and market towns. The Centre also houses the Secret Hills Gallery which features changing displays of craft and artworks that celebrate Shropshire's creative industry. Try GEOcaching, a kind of treasure-hunt that uses hand-held GPS.

Times: Open all year, daily from 10. (Last admission 3.30 Nov-Mar, 4.30 Apr-Oct). **Fee:** £4.50 (ch £3 & ch under 5 free, pen £4). Family ticket £13.50. Groups 20+ £3.75 each, ch £2.50 each. **Facilities:** ❷ ❣
🍴 licensed 🍴 ❤ (wheelchair available) toilets for disabled shop
⊗ (ex guide dogs) 🏴

HAUGHMOND ABBEY
MAP 07 SJ51

Haughmond Abbey

Upton Magna SY4 4RW

⮑ *(off B5062)*

☎ 01743 709661

web: www.english-heritage.org.uk

Absorb these extensive 12th-century Augustinian abbey ruins, and visit the small museum.

Times: Open Apr-May & Sep, Thu-Mon, 10-5; Jun-Aug, daily, 10-6.
Fee: £2.70 (ch £1.40, concessions £2). Prices and opening times are subject to change in Spring 2007. Please check web site or call 0870 333 1181 for the most up to date prices and opening times when planning your visit.
Facilities: ❷ ❤ (limited access for wheelchair users) shop ▦

HODNET
MAP 07 SJ62

Hodnet Hall Gardens

TF9 3NN

⮑ *(Hodnet is on the A442, Telford-Whitchurch road and A53 Shrewsbury-Market Drayton road).*

☎ 01630 685786

e-mail: marlene@heber-percy.freeserve.co.uk

web: www.hodnethallgardens.co.uk

Over sixty acres of brilliantly coloured flowers, magnificent forest trees, sweeping lawns, and a chain of ornamental pools which run along the cultivated garden valley to provide a habitat for waterfowl and other wildlife. Big game trophies adorn the 17th-century tearooms, and plants are usually for sale in the kitchen gardens. The house, rebuilt in Victorian-Elizabethan style, is not open.

Times: Open Apr-Sep, Tue-Sun & BH Mon 12-5. Oct, Sun only 12-dusk
Facilities: ❷ 🍴 licensed 🍴 ❤ (2 wheelchairs available) toilets for disabled shop garden centre

IRONBRIDGE
MAP 07 SJ60

Ironbridge Gorge Museums

Coach Rd TF8 7DQ

⮑ *(M54 junct 4, signed)*

☎ 01952 884391 & 0800 590258

e-mail: tic@ironbridge.org.uk

web: www.ironbridge.org.uk

Ironbridge is the site of the world's first iron bridge. It was cast and built here in 1779, to span a narrow gorge over the River Severn. Now Ironbridge is the site of a remarkable series of museums relating the story of the bridge, recreating life in Victorian times and featuring ceramics and social history displays.

Times: ✱ Open all year, 10-5. Some small sites closed Nov-Mar. Telephone for exact winter details. **Facilities:** ❷ ❣ 🍴 licensed ❤ (wheelchairs, potters wheel, Braille guide, hearing loop) toilets for disabled shop
⊗ (ex Blists Hill & guide dogs) 🏴

LILLESHALL · MAP 07 SJ71

Lilleshall Abbey · FREE

TF10 9HW

➲ *(off A518 on unclass road)*

☎ 0121 625 6820

web: www.english-heritage.org.uk

In the beautiful grounds of Lilleshall Hall, ruined Lilleshall Abbey was founded shortly before the middle of the 12th century and from the high west front visitors can look down the entire 228ft length of the abbey church.

Times: Open Apr-Sep, daily 10-5. **Facilities:** ⌗

LUDLOW · MAP 07 SO57

Ludlow Castle

Castle Square SY8 1AY

➲ *(A49 to town centre)*

☎ 01584 873355

e-mail: hduce@ludlowcastle.plus.com

web: www.ludlowcastle.com

Ludlow Castle dates from about 1086. In 1473, Edward IV sent the Prince of Wales and his brother - later to become the Princes in the Tower - to live here, and Ludlow Castle became a seat of government. John Milton's *Comus* was first performed at Ludlow Castle in 1634; now contemporary performances of Shakespeare's plays, together with concerts, are put on in the castle grounds during the Ludlow Festival (end June-early July). Please telephone for details of events running throughout the year.

Times: Open all year, Jan Sat-Sun 10-4; Feb-Mar & Oct-Dec daily 10-4; Apr-Jul & Sep daily 10-5; Aug daily 10-7 (last admission 30 minutes before closing). Closed 25 Dec. **Fee:** £4 (ch under 6 free, ch £2, pen £3.50). Family ticket £11. **Facilities:** ℗ (100yds) 🍽 ⑩ licensed ⏚ & toilets for disabled shop ▪

MORETON CORBET · MAP 07 SJ52

Moreton Corbet Castle · FREE

➲ *(off B5063, in Moreton Corbet)*

web: www.english-heritage.org.uk

Inherited by the Corbets in 1235, who are thought to have remodelled the great keep, this castle may already have been standing for over 100 years. It was remodelled in the 16th century and then partially demolished to make way for a great Elizabethan mansion House. Although damaged in the civil war, the castle and mansion stand today as one of the most picturesque ruins of the Shropshire Marches.

Times: Open at any reasonable time **Facilities:** ℗ & ⌗

MUCH WENLOCK · MAP 07 SO69

Wenlock Priory

TA3 6HS

☎ 01952 727466

web: www.english-heritage.org.uk

Experience the ruins of this large Cluniac priory and the atmospheric remains of the 13th-century church and Norman chapter house. The

continued

audio tour offers a fascinating insight into its history. Impressive topiary figures guard the priory ruins.

Times: Open all year, Mar-Apr & Sep-Oct, Thu-Mon, 10-5; May-Jun, daily, 10-5; Jul-Aug, daily, 10-6; Nov-Feb, Thu-Sun, 10-4. Closed 24-26 Dec & 1 Jan. **Fee:** £3.30 (ch £1.70, concessions £2.50). Prices and opening times are subject to change in Spring 2007. Please check web site or call 0870 333 1181 for the most up to date prices and opening times when planning your visit. **Facilities:** ℗ ⌗

OSWESTRY · MAP 07 SJ22

Old Oswestry Hill Fort · FREE

➲ *(1m N of Oswestry, off an unclass road off A483)*

web: www.english-heritage.org.uk

An impressive Iron Age hill-fort of 68 acres, defended by a series of five ramparts, with an elaborate western entrance and unusual earthwork cisterns.

Times: Open at any reasonable time. **Facilities:** ⌗

QUATT · MAP 07 SO78

Dudmaston

WV15 6QN

➲ *(4m SE of Bridgnorth on A442)*

☎ 01746 780866

e-mail: dudmaston@nationaltrust.org.uk

The 17th-century flower paintings which belonged to Francis Darby of Coalbrookdale are exhibited in this house of the same period, with modern works, botanical art and fine furniture. The house stands in an extensive parkland garden and there are dingle and lakeside walks.

Times: Open Apr-Sep, Tue, Wed & Sun & BH Mons, 2-5.30. Garden Mon-Wed noon-6. Closed Good Fri. **Fee:** ✱ House & Garden £5. Garden only £4. Family ticket £12.50. **Facilities:** ℗ 🍽 ⏚ & (Braille guides, taped tours) toilets for disabled shop ⊗ (ex in grounds, & guide dogs) ▪ ▪

SHREWSBURY · MAP 07 SJ41

Shrewsbury Castle and Shropshire Regimental Museum

The Castle, Castle St SY1 2AT

➲ *(located in town centre, adjacent to railway station)*

☎ 01743 358516

e-mail: shropsrm@zoom.co.uk

web: www.shrewsburymuseums.com

The museum of The King's Shropshire Light Infantry and The Shropshire Yeomanry is housed in the main surviving building of Shrewsbury Castle which once dominated the town. The grounds contain the medieval 'motte' and the romantic 'Laura's Tower'. Please telephone or visit website for details of events running throughout the year.

Times: Open 27 May-10 Sep: Mon-Sat, 10-5: Sun 10-4. 11 Sep-22 Dec: Tue-Sat, 10-4 **Fee:** ✱ £2.50 (£1.25 concessions). All local residents, ch under 18 or in full time education free. **Facilities:** ℗ (3 mins NCP) (metered on street parking) ⏚ & (please ask staff for assistance) toilets for disabled shop ⊗ (ex guide dogs)

England

STOKESAY   MAP 07 SO48

Stokesay Castle

SY7 9AH

➲ *(1m S of Craven Arms off A49)*

☎ 01588 672544

web: www.english-heritage.org.uk

Most perfectly preserved 13th-century fortified manor house. See its superb timber-framed Jacobean gatehouse and stroll through the impressive great hall. Delightful cottage gardens.

Times: Open all year, Mar-Apr & Sep-Oct, Thu-Mon, 10-5; May-Aug, daily, 10-6; Nov-Feb, Fri-Mon, 10-4. Closed 24-26 Dec & 1 Jan. **Fee:** £4.80 (ch £2.40, concessions £3.60) Family £12. Prices and opening times are subject to change in Spring 2007. Please check web site or call 0870 333 1181 for the most up to date prices and opening times when planning your visit. **Facilities:** ❷ ♿ (tape tour for visually handicapped, ramp for wheelchairs) toilets for disabled ⊗ ♨

TELFORD   MAP 07 SJ60

Hoo Farm Animal Kingdom   **2 for 1**

Preston-on-the-Weald Moors TF6 6DJ

➲ *(M54 junct 6, follow brown tourist signs)*

☎ 01952 677917

e-mail: info@hoofarm.com

web: www.hoofarm.com

Hoo Farm is a real children's paradise where there is always something happening. A clean, friendly farm that appeals to all ages and offers close contact with a wide variety of animals from fluffy yellow chicks and baby lambs to foxes, llamas, deer and ostriches. A daily programme of events encourages audience participation in the form of bottle feeding lambs, pig feeding and collecting the freshly laid eggs. New for this year is ferret racing! The Craft Area offers the chance to try your hand at candle dipping, glass or pottery painting or even throwing a pot on the potters wheel. There are Junior Quad Bikes and a Rifle Range, Pony Rides, powered mini tractors as well as indoor and outdoor play areas and a new games room. Please telephone for details of special events running throughout the year.

Times: Open: 19 Mar-9 Sep, Tue-Sun 10-6. 10 Sep-26 Nov, Tue-Sun, 10-5. 26 Nov-24 Dec, daily 10-5 closes at 1 on 24 Dec. Closed 25 Dec to mid March. **Fee:** £5.25 (ch £4.75 & pen £4.50). Family ticket (2ad+3ch) £21. **Facilities:** ❷ ♥ ▤ ♿ toilets for disabled shop ⊗ (ex guide dogs) ➡

WELLINGTON   MAP 07 SJ61

Sunnycroft NEW

200 Holyhead Rd TF1 2DR

➲ *(3m W of Telford in Wellington off B5061)*

☎ 01952 242884

A Victorian gentleman's villa, typical of houses built for prosperous business and professional people on the fringe of towns and cities. The house is a time capsule of early 20th century life both above and below stairs, when it was home to the Lander family. Displays of embroidery by Joan Lander can be seen within the house.

Times: House open 23 Mar-29 Oct, Fri, Sun & Mon, 1-5 (last admission 4). Also open Good Fri & BH Mons. Entry by guided tour only. **Fee:** ✱ House & Garden £5 (ch £2.50). Family £12.50. Garden £2.50 (ch £1.25). Family £6.30 **Facilities:** ❷ ⊗ (ex on leads in grounds) 🐾

WESTON-UNDER-REDCASTLE MAP 07 SJ52

Hawkstone Historic Park & Follies

SY4 5UY

➲ *(3m from Hodnet off A53, follow brown heritage signs)*

☎ 01939 200611

e-mail: info@hawkstone.co.uk

web: www.hawkstone.co.uk

Created in the 18th century by the Hill family, Hawkstone was once one of the greatest historic parklands in history. After almost one hundred years of neglect it has now been restored and designated a Grade 1 historic park. Visitors can once again experience the magical world of intricate pathways, arches and bridges, towering cliffs and follies, and an awesome grotto. The Grand Valley and woodlands have centuries-old oaks, wild rhododendrons and lofty monkey puzzles. The park covers nearly 100 acres of hilly terrain and visitors are advised to wear sensible shoes and clothing and to bring a torch. Allow 3-4 hours for the tour, which is well signposted and a route map is provided in the admission price. Attractions include 'Hear King Arthur' and meeting the Duke of Wellington in the White Tower to discuss the Battle of Waterloo.

Times: ✱ Open from 10, Jan-Mar, Sat & Sun; Apr-May, & Sep-Oct, Wed-Sun; Jun-Aug, daily. Closed Nov & Dec. **Facilities:** ❷ ♥ ▯ licensed ♿ (no access to follies due to terrain access Valley only) toilets for disabled shop ➡

WROXETER   MAP 07 SJ50

Wroxeter Roman City

SY5 6PH

➲ *(5m E of Shrewsbury, 1m S of A5)*

☎ 01743 761330

web: www.english-heritage.org.uk

Discover what urban life was like 2,000 years ago in the forth largest city in Roman Britain. See the remains of the impressive 2nd-century municipal baths and view the excavated treasures in the museum.

Times: Open all year, Mar-May & Sep-Oct, daily, 10-5; Jun-Aug, daily, 10-6; Nov-Feb, Wed-Sun, 10-4. Closed 24-26 Dec & 1 Jan. **Fee:** £4 (ch £2, concessions £3). Family £10. Prices and opening times are subject to change in Spring 2007. Please check web site or call 0870 333 1181 for the most up to date prices and opening times when planning your visit. **Facilities:** ❷ ♿ shop ♨

The National Trust: For over a hundred years, the NT has been acquiring and protecting threatened coastline, countryside and buildings. To find out more about this organisation, its sites, and policies, visit their website: **www.nationaltrust.org.uk**

Somerset

Exmoor National Park,
Exmoor

Somerset has what must be England's prettiest name. Coming from the Saxon, it literally means 'Land of the Summer People'. It is rich in history and legend, as well as having some wonderful countryside including Exmoor National Park. Glastonbury Tor is one of the county's most notable sites and the area is deep in legend involving Joseph of Arimathea and King Arthur. Bath, with its delightful buildings of golden Bath stone, retains the air of elegance associated with its 18th century past.

AXBRIDGE

MAP 03 ST45

King John's Hunting Lodge

The Square BS26 2AP

➲ (on corner of Axbridge High St, in the Square)

☎ 01934 732012

web: www.nationaltrust.org.uk

Nothing to do with King John or with hunting, this jettied and timber-framed house was built around 1500. It gives a good indication of the wealth of the merchants of that time and is now a museum of local history, with old photographs, paintings and items such as the town stocks and constables' staves.

Times: ✱ Open Apr-Sep, daily 1-4. **Fee:** ✱ Donations welcome
Facilities: & shop ⊗ ✖

BARRINGTON

MAP 03 ST31

Barrington Court Garden

TA19 0NQ

➲ (5m NE of Ilminster on B3168)

☎ 01460 241938 & 242614

e-mail: barringtoncourt@nationaltrust.org.uk

web: www.nationaltrust.org.uk

The house is a Tudor Manor, the interior of which is now let out to Stuart Interiors as showrooms with antique furniture for sale. The gardens were created in the 1920s, with the help (through the post) of Gertrude Jekyll. They are laid out in 'rooms' and there is a large walled kitchen garden supplying fresh fruit and vegetables to the restaurant.

Times: Open Mar, Thu-Tue 11-4.30; Apr-Sep daily (ex Wed) 11-5; Oct Thu-Tue 11-4.30. **Fee:** ✱ £7 (ch £3). Family £17. Groups £6 **Facilities:** ℗ 🍴 licensed & (Batricars, Braille and large print guides, w/chairs) toilets for disabled shop garden centre ⊗ (except guide dogs) ✖

BATH

MAP 03 ST76

American Museum

Claverton Manor BA2 7BD

➲ (2.5m SE)

☎ 01225 460503

e-mail: info@americanmuseum.org

web: www.americanmuseum.org

Claverton Manor is just two miles south east of Bath, in a beautiful setting above the River Avon. The house was built in 1820 by Sir Jeffrey Wyatville, and is now a museum of American decorative arts. The gardens are well worth seeing, and include an American arboretum and a replica of George Washington's garden at Mount Vernon. The Folk Art Gallery and the New Gallery are among the many exhibits in the grounds along with seasonal exhibitions.

Times: Open mid Mar-Oct, Tue-Sun 2-5. Gardens 12-6. Open Mon in Aug & BHs. **Facilities:** ℗ 🍴 & toilets for disabled shop 🍴

Bath Abbey

Abbey Churchyard BA1 1LT

➲ (centre of Bath, next to Pump Rooms & The Roman Baths. Orange grove drop off and collection point for coaches-east end)

☎ 01225 422462 & 446300

e-mail: office@bathabbey.org

web: www.bathabbey.org

The 15th-century abbey church was built on the site of the Saxon abbey where King Edgar was crowned in 973. The church is Perpendicular style with Norman arches and superb fan-vaulting. The famous West Front carvings represent the founder-bishop's dream of angels ascending and descending from heaven.

Times: Open Apr-Oct, Mon-Sat, 9-6. Nov-Mar, Mon-Sat, 9-4.30. Closed 25 Dec and Good Fri, except for services. **Fee:** Visitors invited to donate £2.50 each. **Facilities:** ℗ (3-4 mins) (limited street parking) 🍴 & (level access, induction loop, large print leaflet) toilets for disabled shop ⊗ (ex guide & hearing dogs)

Bath Aqua Theatre of Glass NEW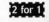

105-107 Walcot St BA1 5BW

☎ 01225 428146

e-mail: sales@bathaquaglass.com

web: www.bathaquaglass.com

View old stained glass windows renovated from Bath Abbey Chambers. In the heart of the citys artisan quarter, this is an ideal centre to learn about the history of glass and watch the ancient craft of free glass blowing.

Times: Open all year, daily, 9.30-5. Closed Sun, Oct-Etr. **Fee:** ✱ £3.50 (ch & concessions £2). Family of 4 £8. **Facilities:** & toilets for disabled shop ⊗ 🍴

Bath Postal Museum

27 Northgate St BA1 1AJ

➲ (on entering city fork left at mini rdbt. After all traffic lights into Walcot St. Podium car park facing)

☎ 01225 460333

e-mail: info@bathpostalmuseum.org

web: www.bathpostalmuseum.org

Discover how 18th-century Bath influenced and developed the Postal System, including the story of the Penny Post. The first letter sent with a stamp was sent from Bath. Visitors can explore the history of written communication from Egyptian clay tablets, thousands of years ago, to the first Airmail flight from Bath to London in 1912. See the Victorian Post Office and watch continuous video films including the in-house production entitled 'History of Writing'. Visit the children's activity room and shop.

Times: Open all year, Mon-Sat 11-4.30. (Last admission Mar-Oct 4.30, Oct-Mar 4). Closed Sun, 25-26 Dec & 1 Jan. **Fee:** £2.90 (ch under 5 free, ch £1.50, students £1.90 & pen £2.40). Family and Party 10+ tickets available. **Facilities:** ℗ (50yds) (no on street parking) & (films and computer games for hearing impaired) shop ⊗ (ex guide dogs) 🍴

England

The Building of Bath Museum

Countess of Huntingdons Chapel, The Vineyards, The Paragon BA1 5NA

➲ *(Take A4, 2nd exit at mini rdbt. Along road on right)*

☎ 01225 333895

e-mail: enquiries@bathmuseum.co.uk

web: www.bath-preservation-trust.org.uk

This new museum relates the fascinating story of how Georgian Bath was created. 17th-century Bath was a medieval market town but in the space of 100 years it was transformed into one of the most beautiful and glamorous cities in Europe. The exhibition depicts elegant society life in "Beau" Nash's spa resort and explains how the houses were constructed. After a visit, the street scene outside seems like an extension of the exhibition. Ring for details of special events such as concerts and lectures.

Times: Open 15 Feb-30 Nov, Tue-Sun & BHs 10.30-5. **Fee:** £4 (ch £2, concessions £3, children under 6 free). Family ticket £10. Party 10+
Facilities: ℗ (500mtrs) 🍴 ♿ shop ⊗ (ex guide dogs) ▬

Holburne Museum of Art

Great Pulteney St BA2 4DB

➲ *(M4 junct 18 to A4 and follow brown signs)*

☎ 01225 466669

e-mail: holburne@bath.ac.uk

web: www.bath.ac.uk/holburne

This jewel in Bath's crown was once the Georgian Sydney Hotel, whose glittering society Jane Austen watched from her house opposite. It displays the treasures collected by Sir William Holbourne: superb English and continental silver, porcelain, maiolica, glass and Renaissance bronzes. Since Sir William's time the collection has been greatly expanded and now includes landscapes by Guardi and Turner, and portraits by Stubbs, Ramsay, Raeburn, Zoffany and Bath's own artists Gainsborough, Hoare, and the Barkers of Bath.

Times: ✱ Open mid Feb-mid Dec, Tue-Sat 10-5, Sun 11-5. (Closed Mon ex group bookings by appointment). **Facilities:** ❷ 🍴 (lift to 1st floor) shop ⊗ (ex guide dogs) ▬

The Jane Austen Centre

40 Gay St, Queen Square BA1 2NT

➲ *(in heart of Bath by Queen Square)*

☎ 01225 443000

e-mail: info@janeausten.co.uk

web: www.janeausten.co.uk

Celebrating Bath's most famous resident, the centre offers a snapshot of life during Regency times and explores how living in this city affected Jane Austen's life and writing. Every September, Bath holds a Jane Austen festival.

Times: Open all year, daily 10-5.30. Closed 24-25 Dec & 1 Jan. **Fee:** £5.95 (ch £2.95, concessions £4.50) **Facilities:** ℗ (50mtrs) 🍴 ♿ shop ⊗ (ex guide dogs) ▬

Museum of Bath at Work   2 for 1

Julian Rd BA1 2RH

➲ *(from city centre, off Lansdown Rd into Julian Rd. Museum next to church on right)*

☎ 01225 318348

e-mail: mobaw@hotmail.com

web: www.bath-at-work.org.uk

Two thousand years of Bath's commercial and industrial development are explored with exhibits on 'The Story of Bath Stone', a Bath cabinet makers workshop, a 1914 Horstmann car and a reconstruction of J B Bowlers' engineering and mineral water business. A computer info point is available. 2007 exhibition: How We Work Now: Bath at Work Today.

Times: Open all year, Etr-1 Nov, daily 10.30-5; Nov-Etr, wknds 10.30-5. Closed 25-26 Dec. **Fee:** ✱ £4 (concessions £3). Family ticket £10. **Facilities:** ℗ (0.25m) 🍴 ♿ (audio guides, ramps) shop ⊗ (ex guide dogs)

Museum of Costume

Bennett St BA1 2QH

➲ *(Museum near city centre. Parking in Charlotte Street Car park.)*

☎ 01225 477173

e-mail: costume_bookings@bathnes.gov.uk

web: www.museumofcostume.co.uk

The Museum of Costume is one of the finest collections of fashionable dress in the world, covering the period from the late 16th-century to the present day. It is housed in Bath's famous 18th-century Assembly Rooms designed by John Wood the Younger in 1771. Entrance to the Assembly Rooms is free.

Times: Open all year, daily Jan-Feb 11-4; Mar-Oct 11-5; Nov-Dec 11-4. Closed 25&26 Dec. **Fee:** ✱ £6.50 (ch £4.50). Family ticket £18. Combined ticket with Roman Baths, £13 (ch £7.60). **Facilities:** ℗ (5 mins walk) (park & ride recommended) 🍴 ♿ (audio guides available) toilets for disabled shop ⊗ (ex guide dogs) ▬

England

No 1 Royal Crescent

No 1 Royal Cresent BA1 2LR

➲ (1st house in Royal Crescent situated above Victoria Ave & Victoria Park, Charlotte St car park)

☎ 01225 428126

e-mail: no1museum@bptrust.org.uk

web: www.bath-preservation-trust.org.uk

Bath is very much a Georgian city, but most of its houses have naturally altered over the years to suit changing tastes and lifestyles. Built in 1768 by John Wood the Elder, No 1 Royal Crescent has been restored to look as it would have done some 200 years ago. Visitors can see a grand townhouse of the late 18th-century with authentic furniture, paintings and carpets. On the ground floor are the study and dining room and on the first floor a lady's bedroom and drawing room. In the basement a period kitchen and museum shop.

Times: Open 10 Feb-27 Oct, 10.30-5 28 Oct-25 Nov, 10.30-4. Open BH Mon. Open wknds 1-2, 8-9 Dec. Closed Good Fri. (Last admission 30 mins before closing). **Fee:** ✱ £5 (concessions £3.50). Family ticket £12. Party 10+ £3 each. Schools £2.50 each **Facilities:** Ⓟ (5 mins walk) (street parking with card £1 per hour) 🍴 (virtual tour, induction loop, Braille guide) shop ⊗ (ex guide dogs)

Prior Park Landscape Garden

Ralph Allen Dr BA2 5AH

➲ (in city centre)

☎ 01225 833422 & 0900 133 5242

e-mail: priorpark@nationaltrust.org.uk

web: www.nationaltrust.org.uk

Created by local entrepreneur Ralph Allen with advice from Alexander Pope and 'Capability' Brown, this garden in set in a sweeping valley with magnificent views of the city of Bath. Many interesting features include a Palladian Bridge (250 years old in 2005), three lakes, and lovely wooded glades.

Times: Open Feb-29 Nov, Wed-Mon 11-5.30; 3 Dec-Jan, Fri-Sun 11-dusk. (BHs 11-5.30) Closed 25-26 Dec and 1 Jan. **Fee:** ✱ £4.50 (ch £2.50). Family (2ad+2ch) £11.50. **Facilities:** Ⓟ (park & ride) ♿ (Braille, large print guides, designated parking) toilets for disabled

Roman Baths & Pump Room

Abbey Church Yard BA1 1LZ

➲ (M4 junct 18, A46 into city centre)

☎ 01225 477785

e-mail: romanbaths_bookings@bathnes.gov.uk

web: www.romanbaths.co.uk

The remains of the Roman baths and temple give a vivid impression of life nearly 2000 years ago. Built next to Britain's only hot spring, the baths served the sick, and the pilgrims visiting the adjacent Temple of Sulis Minerva. Above the Temple Courtyard, the Pump Room became a popular meeting place in the 18th century. The site still flows with natural hot water and no visit is complete without a taste of the famous hot spa water.

Roman Baths & Pump Room

Times: Open all year, Mar-Jun & Sep-Oct, daily 9-5; Jul & Aug daily 9am-9pm; Jan-Feb & Nov-Dec, daily 9.30-4.30. Closed 25-26 Dec. (Last exit 1hr after closing). **Fee:** ✱ £10 (£11 Jul-Aug) (ch £6). Family ticket £28. Combined ticket with Museum of Costume £13 (ch £7.60). Disabled visitors free admission to ground floor areas. **Facilities:** Ⓟ (5 mins walk) (park & ride recommended) 🍴 licensed 🍴 ♿ (sign language & audio tours) toilets for disabled shop ⊗ (ex guide dogs) 🍴

Sally Lunn's Refreshment House & Museum

4 North Pde Passage BA1 1NX

➲ (centre of Bath, follow signs, next to Bath Abbey)

☎ 01225 461634

e-mail: enquiries@sallylunns.co.uk

web: www.sallylunns.co.uk

This Tudor building is Bath's oldest house and was a popular 17th-century meeting place. The traditional 'Sally Lunn' is similar to a brioche, and it is popularly believed to carry the name of its first maker who came to Bath in 1680. The bun is still served in the restaurant, and the original oven, Georgian cooking range and a collection of baking utensils are displayed in the museum.

Times: Open all year, Museum - Mon-Fri 10-6, Sat 10-5, Sun 11-5. Closed 25-26 Dec & 1 Jan. **Fee:** ✱ 30p (concessions free). **Facilities:** Ⓟ (2-3 min walk) (cards required for street parking) 🍴 🍴 licensed 🍴 ♿ (Braille menu available) shop ⊗ (ex guide dogs) 🍴

The William Herschel Museum NEW 2 for 1

19 New King St BA1 2BL

➲ (in Bath city centre)

☎ 01225 446865

e-mail: admin@herschelbpt.fsnet.co.uk

web: www.bath-preservation-trust.org.uk

18th-century town house, celebrates the achievements of William Herschel and his sister Caroline, both distinguished astronomers. Decorated and furnished in the style of the period of Georgian Bath. The gardens are semi formal in design and include different plants and herbs popular at the time.

Times: Open Feb-16 Dec, Mon-Tue & Thu-Fri, 1-5, Sat, Sun & BHs 11-5. **Fee:** ✱ £3.50, (ch £2, under 5 free, students £2.50, concessions £3) **Facilities:** Ⓟ (some 2 hour free spaces) (audio tours, handling collections, sub titles) shop ⊗ (ex assist dogs)

Are there any excellent Days Out that we have missed? Use the Readers' Report form at the back of the book to tell us about them.

CASTLE CARY
MAP 03 ST63

Hadspen Garden & Nursery

Hadspen House BA7 7NG

➲ *(2m SE off A371)*

☎ 01749 813707

e-mail: pope@hadspengarden.co.uk

web: www.hadspen.co.uk

Situated within a 17th-century curved wall, this five acre garden has borders planted with roses and herbaceous plants, many of which have been developed here. Plants grown in the garden are available in the adjoining nursery.

Times: ✱ Open 4 Mar-26 Sep, Thu-Sun & BHs 10-5. **Facilities:** 𝐏 ❍I 📶 ♿ garden centre ⊗ (ex guide dogs) ◀

CHARD
MAP 03 ST30

Forde Abbey
2 for 1

TA20 4LU

➲ *(5m SE of Chard, signed from A30 and A358)*

☎ 01460 221290

e-mail: info@fordeabbey.co.uk

web: www.fordeabbey.co.uk

As one of the top gardens in England, Forde Abbey has much to offer keen gardeners. The 30 acres include a colourful bog garden, a walled kitchen garden, cascades, ponds, Ionic temple, rockery, herbaceous borders and the Centenary Fountain, the highest powered fountain in England. The privately owned magnificent 12th-century house contains outstanding Mortlake tapestries, spectacularly decorated plaster ceilings and fine furniture and paintings.

Times: Gardens, open all year, daily 10-4.30. House Apr-Oct, Tue-Fri, Sun & BH 12-4. **Fee:** ✱ Gardens £5.60 (under 15's free, pen £5.10). House & Gardens £7.70 (ch free, pen £7.20). **Facilities:** 𝐏 💺 ❍I licensed 📶 ♿ (large print guide, wheelchair & batricar) toilets for disabled shop garden centre ◀

CLEVEDON
MAP 03 ST47

Clevedon Court

Tickenham Rd BS21 6QU

➲ *(off B3130 1.5m E of Clevedon)*

☎ 01275 872257

web: www.nationaltrust.org.uk

Clevedon Court is a remarkably complete manor house of around 1320. Additions have been made in each century, so it has a pleasing variety of styles, with an 18th-century, terraced garden.

Times: Open 2 Apr-28 Sep, Wed-Thu, Sun & BH Mon 2-5. Car park & Gardens will open at 1.15. **Fee:** ✱ £5.50 (ch £2.50). Party 20+ by arrangement. **Facilities:** 𝐏 ♿ (access via steps, Braille/large print guide) ⊗ 🐾

CRICKET ST THOMAS
MAP 03 ST30

The Wildlife Park at Cricket St Thomas

TA20 4DB

➲ *(3m E of Chard on A30, follow brown heritage signs.)*

☎ 01460 30111

e-mail: wildlifepark.cst@bourne-leisure.co.uk

web: www.wild.org.uk

The Wildlife Park offers you the chance to see more than 60 species of animals at close quarters. Visitors can learn about what is being

continued

done to save endangered species, take a walk through the Lemur Wood, ride on the Safari Train or visit the Children's Farm. During peak season, park mascot Larry the Lemur stars in his own show.

Times: Open all year, daily 10-6 last admission 4, (10-4.30, last admission 3 in winter). Closed 25 Dec. **Fee:** £8.25 (ch 3-14 £6.25, under 3's free, pen £7.25). Family ticket £26 (2ad+3ch). **Facilities:** 𝐏 💺 ❍I licensed ♿ (some steep slopes) shop ⊗ (ex guide dogs) ◀

DUNSTER
MAP 03 SS94

Dunster Castle

TA24 6SL

➲ *(3m SE of Minehead, approach from A39. Approx 2m from Dunster Stn)*

☎ 01643 821314 & 823004

e-mail: dunstercastle@nationaltrust.org.uk

web: www.nationaltrust.org.uk

The castle's picturesque appearance is largely due to 19th-century work, but older features can also be seen, the superb 17th-century oak staircase for example. Sub-tropical plants flourish in the 28-acre park and the terraced gardens are noted for exotica such as a giant lemon tree, yuccas, mimosa and palms as well as the National Collection of Strawberry Trees.

Times: Castle: 18 Mar-29 Oct, Sat-Wed 11-5; 30 Oct-5 Nov, Sat-Wed 11-4. Garden & Park: Jan-17 Mar & 30 Oct-Dec, all week, 11-4, 18 Mar-29 Oct, all week, 10-5. **Fee:** ✱ Castle, Garden & Park £7.50 (ch under 16 £3.80). Family ticket £18.50. Garden & Park only £4.10 (ch under 16 £2). Family ticket £10. **Facilities:** 𝐏 ♿ (Braille, large print guides, Batricar & 2 w/chairs) toilets for disabled shop ⊗ (ex in park) 🐾

EAST LAMBROOK
MAP 03 ST41

East Lambrook Manor Garden

TA13 5HH

➲ *(signed off A303, at South Petherton rdbt)*

☎ 01460 240328

e-mail: enquiries@eastlambrook.com

web: www.eastlambrook.com

It was the late Margery Fish who created the concept of 'cottage gardening' in the 1940s. Her wonderful Grade I listed gardens are known to garden lovers throughout the world. The gardens now house a collection of Geraniums, a specialist plant nursery, an award-winning tea shop and art gallery.

Times: Open daily 10-5 Closed 2 wks at Xmas. **Fee:** ✱ £3.95 (ch £1 & pen £3.50). Group rate available. **Facilities:** 𝐏 💺 📶 ♿ (gardens partly accessible) shop garden centre ⊗ (ex guide dogs) ◀

FARLEIGH HUNGERFORD
MAP 03 ST85

Farleigh Hungerford Castle

BA2 7RS

➲ *(3.5m W of Trowbridge on A366)*

☎ 01225 754026

web: www.english-heritage.org.uk

Set in a picturesque valley, this castle hides many secrets and a sinister past. An audio tour reveals all.

Times: Open all year, Apr-Jun & Sep, daily 10-5; Jul-Aug, daily 10-6; Oct, daily 10-4; Nov-Mar, Sat-Sun 10-4. Closed 24-26 Dec & 1 Jan. **Fee:** £3.50 (ch £1.80, concessions £2.60). Prices and opening times are subject to change in Spring 2007. Please check web site or call 0870 333 1181 for the most up to date prices and opening times when planning your visit. **Facilities:** 𝐏 ♿ shop ⊗ ♯

England

GLASTONBURY
MAP 03 ST43

Glastonbury Abbey
2 for 1

Abbey Gatehouse, Magdalene St BA6 9EL
➲ *(on A361 between Frome & Taunton.)*
☎ 01458 832267
e-mail: info@glastonburyabbey.com
web: www.glastonburyabbey.com

Few places in Britain are as rich in myth and legend as Glastonbury. Tradition maintains that the impressive ruins mark the birth place of Christianity in Britain. Joseph of Arimathea is said to have founded a chapel here in AD61, planting his staff in the ground where it flowered both at Christmas and Easter. Later, it is said, King Arthur and Guinevere were buried here, and the abbey has been a place of pilgrimage since the Middle Ages. The present abbey ruins date mostly from the 12th and 13th centuries, fell into decay after the Dissolution. The display area contains artefacts and a model of the Abbey as it might have been in 1539. During the summer months meet a character from the past, who will tell you something of this wonderful place. Thirty-six acres of grounds including two ponds, an orchard and wildlife areas.

Times: Open all year, daily, Jun-Aug 9-6; Sep-May 9.30-6 or dusk, whichever is the earliest. Dec-Feb open at 10. Closed 25 Dec. **Fee:** £4.50 (ch 5-15 £3, concessions £4). Family ticket £12.50 (2ad+2ch) **Facilities:** ❷ (charged) 💻 ♿ (audio tape, deaf loop, wheelchairs, lge print leaflet) toilets for disabled shop ⊗ (ex on leads) ◼

KINGSDON
MAP 03 ST52

Lytes Cary Manor

TA11 7HU
➲ *(off A303, signed from Padimore rdbt at junct of A303 & A37, take A372)*
☎ 01458 224471
e-mail: lytescarymanor@nationaltrust.org.uk
web: www.nationaltrust.org.uk

Fine medieval manor house and delightful 14th-century chapel, surrounded by gardens with an enchanting mixture of formality and simplicity. Much of the present house was built in the 16th century although the oldest part, the chapel, dates from 1343. The Great Hall was a 15th-century addition. Unfortunately the gardens did not survive, but the present formal gardens are being restocked with plants that were commonly grown at the time of building, according to the '*Lytes Cary Herbal*' a manuscript still on display within the

continued

property. High yew topiary hedges enclose large borders and hidden paths.

Times: Open end Mar-Oct, Wed & Fri-Sun 11-5. Open BH. Closes at dusk if earlier than 5. **Fee:** ✱ £5 (ch £2). Family £12. Garden only £3.50 Ch £1.50. **Facilities:** ❷ ♿ (Braille guide, scented plants) toilets for disabled ⊗ (ex guide dogs) ◼

MONTACUTE
MAP 03 ST41

Montacute House

TA15 6XP
➲ *(4m W of Yeovil, on S side of A3088)*
☎ 01935 823289
e-mail: montacute@nationaltrust.org.uk
web: www.nationaltrust.org.uk

Set amidst formal gardens, Montacute House was built by Sir Edward Phelips. He was a successful lawyer, and became Speaker of the House of Commons in 1604. Inside there are decorated ceilings, ornate fireplaces, heraldic glass and fine wood panelling. The Long Gallery displays a permanent collection of Tudor and Jacobean portraits from the National Portrait Gallery in London. Montacute has been used as the setting for successful films such as '*Sense and Sensibility*'.

Times: House: 22 Mar-29 Oct, Wed-Mon, 11-5. Garden: Jan-19 Mar, Wed-Sun, 11-4. 22 Mar-29 Oct, Wed-Mon, 11-6. Nov-17 Mar, Wed-Sun, 11-4. Shop: 1-19 Mar, Wed-Sun 11-4. 22 Mar-29 Oct, Wed-Mon, 11-5.30. Nov-17 Dec, Wed-Sun. 11-4. Restaurant: 5-19 Mar, Sun. 11-4. 22 Mar-29 Oct, Wed-Mon, 12-3. 5 Nov-17 Dec, Sun, 11-4. **Fee:** ✱ House, Garden & Park £8 (ch £4). Family ticket £20. Garden & Park only £4.50 (ch £2), 3 Nov-Mar, £2 (ch £1). **Facilities:** ❷ 💻 🍴 licensed ♿ (Braille guide, 3 manual wheelchairs) toilets for disabled shop garden centre ⊗ (ex in park) ◼

MUCHELNEY
MAP 03 ST42

Muchelney Abbey

TA10 0DQ
☎ 01458 250664
web: www.english-heritage.org.uk

The monastery was first established at Muchelney by Ine, a 7th-century king of Wessex. It did not survive the Viking invasions, but the abbey was re-founded about AD950 and lasted for nearly six centuries. The present remains date largely from the 12th-century. The best preserved feature of the site today is the Abbot's lodging, which had only just been completed in 1539 when the abbey was surrendered to Henry VIII.

Times: Open Apr-Jun & Sep, daily 10-5; Jul-Aug, daily 10-6; Oct, daily 10-4. **Fee:** £3.20 (ch £1.60, concessions £2.40). Prices and opening times are subject to change in Spring 2007. Please check web site or call 0870 333 1181 for the most up to date prices and opening times when planning your visit. **Facilities:** ❷ ♿ shop ⊗ ⊞

NETHER STOWEY
MAP 03 ST13

Coleridge Cottage

35 Lime St TA5 1NQ
➲ *(at W end of Nether Stowey, on S side of A39, 8m W of Bridgwater)*
☎ 01278 732662
web: www.nationaltrust.org.uk

It was in this small cottage that Coleridge was most inspired as a poet and here that he wrote *The Rime of the Ancient Mariner*, part of

continued

Christabel, Frost at Midnight and *Kubla Khan*. The Coleridge family moved to Nether Stowey in 1797 and became friendly with the Wordsworths who lived nearby.

Times: Open Apr-24 Sep, Thu-Sun & BHs 2-5. **Fee:** ✱ £3.50 (ch £1.70). **Facilities:** Ⓟ (500yds) (steps to entrance, Braille & large print guides) ⊗ ⛄

NUNNEY   MAP 03 ST74

Nunney Castle   FREE

➲ *(3.5m SW of Frome, off A361)*
web: www.english-heritage.org.uk

Built in 1373, and supposedly modelled on France's Bastille, this crenellated manor house has one of the deepest moats in England. It was ruined by Parliamentarian forces in the Civil War.

Times: Open at any reasonable time. **Facilities:** ₺ ♨

SPARKFORD   MAP 03 ST62

Haynes International Motor Museum

BA22 7LH
➲ *(from A303 follow A359 towards Castle Cary, museum clearly signed)*
☎ 01963 440804
e-mail: info@haynesmotormuseum.co.uk
web: www.haynesmotormuseum.co.uk

Spectacular collection of historic cars, motorcycles and motoring memorabilia. Vehicles range from a 1903 Oldsmobile to sports cars of the 50s and 60s and modern day classics. Also at the Museum is a 70 seat video cinema, the Hall of Motorsports, a millennium hall and a picnic area and children's adventure playground.

Times: Open all year, Mar-Oct, daily 9.30-5.30; Nov-Feb, 10-4.30. Closed 24-26 Dec & 1 Jan. **Facilities:** ❷ 🍽 licensed 🗐 ₺ (ramps & loan wheelchairs available) toilets for disabled shop ⊗ (ex guide dogs & in grounds) 📧

STOKE ST GREGORY   MAP 03 ST32

Willow & Wetlands Visitor Centre   2 for 1

Meare Green Court TA3 6HY
➲ *(between North Curry & Stoke St Gregory, signed from A361 & A378)*
☎ 01823 490249
e-mail: info@englishwillowbaskets.co.uk
web: www.englishwillowbaskets.co.uk

The centre is owned and run by Somerset Basketmakers and willow growers P H Coate & Son. The environmental exhibition gives a fascinating insight into the Somerset Levels and Moors. Guided tours of the yard and workshops are available.

Times: Open all year, Mon-Fri 9-5 (guided tours 10-4), Sat (no tours) 9-5. Closed Sun. **Fee:** ✱ Admission free, tour charge: £3.50 (ch £1.75, pen £3). Family ticket £8. Credit cards accepted if total admission price exceeds £10. **Facilities:** ❷ 💻 🗐 ₺ (some areas of gardens accessible) toilets for disabled shop 📧

STOKE-SUB-HAMDON   MAP 03 ST41

Stoke-Sub-Hamdon Priory   FREE

North St TA4 6QP
➲ *(between A303 & A3088)*
☎ 01935 823289
web: www.nationaltrust.org.uk

A complex of buildings, begun in the 14th century for the priests of the Chantry Chapel of St Nicholas (now destroyed).

Times: Open 26 Mar-Oct, daily 10-6 or dusk if earlier.
Facilities: Ⓟ ⊗ 🚌(on road parking only) ⛄

STREET   MAP 03 ST43

The Shoe Museum   FREE

C & J Clark Ltd, High St BA16 0YA
➲ *(A39 to Street, follow signs for Clarks Village)*
☎ 01458 842169

The museum is in the oldest part of the shoe factory set up by Cyrus and James Clark in 1825. It contains shoes from Roman times to the present, buckles, engravings, fashion plates, machinery, hand tools and advertising material.

Times: Open all year, Mon-Fri 10-4.45. Closed 10 days over Christmas and BH. **Facilities:** Ⓟ At Clarks Village ₺ (access wkdays only) shop ⊗ (ex guide dogs)

See advert on page 239

TAUNTON   MAP 03 ST22

Hestercombe Gardens

Cheddon Fitzpaine TA2 8LG
➲ *(3m N of Taunton near Cheddon Fitzpaine. Signed from all main roads)*
☎ 01823 413923
e-mail: info@hestercombegardens.com
web: www.hestercombegardens.com

There are three period gardens to enjoy at Hestercombe: the 40-acre Georgian pleasure grounds with woodland walks, temples, Witch House and Great Cascade; the Victorian terrace and newly established Victorian shrubbery; and the Edwardian gardens, where the work of Gertrude Jekyll and architect Edwin Lutyens are shown off to full effect.

continued

Times: Open daily, 10-6 (last admission 5). Closed 25 Dec.
Facilities: ♿ ⦿ licensed ♿ (gardens partially accessible) toilets for disabled shop garden centre (open Apr-Oct) ⊗ (ex on lead) ▬

TINTINHULL   MAP 03 ST41

Tintinhull House Garden
Farm St BA22 8PZ
➲ *(0.5m S off A303. Follow signs to Tintinhull village, garden is well signed)*
☎ 01935 826357
e-mail: tintinhull@nationaltrust.org.uk
web: www.nationaltrust.org.uk

An attractive, mainly 17th-century manor house with a Queen Anne façade, it stands in two acres of beautiful formal gardens. The gardens were largely created by Mrs Reiss, who gave the property to the National Trust in 1953.

Times: Open 22 Mar-29 Oct, Wed-Sun & BH Mons 11-5. Tea room: as garden. **Fee:** ✱ £5 (ch £2.50). Family £12.50 **Facilities:** ♿ ▬ ♿ (1 Wheelchair, Braille and large print guide) ⊗ (ex guide dogs) ✻

WASHFORD   MAP 03 ST04

Cleeve Abbey
TA23 0PS
➲ *(0.25m S of A39)*
☎ 01984 640377
web: www.english-heritage.org.uk

This 13th-century monastic site features some of the finest cloister buildings in England; medieval wall paintings, a mosaic tiled floor and an interesting exhibition.

Times: Open Apr-Jun & Sep, daily 10-5; Jul-Aug, daily 10-6; Oct, daily 10-4. **Fee:** £3.40 (ch £1.70, concessions £2.60). Prices and opening times are subject to change in Spring 2007. Please check web site or call 0870 333 1181 for the most up to date prices and opening times when planning your visit. **Facilities:** ♿ ♿ shop ⌗

Tropiquaria Animal and Adventure Park
TA23 0QB

➲ *(on A39, between Williton and Minehead)*
☎ 01984 640688
e-mail: office@tropiquaria.co.uk
web: www.tropiquaria.co.uk

Housed in a 1930s BBC transmitting station, the main hall has been converted into an indoor jungle with a 15-foot waterfall, tropical plants and free-flying birds. (Snakes, lizards, iguanas, spiders, toads and terrapins are caged!) Downstairs is the submarine crypt with local and tropical marine life. Other features include landscaped gardens, the Shadowstring Puppet Theatre, and 'Wireless in the West' museum. Also two new full size pirate adventure ships are moored on the front lawn accessible to pirates of all ages! The park has an indoor playcastle for adventure and fun whatever the weather.

Times: Open Apr-Sep, daily 10-6 (last entry 4.30); Oct daily 11-5 (last entry 4); Nov-Mar wknds 11-4 (last entry 3). **Fee:** ✱ £6.95 (ch & pen £5.95). **Facilities:** ♿ ▬ ♿ (ramp to pirate galleon & indoor castle) toilets for disabled shop ⊗ (ex guide dogs) ▬

WELLS   MAP 03 ST54

The Bishop's Palace
Henderson Rooms BA5 2PD
➲ *(Follow city centre signs, turn left into Market Pl and enter archway between National Trust shop and post office)*
☎ 01749 678691
e-mail: info@bishopspalacewells.co.uk
web: www.bishopspalacewells.co.uk

Close to the cathedral is the moated bishop's palace. The early part of the palace, the bishop's chapel and the ruins of the banqueting hall date from the 13th century and the undercroft remains virtually unchanged from this time. There are several state rooms and a long gallery which houses portraits of former Bishops. Events include a Living History re-enactment.

Times: Open Apr-Oct, Mon-Fri 10.30-5, Sun noon-5 **Facilities:** ℗ (100yds) ▬ ⦿ licensed ▦ ♿ (free use of electric wheelchair) shop

---

WESTON-SUPER-MARE   MAP 03 ST36

The Helicopter Museum
The Heliport, Locking Moor Rd BS24 8PP
➲ *(outskirts of town on A371, nr M5 junct 21)*
☎ 01934 635227
e-mail: office@helimuseum.fsnet.co.uk
web: www.helicoptermuseum.co.uk

The world's largest rotary-wing collection and the only helicopter museum in Britain. More than 70 helicopters and autogyros are on display - including examples from France, Germany, Poland, Russia and the United States, from 1935 to the present day - with displays of models, engines and other components explaining the history and development of the rotocraft. Special events include 'Open Cockpit Days', when visitors can learn more about how the helicopter works.

Times: Open all year, Nov-Mar, Wed-Sun 10-4.30; Apr-Oct 10-5.30. Open daily during Etr & Summer school hols 10-5.30. Closed 24-26 Dec & 1 Jan. **Fee:** ✱ £5.30 (ch under 5 free, ch 5-16 £3.30, pen £4.30). Family ticket (2ad+2ch) £14.50, (2ad+3ch) £16.50. Party 12+. **Facilities:** ♿ ▬ ♿ (large print and Braille information sheet) toilets for disabled shop ▬

North Somerset Museum
Burlington St BS23 1PR
➲ *(in centre of Weston-super-Mare)*
☎ 01934 621028
e-mail: museum.service@n-somerset.gov.uk
web: www.n-somerset.gov.uk/museum

This museum, housed in the former workshops of the Edwardian Gaslight Company, has displays on the seaside holiday, an old chemist's shop, a dairy and Victorian pavement mosaics. Adjoining the museum is Clara's Cottage, a Westonian home of the 1900s with period kitchen, parlour, bedroom and back yard. One of the rooms has an additional display of Peggy Nisbet dolls. Other displays include wildlife gallery, Mendip minerals, mining and local archaeology, costume, ceramics and cameras.

Times: Open all year: Mon-Sat 10-4.30. Closed 25-27 Dec & 1 Jan. **Fee:** ✱ £3.90 (ch free when accompanied by an adult, pen £2.85) **Facilities:** ℗ (800yds) (1 disabled parking outside museum) ▬ ♿ (Hearing loop at reception) toilets for disabled shop ⊗ (ex guide dogs) ▬

England

WOOKEY HOLE
MAP 03 ST54

Wookey Hole Caves & Papermill
2 for 1

BA5 1BB

➲ (M5 junct 22 follow signs via A38 & A371, from Bristol & Bath A39 to Wells then 2m to Wookey Hole)

☎ 01749 672243

e-mail: witch@wookey.co.uk

web: www.wookey.co.uk

Britain's most spectacular caves and legendary home of the infamous Witch of Wookey. The 19th-century paper mill houses a variety of fascinating attractions including a Cave Museum, Victorian Penny Arcade, Magical Mirror Maze, Haunted Corridor of Crazy Mirrors, and the Wizard's Castle play area. Visitors can also see paper being made in Britain's only surviving handmade paper mill. Puppet theatre shows, magic lessons, an enchanted fairy garden and Dinosaur Valley round off this family day out in Wookey Gorge.

Times: Open all year, Nov-Mar, daily 10-4; Apr-Oct, daily 10-5. Closed 25 Dec. **Fee:** ✱ £10.90 (ch 4-14 & concessions £8.50, under 4's free). **Facilities:** ❷ ⭐ licensed 🍴 ♿ (papermill only accessible) toilets for disabled shop ⊗ (ex guide dogs) 🎧

YEOVILTON
MAP 03 ST52

Fleet Air Arm Museum
2 for 1

Royal Naval Air Station BA22 8HT

➲ (on B3151, just off junct of A303 and A37)

☎ 01935 840565

e-mail: info@fleetairarm.com

web: www.fleetairarm.com

The Fleet Air Arm Museum has the largest collection of naval aircraft anywhere in Europe. Situated alongside Europe's largest naval air station, visitors may see Sea Harriers and helicopters going through their rigorous training procedures. Inside the museum you will have the opportunity of going on board Concorde, and being transported by a simulated helicopter flight to the replica flight deck of the aircraft carrier HMS Ark Royal, where you can experience the thrills of a working flight deck, and even see a nuclear bomb! The site includes an adventure playground, a licensed restaurant, and a shop.

Times: Open all year, daily Apr-Oct 10-5.30; Nov-Mar, Wed-Sun 10-4.30. Closed 24-26 Dec. **Fee:** ✱ £10 (ch under 5 free, ch 5-16 £7, concessions £8). Family ticket (2ad+3ch) £30. **Facilities:** ❷ ⭐ licensed 🍴 ♿ (wheelchairs available) toilets for disabled shop ⊗ (ex guide dogs) 🎧

See advert on this page

Staffordshire

Foxfield

For many visitors the main attractions of Staffordshire are the roller coaster
entertainment of Alton Towers, or the craftsmanship of the world-famous
potteries in Stoke-on-Trent. However, the county has very much more for
the visitor— including a choice of steam railway attractions. There is beautiful
countryside, particularly where the Peak District National Park crosses into
the North East of the county while Cannon Chase, thirty thousand acres of
forest and heathland, lies to the South.

ALTON   MAP 07 SK04

Alton Towers

ST10 4DB

⮑ (from S - M1 junct 23a or M6 junct 15. From N - M1 junct 28 or M6 junct 16)

☎ 08705 204060

e-mail: info@alton-towers.com

web: www.altontowers.com

Alton Towers is a fantastic day out for all the family. With world first rides and attractions as well as some beautiful gardens, this is more than just a theme park. Recent additions include the Spinball Whizzer, a spinner coaster, as well as The Flume, in which visitors now travel in red bath tubs, rather than rustic logs.

Times: ✱ Open daily 12 Mar-30 Oct **Fee:** Advance book, Adults from £23 (ch from £16) **Facilities:** ❷ (charged) ⬛ ⅟◎⅟ licensed ᕮ (disabled guest guide books) toilets for disabled shop. ⊗ (ex guide dogs) ◀

BIDDULPH   MAP 07 SJ85

Biddulph Grange Garden

Grange Rd ST8 7SD

⮑ (access from A527, Tunstall-Congleton road. Entrance on Grange Rd 0.5m N of Biddulph)

☎ 01782 517999

e-mail: biddulphgrange@nationaltrust.org.uk

web: www.nationaltrust.org.uk

This exciting and rare survival of a high Victorian garden has undergone extensive restoration. Conceived by James Bateman, the fifteen acres are divided into a number of smaller gardens which were designed to house specimens from his extensive plant collection.

Times: Open mid Mar-Oct, Wed-Sun & BH 11-5.30 (last admission 5.30 or dusk if earlier); early Nov-mid Dec, Sat-Sun 11-3 or dusk. **Fee:** ✱ Mar-Oct: £5.30 (ch £2.60), Family ticket £13; Nov-Dec: £2 (ch £1), Family ticket £5. **Facilities:** ❷ ⬛ ᕮ (not suitable for people with mobility problems) shop ⊗ (ex guide & hearing dogs) ⅟⅃ ◀

BURTON-UPON-TRENT   MAP 08 SK22

Coors Visitor Centre & Museum of Brewing   `2 for 1`

PO Box 220, Horninglow St DE14 1YQ

⮑ (off A38 at Burton-on-Trent, well signed)

☎ 0845 600 0598

e-mail: enquiries@coorsvisitorcentre.com

web: www.coorsvisitorcentre.com

Beer has been brewed in Burton upon Trent for centuries and the Museum of Brewing at the Coors Visitor Centre charts its fantastic heritage. Learn all about the history of brewing, meet the famous Coors Shire horses and explore the collection of restored vintage vehicles.

Times: Open all year, daily 10-5. (Last admission 4). Closed 25-26 Dec & 1 Jan. **Fee:** ✱ £6 (ch over 5yrs £3, concessions £4). Family ticket £17.50 (2ad+3ch); admission includes complimentary half pint of lager or beer or tea, coffee or soft drink. **Facilities:** ❷ ⬛ ⅟◎⅟ ⅟⅃ ᕮ (ramps, lift) toilets for disabled shop ⊗ (ex guide dogs) ◀

CHEDDLETON   MAP 07 SJ95

Cheddleton Flint Mill

Beside Caldon Canal, Leek Rd ST13 7HL

⮑ (3m S of Leek on A520)

☎ 01782 502907

web: www.people.ex.ac.uk/akoutram/cheddleton-mill

Twin water-wheels on the River Churnet drive flint-grinding pans in the two mills. Museum collection of machinery used in the preparation of materials for the ceramic industry. This includes a 100 HP Robey horizontal steam engine, model Newcomen beam engine, edge-runner mill, and the narrow boat Vienna, moored on the Caldon Canal. Display panels explain the processes of winning and treating clays, stone and flint for the pottery industry.

Times: Open all year, Sat & Sun 2-5, Mon-Fri 10-5 (by arrangement). Phone to check **Fee:** All donations gratefully accepted. **Facilities:** ❷ ⅟⅃ ᕮ toilets for disabled

Churnet Valley Railway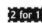

The Station ST13 7EE

⮑ (3m S from Leek, 3m N from Cellarhead along A520. Kingsley & Froghall Station is situated on the Stoke to Ashbourne road, A52)

☎ 01538 360522

e-mail: enquiries@churnetvalleyrailway.co.uk

web: www.churnetvalleyrailway.co.uk

The Churnet Valley Railway runs through the hidden countryside between Cheddleton, with its grade II Victorian station, Kingsley and Froghall, with the newly built station and Canal Wharf. The journey incorporates Consall, which has a sleepy rural station and nature reserve, and Leekbrook with one of the longest tunnels on a preserved railway. 2-for-1 voucher is not valid on Special Event days. Special Events: 1940's wknd Apr, Ghost Train Oct, Santa & Steam Dec, Day out with Thomas Feb and Jul.

Times: Open every Sun, Mar-Oct; all BH's Wed & Sat, Jun-Aug; Diesel trains every Tue & Thu in Aug and every Sat Mar-Oct. **Fee:** All day travel: £9 (ch £5, pen £7) **Facilities:** ❷ ⬛ ᕮ (ramps) toilets for disabled shop ◀

England

Halfpenny Green Vineyards   `FREE`

DY7 5EP

➲ *(0.5m off B4176 Dudley to Telford road)*

☎ 01384 221122

e-mail: enquiries@halfpenny-green-vineyards.co.uk

web: www.halfpenny-green-vineyards.co.uk

Using German, French and hybrid varieties that can prosper even in the poorest British summer, this vineyard offers "The complete English wine experience." This includes a self-guided vineyard trail as well as guided tours, wine-tasting, a craft centre and a visitor centre. Visitors can purchase wines with personalised labels for special occasions. Coarse fishing is also available.

Times: Open all year, daily 10.30-5. **Facilities:** 🅿 💻 🍴 licensed 🗊 ♿ toilets for disabled shop ⊗ (ex guide dogs) ⛴

Himley Hall & Park

DY3 4DF

➲ *(off A449, on B4176)*

☎ 01384 817817

e-mail: himley.hall@dudley.gov.uk

The extensive parkland offers a range of attractions, including a nine-hole golf course and coarse fishing. The hall is open to the public when exhibitions are taking place. Permanent orienteering course, a charge is made for the maps. Guided tours at the hall available by prior arrangement. The Hall is available for private hire. There are also a large variety of outdoor events and concerts.

Times: ✱ Open Hall: early Sep-mid Sep, 2-5. Closed Mon ex BH. Park open all year. **Facilities:** 🅿 (charged) 💻 🗊 ♿ toilets for disabled ⊗ (ex guide dogs & in park)

Blackbrook Zoological Park

Winkhill ST13 7QR

➲ *(off A523 Leek to Ashbourne road)*

☎ 01538 308293

e-mail: enquiries@blackbrookzoologicalpark.co.uk

web: www.blackbrookzoologicalpark.co.uk

Blackbrook Zoological Park is a fun and educational day for all. A continually growing attraction, always with something new to see. The zoo features: rare birds, reptiles, insects and aquatics; owl flights, Pelican and Lemur feeds. Blackbrook Zoological Park is fully accessible for pushchairs and wheelchairs.

Times: Open daily 10.30-5.30; Winter 10.30-dusk **Fee:** £6.95 (ch £4.25, pen £5.75) **Facilities:** 🅿 💻 🗊 ♿ (fully accessible) toilets for disabled shop ⊗ (ex guide dogs) ⛴

Erasmus Darwin House   `2 for 1`

Beacon St WS13 7AD

➲ *(signed to Lichfield Cathedral. Access by foot through cathedral close at West End)*

☎ 01543 306260

e-mail: enquiries@erasmusdarwin.org

web: www.erasmusdarwin.org

The House is dedicated to Erasmus Darwin, the grandfather of Charles Darwin, and a talented doctor, inventor, philosopher, poet and founder member of the Lunar Society. A resident of Lichfield for more than 20 years, the displays are contained within his beautiful 18th-century home, and recreate the story of Erasmus' life, ideas and inventions, through period rooms, audio visual and interactive displays.

Times: Open Apr-Sep: Tue-Sun noon-5, Oct-Mar: Thu-Sun noon-5. (Last admission 4.15). **Fee:** £2.50 (concessions £2). Family ticket (2ad+2ch) £6. **Facilities:** 🅿 (200mtrs) (Pay and Display) ♿ (audio tour) toilets for disabled shop ⊗ (ex guide dogs)

Lichfield Cathedral

WS13 7LD

➲ *(signed from all major roads and within city).*

☎ 01543 306240 & 306100

e-mail: enquiries@lichfield-cathedral.org

web: www.lichfield-cathedral.org

The Cathedral's three spires, known as the Ladies of the Vale, dominate the landscape. The first cathedral here was founded in AD700 to house the shrine of St Chad. The present building, with its elaborate carvings, has been much restored since it was attacked during the Civil War. Among its treasures are an 8th-century illuminated manuscript, the St Chad Gospels, a collection of modern silver and the 16th-century Flemish glass in the Lady Chapel. Many musical events take place here.

Times: Open daily 7.45-6.30. **Fee:** ✱ Suggested donation of £4 for each adult visitor. **Facilities:** 🅿 (200mtrs) (no parking ex disabled in close) 💻 🍴 licensed 🗊 ♿ (touch & hearing centre for blind) toilets for disabled shop ⊗ (ex guide/hearing dogs)

Lichfield Heritage Centre

Market Square WS13 6LG

➲ *(in city centre)*

☎ 01543 256611

e-mail: info@lichfieldheritage.org.uk

web: www.lichfieldheritage.org.uk

A colourful new exhibition, 'The Lichfield Story' gives a vivid account of Lichfield's rich and varied history over 2000 years. It is the home to the Staffordshire Millennium Embroideries which are displayed within their own gallery. In addition, the Exhibition houses fine examples of City, Diocesan and Regimental silver, ancient Charters and archives. Two audio visual presentations, a Family Trail and for younger children a Mouse Hole Trail provide interest and fun for all the family as they tour the Exhibition.

Times: ✱ Open all year, daily 10-5, Sun 10.30-5. (Last admission 4). Closed Xmas & New Year. **Facilities:** 🅿 (200yds) 💻 🗊 ♿ (lift to first floor) toilets for disabled shop ⊗ (ex guide dogs) ⛴

Samuel Johnson Birthplace Museum FREE

Breadmarket St WS13 6LG

➲ *(located in city centre market place)*

☎ 01543 258441

e-mail: sjmuseum@lichfield.gov.uk

web: www.lichfield.gov.uk/sjmuseum

Dr Samuel Johnson, author of the famous English dictionary of 1755, lexicographer, poet, critic, biographer and personality. One of England's greatest writers, Dr Johnson was born in this house in 1709. The birthplace now houses a museum dedicated to his extraordinary life, work and personality. Five floors of exhibits featuring period room settings, introductory video and personal items owned by Johnson, his family and his famous friends.

Times: ✱ Open daily Apr-Sep 10.30-4.30; Oct-Mar 12-4.30. (Last admission 4). **Facilities:** ℗ (500yds) ৬ (large print text literature, induction loop system) shop ⊗ (ex guide dogs)

SHUGBOROUGH   MAP 07 SJ92

Shugborough Estate

ST17 OXB

➲ *(6m E of Stafford off A513, signed from M6 junct 13)*

☎ 01889 881388

e-mail: shugborough.promotions@staffordshire.gov.uk

web: www.shugborough.org.uk

Set on the edge of Cannock Chase, Shugborough is the magnificent 900-acre seat of the Earls of Lichfield. The 18th-century mansion house contains fine collections of ceramics, silver, paintings and French furniture. Part of the house is still lived in by the Lichfield family. Visitors can enjoy the Grade I listed historic garden and a unique collection of neo-classical monuments. Other attractions include the museum and the original servants' quarters, the laundry, kitchens, brewhouse and coachhouses which have all been restored and are fully operational. Costumed characters help to recreate the past and there is a varied programme of events each year.

Times: Open 18 Mar-28 Oct, daily 11-5. Site open all year to pre-booked parties. **Fee:** ✱ £10 (ch £6, concessions £7). Family Ticket £25. Parking fee (£3) refunded on purchase of all site ticket. **Facilities:** ℗ (charged) 🍴 licensed ৬ (step climber for wheelchairs, 2 Batricars) toilets for disabled shop ⊗ (ex guide dogs & in parkland) 🎒

STAFFORD   MAP 07 SJ92

Shire Hall Gallery FREE

Market Square ST16 2LD

➲ *(M6 junct 13, follow signs to Stafford town centre & gallery is signed from there)*

☎ 01785 278345

e-mail: shirehallgallery@staffordshire.gov.uk

web: www.staffordshire.gov.uk/sams

A fine gallery housed in the 18th-century Shire Hall - one of Staffordshire's most magnificent buildings. It holds exhibitions of contemporary arts, contains historic courtrooms and a Crafts Council selected craft shop.

Times: Open all year Mon & Wed-Sat, 9.30-5; Tue 10-5; Sun 1-4. Gallery closes for exhibition changes and at BHs, please call for further details. **Facilities:** ℗ (5 mins walk) 💷 🍴 🥃 ৬ (Wheelchair lifts to some areas of the building) toilets for disabled shop ⊗ (ex guide dogs) 🎒

STOKE-ON-TRENT   MAP 07 SJ84

Ceramica

Market Place, Burslem ST6 3DS

➲ *(A4527 (signposted Tunstall). After 0.5m right onto B5051 for Burslem. Ceramica is in Old Town Hall in centre of town.)*

☎ 01782 832001

e-mail: info@ceramicauk.com

web: www.ceramicauk.com

A unique experience for all the family, Ceramica is housed in the Old Town Hall in the centre of Burslem, Mother Town of the Potteries. Explore the hands-on activities in Bizarreland, and learn how clay is transformed into china. Dig into history with the time team and take a magic carpet ride over the town. Discover the past, present and future of ceramics with the interactive displays in the Pavillions. Explore the Memory Bank and read the local news on Ceramica TV.

Times: ✱ Open all year Mon-Sat 9.30-5, Sun 10.30-4.30. For Xmas opening please telephone. **Facilities:** ℗ (charged) 🥃 ৬ (ramps, lift to all floors, tactile displays) toilets for disabled shop ⊗ (ex guide dogs) 🎒

Gladstone Working Pottery Museum

Uttoxeter Rd, Longton ST3 1PQ

➲ *(A50 then follow brown heritage signs.)*

☎ 01782 319232

e-mail: gladstone@stoke.gov.uk

web: www.stoke.gov.uk/gladstone

Located at the heart of the Potteries, Gladstone Pottery Museum is the last remaining Victorian Pottery industry. Whilst touring the original factory building discover what it was like for the men, women and children to live and work in a potbank during the era of the coal firing bottle ovens. In original workshops working potters can be found demonstrating traditional pottery skills. There are also lots of opportunities for you to have a go at pottery making, throw your own pot on the potters wheel, make china flowers and decorate pottery items to take home. Also explore Flushed with Pride, dedicated to the story of the development of the toilet, and The Tile Gallery, a fine collection which traces the development of decorative tiles.

Times: ✱ Open all year, daily 10-5 (last admission 4). Limited opening Xmas & New Year. **Facilities:** ℗ 💷 🍴 licensed ৬ (electric buggy available to loan) toilets for disabled shop ⊗ (ex guide dogs) 🎒

England

The Potteries Museum & Art Gallery `FREE`
Bethesda St, Hanley ST1 3DW

➲ *(M6 junct 15/16 take A500 to Stoke-on-Trent. Follow signs for city centre (Hanley), Cultural Quarter & The Potteries Museum)*

☎ 01782 232323
e-mail: museums@stoke.gov.uk
web: www.stoke.gov.uk/museums

The history of the Potteries under one roof, including a dazzling display of the world's finest collection of Staffordshire ceramics. Other displays introduce natural, local and archaeological history from in and around The Potteries, and a Mark 16 Spitfire commemorating its locally born designer - Reginald Mitchell.

Times: ✱ Open Mar-Oct, Mon-Sat 10-5, Sun 2-5; Nov-Feb, Mon-Sat 10-4, Sun 1-4. Closed 25 Dec-1 Jan. **Facilities:** ❷ (charged) ☕ ♿ (lift, induction loop, 2 wheelchairs available) toilets for disabled shop ⊗ (ex guide/assist dogs) ◀

Wedgwood Visitor Centre `2 for 1`
Barlaston ST12 9ES

➲ *(from M1, via A50 follow tourist signs to Stoke)*

☎ 01782 282986
e-mail: bookings@wedgwood.com
web: www.thewedgwoodvisitorcentre.com

At the Wedgwood Visitor Centre the whole family can share in almost 250 years of history and heritage that is still being lived today. Nothing

continued

is stage-managed or recreated just for visitors. What you see is the continuing life of this successful English manufacturer and exporter of fine quality ceramics. The tour features a film theatre, two exhibition areas, and a hands-on area.

Times: Open all year, Mon-Fri 9-5, Sat & Sun 10-5. Closed 24 Dec-1Jan inclusive. **Fee:** ✱ £8 (ch £6) £27 family. **Facilities:** ❷ ☕ ◉ licensed ♿ (fully wheelchair accessible/hearing loops) toilets for disabled shop ⊗ (ex guide dogs) ◀

TAMWORTH   MAP 07 SK20

Drayton Manor Theme Park
B78 3TW

➲ *(M42 junct 9/10, on A4091. Exit at T2 of M6 toll)*

☎ 08708 752252
e-mail: info@draytonmanor.co.uk
web: www.draytonmanor.co.uk

A popular family theme park with over 100 rides and attractions set in 280 acres of parkland and lakes. Drayton Manor features world-class rides like 'Apocalypse'- the world's first stand-up tower drop, 'Stormforce 10' - the best water ride in the country and 'Shockwave' - Europe's only stand-up rollercoaster. A new rollercoaster sensation is G-Force. Plus a host of family attractions, children's rides, zoo, museum, shops and attractions.

Times: Park open end Mar-Oct. Rides from 10.30-5 or 6. Zoo open all year. **Fee:** Please telephone or visit website for details. **Facilities:** ❷ ☕ ◉ licensed ♿ (ramps or lifts to most rides, some rides limited access) toilets for disabled shop garden centre ⊗ (ex in park & guide dogs) ◀

Tamworth Castle `2 for 1`
Tamworth Borough Council, Marmion House, Lichfield St B79 7NA

➲ *(M42 junct 10 & M6 junct 12, access via A5)*

☎ 01827 709629 & 709626
e-mail: heritage@tamworth.gov.uk
web: www.tamworthcastle.co.uk

The dramatic Norman motte and bailey castle was once the home of England's Royal Champions and today is (reputedly) haunted by two lady ghosts. Quizzes, dressing-up, brass rubbing and puzzles make it a great family destination. Special events throughout the year. Tamworth Castle was purchased from the town corporation 110 years ago in 2007.

continued

Tamworth Castle

Times: Open mid Feb-Oct: Tue-Sun 12-5.15, (last admission 4.30). Nov-mid Feb: Thu-Sun 12-5.15, (last admission 4.30). **Fee:** ✱ £4.95 (ch £2.95 & pen £3.95). Family £13. Prices subject to change. **Facilities:** Ⓟ (100yds & 400yds) ☕ 🍴 ♿ (one wheelchair for use inside the castle) shop ⊗ (ex guide dogs & hearing dogs) 📞

WALL   MAP 07 SK10

Wall Roman Site

Watling St WS14 0AW

➲ *(off A5)*

☎ 01543 480768

web: www.english-heritage.org.uk

Explore the haunting remains of a 2,000 year old wayside staging post situated along Watling Street, the famous Kent to North Wales Roman road.

Times: Open Apr-May & Sep-Oct, Wed-Sun, 10-5; Jun-Aug, daily, 10-6.
Fee: £3 (ch £1.50, concessions £2.30). Prices and opening times are subject to change in Spring 2007. Please check web site or call 0870 333 1181 for the most up to date prices and opening times when planning your visit.
Facilities: Ⓟ shop ⚏ ⚒

WESTON PARK   MAP 07 SJ81

Weston Park

TF11 8LE

➲ *(on A5 at Weston-under-Lizard, 30min from central Birmingham 3m off M54 junct 3 and 8m off M6 junct 12).*

☎ 01952 852100

e-mail: enquiries@weston-park.com

web: www.weston-park.com

Built in 1671, this fine mansion stands in elegant gardens and a vast park designed by 'Capability' Brown. Three lakes, a miniature railway, and a woodland adventure playground are to be found in the grounds, and in the house itself there is a magnificent collection of pictures, furniture and tapestries. There is also an animal centre and Deer Park.

Times: Open wknds from 15 Apr-Jul, then daily until 3 Sep. **Fee:** ✱ Park & Gardens £2.50 (ch 3-14 £1.50, pen £2). House, £2.25 (ch 3-14 £1.25, pen £1.75). Family ticket (2 ad & 3 ch) inc house, park & gardens £9.50.
Facilities: Ⓟ ☕ 🍴 licensed 🍴 ♿ (disabled route, access to restaurant & shop) toilets for disabled shop 📞

WHITTINGTON   MAP 07 SK10

Staffordshire Regiment Museum

Whittington Barracks WS14 9PY

➲ *(on A51 between Lichfield/Tamworth)*

☎ 01543 434390

e-mail: museum@rhqstaffords.fsnet.co.uk

Located next to Whittington Barracks, the museum tells the story of the soldiers of the Staffordshire Regiment and its predecessors. Exhibits include vehicles, uniforms, weapons, medals and memorabilia relating to three hundred years of regimental history, including distinguished service in the First and Second World Wars and the Gulf War. Visitors can experience a World War I trench system with sound effects and a World War II Anderson shelter.

Times: Open all year, Tue-Fri 10-4.30 (last admission 4); also Apr-Oct wknds and BH 12.30-4.30. Closed Xmas-New Year. Parties at other times by arrangement. **Fee:** ✱ £2.50 (ch £1, concessions £1.50) Family ticket £5. Regimental Association Members & serving soldiers free. **Facilities:** Ⓟ 🍴 ♿ (ramps, lowered kerbs, graded access to attraction) toilets for disabled shop ⊗ (ex guide dogs)

WILLOUGHBRIDGE   MAP 07 SJ74

The Dorothy Clive Garden

TF9 4EU

➲ *(on A51 between Nantwich & Stone)*

☎ 01630 647237

e-mail: info@dorothyclivegarden.co.uk

web: www.dorothyclivegarden.co.uk

This 200-year-old gravel quarry has been converted into a delightful woodland garden. The quarry is at the top of a small hill and the garden has fine views of the countryside and adjoining counties. There is a variety of rare trees and shrubs. The garden provides colour and interest throughout the seasons from spring to glowing autumn tints. Below the woodland garden is the hillside garden with daffodil and tulip walks and colourful borders.

Times: Open Etr-Oct, daily 10-5.30. **Facilities:** Ⓟ ☕ ♿ (wheelchairs for use, special route) toilets for disabled 📞

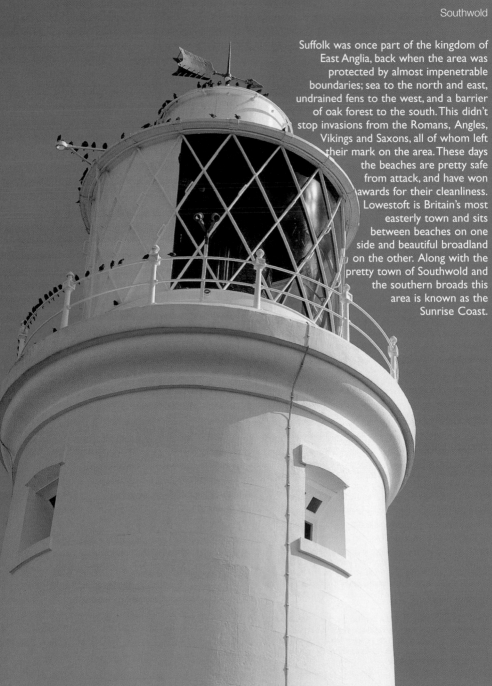

Suffolk

Southwold

Suffolk was once part of the kingdom of East Anglia, back when the area was protected by almost impenetrable boundaries; sea to the north and east, undrained fens to the west, and a barrier of oak forest to the south. This didn't stop invasions from the Romans, Angles, Vikings and Saxons, all of whom left their mark on the area. These days the beaches are pretty safe from attack, and have won awards for their cleanliness. Lowestoft is Britain's most easterly town and sits between beaches on one side and beautiful broadland on the other. Along with the pretty town of Southwold and the southern broads this area is known as the Sunrise Coast.

BUNGAY MAP 05 TM38

Otter Trust

Earsham NR35 2AF

⮑ (off A143, 1m W of Bungay)

☎ 01986 893470

The Otter Trust is the largest otter conservation organisation in Britain. Covering 23 acres, British and Asian otters can be seen under near natural conditions. There are three lakes and walks along the banks of the River Waveney. Hand-reared fallow deer are very tame and walk free in the grounds.

Times: Open Apr (or Good Fri if earlier)-Sep, daily 10.30-6. Last entry 5 **Fee:** £6 (ch over 3 £3). Disabled person in wheelchair free. **Facilities:** ❷ ☕ ♿ toilets for disabled shop ⊗ (ex guide dogs) ⊂

BURY ST EDMUNDS MAP 05 TL86

Moyse's Hall Museum

Cornhill IP33 1DX

⮑ (take Bury central exit from A14, follow signs for town centre, museum situated in town centre)

☎ 01284 706183

e-mail: moyses.hall@stedsbc/gov.uk

web: www.stedmundsbury.gov.uk/moyses.htm

Moyse's Hall is a 12th-century Norman house built of flint and stone which now serves as a local history museum, and among the fascinating exhibits are memorabilia of the notorious William Corder "Murder in the Red Barn". Other collections include the history of the town, archaeology and the Suffolk Regiment.

Times: Open all year, Mon-Fri 10.30-4.30, Sat & Sun 11-4. Closed 25-27 Dec and all BH. **Fee:** ✱ £2.60 (ch & concessions £2.10). Free for residents of St Edmundsbury. **Facilities:** ℗ (200yds 1hr max) Long term parking, short walk 🍴 ♿ (stairlift, lift, hearing loop, w/chair) toilets for disabled shop ⊗ (ex guide dogs)

EASTON MAP 05 TM25

Easton Farm Park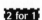

IP13 0EQ

⮑ (signed from A12 at Wickam Market, and from A1120)

☎ 01728 746475

e-mail: info@eastonfarmpark.co.uk

web: www.eastonfarmpark.co.uk

Award winning Farm Park on the banks of the River Deben. There are lots of breeds of farm animals, including Suffolk Punch horses, ponies, pigs, lambs, calves, goats, rabbits, guinea pigs and poultry. Chicks hatching and egg collecting daily. Free hug-a-bunny and pony rides every day.

Times: Open Mar-end Sep, daily 10.30-6. Also open Feb & Oct half term hols and wknds in Dec. **Fee:** £6.25 (ch under 1 free, ch 1-16 £4.75 pen £5.75). Family £20. **Facilities:** ❷ ☕ 🍴 ♿ (special parking and wheelchairs) toilets for disabled shop ⊂

EUSTON MAP 05 TL87

Euston Hall

IP24 2QP

⮑ (on A1088, 3m S of Thetford)

☎ 01842 766366

e-mail: lcampbell@euston-estate.co.uk

web: www.eustonhall.co.uk

Home of the Duke and Duchess of Grafton, this 18th-century house is notable for its fine collection of pictures, by Stubbs, Lely, Van Dyck and other Masters. The grounds were laid out by John Evelyn, William Kent and 'Capability' Brown, and include a 17th-century church in the style of Wren and a river walk to the newly restored watermill.

Times: Open 15 Jun-14 Sep, Thu only. Also open Sun 25 Jun, 16 Jul & 3 Sep, 2.30-5. **Fee:** ✱ £5 (ch 5-16 £2, concessions £4). Parties 12+ £4 each. Ground only £3. **Facilities:** ❷ ☕ ♿ toilets for disabled shop ⊗ (ex guide dogs)

FLIXTON MAP 05 TM38

Norfolk & Suffolk Aviation Museum

Buckeroo Way, The Street NR35 1NZ

⮑ (off A143, take B1062, 2m W of Bungay)

☎ 01986 896644

e-mail: nsam.flixton@virgin.net

web: www.aviationmuseum.net

Situated in the Waveney Valley, the museum has over 50 historic aircraft. There is also a Bloodhound surface-to-air missile, the 446th Bomb Group Museum, RAF Bomber Command Museum, the Royal Observer Corps Museum, RAF Air-Sea Rescue and Coastal Command and a souvenir shop. Among the displays are Decoy Sites and Wartime Deception, Fallen Eagles - Wartime Luftwaffe Crashes and an ex-Ipswich airport hangar made by Norwich company Boulton and Paul Ltd.

Times: Open Apr-Oct, Sun-Thu 10-5 (last admission 4); Nov-Mar, Tue, Wed & Sun 10-4 (last admission 3). Closed late Dec-early Jan. **Facilities:** ❷ ☕ ♿ (helper advised, ramps/paths to all buildings) toilets for disabled shop

FRAMLINGHAM MAP 05 TM26

Framlingham Castle

IP8 9BT

⮑ (on B1116)

☎ 01728 724189

web: www.english-heritage.org.uk

Walk the 12th-century battlements that encircle the castle site with their impressive thirteen towers. Exceptional views over the countryside and a very popular audio tour.

Times: Open all year, Apr-Sep, daily 10-6; Oct-Mar Thu-Mon, 10-4. Closed 24-26 Dec & 1 Jan. **Fee:** £4.50 (ch £2.30, concessions £3.40). Family ticket £11.30. Prices and opening times are subject to change in Spring 2007. Please check web site or call 0870 333 1181 for the most up to date prices and opening times when planning your visit. **Facilities:** ❷ ♿ shop ♨

HORRINGER   MAP 05 TL86

Ickworth House, Park & Gardens

IP29 5QE

➲ *(2.5m SW of Bury St Edmunds in village of Horringer on A143)*

☎ 01284 735270

e-mail: ickworth@ntrust.org.uk

web: www.nationaltrust.org.uk/ickworth

The eccentric Earl of Bristol created this equally eccentric house, begun in 1795, to display his collection of European art. The Georgian Silver Collection is considered the finest in private hands. 'Capability' Brown designed the parkland, and also featured are a vineyard, waymarked walks and an adventure playground. 2007 sees the 50th anniversary of the opening of Ickworth by the National Trust. Birthday celebrations will take place throughout the year.

Times: Open: House 19 Mar-4 Nov, Mon, Tue, Fri, wknds and BHs, 1-5 (4.30 in Oct and Nov) Garden: 19 Mar-4 Nov, Mon, Tue, Fri, wknds and BHs, 10-5. Oct-17 Mar, Mon, Tue, Fri, wknds and BHs, 11-4. Park: daily 8-8. **Fee:** ✱ House, Garden & Park £6.70 (National Trust members & ch under 5 free, ch £3) Garden & park £3.10 (ch 90p). Discount for pre-booked parties. **Facilities:** ❷ ○❙ licensed ▥ ♿ (Braille guide, batricars, hearing loop, large print guides) toilets for disabled shop ⊗ (ex guide dogs and on lead) ❦ ◀

IPSWICH   MAP 05 TM14

Christchurch Mansion   **FREE**

Soane St IP4 2BE

➲ *(S side of Christchurch Park, close to town centre)*

☎ 01473 433554 & 213761

e-mail: christchurch.mansion@ipswich.gov.uk

web: www.ipswich.gov.uk

The house was built in 1548 on the site of an Augustinian priory. Set in a beautiful park, it displays period rooms and an art gallery which has changing exhibitions. The Suffolk Artists' Gallery has a collection of paintings by Constable and Gainsborough.

Times: Open all year, Tue-Sat 10-5 (dusk in winter), Sun 12-4.30 (dusk in winter). Closed Good Fri, 24-26 Dec & 1-2 Jan. Open BH Mon. **Facilities:** ❷ (10 min walk) ▥ ♿ (tape guide for partially sighted) toilets for disabled shop ⊗

Ipswich Museum   **FREE**

High St IP1 3QH

➲ *(follow tourist signs to Crown St car park. Museum 3 mins walk from here)*

☎ 01473 433550

e-mail: museum.service@ipswich.gov.uk

The Museum has sections on Victorian Natural History, Suffolk wildlife, Suffolk geology, Roman Suffolk, Anglo-Saxon Ipswich and Peoples of the World. There is also one of the best bird collections in the country.

Times: Open all year, Tue-Sat 10-5. Closed Sun, BHs, 24-26 Dec & 1 Jan. **Facilities:** ❷ (3 min walk) ▥ ♿ (lift) toilets for disabled shop ⊗ (ex guide dogs)

LAVENHAM   MAP 05 TL94

Lavenham Guildhall

Market Place CO10 9QZ

➲ *(Lavenham Market Place. A1141 & B1071)*

☎ 01787 247646

e-mail: jane.gosling@nationaltrust.org.uk

web: www.nationaltrust.org.uk/regions/eastofengland

The Guildhall of Corpus Christi is one of the finest timber framed buildings in Britain. It was built around 1530 by the prosperous Corpus Christi Guild, for religious rather than commercial reasons. The hall now houses a local history museum telling the story of Lavenham's 15th- and 16th-century cloth-trade riches. Visitors can also see the walled garden with its 19th-century lock-up and mortuary.

Times: Open Mar & Nov, Sat & Sun 11-4; Apr, Wed-Sun 11-5; May-Oct daily 11-5. (Closed Good Fri but open BH Mon) **Fee:** ✱ £3.50 (ch £1.50). Parties £3 each. School parties by arrangement £1 per ch. **Facilities:** ❷ (adjacent) ▥ ♿ (photo album of museum, Braille guide) shop ⊗ (ex guide dogs) ❦

LEISTON   MAP 05 TM46

Leiston Abbey   **FREE**

IP16 4TB

➲ *(N of Leiston, off B1069)*

☎ 01728 831354 832500

e-mail: admin@leistonabbey.co.uk

web: www.leistonabbey.co.uk

For hundreds of years this 14th-century abbey was used as a farm and its church became a barn. A Georgian house, now used as a school for young musicians, was built into its fabric and remains of the choir, the church transepts and parts of the cloisters still stand.

Times: Open at any reasonable time. **Facilities:** ❷ ▥ ♿ ⊗ (ex on lead)

Long Shop Museum   **2 for 1**

Main St IP16 4ES

➲ *(Turn off A12, follow B1119 from Saxmundham to Leiston. Museum is in the middle of town)*

☎ 01728 832189

e-mail: longshop@care4free.net

web: www.longshop.care4free.net

Discover the Magic of Steam through a visit to the world famous traction engine manufacturers. Trace the history of the factory and Richard Garrett engineering. See the traction engines and road rollers in the very place that they were built. Soak up the atmosphere of the Long Shop, built in 1852 as one of the first production line engineering halls in the world. An award-winning museum with five exhibition halls full of items from the glorious age of steam and covering 200 years of local, social and industrial history.

Times: Open Apr-Oct, Mon-Sat 10-5, Sun 11-5. **Fee:** £4 (ch under 5 free, ch £2, concessions £3.50) Family £10. **Facilities:** ❷ ▥ ♿ (wheelchair available) toilets for disabled shop ⊗ (ex guide dogs)

LINDSEY MAP 05 TL94

Lindsey Chapel FREE
Rose Green

⮕ *(on unclass road 0.5m E of Rose Green)*
web: www.english-heritage.org.uk

Built mainly in the 13th century, this small thatched, flint-and-stone chapel incorporates some earlier work.

Times: Open all year, daily 10-4. **Facilities:** ৬ ⊛ ♯

LONG MELFORD MAP 05 TL84

Kentwell Hall
CO10 9BA

⮕ *(signposted off A134, between Bury St Edmunds & Sudbury)*
☎ 01787 310207
e-mail: info@kentwell.co.uk
web: www.kentwell.co.uk

Kentwell Hall is a moated red brick Tudor manor with gardens, woodland walks and a rare breeds farm. Restoration started in 1971 and still continues today. The house and grounds are open to the public at certain times of the year, and recreations of Tudor and 1940s life take place at weekends. Ring for details.

Times: Open: Gardens & Farm: Mar, Sun, 11-4. House, Gardens and Farm: Apr-Jun, Sun-Wed and daily in Jul, Aug and Sep 12-5. Open: BH and school hols. **Fee:** ✱ House, Garden & Farm £7.15 (ch £4.60, pen £6.15). Garden & Farm only £5 (ch £3.30, pen £4.30). **Facilities:** ❷ ▣ ⊞ ৬ (wheelchair ramps & 3 wheelchairs for loan) toilets for disabled shop ⊛ (ex guide dogs) ◀

Melford Hall
CO10 9AA

⮕ *(off A134, 3m N of Sudbury, next to village green)*
☎ 01787 379228 & 376395
e-mail: melford@nationaltrust.org.uk
web: www.nationaltrust.org.uk

Set in the unspoilt village of Long Melford, the house has changed little externally since 1578 when Queen Elizabeth I was entertained here, and retains its original panelled banqueting hall. It has been the home of the Hyde Parker Family since 1786. There is a Regency library, Victorian bedrooms, good collections of furniture and porcelain

continued

and a small display of items connected with Beatrix Potter, who was related to the family. The garden contains some spectacular specimen trees and a banqueting house and there is an attractive walk through the park.

Times: Open Apr (Sat & Sun) & 11-13 Apr. May-Sep (Wed-Sun); Oct (Sat & Sun); BH Mon. Closed Good Fri; 1.30-5. **Fee:** £5.20 (ch £2.60) Family £13. National Trust Members free. **Facilities:** ❷ ▣ ৬ (stairlift, ramp, Braille & large print guides) toilets for disabled garden centre ⊛ (ex guide dogs) ▨

LOWESTOFT MAP 05 TM59

East Anglia Transport Museum
Chapel Rd, Carlton Colville NR33 8BL

⮕ *(3m SW of Lowestoft, follow brown signs from A12, A146 & B1384)*
☎ 01502 518459
e-mail: enquiries@eatm.org.uk
web: www.eatm.org.uk

A particular attraction of this museum is the reconstructed 1930s street scene which is used as a setting for working vehicles: visitors can ride by tram, trolley bus and narrow gauge railway. Other motor, steam and electrical vehicles are exhibited. There is also a woodland picnic area served by trams.

Times: Open: Apr-Sep, Sun and BH 11-5. From Jun, Thu and Sat, 2-4. **Fee:** £5 (ch 5-15 £3.50) pen £4. Price includes rides. Party rates available. **Facilities:** ❷ ▣ ৬ toilets for disabled shop ◀

Maritime Museum
Sparrow Nest Gardens, Whapload Rd
NR32 1XG

⮕ *(on A12, 100mtrs N of Lowestoft Lighthouse, turn right down Ravine)*
☎ 01502 561963

Models of ancient and modern fishing and commercial boats, fishing gear and shipwrights' tools are among the exhibits. There is also an exhibition of the evolution of lifeboats, and a replica of the aft cabin of a steam drifter, as well as an art gallery.

Times: Open 6-15 Apr; 29 Apr-28 Oct, daily 10-5. **Fee:** 75p (ch & students 25p, pen 50p). **Facilities:** ❷ ⊞ ৬ (hear for all) toilets for disabled shop ⊛ (ex guide dogs)

New Pleasurewood Hills
Leisure Way, Corton NR32 5DZ

⮕ *(off A12 at Lowestoft)*
☎ 01502 586000 (admin) & 508200 (info)
e-mail: info@pleasurewoodhills.co.uk
web: www.pleasurewoodhills.co.uk

There are over 40 rides, shows and attractions at New Pleasurewood Hills, set in 50 acres of beautiful parkland. Old favourites such as the Tidal Wave Watercoaster and the Fairytale Fantasy Ride combine with more recent attractions such as Formula K Raceway Go-Karts, the new 100ft Drop Tower, the Crazy Coaster and the Double Decker Carousel.

Times: ✱ Open Apr-Oct & Xmas. Telephone for details. **Facilities:** ❷ ▣ ⓞ licensed ⊞ ৬ (all shows accessible, most ride operators able to assist) toilets for disabled shop ⊛ (ex guide dogs) ◀

England

NEWMARKET
MAP 05 TL66

National Horseracing Museum and Tours
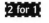
99 High St CB8 8JH

⮑ *(located in centre of High St)*
☎ 01638 667333
web: www.nhrm.co.uk

This friendly award-winning museum tells the story of the people and horses involved in racing in Britain. Have a go on the horse simulator in the hands-on gallery and chat to retired jockeys and trainers about their experiences. Special mini bus tours visit the gallops, a stable and yard and horses' swimming pool.

Times: Open Etr-end Oct, Tue-Sun (also BH Mons & Mons in Jul & Aug) 11-5. 10 opening on race days. **Fee:** ✱ £4.50 (ch £1.50, concessions £3.50). Family ticket £10 (2ad+2ch). **Facilities:** ℗ (300yds) (coach drop off in front of museum) 🍽 ⓘ licensed & (ramps & lift) toilets for disabled shop ⊗ (ex guide dogs) 🍴

ORFORD
MAP 05 TM45

Orford Castle
IP12 2ND

⮑ *(on B1084)*
☎ 01394 450472
web: www.english-heritage.org.uk

A great keep of Henry II with three huge towers and commanding views over Orford Ness. Climb the spiral staircase leading to a maze of rooms and passageways.

Times: Open all year, Apr-Sep, daily 10-6; Oct-Mar, Thu-Mon, 10-4. Closed 24-26 Dec & 1 Jan **Fee:** £4.50 (ch £2.30, concessions £3.40) Family £11.30. Prices and opening times are subject to change in Spring 2007. Please check web site or call 0870 333 1181 for the most up to date prices and opening times when planning your visit. **Facilities:** ❷ shop ⊗ ⊞

SAXTEAD GREEN
MAP 05 TM26

Saxtead Green Post Mill
The Mill House IP13 9QQ

⮑ *(2.5m NW of Framlingham on A1120)*
☎ 01728 685789
web: www.english-heritage.org.uk

A post mill since 1287, Saxtead Green Post Mill is still in working order. Climb the wooden stairs to the various floors full of fascinating mill machinery. An audio tour explains the workings of the mill.

Times: Open Apr-Sep, Fri-Sat & BHs 12-5 **Fee:** £2.70 (ch £1.40, concessions £2). Prices and opening times are subject to change in Spring 2007. Please check web site or call 0870 333 1181 for the most up to date prices and opening times when planning your visit. **Facilities:** shop ⊗ ⊞

We endeavour to be as accurate as possible, but changes to times and other information can occur after the guide has gone to press.

STOWMARKET
MAP 05 TM05

Museum of East Anglian Life
IP14 1DL

⮑ *(located in centre of Stowmarket, signed from A14 & B1115)*
☎ 01449 612229
e-mail: enquiries@eastanglianlife.org.uk
web: www.eastanglianlife.org.uk

This 70-acre, all-weather museum is set in an attractive river-valley site with 3km of woodland and riverside nature trails. There are reconstructed buildings, including a working water mill, a smithy and also a wind pump, and the Boby Building houses craft workshops. There are displays on Victorian domestic life, gypsies, farming and industry. These include working steam traction engines, the only surviving pair of Burrell ploughing engines of 1879, and a working Suffolk Punch horse. The William Bone Building, illustrates the history of Ransomes of Ipswich.

Times: Open late March-end Oct. **Fee:** £6.50 (ch 4-16 £3.50, concessions £5.50). Family ticket (2ad+2/3ch) £17.50. 1ad family £11. Party 10+. **Facilities:** ℗ (adjacent) 🍽 ⓘ & (w/chairs & 2 buggies available, special vehicle facilities) toilets for disabled shop ⊗ (ex on a lead) 🍴

SUDBURY
MAP 05 TL84

Gainsborough's House
46 Gainsborough St CO10 2EU

⮑ *(situated in centre of Sudbury. Follow pedestrian signs from town centre car parks or from train stn)*
☎ 01787 372958
e-mail: mail@gainsborough.org
web: www.gainsborough.org

The birthplace of Thomas Gainsborough RA (1727-88). The Georgian-fronted town house, with an attractive walled garden, displays more of the artist's work than any other gallery, together with 18th-century furniture and memorabilia. There's a varied programme of exhibitions throughout the year including fine art, craft, photography, printmaking and sculpture.

Times: Open all year. Mon-Sat 10-5. closed Sun, Good Fri & Xmas-New Year. **Fee:** £4 (concessions £3.20, ch and students £1.50). Family £8. **Facilities:** ℗ (300yds) (no parking in Gainsborough Street) 🍽 ⓘ & (lift to first floor) toilets for disabled shop ⊗ (ex guide dogs) 🍴

SUFFOLK WILDLIFE PARK
MAP 05 TM58

Africa Alive!
Kessingland NR33 7TF

⮑ *(25min S of Gt. Yarmouth just S of Lowestoft off A12)*
☎ 01502 740291
e-mail: info@africa-alive.co.uk
web: www.africa-alive.co.uk

Set in 80 acres of dramatic coastal parkland, visitors can explore the sights and sounds of Africa at Africa Alive! There are giraffes, rhinos, cheetah, hyenas and many more, including a birds eye view of the new lion enclosure. There are lots of daily feeding talks and animal encounter sessions, a magnificent bird of prey display, and free journey round the park with live commentary.

Times: Open all year, daily from 10. Closed 25-26 Dec. **Fee:** ✱ Please call park reception for full admission prices **Facilities:** ❷ 🍽 🍽 & (wheelchairs available for hire) toilets for disabled shop ⊗ 🍴

WESTLETON
MAP 05 TM46

RSPB Nature Reserve Minsmere
IP17 3BY

⮞ *(signed from A12 at Yoxford & Blythburgh and from Westleton Village)*

☎ 01728 648281
e-mail: minsmere@rspb.org.uk
web: www.rspb.org.uk/reserves/minsmere

Set on the beautiful Suffolk coast, Minsmere offers an enjoyable day out for all. Nature trails take you through a variety of habitats to the excellent birdwatching hides. Spring is a time for birdsong, including nightingales and booming bitterns. In summer, you can watch breeding avocets and marsh harriers. Autumn is excellent for migrants, and in winter, hundreds of wildfowl visit the reserve. Look out for otters and red deer. The visitor centre has a well-stocked shop and licensed tearoom, and you can find out more about the reserve. There is a programme of events throughout the year, including several for children and families. Self-guided activity booklets for families.

Times: Open daily (ex 25-26 Dec) 9-9 (or dusk if earlier). Visitor centre: 9-5 (9-4 Nov-Jan). **Fee:** £5 (ch £1.50, concessions £3). Family ticket £10. RSPB members free **Facilities:** ♿ 🖥 🖼 ♿ (batricar available for loan, booking advised) toilets for disabled shop ⊗ (ex guide dogs) 🍴

WEST STOW
MAP 05 TL87

West Stow Anglo Saxon Village

West Stow Country Park, Icklingham Rd
IP28 6HG

⮞ *(off A1101, 7m NW of Bury St Edmunds. Follow brown heritage signs)*

☎ 01284 728718
e-mail: weststow@stedsbc.gov.uk
web: www.stedmundsbury.gov.uk/weststow.htm

The village is a reconstruction of a pagan Anglo-Saxon settlement dated 420-650 AD. Seven buildings have been reconstructed on the site of the excavated settlement. There is a Visitors' Centre and a children's play area. A new Anglo-Saxon Centre houses the original objects found on the site. The village is located in the West Stow Country Park. The park is 125 acres with river, lake, woodland and heath and has many trails and paths.

Times: Open all year, daily 10-5. Last entry 4 (3.30 in Winter) Except Xmas period. **Fee:** ✱ £5 (ch £4). Family ticket £15. (Prices subject to change for special events) **Facilities:** ♿ 🖥 ♿ (ramps) toilets for disabled shop ⊗ (ex guide dogs) 🍴

WOODBRIDGE
MAP 05 TM24

Sutton Hoo
2 for 1

IP12 3DJ

⮞ *(off B1083 Woodbridge to Bawdsey road. Follow signs from A12 avoiding Woodbridge itself)*

☎ 01394 389700
e-mail: suttonhoo@nationaltrust.org.uk
web: www.nationaltrust.org.uk

Discovered in 1939 and described as page one of English history, this is the site of one of the most important archaeological finds in Britain's history: the complete 7th-century ship burial of an Anglo-Saxon king, which had been missed by grave-robbers, and lay undisturbed for 1300 years. Sutton Hoo displays reveal how Anglo-Saxon nobles lived, went to war and found a new kingdom in East Anglia. The centre-piece is a full sized replica of an Anglo-Saxon warrior king's burial chamber. The discoveries at Sutton Hoo changed forever our perceptions of the dark ages, by revealing a culture rich in craftsmanship, trade and legend.

Times: Open: Jun, Wed-Sun, 11-5. Jul-Aug, daily. 11-5. Sep-Oct, Wed-Sun, 11-5. Nov-Feb, Sat-Sun, 11-4. Open: BH and School hols. **Fee:** ✱ £5.50 (ch £2.50) Family £13.50. Free to NT members **Facilities:** ♿ 🍴 licensed 🖼 ♿ (ramps, electric buggy hire) toilets for disabled shop 🐾 🍴

Woodbridge Tide Mill
Tide Mill Way IP12

⮞ *(follow signs for Woodbridge off A12, 7m E of Ipswich Tide Mill is on riverside)*

☎ 01728 746959
e-mail: wtm@redpoll.co.uk
web: www.tidemill.org.uk

The machinery of this 18th-century mill has been completely restored. There are photographs and working models on display. Situated on a busy quayside, the unique building looks over towards the historic site of the Sutton Hoo Ship Burial. Every effort is made to run the machinery for a while whenever the mill is open and the tides are favourable.

Times: Open Etr, then daily May-Sep; Apr, Oct wknds only, 11-5.
Facilities: ♿ (400yds) (no parking or turning in Tide Mill Way) 🖼 ♿ shop ⊗ (ex guide dogs)

Surrey

River Thames,
Hampton Court

Despite its proximity to London, Surrey has the
reputation of being Britain's most wooded county,
hence the description 'leafy Surrey', and can boast some
of England's most beautiful countryside. The North
Downs provide spectacular views across river valleys,
woods and forestry – on a clear day the Channel coast
can be seen from Leith Hill. In the northern part of the
county the River Thames passes through Runnymede,
where the Magna Carta was signed in 1215, on its way
through London to the sea.

ASH VALE   MAP 04 SU85

Army Medical Services Museum   **FREE**
Keogh Barracks GU12 5RQ
➲ *(M3 junct 4 on A331 to Mytchett then follow tourist signs)*
☎ 01252 868612
e-mail: armymedicalmuseum@btinternet.com
web: www.ams-museum.org.uk

The museum traces the history of Army medicine, nursing, dentistry and veterinary science from 1660 until the present day. Medical equipment and ambulances complement displays including uniforms and medals.

Times: Open all year, Mon-Fri 10-3.30. Closed Xmas, New Year & BH. Wknds by appointment only. **Facilities:** ♿ 🅿️ & (hand rails, wide doors, audio guide, Braille guides) toilets for disabled shop ✖ (ex guide dogs)

CHERTSEY   MAP 04 TQ06

Thorpe Park
Staines Rd KT16 8PN
➲ *(M25 junct 11 or 13 and follow signs via A320 to Thorpe Park)*
☎ 0870 444 4466
web: www.thorpepark.com

Fun-loving families and thrill-seekers come alive at Thorpe Park, home to some of the most exciting rollercoaster experiences in Europe. There are over 25 rides, including Stealth, Europes fastest and tallest launch rollercoaster. Another unique ride is Colossus, the worlds first 10-loop roller.

Times: Open: 15 Mar-5 Nov (ex 2-5, 9-12 Oct). Opening times vary throughout, check in advance. **Fee:** ✱ From £28.50 (ch under 1m free, ch 4-11 from £20). **Facilities:** 🅿️ 🚭 🍴 licensed & (some rides not accessible, wheelchair hire available) toilets for disabled shop ✖ (ex assist dogs) ◀

EAST CLANDON   MAP 04 TQ05

Hatchlands Park
GU4 7RT
➲ *(E of Guildford, off A246)*
☎ 01483 222482
e-mail: hatchlands@nationaltrust.org.uk
web: www.nationaltrust.org.uk/hatchlands

Built in the 1750s for Admiral Boscawen, hero of the battle of Louisburg and set in a beautiful 430-acre Repton Park offering a variety of park and woodlands walks, Hatchlands boasts the earliest known decorative works by Robert Adam. Hatchlands is home to the Cobbe collection, the world's largest group of keyboard instruments associated with famous composers. There is also a small garden by Gertrude Jekyll and a beautiful bluebell wood in May.

Times: ✱ House & Gardens: Apr-Oct, Tue-Thu & Sun, 2-5.30 (also open BH & Fri in Aug). Park Walks open Apr-Oct, daily, 11-6. **Fee:** ✱ £6 (ch £3). Park walks £3 (ch £1.50). Family ticket £15. Combined ticket with Clandon Park £9 (ch £4.50). Family £22.50. **Facilities:** 🅿️ 🍴 licensed 🚭 & (wheelchair available & parking) toilets for disabled shop 🌿 ◀

FARNHAM   MAP 04 SU84

Birdworld & Underwaterworld
Holt Pound GU10 4LD
➲ *(3m S of Farnham on A325)*
☎ 01420 22140
e-mail: bookings@birdworld.co.uk
web: www.birdworld.co.uk

Birdworld is the largest bird collection in the country and includes toucans, pelicans, flamingoes, ostriches and many others. Underwater World is a tropical aquarium with brilliant lighting that shows off collections of marine and freshwater fish, as well as the swampy depths of the alligator exhibit. Visitors can also visit some beautiful gardens, the Jenny Wren farm and the Heron Theatre.

Times: Open daily, 10-6 (summer), 10-4.30 (winter). **Fee:** ✱ £9.95 (ch 3-14 £8.25, pen £8.25). Family ticket (2ad+2ch) £32.95 **Facilities:** 🅿️ 🍴 🚭 & (wheelchairs available) toilets for disabled shop garden centre ✖ (ex guide dogs) ◀

Farnham Castle Keep
Castle Hill GU6 0AG
➲ *(0.5m N on A287)*
☎ 01252 713393
web: www.english-heritage.org.uk

A motte and bailey castle, once one of the seats of the Bishop of Winchester, has been in continuous occupation since the 12th-century.

Times: Open Apr-Sep, 12-5, Fri-Sun & BHs **Fee:** £2.80 (ch £1.40, concessions £2.10). Prices and opening times are subject to change in Spring 2007. Please check web site or call 0870 333 1181 for the most up to date prices and opening times when planning your visit. **Facilities:** 🅿️ shop ♿

GODSTONE

MAP 05 TQ35

Godstone Farm

RH9 8LX

⮠ *(M25 junct 6, S of village, signed)*

☎ 01883 742546

e-mail: havefun@godstonefarm.co.uk

web: www.godstonefarm.co.uk

An ideal day out for children, Godstone Farm has lots of friendly animals, big sand pits and play areas. The Indoor Play Barn costs 80p extra on rainy days.

Times: Open Mar-Oct, 10-6 (last admission 5); Nov-Feb 10-5 (last admission 4). Closed 25 & 26 Dec. **Fee:** ✱ Contact for admission prices. **Facilities:** ❷ ☕ 🗐 ♿ toilets for disabled shop ⊗ (ex guide dogs) ◼

GREAT BOOKHAM

MAP 04 TQ15

Polesden Lacey

RH5 6BD

⮠ *(2m S off A246 from village of Bookham)*

☎ 01372 452048

e-mail: polesdenlacey@nationaltrust.org.uk

web: www.nationaltrust.org.uk/polesdenlacey

King George VI and Queen Elizabeth (the Queen Mother) spent part of their honeymoon here, and photographs of other notable guests can be seen. The house is handsomely furnished and full of charm, and it is set in spacious grounds. There is also a summer festival, where concerts and plays are performed. Please phone 01372 452048 for details of special events.

Times: Open all year. Grounds, Garden & Landscape walks: daily 11-6. House: 12 Apr-29 Oct, Wed-Sun 11-5. Grounds, garden and landscape walks daily 11-5. Also BH Mon 11-5 (last admission 30mins before closing) **Fee:** ✱ Ground, Garden & Landscape walks: £6 (ch under 17 half price, ch under 5 free). Family ticket £15; House: £3 extra. Family £7.50 extra. Party 15+ **Facilities:** ❷ ☕ 🍽 licensed 🗐 ♿ (Braille guide & disabled parking by arrangement) toilets for disabled shop garden centre ⊗ (ex on lead) 🐾 ◼

GUILDFORD

MAP 04 SU94

Dapdune Wharf

Wharf Rd GU1 4RR

⮠ *(off Woodbridge Rd to rear of Surrey County Cricket Ground)*

☎ 01483 561389

e-mail: riverwey@nationaltrust.org.uk

web: www.nationaltrust.org.uk/riverwey

The visitor centre at Dapdune Wharf is the centrepiece of one of the National Trust's most unusual properties, the River Way Navigations. A series of interactive exhibits and displays allow you to discover the fascinating story of Surrey's secret waterway, one of the first British rivers to be made navigable. See where huge Wey barges were built and climb aboard *Reliance*, one of the last surviving barges. Children's trails and special events run throughout the season.

Times: Open Apr-Oct, Thu-Mon 11-5. River trips Thu-Mon 11-5 (conditions permitting) **Fee:** ✱ £3.50 (ch £2). Family ticket £10. National Trust Members free. **Facilities:** ❷ ☕ 🗐 ♿ (Braille guide) toilets for disabled shop ⊗ (ex on leads) 🐾

Guildford House Gallery

FREE

155 High St GU1 3AJ

⮠ *(N side of High St, opposite Sainsbury's)*

☎ 01483 444740

e-mail: guildfordhouse@guildford.gov.uk

web: www.guildfordhouse.co.uk

An impressive building in its own right, Guildford House dates from 1660 and has been Guildford's art gallery since 1959. A changing selection from the Borough's Art Collection is on display, including pastel portraits by John Russell, topographical paintings and contemporary craftwork, as well as temporary exhibitions.

Times: Open Tue-Sat 10-4.45. Closed Good Fri, 25-26 Dec **Facilities:** ℗ (100yds) ☕ 🍽 🗐 ♿ (ramps available for w/chair access to ground floor) shop ⊗ (ex guide dogs) ◼

Loseley Park

2 for 1

GU3 1HS

⮠ *(2m SW of Guildford, off A3 onto B3000)*

☎ 01483 304440 & 505501

e-mail: enquiries@loseley-park.com

web: www.loseley-park.com

Magnificent Elizabethan mansion, home of the More-Molyneux family for over 450 years. Set in magnificent parkland scenery. Based on a Gertude Jekyll design. The walled garden contains five gardens each with its own theme and character. These include the award-wining Rose Garden, Vine Walk, Fruit, Flower Garden and the Serene White Fountain Garden.

Times: Open Grounds and Walled Garden: May-Sep, Tue-Sun & BH 11-5. House May-Aug, Tue-Thu, Sun & BH 1-5. **Fee:** ✱ House & Gardens £7 (ch £3.50, ch under 5 free, concessions £6.50). Gardens only £4 (ch £2, concessions £3.50). Discount for pre-booked groups. Garden season ticket £12 (admits ticket holder & guest from May-Sep) **Facilities:** ❷ ☕ 🍽 licensed ♿ (wheelchair available, parking outside shop) toilets for disabled shop garden centre ⊗ (ex guide dogs) ◼

HASCOMBE

MAP 04 SU94

Winkworth Arboretum

Hascombe Rd GU8 4AD

⮠ *(2m SE of Godalming, E side of B2130, follow brown tourist signs from Godalming)*

☎ 01483 208477

e-mail: winkwortharboretum@nationaltrust.org.uk

web: www.nationaltrust.org.uk/winkwortharboretum

This lovely woodland covers a hillside of nearly 100 acres, with fine views over the North Downs. The best times to visit are April and May, for the azaleas, bluebells and other flowers, and October for the autumn colours. A delightful Victorian boathouse is open Apr-Oct with fine views over Rowes Flashe lake. Many rare trees and shrubs in group plantings for spring and autumn colour effect.

Times: Open all year, daily during daylight hours. (Could close when weather is bad) **Fee:** ✱ £4.50 (ch £2). Family ticket £10, additional family member £1.75. **Facilities:** ❷ ☕ 🗐 ♿ (suggested route, free entry for helpers) toilets for disabled shop ⊗ (ex on lead) 🐾 ◼

OUTWOOD — MAP 04 TQ34

Outwood Windmill

Outwood Common RH1 5PW

➲ (M25 junct 6, take A25 through Godstone towards Redhill, after 1m turn S off A25 at Bletchingly, between The Prince Albert & The White Hart. Mill 3m on left)

☎ 01342 843458 & 843644

e-mail: info@outwoodwindmill.co.uk

web: www.outwoodwindmill.co.uk

This award-winning example of a post-mill dates from 1665 and is the oldest working windmill in England and one of the best preserved in existence. Standing 400ft above sea level, it is surrounded by common land and National Trust property. Ducks and geese wander freely in the grounds.

Times: Open: Every Sun from Etr-Sep and BH. Mon and Wed for booked parties. **Fee:** £3 (ch £2). **Facilities:** ℗ (10yds) ⬚ ♿ toilets for disabled shop

PAINSHILL PARK — MAP 04 TQ06

Painshill Park   `2 for 1`

Portsmouth Rd KT11 1JE

➲ (W of Cobham on A245)

☎ 01932 868113

e-mail: info@painshill.co.uk

web: www.painshill.co.uk

Within its 160 acres created by Charles Hamilton as a series of subtle and surprising vistas, its landscapes (The Hamilton Landscapes) include authentic 18th-century plantings, working vineyard, Gothic Temple, Chinese Bridge, Crystal Grotto, Turkish Tent, restored Hermitage and Gothic Tower. The 2 for 1 voucher is not valid for special events.

Times: Open: Apr-Oct, 10.30-6. Nov-Mar, 10.30-4. Closed 25-26 Dec. **Fee:** £6.60 (ch 5-16 £3.85, concessions £5.80). Pre-booked adult groups 10+ £5.80. Please phone 01932 868113 for prices. For more details check website. **Facilities:** ℗ ⬛ ⬚ ♿ (wheelchairs & buggies available - pre-booked) toilets for disabled shop ⊗ (ex on lead) ⬛

REIGATE — MAP 04 TQ24

Reigate Priory Museum   `2 for 1`

Bell St RH2 7RL

➲ (in Priory Park close to town centre, use Bell St car park on A217)

☎ 01737 222550

web: www.reigatepriorymuseum.org.uk

The Priory Museum is housed in Reigate Priory which was originally founded before 1200, this Grade I listed building was converted to a mansion in Tudor times. Notable features include the magnificent Holbein fireplace, 17th-early 18th century oak staircase and murals. The small museum has changing exhibitions on a wide range of subjects, designed to appeal to both adults and children. The collection includes domestic bygones, local history and costume.

Times: Open Etr-early Dec, Wed & Sat, 2-4.30 in term time. **Fee:** ✱ Donations welcome. **Facilities:** ℗ (50yds) ⬚ ♿ (hands on facilities) shop ⊗ (ex assist dogs)

TILFORD — MAP 04 SU84

Rural Life Centre   `2 for 1`

Reeds Rd GU10 2DL

➲ (off A287, 3m S of Farnham, signed)

☎ 01252 795571

e-mail: rural.life@lineone.net

web: www.rural-life.org.uk

The museum covers village life from 1750 to 1960. It is set in over ten acres of garden and woodland and incorporates purpose-built and reconstructed buildings, including a chapel. Displays show village crafts and trades, such as wheelwrighting, thatching, ploughing and gardening. The historic village playground provides entertainment for children and there is an arboretum featuring over 100 trees from around the world.

Times: Open mid Mar-end Oct, Wed-Sun & BH 10-5; Winter Wed & Sun only 11-4 **Fee:** £5.50 (ch £3.50 & pen £4.50). Family ticket £16 (2ad+2ch) **Facilities:** ℗ ⬛ ⑩ licensed ⬚ ♿ (3 wheelchairs for use) toilets for disabled shop ⬛

WEST CLANDON — MAP 04 TQ05

Clandon Park

GU4 7RQ

➲ (E of Guildford on A247)

☎ 01483 222482

e-mail: clandonpark@nationaltrust.org.uk

web: www.nationaltrust.org.uk/clandonpark

A grand Palladian mansion built c.1730 by the Venetian architect Giacomo Leoni, and notable for its magnificent marble hall. The house is filled with the superb Gubbay collection of 18th-century furniture, porcelain, textiles and carpets. The attractive gardens contain a parterre, grotto, sunken Dutch garden and a Maori meetinghouse.

Times: House and Garden open Apr-Oct, Tue-Thu & Sun 11-5 (also BHs) **Fee:** ✱ House & Garden £6.50 (ch £3.20). Family ticket £16. Combined ticket with Hatchlands Park £9 (ch £4.50). Family £22.50 **Facilities:** ℗ ⑩ licensed ⬚ ♿ (wheelchairs, Braille guide & disabled parking) toilets for disabled shop ⊗ (ex guide dogs) ⬥ ⬛

WEYBRIDGE

MAP 04 TQ06

Brooklands Museum

Brooklands Rd KT13 0QN

➲ *(M25 junct 10/11, museum off B374)*

☎ 01932 857381

e-mail: info@brooklandsmuseum.com

web: www.brooklandsmuseum.com

Brooklands racing circuit was the birthplace of British motorsport and aviation. From 1907 to 1987 it was a world-renowned centre of engineering excellence. The Museum features old banked track and the 1-in-4 Test Hill. Many of the original buildings have been restored including the Clubhouse, the Shell and BP Petrol Pagodas, and the Malcolm Campbell Sheds in the Motoring Village. Many motorcycles, cars and aircraft are on display. Ring for details of special events.

Times: Open Mon-Sun & BHs 10-5 (4 in winter). **Fee:** ✱ £7 (ch under 5 free, ch 6-16 £5, concessions £6). Family ticket (2ad+3ch) £20.
Facilities: ⬀ 🍽 ⴴ toilets for disabled shop ⊗ (ex guide dogs) ◼

WISLEY

MAP 04 TQ05

RHS Garden Wisley

GU23 6QB

➲ *(on A3, close to M25 junct 10)*

☎ 01483 224234

web: www.rhs.org.uk

Covering over 240 acres, Wisley is the flagship of the Royal Horticultural Society demonstrating the very best in gardening practices. The gardens have a wide variety of trees, shrubs and plants, many of which are unusual in Britain. Whatever the season the garden serves as a working encyclopedia for gardeners of all levels.

Times: Open all year, Mon-Fri 10-6 (4.30 Nov-Feb), Sat-Sun, 9-6 (4.30 Nov-Feb). Closed 25 Dec. **Fee:** ✱ £7 (ch 6-16 £2) Group bookings 10+ £5.50 (ch £1.60) **Facilities:** ⬀ 🍽 licensed 🛒 ⴴ (free wheelchairs, mobility buggy, wheelchair route) toilets for disabled shop garden centre ⊗ (ex guide dogs) ◼

Boats moored along the Wey Navigation, Guildford

East Sussex

Pevensey Castle,
Pevensey

Best known for its coastal resorts, this is also a county of battles and
castles. The famous battle of 1066 took place closer to the town of
Battle than Hastings, but the whole area is great for history buffs.
Brighton, Hastings and Eastbourne have much to attract the visitor,
and Brighton has the added advantage of a vibrant modern nightlife
and plenty of artistic activity. Eastbourne may have a gentler
atmosphere, but it enjoys one of the highest sunshine rates in Britain.

ALFRISTON
MAP 05 TQ50

Alfriston Clergy House
The Tye BN26 5TL

↪ (4m NE of Seaford, E of B2108, next to church)

☎ 01323 870001

e-mail: alfriston@nationaltrust.org.uk

web: www.nationaltrust.org.uk

This 14th-century thatched Wealden 'hall house' was the first building to be acquired by the National Trust in 1896. It has an unusual chalk and sour milk floor, and its pretty cottage garden is in an idyllic setting beside Alfriston's parish church, with views across the meandering River Cockmere. Please telephone for details of events running throughout the year.

Times: Open 4-19 Mar, Sat-Sun 11-4; 25 Mar-29 Oct, Sat-Mon, daily (ex Tue & Fri), 10-5; 30 Nov-17 Dec daily (ex Tue & Fri) 11-4. **Fee:** ✱ £3.25 (ch £1.60). Family ticket £8.10. **Facilities:** ℗ (0.25m) 🍴 ♿ (Braille/large print guides, sensory guide) shop ⊗ (ex guide dogs) 🐾 ▬

Drusillas Park
BN26 5QS

↪ (off A27 near Alfriston 12m from Brighton & 7m from Eastbourne)

☎ 01323 874100

e-mail: info@drusillas.co.uk

web: www.drusillas.co.uk

Situated amidst the stunning scenery of the Cuckmere Valley at Alfriston, Drusillas is widely recognised as the best small zoo in England. There are over 100 animal species in naturalistic environments, including meerkats, bats, penguins, monkeys, reptiles and creepy crawlies. The large adventure play area is paradise for anyone who needs to let off steam. There are also beautiful gardens, Panning for Gold, a Wacky Workshop, Jungle Adventure Golf, Explorers Lagoon, Mokomo's Jungle Rock, Vertical Limit, Penguin Plunge, a train that goes through the llama paddock and Amazon Adventure - a vast indoor play area.

Times: Open all year, daily 10-6 (winter 10-5). Closed 24-26 Dec. **Fee:** ✱ Family super saver tickets: Family of 3 £31.50, family of 4 £42, family of 5 £52.50 **Facilities:** ℗ 🍴 🍽 licensed 🍴 ♿ (rear train carriage & sensory trails) toilets for disabled shop ⊗ (ex guide dogs) ▬

BATTLE
MAP 05 TQ71

Battle Museum of Local History
[2 for 1]
The Almonry, High St TN33 0EA

↪ (A21 towards Hastings. Right onto A2001. Museum on High St adjacent to Market Sq, N end of town)

☎ 01424 775955

e-mail: enquiries@battlemuseum.org.uk

web: www.battlemuseum.org.uk

The focal point of this museum is the only battle-axe head yet from the Battle of Hastings and a reproduction of the Bayeux Tapestry. There are also local history exhibits. There is a special exhibition displaying the wealth of finds at the Beauport Park Roman Bath House excavated just outside Battle. The museum holds a temporary exhibition each year.

Times: Open Apr-Oct, daily 10.30-4.30 (Sun 2-5). **Fee:** £1 (ch accompanied free). **Facilities:** ℗ (20yds) 🍴 ♿ (single storey building) toilets for disabled shop ⊗ (ex guide dogs)

1066 Battle of Hastings Abbey & Battlefield
TN33 0AD

↪ (A21 onto A2100)

☎ 01424 773792

web: www.english-heritage.org.uk

Explore the site of the Battle of Hastings, where on 14th October 1066, one of the most famous events in English history took place. Free interactive wand tour of the battlefield and atmospheric abbey ruins.

Times: Open all year, Apr-Sep, daily 10-6; Oct-Mar, daily 10-4. Closed 24-26 Dec & 1 Jan. **Facilities:** ℗ (charged) ♿ shop ⊞

Yesterday's World
[2 for 1]
89-90 High St TN33 0AQ

↪ (M25 junct 5, A21 onto A2100 towards Battle, opposite Battle Abbey Gatehouse)

☎ 01424 775378 & 774269

e-mail: info@yesterdaysworld.co.uk

web: www.yesterdaysworld.co.uk

A fun day out for all the family, as the past is brought to life. Walk down the cobbled streets of yesteryear and meet the colourful characters in over 30 shop and room settings including a 1930s grocer's and a Victorian kitchen. The exhibition contains many rarities from the 1850s onwards, including some of Queen Victoria's personal effects and letters written by the present queen. The museum is housed in beautiful gardens with children's play village, miniature golf and summer tea rooms. Please visit website for details of events running throughout the year.

Times: Open all year, Winter, daily 9.30-5.30 ; Summer, daily 9.30-6. Closed 25-26 Dec and 1 Jan. **Fee:** ✱ £5.95 (ch £3.95, pen £4.95). Family ticket £16.99. Discount for groups of 15+. **Facilities:** ℗ (100yds) (£2.50 per day) 🍽 🍴 ♿ (limited access for wheelchairs) toilets for disabled shop ▬

BODIAM   MAP 05 TQ72

Bodiam Castle

TN32 5UA

⮡ *(2m E of A21 Hurst Green)*

☎ 01580 830436

e-mail: bodiamcastle@nationaltrust.org.uk
web: www.nationaltrust.org.uk/places/bodiamcastle

With its tall round drum towers at each corner, Bodiam is something
of a fairytale castle. It was built in 1386 by Sir Edward Dalnygrigge, for
comfort and defence. The walls measure some 6ft 6in thick, and the
great gatehouse was defended by gun loops and three portcullises.

Times: Open 10 Feb-Oct, daily 10.30-6 (dusk if earlier); Nov-Feb, Sat & Sun
10.30-4 (dusk if earlier). (Last admission 1 hour before closing).
Fee: ✱ £4.20 (ch £2.10). Family ticket £10.50. Group 15+ £3.60, (ch £1.80).
Car £2, Coach £5. **Facilities:** ♿ (charged) 🍴 ♿ (Braille/large print guides,
parking on request) toilets for disabled shop ⊗ (ex guide dogs) ⛟ ◾

BRIGHTON   MAP 04 TQ30

Booth Museum of Natural History   FREE

194 Dyke Rd BN1 5AA

⮡ *(from A27 Brighton by pass, 1.5m NW of town centre,
opposite Dyke Rd Park)*

☎ 01273 292777

e-mail: boothmuseum@brighton-hove.gov.uk
web: www.virtualmuseum.info

The museum was built in 1874 to house the bird collection of Edward
Thomas Booth (1840-1890). His collection is still on display, but the
museum has expanded considerably since Booth's day and now
includes thousands of butterfly and insect specimens, geology
galleries with fossils, rocks and local dinosaur bones, a magnificent
collection of animal skeletons, largely collected by the Brighton
solicitor F W Lucas (1842-1932), and an interactive discovery gallery.

Times: Open all year, Mon-Sat (ex Thu) 10-5, Sun 2-5. Closed Good Fri,
Xmas & 1 Jan. **Facilities:** ♿ (road opposite) (2 hr limit) 🍴 ♿ toilets for
disabled shop ⊗ (ex guide dogs) ◾

Brighton Museum & Art Gallery   FREE

Royal Pavilion Gardens BN1 1EE

⮡ *(A23/M23 from London. In city centre near seafront.
New entrance in Royal Pavilion Gardens)*

☎ 01273 290900

e-mail: museums@brighton-hove.gov.uk
web: www.brighton.virtualmuseum.info

A £10 million redevelopment has transformed Brighton museum into
a state-of-the-art visitor attraction. Dynamic and innovative new
galleries, including fashion, 20th-century design and world art,
featuring exciting interactive displays appealing to all ages. The
museum also benefits from a spacious new entrance located in the
Royal Pavilion gardens and full disabled access.

Times: Open Tue-Sat 10-5, Sun 2-5. (Closed Mon ex BHs).
Facilities: ♿ (5 mins walk) (Church St NCP & on street) 🍴 ♿ (lift, tactile
exhibits, induction loops, ramps, automatic door) toilets for disabled shop
⊗ (ex guide dogs)

Brighton Toy and Model Museum   NEW

52-55 Trafalgar St BN1 4EB

⮡ *(underneath Brighton Railway Station)*

☎ 01273 749494

e-mail: info@brightontoymuseum.co.uk
web: www.brightontoymuseum.co.uk

A fascinating collection of over 10,000 exhibits, includes collections of
toys from the last one hundred years. Toys from the top toy makers
and a priceless model train collection are some examples to be
viewed.

Times: Open all year, Tue-Fri 10-5, Sat 11-5. Closed Sun & Mon.
Fee: ✱ £3.50 (ch & concessions £2.50). Family £10. **Facilities:** ♿ (10 mins
walk) (no on street parking) ♿ (ramp, wide door, rails & bars) toilets for
disabled shop ⊗ (ex assist dogs)

Preston Manor

Preston Drove BN1 6SD

⮡ *(off A23, 2m N of Brighton)*

☎ 01273 292770

e-mail: museums@brighton-hove.gov.uk
web: www.prestonmanor.virtualmuseum.info

This charming Edwardian manor house is beautifully furnished with
notable collections of silver, furniture and paintings and presents a
unique opportunity to see an Edwardian home both 'upstairs' and
'downstairs'. The servants' quarters can be seen, featuring kitchen,
butler's pantry and boot hall. The house is set in beautiful gardens,
which include a pet cemetery and the 13th-century parish church of St
Peter. The restored walled garden enables disabled people to explore
the garden for the first time.

Times: Open Apr-Sep, Tue-Sat 10-5, Sun 2-5. Closed Mon. **Fee:** ✱ £3.90
(ch £2.25, concessions £3.20). Family ticket £6.15-£10. Party 20+ £3.30 each.
Facilities: ♿ 🍴 ♿ (call prior to visit to discuss access requirements) shop
⊗ (ex guide dogs)

Royal Pavilion

BN1 1EE

⮡ *(M23/A23 from London. In city centre near seafront.
15 min walk from rail station)*

☎ 01273 290900

e-mail: visitor.services@brighton-hove.gov.uk
web: www.royalpavilion.org.uk

Acclaimed as one of the most exotically beautiful buildings in the
British Isles, the Royal Pavilion was the magnificent seaside residence
of George IV. This breathtaking Regency palace is decorated in
Chinese style, with a romanticised Indian exterior, and surrounded by
restored Regency gardens.

Times: Open all year, Apr-Sep, daily 9.30-5.45 (last admission 5); Oct-Mar,
daily 10-5.15 (last admission 4.30). Closed 25&26 Dec. **Fee:** ✱ £7.50
(ch £5, concessions £5.75) Family ticket (1ad+upto 2ch) £11.50 (2ad+upto
2ch) £19. Groups 20+ £6.20 each. **Facilities:** ♿ (5 mins walk) (NCP & on
Church St) 🍴 ♿ (wheelchairs, audio guides) toilets for disabled shop
⊗ (ex guide dogs) ◾

England

Sea Life Centre **2 for 1**
Marine Pde BN2 1TB
➲ *(next to Brighton Pier between Marine Parade & Madeira Drive)*
☎ 01273 604234
e-mail: slcbrighton@merlinentertainments.biz
web: www.sealife.co.uk

Experience spectacular marine displays, set in the world's oldest functioning aquarium. Take a look at over 100 species in their natural habitat, including seahorses, sharks and rays. Over forty exhibits include Adventures at 20,000 Leagues complete with NASA-designed walkthrough observation tunnel. Features also include a Captain Pugwash quiz trail, a soft play area, a cafe and a giftshop.

Times: Open all year, daily 10-5. (Last admission 4). Open later on wknds in summer & school hols. Closed 25 Dec. **Fee:** ✱ £9.95 (ch £7.50, concessions £8.50). **Facilities:** Ⓟ (200yds) (pay & display) 🍽 📷 ♿ (Access in majority of Centre) toilets for disabled shop ⊗ (ex guide dogs) ◼

BURWASH MAP 05 TQ62

Bateman's
TN19 7DS
➲ *(0.5m SW off A265)*
☎ 01435 882302
e-mail: batemans@nationaltrust.org.uk
web: www.nationaltrust.org.uk

Rudyard Kipling lived for over 34 years in this 17th-century manor house and it remains much the same as it was during his lifetime. His 1928 Rolls Royce Phantom is on display, and the watermill at the bottom of the garden grinds wheat into flour on Saturday afternoons and Wednesdays.

Times: Open 18 Mar-29 Oct, Sat-Wed 11-5, also open Good Fri, (last admission 4.30). House closes at 5. **Fee:** ✱ £6.20 (ch £3.10). Family ticket £15.50 Party £5.20 (ch £2.60) **Facilities:** Ⓟ 🍽 🍴 licensed 📷 ♿ (Braille guide, touch test, computerised tour of upper floors) toilets for disabled shop ⊗ (ex guide/hearing dogs) 🐾 ◼

EASTBOURNE MAP 05 TV69

"How We Lived Then" Museum of Shops & Social History
20 Cornfield Ter BN21 4NS
➲ *(just off seafront, between town centre & theatres, signed)*
☎ 01323 737143
e-mail: howwelivedthen@btconnect.com
web: www.how-we-lived-then.co.uk

Over the last 50 years, Jan and Graham Upton have collected over 100,000 items which are now displayed on four floors of authentic old shops and room-settings, transporting visitors back to their grandparents' era. Other displays, such as seaside souvenirs, wartime rationing and Royal mementoes, help to capture 100 years of social history.

Times: Open all year, daily, 10-5.30 (last entry 5). Winter times subject to change, telephone establishment. **Fee:** ✱ £4 (ch 5-15 £3, under 5's free, pen £3.50). Party 10+. **Facilities:** Ⓟ (outside) 📷 ♿ (no charge) shop

---

EAST DEAN MAP 05 TV59

Seven Sisters Sheep Centre NEW
Gilberts Dr BN20 0AA
☎ 01323 423302
e-mail: sevensisters.sheepcentre@talk21.com
web: www.sheepcentre.co.uk

Possibly the largest collection of sheep in the world, where over 40 different breeds can be visited at this family run farm. See lambs being born, sheep sheared and milked, cheese making and spinning. Take in the agricultural heritage and history of sheep on the South Downs.
Times: ✱ Open 3 Mar-7 May & 30 Jun-2 Sep, 2-5 (11-5 wknds/E Sussex school holidays). **Fee:** £4 (ch £3, concessions £3.50) **Facilities:** Ⓟ 🍽 ♿ ⊗ (ex guide dogs)

FIRLE MAP 05 TQ40

Firle Place
BN8 6LP
➲ *(off A27, Eastbourne to Brighton road near Lewes)*
☎ 01273 858307
e-mail: gage@firleplace.co.uk
web: www.firleplace.co.uk

Home of the Gage family for over 500 years, the house has a Tudor core but was remodelled in the 18th century. Its treasures include important European and English Old Master paintings, fine English and French furniture, and porcelain, including notable examples from Sèvres and English factories. There are family monuments and brasses in the church at West Firle.

Times: Open May-Sep, Sun, Wed, Thu & BHs 2-4.30. **Fee:** £6 (ch £3, concessions £5.50). Groups 25+. Connoisseurs Day £7.50 each. Family £15, Season £12. **Facilities:** Ⓟ 🍴 licensed ♿ (virtual tour video) toilets for disabled shop. ⊗ (ex in garden) ◼

FOREST ROW   MAP 05 TQ43

Ashdown Forest Llama Park
Wych Cross RH18 5JN
⮕ *(on A22 between Uckfield & East Grinstead, 250mtrs S of junct with A275)*
☎ 01825 712040
e-mail: info@llamapark.co.uk
web: www.llamapark.co.uk

One of the leading llama breeding centres in the country. Walk around three 18th-century barns and a new visitor centre to discover over 100 llamas and alpacas. Llamas and alpacas were first domesticated in South America more than 5,000 years ago, and visitors can learn all about their contribution to these societies at the museum. Visitors can also walk with llamas in the grounds, but these walks do need to be booked and paid for in advance. Contact the park for more details.

Times: Open daily 10-5. Closed 25 & 26 Dec and 1 Jan **Fee:** £4.75 (ch £4, pen & concessions) **Facilities:** ❷ 💷 ♿ (ramps, wheelchairs provided for free) toilets for disabled shop ⊗ ◀

GLYNDE   MAP 05 TQ40

Glynde Place
BN8 6SX
⮕ *(off A27 between Lewes & Eastbourne)*
☎ 01273 858224
e-mail: hampden@glyndeplace.co.uk
web: www.glyndeplace.com

A lovely Elizabethan manor with 18th-century additions, in a beautiful downland setting. Glynde Place is the family home of Viscount and Viscountess Hampden whose forebears built the house in 1569 using a mixture of flint and stone. Portraits, furniture, silver, embroidery and books testify to 400 years of family life.

Times: ✱ Open May-Aug, Wed, Sun & Aug BH 2-4.45. **Facilities:** ❷ 💷 📶 ♿ toilets for disabled shop ⊗ (ex guide dogs)

HAILSHAM   MAP 05 TQ50

Michelham Priory
Upper Dicker BN27 3QS
⮕ *(off A22 & A27, 2m W of Hailsham, 8m NW of Eastbourne, signed from A27 & A22)*
☎ 01323 844224
e-mail: adminmich@sussexpast.co.uk
web: www.sussexpast.co.uk

Set on a moated island surrounded by glorious gardens, Michelham Priory is one of the most beautiful historic houses in Sussex. Founded in 1229 for Augustinian canons, the Priory is approached through a 14th-century gatehouse spanning the longest water-filled medieval moat in the country. Most of the original priory was demolished during the Dissolution, but the remains were incorporated into a Tudor farm that became a country house. Outside, the gardens are enhanced by a working watermill, physic garden, smithy, rope museum and the dramatic Elizabethan Great Barn.

Times: Open Mar-Oct, Tue-Sun (daily in Aug & BH Mons). Mar & Oct 10.30-4.30, Apr-Jul & Sep 10.30-5, Aug 10.30-5.30. **Fee:** ✱ £5.60 (ch 5-15 £2.90, concessions £4.70). Family ticket (2ad+2ch) £14.30. Disabled/carer £2.80 each. **Facilities:** ❷ 💷 🍽 licensed ♿ (pre-booked wheelchairs, Braille guide & tactile tours) toilets for disabled shop ⊗ (ex guide dogs) ◀

HALLAND   MAP 05 TQ51

Bentley Wildfowl & Motor Museum
BN8 5AF
⮕ *(7m NE of Lewes, signposted off A22, A26 & B2192)*
☎ 01825 840573
e-mail: barrysutherland@pavilion.co.uk
web: www.bentley.org.uk

Hundreds of swans, geese and ducks from all over the world can be seen on lakes and ponds along with flamingoes and peacocks. There is a fine array of Veteran, Edwardian and Vintage vehicles, and the house has splendid antiques and wildfowl paintings. The gardens specialise in old-fashioned roses. Other attractions include woodland walks, a nature trail, education centre, adventure playground and a miniature train.

Times: ✱ Open 17 Mar-Oct, daily 10.30-4.30. House open from noon, Apr-Nov, Feb & part of Mar, wknds only. Estate closed Dec & Jan. House closed all winter. **Facilities:** ❷ 💷 📶 ♿ (wheelchairs available) toilets for disabled shop ⊗ (ex guide dogs) ◀

HASTINGS   MAP 05 TQ80

Old Town Hall Museum of Local History   `FREE`
Old Town Hall, High St TN34 3EW
⮕ *(off A259 coast road into High St in Hastings old town. Signed)*
☎ 01424 781166
e-mail: oldtownmuseum@hastings.gov.uk
web: www.hmag.org.uk

Situated in the heart of Hastings Old Town, the museum was originally a Georgian Town Hall built in 1823. Refurbished displays tell the story of Hastings Old Town as a walk back in time, with features including a Cinque Ports ship, and interactive displays.

Times: Winter: Oct-Mar, Mon-Fri 10-4 Sat-Sun 11-4. Summer: Apr-Sep Mon-Sat 10-5 Sun 11-5. **Facilities:** ℗ (150yds) (parking meters in operation) 📶 ♿ (lift, evac chair, low-level displays, audio tour) toilets for disabled shop ⊗ (ex guide dogs)

Smugglers Adventure
St Clements Caves, West Hill TN34 3HY
⮕ *(follow brown signs on A259, coast road, through Hastings. Use seafront car park, then take West Cliff railway or follow signed footpath)*
☎ 01424 422964
e-mail: smugglers@discoverhastings.co.uk
web: www.discoverhastings.co.uk

A Smuggler's Adventure is a themed experience housed in a labyrinth of caverns and passages deep below the West Hill. Visitors first tour a comprehensive exhibition and museum, followed by a video theatre, before embarking on the Adventure Walk - a trip through several acres of caves with life-size tableaux, push-button automated models and dramatic scenic effects depicting life in the days of 18th-century smuggling.

Times: ✱ Open all year daily, Etr-Sep 10-5.30; Oct-Etr 11-4.30. Closed 24-26 Dec. **Facilities:** ℗ (500yds) (parking meters on some streets) 📶 shop ⊗ (ex guide dogs) ◀

1066 Story in Hastings Castle

Castle Hill Rd, West Hill TN34 3RG

➲ *(close to A259 seafront, 2m from B2093)*

☎ 01424 781111 & 781112 (info line)

e-mail: bookings@discoverhastings.co.uk

web: www.hastings.gov.uk

The ruins of the Norman castle stand on the cliffs, close to the site of William the Conqueror's first motte-and-bailey castle in England. It was excavated in 1825 and 1968, and old dungeons were discovered in 1894. An unusual approach to the castle can be made via the West Hill Cliff Railway.

Times: ✱ Open daily, Oct-26 Mar 11-3.30, 27 Mar-Sep 10-5. Closed 24-26 Dec. **Facilities:** Ⓟ (seafront) (time restrictions, pay & display) ♿ (concrete slope, some uneven ground) shop ⊗ (ex guide dogs)

HERSTMONCEUX   MAP 05 TQ61

The Observatory Science Centre

BN27 1RN

➲ *(0.75m N of Wartling village)*

☎ 01323 832731

e-mail: info@the-observatory.org

web: www.the-observatory.org

From the 1950s to the 1980s this was part of the Royal Greenwich Observatory, and was used by astronomers to observe and chart movements in the night sky. Visitors can learn about not only astronomy, but also other areas of science in a series of interactive and engaging displays. There are also exhibitions, a discovery park, and a collection of unusual giant exhibits.

Times: Open daily from 28 Jan-3 Dec. Open wknds of Jan 7/8, 14/15, 21/22 and Dec 9/10. **Fee:** ✱ £6.50 (ch 4-15 £4.75) Family ticket (2ad + 3ch or 1ad + 4ch £19.50, family of 5 £22.30. **Facilities:** ❶ 🅿 🔳 ♿ (ramps & disabled entrance, lift to 1st floor) toilets for disabled shop ⊗ (ex guide dogs) 🔶

The Truggery   FREE

Coopers Croft BN27 1QL

➲ *(from A22 at Hailsham, Boship rdbt, take A271 towards Bexhill for 4m)*

☎ 01323 832355

e-mail: sarah@truggery.fsnet.co.uk

web: www.truggery.co.uk

The art of Sussex trug making can be seen through all the work processes including preparing timber, use of the draw knife and assembly of trugs.

Times: Open all year Mon-Fri 10-5, Sat 10-1. Closed Sun. Jan-Apr opening times may vary. **Facilities:** ❶ 🔳 ♿ shop 🔶

LEWES   MAP 05 TQ41

Anne of Cleves House

52 Southover High St BN7 1JA

➲ *(S of town centre off A27/A26/A275)*

☎ 01273 474610

e-mail: anne@sussexpast.co.uk

web: www.sussexpast.co.uk

Henry VIII gave this beautiful timber-framed house to Anne of Cleves, his fourth wife, as part of her divorce settlement. Today there are collections of early English furniture, Sussex pottery and stone from Lewes Priory, plus a local social history exhibition. The Wealden Iron Gallery tells the story of the industrial past of Sussex and contains a large collection of iron artefacts.

Times: Open Jan-Feb & Nov-Dec, Tue-Sat 10-5; Mar-Oct, Tue-Sat 10-5, Sun, Mon & BHs 11-5. Closed 24-26 Dec. **Fee:** ✱ £3.10 (ch 5-15 £1.55, concessions £2.80). Family ticket £7.90 (2ad+2ch), £6.30 (1ad+4ch). Disabled/Carer £1.55 each **Facilities:** Ⓟ (25yds) (on street-2hr restriction) ♿ shop ⊗ (ex guide dogs) 🔶

Charleston NEW

Firle BN8 6LL

➲ *(Signed off A27, 7m E of Lewes between the villages of Firle and Selmeston)*

☎ 01323 811265 & 811626

e-mail: info@charleston.org.uk

web: www.charleston.org.uk

From 1916 Charleston was the home of the artists Vanessa Ball and Duncan Grant, and a rural retreat for the Bloomsbury Group. Over the years the house was transformed and filled with furniture, textiles and art by them and their contemporaries including Picasso, Renoir, Sickert, Derain and Lamb. The Downland setting captures their pioneering, creative and Bohemian way of life. The walled garden was redesigned in a style reminiscent of southern Europe, with mosaics, box hedges, gravel pathways and ponds, but with a touch of Bloomsbury humour in the placing of the statuary.

Times: Open Wed & Sat 11.30-6, Thu, Fri, Sun & BH 2-6 (Thu & Fri 11.30-6 Jul-Aug) **Fee:** ✱ House and grounds £6.50 (ch 6-16 £4.50) Family ticket 1 or 2 ad & up to 4 ch £17.50. Gardens only £2.50 (ch £1) **Facilities:** ❶ 🔳 ⊗ (ex assist dogs)

Lewes Castle & Barbican House Museum

169 High St BN7 1YE

➲ *(N of High St off A27/A26/A275)*

☎ 01273 486290

e-mail: castle@sussexpast.co.uk

web: www.sussexpast.co.uk

High above the medieval streets stands Lewes Castle, begun soon after the Norman Conquest by William de Warenne as his stronghold in Sussex and added to over the next 300 years, culminating in the magnificent Barbican. Thomas Read Kemp and his family owned and updated the ruins during Georgian times. Barbican House is next to the castle, and now houses a museum covering the area from pre-history to the late medieval period. Visitors can climb to the top of the castle, from where they are rewarded by stunning views. A 'sound and light' show in the museum below tells the story of the town of Lewes through the ages.

Times: Open daily, Tue-Sat 10-5.30, Sun, Mon & BHs 11-5.30. (Last admission 30 mins before closing). Closed Xmas & Mon in Jan.

Fee: ✱ £4.50 (ch (5-15) £2.25, concessions £4). Family ticket (2ad+2ch) £11.70, (1ad+4ch) £9.20. Disabled/Carer £2.25 each. **Facilities:** Ⓟ (on street parking) shop ⊗ (ex guide dogs) ◀

NEWHAVEN — MAP 05 TQ40

Paradise Park & Gardens   `2 for 1`

Avis Rd BN9 0DH

➲ *(signed off A26 & A259)*

☎ 01273 512123

e-mail: promotions@paradisepark.co.uk

web: www.paradisepark.co.uk

A perfect day out for plant lovers whatever the season. Discover the unusual garden designs with waterfalls, fountains and lakes, including the Caribbean garden and the tranquil Oriental garden. The Conservatory Gardens complex contains a large variety of the world's flora divided into several zones. There's also a Sussex history trail and Planet Earth with moving dinosaurs and interactive displays, plus rides and amusements for children.

Times: Open all year, daily 9-6. Closed 25-26 Dec. **Fee:** ✱ £7.99 (ch £5.99). Family ticket £19.99 (2ad+2ch). **Facilities:** Ⓟ ⬤ 〒 ⛾ 📶 ⛬ ⬤ (all areas level or ramped) toilets for disabled shop garden centre ⊗ (ex guide dogs) ◀

NORTHIAM — MAP 05 TQ82

Great Dixter House & Gardens

TN31 6PH

➲ *(off A28, signed)*

☎ 01797 252878

e-mail: office@greatdixter.co.uk

web: www.greatdixter.co.uk

Birthplace and home of Christopher Lloyd, gardening writer, Great Dixter was built in 1460 and boasts one of the largest timber-framed buildings in the country. Lutyens was employed to restore both the house and gardens in 1910. The gardens are now a combination of meadows, ponds, topiary and notably the Long Border and Exotic Garden.

Times: Open Apr-May, Tue-Sun & BH Mon, 2-5 (last admission 5); May - Sep Gardens open from 11 on Sun & Mon BH wknds only. **Fee:** ✱ House & Gardens £7.50 (ch £3). Gardens only £6 (ch £2.50). Party 25+. **Facilities:** Ⓟ ⛬ (2 wheelchairs available free of charge) toilets for disabled shop garden centre ⊗ (ex guide dogs) ◀

PEVENSEY — MAP 05 TQ60

Pevensey Castle

BN24 5LE

➲ *(off A259)*

☎ 01323 762604

web: www.english-heritage.org.uk

William the Conqueror landed here in 1066 and established his first stronghold. Discover the history of the Norman castle and the remains of an unusual keep through the free audio tour.

Times: Open Apr-Sep, daily, 10-6; Oct, daily, 10-4; Nov-Mar, Sat-Sun, 10-4.

Fee: £3.90 (ch £2, concessions £2.90). Prices and opening times are subject to change in Spring 2007. Please check web site or call 0870 333 1181 for the most up to date prices and opening times when planning your visit.

Facilities: Ⓟ (charged) ☕ ⛬ shop ⊞

RYE — MAP 05 TQ92

Lamb House

West St TN31 7ES

➲ *(facing W end of Church)*

☎ 01580 762334

web: www.nationaltrust.org.uk

This 18th-century house was the home of novelist Henry James from 1898 until his death in 1916, and was later occupied by the writer, E F Benson. Some of James' personal posessions can be seen. There is also a charming walled garden.

Times: Open 24 Mar-28 Oct, Thurs & Sat 2-6, (last admission 5.30).

Fee: ✱ £2.90 (ch £1.40). Family ticket £7.25. Groups £2.50 per person

Facilities: Ⓟ (500mtrs) 📶 ⛬ (scented plants & herbs, some steps to house) ⊗ (ex guide dogs) ⚘

Rye Castle Museum

3 East St TN31 7JY

➲ *(in town centre, on A259)*

☎ 01797 226728

e-mail: info@ryemuseum.co.uk

web: www.ryemuseum.co.uk

Part of the museum is housed in a stone tower built as a fortification in 1249. The museum's collection of ironwork, medieval pots and smuggling items are on display here, while the East Street site contains the rest of the collection, including pottery made in Rye, fashions, an eighteenth-century fire engine, toys, cinque port regalia, a special exhibition on Rye between the wars, descriptions of the changes to the harbour and shipbuilding in Rye, and businesses and leisure in Rye during the 19th and 20th centuries.

Times: Open all year Nov-Mar wknds only 10.30-3; Apr-Oct Thu-Mon 10.30-5 (last entry 4.30). Closed between 1-2. **Fee:** ✱ Entrance to both sites: £2.90 (ch under 7 free, ch 7-16 £1.50, concessions £2). Family ticket £5.90. Single entry only: £1.90 (ch under 7 free, ch 7-16 £1, concessions £1.50). Family ticket £4.50. Party 8+. Subject to change.

Facilities: Ⓟ (30yds) (street 1hr) (long stay 10mins away) 📶 ⛬ (only East Street accessible, part of garden) toilets for disabled shop ⊗ (ex guide dogs)

SHEFFIELD PARK   MAP 05 TQ42

Sheffield Park Garden

TN22 3QX

➲ (midway between East Grinstead & Lewes, 5m NW of Uckfield, on E side of A275, between A272 & A22)

☎ 01825 790231

e-mail: sheffieldpark@nationaltrust.org.uk

web: www.nationaltrust.org.uk/sheffieldpark

Sheffield Park was originally landscaped by 'Capability' Brown, in about 1775 to create a beautiful park with four lakes and cascades. Further extensive planting was done at the beginning of the 20th century, to give emphasis to autumn colour among the trees. In May and June masses of azaleas and rhododendrons bloom and later there are magnificent waterlilies on the lakes. Autumn brings stunning colours from the many rare trees and shrubs. Special events throughout the season.

Times: Open all year. Please phone for details. **Fee:** ✱ £6.20 (ch £3.10, ch under 5 free). Family ticket £15.50. NT members free. **Facilities:** ♿ ☕ 🍴 ♿ (powered self drive cars & wheelchairs pre-book) toilets for disabled shop garden centre ⊗ (ex guide/hearing dogs) ♿ 📷

SHEFFIELD PARK STATION   MAP 05 TQ42

Bluebell Railway

Sheffield Park Station TN22 3QL

➲ (4.5m E of Haywards Heath, off A275, 10m S of East Grinstead A22-A275)

☎ 01825 720800 & 722370

e-mail: info@bluebell-railway.co.uk

web: www.bluebell-railway.co.uk

A volunteer-run heritage steam railway with nine miles of track running through pretty Sussex countryside. Please note that there is no parking at Kingscote Station. If you wish to board the train here, catch the bus (service 473) which connects Kingscote and East Grinstead.

Times: Open all year, Sat & Sun, daily May-Sep & during school holidays. Santa Specials run Dec. For timetable and information regarding trains contact above. **Fee:** ✱ 3rd class return fare £9.50 (ch £4.70). Family ticket £27. Admission to Sheffield Park Station only £1.60 (ch 80p). Other tickets available on request. Maybe subject to change, please telephone for details. **Facilities:** ♿ ☕ 🍴 licensed ♿ (special carriage for wheelchairs & carers with lift) toilets for disabled shop 📷

TICEHURST   MAP 05 TQ63

Pashley Manor Gardens

TN5 7HE

➲ (on B2099 between A21 and Ticehurst village, follow brown tourist signs)

☎ 01580 200888

e-mail: info@pashleymanorgardens.com

web: www.pashleymanorgardens.com

Once belonging to the family of Anne Boleyn, Pashley Manor has a beautiful traditional English garden. Visitors can wander among fine old trees, fountains, springs and large ponds, all surrounded by romantic landscaping and imaginative plantings, and interspersed with statues and sculptures by leading European sculptors. A series of craft and speciality plant fairs take place throughout the year. Please telephone for details.

Times: Open 4 Apr-Sep, Tue-Thu, Sat & BH Mon 11-5; Garden only Oct, Mon-Fri 10-4. **Fee:** ✱ £6 (ch £5.50) pen £5.50 **Facilities:** ♿ 🍴 licensed ♿ toilets for disabled shop ⊗ (ex guide dogs) 📷

West Sussex

Chichester

This is a lush county with plenty of coastline. Chichester is famous for its 900-year-old cathedral, while Selsey Bill is the ideal headland for bird-spotting. But it's Bognor Regis or Worthing that holidaymakers usually aim for. Bognor was one of the first bathing resorts back in the 18th century, and the 'Regis' was added after George V convalesced there in 1929. This is also a good place for bird-spotting, especially if you count the annual Birdman competition, which sees hopeful contestants launch themselves from the end of the pier in an attempt to fly.

AMBERLEY   MAP 04 TQ01

Amberley Working Museum
BN18 9LT
➲ (on B2139, between Arundel and Storrington, adjacent to Amberley railway station)
☎ 01798 831370
e-mail: office@amberleymuseum.co.uk
web: www.amberleymuseum.co.uk

36 acre open-air museum dedicated to the industrial heritage of the south east of England. Traditional craftspeople on site (including a blacksmith and potter), working narrow-gauge railway and vintage bus collection, Connected Earth telecommunications display, Seeboard Electricity Hall, stationary engines, print workshop, woodturners, wheelwrights, nature trails, restaurant, shop and much more.

Times: ✳ Open 12 Mar-2 Nov, Wed-Sun & BH Mon 10-5.30 (last admission 4.30). Also open daily during school hols. **Facilities:** ❷ 🍽 🎐 📶
♿ (wheelchairs available for loan & large print guides) toilets for disabled shop ◀

ARDINGLY   MAP 05 TQ32

Wakehurst Place & Millennium Seed Bank
Royal Botanic Gardens RH17 6TN
➲ (M23 junct 10, 1.5m NW of Ardingly, on B2028, follow brown tourist signs)
☎ 01444 894066
e-mail: wakehurst@kew.org
web: www.kew.org

Woodland and lakes linked by a pretty watercourse make this large garden a beautiful place to walk, and it also has an amazing variety of interesting trees and shrubs, a winter garden, and a rock walk. It is administered and maintained by the Royal Botanic Gardens, Kew.

Times: Open Jan-Feb 10-4, Mar-Oct 10-6, Nov-Oct 10-4. Closed 24-25 Dec. **Facilities:** ❷ 🍽 🎐 licensed 🎐 ♿ (manual and electric wheelchairs available) toilets for disabled shop garden centre ⊗ (ex guide dogs) ◀

ARUNDEL   MAP 04 TQ00

Arundel Castle   2 for 1
BN18 9AB
➲ (on A27 between Chichester & Worthing)
☎ 01903 882173
e-mail: info@arundelcastle.org
web: www.arundelcastle.org

Set high on a hill in West Sussex, this magnificent castle and stately home, seat of the Dukes of Norfolk for nearly 1000 years, commands stunning views across the river Arun and out to sea. Climb to the keep and battlements; marvel at a fine collection of 16th-century furniture; portraits by Van Dyke, Gainsborough, Canaletto and others; tapestries and the personal possessions of Mary, Queen of Scots; wander in the grounds and renovated Victorian flower and vegetable gardens.

continued

Arundel Castle

Times: Open Apr-Oct, Sun-Fri 11-5, Castle open 12-5. (Last admission 4). Closed Sat. **Fee:** ✳ £12 (ch 5-16 £7.50, pen £9.50). Family ticket £32. Party 20+. **Facilities:** ❷ (charged) 🍽 🎐 ♿ (chair lift) toilets for disabled shop ⊗ (ex assist dogs) ◀

WWT Arundel   2 for 1
Mill Rd BN18 9PB
➲ (signed from A27 & A29)
☎ 01903 883355
e-mail: arundel@wwt.org.uk
web: www.wwt.org.uk

More than a thousand ducks, geese and swans from all over the world can be found here, many of which are so friendly that they will eat from your hand. The wild reserve attracts a variety of birds and includes a reedbed habitat considered so vital to the wetland wildlife it shelters that it has been designated a Site of Special Scientific Interest. Visitors can walk right through this reedbed on a specially designed boardwalk. There is a packed programme of events and activities throughout the year.

Times: Open all year, daily; summer 9.30-5; winter 9.30-4.30. (Last admission summer 5; winter 4). Closed 25 Dec. **Fee:** ✳ £6.75 (ch £3.25, pen £5.25). Family ticket £17. **Facilities:** ❷ 🍽 🍽 licensed 🎐 ♿ (level paths, free wheelchair loan) toilets for disabled shop ⊗ (ex guide & hearing dogs) ◀

ASHINGTON   MAP 04 TQ11

Holly Gate Cactus Garden   2 for 1
Billingshurst Rd RH20 3BB
➲ (off A24, towards Ashington then B2133 towards Billingshurst for 0.5m)
☎ 01903 892930
e-mail: info@hollygatecactus.co.uk
web: www.hollygatecactus.co.uk

A mecca for the cactus enthusiast, with more than 30,000 succulent and cactus plants, including many rare types. They come from both arid and tropical parts of the world, and are housed in over 10,000 sq ft of greenhouses.

Times: Open all year, daily 9-5 (Nov-Feb, 9-4). Closed 25-26 Dec. **Fee:** £2 (ch & pen £1.50). Family ticket £6. Party 20+ 25p deduction. **Facilities:** ❷ ♿ shop garden centre ⊗ (ex guide dogs) ◀

BIGNOR
MAP 04 SU91

Bignor Roman Villa & Museum
RH20 1PH

➲ (6m S of Pulborough & 6m N of Arundel on A29, signed. 8m S of Petworth on A285, signed)

☎ 01798 869259

e-mail: bignorromanvilla@care4free.net

web: www.pyrrha.demon.co.uk

Rediscovered in 1811, this Roman house was built on a grand scale. It is one of the largest known, and has spectacular mosaics. The heating system can also be seen, and various finds from excavations are on show. The longest mosaic in Britain (82ft) is on display here in its original position.

Times: Open Mar-Apr, Tue-Sun & BH 10-5; May daily 10-5; Jun-Sep daily 10-6, Oct daily 10-5 **Fee:** ✱ £4.35 (ch 5-15 £1.85, pen £3.10). Party 10+ 20% discount. Guided tours by arrangement. **Facilities:** ℗ 🖤 🍴 ♿ (most areas accessible) shop ⊗ (ex guide dogs) 🍴

BRAMBER
MAP 04 TQ11

Bramber Castle
FREE

BN4 3FB

➲ (on W side of village off A283)

web: www.english-heritage.org.uk

The remains of a Norman motte and bailey castle. The gatehouse, still standing almost to its original height, and walls are still visible.

Times: Open any reasonable time. **Facilities:** ℗ 🦌

CHICHESTER
MAP 04 SU80

Chichester Cathedral
FREE

West St PO19 1PX

➲ (in city centre)

☎ 01243 782595

e-mail: visitors@chichestercathedral.org.uk

web: www.chichestercathedral.org.uk

The beauty of the 900-year-old cathedral, site of the shrine of St Richard, is enhanced by many art treasures, ancient and modern.

Times: Open end Mar-end Sep daily 7.15-7; end Sep-end Mar 7.15-6. **Facilities:** ℗ (within city walls) 🖤 🍴 licensed ♿ (touch & hearing centre, loop system) toilets for disabled shop ⊗ (ex guide dogs)

Mechanical Music & Doll Collection
Church Rd, Portfield PO19 4HN

➲ (1m E of Chichester, signed off A27)

☎ 01243 372646

A unique opportunity to see and hear barrel organs, polyphons, musical boxes, fair organs etc - all fully restored and playing. A magical musical tour to fascinate and entertain all ages. The doll collection contains fine examples of Victorian china and wax dolls, and felt and velvet dolls of the 1920s.

Times: Open Jun-Sep, Wed 1-4; Group bookings anytime in the year by prior arrangement. **Fee:** ✱ £2.50 (ch £1.25). **Facilities:** ℗ ♿ shop ⊗ (ex guide dogs)

Pallant House Gallery
2 for 1

9 North Pallant PO19 1TJ

➲ (from city centre (the Cross) take East St turning right at Superdrug. Gallery at end of North Pallant on left)

☎ 01243 774557

e-mail: info@pallant.org.uk

web: www.pallant.org.uk

A Queen Anne townhouse and a modern building have been combined to house a fine collection of 20th-century British art. The permanent collection includes pieces by: Auerbach, Blake, Bomberg, Caulfield, Freud, Hamilton, Hitchens, Leger, Moore, Nash, Nicholson, Piper, Richards, Severini, Sickert and Sutherland. Telephone or visit website for details of temporary exhibitions.

Times: Open Tue-Sat, 10-5, Sun & BHs, 12.30-5. Closed Mon. **Fee:** £6.50 (ch £2, student £3.50). Family ticket £15. Cheap Tuesday - half price. **Facilities:** ℗ (100 yds) 🖤 🍴 licensed 🍴 ♿ toilets for disabled shop ⊗ (ex guide dogs) 🍴

EAST GRINSTEAD
MAP 05 TQ33

Standen
West Hoathly Rd RH19 4NE

➲ (2m S of East Grinstead, signed from B2110)

☎ 01342 323029

e-mail: standen@nationaltrust.org.uk

web: www.nationaltrust.org.uk/standen

Standen is a showpiece of the 19th-century Arts and Crafts Movement. It was designed by Philip Webb for the Beale family, and is decorated throughout with William Morris wallpapers and fabrics. The interior has been carefully preserved. Webb also designed some of the furniture and details. There is a hillside garden and two woodland walks. Telephone for details of special events.

Times: House open mid Mar-Oct, Wed-Sun & BH 11-4.30 (last entry 4). Garden open same dates as house 11-5.30 & Nov-mid Dec, Sat-Sun 11-3. **Fee:** ✱ House & garden £6.50. Garden only £3.90 (ch half price). Family ticket £15. Joint ticket which includes same day entry to Nymans garden £10, available Wed-Fri. **Facilities:** ℗ 🍴 licensed 🍴 ♿ (Braille guide & touch list & large print guide) toilets for disabled shop ⊗ (ex guide dogs & on wood walk) 🦌 🍴

FISHBOURNE
MAP 04 SU80

Fishbourne Roman Palace
Salthill Rd PO19 3QR

➲ (off A27 onto A259 into Fishbourne. Turn right into Salthill Rd & right into Roman Way)

☎ 01243 785859

e-mail: adminfish@sussexpast.co.uk

web: www.sussexpast.co.uk

This is the largest known Roman residence in Britain. It was occupied from the 1st to the 3rd centuries AD, and has many beautiful mosaic floors. 25 of these can still be seen in varying states of completeness, including others rescued from elsewhere in the area. Outside, part of the garden has been replanted to its original 1st-century plan. The museum displays a collection of finds from the excavations and tells the story of the site's discovery. A computer-generated, audio-visual presentation helps bring the site back to life, as it would have been many centuries ago.

continued

Times: Open all year, daily Feb-15 Dec. Feb, Nov-Dec 10-4; Mar-Jul & Sep-Oct 10-5; Aug 10-6. Winter wknds 10-4. **Fee:** ✱ £6.50 (ch 5-15 £3.40, concessions £5.50, registered disabled £4.90). Family ticket £16.60 (2ad+2ch). **Facilities:** ♿ 💺 📷 ♿ (self guiding tapes & tactile objects for the blind) toilets for disabled shop ⊗ (ex guide dogs) ◀

FONTWELL   MAP 04 SU90

Denmans Garden   `2 for 1`

Denmans Ln BN18 0SU

⤷ *(5m E of Chichester off A27 W between Chichester and Arundel, adjacent to Fontwell racecourse)*

☎ 01243 542808

e-mail: denmans@denmans-garden.co.uk

web: www.denmans-garden.co.uk

The garden, jointly owned by John Brookes MBE and Michael Neve, is planted for all-year interest with emphasis on shape, colour and texture, and although four acres in size, is full of planting and design ideas that can be adapted to suit any size of garden. Gravel is used extensively in the garden, both to walk on and as a growing medium, so that you can walk through plantings rather than past them. Individual plants are allowed to self-seed and ramble.

Times: Open all year daily 9-5. Closed 24-26 Dec & 1 Jan **Fee:** ✱ £3.95 (ch £2.25, ch under 4 free, pen £3.45). Family ticket £11 Party 15+ £3.25 each. **Facilities:** ♿ 💺 📷 ♿ toilets for disabled shop garden centre ⊗ (ex guide dogs) ◀

GOODWOOD   MAP 04 SU81

Goodwood House

PO18 0PX

⤷ *(3m NE of Chichester)*

☎ 01243 755048

e-mail: curator@goodwood.co.uk

web: www.goodwood.co.uk

The Sussex Downs and 12000 acre working country estate provide a glorious backdrop to the magnificent Regency house, which has been the home of the Dukes of Richmond for over 300 years. The gilded, richly-decorated State Apartments include the luxurious Yellow Drawing Room and the unique Egyptian Dining Room. The art collection includes paintings by George Stubbs and Canaletto.

Times: Open end Mar-Sep, Sun & Mon, 1-5; Aug, Sun-Thu. Closed for occasional events. **Fee:** £8 (ch under 12 free, ch & student £4, pen £7). Groups 20+ £7 each. **Facilities:** ♿ 💺 ♿ (ramp at front of house, disabled parking area) toilets for disabled shop ⊗ (ex guide dogs) ◀

HANDCROSS   MAP 04 TQ22

Nymans Garden

Staplefield Rd RH17 6EB

⤷ *(on B2114 at Handcross, 4.5m S of Crawley)*

☎ 01444 400321

e-mail: nymans@nationaltrust.org.uk

web: www.nationaltrust.org.uk/nymans

Nymans is one of the great gardens of the Sussex Weald. It has a fascinating and exotic plant collection, partially ruined mansion and woodland walks. There are great opportunities to enjoy Nymans and the surrounding estate in any season.

Times: Open Garden: 16 Feb-30 Oct, Wed-Sun & BH. Nov-Mar, wknds 11-4 (restricted access due to ground conditions). House open 16 Mar-30 Oct, 11.30-5. Closed 25-26 Dec & 1-2 Jan. **Fee:** ✱ £6.70 (ch £3.30), Family ticket £16.70; Winter: £3.30 (ch £1.60), Family ticket £8 **Facilities:** ♿ 💺 📷 ♿ (wheelchair route, Batricar, Braille guide) toilets for disabled shop garden centre ⊗ (ex guide & hearing dogs) ♨ ◀

HAYWARDS HEATH   MAP 05 TQ32

Borde Hill Garden

Balcombe Rd RH16 1XP

⤷ *(0.5m N of Haywards Heath on Balcombe Rd, 3m from A23)*

☎ 01444 450326

e-mail: info@bordehill.co.uk

web: www.bordehill.co.uk

This glorious garden flows into linked garden rooms, boasting their own distinctive character and style. Year-round colour and interest with spring flowering rhododendrons, azaleas, camellias, magnolias and the many champion trees. The Rose and Italian Gardens with the herbaceous borders provide colour for summer and into autumn. Set in 200 acres of parkland with panoramic views, woodland and lakeside walks.

Times: Open Apr-Oct, 10-6. **Fee:** ✱ £6 (ch £3.50, pen & group £5) **Facilities:** ♿ 💺 🍴 licensed ♿ (wheelchairs available, audio/Braille guides) toilets for disabled shop ◀

HIGHDOWN   MAP 04 SU91

Highdown   `FREE`

Highdown Gardens BN12 6PE

⤷ *(N off A259 between Worthing & Littlehampton. Access off dual carriageway, when coming from E proceed to rdbt)*

☎ 01903 501054

e-mail: chris.beardsley@worthing.gov.uk

web: www.worthing.gov.uk/wbc

Set on downland countryside this unique garden overlooks the sea, and has been deemed a National collection due to the unique assortment of rare plants and trees. The garden was the achievement of Sir Frederick and Lady Stern, who worked for fifty years to prove that plants could grow on chalk. Many of the original plants were collected in China and the Himalayas.

Times: Open all year: Apr-Sep, Mon-Fri 10-6. Winter: Oct-Nov & Feb-Mar, Mon-Fri, 10-4.30; Dec-Jan, 10-4. **Facilities:** ♿ ♿ toilets for disabled ⊗ (ex guide dogs)

LITTLEHAMPTON   MAP 04 TQ00

Look & Sea! Visitor Centre   [2 for 1]
63-65 Surrey St BN17 5AW
➲ *(on harbour front 10 mins walk from Littlehampton Station)*
☎ 01903 718984
e-mail: info@lookandsea.co.uk
web: www.lookandsea.co.uk

An interactive museum exploring the history and geography of Littlehampton and the surrounding area. Inside the modern waterfront building you can meet the 500,000 year old Boxgrove Man, become a ship's captain in an interactive computer game, and enjoy spectacular panoramic views of the Sussex coast from the circular glass tower.

Times: Open all year, daily 9-5 **Fee:** ✱ £2.95 (ch £2.50, concessions £2.50). **Facilities:** ℗ (20 mtrs) 🍽 licensed 🎫 ♿ toilets for disabled shop ⊗ (ex guide dogs) 🎟

LOWER BEEDING   MAP 04 TQ22

Leonardslee Lakes & Gardens
RH13 6PP
➲ *(4m SW from Handcross, at junct of B2110 & A281)*
☎ 01403 891212
e-mail: gardens@leonardslee.com
web: www.leonardslee.com

This Grade I listed garden is set in a peaceful valley with walks around seven beautiful lakes. It is a paradise in spring, with banks of rhododendrons and azaleas along paths lined with bluebells. Wallabies live in parts of the valley, deer in the parks and wildfowl on the lakes. Enjoy the Rock Garden, the fascinating Bonsai, the new 'Behind the Doll's House' exhibition and the collection of Victorian Motorcars (1889-1900).

Times: Open Apr-Oct, daily 9.30-6 **Facilities:** ℗ 🍽 licensed shop garden centre ⊗ 🎟

PETWORTH   MAP 04 SU92

Petworth House & Park
GU28 0AE
➲ *(in town centre, A272/283)*
☎ 01798 342207 & 343929
e-mail: petworth@nationaltrust.org.uk
web: www.nationaltrust.org.uk/petworth

Petworth house is an impressive 17th-century mansion set in a 700 acre Deer Park, landscaped by 'Capability' Brown, and immortalised in Turner's paintings. At Petworth you will find the National Trust's finest art collection including work by Van Dyck, Titian, and Turner, as well as sculpture, ceramics and fine furniture. Fascinating Servants' Quarters show the domestic side of life of this great estate.

Times: Open Apr-Oct 11-5 last entry 4.30 (closed Thu-Fri) **Fee:** ✱ £8 (ch £4). Family ticket £20. Party 15+ £7 each. NT members free. Pleasure Ground £3 (ch £1.50). **Facilities:** ℗ 🍽 licensed 🎫 ♿ (wheelchairs available, Braille guide, virtual tour) toilets for disabled shop ⊗ (ex guide/hearing dogs) ⛟ 🎟

PULBOROUGH   MAP 04 TQ01

Parham House & Gardens
Parham Park, Storrington RH20 4HS
➲ *(midway between A29 & A24, off A283 between Pulborough & Storrington)*
☎ 01903 744888 & 742021
e-mail: enquiries@parhaminsussex.co.uk
web: www.parhaminsussex.co.uk

Surrounded by a deer park, fine gardens and 18th-century pleasure grounds in a beautiful downland setting, this Elizabethan family home contains an important collection of paintings, furniture, carpets and rare needlework. There are four acres of walled garden with huge herbaceous borders, greenhouse, orchard and herb garden. A brick and turf maze has been created in the grounds - designed with children in mind, it is called 'Veronica's Maze'.

Times: Open Etr Sun-Sep, Wed, Thu, Sun & BH Mons (also open Tue & Fri in Aug). Gardens open 12-6; House 2-6 (last entry 5). **Fee:** ✱ House & Gardens £6.50 (ch 5-15 £2.50, pen & disabled visitors £5.50). Family ticket £15.50. Garden only £5 (ch £1). Party rates available. **Facilities:** ℗ 🍽 🎫 ♿ (wheelchairs, ramps, recorded tour tape, parking) toilets for disabled shop garden centre ⊗ (ex guide dogs & in grounds) 🎟

RSPB Pulborough Brooks Nature Reserve

Uppertons Barn Visitor Centre, Wiggonholt RH20 2EL

➲ *(signed on A283, 2m SE of Pulborough & 2m NW of Storrington)*

☎ 01798 875851

e-mail: pulborough.brooks@rspb.org.uk

web: www.rspb.org.uk

Set in the scenic Arun Valley and easily reached via the visitor centre at Wiggonholt, this is an excellent reserve for year-round family visits. A nature trail winds through hedgerow-lined lanes to viewing hides overlooking water-meadows. Breeding summer birds include nightingales and warblers, ducks and wading birds, and nightjars and hobbies on nearby heathland. Unusual wading birds and hedgerow birds regularly pass through on spring and autumn migration.

Times: ✶ Open daily, Reserve: 9-9, (or sunset if earlier). Visitor centre: 10-5. Reserve closed 25 Dec, Visitor Centre closed 25-26 Dec.

Facilities: ❷ ➓ 🍴 ♿ (free hire electric buggy and wheelchair) toilets for disabled shop ⊗ (ex guide dogs) ◀

SINGLETON
MAP 04 SU81

Weald & Downland Open Air Museum

PO18 0EU

➲ *(6m N of Chichester on A286)*

☎ 01243 811348

e-mail: office@wealddown.co.uk

web: www.wealddown.co.uk

A showcase of English architectural heritage, where historic buildings have been rescued from destruction and rebuilt in a parkland setting. Vividly demonstrating the evolution of building techniques and use of local materials, these fascinating buildings bring to life the homes, farms and rural industries of the south east of the past 500 years.

Times: Open all year, Mar-Oct, daily 10.30-6. Call or see website for winter opening. **Fee:** ✶ £7.95 (ch £4.25, pen £6.95). Family ticket (2ad+3ch) £21.95. **Facilities:** ❷ ➓ 🍴 ♿ (separate entrance and ramps available for some buildings) toilets for disabled shop ⊗ (ex on lead) ◀

SOUTH HARTING
MAP 04 SU71

Uppark

GU31 5QR

➲ *(A3 take A272, B2146 to South Harting, follow signs to Uppark)*

☎ 01730 825415 825857

e-mail: uppark@nationaltrust.org.uk

web: www.nationaltrust.org.uk/uppark

A late 17th-century house set high on the South Downs with magnificent sweeping views to the sea. An extensive exhibition tells the dramatic story of the 1989 fire and subsequent restoration of the house and its collections. The elegant Georgian interior houses a famous Grand Tour collection that includes paintings, furniture and ceramics. An 18th-century dolls' house with original features is one of the more impressive items. The servants' quarters appear as they did in Victorian days, when H G Wells' mother was housekeeper, while the garden is restored in the early 19th-century 'Picturesque' style.

Times: Open end Mar-end Oct, Sun-Thu. Restoration exhibition, gardens, shop and restaurant: 11.30-5. House: 12.30-4. **Fee:** £6.50 (ch £3.25) family £16. **Facilities:** ❷ ➓ 🍴 licensed 🍴 ♿ (ramps, lift to basement, chair lift in exhibition) toilets for disabled shop ⊗ (ex woodland walk & car park) 🐾 ◀

TANGMERE
MAP 04 SU90

Tangmere Military Aviation Museum Trust

PO20 2ES

➲ *(off A27, 3m E of Chichester towards Arundel)*

☎ 01243 775223

e-mail: info@tangmere-museum.org.uk

web: www.tangmere-museum.org.uk

Based at an airfield that played an important role during the World Wars, this museum spans 80 years of military aviation. There are photographs, documents, aircraft and aircraft parts on display along with a Hurricane replica, Spitfire replica and cockpit simulator. A hangar houses a Supermarine Swift and the record-breaking aircraft Meteor and Hunter. Aircraft outside include; Lockheed T33, English Electric Lightning, De Havilland Sea Vixen, McDonnell Douglas Phantom F4, Gloster Meteor and a Westland Whirlwind helicopter.

Times: Open Mar-Oct, daily 10-5.30; Feb & Nov, daily 10-4.30. **Fee:** ✶ £5 (ch £1.50 & pen £4) Family £11.50 (2ad+2ch). **Facilities:** ❷ ➓ 🍴 ♿ (wheelchairs available) toilets for disabled shop ⊗ (ex guide dogs)

WEST DEAN
MAP 04 SU81

West Dean Gardens
PO18 0QZ
➲ *(6m N of Chichester and 7m S of Midhurst on A286)*
☎ 01243 818210 & 811301
e-mail: gardens@westdean.org.uk
web: www.westdean.org.uk

Award winning historic garden of 35 acres in a tranquil downland setting. Noted for its 300ft long Harold Peto pergola, mixed and herbaceous borders, rustic summerhouses and specimen trees. Walled kitchen garden with magnificent collection of 16 Victorian glasshouses and frames. The visitors' centre provides a high level of facilities with a beautiful prospect of the River Lavant and West Dean Park.

Times: Open Mar-Oct, daily 10.30-5, Nov-Feb, 10.30-4, Wed-Sun only 3 hours. Closed 24 Dec-2 Jan. **Fee:** ✱ Mar-Oct, £6 (concessions £2.50). Family ticket £14.25. Nov-Feb, £3 (ch £1.25). Family ticket £7.25. Adult season ticket £22.50, family season ticket £50. **Facilities:** ❷ ⭐ licensed 🍴 ᪲ (reserved parking, 2 wheelchairs available) toilets for disabled shop ⊗ (ex guide dogs) ▬

WISBOROUGH GREEN
MAP 04 TQ02

Fishers Farm Park NEW
Newpound Ln RH14 0EG
➲ *(follow brown & white tourist boards on all roads approaching Wisborough Green)*
☎ 01403 700063
e-mail: info@fishersfarmpark.co.uk
web: www.fishersfarmpark.co.uk

All weather, all year farm and adventure park, providing a mixture of farmyard and dynamic adventure play.

Times: Open all year, daily, 10-5. Closed 26-26 Dec. **Fee:** ✱ From £7.75 (ch 2 yrs from £4, ch 3-16 yrs from £7.25, concessions from £6.25) **Facilities:** ❷ ⭐ ⭐ licensed ᪲ toilets for disabled shop ⊗ ▬

Chichester Cathedral

Tyne & Wear

River Ty
Newcastle Upon T

The vibrant city of Newcastle Upon Tyne has see
great deal of recent investment and redevelopme
especially the Quayside area. Its famous brid
include the innovative Gateshead Millennium Brid
nicknamed the Blinking Eye, and the iconic T
Bridge, built in 1849 by Robert Stephenson, the
road and rail bridge in the wo

England

GATESHEAD   MAP 12 NZ26

Baltic Centre for Contemporary Art   FREE
South Shore Rd, Gateshead Quays NE8 3BA

➲ *(follow signs for Quayside, Millennium Bridge. 15 mins' walk from Gateshead Metro & Newcastle Central Station)*

☎ 0191 478 1810 & 440 4944
e-mail: info@balticmill.com
web: www.balticmill.com

Once a 1950s grain warehouse, part of the old Baltic Flour Mills, the Baltic Centre for Contemporary Art is an international centre presenting a dynamic and ambitious programme of complementary exhibitions and events. It consists of five art spaces, cinema, auditorium, library and archive, eating and drinking areas and a shop. Check website for current events information.

Times: Please see website for details **Facilities:** ☉ (charged) ☕ ⌑ licensed ⊟ ♿ (wheelchairs/scooters, Braille/large-print guides) toilets for disabled shop ⊗ (ex guide & hearing dogs)

JARROW   MAP 12 NZ36

Bede's World   2 for 1
Church Bank NE32 3DY

➲ *(off A185 near S end of Tyne tunnel)*

☎ 0191 489 2106
e-mail: visitor.info@bedesworld.co.uk
web: www.bedesworld.co.uk

The Venerable Bede lived over 1300 years ago and was one of early Britain's greatest scholars, author of the *Historia Ecclesiastica Gentis Anglorum* - the definitive history of the early medieval period. As well as exhibits detailing Bede's monastic life and work, the museum re-creates an Anglo-Saxon farm and incorporates the ruins of the medieval monastery.

Times: Open all year, Apr-Oct, Mon-Sat 10-5.30, Sun noon-5.30; Nov-Mar, Mon-Sat 10-4.30 & Sun 12-4.30; Xmas-New Year opening times vary. **Fee:** ✱ £4.50 (ch & concessions £3). Family ticket £10. Concession Family ticket £7. Party rates 15+. **Facilities:** ☉ ☕ ⌑ licensed ⊟ ♿ (wheelchair & elec. wheelchair on request, disabled parking) toilets for disabled shop ⊗ (ex guide dogs) ⌑

NEWCASTLE UPON TYNE   MAP 12 NZ26

Centre for Life   2 for 1
Times Square NE1 4EP

➲ *(A1M, A69, A184, A1058 & A167, follow signs to Centre for Life or Central Station)*

☎ 0191 243 8210
e-mail: info@life.org.uk
web: www.life.org.uk

The Life Science Centre is an interactive, action-packed day out that takes the visitor to the beginning of life and back again. From single-celled organisms to dinosaurs, from 4 billion years ago to today, this is a fascinating attraction that deals with perhaps the most fundamental subject of all: Life Itself.

Times: Open all year Mon-Sat 10-6, Sun 11-6 . Closed 25 Dec & 1 Jan. (Last entry subject to seasonal demand). **Fee:** £6.95 (ch £4.50, concessions £5.50). Family ticket £19.95. **Facilities:** ☉ (charged) ☕ ⌑ licensed ♿ (ramps, wheelchairs, induction loops) toilets for disabled shop ⊗ (ex guide dogs) ⌑

Museum of Antiquities   FREE
The University NE1 7RU

➲ *(Situated on main campus of Newcastle University between The Haymarket & Queen Victoria Rd)*

☎ 0191 222 7849
e-mail: m.o.antiquities@ncl.ac.uk
web: www.ncl.ac.uk/antiquities

Artefacts from north east England from prehistoric times to AD 1600 are on display here. The principal museum for Hadrian's Wall, this collection includes models of the wall, life-size Roman soldiers and a newly refurbished reconstruction of the Temple of Mithras.

Times: Open all year, daily (ex Sun), 10-5. Closed Good Fri, 24-26 Dec & 1 Jan. **Facilities:** ℗ (400yds) ⊟ ♿ (large print guide) shop ⊗ (ex guide dogs) ⌑

ROWLANDS GILL   MAP 12 NZ15

Gibside
NE16 6BG

➲ *(3m W of Metro Centre & 6m SW of Gateshead, on B6314, clearly signposted from the A1)*

☎ 01207 541820
e-mail: gibside@nationaltrust.org.uk
web: www.nationaltrust.org.uk

This 18th-century landscaped garden is the former home of the Bowes-Lyon family, with miles of walks through the wooded slopes and riverside of the Derwent valley. Discover hidden vistas, wildlife or wild flowers, or just enjoy a Georgian style lunch in the tea room. Lots of events and activities for children and families, and those interested can hold an Anglican wedding in the unique Palladian Chapel.

Times: Grounds open: all year daily 6 Mar-22 Oct 10-6 (last entry 4.30); 23 Oct-4 Mar 10-4 (last entry 3.30) closed 23-26 Dec, 30 Dec-2 Jan; Chapel open 6 Mar-22 Oct 11-4.30; Shop & tea room open 26 Mar-22 Oct 11-5; 23 Oct-4 Mar 11-4 **Fee:** ✱ £5 (ch £3). Family (2ad+4ch), £15, family (1ad+3ch), £10 **Facilities:** ☉ ☕ ♿ (Braille guide, w/chairs and carriers, induction loop) toilets for disabled shop ⧆ ⌑

SOUTH SHIELDS   MAP 12 NZ36

Arbeia Roman Fort & Museum
Baring St NE33 2BB

➲ *(5 mins' walk from town centre)*

☎ 0191 456 1369
web: www.twmuseums.org.uk

In South Shields town are the extensive remains of Arbeia, a Roman fort in use from the 2nd to 4th century. It was the supply base for the Roman army's campaign against Scotland. On site there are full size reconstructions of a fort gateway, a barrack block and part of the commanding officer's house. Archaeological evacuations are in progress throughout the summer.

Times: Open all year, Apr-Oct, Mon-Sat 10-5.30, Sun 1-5; Nov-Mar, Mon-Sat 10-3.30. Closed 25-26 Dec & 1 Jan **Fee:** Fort & Museum free of charge ex for 'Timequest' Archaeological Interpretation Gallery £1.50 (ch & concessions 80p). **Facilities:** ℗ (on road outside) ♿ (pre-visit info pack and portable induction loop) toilets for disabled shop ⌑

England

SUNDERLAND   MAP 12 NZ35

National Glass Centre
Liberty Way SR6 0GL
➲ *(A19 onto A1231, signposted from all major roads)*
☎ 0191 515 5555
e-mail: info@nationalglasscentre.com
web: www.nationalglasscentre.com

Housed in a striking modern building, the National Glass Centre celebrates the unique material and explains its history. Visitors can see the changing exhibitions of glass art, featuring pieces by leading artists. There is also the opportunity to witness the glass-making process and learn how it impacts on our lives. The brave can even walk on the glass roof 30 feet above the riverside.

Times: Open daily 10-5 (last admission to glass tour 4). Closed 25 Dec & 1 Jan. **Fee:** ✱ £3 (concessions £1.50). Family ticket £6.
Facilities: ❷ ⏱ licensed ♿ (lifts, ramps, parking facilites) toilets for disabled shop ⊗ (ex guide dogs) ◀

Sunderland Museum & Winter Gardens
Burdon Rd SR1 1PP
➲ *(in city centre on Burdon Rd, short walk from Sunderland metro and mainline stations)*
☎ 0191 553 2323
e-mail: sunderland@twmuseums.org.uk
web: www.twmuseums.org.uk/sunderland

An award-winning attraction with wide-ranging displays and many hands-on exhibits that cover the archaeology and geology of Sunderland, the coal mines and shipyards of the area and the spectacular glass and pottery made on Wearside. Other galleries show the changes in the lifestyles of Sunderland women over the past century, works by LS Lowry and wildlife from all corners of the globe. The Winter Gardens are a horticultural wonderland where exotic plants from around the world can be seen growing to their full natural height in a spectacular glass and steel rotunda.

Times: Open all year, Mon-Sat 10-5, Sun 2-5. **Facilities:** ⓟ (150 yds) 🍴 ⏱ licensed ▦ ♿ (lifts to all floors, induction loops) toilets for disabled shop ⊗ (ex guide dogs) ◀

TYNEMOUTH   MAP 12 NZ36

Blue Reef Aquarium
Grand Pde NE30 4JF
➲ *(follow A19, taking A1058 (coast road), signed Tynemouth. Situated on seafront)*
☎ 0191 258 1031
e-mail: tynemouth@bluereefaquarium.co.uk
web: www.bluereefaquarium.co.uk

From its position overlooking one of the North East's prettiest beaches, Blue Reef is home to a dazzling variety of creatures including seahorses, puffer fish, octopi, crabs, and even the deadly piranha. Visitors can walk through an underwater tunnel in a 250,000 litre tropical ocean tank. This offers close encounters with all manner of undersea wonders like sharks and stingrays.

Times: Open all year, daily from 10. Closed 25 Dec **Fee:** £5.99 (ch 3-16 £3.99, concessions £4.99). Family ticket (2ad+2ch) £17.50, (2ad+3ch) £21.50. **Facilities:** ❷ (charged) 🍴 ▦ ♿ (wheelchair available) toilets for disabled shop ⊗ (ex guide dogs) ◀

Tynemouth Priory and Castle
NE30 4BZ
➲ *(near North Pier)*
☎ 0191 257 1090
web: www.english-heritage.org.uk

Discover a rich and varied history as you explore the priory, castle and underground chambers beneath a World War I gun battery.

Times: Open all year, Apr-Sep, daily 10-5; Oct, daily 10-4; Nov-Mar, Thu-Mon 10-4. Gun Battery:Access limited, please ask site staff for details. Closed 24-26 Dec & 1 Jan. **Fee:** £3.40 (ch £1.70, concessions £2.60. Family £8.50). Prices and opening times are subject to change in Spring 2007. Please check web site or call 0870 333 1181 for the most up to date prices and opening times when planning your visit. **Facilities:** ♿ (wheelchair access to priory) shop ⊞

WALLSEND   MAP 12 NZ26

Segedunum Roman Fort, Baths & Museum
Buddle St NE28 6HR
➲ *(A187 from Tyne Tunnel, signposted)*
☎ 0191 236 9347
e-mail: segedunum@twmuseums.org.uk
web: www.twmuseums.org.uk

Hadrian's Wall was built by the Roman Emperor, Hadrian in 122AD, Segedunum was built as part of the Wall, serving as a garrison for 600 soldiers until the collapse of Roman rule around 410AD. This major historical venture shows what life would have been like then, using artefacts, audio-visuals, reconstructed buildings and a 34m high viewing tower. Plenty of special events including puppet shows, workshops, and Saturnalia. Contact for details.

Times: Open all year, Apr-Oct 10-5.30, Nov-Mar, 10-3. **Fee:** ✱ £3.95 (ch, pen & concessions £2.25). (ch 16 and under free) **Facilities:** ❷ 🍴 ▦ ♿ (lifts) toilets for disabled shop ⊗ (ex guide dogs) ◀

WASHINGTON   MAP 12 NZ35

Washington Old Hall
The Avenue, Washington Village NE38 7LE
➲ *(7m S of Newcastle-upon-Tyne. From A1 and A19 follow signs to A1231 to Washington, then District 4. The Avenue, next to Holy Trinity Church)*
☎ 0191 416 6879
e-mail: washington.oldhall@nationaltrust.org.uk
web: www.nationaltrust.org.uk

Sitting next to Washington's Holy Trinity church, the Old Hall was the home of George Washington's ancestors from 1183 to 1613, and was originally a medieval manor, but was rebuilt in the 17th century. The house has been restored and filled with period furniture, and contains displays on George Washington and the history of American Independence. Enjoy a peaceful walk in the formal Jacobean garden.

Times: Open Apr-Oct, Sun-Wed & Good Fri 11-5. House: 11-5. Garden: 10-5. Tea-room: 11-4. **Fee:** ✱ £4 (ch £2.50). Family ticket £10.50. **Facilities:** ❷ 🍴 ♿ (Braille guide, sensory scented gdns, induction loop, w/chair) toilets for disabled shop ⊗ (ex guide dogs) ✤

WWT Washington

2 for 1

District 15 NE38 8LE

➲ *(signposted off A195, A1231 & A182)*

☎ 0191 416 5454

e-mail: washington@wwt.org.uk

web: www.wwt.org.uk

In a parkland setting, on the north bank of the River Wear, WWT Washington is the home of a wonderful collection of exotic wildfowl from all over the world. There is also a heronry where visitors can watch a colony of wild Grey Herons on CCTV. The 100-acre site includes an area for wintering wildfowl which can be observed from hides, and a flock of Chilean Flamingos. Other features include a discovery centre, waterfowl nursery, picture windows and a viewing gallery from which to observe the birds.

Times: Open all year, daily 9.30-5 (summer) or 9.30-4 (winter). Closed 25 Dec. **Fee:** ✱ £5.95 (ch £3.75, concessions £4.75). Family £15.50 **Facilities:** ❷ ☕ ⑩ licensed ♿ (lowered windows in certain hides, wheelchairs to hire free) toilets for disabled shop ⊗ (ex guide/hearing dogs) 🍴

WHITBURN

MAP 12 NZ46

Souter Lighthouse

Coast Rd SR6 7NH

➲ *(on A183 coast road, 2m S of South Shields, 3m N of Sunderland)*

☎ 0191 529 3161 & 01670 773966

e-mail: souter@nationaltrust.org.uk

web: www.nationaltrust.org.uk

When it opened in 1871, Souter was the most advanced lighthouse in the world, and warned shipping off the notorious rocks in the river approaches of the Tyne and Wear. Painted red and white and standing at 150ft high, it is a dramatic building and hands-on displays and volunteers help bring it to life. Visitors can explore the whole building with its engine room and lighthouse keeper's cottage. You can take part in hands-on activities concerning shipwrecks and the workings of the lighthouse, and see coastal creatures in the Rockpool Fishtank. Climb to the top of the lighthouse, or walk along the Leas, a 2.5 mile stretch of spectacular coastline.

Times: Open Apr-29 Oct daily ex Fri (open Good Fri) 11-5 (last entry 30mins before closing). **Fee:** ✱ £4 (ch £2.50) Family ticket £10.50. **Facilities:** ❷ ⑩ 📗 ♿ (Braille guide, induction loops, tactile exhibits) toilets for disabled shop ⊗ (ex guide dogs) 🍴

Tynemouth Priory

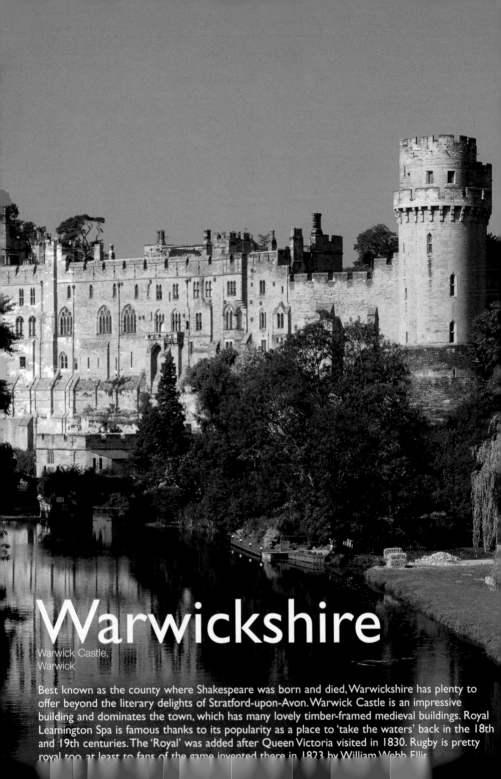

Warwickshire

Warwick Castle,
Warwick

Best known as the county where Shakespeare was born and died, Warwickshire has plenty to offer beyond the literary delights of Stratford-upon-Avon. Warwick Castle is an impressive building and dominates the town, which has many lovely timber-framed medieval buildings. Royal Leamington Spa is famous thanks to its popularity as a place to 'take the waters' back in the 18th and 19th centuries. The 'Royal' was added after Queen Victoria visited in 1830. Rugby is pretty royal too, at least to fans of the game invented there in 1823 by William Webb Ellis.

ALCESTER   MAP 04 SP05

Ragley Hall

B49 5NJ

➲ (8m SW of Stratford-upon-Avon, off A46/A435, follow brown tourist signs)

☎ 01789 762090

e-mail: info@ragleyhall.com

web: www.ragleyhall.com

Built in 1680, Ragley is the family home of the Marquess and Marchioness of Hertford and houses a superb collection of 18th century paintings, porcelain and furniture. Set in 27 acres of gardens and 400 acres of parkland, The house contains a stunning mural by Graham Rust *The Temptation* and England's finest Baroque plasterwork dated 1750. Ticket includes the house, Terrace Tea rooms overlooking the rose garden, gift shop, adventure playground, unique 3D maze, lakeside picnic area, woodland walk and stables containing equestrian memorabilia. Location for BBC production of *Scarlet Pimpernel*.

Times: ✱ Open mid Apr-end Sep, Thu-Sun & BH Mon. Park & Garden open daily, mid Jul-end Aug. **Facilities:** ♿ 💺 ♿ (lift to first floor) toilets for disabled shop

---

BADDESLEY CLINTON   MAP 04 SP27

Baddesley Clinton Hall

B93 0DQ

➲ (0.75m W off A4141, 7.5m NW of Warwick)

☎ 01564 783294

e-mail: baddesleyclinton@nationaltrust.org.uk

web: www.nationaltrust.org.uk

A romantically-sited medieval moated house, dating from the 14th century, that has changed very little since 1634. With family portraits, priest's holes, chapel, garden, ponds, nature trail and lake walk.

Times: Open Garden, Restaurant & Shop: Mar-Apr & Oct-5 Nov, Wed-Sun 12-5; May-Sep, Wed-Sun 12-5.30; 8 Nov-10 Dec, Wed-Sun 12-4.30. House: Mar-Apr & Oct-5 Nov, Wed-Sun 1.30-5; May-Sep, Wed-Sun 1.30-5.30. BH Mon Good Fri. **Fee:** ✱ Garden only £3.40 (ch £1.70). House & Garden £6.80 (ch £3.40). Family ticket £17. Joint ticket with Packwood House £9.80 (ch £4.90). Family ticket £24.50. Joint ticket for gardens only £4.90 (ch £2.45). National Trust members and children under 5 free.

Facilities: ♿ 🍴 licensed 📷 ♿ (4 wheelchairs available, Braille guides, tactile route) toilets for disabled shop ⊗ (ex guide dogs) ♨ 🍽

CHARLECOTE   MAP 04 SP25

Charlecote Park   [2 for 1]

CV35 9ER

➲ (5m E of Stratford, 1m W of Wellesbourne, off B4086)

☎ 01789 470277 Events 07788 658495

e-mail: charlecote.park@nationaltrust.org.uk

web: www.nationaltrust.org.uk

Queen Elizabeth I and William Shakespeare knew Charlecote Park well. Follow in their footsteps at this impressive Warwickshire house and ancient deer park. Special events held every week, from outdoor picnic concerts to family events, outdoor theatre and specialist tours. Call for event details.

Times: Open 4 Mar-29 Oct, Fri-Tue; Grounds 10.30-5.30, (Park until 6), House noon-5. Open wknds Nov & Dec **Fee:** ✱ House & Grounds; £6.90 (ch £3.50), Family £17, Groups £5.90. Grounds only; £3.50 (ch £1.85). NT members free. **Facilities:** ♿ 💺 🍴 licensed 📷 ♿ (Braille guides, induction loop) toilets for disabled shop ⊗ (ex assist dogs) ♨

COMPTON VERNEY   MAP 04 SP35

Compton Verney   [2 for 1]

CV35 9HZ

➲ (7m E of Stratford-upon-Avon on B4086 between Wellesbourne & Kineton)

☎ 01926 645500

e-mail: info@comptonverney.org.uk

web: www.comptonverney.org.uk

Warwickshire largest gallery, housed in an 18th-century Grade I Robert Adam mansion house, set in 120 acres of 'Capability' parkland. Six permanent collections include; Naples 1600-1800, Germany 1450-1650, British portraits, China, British Folk Art and the Marx-Lambert collection. There is also a programme of changing exhibitions, special events, tours and workshops.

Times: Open: 24 Mar-9 Dec, Tue-Sun, 10-5. Closed Mon except BH. **Fee:** ✱ £7 (ch under 5's free, 5-16 £2, concessions £4) Family £16 (2 ad + up to 4 ch). **Facilities:** ♿ 💺 🍴 licensed 📷 ♿ (w/chairs, large print guides, hearing loop) toilets for disabled shop ⊗ (ex assist dogs) 🍽

COUGHTON   MAP 04 SP06

Coughton Court

B49 5JA

➲ (2m N of Alcester on E side of A435)

☎ 01789 400777 400702

web: www.nationaltrust.org.uk

This imposing Tudor house is set in beautiful gardens, and has been home to the Throckmortons for hundreds of years. The house contains many family portraits, and much in the way of fascinating furniture, fabrics and ornaments. The estate has two churches, a 19th-century Catholic church, and the parish church of St Peters. A special exhibition outlines the involvement of the family in the Gunpowder Plot of 1605.

Times: Open: Apr-Sep, Wed-Sun. 10 Oct-29 Oct, Sat-Sun. Open BH Mon and Tue. Closed: 24 Jun and 15 Jul. **Fee:** ✱ House and Garden: £8.60 (ch £4.30). Family ticket £21.50. Garden only: £5.90 (ch £2.95). Family ticket £15. **Facilities:** ♿ 🍴 licensed 📷 ♿ (Braille guide, parking, 3 w/chairs available) toilets for disabled shop ⊗ (ex guide dogs) ♨ 🍽

England

FARNBOROUGH

MAP 04 SP44

Farnborough Hall

OX17 1DU
⮕ *(6m N of Banbury, 0.5m W of A423)*
☎ 01295 690002
web: www.nationaltrust.org.uk

A classical mid 18th-century stone house with notable plasterwork; the entrance hall, staircase and two principal rooms are shown. The grounds contain charming 18th-century temples, a 0.75m terrace walk and an obelisk.

Times: House, grounds & terrace walk open Apr-Sep, 2-5.30. (Last admission 5). **Fee:** ✱ House, Garden & Terrace walk £4.20 (ch £2.10), Family £11.50. Terrace walk £1.80. Terrace walk only (Thu & Fri) £2.10. **Facilities:** ❶ 🍴 ⅗ ✿ (ex guide dogs) ⛄

GAYDON

MAP 04 SP35

Heritage Motor Centre `2 for 1`

Banbury Rd CV35 0BJ
⮕ *(M40 junct 12 and take B4100. Attraction signed)*
☎ 01926 641188
e-mail: enquiries@heritage-motor-centre.co.uk
web: www.heritage-motor-centre.co.uk

Home to the largest collection of historic British cars in the world, the Heritage Motor Centre is set in 65 acres of grounds. Attractions at the Centre include the Time Road, a fascinating journey through Britain's motoring and social history, the motoring cinema, and the 'Get Behind the Wheel' zone, where visitors get the chance to sit in a variety of cars from the collection. Outside features include; Land Rover 4x4 off-roading, go-karting, and children's miniature roadway.

Times: Open all year daily 10-5. (Closed 24-26 Dec). **Fee:** ✱ £8 (ch 5-16 £6, under 5 free, & pen £7). Family ticket £25. Additional charges apply to outdoor activities **Facilities:** ❶ 🅿 🍴 ⅗ (lift to all floors, limited number of manual wheelchairs) toilets for disabled shop ✿ (ex guide/hearing dogs) ⛄

See advert on opposite page

KENILWORTH

MAP 04 SP27

Kenilworth Castle

CV8 1NE
☎ 01926 852078
web: www.english-heritage.org.uk

Explore the largest and most extensive castle ruin in England, with a past rich in famous names and events in history. Its massive red sandstone towers, keep and wall glow brightly in the sunlight. Discover the history of Kenilworth through the interactive model in Leicester's Barn.

Times: Open all year, Apr-May & Sep-Oct daily, 10-5; Jun-Aug, daily, 10-6; Nov-Feb, daily, 10-4. Closed 24-26 Dec & 1 Jan. Gatehouse may close early Sat for private events **Fee:** £5.90 (ch £3, concessions £4.40) Family £14.80. Prices and opening times are subject to change in Spring 2007. Please check web site or call 0870 333 1181 for the most up to date prices and opening times when planning your visit. **Facilities:** ❶ 🍴 ⅗ shop ⛽

Stoneleigh Abbey

CV8 2LF
⮕ *(entrance off B4115 close to junct of A46 and A452)*
☎ 01926 858535 & 858585
e-mail: enquire@stoneleighabbey.org
web: www.stoneleighabbey.org

Stoneleigh Abbey is one of the finest country house estates in the Midlands and has been the subject of considerable restoration work. The abbey, founded in the reign of Henry II, is now managed by a charitable trust. Visitors will experience a wealth of architectural styles spanning more than 800 years. The magnificent state rooms and chapel, the medieval Gatehouse and the Regency stables are some of the major areas to be admired. Set in 690 acres of parkland.

Times: Open Good Fri-Oct, Tue-Thu, Sun & BHs for guided tours at 11, 1 & 3. Grounds open 10-5. **Fee:** Grounds only, £3. Guided tour of house, £6.50 (1ch 5-12 free, additional ch £3) pen £5. **Facilities:** ❶ 🍴 🅿 ⅗ (Lift acces to state rooms) toilets for disabled shop ✿ (ex assist dogs)

MIDDLETON

MAP 07 SP19

Ash End House Childrens Farm

Middleton Ln B78 2BL
⮕ *(signed from A4091)*
☎ 0121 329 3240
e-mail: contact@thechildrensfarm.co.uk
web: www.childrensfarm.co.uk

Ideal for young children, this is a small family-owned farm with many friendly animals to feed and stroke, including some rare breeds. Café, new farm shop stocking local produce, play areas, picnic barns and lots of undercover activities.

Times: Open daily 10-5 or dusk in winter. Closed 25 Dec-1 Jan and wkdays in Jan. **Fee:** £4.50 (ch £4.90 includes animal feed, farm badge & all activities). **Facilities:** ❶ 🍴 🅿 ⅗ toilets for disabled shop ✿ (ex guide dogs) ⛄

Middleton Hall

B78 2AE

⮕ *(M42 junct 9, on A4091 midway between Belfry & Drayton Manor, follow brown heritage signs)*

☎ 01827 283095

e-mail: middletonhall@btconnect.com

web: www.middletonhalltrust.co.uk

Once the home of two great 17th-century naturalists, Francis Willughby and John Ray, the Hall shows several architectural styles, from c1300 to a Georgian west wing. The grounds include a nature reserve, lake, meadow, orchard and woodland, all Sites of Special Scientific Interest. Please telephone or visit website for details of events running throughout the year.

Times: Open Apr-13 Oct, Sun 2-5, BH Sun 11-5. **Fee:** £2.50 (ch free, pen £1.50). BH & some Sun £5 (ch £1, pen £3.50) **Facilities:** ℗ ☕ 🍴 ♿ (wheelchair available) toilets for disabled shop

NUNEATON   MAP 04 SP39

Arbury Hall

CV10 7PT

⮕ *(2m SW of Nuneaton, off B4102 Meriden road)*

☎ 024 7638 2804

e-mail: brenda.newell@arburyhall.net

The 16th-century Elizabethan house, Gothicised in the 18th century, has been the home of the Newdegate family for over 450 years. It is the finest complete example of Gothic revival architecture in existence, and contains pictures, furniture, and beautiful plasterwork ceilings. The 17th-century stable block, with a central doorway by Wren, houses the tearooms and lovely gardens with lakes and wooded walks.

Times: Open Apr-Sep. Hall & Gardens: Sun & Mon of BH wknds only. For other opening days & times, contact Administrator. **Fee:** ✱ £6.50 (ch £4) Gardens only £5 (ch £3.50) **Facilities:** ℗ ☕ ♿ toilets for disabled shop ⊗ (ex guide dogs & in grounds)

PACKWOOD HOUSE   MAP 07 SP17

Packwood House

B94 6AT

⮕ *(on unclass road off A3400)*

☎ 01564 782024

e-mail: packwood@nationaltrust.org.uk

web: www.nationaltrust.org.uk

Dating from the 16th century, Packwood House has been extended and much changed over the years. An important collection of tapestries and textiles is displayed. Equally important are the stunning gardens with renowned herbaceous borders, attracting many visitors, and the almost surreal topiary garden based on the Sermon on the Mount.

Times: Open Gardens: Mar-5 Nov Wed-Sun, BH Mon, Good Fri. Mar/Oct/Nov 11-4.30. May-Sep 11-5.30; House Mar-Nov 12-4.30 **Fee:** ✱ House & Garden £6.20 (ch £3.10). Family ticket £15.50. Garden only £3.20 (ch £1.60). Joint ticket with Baddesley Clinton £9.80 (ch £4.90). Family ticket £24.50, joint ticket for gardens only £4.90 (ch 2.45). National trust members and ch under 5 go free. **Facilities:** ℗ 🍴 ♿ (2 w/chairs available, tactile tour, Braille guide) toilets for disabled shop ⊗ (ex guide dogs) 🐾 ◼

RUGBY   MAP 04 SP57

The Webb Ellis Rugby Football Museum   FREE

5 Saint Matthew's St CV21 3BY

⮕ *(on A428 opposite Rugby School)*

☎ 01788 567777

e-mail: service@webb-ellis.co.uk

web: www.webb-ellis.co.uk

An intriguing collection of Rugby football memorabilia is housed in the shop in which rugby balls have been made since 1842. Visitors can watch a craftsman at work, hand-stitching the footballs. Situated near to Rugby School and its famous playing field.

Times: Open all year, Mon-Sat 9-5. Phone for holiday opening times. **Facilities:** ℗ (500yds) ♿ shop ⊗ (ex guide dogs)

RYTON-ON-DUNSMORE   MAP 04 SP37

Ryton Organic Gardens

CV8 3LG

⮕ *(5m SE of Coventry signed off A45, on road to village of Wolston)*

☎ 024 7630 3517

e-mail: enquiry@gardenorganic.org.uk

web: www.gardenorganic.org.uk

Ten acres of glorious gardens show how you can grow flowers, fruit and vegetables nature's way without added chemicals. More than

continued

England

thirty individual gardens to look at and enjoy, plus 'The Vegetable Kingdom' - learn all about vegetables, their history, varieties, and how they help to keep us healthy, in a fully interactive visitor centre. Garden Organic Ryton is the home of Garden Organic, the national charity for organic growing. Special events, tours, restaurant and coffee shop.

Times: Open daily 9-5. Closed Xmas. **Fee:** ✱ £5 (ch £2.50, concessions £4.50). **Facilities:** ❷ ♨ ⍟ licensed 🛍 ♿ (wheelchairs available & scooter) toilets for disabled shop garden centre ⊗ (ex guide dogs) ◀

SHOTTERY   MAP 04 SP15

Anne Hathaway's Cottage
Cottage Ln CV37 9HH

➲ *(House in Shottery Village, 1m from Stratford)*

☎ 01789 292100

e-mail: info@shakespeare.org.uk

web: www.shakespeare.org.uk

This world-famous thatched cottage was the childhood home of Anne Hathaway, William Shakespeare's wife. The cottage still contains many family items including the beautiful Hathaway Bed. In the stunning grounds there is a quintessential English cottage garden, orchard, sculpture garden, a romantic willow cabin and a maze.

Times: Open Nov-Mar, daily 10-4; Apr-May & Oct-Nov, Mon-Sat 9.30-5, Sun 10-5; Jun-Aug, Mon-Sat 9-5, Sun 9.30-5. **Fee:** ✱ £5.50 (ch £2, concessions £4.50). Family ticket £13. All five Shakespeare Houses £14 (ch £6.50, concessions £12) Family ticket £29. **Facilities:** ❷ ♨ ♿ (access room with virtual reality tours of cottage) toilets for disabled shop ⊗ (ex assist dogs) ◀

STRATFORD-UPON-AVON   MAP 04 SP25

Hall's Croft
Old Town CV37 6EP

➲ *(located in the centre of Stratford upon Avon)*

☎ 01789 292107

e-mail: info@shakespeare.org.uk

web: www.shakespeare.org.uk

This elegant 17th-century house belonged to Shakespeare's eldest daughter, Susanna and her husband, the physician John Hall. It is an impressive building with many exquisite furnishing and paintings of the period, and an exhibition on early medicine.

Times: Open Nov-Mar, daily 11-4; Apr-May and Sep-Oct, daily 11-5; Jun-Aug, Mon-Sat 9.30-5, Sun 10-5. **Fee:** ✱ £3.75 (ch £1.75, concessions £3) Family ticket £10. All five Shakespeare Houses £14 (ch £6.50, concessions £12) Family ticket £29. Three in Town Shakespeare Houses £11 (ch £5.50, concessions £9) Family ticket £23. **Facilities:** ℗ ♨ ♿ toilets for disabled shop ⊗ (ex assist dogs) ◀

New Place / Nash's House
Chapel St CV37 6EP

➲ *(located in centre of Stratford upon Avon)*

☎ 01789 292325

e-mail: info@shakespeare.org.uk

web: www.shakespeare.org.uk

The elegant home of Shakespeare's granddaughter, Elizabeth Hall's first husband Thomas Nash. The adjacent site of New Place, where

continued

Shakespeare retired and subsequently died in 1616, is now preserved as a picturesque garden space with an attractive Elizabethan knot garden. There is a Complete Works of Shakespeare exhibition from May 2006 to December 2007.

Times: Open Nov-Mar, daily 11-4; Apr-May & Sep-Oct, daily 11-5; Jun-Aug, Mon-Sat 9.30-5, Sun 10-5.30. **Fee:** ✱ £3.75 (ch £1.75, concessions £3) Family ticket £10. All five Shakespeare Houses £14 (ch £6.50, concessions £12) Family ticket £29. All three Town Shakespeare Houses £11 (ch £5.50, concessions £9) Family ticket £23. **Facilities:** ℗ (250yds) ♿ toilets for disabled shop ⊗ (ex assist dogs) ◀

Royal Shakespeare Company
Collection

Royal Shakespeare Theatre, Waterside CV37 6BB

➲ *(M40 junct 14 take A46 S. At 1st rdbt take 1st exit (A439). Park in town centre, follow RSC signs)*

☎ 01789 262870

e-mail: info@rsc.org.uk

web: www.rsc.org.uk

The RSC gallery opened in 1881, and was part of the first Shakespeare Memorial Theatre. In 1926 fire destroyed the theatre leaving only a semi circular wall and the gallery. The exhibition space now displays costumes from past RSC productions, paintings and other Theatre Memorabilia.

Times: Open all year, Mon-Fri 1.30-6.30, Sat 10.30-6.30 & Sun (Nov-Mar) 11.30-4.30. Closed 24-25 Dec. Theatre tours usually Mon-Fri (ex matinee days), 1.30 & 5.30, Sun 12, 1, 2 & 3. **Facilities:** ❷ (charged) ♨ ⍟ licensed 🛍 ♿ (services for hearing impaired, reading room) toilets for disabled shop ⊗ (ex guide dogs)

Shakespeare's Birthplace
Henley St CV37 6QW

➲ *(in town centre)*

☎ 01789 204016

e-mail: info@shakespeare.org.uk

web: www.shakespeare.org.uk

Shakespeare was born in the half-timbered house in 1564. Containing original and replica artefacts, it is now presented as it may have been when he was a boy. The ticket price includes entrance to an exhibition

continued

of the author's life, including a first edition of his complete works from 1623.

Shakespeare's Birthplace

Times: Open Nov-Mar, Mon-Sat 10-4, Sun 10.30-4; Apr-May & Sep-Oct, Mon-Sat 10-5, Sun 10-5; Jun-Aug, Mon-Sat 9-5, Sun 9.30-5. **Fee:** ✻ £7 (ch £2.75, concessions £6) Family ticket £17. All five Shakespeare Houses £14 (ch £6.50, concessions £12) Family ticket £29. All three Town Shakespeare Houses £11 (ch £5.50, concessions £9) Family ticket £23. **Facilities:** Ⓟ (coach park 100m drop off only) (max 30 mins) ♿ (computer based virtual reality tour of upper floor) toilets for disabled shop ⊗ (ex assist dogs) 🅿

See advert on this page

Stratford Butterfly Farm

2 for 1

Tramway Walk, Swan's Nest Ln CV37 7LS
➲ *(south bank of River Avon opposite RSC)*
☎ 01789 299288
e-mail: sales@butterflyfarm.co.uk
web: www.butterflyfarm.co.uk

Europe's largest live Butterfly and Insect Exhibit. Hundreds of the world's most spectacular and colourful butterflies, in the unique setting of a lush tropical landscape, with splashing waterfalls and fish-filled pools. See also the strange and fascinating Insect City, a bustling metropolis of ants, stick insects, beetles and other remarkable insects. See the dangerous and deadly in Arachnoland!

Times: Open all year daily 10-6 (winter 10-dusk). Closed 25 Dec.
Fee: £4.95 (ch £3.95) concessions £4.45. Family £14.95
Facilities: Ⓟ (opposite entrance) (site parking orange badge holders only) 🍴 ♿ shop ⊗ 🅿

The Teddy Bear Museum

2 for 1

19 Greenhill St CV37 6LF
➲ *(M40 junct 15, follow signs to town centre)*
☎ 01789 293160
e-mail: info@theteddybearmuseum.com
web: www.theteddybearmuseum.com

Collection of some of the oldest and rarest teddy bears in the world, displayed in a house once owned by Henry VIII. Lots of modern teddy bear stars too, including the original Fozzie Bear, Paddington Bear from the earliest television series, Mr Bean's bear, and many more.

continued

Times: Open all year, daily 9.30-5.30 (ex Jan & Feb 10-4.30). Closed 25-26 Dec. **Fee:** ✱ £2.95 (ch £1.95, concessions £2.45). Family ticket £9.50 (2ad + 3ch or 1ad + 4ch) **Facilities:** Ⓟ (30yds & 200yds) ⬛ ⊗ (access to ground floor shop only) shop ⊗ (ex guide dogs) ◼

UPTON HOUSE   MAP 04 SP34

Upton House

OX15 6HT

➲ *(M40 junct 12, on A422, 7m NW of Banbury, 12m SE of Stratford)*

☎ 01295 670266

e-mail: uptonhouse@nationaltrust.org.uk
web: www.nationaltrust.org.uk

The house, built of mellow local stone, dates from 1695, and contains an outstanding collection of paintings by English and Continental Old Masters, Brussels tapestries, Sèvres porcelain, Chelsea figures, 18th-century furniture, and a collection of original artwork used to advertise Shell oil during the 1920s and 30s. Viscount Bearsted, the donor of Upton, was chairman of Shell and the son of its founder.

Times: Open 4 Nov-17 Dec, Sat & Sun 12-4. 18 Mar-1 Nov, Sat-Wed; House 1-5, Garden 12-5, (Sat & Sun 11-5 garden) **Fee:** ✱ £7 (ch £3.70) Family £17. Garden only £4.20 (ch £2.10, under 5's free) Party 15+ £5.60 (£3.50 garden only). **Facilities:** Ⓟ ⬛ ⊩◎⬛ ⬛ ⬛ (Braille guide, close parking, buggy w/chair, virtual tour) toilets for disabled shop ⊗ (ex assist dogs) ⬛ ◼

WARWICK   MAP 04 SP26

Warwick Castle

CV34 4QU

➲ *(2m from M40 junct 15)*

☎ 0870 442 2000

e-mail: customer.information@warwick-castle.com
web: www.warwick-castle.co.uk

From the days of William the Conqueror to the reign of Queen Victoria, Warwick Castle has provided a backdrop for many turbulent times. Attractions include Kingmaker, Death or Glory, and Birds of Prey. Please telephone for details of events running throughout the year.

continued

Times: Open all year, daily 10-6 (5pm Nov-Mar). Closed 25 Dec. **Fee:** ✱ £13.95-£17.95 (ch 4-16 £8.95-£10.95, pen £9.95-£12.95, students £10.75-£12.95). Family ticket (2ad+2ch) £38-£48. Wheelchair bound visitors free. Group discounts are available if pre-booked. **Facilities:** ❷ (charged) ⬛◎⬛ licensed ⬛ ⬛ (hearing loop, large print guides, DVD, audio guides) toilets for disabled shop ⊗ (ex assistance dogs) ◼

Warwickshire Yeomanry Museum

The Court House Vaults, Jury St CV34 4EW

➲ *(situated on corner of Jury St & Castle St, 2m E of M40 junct 15)*

☎ 01926 492212

The vaults of the courthouse display militaria from the county Yeomanry, dating from 1794 to 1945. It includes regimental silver, paintings, uniforms and weapons. A small room in the cellars now houses the HUJ Gun project, a field gun captured by the Yeomanry in 1917.

Times: ✱ Open Etr-Oct, Sat-Sun & BHs, 10-1 & 2-4. Other times by prior arrangement. **Facilities:** Ⓟ (300yds) (2hr max in nearby streets) shop ⊗

WILMCOTE   MAP 04 SP15

Mary Arden's House and the Shakespeare Countryside Museum

Station Rd CV37 9UN

➲ *(3m NW of Stratford-upon-Avon off A3400)*

☎ 01789 293455

e-mail: info@shakespeare.org.uk
web: www.shakespeare.org.uk

This picturesque, half-timbered Tudor house was the childhood home of Shakespeare's mother, Mary Arden. The site also includes Palmers Farm - a working farm with rare breed farm animals, including Gloucester Old Spot Pigs, Cotswold Sheep and Longhorn cattle. Falconry displays take place and there is a children's adventure playground.

Times: Open Nov-Mar, Mon-Sun 10-4, Apr-May & Sep-Oct, Mon-Sun 10-5, Jun-Aug, Mon-Sun 9.30-5. **Fee:** ✱ £6 (ch £2.50, concessions £5) Family ticket £15. All five Shakespeare Houses £14 (ch £6.50, concessions £12) Family ticket £29. **Facilities:** Ⓟ ⬛ ⬛ toilets for disabled shop ⊗ (ex assist dogs) ◼

Castle ruins at Kenilworth

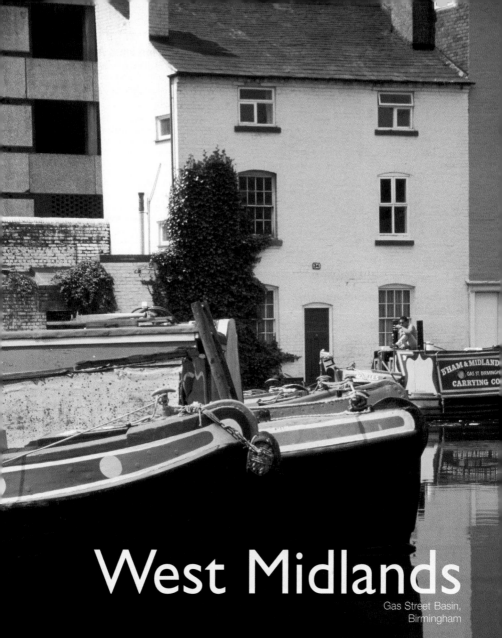

West Midlands

Gas Street Basin,
Birmingham

Sitting at the centre of England, the West Midlands is a metropolitan county.
Birmingham is the biggest city in the county, and also Britain's second largest, its
position at the hub of things emphasised by the miles of canals criss-crossing the
city, and its amazing tangle of flyovers, part of which is dubbed 'Spaghetti Junction'.
It's not all industry though, there are extensive areas of moorland and hills, stately
homes, gardens and picturesque villages. The village of Meriden is said to be the
centre of England, and there is a monument to mark the exact spot.

England

BIRMINGHAM   MAP 07 SP08

Aston Hall

Trinity Rd, Aston B6 6JD

⮞ *(M6 junct 6 follow A38(M) Aston Expressway towards city centre. Leave at Aston Waterlinks and follow brown signs to Aston Hall)*

☎ 0121 327 0062

e-mail: bmag-enquiries@birmingham.gov.uk

web: www.bmag.org.uk

Built by Sir Thomas Holte, Aston Hall is a fine Jacobean mansion complete with a panelled Long Gallery, balustraded staircase and magnificent plaster friezes and ceilings. King Charles I spent a night here during the Civil War and the house was damaged by Parliamentary troops. It was also leased to James Watt Junior, the son of the great industrial pioneer.

Times: Open Etr-Oct, Tue-Sun 11.30-4. Closed Mon ex BHs.
Facilities: ❷ ⬛ & (ground floor only partially accessible) shop ⊗ (ex guide dogs)

Birmingham Botanical Gardens & Glasshouses [2 for 1]

Westbourne Rd, Edgbaston B15 3TR

⮞ *(2m W of city centre, follow signs for Edgbaston, then brown heritage signs)*

☎ 0121 454 1860

e-mail: admin@birminghambotanicalgardens.org.uk

web: www.birminghambotanicalgardens.org.uk

Originally opened in 1832, the gardens include the Tropical House, which has a 24ft-wide lily pool and lush vegetation. The Mediterranean house features a wide variety of citrus fruits and the Arid House has a desert scene with its giant agaves and opuntias. Outside, a tour of the gardens includes rhododendrons and azalea borders and a collection of over 200 trees. Young children's discovery garden and a sculpture trail.

Times: Open daily all year, wkdays 9-7 or dusk, Sun 10-7 or dusk whichever is earlier. Closed 25 Dec. **Fee:** ✱ £6.10 (concessions £3.60); £6.40 summer Sun & BHs. Family £18 (£19 summer & BHs) Groups 10+ £5 (concessions £3.20) **Facilities:** ❷ ⬛ ⭐ licensed 🏠 & (3 wheelchairs, 2 electric scooters & Braille guides) toilets for disabled shop garden centre ⊗ (ex guide dogs) ◼

Birmingham Museum & Art Gallery

Chamberlain Sq B3 3DH

☎ 0121 303 2834

e-mail: bmag-enquiries@birmingham.gov.uk

web: www.bmag.org.uk

One of the world's best collections of Pre-Raphaelite paintings can be seen here, including important works by Burne-Jones, a native of Birmingham. Also on display are fine silver, ceramics and glass. The archaeology section has prehistoric Egyptian, Greek and Roman antiquities, and also objects from the Near East, Mexico and Peru. New galleries explore the creation of art, while the Touch gallery includes talking sculptures, and Samurai armour. The Bull Ring explores the 800 year history of this well-known area.

Times: Open all year, Mon-Thu & Sat 10-5, Fri 10.30-5 and Sun 12.30-5.
Facilities: ℗ (city carparks nearby) ⬛ ⭐ licensed & (lift) toilets for disabled shop ⊗ ◼

Blakesley Hall

Blakesley Rd, Yardley B25 8RN

⮞ *(A4040 onto Blakesley Rd, Hall 100yds on right)*

☎ 0121 464 2193

e-mail: laura_r_cox@birmingham.gov.uk

web: www.bmag.org.uk

Blakesley Hall is a fine Yeoman farmers residence, built by Richard Smalbroke in 1590. It has a half-timbered exterior and a Stuart interior, with a wonderful herb garden. The visitor centre has a varied exhibition programme, tea room and gift shop. Regular weekend events take place throughout the open season.

Times: Open Apr-Oct, Tue-Sun & BHs, 11.30-4 **Facilities:** ❷ ⬛ 🏠 shop ⊗

Museum of the Jewellery Quarter

75-79 Vyse St, Hockley B18 6HA

⮞ *(off A41 into Vyse St, museum on left after 1st side street)*

☎ 0121 554 3598

e-mail: bmag-enquiries@birmingham.gov.uk

web: www.bmag.org.uk

The Museum tells the story of jewellery making in Birmingham from its origins in the Middle Ages right through to the present day. Discover the skill of the jeweller's craft and enjoy a unique tour of an original jewellery factory frozen in time. For over eighty years the family firm of Smith and Pepper produced jewellery from the factory. This perfectly preserved 'time capsule' workshop has changed little since the beginning of the century. The Jewellery Quarter is still very much at the forefront of jewellery manufacture in Britain and the Museum showcases the work of the city's most exciting new designers.

Times: Open Etr-Oct, Tue-Sun 11.30-4. (Closed Mon ex BH Mon)
Facilities: ℗ (limited 2hr stay/pay & display) ⬛ & (tours for hearing/visually impaired booked in advance) toilets for disabled shop ⊗ (ex guide dogs) ◼

RSPB Sandwell Valley Nature Reserve `FREE`

20 Tanhouse Av, Great Barr B43 5AG

⤷ (off B4167 Hamstead Rd into Tanhouse Ave)

☎ 0121 357 7395

web: www.rspb.org.uk

Opened in 1983 on the site of an old colliery, Sandwell Valley is home to hundreds of bird, animal and insect species in five different habitats. Summer is the best time to see the yellow wagtail or reed warblers, while wintertime attracts goosanders, snipe, and redshanks. There are guided walks and bug hunts for the kids in summer, and a shop and visitor centre all year round.

Times: ✱ Open Tue-Fri 9-5, Sat & Sun 10-5 (closes at dusk in winter). Closed Mon, 24 Dec-2 Jan **Facilities:** ❷ 🚽 ♿ toilets for disabled shop

Sarehole Mill `FREE`

Cole Bank Rd, Hall Green B13 0BD

⤷ (A34 towards Birmingham. After 5m turn left on B4146, attraction on left)

☎ 0121 777 6612

e-mail: bmag-enquiries@birmingham.gov.uk

web: www.bmag.org.uk

Home to Birmingham's only working watermill; Sarehole Mill was built in the 1760s. Used for both flour production and metal rolling up to the last century, the Mill can still be seen in action during the summer months. Restored with financial backing from JRR Tolkien, who grew up in the area and cites Sarehole as an influence for writing *The Hobbit* and *Lord of the Rings*.

Times: Open Etr-Oct, Tue-Sun 11.30-4. (Closed Mon, ex BH Mon) **Facilities:** ❷ ⊗ (ex guide dogs)

Selly Manor Museum

Maple Rd, Bournville B30 2AE

⤷ (off A38)

☎ 0121 472 0199

e-mail: gillianellis@bvt.org.uk

These two timber-framed manor houses date from the 13th and early 14th centuries, and have been re-erected in the 'garden suburb' of Bournville. There is a herb garden and events are held all year.

Times: ✱ Open mid Jan-mid Dec, Tue-Fri 10-5; Apr-Sep & BH, Sat-Sun 2-5. **Facilities:** ❷ ♿ toilets for disabled shop

Soho House `FREE`

Soho Av, Handsworth B18 5LB

⤷ (from city centre follow A41 to Soho Rd, follow brown heritage signs to Soho Ave)

☎ 0121 554 9122

e-mail: bmag-enquiries@birmingham.gov.uk

web: www.bmag.org.uk

Soho House was the elegant home of industrial pioneer Matthew Boulton between 1766 and 1809. Here, he met with some of the most important thinkers and scientists of his day. The house has been carefully restored and contains many of Boulton's possessions including furniture, clocks, silverware and the original dining table where the Lunar Society met.

Times: Open Etr-Oct, Tue-Sun 11.30-4. (Closed Mon ex BH Mons) **Facilities:** ❷ 🚽♿ (induction loop) toilets for disabled shop ⊗ (ex guide dogs) 🗺

Thinktank at Millennium Point

Millennium Point, Curzon St B4 7XG

☎ 0121 202 2222

e-mail: findout@thinktank.ac

web: www.thinktank.ac

Thinktank is the award winning, Birmingham Museum of Science and Discovery. Four floors with ten themed galleries are packed with interactive exhibits that explore everything from locomotives and aircraft to intestines and taste buds to emotional robots! Themed events, exhibitions, talks and tours run throughout the year.

Times: ✱ Open daily 10-5 (last entry 4). Closed 24-26 Dec **Facilities:** ❷ (charged) 🚽 ♿ induction loop, wheelchair loan, BSL events, parking toilets for disabled shop science kits, talking clocks, puzzles ⊗ (ex guide dogs) 🗺

BOURNVILLE   MAP 07 SP08

Cadbury World

Linden Rd B30 2LU

⤷ (1m S of A38 Bristol Rd, on A4040 Ring Rd. Follow brown signs from M5 junct 2 and junct 4)

☎ 0845 450 3599

e-mail: cadbury.world@csplc.com

web: www.cadburyworld.co.uk

Lots of recent changes have meant Cadbury World now has much more to see, do and taste. There is the chance to get involved in the chocolate making process, and to find out how the chocolate is used to make famous confectionery. Visitors can learn about the early struggles and triumphs of the Cadbury business, and follow the history of Cadbury television advertising. There are two new attractions: Essence, where visitors can create their own unique product by combining liquid chocolate with different tastes, and Purple Planet, where you can chase a crème egg, grow cocoa beans, and see yourself moulded in chocolate.

Times: Opening times vary throughout the year please contact the information line 0845 450 3599. **Fee:** ✱ £12.50 (ch 4-15 yrs £9.50, concessions £9.95) **Facilities:** ❷ 🚽 🍴 licensed 🏧 ♿ (adapted ride & lift to 2nd floor, subtitles) toilets for disabled shop ⊗ (ex guide dogs) 🗺

England

CASTLE BROMWICH   MAP 07 SP18

Castle Bromwich Hall Gardens

Chester Rd B36 9BT

➲ *(M6 junct 5, follow brown tourist signs)*

☎ 0121 749 4100

e-mail: admin@cbhgt.org.uk

web: www.cbhgt.org.uk

This recently-restored 17th-century formal garden illustrates a period of history in an unusual and fascinating way. Although the garden is an accurate reconstruction of the garden as it was around 1680-1740, there is an addition: the holly maze, which was created in the 19th century, based on 17th-century plans.

Times: Open: Apr-1 Oct, Wed-Fri 1.30-4.30; Sat, Sun & BH Mon 1.30-5.30 **Fee:** ✱ £3.50 (ch 50p, concessions £3) **Facilities:** ℗ ⯐ 🏛 ♿ (wheelchairs available for free) toilets for disabled shop garden centre ⊗ (ex on a lead)

COVENTRY   MAP 04 SP37

Coventry Cathedral & Visitor Centre

7 Priory Row CV1 5ES

➲ *(signposted on all approaches to the city)*

☎ 024 7622 7597

e-mail: information@coventrycathedral.org

web: www.coventrycathedral.org

Coventry's old cathedral was bombed during an air raid of November 1940 which devastated the city. The remains have been carefully preserved. The new cathedral was designed by Sir Basil Spence and consecrated in May 1962. It contains outstanding modern works of art, including a huge tapestry designed by Graham Sutherland, the west screen (a wall of glass engraved by John Hutton with saints and angels), bronzes by Epstein, and the great baptistry window by John Piper.

Times: ✱ Open all year, daily, Etr-Oct 8.30-6, Oct-Etr 8.30-5.30. **Facilities:** ℗ (250yds) ⯐♿ (lift, touch and hearing centre, paved wheelchair access) toilets for disabled shop ⊗ (ex guide dogs)

Coventry Transport Museum   FREE

Millennium Place, Hales St CV1 1PN

➲ *(just off junct 1, Coventry ring road, Tower St in city centre)*

☎ 024 7623 4270

e-mail: enquiries@transport-museum.com

web: www.transport-museum.com

Coventry is the traditional home of the motor industry, and the museum's world-renowned collection displays over 150 years of its history. You can design your own car, feel what its like to break the sound barrier at 763mph and even travel into the future.

Times: Open all year, daily 10-5. Closed 24-26 Dec. **Facilities:** ℗ (adjacent) (pay & display) ⯐♿ (audio tour, tactile floor & models, wheelchairs for hire) toilets for disabled shop ⊗ (ex guide dogs) ◀

Herbert Art Gallery & Museum

Jordan Well CV1 5QP

➲ *(in city centre near Cathedral)*

☎ 024 7683 2381 & 2565

e-mail: artsandheritage@coventry.gov.uk

web: www.coventrymuseum.org.uk

The Herbert is currently undergoing a major redevelopment, which is due for completion in 2008. During the time of the redevelopment there will be an active programme of temporary exhibitions, and plenty of events and activities for children.

Times: Open all year, Mon-Sat 10-5.30, Sun 12-5. Closed 24-26, 31 Dec & 1 Jan **Facilities:** ℗ (500yds) ⯐ 🏛 ♿ (disabled parking, automatic doors) toilets for disabled shop ⊗ (ex guide/assistance dogs)

Jaguar Daimler Heritage Centre   FREE

Browns Ln, Allesley CV5 9DR

➲ *(on A45, follow signs for Browns Lane Plant)*

☎ 024 7620 3322

e-mail: jagtrust@jaguar.com

web: www.jdht.com

Established in 1983, the Jaguar-Daimler Heritage Trust maintains a unique collection of motor vehicles and artefacts manufactured by Jaguar Cars Ltd, and the many other renowned marques associated with the company.

Times: Wkdays by appointment, no appointment required on last Sun of the month. **Facilities:** ℗ ⯐ 🏛 ♿ toilets for disabled shop ⊗ (ex guide dogs)

Lunt Roman Fort

Coventry Rd, Baginton CV8 3AJ

➲ *(S side of city, off Stonebridge highway, A45)*

☎ 024 7678 5173 & 7683 2565

e-mail: info@theherbert.org

web: www.theherbert.org

The turf and timber Roman fort from around the end of the 1st century has been faithfully reconstructed. An Interpretation Centre is housed in the granary.

Times: Open 27 Mar-Oct, Sat-Sun & BH Mon 10-5; mid Jul-end Aug, Thu-Tue 10-5; Spring BH wk, Thu-Tue 10-5. **Fee:** ✱ £2 (concessions £1). **Facilities:** ℗ ♿ (ramp to Granary Interpretation Centre) toilets for disabled shop ⊗ (ex guide/assistance dogs)

Priory Visitor Centre   FREE

Priory Row CV1 5EX

➲ *(in city centre near Cathedral)*

☎ 024 7655 2242

e-mail: prioryvisitorscentre@coventry.gov.uk

web: www.theherbert.org

Earl Leofric and his wife Lady Godiva founded a monastery in Coventry in the 11th century. This priory disappeared somewhere beneath the cathedral that was built on the site, until this cathedral was in turn demolished by Henry VIII in the 16th century. Soon after that most of the buildings on the site had been reduced to ground level, leaving modern archaeologists to discover the outlines of history. This visitor centre displays finds from the site as well as telling the story of Coventry's first cathedral.

Times: Open Mon-Sat 10-5.30, Sun noon-4 **Facilities:** ℗ (500yds) 🏛 ♿ toilets for disabled shop ⊗ (ex guide/assistance dogs)

St Mary's Guildhall `FREE`

Bayley Ln CV1 5QP

⮑ *(in city centre near ruined Cathedral)*

☎ 024 7683 2386

e-mail: info@theherbert.org

web: www.theherbert.org

This impressive medieval Guildhall has stood in the heart of Coventry for over 650 years, and has played its part in the history of the area. It served as Henry VI's court during the War of the Roses, was a prison to Mary Queen of Scots, and was used as a setting by George Eliot in her novel *Adam Bede*. The Great Hall contains a Tournai tapestry commissioned for the visit of Henry VII and Queen Elizabeth in 1500.

Times: Open Etr Sun-Sep, Sun-Thu 10-4 **Facilities:** Ⓟ (600yds) ⓘⓞ⅃ & shop ⊗ (ex guide/assistance dogs)

DUDLEY MAP 07 SO99

Black Country Living Museum `2 for 1`

Tipton Rd DY1 4SQ

⮑ *(on A4037, near Showcase cinema)*

☎ 0121 557 9643 & 520 8054

e-mail: info@bclm.co.uk

web: www.bclm.co.uk

On the 26-acre site is a recreated canal-side village, with shops, houses and workplaces. Meet the costumed guides and find out what life was like around 1900. Ride on a tramcar, take a trip down the underground mine, venture into the limestone caverns or visit the olde tyme fairground (additional charge). There are also demonstrations of chainmaking, glass engraving and sweet-making. Watch a silent movie in the Limelight cinema, taste fish and chips cooked on a 1930s range, and finish your visit with a glass of real ale in the Bottle and Glass Inn.

Times: Open all year, Mar-Oct daily 10-5; Nov-Feb, Wed-Sun 10-4. (Telephone for Xmas closing) **Fee:** ✱ £11 (ch 5-18 £6, pen £9). Family ticket (2ad+3ch) £30. **Facilities:** Ⓟ (charged) 🍴 ⓞ⅃ licensed & (ramps available) toilets for disabled shop ⊗ (ex guide dogs) 🛥

Dudley Zoological Gardens `2 for 1`

2 The Broadway DY1 4QB

⮑ *(M5 junct 2 towards Wolverhampton/Dudley, signed)*

☎ 01384 215313

e-mail: marketing@dudleyzoo.org.uk

web: www.dudleyzoo.org.uk

From lions and tigers to snakes and spiders, enjoy animal encounters and feeds. Get closer to some furry, and some not so furry creatures, and have fun on the fair rides, land train, and the adventure playground. Step back in time and see history come to life in the castle. 2 for 1 voucher cannot be used on BHs.

Times: Open all year, Etr-mid Sep, daily 10-4; mid Sep-Etr, daily 10-3. Closed 25 Dec. **Fee:** ✱ £9.95 (ch 4-15 £6.75, concessions £7.25). Family ticket £31 (2ad+3ch) **Facilities:** Ⓟ (charged) 🍴 ⓞ⅃ licensed ⓘ & (land train from gates-castle, w/chair pre book) toilets for disabled shop ⊗ (ex guide dogs) 🛥

Museum & Art Gallery `FREE`

St James's Rd DY1 1HU

⮑ *(M5 N junct 2. Take A4123 signed to Dudley)*

☎ 01384 815575

e-mail: museum.pls@mbc.dudley.gov.uk

web: www.dudley.gov.uk

The museum houses the Brooke Robinson collection of 17th-, 18th- and 19th-century European painting, furniture, ceramics and enamels. A fine geological gallery, 'The Time Trail' has spectacular displays of fossils from the local Wenlock limestone and coal measures.

Times: ✱ Open all year, Mon-Sat 10-4. Closed BHs. **Facilities:** Ⓟ (25mtrs) ⓘ & (Braille & large print text. Tactile objects) shop ⊗ (ex guide dogs)

KINGSWINFORD MAP 07 SO88

Broadfield House Glass Museum `FREE`

Compton Dr DY6 9NS

⮑ *(Off A491 Stourbridge to Wolverhampton road, just S of Kingswinford Village Centre)*

☎ 01384 812745

e-mail: glass.museum@dudley.gov.uk

web: www.glassmuseum.org.uk

Situated in the historic Stourbridge Glass Quarter, Broadfield House Glass Museum is one of the best glass museums in the world. Home to a magnificent collection of British glass from the 17th century to the present day, the museum hosts an exciting programme of exhibitions and events, and is a main venue for the International Festival of Glass, which is held in August. The museum also has a gift shop, and a hot glass studio.

Times: Open all year, Tue-Sun & BHs 12-4. Please phone for Xmas/Etr openings **Facilities:** Ⓟ & toilets for disabled shop ⊗ (ex guide dogs) 🛥

SOLIHULL MAP 07 SP17

National Motorcycle Museum

Coventry Rd, Bickenhill B92 0EJ

⮑ *(M42 junct 6, off A45 near NEC)*

☎ 01675 443311

web: www.nationalmotorcyclemuseum.co.uk

Five exhibition halls showing British motorcycles built during the Golden Age of motorcycling. Spanning 90 years, the immaculately restored machines are the products of around 150 different factories. Over 700 machines are on show, most are owned by the museum, while others are from collections or private owners. Restoration work is carried out by enthusiasts, and new motorcycles are acquired from all over the world.

Times: Open all year, daily 10-6. Closed 24-26 Dec. **Fee:** ✱ £6.95 (ch 12 & pen £4.95). Party 20+ £5.95 **Facilities:** Ⓟ ⓞ⅃ licensed & toilets for disabled shop ⊗ (ex guide dogs) 🛥

England

STOURBRIDGE
MAP 07 SO88

The Falconry Centre
 2 for 1

Hurrans Garden Centre, Kidderminster Rd
South, Hagley DY9 0JB
➲ (off A456)
☎ 01562 700014
e-mail: info@thefalconrycentre.co.uk
web: www.thefalconrycentre.co.uk

The centre houses some 70 birds of prey including owls, hawks and
falcons and is also a rehabilitation centre for sick and injured birds of
prey. Spectacular flying displays are put on daily from midday. There
are picnic areas, special fun days and training courses available.

Times: Open all year, daily 10-5 & Sun 11-5. Closed 25, 26 Dec & Etr Sun.
Fee: ✱ £3.50 (ch, pen & disabled £2.50). Party 25+ 10% discount.
Facilities: ℗ ☕ ㄟ (Ramps in most places) toilets for disabled shop
garden centre ⊗ (ex guide dogs) ◂

WALSALL
MAP 07 SP09

New Art Gallery Walsall
FREE

Gallery Square WS2 8LG
➲ (signed from all major routes into town centre)
☎ 01922 654400
e-mail: info@artatwalsall.org.uk
web: www.artatwalsall.org.uk

Opened in 2000, this exciting new art gallery has at its core the
Garman Ryan Collection, and a Children's Discovery Gallery that offers
access to the very best in contemporary art in the only interactive art
gallery designed especially for young people.

Times: Open all year, Tue-Sat 10-5, Sun noon-5. Closed Mon ex BH Mon,
25-28 Dec & 1 Jan. Please telephone to confirm. **Facilities:** ℗ (5 minutes
on foot) (free on site for disabled) ☕ 📷 ㄟ (lift access to facilties,
induction loop, large print) toilets for disabled shop ⊗ (ex guide dogs)

Walsall Leather Museum
FREE

Littleton St West WS2 8EQ
➲ (On Walsall ring-road A4148 on N side of town)
☎ 01922 721153
e-mail: leathermuseum@walsall.gov.uk
web: www.walsall.gov.uk/leathermuseum

Award winning working museum in the saddlery and leathergoods
'capital' of Britain. Watch skilled craftsmen and women at work in this
restored Victorian leather factory. Displays tell the story of Walsall's
leatherworkers past and present. Large shop stocks range of Walsall
made leathergoods, many at bargain prices. Saddle Room Café serves
delicious home-cooked cakes and light lunches. Groups very welcome,
guided tours available.

Times: Open all year, Tue-Sat 10-5 (Nov-Mar 4), Sun noon-5 (Nov-Mar 4).
Open BH Mon. Closed 24-26 Dec, 1 Jan, Good Fri, Etr Sun & May Day.
Facilities: ℗ (10mtrs) ☕ ㄟ (staff with sign language skills, tactile activities,
parking) toilets for disabled shop ⊗ (ex guide dogs) ◂

WOLVERHAMPTON
MAP 07 SO99

Bantock House and Park
FREE

Finchfield Rd WV3 9LQ
➲ (follow signs for Wolverhampton. Bantock House 1m
out of city & well signed from ring road)
☎ 01902 552195
e-mail: bantockhouse@dial.pipex.com
web: www.wolverhampton.gov.uk

A rare survival of a Georgian farmhouse that was extended in the early
19th century to double its size. The current interior represents the
Edwardian era, when the décor was radically altered. The ground floor
is set out as the family home, while upstairs visitors can discover
Wolverhampton's history. The gardens have been restored to their
Edwardian designs and include a rose garden, Dutch garden and
woodland pond.

Times: Open Apr-end Oct, 11-5; Nov-end Mar, 12-4. Closed Mon except
BH **Facilities:** ℗ ☕ 📷 ㄟ (wheelchair, induction loop, Braille guide)
toilets for disabled shop ⊗ (ex assist dogs)

Moseley Old Hall

Fordhouses WV10 7HY
➲ (4m N of Wolverhampton, off A460 and A449)
☎ 01902 782808
e-mail: moseleyoldhall@nationaltrust.org.uk
web: www.nationaltrust.org

In 1651, the Prince of Wales, (later King Charles II) hid at Moseley Old
Hall following his defeat at the Battle of Worcester. This romantic and
daring story of the uncrowned king's escape is brought to life for
visitors who enjoy stories from one of England's most turbulent times.
Visitors can see the bed Charles slept on and the priest hole that
concealed him. The impressive knot garden is based on a design of
1640. For details of special events please send a 9" x 4" envelope.

Times: Open 18 Mar-29 Oct, Sat, Sun & Wed 1-5; 5 Nov-17 Dec, Sun 1-4.
Fee: ✱ £5 (ch £2.50). Family ticket £12.50. **Facilities:** ℗ ☕ 📷 ㄟ (Braille
& large print, 1 wheelchair, thick handled cutlery) toilets for disabled
shop ♿ ◂

Wightwick Manor

WV6 8EE

➲ *(3m W, beside Mermaid Inn off A454 Bridgnorth)*

☎ 01902 761400

e-mail: wightwickmanor@nationaltrust.org.uk

web: www.nationaltrust.org.uk

This house was begun in 1887 and is one of the finest examples of 19th-century decorative style. All aspects of William Morris's talents are shown in the house - wallpapers, textiles, carpets, tiles, embroidery and even books. The garden reflects late Victorian and Edwardian design.

Times: Open Mar-end Dec, Thu, Fri, Sat & BH Sun & Mon 1.30-5. (Last admission 4.30). Garden & servant tours throughout the year, please phone for details. **Fee:** £6.80 (accompanied ch & students £3.30). Gardens only £3.30 (ch free in garden) **Facilities:** ♿ 🍽 ♿ (car parking call 01902 761400 for details) toilets for disabled shop ⊗ (ex assist dogs & in gardens) ⛟

WORDSLEY   MAP 07 SO88

The Red House Glass Cone   `2 for 1`

High St DY8 4AZ

➲ *(A491 just N of Stourbridge)*

☎ 01384 812750

e-mail: redhouse.cone@dudley.gov.uk

web: www.redhousecone.co.uk

One of only four cones left in the UK and one of the most complete glass cone sites in Europe, over one hundred feet tall. Explore the fascinating history, watch glassmakers in action and discover the underground tunnels. 2-for-1 voucher may be used for audio guides.

Times: Nov-Mar, Mon-Sun, 10-4, Apr-Oct, Mon-Sat, 10-5, Sun 10-4

Fee: Admission free. Audio guides charged £1.50. **Facilities:** ♿ 🍽 ♿ (lift from first floor to gallery) toilets for disabled shop ⊗ (ex guide dogs & in grounds) 🍴

Birmingham's 19th-century Council House

Isle of Wight

The Needles

Despite being less than 39km (23 miles) across at its widest point, the Isle of Wight offers plenty of variety, with lovely countryside, holiday resorts and mild climate. A chalk ridge runs east to west of the island, and is popular with walkers for the fine views afforded from its vantage points. The resorts of Ryde, Sandown, Shanklin and Ventnor all have good sandy beaches, and the town of Newport is great for shopping and sightseeing.

ALUM BAY
MAP 04 SZ38

The Needles Old Battery
West High Down PO30 0JH

⮑ *(at Needles Headland, W of Freshwater Bay and Alum Bay, B3322)*

☎ 01983 754772

e-mail: isleofwight@nationaltrust.org.uk

web: www.nationaltrust.org.uk/isleofwight

The threat of a French invasion prompted the construction in 1862 of this spectacularly sited fort, which now contains exhibitions on the Battery's involvement in both World Wars, as well as the Headland's intriguing past as part of the secret rocket testing programme. Two of the original gun barrels are displayed in the parade ground and a 60-yard tunnel leads to a searchlight emplacement perched above the Needles Rocks giving magnificent views of the Dorset coastline beyond.

Times: Open 26 Mar-29 Oct Sat-Thu 10.30-5. Jul-Aug daily. **Fee:** ✱ £3.90 (ch £1.95). Family ticket £8.90. May be subject to change.
Facilities: ℗ (0.5m) 💺 📗 ♿ (ramp & audio tours, hearing loops) toilets for disabled shop 👶 ☜

The Needles Park
PO39 0JD

⮑ *(signed on B3322)*

☎ 0870 458 0022

e-mail: info@theneedles.co.uk

web: www.theneedles.co.uk

Overlooking the Needles on the western edge of the island, the park has attractions for all the family: included in the wide range of facilities is the spectacular chair lift to the beach to view the famous coloured sand cliffs, Needles Rocks and lighthouse. Other popular attractions are Alum Bay Glass and the Isle of Wight Sweet Manufactory. Kids will enjoy the Junior Driver roadway, and the Jurassic Golf course.

Times: Open Apr-30 Oct, daily 10-5. Hours extended in high season & on special event days **Fee:** ✱ No admission charged for entrance to Park. All day car park charge £3. Pay as you go attractions or Supersaver Attraction discount ticket. **Facilities:** ℗ (charged) 💺 🍴 licensed ♿ (designated parking) toilets for disabled shop ☜

ARRETON
MAP 04 SZ58

Arreton Manor
`2 for 1`

PO30 3AA

⮑ *(on main Sandown to Newport road)*

☎ 01983 522604

e-mail: info@arretonmanor.co.uk

web: www.arretonmanor.co.uk

Set in five acres on the Arreton Downs, the manor was first mentioned in Alfred the Great's will in 885. Historical records in 1050 say it was owned by Edward the Confessor and the manor was mentioned thirty six years later in the Domesday Book. Although parts of the property are Jacobean, it still possesses many Tudor designs and features. Now a lived in family home.

Times: Open Etr hols & Jun-Sep, daily 10-5 (last tour 4.30) **Fee:** ✱ £5 (ch £2, pen £4.50) Garden only £3 **Facilities:** ℗ 💺 ♿ toilets for disabled shop ⊗ (exc guide dogs)

Robin Hill Country Park
Downend PO30 2NU

⮑ *(0.5m from Arreton next to Hare & Hounds pub)*

☎ 01983 527352

e-mail: dj@robin-hill.com

web: www.robin-hill.com

Set in 88 acres of woodland and countryside Robin Hill has a wide variety of activities and attractions including; Tree Top Trail, Mazes, Snake Slides, Troll Island, Squirrel Tower, Toboggan Run. A 5 year garden project is underway and the new Woodland Centre offers nature displays and wildlife cameras.

Times: Open 26 Mar-29 Oct, daily 10-5 (last admission 4). **Fee:** ✱ £7.50, pen £5.50, disabled £4. Saver ticket for 4 £27. **Facilities:** ℗ 💺 🍴 ♿ (most areas are accessible, ramps access) toilets for disabled shop ⊗ (ex on lead) ☜

BEMBRIDGE
MAP 04 SZ68

Bembridge Windmill
PO35 5SQ

⮑ *(0.5m S of Bembridge on B3395)*

☎ 01983 873945

e-mail: isleofwight@nationaltrust.org.uk

web: www.nationaltrust.org.uk/Isleofwight

Built around 1700, this is the only surviving windmill on the island and has much of its original machinery intact. It was last used in 1913, and the stone-built tower with its wooden cap and machinery has been restored so that visitors can explore its four floors. The mill also provides breathtaking views across glorious, unspoilt countryside.

Times: Open 27 Mar-29 Oct, Sun-Fri, 10-4.30. Jul, Aug & Sep daily. May be subject to change. **Fee:** ✱ £2.10 (ch £1.05) Family £6
Facilities: ℗ (200yds) 💺 📗 ♿ (hearing loop, pictorial guide, audio guide, Braille guide) shop ⊗ (ex guide dogs) 👶 ☜

BLACKGANG
MAP 04 SZ47

Blackgang Chine Fantasy Park
PO38 2HN

⮑ *(follow signs from Ventnor for Whitnell & Niton. From Niton follow signs for Blackgang)*

☎ 01983 730330

e-mail: info@blackgangchine.com

web: www.blackgangchine.com

Opened as scenic gardens in 1843 covering some 40 acres, the park has imaginative play areas, water gardens, maze and coastal gardens. Set on the steep wooded slopes of the chine are the themed areas Smugglerland, Nurseryland, Dinosaurland, Fantasyland and Frontierland. St Catherine's Quay has a maritime exhibition showing the history of local and maritime affairs.

Times: Open mid Mar-end Oct daily, 10-5; late Jul-early Sep open until 10. **Fee:** ✱ Combined ticket (as from 15 May) to chine, sawmill & quay £8.50. Saver ticket (4 people) £31. **Facilities:** ℗ (charged) 💺 📗 ♿ toilets for disabled shop ☜

England

BRADING
MAP 04 SZ68

Brading The Experience
46 High St PO36 0DQ
➲ *(on A3055, in Brading High St)*
☎ 01983 407286
e-mail: info@bradingtheexperience.co.uk
web: www.bradingtheexperience.co.uk

Brading The Experience is more than just a waxworks! Comprising Great British Legends Gallery, 16th Century Rectory Mansion filled with famous and infamous characters from the past, Chamber of Horrors, award-winning Courtyards, Animal World, World of Wheels and The Pier.

Times: Open all year, Summer 10-5.30, Winter 10.30-5 (last admission 1.5hrs before closing) **Fee:** £6.75 (ch 5-15, £4.75, under 5 free, pen. £5.75) Family £21 (2ad+2ch), Family £25 (2ad+3ch). Party 20+. **Facilities:** ♿ 💺 🍴 ♿ (disabled route planner) shop. ◀

Lilliput Antique Doll & Toy Museum
High St PO36 0DJ
➲ *(A3055 Ryde/Sandown road, in Brading High Street)*
☎ 01983 407231
e-mail: lilliput.museum@btconnect.com
web: www.lilliputmuseum.com

This private museum contains one of the finest collections of antique dolls and toys in Britain. There are over 2000 exhibits, ranging in age from 2000BC to 1945 with examples of almost every seriously collectable doll, many with royal connections. Also dolls' houses, teddy bears and rare and unusual toys.

Times: Open all year, daily, 10-5. **Fee:** ✱ £1.95 (ch & pen £1.15, ch under 5 free). Party on request. **Facilities:** ℗ (200 yds) 🍴 ♿ (ramps provided on request) shop collectables, wooden toys ◀

Morton Manor
2 for 1
PO36 0EP
➲ *(off A3055 in Brading, well signed)*
☎ 01983 406168
e-mail: mortonmanor-iow@amserve.com

The manor dates back to 1249, but was rebuilt in 1680 with further changes during the Georgian period. The house contains furniture of both the 18th and 19th centuries, but its main attraction lies in the gardens. The garden is landscaped into terraces, with ornamental ponds, a sunken garden and a traditional Elizabethan turf maze.

Times: Open Apr-Oct, daily 10-5.30. Closed Sat. (Last admissions 4.30). **Fee:** £5 (ch £2.50, pen £4.50) Party 15+ £4 each. **Facilities:** ♿ 💺 🍴 licensed 🍴 ♿ shop garden centre ⊗ (ex guide dogs)

Nunwell House & Gardens
2 for 1
Coach Ln PO36 0JQ
➲ *(Off Ryde-Sandown Rd, A3055, follow brown tourist signs)*
☎ 01983 407240

Set in beautiful gardens, Nunwell is an impressive, lived-in and much loved house where King Charles I spent his last night of freedom. It has fine furniture and interesting collections of family militaria. In

continued

summer, concerts are occasionally held in the music room. There are also five acres of gardens with some lovely views.

Times: Open 28-29 May, 3 Jul-6 Sep, Mon-Wed 1-5. Tours of House 1.30, 2.30 & 3.30 **Fee:** ✱ £4 inc guide book (ch under 10 £1, concessions £3.50) **Facilities:** ♿ shop ⊗ (ex guide dogs)

BRIGHSTONE
MAP 04 SZ48

Brighstone Shop and Museum
FREE
North St PO30 4AX
➲ *(off B3399 in Brighstone onto North Street, next to Post Office)*
☎ 01983 740689
e-mail: isleofwight@nationaltrust.org.uk
web: www.nationaltrust.org.uk/isleofwight

Situated within a row of attractive, thatched cottages you will find this museum which contains an evocative tableau and an interesting exhibition on village life in the 19th century.

Times: Open 28 May-1 Oct daily. Mon-Sat 10-5. Sun 12-5. 2 Oct-23 Dec. Mon-Sat 10-4. 28-30 Dec Thu-Sat 10-1. **Facilities:** ℗ (100m) ♿ (hearing loop) shop ⊗ (ex guide dogs) 🐾 ◀

CARISBROOKE
MAP 04 SZ48

Carisbrooke Castle
PO30 1XY
➲ *(1.25m SW of Newport, off B3401)*
☎ 01983 522107
web: www.english-heritage.org.uk

A royal fortress and prison to King Charles I, Carisbrooke is set on a sweeping ridge at the heart of the Isle of Wight. Don't miss the donkeys that can be seen working a 16th-century wheel to draw water from the well.

Times: Open all year, Apr-Sep, daily 10-5; Oct-Mar, daily 10-4. Closed 24-26 Dec & 1 Jan. **Fee:** £5.50 (ch £2.80, concessions £4.10). Family £13.80. Prices and opening times are subject to change in Spring 2007. Please check web site or call 0870 333 1181 for the most up to date prices and opening times when planning your visit. **Facilities:** ♿ 💺 ♿ shop ✿

FRESHWATER
MAP 04 SZ38

Dimbola Lodge Museum
Terrace Ln, Freshwater Bay PO40 9QE
➲ *(off A3054, visible from Freshwater Bay)*
☎ 01983 756814
e-mail: administrator@dimbola.co.uk
web: www.dimbola.co.uk

Home of Julia Margaret Cameron, the pioneer Victorian portrait photographer. The house has the largest permanent collection of Cameron prints on display in the UK, as well as galleries exhibiting work by young, up and coming, and acclaimed modern photographers; and a large display of cameras and accessories.

Times: Open all year Tue-Sun. Closed 5 days at Xmas. Open BH Mons and daily during school Summer hols. **Fee:** ✱ £4 (ch 16 free) £3.50 student rate upon showing NUS card. **Facilities:** ♿ 🍴 licensed 🍴 ♿ (chairlifts) toilets for disabled shop ⊗ (ex guide dogs) ◀

MOTTISTONE — MAP 04 SZ48

Mottistone Manor Garden

PO30 4ED

⮡ *(2m W of Brighstone on B3399)*

☎ 01983 741302

e-mail: isleofwight@nationaltrust.org.uk

web: www.nationaltrust.org.uk/isleofwight

This magical garden is set in a sheltered valley with views to the sea, and surrounds an Elizabethan manor house, which is tenanted. With its colourful borders, shrub-filled banks and grassy terraces, it provides a tranquil and interesting place to visit. There is also a small organic kitchen garden, and there are some delightful walks onto the downs across the adjoining Mottistone Estate.

Times: Open 27 Mar-29 Oct, Sun-Thu 11-5.30 **Fee:** ✱ £3.10 (ch £1.55) Family £7.75. **Facilities:** ❷ 🖳 📶 ♿ (limited access, hearing loop, large print menu) toilets for disabled shop garden centre 🐾 ⬛

NEWTOWN — MAP 04 SZ49

Old Town Hall

Town Ln PO30 4PA

⮡ *(1m N of A3054 between Yarmouth & Newport)*

☎ 01983 531785

e-mail: isleofwight@nationaltrust.org.uk

web: www.nationaltrust.org.uk/isleofwight

The small, now tranquil, village of Newtown once sent two members to parliament and the Town Hall was the setting for often turbulent elections. This historic building contains exhibits on local history including the exploits of Fergusons Gang, a mysterious group of anonymous benefactors. There are splendid views across unspoilt countryside to the town and footpaths leading to the nearby estuary.

Times: Open 27 Apr-25 Oct, Mon, Wed & Sun, 2-5 (also open Good Fri & Etr Sat) Jul & Aug, Sun-Thu, 2-5. **Fee:** ✱ £1.80 (ch 90p). Family £4.50. **Facilities:** ❷ 📶 ♿ toilets for disabled ⊗ (ex guide dogs) 🐾

OSBORNE HOUSE — MAP 04 SZ59

Osborne House

PO32 6JY

⮡ *(1m SE of East Cowes)*

☎ 01983 200022

web: www.english-heritage.org.uk

The beloved seaside retreat of Queen Victoria offers a glimpse into the private life of Britain's longest reigning monarch. The royal apartments are full of treasured mementos; and Queen Victoria's role as Empress of India is celebrated in the decoration of the Durbar Room. Visit the gardens and the charming Swiss Cottage.

Times: Open House: Apr-Sep, daily, 10-5; Oct, daily, 10-4; Nov-Mar, 10-4, Wed-Sun (guided tours only, must pre-book, last tour 2.30. House & grounds close 4. During Xmas tour season 11 Nov-7 Jan, last tour time is 3). Closed 24-26 Dec & 1 Jan. On 22-23, 28-29 Jul and 3 Aug the house closes at 3 (grounds close 4). For special events please call for details **Fee:** House & Gardens: £9.50 (ch £4.80, concessions £7.10). Family £23.80. Garden only: £5.50 (ch £2.80, concessions £4.10). Family £13.80. Prices and opening times are subject to change in Spring 2007. Please check web or call 0870 333 1181 for the most up to date prices and opening times.

Facilities: ❷ 🖳 ♿ shop ⊗ 🚻

PORCHFIELD — MAP 04 SZ49

Colemans Animal Farm

Colemans Ln PO30 4LX

⮡ *(A3054 Newport to Yarmouth road, follow brown tourist signs)*

☎ 01983 522831

e-mail: info@colemansfarm.net

web: www.colemansfarm.com

Ideal for young children, this extensive petting farm has donkeys, goats, rabbits, guinea pigs, pigs, Highland cattle, Shetland ponies, chickens, ducks and geese. There is also a fun barn with slides and swings, an adventure playground, a Tractor Fun Park, and an Old Barn Café for adults who need to relax. Visitors can cuddle, stroke and feed the animals at special times throughout the day. Other special events run all day.

Times: Open mid Mar-end Oct, Tue-Sun, 10-4.30 (last admission recommended 3.30). (Closed Mon, ex during school and BHs). Open for pre-booked events out of season. **Fee:** £5.95 (ch £4.95, concessions £4.50), family ticket £18. **Facilities:** ❷ 🖳 ♿ toilets for disabled ⬛

SANDOWN — MAP 04 SZ58

Dinosaur Isle 〔2 for 1〕

Culver Pde PO36 8QA

☎ 01983 404344

e-mail: dinosaur@iow.gov.uk

web: www.dinosaurisle.com

Britain's first purpose built dinosaur attraction where, in a building reminiscent of a Pterosaur flying across the Cretaceous skies, you can walk back through fossilised time. In recreated landscape meet life sized models of the island's famous five - Neovenator, Eotyrannus, Iguanodon, Hypsilophodon and Polacanthus. Look out for the flying Pterodactyls and skeletons as they are found, watch volunteers preparing the latest finds or try the many hands-on activities.

Times: Open all year daily, Apr-Sep 10-6; Oct 10-5; Nov-Mar 10-4. Closed 24-26 Dec & 1 Jan, please phone to confirm opening Jan-10 Feb. Last admission 1hr before closing. **Fee:** ✱ £4.75 (ch 3-15 £2.75, concessions £3.50) Family £13 (2+2) **Facilities:** ❷ (charged) 📶 ♿ toilets for disabled shop ⊗ (assist dogs) ⬛

SHANKLIN   MAP 04 SZ58

Shanklin Chine   **2 for 1**
12 Pomona Rd PO37 6PF
➲ *(turn off A3055 at lights, left into Hope Rd & continue onto Esplanade for entrance)*
☎ 01983 866432
e-mail: jillshanklinchine1@msn.com
web: www.shanklinchine.co.uk

This scenic gorge at Shanklin is a magical world of unique beauty and a haven for rare plants and wildlife. A path winds through the ravine with overhanging trees, ferns and other flora covering the steep sides. 'The Island-Then and Now' is an exhibition detailing the history of the Isle of Wight, including its military importance in WWII.

Times: 31 Mar-25 May , 10-5. 26 May-10 Sep, 10-10. 11 Sep-29 Oct, 10-5.
Fee: ✱ £3.75 (ch under 14 £2, concessions £2.75). Family ticket £9.50 (2ad+2ch), £11.50 (2ad +3ch). Group rates available.
Facilities: Ⓟ (450yds) ♨ ♿ (access via lower entry only) shop

---

VENTNOR   MAP 04 SZ57

Ventnor Botanic Garden
Undercliff Dr PO38 1UL
➲ *(on A3055 coastal road, 1.5m W of Ventnor)*
☎ 01983 855397
e-mail: alison.ellsbury@iow.gov.uk
web: www.botanic.co.uk

Due to the unique microclimate of the 'Undercliff', plants that can only survive in a Mediterranean climate thrive on the Isle of Wight. Built on the site of a Victorian hospital for TB sufferers, the garden was founded in 1970 by Sir Harold Hillier, and opened in 1972 by Earl Mountbatten. The garden has plants from Australasia, Africa, America, the Mediterranean, and the Far East, and is a great day out for anyone remotely interested in exotic flora.

Times: Gardens: open all year; Visitor Centre & Green House: Mar-Oct, daily 10-5 & Nov-Feb, wknds only 10-4 **Fee:** Free admission to Gardens & Visitor Centre; Green House £1 **Facilities:** Ⓟ (charged) ♨ ⓝ ♿ (lifts in visitor centre, wheelchairs, 2 lifts) toilets for disabled shop garden centre ⊗ (guide dogs) ◀

WROXALL   MAP 04 SZ57

Appuldurcombe House
PO38 3EW
➲ *(off B3327, 0.5 miles W)*
☎ 01983 852484
web: www.english-heritage.org.uk

The shell of Appuldurcombe, once the grandest house on the Isle of Wight, stands in its own grounds, designed by 'Capability' Brown. An exhibition of prints and photographs depicts the house and its history.

Times: Open Apr-Jun & Sep-Oct, daily 10-4; Jul-Aug, daily 10-5. Last admission to property 1hr before closing. **Fee:** £3 (ch £2 & concessions £2.75). Family ticket £9. **Facilities:** Ⓞ ♿ shop ⊗ (ex on leads) ⚏

YARMOUTH   MAP 04 SZ38

Yarmouth Castle
Quay St PO4 1OP
➲ *(adjacent to car ferry terminal)*
☎ 01983 760678
web: www.english-heritage.org.uk

The last addition to Henry VIII's coastal defences completed in 1547, the Tudor castle is set in a beautiful old seaside town. See the Isle of Wight paintings and memorable photographs of Old Yarmouth.

Times: Open Apr-Sep, Sun-Thu, 11-4. **Fee:** £2.80 (ch £1.40, concessions £2.10). Prices and opening times are subject to change in Spring 2007. Please check web site or call 0870 333 1181 for the most up to date prices and opening times when planning your visit. **Facilities:** Ⓟ (200yds) ♿ shop ⚏

The National Trust: For over a hundred years, the NT has been acquiring and protecting threatened coastline, countryside and buildings. To find out more about this organisation, its sites, and policies, visit their website: **www.nationaltrust.org.uk**

Wiltshire

Stonehenge,
Salisbury Plain

To many visiting the county, Wiltshire has three major attractions: Salisbury, Stonehenge and Longleat. While these are all exceptional, there's plenty more to discover. For example, the standing stones at Avebury, an earthwork camp at Windmill Hill, the huge and mysterious mound of Silbury Hill, and the burial mound of West Kennet Long Barrow. A more recent claim to fame comes from the beautiful village of Lacock, where, in 1831, William Henry Fox Talbot produced what many consider to be the first photographic negative and there is now a museum dedicated to early photography.

England

AVEBURY MAP 04 SU06

Alexander Keiller Museum
High St SN8 1RF

⮡ *(6m W of Marlborough. 1m N of Bath Rd (A4) on A4361 and B4003)*

☎ 01672 539250

e-mail: avebury@nationaltrust.org.uk

web: www.nationaltrust.org.uk

This is one of the most important megalithic monuments in Europe, and was built before Stonehenge. The museum, including an exhibition in the 17th-century threshing barn, presents the full archaeological story of the stones using finds from the site, along with inter-active and audio-visual displays.

Times: Open Apr-Oct, daily 10-6; Nov-Mar 10-4 .Closed 24-26 Dec
Fee: ✱ £4.20 (ch £2.10) Family £10.50 (2ad+3ch) Family £7.50 (1ad+3ch). Groups £3.60 (ch 1.80). **Facilities:** ℗ (charged) ☕ 🍴 licensed 🏪 ᴔ (Braille guide, large print guide, drop off point) toilets for disabled shop ⊗ (ex guide dogs) ⏧ ➹

Avebury Manor
SN8 1RF

⮡ *(from A4 take A4361/B4003)*

☎ 01672 539250

e-mail: avebury@nationaltrust.org.uk

web: www.nationaltrust.org.uk

Avebury Manor has a monastic origin, and has been much altered since then. The present buildings date from the early 16th century, with notable Queen Anne alterations and Edwardian renovation. The flower gardens contain medieval walls, and there are examples of topiary.

Times: Open: House 2 Apr-Oct, Sun-Tue, 2-4.40, BH Mon 2-5.30 (last admission 4.40). Garden Apr-Oct daily (ex Wed & Thu) 11-5.
Fee: ✱ Manor & Garden £4 (ch £2). Garden £3 (ch £1.50).
Facilities: ℗ (charged) ☕ 🍴 ᴔ (audio visual, Braille/large print guide, induction loop) toilets for disabled shop ⊗ ⏧ ➹

BRADFORD-ON-AVON MAP 03 ST86

Bradford-on-Avon Tithe Barn `FREE`
⮡ *(0.25m S of town centre, off B3109)*

web: www.english-heritage.org.uk

This impressive tithe barn, over 160ft long by 30ft wide, once belonged to Shaftesbury Abbey. The roof is of stone slates, supported outside by buttresses and inside by massive beams and a network of rafters.

Times: Open all year, daily 10.30-4. Closed 25 Dec.
Facilities: ℗ (charged) ᴔ ⊗ ⌗

Great Chalfield Manor
SN12 8NH

⮡ *(3m SW of Melksham off B3107 via Broughton Gifford Common)*

☎ 01225 782239

web: www.nationaltrust.org.uk

Built during the Wars of the Roses, the manor is a beautiful, mellow, moated house restored in the 1920s. There is a small 13th-century church next to the house.

Times: Open 2 Apr-29 Oct, Tue-Thu & Sun, guided tours only at 12.15, 2.15, 3, 3.45, 4.30. (Sun 2-5 only) **Fee:** ✱ £4.80 (ch £2.40). Family ticket £12.20. Groups £4.30 (ch £2.20). Garden only £3. **Facilities:** ℗ ᴔ (drop off point, wheelchair, Braille guide) ⊗ ➹

The Peto Garden at Iford Manor
Iford Manor BA15 2BA

⮡ *(Brown tourist signs 0.5m S of Bradford-on-Avon on B3109)*

☎ 01225 863146

e-mail: ifordmanor@countryside.uk.net

web: www.ifordmanor.co.uk

An award-winning garden in the romantic setting of the Frome Valley. Designed by Harold Peto between 1899 and 1933, this Italian style garden features terraces, statues and ponds. Recitals and operas take place in the garden throughout the summer season as part of the Iford Arts programme

Times: Open May-Sep, Tue-Thu, Sat & Sun. Apr & Oct open Sun only 2-5. Closed Mon & Fri except BH Mons. **Fee:** ✱ £4.50 (ch under 10 free, concessions £4) **Facilities:** ℗ ☕ 🏪 ⊗ (ex on leads)

CALNE MAP 03 ST97

Bowood House & Gardens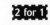
SN11 0LZ

⮡ *(off A4 Chippenham to Calne road, in Derry Hill village)*

☎ 01249 812102

e-mail: houseandgardens@bowood.org

web: www.bowood.org

Built in 1624, the house was finished by the first Earl of Shelburne, who employed celebrated architects, notably Robert Adam, to complete the work. Adam's library is particularly admired, and also in the house is the laboratory where Dr Joseph Priestley discovered the existence of oxygen in 1774. The house overlooks terraced gardens towards the 40-acre lake and some beautiful parkland. The gardens were laid out by 'Capability' Brown in the 1760s, and are carpeted with daffodils, narcissi and bluebells in spring. There is also an adventure playground and new soft play area. 2 for 1 voucher not valid for special events.

Times: Open mid Apr-Oct, daily 11-6, including BH. Rhododendron Gardens (separate entrance off A342) open 6 weeks during mid Apr-early Jun, 11-6. **Fee:** ✱ House & Gardens £7.50 (ch 2-4 £3.80; 5-15 £5; pen £6.50). Family ticket (2ad+2ch) £22.50. Rhododendrons only £4.80 (pen £4.30). £1 discount if house visited on same day. **Facilities:** ℗ ☕ ᴔ (parking by arrangement, DVD tour of upstairs) toilets for disabled shop ⊗ (ex assisstance dogs) ➹

CORSHAM   MAP 03 ST87

Corsham Court
SN13 0BZ
➲ *(4m W of Chippenham off the A4)*
☎ 01249 701610
web: www.corsham-court.co.uk

The Elizabethan manor was built in 1582, and then bought by the Methuen family in the 18th century to house their collections of paintings and statues. 'Capability' Brown made additions to the house and laid out the park, and later John Nash made further changes. There is furniture by Chippendale, Adam, Cobb and Johnson inside, as well as the Methuen collection of Old Master paintings. The garden has flowering shrubs, herbaceous borders, a Georgian bath house and peacocks.

Times: Open 20 Mar-Sep daily (ex Mon & Fri), but incl BHs 2-5.30. Oct-19 Mar open wknds only 2-4.30. (Last admission 30 minutes before closing). Closed Dec. Open throughout year by appointment for groups 15+. **Fee:** £6.50 (ch 5-15 £3, pen £5) Group rate £5 **Facilities:** ♿ & (stair lift) toilets for disabled shop ⊗ (ex guide dogs)

See advert on page 299

HOLT   MAP 03 ST86

The Courts
BA14 6RR
➲ *(3m SW of Melksham, 2.5m E of Bradford on Avon, on south side of B3107 follow signs to Holt)*
☎ 01225 782875
e-mail: courtsgarden@nationaltrust.org.uk
web: www.nationaltrust.org.uk

The house is not open, but it makes an attractive backdrop to the gardens - a network of stone paths, yew hedges, pools and borders with a strange, almost magical atmosphere. The peaceful water gardens are planted with irises and lilies.

Times: Open 29 Mar-15 Oct, daily (ex Wed) 11-5.30; out of season by appointment only. **Fee:** ✳ £5 (ch £2.50). Family ticket £12.80. Groups £4.50 (ch £2.30). **Facilities:** ♿ 🖤 📷 & (wheelchair, Braille & large print guide) toilets for disabled ⊗ (ex guide dogs) 🌿

LACOCK   MAP 03 ST96

Lacock Abbey, Fox Talbot Museum & Village
SN15 2LG
➲ *(3m S of Chippenham, E of A350, car park signed)*
☎ 01249 730227 (abbey) 730459
web: www.nationaltrust.org.uk

This fascinating museum dedicated to the 'Father of Modern Photography' is set in a medieval cloistered abbey which has been converted into a fine country house. Best known these days as a 'Harry Potter' location.

Times: Museum, Cloisters & Grounds, Mar-Oct, daily 11-5.30. Closed Good Fri. Abbey, 27 Mar-Oct daily, ex Tue, 1-5.30. Closed Good Fri. **Fee:** ✳ Museum, Abbey, Grounds & Cloisters £7.80 (ch £3.90) Family ticket £20 (2ad+2ch). Garden, Cloisters & Museum £4.80 (ch £2.40) Family ticket £12.20 (2ad+2ch). Abbey, Cloisters & Grounds £6.30 (ch £3.20) Family ticket £16.10 (2ad+2ch). Museum (winter) £3.40 (ch £1.70) Family ticket £8.70 (2ad+2ch). **Facilities:** ♿ (charged) & (manual wheelchairs, Braille/large print & audio guides) toilets for disabled shop ⊗ 🌿

LONGLEAT   MAP 03 ST84

Longleat
The Estate Office BA12 7NW
➲ *(turn off A36 Bath-Salisbury road onto A362 Warminster-Frome road)*
☎ 01985 844400
e-mail: enquiries@longleat.co.uk
web: www.longleat.co.uk

Nestling within magnificent 'Capability' Brown landscaped grounds in the heart of Wiltshire, Longleat House is widely regarded as one of the most beautiful stately homes open to the public. Longleat House was built by Sir John Thynne and completed in 1580. It has remained the home of the same family ever since. Many treasures are contained within the house: paintings by Tintoretto and Wooton, exquisite Flemish tapestries, fine French furniture and elaborate ceilings by John Dibblee Crace. The murals in the family apartments in the West Wing were painted by Alexander Thynne, the present Marquess, and are fascinating and remarkable additions to the collection. Apart from the ancestral home, Longleat is also renowned for its safari park, the first of its kind in the UK. Here, visitors have the rare opportunity to see

continued

hundreds of animals in natural woodland and parkland settings. Among the most magnificent sights are the famous pride of lions, wolves, rhesus monkeys and zebra. Other attractions which ensure a fun family day out include the 'Longleat Hedge Maze', the 'Adventure Castle', 'Longleat Railway', 'Pets' Corner' and the 'Safari Boats'.

Times: Daily Apr-5 Nov. Telephone for opening times **Fee:** ✱ Longleat passport: £19 (ch 3-14 yrs & pen £15) **Facilities:** ❷ ⬛ 🍴 licensed 🍴 ♿ (informative leaflet available or see website) toilets for disabled shop ⬛

LUDGERSHALL   MAP 04 SU25

Ludgershall Castle and Cross   `FREE`
SP11 9QR
➲ *(7m NW of Andover on A342)*
web: www.english-heritage.org.uk

Ruins of an early 12th-century royal hunting palace and medieval cross. The visitor can see large earthworks of the Norman motte-and-bailey castle and the flint walls of the later hunting palace. The stump of a medieval cross stands in the village street.

Times: Open at any reasonable time. **Facilities:** ❷ ♿ ✜

LYDIARD PARK   MAP 04 SU18

Lydiard Park
Lydiard Tregoze SN5 3PA
➲ *(M4 junct 16, follow brown tourist signs)*
☎ 01793 770401
e-mail: lydiardpark@swindon.gov.uk
web: www.swindon.gov.uk

Set in country parkland, Lydiard Park belonged to the St John family (the Bolingbrokes) for 500 years up until 1943 when the Swindon Corporation purchased it. Since then the house has been restored and many of the original furnishings returned, together with a family portrait collection dating from Elizabethan to Victorian times. Exceptional plasterwork, early wallpaper, a rare painted glass window, and a room devoted to the talented 18th-century amateur artist, Lady Diana Spencer (Beauclerk), can also be seen.

Times: Open all year, House: Mon-Sat 10-5, Sun 2-5. Winter closing 4 (Nov-Feb). Park: all year, daily closing at dusk each day. **Fee:** ✱ £2.20 (ch £1, pen £2) **Facilities:** ❷ ⬛ 🍴 ♿ (audio box in state room) toilets for disabled shop ⊗ (ex guide dogs in house)

MARLBOROUGH   MAP 04 SU16

Crofton Beam Engines
Crofton Pumping Station, Crofton SN8 3DW
➲ *(signed from A4/A338/A346 & B3087 at Burbage)*
☎ 01672 870300
e-mail: enquiries@croftonbeamengines.org
web: www.croftonbeamengines.org

The oldest working beam engine in the world still in its original building and still doing its original job, the Boulton and Watt 1812, can be found in this rural spot. Its companion is a Harvey's of Hayle of 1845. Both are steam driven, from a hand-stoked, coal-fired boiler, and pump water into the summit level of the Kennet and Avon Canal with a lift of 40ft.

Times: Open daily 6 Apr-Sep, 10.30-5 (last entry 4.30). 'In Steam' Etr, BH wknds & last wknd of Jun, Jul & Sep. **Fee:** ✱ In Steam wknd: £5 (ch £1, under 5 free & pen £4). Family ticket £10. Non-In Steam days £3 (ch £1, pen £2.50) Family £7 **Facilities:** ❷ (charged) ⬛♿ (phone warden in advance, sighted guides provided) shop ⬛

MIDDLE WOODFORD   MAP 04 SU13

Heale Gardens, Plant Centre & Shop
SP4 6NT
➲ *(4m N of Salisbury, between A360 & A345)*
☎ 01722 782504

Heale House and its eight acres of beautiful garden lie beside the River Avon at Middle Woodford. Much of the house is unchanged since King Charles II sheltered here after the Battle of Worcester in 1651. The garden provides a wonderfully varied collection of plants, shrubs, and musk and other roses, growing in the formal setting of clipped hedges and mellow stonework. Special Event: Snowdrop Sundays in Feb.

Times: Open: Plant centre daily, 10-5. Gardens daily (closed Mon ex BHs) **Facilities:** ❷ ⬛ 🍴 ♿ (most parts accessible) shop garden centre ⊗ (ex guide dogs) ⬛

SALISBURY   MAP 04 SU12

The Medieval Hall (Secrets of Salisbury)
Cathedral Close SP1 2EY
➲ *(look for signs within Salisbury Cathedral Close)*
☎ 01722 412472 & 324731
e-mail: medieval.hall@ntworld.com
web: www.medieval-hall.co.uk

Visit the historic 13th-century Medieval Hall and watch the fascinating 40 minute sound and picture guide to the city and region. A witty and informative soundtrack, (available in six different languages) specially composed music and some startling effects accompany hundreds of images to provide an insight into Salisbury's extraordinary past, the colourful city of today, and many of the attractions in the area. Enjoy refreshments 'while you watch'. Contact the Hall for full details of special events.

Times: Open Apr-Sep, 11-5. Also open throughout year for pre-booked groups. Occasionally closed for special events. **Fee:** ✱ £2.25 (ch under 18 £1.75, ch under 6 free). Family tickets available **Facilities:** ❷ (charged) ⬛ ♿ (ramp access) shop

Mompesson House
The Close SP1 2EL
➲ *(on N side of Choristers Green in Cathedral Close, near High St Gate)*
☎ 01722 335659
e-mail: mompessonhouse@nationaltrust.org.uk
web: www.nationaltrust.org.uk

With its high wrought-iron railings and perfect proportions, this Queen Anne house makes an impressive addition to the elegant Cathedral Close in Salisbury. Inside are stucco ceilings, a carved oak staircase and period furniture plus an important collection of 18th-century glasses, china and some outstanding paintings.

Times: Open 25 Mar-29 Oct, daily (ex Thu & Fri) 11-5. Open Good Fri. **Fee:** ✱ £4.40 (ch £2.20). Group rate £3.90. Garden only £1. Family £10.90. **Facilities:** ℗ (260 yds) (limited disabled parking available) ⬛ ♿ (ramps, Braille & large print guide) toilets for disabled shop ⊗ ⬛

England

Old Sarum

Castle Rd SP1 3SD

➲ *(2m N on A345)*

☎ 01722 335398

web: www.english-heritage.org.uk

The site of the original city of Salisbury. The 56-acre ruins of this once bustling town are rich in history and woodland. Founded in the Iron Age and occupied until the 16th-century. Romans, Saxons and Normans have all left their mark.

Times: Open Apr-Jun & Sep, daily 10-5; Jul-Aug, daily 9-6; Mar & Oct, daily, 10-4. Nov-Feb, daily, 11-3. Closed 24-26 Dec & 1 Jan **Fee:** £2.90 (ch £1.50, concessions £2.20). Prices and opening times are subject to change in Spring 2007. Please check web site or call 0870 333 1181 for the most up to date prices and opening times when planning your visit.
Facilities: ❷ ⓹ (assess to outer bailey and grounds only) shop ⊞

Salisbury Cathedral

33 The Close SP1 2EJ

➲ *(S of city centre & Market Sq)*

☎ 01722 555120

e-mail: visitors@salcath.co.uk

web: www.salisburycathedral.org.uk

Built in one phase between 1220 and 1258, the Cathedral is probably Britain's finest piece of medieval architecture. The spire is 123 metres tall, making it the tallest in England. The Chapter House displays a frieze depicting scenes from Genesis and Exodus, also the finest surviving Magna Carta. The Choir continues a tradition that began around 800 years ago, with performances at daily services. They are accompanied by Europe's finest romantic church organ. The surrounding Cathedral Close contains two museums, two small stately homes and acres of lawn.

Times: Open all year, daily 7.15am-6.15pm; Jun-Aug, Mon-Sat 7.15am-7.15pm. **Fee:** Suggested voluntary donations: £4 (ch 5-17 £2, concessions £3.50). Family £8.50. **Facilities:** ⓟ (100yds) 🍽 🍴 licensed 📗 ⓹ (loop system, interpretative model for blind, wheelchairs) toilets for disabled shop 🛍

Salisbury & South Wiltshire Museum

The King's House, 65 The Close SP1 2EN

➲ *(in Cathedral Close)*

☎ 01722 332151

e-mail: museum@salisburymuseum.org.uk

web: www.salisburymuseum.org.com

One of the most outstanding of the beautiful buildings in Cathedral Close houses this local museum. Galleries feature Stonehenge, History of Salisbury, the Pitt Rivers collection, ceramics and pictures and the Wedgwood room, a reconstruction of a pre-NHS surgery, and a costume, lace and embroidery gallery.

Times: Open all year Mon-Sat 10-5; also Suns Jul & Aug, 2-5. Closed Xmas. **Fee:** ✱ £4 (ch £1.50, concessions £3). Family ticket £9.50. Season saver tickets available. **Facilities:** ⓟ (100mtrs) (nearby parking charge) 🍽 📗 ⓹ (parking, induction loop, wheelchair, interactive computers) toilets for disabled shop ⊗ (ex guide dogs) 🛍

STONEHENGE   **MAP 04 SU14**

Stonehenge

SP4 7DE

➲ *(2m W of Amesbury on junct A303 and A344/A360)*

☎ 01980 624715

web: www.english-heritage.org.uk

Britain's greatest prehistoric monument and a World Heritage Site. What visitors see today are the substantial remains of the last in a series of monuments erected between c3000 and 1600BC.

continued

CORSHAM COURT

HOME OF THE METHUEN FAMILY

Corsham Court is one of England's finest Stately Homes. It was a Royal Manor in the days of the Saxon Kings, and the present building is based upon an Elizabethan Manor dating from 1582. Magnificent Georgian State Rooms were added in 1760. It houses one of the oldest and most distinguished collections of Old Masters and Furniture in the country, and with its 'Capability' Brown gardens and arboretum, and architecture by John Nash and Thomas Bellamy, Corsham Court provides the visitor with a wonderful opportunity to enjoy the many delights of the historic and beautiful Stately Home.

Tel/Fax: 01249 701610
www.corsham-court.co.uk
For opening times see gazetteer entry

Times: Open all year, mid Mar-May, daily 9.30-6; Jun-Aug, daily 9-7; Sep-mid Oct, daily 9.30-6; mid Oct-mid Mar, daily 9.30-4. Closed 24-26 Dec & 1 Jan. Note: Usual facilities may not apply around Summer Solstice 20-22 June, please check **Fee:** £5.90 (ch £3, concessions £4.40). Family ticket £14.80. Prices and opening times are subject to change in Spring 2007. Please check web site or call 0870 333 1181 for the most up to date prices and opening times when planning your visit. **Facilities:** ❷ 💻 ⬥ shop ⊗ (ex guide & hearing dogs) ⯏

STOURHEAD   MAP 03 ST73

Stourhead Garden & House

Stourhead Estate Office BA12 6QD

➲ *(At Stourton off B3092, 3m NW Mere A303, follow brown tourist signs)*

☎ 01747 841152

e-mail: stourhead@nationaltrust.org.uk

web: www.nationaltrust.org.uk

An outstanding example of the English landscape style, this splendid garden was designed by Henry Hoare II and laid out between 1741 and 1780. Classical temples, including the Pantheon and Temple of Apollo, are set around the central lake at the end of a series of vistas, which change as the visitor moves around the paths and through the mature woodland with its extensive collection of exotic trees.

Times: Garden open all year 9-7 (or dusk if earlier). House open 18 Mar-Oct ,11.30-4.30 (closed Wed & Thu); King Alfred tower open 18 Mar-Oct, daily 11.30-4.30. **Fee:** ✱ Garden & House £10.40 (ch £5.20) Family ticket £24.70, groups £9.90, Garden or House £6.20, ch £3.40, King Alfred Tower £2.30, ch £1.20. **Facilities:** ❷ 💻 🍴 licensed ⬥ (wheelchairs, electric buggy, telephone in advance) toilets for disabled shop garden centre ⊗ (ex in gardens Nov-Feb only) 🧺 🍴

STOURTON   MAP 03 ST73

Stourton House Flower Garden   2 for 1

Stourton House BA12 6QF

➲ *(3m NW of Mere, on A303)*

☎ 01747 840417

Set in the attractive village of Stourton, the house has more than four acres of beautifully maintained flower gardens. Many grass paths lead

continued

---

through varied and colourful shrubs and trees. Stourton House also specialises in unusual plants and dried flowers, many of which are for sale. It also has collections of daffodils, delphiniums and hydrangeas, along with a nature garden where visitors can sit and watch the birds, butterflies and other wildlife.

Times: Open last 2 Sun Feb & Apr-end Nov, Wed, Thu, Sun & BH Mon 11-6 (or dusk if earlier). Also open Dec-Mar, wkdays for plant/dried flower sales. **Fee:** ✱ £3.50 (ch 50p). **Facilities:** ❷ 💻 ⬥ (wheelchairs available) toilets for disabled shop garden centre ⊗ (ex by arrangement)

SWINDON   MAP 04 SU18

STEAM - Museum of the Great Western Railway 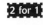

Kemble Dr SN2 2TA

➲ *(from M4 junct 16 & A420 follow brown signs to 'Outlet Centre' & Museum)*

☎ 01793 466646

e-mail: steampostbox@swindon.gov.uk

web: www.swindon.gov.uk/steam

This fascinating day out tells the story of the men and women who built, operated and travelled on the Great Western Railway. Hands-on displays, world-famous locomotives, archive film footage and the testimonies of ex-railway workers bring the story to life. A reconstructed station platform, posters and holiday memorabilia recreate the glamour and excitement of the golden age of steam. Located next door to the McArthurGlen Designer Outlet Great Western, STEAM offers a great day out for all. Good value group packages, special events and exhibitions and shop.

Times: Open daily 10-5. Closed 25-26 Dec & 1 Jan **Fee:** £5.95 (ch £3.80, pen £3.90) Family ticket £14.70 (2ad+2ch) **Facilities:** ℗ (100 yds) (disabled parking 20yds) 🍴 ⬥ (wheelchair or scooter can be pre-booked) toilets for disabled shop ⊗ (ex guide dogs) 🍴

Swindon & Cricklade Railway NEW

Blunsdon Station, Tadpole Ln, Blunsdon SN25 2DA

➲ *(M4 junct 15, take A419 to lights at Blunsdon Stadium. Railway in 1m along minor road to stadium)*

☎ 01793 771615

e-mail: randallchri@yahoo.co.uk

web: www.swindon-cricklade-railway.org

Heritage railway in the process of being restored. Steam and diesel locomotives, historic carriages, wagons and a large variety of railway structures from a past era.

Times: Open Etr-end Oct, Sat-Sun, 11-4. Nov-Etr, Sun only. Also open BHs & Xmas & Wed in local school hols. **Fee:** ✱ £3.50 (ch £2.50). Family £10. Different prices apply for some special events. **Facilities:** ❷ 💻 ⬥ toilets for disabled shop

Directions are provided by the attractions.

TEFFONT MAGNA MAP 03 ST93

Farmer Giles Farmstead
SP3 5QY
➲ *(11m W of Stonehenge, off A303 to Teffont. Follow brown signs)*
☎ 01722 716338
e-mail: tdeane6995@aol.com
web: www.farmergiles.co.uk

Forty acres of Wiltshire downland with farm animals to feed, ponds, inside and outside play areas, exhibitions, tractor rides, and giftshop.

Times: ✱ Open 18 Mar-5 Nov, daily 10-6, wknds in winters, 10-dusk. Party bookings all year. **Facilities:** ℗ ⭑◎⭑ licensed ♿ (complete access for disabled/wheelchairs available for use) toilets for disabled shop ◀

TISBURY MAP 03 ST92

Old Wardour Castle
SP3 6RR
➲ *(2m SW)*
☎ 01747 870487
web: www.english-heritage.org.uk

This 14th-century castle stands in a romantic lakeside setting. Landscaped grounds and elaborate rockwork grotto surround the unusual hexagonal ruins. Scenes from *Robin Hood, Price of Thieves*, starring Kevin Costner were filmed here.

Times: Open all year, Apr-Jun & Sep, daily 10-5; Jul-Aug, daily 10-6; Oct, daily 10-4; Nov-Mar, Sat-Sun 10-4. Closed 24-26 Dec & 1 Jan. **Fee:** £3.20 (ch £1.60, concessions £2.40). Prices and opening times are subject to change in Spring 2007. Please check web site or call 0870 333 1181 for the most up to date prices and opening times when planning your visit. **Facilities:** ℗ ♿ ⌗

TOLLARD ROYAL MAP 03 ST91

Larmer Tree Gardens
SP5 5PT
➲ *(off A354 Blandford to Salisbury road, follow brown signs with flower)*
☎ 01725 516228
e-mail: events@larmertreegardens.co.uk
web: www.larmertreegardens.co.uk

Created by General Pitt Rivers in 1880 as a pleasure ground for 'public enlightenment and entertainment' the gardens are an extraordinary example of Victorian extravagance and vision. The garden contains a wonderful collection of ornate buildings, majestic trees and intimate arbours, retained in an enchanted and tranquil atmosphere.

Times: ✱ Garden open: Feb-Nov, Mon-Thu 11-5 (Sun from Etr-Oct). Tea Pavilion Sun & BHs Etr-Sep 11-5 **Facilities:** ℗ ⭑◎⭑ licensed ♿ toilets for disabled shop ⊗ (ex guide dogs) ◀

WESTBURY MAP 03 ST85

Brokerswood Country Park
Brokerswood BA13 4EH
➲ *(off A36 at Bell Inn, Standerwick. Follow brown signs from A350)*
☎ 01373 822238 & 823880
e-mail: woodland.park@virgin.net
web: www.brokerswood.co.uk

Brokerswood Country Park's nature walk leads through 80 acres of woodlands, with a lake and wildfowl. Facilities include a woodland visitor centre (covering wildlife and forestry), two children's adventure playgrounds (Etr-Oct school holidays & wknds only), guided walks and the woodland railway, over a third of a mile long.

Times: ✱ Open all year; Park open daily 10-5. Closed 24-26 Dec & 1 Jan. Ring for museum opening hours. **Fee:** ✱ £3.50 (ch 3-16 yrs £2.50, pen £3). Family £10. Different prices apply for some special events. **Facilities:** ℗ ⭑◎⭑ ♿ (ramp access to cafe) toilets for disabled shop ◀

WESTWOOD   MAP 03 ST85

Westwood Manor

BA15 2AF

➲ *(1.5m SW of Bradford on Avon, off B3109)*

☎ 01225 863374

web: www.nationaltrust.org.uk

This late 15th-century stone manor house was altered in the early 17th century and has late Gothic and Jacobean windows and fine plasterwork. There is a modern topiary garden.

Times: Open 2 Apr-27 Sep, Tue, Wed & Sun, 2-5. **Fee:** ✱ £4.80 (ch £2.40). Family ticket (2ad+2ch) £12.25. **Facilities:** ❷ ⴲ (drop off point, Braille & large print guide) ⊗ 🚐 🕭

WILTON (NEAR SALISBURY)   MAP 04 SU03

Wilton House

SP2 0BJ

➲ *(3m W of Salisbury, on A30, 10m from Stonehenge & A303)*

☎ 01722 746720 & 746729(24 hr line)

e-mail: tourism@wiltonhouse.com

web: www.wiltonhouse.com

This fabulous Palladian mansion amazes visitors with its treasures, including magnificent art, fine furniture and interiors by Inigo Jones. The traditional and modern gardens, some designed by the 17th Earl, are fabulous throughout the season and continue to delight visitors, whilst the adventure playground is a firm favourite with children.

Times: ✱ Open 2 Apr-Oct, daily, 10.30-5.30. (Last admission 4.30). House closed Mon, ex BHs. **Facilities:** ❷ 🖳 ⊞ ⴲ (induction loop) toilets for disabled shop garden centre ⊗ (ex assist dogs) 🍴

WOODHENGE   MAP 04 SU14

Woodhenge   FREE

➲ *(1.5m N of Amesbury, off A345 just S of Durrington)*

web: www.english-heritage.org.uk

A Neolithic ceremonial monument dating from about 2300 BC, consisting of six concentric rings of timber posts, now marked by concrete piles. The long axis of the rings, which are oval, points to the rising sun on Midsummer Day.

Times: Open all reasonable times. Usual facilities may not apply around Summer Solstice 20-22 Jun. Please check **Facilities:** ❷ ⴲ ⌗

White Horse at Westbury

Worcestershire

Broadway Tower

In Worcestershire, the fertile plains of the Vale of Evesham and the Severn Valley climb to the Malvern Hills in the west, and the Cotswolds in the south. To the north of the county lies the industrialised area of the Black Country, in sharp contrast to the south's rural idyll. From its elevated position, the unique Broadway Tower offers fine views and houses exhibitions depicting its colourful past.

England

BEWDLEY
MAP 07 SO77

Severn Valley Railway
Comberton Hill DY10 1QN
☎ 01299 403816
web: www.svr.co.uk
(For full entry see Kidderminster)

West Midland Safari & Leisure Park
Spring Grove DY12 1LF
⊃ (on A456 between Kidderminster & Bewdley)
☎ 01299 402114
e-mail: info@wmsp.co.uk
web: www.wmsp.co.uk

Located in the heart of rural Worcestershire, this 200-acre site is the home to a drive-through safari and an amazing range of exotic animals. Animal attractions include the new Leopard Valley, Twilight Cave, Creepy Crawlies, the Reptile House, Sealion Theatre, and the new buffalo, Boma. There are also a variety of rides, amusements and live shows suitable for all members of the family.

Times: Mid Feb-early Nov. Times may change refer to website.
Fee: ✱ £8.99 (ch 4 free). Multi ride wristband £8.75. Ride tickets £4 for three tickets from machines (various no of tickets per ride).
Facilities: ❷ ♨ �🍴 licensed 🟢 ♿ (most area accessible slopes/tarmac paths) shop ⊗ (ex guide dogs) ◀

BROADWAY
MAP 04 SP03

Broadway Tower & Animal Park   2 for 1
WR12 7LB
⊃ (off A44, 1m SE of village)
☎ 01386 852390
e-mail: info@broadwaytower.co.uk
web: www.broadwaytower.co.uk

The 65ft tower was designed by James Wyatt for the 6th Earl of Coventry, and built in 1799. The unique building now houses exhibitions depicting its colourful past and various uses such as holiday retreat to artist and designer William Morris. The viewing platform is equipped with a telescope, giving wonderful views over 13 counties.

Times: Open Apr-Oct, daily 10.30-5. Nov-Mar (tower only) wknds weather permitting 11-3 or by prior booking. **Fee:** Tower, £3.80 (ch 4-4 £2.30, concessions £3) Family £10 (2ad+2ch) **Facilities:** ❷ ♨ 🍴 licensed shop ◀

BROMSGROVE
MAP 07 SO97

Avoncroft Museum of Historic Buildings   2 for 1
Stoke Heath B60 4JR
⊃ (2m S, off A38)
☎ 01527 831886 & 831363
e-mail: admin@avoncroft.org.uk
web: www.avoncroft.org.uk

A visit to Avoncroft takes you through nearly 700 years of history. Here you can see 25 buildings rescued from destruction and authentically restored on a 15 acre rural site. There are 15th and 16th-century timber framed buildings, 18th-century agricultural buildings and a cockpit. There are industrial buildings and a working windmill from the 19th century, and from the 20th fully furnished pre-fab.

continued

Times: Open Jul-Aug daily 10.30-5; Apr-Jun, Tue-Fri 10.30-4.30, Sat-Sun 10.30-5; Sep-Oct, Tue-Fri 10.30-4.30, Sat-Sun 10.30-5; Mar, Tue-Thu, Sat-Sun 10.30-4 **Fee:** £6 (ch £3, pen £5). Family ticket £15 (2ad+3ch)
Facilities: ❷ ♨ 🟢 ♿ (ramps, wheelchair available) toilets for disabled shop ⊗ (ex on lead) ◀

EVESHAM
MAP 04 SP04

The Almonry Heritage Centre
Abbey Gate WR11 4BG
⊃ (on A4184, opposite Merstow Green, main N/S route through Evesham)
☎ 01386 446944
e-mail: tic@almonry.ndo.co.uk
web: www.evesham.uk.com

The 14th-century stone and timber building was the home of the Almoner of the Benedictine Abbey in Evesham. It now houses exhibitions relating to the history of Evesham Abbey, the Battle of Evesham, and the culture and trade of Evesham. Evesham Tourist Information Centre is also located here.

Times: Open all year, Mon-Sat & BHs, 10-5, Sun 2-5. Closed Xmas & Sun in Nov-Feb. **Fee:** £2.50 (ch 16 free, concessions £1.50)
Facilities: ℗ (110yds) shop ⊗

GREAT WITLEY
MAP 03 SO76

Witley Court
WR6 6JT
⊃ (on A433)
☎ 01299 896636
web: www.english-heritage.org.uk

Discover the magnificent ruins of this once-great house destroyed by fire in 1937. Explore the magnificent landscaped gardens which feature the stunning Perseus and Andromeda fountains and contemporary sculpture. Step back in time with the audio tour.

Times: Open all year, Mar-May & Sep-Oct, daily, 10-5; Jun-Aug, daily, 10-6; Nov-Feb, Thu-Mon, 10-4. Closed 24-26 Dec & 1 Jan. **Fee:** £5.20 (ch £2.60, concessions £3.90). Family £13. Prices and opening times are subject to change in Spring 2007. Please check web site or call 0870 333 1181 for the most up to date prices and opening times when planning your visit.
Facilities: ❷ ♨ ♿ shop ⊗ ⌗

HANBURY
MAP 03 SO96

Hanbury Hall
School Rd WR9 7EA
⊃ (4.5m E of Droitwich, 1m N of B4090 and 1.5m W of B4091)
☎ 01527 821214
e-mail: hanburyhall@nationaltrust.org.uk
web: www.nationaltrust.org.uk

This William and Mary style red-brick house, completed in 1701, was built by a prosperous local family. The house contains outstanding painted ceilings and staircase by Thornhill, and the Watney collection of porcelain. The 18th-century garden has recently been restored with many features including parterre, bowling green and working orangery.

Times: Open Mar-Oct, Sat-Wed 11-5.30. (Last entry 4.30). Grounds open: weekends Nov-10 Dec **Fee:** ✱ House & Garden £6. Family ticket £15. Garden only £4. **Facilities:** ❷ ♨ ♿ (Braille guide, 2 wheelchairs) toilets for disabled shop ⊗ (ex guide dogs & in the park) ✄ ◀

KIDDERMINSTER

MAP 07 SO87

Bodenham Arboretum & Earth Centre NEW

2 for 1

Wolvesley DY11 5SY

➲ *(follow brown signs W from Wolverley Church island along the B4189)*

☎ 01562 852444 & 850456

web: www.bodenham-arboretum.co.uk

An award winning arboretum, over 2,700 species of trees and shrubs, attractively landscaped in 156 acres. The arboretum is incorporated into a working farm. Five miles of paths lead through dells, glades around lakes, pools and grazing fields.

Times: Open Mar-23 Dec, Wed-Sun, 11-5. Oct, daily. Also open Jan-Feb wknds only. **Fee:** ✱ £5 (ch 5-16 & w/chair users £2) **Facilities:** ♿ 💺 🍴 ♿ toilets for disabled shop ⊗ (ex on leads) 🎫

Severn Valley Railway

Comberton Hill DY10 1QN

➲ *(on A448, clearly signed)*

☎ 01299 403816

web: www.svr.co.uk

The leading standard gauge steam railway, with one of the largest collections of locomotives and rolling stock in the country. Services operate from Kidderminster and Bewdley to Bridgnorth through 16 miles of picturesque scenery along the River Severn. Special steam galas and "Day out with Thomas" Weekends take place during the year along with Santa Specials.

Times: Trains operate wknds throughout year, daily, early May end of Sep, school hols & half terms, Santa Specials, phone for details. **Fee:** ✱ Subject to Review. (Train fares vary according to journey. Main through ticket £11.80 return, Family ticket £31) **Facilities:** ♿ (charged) 💺 🍴 ♿ (some specially adapted trains, call for details) toilets for disabled shop (at Kidderminster/Bridgnorth) 🎫

See advert on this page

Worcestershire County Museum

2 for 1

Hartlebury Castle, Hartlebury DY11 7XZ

➲ *(4m S of Kidderminster clearly signed from A449)*

☎ 01299 250416

e-mail: museum@worcestershire.gov.uk

web: http://www.worcestershire.gov.uk/museum

Housed in the north wing of Hartlebury Castle, the County Museum contains a delightful display of crafts and industries. There are unique collections of toys and costume, displays on domestic life, period room settings and horse-drawn vehicles. Visitors can also see a reconstructed forge, a schoolroom, a wheelwright's and tailor's shop.

continued

Admission to the Museum now includes access to the buildings magnificent State Rooms, where previous Bishops of Worcester have lived and entertained visitors to the castle.

Times: Open Feb-Dec, Tue-Fri 10-5; Sat, Sun & BHs 11-5. Closed Good Fri. **Fee:** £4 (ch & pen £2). Family ticket £11. **Facilities:** ℗ 💻 🍴 ⚅ (car parking spaces, close to main building, lift) toilets for disabled shop ⊗ (ex guide dogs & in grounds) 🚩

REDDITCH   MAP 04 SP06

Forge Mill Needle Museum & Bordesley Abbey Visitor Centre

Forge Mill, Needle Mill Ln, Riverside B98 8HY
➲ *(N side of Redditch, off A441.)*
☎ 01527 62509
e-mail: museum@redditchbc.gov.uk
web: www.redditchbc.gov.uk

The Needle Museum tells the fascinating and sometimes gruesome story of how needles are made. Working, water-powered machinery can be seen in an original needle-scouring mill. The Visitor Centre is an archaeological museum showing finds from excavations at the nearby Bordesley Abbey. Children can become an archaeologist for the day and explore the ruins of this fascinating ancient monument.

Times: ✱ Open Etr-Sep, Mon-Fri 11-4.30, Sat-Sun 2-5; Feb-Etr & Oct-Nov, Mon-Thu 11-4 & Sun 2-5. Parties by arrangement. **Facilities:** ℗ 🍴 ⚅ (wheelchair, museum audio tour, Braille guide, hearing loop) toilets for disabled shop ⊗ (ex guide dogs) 🚩

SEVERN STOKE   MAP 03 SO84

Croome Park

Builders Yard, High Green WR8 9JS
➲ *(8m S of Worcester signposted off A38 and B4084).*
☎ 01905 371006
e-mail: croomepark@nationaltrust.org.uk
web: www.nationaltrust.org.uk

'Capability' Brown's first complete landscape design. A decade of restoration has transformed the park to its 18th-century splendour.

Times: 3 Mar-Apr, 10-5.30, Wed-Sun. May-3 Sep, 10-5.30, Mon-Sun. 6 Sep-29 Oct, 10-5.30, Wed-Sun. Nov-17 Dec, 10-4, Wed-Sun. **Fee:** ✱ £3.90 (ch £1.90) Family £9.50. **Facilities:** ℗ 🍴 ⚅ (w/chair, Braille & large print guides, induction loop) toilets for disabled garden centre 🌿

SPETCHLEY   MAP 03 SO85

Spetchley Park Gardens

Spetchley Park WR5 1RS
➲ *(2m E of Worcester on A44)*
☎ 01905 345213 or 345224
e-mail: hb@spetchleygardens.co.uk
web: www.spetchleygardens.co.uk

The 110-acre deer park and the 30-acre gardens surround an early 19th-century mansion (not open), with sweeping lawns and herbaceous borders, a rose lawn and enclosed gardens with low box and yew hedges. There is a large collection of trees (including 17th-century Cedars of Lebanon), shrubs and plants, many of which are rare or unusual.

Times: Open all year: Wed-Sun, 11-6. BH Mon, 11-6. Other days by appointment **Fee:** ✱ £5 (ch free). Party 25+ £4.50. **Facilities:** ℗ 💻 🍴 ⚅ (most of garden accessible) ⊗ (ex guide dogs)

STONE   MAP 07 SO87

Stone House Cottage Gardens   2 for 1

DY10 4BG
➲ *(2m SE of Kidderminster, on A448)*
☎ 01562 69902
e-mail: louisa@shcn.co.uk
web: www.shcn.co.uk

A beautiful walled garden with towers provides a sheltered area of about one acre for rare shrubs, climbers and interesting herbaceous plants. Adjacent to the garden is a nursery with a large selection of unusual plants.

Times: Open mid Mar-mid Sept, Wed-Sat, 10-5. **Fee:** ✱ £3 (ch free). **Facilities:** ℗ garden centre ⊗

WICHENFORD   MAP 03 SO76

Wichenford Dovecote NEW

➲ *(N of B4204)*
☎ 01527 821214
web: www.nationaltrust.org.uk

17th-century half-timbered black-and-white dovecote, in a picturesque riverside location.

Times: Open Apr-Oct, Mon-Sun, 9-6. **Fee:** ✱ £1 **Facilities:** 🌿

WORCESTER   MAP 03 SO85

City Museum & Art Gallery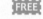

Foregate St WR1 1DT
➲ *(in city centre, 150m from Foregate St Train Station)*
☎ 01905 25371
e-mail: artgalleryandmuseum@cityofworcester.gov.uk
web: www.worcestercitymuseums.org.uk

The gallery has temporary art exhibitions from both local and national sources. Museum exhibits cover geology, local and natural history. Of particular interest is a complete 19th-century chemist's shop. There are collections relating to the Worcestershire Regiment and the Worcestershire Yeomanry Cavalry.

Times: Open all year, Mon-Fri 9.30-5.30, Sat 9.30-5. Closed Sun, 25-26 Dec, 1 Jan & Good Fri, Easter Mon and Whitsun BH Mon. **Facilities:** ℗ (city centre) 💻 🍴 ⚅ (lift, induction loop) toilets for disabled shop ⊗ 🚩

Elgar's Birthplace Museum   2 for 1

Crown East Ln, Lower Broadheath WR2 6RH
➲ *(3m W of Worcester, signed off A44 to Leominster)*
☎ 01905 333224
e-mail: birthplace@elgarmuseum.org
web: www.elgarmuseum.org

In 2000, the Elgar Centre was opened, to complement the historic Birthplace Cottage and to provide additional exhibition space for more treasures from this unique collection, telling the story of Elgar's musical development and inspirations. Listen to his music as the audio tour guides you round the easily accessible displays. 2007 is the 150th Anniversary of Elgar's birth, so there will be special events and concerts. Contact for details

Times: Open daily, last admission 4.15. Closed 23 Dec-end Jan. **Fee:** ✱ £5 (ch £2 & pen £4.50) concessions £3 **Facilities:** ℗ 🍴 ⚅ (large print guides, audio facilities, wheelchair) toilets for disabled shop ⊗ (ex guide dogs) 🚩

England

The Greyfriars NEW

Friar St WR1 2LZ

➲ (in city centre, use public car park on Friar St)

☎ 01905 23571

e-mail: greyfriars@nationaltrust.org.uk
web: www.nationaltrust.org.uk

Built in 1480, this is a beautiful timbered framed merchants house in the city centre. Rescued from demolition and carefully restored. The panelled interior contains interesting textiles and furnishings. An archway leads through to a pleasant walled garden.

Times: Open Mar-1 Jul & 30 Aug-16 Dec, Wed-Sat, 1-5; 2 Jul-27 Aug, Wed-Sun, 1-5. **Fee:** ✱ £3.60 (ch £1.90). Family £9. **Facilities:** ℗ (200yds) ☕ ⊗ ♨ ▅

Hawford Dovecote

➲ (3m N of Worcester, 0.5m E of A449).

☎ 01527 821214

e-mail: hanburyhall@nationaltrust.org
web: www.nationaltrust.org.uk

An unusual square, half-timbered 16th-century dovecote. Access on foot only via the entrance drive to the adjoining house.

Times: Open Apr-Oct, daily 9-6 or sunset. (Closed Good Fri). Other times by prior appointment only. **Fee:** ✱ £1 **Facilities:** ℗ 50yds (on street parking) ⊗ 🚌 ♨

Museum of Worcester Porcelain `2 for 1`

Severn St WR1 2NE

➲ (M5 junct 7, follow signs to city centre, at 7th set of lights take 1st left into Edger St & bear left with road into Severn St. At T Junct bear right & after 700yds take 1st left. Museum on left)

☎ 01905 746000

e-mail: museum@royal-worcester.co.uk
web: www.worcesterporcelainmuseum.org

An informative and entertaining audio tour features Henry Sandon, museum patron and BBC *Antiques Roadshow* expert, along with skilled craftsmen, is free with entry and tells the story of the factory and its workforce. Gallery displays range from Oriental simplicity to Victorian extravagance.

Times: Open: Mar-Nov, Mon-Sat 10-5.30, Sun 11-5. Dec-Feb, Mon-Sat, 10-4, Sun, 11-5. Closed 25-26 Dec & Etr Sun. **Fee:** ✱ Museum: £5 **Facilities:** ℗ (charged) ☕ 🍴 📋 ♿ (ex factory) toilets for disabled shop ⊗ ▅

Worcester Cathedral

WR1 2LH

➲ (city centre, signed from M5 junct 7)

☎ 01905 28854 & 21004

e-mail: info@worcestercathedral.org.uk
web: www.cofe-worcester.org.uk

Worcester Cathedral is one of England's loveliest cathedrals, with Royal Tombs, medieval cloisters, an ancient crypt and Chapter House and magnificent Victorian stained glass. The tower is open in the summer. There are a number of different celebrations each year, including the Heart of England Food Fair and many concerts.

Times: ✱ Open all year, daily 7.30-6. **Facilities:** ℗ (500yds) ☕ 📋 ♿ (access from College Green) toilets for disabled shop ⊗ (ex guide dogs) ▅

Malvern Hills

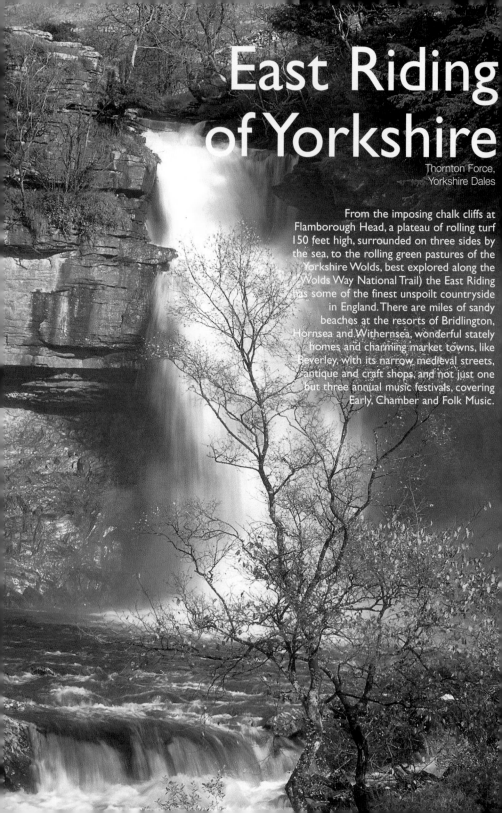

East Riding of Yorkshire

Thornton Force,
Yorkshire Dales

From the imposing chalk cliffs at
Flamborough Head, a plateau of rolling turf
150 feet high, surrounded on three sides by
the sea, to the rolling green pastures of the
Yorkshire Wolds, best explored along the
Wolds Way National Trail) the East Riding
has some of the finest unspoilt countryside
in England. There are miles of sandy
beaches at the resorts of Bridlington,
Hornsea and Withernsea, wonderful stately
homes and charming market towns, like
Beverley, with its narrow medieval streets,
antique and craft shops, and not just one
but three annual music festivals, covering
Early, Chamber and Folk Music.

England

BEMPTON   MAP 08 TA17

RSPB Nature Reserve
YO15 1JD
⊃ *(take cliff road from B1229, Bempton Village and follow brown tourist signs)*
☎ 01262 851179

Part of the spectacular chalk cliffs that stretch from Flamborough Head to Speeton. This is one of the best sites in England to see thousands of nesting seabirds including gannets and puffins at close quarters. Viewpoints overlook the cliffs, which are best visited from April to July. Over 2 miles of chalk cliffs rising to 400ft with numerous cracks and ledges. Enormous numbers of seabirds nest on these cliffs including guillemots, razorbills, kittiwakes, fulmars, herring gulls and several pairs of shag. This is the only gannetry in England and is growing annually. Many migrants pass off-shore including terns, skuas and shearwaters. Wheatears, ring ouzels and merlins frequent the clifftop on migration. Grey seal and porpoise are sometimes seen offshore.

Times: Visitor centre open daily, Mar-Oct 10-5. Nov -Dec 9.30-4.
Fee: ✱ £3.50 per car, £6 per minibus, £10 per coach.
Facilities: ❷ (charged) 🖵 ⛅ large print guide toilets for disabled shop 🔲

BEVERLEY   MAP 08 TA03

The Guildhall
Register Sq HU17 9AU
⊃ *(in Register Sq, next to post office)*
☎ 01482 392776
e-mail: stefan.ramsden@eastriding.gov.uk

A Guildhall has been on this site since 1500, although parts of the building date back to a private dwelling of 1320. Largely remodelled in the Palladian style in the 1760s, the Courtroom features a magnificent stucco work ceiling, and the Magistrate's Room houses rare 17th-century Civic furniture.

Times: ✱ Open every Fri, 10-4. Please phone for guide tours at other times. **Facilities:** ⛅ (disabled parking 100yds) ⊗ (ex guide dogs)

BURTON AGNES   MAP 08 TA16

Burton Agnes Hall
Estate Office YO25 0ND
⊃ *(on A614)*
☎ 01262 490324
e-mail: burton.agnes@farmline.com
web: www.burton-agnes.com

Built in 1598, this is a magnificent Elizabethan house, with furniture, pictures and china amassed by the family owners over four centuries. There is a walled garden with maze, potager, herbaceous borders, clematis, campanula and geranium collections, and jungle garden, as well as woodland walks.

continued

Burton Agnes Hall

Times: Open Apr-Oct, 17 Nov- 16 Dec, daily 11-5. 10-25 Feb open daily 11-4. **Fee:** ✱ Hall & grounds £5.50 (ch £2.75, pen £5). Grounds only £2.75 (ch £1.30, pen £2.50). Party 30+. **Facilities:** ❷ 🖵 ⛅ (scented garden for the blind) toilets for disabled shop garden centre 🔲

Burton Agnes Manor House
⊃ *(in Burton Agnes, 5m SW of Bridlington on A166)*
web: www.english-heritage.org.uk

A rare and well-preserved example of a Norman house. Some interesting Norman architectural features can still be seen, but the building was encased in brick during the 17th and 18th centuries. The house is near Burton Agnes Hall and the gardens are privately owned and not managed by English Heritage.

Times: Open Apr-Oct, daily 11-5. **Facilities:** ⌗

GOOLE   MAP 08 SE72

The Waterways Museum
Dutch River Side DN14 5TB
⊃ *(M62 junct 36, enter Goole, turn right at next 3 sets of lights onto Dutch River Side. 0.75m and follow brown signs)*
☎ 01405 768730
e-mail: waterwaysmuseum@btinternet.com
web: www.waterwaysmuseumandadventurecentre.co.uk

Discover the story of the Aire & Calder Navigation and the growth of the 'company town' of Goole and its busy port. Find out how to sail and, in the interactive gallery, see how wooden boats were built. Enjoy the unique 'Tom Pudding' story, brought to life through the vessels on the canal and the boat hoist in South Dock. Rediscover the Humber keels and sloops, and Goole's shipbuilding history through the objects, photos and memories of Goole people.

Times: Open Mon-Fri 9-4.30 (Apr-Sep, Sun 12-5) **Facilities:** ❷ 🖵 📷 ⛅ (disabled access on boats, nature trail, wheelchair) toilets for disabled shop ⊗ (ex guide dogs)

England

Hornsea Museum   `2 for 1`

11 Newbegin HU18 1AB
➲ *(turn off A165 onto B1244)*
☎ 01964 533443
web: www.hornseamuseum.com

A former farmhouse whose outbuildings now illustrate local life and history. There are 19th-century period rooms and a dairy, plus craft tools and farming implements. Photographs, local personalities and industries are also featured along with a large display of Hornsea pottery.

Times: Open Etr-Sep & Oct half-term hols, Tue-Sat 11-5, Sun 2-5 (last admission 4). Also open BH Mon. **Fee:** £2.50 (concessions £2). Family ticket £7.50 **Facilities:** Ⓟ (50yds) 🍴 ♿ (audio interpretation for blind/partially sighted) toilets for disabled shop ⊗ (ex guide dogs)

Maister House   `FREE`

160 High St HU1 1NL
➲ *(Hull city centre)*
☎ 01482 324114
web: www.nationaltrust.org.uk

The house is a mid-18th-century rebuilding, notable for its splendid stone and wrought-iron staircase, ornate stucco work and finely carved doors. Only the staircase and entrance hall are open as the house is now let as offices.

Times: Open all year, Mon-Fri 10-4 (Closed BH). **Facilities:** Ⓟ ⊗ 🚌 ✹

Maritime Museum   `FREE`

Queen Victoria Square HU1 3DX
➲ *(follow A63 to town centre, museum is within pedestrian area)*
☎ 01482 613902
e-mail: museums@hullcc.gov.uk
web: www.hullcc.gov.uk/museums

Hull's maritime history is illustrated here, with displays on whales and whaling, ships and shipping, and other aspects of this Humber port. There is also a Victorian court room which is used for temporary exhibitions. The restored dock area, with its fine Victorian and Georgian buildings, is well worth exploring too.

Times: ✱ Open all year, Mon-Sat 10-5 & Sun 1.30-4.30. Closed 25 Dec-2 Jan & Good Fri) **Facilities:** Ⓟ (100yds) 🍴 ♿ shop ⊗ (ex guide dogs)

'Streetlife' - Hull Museum of Transport   `FREE`

High St HU1 1PS
➲ *(A63 from M62, follow signs for Old Town)*
☎ 01482 613902
e-mail: museums@hullcc.gov.uk
web: www.hullcc.gov.uk/museums

This purpose built museum uses a 'hands-on' approach to trace 200 years of transport history. With a vehicle collection of national importance, state-of-the-art animatronic displays and authentic scenarios, you can see Hull's Old Town brought vividly to life. The mail coach ride uses the very latest in computer technology to recreate a Victorian journey by four-in-hand.

Times: ✱ Open all year, Mon-Sat 10-5, Sun 1.30-4.30. Closed 24-25 Dec & Good Fri **Facilities:** Ⓟ (500mtrs) 🍴 ♿ toilets for disabled shop ⊗ (ex guide dogs)

The Deep

HU1 4DP
➲ *(follow signs from city centre)*
☎ 01482 381000
e-mail: info@thedeep.co.uk
web: www.thedeep.co.uk

The Deep tells the story of the world's oceans using live animals and hands-on activities, with over 3000 fish and more than 40 sharks. Now featuring The Twilight Zone, an exhibition all about the weird and alien creatures from the deep sea like giant pacific octopus, wolf eels and giant Japanese spider crabs.

Times: Open all year, daily 10-6. Closed 24-25 Dec **Fee:** ✱ £8 (ch under 16 £6, pen £6). Family ticket (2ad+2ch) £25, (2ad+3ch) £30 **Facilities:** Ⓟ (charged) 🎧 ﾃ licensed 🍴 ♿ (signing for the deaf if booked in advance, tactile guides) toilets for disabled shop ⊗ (ex guide dogs) ◀

England

Wilberforce House

 FREE

23-25 High St HU1 1NE

➲ *(A63 from M62 or A1079 from York, follow signs for Old Town)*

☎ 01482 613902

e-mail: museums@hullcc.gov.uk

web: www.hullcc.gov.uk/museums

The early 17th-century Merchant's house was the birthplace of William Wilberforce, who became a leading campaigner against slavery. There are Jacobean and Georgian rooms and displays on Wilberforce and the anti-slavery campaign. The house also has secluded gardens. There are special exhibitions throughout the year.

Times: ✱ Open all year, Mon-Sat 10-5 & Sun 1.30-4.30. Closed 25-26 Dec, 1 Jan & Good Fri. **Facilities:** ℗ (500mtrs) (meters on street) ♿ (large print, video area & audio guides) shop ⊗ (ex guide dogs)

POCKLINGTON   MAP 08 SE84

Burnby Hall Garden & Stewart Collection

33, The Balk YO42 2QF

➲ *(off A1079 at turning for Pocklington off B1247, follow brown signs)*

☎ 01759 307125

e-mail: briah@brianpetrie.plus.com

web: www.burnbyhallgardens.com

The two lakes in this garden have an outstanding collection of 80 varieties of hardy water lilies, designated a National Collection. The lakes stand within nine acres of beautiful gardens including heather beds, a rock garden, a spring and summer bedding area, woodland walk and Victorian garden. The museum contains sporting trophies and ethnic material gathered on world-wide travels. There are band concerts every other Sunday.

Times: Open Apr-Sep, daily 10-6 (last admission 5). **Fee:** ✱ £3.50 (ch 5-15 £1.60, pen £2.75). Party 20+.£2.50 each **Facilities:** ℗ 🍴 ♿ (free wheelchair hire, viewing platform for wheelchairs) toilets for disabled shop ⊗ (ex guide dogs) 🍴

SEWERBY   MAP 08 TA16

Sewerby Hall & Gardens

Church Ln, Sewerby YO15 1EA

➲ *(2m NE of Bridlington on B1255 towards Flamborough)*

☎ 01262 673769

e-mail: sewerby.hall@eastring.gov.uk

web: www.sewerby-hall.co.uk

Sewerby Hall and Gardens, set in 50 acres of parkland overlooking Bridlington Bay, dates back to 1715. The Georgian House, with its 19th-century Orangery, contains art galleries, archaeological displays and an Amy Johnson Room with a collection of her trophies and mementoes. The grounds include magnificent walled Old English and Rose gardens and host many events throughout the year. Activities for all the family include a Children's Zoo and play areas, golf, putting, bowls, plus woodland and clifftop walks. Phone for details of special events.

Times: Estate open all year, dawn-dusk. Hall open Etr-end Oct. Please contact for further details. **Fee:** £3.10 (ch 5-15 £1.50, pen £2.80). Family ticket £9. Group 10+ **Facilities:** ℗ 🍴 🍴 ♿ toilets for disabled shop 🍴

SPROATLEY   MAP 08 TA13

Burton Constable Hall

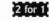

HU11 4LN

➲ *(Follow signs for A165 Bridlington Road towards Sirlaugh, then right towards Hornsea and follow brown historic house signs to Burton Constable)*

☎ 01964 562400

web: www.burtonconstable.com

This superb Elizabethan house was built in 1570, but much of the interior was remodelled in the 18th century. There are magnificent reception rooms and a Tudor long gallery with a pendant roof: the contents range from pictures and furniture to a unique collection of 18th-century scientific instruments. Outside are 200 acres of parkland landscaped by 'Capability' Brown, with oaks and chestnuts, and a lake with an island.

Times: Open, Hall & Grounds Etr Sat-end Oct. Grounds 12.30-5, Hall 1-5. (Last admission 4). Closed Fri. **Fee:** House £5.50 (ch £2.50, pen £5). Family ticket £12.50. Grounds only £1.50 (ch 75p) **Facilities:** ℗ 🍴 🍴 ♿ (stair lift to first foor, wheelchairs) toilets for disabled shop ⊗ (ex assist dogs)

North Yorkshire

River Ouse,
York

Far and away the largest county in England,
North Yorkshire has a stunning landscape,
covering part of the Pennines, the rolling
farmlands of the Vale of York, the Cleveland
Hills, and the North York Moors, plus the
Yorkshire Dales National Park, which includes
Swaledale and Wensleydale. The beautiful
remains of Fountains Abbey, Britain's largest
monastic ruin and a World Heritage Site, are
amongst many reminders in the county of
Henry VIII's Dissolution of the Monasteries.
Along the coast are fishing villages like
Staithes and Robin Hood's Bay, as well as the
resort towns of Scarborough and Whitby. The
city of York, with the River Ouse meandering
through, has been an important British centre
since the Romans built a fort there in AD71,
and York Minster is the largest medieval
Gothic cathedral north of the Alps.

ALDBOROUGH   MAP 08 SE46

Aldborough Roman Site
YO5 9ES

⮑ *(0.75m SE of Boroughbridge, on minor road off B6265 within 1m of junct of A1 & A6055)*

☎ 01423 322768

web: www.english-heritage.org.uk

View two spectacular mosaic pavements and discover the remains of the once principal Roman town.

Times: Open 19 Mar-Jul, Thu-Mon, 10-5; Aug, daily, 10-5; Sep, Thu-Mon, 10-5. **Facilities:** shop ♯

AYSGARTH   MAP 07 SE08

National Park Centre   FREE
DL8 3TH

⮑ *(off A684, Leyburn to Hawes road at Falls junct, Palmer Flatt Hotel & continue down hill over river, centre 500yds on left)*

☎ 01969 662910

e-mail: aysgarth@ytbtic.co.uk

web: www.yorkshiredales.org.uk

A visitor centre for the Yorkshire Dales National Park, with maps, guides, walks and local information. Interactive displays explain the history and natural history of the area. Plan the day ahead with a light lunch in the coffee shop. Various guided walks begin here throughout the year.

Times: Open Apr-Oct, daily 10-5; Winter open Fri-Sun, 10-4.
Facilities: ❷ (charged) ♿ & (viewing platform at Falls) toilets for disabled shop ⊗ (ex guide dogs) ◀

BEDALE   MAP 08 SE28

Bedale Museum   FREE
DL8 1AA

⮑ *(on A684, 1.5m W of A1 at Leeming Bar. Opposite church, at N end of town)*

☎ 01677 423797

Situated in a building dating back to the 17th-century, the Bedale is a fascinating museum. The central attraction is the Bedale fire engine, which dates back to 1742. Other artefacts include documents, toys, craft tools and household utensils, which all help to give an absorbing picture of the lifestyle of the times.

Times: Open all year Tue & Fri 10-12.30 & 2-4, Wed 2-4, Thu-Sat 10-12
Facilities: ❷ & toilets for disabled shop ⊗ (ex guide dogs)

BENINGBROUGH   MAP 08 SE55

Beningbrough Hall & Gardens
YO6 1DD

⮑ *(off A19, 8m NW of York)*

☎ 01904 470666

e-mail: beningbrough@nationaltrust.org.uk

web: www.nationaltrust.org.uk

Beningbrough was built around 1716. It houses 100 portraits from the National Portrait Gallery in London. Ornately carved wood panelling is a feature of several of the rooms. There is also a fully equipped Victorian Laundry and walled garden.

Times: Open early Mar-end Oct daily (ex Thu & Fri) open Good Fri, Jul-Aug daily (ex Thu) 12-5. Grounds 11-5.30. Galleries & Grounds winter wkds Nov-Feb, Sat & Sun 11-3. **Fee:** ✱ Summer: £7 (ch £3.50) Winter : £4.50 (ch £2.50) **Facilities:** ❷ 🍽 licensed ▤ & (access to Victorian laundry, shop & restaurant) toilets for disabled shop ⊗ ❄

BRIMHAM   MAP 08 SE26

Brimham Rocks
Summerbridge HG3 4DW

⮑ *(10m NW of Harrogate, off B6265)*

☎ 01423 780688

e-mail: brimhamrocks@nationaltrust.org.uk

web: www.nationaltrust.org.uk

The rocks stand on National Trust open moorland at a height of 987ft, enjoying spectacular views over the surrounding countryside. The area is filled with strange and fascinating rock formations and is rich in wildlife. Brimham House is now an information point and shop.

Times: Open 8-dusk, (facilities may close in bad weather): shop with exhibition room, kiosk mid Mar-end May & Oct, Sat & Sun 11-5, end May-end Sep daily 11-5, early Nov-mid Dec, Sun 11-5. Also open daily; local school hols, BHs, 25 Dec & 1 Jan (weather permitting). **Fee:** Cars (up to 4hrs £3, over 4hrs £4). Minibuses £7. Coaches £12. Motorcycles free. Nat Trust members free. Cars up to 4 hours £3.50. Cars over 4 hours £4.50.
Facilities: ❷ (charged) ♿ ▤ & (adapted path steep in places, Braille/large print guide) toilets for disabled shop ❄ ◀

CASTLE BOLTON   MAP 07 SE09

Bolton Castle
DL8 4ET

⮑ *(off A684, 6m W of Leyburn)*

☎ 01969 623981

e-mail: harry@boltoncastle.co.uk

web: www.boltoncastle.co.uk

Medieval castle completed in 1399, overlooking Wensleydale. Stronghold of the Scrope family. Mary Queen of Scots was imprisoned here for six months during 1568 and 1569. The castle was besieged and taken by Parliamentary forces in 1645. Tapestries, tableaux, arms and armour can be seen. Medieval gardens including maze. Events throughout the year, please telephone for details.

Times: Open Apr-Oct, 10-5; Nov-Mar, 10-4/dusk. Phone for winter opening times. **Fee:** ✱ £5 (ch, concessions £3.50). Family ticket £12.
Facilities: ❷ ♿ ▤ shop ⊗ (ex guide dogs) ◀

CASTLE HOWARD
See **Malton**

COXWOLD
MAP 08 SE57

Byland Abbey
YO6 4BD

➲ *(2m S of A170 between Thirsk & Helmsley, near Coxwold village)*

☎ 01347 868614

web: www.english-heritage.org.uk

A hauntingly beautiful monastic ruin set in peaceful meadows in the shadow of the Hambleton Hills. Marvel at the collection of medieval floor tiles still in their original setting.

Times: Open Apr-Jul & Sep, Thu-Mon, 10-5; Aug, daily, 10-5. **Fee:** £3 (ch £1.50, concessions £2.30). Prices and opening times are subject to change in Spring 2007. Please check web site or call 0870 333 1181 for the most up to date prices and opening times when planning your visit.
Facilities: ❷ ▤ ♿ (garden/grounds partly accessible) toilets for disabled ⚏ ◀

DANBY
MAP 08 NZ70

Moors Centre
FREE

Lodge Ln YO21 2NB

➲ *(turn S off A171, follow Moors Centre Danby signs . Left at crossroads in Danby and then 2m, Centre at bend on right)*

☎ 01439 772737

e-mail: moorscentre@ytbtic.co.uk

web: www.moors.uk.net

The ideal place to start exploring the North York Moors National Park. There is an exhibition about the area as well as events, video, a shop and local walks. The Moorsbus service also operates from this site - phone for details.

Times: Open all year, Apr-Oct, daily 10-5. Nov-Feb wknds only 11-4, Mar daily 11-4. Closed 25-26 Dec **Facilities:** ❷ (charged) ▰ ▤ ♿ (woodland & garden trails, motorised & manual wheelchairs) toilets for disabled shop ⊗ (ex guide dogs & in grounds) ◀

EASBY
MAP 08 NZ10

Easby Abbey
FREE

➲ *(1m SE of Richmond off B6271)*

web: www.english-heritage.org.uk

Set beside the River Swale, this Premonstratensian Abbey was founded in 1155 and dedicated to St Agatha. Extensive remains of the monks' domestic buildings can be seen.

Times: Open Apr-Sep, daily, 10-6; Oct, daily, 10-5; Nov-Mar, daily, 10-4. Closed 24-25 Dec. & 1 Jan **Facilities:** ❷ ⚏

ELVINGTON
MAP 08 SE74

Yorkshire Air Museum & Allied Air Forces Memorial
2 for 1

Halifax Way YO41 4AU

➲ *(from York take A1079 then immediate right onto B1228, museum is signposted on right)*

☎ 01904 608595

e-mail: museum@yorkshireairmuseum.co.uk

web: www.yorkshireairmuseum.co.uk

This award-winning museum and memorial is based around the largest authentic former WWII Bomber Command Station open to the public. There is a restored tower, an air gunners museum, archives, an Airborne Forces display, Squadron memorial rooms, and much more. Among the exhibits are replicas of the pioneering Cayley Glider and Wright Flyer, along with the Halifax Bomber and modern jets like the Harrier GR3, Tornado GR1 and GR4.

Times: Open daily, 10-5 (summer), 10-3.30 (winter). Closed 25 & 26 Dec. **Fee:** ✱ £5 (ch £3 & pen £4). **Facilities:** ❷ ▰ ℐ licensed ♿ (Access to all except top control tower) toilets for disabled shop ◀

See advert on page 323

FAIRBURN
MAP 08 SE42

RSPB Nature Reserve
FREE

Fairburn Ings, The Visitor Centre, Newton Ln WF10 2BH

➲ *(W of A1, N of Ferrybridge. Signed from Allerton Bywater off A656. Signed Fairburn Village off A1)*

☎ 01977 603796

e-mail: james.dean@rspb.org.uk

One-third of the 700-acre RSPB reserve is open water, and over 270 species of birds have been recorded. A visitor centre provides information, and there is an elevated boardwalk, suitable for disabled visitors.

Times: Access to the reserve via car park, open 9-dusk. Centre open 9.30-5 everyday. Car park open: 9-5. Closed 25-26 Dec. **Facilities:** ❷ ♿ (raised boardwalk for wheelchair) toilets for disabled shop ⊗ (ex guide dogs & in reserve)

GRASSINGTON

MAP 07 SE06

National Park Centre

Hebden Rd BD23 5LB

➲ *(situated on B6265 in the main Grassington car park)*

☎ 01969 751690

e-mail: grassington@yorkshiredales.org.uk

web: www.yorkshiredales.org.uk

The centre is a useful introduction to the Yorkshire Dales National Park. It has a video and a display on 'Wharfedale - Gateway to the Park', and maps, guides and local information are available. There is also a 24-hr public access information service through computer screens and a full tourist information service.

Times: Open Apr-Oct daily, 10-5; Nov-Mar, Fri, & Sat-Sun, 10-4 (also daily in school hols). **Facilities:** ℗ (charged) ﷼ toilets for disabled shop ⬛

GUISBOROUGH

MAP 08 NZ61

Gisborough Priory

TS14 6HG

➲ *(next to parish church)*

☎ 01287 633801

e-mail: guisboroughtic@redcar-cleveland.gov.uk

web: www.redcar-cleveland.gov.uk

The remains of the east end of the 14th-century church make a dramatic sight here. The priory was founded in the 12th century for Augustinian canons.

Times: Open Jun-Sep, Tue-Sun, 9-5; Oct-May, Wed-Sun, 9-5. **Fee:** ✱ £1.10 (ch 55p, concessions 75p). Opening times and prices are subject to change, for further details please phone 0870 333 1181 **Facilities:** ℗ ﷼ ﷼ ⬛

HARROGATE

MAP 08 SE35

RHS Garden Harlow Carr

Crag Ln, Otley Rd HG3 1QB

➲ *(off B6162 Otley Rd, 1.5m from Harrogate centre)*

☎ 01423 565418

e-mail: admin-harlowcarr@rhs.org.uk

web: www.rhs.org.uk/harlowcarr

Established in1950, RHS Garden Harlow Carr provides a beautiful garden setting covering 58 acres, including 'Gardens Through Time', streamside garden, contemporary herbaceous borders, scented and kitchen gardens, woodland and flower meadow, extensive plant centre and Bettys Café Tea Rooms. Events throughout the year include; outdoor theatre, festivals, workshops and children's activities. There is also a Museum of Gardening, library on site and a childrens play area.

Times: Open all year, daily 9.30-6, or 4 Nov-Mar. (Last admission 1hr before closing). **Fee:** £6 (ch under 16 £2) Child under 6 - free. RHS members+1 guest free. **Facilities:** ℗ ⬛ ﷼ ﷼ (electric and push wheelchairs available, scented garden) toilets for disabled shop garden centre ⊗ (ex guide dogs) ⬛

The Royal Pump Room Museum

Crown Place HG1 2RY

➲ *(A61 into town centre and follow brown heritage signs)*

☎ 01423 556188

e-mail: museums@harrogate.gov.uk

web: www.harrogate.gov.uk/museums

Housed in an early Victorian pump room over the town's sulphur wells, the museum tells the story of Harrogate's heyday as England's European spa. Visitors discover some of the amazing spa treatments; taste the sulphur water; and explore stories of Russian royalty, communal ox-roasts and early bicycles, among many others. From May 2006 to February 2007 there is a special behind the scenes exhibition, and from March 2007 there is an exploration of many aspects of Victorian life, which includes the work of local Victorian artist, William Powell Frith.

Times: Open all year, Mon-Sat 10-5, Sun 2-5, (Nov-Mar close at 4). Closed 24-26 Dec, 15-17 May, 1 & 8-19 & 19-21 Feb for works. **Fee:** ✱ £2.80 (ch £1.50, concessions £1.70). Family rate £8 (2ad+2ch). Party. Combined seasonal tickets available for The Royal Pump Room Museum & Knaresborough Castle & Museum £10 **Facilities:** ℗ (100yds) (restricted to 3hrs, need parking disc) ﷼ ﷼ toilets for disabled shop ⊗ (ex guide dogs) ⬛

HAWES

MAP 07 SD88

Dales Countryside Museum Centre & TIC

Station Yard DL8 3NT

➲ *(off A684 in Old Station Yard)*

☎ 01969 667450 & 667494

e-mail: hawes@ytbtic.co.uk

web: www.yorkshiredales.org.uk

Fascinating museum telling the story of the people and landscape of the Yorkshire Dales. Static steam loco and carriages with video and displays. Added features include hands-on interactive displays for children, temporary exhibitions & events.

Times: ✱ Open all year daily 10-5. **Facilities:** ℗ (charged) ﷼ ﷼ (lifts, ramps and parking) toilets for disabled shop ⊗ (ex guide dogs) ⬛

HELMSLEY

MAP 08 SE68

Duncombe Park

YO62 5EB

➲ *(located within North York Moors National Park, off A170 Thirsk-Scarborough road, 1m from Helmsley market place)*

☎ 01439 778625

e-mail: liz@duncombepark.com

web: www.duncombepark.com

Duncombe Park stands at the heart of a spectacular 30-acre early 18th-century landscape garden which is set in 300 acres of dramatic parkland around the River Rye. The house, originally built in 1713, was gutted by fire in 1879 and rebuilt in 1895. Its principal rooms are a fine example of the type of grand interior popular at the turn of the century. Home of the Duncombes for 300 years, for much of this century the house was a girls' school. In 1985 the present Lord and Lady Feversham decided to make it a family home again and after major restoration, opened the house to the public in 1990. Part of the

continued

garden and parkland were designated a 250-acre National Nature Reserve in 1994. Special events include a Country Fair (May), an Antiques Fair (June), Steam Fair (July), Antiques Fair (November). Please telephone for details.

Times: Open: May-end Oct, Sun-Thu; Gardens, Parkland Centre tea room & shop & Parkland walks 11-5.30. House by guided tour only every hour from 12.30-3.30. **Fee:** House & Gardens £7.25 (ch 10-16, £3.25, concessions £5.50) Gardens & Parkland £4 (ch £2, concessions £3.50) Parkland only £2 (ch £1). **Facilities:** ☉ ⏀ licensed ▥ ⚬ (portable ramp, lift, wheelchair for loan) toilets for disabled shop ⊗ (ex guide dogs) ◀

Helmsley Castle

YO6 5AB

☎ 01439 770442

web: www.english-heritage.org.uk

An atmospheric ruin with formidable double earthworks. Also, an exhibition of the history of the castle.

Times: Open all year, Apr-Sep, daily 10-6; Oct, daily, 10-5; Nov-Mar, daily, 10-4. Closed 24-26 Dec & 1 Jan. **Fee:** £4 (ch £2, concessions £3) Family £10. Prices and opening times are subject to change in Spring 2007. Please check web site or call 0870 333 1181 for the most up to date prices and opening times when planning your visit. **Facilities:** ☉ (charged) shop ⌗

Flamingo Land Theme Park & Zoo

The Rectory YO17 6UX

➲ (turn off A64 onto A169, Pickering to Whitby road)

☎ 01653 668287

e-mail: info@flamingoland.co.uk

web: www.flamingoland.co.uk

Set in 375 acres of North Yorkshire countryside with over 100 rides and attractions there's something for everyone at Flamingo Land. Enjoy the thrills and spills of 12 white knuckle rides or enjoy a stroll through the extensive zoo where you'll find tigers, giraffes, hippos and rhinos. The theme park also boasts 6 great family shows.

Times: Open daily, 30 Mar-28 Oct **Fee:** ✱ £19 (ch 4-11 £16.50, ch under 3 free, pen £9.50). Family ticket (4 people) £70. **Facilities:** ☉ ♨ ⏀ licensed ▥ ⚬ (parking, wheelchair hire) toilets for disabled shop ◀

Kirkham Priory

Whitwell-on-the-Hill YO6 7JS

➲ (5m SW of Malton on minor road off A64)

☎ 01653 618768

web: www.english-heritage.org.uk

Discover the ruins of this Augustinian priory, which includes a magnificent carved gatehouse, set in a peaceful and secluded valley by the River Derwent.

Times: Open Apr-Aug, daily 10-6; Sep, Thu-Mon, 10-4; Oct, Sat-Sun, 10-4. **Fee:** £3 (ch £1.50, concessions £2.30). Prices and opening times are subject to change in Spring 2007. Please check web site or call 0870 333 1181 for the most up to date prices and opening times when planning your visit. **Facilities:** ☉ ⚬ ⌗

Knaresborough Castle & Museum

Castle Yard HG5 8AS

➲ (off High St towards Market Square, right at police station into Castle Yard)

☎ 01423 556188

e-mail: museums@harrogate.gov.uk

web: www.harrogate.gov.uk/museums

Towering high above the town of Knaresborough, the remains of this 14th-century castle look down over the gorge of the River Nidd. This imposing fortress was once the hiding place of Thomas Becket's murderers and served as a prison for Richard II. Remains include the keep, the sally-port, parts of the curtain wall and the Old Court of Knaresborough. It now houses a local museum, and entrance is part of the combined ticket price.

Times: Open Good Fri-end Sep, daily 10.30-5. Guided tours regularly available **Fee:** ✱ £2.50 (ch £1.25, concessions £1.50). Family ticket (2ad+2ch) £7 Party 10+. Joint & season tickets available for Knaresborough Castle & Museum & The Royal Pump Room Museum.

Facilities: ☉ (charged) ▥ ⚬ toilets for disabled shop ⊗ (ex guide dogs)

Yorkshire Dales Falconry & Wildlife Conservation Centre

Crows Nest LA2 8AS

➲ (on A65 follow brown signs)

☎ 01729 822832

e-mail: mail@falconryandwildlife.com

web: www.falconryandwildlife.com

The first privately owned falconry centre in the north of England. The main aim of the centre is to educate and promote awareness that many of the world's birds of prey are threatened with extinction. Successful captive breeding and educational programmes will help to safeguard these creatures. Regular free flying demonstrations throughout the day with strong encouragement for audience participation.

Times: Open all year summer 10-6; winter 10-4. Closed 25-26 Dec **Fee:** £5.50 (ch & pen £3.50) Family ticket £16. Group 15+ Adults £4.50 (ch £2.95)1 Ad free with 10 ch. **Facilities:** ☉ ♨ ⚬ (Ramp for w/chair into tea room, and giftshop access) toilets for disabled shop ⊗ (ex guide dogs) ◀

Malham National Park Centre　　　FREE

BD23 4DA

➲ (off A65 at Gargrave opposite petrol station. Malham 7m)

☎ 01969 652381

e-mail: malham@yorkshiredales.org.uk

web: www.yorkshiredales.org.uk

The national park centre has maps, guides and local information together with displays on the remarkable natural history of the area, local community and work of conservation bodies. Audio-visuals are provided for groups and a 24-hour teletext information service is available.

Times: Open Apr-Oct, daily 10-5; Winter, Sat-Sun, 10-4. Daily in school hols. **Facilities:** ☉ (charged) ▥ ⚬ (Radar key scheme for toilet) toilets for disabled shop ◀

MALTON   MAP 08 SE77

Castle Howard

YO60 7DA

⮑ *(15m NE of York, off A64, follow brown heritage signs)*

☎ 01653 648333

e-mail: house@castlehoward.co.uk

web: www.castlehoward.co.uk

Castle Howard is a magnificent 18th-century house with extensive collections and breathtaking grounds featuring temples, lakes and fountains. Attractions include historical character guides, outdoor tours, exhibitions, event programme plus lakeside adventure playground.

Times: Open Mar-Oct. House open from 11 (last admission 4).Grounds & Stable courtyard open from 10. **Fee:** ✱ £9.50 (ch £6.50, pen £8.50). Grounds only £6.50 (ch £4.50, pen £6). **Facilities:** ℗ ⬛ ⓘⓞⓘ licensed ♿ (wheelchair lift, free adapted transport to house) toilets for disabled shop garden centre (ex guide dogs) ⬛

Eden Camp Modern History Theme Museum   2 for 1

Eden Camp YO17 6RT

⮑ *(junct of A64 & A169, between York & Scarborough)*

☎ 01653 697777

e-mail: admin@edencamp.co.uk

web: www.edencamp.co.uk

The story of the people's war unfolds in this museum devoted to civilian life in World War II. The displays, covering the blackout, rationing, the Blitz, the Home Guard and others, are housed in a former prisoner-of-war camp built in 1942 for German and Italian soldiers. Hut 13, covers the conflicts that Britain has been involved with from 1945 to present day. Huts 24-29 cover the military and political events of the war, whilst Hut 11 is dedicated to telling the story of World War I. The Museum also houses an extensive collection of military vehicles and equipment. Special Events: Escapers and Evaders April, All Services Commemorative Day and Parade 2nd Sun after August BH, Palestine Veterans Reunion Day 3rd Sat in Oct.

Times: Open 2nd Mon in Jan-23 Dec, 7 days a week, daily 10-5. (Last admission 4) **Fee:** £4.50 (ch & pen £3.50) Party 10+.£3.50 - £1 discount on individual admission prices. **Facilities:** ℗ ⬛ ⓘ ♿ (taped tours, Braille guides) toilets for disabled shop

Malton Museum

Old Town Hall, Market Place YO17 7LP

⮑ *(leave A64, follow signs for Malton town centre)*

☎ 01653 695136

web: www.maltonmuseum.co.uk

The extensive Roman settlements in the area are represented and illustrated in this museum, including collections from the Roman fort of Derventio. There are also displays of local prehistoric and medieval finds plus changing exhibitions of local interest. Special Event: Jul 2005-Oct 2007 'Wharram Percy, Life in a Medieval Village' exhibition.

Times: Open Etr Sat-Oct, Mon-Sat 10-4. **Fee:** ✱ £1.50 (ch, concessions £1) Family ticket £4 (2ad+2ch) **Facilities:** ℗ (adjacent) (pay & display-2hrs) ⓘ ♿ shop ⊗ (ex guide dogs)

MASHAM   MAP 08 SE28

Theakston Brewery & Visitor Centre   2 for 1

The Brewery HG4 4YD

⮑ *(on the A6108, in town centre. Parking for Brewery visitors is in the market place. Follow Brown and White Pedestrian signposts. Approx 2 minute walk)*

☎ 01765 680000

e-mail: info@theakstons.co.uk

web: www.theakstons.co.uk

Visit the Theakston Brewery in Masham, home of the legendary 'Old Peculier' and witness the creation of real taste first-hand. Discover how traditional brewing techniques are still being applied to create today's award winning pint. As these tours are thirsty work, you'll be invited, to round off your visit in the bar with a glass of Theakston beer.

Times: Open all year daily 10.30-4 Closed Xmas hols **Fee:** ✱ £4.75 (ch £2.50, student £4.50 & pen £4). Family ticket £12.50 (2ad+2ch). **Facilities:** ℗ (400yds) ⬛ ♿ (ex brewery tours, stair lift to visitor centre) toilets for disabled shop ⊗ (ex guide dogs) ⬛

England

MIDDLEHAM MAP 07 SE18

Middleham Castle

DL8 4RJ

⮑ *(2m S of Leyburn on A6108)*

☎ 01969 623899

web: www.english-heritage.org.uk

Explore the maze of rooms and passageways at this impressive castle, once the boyhood home of the ill-fated Richard III. Oak viewing gallery of the magnificent views of the 12th-century keep and exhibition.

Times: Open all year, Apr-Sep, daily 10-6; Oct-Mar, Thu-Mon, 10-4. Closed 24-26 Dec & 1 Jan **Fee:** £3.50 (ch £1.80, concessions £2.60). Prices and opening times are subject to change in Spring 2007. Please check web site or call 0870 333 1181 for the most up to date prices and opening times when planning your visit. **Facilities:** ℗ ♿ (ex tower) shop ⊞

MIDDLESBROUGH MAP 08 NZ42

Captain Cook Birthplace Museum

Stewart Park, Marton TS7 8AT

⮑ *(3m S on A172)*

☎ 01642 311211

e-mail: captcookmuseum@middlesbrough.gov.uk

web: www.middlesbrough.gov.uk

Opened to mark the 250th anniversary of the birth of the voyager in 1728, this museum illustrates the early life of James Cook and his discoveries with permanent and temporary exhibitions. Located in spacious and rolling parkland, the site also offers outside attractions for the visitor. Recently refurbished, the museum has a special resource centre which has fresh approaches to presentation with computers, films, special effects, interactives and educational aids.

Times: ✱ Open all year: Mar-Oct, Tue-Sun, 10-5.30. Nov-Feb 9-3.30. (Last entry 45 mins before closure). Closed Mon except BH, 24-28 Dec & 31 Dec-7 Jan. **Facilities:** ℗ ☕ ⑂ ▥ ♿ (lift to all floors, car parking) toilets for disabled shop ⊗ (ex guide dogs) ◀

NEWBY HALL & GARDENS MAP 08 SE36

Newby Hall & Gardens

HG4 5AE

⮑ *(4m SE of Ripon & 2m W of A1M, off B6265, between Boroughbridge and Ripon)*

☎ 01423 322583

e-mail: info@newbyhall.com

web: www.newbyhall.com

A late 17th-century house with beautifully restored Robert Adam interiors containing an important collection of classical sculpture, Chippendale furniture and Gobelin tapestries. 25 acres of award-winning gardens include a miniature railway, an adventure garden for

continued

children and a woodland discovery walk with contemporary sculpture park (Jun-Sep).

Newby Hall & Gardens

Times: ✱ Open Apr-Sep, Tue-Sun & BHs, also Mon in Jul & Aug; Gardens 11-5.30; House 12-5. (Last admission 5 Gardens, 4.30 House)

Facilities: ℗ ☕ ⑂ licensed ♿ (wheelchairs available, maps of wheelchair routes) toilets for disabled shop garden centre ⊗ (ex guide dogs) ◀

NORTH STAINLEY MAP 08 SE27

Lightwater Valley Theme Park `2 for 1`

HG4 3HT

⮑ *(3m N of Ripon on A6108)*

☎ 0870 458 0040

e-mail: leisure@lightwatervalley.co.uk

web: www.lightwatervalley.co.uk

The family sized theme park with thrills of all sizes, from Europe's longest rollercoaster 'The Ultimate' and 'The Grizzly Bear', to family favourites such as the 'ladybird' rollercoaster and Grand Prix Go Karting along with spinning teacups, vintage cars and much more for younger children. New rides include the Eagles Claw, and the Skyride. You just pay once and enjoy the fun all day long!

Times: Open 31 Mar-15 Apr, wknds only; 21 Apr-27 May inc BH Mon; daily from 2 Jun-2 Sep, wknds only, 8 Sep-21 Oct, daily 22 Oct-28 Oct. Gates open at 10, closes 4.30, depending on time of year. **Fee:** ✱ £15.95 over 1.2mtrs, £14.50 under 1.2mtrs, free under 1m; pen £7.95. Family ticket £58 (2ad+2ch) or (1ad+3ch under 16) **Facilities:** ℗ ☕ ⑂ licensed ♿ (even pathways) toilets for disabled shop garden centre ⊗ (ex guide dogs) ◀

NUNNINGTON MAP 08 SE67

Nunnington Hall

YO62 5UY

⮑ *(4.5m SE of Helmsley)*

☎ 01439 748283

e-mail: nunningtonhall@nationaltrust.org.uk

web: www.nationaltrust.org

This large 16th to 17th-century house has panelled rooms and a magnificent staircase. The Carlisle collection of miniature rooms is on display. Changing programme of temporary exhibitions.

Times: ✱ Open mid Mar-May, Wed-Sun 1.30-5. Jun-Aug Tue-Sun 1.30-5.30. Sep, Wed-Sun 1.30-5.30. **Facilities:** ℗ ☕ ▥ ♿ (wheelchairs, Braille guide, scented garden) toilets for disabled shop ⅏

ORMESBY MAP 08 NZ51

Ormesby Hall

TS7 9AS

⊃ *(3m SE of Middlesborough, W of A19 take the A174 to the A172 . Follow signs for Ormesby Hall. Car entrance on Ladgate Lane B1380)*

☎ 01642 324188

e-mail: ormesbyhall@ntrust.org.uk

web: www.nationaltrust.org.uk

An 18th-century mansion, Ormesby Hall has stables attributed to John Carr of York. Plasterwork, furniture and 18th-century pictures are on view. Exhibiting a large model railway.

Times: Open end Mar-end Oct, Fri-Mon 1.30-5 **Fee:** ✱ House & Gardens £4 (ch £2.50) Family ticket £10.50 (2+3). Party £3.50. NT members free. **Facilities:** ❷ ⬛ 🔲 ⬤ (parking, Braille guide, special tours, sensory list) toilets for disabled ⬛

OSMOTHERLEY MAP 08 SE49

Mount Grace Priory

DL6 3JG

⊃ *(1m NW)*

☎ 01609 883494

web: www.english-heritage.org.uk

The best preserved Carthusian monastery in the country, set in breathtakingly beautiful woodland surroundings and gardens, including fully reconstructed Monks cells and herb garden, illustrating the solitary life of the monk.

Times: Open Apr-Sep, Thu-Mon, 10-6; Oct-Mar, Thu-Sun, 10-4. Closed 24-26 Dec & 1 Jan. **Fee:** ✱ £4 (ch £2, concessions £3) Family £10.00. National Trust members free except on event days. Prices and opening times are subject to change in Spring 2007. Please check website or call 0870 3331181 for the most up to date prices and opening times when planning your visit. **Facilities:** ❷ shop ⊗ ⬛ ⬛

PARCEVALL HALL GARDENS MAP 07 SEO6

Parcevall Hall Gardens

BD23 6DE

⊃ *(Off B6265 between Grassington and Pateley Bridge)*

☎ 01756 720311

e-mail: info@parcevallhallgardens.co.uk

web: www.parcevallhallgardens.co.uk

Enjoying a hillside setting east of the main Wharfedale Valley, these beautiful gardens surround a Grade II listed house which is used as the Bradford Diocesan Retreat House (not open to the public).

Times: Open Apr-Oct, daily 10-6. Winter visitors by appointment. (Last entry 5) **Fee:** £5 (ch up to 16, 75p). **Facilities:** ❷ ⬛ 🔲 shop garden centre

PATELEY BRIDGE MAP 07 SE16

Stump Cross Caverns

Greenhow HG3 5JL

⊃ *(on B6265 between Pateley Bridge & Grassington)*

☎ 01756 752780

web: www.stumpcrosscaverns.co.uk

Discovered by the brothers Mark and William Newbould in 1860, Stump Cross Caverns have been an attraction for visitors since 1863 when one shilling was charged for entrance. Among the few limestone show caves in Britain, these require no special clothing, experience or equipment, as walkways are gravel and concrete and floodlighting is provided. Stalagmites, stalactites and calcite precipitation make this an eerie day out.

Times: Open daily, Mar-end of Nov, then wknds and school hols Dec, Jan, Feb 10-5. **Fee:** ✱ £5 (ch £3.95, ch under 4 free) free gift for ch in school hols **Facilities:** ❷ ⬛ 🍴 licensed ⬤ (Ground floor and gardens accessible) shop ⊗ (ex guide dogs) ⬛

PICKERING MAP 08 SE78

North Yorkshire Moors Railway

Pickering Station YO18 7AJ

⊃ *(from A169 take road towards Kirkbymoorside, right at traffic lights, station 400yds on left)*

☎ 01751 472508

e-mail: admin@nymr.pickering.fsnet.co.uk

web: www.northyorkshiremoorsrailway.com

Operating through the heart of the North York Moors National Park between Pickering and Grosmont, steam trains cover a distance of 18 miles. The locomotive sheds at Grosmont are open to the public. Events throughout the year include Day Out with Thomas, Steam Gala, Santa Specials.

Times: Open 29 Mar-Oct, daily; Dec, Santa specials and Xmas-New Year running. Further information available from Pickering Station. **Fee:** ✱ Return: £13 (ch £6.50, pen £11). Family ticket £28 (2ad+3ch), others on request. Party 20+. **Facilities:** ❷ (charged) ⬛ 🍴 licensed 🔲 ⬤ (ramp for trains) toilets for disabled shop (at Pickering, Goathland & Grosmont) ⬛

England

Pickering Castle

YO6 5AB

☎ 01751 474989

web: www.english-heritage.org.uk

Splendid 12th-century castle, on the edge of the Yorkshire Moors, originally built by William the Conqueror. Visit the exhibition on the castle's history and take in the views from the keep.

Times: Open Apr-Sep, daily, 10-6; Oct, Thu-Mon, 10-5. **Fee:** £3 (ch £1.50, concessions £2.30). Family £7.50. Prices and opening times are subject to change in Spring 2007. Please check web site or call 0870 333 1181 for the most up to date prices and opening times when planning your visit. **Facilities:** ❷ & (ex motte) shop ♯

REDCAR   MAP 08 NZ62

RNLI Zetland Museum   FREE

5 King St TS10 3AH

➲ *(on corner of King St and The Promenade)*

☎ 01642 485370 & 471813

The museum portrays the lifeboat, maritime, fishing and local history of the area, including its main exhibit 'The Zetland' - the oldest lifeboat in the world, dating from 1802. There is also a replica of a fisherman's cottage c1900 and almost 2000 other exhibits. The museum is housed in an early lifeboat station, now a listed building.

Times: ✱ Open May Wed 11-4, Sat-Sun 12-4. Jun-Sep Tue-Fri 11-4, Sat-Sun 12-4. Closed Mon. **Facilities:** ℗ (20m) (60p per hour) 🍴 & (ground floor accessible only) shop

---

RICHMOND   MAP 07 NZ10

Green Howards Museum

Trinity Church Square, Market Place DL10 4QN

➲ *(take any turning on the A1, between Catterick & South Corner, signed to Richmond. Located in centre cobbled market square, in Holy Trinity Church)*

☎ 01748 826561

e-mail: greenhowardsmus@aol.com

web: www.greenhowards.org.uk

This award-winning museum traces the military history of the Green Howards from the late 17th century onwards. The exhibits include uniforms, weapons, medals and a special Victoria Cross exhibition. Regimental and civic plate is displayed, and there is CD ROM and touch screen video of the First World War Western Front and the Green Howards in the Second World War. Audio guide available.

Times: Open Feb, Mon-Fri 9-4.30; Mar, Mon-Fri 9-4.30; mid Apr-Oct, Mon-Sat 9-4.30 & Sun 2-4.30; Nov, Mon-Sat 9-4.30. Closed from 1 Oct 2006 to 1 Apr 2007 for refurbishment of shop & ground floor. **Fee:** £3 (unaccompanied ch £1.50, pen £2.50). Family ticket £5. Richmondshire residents and accompanied children free. **Facilities:** ℗ (in market place) (disk parking, 2hr max) 🍴 & (stairlift for access to all floors, lightweight wheelchair) shop ⊗ (ex guide dogs)

Richmond Castle

DL10 4QW

☎ 01748 822493

web: www.english-heritage.org.uk

Overlooking the River Swale and market town of Richmond, the views from the keep are stunning. Built by William the Conqueror to subdue the rebellious North, the castle now houses an exciting interactive exhibition.

Times: Open all year, Apr-Sep, daily, 10-6; Oct-Mar, Thu-Mon, 10-4. Closed 24-26 Dec & 1 Jan. **Fee:** £3.60 (ch £1.80, concessions £2.70) Family £9. Prices and opening times are subject to change in Spring 2007. Please check web site or call 0870 333 1181 for the most up to date prices and opening times when planning your visit. **Facilities:** ℗ (800 yds) & toilets for disabled shop ♯

RIEVAULX   MAP 08 SE58

Rievaulx Abbey

➲ *(2.25m W of Helmsley on minor road off B1257)*

☎ 01439 798228

web: www.english-heritage.org.uk

Explore the magnificent romantic ruin set in a tranquil wooded valley of the River Rye. Find out about monastic life with the help of our audio tour and exhibition.

Times: Open Apr-Sep, daily, 10-6; Oct, Thu-Mon, 10-5; Nov-Mar, Thu-Mon, 10-4. Closed 24-26 Dec & 1 Jan **Fee:** £4.20 (ch £2.10, concessions £3.20). Prices and opening times are subject to change in Spring 2007. Please check web site or call 0870 333 1181 for the most up to date prices and opening times when planning your visit. **Facilities:** ❷ & shop 🚌 ♯

Rievaulx Terrace & Temples

YO62 5LJ

➲ *(2m NW of Helmsley on B1257)*

☎ 01439 798340

e-mail: nunningtonhall@nationaltrust.org.uk

web: www.nationaltrust.org.uk

This curved terrace, half a mile long, overlooks the abbey, with views of Ryedale and the Hambleton Hills. It has two mock-Greek temples, one built for hunting parties, the other for quiet contemplation. There are also remarkable frescoes by Borgnis, and an exhibition on English landscape design.

Times: ✱ Open mid Mar-end Sep, daily 10.30-6. Oct daily, 10.30-5. **Facilities:** ❷ 🍴 & (w/chair/runaround vehicle/Braille guide/ramp) shop ♨

RIPLEY   MAP 08 SE26

Ripley Castle

HG3 3AY

➲ *(off A61, Harrogate to Ripon road)*

☎ 01423 770152

e-mail: enquiries@ripleycastle.co.uk

web: www.ripleycastle.co.uk

Ripley Castle has been home to the Ingilby family since 1320, and stands at the heart of an estate with deer park, lake and Victorian walled gardens. The Castle has a rich history and a fine collection of Royalist armour housed in the 1555 tower. There are also walled

continued

gardens, tropical hot houses, woodland walks, pleasure grounds and the National Hyacinth collection in spring.

Ripley Castle

Times: Open Oct-Nov & Mar-May, Tue, Thu, Sat & Sun 10.30-3, Jun-Sep daily 10.30-3, Dec-Feb wknds only, also BH and school hols. Groups all year by prior arrangement. Gardens open daily 9-5.30. **Fee:** Castle & Gardens £6.50 (ch £4, pen £5.50). Gardens only £4 (ch £2.50, pen £3.50). Party £3.50. **Facilities:** ❷ 💺 🍴 licensed ♿ (mobility buggy for hire, audio loop) toilets for disabled shop garden centre ❽ (ex guide dogs) 🛒

RIPON
MAP 08 SE37

Fountains Abbey & Studley Royal
HG4 3DY
➲ *(4m W of Ripon off B6265)*
☎ 01765 608888
e-mail: fountainsenquiries@nationaltrust.org.uk
web: www.fountainsabbey.org.uk

A world heritage site comprising of the ruin of a 12th-century Cistercian Abbey and monastic watermill, an Elizabethan mansion and one of the best surviving examples of a Georgian water garden. Elegant ornamental lakes, canals, temples and cascades provide eye-catching vistas. The site also contains a Victorian St. Mary's Church and medieval deer park.

Times: ✱ Open daily all year: Nov-Feb 10-4, Mar-Oct 10-5. Closed Fri Nov-Jan. **Facilities:** ❷ 💺 🍴 licensed 🍴 ♿ (pre-bk wheelchairs & batricars. Braille/large print guides) toilets for disabled shop 🌿 🛒

Norton Conyers
Watt HG4 5EQ
➲ *(from Ripon take A61 to Thirsk. At top of hill just outside Ripon, turn sharp left onto Wath Road)*
☎ 01765 640333
e-mail: norton.conyers@bronco.co.uk

This charming late medieval house has belonged to the Grahams since 1624, and is now the home of Sir James and Lady Graham. Of medieval origins, it was altered in Stuart times, and again in the 18th century. Its interior, pictures and furniture reflect nearly four hundred years of occupation by the same family. Famous visitors include Charles I in 1633, James II and his wife in 1679, and Charlotte Brontë in 1839. The last of these is said to have been inspired by a local

continued

legend of a mad woman in the attic to create mad Mrs Rochester in her novel *Jane Eyre*. The house is set in a fine park with an 18th-century walled garden.

Times: Open - House & Garden, Etr Sun & Mon, BH Sun & Mon; 23 Apr-30 Jul and daily 3-8 July. Sun only; 3-8 Jul daily, House 2-5, Garden 10-4. House closed all Aug for urgent repairs. Garden open Aug Sun and BH Mon. **Fee:** £5.50 (ch under 16 free, pen £4). Garden entry is free, with donations welcome, although a charge is made at garden charity openings. **Facilities:** ❷ 🍴 ♿ (ramp at entrance) toilets for disabled shop ❽ (ex guide dogs)

SALTBURN-BY-THE-SEA
MAP 08 NZ62

Saltburn Smugglers Heritage Centre `2 for 1`
Old Saltburn TS12 1HF
➲ *(adjoining Ship Inn, on A174)*
☎ 01287 625252
web: www.redcar-cleveland.gov.uk

Set in old fisherman's cottages, this centre skillfully blends costumed characters with authentic sounds and smells. Follow the story of John Andrew "King of Smugglers", who was at the heart of illicit local trade 200 years ago.

Times: Open Apr-Sep, daily 10-6: Winter open by arrangement only telephone 01642 471069. **Fee:** ✱ £1.95 (ch £1.45). Family ticket £5.80. Party. **Facilities:** ❷ (200 mtrs) (charged) 🍴 shop ❽ (ex assist dogs)

SCARBOROUGH
MAP 08 TA08

Scarborough Castle
Castle Rd YO11 1HY
➲ *(E of town centre)*
☎ 01723 372451
web: www.english-heritage.org.uk

This 12th-century fortress housed many important figures in history. Enjoy the spectacular coastal view and see the remains of the great keep still standing over three storeys high. Discover the castle's exciting history through the free audio tour.

Times: Open all year, Apr-Sep, daily 10-6; Oct, Thu-Mon, 10-5; Nov-Mar, Thu-Mon, 10-4. Closed 24-26 Dec & 1 Jan. **Fee:** £3.50 (ch £1.80, concessions £2.60). Family £8.80. Prices and opening times are subject to change in Spring 2007. Please check web site or call 0870 333 1181 for the most up to date prices and opening times when planning your visit. **Facilities:** ❷ (100yds) ♿ (ex in keep) 🚻

Sea Life & Marine Sanctuary
Scalby Mills Rd, North Bay YO12 6RP
➲ *(follow brown tourist signs after entering Scarborough. Centre in North Bay Leisure Parks area of town)*
☎ 01723 376125
web: www.sealife.co.uk

Made up of three large white pyramids, this impressive marine sanctuary overlooks the white sandy beaches of the North Bay, Scarborough's Castle, and Peasholm Park. The sanctuary features Jurassic seas, jellyfish, Otter River, penguins, and sea turtles.

Times: ✱ Open all year daily. Closed 25 Dec. **Facilities:** ❷ (charged) 💺 🍴 ♿ (lift to cafe) toilets for disabled shop ❽ (except guide dogs) 🛒

England

SKINNINGROVE   MAP 08 NZ71

Cleveland Ironstone Mining Museum   **2 for 1**

Deepdale TS13 4AP

⮑ *(in Skinningrove Valley, just off A174 near coast between Saltburn and Whitby)*

☎ 01287 642877

e-mail: visits@ironstonemuseum.co.uk

web: www.ironstonemuseum.co.uk

On the site of the old Loftus Mine, this museum offers visitors a glimpse into the underground world of Cleveland's ironstone mining past. Discover the special skills and customs of the miners who helped make Cleveland the most important ironstone mining district in Victorian and Edwardian England.

Times: Open Apr-Oct, Mon-Sat from 1 (last admission 4). Open main Summer school hols daily , also open Sun pm's. **Fee:** £4 (ch £2). Family ticket (2ad+2ch) £10. **Facilities:** ❷ 🗐 ♿ (2 wheelchairs on site. Induction loop) toilets for disabled shop ⊗ (ex guide dogs)

SKIPTON   MAP 07 SD95

Skipton Castle

BD23 1AW

⮑ *(in town centre at head of High Street)*

☎ 01756 792442

e-mail: info@skiptoncastle.co.uk

web: www.skiptoncastle.co.uk

Skipton is one of the most complete and well-preserved medieval castles in England. Some of the castle dates from the 1650s when it was rebuilt after being partially damaged following the Civil War. However, the original castle was erected in Norman times and became the home of the Clifford family in 1310 and remained so until 1676. Illustrated tour sheets are available in a number of languages. Please see website for special events.

Times: Open daily from 10, (Sun from noon). Last admission 6 (4pm Oct-Feb). Closed 25 Dec. **Fee:** ✱ £5.40 (inc illustrated tour sheet) (ch under 18 £2.90, under 5 free, concessions £4.80). Family ticket £15.90. Party 15+. **Facilities:** ℗ (200m) 🍽 🗐 shop garden centre ⊗ (ex on a lead) 🍴

SUTTON-ON-THE-FOREST   MAP 08 SE56

Sutton Park

YO61 1DP

⮑ *(off A1237 onto B1363 York to Helmsley road. 8m N of York city centre)*

☎ 01347 810249 & 811239

e-mail: suttonpark@fsbdial.co.uk

web: www.statelyhome.co.uk

The early Georgian house contains fine furniture, paintings and porcelain. The grounds have superb, award-winning terraced gardens, a lily pond and a Georgian ice house. There are also delightful woodland walks as well as spaces for caravans.

Times: ✱ Open Gardens 2 Apr-end Sep, daily 11-5. House open 2 Apr-27 Sep, Wed & Sun, also Good Fri, Etr Mon and all BH Mons. **Facilities:** ❷ 🍽 🗐 ♿ (wheelchair and lift in house, ramps in garden) toilets for disabled shop ⊗ (ex guide dogs in garden)

THIRSK   MAP 08 SE48

Falconry Centre NEW

Sion Hill Hall, Kirby Wiske YO7 4EU

⮑ *(follow brown tourist signs)*

☎ 01845 587522

e-mail: mail@falconrycentre.co.uk

web: www.falconrycentre.co.uk

Set up to ensure that birds of prey would survive to provide the public with a rare opportunity to see and enjoy these beautiful birds. Enjoy the excitement of falconry with over 70 birds and 30 species.

Times: Open Mar-Oct, daily, 10.30-5.30. **Fee:** ✱ £5 (ch £3, under 3 free). Family ticket £14 (2ad+2ch) **Facilities:** ❷ 🍽 ♿ toilets for disabled shop ⊗ 🍴

Monk Park Farm Visitor Centre NEW

Bagby YO7 2AG

⮑ *(just off A170 Scarborough road or A19 from York)*

☎ 01845 597730

web: www.monkpark.co.uk

Monk Park, once a haven for monks who made their living from the land, is now a favourite for children. There is something for all ages to see and do, with indoor and outdoor viewing and feeding areas. The park has also been the venue for filming *Blue Peter* and *Vets in Practice*.

Times: Open Feb half term-Oct, daily, 11-5.30. **Fee:** ✱ £4 incl ch & concessions **Facilities:** ❷ 🍽 ♿ (ramps) toilets for disabled shop ⊗ (ex assist dogs)

WHITBY   MAP 08 NZ81

Whitby Abbey

YO22 4JT

⮑ *(on clifftop E of Whitby town centre)*

☎ 01947 603568

web: www.english-heritage.org.uk

Uncover the full story of these atmospheric ruins in their impressive clifftop location above the picturesque fishing town with associations ranging from Victorian jewellery and whaling, to Count Dracula.

Times: Open all year, Apr-Sep, daily, 10-6; Oct, daily 10-5; Nov-Mar, Thu-Mon, 10-4. Closed 24-26 Dec & 1 Jan. **Fee:** £4.20 (ch £2.10, concessions

continued

£3.20). Family £10.50. Prices and opening times are subject to change in Spring 2007. Please check web site or call 0870 333 1181 for the most up to date prices and opening times when planning your visit.
Facilities: ℗ (charged) ☐ shop ⛶

WINTRINGHAM — MAP 08 SE87

Wolds Way Lavender 〔2 for 1〕 〔FREE〕

Deer Farm Park, Sandy Ln, Wintringham YO17 8HW

⤷ *(off A64 between Malton & Scarborough, follow brown signs)*

☎ 01944 758641
e-mail: admin@woldswaylavender.co.uk
web: www.woldswaylavender.co.uk

The medicinal and therapeutic benefits of lavender are extolled at this 12-acre site close to the Yorkshire Wolds. Four acres are currently planted with lavender, and a wood-burning still for the extraction of lavender oil. Visitors can be calmed by the Sensory Areas, enjoy a cuppa in the tearoom, and purchase all manner of lavender items at the farm shop. 2-for-1 offer applies to tea/coffee and lavender scone.

Times: Open daily, wk before 21 Mar- 30 Oct, 10-4. May-Aug 10-5
Facilities: ℗ ☐ ☐ ⅙ (sensory garden, raised flower beds) shop garden centre ⊗ (ex guide dogs) ⊜

YORK — MAP 08 SE65

Clifford's Tower

Tower St YO1 1SA
☎ 01904 646940
web: www.english-heritage.org.uk

Visit this proud symbol of the might of England's medieval kings - and enjoy magnificent views over York. The original wooden tower was built to help William the Conqueror subdue the North. It was burned down during the persecution of the Jewish community in 1190 and rebuilt in a rare design of interlocking circles by Henry III in the 13th-century.

Times: Open Apr-Sep, daily 10-6; Oct, daily 10-5; Nov-Mar, daily 10-4. Closed 24-26 Dec & 1 Jan. **Fee:** £3 (ch £1.50, concessions £2.30) Family £7.50. Prices and opening times are subject to change in Spring 2007. Please check web site or call 0870 333 1181 for the most up to date prices and opening times when planning your visit. **Facilities:** ℗ shop ⊗ ⊜ ⛶

DIG

St Saviourgate YO1 8NN

⤷ *(follow A19 or A64 to city centre then pedestrian signs for attraction)*

☎ 01904 654324
e-mail: enquiries@vikingjorvik.com
web: www.digyork.co.uk

Dig is the place to experience an unusual way of discovering York's Viking history. Visitors of all ages can get their hands dirty unearthing the secrets of the past with a trusty trowel, as well as learn about how archaeology is conducted in the field, and see what happens in a conservation lab.

Times: Open daily ex 24-25 Dec. Apr-Oct 10-6, Nov-Mar 10-5.
Fee: ✳ £5.50. (ch, concessions £5) Family of 4 £16. Group rates available on request. **Facilities:** ℗ (50yds) (NCP) ☐ ⅙ (induction loop, sensory garden, hearing posts) toilets for disabled shop ⊗ (ex guide dogs) ⊜

Fairfax House

Castlegate YO1 9RN

⤷ *(city centre, close to Jorvik Centre and Cliffords Tower)*

☎ 01904 655543
e-mail: peterbrown@fairfaxhouse.co.uk
web: www.fairfaxhouse.co.uk

An outstanding mid 18th-century house with a richly decorated interior, Fairfax House was acquired by the York Civic Trust in 1983 and restored. The house contains fine examples of Georgian furniture, porcelain, paintings and clocks which were donated by Mr Noel Terry, the great grandson of the founder of the York-based confectionery business. There is a special display of a recreated meal dating from 1763 in the dining room and kitchen.

Times: ✳ Open 7 Feb-5 Jan, Mon-Sat 11-5, (Fri guided tours only at 11& 2). Sun 1.30-5. (Last admission 4.30) **Facilities:** ℗ (50yds) (3hr short stay) ☐ ⅙ (with assistance, phone before visit) shop ⊗ (ex guide dogs) ⊜

Guildhall 〔FREE〕

Coney St YO1 9QN

⤷ *(5-10mins walk from rail station)*

☎ 01904 613161
web: www.york.gov.uk

The present Hall dates from 1446 but in 1942 an air raid virtually destroyed the building. The present Guildhall was carefully restored as an exact replica and was re-opened in 1960. There is an interesting arch-braced roof decorated with colourful bosses and supported by 12 solid oak pillars. There are also some beautiful stained-glass windows.

Times: Open all year, May-Oct, Mon-Fri 9-5, Sat 10-5, Sun 2-5; Nov-Apr, Mon-Fri 9-5. **Facilities:** ℗ (15-20 mins walk) ⅙ (electric chair lift & ramps) toilets for disabled ⊗ (ex guide dogs) ⛟

England

Jorvik

Coppergate YO1 9WT

➲ *(follow A19 or A64 to York. Jorvik in Coppergate shopping area (city centre) signed)*

☎ 01904 543402

e-mail: enquiries@vikingjorvik.com

web: www.vikingjorvik.com

Explore York's Viking history on the very site where archaeologists discovered remains of the city of Jorvik. Encounter Viking residents, learn what life was like here 1000 years ago, and journey through a reconstruction of actual Viking streets. The 'Fearsome Craftsmen' exhibit reveals the skills and artistry of the Vikings, while 'Unearthed' tells how the people of ancient York lived and died, as revealed by real bone material. Special events throughout the year.

Times: Open all year, Apr-Oct daily 10-5; and Viking festival Nov-Mar daily 10-4. Closed 25 Dec. Opening times subject to change, please telephone for up to date details. **Fee:** £7.75 (ch 5-15 £5.50, under 5 free, concessions £6.60) Family of 4 £21.95 & family of 5 £26.50. Telephone bookings on 01904 543403 (£1 booking fee per person at peak times). **Facilities:** Ⓟ (400 yds) (limited to 3 hours) 🍽 🗻 ⓺ (lift & time car designed to take wheelchair, hearing loop) toilets for disabled shop ⊗ (ex guide dogs) 🢀

Merchant Adventurers' Hall

Fossgate YO1 9XD

➲ *(located in town centre, between Piccadilly and Fossgate)*

☎ 01904 654818

e-mail: enquiries@theyorkcompany.co.uk

web: www.theyorkcompany.co.uk

The medieval guild hall of the powerful Merchant Adventurers' Company was built 1357-1361 and is one of the finest in Europe. The Hall consists of a Great Hall where the merchant adventurers dined; an Undercroft which served as a hospital for the poor; and a Chapel. Today it operates as a museum. The Hall contains early furniture, one piece dating from the 13th century, paintings, silver, and weights and measures.

Times: Open Etr-Sep, Mon-Thu, 9-5, Fri & Sat, 9-3.30. Sun 12-4. Oct-Etr, Mon-Sat, 9-3.30, Sun & Xmas period closed. **Fee:** ✱ £2.50 (ch under 7 free, ch 7-17yrs £1, concessions £2). **Facilities:** Ⓟ (500yds) 🗻 ⓺ (access from Fossgate, lift) toilets for disabled ⊗ (ex guide dogs)

National Railway Museum

Leeman Rd YO26 4XJ

➲ *(behind rail station. Signed from all major roads and city centre.*

☎ 01904 621261

e-mail: nrm@nmsi.ac.uk

web: http://www.nrm.org.uk

The National Railway Museum is the world's largest railway museum. Housing: *The Flying Scotsman*, three enormous galleries, interactive exhibits and daily events, the National Railway Museum mixes education with fun. This attraction is also free. Until Jan 2009, visitors to the NRM can take a ride on the London Eye-style Norwich Union Yorkshire Wheel. NB: There is a charge for the wheel.

Times: Open all year, daily 10-6. Closed 24-26 Dec. **Facilities:** Ⓟ (charged) 🍽 🗻 licensed ⓺ ("Please Touch" evenings usually in June) toilets for disabled shop garden centre ⊗ (ex guide/hearing dogs) 🢀

St Williams College

5 College St YO1 7JF

➲ *(adjacent to York Minster at east end)*

☎ 01904 557233

e-mail: conference@yorkminster.org

web: www.yorkminster.org

St Williams College, a 15th-century timber-framed building, housed chantry priests until 1549. It now contains York Minster's Conference and Banquet Centre, shop, restaurant and the medieval rooms are open to view when not being used for functions; an ideal venue for wedding receptions and medieval banquets. Craft Fairs most weekends.

Times: ✱ Open all year 10-5 for viewing of medieval rooms subject to private bookings - phone for details. Closed 24-26 Dec & Good Fri. **Facilities:** Ⓟ 5min walk 🍽 🗻 licensed 🗻 shop ⊗ assist dogs

Treasurer's House

Minster Yard YO1 7JL

➲ *(in Minster Yard, on N side of Minster, in the centre of York)*

☎ 01904 624247

e-mail: treasurershouse@nationaltrust.org.uk

web: www.nationaltrust.org.uk

Named after the Treasurer of York Minster and built over a Roman Road, the house is not all it seems. Nestled behind the Minster, the size, splendour and contents of the house are a constant surprise to visitors - as are the famous ghost stories. Children's trails and access to the tea room free.

Times: ✱ Open mid Mar-end Oct, daily except Fri, 11-5. **Facilities:** Ⓟ (800 mtrs) 🍽 🗻 ⓺ (Braille guide/tactile pictures/induction loop/scented path) ⊗ (ex guide dogs) 🦌

The York Brewery Co Ltd

12 Toft Green YO1 6JT

➲ *(5 min walk from York train station. Turn right out of station, right at lights. Walk under Mickelgate Bar, then left into Toft Green. Brewery is 300yds on right)*

☎ 01904 621162

e-mail: tony@yorkbrew.co.uk

web: www.yorkbrew.co.uk

One of the North's finest independent breweries now offers a tour of its premises inside the city walls. Visitors can observe all the processes

continued

that go into producing beers like *Centurion's Ghost*, *Yorkshire Terrier*, *Guzzler*, and *Stonewall*. Those made intolerably thirsty by the sight of all this brewing expertise will be glad to know that the adult ticket price includes one pint of beer.

Times: Open daily tours at 12.30, 2, 3.30 and 5 Mon-Sat (Sun, May-Sep) **Fee:** £5 (£4.50 pen & ch 14-17yrs £3). **Facilities:** ℗ (50yds) (£1.40 p/hr) shop ⊗ (ex guide dogs) ◼

York Castle Museum

The Eye of York YO1 1RY
➲ *(city centre, next to Clifford's Tower)*
☎ 01904 653611
web: http://www.york.gov.uk

Fascinating exhibits that bring memories to life, imaginatively displayed through reconstructions of period rooms and two indoor streets, complete with cobbles, a Hansom cab and a park. The museum is housed in the city's former prison and is based on an extensive collection of 'bygones' acquired at the beginning of the twentieth century. It is one of the first folk museums to display a huge range of everyday objects in an authentic scene. The Victorian street includes a pawnbroker, a tallow candle factory and a haberdasher's. There is even a reconstruction of the original sweet shop of the York chocolate manufacturer, Joseph Terry. An extensive collection of many other items ranging from musical instruments to costumes and a gallery of domestic gadgets from Victorian times to the 1960s (entitled 'Every home should have one') are further attractions to this remarkable museum. The museum also has one of Britain's finest collections of Militaria; this includes a superb example of an Anglo-Saxon helmet - one of only three known. A special exhibition called 'Seeing it Through' explores the life of York citizens during the Second World War. The museum includes the cell where highwayman Dick Turpin was held. Please contact the museum for deatils of exhibition and events.

Times: ✱ Open all year, Apr-Oct Mon-Sat 9.30-5.30, Sun 10-5.30; Nov-Mar, Mon-Sat 9.30-4, Sun 10-4. Closed 25-26 Dec & 1 Jan. **Facilities:** ⬛ & toilets for disabled shop ⊗ ◼

York City Art Gallery `FREE`

Exhibition Square YO1 7EW
➲ *(3min walk from the minster in the centre of York).*
☎ 01904 687687
e-mail: www.york.trust.museum
web: www.york.trust.museum

The gallery is remarkable for the range and quality of its collections that provide a survey of most developments in Western European painting over the past six centuries. Works by Parmigianino, Bellotto, Lely, Reynolds, Frith, Boudin, Lowry and Nash and nudes by Etty are on permanent display. There are also fine collections of watercolours and pottery.

Times: Open all year, daily 10-5. (Closed 25 & 26 Dec & 1 Jan). **Facilities:** ℗ (500mtrs) ⬛ (chair lift) shop ⊗ (ex guide dogs) ◼

The York Dungeon

12 Clifford St YO1 9RD
➲ *(A64/A19/A59 to city centre)*
☎ 01904 632599
e-mail: yorkdungeons@merlinentertainments.biz
web: www.thedungeons.com

Deep in the heart of historic York lies the York Dungeon bringing more than 2,000 years of gruesomely authentic history vividly back to life. Be warned, in the dungeon's dark catacombs it always pays to keep your wits about you. The 'exhibits' have an unnerving habit of coming
continued

back to life. The journey includes Dick Turpin, Guy Fawkes, Witch Trials, Clifford's Tower, Pit of Despair, Guy Fawkes and Gorvik - the real Viking experience. The most recent addition is the Labyrinth of the Lost, which explores the Roman presence in York.

Times: Open Apr-Sep 10.30-5 (last admission); Nov-Jan 11-4; Oct, Feb & Mar 10.30-4.30; Etr & Summer hols 10-5.30 **Fee:** ✱ £10.95 (ch £7.95, concessions £8.95) Family ticket (2ad+2ch) £33.95 **Facilities:** ℗ (500yds) 🏛 & (wheelchair ramps, stairlifts, award winning access) toilets for disabled shop ⊗ (ex guide dogs) ◼

York Minster

Deangate YO1 7HH
➲ *(easy access via A19, A1 or A64)*
☎ 01904 557216
e-mail: visitors@yorkminster.org
web: www.yorkminster.org

Enjoy the peaceful atmosphere of the largest Gothic cathedral in Northern Europe, a place of worship for over 1,000 years, and a treasure house of stained glass. Take an audio tour of the Undercroft to find out more about the Minster's fascinating history and climb the Tower for amazing views.

Times: Open from 7 for services. Visitors Mon-Sat 9-5 (9.30 in winter), Sun noon-3.45. Phone for 2007 details. **Fee:** ✱ £5 (ch16 free, concessions £4). Small charge also for the Undercroft and Tower. **Facilities:** ℗ (440yds) & (tactile model, Braille & large print guide) toilets for disabled shop ⊗ (ex assist dogs) ◼

Yorkshire Museum

Museum Gardens YO1 7FR
➲ *(park & ride service from 4 sites near A64/A19/A1079 & A166, also 3 car parks within short walk)*
☎ 01904 551800
e-mail: yorkshire.museum@york.gov.uk
web: http://www.york.gov.uk

The Yorkshire Museum is set in 10 acres of botanical gardens in the heart of the historic City of York, and displays some of the finest Roman, Anglo-Saxon, Viking and Medieval treasures ever discovered in Britain. The Middleham jewel, a fine example of English Gothic jewellery, is on display, and in the Roman Gallery, visitors can see a marble head of Constantine the Great. The Anglo-Saxon Gallery houses the delicate silver-gilt Ormside bowl and the Gilling sword.

Times: ✱ Open all year, daily 10-5. **Facilities:** ℗ (5 mins walk) 🏛 & (ramps & lift) toilets for disabled shop ⊗ ◼

South Yorkshire

Conisbrough Castle,
Conisbrough

South Yorkshire is historically an industrial area of steel and coal production and the decline of
these industries has resulted in some impressive industrial visitor attractions. Beautiful
countryside includes part of the Trans-Pennine Trail and the fine medieval architecture of
Conisbrough Castle. The county also claims part of the Peak District National Park, whose hills
and dales provide excellent walking. The city of Sheffield has a good range of art galleries and
museums which can be easily reached using the Sheffield 'state-of-the-art' electric Supertram.

BARNSLEY   MAP 08 SE30

Monk Bretton Priory

S71 5QD

⮑ *(1m E of town centre, off A633)*

web: www.english-heritage.org.uk

The priory was an important Cluniac house, founded in 1153. The considerable remains of the gatehouse, church and other buildings can be seen.

Times: Open all year, Apr-Sep, daily 10-6; Oct, daily 10-5; Nov-Mar, daily 10-4 (managed by a key keeper). Closed 24-26 Dec & 1 Jan.
Fee: Admission free. Charge may apply on event days **Facilities:** ❷ ♿

CONISBROUGH   MAP 08 SK59

Conisbrough Castle   FREE

DN12 3HH

⮑ *(NE of town centre off A630)*

☎ 01709 863329

web: www.english-heritage.org.uk

The white, circular keep of this 12th-century castle is a spectacular structure. Made of magnesian limestone, it is the oldest of its kind in England. Recently restored, with two new floors and a roof, it is a fine example of medieval architecture and was an inspiration for Sir Walter Scott's classic novel *Ivanhoe*.

Times: Open all year, Apr-Sep, daily 10-5 (last admission 4.20); Oct-Mar, daily 10-4 (last admission 3.20). Closed over Xmas period. Please call for details **Facilities:** ❷ 💺♿ (wheelchair access limited) shop ⊗

DONCASTER   MAP 08 SE50

Brodsworth Hall & Gardens

Brodsworth DN5 7XJ

⮑ *(between A635 & A638)*

☎ 01302 722598

web: www.english-heritage.org.uk

This Victorian country house has survived largely intact. Imagine how the serving classes fared below stairs, then experience, in contrast, the opulent 'upstairs' apartments. Outside, visitors can enjoy a leisurely stroll around the extensive newly restored gardens.

Times: House: open Apr-29 Sep, Tue-Sun & BHs, 1-5; 30 Sep-29 Oct, Sat-Sun, 12-4. Gardens: open Apr-29 Oct, daily 10-5.30. Garden, Tearoom, Shop & Servants Wing: open 30 Oct-Mar, Sat-Sun 10-4. Closed 23-24 & 30-31 Dec. Last admission half hour before closing **Fee:** House & Gardens; £6.60 (ch £3.30, concessions £5). Gardens only; £4.60 (ch £2.30, concessions £3.50). Prices and opening times are subject to change in Spring 2007. Please check web site or call 0870 333 1181 for the most up to date prices and opening times when planning your visit. **Facilities:** ❷ 💺 ♿ toilets for disabled shop ⊗ ♿ 🍴

Doncaster Museum & Art Gallery   FREE

Chequer Rd DN1 2AE

⮑ *(off inner ring road)*

☎ 01302 734293

e-mail: museum@doncaster.gov.uk

web: www.doncaster.gov.uk/museums

The wide-ranging collections include fine and decorative art and sculpture. Also ceramics, glass, silver, and displays on history, archaeology and natural history. The historical collection of the Kings Own Yorkshire Light Infantry is housed here. A recent addition is the By River and Road gallery, which details the history of the Doncaster area. Temporary exhibitions are held.

Times: Open all year, Mon-Sat 10-5, Sun 2-5. Closed Good Fri, 25-26 Dec & 1 Jan. **Facilities:** ❷ 💺 ♿ (lift, hearing loop in lecture room) toilets for disabled shop ⊗ (ex guide dogs)

MALTBY   MAP 08 SK59

Roche Abbey

S66 8NW

⮑ *(1.5m S off A634)*

☎ 01709 812739

web: www.english-heritage.org.uk

Visit the enchanting valley designed by 'Capability' Brown and discover the fascinating ruins of Roche Abbey, founded in 1147 by the Cistercians.

Times: Open Apr-Jul & Sep, Thu-Mon, 10-5; Aug, daily, 10-5. **Fee:** £3 (ch £1.50, concessions £2.30). Prices and opening times are subject to change in Spring 2007. Please check web site or call 0870 333 1181 for the most up to date prices and opening times when planning your visit. **Facilities:** ❷ ♿ shop ♿

ROTHERHAM   MAP 08 SK49

Magna Science Adventure Centre   2 for 1

Sheffield Rd, Templeborough S60 1DX

⮑ *(M1 junct 33/34, follow Templeborough sign off rdbt, then brown heritage signs)*

☎ 01709 720002

e-mail: ebodley@magnatrust.co.uk

web: www.visitmagna.co.uk

Magna is the UK's first Science Adventure Centre, an exciting exploration of Earth, Air, Fire and Water. A chance for visitors to create their own adventure through hands-on interactive challenges. Visit the four Adventure Pavilions, two shows and Sci-Tec outdoor adventure playground and have fun unearthing the mysteries of our world.

Times: ✱ Open all year, daily (ex some Mons), 10-5 **Fee:** ✱ £9.95 (ch & concessions £7.95). Family ticket (2ad + 1ch) £25 **Facilities:** ❷ 💺 🍴 licensed ♿ (lifts, portable seating, wheelchair hire) toilets for disabled shop ⊗ (ex guide dogs) 🍴

England

SHEFFIELD

MAP 08 SK38

Kelham Island Museum

2 for 1

Alma St S3 8RY

➲ (0.5m NW of city centre, take A61 N to West Bar, follow signs)

☎ 0114 272 2106

e-mail: postmaster@simt.co.uk

web: www.simt.co.uk

The story of Sheffield, its industry and life, with the most powerful working steam engine in Europe, reconstructed workshops, and craftspeople demonstrating traditional 'made in Sheffield' skills - this is a 'living' museum. During the year Kelham Island stages events, displays and temporary exhibitions culminating in the annual Christmas Victorian Market.

Times: Open Mon-Thu 10-4, Sun 11-4.45. Closed Fri and Sat. Check opening days/times at Xmas & New Year before travelling. **Fee:** £4 (concessions £3). Family ticket £8. **Facilities:** ℗ 🍴 ♿ (wheelchair on request) toilets for disabled shop ⊗

Millennium Galleries

FREE

Arundel Gate S1 2PP

☎ 0114 278 2600

e-mail: info@sheffieldgalleries.org.uk

web: www.sheffieldgalleries.org.uk

With four different galleries under one roof, the Millennium Galleries has something for everyone. Enjoy new blockbuster exhibitions drawn from the collections of Britain's national galleries and museums, including the Victoria & Albert Museum and Tate Gallery. See the best of contemporary craft and design in a range of exhibitions by established and up-and-coming makers. Be dazzled by Sheffield's magnificent and internationally important collection of decorative and domestic metalwork and silverware. Discover the Ruskin Gallery with its wonderful array of treasures by Victorian artist and writer John Ruskin.

Times: ✱ Open daily Mon-Sat 10-5, Sun 11-5. **Facilities:** ℗ 🍴 🍴 licensed ♿ (hearing loop) toilets for disabled shop ⊗ (ex guide dogs) 🍴

Roche Abbey, founded in the 12th century, with grounds landscaped by Capability Brown in the 18th century

West Yorkshire

Harewood House

Traditional, bustling market towns like Ilkley and Wetherby contrast well with lively modern cities. Leeds is well known for some of the best shopping outside London, while the county offers plenty of outdoor activities, from caving, climbing and sailing to wonderful walks in spectacular scenery and visiting stately homes such as Harewood House. The wild and dramatic moors inspired the Brontë sisters to write some of the most enduring works of English literature, and the cobbled main street of Haworth, and its Parsonage, where they lived, attract visitors from all over the world.

England

BRADFORD
MAP 07 SE13

Bolling Hall
FREE

Bowling Hall Rd BD4 7LP

➲ *(1m from city centre off A650)*

☎ 01274 431826

web: www.bradfordmuseums.org

A classic West Yorkshire manor house, complete with galleried 'housebody' (hall), Bolling Hall dates mainly from the 17th century but has medieval and 18th-century sections. It has panelled rooms, plasterwork in original colours, heraldic glass and a rare Chippendale bed.

Times: Open all year, Wed-Fri 11-4, Sat 10-5, Sun 12-5. Closed Mon ex BH, Good Fri, 25-26 Dec. **Facilities:** ℗ ▣ & shop ⊗ (ex guide dogs)

Bradford Industrial Museum and Horses at Work
FREE

Moorside Mills, Moorside Rd, Eccleshill BD2 3HP

➲ *(off A658)*

☎ 01274 435900

web: www.bradfordmuseums.org

Moorside Mills is an original spinning mill, now part of a museum that brings vividly to life the story of Bradford's woollen industry. There is the machinery that once converted raw wool into cloth, and the mill yard rings with the sound of iron on stone as shire horses pull trams, haul buses and give rides. Daily demonstrations and changing exhibitions.

Times: Open all year, Tue-Sat 10-5, Sun 12-5. Closed Mon ex BH, Good Fri, 25-26 Dec **Facilities:** ℗ ▣ ▣ & (induction loop in lecture theatre, lift) toilets for disabled shop ⊗ (ex guide dogs)

Cartwright Hall Art Gallery
FREE

Lister Park BD9 4NS

➲ *(1m from city centre on A650)*

☎ 01274 431212

e-mail: cartwright.hall@bradford.gov.uk

web: www.bradfordmuseums.org

Built in dramatic Baroque style in 1904, the gallery has permanent collections of 19th and 20th-century British art, contemporary prints, and older works by British and European masters.

Times: Open all year, Tue-Sat 10-5, Sun 1-5. Closed Mon ex BH, Good Fri, 25-26 Dec. **Facilities:** ℗ & (wheelchair available, lift) toilets for disabled shop ⊗ (ex guide dogs)

Colour Museum
2 for 1

Perkin House, 1 Providence St BD1 2PW

➲ *(from city centre follow signs B6144 (Haworth), then brown heritage signs)*

☎ 01274 390955

e-mail: museum@sdc.org.uk

web: www.colour-experience.org

Europe's only Museum of Colour comprises two galleries packed with visitor-operated exhibits demonstrating the effects of light and colour, including optical illusions, and the story of dyeing and textile printing. There is a programme of special exhibitions and events. Please telephone for details.

Times: Open 2 Jan-18 Dec, Tue-Sat, 10-4. **Fee:** ✱ £2 (concessions £1.50). Family ticket £4 **Facilities:** ℗ (200 yds) ▣ & (lifts, ramps at door) toilets for disabled shop ⊗ (ex guide dogs) ◀

National Museum of Photography, Film & Television

BD1 1NQ

➲ *(2m from end of M606, follow signs for city centre)*

☎ 0870 7010200

e-mail: talk.nmpft@nmsi.ac.uk

web: www.nmpft.org.uk

Experience the past, present and future of photography, film and television with amazing interactive displays and spectacular 3D IMAX cinema.

Times: ✱ Open all year, Tue-Sun, BHs & main school hols 10-6. Closed Mon. **Facilities:** ℗ (adjacent) ▣ ▣◀ licensed ▣ & (tailored tours, Braille signs, induction loop, cinema seating) toilets for disabled shop ⊗ (ex guide dogs) ◀

BRAMHAM
MAP 08 SE44

Bramham Park

LS23 6ND

➲ *(on A1, 4m S of Wetherby, take Bramham/Thorner slip road and follow signs)*

☎ 01937 846000

e-mail: enquiries@bramhampark.co.uk

web: www.bramhampark.co.uk

This fine Queen Anne house was built by Robert Benson and is the home of his descendants. The garden has ornamental ponds, cascades, temples and avenues.

Times: ✱ Open Apr-Sep, daily 11.30-4.30. Closed 7-14 Jun & 16 Aug-4 Sep **Facilities:** ℗ & toilets for disabled

GOMERSAL
MAP 08 SE22

Red House
FREE

Oxford Rd BD19 4JP

➲ *(M62 junct 26, take A58 towards Leeds then right onto A651 towards Gomersal. Red House is on right hand side)*

☎ 01274 335100

web: www.kirkleesmc.gov.uk/community/museums.museum.shtml

Delightful redbrick house displayed as the 1830s home of a Yorkshire wool clothier and merchant. The house and family was frequently visited by Charlotte Brontë in the 1830s and featured in her novel *Shirley*. The gardens have been reconstructed in the style of the period and there are exhibitions on the Brontë connection and local history in restored barn and cartsheds.

Times: ✱ Open all year, Mon-Fri 11-5, Sat-Sun 12-5. Telephone for Xmas opening. Closed Good Fri & 1 Jan. **Facilities:** ℗ ▣ & (Braille & T-setting hearing aid available) toilets for disabled shop ⊗ (ex guide dogs) ◀

HALIFAX   MAP 07 SE02

Bankfield Museum   FREE
Boothtown Rd, Akroyd Park HX3 6HG
➲ *(on A647 Bradford via Queensbury road, 0.5m from Halifax town centre)*
☎ 01422 354823 & 352334
e-mail: bankfield-museum@calderdale.gov.uk
web: www.calderdale.gov.uk

Built by Edward Akroyd in the 1860s, this Renaissance-style building is set in parkland on a hill overlooking the town. It has an outstanding collection of costumes and textiles from many periods and parts of the world, including a new gallery featuring East European textiles. There is also a section on toys, and the museum of the Duke of Wellington's Regiment is housed here. Temporary exhibitions are held and there is a lively programme of events, workshops and activities. Please ring for details.

Times: Open all year, Tue-Sat 10-5, Sun 1-4, BH Mon 10-5.
Facilities: ❷ 🍴 ♿ (audio guide & tactile objects) toilets for disabled shop ✸ (ex guide dogs) 🍽

Eureka! The Museum for Children   2 for 1
Discovery Rd HX1 2NE
➲ *(M62 junct 24 follow brown heritage signs to Halifax centre - A629)*
☎ 01422 330069
e-mail: info@eureka.org.uk
web: www.eureka.org.uk

With over 400 'must touch' exhibits, interactive activities and challenges, visitors are invited to embark upon a journey of discovery through four main gallery spaces: Me and My Body, Living and Working Together, Our Global Garden and SoundSpace, an interactive music gallery inviting children to explore the science behind sound, rhythm and technology. They can find out how their bodies and senses work, discover the realities of daily life, travel from the familiar 'backyard' to amazing and faraway places and experiment in many other ways. Now with two new galleries designed especially for children under five: Sound Garden and Desert Discovery, which provide babies and small children with an introduction to the natural world. A brand new outdoor Maze of Illusions is open in the summer.

Times: Open all year, daily 10-5. Closed 24-26 Dec **Fee:** £6.50 (ch under 3 £1.95, ch under 1 free) Family Saver ticket admits 5 £29.50. Special group rates available. **Facilities:** ❷ (charged) 🍽♿ (lift, staff trained in basic sign language, large print) toilets for disabled shop ✸ (ex guide dogs) 🍽

Halifax Visitor Centre and Art Gallery   FREE
HX1 1RE
➲ *(follow brown tourist signs, close to railway station)*
☎ 01422 368725
e-mail: halifax@ytbtic.co.uk
web: www.calderdale.gov.uk

The merchants of Halifax built the elegant and unique hall in 1770, and it has over 300 merchant's rooms around a courtyard, now housing an art gallery and visitor centre. There are around eight temporary exhibitions each year.

Times: Open all year daily. Closed 25-26 Dec. Art Gallery, Tue-Sun & BH Mon 10-5. **Facilities:** ℗ (50 yds) 🍽 🍴 ♿ (lifts, shopmobility on site & audio guide available) toilets for disabled shop ✸ (ex guide dogs) 🍽

Shibden Hall   2 for 1
Lister's Rd HX3 6XG
➲ *(2km E of Halifax on A58)*
☎ 01422 352246 & 321455
e-mail: shibden.hall@calderdale.gov.uk
web: www.calderdale.gov.uk

The house dates back to the early 15th century, and its rooms have been laid out to illustrate life in different periods of its history. Craft weekends, featuring over 30 craftworkers demonstrating historic skills, are held, and there's a lively programme of craft events, workshops and family activities. Please apply for details.

Times: Open Mar-Nov, Mon-Sat 10-5, Sun 12-5. Dec-Feb, Mon-Sat 10-4, Sun 12-4. **Fee:** ✱ £3.50 (ch & concessions £2.50) Family ticket £10. **Facilities:** ❷ 🍽 🍴 ♿ (garden only partially accessible) toilets for disabled shop ✸ (ex guide dogs) 🍽

HAREWOOD   MAP 08 SE34

Harewood House & Bird Garden
LS17 9LG
➲ *(junct A61/A659 Leeds to Harrogate road)*
☎ 0113 218 1010
e-mail: business@harewood.org
web: www.harewood.org

Designed in 1759 by John Carr, Harewood House is home to the Queen's cousin, the Earl of Harewood. His mother, HRH Princess Mary, Princess Royal lived at Harewood for 35 years and much of her memorabilia is still displayed. The House, renowned for its stunning architecture and exquisite Adam interiors, contains a rich collection of Chippendale furniture, fine porcelain and outstanding art collections from Italian Renaissance masterpieces and Turner watercolours to contemporary works. The old kitchen contains the best collection of noble household copperware in the country giving visitors a glimpse into below stairs life. The grounds include a restored parterre terrace, oriental rock garden, walled garden, lakeside and woodland walks, a bird garden and for youngsters, an adventure playground.

Times: Open 4 Feb-30 Oct, (grounds until 17 Dec), Grounds (inc Bird Gardens) daily from 10, House from 11. **Fee:** Mon-Fri £12.50. Sat-Sun, £14.50. ch and student, Mon-Fri, £7.20, Sat-Sun, £9, pen Mon-Fri, £11, Sat-Sun, £13.50) Family, Mon-Fri, £41.50, Sat-Sun, £49. **Facilities:** ❷ 🍽 🍴 licensed 🍴 ♿ (electric ramp, lift) toilets for disabled shop ✸ (ex guide dogs or in gardens) 🍽

England

HAWORTH MAP 07 SE03

Brontë Parsonage Museum

BD22 8DR

⮕ *(A629 & A6033 follow signs for Haworth, take Rawdon Rd, pass 2 car parks, next left, then right)*

☎ 01535 642323

e-mail: bronte@bronte.org.uk

web: www.bronte.info

Haworth Parsonage was the lifelong family home of the Brontës. An intensely close-knit family, the Brontës saw the parsonage as the heart of their world and the moorland setting provided them with inspiration for their writing. The house contains much personal memorabilia, including the furniture Charlotte bought with the proceeds of her literary success, Branwell's portraits of local worthies, Emily's writing desk and Anne's books and drawings.

Times: Open Apr-Sep, daily 10-5.30; Oct-Mar daily 11-5 (final admission 30 min before closing). Closed 24-27 Dec & 2-31 Jan. **Fee:** ✸ £5.50 (ch 5-16 £2.20 concessions £4.20). Family ticket £13.20. **Facilities:** ⓟ (charged) 🏪 ⴳ (Info in large type & Braille, loop induction system) shop ⊗ (ex guide dogs) 🚢

Keighley & Worth Valley Railway & Museum

Keighley BD22 8NJ

⮕ *(1m from Keighley on A629 Halifax road, follow brown signs)*

☎ 01535 645214 & 677777

e-mail: admin@kwvr.co.uk

web: www.kwvr.co.uk

The line was built mainly to serve the valley's mills, and passes through the heart of Brontë country. Beginning at Keighley (shared with Network Rail), it climbs up to Haworth, and terminates at Oxenhope, which has a storage and restoration building. At Haworth there are locomotive workshops and at Ingrow West, an award-winning museum.

Times: ✸ Open every wknd, please phone for other times. **Facilities:** ⓟ (charged) 🍽 ⴳ (level access to all sites, ramps on trains and stations) toilets for disabled shop 🚢

HUDDERSFIELD MAP 07 SE11

Tolson Memorial Museum `FREE`

Ravensknowle Park, Wakefield Rd HD5 8DJ

⮕ *(on A629, 1m from town centre)*

☎ 01484 223830

e-mail: tolson.museum@kirkdees.gov.uk

web: tolson.museum.co.uk

Displays on the development of the cloth industry and a collection of horse-drawn vehicles, together with natural history, archaeology, toys and folk exhibits. There is a full programme of events and temporary exhibitions.

Times: ✸ Open all year. Mon-Fri 11-5, Sat & Sun noon-5. Closed Xmas. **Facilities:** ⓟ ⴳ (mini-com, partial stairlift, induction loop, parking) toilets for disabled shop ⊗ (ex registered assist dogs) 🚢

ILKLEY MAP 07 SE14

Manor House Gallery & Museum `FREE`

Castle Yard, Church St LS29 9DT

⮕ *(behind Ilkley Parish Church, on A65)*

☎ 01943 600066

web: www.bradfordmuseums.org

This Elizabethan manor house, one of Ilkley's few buildings to pre-date the 19th century, was built on the site of a Roman fort. Part of the Roman wall can be seen, together with Roman objects and displays on archaeology. There is a collection of 17th and 18th-century farmhouse parlour and kitchen furniture, and the art gallery exhibits works by contemporary artists and craftspeople.

Times: Open all year, Tue-Sat 1-5, Sun 1-4. Open BH Mon. Closed Good Fri, 25-28 Dec. **Facilities:** ⓟ (5mins) ⴳ shop ⊗ (ex guide dogs)

KEIGHLEY MAP 07 SE04

Cliffe Castle Museum & Gallery

Spring Gardens Ln BD20 6LH

⮕ *(NW of town off A629)*

☎ 01535 618230

web: www.bradfordmuseums.org

Built as a millionaires mansion, the house displays Victorian interiors, together with collections of local and natural history, ceramics, dolls, geological items and minerals. The grounds have a play area and an aviary. Temporary Exhibitions throughout the year.

Times: Open all year, Tue-Sat 10-5, Sun 12-5. Open BH Mon. Closed Good Fri & 25-28 Dec. **Facilities:** ⓟ 🍽 🏪 ⴳ toilets for disabled shop garden centre ⊗ (ex guide dogs)

East Riddlesden Hall

Bradford Rd BD20 5EL

⮕ *(1m NE of Keighley on S side of Bradford Rd)*

☎ 01535 607075

e-mail: eastriddlesden@nationaltrust.org.uk

web: www.nationaltrust.org.uk

The interior of this 17th-century manor house is furnished with textiles, Yorkshire oak and pewter, together with fine examples of 17th-century embroidery. The honeysuckle and rose covered façade ruin of the Starke Wing, provides the backdrop to the garden. Wild flowers, perennials, and a fragrant herb border provide a transition of colour throughout the year.

Times: ✸ Open mid Mar-late Oct daily (ex Mon, Thu & Fri). Open Good Fri, BH Mons and Mons in Jul & Aug 12-5, Sat 1-5 **Facilities:** ⓟ 🍽 🏪 ⴳ (Braille and large print guides, sensory photo album) shop ⊗ 🐾

LEEDS MAP 08 SE33

Abbey House Museum

Abbey Walk, Abbey Rd, Kirkstall LS5 3EH

⮕ *(3m W of city centre on A65)*

☎ 0113 230 5492

e-mail: abbey.house@leeds.gov.uk

web: www.leeds.gov.uk

Displays at this museum include an interactive childhood gallery, a look at Kirkstall Abbey, and an exploration of life in Victorian Leeds. Three reconstructed streets allow the visitor to immerse themselves in

continued

the sights and sounds of the late 19th century, from the glamourous art furnishers shop to the impoverished widow washerwoman.

Times: Open all year Tue-Fri 10-5, Sat noon-5, Sun 10-5. Closed Mon ex BH Mon (open 10-5) **Fee:** £3.50 (ch £1.50 accompanied by an adult, concessions £2.50). Family ticket £5 **Facilities:** ℗ 💺 🍴 licensed ♿ (Braille plaques on wall, tactile tours by request) toilets for disabled shop ⊗ (ex guide dogs) ◀

Kirkstall Abbey   `FREE`

Abbey Rd, Kirkstall LS5 3EH

⮁ *(off A65, W of city centre)*

☎ 0113 230 5492

e-mail: abbey.house@leeds.gov.uk

web: www.leeds.gov.uk

The most complete 12th-century Cistercian Abbey in the country stands on the banks of the River Aire. Many of the original buildings can still be seen, including the cloister, church and refectory. Regular tours take visitors to areas not normally accessible to the public. During the summer the Abbey hosts plays, fairs and musical events. A new visitor centre at the Abbey gives an insight into the history of the Abbey.

Times: Open all year. Abbey site open dawn to dusk. The visitor centre is open: Summer, Tue-Sun, 11-4. Winter, Tue-Sun, 11-3.
Facilities: ℗ ♿ toilets for disabled shop

Leeds City Art Gallery   `FREE`

The Headrow LS1 3AA

⮁ *(in city centre, next to town hall and library)*

☎ 0113 247 8248

e-mail: city.art.gallery@leeds.gov.uk

web: www.leeds.gov.uk/artgallery

Home to one of the best collections of 20th-century British art outside London, as well as Victorian and late 19th-century pictures, an outstanding collection of English watercolours, a display of modern sculpture and temporary exhibitions focusing on contemporary art. The gallery holds an active events programme with talks, demonstrations and workshops regularly planned.

Times: Open all year, Mon-Sat 10-5, Wed until 8, Sun 1-5. Closed BHs.
Facilities: ℗ (street parking) 💺 🍴 licensed 🎒 ♿ (restricted access to upper floor, access ramp) toilets for disabled shop ⊗ (ex guide dogs)

Leeds Industrial Museum at Armley Mills

Canal Rd, Armley LS12 2QF

⮁ *(2m W of city centre, off A65)*

☎ 0113 263 7861

web: www.leeds.gov.uk

Once the world's largest woollen mill, Armley Mills evokes memories of the 18th-century woollen industry, showing the progress of wool from the sheep to knitted clothing. The museum has its own 1930s cinema illustrating the history of cinema projection, including the first moving pictures taken in Leeds. There are demonstrations of static engines and steam locomotives, a printing gallery and a journey through the working world of textiles and fashion.

Times: Open all year, Tue-Sat 10-5, Sun 1-5. (Last entry 1 hr before closing). Closed Mon ex BHs. **Fee:** £3 (ch £1, concessions £1.50). **Facilities:** ℗ ♿ (chair-lifts between floors) toilets for disabled shop ⊗ ◀

Middleton Railway

Moor Rd, Hunslet LS10 2JQ

⮁ *(M621 junct 5 or follow signs from A61)*

☎ 0113 271 0320 (ansaphone)

e-mail: info@middletonrailway.org.uk

web: www.middletonrailway.org.uk

This was the first railway authorised by an Act of Parliament (in 1758) and the first to succeed with steam locomotives (in 1812). Steam trains run each weekend in season from Tunstall Road roundabout to Middleton Park. There is a programme of special events.

Times: ✱ Moor Road Station open for viewing every wknd. Trains run Apr-Dec, Sat-Sun & BH **Facilities:** ℗ 💺 🎒 ♿ (ramped access to all areas) toilets for disabled shop ◀

Royal Armouries Museum   `FREE`

Armouries Dr LS10 1LT

⮁ *(off A61 close to Leeds centre, follow brown heritage signs.)*

☎ 0113 220 1999 & 0990 106 666

e-mail: enquiries@armouries.org.uk

web: www.royalarmouries.org

The museum is an impressive contemporary home for the renowned national collection of arms and armour. The collection is divided between five galleries: War, Tournament, Self-Defence, Hunting and Oriental. The Hall of Steel features a 100ft-high mass of 3000 pieces of arms and armour. Visitors are encouraged to take part in and handle some of the collections. Live demonstrations and interpretations take place throughout the year.

Times: Open daily, from 10-5. Closed 24-25 Dec **Facilities:** ℗ (charged) 💺 🍴 licensed 🎒 ♿ (induction loops, wheelchairs, signers, low level counter) toilets for disabled shop ⊗ (ex guide & hearing dogs) ◀

Temple Newsam House & Park

LS15 0AE

⮁ *(4m from city centre on A63 or 2m from M1 junct 46)*

☎ 0113 264 7321 (House) & 5535 (Park)

web: www.leeds.gov.uk

This Tudor and Jacobean mansion boasts extensive collections of decorative arts in their original room settings, including an incomparable Chippendale collection. Set in 1500 acres of parkland (landscaped by 'Capability' Brown), there is a Rare Breeds Centre, and the gardens have a magnificent display of rhododendrons. Free audio guides tour you around the house and tell you more about the people who lived there. On special days, visitors can join in with the laundry maids washing at the dolly tub, watch the blacksmith hammer out shoes and see logs cut at the saw-mill.

Times: Open all year. House: Tue-Sat 10-5, Sun 1-5; Nov-28 Dec & Mar, Tue-Sat 10-4, Sun 12-5. Open Bank Hols. Home Farm: Tue-Sun, 10-4 (3 in winter); Gardens: 10-dusk. Estate: daily, dawn-dusk. Closed Jan-Feb re-opens 28 Feb. **Fee:** House: £3.50, Farm: £3, Joint, £5.50. Ch; House: £2.50, Farm: £2, Joint: £3.50. Family; House: £9, Farm: £8, Joint: £14. **Facilities:** ℗ (charged) 💺 ♿ (ramps for full access to parkland, electric wheelchairs) toilets for disabled shop ⊗ (ex guide dogs) ◀

England

Thackray Museum
2 for 1

Beckett St LS9 7LN

➲ *(M1 junct 43, onto M621 junct 4. Follow signs for York & St James Hospital, then brown tourist signs)*

☎ 0113 244 4343

e-mail: info@thackraymuseum.org

web: www.thackraymuseum.org

Housed in a large Victorian building, next to the famous St James's Hospital, the Thackray Museum offers a unique hands-on experience. A cow from Gloucester, green mould and smelly toilets - all these things have helped transform our lives. Find out how by walking back in time and exploring the sights, sounds and smells of Victorian slum life. Also the interactive Bodyworks Gallery offers the chance to explore the workings of the human body.

Times: Open all year, daily 10-5.(last admission 3) Closed 24-26 & 31 Dec & 1 Jan **Fee:** ✱ £5.50 (ch 4-16 £4, concessions £4.50). Family ticket (2ad+3ch) £18. Group rates available. **Facilities:** ❷ (charged) ☕ ♿ (wheelchairs, induction loop, large texts) toilets for disabled shop ⊗ (ex guide dogs) ◀

Tropical World

Canal Gardens, Roundhay Park LS8 2ER

➲ *(3m N of city centre off A58 at Oakwood)*

☎ 0113 266 1850

web: www.leeds.gov.uk

The atmosphere of the tropics is recreated here as visitors walk on the beach among exotic trees. A waterfall cascades into a rock-pool and other pools contain terrapins and carp. There are reptiles, insects and more than 30 species of butterfly. Feel the dry heat of the desert and the darkness of the nocturnal zone, and watch out for the piranhas and other exotic fish in the depths of the aquarium.

Times: Open Winter (GMT), daily 10-4 (last admission 3.30); Summer (BST), 10-6 (last admission 5.30) **Fee:** ✱ £3 (ch 8-15 £2, under 8's & Leeds card holders free) **Facilities:** ❷ ☕ ♿ toilets for disabled shop ⊗ (ex guide dogs) ◀

LOTHERTON HALL
MAP 08 SE43

Lotherton Hall

Aberford LS25 3EB

➲ *(off the A1, 0.75m E of junct with B1217)*

☎ 0113 281 3259

web: www.leeds.gov.uk

Built in Edwardian times, the museum contains furniture, pictures, silver and ceramics from the Gascoigne collection, and works of art on loan from Leeds galleries. Outside, the Edwardian garden, bird garden and deer park are delightful places in which to stroll.

Times: Open Tue-Sat 10-5. Sun 1-5. BHs. Nov-Dec & Mar Tue-Sat 10-4, Sun 12-4. **Fee:** £3.50 (ch £1, concessions £1.50). Leeds card 20% discount. **Facilities:** ❷ (charged) ☕ 🍴 licensed ♿ shop ⊗ (ex in park) ◀

MIDDLESTOWN
MAP 08 SE21

National Coal Mining Museum For England
FREE

Caphouse Colliery, New Rd WF4 4RH

➲ *(on A642 between Huddersfield & Horbury)*

☎ 01924 848806

e-mail: info@ncm.org.uk

web: www.ncm.org.uk

A unique opportunity to go 140 metres underground down one of Britain's oldest working mines. Take a step back in time with one of the museum's experienced local miners who will guide parties around the underground workings, where models and machinery depict methods and conditions of mining from the early 1800s to present day. Other attractions include the Hope Pit, pithead baths, Victorian steam winder, nature trail and adventure playground and meet the last ever working pit ponies. You are strongly advised to wear sensible footwear and warm clothing.

Times: Open all year, daily 10-5. Closed 24-26 Dec & 1 Jan. **Facilities:** ❷ ☕ 🍴 licensed 📷 ♿ (induction loop, audio tours, 2 w'chairs for underground) toilets for disabled shop ⊗ (ex guide dogs) ◀

NOSTELL PRIORY
MAP 08 SE41

Nostell Priory

Doncaster Rd WF4 1QE

➲ *(5m SE of Wakefield towards Doncaster, on A638)*

☎ 01924 863892

e-mail: nostellpriory@nationaltrust.org.uk

web: www.nationaltrust.org.uk/nostellpriory/

Built by James Paine in the middle of the 18th century, the priory has an additional wing built by Robert Adam in 1766. It contains a notable saloon and tapestry room, and displays pictures and Chippendale furniture. There are lakeside walks within the grounds with rhododendrons and azaleas in bloom in late spring.

Times: ✱ Open mid Mar-early Nov, Wed-Sun 1-5, Grounds 11-6. **Facilities:** ❷ ☕ 📷 ♿ (lift, Braille guide/tactile books, wheelchair) toilets for disabled shop 🐾

OAKWELL HALL   MAP 08 SE22

Oakwell Hall

Nutter Ln, Birstall WF17 9LG

➲ *(6m SE of Bradford, off M62 junct 26/27, follow brown heritage signs, turn off A652 onto Nutter Lane)*

☎ 01924 326240

e-mail: oakwell.hall@kirklees.gov.uk

web: www.oakwellhallcountrypark.co.uk

A moated Elizabethan manor house, furnished as it might have looked in the 1690s. Extensive 110-acre country park with visitor information centre, period gardens, nature trails, arboretum and children's adventure playground.

Times: Open all year, daily Mon-Fri 11-5; Sat & Sun 12-5. Closed Good Fri & 24 Dec-1 Jan. **Fee:** ✱ Hall £1.50 (ch & wheelchair users 60p). Family ticket £3.30. Charges Mar-Oct. Free admission Nov-Feb. Vistor centre and park free all year. **Facilities:** ♥ ♨ 🍴 ♿ (large print & Braille guide, induction loops) toilets for disabled shop ⊗ (ex guide dogs) 🍴

WAKEFIELD   MAP 08 SE32

Wakefield Art Gallery   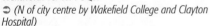 FREE

Wentworth Ter WF1 3QW

➲ *(N of city centre by Wakefield College and Clayton Hospital)*

☎ 01924 305796

e-mail: museumsandarts@wakefield.gov.uk

web: www.wakefield.gov.uk/cultureandleisure

Wakefield was home to two of Britain's greatest modern sculptors - Barbara Hepworth and Henry Moore. The art gallery, which has an important collection of 20th-century paintings and sculptures, has a special room devoted to these two local artists. There are frequent temporary exhibitions of both modern and earlier works.

Times: Open all year, Tue-Sat 10.30-4.30, Sun 2-4.30. **Facilities:** ℗ (on street parking restricted to 2hrs) ♿ shop ⊗ (ex guide dogs)

WEST BRETTON   MAP 08 SE21

Yorkshire Sculpture Park

WF4 4LG

➲ *(M1 junct 38, follow brown heritage signs to A637. Left at rdbt, attraction signed)*

☎ 01924 832631

e-mail: info@ysp.co.uk

web: www.ysp.co.uk

Set in the beautiful grounds and gardens of a 500 acre, 18th-century country estate, Yorkshire Sculpture Park is one of the world's leading open-air galleries and presents a changing programme of international sculpture exhibitions. The landscape provides a variety of magnificent scenic vistas of the valley, lakes, estate buildings and bridges. By organising a number of temporary exhibitions each year, the park ensures that there is always something new to see. The Visitor Centre provides all-weather facilities including a large restaurant, shop, coffee bar, audio-visual auditorium and meeting rooms. The Underground Gallery with a 50 metre concourse to light-filled galleries.

Times: Open all year 10-6 (summer) 10-5 (winter). Please phone for details of Xmas closures **Fee:** ✱ Free. (Donations welcome). Car parking £3, coaches £8 **Facilities:** ♥ (charged) ♨ 🍴 licensed 🍴 ♿ (free scooters, parking, trail accessible for wheelchairs) toilets for disabled shop ⊗ (ex assist dogs)

The National Trust: For over a hundred years, the NT has been acquiring and protecting threatened coastline, countryside and buildings. To find out more about this organisation, its sites, and policies, visit their website: **www.nationaltrust.org.uk**

Guernsey

Petit Pot Bay

If it's sunshine, shopping and sea you're interested in, then the island of Guernsey is the ideal location, combining the feeling of being abroad with the familiarity of the English language, British ways of life and tax-free shopping. The island enjoys around 2,000 hours of sunshine a year. This makes its 27 beaches great places to spend your time, and no matter which way the wind is blowing, you'll be sure to find one that's sheltered.

FOREST   MAP 16

German Occupation Museum
GY8 0BG
➲ *(Behind Forest Church near the airport)*
☎ 01481 238205

The museum has the Channel Islands' largest collection of Occupation items, with tableaux of a kitchen, bunker rooms and a street during the Occupation. Liberation Day 9th May will be celebrated with special events and exhibitions.

Times: Open Apr-Oct 10-4.30, Nov-Mar 10-12.30 (Closed Mon). **Fee:** £3.75 (ch £2). Free admission for disabled. **Facilities:** ♿ 🅿 🍴 ♿ (ramps & handrails) ⊗ (ex assist dogs)

ROCQUAINE BAY   MAP 16

Fort Grey and Shipwreck Museum `2 for 1`
GY7 9BY
➲ *(on coast road at Rocquaine Bay)*
☎ 01481 265036
e-mail: admin@museums.gov.gg
web: www.museum.guernsey.net

The fort is a Martello tower, built in 1804, as part of the Channel Islands' extensive defences. It is nicknamed the 'cup and saucer' because of its appearance, and houses a museum devoted to ships wrecked on the treacherous Hanois reefs nearby.

Times: Open Etr-Oct, 10-5 **Fee:** ✱ Fort Grey, £2.50 (pen £1.25), 3 Venue Ticket £9 (pen £5) **Facilities:** Ⓟ (opposite fort) 🏪 shop ⊗ (ex guide dogs) ◀

ST ANDREW   MAP 16

German Military Underground Hospital & Ammunition Store
La Vassalerie GY6 8XR
➲ *(St Andrews Parish, centre of island)*
☎ 01481 239100

The largest structure created during the German Occupation of the Channel Islands, a concrete maze of about 75,000 sq. ft, which took slave workers three-and-a-half years to complete, at the cost of many lives. Most of the equipment has been removed, but the central heating plant, hospital beds and cooking facilities can still be seen.

Times: ✱ Open Jul-Aug, daily 10-noon & 2-4.30; May-Jun & Sep, daily 10-noon & 2-4; Apr & Oct, daily 2-4; Mar & Nov, Sun & Thu 2-3. **Facilities:** ♿ 🏪 ♿ shop

Are there any excellent Days Out that we have missed? Use the Readers' Report form at the back of the book to tell us about them.

ST MARTIN   MAP 16

Sausmarez Manor `2 for 1`
Sausmarez Rd GY4 6SG
➲ *(halfway between airport & St Peter Port)*
☎ 01481 235571
e-mail: sausmarezmanor@cwgsy.net
web: www.sausmarezmanor@cwgsy.co.uk

The Manor has been owned and lived in by the same family for centuries. The style of each room is different, with collections of Oriental, French and English furniture and paintings. Outside the Formal Garden has herbaceous borders, and the Woodland Garden, set around two small lakes and a stream, is planted with colourful shrubs, bulbs and wild flowers from the subtropics. Also on view, a sculpture park which is now the most comprehensive in Britain.

Times: Open Etr-Oct 10.30 & 11.30, Mon-Thu; Jun-Aug 10.30, 11.30 & 2 Mon-Thu; or by appointment. **Fee:** ✱ House £5.90 (ch £2, pen £4.50). Woodland Garden £4.50 (accompanied ch & pen £3, disabled free). Sculpture Park £4.50 (accompanied ch & pen £3, disabled free). **Facilities:** ♿ 🅿 🍴 🏪 ♿ (free admission, partial access to garden, wheelchair loan) shop ⊗ (ex assist dogs)

ST PETER PORT   MAP 16

Castle Cornet `2 for 1`
GY1 1AU
➲ *(5 mins walk from St Peter Port bus terminus)*
☎ 01481 721657
e-mail: admin@museums.gov.gg
web: www.museum.guernsey.net

The history of this magnificent castle spans eight centuries and its buildings now house several museums, the Refectory Café and a shop. Soldiers fire the noonday gun in a daily ceremony. Look for the Maritime Museum that charts Guernsey's nautical history, the 'Story of Castle Cornet' with its mystery skeleton and the 201 squadron RAF Museum.

Times: Open Etr-end Oct, daily 10-5. **Fee:** ✱ £6 (pen £4). 3 venue ticket £9 (pen £5) **Facilities:** Ⓟ (100 yds) time limit 🍴 🏪 shop ⊗ (ex guide dogs) ◀

England

Guernsey Museum & Art Gallery   `2 for 1`

Candie Gardens GY1 1UG

➲ *(On the outskirts of St Peter Port set in the Victorian 'Candie gardens')*

☎ 01481 726518

e-mail: admin@museums.gov.gg

web: www.museum.guernsey.net

The museum, designed around a Victorian bandstand, tells the story of Guernsey and its people. There is an audio-visual theatre and an art gallery, and special exhibitions are arranged throughout the year. It is surrounded by beautiful gardens with superb views over St Peter Port harbour.

Times: Open Feb-Dec daily 10-5 (Winter 10-4) **Fee:** ✱ £3.50 (pen £2.50). 3 venue ticket £9 (pen £5) **Facilities:** ℗ (street parking) (2hr & 5hr) 💺 📋 ♿ toilets for disabled shop ⊗ (ex guide dogs) ◀

VALE   MAP 16

Rousse Tower   `FREE`

Rousse Tower Headland

➲ *(on Island's W coast, signed)*

☎ 01481 726518 & 726965

e-mail: p.sarl@museums.gov.gg

web: www.museum.guernsey.net

One of the original fifteen towers built in 1778-9 in prime defensive positions around the coast of Guernsey. They were designed primarily to prevent the landing of troops on nearby beaches. Musket fire could be directed on invading forces through the loopholes. An interpretation centre displays replica guns.

Times: Open Apr-Oct 9-dusk, Nov-Mar Wed, Sat & Sun 9-4. **Facilities:** ℗ ⊗ (ex guide dogs)

Jerbourg Point, St Martin

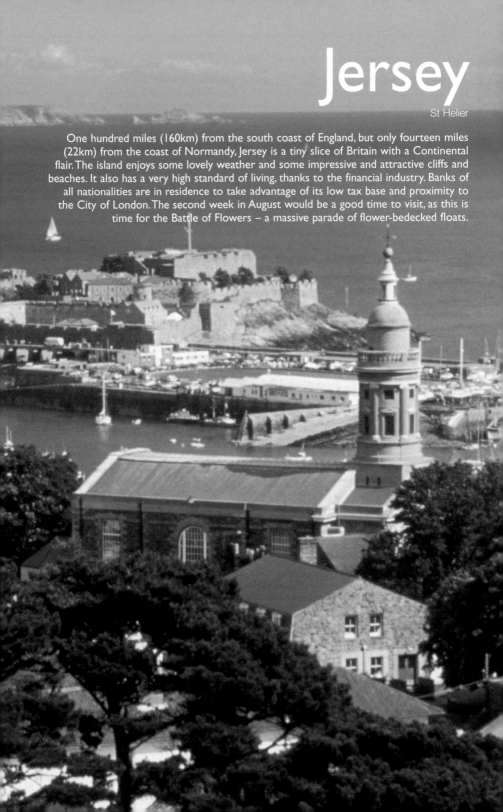

Jersey

St Helier

One hundred miles (160km) from the south coast of England, but only fourteen miles (22km) from the coast of Normandy, Jersey is a tiny slice of Britain with a Continental flair. The island enjoys some lovely weather and some impressive and attractive cliffs and beaches. It also has a very high standard of living, thanks to the financial industry. Banks of all nationalities are in residence to take advantage of its low tax base and proximity to the City of London. The second week in August would be a good time to visit, as this is time for the Battle of Flowers – a massive parade of flower-bedecked floats.

GOREY MAP 16

Mont Orgueil Castle

JE3 6ET

➲ *(A3 or coast road to Gorey)*

☎ 01534 853292

e-mail: marketing@jerseyheritagetrust.org

web: www.jerseyheritagetrust.org

Standing on a rocky headland, on a site which has been fortified since the Iron Age, this is one of the best-preserved examples in Europe of a medieval concentric castle, and dates from the 12th and 13th centuries.

Times: Open daily: Apr-Nov, 10-6. **Fee:** ✱ £6 (ch 10-16, ch under 6 free, concessions £5.20). Family and discount tickets
Facilities: ❷ ⭐ ⊗ (ex guide dogs) ◼

LA GREVE DE LECQ MAP 16

Greve de Lecq Barracks `FREE`

➲ *(on right hand side of valley, overlooking beach)*

☎ 01534 483193 & 482238

e-mail: enquiries@nationaltrustjersey.org.je

web: www.nationaltrustjersey.org.je

Originally serving as an outpost of the British Empire, these barracks, built in 1810, were used for civilian housing from the end of WWI to 1972, when they were bought by the National Trust and made into a museum that depicts the life of soldiers who were stationed here in the 19th century. Also includes a collection of old horse-drawn carriages.

Times: Open: 4 Jun-25 Sept, Sun only. **Facilities:** ❷ ᗝ (wheelchair ramps) toilets for disabled shop ⊗ (ex guide dogs) ▦

GROUVILLE MAP 16

La Hougue Bie

JE2 7UA

➲ *(A6 or A7 to Five Oaks, at mini-rdbt take B28 to site)*

☎ 01534 853823

e-mail: marketing@jerseyheritagetrust.org

web: www.jerseyheritagetrust.org

This Neolithic burial mound stands 40ft high, and covers a stone-built passage grave that is still intact and may be entered. The passage is 50ft long, and built of huge stones, the mound is made from earth, rubble and limpet shells. On top of the mound are two medieval chapels, one of which has a replica of the Holy Sepulchre in Jerusalem below. Also on the site is an underground bunker built by the Germans as a communications centre, now a memorial to the slave workers of the Occupation.

Times: Open Apr-Nov, daily 10-5. **Fee:** ✱ £5.40 (ch under 6 free, student & concessions £4.60). Discount & family tickets. **Facilities:** ❷ shop ⊗ (ex guide dogs) ◼

ST BRELADE MAP 16

Jersey Lavender Farm

Rue du Pont Marquet JE3 8DS

➲ *(on B25 from St Aubin's Bay to Redhouses)*

☎ 01534 742933

e-mail: admin@jerseylavender.co.uk

web: www.jerseylavender.co.uk

Jersey Lavender grows nine acres of lavender, distils out the essential oil and creates a range of fine toiletry products. Visitors are able to see the whole process from cultivating, through to harvesting, distillation and the production of the final product. There is a national collection of lavenders, extensive gardens, herb beds and walks among the lavender fields. There are also other herbs that are grown and distilled, namely eucalyptus, rosemary and tea tree.

Times: ✱ Open 10 May-18 Sep, Tue-Sun 10-5. **Facilities:** ❷ ⭐ ⬚ ᗝ (free wheelchair loan) toilets for disabled shop garden centre ◼

ST CLEMENT MAP 16

Samarès Manor `2 for 1`

JE2 6QW

➲ *(2m E of St Helier on St Clements Inner Rd)*

☎ 01534 870551

e-mail: enquiries@samaresmanor.com

web: www.samaresmanor.com

The manor stands in 14 acres of beautiful gardens. The Japanese Garden occupies an artificial hill, and has a series of waterfalls cascading over Cumberland limestone. There are farm animals, a craft centre, a children's play area, tours of the manor house, and a childrens nature trail. The Jersey Royal Rifle and Carriage Museum is situated in the manor's early Victorian courtyard.

Times: Open 8 Apr-14 Oct. **Fee:** ✱ £5.60 (ch under 16 £1.95, pen £5.20). **Facilities:** ❷ ⭐ ⬚ licensed ⬚ ᗝ toilets for disabled shop garden centre ⊗ (ex guide dogs) ◼

ST HELIER MAP 16

Elizabeth Castle

JE2 3WU

➲ *(access by causeway or amphibious vehicle)*

☎ 01534 723971

e-mail: marketing@jerseyheritagetrust.org

web: www.jerseyheritagetrust.org

The original Elizabethan fortress was extended in the 17th and 18th centuries, and then refortified by the Germans during the Occupation. Please telephone for details of events.

Times: Open 2 Apr-5 Nov, daily 10-6. **Fee:** ✱ £5.40 (ch under 6 free, concessions & students £4.60). Discounts and family tickets
Facilities: ℗ (paycards required) ⭐ ᗝ toilets for disabled shop ⊗ (ex guide dogs) ◼

England

Jersey Museum

The Weighbridge JE2 3NF
➲ *(near bus station on weighbridge)*
☎ 01534 633300
e-mail: marketing@jerseyheritagetrust.org
web: www.jerseyheritagetrust.org

Home to 'The Story of Jersey', Jersey's art gallery, an exhibition gallery which features a changing programme, a lecture theatre, and an audio-visual theatre. Special exhibitions take place throughout the year.

Times: Open all year, daily 10-5. Winter daily 10-4. Closed 24-26 Dec & 1 Jan. **Fee:** ✱ £5.40 (ch under 6 free, students & concessions £4.60). Discount and family tickets **Facilities:** ℗ (100yds) (paycard at most public parking) ◉ licensed 📖 ♿ (audio loop,car park,magnilink viewer,lift) toilets for disabled shop ⊗ (ex guide dogs) 🛥

Maritime Museum & Occupation Tapestry Gallery

New North Quay JE2 3ND
➲ *(alongside Marina, opposite Liberation Square)*
☎ 01534 811043
e-mail: marketing@jerseyheritagetrust
web: www.jerseyheritagetrust.org

This converted 19th-century warehouse houses the tapestry consisting of 12 two-metre panels that tells the story of the occupation of Jersey during World War II. Each of the 12 parishes took responsibility for stitching a panel, making it the largest community arts project ever undertaken on the island. The Maritime Museum celebrates the relationship of islanders and the sea, including an award winning hands-on experience, especially enjoyed by children.

Times: Open all year, daily 10-5. Winter closing at 4. **Fee:** ✱ £6 (ch under 6 free, concessions £5.20). Discount and family tickets **Facilities:** ℗ (paycards in public car parks) ♿ (Braille books, audio guide etc) toilets for disabled shop ⊗ (ex guide dogs) 🛥

ST LAWRENCE   MAP 16

German Underground Hospital

Les Charrieres Malorey JE3 1FU
➲ *(bus route 8A from St Helier)*
☎ 01534 860808
e-mail: info@jerseywartunnels.com
web: www.jerseywartunnels.com

On 1 July 1940 the Channel Islands were occupied by German forces, and this vast complex dug deep into a hillside is the most evocative reminder of that Occupation. A video presentation, along with a large collection of memorabilia, illustrates the lives of the islanders at war and a further exhibition records their impressions during 1945, the year of liberation.

Times: ✱ Open 14 Feb-19 Dec, daily 9.30-5.30 (last admission 4). **Facilities:** ℗ 🅿 ◉ licensed 📖 ♿ (ramp to restaurant & lift in Visitor Centre to restaurant) toilets for disabled shop ⊗ (ex guide dogs) 🛥

Hamptonne

La Rue de la Patente JE3 1HS
➲ *(5m from St Helier on A1, A10 & follow signs)*
☎ 01534 863955
e-mail: marketing@jerseyheritagetrust.org
web: www.jerseyheritagetrust.org

Here visitors will find a medieval 17th-century home, furnished in authentic style and surrounded by 19th-century farm buildings. Guided tours every weekday. Living history interpretation and daily demonstrations.

Times: Open Apr-early Nov, daily 10-5. **Fee:** ✱ £5.40 (ch under 6 free, student & concessions £4.60). Discount and family tickets. **Facilities:** ℗ ◉ licensed ♿ (Sensory Garden, designated parking, tapes for tours) toilets for disabled shop ⊗ (ex guide dogs) 🛥

ST OUEN   MAP 16

The Channel Islands Military Museum

Five Mile Rd
➲ *(N end of 5 Mile Rd, at rear of Jersey Woollen Mill & across rd from Jersey Pearl)*
☎ 01534 723136
e-mail: damienhorn@jerseymail.co.uk

The museum is housed in a German coastal defence bunker, which formed part of Hitler's Atlantic Wall. It has been restored, as far as possible, to give the visitor an idea of how it looked. The visitor can also see German uniforms, motorcycles, weapons, documents, photographs and other items from the 1940-45 occupation.

Times: Open wk before Etr-Oct **Fee:** ✱ £4 (ch £2) Groups by arrangement. **Facilities:** ℗ 🅿 ♿ (all parts accessible ex 1 small room) toilets for disabled shop ⊗ (ex guide dogs)

Kempt Tower Visitor Centre   FREE

Five Mile Rd
☎ 01534 483651 & 483140

The centre has displays on history and the wildlife of St Ouen's Bay, including Les Mielles, which is Jersey's miniature national park. Nature walks are held every Thursday (May to September). Check local press for details.

Times: ✱ Open BHs, Apr & Oct, Thu & Sun only 2-5; May-Sep, daily (ex Mon) 2-5. **Facilities:** ℗ shop ⊗

English Heritage: Find out more about English Heritage sites, their policies and the work they do, at their website: **www.english-heritage.org.uk**

ST PETER
MAP 16

The Living Legend
Rue de Petit Aleval JE3 7ET

⮑ *(from St Helier, along main esplanade & right to Bel Royal. Left and follow road to attraction, signed from German Underground Hospital)*

☎ 01534 485496
e-mail: info@jerseyslivinglegend.co.je
web: www.jerseyslivinglegend.co.je

Pass through the granite archways into the landscaped gardens and the world of the Jersey Experience where Jersey's exciting past is recreated in a three dimensional spectacle featuring Stephen Tompkinson, Tony Robinson and other well-known names. Learn of the heroes and villains, the folklore and the story of the island's links with the UK and its struggles with Europe. Other attractions include an adventure playground, street entertainment, the Jersey Craft and Shopping Village, a range of shops and the Jersey Kitchen Restaurant. Two 18-hole adventure golf courses are suitable for all ages. Jersey Karting is a formula one style experience. A unique track featuring adult and cadet karts.

Times: Open daily, Mar-Nov 9.30-5, Sat-Sun 10-5 **Fee:** ✱ £7.10 (ch 7-13 £4.85, pen £6.80, student £5.50, disabled £5.60). **Facilities:** ❷ ➳ ❤❁ licensed ♿ (wheelchair available) toilets for disabled shop ⊗ (ex guide dogs) ⬛

Le Moulin de Quetivel
St Peters Valley, Le Mont Fallu

⮑ *(A11 through St Peter's Valley. Attraction located on left, with junct of Le Mont Fallu B58)*

☎ 01534 483193 & 745408
e-mail: enquiries@nationaltrustjersey.org.je
web: www.nationaltrustjersey.org.je

There has been a water mill on this site since 1309. The present granite-built mill was worked until the end of the 19th century, when it fell into disrepair; during the German Occupation it was reactivated for grinding locally grown corn, but after 1945 a fire destroyed the remaining machinery, roof and internal woodwork. In 1971 the National Trust for Jersey began restoration, and the mill is now producing stoneground flour again.

Times: 20 May-23 Sept, Sat only. **Fee:** ✱ £2 (ch under 16 free, concessions £1.50). Free entry UK National Trust card.
Facilities: ❷ ♿ shop ⊗ (ex guide dogs) ⬛

TRINITY
MAP 16

Durrell Wildlife Conservation Trust
Les Augres Manor, La Profunde Rue JE3 5BP

☎ 01534 860000
e-mail: info@durrell.org
web: www.durrell.org

Gerald Durrell's unique sanctuary and breeding centre for many of the world's rarest animals. Visitors can see these remarkable creatures, some so rare that they can only be found here, in modern, spacious enclosures in the gardens of the 16th-century manor house. Major attractions are the magical Aye-Ayes from Madagascar and the world-famous family of Lowland gorillas. There is a comprehensive programme of keeper talks, animal displays and activities.

Times: ✱ Open all year, daily 9.30-6 (summer); 9.30-5 (winter). Closed 25 Dec. **Facilities:** ❷ ➳ ❤❁ ♿ toilets for disabled shop ⊗ ⬛

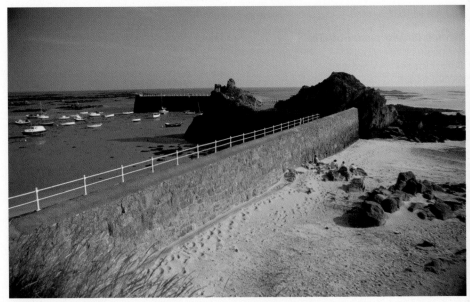

La Rocque

Isle of Man

Great Laxey Wheel

Despite its size (just 33 miles by 13 (48km by 21km)), this island in
the middle of the Irish Sea packs in plenty of history and culture.
As well as its kippers, tailless cats, famous Great Laxey Wheel and
narrow-gauge steam and electric railways, the island is known for
the annual motorcycle races, the Isle of Man Tourist Trophy (TT).
These take place on the island's roads, attracting racers and
spectators from all over the world, and celebrate their centenary
in 2007. The island has the world's oldest continuous parliament
(the Tynwald), thanks to the Vikings who had a huge impact on the
island's culture, and you'll also find picturesque castles, dramatic
scenery, craggy coastline and beautiful golden beaches.

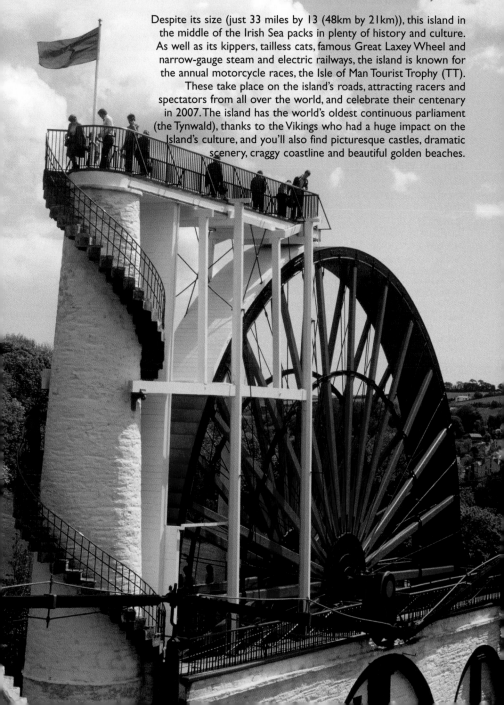

BALLASALLA   MAP 06 SC27

Rushen Abbey

IM9 3DB

➲ *(right at Whitestone Inn, left at next rdbt, then 1st right over bridge, car park on left)*

☎ 01624 648000

e-mail: enquiries@mnh.gov.im

web: www.storyofmann.com

The most substantial and important medieval religious site in the Isle of Man. Remains of medieval buildings, exhibitions and displays, set in beautifully landscaped gardens.

Times: Open Etr-late Oct, daily 10-5. **Fee:** £3.30 (ch £1.70) Family ticket £8.30. Groups from £2.60. **Facilities:** ❷ & toilets for disabled shop ❽ (ex guide dogs) ◀

BALLAUGH   MAP 06 SC39

Curraghs Wild Life Park

IM7 5EA

➲ *(on main road halfway between Kirk Michael & Ramsey)*

☎ 01624 897323

e-mail: curraghswlp@gov.im

web: www.gov.im/wildlife

This park has been developed adjacent to the reserve area of the Ballaugh Curraghs and a large variety of animals and birds can be seen. A walk-through enclosure lets visitors explore the world of wildlife, including local habitats along the Curraghs nature trail. The miniature railway runs on Sundays.

Times: Open all year Etr-Oct, daily 10-6. (Last admission 5). Oct-Etr, Sat & Sun 10-4. **Fee:** ✱ £5 (ch £2.50, under 5's free, pen £3). Party. **Facilities:** ❷ ▣ & (loan of wheelchair & electric wheelchair) toilets for disabled shop ❽ (ex guide dogs by arrangement) ◀

CASTLETOWN   MAP 06 SC26

Castle Rushen

The Quay IM9 1LD

➲ *(centre of Castletown)*

☎ 01624 648000

e-mail: enquiries@mnh.gov.im

web: www.storyofmann.com

One of Europe's best preserved medieval castles, Castle Rushen is a limestone fortress rising out of the heart of the old capital of the island, Castletown. Once the fortress of the Kings and Lords of Mann, Castle Rushen is bought alive with rich decorations, and the sounds and smells of a bygone era.

Times: Open daily, Etr-Oct, 10-5. **Fee:** £4.80 (ch £2.40) Family £12. Group from £3.80 each. **Facilities:** ℗ (100 yds) (disc zone parking) ▥ & shop ❽ (ex guide dogs) ◀

Nautical Museum

➲ *(From Castletown centre, cross footbridge over harbour. Museum on right)*

☎ 01624 648000

e-mail: enquiries@mnh.gov.im

web: www.storyofmann.com

Set at the mouth of Castletown harbour The Nautical Museum is home to an 18th-century armed yacht, *The Peggy*, built by a Manxman in 1791. A replica sailmaker's loft, ship model and photographs bring alive Manx maritime life and trade in the days of sail.

Times: Open daily, Etr-Oct, 10-5. **Fee:** £3.30 (ch £1.70). Family £8.30. Groups from £2.60 **Facilities:** ℗ (50 yds) ▥ & shop ❽ (ex guide dogs) ◀

Old Grammar School   [FREE]

IM9 1LE

➲ *(centre of Castletown, opposite the castle)*

☎ 01624 648000

e-mail: enquiries@mnh.gov.im

web: www.storyofmann.com

Built around 1200AD, the former capital's first church, St Mary's, has had a significant role in Manx education. It was a school from 1570 to 1930 and evokes memories of Victorian school life.

Times: Open daily, Etr-late Oct, 10-5. **Facilities:** ❷ ▥ shop ❽ (ex guide dogs)

The Old House of Keys

IM9 1LA

➲ *(opposite Castletown Rushen in centre of Castletown)*

☎ 01624 648000

e-mail: enquiries@mnh.gov.im

web: www.storyofmann.com

The Old House of Keys is a portrayal of the long and often turbulent history of Manx politics. It has been restored to its appearance in 1866 and visitors are invited to participate in a lively debate with interactive Members of Tynwald, the Manx parliament.

Times: Open daily, Apr-late Oct, 10-5. **Fee:** £3 (ch £1.50) Family ticket £7.50 **Facilities:** ℗ (30yds) (disc zone parking) & ❽ (ex guide dogs)

CREGNEASH   MAP 06 SC16

Cregneash Village Folk Museum

➲ *(2m from Port Erin/Port St Mary, signed)*

☎ 01624 648000

e-mail: enquiries@mnh.gov.im

web: www.storyofmann.com

The Cregneash story begins in Cummal Beg - the village information centre where you can experience what life was really like in a Manx crofting village during the early 19th century. As you stroll around this attractive village, set in beautiful countryside, call into Harry Kelly's cottage, a Turner's shed, a Weaver's house, and the Smithy. The Manx Four-horned Loghtan Sheep can be seen grazing along with other animals from the village farm.

Times: Open Etr-Oct, daily, 10-5. **Fee:** £3.30 (ch £1.70) Family £8.30. Group rates from £2.60 **Facilities:** ❷ ▣ ▥ & toilets for disabled shop ❽ (ex guide dogs) ◀

DOUGLAS   MAP 06 SC37

Manx Museum   FREE
IM1 3LY

➲ (signed in Douglas)

☎ 01624 648000

e-mail: enquiries@mnh.gov.im

web: www.storyofmann.com

The Island's treasure house provides an exciting introduction to the "Story of Mann" where a specially produced film portrayal of Manx history complements the award winning displays. Galleries depict natural history, archaeology and the social development of the Island. There are also examples of famous Manx artists in the National Art Gallery together with the Island's National archive and reference library

Times: Open daily all year, Mon-Sat, 10-5. Closed 25-26 Dec & 1 Jan. **Facilities:** ❷ ➟ ⱺ licensed 🎦 ♿ (lift) toilets for disabled shop ⊗ (ex guide dogs) ◀

Snaefell Mountain Railway
Banks Circus IM1 5PT

➲ (Manx Electric Railway from Douglas and change at Laxey)

☎ 01624 663366

e-mail: info@busandrail.dtl.gov.im

web: www.iombusandrail.info

Snaefell is the Isle of Man's highest mountain. Running up it is Britain's oldest working mountain railway, which was laid in 1895. From the top of Snaefell, on a clear day, England, Ireland, Scotland and Wales are all visible.

Times: Open 30 Apr-Sep. **Fee:** ✱ Laxey-Summit: Return £7.40, Single, £4.40 (ch half fare). **Facilities:** ❷ ➟ shop ◀

LAXEY   MAP 06 SC48

Great Laxey Wheel & Mines Trail

➲ (signed in Laxey village)

☎ 01624 648000

e-mail: enquiries@mnh.gov.im

web: www.storyofmann.com

Built in 1854, the Great Laxey Wheel, 22 metres in diameter, is the largest working water wheel in the world. It was designed to pump water from the lead and zinc mines and is an acknowledged masterpiece of Victorian engineering. The wheel was christened by Lady Isabella, the wife of the Lieutenant Governor of the Isle of Man.

Times: Open Etr-Oct, daily, 10-5. **Fee:** £3.30 (ch £1.70) Family £8.30. Group rates from £2.60 **Facilities:** ❷ 🎦 ♿ shop ⊗ (ex guide dogs) ◀

PEEL   MAP 06 SC28

House of Manannan
Mill Rd IM5 1TA

➲ (signed in Peel)

☎ 01624 648000

e-mail: enquiries@mnh.gov.im

web: www.storyofmann.com

This £6 million centre is an unforgettable experience. Reconstructions, interactive displays, audio visual presentations and original material explore the Celtic, Viking and maritime traditions of the Isle of Man. A

visit will leave you in awe of the diversity of Manx heritage and eager to learn more.

Times: Open daily, 10-5. Closed 25-26 Dec & 1 Jan. **Fee:** £5.50 (ch £2.80) Family £13.80. Group rates from £4.40. **Facilities:** ❷ 🎦 ♿ toilets for disabled shop ⊗ (ex guide dogs) ◀

Peel Castle
IM5 1TB

➲ (on St Patrick's Isle, facing Peel Bay, signed)

☎ 01624 648000

e-mail: enquiries@mnh.gov.im

web: www.storyofmann.com

One of the Island's principle historic centres, this great natural fortress with its imposing curtain wall set majestically at the mouth of Peel Harbour is steeped in Viking heritage. The sandstone walls of Peel Castle enclose an 11th-century church and Round Tower, the 13th-century St German's Cathedral and the later apartments of the Lords of Mann.

Times: Open Etr-Oct, daily, 10-5. **Fee:** £3.30 (ch £1.70). Family £8.30. Group rates from £2.60. **Facilities:** Ⓟ (100yds) 🎦 ⊗ (ex guide dogs)

PORT ST MARY   MAP 06 SC26

Sound Visitor Centre   FREE
The Sound IM1 3LY

➲ (follow coastal road towards Port Erin/Port St Mary. Past Cregneash village towards most S point of Island)

☎ 01624 648000 & 838123

e-mail: enquiries@mnh.gov.im

web: www.storyofmann.com

The Sound Visitor Centre is set in one of the Island's most scenic areas overlooking the natural wonders of the Sound and the Calf of Man. Along with information and audio presentations about the area, a new car park and high quality refreshments are provided for the enjoyment and convenience of visitors.

Times: Open daily, Etr-Oct 10-5. For Winter opening times telephone 01624 838123. **Facilities:** ❷ ➟ ⱺ licensed 🎦 ♿ toilets for disabled

RAMSEY   MAP 06 SC49

The Grove
IM8 3UA

➲ (on W side of Andreas Rd. Signed in Ramsey)

☎ 01624 648000

e-mail: enquiries@mnh.gov.im

web: www.storyofmann.com

This Victorian time capsule was a country house built as a summer retreat for a Liverpool shipping merchant. Rooms are filled with period furnishings together with a costume exhibition. In the adjacent farmyard are buildings containing displays on farming and 19th century vehicles. Around the grounds you may see Loghtan sheep, ducks and perhaps a Manx cat.

Times: Open Etr-late Oct, daily, 10-5. **Fee:** ✱ £3.30 (ch £1.70). Family £8.30. Group rates from £2.60. **Facilities:** ❷ ➟ ⱺ 🎦 ♿ shop ⊗ (ex guide dogs) ◀

continued

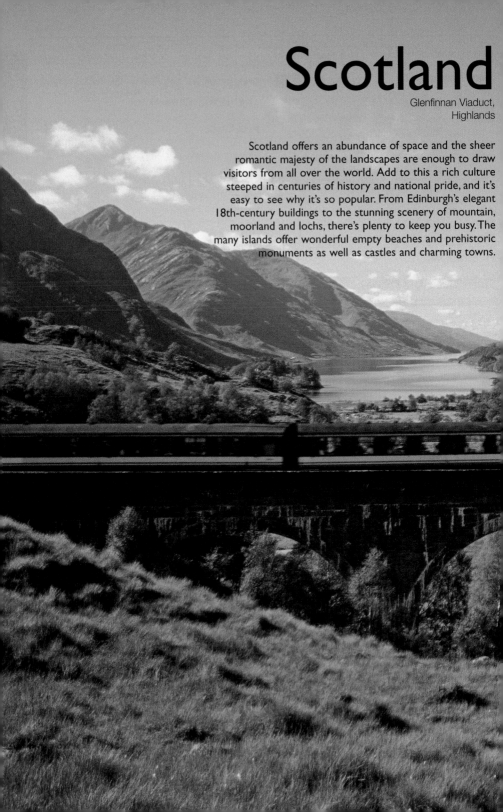

Scotland

Glenfinnan Viaduct,
Highlands

Scotland offers an abundance of space and the sheer romantic majesty of the landscapes are enough to draw visitors from all over the world. Add to this a rich culture steeped in centuries of history and national pride, and it's easy to see why it's so popular. From Edinburgh's elegant 18th-century buildings to the stunning scenery of mountain, moorland and lochs, there's plenty to keep you busy. The many islands offer wonderful empty beaches and prehistoric monuments as well as castles and charming towns.

Scotland

ABERDEEN CITY

ABERDEEN   MAP 15 NJ90

Aberdeen Art Gallery   `FREE`

Schoolhill AB10 1FQ
➲ *(located in city centre)*
☎ 01224 523700
e-mail: info@aagm.co.uk
web: http://www.aagm.co.uk

One of the city's most popular tourist attractions Aberdeen's splendid art gallery houses an important fine art collection with many 19th and 20th century works.

Times: ✳ Open all year Mon-Sat 10-5, Sun 2-5. Closed Xmas & New Year
Facilities: ℗ (500yds) ☕ & (ramp, lift) toilets for disabled shop
⊗ (ex guide dogs)

Aberdeen Maritime Museum   `FREE`

Shiprow AB11 5BY
➲ *(located in city centre)*
☎ 01224 337700
e-mail: info@aagm.co.uk
web: www.aagm.co.uk

The museum is in Provost Ross's House, Aberdeen's oldest building (1593). It highlights the city's maritime history, its oil industry, and its shipbuilding.

continued

Times: ✳ Open all year Mon-Sat 10-5, Sun 12-3. Closed Xmas & New Year.
Facilities: ℗ (250yds) ☕ ⑩ licensed ⏰ & (ramps, lifts) toilets for disabled shop ⊗ ◤

Cruickshank Botanic Garden   `FREE`

University of Aberdeen, St Machar Dr AB24 3UU
➲ *(enter by gate in Chanonry, in Old Aberdeen)*
☎ 01224 272704
e-mail: pss@abdn.ac.uk
web: http://www.abdn.ac.uk/pss/cruickshank

Developed at the end of the 19th century, the 11 acres include rock and water gardens, a rose garden, a fine herbaceous border, an arboretum and a patio garden. There are collections of spring bulbs, gentians and alpine plants, and a fine array of trees and shrubs.

Times: Open all year, Mon-Fri 9-4.30; also Sat & Sun, May-Sep 2-5.
Facilities: ℗ (200mtrs) ⏰ & ⊗

The Gordon Highlanders Museum

St Luke's, Viewfield Rd AB15 7XH
☎ 01224 311200
e-mail: museum@gordonhighlanders.com
web: www.gordonhighlanders.com

Presenting a large collection of artefacts, paintings, films and reconstructions, the Gordon Highlanders Museum is the perfect day out for anyone interested in British military history. The exhibition includes interactive maps, original film footage, scaled reproductions, life-size models, touch screens, uniforms, medals and more. The grounds also contain a tea-room, shop, the home and paintings of Scottish artist, Sir George Reid, and gardens.

Times: Open Apr-Oct, Tue-Sat 10.30-4.30, Sun 12.30-4.30. (Closed Mon). Open by appointment only at other times. **Fee:** ✳ £3.50 (ch £1.50, concessions £2.50). **Facilities:** ❷ ☕ ⏰ & (low level cases, hearing loop) toilets for disabled shop ⊗ (ex guide dogs) ◤

Provost Skene's House   `FREE`

Guestrow, off Broad St AB10 1AS
☎ 01224 641086
e-mail: info@aagm.co.uk
web: www.aagm.co.uk

Experience the epitome of style and elegance in this 16th-century townhouse, furnished and decorated in the styles of earlier times. See

continued

changing fashions in the Costume Gallery and view an important cycle of religious paintings in the gallery.

Times: ✱ Open all year Mon-Sat 10-5, Sun 1-4. Closed Xmas & New Year. Telephone for details. **Facilities:** Ⓟ (200yds) 🍽 ⊗ (ex guide dogs)

Satrosphere Science Centre

179 Constitution St AB24 5TU

➲ *(located very close to Beach Esplanade. Follow signs to fun beach, then attraction)*

☎ 01224 640340

e-mail: info@satrosphere.net

web: www.satrosphere.net

Satrosphere, the Discovery Place, is different from many museums or exhibition centres. It is an Interactive Centre where everything is 'hands-on'. Visitors can learn through discovery and exploration, from more than fifty exhibits which will challenge and amaze. There are also special weekend events that combine fun-packed experiments, live shows and spectacular demonstrations that bring science alive. Things are always changing, so every visit is different.

Times: Open daily, 10-5. Closed 25-26 Dec and 1-2 Jan. **Fee:** ✱ £5.75 (under 3's free, ch & concessions £4.50). **Facilities:** Ⓟ 🍽 & toilets for disabled shop ⊗ (ex guide dogs) 🍴

PETERCULTER   **MAP 15 NJ80**

Drum Castle

AB31 5EY

➲ *(3m W, off A93)*

☎ 01330 811204

e-mail: drum@nts.org.uk

web: www.nts.org.uk

The great 13th-century Square Tower is one of the three oldest tower houses in Scotland and has associations with Robert the Bruce. The handsome mansion, added in 1619, houses a collection of family memorabilia. The grounds contain the 100-acre Old Wood of Drum, a natural oak wood and an old rose garden.

Times: ✱ Open Apr-May & Sep, daily 12.30-5.30, Jun-Aug, daily 10-5.30. Grounds all year, daily 9.30-sunset. Times may change for 2007 please telephone or check website **Facilities:** Ⓟ 🍽 & (wheelchair available) shop ⊗ (ex guide dogs) 🍴

ABERDEENSHIRE

ALFORD   **MAP 15 NJ51**

Alford Valley Railway

AB33 8AD

➲ *(A944 Alford Village)*

☎ 019755 62326 & 62811

Narrow-gauge passenger railway between Alford and Haughton Park, approx one mile. Diesel traction. Exhibitions.

Times: Open Apr, May & Sep wknds 1-5, Jun-Aug daily from 1 (30 min service). Party bookings also available at other times. **Fee:** £2.50 (ch £1) return fare. **Facilities:** Ⓟ 🍴 & (ramps at station platforms) toilets for disabled shop

Craigievar Castle

AB33 8JF

➲ *(on A980, 6m S of Alford)*

☎ 013398 83635

e-mail: craigievarcastle@nts.org.uk

web: www.nts.org.uk

A fairytale like castle, the Great Tower completed in 1626. The collection includes family portraits and 17th and 18th century furniture.

Times: ✱ Open Apr-Sep, Fri-Tue 12-5.30. Guided tours only. Grounds all year, daily 9.30-sunset. Times may change for 2007 please telephone or check website **Facilities:** 🍴

BALMORAL   **MAP 15 NO29**

Balmoral Castle Grounds & Exhibition

AB35 5TB

➲ *(on A93 between Ballater & Braemar)*

☎ 013397 42534

e-mail: info@balmoralcastle.com

web: www.balmoralcastle.com

Queen Victoria and Prince Albert first rented Balmoral Castle in 1848, and Prince Albert bought the property four years later. He commissioned William Smith to build a new castle, which was completed by 1856 and is still the Royal Family's Highland residence. Country walks and pony trekking can be enjoyed, and an exhibition of paintings and other works of art can be seen in the castle ballroom, together with a Travel and Carriage exhibition and a wildlife exhibition.

Times: ✱ Open Apr-Jul, daily 10-5. **Facilities:** Ⓟ (100yds) 🍽 🖼 & (wheelchairs & battricars available, reserved parking) toilets for disabled shop ⊗ (ex guide dogs/in grounds) 🍴

BANCHORY   **MAP 15 NO69**

Banchory Museum   `FREE`

Bridge St AB31 5SX

➲ *(in Bridge St beside tourist information centre)*

☎ 01771 622807

e-mail: heritage@aberdeenshire.gov.uk

The museum has displays on Scott Skinner (The 'Strathspey King'), natural history, royal commemorative china, local silver artefacts and a variety of local history displays.

Times: Open May, Jun & Sep, Oct, Mon, Fri, Sat 11-1 & 2-4; Jul-Aug, Mon-Wed, Fri-Sat, 11-1, 2-4. **Facilities:** Ⓟ (100yds) (limited) & toilets for disabled ⊗ (ex guide dogs)

BANFF   **MAP 15 NJ66**

Banff Museum   `FREE`

High St AB45 1AE

☎ 01771 622807

e-mail: heritage@aberdeenshire.gov.uk

Displays of geology, natural history, local history, Banff silver, arms and armour, and displays relating to James Ferguson (18th-century astronomer) and Thomas Edward (19th-century Banff naturalist).

Times: Open Jun-Sep, Mon-Sat 2-4.30. **Facilities:** Ⓟ (200yds) & ⊗ (ex guide dogs)

Scotland

Duff House

AB45 3SX

⮫ *(0.5m S, access S of town)*

☎ 01261 818181

web: www.historic-scotland.gov.uk

The house was designed by William Adam for William Duff, later Earl of Fife. The main block was roofed in 1739, but the planned wings were never built. Although it is incomplete, the house is still considered one of Britain's finest Georgian baroque buildings. Duff House is a Country House Gallery of the National Galleries of Scotland.

Times: Telephone for details of opening dates and times.
Fee: ✱ Telephone for details of admission charges.
Facilities: ❷ ⑩ ♿ toilets for disabled shop ⊗ ♠

CORGARFF   **MAP 15 NJ20**

Corgarff Castle

AB36 8YL

⮫ *(8m W of Strathdon village)*

☎ 01975 651460

web: www.historic-scotland.gov.uk

The 16th-century tower was besieged in 1571 and is associated with the Jacobite risings of 1715 and 1745. It later became a military barracks. Its last military use was to control the smuggling of whisky between 1827 and 1831.

Times: Open all year, Apr-Sep, daily 9.30-6.30; Oct-Mar, wknds only 9.30-4.30. Closed 25-26 Dec & 1-2 Jan. **Fee:** ✱ £4 (ch £1.60, concessions £3). Please phone or check website for further details. **Facilities:** ❷ shop ♠

CRATHES   **MAP 15 NO79**

Crathes Castle & Garden

AB31 5QJ

⮫ *(On A93, 3m E of Banchory)*

☎ 01330 844525

e-mail: crathes@nts.org.uk

web: www.nts.org.uk

This impressive 16th-century castle with magnificent interiors has royal associations dating from 1323. There is a large walled garden and a notable collection of unusual plants, including yew hedges dating from 1702. The grounds contain six nature trails, one suitable for disabled visitors, and an adventure playground.

Times: ✱ Open: Castle & Visitor Centre: Apr-Sep, daily 10-5.30, Oct daily 10-4.30. To help enjoy your visit & for safety reasons, admission to the castle is by timed ticket (limited numbers: entry may be delayed). Garden & grounds all year, daily 9-sunset. Times may change for 2007 please telephone or check website **Facilities:** ❷ ⑩ licensed ♿ (tape for visually impaired) toilets for disabled shop ⊗ (ex guide dogs) 🐾

HUNTLY   **MAP 15 NJ53**

Brander Museum   FREE

The Square AB54 8AE

⮫ *(in centre of Huntly, sharing building with library, museum on ground floor)*

☎ 01771 622807

e-mail: heritage@aberdeenshire.gov.uk

The museum has displays of local and church history, plus the 19th-century Anderson Bey and the Sudanese campaigns. Exhibits

continued

---

connected with George MacDonald, author and playwright, can also be seen.

Times: Open all year, Tue-Sat 2-4.30. **Facilities:** ⓟ (25yds) ♿ (access difficult due to 3 large steps at entrance) ⊗ (ex guide dogs)

Huntly Castle

AB54 4SH

☎ 01466 793191

web: www.historic-scotland.gov.uk

The original medieval castle was rebuilt a number of times and destroyed, once by Mary, Queen of Scots. It was rebuilt for the last time in 1602, in palatial style, and is now an impressive ruin, noted for its ornate heraldic decorations. It stands in wooded parkland.

Times: Open all year, Apr-Sep, daily 9.30-6.30; Oct-Mar, Mon-Wed & Sat-Sun 9.30-4.30. Closed 25-26 Dec & 1-2 Jan. **Fee:** ✱ £4 (ch £1.60, concessions £3). Please phone or check website for details.
Facilities: ❷ shop ♠

INVERURIE   **MAP 15 NJ72**

Carnegie Museum   FREE

Town House, The Square AB51 3SN

⮫ *(in centre of Inverurie, on left side of townhouse building, above library)*

☎ 01771 622807

e-mail: heritage@aberdeenshire.gov.uk

This fine museum contains displays on local history and archaeology, including Pictish stones, Bronze Age material and the Great North of Scotland Railway.

Times: Open all year, Mon & Wed-Fri 2-4.30, Sat 10-1 & 2-4. Closed Tue & public hols. **Facilities:** ⓟ (50yds) ⊗ (ex guide dogs)

KEMNAY   **MAP 15 NJ71**

Castle Fraser

AB51 7LD

⮫ *(off A944, 4m N of Dunecht)*

☎ 01330 833463

e-mail: castlefraser@nts.org.uk

web: www.nts.org.uk

The massive Z-plan castle was built between 1575 and 1636 and is one of the grandest of the Castles of Mar. The interior was remodelled in 1838 and decoration and furnishings of that period survive in some of the rooms. A formal garden inside the old walled garden, estate trails, a children's play area and a programme of concerts are among the attractions.

Times: ✱ Open Apr-Jun & Sep, Fri-Tue 12-5.30, Jul-Aug, daily 11-5.30. Times may change for 2007 please telephone or check website
Facilities: ❷ 🍴 ♿ shop garden centre ⊗ (ex guide dogs, certain areas) 🐾

KILDRUMMY   **MAP 15 NJ41**

Kildrummy Castle

AB54 7XT

⮫ *(10m SW of Alford)*

☎ 01975 571331

web: www.historic-scotland.gov.uk

An important part of Scottish history, at least until it was dismantled in 1717, this fortress was the seat of the Earls of Mar. Now it is a ruined,

continued

but splendid, example of a 13th-century castle, with four round towers, hall and chapel all discernible. Some parts of the building, including the Great Gatehouse, are from the 15th and 16th centuries.

Times: Open Apr-Sep, daily 9.30-6.30. **Fee:** ✱ £3 (ch £1.30, concessions £2.30). Please phone or check website for further details. **Facilities:** ℗ ✓ toilets for disabled shop ▮

Kildrummy Castle Gardens

AB33 8RA

➲ *(on A97 off A944. 10m W of Alford)*

☎ 019755 71277 & 71203

e-mail: information@kildrummy-castle-gardens.co.uk
web: www.kildrummy-castle-gardens.co.uk

With the picturesque ruin as a backdrop, these beautiful gardens include an alpine garden in an ancient quarry and a water garden. There's a small museum and a children's play area.

Times: ✱ Open Apr-Oct, daily 10-5. **Facilities:** ℗ ✓ toilets for disabled shop garden centre

---

MACDUFF   MAP 15 NJ76

Macduff Marine Aquarium

11 High Shore AB44 1SL

➲ *(off A947 and A98 to Macduff, aquarium signed)*

☎ 01261 833369

e-mail: macduff.aquarium@aberdeenshire.gov.uk
web: www.macduff-aquarium.org.uk

Exciting displays feature local sealife. The central exhibit, unique in Britain, holds a living kelp reef. Divers feed the fish in this tank. Other displays include an estuary exhibit, splash tank, rock pools, deep reef tank and ray pool. Young visitors especially enjoy the touch pools. There are talks, video presentations and feeding shows throughout the week.

Times: Open 10-5 daily (last admission 4.15). Closed 25-26 Dec & 31 Dec-2 Jan **Fee:** ✱ £5 (ch £2.50, concessions £3). Family ticket (2ad+2ch) £13.75. Groups 10+ **Facilities:** ℗ 🎧 ✓ (audio tour for visually impaired) toilets for disabled shop ⊗ (ex guide dogs) 🍴

MARYCULTER   MAP 15 NO89

Storybook Glen

AB12 5FT

➲ *(5m W of Aberdeen on B9077)*

☎ 01224 732941

web: www.storybookglenaberdeen.co.uk

This is a child's fantasy land, where favourite nursery rhyme and fairytale characters are brought to life. Grown-ups can enjoy the nostalgia and also the 20 acres of Deeside country, full of flowers, plants, trees and waterfalls.

Times: Open Mar-Oct, daily 10-6; Nov-Feb, daily 10-4. **Fee:** ✱ £4.85 (ch £3.50, pen £3.60). **Facilities:** ℗ 🍴 🍴 licensed ✓ toilets for disabled shop garden centre ⊗ (ex guide dogs) 🍴

METHLICK   MAP 15 NJ83

Haddo House

AB41 7EQ

➲ *(off B999, 4m N of Pitmedden)*

☎ 01651 851440

e-mail: haddo@nts.org.uk
web: www.nts.org.uk

Haddo House is renowned for its association with the Haddo Choral Society and is the venue for international concerts. It is a splendid Palladian-style mansion built in the 1730s to designs by William Adam. Home to the Earls of Aberdeen, the house was refurbished in the 1880s in the 'Adam Revival' style. The adjoining country park offers beautiful woodland walks.

Times: ✱ Open, House: Jun, Fri-Mon 11-4.30; Jul-Aug, daily 11-4.30. Guided tours only, departing set times. Garden open all year, daily 9.30-6. Times may change for 2007 please telephone or check website **Facilities:** ℗ 🍴 ✓ (lift to first floor of house & wheelchair) toilets for disabled shop ⊗ (ex in grounds & guide dogs) 🍴

MINTLAW   MAP 15 NJ94

Aberdeenshire Farming Museum

Aden Country Park AB42 5FQ

➲ *(1m W of Mintlaw on A950)*

☎ 01771 622807

e-mail: heritage@aberdeenshire.gov.uk
web: www.aberdeenshire.gov.uk/heritage

Housed in 19th-century farm buildings, once part of the estate which now makes up the Aden Country Park. Two centuries of farming history and innovation are illustrated, and the story of the estate is also told. The reconstructed farm of Hareshowe shows how a family in the north-east farmed during the 1950s - access by guided tour only.

Times: Open May-Sep, daily 11-4.30; Apr & Oct, wknds only noon-4.30. (Last admission 30 mins before closing). Park open all year, Apr-Sep 7-10, winter 7-7. **Facilities:** ℗ (charged) 🍴 ✓ (sensory garden) toilets for disabled ⊗ (ex guide dogs)

OLD DEER   MAP 15 NJ94

Deer Abbey   FREE

➲ *(2m W of Mintlaw on A950)*

☎ 01466 793191

web: www.historic-scotland.gov.uk

The remains of the Cistercian Abbey, founded in 1218, include the infirmary, Abbot's House and the southern claustral range. The University Library at Cambridge now houses the famous Book of Deer.

Times: Open at all reasonable times. **Facilities:** ℗ ⊗ ▮

OYNE   MAP 15 NJ62

Archaeolink

Berryhill AB52 6QP

➲ *(1m off A96 on B9002)*

☎ 01464 851500

e-mail: info@archaeolink.co.uk
web: www.archaeolink.co.uk

A stunning audio-visual show, a Myths and Legends Gallery and a whole range of interpretation techniques help visitors to explore what it was like to live 6000 years ago. In addition there are landscaped
continued

walkways, and outdoor activity areas including an Iron Age farm, Roman marching camp and Stone Age settlement in the 40-acre park. Enjoy daily hands-on activities for all ages, guided tours with costumed guides or relax in the coffee shop. Special weekend events held regularly.

Times: ✱ Open all year daily, Apr-Oct 10-5, Nov-Mar 11-4.
Facilities: ☉ ⬛ ⃠ licensed ⬛ ᕒ (induction loop in theatre, wheelchair) toilets for disabled shop ⊗ (ex guide dogs) ⬛

PETERHEAD   MAP 15 NK14

Arbuthnot Museum & Art Gallery   FREE

St Peter St AB42 1QD

➲ *(at St.Peter St & Queen St x-roads, above library)*

☎ 01771 622807

e-mail: heritage@aberdeenshire.gov.uk

Specialising in local exhibits, particularly those relating to the fishing industry, this museum also displays Arctic and whaling specimens and a British coin collection. The regular programme of exhibitions changes approximately every six weeks.

Times: Open all year, Mon, Tue & Thu-Sat 11-1 & 2-4.30, Wed 11-1. Closed Sun and BHs. **Facilities:** Ⓟ (150 yds) ⊗ (ex guide dogs)

PITMEDDEN   MAP 15 NJ82

Pitmedden Garden

AB41 7PD

➲ *(1m W of Pitmedden on A920)*

☎ 01651 842352

e-mail: aclipson@nts.scot.demon.co.uk

web: www.nts.org.uk

The fine 17th-century walled garden, with sundials, pavilions and fountains dotted among the parterres, has been authentically restored, and there is a Museum of Farming Life and a woodland walk.

Times: ✱ Open May-Sep, daily 10-5.30. Grounds: all year, daily. Times may change for 2007 please telephone or check website **Facilities:** ☉ ⬛ ᕒ (2 wheelchairs available) toilets for disabled shop ⌚

Tolquhon Castle

AB41 7LP

➲ *(2m NE off B999)*

☎ 01651 851286

web: www.historic-scotland.gov.uk

Now roofless, this late 16th-century quadrangular mansion encloses an early 15th-century tower. There is a fine gatehouse and a splendid courtyard.

Times: Open all year, Apr-Sep, daily 9.30-6.30; Oct-Mar, wknds only 9.30-6.30. Closed 25-26 Dec & 1-2 Jan. **Fee:** ✱ £3 (ch £1.30, concessions £2.30). Please phone or check website for further details.
Facilities: ☉ ᕒ toilets for disabled shop ⊗ ⃠

RHYNIE   MAP 15 NJ42

Leith Hall & Garden

Kennethmont AB54 4NQ

➲ *(on B9002, 1m W of Kennethmont)*

☎ 01464 831216

e-mail: leithhall@nts.org.uk

web: www.nts.org.uk

Home of the Leith family for over 300 years, the house dates back to 1650, and has a number of Jacobite relics and fine examples of needlework. It is surrounded by charming gardens and extensive grounds.

Times: ✱ Open House: Good Fri-Etr Mon, daily 12-5; May-Sep, Fri-Tue 12-5. Garden & grounds all year, daily 9.30-sunset. Times may change for 2007 please telephone or check website **Facilities:** ☉ ⬛ ᕒ (parking next to hall, scented garden for the blind) toilets for disabled ⊗ (ex guide dogs) ⌚

STONEHAVEN   MAP 15 NO88

Dunnottar Castle

AB39 2TL

➲ *(2m S of Stonehaven on A92)*

☎ 01569 762173

This once-impregnable fortress, now a spectacular ruin, was the site of the successful protection of the Scottish Crown Jewels from the might of Cromwell. A must for anyone who takes Scottish history seriously.

Times: Open all year, summer Mon-Sat 9-6, Sun 2-5; winter open Fri-Mon only. (Last entry 30mins before closing). Closed 25-26 Dec & New Year.
Fee: ✱ £4 (ch 5-15 £1) **Facilities:** ☉ ⬛ ⊗ (ex on a lead)

Tolbooth Museum   FREE

Old Pier AB39 2JU

➲ *(on harbour front)*

☎ 01771 622807

e-mail: heritage@aberdeenshire.gov.uk

Built in the late 16th century as a storehouse for the Earls Marischal at Dunnottar Castle, the building was the Kincardineshire County Tollbooth from 1600-1767. Displays feature local history and fishing.

Times: Open May-16 Oct, Wed-Mon, 1.30-4.30. Closed Tue.
Facilities: Ⓟ (20yds) ᕒ ⊗ (ex guide dogs)

TURRIFF   MAP 15 NJ75

Fyvie Castle

Fyvie AB53 8JS

➲ *(8m SE of Turriff on A947)*

☎ 01651 891266

e-mail: aclipson@nts.scot.demon.co.uk

web: www.nts.org.uk

This superb castle, founded in the 13th century, has five towers, each built in a different century, and is one of the grandest examples of Scottish Baronial. It contains the finest wheel stair in Scotland, and a 17th-century morning room, lavishly furnished in Edwardian style. The collection of portraits is exceptional, and there are also displays of arms and armour and tapestries.

Times: ✱ Open Apr-Jun & Sep, Fri-Tue 12-5; Jul-Aug, daily 11-5. Grounds all year, daily, 9.30-sunset. Times may change for 2007 please telephone or check website **Facilities:** ☉ ⬛ ᕒ (small lift, Braille sheets) toilets for disabled shop ⊗ (ex guide dogs) ⌚

ANGUS

ARBROATH
MAP 12 NO64

Arbroath Abbey
DD11 1EG
☎ 01241 878756
web: www.historic-scotland.gov.uk

The 'Declaration of Arbroath' - declaring Robert the Bruce as king - was signed at the 12th-century abbey on 6 April 1320. The abbot's house is well preserved, and the church remains are also interesting.

Times: Open all year, Apr-Sep, daily 9.30-6.30; Oct-Mar, daily 9.30-4.30. Closed 25-26 Dec & 1-2 Jan. **Fee:** ✱ £4 (ch £1.60, concessions £3). Please phone for further details or or alternatively check website
Facilities: ❷ & ⊗ 戸

Arbroath Museum   FREE
Signal Tower, Ladyloan DD11 1PU
➲ (on A92 adjacent to harbour. 16m NE of Dundee)
☎ 01241 875598
e-mail: signal.tower@angus.gov.uk
web: www.angus.gov.uk/history/museums

Fish and Arbroath Smokies, textiles and engineering feature at this local history museum housed in the 1813 shore station of Stevenson's Bell Rock lighthouse. 2007 is the 200th anniversary of the commencement of building of Bell Rock lighthouse.

Times: ✱ Open all year, Mon-Sat 10-5; Jul-Aug, Sun 2-5. Closed 25-26 Dec & 1-2 Jan. **Facilities:** ❷ 戸 & (induction loop) shop ⊗ (ex guide dogs)

BRECHIN
MAP 15 NO66

Brechin Town House Museum   FREE
28 High St DD9 7AA
➲ (off A90 at sign for Brechin, 2m into town centre)
☎ 01356 625536
e-mail: brechin.museum@angus.gov.uk
web: www.angus.gov.uk/history/museum

Within a former courtroom, debtor's prison and seat of local government, this museum covers the history of the little City of Brechin from the earliest settlement, through the market town to the industrialisation in the form of flax, jute mills, distilling, weaving and engineering. Brechin's fascinating history of development is portrayed in vivid displays.

Times: ✱ Open Mon-Tue & Thu-Sat 10-5, Wed 10-1
Facilities: ℗ (150yds) (2hrs max in free car park) 戸 & toilets for disabled shop ⊗ (ex guide dogs)

Pictavia Visitor Centre
Brechin Castle Centre, Haughmuir DD9 6RL
➲ (off A90 at Brechin)
☎ 01356 626241
e-mail: ecdev@angus.gov.uk
web: www.pictavia.org.uk

Find about more about the ancient pagan nation of the Picts, who lived in Scotland nearly 2000 years ago. Visitors can learn about Pictish

continued

culture, art and religion through film, interactive displays and music. There are also nature and farm trails, a pets' corner, and an adventure playground.

Times: Open daily, Etr-mid Oct, Mon-Sat 9.30-5.30, Sun 10.30-5.30; mid Oct-Etr, Mon-Sat 9.30-5, Sun 10-5. Closed 25-26 Dec & 1-2 Jan
Fee: ✱ £3.25 (ch & concessions £2.25) **Facilities:** ❷ ♨ ⏹ licensed 戸 & toilets for disabled shop garden centre ⊗ (ex assist dogs) ◀

CARNOUSTIE
MAP 12 NO53

Barry Water Mill
Barry DD7 7RJ
➲ (N of Barry village between A92 & A930, 2m W of Carnoustie)
☎ 01241 856761
web: www.nts.org.uk

This restored 18th-century mill works on a demonstration basis. Records show that the site has been used for milling since the 16th century. Displays highlight the important place the mill held in the community. There is a waymarked walk and picnic area.

Times: ✱ Open Apr-Oct, Fri-Tue, 12-5. Times may change for 2007 please telephone or check website **Facilities:** ❷ & (ramp from car park to mill) toilets for disabled ♨

EDZELL
MAP 15 NO56

Edzell Castle
DD9 7UE
➲ (on B966)
☎ 01356 648631
web: www.historic-scotland.gov.uk

The 16th-century castle has a remarkable walled garden built in 1604 by Sir David Lindsay. Flower-filled recesses in the walls are alternated with heraldic and symbolic sculptures of a sort not seen elsewhere in Scotland. There are ornamental and border gardens and a garden house.

Times: Open all year, Apr-Sep, daily 9.30-6.30; Oct-Mar, Mon-Wed & Sat-Sun 9.30-4.30. Closed 25-26 Dec & 1-2 Jan. **Fee:** ✱ £4 (ch £1.60, concessions £3). Please phone or check website for further details.
Facilities: ❷ & shop 戸

FORFAR
MAP 15 NO45

The Meffan Art Gallery & Museum   FREE
20 West High St DD8 1BB
➲ (off A90, 13m N of Dundee. Attraction in town centre)
☎ 01307 464123 467017
e-mail: the.meffan@angus.gov.uk
web: www.angus.gov/history/museum

This lively, ever-changing contemporary art gallery and museum are full of surprises. Walk down a cobbled street full of shops, ending up at a witch-burning scene! Carved Pictish stones and a diorama of an archaeological dig complete the vibrant displays.

Times: Open all year. Closed 25-26 Dec & 1-2 Jan. **Facilities:** ℗ (150yds) (30 mins limit on street) 戸 & (handrails, wide door, portable ramp) toilets for disabled shop ⊗ (ex guide dogs) ◀

Scotland

Scotland

GLAMIS   MAP 15 NO34

Angus Folk Museum

Kirkwynd Cottages DD8 1RT

➲ *(off A94, in Glamis)*

☎ 01307 840288

web: www.nts.org.uk

A row of stone-roofed, late 18th-century cottages now houses the splendid Angus Folk Collection of domestic equipment and cottage furniture. Across the wynd, an Angus stone steading houses 'The Life on the Land' exhibition.

Times: ✹ Open Apr-Jun & Sep, Fri-Tue 12-5; Jul & Aug 12-5. Times may change for 2007 please telephone or check website **Facilities:** ❷ ⓹ toilets for disabled ⓧ (ex guide dogs) ⚑

Glamis Castle   2 for 1

DD8 1RJ

➲ *(5m W of Forfar on A94)*

☎ 01307 840393

e-mail: enquires@glamis-castle.co.uk

web: www.glamis-castle.co.uk

Glamis Castle is the family home of the Earls of Strathmore and Kinghorne and has been a royal residence since 1372. It is the childhood home of the late Queen Mother, the birthplace of her daughter the late Princess Margaret and the setting for Shakespeare's play *Macbeth*. Though the Castle is open to visitors it remains the home of the Strathmore family. Each year there are Highland games, a transport extravaganza, the Scottish Prom, and a countryside festival. Contact for exact dates.

Times: Open Mar-Oct, 10-6. Nov-Dec as advertised. (Last admission 4.30). **Fee:** ❹ Castle & grounds £7.30 (ch £4.10, pen & students £6.10). Family ticket £21. Grounds only £3.50 (ch, pen & students £2.50). Group 20+ **Facilities:** ❷ ⓣⓞⓘ licensed ▩ ⓹ (castle tour not suitable due to stairs) toilets for disabled shop ⓧ (ex in grounds, guide dogs) ◀

KIRRIEMUIR   MAP 15 NO35

J M Barrie's Birthplace

9 Brechin Rd DD8 4BX

➲ *(on A90/A926, 6m NW of Forfar)*

☎ 01575 572646

e-mail: aclipson@nts.scot.demon.co.uk

web: ww.nts.org.uk

The creator of Peter Pan, Sir James Barrie, was born in Kirriemuir in 1860. The upper floors of No 9 Brechin Road are furnished as they may have been when Barrie lived there, and the adjacent house, No 11, houses an exhibition about him. The wash-house outside was his first 'theatre' and gave him the idea for Wendy's house in *Peter Pan*.

Times: ✹ Open Apr-Jun & Sep, Fri-Tue 12-5; Jul-Aug, daily 12-5. Times may change for 2007 please telephone or check website **Facilities:** ⓟ (100yds) ▱ ⓹ (stairlift, audio programmes) shop ⓧ (ex guide dogs) ⚑

Kirriemuir Gateway to Glens Museum

The Town House, 32 High St DD8 4BB

➲ *(in town centre square, 30mins from Dundee, N on A90)*

☎ 01575 575479

e-mail: kirrie.gateway@angus.gov.uk

web: www.angus.gov.uk/history/museum

Housed in the town house dating from 1604, this museum covers the history of Kirriemuir and the Angus Glens from prehistoric times. A realistic model of Kirriemuir on market day in 1604 can be seen and local voices can be heard telling their part in the area's history from sweet making to linen weaving. Animals and birds can be seen at close range in the Wildlife diorama.

Times: Open Mon-Wed, Fri & Sat 10-5, Thu 2-5 **Facilities:** ⓟ (200yds) (free car park) ⓹ toilets for disabled shop ⓧ (ex guide dogs)

MONTROSE   MAP 15 NO75

House of Dun

DD10 9LQ

➲ *(on A935, 3m W of Montrose)*

☎ 01674 810264

e-mail: houseofdun@nts.org.uk

web: www.nts.org.uk

This Georgian house, overlooking the Montrose Basin, was built for Lord Dun in 1730 and is noted for the exuberant plasterwork of the interior. Family portraits, fine furniture and porcelain are on display, and royal mementos connected with a daughter of King William IV and the actress Mrs Jordan, who lived here in the 19th century. There is a walled garden and woodland walks.

Times: ✹ Open House: Apr-Jun, & Sep, Fri-Tue 12-5, Jul-Aug, daily 12-5. Garden & grounds all year daily 9.30-sunset. Times may change for 2007 please telephone or check website **Facilities:** ❷ ⓣⓞⓘ ⓹ (Braille sheets, house wheelchair & stair lift) toilets for disabled shop ⓧ (ex guide dogs) ⚑

Montrose Museum & Art Gallery

Panmure Place DD10 8HE

➲ *(opposite Montrose Academy in town centre, approach via A92 from Aberdeen or Dundee)*

☎ 01674 673232

e-mail: montrose.museum@angus.gov.uk

web: www.angus.gov.uk/history/museum

Extensive local collections cover the history of Montrose from prehistoric times, the maritime history of the port, the natural history of Angus, and local art.

Times: Open all year, Mon-Sat 10-5. Closed 25-26 Dec & 1-2 Jan. **Facilities:** ⓟ 20yds ▩ ⓹ shop ⓧ (ex guide dogs)

ARGYLL & BUTE

ARDUAINE   MAP 10 NM71

Arduaine Garden

PA34 4XQ

➲ (20m S of Oban, on A816)

☎ 01852 200366

web: www.nts.org.uk

An outstanding 18-acre garden on a promontory bounded by Loch Melfort and the Sound of Jura, climatically favoured by the North Atlantic Drift. It is famous for its rhododendrons and azalea species and other rare trees and shrubs.

Times: ✱ Open all year, daily 9.30-sunset. Reception Apr-Sep 9.30-4.30. Times may change for 2007 please telephone or check website **Facilities:** 🅿 ⅙ toilets for disabled ⊗ (ex guide dogs) ⅋

ARROCHAR   MAP 10 NN20

Argyll Forest Park   `FREE`

Forestry Commission, Ardgartan Visitor Centre

G83 7AR

➲ (on A83 at foot of "The Rest and Be Thankful")

☎ 01301 702597

e-mail: robin.kennedy@forestry.gsl.gov.uk

This park extends over a large area of hill ground and forest, noted for its rugged beauty. Numerous forest walks and picnic sites allow exploration; the Arboretum walks and the route between Younger Botanic Gardens and Puck's Glen are particularly lovely.

Times: Open all year. **Facilities:** 🅿 📕 shop ◀

AUCHINDRAIN   MAP 10 NN00

Auchindrain Museum   `2 for 1`

PA32 8XN

➲ (6m SW of Inverarary on A83)

☎ 01499 500235

e-mail: manager@auchindrain-museum.org.uk

web: www.auchindrain-museum.org.uk

Auchindrain is an unusual attraction that brings an original Township or farming village back to life. On entering the Museum visitors step back in time to witness how the local community lived, worked and played. The original Township buildings are furnished and give a fascinating glimpse into the lives of the people who once lived and worked at Auchindrain.

Times: Open Apr-Oct, daily 10-5. **Fee:** ✱ £4.50 (ch £2.20, pen £3.50). Family ticket £12. **Facilities:** 🅿 💷 📕 shop

BARCALDINE   MAP 10 NM94

Scottish Sea Life Sanctuary

PA37 1SE

➲ (10m N of Oban on A828 towards Fort William)

☎ 01631 720386

e-mail: obansealife@merlinentertainments.biz

web: www.sealsanctuary.co.uk

Set in one of Scotland's most picturesque locations, the Scottish Sea Life Sanctuary provides dramatic views of native undersea life

continued

---

including stingrays, seals, octopus and catfish. There are daily talks and feeding demonstrations and during the summer young seals can be viewed prior to their release back into the wild. Recent additions include Otter Creek - a large naturally landscaped enclosure with deep diving pool with underwater viewing and cascading streams through other pools and 'Into the Deep', a themed interactive area displaying living creatures from the deep. There is a restaurant, gift shop, children's play park and a nature trail.

Times: Open all year, mid Feb-Nov, daily 10-5. Dec & Jan; Sat-Sun & school hols only **Facilities:** 🅿 💷 🍴 📕 ⅙ (assistance available for wheelchairs) toilets for disabled shop ⊗ (ex guide dogs) ◀

BENMORE   MAP 10 NS18

Benmore Botanic Garden

PA23 8QU

➲ (7m N of Dunoon on A815)

☎ 01369 706261

e-mail: benmore@rbge.org.uk

web: www.rbge.org.uk

From the formal gardens, through the hillside woodlands, follow the paths to a stunning viewpoint with a spectacular outlook across the garden and the Holy Loch to the Firth of Clyde and beyond. Amongst many highlights are the stately conifers, the magnificent avenue of giant redwoods, and an extensive magnolia and rhododendron collection.

Times: Open Mar & Oct daily 10-5, Apr-Sep daily 10-6 **Fee:** ✱ £3.50 (ch £1, concessions £3). Family £8. Party rates. **Facilities:** 🅿 💷 🍴 licensed 📕 ⅙ toilets for disabled shop garden centre ⊗ (ex guide dogs) ◀

CARNASSERIE CASTLE   MAP 10 NM80

Carnasserie Castle   `FREE`

PA31 8RQ

➲ (2m N of Kilmartin off A816)

web: www.historic-scotland.gov.uk

A handsome combined tower house and hall, home of John Carswell, first Protestant Bishop of the Isles and translator of the first book printed in Gaelic. Very fine architectural details of the late 16th century.

Times: Open at all reasonable times. **Facilities:** ⊗ 🚩

HELENSBURGH   MAP 10 NS28

The Hill House

Upper Colquhoun St G84 9AJ

➲ (off B832, between A82 & A814)

☎ 01436 673900

web: www.nts.org.uk

The Hill House is a handsome example of Charles Rennie Mackintosh's work, modern but part-inspired by Scottish tower houses. It was commissioned by the publisher Walter Blackie. The gardens are being restored to Blackie's design, with features reflecting the suggestions of Mackintosh. There is also a special display about Mackintosh.

Times: ✱ Open Apr-Oct, daily 1.30-5.30. Morning visits available for pre-booked groups. Times may change for 2007 please telephone or check website **Facilities:** 🅿 💷 shop ⊗ ⅋

Scotland

Scotland

INVERARAY

MAP 10 NN00

Bell Tower of All Saints' Church

The Avenue PA32 8YX

➲ (through the arches on Front St, into Avenue car park)

☎ 01838 200293

e-mail: dean.sedati@virgin.net

The tower stands next to All-Saints Church but is separate from it. Built by the 10th Duke of Argyll as a war memorial to the dead of Clan Campbell, it was completed in 1931. It has the second heaviest peal of bells in the world, and these are rung once a month. The tower is 126 feet high and has a narrow circular staircase of 176 steps, which are not suitable for the infirm. From the top is a spectacular view of Inveraray, Loch Fyne and the surrounding hills.

Times: Tower open daily, 10-1, 2-5, May-Sept. Church open, Mar-Oct. **Fee: ✱** £2 (ch & pen 75p). Family ticket £4 **Facilities:** Ⓟ (adjacent to church) (pay and display) ♿ (Unsuitable as 176 step stone spiral staircase) ⊗ (ex guide dogs)

Inveraray Castle

`2 for 1`

PA32 8XE

➲ (on A83 Glasgow to Campbeltown road)

☎ 01499 302203

e-mail: enquiries@inveraray-castle.com

web: www.inveraray-castle.com

The Castle is currently home to the Duke of Argyll, Head of the Clan Campbell, whose family have lived in Inveraray since the 15th century. Designed by Roger Morris and decorated by Robert Mylne, the fairytale exterior belies the grandeur of the gracious interior. The Armoury Hall contains some 1300 pieces including Brown Bess muskets, Lochaber axes, 18th-century Scottish broadswords, and swords from the Battle of Culloden. Other rooms contain fine French tapestries, Scottish, English and French furniture, and a wealth of other works of art. There is also a unique collection of china, silver and family artefacts.

Times: Open 1st Sat in Apr-last Sun in Oct. Mon-Sat 10-5.45, Sun 1-5.45. **Fee:** £6.30 (ch under 16 £4.10, concessions £5.20) Family ticket £17. School parties. Groups 20+. 20% discount. School parties £2.10 per child. **Facilities:** ❷ ➠ 🃏 ♿ toilets for disabled shop ⊗ (ex guide dogs and in grounds) ➡

Inveraray Jail

Church Square PA32 8TX

➲ (on A82/A83 Campbeltown road)

☎ 01499 302381

e-mail: Info@Inverarayjail.co.uk

web: www.inverarayjail.co.uk

Enter Inveraray Jail and step back in time. See furnished cells and experience prison sounds and smells. Ask the 'prisoner' how to pick oakum. Turn the heavy handle of an original crank machine, take 40 winks in a hammock or listen to Matron's tales of day-to-day prison life. Visit the magnificent 1820 courtroom and hear trials in progress. Imaginative exhibitions including 'Torture, Death and Damnation' and 'In Prison Today'. Also a fully preserved "Black Maria", built in 1891.

Times: Open all year, Nov-Mar, daily 10-5 (last admisssion 4); Apr-Oct, daily 9.30-6 (last admission 5). Closed 25-26 Dec & 1-2 Jan. **Fee: ✱** £6.25 (ch £3.15, pen £4.15). Family ticket £17.20. **Facilities:** Ⓟ (100 yds) 🃏 ♿ (wheelchair ramp at rear, induction loop in courtroom) toilets for disabled shop ⊗ (ex on leads) ➡

KILMARTIN

MAP 10 NR89

Dunadd Fort

`FREE`

➲ (2m S of Kilmartin on A816)

web: www.historic-scotland.gov.uk

Dunadd was one of the ancient capitals of Dalriada from which the Celtic kingdom of Scotland was formed. Near to this prehistoric hill fort (now little more than an isolated hillock) are carvings of a boar and a footprint; these probably marked the spot where early kings were invested with their royal power.

Times: Open at all reasonable times. **Facilities:** ⊗ 🪧

Kilmartin House Museum

PA31 8RQ

➲ (in centre of village, adjacent to church)

☎ 01546 510278

e-mail: museum@kilmartin.org

web: www.kilmartin.org

Kilmartin may seem to be a quiet Scottish village, but at least 150 prehistoric sites lie within six miles of it. There are mysterious carved rocks, enigmatic standing stones, fascinating burial cairns and the fortress of the earliest Scottish Kings. Thousands of years of history are traced in a museum that explores ancient peoples' struggles for survival, their attempts to understand the world around them, early agriculture, and social strife in the shape of aggression and conflict. There is also an audio-visual extravaganza that uses 12 projectors to project 600 slides in 16 minutes. The presentation deals with the history and beauty of the landscape of Mid Argyll.

Times: Open Mar-Oct, daily, 10-5.30. Reduced days/hours Nov-Feb. **Facilities:** ❷ ➠ 🍴 licensed ♿ toilets for disabled shop ⊗ (ex guide dogs) 🚌(ex small coaches, pre-booked) ➡

LOCHAWE

MAP 10 NN12

Cruachan Power Station

Visitor Centre, Dalmally PA33 1AN

➲ (A85 18m E of Oban)

☎ 01866 822618

e-mail: visit.cruachan@scottishpower.com

web: www.visitcruachan.co.uk

A vast cavern hidden 1km inside Ben Cruachan, which contains a 400,000-kilowatt hydro-electric power station, driven by water drawn from a high-level reservoir up the mountain. A guided tour takes you inside the mountain and reveals the generators in their underground cavern.

Times: Open Etr-Nov, daily 9.30-5 (last tour 4.15). (Winter hours available on request). **Fee: ✱** £5 (ch 6-16 £2, concessions £4.50) **Facilities:** ❷ ➠ ♿ toilets for disabled shop ⊗ (ex guide dogs) ➡

MINARD

MAP 10 NR99

Crarae Gardens

PA32 8YA

➲ (10m S of Inveraray on A83)

☎ 01546 886614

web: www.nts.org.uk

Set beside Loch Fyne, these gardens are among Scotland's loveliest, noted for their rhododendrons, azaleas, conifers and ornamental shrubs, which include a number of rare species.

Times: ✱ Open all year, daily, 9-sunset. Visitor centre, Etr-Oct, daily 10-5. Times may change for 2007 please telephone or check website **Facilities:** ❷ ➠ ♿ toilets for disabled shop garden centre ➡

OBAN   MAP 10 NM83

Dunstaffnage Castle
PA37 1PZ
- *(3m N on peninsula)*
☎ 01631 562465
web: www.historic-scotland.gov.uk

Now ruined, this four-sided stronghold has a gatehouse, two round towers and walls 10ft thick. It was once the prison of Flora MacDonald.

Times: Open all year, Apr-Sep, daily 9.30-6.30; Oct-Mar, Mon-Wed & Sat-Sun daily 9.30-4.30. Closed 25-26 Dec & 1-2 Jan. **Fee:** ✱ £3 (ch £1.30, concessions £2.30). Please phone or check website for further details. **Facilities:** ❷ shop ⌨

TAYNUILT   MAP 10 NN03

Bonawe Iron Furnace
PA35 1JQ
- *(0.75m NE off B845)*
☎ 01866 822432
web: www.historic-scotland.gov.uk

The furnace is a restored charcoal blast-furnace for iron-smelting and making cast-iron. It was established in 1753 and worked until 1876. The works exploited the Forest of Lorne to provide charcoal for fuel.

Times: Open Apr-Sep, daily 9.30-6.30. **Fee:** ✱ £3.50 (ch £1.50, concessions £2.50). Please phone or check website for further details. **Facilities:** ❷ ⌂ toilets for disabled shop ⌨

CITY OF EDINBURGH

BALERNO   MAP 11 NT16

Malleny Garden
EH14 7AF
- *(off A70 Lanark road)*
☎ 0131 449 2283
web: www.nts.org.uk

The delightful gardens are set round a 17th-century house (not open to the public). Shrub roses, a woodland garden, and a group of four clipped yews, survivors of a group planted in 1603, are among its notable features. The National Bonsai Collection for Scotland is also at Malleny.

Times: ✱ Garden: all year daily 10-6 or dusk if earlier. House not open. Times may change for 2007 please telephone or check website **Facilities:** ❷ ⌂ ⊗ (ex guide dogs) ⅋

EDINBURGH   MAP 11 NT27

Brass Rubbing Centre
Trinity Apse, Chalmers Close, High St EH1 1SS
- *(located on the Royal Mile)*
☎ 0131 556 4364
e-mail: admin@museumofchildhood.fsnet.co.uk
web: www.cac.org.uk

Housed in the 15th-century remnant of Trinity Apse, the Centre offers the chance to make your own rubbing from a wide range of replica monumental brasses and Pictish stones. Tuition is available.

Times: Open Apr-Sep, Mon-Sat 10-5 (during Edinburgh Festival Sun 12-5). **Fee:** ✱ Free entry. Charge for brass rubbing. **Facilities:** ℗ (250mtrs) (parking meters, few spaces) shop ⊗ (ex guide dogs)

Camera Obscura & World of Illusions
Castlehill, Royal Mile EH1 2ND
- *(next to Edinburgh Castle)*
☎ 0131 226 3709
e-mail: info@camera-obscura.co.uk

A unique view of Edinburgh - as the lights go down, a brilliant moving image of the surrounding city appears. The scene changes as a guide operates the camera's system of revolving lenses and mirrors.

Times: ✱ Open all year, daily, Apr-Oct 9.30-6; Nov-Mar 10-5. Closed 25 Dec. Open later Jul-Aug, phone for details. **Facilities:** ℗ (300mtrs) shop ⊗ (ex guide dogs) ⌨

City Art Centre
2 Market St EH1 1DE
- *(opposite rear of Waverley Stn)*
☎ 0131 529 3993
e-mail: cac.marketing@edinburgh.gov.uk
web: www.cac.org.uk

The City Art Centre houses the city's permanent fine art collection and stages a constantly changing programme of temporary exhibitions from all parts of the world. It has six floors of display galleries (linked by an escalator). From 30 Nov 2006 to 25 Feb 2007, an exhibition tells the story of Andrew: Scotland's Patron Saint.

Times: Open Mon-Sat 10-5 & Sun 12-5 **Fee:** ✱ Free. Admission charged for some exhibitions. **Facilities:** ℗ (500yds) (single yellow lines) ⌨ ▦ ⌂ (induction loop, lifts, Braille signage, escalator) toilets for disabled shop ⊗ (ex guide dogs) ⌨

Craigmillar Castle
EH16 4SY
- *(2.5m SE, off A68)*
☎ 0131 661 4445
web: www.historic-scotland.gov.uk

Mary, Queen of Scots retreated to this 14th-century stronghold after the murder of Rizzio. The plot to murder Darnley, her second husband, was also hatched here. There are 16th and 17th century apartments.

Times: Open all year, Apr-Sep, daily 9.30-6.30; Oct-Mar, Mon-Wed & Sat-Sun 9.30-4.30. Closed 25-26 Dec & 1-2 Jan. **Fee:** ✱ £3.50 (ch £1.50, concessions £2.50). Please phone or check website for further details. **Facilities:** ❷ ⌂ toilets for disabled shop ⌨

Dean Gallery
73 Belford Rd EH4 3DS
- *(20 min walk from Edinburgh Haymarket stn & Princes St)*
☎ 0131 624 6200
e-mail: enquiries@nationalgalleries.org
web: www.nationalgalleries.org

Opened in March 1999, the Dean Gallery provides a home for the Eduardo Paolozzi gift of sculpture and graphic art, the Gallery of Modern Art's renowned Dada and Surrealist collections, a major library and archive centre, along with temporary exhibition space for modern and contemporary art.

Times: Open all year, daily 10-5. Extended opening during Edinburgh Festival. Closed 25-26 Dec. **Fee:** ✱ Admission to permanent collections free, charge may be made for special exhibitions. **Facilities:** ❷ ⌨ ⌂ (ramps & lift) toilets for disabled shop ⊗ (ex guide dogs) ⌨

Scotland

Dynamic Earth

Holyrood Rd EH8 8AS

➲ *(on edge of Holyrood Park, opposite Palace of Holyrood House)*

☎ 0131 550 7800

e-mail: enquiries@dynamicearth.co.uk

web: www.dynamicearth.co.uk

How the Earth works! Take a walk through Scotland's geological history. Travel back in time to follow the creation of Planet Earth. Be shaken by a volcano, feel the chill of polar ice and get caught in a tropical rainstorm. A new addition is the Journey to the Centre of the Earth. Please visit website for details of events running throughout the year.

Times: Open Apr-Oct daily & Nov-Mar Wed-Sun 10-5, (last entry 3.50); Jul-Aug daily, 10-6, (last entry 4.50). **Fee:** £8.95 (ch £5.45).
Facilities: ❷ (charged) ☕ 🍴 ♿ (audio guides, large print gallery guides) toilets for disabled shop ⊗ (ex guide dogs) ◀

Edinburgh Castle

EH1 2NG

☎ 0131 225 9846

web: www.historic-scotland.gov.uk

This historic stronghold stands on the precipitous crag of Castle Rock. One of the oldest parts is the 11th-century chapel of the saintly Queen Margaret, but most of the present castle evolved later, during its stormy history of sieges and wars, and was altered again in Victorian times. The Scottish crown and other royal regalia are displayed in the Crown Room. Also notable is the Scottish National War Memorial.

Times: Open all year, Apr-Sep daily 9.30-6; Oct-Mar 9.30-5. Closed 25-26 Dec. **Fee:** ✱ £10.30 (ch £4.50, concessions £8.50). Please phone or check website for further details. **Facilities:** ❷ (charged) ☕ 🍴 licensed ♿ (free transport to top of Castle Hill lift) toilets for disabled shop ⊗ 🎌

The Edinburgh Dungeon

2 for 1

31 Market St EH1 1QB

➲ *(close to Waverly Train Station)*

☎ 0131 240 1000 & 240 1002

e-mail: edinburghdungeon@merlinentertainments.biz

web: www.thedungeons.com

From the same team at The London Dungeon, there comes a Scottish "feast of fun with history's horrible bits". A mixture of live actors, rides, shows and special effects take the brave visitor back into a dark past that includes such delights as the Judgement of Sinners, the Plague, Burke & Hare: Bodysnatchers, and Clan Wars, which attempts to recreate the horror of the Glencoe Massacre of 1692. A new attraction is Inferno, which explores the Great Fire of Edinburgh in 1828.

Times: Open all year ex Xmas. Please telephone for times. **Fee:** ✱ £11.95 (ch 5-14 £7.95, concessions £9.95) family £37.75 **Facilities:** ℗ (100mtrs) (metered bays limited to 1-2hrs) 🍴 ♿ toilets for disabled shop ⊗ (ex guide dogs) ◀

Edinburgh Zoo

Murrayfield EH12 6TS

➲ *(3m W of city centre on A8 towards Glasgow)*

☎ 0131 334 9171

e-mail: marketing@rzss.org.uk

web: www.edinburghzoo.org.uk

Scotland's largest wildlife attraction, set in 80 acres of leafy hillside parkland, just ten minutes from the city centre. With over 1,000

animals ranging from the tiny poison arrow frog to massive white rhinos, including many threatened species. See the world's largest penguin pool with underwater viewing, and the Darwin Maze, based on the theme of evolution.

Times: ✱ Open all year, Apr-Sep, daily 9-6; Oct & Mar, daily 9-5; Nov-Feb, daily 9-4.30. **Facilities:** ❷ (charged) ☕ 🍴 licensed 🍴 ♿ (wheelchair loan free, 1 helper free - phone in advance) toilets for disabled shop ⊗ (ex guide dogs) ◀

Georgian House

7 Charlotte Square EH2 4DR

➲ *(2 mins walk W end of Princes St)*

☎ 0131 226 3318

e-mail: thegeorgianhouse@nts.org.uk

web: www.nts.org.uk

The house is part of Robert Adam's splendid north side of Charlotte Square, the epitome of Edinburgh New Town architecture. The lower floors of No 7 have been restored in the style of the early 1800s, when the house was new. There also videos of life in the New Town, and this house in particular.

Times: ✱ Open Apr-Oct, daily 10-5; Mar & Nov-24 Dec daily 11-3. Times may change for 2007 please telephone or check website
Facilities: ℗ (100 yds) (meters, disabled directly outside) ♿ (induction loop, Braille guide) shop ⊗ (ex guide dogs) 🎌

Gladstone's Land

477b Lawnmarket EH1 2NT

➲ *(5 mins walk from Princes St via Mound)*

☎ 0131 226 5856

web: www.nts.org.uk

Built in 1620, this six-storey tenement, once a merchant's house, still has its arcaded front - a rare feature now. Visitors can also see unusual tempera paintings on the walls and ceilings. It is furnished as a typical 17th-century merchant's home, complete with ground-floor shop front and goods of the period.

Times: ✱ Open Apr-Oct, Mon-Sat, 10-5, Sun 2-5. Times may change for 2007 please telephone or check website **Facilities:** ℗ (440yds) (outside for disabled) ♿ (tours for the blind can be arranged) shop ⊗ (ex guide dogs) 🎌

John Knox House

Scottish Story Teller Centre, 43-45 High St EH1 1SR

➲ *(between The Castle and Holyrood House)*

☎ 0131 556 9579

e-mail: reception@scottishstorytellingcentre.com

web: www.scottishstorytellingcentre.co.uk

John Knox the Reformer is said to have died in the house, which was built by the goldsmith to Mary, Queen of Scots. Renovation work has revealed the original floor in the Oak Room, and a magnificent painted ceiling.

Times: Open all year, Mon-Sat 10-6. July-Sep, Sun, 12-6. Closed 25-26 Dec and 1-2 Jan. **Fee:** ✱ £3 (ch £1, under 5's free, concessions £2.50).
Facilities: ℗ (5 min walk) (paying car park) ☕ 🍴 ♿ (transcript of tapes, tours for blind, with notice) toilets for disabled shop ⊗ (ex guide dogs) ◀

continued

Lauriston Castle

Cramond Rd South, Davidson's Mains EH4 5QD

➲ *(NW outskirts of Edinburgh, 1m E of Cramond overlooking the Forth at Silverknowles)*

☎ 0131 336 2060

e-mail: cac.marketing@edinburgh.gov.uk

web: www.cac.org.uk

The castle is a late 16th-century tower house with 19th-century additions but is most notable as a classic example of the Edwardian age. It has a beautifully preserved Edwardian interior and the feel of a country house, and the spacious grounds are very pleasant.

Times: For opening times please contact the steward on 0131 336 2060.
Fee: ✱ For admission prices please contact the steward on 0131 336 2060.
Facilities: ♿ ⭐ toilets for disabled shop ⊗ (ex guide dogs)

Mary King's Close

2 Warriston's Close, High St EH1 1PG

➲ *(off High St, opposite St. Giles Cathedral)*

☎ 08702 430160

e-mail: info@realmarykingsclose.com

web: www.realmarykingsclose.com

Step back in time to walk through a warren of hidden streets, deep beneath The Royal Mile. Meet some of the real characters who used to inhabit these closes and hear tales of extraordinary apparitions as you are guided through dramatic episodes from Edinburgh's hidden past.

Times: Apr-Oct, 10-9 (last tour), Sun-Sat. Nov-Mar, 10-4 (last tour), Sun-Fri, 10-9 (last tour) Sat. Closed 25 Dec. **Fee:** ✱ £8 (ch £6, concessions £7).
Facilities: ♿ ⭐ (hearing loop) toilets for disabled shop ⊗ (ex guide dogs) ◧

Museum of Childhood FREE

42 High Street, Royal Mile, EH1 1TG

➲ *(On the Royal Mile)*

☎ 0131 529 4142

e-mail: admin@museumofchildhood.fsnet.co.uk

web: www.cac.org.uk

One of the first museums of its kind, this was the brainchild of a local councillor and first opened in 1955. It has a wonderful collection of toys, games and other belongings of children through the ages, to delight visitors both old and young. Ring for details of special events.

Times: Open all year, Mon-Sat 10-5, Sun 12-5. **Facilities:** ♿ ⭐ (3 floors only) toilets for disabled shop ⊗ (ex guide dogs)

Museum of Edinburgh FREE

142 Canongate, Royal Mile EH8 8DD

➲ *(on the Royal Mile)*

☎ 0131 529 4143

e-mail: cac.marketing@edinburgh.gov.uk

web: www.cac.org.uk

Housed in one of the best-preserved 16th-century buildings in the Old Town. It was built in 1570 and later became the headquarters of the Incorporation of Hammermen. Now a museum of local history, it has collections of silver, glassware, pottery, and other items such as street signs.

Times: Open all year, Mon-Sat 10-5. Sun in Aug noon-5.
Facilities: ♿ (200yds) (parking meters, limited spaces) ⭐ shop ⊗ (ex guide dogs)

Museum of Scotland FREE

Chambers St EH1 1JF

➲ *(Situated in Chambers Street in the Old Town. A few mins walk from Princes Street and The Royal Mile)*

☎ 0131 247 4422

e-mail: info@nms.ac.uk

web: www.nms.ac.uk

The museum is a striking landmark in Edinburgh's historic Old Town. It houses more than 10,000 of the nation's most precious artefacts, as well as everyday objects which throw light on life in Scotland through the ages. Admission to the Royal Museum which is adjacent to the Museum of Scotland is also free. Telephone for details of special events.

Times: Open all year, Mon-Sun 10-5. Closed 25 Dec. Please telephone for times on 26 Dec and 1 Jan. **Facilities:** ♿ (off street metered parking) ⬛ ⭐ licensed ◫ ⭐ toilets for disabled shop ⊗ (ex assist dogs) ◧

National Gallery of Scotland

The Mound EH2 2EL

➲ *(off Princes St)*

☎ 0131 624 6200

e-mail: enquiries@nationalgalleries.org

web: www.nationalgalleries.org

Occupying a handsome neo-classical building designed by William Playfair, the gallery is home to Scotland's greatest collection of European paintings and sculpture from the Renaissance to Post-

continued

Impressionism. It contains notable collections of works by Old Masters, Impressionists and Scottish artists.

Times: Open all year, daily 10-5, Thu until 7. New Year' Day noon-5. Closed 25-26 Dec. **Fee:** ✱ Free. Admission charged to some major exhibitions. **Facilities:** Ⓟ (150yds) (pay and display) 🍽️ 🍴 licensed 🛗 ♿ (ramps & lift, room A1 not accessible) toilets for disabled shop ⊗ (ex guide dogs) ◀

National War Museum of Scotland

Edinburgh Castle EH1 2NG

➲ *(at Edinburgh Castle, a few minutes walk up the Royal Mile to Castlehill)*

☎ 0131 247 4413

e-mail: info@nms.ac.uk

web: www.nms.ac.uk

Explore the Scottish experience of war and military service over the last 400 years. A chance to experience the poignant stories of the Scots who went to war, through their letters and personal treasures.

Times: Open all year, daily, Apr-Oct, 9.45-5.45; Nov-Mar, daily, 9.45-4.45 Closed 25-26 Dec. **Fee:** ✱ £10.30 (ch £4.50, ch under 5 free, concessions £8.50) NMS members £8.30. **Facilities:** Ⓟ ♿ (courtesy vehicle runs from the Castle ticket kiosk) toilets for disabled shop ⊗ (ex assist dogs)

Nelson Monument

Calton Hill EH7 5AA Calton Hill

➲ *(Overlooking end of city)*

☎ 0131 556 2716

e-mail: cac.marketing@edinburgh.gov.uk

web: www.cac.org.uk

Designed in 1807 the monument dominates the east end of Princes Street. The views are superb, and every day except Sunday the time ball drops at 1pm as the gun at the castle goes off.

Times: Open all year, Apr-Sep, Mon 1-6 & Tue-Sat 10-6; Oct-Mar Mon-Sat 10-3. **Fee:** ✱ £3 **Facilities:** ❷ shop ⊗ (ex guide dogs)

Palace of Holyroodhouse

EH8 8DX

➲ *(at east end of Royal Mile)*

☎ 0131 556 5100

e-mail: bookinginfo@royalcollection.org.uk

web: www.royalcollection.org.uk

The Palace grew from the guest house of the Abbey of the Holyrood, said to have been founded by David I after a miraculous apparition. Mary, Queen of Scots had her court here from 1561 to 1567, and 'Bonnie' Prince Charlie held levees at the Palace during his occupation of Edinburgh. Today the Royal Apartments are used by HM The Queen for state ceremonies and official entertaining, and are finely decorated with works of art from the Royal Collection.

Times: Open daily, Apr-Oct 9.30-6 (last admission 5); Nov-Mar 9.30-4.30 (last admission 3.30). Closed Good Fri, 25-26 Dec and when The Queen is in residence. **Fee:** £8.80 (ch under 17 £4.80, concessions £7.80). Family ticket (2ad+3ch) £22.50. **Facilities:** ❷ (charged) 🍽️ ♿ (first floor by lift, wheelchair available) toilets for disabled shop ⊗ (ex guide dogs) ◀

Parliament House `FREE`

Supreme Courts, 2-11 Parliament Square EH1 1RQ

➲ *(behind St Giles Cathedral on the high street)*

☎ 0131 225 2595

e-mail: emackenzie@scotcourts.gov.uk

web: www.scotcourts.gov.uk

Scotland's independent parliament last sat in 1707, in this 17th-century building hidden behind an 1829 façade, now the seat of the Supreme Law Courts of Scotland. A large stained glass window depicts the inauguration of the Court of Session in 1540.

Times: Open all year, Mon-Fri 10-4. **Facilities:** Ⓟ (400mtrs) (metered parking in high street) 🍽️ 🍴 ♿ (stair lift to restaurant) toilets for disabled ⊗ (ex guide dogs)

The People's Story `FREE`

Canongate Tolbooth, 163 Canongate, Royal Mile EH8 8BN

➲ *(on the Royal Mile)*

☎ 0131 529 4057

e-mail: cac.marketing@edinburgh.gov.uk

web: www.cac.org.uk

The museum, housed in the 16th-century tolbooth, tells the story of the ordinary people of Edinburgh from the late 18th century to the present day. Reconstructions include a prison cell, 1930s pub and 1940s kitchen supported by photographs, displays, sounds and smells.

Times: Open all year Mon-Sat 10-5. Also open Sun in Aug 12-5. **Facilities:** Ⓟ (100yds) (parking meters) ♿ (lift, induction loop in video room, touch facilities) toilets for disabled shop ⊗ (ex guide dogs)

Royal Botanic Garden Edinburgh `FREE`

Inverleith Row EH3 5LR

➲ *(1m N of city centre, off A902)*

☎ 0131 552 7171

e-mail: info@rbge.org.uk

web: www.rbge.org.uk

Established in 1670, on an area the size of a tennis court, the Garden is now over 70 acres of beautifully landscaped grounds. Spectacular features include the Rock Garden and the Chinese Hillside. The amazing glasshouses feature Britain's tallest palm house and the magnificent woodland gardens and arboretum.

Times: Open all year, daily; Apr-Sep, 10-7; Mar & Oct, 10-6; Nov-Feb, 10-4. Closed 25 Dec & 1 Jan. (Facilities close 30 mins before Garden) **Facilities:** Ⓟ (free on street) (restricted at certain times) 🍽️ 🍴 licensed 🛗 ♿ (wheelchairs available at east/west gates) toilets for disabled shop garden centre ⊗ (ex guide dogs) ◀

Royal Museum `FREE`

Chambers St EH1 1JF

➲ *(situated in Chambers Street, in the Old Town, a few mins walk from Princes Street and the Royal Mile)*

☎ 0131 247 4422

e-mail: info@nms.ac.uk

web: www.nms.ac.uk

This magnificent museum houses extensive international collections covering the Decorative Arts, Natural History, Science, Technology and Working Life, and Geology. Temporary exhibitions, films, lectures and

continued

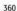

concerts take place throughout the year. March to May 2007: Pixar: 20 Years of Animation.

Royal Museum

Times: Open all year, Mon-Sun 10-5. Closed 25 Dec. Phone for times on 26 Dec/1 Jan. **Facilities:** Ⓟ (on street, metered) 💄 🍴 licensed 🔊 (induction loops) toilets for disabled shop ⊗ (ex assist dogs) ◀

The Royal Yacht Britannia

Ocean Terminal, Leith EH6 6JJ
⤳ *(follow signs to North Edinburgh & Leith. Situated within Ocean Terminal)*
☎ 0131 555 5566
e-mail: enquiries@tryb.co.uk
web: www.royalyachtbritannia.co.uk

Visit the Royal Yacht Britannia, now in Edinburgh's historic port of Leith. The experience starts in the Visitor Centre where you can discover Britannia's fascinating story. Then step aboard for a self-led audio tour which takes you around five decks giving you a unique insight into what life was like for the Royal Family, officers and yachtsmen. Highlights include the State Apartments, Admiral's Cabin, Engine Room, Laundry, Sick Bay and Royal Marine's Barracks.

Times: Open Jan-Mar & Oct-Dec: 10-3.30 (last admission). Apr-Sep 9.30-4.30 (last admission). Closed 25 Dec & 1 Jan. **Fee:** ✱ £9 (ch 5-17 £5, concessions £7). Family ticket (2ad+3ch) £25. **Facilities:** Ⓟ ⅙ (lift to ship, all areas ramped, written scripts) toilets for disabled shop ⊗ (ex guide dogs) ◀

Scotch Whisky Heritage Centre

354 Castlehill, The Royal Mile EH1 2NE
⤳ *(next to Edinburgh Castle)*
☎ 0131 220 0441
e-mail: enquiry@whisky-heritage.co.uk
web: www.whisky-heritage.co.uk

This fascinating heritage centre reveals the history of the Scottish Whisky industry. The tour has four main areas: The Making of Scotch Whisky, The Distillery, The Blender's Ghost, and Whisky Barrel Ride. The Whisky Bond Bar has over 280 different whiskies available.

Times: Open daily, 10-5.30 (extended in summer). Closed 25 Dec. **Fee:** ✱ £8.95 (ch 5-17 £4.95, concessions £6.95). **Facilities:** Ⓟ (100m) (metered parking & NCP) 💄 🍴 licensed 🔊 ⅙ (Braille script) toilets for disabled shop ⊗ (ex guide dogs) ◀

Scottish National Gallery of Modern Art

Belford Rd EH4 3DR
⤳ *(in West End, 20min walk from Haymarket station)*
☎ 0131 624 6200
e-mail: enquiries@nationalgalleries.org
web: www.nationalgalleries.org

An outstanding collection of 20th-century painting, sculpture and graphic art. Includes major works by Matisse, Picasso, Bacon, Moore and Lichtenstein and an exceptional group of Scottish paintings. Set in leafy grounds with a sculpture garden.

Times: Open all year, daily 10-5. New Year's Day noon-5. Closed 25-26 Dec. **Fee:** ✱ Free. Admission charged to some major exhibitions. **Facilities:** Ⓟ 💄 🔊 ⅙ (ramps & lift) toilets for disabled shop ⊗ (ex guide dogs) ◀

Scottish National Portrait Gallery

1 Queen St EH2 1JD
⤳ *(parallel to Princes St, just behind St Andrew Square)*
☎ 0131 624 6200
e-mail: enquiries@nationalgalleries.org
web: www.nationalgalleries.org

The collection provides a visual history of Scotland from the 16th century to the present day, told through the portraits of the people who shaped it. Among the most famous are Mary, Queen of Scots, Ramsay's portrait of David Hume and Raeburn's portrait of Sir Walter Scott. The building also houses the National Collection of Photography.

Times: Open all year, daily, 10-5, Thu until 7. New Year's Day noon-5. Closed 25-26 Dec. **Fee:** ✱ Free. Admission charged to some major exhibitions. **Facilities:** Ⓟ (200yds) (pay and display) 💄 🔊 ⅙ (ramps & lift) toilets for disabled shop ⊗ (ex guide dogs) ◀

The Writers' Museum   `FREE`

Lady Stair's House, Lady Stair's Close, Lawnmarket EH1 2PA
⤳ *(off the Royal Mile)*
☎ 0131 529 4901
e-mail: enquiries@writersmuseum.demon.co.uk
web: www.cac.org.uk

Situated in the historic Lady Stair's House which dates from 1622, the museum houses various objects associated with Robert Burns, Sir Walter Scott and Robert Louis Stevenson. Temporary exhibitions are planned throughout the year.

Times: Open all year, Mon-Sat 10-5. (Aug only, Sun 12-5). **Facilities:** Ⓟ (500mtrs) (parking meters) 🔊 shop ⊗ (ex guide dogs)

Scotland

GOGAR
MAP 11 NT17

Suntrap Garden
43 Gogarbank EH12 9BY
➲ *(between A8 & A71 W of city bypass)*
☎ 0131 339 7283
e-mail: suntrap@btopenworld.com
web: www.suntrap-garden.org.uk

The three-acre garden comprises of many gardens within a single garden, including Italian, Rock, Peat and Woodland.

Times: Open all year Oct-Apr, 10-4; May-Sep, 10-6 **Facilities:** ❷ 🍴 ♿ (limited access to toilet facilities at wknds) toilets for disabled garden centre ⊗ (ex on lead)

SOUTH QUEENSFERRY
MAP 11 NT17

Dalmeny House
EH30 9TQ
☎ 0131 331 1888
e-mail: events@dalmeny.co.uk
web: www.dalmeny.co.uk

This is the home of the Earl and the Countess of Rosebery, whose family have lived here for over 300 years. The house, however, dates from 1815 when it was built in Tudor Gothic style. There is fine French furniture, tapestries and porcelain from the Rothschild Mentmore collection. Early Scottish furniture is also shown, with 18th-century portraits, Rosebery racing mementoes, a display of pictures and one of the world's most important Napoleonic collections.

Times: Open Jul-Aug, Sun-Tue 2-5.30. (Last admission 4.30). Open other times by arrangement for groups. **Fee:** ✱ £5 (ch 10-16 £3, concessions £4). Party 20+. **Facilities:** ❷ 🍽 🍴 ♿ toilets for disabled ⊗ (ex guide dogs or in grounds)

Hopetoun House
2 for 1
EH30 9SL
➲ *(2m W of Forth Road Bridge, off A904)*
☎ 0131 331 2451
e-mail: marketing@hopetounhouse.com
web: www.hopetounhouse.com

Hopetoun House at South Queensferry is just a short drive from Edinburgh and has all the ingredients for a great family day out. Whether it is a leisurely stroll, afternoon tea or a touch of nostalgia you crave, Hopetoun will fit the bill. Built some 300 years ago, it is a delight to wander the corridors and historical rooms of one of the most splendid examples of the work of Scottish architects, Sir William Bruce and William Adam. It shows some of the finest examples in Scotland of carving, wainscoting and ceiling painting. With 100 acres of parkland including a deer park, the gardens are a colourful carpet of seasonal flowers. After a gentle walk, indulge yourself with a traditional tea and a browse through our shop.

Times: Open daily Etr-Sep, 11-5.30. **Fee:** ✱ £8 (ch £4.25). Grounds £3.70 (ch £2.20). **Facilities:** ❷ 🍽 🍴 ♿ (ramps) toilets for disabled shop ⊗ (ex on leads) 🚢

Inchcolm Abbey
Inchcolm Island
➲ *(1.5m S of Aberdour. Access by ferry Apr-Sep)*
☎ 01383 823332
web: www.historic-scotland.gov.uk

Situated on a green island on the Firth of Forth, the Augustinian abbey was founded in about 1192 by Alexander I. The well-preserved remains include a fine 13th-century octagonal chapter house and a 13th-century wall painting.

Times: Open Apr-Sep, daily 9.30-6.30. **Fee:** ✱ £4 (ch £1.60, concessions £3). Additional charge for ferry trip. Please phone or check website for further details. **Facilities:** ♿ toilets for disabled shop ⊗ 🇮

Queensferry Museum
FREE
53 High St EH30 9HP
➲ *(A90 from Edinburgh)*
☎ 0131 331 5545
web: www.cac.org.uk

The museum commands magnificent views of the two great bridges spanning the Forth and traces the history of the people of Queensferry and Dalmeny, the historic passage to Fife, the construction of the rail and road bridges and the wildlife of the Forth estuary. An ancient annual custom, in August, is Burry Man, who is clad from head to toe in burrs, and parades through the town. See the full size model of the Burry Man in the museum.

Times: Open all year, Mon & Thu-Sat 10-1, 2.15-5, Sun noon-5. (Last admission 1/2 hour before closing). Closed 25-26 Dec & 1-2 Jan **Facilities:** ℗ (0.25m) (induction loop at reception) shop ⊗ (ex guide dogs)

CITY OF GLASGOW

GLASGOW
MAP 11 NS56

Burrell Collection

2060 Pollokshaws Rd G43 1AT
➲ *(3.5m S of city centre)*
☎ 0141 287 2550
e-mail: museums@cls.glasgow.gov.uk
web: www.glasgowmuseums.com

Set in Pollok Country Park, this award-winning building makes the priceless works of art on display seem almost part of the woodland setting. Shipping magnate Sir William Burrell's main interests were medieval Europe, Oriental art and European paintings. Colourful paintings and stained glass show the details of medieval life. Furniture, paintings, sculpture, armour and weapons help to complete the picture. Rugs, ceramics and metalwork represent the art of Islam. There is also a strong collection of Chinese and other Oriental ceramics. Paintings on display include works by Bellini, Rembrandt and the French Impressionists.

Times: ✱ Open all year, Mon-Thu & Sat 10-5, Fri & Sun 11-5. Closed 24-25 & 31 [pm] Dec & 1-2 Jan **Facilities:** ❷ (charged) 🍽 🍽 licensed 🍴 ♿ (wheelchairs available, tape guides, lifts) toilets for disabled shop ⊗

Clydebuilt - Scottish Maritime Museum at Braehead

Braehead Shopping Centre, King Inch Rd G51 4BN

➲ *(M8 junct 25A, 26, follow signs for Braehead Shopping Centre, then Green car park)*

☎ 0141 886 1013

e-mail: clydebuilt@tinyworld.co.uk

web: www.scottishmaritimemuseum.org

On the banks of the River Clyde, home of the Scottish shipbuilding industry, visitors can discover how Glasgow's famous ships were built, from the design stages through to the launch. There are also displays on the textile and cotton industries, iron and steel, and tobacco. Hands-on activities allow you to operate a real ship's engine, become a ship's riveter, and steer a virtual ship up the Clyde.

Times: Open Mon-Sat 10-5.30; Sun 11-5. **Fee:** ✱ £4.25 (ch £2.50, concessions £3). Family ticket £10 **Facilities:** ☻ ▯ ♿ (lift/ramps/wheelchairs from shopping centre) toilets for disabled shop ⊗ (ex guide dogs)

Gallery of Modern Art   FREE

Royal Exchange Square G1 3AH

➲ *(just off Buchanan St & close to Central Station & Queen St Stn)*

☎ 0141 229 1996

e-mail: museums@cls.glasgow.gov.uk

web: www.glasgowmuseums.com

GoMA offers a thought-provoking programme of temporary exhibitions and workshops. It displays work by local and international artists, as well as addressing contemporary social issues through its major bi-annual projects.

Times: ✱ Open all year, Mon-Tue & Sat 10-5, Thu 10-8, Fri & Sun 11-5. **Facilities:** ☻ (200yds) ▯ ▯ ♿ toilets for disabled shop ⊗ (ex guide dogs)

Glasgow Botanic Gardens   FREE

730 Great Western Rd G12 0UE

➲ *(From M8 junct 17 onto A82 Dumbarton. Approx 2-3m the Botanic Gardens are on the right)*

☎ 0141 334 2422

e-mail: gbg@land.glasgow.gov.uk

Home of the national collections of Dendrobium Orchids, Begonias and tree ferns. The Gardens consist of an arboretum, herbaceous borders, a herb garden, rose garden, and unusual vegetables. The Kibble Palace contains carnivorous plants, island flora and temperate plant collections.

Times: Open all year. Gardens open daily 7-dusk, Glasshouses 10-4.45 (4.15 in winter). **Facilities:** ☻ (street parking) ▯ ♿ toilets for disabled ⊗

Glasgow Cathedral   FREE

Castle St G4 0QZ

➲ *(M8 junct 15, in centre of Glasgow)*

☎ 0141 552 6891

web: www.historic-scotland.gov.uk

The only Scottish mainland medieval cathedral to have survived the Reformation complete (apart from its western towers). Built during the 13th to 15th centuries over the supposed site of the tomb of St Kentigern. Notable features in this splendid building are the elaborately vaulted crypt, which included an introductory display and

collection of carved stones, the stone screen of the early 15th century and the unfinished Blackadder Aisle.

Times: Open all year, Apr-Sep daily 9.30-6, Sun 1-5; Oct-Mar daily 9.30-4, Sun 1-4. Closed 25-26 Dec & 1-2 Jan. **Facilities:** ♿ (telephone for disabled access details) shop ⊗ ▯

Glasgow Museums Resource Centre   FREE

200 Woodhead Rd, South Nitshill Ind Estate G53 7NN

➲ *(on S side, close to Rail Stn)*

☎ 0141 276 9300

web: www.glasgowmuseums.com

GMRC is the first publicly-accessible store for the city's museum service, offering a behind-the-scenes look at 200,000 treasures held in storage. Please note that access to the stores is by guided tour only. Viewings of a specific object can be arranged, with two weeks prior notice. Activities, tours and talks are held throughout the year - see website or phone for details.

Times: Open all year Mon-Thu & Sat 10-5, Fri-Sun 11-5. Guided tours for public at 2.30 Access is only by guided tours. **Facilities:** ☻ ♿ toilets for disabled ⊗ (ex guide dogs)

Glasgow Science Centre

50 Pacific Quay G51 1EA

➲ *(M8 junct 24 or M77 junct 21, follow brown signs, across Clyde from SECC)*

☎ 0871 540 1000

e-mail: admin@glasgowsciencecentre.org

web: www.glasgowsciencecentre.org

The centre is home to many entertaining and exciting attractions and contains hundreds of interactive exhibits. Highlights include the Scottish Power Planetarium, Scotland's only IMAX cinema and the 127m Glasgow Tower, a remarkable free-standing structure that gives breathtaking views of the city (check availability before visiting). GSC presents the world of science and technology in new and exciting ways.

Times: Open 2 Jan-26 Mar, 10-6. 27 Mar daily 10-6 **Fee:** Science Mall* or Imax: £6.95 (ch & concessions £4.95). Science Mall & Imax: £9.95 (ch & concessions £7.95). 10% off for groups 4+. * Scottish Power Planeterium extra £2. **Facilities:** ☻ (charged) ▯ ♿ (induction loops) toilets for disabled shop ⊗ (ex guide/hearing dogs) ◀

Greenbank Garden

Flenders Rd, Clarkston G76 8RB

➲ *(off A726 on southern outskirts of city)*

☎ 0141 639 3281

web: www.nts.org.uk

The spacious, walled woodland gardens are attractively laid out in the grounds of an elegant Georgian house, and best seen between April and October. A wide range of flowers and shrubs are grown, with the idea of helping private gardeners to look at possibilities for their own gardens. A greenhouse and garden designed for the disabled gardener also displays specialised tools.

Times: ✱ Open daily 9.30-sunset. Times may change for 2007 please telephone or check website **Facilities:** ☻ ▯ ♿ (wheelchairs available) toilets for disabled shop ⊗ (ex guide dogs) ⚘

continued

Scotland

Holmwood House

61-63 Netherlee House, Cathcart G44 3YG

⮑ *(off Clarkston Rd)*

☎ 0141 637 2129

web: www.nts.org.uk

Built in the mid 19th century, the architectural style of the house is an adaptation of classical Greek. Many rooms are richly ornamented in wood, plaster and marble.

Times: ✱ Open Apr-Oct, daily 12-5. Morning visits available for pre-booked groups. Times may change for 2007 please telephone or check website **Facilities:** ☒

House for an Art Lover

10 Dumbreck Rd, Bellahouston Park G41 5BW

⮑ *(M8 W junct 23 signed B768, left at top of slip road onto Dumbreck Rd. Bellahouston Park on right)*

☎ 0141 353 4770

e-mail: info@houseforanartlover.co.uk

web: www.houseforanartlover.co.uk

Inspired by a portfolio of drawings by Charles Rennie Mackintosh in 1901, this fascinating artistic attraction and private dining venue opened in 1996. Visitors can view the Mackintosh suite of rooms and learn from a DVD presentation about the development of the building and its contents. There is a full programme of changing art exhibitions, dinner concerts and afternoon musical recitals. Contact for more details.

Times: Open Apr-Sep, Mon-Wed 10-4 & Thu-Sun 10-1; Oct-Mar, Sat-Sun 10-1, telephone for wkday opening details. **Fee:** £3.50 (ch under 10 free, concessions £2.50). **Facilities:** ☻ ☻ ☻ ☒ (lift to 2nd floor) toilets for disabled shop ☒ (ex guide dogs) ◀

Hunterian Art Gallery

82 Hillhead St, The University of Glasgow G12 8QQ

⮑ *(on University of Glasgow Campus in Hillhead District, 2m W of city centre)*

☎ 0141 330 5431

e-mail: hunter@museum.gla.ac.uk

web: www.hunterian.gla.ac.uk

The founding collection is made up of paintings bequeathed in the 18th century by Dr William Hunter, including works by Rembrandt and Stubbs. The Gallery now has works by James McNeill Whistler, major displays of paintings by the Scottish Colourists, and a graphics collection holding some 300,000 prints. A popular feature of the Charles Rennie Mackintosh collection is the re-construction of the interiors of The Mackintosh House.

Times: ✱ Open Mon-Sat 9.30-5. Telephone for BH closures. **Facilities:** ☻ (500 yds) (pay & display) ☒ ☒ (lift, wheelchair available) toilets for disabled shop ☒ (ex guide dogs) ◀

Hunterian Museum   `FREE`

Gilbert Scott Building, The University of Glasgow G12 8QQ

⮑ *(on University of Glasgow campus in Hillhead District, 2m W of city centre)*

☎ 0141 330 4221

e-mail: hunter@museum.gla.ac.uk

web: www.hunterian.gla.ac.uk

Named after the 18th-century physician, Dr William Hunter, who bequeathed his large and important collections of coins, medals, fossils, geological specimens and archaeological and ethnographic items to the university. The exhibits are shown in the main building of the university, and temporary exhibitions are held.

Times: ✱ Open all year, Mon-Sat 9.30-5. Closed certain BHs phone for details. **Facilities:** ☻ (100yds) (pay & display) ☒ (lift) toilets for disabled shop ☒ (ex guide dogs) ◀

Hutchesons' Hall

158 Ingram St G1 1EJ

⮑ *(near SE corner of George Square)*

☎ 0141 552 8391

e-mail: hutchesonshall@nts.org.uk

web: www.nts.org.uk

This handsome early 19th-century building was designed by David Hamilton and houses a visitor centre and shop. There is a video about Glasgow's merchant city, and the Hall can be booked for functions. Telephone for details of concerts, recitals, etc.

Times: ✱ Gallery: open Mon-Sat, 10-5. Closed 24 Dec-mid Jan. Hall: open subject to functions. Times may change for 2007 please telephone or check website **Facilities:** ☻ (on street) (meters)(outside for disabled) ☒ ☒ toilets for disabled shop ☒ ☒

The Lighthouse NEW

11 Mitchell Ln G1 3NU

⮑ *(in city centre)*

☎ 0141 221 6362

e-mail: enquiries@thelighthouse.co.uk

web: www.thelighthouse.co.uk

Scotlands National Centre for Architecture, Design and the City. Extending over six floors and one of the biggest centres of its kind in Europe. Home to the award-winning Mackintosh Centre, devoted to the art, architecture and design of Charles Rennie Mackintosh. There are also temporary exhibition spaces with a thought provoking programme. A place of discovery and learning, another feature of The Lighthouse is the uninterrupted view over Glasgow's cityscape. Climb the helical staircase in the Mackintosh Tower or use the lift to the Level 6 Viewing Platform and spot some significant buildings that make up Glasgow's architectural tapestry.

Times: Open all year, Mon & Wed-Sat, 10.30-5, Tue 11-5, Sun noon-5. **Fee:** ✱ £3 (ch £1, concessions £1.50) **Facilities:** ☻ (50mtrs) ☒ licensed ☒ (induction loop) toilets for disabled shop ☒ (ex assist dogs) ◀

McLellan Galleries   `FREE`

270 Sauchiehall St G2 3EH

⮑ *(N side of Sauchiehall St, close to Glasgow School of Art)*

☎ 0141 565 4137

e-mail: museums@cls.glasgow.gov.uk

web: www.glasgowmuseums.com

The McLellan Galleries first opened in 1854 and featured the personal collection of Glasgow industrialist and coachbuilder Archibald McLellan. With over 1,200 sq metres of top gallery space, the McLellan Galleries provide Glasgow Museums with the opportunity to hold major exhibitions and establish Glasgow as Britain's second art city.

Times: ✱ Open all year, Mon-Thu & Sat 10-5, Fri & Sun 11-5. Closed 24-25 & 31 Dec [pm] & 1-2 Jan **Facilities:** ☻ (500mtrs) ☒ ☒ ☒ (assistance available, lift) toilets for disabled shop ☒

continued

Museum of Transport

FREE

1 Bunhouse Rd G3 8DP
➲ (1.5m W of city centre)
☎ 0141 287 2720
e-mail: museums@cls.glasgow.gov.uk
web: www.glasgowmuseums.com

Visit the Museum of Transport and the first impression is of gleaming metalwork and bright paint. All around you there are cars, caravans, carriages and carts, fire engines, buses, steam locomotives, prams and trams. The museum uses its collections of vehicles and models to tell the story of transport by land and sea, with a unique Glasgow flavour. Visitors can even go window shopping along the recreated Kelvin Street of 1938. Upstairs 250 ship models tell the story of the great days of Clyde shipbuilding. The Museum of Transport has something for everyone.

Times: ✱ Open all year, Mon-Thu & Sat 10-5, Fri & Sun 11-5.
Facilities: ❷ (charged) ♨ 🍴 ♿ (assistance available) toilets for disabled shop ⊗ (ex guide dogs)

People's Palace and Winter Gardens

FREE

Glasgow Green G40 1AT
➲ (1m SE of city centre)
☎ 0141 271 2951
e-mail: museums@cls.glasgow.gov.uk
web: www.glasgowmuseums.com

Glasgow grew from a medieval town located by the Cathedral to the Second City of the British Empire. Trade with the Americas, and later industry, made the city rich. But not everyone shared in Glasgow's wealth. The People's Palace on historic Glasgow Green shows how ordinary Glaswegians worked, lived and played. Visitors can discover how a family lived in a typical one-room Glasgow 'single end' tenement flat, see Billy Connolly's amazing banana boots, learn to speak Glesga, take a trip 'doon the watter' and visit the Winter Gardens.

Times: ✱ Open all year, Mon-Thu & Sat 10-5, Fri & Sun 11-5. Closed 24-25 & 31 Dec [pm] & 1-2 Jan **Facilities:** ❷ (50yds) ♨ ♿ (lifts) toilets for disabled shop garden centre ⊗

Pollok House

Pollok Country Park, 2060 Pollokshaws Rd G43 1AT
➲ (3.5m S of city centre, off M77 junct 2, follow signs for Burrell Collection)
☎ 0141 616 6410
e-mail: pollokhouse@nts.org.uk
web: www.nts.org.uk

The house is one of Glasgow's most elegant, and was built by the Maxwell family in the 18th century and expanded between 1890 and 1901, including extensive servants' quarters. The rooms are decorated with 18th-century plasterwork, fine furniture and the Stirling Maxwell art collection, including works by El Greco, Goya and William Blake.

Times: ✱ House: open daily 10-5. Closed 25 & 26 Dec & 1 & 2 Jan.
Facilities: ❷ 🍴 licensed ♿ (lifts) toilets for disabled shop ⊗

Provand's Lordship

FREE

3 Castle St G4 0RB
➲ (1m E of city centre)
☎ 0141 552 8819
e-mail: museums@cls.glsgow.gov.uk
web: www.glasgowmuseums.com

Provand's Lordship is the only house to survive from Medieval Glasgow. For over 500 years it has watched the changing fortunes of the city and the nearby Cathedral. Bishop Andrew Muirhead built the house as part of St Nicholas' Hospital in 1971. The prebendary of Barlanark later bought it for use as a manse. Inside, the displays recreate home life in the middle ages. Behind the house is the St Nicholas Garden, built in 1997. It is a medical herb garden, in keeping with the original purpose of the house.

Times: ✱ Open all year, Mon-Thu & Sat 10-5, Fri & Sun 11-5.
Facilities: ❷ (50 yds) ♨ 🍴 ♿ (please contact for details) shop ⊗ (ex guide dogs)

St Mungo Museum of Religious Life & Art

FREE

2 Castle St G4 0RH
➲ (1m NE of city centre)
☎ 0141 553 2557
e-mail: museums@cls.glasgow.gov.uk
web: www.glasgowmuseums.com

The award-winning St Mungo Museum explores the importance of religion in peoples' everyday lives and art. It aims to promote understanding and respect between people of different faiths and of none. Highlights of the collection include the Salvador Dali painting Christ of St John of the Cross. The museum also features stained glass, objects, statues and video footage. Within the grounds is Britain's first Japanese Zen garden.

Times: ✱ Open all year, Mon-Thu & Sat 10-5, Fri & Sun 11-5.
Facilities: ❷ (50yds) ♨ 🍴 ♿ (taped information & lift) toilets for disabled shop ⊗ (ex guide dogs)

The Scottish Football Museum

2 for 1

Hampden Park G42 9BA
➲ (3m S of city centre, follow brown tourist signs)
☎ 0141 616 6139
e-mail: info@scottishfootballmuseum.org.uk
web: www.scottishfootballmuseum.org.uk

Using 2500 pieces of footballing memorabilia, the Scottish Football Museum covers such themes as football's origins, women's football, fan culture, other games influenced by football, and even some social history. The exhibits include the world's oldest football, trophy and ticket, a reconstructed 1903 changing room and press box, and items of specific import, such as Kenny Dalglish's silver cap, Jimmy

continued

We endeavour to be as accurate as possible, but changes to times and other information can occur after the guide has gone to press.

McGrory's boots, and the ball from Scotland's 5-1 win over England in 1928.

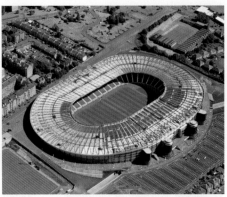

The Scottish Football Museum

Times: Open Mon-Sat 10-5, Sun 11-5. Closed match days, special events and Xmas/New Year, please telephone in advance for confirmation **Fee:** Museum £5.50 (ch under 16 & concessions £2.75) Stadium £6 (ch under 16 & concessions £3) Combined Ticket £8.50 (ch under 16 & concessions £4.25) Ch under 5 are free. **Facilities:** ❷ ☑ ⬛ ₲ (ramps throughout) toilets for disabled shop ❽ (ex guide dogs) ◀

The Tall Ship at Glasgow Harbour   `2 for 1`
100 Stobcross Rd G3 8QQ
➲ *(from M8 junct 19 onto A814 follow signs for attraction)*
☎ 0141 222 2513
e-mail: info@thetallship.com
web: www.thetallship.com

Visit The Tall Ship at Glasgow Harbour and step back in time to the days of sail. Experience Glasgow's maritime history at first hand and explore the UK's only remaining Clydebuilt sailing ship, the Glenlee. Exhibitions on board and in the visitor centre on the quayside tell the story of the ship and the Glasgow Harbour area. If you have ever wondered what it would have been like to be a sailor on a tall ship, this is your chance to find out! Children can have fun by joining in the hunt for Jock, the ship's cat. An unmissable experience, The Tall Ship offers guided tours, changing exhibitions, children's activities, a nautical gift shop and cafe.

Times: Open daily Mar-Oct 10-5, Nov-Feb 10-4. **Fee:** ✱ £4.95 (concessions £3.75, 1 ch free with paying adult/concession, additional ch £2.50). **Facilities:** ❷ ☑ ⬛ ₲ toilets for disabled shop ◀

Tenement House
145 Buccleuch St, Garnethill G3 6QN
➲ *(N of Charing Cross)*
☎ 0141 333 0183
e-mail: tenementhouse@nts.org.uk
web: www.nts.org.uk

This shows an unsung but once-typical side of Glasgow life: it is a first-floor flat, built in 1892, with a parlour, bedroom, kitchen and bathroom, furnished with the original recess beds, kitchen range, sink, and coal bunker, among other articles. The home of Agnes Toward from 1911 to 1965, the flat was bought by an actress who preserved it as a 'time capsule'. The contents vividly portray the life of one section of Glasgow society.

continued

Times: ✱ Open Mar-Oct, daily 2-5. Wkday morning visits available for pre-booked educational & other groups. Times may change for 2007 please telephone or check website **Facilities:** ℗ (100yds) (restricted, recommend parking in town) ₲ (Braille guide) ❽ (ex guide dogs) ☷

Trades Hall   `2 for 1`
85 Glassford St G1 1UH
➲ *(in city centre in Merchant City. Accessible from George Square & Argyle St)*
☎ 0141 552 2418
e-mail: info@tradeshallglasgow.co.uk
web: www.tradeshallglasgow.co.uk

The Trades Hall is one of Glasgow's most historic buildings and was home to the 14 incorporated crafts who regulated trade and played a vital role in shaping and making Glasgow the city it is today. Visitors can explore the impressive rooms of the building taking in the Grand Hall with its spectacular soaring windows, baroque chandeliers and striking dome, and the Saloon which features an original Adam fireplace and beautiful stained glass windows.

Times: Open Apr-Oct, by appointment Mon-Sat, 9-6, subject to availability **Fee:** ✱ £1.50 (ch under 5 free) **Facilities:** ℗ (NCP 100yds) (half price at NCP if visiting building) ₲ (electronic ramps for rise in levels of 3 & 4 stairs) toilets for disabled ❽ (ex guide dogs)

University of Glasgow Visitor Centre
University Av G12 8QQ
➲ *(M8 junct 19 E or junct 18 W)*
☎ 0141 330 5511
e-mail: visitorcentre@gla.ac.uk
web: www.gla.ac.uk/visitors

The Visitor Centre is spacious and pleasant, with leaflets, publications and video displays explaining how the university works and its history, plus what courses are available and which university events are open to the public. Historic attractions include the Memorial Chapel, Professors' Square and Lion and Unicorn Staircase. Hunterian Museum is not part of the tour but visitors are welcome to view the museum on their own.

Times: ✱ Open all year, Mon-Sat 9.30-5. Also May-Sep, Sun 2-5. **Facilities:** ℗ (880yds) (few spaces available) ☑ ⬛ ₲ (designated seating) toilets for disabled shop ❽ (ex guide dogs) ◀

CLACKMANNANSHIRE

ALLOA   MAP 11 NS89

Alloa Tower
Alloa Park FK10 1PP
➲ *(on A907)*
☎ 01259 211701
web: www.nts.org.uk

Beautifully restored, the tower, completed in 1467, is the only remaining part of the ancestral home of the Earls of Mar. The structure retains rare medieval features, notably the complete timber roof structure and groin vaulting. A superb loan collection of portraits and chattels of the Erskine family includes paintings by Raeburn.

Times: ✱ Open Apr-Oct, daily 1-5. Wkday morning visits available for pre-booked groups. Times may change for 2007 please telephone or check website **Facilities:** ❷ ₲ toilets for disabled ❽ ☷

ALVA   MAP 11 NS89

Mill Trail Visitor Centre   FREE
Glentana Mill, West Stirling St FK12 5EN
➲ (on A91 approx 8m E of Stirling)
☎ 01259 769696

In the heart of Scotland's woollen mill country, the Centre recounts the history of Scotland's woollen and tweed traditions, and features machines from spinning wheels to large motorised looms of the type in use today. Hear 12 year-old Mary describe her working day as a mill girl 150 years ago, and then contrast her story with our modern working woollen mill. Factory bargains and local crafts, tourist information centre, café.

Times: ✱ Open all year, Jan-Jun 10-5; Jul-Aug 9-5; Sep-Dec 10-5.
Facilities: ❷ ⬛ ♿ toilets for disabled shop ⊗ (ex guide dogs) ▄

DOLLAR   MAP 11 NS99

Castle Campbell
FK14 7PP
➲ (10m E of Stirling on A91)
☎ 01259 742408
web: www.historic-scotland.gov.uk

Traditionally known as the 'Castle of Gloom', the 15th to 17th-century tower stands in the picturesque Ochil Hills, gives wonderful views, and can be reached by a walk through the magnificent Dollar Glen. Care must be taken in or after rain when the path may be dangerous.

Times: Open all year, Apr-Sep, daily 9.30-6.30; Oct-Mar, Mon-Wed & Sat-Sun 9.30-4.30. Closed 25-26 Dec & 1-2 Jan. **Fee:** ✱ £4 (ch £1.60, concessions £3). Please phone or check website for further details.
Facilities: ❷ ⭘⃝ shop ▐ ♨

DUMFRIES & GALLOWAY

ARDWELL   MAP 10 NX14

Ardwell House Gardens
DG9 9LY
➲ (10m S of Stranraer, on A716)
☎ 01776 860227

Country house gardens and grounds with flowering shrubs and woodland walks. Plants for sale. House not open to the public.
Times: Open Mar-Oct, 10-5. Walled garden & greenhouses close at 5.
Fee: ✱ £3 (ch & pen £2). **Facilities:** ❷ ▦ garden centre

CAERLAVEROCK   MAP 11 NY06

Caerlaverock Castle
Glencaple DG1 4RU
➲ (8m SE of Dumfries, on B725)
☎ 01387 770244
web: www.historic-scotland.gov.uk

This ancient seat of the Maxwell family is a splendid medieval stronghold dating back to the 13th century. It has high walls and round towers, with machicolations added in the 15th century.

Times: Open all year, Apr-Sep, daily 9.30-6.30; Oct-Mar, daily 9.30-4.30. Closed 25-26 Dec & 1-2 Jan. **Fee:** ✱ £4.50 (ch £2, concessions £3.50). Please phone or check website for further details.
Facilities: ❷ ⭘⃝ ♿ toilets for disabled shop ▐

WWT Caerlaverock   2 for 1
Eastpark Farm DG1 4RS
➲ (9m SE of Dumfries, signed from A75)
☎ 01387 770200
e-mail: caerlaverock@wwt.org.uk
web: www.wwt.org.uk

This internationally important wetland is the winter habitat of the entire Svalbard population of Barnacle Geese which spends the winter on the Solway Firth. Observation facilities include 20 hides, 3 towers and a heated observatory. A wide variety of other wildlife can be seen, notably the rare Natterjack Toad and a family of Barn Owls which can be observed via a CCTV system.

Times: Open daily 10-5. Closed 25 Dec. **Fee:** £4.40 (ch £2.70 & concessions £3.60). Family ticket £11.50 **Facilities:** ❷ ⬛ ♿ toilets for disabled shop ⊗ (ex guide dogs)

CARDONESS CASTLE   MAP 11 NX55

Cardoness Castle
DG7 2EH
➲ (1m SW of Gatehouse of Fleet, off A75)
☎ 01557 814427
web: www.historic-scotland.gov.uk

A 15th-century stronghold overlooking the Water of Fleet. It was once the home of the McCullochs of Galloway. The architectural details inside the tower are of very high quality.

Times: Open Apr-Sep, daily 9.30-6.30; (Oct closed Thu & Fri) Nov-Mar open wknds only. Closed 25-26 Dec & 1-2 Jan. **Fee:** ✱ £3 (ch £1.30 concessions £2.30). Please phone or check website for further details.
Facilities: ❷ shop ▐

CASTLE DOUGLAS   MAP 11 NX76

Threave Castle
DG7 1RX
➲ (3m W on A75)
☎ 0411 223101
web: www.historic-scotland.gov.uk

Archibald the Grim built this lonely castle in the late 14th century. It stands on an islet in the River Dee, and is four storeys high with round towers guarding the outer wall. The island is reached by boat.

Times: Open Apr-Sep, daily 9.30-6.30. **Fee:** ✱ £3.50 (ch £1.50, concessions £2.50). Charge includes ferry trip. Please phone or check website for further details. **Facilities:** ❷ ⊗ ▐

Scotland

Threave Garden & Estate

DG7 1RX

➲ *(1m W of Castle Douglas, off A75)*

☎ 01556 502575

e-mail: threave@nts.org.uk

web: www.nts.org.uk

The best time to visit is in spring when there is a dazzling display of daffodils. The garden is a delight in all seasons, however, and is home to the National Trust for Scotland's School of Practical Gardening.

Times: ✱ Estate & Garden: all year, daily 9.30-sunset. Walled Garden & Glasshouse daily 9.30-5. Visitor Centre, Countryside Centre & exhibition Feb-Mar & Nov-23 Dec, daily 10-4; Apr-Oct, daily 9.30-5.30. House Mar-Oct, Wed-Fri & Sun, 11-4 (guided tours only, admission by timed ticket).Times may change for 2007 please telephone or check website **Facilities:** ✿ ⏃◯⏃ licensed ♿ (wheelchairs available incl. electric wheelchair) toilets for disabled shop garden centre ⊗ (ex guide dogs) ♨

CREETOWN   MAP 11 NX45

Creetown Gem Rock Museum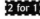

Chain Rd DG8 7HJ

➲ *(follow signs from A75 at Creetown bypass)*

☎ 01671 820357 & 820554

e-mail: gem.rock@btinternet.com

web: www.gemrock.net

The Gem Rock is the leading independent museum of its kind in the UK, and is renowned worldwide. Crystals, gemstones, minerals, jewellery and fossils, the Gem Rock displays some of the most breathtaking examples of nature's wonders. See the audio-visual 'Fire in the Stones', explore the Crystal Cave, and relax in the Prospector's Study.

Times: Open Etr-Sep, daily 9.30-5.30; Oct-Nov & Feb, Mar-Etr, daily 10-4; Dec, wknds 10-4 or by appointment wkdays. Closed 23 Dec-Jan. **Fee:** £3.75 (ch £2.25 under 5 free, concessions £3.25). Family ticket £9.75 (2ad+3ch). **Facilities:** ✿ ⏃ ⏃ ♿ (ideal attraction for wheelchair users) toilets for disabled shop ⊗ (ex guide dogs) ⊠

DRUMCOLTRAN TOWER   MAP 11 NX86

Drumcoltran Tower   **FREE**

➲ *(7m NE of Dalbeattie, in farm buildings off A711)*

web: www.historic-scotland.gov.uk

A well-preserved tower of mid 16th-century date simply planned and built, sitting within a busy modern farmyard.

Times: Open at any reasonable time. **Facilities:** ✿ ⊗ ⏃

DUMFRIES   MAP 11 NX97

Burns Mausoleum   **FREE**

St Michael's Churchyard

➲ *(at junct of Brooms Rd [ATS] and St Michael's St [B725])*

☎ 01387 255297

e-mail: dumfriesmuseum@dumgal.gov.uk

web: www.dumgal.gov.uk/museums

The mausoleum is in the form of a Greek temple, and contains the tombs of Robert Burns, his wife Jean Armour, and their five sons. A sculptured group shows the Muse of Poetry flinging her cloak over Burns at the plough.

continued

Times: Unrestricted access to exterior. Guided tours, and access to interior available from Robert Burns House. Please phone 01387 255297 for details. **Facilities:** ⓟ (50yds) ♿ (visitors with mobility difficulties tel 01387 255297)

Dumfries Museum & Camera Obscura

The Observatory, Rotchell Rd DG2 7SW

➲ *(A75 from S Carlisle or SW from Castle Douglas, museum in Maxwellton area of Dumfries)*

☎ 01387 253374

e-mail: dumfriesmuseum@dumgal.gov.uk

web: www.dumgal.gov.uk/museums

Situated in and around the 18th-century windmill tower, the museum's collections were started over 150 years ago and exhibitions trace the history of the people and landscape of Dumfries & Galloway. The Camera Obscura is to be found on the top floor of the windmill tower. 2 for 1 voucher valid at Camera Obscura.

Times: Open all year, Apr-Sep Mon-Sat 10-5, Sun, 2-5; Oct-Mar, Tue-Sat 10-1 & 2-5. **Fee:** ✱ Free except Camera Obscura £1.90 (concessions 95p) **Facilities:** ✿ ⏃ ♿ (parking available) shop

Old Bridge House Museum

Mill Rd DG2 7BE

➲ *(at W end of Devorgilla's Bridge)*

☎ 01387 256904

e-mail: dumfriesmuseum@dumgal.gov.uk

web: www.dumgal.gov.uk/museums

The Old Bridge House was built in 1660, and is the oldest house in Dumfries. A museum of everyday life in the town, it has an early 20th-century dentist's surgery, a Victorian nursery and kitchens of the 1850s and 1900s.

Times: Open Apr-Sep, Mon-Sat 10-5 & Sun 2-5. **Fee:** Donations welcome **Facilities:** ✿ ⏃ shop

Robert Burns Centre

Mill Rd DG2 7BE

➲ *(on Westbank of River Nith)*

☎ 01387 264808

e-mail: dumfriesmuseum@dumgal.gov.uk

web: www.dumgal.gov.uk/museums

This award-winning centre explores the connections between Robert Burns and the town of Dumfries. Situated in the town's 18th-century watermill, the centre tells the story of Burns' last years spent in the busy streets and lively atmosphere of Dumfries in the 1790s. In the evening the centre shows feature films in the Film Theatre. 2 for 1 voucher valid on audio visual presentations.

Times: Open all year, Apr-Sep, daily 10-8 (Sun 2-5); Oct-Mar, Tue-Sat 10-1 & 2-5. **Fee:** ✱ Free admission to museum, audio-visual theatre £1.60 (concessions 80p). **Facilities:** ✿ ⏃◯⏃ ⏃ ♿ (induction loop hearing system in auditorium, chairlift) toilets for disabled shop ⊠

Robert Burns House

Burns St DG1 2PS

➲ *(signed from Brooms Rd [ATS] car park)*

☎ 01387 255297

e-mail: dumfriesmuseum@dumgal.gov.uk

web: www.dumgal.gov.uk/museums

It was in this house that Robert Burns spent the last three years of his

continued

short life; he died here in 1796. It retains much of its 18th-century character and contains many fascinating items connected with the poet. There is the chair in which he wrote his last poems, many original letters and manuscripts, and the famous Kilmarnock and Edinburgh editions of his work.

Times: Open all year, Apr-Sep, Mon-Sat 10-5, Sun 2-5; Oct-Mar Tue-Sat 10-1 & 2-5. **Fee:** ✻ Donations welcome **Facilities:** Ⓟ (opposite) 🛍 shop

---

DUNDRENNAN   MAP 11 NX74

Dundrennan Abbey
DG6 4QH
➲ *(6.5m SE of Kirkcudbright, on A711)*
☎ 01557 500262
web: www.historic-scotland.gov.uk

The now ruined abbey was founded for the Cistercians. The east end of the church and the chapter house are of exceptional architectural quality. Mary, Queen of Scots is thought to have spent her last night in Scotland here on 15 May 1568, before seeking shelter in England, where she was imprisoned and eventually executed.

Times: Open, Apr-Sep, daily 9.30-6.30; Oct open daily 9.30-4.30 closed Thu & Fri. Nov-Mar wknds only 9.30-4.30. Closed 25-26 Dec & 1-2 Jan. **Fee:** ✻ £2.50 (ch £1, concessions £2). Please phone or check website for further details. **Facilities:** Ⓟ �潱 ⊗ ♦

GLENLUCE   MAP 10 NX15

Glenluce Abbey
DG8 0AF
➲ *(2m NW, off A75)*
☎ 01581 300541
web: www.historic-scotland.gov.uk

The abbey was founded for the Cistercians in 1192 by Roland, Earl of Galloway. The ruins include a vaulted chapter house, and stand in a beautiful setting.

Times: Open all year, Apr-Sep daily 9.30-6.30; Oct closed Thu & Fri. Nov-Mar wknds only. Closed 25-26 Dec & 1-2 Jan. **Fee:** ✻ £2.50 (ch £1, concessions £2). Please phone or check website for further details. **Facilities:** Ⓟ 潱㄰ ⊗ ♦

KIRKCUDBRIGHT   MAP 11 NX65

Broughton House & Garden
12 High St DG6 4JX
➲ *(off A711/A755)*
☎ 01557 330437
e-mail: aclipson@nts.scot.demon.co.uk
web: www.nts.org.uk

An 18th-century town house where Edward A Hornel, one of the 'Glasgow Boys' group of artists, lived and worked from 1901-1933. It features a collection of his work, an extensive library of local history, including rare editions of Burns' works, and a Japanese-style garden that he created.

Times: ✻ Garden only Feb-Mar, Mon-Fri, 11-4. House & garden: Good Fri-Sep, Thu-Mon, 12-5. Times may change for 2007 please telephone or check website **Facilities:** Ⓟ (on street) (limited space) ⊗ (ex guide dogs) ☙

Galloway Wildlife Conservation Park NEW

Lochfergus Plantation DG6 4XX
➲ *(follow brown signs from A75, 1m from Kirkcudbright on B727)*
☎ 01557 331645
e-mail: info@gallowaywildlife.co.uk
web: www.gallowaywildlife.co.uk

The wild animal conservation centre for southern Scotland, set in 27 acres of mixed woodland. A varied zoological collection of over 150 animals from all over the world. Close animal encounters and bird of prey displays are some of the features giving an insight into wildlife conservation.

Times: Open Feb-Nov, daily, 10-6 (last admission 5); Dec-Jan, wknds, 10-4 (last admission 3). **Fee:** £5 (ch 4-15 £3.50, under 4 free, concessions £4.50) **Facilities:** Ⓟ 潱㄰ ⊗ (British sign language) shop ⊗ (ex assist dogs) ◀

MacLellan's Castle
➲ *(in Kirkcudbright on A711)*
☎ 01557 331856
web: www.historic-scotland.gov.uk

This handsome structure has been a ruin since the mid 18th-century. It was once an imposing castellated mansion, elaborately planned with fine architectural detail. Something of its 16th-century grandeur still remains.

Times: Open Apr-Sep, daily 9.30-6.30. **Fee:** ✻ £3 (ch £1.30, concessions £2.30). Please phone or check website for further details. **Facilities:** Ⓟ shop ⊗ ⟐ ♦

Stewartry Museum   FREE
St Mary St DG6 4AQ
➲ *(from A711 through town, pass parish church, museum approx 200mtrs on right)*
☎ 01557 331643
e-mail: david@dumgal.gov.uk
web: www.dumgal.go.uk/museums

A large and varied collection of archaeological, social history and natural history exhibits relating to the Stewartry district.

Times: Open May, Jun & Sep, Mon-Sat 11-5 Sun 2-5; Jul-Aug, Mon-Sat 10-5 Sun 2-5; Oct Mon-Sat 11-4 Sun 2-5; Nov-Apr Mon-Sat 11-4 **Facilities:** Ⓟ (outside) 🛍 ㄰ shop ⊗ (ex guide dogs)

Scotland

Tolbooth Art Centre
FREE

High St DG6 4JL

➲ *(from A711, through town pass parish church & Stewartry Museum, 1st right into High St)*

☎ 01557 331556

e-mail: DavidD@dumgal.gov.uk

web: www.dumgal.gov.uk/museums

Dating from 1629, the Tolbooth was converted into an art centre and provides an interpretive introduction to the Kirkcudbright artists's colony, which flourished in the town from the 1880s. It also provides studio and exhibition space for contemporary local and visiting artists. There is a programme of exhibitions from March to October.

Times: Open May, Jun & Sep, Mon-Sat 11-5 Sun 2-5; Jul & Aug, Mon-Sat 10-5, Sun 2-5; Oct, Mon-Sat 11-4 Sun 2-5; Nov-Apr, Mon-Sat 11-4
Facilities: Ⓟ (on street parking) 🅿️ ♿ (lift for access to upper floors) toilets for disabled shop ⊗ (ex guide dogs)

NEW ABBEY   **MAP 11 NX96**

New Abbey Corn Mill

DG2 8BX

➲ *(7m S of Dumfries on A710)*

☎ 01387 850260

web: www.historic-scotland.gov.uk

Built in the late 18th century, this water-driven corn mill is still in working order, and regular demonstrations are held.

Times: Open all year, Apr-Sep, daily 9.30-6.30; Oct-Mar, Mon-Wed & Sat-Sun 9.30-4.30. Closed 25-26 Dec & 1-2 Jan. **Fee:** ✱ £3.50 (ch £1.50, concessions £2.50). Please phone or check website for details.
Facilities: Ⓟ (100yds) shop ⊗ 🗮

Shambellie House Museum of Costume
FREE

DG2 8HQ

➲ *(7m S of Dumfries, on A710)*

☎ 01387 850375

e-mail: info@nms.ac.uk

web: www.nms.ac.uk/costume

Shambellie House is a beautiful Victorian country house set in attractive wooded grounds. You are invited to step back in time and

experience Victorian and Edwardian grace and refinement. See period costume from the 1850s to the 1950s displayed in appropriate room settings with accessories, furniture and decorative art. Telephone for details of special events.

Times: Open Apr-Oct, daily, 10-5. **Facilities:** Ⓟ 🅿️ ♿ (ramp and w/chair lift at main entrance) shop ⊗ (ex guide/hearing dogs) 🗮

Sweetheart Abbey

DG2 8BU

➲ *(on A710)*

☎ 01387 850397

web: www.historic-scotland.gov.uk

Lady Devorgilla of Galloway founded Balliol College, Oxford in memory of her husband John Balliol; she also founded this abbey in his memory in 1273. When she died in 1289 she was buried in front of the high altar with the heart of her husband resting on her bosom; hence the name 'Sweetheart Abbey'. The abbey features an unusual precinct wall of enormous boulders.

Times: Open all year, Apr-Sep, daily 9.30-6.30; Oct-Mar, Mon-Wed & Sat-Sun 9.30-4.30. Closed 25-26 Dec & 1-2 Jan. **Fee:** ✱ £2.50 (ch £1, concessions £2). Please phone or check website for further details.
Facilities: Ⓟ ♿ (with assistance) ⊗ 🗮

PALNACKIE   **MAP 11 NX85**

Orchardton Tower
FREE

➲ *(6m SE of Castle Douglas on A711)*

web: www.historic-scotland.gov.uk

A charming little tower house of mid-15th-century date. It is, uniquely, circular in plan.

Times: Open all reasonable times. Closed 25-26 Dec. **Facilities:** Ⓟ ⊗ 🗮

PORT LOGAN   **MAP 10 NX04**

Logan Botanic Garden

DG9 9ND

➲ *(on B7065, 14m S of Stranraer)*

☎ 01776 860231

e-mail: logan@rbge.org.uk

web: www.rbge.org.uk

Logan's exceptionally mild climate allows a colourful array of tender plants to thrive out-of-doors. Amongst the many highlights are tree ferns, cabbage palms, unusual shrubs, climbers and tender perennials found within the setting of the walled, water, terrace and woodland gardens.

Times: Open Mar-Oct, Mar & Oct daily 10-5. Apr-Sep 10-6 **Fee:** ✱ £3.50 (ch £1, concessions £3). Family £8 **Facilities:** Ⓟ 🍴 licensed 🅿️ ♿ (access limited, wheelchairs available for loan) toilets for disabled shop garden centre ⊗ (ex guide dogs) 🗮

continued

RUTHWELL   MAP 11 NY16

Ruthwell Cross   `FREE`

➲ *(sited within the parish church on B724)*
web: www.historic-scotland.gov.uk

Now in a specially built apse in the parish church, the carved cross
dates from the 7th or 8th centuries. Two faces show scenes from the
Life of Christ; the others show scroll work, and parts of an ancient
poem in Runic characters. It was broken up in the 18th century, but
pieced together by a 19th-century minister.

Times: Open all reasonable times. Contact Key Keeper for access on 01387
870249. **Facilities:** ♿ ⊗ 🔔

Savings Banks Museum   `FREE`
DG1 4NN

➲ *(off B724, 10m E of Dumfries & 7m W of Annan)*
☎ 01387 870640
e-mail: tsbmuseum@btinternet.com
web: www.lloydstsb.com/savingsbankmuseum

Housed in the building where Savings Banks first began, the museum
traces their growth and development from 1810 up to the present day.
The museum also traces the life of Dr Henry Duncan, father of savings
banks, and restorer of the Ruthwell Cross. Multi-lingual leaflets available.

Times: Open, Tue-Sat, Apr-Sep, Thu-Sat, Oct-Mar, 10-4; Open on BHs
except Xmas & New Year **Facilities:** ♿ 🍴 ♿ (touch facilities for blind,
guide available) ⊗ (ex guide dogs)

SANQUHAR   MAP 11 NS70

Sanquhar Tolbooth Museum   `FREE`
High St DG4 6BN

➲ *(on A76 Dumfries-Kilmarnock road)*
☎ 01659 250186
e-mail: dumfriesmuseum@dumgal.gov.uk
web: www.dumgal.gov.uk/museums

Housed in the town's fine 18th-century tolbooth, the museum tells the
story of the mines and miners of the area, its earliest inhabitants,
native and Roman, the history and customs of the Royal Burgh of
Sanquhar and local traditions.

Times: Open Apr-Sep, Tue-Sat 10-1 & 2-5, Sun 2-5. **Facilities:** ♿ 🍴
♿ (museum up steps, phone for info) shop

STRANRAER   MAP 10 NX06

Castle Kennedy Gardens   2 for 1
Stair Estates, Rephad DG9 8BX

➲ *(5m E of Stranraer on A75, signed at Castle Kennedy
Village)*
☎ 01776 702024 & 01581 400225
e-mail: info@castlekennedygardens.co.uk
web: www.castlekennedygardens.co.uk

Situated on a peninsula between two lochs, the gardens around the Old
Castle were first laid out in the early 18th century. Noted for their
rhododendrons and azaleas (at their best May and early Jun) and walled
kitchen garden with fine herbaceous borders (best in Aug and Sep). The
gardens contain many avenues and walks amid beautiful scenery.

Times: Open Etr-Sep, daily 10-5 **Fee:** ✱ £4 (ch £1, pen £3). Party 20+ 10%
discount. **Facilities:** ♿ 🍴 🍴 ♿ (tearoom to enable access) toilets for
disabled shop garden centre ⊗ (ex on a lead) 🔊

Glenwhan Gardens   2 for 1
Dunragit DG9 8PH

➲ *(7m E of Stranraer, signed)*
☎ 01581 400222
e-mail: tess@glenwhan.freeserve.co.uk
web: www.glenwhangardens.co.uk

Enjoying spectacular views over the Mull of Galloway and Luce Bay,
Glenwhan is a beautiful 12-acre garden set on a hillside. There are two
lakes filled with rare species, alpines, scree plants, heathers, conifers,
roses, woodland walks and fascinating garden sculpture.

Times: Open Apr-Sep, daily 10-5 **Fee:** ✱ £4 (ch £2, concessions £3).
Family £9. Season £10 **Facilities:** ♿ 🍴 🍴 licensed ♿ (wheelchairs
provided) toilets for disabled shop garden centre

THORNHILL   MAP 11 NX89

Drumlanrig Castle
DG3 4AQ

➲ *(4m N of Thornhill off A76)*
☎ 01848 331555
e-mail: bre@drumlanrigcastle.org.uk
web: www.drumlanrig.com

This unusual pink sandstone castle was built in the late 17th century in
Renaissance style. It contains a outstanding collection of fine art. There
is also French furniture, as well as silver and relics of Bonnie Prince
Charlie. The old stable block has a craft centre with resident craft
workers, and the grounds offer an extensive garden plant centre,
working forge, mountain bike hire and woodland walks. For details of
special events phone 01848 331555.

Times: Open early May-late Aug, Castle open daily. Guided tours and
restricted route may operate at various times, please verify before visiting.
Fee: ✱ £7 (ch £4 & pen £6). Grounds only £4. Party 20+ £5 each.
Facilities: ♿ 🍴 licensed ♿ (lift for wheelchair users) toilets for disabled
shop garden centre ⊗ (ex in park on lead) 🔊

WANLOCKHEAD   MAP 11 NS81

Museum of Scottish Lead Mining   `2 for 1`
ML12 6UT
➲ *(signed from M74 and A76)*
☎ 01659 74387
e-mail: miningmuseum@hotmail.com
web: www.leadminingmuseum.co.uk

Wanlockhead is Scotland's highest village, set in the beautiful Lowther Hills. Visitors can see miners' cottages, the miners' library as well as the 18th-century lead mine. Visitors can also pan for gold.

Times: Open Apr-2 Nov, daily 10.30-4.30; Jul & Aug 10-5. **Fee:** ✱ £5 (ch £3.50, concessions £3.75). Family ticket £13.50 **Facilities:** ♿ ☕ ⭗ licensed 🏠 ♿ (induction loops) toilets for disabled shop ⊗ (ex guide dogs) 🍴

WHITHORN   MAP 10 NX44

Whithorn-Cradle of Christianity
45-47 George St DG8 8NS
➲ *(follow directions S from junct at Newton Stewart & Glenluce A75. Centre on main street in centre of Whithorn)*
☎ 01988 500508
e-mail: enquiries@whithorn.com
web: www.whithorn.com

The Whithorn Dig is the site of the first Christian settlement in Scotland - the Candida Casa of St Ninian. Friendly guides explain the excavation, and there's a museum of Early Christian stones.

Times: ✱ Open daily, Apr-Oct 10.30-5. **Facilities:** ℗ ☕ 🏠 ♿ (one short staircase with 'stairmatic') toilets for disabled shop 🍴

Whithorn Priory
DG8 8PY
➲ *(on A746)*
☎ 01988 500508
web: www.historic-scotland.gov.uk

The first Christian church in Scotland was founded here by St Ninian in 397AD, but the present ruins date from the 12th century. These

continued

ruins are sparse but there is a notable Norman door, the Latinus stone of the 5th century and other early Christian monuments.

Times: Open Apr-Oct, daily 10.30-5. **Fee:** ✱ £3 (ch £1.50 & concessions £2). Please phone or check website for further details.
Facilities: ♿ ☕ ⭗ 🎫

DUNDEE CITY

DUNDEE   MAP 11 NO43

Broughty Castle Museum   `FREE`
Castle Approach, Broughty Ferry DD5 2TF
➲ *(turn S off A930 at traffic lights by Eastern Primary School in Broughty Ferry)*
☎ 01382 436916
e-mail: broughty@dundeecity.gov.uk
web: www.dundeecity.gov.uk/broughtycastle

The 15th-century castle was rebuilt to defend the Tay estuary in the 19th century. It now houses fascinating displays on Dundee's whaling history, arms and armour, local history and seashore life. There are superb views across the Tay estuary from the observation room.

Times: Open all year Apr-Sep, Mon-Sat 10-4, Sun 12.30-4; Oct-Mar, Tue-Sat 10-4, Sun 12.30-4. Closed Mons, 25-26 Dec & 1-3 Jan. **Facilities:** ♿ ☕ 🏠 ♿ (unsuitable for wheelchairs) shop ⊗ (ex guide dogs)

Camperdown Country Park
Coupar Angus Rd DD2 4TF
➲ *(A90 to Dundee then onto A923 (Coupar-Angus road), left at 1st rdbt to attraction)*
☎ 01382 431818
e-mail: camperdown@dundeecity.gov.uk
web: www.camperdownpark.com

Camperdown is Dundees largest park, covers an area of over 400 acres and is home to some 190 species of tree. There is a good range of facilities, including an 18-hole golf course, a putting green, boating pond, childrens play area, footpaths and woodland trails, and Camperdown Wildlife Centre. There is also a year-round calendar of special events, contact for details.

Times: Open Park: all year. Wildlife Centre: Mar-Sep, daily 10-4.30 (last admission 3.45), Oct-Mar 10-3.30 (last admission 2.45). **Fee:** Park-Free admission. Wildlife Centre charged. **Facilities:** ♿ ☕ ♿ (ramps) toilets for disabled shop ⊗ (ex guide dogs and on leads)

Discovery Point & RRS Discovery
Discovery Quay DD1 4XA
➲ *(follow brown heritage signs for Historic Ships)*
☎ 01382 201245
e-mail: info@dundeeheritage.sol.co.uk
web: www.rrsdiscovery.com

Discovery Point is the home of *RRS Discovery*, Captain Scott's famous Antarctic ship. Spectacular lighting, graphics and special effects re-create key moments in the Discovery story. The restored bridge gives a captain's view over the ship and the River Tay. Learn what happened to the ship after the expedition, during the First World War and the Russian Revolution, and find out about her involvement in the first survey of whales' migratory patterns.

continued

Discovery Point & RRS Discovery

Times: Open Apr-Oct, Mon-Sat 10-6. Sun 11-6; Nov-Mar, Mon-Sat 10-5. Sun 11-5. **Fee:** ✱ £6.45 (ch £3.85, pen & concessions £4.90). Group £5.15 (ch £3.50, pen & concessions £4) **Facilities:** ❷ (charged) ⑩ licensed ♿ (in-house wheelchairs & lifts, parking, ramps onto ship) toilets for disabled shop ⊗ (ex guide & hearing dogs) ◀

HM Frigate Unicorn
Victory Dock DD1 3BP
➲ *(from W follow A85 from A90 at Invergowrie. From E follow A92. Near N end of Tay Road Bridge. Follow signs for City Quay).*
☎ 01382 200900 & 200893
e-mail: frigateunicorn@hotmail.com
web: www.frigateunicorn.org
The *Unicorn* is the oldest British-built warship afloat, and Scotland's only example of a wooden warship. Today she houses a museum of life in the Royal Navy during the days of sail, with guns, models and displays.

Times: Open all year Apr-Oct, daily 10-5; Nov-Mar, Wed-Fri 12-4, Sat & Sun 10-4.Closed Mon-Tue & 2 weeks at Xmas & New Year. **Fee:** £4 (concessions £3). Family ticket £9-£11. Groups 10+ £2.50 each. **Facilities:** ❷ 🛒 📷 ♿ (audio visual presentations, introductory video) shop ⊗ (Guide dogs on deck area only) ◀

Mills Observatory
Balgay Park, Glamis Rd DD2 2UB
➲ *(1m W of city centre, in Balgay Park, on Balgay Hill. Vehicle entrance at Glamis Rd gate to Balgay Park)*
☎ 01382 435967
e-mail: mills.observatory@dundeecity.gov.uk
web: www.dundeecity.gov.uk/mills
The observatory was built in 1935, and has a Victorian 10in Cooke refracting telescope among its instruments. The gallery has displays on astronomy and space exploration; visitors can view a safe projection of the sun on bright days. There is a small planetarium for booked groups only. Open nights during the winter months, children's activities during the summer holidays.

Times: Open all year, Apr-Sep, Tue-Fri 11-5, Sat & Sun 12.30-4; Oct-Mar, Mon-Fri 4-10, Sat & Sun 12.30-4. Closed 25-26 Dec & 1-3 Jan. **Fee:** Free except for planetarium shows extra, £1 (ch 50p) Groups £10.
Facilities: ❷ 📷 ♿ (portable telescopes available, images on screen) toilets for disabled shop ⊗ (ex guide dogs) ◀

Verdant Works
West Henderson's Wynd DD2 5BT
➲ *(follow brown tourist signs)*
☎ 01382 225282
e-mail: info@dundeeheritage.sol.co.uk
web: www.verdantworks.com

Dating from 1830, this old Jute Mill covers 50,000 sq ft and has been restored as a living museum of Dundee and Tayside's textile history and award-winning European Industrial Museum. Phase I explains what jute is, where it comes from and why Dundee became the centre of its production. Working machinery illustrates the production process from raw jute to woven cloth. Phase II deals with the uses of jute and its effects on Dundee's social history.

Times: Open Apr-Oct; Mon-Sat 10-5, Sun 11-5. Nov-Mar; Mon-Sat 10-4, Sun 11-4. Venue closes 1hr after last entry. Please check for winter opening times. Closed 25-26 Dec & 1-2 Jan **Fee:** ✱ £5.95 (ch £3.85, pen & concessions £4.45). Family ticket (2ad+2ch) £17. **Facilities:** ❷ (charged) ♿ (wheelchairs, induction loops) toilets for disabled shop ⊗ (ex guide & hearing dogs) ◀

GALSTON   **MAP 11 NS53**

Loudoun Castle Theme Park
KA4 8PE
➲ *(signed from A74(M), from A77 and from A71)*
☎ 01563 822296
e-mail: loudouncastle@btinternet.com
web: www.loudouncastle.co.uk
Loudoun Castle Theme Park is a great day out for the whole family. Theme park rides, live entertainment and McDougals Farm are just a taster of what's on offer.

Times: Open Etr-end of Sep. Please phone for further details.
Facilities: ❷ 🛒 ⑩ licensed 📷 ♿ toilets for disabled shop ⊗ (ex guide dogs) ◀

Scotland

KILMARNOCK
MAP 10 NS43

Dick Institute Museum & Art Galleries
Elmbank Ave KA1 3BU
➲ *(follow brown tourist signs from A77 S of Glasgow, into town centre)*
☎ 01563 554343
web: www.east-ayrshire.gov.uk

Temporary and permanent exhibitions spread over two floors of this grand Victorian building. Fine art, social and natural history feature upstairs, whilst the downstairs galleries house temporary exhibitions of art and craft.

Times: Open all year, Tue-Sat 11-5. Closed Sun, Mon and Public Hols. **Fee:** Free except for special exhibitions when a charge may be made. **Facilities:** ❷ ♿ (wheelchair available) toilets for disabled shop ⊗ (ex guide dogs)

EAST DUNBARTONSHIRE

BEARSDEN
MAP 11 NS57

Antonine Wall: Bearsden Bath-house `FREE`
Roman Rd G61 2SG
➲ *(signed from Bearsden Cross on A810)*
web: www.historic-scotland.gov.uk

Considered to be the best surviving visible Roman building in Scotland, the bath-house was discovered in 1973 during excavations for a construction site. It was originally built for use by the Roman garrison at Bearsden Fort, which is part of the Antonine Wall defences. This building dates from the 2nd century AD. Visitors should wear sensible footwear.

Times: Open all reasonable times. **Facilities:** ♿ ⊗ ⅋

EAST LOTHIAN

ABERLADY
MAP 12 NT47

Myreton Motor Museum `2 for 1`
EH32 0PZ
➲ *(1.5m from A198, 2m from A1)*
☎ 01875 870288 & 07947 066666
e-mail: myreton.motor.museum@aberlady.org

The museum has on show a large collection, from 1899, of cars, bicycles, motor cycles and commercials. There is also a large collection of period advertising, posters and enamel signs etc.

Times: Open, Mar-Nov daily 11-4, Dec-Feb, wknds only 11-3 **Fee:** £6 (ch £3). **Facilities:** ❷ ♿ ⊗ (ex guide dogs)

DIRLETON
MAP 12 NT58

Dirleton Castle
EH39 5ER
➲ *(on A198)*
☎ 01620 850330
web: www.historic-scotland.gov.uk

The oldest part of this romantic castle dates from the 13th century. It was besieged by Edward I in 1298, rebuilt and expanded, and then

continued

destroyed in 1650. Now the sandstone ruins have a beautiful mellow quality. Within the castle grounds is a garden established in the 16th century, with ancient yews and hedges around a bowling green.

Times: Open all year, Apr-Sep daily 9.30-6.30; Oct-Mar daily 9.30-4.30. Closed 25-26 Dec & 1-2 Jan. **Fee:** ✱ £4 (ch £1.60, concessions £3). Please phone or check website for further details. **Facilities:** ❷ shop ⅋

EAST FORTUNE
MAP 12 NT57

Museum of Flight
East Fortune Airfield EH39 5LF
➲ *(signed from A1 near Haddington. Onto B1347, past Athelstaneford, 20m E of Edinburgh)*
☎ 01620 897240
e-mail: info@nms.ac.uk
web: www.nms.ac.uk

The Museum of Flight is situated on 63 acres of one of Britain's best preserved wartime airfields, the museum has four hangars, with more than 50 aeroplanes, plus engines, rockets and memorabilia. Items on display include two Spitfires, a Vulcan bomber and Britain's oldest surviving aeroplane, built in 1896; recent exhibits also include a Phantom jet fighter, and a Harrier jump-jet. The Concorde Experience explores the story of this historic plane through the lives of those who worked or travelled on it. The Experience is free with admission, but a charge is made to go on board the plane, and pre-booking for this is essential.

Times: Open Apr-Oct, daily, 10-5. Jul-Aug, daily, 10-6. Nov-Mar, wknds only, 10-4. Open 28-31 Dec, 3-7 Jan, 12-18 Feb. **Fee:** ✱ £5, (ch under 12 free, concessions £4). NMS members free. To include Concorde Boarding Pass; +£3 ad, +£2 ch & concessions. **Facilities:** ❷ ♨ ♿ toilets for disabled shop ⊗ (ex assist dogs) ⬛

EAST LINTON
MAP 12 NT57

Hailes Castle `FREE`
➲ *(1.5m SW of East Linton on A1)*
web: www.historic-scotland.gov.uk

A beautiful sited ruin incorporating a fortified manor of 13th-century date, extended in the 14th and 15th centuries. There are two vaulted pit-prisons.

Times: Open at all reasonable times. **Facilities:** ❷ ⊗ ⅋

Preston Mill & Phantassie Doocot

EH40 3DS

➲ *(signed from A1)*

☎ 01620 860426

web: www.nts.org.uk

This attractive mill, with conical, pantiled roof, is the oldest working water-driven meal mill to survive in Scotland, and was last used commercially in 1957. Nearby is the charming Phantassie Doocot (dovecote), built for 500 birds.

Times: ✱ Open Apr-Sep, Thu-Mon 12-5, Sun 1-5. Times may change for 2007 please telephone or check website **Facilities:** ❷ ♿ toilets for disabled shop ⊗ (ex guide dogs) ♨

INVERESK   MAP 11 NT37

Inveresk Lodge Garden

EH21 7TE

➲ *(A6124, S of Musselburgh)*

☎ 01721 722502

web: www.nts.org.uk

This charming terraced garden, set in the historic village of Inveresk, specialises in plants, shrubs and roses suitable for growing on small plots. The 17th-century house makes an elegant backdrop.

Times: ✱ Open all year daily 10-6 or dusk if earlier. Times may change for 2007 please telephone or check website **Facilities:** ❷ ♿ ⊗ (ex guide dogs) ♨

NORTH BERWICK   MAP 12 NT58

Scottish Seabird Centre

The Harbour EH39 4SS

➲ *(A1 from Edinburgh, then A198 to North Berwick. Brown heritage signs clearly marked from A1)*

☎ 01620 890202

e-mail: info@seabird.org

web: www.seabird.org

Get close to nature with a visit to this award-winning centre. With panoramic views over the islands of the Firth of Forth and sand-fringed bays of North Berwick, the area is a haven for wildlife. Use state-of-the-art 'Big Brother' cameras to see wide variety of wildlife action live - including gannet colony, hundreds of puffins seals and sometimes bottlenose dolphins. Wildlife boat safari with landings on the islands and passenger ferry to Fife (summer). New features include the Environmental Discovery Centre and Migration Tunnel.

Times: Open all year, Apr-Oct 10-6 daily, Nov-Jan 10-4 (Mon-Fri) 10-5.30 (Sat & Sun), Feb-Mar 10-5 (Mon-Fri) 10-5.30 (Sat & Sun). Closed 25 Dec **Facilities:** ❷ 🖳 🍴 📷 ♿ (1 w/chair, parking on site, walking frame available) toilets for disabled shop ⊗ (ex guide dogs) 🍴

Tantallon Castle

EH39 5PN

➲ *(3m E, off A198)*

☎ 01620 892727

web: www.historic-scotland.gov.uk

A famous 14th-century stronghold of the Douglases facing towards the lonely Bass Rock from the rocky Firth of Forth shore. Nearby 16th and 17th century earthworks.

Times: Open all year, Apr-Sep, daily 9.30-6.30; Oct-Mar, Mon-Wed & Sat-Sun 9.30-4.30. Closed 25-26 Dec & 1-2 Jan. **Fee:** ✱ £4 (ch £1.60, concessions £3). Please phone or check website for further details. **Facilities:** ❷ shop ⊗ 🚻

PRESTONPANS   MAP 11 NT37

Prestongrange Museum   FREE

Prestongrange

➲ *(on B1348)*

☎ 0131 653 2904

e-mail: elms@eastlothian.gov.uk

web: www.eastlothian.gov.uk/museums

The oldest documented coal mining site in Scotland, with 800 years of history, this museum shows a Cornish Beam Engine and on-site evidence of associated industries such as brickmaking and pottery. It is located next to a 16th-century customs port. Special Events - weekend events for families and children in July/August.

Times: Open end Mar-mid Oct, daily 11-4. **Facilities:** ❷ 🖳 ♿ (grounds partly accessible) toilets for disabled shop ⊗ (ex guide dogs)

FALKIRK

BIRKHILL   MAP 11 NS97

The Birkhill Fireclay Mine

EH51 9AQ

➲ *(A706 from Linlithgow, A904 from Grangemouth, follow brown signs to Steam Railway & Fireclay Mine. Main access is by train from Bo'ness)*

☎ 01506 825855

e-mail: mine@srps.org.uk

web: www.srps.org.uk

Tour guides will meet you at Birkhill Station and lead you down into the ancient woodland of the beautiful Avon Gorge, and then into the caverns of the Birkhill Fireclay mine. See how the clay was worked, what it was used for and find the 300-million-year-old fossils in the roof of the mine.

Times: Open Etr-Oct, wknds only; Jul-Aug, daily. **Fee:** ✱ Mine and Train £8 (ch £4.50, concessions £6.50) Family ticket (2ad+2ch) £21. Mine only £3 (ch £2, concessions £2.50) Family ticket £8 **Facilities:** ❷ 🖳

BO'NESS   MAP 11 NT08

Bo'ness & Kinneil Railway

Bo'ness Station, Union St EH51 9AQ

➲ *(A904 from all directions, signed)*

☎ 01506 825855

e-mail: railway@srps.org.uk

web: www.srps.org.uk

Historic railway buildings, including the station and train shed, have been relocated from sites all over Scotland. The Scottish Railway Exhibition tells the story of the development of railways and their impact on the people of Scotland. Take a seven mile return trip by steam train to the tranquil country station at Birkhill. Special events take place throughout the year.

Times: Open Apr-Jun & Sep-Oct, Sat-Sun; Jul-Aug, Tue-Sun; Dec wknds only. Steam trains daily, depart 11, 12.15, 1.45 & 3, diesel departs at 4.15. Ring for details of special events. **Fee:** ✱ Return fare £5 (ch 3-15 £2.50, concessions £4). Family ticket £13. Ticket for return train fare & tour of Birkhill Fireclay Mine £8 (ch £4.50, concessions £6.50), Family ticket £21. **Facilities:** ❷ 🖳 ♿ (ramps to station & adapted carriage) toilets for disabled shop 🍴

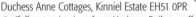

Kinneil Museum & Roman Fortlet [FREE]

Duchess Anne Cottages, Kinniel Estate EH51 0PR

➲ *(follow tourist signs from Heritage Railway, off M9. Establishment at E end of town accessed via Dean Rd)*

☎ 01506 778530

web: www.falkirk.gov.uk/cultural

The museum is in a converted stable block of Kinneil House. The ground floor has displays on the industrial history of Bo'ness, while the upper floor looks at the history and environment of the Kinneil Estate. The remains of the Roman fortlet can be seen nearby. An audio visual presentation shows 2000 years of history.

Times: Open all year, Mon-Sat 12.30-4. **Facilities:** ℗ & shop ⊗ (ex assist dogs)

FALKIRK   MAP 11 NS88

Callendar House [FREE]

Callendar Park FK1 1YR

➲ *(On southside of town centre, Callendar House is signposted. Easily accessible from M9)*

☎ 01324 503770

e-mail: callendar.house@falkirk.gov.uk

web: www.falkirk.gov.uk/cultural

Mary, Queen of Scots, Oliver Cromwell, Bonnie Prince Charlie, noble earls and wealthy merchants all feature in the history of Callendar House. Costumed interpreters describe early 19th-century life in the kitchens and the 900-year history of the house is illustrated in the 'Story of Callendar House' exhibition. The house is set in parkland, offering boating and woodland walks. Regular temporary heritage, natural history and visual arts exhibitions in Callendar House's Large and Small Galleries.

Times: Open all year, Mon-Sat, 10-5. Apr-Sep, Sun, 2-5. **Facilities:** ℗ 💺 & (lifts) toilets for disabled shop ⊗ (ex assist dogs) 🍴

Rough Castle [FREE]

➲ *(1m E of Bonnybridge, signed from B816)*

web: www.historic-scotland.gov.uk

The impressive earthworks of a large Roman fort on the Antonine Wall can be seen here. The buildings have disappeared, but the mounds and terraces are the sites of barracks, and granary and bath buildings. Running between them is the military road, which once linked all the forts on the wall and is still well defined.

Times: Open any reasonable time. **Facilities:** ℗ ⊗ 🚻

FIFE

ABERDOUR   MAP 11 NT18

Aberdour Castle

KY3 0SL

➲ *(in Aberdour, 5m E of Forth Bridge on A921)*

☎ 01383 860519

web: www.historic-scotland.gov.uk

The earliest surviving part of the castle is the 14th-century keep. There are also later buildings, and the remains of a terraced garden, a bowling green and a fine 16th-century doocot (dovecote).

continued

Times: Open all year, Apr-Sep, daily 9.30-6.30; Oct-Mar, daily 9.30-4.30. Closed Thu-Fri & 25-26 Dec & 1-2 Jan. **Fee:** ✱ £3.50 (ch £1.50, concessions £2.50). Please telephone for further details or check website **Facilities:** ℗ 🍽 & (wheelchairs) toilets for disabled shop 🚻

ANSTRUTHER   MAP 12 NO50

Scottish Fisheries Museum [2 for 1]

St Ayles, Harbour Head KY10 3AB

➲ *(A917 through St Monans & Pittenweem to Anstruther)*

☎ 01333 310628

e-mail: info@scotfishmuseum.org

web: www.scotfishmuseum.org

This award-winning national museum tells the story of Scottish fishing and its people from the earliest times to the present. With 10 galleries, 2 large boatyards, and a restored fisherman's cottage, which contain many fine paintings and photographs, boat models and actual boats, clothing and items of daily life to see, a visit to the museum makes for an exceptional day out.

Times: Open all year, Apr-Sep, Mon-Sat 10-5.30, Sun 11-5; Oct-Mar, Mon-Sat 10-4.30, Sun 12-4.30. Closed 25-26 Dec & 1-2 Jan. (Last admission 1 hr before closing). **Fee:** ✱ £4.50 (concessions £3.50). Party 12+ £3 (primary ch £1, accompanied ch free, concessions £2) **Facilities:** ℗ (20yds) (charge in summer) 💺 & (ramps throughout to provide full access) toilets for disabled shop ⊗ (ex guide dogs) 🍴

BURNTISLAND   MAP 11 NT28

Burntisland Edwardian Fair Museum [FREE]

102 High St KY3 9AS

➲ *(in the centre of Burntisland)*

☎ 01592 412860

web: kirkcaldy.museum@fife.gov.uk

Burntisland Museum has recreated a walk through the sights and sounds of the town's fair in 1910, based on a painting of the scene by local artist Andrew Young. See reconstructed rides, stalls and side shows of the time.

Times: Open all year, Mon, Wed, Fri & Sat 10-1 & 2-5; Tue & Thu 10-1 & 2-7. Closed PHs) **Facilities:** ℗ (20m) (on street parking) ⊗ (ex guide dogs)

Scotland

CULROSS   MAP 11 NS98

Culross Palace, Town House & The Study
West Green House KY12 8JH
➲ (off A985, 3m E of Kincardine Bridge)
☎ 01383 880359
web: www.nts.org.uk

A royal burgh, Culross dates from the 16th and 17th centuries and has remained virtually unchanged since. It prospered from the coal and salt trades, and when these declined in the 1700s, Culross stayed as it was. It owes its present appearance to the National Trust for Scotland, which has been gradually restoring it. In the Town House is a visitor centre and exhibition; in the building called The Study can be seen a drawing room with a Norwegian painted ceiling, and The Palace has painted rooms and terraced gardens.

Times: ✱ Open Palace, Study & Town House: Good Fri-Sep, daily 12-5. Garden all year 10-6 or sunset if earlier. Times may change for 2007 please telephone or check website **Facilities:** ❷ ♨ & toilets for disabled shop ⊗ (ex guide dogs) ⛟

CUPAR   MAP 11 NO31

Hill of Tarvit Mansionhouse & Garden
KY15 5PB
➲ (2.5m S of Cupar, off A916)
☎ 01334 653127
web: www.nts.org.uk

Built in the first decade of the 20th century, the Mansionhouse is home to a notable collection of paintings, tapestries, furniture and Chinese porcelain. The grounds include formal gardens, and there is a regular programme of concerts and art exhibitions.

Times: ✱ Open Apr-Sep, daily 1-5; Oct wknds 1-5. Garden & grounds all year, daily 9.30-sunset. Times may change for 2007 please telephone or check website **Facilities:** ❷ ♨ & toilets for disabled shop ⊗ (ex guide dogs) ⛟

The Scottish Deer Centre   [2 for 1]
Bow-of-Fife KY15 4NQ
➲ (3m W of Cupar on A91)
☎ 01337 810391

Guided tours take about 30 minutes and allow you to meet and stroke deer. There are indoor and outdoor adventure play areas. Other features include regular falconry displays, viewing platform and a tree top walkway. European Grey Wolves are fed everyday (except Friday) at 3pm.

Times: Open daily, Etr-Oct 10-6, Nov-Etr 10-5. **Fee:** ✱ £5.50 (ch 3-15 £3.95) **Facilities:** ❷ ♨ & (special parking bay, loan of wheelchairs) toilets for disabled shop ⊗ (ex guide dogs) ⛟

DUNFERMLINE   MAP 11 NT08

Abbot House Heritage Centre
Abbot House, Maygate KY12 7NE
➲ (in city centre)
☎ 01383 733266
e-mail: dht@abbothouse.fsnet.co.uk
web: www.abbothouse.co.uk

For the better part of a millennium, pilgrims have beaten a path to Dumfermline's door. Today visitors can still share the rich royal

continued

heritage of the capital of Fife's Magic Kingdom. The volunteer-run Abbot House Heritage Centre - dubbed 'The People's Tardis' - propels the traveller through time from the days of the Picts - a time warp peopled by a veritable Who's Who of characters from Dumfermline's past: Scotland's royal saint, Braveheart's Wallace and Bruce, Scotland's Chaucer, steel magnate Andrew Carnegie and a whole panoply of kings, ending with the birth of ill-starred Charles I.

Times: Mar-Oct, daily, 10-5. Nov-Feb, Sun-Fri, 10-4, Sat, 10-5. **Fee:** £4 (accompanied ch under 16 free, concessions £3). Party 20+
Facilities: ℗ (150yds) ♨ & (parking on site, videos of inaccesible areas) toilets for disabled shop ⊗ (ex guide dogs) ⛟

Andrew Carnegie Birthplace Museum
Moodie St KY12 7PL
➲ (400yds S from Abbey)
☎ 01383 724302
e-mail: carnegiebirthplace@hotmail.com
web: www.carnegiebirthplace.com

The museum tells the story of the handloom weaver's son, born here in 1835, who created the biggest steel works in the USA and then became a philanthropist on a huge scale. The present-day work of the philanthropic Carnegie Trust is also explained.

Times: Open Apr-Oct, Mon-Sat 11-5, Sun 2-5. **Fee:** £2 (ch under 16 free, concessions £1). **Facilities:** ❷ 🗓 & (photo album) toilets for disabled shop ⊗ (ex guide dogs)

Dunfermline Abbey
Pittencrieff Park
☎ 01383 739026
web: www.historic-scotland.gov.uk

The monastery was a powerful Benedictine house, founded by Queen Margaret in the 11th century. A modern brass in the choir marks the grave of King Robert the Bruce. The monastery guest house became a royal palace, and was the birthplace of Charles I.

Times: Open all year, Apr-Sep, daily 9.30-6.30; Oct-Mar, daily 9.30-4.30, closed Thu (pm), Fri & Sun (am). Closed 25-26 Dec & 1-2 Jan. **Fee:** ✱ £3 (ch £1.30, concessions £2.30). Please phone or check website for further details. **Facilities:** ℗ shop ⊗ 🚩

Pittencrieff House Museum
Pittencrieff Park KY12 8QH
➲ (off A994 into Pittencriefff Park Car Park. Attraction on W edge of town)
☎ 01383 722935 & 313838
e-mail: dunfermline.museum@fife.gov.uk

A fine 17th-century house standing in the beautiful park gifted to the town by Andrew Carnegie. Accessible displays tell the story of the park's animals and plants, with plenty of photographs of people enjoying the park over the last 100 years.

Times: Open all year daily Jan-Mar 11-4; Apr-Sep 11-5; Oct-Dec 11-4
Facilities: ℗ (800yds) 🗓 & (ramp) toilets for disabled shop ⊗ (ex guide dogs)

Scotland

Falkland Palace & Garden

KY15 7BU

➲ (off A912, 11m N of Kirkaldy)

☎ 01337 857397

web: www.nts.org.uk

The hunting palace of the Stuart monarchs, this fine building, with a French-Renaissance style south wing, stands in the shelter of the Lomond Hills. The beautiful Chapel Royal and King's Bedchamber are its most notable features, and it is also home to the oldest royal tennis court in Britain (1539). The garden has a spectacular delphinium border. Recorded sacred music is played hourly in the Chapel. Please telephone for details of concerts, recitals etc.

Times: ✱ Open Mar-Oct, Mon-Sat 10-6, Sun 1-5. Times may change for 2007 please telephone or check website **Facilities:** ❷ ⅋ shop ⊗ (ex guide dogs) ⛾

Kellie Castle & Gardens

KY10 2RF

➲ (3m NW of Pittenweem on B9171)

☎ 01333 720271

e-mail: aclipson@nts-scot.demon.co.uk

web: www.nts.org.uk

The oldest part dates from about 1360, but it is for its 16th and 17th-century domestic architecture that Kellie is renowned. It has notable plasterwork and painted panelling, and there are also interesting Victorian gardens.

Times: ✱ Open Good Fri-Etr Mon & Jun-Sep, daily 1-5. Garden & grounds all year, daily 9.30-sunset. **Facilities:** ❷ ⬛ ⅋ (induction loop for hard of hearing) shop ⊗ (ex guide dogs) ⛾

Kirkcaldy Museum & Art Gallery `FREE`

War Memorial Gardens KY1 1YG

➲ (next to train station)

☎ 01592 412860

e-mail: kirkcaldy.museum@fife.gov.uk

web: www.fifedirect.org.uk/museums

Set in the town's lovely memorial gardens, the museum houses a collection of fine and decorative art, including 18th to 21st-century Scottish paintings, among them the works of William McTaggart and S J Peploe. An award-winning display 'Changing Places' tells the story of the social, industrial and natural heritage of the area.

Times: Open all year, Mon-Sat 10.30-5, Sun 2-5. Closed local hols **Facilities:** ❷ ⬛ ⅋ (ramp to main entrance & lift to 1st floor galleries) toilets for disabled shop ⊗ (ex guide dogs)

Deep Sea World

KY11 1JR

➲ (from N, M90 take exit for Inverkeithing. From S follow signs to Forth Rd Bridge, 1st exit left)

☎ 01383 411880

e-mail: info@deepseaworld.co.uk

web: www.deepseaworld.com/

The world's longest underwater tunnel gives you a diver's eye view of an underwater world. Come face to face with Sand Tiger sharks, and watch divers hand feed a wide array of sea life. Visit the Amazon Experience with ferocious piranhas and the amazing amphibian display featuring the world's most poisonous frog. Also featuring the newly opened Seal Sanctuary, dedicated to the rehabilitation and release of injured and orphaned seal pups. Please telephone or visit website for details of events running throughout the year.

Times: ✱ Open all year daily, Nov-Mar 10-5, Apr-Oct 10-6 wknds & school hols 10-6 **Facilities:** ❷ ⬛ 🗐 ⅋ (ramps & disabled parking, hearing loop) toilets for disabled shop ⊗ (ex guide dogs)

British Golf Museum

Bruce Embankment KY16 9AB

➲ (opposite Royal & Ancient Golf Club)

☎ 01334 460046 & 460053

e-mail: alisonwood@randa.org

web: www.britishgolfmuseum.co.uk

Where better to find out about golf than in St Andrews, the home of golf. Using diverse and exciting interactive displays, this museum explores the history of British golf from its origins to the personalities of today. The 18th Hole is fun for all the family, with dressing up, a mini-putting green and loads to do!

Times: Open Mar-Oct, Mon-Sat 9.30-5.30, Sun 10-5. Nov-Mar, Mon-Sun 10-4. **Fee:** ✱ £5 (ch 6-15 £2.75, concessions £4) Family ticket £12.75. **Facilities:** ❷ (charged) 🗐 ⅋ toilets for disabled shop ⊗ (ex guide dogs) ◀

Castle & Visitor Centre

KY16 9AR

☎ 01334 477196

web: www.historic-scotland.gov.uk

This 13th-century stronghold castle was the scene of the murder of Cardinal Beaton in 1546. The new visitor centre incorporates an exciting multi-media exhibition describing the history of the castle and nearby cathedral.

Times: ✱ Open all year, Apr-Sep, daily 9.30-6.30; Oct-Mar, daily 9.30-4.30. Closed 25-26 Dec & 1-2 Jan. **Facilities:** ℗ ⅋ toilets for disabled shop ⊗ 🗮

Cathedral (& Museum)

KY16 9QU

☎ 01334 472563

web: www.historic-scotland.gov.uk

The cathedral was the largest in Scotland, and is now an extensive ruin. The remains date mainly from the 12th and 13th centuries, and large parts of the precinct walls have survived intact. Close by is St Rule's church, which the cathedral was built to replace. St Rule's probably dates from before the Norman Conquest, and is considered the most interesting Romanesque church in Scotland.

Times: ✱ Open all year, Apr-Sep, daily 9.30-6.30; Oct-Mar, daily 9.30-4.30. Closed 25-26 Dec & 1-2 Jan. **Facilities:** ℗ shop ⊗ 🗮

St Andrews Aquarium

The Scores KY16 9AS

⮑ *(signed in town centre)*

☎ 01334 474786

web: www.standrewsaquarium.co.uk

This continually expanding aquarium is home to shrimps, sharks, eels, octopi, seals and much much more. Special features include the Seahorse Parade, and the Sea Mammal Research Unit, which is committed to the care of sea mammals and their environment.

Times: ✱ Open daily from 10. Please phone for winter opening
Facilities: ⓟ (charged) 💺 🍴 licensed ♿ toilets for disabled shop ⊗ (ex guide dogs) 🍴

HIGHLAND

AVIEMORE   MAP 14 NH81

Strathspey Steam Railway

Aviemore Station, Dalfaber Rd PH22 1PY

⮑ *(from A9 take B970 for Coylumbridge, on B9152, left after railway bridge, car park 0.25m on left. Other stations: Boat of Garten in village; Broomhill, off A95, 3.5m S of Grantown-on-Spey)*

☎ 01479 810725

e-mail: strathtrains@strathspeyrailway.co.uk

web: www.strathspeyrailway.co.uk

This steam railway covers the ten miles from Aviemore via Boat of Garten to Broomhill. The journey takes about 40 minutes, but allow around two hours for the round trip. Shorter trips are possible and timetables are available from the station and the tourist information centre. Telephone, visit website or see local press for details of events running throughout the year.

Times: Open Etr, 1-9 Apr & Jun-Sep, daily; Apr-May & Oct, Wed-Thu, Sat-Sun & BH Mon. **Fee:** £9.50 basic roundtrip (ch £4.75); £25 Family roundtrip. Day Rover £12 (ch £6) Family £30 **Facilities:** ⓟ 💺 🍴 licensed ♿ (ramps) toilets for disabled shop 🍴

BALMACARA   MAP 14 NG82

Balmacara Estate & Lochalsh Woodland Garden

IV40 8DN

⮑ *(3m E of Kyle of Lochalsh, off A87)*

☎ 01599 566325

e-mail: balmacara@nts.org.uk

web: www.nts.org.uk

The Balmacara Estate comprises some 5,600 acres and seven crofting villages, including Plockton, a conservation area. There are excellent views of Skye, Kintail and Applecross. The main attraction is the Lochalsh Woodland Garden, but the whole area is excellent for walking.

Times: ✱ Open Estate: all year. Woodland garden daily 9-sunset. Balmacara Square Visitor Centre, Apr-Sep, daily, 9-5 (Fri 9-4). Times may change for 2007 please telephone or check website **Facilities:** ⓟ ▾

BETTYHILL   MAP 14 NC76

Strathnaver Museum

KW14 7SS

⮑ *(By the A386 on outskirts of Bettyhill on the E of the village)*

☎ 01641 521418

e-mail: strathnavermus@ukonline.co.uk

The museum has displays on the Clearances, with a fine collection of Strathnaver Clearances furnishings, domestic and farm implements, and local books. There is also a Clan Mackay room. The museum's setting is a former church, a handsome stone building with a magnificent canopied pulpit dated 1774. The churchyard contains a carved stone known as the Farr Stone, which dates back to the 9th century and is a fine example of Pictish art.

Times: Open Apr-Oct, Mon-Sat 10-1 & 2-5; Nov-Mar restricted opening. **Fee:** £2 (ch 50p, under 5's free, concessions £1.50, student/groups £1). **Facilities:** ⓟ ♿ (DVD) shop ⊗ (ex guide dogs)

BOAT OF GARTEN   MAP 14 NH91

Loch Garten Osprey Centre

RSPB Reserve Abernethy Forest, Forest Lodge, Nethybridge PH25 3EF

⮑ *(signed from B970 & A9 at Aviemore, follow 'RSPB Ospreys' signs)*

☎ 01479 821894

Home of the Loch Garten Osprey site, this reserve holds one of most important remnants of Scots Pine forest in the Highlands. Within its 30,760 acres are forest bogs, moorland, mountain top, lochs and crofting land. In addition to the regular pair of nesting ospreys, there are breeding Scottish crossbills, capercaillies, black grouse and many others. The ospreys can be viewed through telescopes and there is a live TV link to the nest. Please telephone for details of special events running throughout the year.

Times: Osprey Centre open daily, Apr-Aug 10-6. **Facilities:** ⓟ 🍽 ♿ (low level viewing slots & optics) toilets for disabled shop ⊗ (ex guide dogs in centre) 🍴

CARRBRIDGE   MAP 14 NH92

Landmark Forest Theme Park

PH23 3AJ

⮑ *(off A9 between Aviemore & Inverness)*

☎ 01479 841613 & 0800 731 3446

e-mail: landmarkcentre@btconnect.com

web: www.landmark-centre.co.uk

This innovative centre is designed to provide a fun and educational visit for all ages. Microworld takes a close-up look at the incredible microscopic world around us. There is a 70ft forest viewing tower and a treetop trail. There are demonstrations of timber sawing, on a steam-powered sawmill and log hauling by a Clydesdale horse throughout the day. Attractions include a 3-track Watercoaster, a maze and a large covered adventure play area, mini electric cars and remote controlled truck arena. New features include; RopeworX, an aerial highwire obstacle course, and Skydive, a parachute jump simulator.

Times: Open all year, daily, Apr-mid Jul 10-6; mid Jul-mid Aug 10-7; Sep-Oct 10-5.30; Nov-Mar 10-5. Closed 25 Dec and 1 Jan. **Fee:** ✱ Apr-Oct: £8.95 (ch £6.90); Multi-visit week, £12.95 (ch £10.90), Year £14.95 (ch £12.90) **Facilities:** ⓟ 💺 🍴 licensed 🍴 ♿ (ramps) toilets for disabled shop 🍴

Scotland

CAWDOR
MAP 14 NH85

Cawdor Castle
IV12 5RD

➲ (on B9090, off A96)

☎ 01667 404401

e-mail: info@cawdorcastle.com

web: www.cawdorcastle.com

Home of the Thanes of Cawdor since the 14th century, this lovely castle has a drawbridge, an ancient tower built round a tree, and a freshwater well inside the house. Gardens Weekend takes place in June - guided tours of gardens with the head gardener.

Times: Open May-7 Oct, daily 10-5.30. Last admission 5. **Fee:** ✱ £7 (ch 5-15 £4.30, pen £6). Family ticket £22 Party 20+ £6.10 each. Gardens, grounds & nature trails only £3.70. **Facilities:** ℗ 🖳 🍴 licensed 🛒 ♿ (ramps to restaurants, shops and gardens) shop ⊗ (ex guide dogs) �

CLAVA CAIRNS
MAP 14 NH74

Clava Cairns
FREE

➲ (6m E of Inverness, signed from B9091)

☎ 01667 460232

web: www.historic-scotland.gov.uk

A well-preserved Bronze Age cemetery complex of passage graves, ring cairns, kerb cairn and standing stones in a beautiful setting. In addition, the remains of a chapel of unknown date can be seen at this site.

Times: Open at all reasonable times. **Facilities:** ℗ ⊗ ♮

CROMARTY
MAP 14 NH76

Hugh Miller's Cottage
Church St IV11 8XA

➲ (on A832)

☎ 01381 600245

web: www.nts.org.uk

The cottage houses an exhibition on the life and work of Hugh Miller, a stonemason born here in 1802 who became an eminent geologist and writer. It was built by his great-grandfather around 1698, and now has a charming cottage garden.

Times: ✱ Open Good Fri-Sep, daily 12-5; Oct, Sun-Wed 12-5. Times may change for 2007 please telephone or check website **Facilities:** ℗ (5mins) (disabled is directly outside) ♿ ⊗ (ex guide dogs) 🚾

CULLODEN MOOR
MAP 14 NH74

Culloden Battlefield
IV2 5EU

➲ (B9006, 5m E of Inverness)

☎ 01463 790607

e-mail: culloden@nts.org.uk

web: www.nts.org.uk

A cairn recalls this last battle fought on mainland Britain, on 16 April 1746, when the Duke of Cumberland's forces routed 'Bonnie' Prince Charles Edward Stuart's army. The battlefield has been restored to its state on the day of the battle, and in summer there are 'living history' enactments. This is a most atmospheric evocation of tragic events.

continued

Telephone for details of guided tours.

Times: ✱ Open Site: all year, daily. Visitor Centre: Feb-Mar & Nov-Dec, daily 11-4; Apr-Jun & Sep-Oct, daily 9-6; Jul-Aug, daily 9-7. Times may change for 2007 please telephone or check website **Facilities:** ℗ 🍴 ♿ (wheelchair, induction loop, raised map) toilets for disabled shop ⊗ (ex guide dogs) 🚾

DRUMNADROCHIT
MAP 14 NH52

Official Loch Ness Exhibition Centre, Loch Ness 2000

IV3 6TU

➲ (on A82, 12m S Inverness)

☎ 01456 450573 & 450218

e-mail: brem@loch-ness-scotland.com

web: www.loch-ness-scotland.com

A fascinating and popular multi-media presentation lasting 30 minutes. Seven themed areas cover the story of the Loch Ness Monster, from the pre-history of Scotland, through the cultural roots of the legend in Highland folklore, and into the 50-year controversy which surrounds it. Using latest technology in computer animation, lasers and multi-media projection systems.

Times: Open all year; Etr-May 9.30-5.30; Jun-Sep 9.30-6 (9-8.30 Jul & Aug); Winter 10-4. (Last admission 30mins before closing). **Fee:** ✱ £5.95 (ch £3.50, ch under 7 & disabled free, concessions £4.50). Family ticket £14.95. Group. **Facilities:** ℗ 🖳 🍴 licensed ♿ (parking) toilets for disabled shop ⊗ (ex in grounds/guide dogs) 🚾

Urquhart Castle
IV63 6XJ

➲ (on A82)

☎ 01456 450551

web: www.historic-scotland.gov.uk

The castle was once Scotland's biggest and overlooks Loch Ness. It dates mainly from the 14th century, when it was built on the site of an earlier fort, and was destroyed before the 1715 Jacobite rebellion.

Times: Open all year, Apr-Sep, daily 9.30-6.30; Oct-Mar, daily 9.30-4.30. Closed 25-26 Dec. **Fee:** ✱ £6.50 (ch £2.50, concessions £5). Please phone or check website for further details. **Facilities:** ℗ shop ⊗ ♮

DUNBEATH
MAP 15 ND12

Laidhay Croft Museum
KW6 6EH

➲ (1m N of Dunbeath on A9)

☎ 01593 731244

The museum gives visitors a glimpse of a long-vanished way of life. The main building is a thatched Caithness longhouse, with the dwelling quarters, byre and stable all under one roof. It dates back some 200 years, and is furnished as it might have been 100 years ago. A collection of early farm tools and machinery is also shown. Near the house is a thatched winnowing barn with its roof supported on three 'Highland couples', or crucks.

Times: Open Etr-Oct, daily 9-5 **Fee:** £2 (ch 50p) **Facilities:** ℗ 🖳 🛒 ♿ toilets for disabled

ELPHIN
MAP 14 NC21

Highland & Rare Breeds Farm
IV27 4HH
➲ (on A835 in Elphin)
☎ 01854 666204

There are highland cattle, traditional 4-horned sheep with coloured fleeces, traditional Scottish ewes and lambs, rare breeds of pigs and goats. Many types of poultry, duck ponds, and a farm walk among the animals. Also on display are farm tools, crofting history, wool crafts and hand-spinning.

Times: ✻ Open Jul & Aug only **Facilities:** ◗ 🕮 ⓹ (assistance available) toilets for disabled shop ⊗ ◥

FORT GEORGE
MAP 14 NH75

Fort George
IV1 2TD
➲ (11m NE of Inverness)
☎ 01667 462777
web: www.historic-scotland.gov.uk

Built following the Battle of Culloden as a Highland fortress for the army of George II, this is one of the outstanding artillery fortifications in Europe and still an active army barracks.

Times: Open all year, Apr-Sep daily 9.30-6.30; Oct-Mar daily 9.30-4.30. Closed 25-26 Dec. **Fee:** ✻ £6.50 (ch £2.50, concessions £5). Please phone or check website for further details. **Facilities:** ◗ 🍴 ⓹ toilets for disabled shop ⊗ 🏴

Queen's Own Highlanders Regimental Museum Collection
IV2 7TD
➲ (off A96 5m from Inverness)
☎ 01463 224380

Fort George has been a military barracks since it was built in 1748-69, and was the Depot of the Seaforth Highlanders until 1961. The museum of the Queen's Own Highlanders (Seaforth and Camerons) is sited in the former Lieutenant Governor's house, where uniforms, medals and pictures are displayed.

Times: Open Apr-Sep, daily 10-6; Oct-Mar, Mon-Fri 10-4. Closed Xmas, New Year & BH. **Fee:** ✻ Free. (Admission charged by Historic Scotland for entry to Fort George). **Facilities:** ◗ ⓹ (stair lift to 1st floor, wheelchair on 1st floor) toilets for disabled shop ⊗ (ex guide dogs)

FORT WILLIAM
MAP 14 NN17

Inverlochy Castle
FREE
PH33 6SN
➲ (2m NE of Fort William, off A82)
web: www.historic-scotland.gov.uk

A fine well-preserved 13th-century castle of the Comyn family; in the form of a square, with round towers at the corners. The largest tower was the donjon or keep. This is one of Scotland's earliest castles.

Times: Open at all reasonable times. **Facilities:** ◗ ⊗ 🏴

West Highland Museum
Cameron Square PH33 6AJ
➲ (museum next door to tourist office)
☎ 01397 702169
e-mail: info@westhighlandmuseum.org.uk
web: www.westhighlandmuseum.org.uk

The displays illustrate traditional Highland life and history, with numerous Jacobite relics. One of them is the 'secret portrait' of Bonnie Prince Charlie, which looks like meaningless daubs of paint but reveals a portrait when reflected in a metal cylinder.

Times: Open all year Jun-Sep, Mon-Sat 10-5 (also July-Aug, Sun 2-5); Oct-May, Mon-Sat 10-4. **Fee:** £3 (ch 50p, concessions £2) **Facilities:** Ⓟ (100yds) (charge all year) ⓹ toilets for disabled shop ⊗ (ex guide dogs)

GAIRLOCH
MAP 14 NG87

Gairloch Heritage Museum
2 for 1
Achtercairn IV21 2BP
➲ (on junct of A382 & B8021 near police station & public car park)
☎ 01445 712287
e-mail: info@gairlochheritagemuseum.org.uk
web: www.gairlochheritagemuseum.org.uk

A converted farmstead now houses the award-winning museum, which shows the way of life in this typical West Highland parish from early times to the 20th century. There are hands-on activities for children and reconstructions of a croft house room, a school room, a shop, and a smugglers' cave. You can also view Gairloch through one of the largest lenses assembled by the Northern Lighthouse Board. Please visit website for details of regular events, such as craft demonstrations, free open evenings and special exhibitions.

Times: Open Apr-Sep, Mon-Sat 10-5; Oct, Mon-Fri 10-1.30 (last admission 4.30). Winter months by arrangement. **Fee:** £3 (ch 50p, concessions £2). Group rates available **Facilities:** ◗ 🍴 🕮 ⓹ (Computer access to archive photographs) shop ⊗ (ex guide dogs)

GLENCOE
MAP 14 NN15

Glencoe & North Lorn Folk Museum
PH49 4HS
➲ (turn off A82 at Glencoe x-roads then immediately right into Glencoe village)
☎ 01855 811664
e-mail: glencoemuseum@btconnect.com
web: www.glencoemuseum.com

Two heather-thatched cottages in the main street of Glencoe now house items connected with the Macdonalds and the Jacobite risings. A variety of local domestic and farming exhibits, dairying and slate-working equipment, costumes and embroidery are also shown.

Times: Open Apr-Oct, Mon-Sat 10-5.30. **Fee:** ✻ £2 (ch free, concessions £1.50). **Facilities:** ◗ ⓹ shop

Glencoe Visitor Centre
PA39 4HX
➲ (on A82, 17m S of Fort William)
☎ 01855 811307 & 811729

Glencoe has stunning scenery and some of the most challenging climbs and walks in the Highlands. Red deer, wildcats, eagles and ptarmigan are among the wildlife. It is also known as a place of

continued

treachery and infamy. The Macdonalds of Glencoe were hosts to a party of troops who, under government orders, fell upon the men, women and children, in a bloody massacre in 1692. The Visitor Centre tells the story.

Times: ✱ Open: Site all year, daily. Visitor Centre Apr-Aug, 9.30-5.30; Mar-Apr & Sep-Oct, daily 10-5; Nov-Feb, Fri-Mon 10-4 (last admission 30 mins before closing). Times may change for 2007 please telephone or check website **Facilities:** ❷ ◗ ㋴ (induction loop in video programme room) toilets for disabled shop ❽ (ex guide dogs) ㊉

GLENFINNAN　　　　MAP 14 NM98

Glenfinnan Monument
PH37 4LT
➲ (on A830, 18.5m W of Fort William)
☎ 01397 722250
e-mail: glenfinnan@nts.org.uk
web: www.nts.org.uk

The monument commemorates the Highlanders who fought for Bonnie Prince Charlie in 1745. It stands in an awe-inspiring setting at the head of Loch Shiel. There is a visitor centre with information (commentary in four languages) on the Prince's campaign.

Times: ✱ Site open all year, daily. Visitor centre: daily Apr-Jun & Sep-Oct 10-5; Jul-Aug 9.30-5.30. Times may change for 2007 please telephone or check website **Facilities:** ❷ ◗ ㋴ (information centre only) shop ㊉

GOLSPIE　　　　MAP 14 NH89

Dunrobin Castle
KW10 6SF
➲ (1m NE on A9, from Golspie)
☎ 01408 633177 & 633268
e-mail: info@dunrobincastle.net
web: www.highlandescape.co.uk

The ancient seat of the Earls and Dukes of Sutherland is a splendid, gleaming, turreted structure, thanks largely to 19th-century rebuilding, and has a beautiful setting overlooking the sea. Paintings, furniture and family heirlooms are on display, and the gardens are on a grand scale to match the house. There are also falconry displays in the gardens.

Times: Open Apr-15 Oct, Mon-Sat 10.30-5.30, Sun 12-5.30. Closes 1 hr earlier Apr, May & Oct. (Last admission half hour before closing). **Fee:** ✱ £6.80 (ch £4.70 & pen £5.80). Family ticket £18.50 Party. **Facilities:** ❷ ◗ 🛒 ㋴ (access by arrangement only) shop ❽ 🍴

HELMSDALE　　　　MAP 14 ND01

Timespan
Dunrobin St KW8 6JX
➲ (off A9 in centre of village, by Telford Bridge)
☎ 01431 821327
e-mail: enquiries@timespan.org.uk
web: www.timespan.org.uk

Located in a historic fishing village, this museum relates to the social and natural history of the area, and the art gallery has changing exhibitions of contemporary art and works by local artists. The garden has over 100 varieties of herbs and plants. There is a gift shop, and a café with beautiful views of the Telford Bridge.

Times: Open Apr-Oct, Mon-Sat 10-5, Sun 12-5. **Fee:** ✱ £4 (ch £2 concessions £3). Family ticket £10. **Facilities:** ❷ ◗ ㋴ (lift) toilets for disabled shop ❽ (ex guide dogs) 🍴

KINCRAIG　　　　MAP 14 NH80

Highland Wildlife Park
PH21 1NL
➲ (on B9152, 7m S of Aviemore)
☎ 01540 651270
e-mail: info@highlandwildlifepark.org
web: www.highlandwildlifepark.org

As you drive through the main reserve, you can see awe-inspiring European bison grazing alongside wild horses, red deer and highland cattle plus a wide variety of other species. Then in the walk-round forest, woodland and moorland habitats prepare for close encounters with animals such as wolves, capercaillie, arctic foxes, wildcats, pine martens, otters and owls. Special events every weekend April to October.

Times: ✱ Open throughout the year, weather permitting. Apr-Oct, 10-6; Jun-Aug 10-7; Nov-Mar 10-4. (Last entry 2 hours before closing). **Facilities:** ❷ ◗ ㋴ toilets for disabled shop ❽ 🍴

KINGUSSIE　　　　MAP 14 NH70

Highland Folk Museum
Duke St PH21 1JG
➲ (12m SW of Aviemore off A9 at Kingussie)
☎ 01540 661307
e-mail: highland.folk@highland.gov.uk
web: www.highlandfolk.com

First established in 1935, this was Britain's first open-air museum. For a glimpse of life in a Blackhouse or a look at farming implements and domestic objects and furniture, this museum offers an internationally renowned collection of items. The Museum Store, not accessible to visitors in previous years, now displays in excess of 1,500 objects.

Times: ✱ Open Apr-Aug, Mon-Sat 9.30-5; Sep & Oct Mon-Fri, 9.30-4 **Facilities:** ❷ ㋴ (ramp, door, rails) toilets for disabled shop ❽ (ex guide dogs) 🍴

Ruthven Barracks　　　FREE
➲ (1m SE from Kingussie, signed from A9 and A86)
☎ 01667 460232
web: www.historic-scotland.gov.uk

An infantry barracks erected in 1719 following the Jacobite rising of 1715, with two ranges of quarters and a stable block. Captured and burnt by Prince Charles Edward Stuart's army in 1746.

Times: Open at any reasonable time. **Facilities:** ❷ ❽ ▦

KIRKHILL　　　　MAP 14 NH54

Moniack Castle (Highland Winery)　
IV5 7PQ
➲ (7m from Inverness on A862, near Beauly, on S side of Beauly Firth)
☎ 01463 831283
e-mail: jg@moniackcastle.co.uk
web: www.moniackcastle.co.uk

Commercial wine-making is not a typically Scottish industry, but nevertheless a wide range of country-style wines is produced, including elderflower and silver birch; mead and sloe gin are also made here. A selection of related products and tours of the

continued

production area are available at this unique attraction, situated in a 16th-century castle.
Times: Open all year, Apr-Oct Mon-Sat 10-5. Nov-Mar, Mon-Fri 11-4.
Fee: ✱ £2 **Facilities:** ❷ shop ⊗ ⬛

NEWTONMORE   MAP 14 NN79

Clan Macpherson House & Museum
Main St PH20 1DE
➲ *(off A9 at junct of Newtonmore and Kingussie, museum on left after entering village)*
☎ 01540 673332
e-mail: museum@clan-macpherson.org
web: www.clan-macpherson.org

Containing relics and memorials of the clan chiefs and other Macpherson families as well as those of Prince Charles Edward Stuart, this museum also displays the Prince's letters to the Clan Chief of 1745 and one to the Prince from his father, the Old Pretender, along with royal warrants and the green banner of the clan. Other interesting historic exhibits include James Macpherson's fiddle, swords, pictures, decorations and medals.
Times: Open Apr-Oct, Mon-Sat 10-5, Sun 12-5pm. Other times by appointment. **Fee:** Free. Donations welcome. **Facilities:** ❷ ♿ (ramp entrance from car park, subtitles on DVD) toilets for disabled shop ⊗ (ex guide dogs) ⬛

Highland Folk Museum
Aultlarie Croft PH20 1AY
➲ *(on A86, follow signs off A9)*
☎ 01540 661307
e-mail: highland.folk@highland.gov.uk
web: www.highlandfolk.com

An early 18th-century farming township with turf houses has been reconstructed at this award-winning museum. A 1930s school houses old world maps, little wooden desks and a Coates library. Other attractions include a working croft with rare breed animals and tailor's workshop. Vintage buses run throughout the site.
Times: Open Apr-Aug, Mon-Sun 10.30-5.30; Sep Mon-Sun, 11-4.30; Oct Mon-Fri, 11-4.30 **Fee:** ✱ £6 (ch & pen £3.50) **Facilities:** ❷ 🅿 ♿ (vintage bus with full disabled access) toilets for disabled shop ⊗ (ex guide dogs) ⬛

POOLEWE   MAP 14 NG88

Inverewe Garden
IV22 2LG
➲ *(6m NE of Gairloch, on A832)*
☎ 01445 781200
e-mail: inverewe@nts.org.uk
web: www.nts.org.uk

The influence of the North Atlantic Drift enables this remarkable garden to grow rare and sub-tropical plants. At its best in early June, but full of beauty from March to October, Inverewe has a backdrop of magnificent mountains and stands to the north of Loch Maree.
Times: ✱ Open: Garden all year, Apr-Oct, daily 9.30-9 (or sunset if earlier). Nov-Mar, 9.30-4. Visitor Centre Apr-Sep, daily 9.30-5; Oct, daily 9.30-4. Times may change for 2007 please telephone or check on website
Facilities: ❷ 🍴 licensed ♿ (some paths difficult) toilets for disabled shop ⊗ (ex guide dogs) 🎏

ROSEMARKIE   MAP 14 NH75

Groam House Museum   `FREE`
High St IV10 8UF
➲ *(off A9 at Tore onto A832)*
☎ 01381 620961 & 01463 811883
e-mail: groamhouse@ecosse.net

Opened in 1980, this community-based museum explores the history, culture and crafts of the mysterious Picts, who faded from history over a thousand years ago. Visitors can see the Rosemarkie Stones, large slabs that show Pictish carvings; paintings, a replica Pictish harp, and a collection of photographs of Pictish stones all over the country. Thanks to a generous donation, the museum now holds the George Bain Collection of Celtic art for the Scottish Nation. Annual exhibitions take place, often as loans from other major museums. 2007 is the year of Highland Culture.
Times: Open Etr week, daily 2-4.30; May-Oct, Mon-Sat, 10-5, Sun 2-4.30; Apr, Sat-Sun 2-4.30. Nov-mid Dec, Sat-Sun 2-4 **Facilities:** ❷ 🅵 ♿ (Key held for disabled public toilets) shop ⊗ (ex guide dogs) ⬛

STRATHPEFFER   MAP 14 NH45

Highland Museum of Childhood
The Old Station IV14 9DH
➲ *(5m W of Dingwall on A834)*
☎ 01997 421031
e-mail: info@highlandmuseumofchildhood.org.uk
web: www.highlandmuseumofchildhood.org.uk

Located in a renovated Victorian railway station of 1885, the museum tells the story of childhood in the Highlands amongst the crofters and townsfolk; a way of life recorded in oral testimony, displays and evocative photographs. An award-winning video, *A Century of Highland Childhood* is shown. There are also doll and toy collections.
Times: Open Apr-Oct, daily 10-5, (Sun 2-5) also Jul & Aug evenings open to 7. Other times by arrangement. **Fee:** £2 (ch, concessions £1.50). Family ticket £5 (2ad+3ch). **Facilities:** ❷ 🅿 🅵 ♿ (tape tour with induction loop for partially sighted) shop ⊗ (ex guide dogs) ⬛

TORRIDON   MAP 14 NG85

Torridon Countryside Centre
The Mains IV22 2EZ
➲ *(N of A896)*
☎ 01445 791221
e-mail: aclipson@nts.scot.demon.co.uk
web: www.nts.org.uk

Set amid some of Scotland's finest mountain scenery, the centre offers audio-visual presentations on the local wildlife. At the Mains nearby visitors may see deer.
Times: ✱ Open Countryside Centre, Good Fri-Sep, daily 10-6. Estate and Deer Museum daily all year. **Facilities:** ❷ ♿ toilets for disabled 🎏

Scotland

WICK — MAP 15 ND35

Castle of Old Wick — FREE

⊃ *(1m S on Shore Rd)*
☎ 01667 460232
web: www.historic-scotland.gov.uk

The ruin of the best-preserved Norse castle in Scotland. Dating from the 12th-century this spectacular site is on a spine of rock projecting into the sea, between two deep, narrow gullies. Visitors must take great care and wear sensible shoes.

Times: Open at all reasonable times. **Facilities:** ⊗ ♖

Wick Heritage Museum

18-27 Bank Row KW1 5EY
⊃ *(close to the harbour)*
☎ 01955 605393
web: wsherit@aol.com

The heritage centre is near the harbour in a complex of eight houses, yards and outbuildings. The centre illustrates local history from Neolithic times to the herring fishing industry. In addition, there is a complete working 19th-century lighthouse, and the famous Johnston collection of photographs.

Times: Open Apr-Oct, Mon-Sat 10-5, last admissions 3.45. (Closed Sun). **Fee:** £2.50 (ch 50p). **Facilities:** ℗ ⚫ toilets for disabled

INVERCLYDE

GREENOCK — MAP 10 NS27

McLean Museum & Art Gallery — FREE

15 Kelly St PA16 8JX
⊃ *(close to Greenock West Railway Station and Greenock Bus Station)*
☎ 01475 715624
e-mail: museum@inverclyde.gov.uk
web: www.inverclyde.gov.uk/museum_gallery

James Watt was born in Greenock, and various exhibits connected with him are shown. The museum also has an art collection, and displays on shipping, local and natural history, Egyptology and ethnography.

Times: Open all year, Mon-Sat 10-5. Closed local & national PHs. **Facilities:** ℗ (200mtrs) 🍴 ⚫ (induction loop) toilets for disabled shop ⊗ (ex guide & assist dogs)

PORT GLASGOW — MAP 10 NS37

Newark Castle

PA14 5NH
⊃ *(on A8)*
☎ 01475 741858
web: www.historic-scotland.gov.uk

The one-time house of the Maxwells, dating from the 15th and 17th centuries. The courtyard and hall are preserved. Fine turrets and the remains of painted ceilings can be seen, and the hall carries an inscription of 1597.

Times: Open Apr-Sep, daily 9.30-6.30. **Fee:** ✱ £3 (ch £1.30, concessions £2.30). Please phone or check website for further details. **Facilities:** ℗ shop ♖

MIDLOTHIAN

CRICHTON — MAP 11 NT36

Crichton Castle

EH37 5QH
⊃ *(2.5m SW of Pathhead, off A68)*
☎ 01875 320017
web: www.historic-scotland.gov.uk

The castle dates back to the 14th century, but most of what remains today was built over the following 300 years. A notable feature is the 16th-century wing built by the Earl of Bothwell in Italian style, with an arcade below.

Times: Open Apr-Sep, daily 9.30-6.30. **Fee:** ✱ £3 (ch £1.30, concessions £2.30). Please phone or check website for further details. **Facilities:** ℗ ♖

DALKEITH — MAP 11 NT36

Edinburgh Butterfly & Insect World

Dobbies Garden World, Lasswade EH18 1AZ
⊃ *(0.5m S of Edinburgh city bypass at Gilmerton junct or Sherrifhall rdbt)*
☎ 0131 663 4932
e-mail: info@edinburgh-butterfly-world.co.uk
web: www.edinburgh-butterfly-world.co.uk

Richly coloured butterflies from all over the world can be seen flying among exotic rainforest plants, trees and flowers. The tropical pools

continued

are filled with giant waterlilies and colourful fish, and are surrounded by lush vegetation. Also scorpions, leaf cutting ants, beetles, tarantulas and other remarkable creatures. There is a unique honeybee display and daily insect handling sessions.

Times: Open Summer daily 9.30-5.30; Winter daily 10-5. Closed 25-26 Dec & 1 Jan. **Fee:** ✱ £5 (ch, concessions & students £3.85). Family ticket £16.50 (2ad+2ch). Party 10+. **Facilities:** ❷ ⬛ 🗐 ♿ toilets for disabled shop garden centre ⊗ (ex guide dogs) ◀

NEWTONGRANGE   MAP 11 NT36

Scottish Mining Museum
Lady Victoria Colliery EH22 4QN
➲ *(10m S of Edinburgh on A7, signed from bypass)*
☎ 0131 663 7519
e-mail: visitorservices@scottishminingmuseum.com
web: www.scottishminingmuseum.com

Based at Scotland's National Coalmining Museum offering an outstanding visit to Britains' finest Victorian colliery. Guided tours with miners, magic helmets, exhibitions, theatres, interactive displays and a visit to the coal face. Home to Scotland's largest steam engine.

Times: Open all year, daily Mar-Oct, 10-5. Nov-Feb, daily, 10-4.
Fee: ✱ £5.95 (ch & concessions £3.95). Family ticket £17.95. Party 20+ (£4.95, ch £3.50) **Facilities:** ❷ ⬛🍴◎ 🗐 ♿ (tactile opportunites, interactive, audio tours) toilets for disabled shop ⊗ (ex guide dogs) ◀

PENICUIK   MAP 11 NT26

Edinburgh Crystal Visitor Centre   FREE
Eastfield EH26 8HB
➲ *(Follow the brown Thistle signs from the Edinburgh City Bypass and the A701/703)*
☎ 01968 675128
e-mail: visitorcentre@edinburgh-crystal.co.uk
web: www.edinburgh-crystal.com

Watch skilled craftsmen as they take molten crystal and turn it into intricately decorated glassware. Not only can you talk to the craftsmen themselves but there is also video footage, story boards, artefacts and audio listening posts to help you understand the 300-year-old history of glassmaking.

Times: Open Mon-Sat 10-5, Sun 11-5. Closed 25-26 Dec and 1-2 Jan.
Facilities: ❷ ⬛🍴◎ licensed 🗐 ♿ (ramp to first floor) toilets for disabled shop ⊗ (ex guide dogs) ◀

MORAY

BALLINDALLOCH   MAP 15 NJ13

The Glenlivet Distillery   FREE
Glenlivet AB37 9DB
➲ *(10m N of Tomintoul, off B9008)*
☎ 01340 821720
e-mail: betty.munro@chivas.com
web: www.theglenlivet.com

The visitor centre includes a guided tour of the whisky production facilities and a chance to see inside the vast bonded warehouses where the spirit matures. The brand new multimedia exhibition and

continued

interactive presentations communicate the unique history, and traditions of Glenlivet Scotch Whisky.

Times: Open 2 Apr-2 Nov. **Facilities:** ❷ ⬛ 🗐 ♿ (cafeteria, lift to exhibition) toilets for disabled shop ⊗ (ex guide dogs) ◀

BRODIE CASTLE   MAP 14 NH95

Brodie Castle
IV36 2TE
➲ *(4.5m W of Forres, off A96)*
☎ 01309 641371
e-mail: brodiecastle@nts.org.uk
web: www.nts.org.uk

The Brodie family lived here for hundreds of years before passing the castle to the NTS in 1980. It contains many treasures, including furniture, porcelain and paintings. The extensive grounds include a woodland walk and an adventure playground. Wheelchairs for disabled visitors are available. Please telephone for details of recitals, concerts, open-air theatre etc.

Times: ✱ Open Apr & Jul-Aug, daily 12-4; May-Jun & Sep, Sun-Thu 12-4. Grounds all year, daily, 9.30-sunset. Times may change for 2007 please telephone or check website **Facilities:** ❷ ⬛ ♿ (audio tape & information sheet in Braille) toilets for disabled shop ⊗ (ex guide dogs) ♉

CRAIGELLACHIE   MAP 15 NJ24

Speyside Cooperage Visitor Centre
Dufftown Rd AB38 9RS
➲ *(1m S of Craigellachie, on A941)*
☎ 01340 871108
e-mail: enquiries@speysidecooperage.co.uk
web: www.speysidecooperage.co.uk

A working cooperage with unique visitor centre, where skilled coopers and their apprentices practise this ancient craft. Each year they repair around 100,000 oak casks which will be used to mature many different whiskies. The 'Acorn to Cask' exhibition traces the history and development of the coopering industry.

Times: Open all year, Mon-Fri 9.30-4. Closed Xmas & New Year.
Fee: ✱ £3.10 (ch £1.80 & pen £2.50). Family ticket £8.50. Party 15+.
Facilities: ❷ ⬛ ♿ (picnic table, disabled viewing point) toilets for disabled shop ⊗ (ex guide dogs) ◀

DUFFTOWN   MAP 15 NJ34

Balvenie Castle
AB55 4DH
➲ *(on A941)*
☎ 01340 820121
web: www.historic-scotland.gov.uk

The ruined castle was the ancient stronghold of the Comyns, and became a stylish house in the 16th century.

Times: Open Apr-Sep, daily 9.30-6.30. **Fee:** ✱ £3 (ch £1.30 concessions £2.30). Please phone for further details or check website
Facilities: ❷ ♿ toilets for disabled ▐

Glenfiddich Distillery `FREE`

AB55 4DH

➲ (N of town, off A941)

☎ 01340 820373

web: www.glenfiddich.com

Set close to Balvenie Castle, the distillery was founded in 1887 by William Grant and has stayed in the hands of the family ever since. Visitors can see the whisky-making process in its various stages, including bottling, and then sample the finished product.

Times: Open all year Mon-Fri 9.30-4.30, also Etr-mid Oct, Sat 9.30-4.30, Sun 12-4.30. Closed Xmas & New Year **Facilities:** ❷ 🍴 ➔ (ramp access to production area & warehouse gallery) toilets for disabled shop ✖ (ex guide dogs)

DUFFUS   MAP 15 NJ16

Duffus Castle `FREE`

➲ (5m NW of Elgin on B9012 to Burghead)

☎ 01667 460232

web: www.historic-scotland.gov.uk

One of the finest examples of a motte and bailey castle in Scotland with a later, very fine, stone hall house and curtain wall. The original seat of the Moray family.

Times: Open at all reasonable times. **Facilities:** ❷ ✖ 🏛

ELGIN   MAP 15 NJ26

Elgin Cathedral

North College St IV30 1EL

☎ 01343 547171

web: www.historic-scotland.gov.uk

Founded in 1224, the cathedral was known as the Lantern of the North and the Glory of the Kingdom because of its beauty. In 1390 it was burnt, along with most of the town. Although it was rebuilt, it fell into ruin after the Reformation. The ruins are quite substantial, however, and there is still a good deal to admire, including the fine west towers and the octagonal chapter house.

Times: Open all year, Apr-Sep, daily 9.30-6.30; Oct-Mar, Mon-Wed & Sat-Sun 9.30-4.30. Closed 25-26 Dec & 1-2 Jan. **Fee:** ✱ £4 (ch £1.60, concessions £3). Please phone or check website for further details. **Facilities:** ℗ ➔ shop 🏛

Elgin Museum `2 for 1`

1 High St IV30 1EQ

➲ (E end of High St, follow brown heritage signs)

☎ 01343 543675

e-mail: curator@elginmuseum.org.uk

web: www.elginmuseum.org.uk

This award-winning museum is internationally famous for its fossil fish and fossil reptiles, and for its Pictish stones. The displays relate to the natural and human history of Moray.

Times: Open Apr-Oct, Mon-Fri 10-5, Sat 11-4. **Fee:** £3 (ch £1, pen, students & UB40 £1.50). Family ticket £6. **Facilities:** ℗ (50mtrs) (limited time) 🍴 ➔ (handrails, case displays at sitting level with large fonts) toilets for disabled shop ✖ (ex guide dogs)

Pluscarden Abbey `FREE`

IV30 8UA

➲ (6m SW of Elgin on unclass road)

☎ 01343 890257

e-mail: monks@pluscardenabbey.org

web: www.pluscardenabbey.org

The original monastery was founded in 1230 by King Alexander II for monks of the Valliscaulian order from Burgundy, but it later became a Benedictine house. Monastic life was abandoned after the Reformation and the house passed through a succession of lay owners until it was bought by the third Marquess of Bute in 1898. His third son, Lord Colum Crichton Stuart gave the monastery to the Benedictines of Prinknash Abbey near Gloucester, and monastic life was recommenced n 1948. Today there are about two dozen monks who lead a life of prayer, study and manual work. The services in the Abbey church are sung in Latin with Gregorian chant and are all open to the public.

Times: Open all year, daily 4.45am-8.30pm **Facilities:** ❷ 🍴 ➔ (induction loop, ramps to shop, garden partially accessible) toilets for disabled shop ✖ (ex guide dogs) 🍴

FOCHABERS   MAP 15 NJ35

Baxters Highland Village `FREE`

IV32 7LD

➲ (1m W of Fochabers on A96)

☎ 01343 820666

e-mail: highland.village@Baxters.co.uk

web: www.baxters.com

The Baxters food firm started here over 130 years ago and now sells its products in over 60 countries. Visitors can see the shop where the story began, watch an audio-visual display, and visit five shops. See the great hall, audio-visual theatre and cooking theatre. A food tasting area is open to visitors.

Times: ✱ Open all year daily, Jan-Mar 10-5; Apr-Dec 9-5.30.
Facilities: ❷ 🍴 licensed 🍴 ➔ (parking facilities) toilets for disabled shop ✖ (ex guide dogs) 🍴

FORRES   MAP 14 NJ05

Dallas Dhu Distillery

IV36 2RR

➲ (1m S of Forres, off A940)

☎ 01309 676548

web: www.historic-scotland.gov.uk

A perfectly preserved time capsule of the distiller's art. It was built in 1898 to supply malt whisky for Wright and Greig's 'Roderick Dhu' blend. Visitors are welcome to wander at will through this fine old Victorian distillery, or to take a guided tour, dram included.

Times: Open all year, Apr-Sep, daily 9.30-6.30; Oct-Mar, Mon-Wed & Sat-Sun 9.30-4.30. Closed 25-26 Dec & 1-2 Jan. **Fee:** ✱ £4.50 (ch £2, concessions £3.50). Please phone or check website for further details. **Facilities:** ❷ ➔ toilets for disabled shop ✖ 🏛

Falconer Museum

Tolbooth St IV36 1PH

➲ *(11m W of Elgin, 26m E of Iverness on A96)*

☎ 01309 673701

e-mail: museums@moray.gov.uk

web: www.moray.gov.uk/museums

Founded by bequests made by two brothers, Alexander and Hugh Falconer. Hugh was a distinguished scientist, friend of Darwin, recipient of many honours and Vice-President of the Royal Society. On display are fossil mammals collected by him, and items relating to his involvement in the study of anthropology. Other displays are on local wildlife, geology, archaeology and history. Also you can see the Forres Quincentennial Time Capsule.

Times: Open all year Feb (provisional)-Oct, Mon-Sat 10-5; Nov-Mar, Mon-Thu 11-12.30 & 1-3.30. Closed Good Fri, May Day, Xmas and New Year. **Fee:** Donations welcome **Facilities:** ♿ 📷 ♿ (induction loop system) shop ⊗ (ex guide dogs)

Sueno's Stone FREE

➲ *(E end of Forres, off A96)*

☎ 01667 460232

web: www.historic-scotland.gov.uk

The most remarkable sculptured monument in Britain, probably a cenotaph, standing over 20 feet high and dating back to the end of the first millennium AD. Covered by a protective glass enclosure.

Times: Open at all reasonable times. **Facilities:** ♿ ⊗ 🚩

KEITH   MAP 15 NJ45

Strathisla Distillery

Seafield Av AB55 5BS

➲ *(A96 Aberdeen to Inverness road, attraction signed midway through town)*

☎ 01542 783044

e-mail: jeanett.grant@chivas.com

web: www.chivas.com

Tour the oldest distillery in the highlands, founded in 1786. A dram of Chivas Regal 12 year old malt is offered on arrival, before viewing the Chivas Brothers DVD and distillery tour.

Times: Open 2 Apr-2 Nov, Mon-Sat 9.30-4, Sun 12-4. **Fee:** £5 per person (ch free, ch under 8 not admitted to production areas, but welcome in centre). Maybe subject to change. **Facilities:** ♿ 📷 ♿ (access is very limited) toilets for disabled shop ⊗ (ex guide dogs) 🍴

MARYPARK   MAP 15 NJ13

Glenfarclas Distillery 2 for 1

AB37 9BD

➲ *(4m S of Aberlour on A95 to Grantown-on-Spey)*

☎ 01807 500245 & 500257

e-mail: info@glenfarclas.co.uk

web: www.glenfarclas.co.uk

Established in 1836, Glenfarclas Distillery is proud of its independence. There is a guided tour illustrating their whisky's history and

production, followed by a dram in the splendour of the Ships Room or a chance to browse in the gift shop.

Times: Open Jan-Mar, Mon-Fri 10-4; Apr-Sep, Mon-Fri 10-5, Jul-Sep also open Sat 10-5; Oct-Dec, Mon-Fri 10-4. Closed Sun. **Fee:** ✱ £3.50. (Free admission to under 18's). **Facilities:** ♿ ♿ (only visitor centre is accessible) toilets for disabled shop ⊗ (ex guide dogs in centre) 🍴

ROTHES   MAP 15 NJ24

Glen Grant Distillery FREE

AB38 7BS

➲ *(on A941 Elgin-Rothes road)*

☎ 01340 832118

e-mail: jennifer.robertson@glengrant.com

Founded in 1840 in a sheltered glen by the two Grant brothers. Discover the secrets of the distillery, including the delightful Victorian garden originally created by Major Grant, and now restored to its former glory, where you can enjoy a dram.

Times: Open Apr-3 Nov, Mon-Sat, 9.30-5, Sun, 12-5. **Facilities:** ♿ 📷 ♿ (reception centre & still house) toilets for disabled shop ⊗ (ex guide dogs) 🍴

SPEY BAY   MAP 15 NJ36

The WDCS Wildlife Centre FREE

IV32 7PJ

➲ *(off A96 onto B9014 at Fochabers, follow road approx 5m to village of Spey Bay. Turn left at Spey Bay Hotel and follow road for 500mtrs)*

☎ 01343 829109

e-mail: enquiries@mfwc.co.uk

web: www.mfwc.co.uk

The centre, owned and operated by the Whale and Dolphin Conservation Society, lies at the mouth of the River Spey and is housed in a former salmon fishing station, built in 1768. There is a free exhibition about the Moray Firth dolphins and the wildlife of Spey Bay. Visitors can browse through a well-stocked gift shop and enjoy refreshments in the cosy tea room.

Times: Open Apr-Oct 10.30-5. Check for winter opening times **Facilities:** ♿ 🍽 📷 ♿ toilets for disabled shop ⊗ (ex guide dogs) 🍴

TOMINTOUL   MAP 15 NJ11

Tomintoul Museum FREE

The Square AB37 9ET

➲ *(on A939, 13m E of Grantown)*

☎ 01309 673701

e-mail: museums@moray.gov.uk

web: www.moray.gov.uk

Situated in one of the highest villages in Britain, the museum features a reconstructed crofter's kitchen and smiddy, with other displays on the local wildlife, the story of Tomintoul, and the local skiing industry.

Times: Open: Mar-May, Mon-Fri, 9.30-12 and 2-4. Jun-Aug, Mon-Sat, 9.30-12 and 2-4.30. Sep, Mon-Sat, 9.30-12 and 2-4. Oct, Mon-Fri, 9.30-12 and 2-4. Closed May day and Good Fri. **Facilities:** ♿ 📷 ♿ (induction loop and sound commentaries) shop ⊗ (ex guide dogs)

Scotland

Scotland

NORTH AYRSHIRE

IRVINE
MAP 10 NS34

Scottish Maritime Museum

Harbourside KA12 8QE

⮞ *(Follow AA signs from Irvine)*

☎ 01294 278283

e-mail: smm@tildesley.fsbusiness.co.uk

web: www.scottishmaritimemuseum.org

The museum has displays that reflect all aspects of Scottish maritime history. Vessels can be seen afloat in the harbour and undercover. Experience life in a 1910 shipyard worker's tenement flat. Visit the Linthouse Engine Shop originally built in 1872, which is being developed and holds a substantial part of the museum's collection in open store.

Times: Open Apr-Oct, 10-5 **Fee:** £3 (ch & pen £2). Family ticket £7. **Facilities:** ❷ 💷 ᕓ (audio tapes for blind) toilets for disabled shop ⊗ (ex guide dogs)

Vennel Gallery

10 Glasgow Vennel KA12 0BD

☎ 01294 275059

e-mail: vennel@north-ayrshire.gov.uk

web: www.north-ayrshire.gov.uk/museums

The Vennel Gallery has a reputation for exciting and varied exhibitions, ranging from international to local artists. Behind the museum is the Heckling Shop where Robert Burns, Scotland's most famous poet, spent part of his youth learning the trade of flax dressing. In addition to the audio-visual programme on Burns, there is a reconstruction of his lodgings at No.4 Glasgow Vennel, Irvine.

Times: Open all year, Thu-Sun 10-1 & 2-5 **Facilities:** ℗ (residential area) ᕓ toilets for disabled shop ⊗ (ex guide dogs)

LARGS
MAP 10 NS25

Kelburn Castle and Country Centre
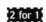
Fairlie KA29 0BE

⮞ *(2m S of Largs, on A78)*

☎ 01475 568685

e-mail: admin@kelburncountrycentre.com

web: www.kelburncountrycentre.com

Historic home of the Earls of Glasgow, Kelburn is famous for its romantic Glen, family gardens, unique trees and spectacular views over the Firth of Clyde. Glen walks, riding and trekking centre, adventure course, activity workshop, Kelburn Story Cartoon Exhibition and a family museum. The "Secret Forest" at the centre, Scotland's most unusual attraction, is a chance to explore the Giant's Castle, maze of the Green Man and secret grotto. Also included is a Falconry Centre, pottery craft studio and an indoor Sawmill Adventure Playground.

Times: Open all year, Etr-end Oct, daily 10-6; Nov-Mar, 11-dusk. Grounds and Sawmill Adventure Playbarn, wknds only **Fee:** ✱ £7 (concessions £4.50). Family ticket £22. **Facilities:** ❷ 💷 ⦿ licensed 🗐 ᕓ (Ranger service to assist disabled) toilets for disabled shop ◄

Vikingar!
Greenock Rd KA30 8QL

⮞ *(on A78, 0.5m into Largs, opposite RNLI lifeboat station)*

☎ 01475 689777

e-mail: cmcnaught@naleisure.co.uk

web: www.naleisure.co.uk

A multi-media experience that takes you from the first Viking raids in Scotland to their defeat at the Battle of Largs.

Times: Open Apr-Sep, daily 10.30-5.30; Oct & Mar, daily 10.30-3.30; Nov & Feb, wknds only 10.30-3.30. Closed Dec & Jan. **Fee:** £4.10 (ch 4-15 £2.30, pen £3.10). Family ticket £12.20. Group 10+ **Facilities:** ❷ 💷 ᕓ toilets for disabled shop ⊗ (ex guide dogs) ◄

SALTCOATS
MAP 10 NS24

North Ayrshire Museum

Manse St, Kirkgate KA21 5AA

☎ 01294 464174

e-mail: namuseum@north-ayrshire.gov.uk

web: www.north-ayrshire.gov.uk/museums

This museum is housed in an 18th-century church, and features a rich variety of artefacts from the North Ayrshire area, including archaeological and social history material. There is a continuing programme of temporary exhibitions.

Times: Open all year, Mon-Sat (ex Sun & Wed) 10-1 & 2-5. **Facilities:** ℗ (100mtrs) 🗐 ᕓ toilets for disabled shop ⊗ (ex guide dogs)

NORTH LANARKSHIRE

MOTHERWELL
MAP 11 NS75

Motherwell Heritage Centre

High Rd ML1 3HU

⮞ *(A723 for town centre. Left at top of hill, after pedestrian crossing and just before railway bridge)*

☎ 01698 251000

e-mail: museums@northlan.gov.uk

web: www.nlcmuseums.bravehost.com

This award-winning audio-visual experience, 'Technopolis', traces the history of the area from Roman times to the rise of 19th-century industry and the post-industrial era. There is also a fine viewing tower, an exhibition gallery and family history research facilities. A mixed programme of community events and touring exhibitions occur throughout the year.

Times: Open all year Wed-Sat 10-5 (Thu 10-7), Sun 12-5. Closed Mon & Tue, ex BHs. Local studies library closed Sun **Facilities:** ❷ 🗐 ᕓ (lifts, audio info & Braille buttons) toilets for disabled shop ⊗ (ex guide dogs)

PERTH & KINROSS

ABERFELDY
MAP 14 NN84

Dewar's World of Whisky
2 for 1
Aberfeldy Distillery PH15 2EB
➲ (from A9 take A827 for Aberfeldy at Ballinluig)
☎ 01887 822010
e-mail: worldofwhisky@dewars.com
web: www.dewarswow.com
Tradition and the latest technology are combined here to tell the story of Dewar's White Label Whisky. Visitors are able to sample the product in the Nosing and Tasting Bar, and have a guided tour of the Aberfeldy distillery, where they can see traditional techniques being employed by skilled craftsmen.

Times: Open Apr-Oct, Mon-Sat 10-6, Sun noon-4; Nov-Mar, Mon-Sat 10-4. Closed Xmas & New Year. **Fee:** ✱ £5.50 (ch £3.50, concessions £4). Family ticket £20 (2ad and up to 5 ch). **Facilities:** ❷ ♿ ♿ (visitor centre only accessible, lift) toilets for disabled shop ⊗ (ex guide dogs) ◀

BLAIR ATHOLL
MAP 14 NN86

Blair Castle
PH18 5TL
➲ (7m NW of Pitlochry, off A9 at Blair Atholl & follow signs to attraction)
☎ 01796 481207
e-mail: office@blair-castle.co.uk
web: www.blair-castle.co.uk

Ancient seat of the Dukes of Atholl and the Atholl Highlanders, the Duke's unique private army. The castle dates back to the 13th century but was altered in the 18th, and later given a castellated exterior. The oldest part is Cumming's Tower, built in about 1270. There are paintings, furniture, porcelain, historic artefacts, Jacobite relics, lace, tapestries, and Masonic regalia. The extensive grounds include a deer park, and a restored 18th-century walled garden. Audio-visual display available. Events are held throughout the year, including the annual parade of the Duke's Private Army (ring for details).

Times: Open all year Nov-end Mar, Tue & Sat 9.30-12.30 (last admission); Apr-end Oct, daily 9.30-4.30 (last admission). **Facilities:** ❷ ♨ ❙◯❙ licensed ⫟ ♿ (scooter, parking) shop ⊗ (ex guide dogs) ◀

CRIEFF
MAP 11 NN82

Innerpeffray Library
PH7 3RF
➲ (4.5m SE on B8062)
☎ 01764 652819
e-mail: library@innerpeff.fsnet.co.uk
web: www.innerpeffraylibrary.co.uk
This is Scotland's oldest free lending library. It was founded in 1680 and is still open every day except Thursdays. It is housed in a late 18th-century building, and contains a notable collection of bibles and rare books. Adjacent is St Mary's Chapel, the original site for the library and the Drummond family burial place.

Times: Open Wed-Sat 10-12.45 & 2-4.45, Sun 2-4. (Closed Mon-Tue). Nov-Feb by appointment only. **Fee:** ✱ £2.50 (ch under 15 50p) **Facilities:** ❷ ♨ ♿ ⊗ (ex guide dogs)

The Famous Grouse Experience
The Hosh PH7 4HA
➲ (1.5m NW off A85)
☎ 01764 656565
e-mail: enquiries@thefamousgrouse.com
web: www.thefamousgrouse.com
A trip to Crieff is incomplete without a visit to The Famous Grouse Experience, set in Scotland's oldest, most visited and award-winning distillery. Opened in July 2002, this attraction is a fun and interesting day out which combines the traditional distillery visit with a unique exciting sensory experience. Spend a relaxing few hours absorbing the history of the brand. Test your senses and see if you have what it takes to become a 'Whisky Nose'. Have lunch, a snack or even a barbecue at the family restaurant. Visit the well-stocked shop or enjoy a peaceful woodland walk over The Brig O' Dram.

Times: Open all year daily 9-6 (last tour 4.30). Closed 25-26 Dec and 1 Jan **Fee:** ✱ £7.50 (concessions £5, ch under 10 free) VIP tour £9.95. **Facilities:** ❷ ♨ ❙◯❙ licensed ⫟ ♿ (lifts in all areas) toilets for disabled shop ⊗ (ex guide dogs) ◀

DUNKELD
MAP 11 NO04

The Ell Shop & Little Houses
FREE
The Cross PH8 0AN
➲ (off A9, 15m N of Perth)
☎ 01350 727460
e-mail: dunkeld@nts.org.uk
web: www.nts.org.uk
The National Trust owns two rows of 20 houses in Dunkeld, and has preserved their 17th/18th-century character. They are not open to the public, but there is a display and audio-visual show in the Information Centre.

Times: ✱ Open Ell Shop mid Mar-Sep, Mon-Sat, 10-5.30, Sun 12.30-5.30. Oct-mid Dec, Mon-Sat 10-4.30, Sun 12.30-4.30. **Facilities:** ℗ (300yds) ♿ toilets for disabled shop ⊗ ♨

Scotland

KILLIECRANKIE　　　　MAP 14 NN96

Killiecrankie Visitor Centre　　FREE
NTS Visitor Centre PH16 5LG
➲ (3m N of Pitlochry on B8079)
☎ 01796 473233
e-mail: killiecrankie@nts.org.uk
web: www.nts.org.uk

The visitor centre features an exhibition on the battle of 1689, when the Jacobite army routed the English, although the Jacobite leader, 'Bonnie Dundee', was mortally wounded in the attack. The wooded gorge is a notable beauty spot, admired by Queen Victoria, and there are some splendid walks.

Times: ✱ Visitor Centre: open Apr-Jun & Sep-Oct, daily 10-5.30, Jul & Aug, daily 9.30-6. Site: open all year daily. Times may change for 2007 please telephone or check website **Facilities:** ℗ ⬛ & (visitor centre only) toilets for disabled shop ✲

KINROSS　　　　MAP 11 NO10

Kinross House Gardens
KY13 8ET
➲ (M90 [Edinburgh to Perth] junct 6 to Kinross, signed in village)
☎ 01577 862900
e-mail: jm@kinrosshouse.com
web: www.kinrosshouse.com

Yew hedges, roses and herbaceous borders are the elegant attractions of these formal gardens. The 17th-century house was built by Sir William Bruce, but is not generally open to the public.

Times: ✱ Gardens only open Apr-Sep, daily 10-7.
Facilities: ℗ & ✲ (ex guide dogs)

Loch Leven Castle
Castle Island KY13 7AR
➲ (on an island in Loch Leven accessible by boat from Kinross)
☎ 01786 450000
web: www.historic-scotland.gov.uk

Mary, Queen of Scots was imprisoned here in this five-storey castle in 1567 - she escaped 11 months later and so gave the 14th-century castle its special place in history.

Times: Open Apr-Sep, daily 9.30-6.30. **Fee:** ✱ £4 (ch £1.60, concessions £3). Charge includes ferry trip. Please phone or check website for further details. **Facilities:** ℗ shop ✲ ⬛

RSPB Nature Reserve Vane Farm
By Loch Leven KY13 9LX
➲ (2m E of M90 junct 5, on S shore of Loch Leven, entered off B9097 to Glenrothes)
☎ 01577 862355
e-mail: vane.farm@rspb.org.uk
web: www.rspb.org.uk

Well placed beside Loch Leven, with a nature trail and hides overlooking the Loch and a woodland trail with stunning panoramic

continued

views. Noted for its pink-footed geese. The area also attracts whooper swans, greylag geese and great spotted woodpeckers amongst others. Details of special events are available from the Visitors' Centre.

Times: ✱ Open all year daily, 10-5. Closed 25-26 Dec & 1-2 Jan.
Facilities: ℗ ⬛ 🔳 & (wheelchair extensions, ramps, telescopes) toilets for disabled shop ✲ (ex guide dogs) ⬛

MILNATHORT　　　　MAP 11 NO10

Burleigh Castle　　FREE
KY13 7XZ
➲ (0.5m E of Milnathort on A911)
web: www.historic-scotland.gov.uk

The roofless but otherwise complete ruin of a tower house of about 1500, with a section of defensive barmkin wall and a remarkable corner tower with a square cap-house corbelled out. This castle was often visited by James IV.

Times: Open summer only. Keys available locally, telephone 01786 45000.
Facilities: ✲ ⬛

MUTHILL　　　　MAP 11 NN81

Drummond Gardens
PH5 2AA
➲ (2m S of Crieff on A822)
☎ 01764 681433
e-mail: thegardens@drummondcastle.sol.co.uk
web: www.drummondcastlegardens.co.uk

The gardens of Drummond Castle were originally laid out in 1630 by John Drummond, 2nd Earl of Perth. In 1830, the parterre was changed to an Italian style. The multi-faceted sundial was designed by John Mylne, Master Mason to Charles I. These are Scotland's largest formal gardens and amongst the finest in Europe.

Times: Open Gardens May-Oct, daily 1-6 (last admission 5). Also Etr for 4 days. **Fee:** £4 (ch £1.50 & pen £3). **Facilities:** ℗ & toilets for disabled shop

PERTH　　　　MAP 11 NO12

Black Watch Regimental Museum
Balhousie Castle, Hay St PH1 5HR
➲ (follow signs to Perth & attraction, approach via Dunkeld Rd)
☎ 0131 310 8530
e-mail: rhq@theblackwatch.co.uk
web: www.theblackwatch.co.uk

The museum of Scotland's oldest highland regiment, which portrays the history of the Black Watch from 1725 to the present day. A memorial room remembers the soldiers of WWI with a lifelike figure in a trench, video footage and many artefacts from the period. Silver, uniforms, weapons and pictures are on display to give visitors an idea of what it was like to be in the regiment.

Times: Open all year. May-Sep, Mon-Sat 10-4.30. Closed last Sat in Jun; Oct-Apr, Mon-Fri, 10-3.30. Closed 23 Dec-6 Jan. Other times & Parties 16+ by appointment. **Fee:** ✱ Donations. **Facilities:** ℗ & (1 bay parking for disabled) toilets for disabled shop ✲ (ex guide dogs) ⬛

Branklyn Garden

116 Dundee Rd PH2 7BB

➲ (on A85)

☎ 01738 625535

e-mail: aclipson@nts.scot.demon.co.uk

web: www.nts.org.uk

The gardens cover two acres and are noted for their collections of rhododendrons, shrubs and alpines. Garden tours and botanical painting courses are held.

Times: ✱ Open Apr & Jul-Sep, Fri-Tue 10-5; May-Jun, daily, 10-5. Times may change for 2007 please telephone or check website
Facilities: ♿ ⊗ (ex guide dogs) ☙

Caithness Glass Factory & Visitor Centre   FREE

Inveralmond PH1 3TZ

➲ (on Perth Western Bypass, A9, at Inveralmond Roundabout)

☎ 01738 492320

e-mail: visitor@caithnessglass.co.uk

web: www.caithnessglass.co.uk

All aspects of paperweight-making can be seen from the purpose-built viewing galleries. Visitors can now enter the glasshouse on a route which enables them to watch the glassmakers closely. There are talks in the glasshouse regularly throughout the day from Monday to Friday. There is also a factory shop, a best shop, children's play area and tourist information centre with internet access.

Times: ✱ Open all year, Factory shop & restaurant, Mon-Sat 9-5, Sun 10-5 (Dec-Feb 12-5). Glassmaking Mon-Sun 9-4.30. **Facilities:** ♿ ⊙ licensed ♿ (wheelchair available) toilets for disabled shop ⊗ (ex guide dogs) ◼

Huntingtower Castle

PH1 3JL

➲ (2m W)

☎ 01738 627231

web: www.historic-scotland.gov.uk

Formerly known as Ruthven Castle and famous as the scene of the so-called 'Raid of Ruthven' in 1582, this structure was built in the 15th and 16th centuries and features a painted ceiling.

Times: Open all year, Apr-Sep, daily 9.30-6.30; Oct-Mar, Mon-Wed & Sat-Sun 9.30-4.30. Closed 25-26 Dec & 1-2 Jan. **Fee:** ✱ £3.50 (ch £1.50, concessions £2.50). Please phone or check website for further details.
Facilities: ♿ shop ⊗ ♫

Perth Museum & Art Gallery   FREE

78 George St PH1 5LB

➲ (in town centre, adjacent to Perth Concert Hall)

☎ 01738 632488

e-mail: museum@pkc.gov.uk

web: www.pkc.gov.uk

Visit Perth Museum and Art Gallery for a fascinating look into Perthshire throughout the ages. Collections cover silver, glass, art, natural history, archaeology and human history.

Times: Open all year, Mon-Sat 10-5. Sun. 1-4.30, May-Sep. Closed Xmas-New Year. **Facilities:** ℗ (800yds) (pay and display) ♿ (ramp, lifts, induction loops) toilets for disabled shop ⊗ (ex guide dogs)

PITLOCHRY   MAP 14 NN95

Edradour Distillery   FREE

PH16 5JP

➲ (2.5m E of Pitlochry on A924)

☎ 01796 472095

web: www.edradour.co.uk

It was in 1825 that a group of local farmers founded Edradour, naming it after the bubbling burn that runs through it. It is Scotland's smallest distillery and is virtually unchanged since Victorian times. Have a dram of whisky while watching an audio-visual in the malt barn and then take a guided tour through the distillery itself.

Times: ✱ Open Jan-Feb, Mon-Sat 10-5, Sun 12.4; Mar-Oct Mon-Sat 9.30-6, Sun 11.30-6; Nov-Dec, Mon-Sat 9.30-5, Sun 12-5. (Last tour 1hr before close, private tours arranged for a fee). **Facilities:** ♿ ♿ toilets for disabled shop ⊗ (ex guide & hearing dogs)

Scottish Hydro Electric Visitor Centre, Dam & Fish Pass

PH16 5ND

➲ (off A9, 24m N of Perth)

☎ 01796 473152

The visitor centre features an exhibition showing how electricity is brought from the power station to the customer, and there is access to the turbine viewing gallery. The salmon ladder viewing chamber allows you to see the fish as they travel upstream to their spawning ground.

Times: Open Apr-Oct, Mon-Fri 10-5.30. Wknd opening Jul, Aug & BHs **Fee:** ✱ £3 (accompanied ch free, concessions £2). **Facilities:** ♿ ▥ ♿ (monitor viewing of salmon fish pass) toilets for disabled shop ⊗ (ex guide dogs)

QUEEN'S VIEW   MAP 14 NN85

Queen's View Visitor Centre   FREE

PH16 5NR

➲ (7m W of Pitlochry on B8019)

☎ 01350 727284

e-mail: peter.fullarton@forestry.gsi.gov.uk

web: www.forestry.gov.uk

Queen Victoria admired the view on a visit here in 1866; it is possibly one of the most famous views in Scotland. The area, in the heart of the Tay Forest Park, has a variety of woodlands that visitors can walk or cycle in.

Times: Open Apr-Nov, daily 10-6. **Facilities:** ♿ (charged) ▰ ♿ toilets for disabled shop ◼

SCONE   MAP 11 NO12

Scone Palace   2 for 1

PH2 6BD

➲ (2m NE of Perth on A93)

☎ 01738 552300

e-mail: visits@scone-palace.co.uk

web: www.scone-palace.co.uk

Scottish kings were crowned at Scone until 1651 and it was the site of the famous coronation Stone of Destiny from the 9th century until the English seized the Stone in 1296. The castellated edifice of the present palace dates from 1803 but incorporates the 16th-century and earlier

continued

Scotland

buildings. The interior houses objets d'art, including French & Scottish furniture, an extensive porcelain collection and paintings. The grounds include a Pinetum, the original Douglas Fir, the unique Murray Star Maze, woodland walks and herbaceous plantings. Also David Douglas Trail.

Times: Open Apr-Oct **Fee:** ✱ Palace & Grounds £7.20 (ch £4.20, concessions £6.20). Family ticket £23. Grounds only £3.80 (ch £2.50, concessions £3.50). Group £6 (ch £4 and concessions £5.30)
Facilities: ❷ ☕ ℺ licensed ▤ ♿ (stairlift which gives access to all state rooms) toilets for disabled shop ⊗ (ex assist dogs & in grounds) ➤

WEEM — MAP 14 NN84

Castle Menzies
PH15 2JD
➲ *(Follow signs from main roads)*
☎ 01887 820982
e-mail: castlem@tiscali.co.uk
web: www.menzies.org

Restored seat of the Chiefs of Clan Menzies, and a fine example of a 16th-century Z-plan fortified tower house. Prince Charles Edward Stuart stayed here briefly on his way to Culloden in 1746. The whole of the 16th-century building can be explored, and there's a small clan museum.

Times: Open Apr-mid Oct, Mon-Sat 10.30-5, Sun 2-5. **Fee:** £4 (ch £2, concessions £3.50). **Facilities:** ❷ ▤ ♿ toilets for disabled shop ⊗ (ex guide dogs)

RENFREWSHIRE

KILBARCHAN — MAP 10 NS46

Weaver's Cottage
The Cross PA10 2JG
➲ *(off A737, 12m SW of Glasgow)*
☎ 01505 705588
e-mail: aclipson@nts.scot.demon.co.uk
web: www.nts.org.uk

The weaving craft is regularly demonstrated at this delightful 18th-century cottage museum, and there is a collection of weaving equipment and other domestic utensils.

Times: ✱ Open Apr-Sep, Fri-Tue, 1-5; morning visits available for pre-booked groups. Times may change for 2007 please telephone or check website **Facilities:** ❷ ⊗ (ex guide dogs) ☙

LANGBANK — MAP 10 NS37

Finlaystone Country Estate
PA14 6TJ
➲ *(on A8 W of Langbank, 10m W of Glasgow Airport, follow Thistle signs)*
☎ 01475 540505
e-mail: info@finlaystone.co.uk
web: www.finlaystone.co.uk

A beautiful country estate, historic formal gardens which are renowned for thier natural beauty, woodland walks and play areas. The 'Dolly Mixture', an international collection of dolls, can be seen in the Visitor Centre.

Times: Open all year. Woodland & Gardens daily, 10-5. **Fee:** ✱ Garden & Woods £3.50 (ch & pen £2.50). 'The Dolly Mixture' Doll Museum free.
Facilities: ❷ ☕ ▤ ♿ (lift to second floor pathways for wheelchairs) toilets for disabled shop ➤

LOCHWINNOCH — MAP 10 NS35

RSPB Lochwinnoch Nature Reserve
Largs Rd PA12 4JF
➲ *(on A760, Largs road, opposite Lochwinnoch station, 16m SW of Glasgow)*
☎ 01505 842663
e-mail: Lochwinnoch@rspb.org.uk
web: www.rspb.org.uk/reserves/lochwinnoch

The reserve, part of Clyde Muirshiel Regional Park and a Site of Special Scientific Interest, comprises two shallow lochs fringed by marsh which in turn is fringed by scrub and woodland. There are two trails with hides and a visitor centre with a viewing area. Please visit website for details of events running throughout the year.

Times: Open all year, daily 10-5. Closed 1-2 Jan & 25-26 Dec.
Fee: ✱ Trails £2 (ch 50p, concessions £1). Family ticket £4.
Facilities: ❷ ▤ ♿ (hides are all wheelchair accessible) toilets for disabled shop ⊗ ➤

PAISLEY — MAP 11 NS46

Coats Observatory — FREE
49 Oakshaw St West PA1 2DE
➲ *(M8 junct 27, follow signs to town centre until Gordon St (A761). Left onto Causeyside St, left onto New St then left onto High St)*
☎ 0141 889 2013
e-mail: museums.els@renfrewshire.gov.uk
web: www.renfrewshire.gov.uk

The Observatory, funded by Thomas Coats and designed by John Honeyman, was opened in 1883. It houses a 5 inch telescope under the dome at the top. Weather recording activities have been carried out here continuously since 1884. There is also earthquake-measuring equipment and the Renfrewshire Astronomical Society holds regular meetings here. There are displays on the solar system, earthquakes and the telescope.

Times: Open all year, Tue-Sat 10-5, Sun 2-5. Last entry 15 minutes before closing. **Facilities:** ℗ (150yds) (meters/limited street parking) ▤ ⊗ (ex guide dogs)

Paisley Museum & Art Galleries — FREE
High St PA1 2BA
➲ *(M8 junct 27 [A741], rdbt 2nd exit [A761-town centre]. At traffic lights take left lane towards Kilbride. Onto Gordon St, right onto Causeyside St, left onto New St, left onto High St)*
☎ 0141 889 3151
e-mail: museums.els@renfrewshire
web: www.renfrewshire.gov.uk

Pride of place here is given to a world-famous collection of Paisley shawls. Other collections illustrate local industrial and natural history, while the emphasis of the art gallery is on 19th-century Scottish artists and an important studio ceramics collection.

Times: ✱ Open all year, Tue-Sat 10-5, Sun 2-5. BH 10-5.
Facilities: ℗ (330yds) ▤ ♿ (parking on site) toilets for disabled shop ⊗ (ex guide dogs)

SCOTTISH BORDERS

COLDSTREAM
MAP 12 NT84

Hirsel
Douglas & Angus Estates, Estate Office, The Hirsel TD12 4LP
➲ *(0.5m W on A697, on N outskirts of Coldstream)*
☎ 01890 882834 & 882965
e-mail: rogerdodd@btconnect.com
web: www.hirselcountrypark.co.uk

The seat of the Home family, the grounds of which are open all year. The focal point is the Homestead Museum, craft centre and workshops. From there, nature trails lead around the lake, along the Leet Valley and into woodland noted for its rhododendrons and azaleas.

Times: Garden & Grounds open all year, daylight hours. Museum 10-5. Craft Centre Mon-Fri, 10-5, wknds noon-5. **Fee:** ✱ £2.50 per car **Facilities:** ❷ (charged) 🍽 ⍾ ⚓ toilets for disabled shop ⊗

DRYBURGH
MAP 12 NT53

Dryburgh Abbey
TD6 0RQ
➲ *(5m SE of Melrose on B6404)*
☎ 01835 822381
web: www.historic-scotland.gov.uk

The abbey was one of the Border monasteries founded by David I, and stands in a lovely setting on the River Tweed. The ruins are equally beautiful, and the church has the graves of Sir Walter Scott and Earl Haig.

Times: Open all year, Apr-Sep daily 9.30-6.30; Oct-Mar daily 9.30-4.30. Closed 25-26 Dec & 1-2 Jan. **Fee:** ✱ £4 (ch £1.60, concessions £3). Please phone or check website for further details. **Facilities:** ❷ ⚓ shop ⊗ ◪

DUNS
MAP 12 NT75

Manderston
TD11 3PP
➲ *(2m E of Duns on A6105)*
☎ 01361 883450 & 882636
e-mail: palmer@manderston.co.uk
web: www.manderston.co.uk

This grandest of grand houses gives a fascinating picture of Edwardian life above and below stairs. Completely remodelled for the millionaire racehorse owner Sir James Miller, the architect was told to spare no expense, and so the house boasts the world's only silver staircase. The staterooms are magnificent, and there are fine formal gardens, with a woodland garden and lakeside walks. Manderston has been the setting for a number of films.

Times: Open mid May-end Sep, Thu & Sun (also late May & Aug English BH Mons). Gardens open, 11.30-dusk. House open, 1.30-4.15 **Fee:** ✱ House & Gardens £7 (ch £3.50); Gardens only £3.50. **Facilities:** ❷ 🍽 ⍾ shop ⊗ (ex guide dogs & on leads)

EYEMOUTH
MAP 12 NT96

Eyemouth Museum
2 for 1
Auld Kirk, Manse Rd TD14 5JE
➲ *(off A1 onto A1107, follow signs to town centre*
☎ 018907 50678

The museum was opened in 1981 as a memorial to the 129 local fishermen lost in the Great Fishing Disaster of 1881. Its main feature is the 15ft Eyemouth tapestry, which was made for the centenary. There are also displays on local history.

Times: Open Apr-Jun & Sep, Mon-Sat 10-5, Sun 10-1; Jul-Aug, Mon-Sat 10-5; Sun 10-2; Oct, Mon-Sat 10-4 (closed Sun) **Fee:** ✱ £2.50 (accompanied ch free, concessions £2). Party on application. **Facilities:** ℗ (250yds) (45min on street outside) ⍾ ⚓ shop ◪

GORDON
MAP 12 NT64

Mellerstain House
2 for 1
TD3 6LG
➲ *(signed on A6089 [Kelso-Gordon road], 1m W)*
☎ 01573 410225
e-mail: enquiries@mellerstain.com
web: www.mellerstain.com

One of Scotland's finest Georgian houses, begun by William Adam and completed by his son Robert in the 1770s. It has beautiful plasterwork, period furniture and pictures, terraced gardens and a lake.

Times: Open Etr & May-Sep, Sun, Mon, Wed, Thurs 12.30-5 (last admission 4.15) & Sun only in Oct **Fee:** ✱ £6 (ch free) Party 20+ £5.50 (if normal opening times) Garden £3.50 **Facilities:** ❷ 🍽 ⍾ ⚓ toilets for disabled shop garden centre ⊗ (ex guide dogs) ◪

Directions are provided by the attractions.

HERMITAGE
MAP 12 NY59

Hermitage Castle
TD9 0LU

➩ *(5.5m NE of Newcastleton, on B6399)*
☎ 01387 376222
web: www.historic-scotland.gov.uk

A vast, eerie ruin of the 14th and 15th centuries, associated with the de Soulis, the Douglases and Mary, Queen of Scots. Much restored in the 19th century.

Times: Open Apr-Sep, daily 9.30-6.30. **Fee:** ✱ £3 (ch £1.30, concessions £2.30). Please phone or check website for further details.
Facilities: ❷ ♿ ▮

INNERLEITHEN
MAP 11 NT33

Robert Smail's Printing Works
7/9 High St EH44 6HA
☎ 01896 830206
e-mail: smails@nts.org.uk
web: www.nts.org.uk

These buildings contain a Victorian office, a paper store with reconstructed waterwheel, a composing room and a press room. The machinery is in full working order and visitors may view the printer at work and experience typesetting in the composing room.

Times: ✱ Open Good Fri-Etr Mon & Jun-Sep, Thu-Mon 12-5, Sun 1-5. Times may change for 2007 please telephone or check website
Facilities: ℗ (300yds) ♿ shop ⊗ (ex guide dogs) ♨

JEDBURGH
MAP 12 NT62

Jedburgh Abbey
☎ 01835 863925
web: www.historic-scotland.gov.uk

Standing as the most complete of the Border monasteries (although it has been sacked and rebuilt many times) Jedburgh Abbey has been described as 'the most perfect and beautiful example of the Saxon and early Gothic in Scotland'. David I founded it as a priory in the 12th century and remains of some of the domestic buildings have been uncovered during excavations.

Times: Open all year, Apr-Sep daily 9.30-6.30; Oct-Mar daily 9.30-4.30. Closed 25-26 Dec & 1-2 Jan. **Fee:** ✱ £4.50 (ch £2, concessions £3.50). Please phone or check website for details. **Facilities:** ❷ ♿ (limited access) toilets for disabled shop ⊗ ▮

Jedburgh Castle Jail & Museum
Castlegate TD8 6BD

➩ *(off A68 towards town centre, follow signs to top of Castlegate)*
☎ 01835 864750
web: www.scotborders.gov.uk/museums

Relive the harsh realities of prison life in the 19th century with a visit to Jedburgh Castle Jail, built in the 1820s on the site of the Royal Burgh's medieval castle. Displays in the cell blocks recreate the lives of prisoners and staff, while the Jailer's House explores the history of the town. A childrens activity guide is available, and there are plenty of hands-on activities for all the family.

Times: Open late Mar-end Oct, Mon-Sat, 10-4.30. Sun 1-4 **Fee:** £2 (ch free, concessions £1) **Facilities:** ❷ ▯ ♿ (audio guide, touch screen tour, hearing loop) toilets for disabled shop ⊗ (ex guide dogs)

KELSO
MAP 12 NT73

Floors Castle
Roxburghe Estates Office TD5 7SF

➩ *(from town centre follow Roxburghe St to main gates)*
☎ 01573 223333
e-mail: marketing@floorscastle.com
web: www.roxburghe.bordernet.co.uk

The home of the 10th Duke of Roxburghe, the Castle's lived-in atmosphere enhances the superb collection of French furniture, tapestries and paintings. The house was designed by William Adam in 1721 and enjoys a magnificent setting overlooking the River Tweed and the Cheviot Hills beyond.

Times: Open 14 Mar-29 Oct, daily 11-5 (last admission 4.30). **Fee:** ✱ £6 (ch £3.25, concessions £5). **Facilities:** ❷ ▯ ⦿ licensed ▯ ♿ (lift) toilets for disabled shop garden centre ⊗ (ex in grounds on leads) ▬

Kelso Abbey
FREE
☎ 0131 668 8800
web: www.historic-scotland.gov.uk

Founded by David I in 1128 and probably the greatest of the four famous Border abbeys, Kelso became extremely wealthy and acquired extensive lands. In 1545 it served as a fortress when the town was attacked by the Earl of Hertford, but now only fragments of the once-imposing abbey church give any clue to its long history.

Times: Open at any reasonable time. **Facilities:** ♿ ▮

LAUDER
MAP 12 NT54

Thirlestane Castle
2 for 1
TD2 6RU

➩ *(off A68, S of Lauder)*
☎ 01578 722430
e-mail: admin@thirlestanecastle.co.uk
web: www.thirlestanecastle.co.uk

This fairy-tale castle has been the home of the Maitland family, the Earls of Lauderdale, since the 12th century. Some of the most splendid plasterwork ceilings in Britain may be seen in the 17th-century state rooms. The family nurseries house a sizeable collection of antique toys and dolls. The informal riverside grounds, with their views of the grouse moors, include a woodland walk, picnic tables and adventure playground. Please visit website for details of events running throughout the year.

Times: May-19 Sep, Wed-Fri & Sun. Jul-Aug Sun-Fri. Open from 10.30, last admission 2.30. **Fee:** ✱ £5.50 (ch £3) Family ticket £15. **Facilities:** ❷ ▯ ▯ shop ⊗ (ex guide dogs) ▬

MELROSE
MAP 12 NT53

Abbotsford
TD6 9BQ

➩ *(2m W off A6091, on B6360)*
☎ 01896 752043
e-mail: enquiries@scottsabbotsford.co.uk
web: www.scottsabbotsford.co.uk

Set on the River Tweed, Sir Walter Scott's romantic mansion remains much the same as it was in his day. Inside there are many mementoes and relics of his remarkable life and also his historical collections, armouries and library, with some 9,000 volumes. Scott built the

continued

mansion between 1811 and 1822, and lived here until his death ten years after its completion.

Times: Open daily from 3rd Mon in Mar-Oct, Mon-Sat 9.30-5. Mar-May & Oct Sun 2-5. Jun-Sep Sun 9.30-5. **Fee:** ✱ £5 (ch £2.50). Party £3.90 (ch £1.95) **Facilities:** ❷ ♨ ♿ (parking at private entrance, ramps at entrance) toilets for disabled shop ⊗ (ex guide & hearing dogs) ▄

Harmony Garden

St Mary's Rd TD6 9LJ

➲ *(opposite Melrose Abbey)*

☎ 01721 722502

web: www.nts.org.uk

Set around the early 19th-century Harmony Hall (not open to visitors), this attractive walled garden has magnificent views of Melrose Abbey and the Eildon Hills. The garden comprises lawns, herbaceous and mixed borders, vegetable and fruit areas, and a rich display of spring bulbs.

Times: ✱ Open Good Fri-Etr Mon & Jun-Sep, Mon-Sat 10-5, Sun 1-5. Times may change for 2007 please telephone or check website **Facilities:** ❷ ♿ ⊗ ♈

Melrose Abbey & Abbey Museum

TD6 9LG

☎ 01896 822562

web: www.historic-scotland.gov.uk

The ruin of this Cistercian abbey is probably one of Scotland's finest, and has been given added glamour by its connection with Sir Walter Scott. The abbey was repeatedly wrecked during the Scottish wars of independence, but parts survive from the 14th century. The heart of Robert the Bruce is buried somewhere within the church.

Times: Open all year, Apr-Sep daily 9.30-6.30; Oct-Mar daily 9.30-4.30. Closed 25-26 Dec & 1-2 Jan. **Fee:** ✱ £4.50 (ch £2, concessions £3.50). Please phone or check website for further details. **Facilities:** ❷ ♿ shop ⊗ ▮

Priorwood Garden & Dried Flower Shop

TD6 9PX

➲ *(off A6091, in Melrose, adjacent to Abbey. On National Cycle Route 1)*

☎ 01896 822493

e-mail: priorwooddriedflowers@nts.org.uk

web: www.nts.org.uk

This small garden specialises in flowers suitable for drying. It is formally designed with herbaceous and everlasting annual borders, and the attractive orchard has a display of 'apples through the ages'. Dried flowers are on sale in the shop.

Times: ✱ Open Good Fri-Etr Mon, May-Jun & Sep-24 Dec, Mon-Sat 12-5, Sun 1-5; Jul-Aug, Mon-Sat 10-5, Sun 1-5. Times may change for 2007 please telephone or check website **Facilities:** ❷ ♿ (ramps, paths) shop ♈

PEEBLES   **MAP 11 NT24**

Kailzie Gardens   〔2 for 1〕

EH45 9HT

➲ *(2.5m SE on B7062)*

☎ 01721 720007

e-mail: info@kailziegardens.com

web: www.kailziegardens.com

These extensive grounds, with their fine old trees, provide a burnside walk flanked by bulbs, rhododendrons and azaleas. A walled garden contains herbaceous, shrub rose borders, greenhouses and a formal rose garden. A garden for all seasons - don't miss the snowdrops. A large stocked trout pond and rod hire available, and an 18-hole putting green, plus an open bait pond, ornamental duck pond and osprey viewing centre.

Times: Open 25 Mar-Oct, daily 11-5.30. Grounds close 5.30. Garden open all year. **Fee:** ✱ mid Mar-Jun £2.50, Jun-Oct £3.50, end Oct-mid Mar £2 honesty box (ch 5-12 80p) **Facilities:** ❷ ♨ ▮⊙▮ licensed ▦ ♿ (ramps in garden) toilets for disabled shop

Neidpath Castle   〔2 for 1〕

EH45 8NW

➲ *(0.5m W of Peebles on A72)*

☎ 01721 720333

e-mail: estateoffice@wemyssandmarch.co.uk

web: www.neidpathcastle.co.uk

Occupying a spectacular position on the Tweed, this 14th-century stronghold was adapted to 17th-century living; it contains a rock-hewn well, a pit prison and a small museum. There are fine walks and a picnic area.

Times: Open Etr wknd, May-Sep Wed-Sat 10.30-5 Sun 12.30-5 (closed Mon & Tue except BHs) **Fee:** ✱ £3 (ch £1, concessions £2.50). Family ticket £7.50. Party 20+. **Facilities:** ❷ ▦ shop

SELKIRK   **MAP 12 NT42**

Bowhill House and Country Park

TD7 5ET

➲ *(3m W of Selkirk off A708)*

☎ 01750 22204

e-mail: bht@buccleuch.com

web: www.heritageontheweb.co.uk

An outstanding collection of pictures, including works by Van Dyck, Canaletto, Reynolds, Gainsborough and Claude Lorraine are displayed here. Memorabilia and relics of people such as Queen Victoria and Sir Walter Scott, and a restored Victorian kitchen add further interest inside the house. Outside, the wooded grounds are perfect for walking. A small theatre provides a full programme of music and drama.

Times: Park open May-Jun 11-5 wknd and BHs only. Jul gardens daily 11-5, house daily 1-5. Aug Sat-Thu 11-5. **Fee:** ✱ House & grounds £6 (ch under 5 & wheelchair users free, pen & groups £4). Grounds only £2. **Facilities:** ❷ ♨ ▮⊙▮ licensed ♿ (guided tours for the blind by appointment) toilets for disabled shop ⊗ (ex in park on leads) ▄

Scotland

Halliwells House Museum `FREE`

Halliwells Close, Market Place TD7 4BC

➲ *(off A7 in town centre)*

☎ 01750 20096

e-mail: museums@scotborders.gov.uk

A row of late 18th-century town cottages converted into a museum. Displays recreate the building's former use as an ironmonger's shop and home, and tell the story of the Royal Burgh of Selkirk. The Robson Gallery hosts a programme of contemporary art and craft exhibitions.

Times: Open Apr-Sep, Mon-Sat 10-5, Sun 10-12; Jul-Aug, Mon-Sat 10-5.30, Sun 10-12; Oct, Mon-Sat 10-4. **Facilities:** ❷ (charged) 🅟 (lift to first floor, large print, interpretation) toilets for disabled shop ❽ (ex guide dogs) ◀

Lochcarron of Scotland Visitor Centre

Waverley Mill, Rodgers Rd TD7 5DX

➲ *(32m S of Edinburgh on A7, follow signs to mill)*

☎ 01750 726000

e-mail: quality@lochcarron.com

web: www.quality@lochcarron.com

The museum brings the town's past to life and the focal point is a display on the woollen industry. Guided tours of the mill take about 40 minutes. Please note that disabled toilets are built for members of staff who are disabled but are not in wheelchairs.

Times: Open all year, Mon-Sat 9-5, Sun (Jun-Sep) 12-5. Mill tours Mon-Thu at 10.30, 11.30, 1.30 & 2.30, Fri am only. **Fee:** ✱ Museum free. Mill tour £2.50 (ch 14 free) group rate £2. **Facilities:** ❷ & toilets for disabled shop ◀

Sir Walter Scott's Courtroom `FREE`

Market Place TD7 4BT

➲ *(on A7 in town centre)*

☎ 01750 20096

e-mail: museums@scotborders.gov.uk

Built in 1803-4 as a sheriff court and town hall this is where the famous novelist, Sir Walter Scott dispensed justice when he was Sheriff of Selkirkshire from 1804-1832. Displays tell of Scott's time as Sheriff, and of his place as a novelist as well as those of his contemporaries, writer, James Hogg and the explorer, Mungo Park.

Times: Open Apr-Sep, Mon-Fri 10-4, Sat 10-2; May-Aug also Sun 10-2; Oct, Mon-Sat 1-4. **Facilities:** ℗ (100mtrs) (30min on street, car park 50p for 2hrs) 🅟 shop ❽ (ex guide dogs) ◀

SMAILHOLM MAP 12 NT63

Smailholm Tower

TD5 7RT

➲ *(6m W of Kelso on B6937)*

☎ 01573 460365

web: www.historic-scotland.gov.uk

An outstanding example of a classic Border tower-house, probably erected in the 15th century. It is 57ft high and well preserved. The tower houses an exhibition of dolls and a display based on Sir Walter Scott's book *Minstrels of the Border.*

Times: Open Apr-Sep, daily 9.30-6.30; Oct, Mon-Wed & Sat-Sun 9.30-4.30. Nov-Mar, wknds only. Closed 25-26 Dec & 1-2 Jan. **Fee:** ✱ £3 (ch £1.30, concessions £2.30). Please phone or check website for further details. **Facilities:** ❷ shop ❽ 🅿

STOBO MAP 11 NT13

Dawyck Botanic Garden

EH45 9JU

➲ *(8m SW of Peebles on B712)*

☎ 01721 760254

e-mail: dawyck@rbge.org.uk

web: www.rbge.org.uk

From the landscaped walks of this historic arboretum an impressive collection of mature specimen trees can be seen - some over 40 metres tall and including the unique Dawyck beech-stand. Notable features include the Swiss Bridge, a fine estate chapel and stonework/terracing produced by Italian craftsmen in the 1820s.

Times: Open daily Feb-Nov. Feb & Nov 10-4. Mar-Oct 10-5. Apr-Sep 10-6 **Fee:** ✱ £3.50 (ch £1, concessions £3). Family ticket £8 **Facilities:** ❷ 🄴 🅟 & toilets for disabled shop garden centre ❽ (ex guide dogs) ◀

TRAQUAIR MAP 11 NT33

Traquair House `2 for 1`

EH44 6PW

➲ *(at Innerleithen take B709, house in 1m)*

☎ 01896 830323 & 830785

e-mail: enquiries@traquair.co.uk

web: www.traquair.co.uk

Said to be Scotland's oldest inhabited house, dating back to the 12th century, 27 Scottish monarchs have stayed at Traquair House. William the Lion Heart held court here, and the house has associations with Mary, Queen of Scots and the Jacobite risings. The Bear Gates were closed in 1745, not to be reopened until the Stuarts should once again ascend the throne. There is croquet, a maze and woodland walks by the River Tweed, craft workshops and a children's mini adventure playground. Also a brewery museum and shop and antique shop.

Times: Open Etr-Oct **Fee:** ✱ Please telephone or visit website for admission costs. **Facilities:** ❷ 🄴 🍽 licensed & toilets for disabled shop ◀

SOUTH AYRSHIRE

ALLOWAY MAP 10 NS31

Burns National Heritage Park `2 for 1`

Murdoch's Lone KA7 4PQ

➲ *(2m S of Ayr)*

☎ 01292 443700

e-mail: info@burnsheritagepark.com

web: www.burnsheritagepark.com

The birthplace of Robert Burns, Scotland's National Poet set in the gardens and countryside of Alloway. An introduction to the life of Robert Burns, with an audio-visual presentation - a multi-screen 3D experience describing the Tale of Tam O'Shanter. This attraction consists of the museum, Burn's Cottage, visitor centre, tranquil landscaped gardens and historical monuments. Please telephone for further details.

Times: Open all year, Apr-Sep 9.30-5.30, Oct-Mar 10-5. Closed 25-26 Dec & 1-2 Jan **Fee:** ✱ £3 (ch & pen £2) **Facilities:** ❷ 🄴 🍽 licensed 🅟 & (wheelchair available) toilets for disabled shop ❽ (ex guide & hearing dogs) ◀

Scotland (vertical text in left margin)

BARGANY
See **Old Dailly**

CULZEAN CASTLE   MAP 10 NS21

Culzean Castle & Country Park
KA19 8LE
➲ *(4m W of Maybole, off A77)*
☎ 01655 884455
e-mail: culzean@nts.org.uk
web: www.culzeancastle.net

This 18th-century castle stands on a cliff in spacious grounds and was designed by Robert Adam for the Earl of Cassillis. It is noted for its oval staircase, circular drawing room and plasterwork. The Eisenhower Room explores the American general's links with Culzean. The 563-acre country park has a wide range of attractions - shoreline, woodland walks, parkland, an adventure playground and gardens.

Times: ✱ Open Castle: Apr-Oct, daily 10.30-5 (last entry 4). Visitor centre: Apr-Oct, daily 9-5.30; Nov-Mar, wknds 11-4. Country Park: open all year 9.30-sunset. Times may change for 2007 please telephone or check website **Facilities:** ✿ 🖱 🍽️ licensed ⅏ (wheelchairs, lift in castle, Braille guides) toilets for disabled shop garden centre ⊗ (ex castle, & guide dogs) 🏵

KIRKOSWALD   MAP 10 NS20

Souter Johnnie's Cottage
Main Rd KA19 8HY
➲ *(on A77, 4m SW of Maybole)*
☎ 01655 760603
e-mail: aclipson@nts.scot.demon.co.uk
web: www.nts.org uk

'Souter' means cobbler and the village cobbler who lived in this 18th-century cottage was the inspiration for Burns' character Souter Johnnie, in his ballad *Tam O'Shanter*. The cottage is now a Burns museum and life-size stone figures of the poet's characters can be seen in the restored ale-house in the cottage garden.

Times: ✱ Open Apr-Sep, Fri-Tue 11.30-5. Times may change for 2007 please telephone or check website **Facilities:** Ⓟ (75yds) ⅏ (only one small step into cottage) ⊗ (ex guide dogs) 🏵

MAYBOLE   MAP 10 NS20

Crossraguel Abbey
KA19 5HQ
➲ *(2m S)*
☎ 01655 883113
web: www.historic-scotland.gov.uk

The extensive remains of this 13th-century Cluniac monastery are impressive and architecturally important. The monastery was founded by Duncan, Earl of Carrick and the church, claustral buildings, abbot's house and an imposing castellated gatehouse can be seen.

Times: Open Apr-Sep, daily 9.30-6.30. **Fee:** ✱ £3 (ch £1.30, concessions £2.30). Please phone or check website for further details.
Facilities: ✿ ⊗ ▮

OLD DAILLY   MAP 10 NX29

Bargany Gardens
KA26 9PH
➲ *(4m NE on B734 from Girvan)*
☎ 01465 871249

Woodland walks with a fine show of azaleas and rhododendrons. Plants on sale from the gardens.

Times: Open Gardens, May 10-5. **Fee:** ✱ £2 (ch under 12 free).
Facilities: ✿ ⅏ (only rock garden not accessible)

TARBOLTON   MAP 10 NS42

Bachelors' Club
Sandgate St KA5 5RB
➲ *(on B744, 7.5m NE of Ayr)*
☎ 01292 541940
web: www.nts.org.uk

In this 17th-century thatched house, Robert Burns and his friends formed a debating club in 1780. Burns attended dancing lessons and was initiated into freemasonry here in 1781. The house is furnished in the style of the period.

Times: ✱ Open Apr-Sep, Fri-Tue 1-5. Morning visits available for pre-booked groups. Times may change for 2007 please telephone or check website **Facilities:** Ⓟ (in village) ⅏ ⊗ (ex guide dogs) 🏵

SOUTH LANARKSHIRE

BIGGAR   MAP 11 NT03

Gladstone Court Museum
ML12 6DT
➲ *(On A702 40m from Glasgow, 30m from Edinburgh, entrance by 113 High St)*
☎ 01899 221050
e-mail: margaret@bmtrust.freeserve.co.uk
web: www.biggar-net.co.uk

An old-fashioned village street is portrayed in this museum, which is set out in a century-old coach-house. On display are reconstructed shops, complete with old signs and advertisements - a bank, telephone exchange, photographer's booth and other interesting glimpses into the recent past.

Times: ✱ Open Etr-Oct, Mon-Sat 11-4.30, Sun 2-4.30.
Facilities: ✿ ⅏ shop ⊗ (ex guide dogs)

Greenhill Covenanters House
Burn Braes ML12 6DT
➲ *(On A702, 30m from Edinburgh, 40m from Glasgow)*
☎ 01899 221050
e-mail: margaret@bmtrust.freserve.co.uk
web: www.biggar-net.co.uk

This 17th-century farmhouse was brought, stone by stone, ten miles from Wiston and reconstructed at Biggar. It has relics of the turbulent 'Covenanting' period, when men and women defended the right to worship in Presbyterian style. Audio presentations.

Times: ✱ Open mid May-Sep, wknds only 2-4.30. **Facilities:** ✿ 🏛 ⅏ ⊗ (ex guide dogs)

Scotland

Moat Park Heritage Centre

ML12 6DT

➤ *(On A702, 30m from Edinburgh, 40m from Glasgow)*

☎ 01899 221050

e-mail: margaret@bmtrust.co.uk

web: ww.biggar-net.co.uk

The centre illustrates the history, archaeology and geology of the Upper Clyde and Tweed valleys with interesting displays.

Times: ✱ Open all year, Apr-Oct, daily 11.30-4.30, Sun 2-4.30; Nov-Feb, wkdays during office hours. Other times by prior arrangement.
Facilities: ❷ 🍴 ♿ (upper floor with assistance on request) toilets for disabled shop ⊗ (ex guide dogs)

BLANTYRE   MAP 11 NS65

David Livingstone Centre

165 Station Rd G72 9BT

➤ *(M74 junct 5 onto A725, then A724, follow signs for Blantyre, right at lights. Centre is at foot of hill)*

☎ 01698 823140

web: www.nts.org.uk

Share the adventurous life of Scotland's greatest explorer, from his childhood in the Blantyre Mills to his explorations in the heart of Africa, dramatically illustrated in the historic tenement where he was born. Various events are planned throughout the season.

Times: ✱ Open Apr-24 Dec, Mon-Sat 10-5, Sun 12.30-5. Times may change for 2007 please telephone or check website **Facilities:** ❷ 💷 ♿ toilets for disabled shop ⊗ (ex guide dogs) 🎋 ◀

BOTHWELL   MAP 11 NS75

Bothwell Castle

G71 8BL

➤ *(approach from Uddingston off B7071)*

☎ 01698 816894

web: www.historic-scotland.gov.uk

Besieged, captured and 'knocked about' several times in the Scottish-English wars, the castle is a splendid ruin. Archibald the Grim built the curtain wall; later, in 1786, the Duke of Buccleuch carved graffiti - a coronet and initials - beside a basement well.

Times: Open all year, Apr-Sep, daily 9.30-6.30; Oct-Mar, daily 9.30-4.30. Closed Thu & Fri in winter, 25-26 Dec & 1-2 Jan. **Fee:** ✱ £3 (ch £1.30 concessions £2.30). Please phone or check website for futher details. **Facilities:** ❷ shop ▮

EAST KILBRIDE   MAP 11 NS65

Museum of Scottish Country Life

Wester Kittochside, Philipshill Rd, (off Stewartfield Way) G76 9HR

➤ *(From Glasgow take A749 to East Kilbride. From Edinburgh follow M8 to Glasgow, turn off junct 6 onto A725 to East Kilbride. Kittochside is signed before East Kilbride)*

☎ 0131 247 4377

e-mail: info@nms.ac.uk

web: www.nms.ac.uk

A fascinating museum built on a 170-acre farm and offering an insight into the working lives of people in rural Scotland. The museum runs a programme of events throughout the year, demonstrating its working collection and contrasting modern and traditional farming methods.

Museum of Scottish Country Life

Times: Open daily 10-5. Closed 25-26 Dec & 1-2 Jan **Fee:** ✱ £4.50 (ch under 18 free, concessions £3) NMS and NTS members free. Charge for some events. **Facilities:** ❷ 💷 ♿ (disabled parking, exhibition building is fully accessible) toilets for disabled shop ⊗ (ex assist dogs) ◀

HAMILTON   MAP 11 NS75

Chatelherault Country Park   `FREE`

Ferniegair ML3 7UE

➤ *(2.5km SE of Hamilton on A72 Hamilton-Larkhall/Lanark Clyde Valley tourist route)*

☎ 01698 426213

e-mail: phyllis.crosbie@southlanarkshire.gov.uk

web: www.southlanarkshire.gov.uk

Designed as a hunting lodge by William Adam in 1732, Chatelherault, built of unusual pink sandstone, has been described as a gem of Scottish architecture. Situated close to the motorway, there is a visitor's centre, shop and adventure playground. Also a herd of white Cadzow cattle.

Times: Visitor Centre, open all year, Mon-Sat 10-5, Sun 12-5. House closed all day Fri & Sat. **Facilities:** ❷ 💷 ♿ (ramps, parking, large print guide) toilets for disabled shop garden centre ⊗ (ex in grounds & guide dogs) ◀

Low Parks Museum   `FREE`

129 Muir St ML3 6BJ

➤ *(off M74 junct 6, by Asda Superstore)*

☎ 01698 328232

e-mail: lowparksmuseum@southlanarkshire.gov.uk

web: www.southlanarkshire.gov.uk

The museum tells the story of both South Lanarkshire and The Cameronians (Scottish Rifles). The Cameronians were unique as they were the only Scottish rifle regiment, and the museum details their fascinating history from 1689 to 1968. Housed in the town's oldest building, dating from 1696, the museum also features a restored 18th-century assembly room and exhibitions on Hamilton Palace and The Covenanters.

Times: Open all year, daily, Mon-Sat 10-5, Sun 12-5. **Facilities:** ❷ 🍴 ♿ toilets for disabled shop ⊗ (ex guide dogs) ◀

continued

NEW LANARK
MAP 11 NS84

New Lanark Visitor Centre
2 for 1

Mill 3, New Lanark Mills ML11 9DB

➲ *(1m S of Lanark. Signed from all major routes. Less than 1hr from Glasgow (M741/A72) and Edinburgh (A70))*

☎ 01555 661345

e-mail: trust@newlanark.org

web: www.newlanark.org

Founded in 1785, New Lanark became well known in the early 19th century as a model community managed by enlightened industrialist and educational reformer Robert Owen. Surrounded by woodland and situated close to the Falls of Clyde, this unique world heritage site explores the philosophies of Robert Owen, using theatre, interactive displays, and the 'Millennium Experience', a magical ride through history. Accommodation is also available at the New Lanark Mill Hotel. Please telephone for details of events running throughout the year.

Times: Open all year daily. Jun-Aug 10.30-5. Sep-May 11-5. Closed 25 Dec and 1 Jan. **Fee:** £5.95 (ch, concessions £4.95) Family ticket (2ad + 2ch) £17.95 Family ticket (2ad + 4ch) £21.95 **Facilities:** ℗ 💷 🍴 licensed 🔲 ♿ (ramps, disabled parking, wheelchairs) toilets for disabled shop ⊗ (ex guide dogs) ◼

STIRLING

BANNOCKBURN
MAP 11 NS89

Bannockburn Heritage Centre
FREE

Glasgow Rd FK7 0LJ

➲ *(2m S of Stirling off M80/M9 junct 9)*

☎ 01786 812664

web: www.nts.org.uk

The Heritage Centre stands close to what is traditionally believed to have been Robert the Bruce's command post before the 1314 Battle of Bannockburn, a famous victory for the Scots and a turning point in Scottish history.

Times: ✱ Site open all year, daily. Heritage Centre Apr-Oct, daily 10-5.30; Feb-Mar & Nov-24 Dec, daily 10.30-4. (Last audio-visual show 30 mins before closing) **Facilities:** ℗ 💷 ♿ (Induction loop) toilets for disabled shop ⊗ (ex site) 🍴

BLAIR DRUMMOND
MAP 11 NS79

Blair Drummond Safari & Leisure Park

FK9 4UR

➲ *(M9 junct 10, 4m on A84 towards Callander)*

☎ 01786 841456 & 841396

e-mail: enquiries@blairdrummond.com

web: www.blairdrummond.com

Drive through the wild animal reserves where zebras, North American bison, antelope, lions, tigers, white rhino and camels can be seen at close range. Other attractions include the sea lion show, a ride on the boat safari through the waterfowl sanctuary and around Chimpanzee Island, an adventure playground, giant astraglide, and pedal boats. There are also African elephants, giraffes and ostriches.

Times: Open 19 Mar-3 Oct, daily 10-5.30. (Last admission 4.30) **Facilities:** ℗ 💷 🍴 licensed 🔲 ♿ (special menus & waitress service if booked in advance) toilets for disabled shop ⊗ (ex assist dogs) ◼

CALLANDER
MAP 11 NN60

Rob Roy and The Trossachs Visitor Centre

Ancaster Square FK17 8ED

➲ *(on A84)*

☎ 01877 330342

e-mail: info@robroyvisitorcentre.com

web: robroyvisitorcentre.com

From Highland hero to Hollywood legend, follow the story of Scotland's most famous Highlander, Rob Roy. Hear his innermost thoughts and witness his exploits. Step back in time and explore a reconstructed 18th-century farmhouse, just as Rob Roy would have experienced it.

Times: Open Apr-May, daily 10-5; Jun-Sep, 10-6; Oct 10-5; Nov-Feb 10-4; Mar 10-5. (Winter openings may vary, please contact) **Fee:** ✱ £3.85 (ch £2.60, concessions £2.90). **Facilities:** ℗ (adjacent to centre) 🔲 ♿ toilets for disabled shop ⊗ ◼

DOUNE
MAP 11 NN70

Doune Castle

FK16 6EA

➲ *(8m S of Callander on A84)*

☎ 01786 841742

web: www.historic-scotland.gov.uk

The 14th-century stronghold with its two fine towers has been restored. It stands on the banks of the River Teith, and is associated with 'Bonnie Prince Charlie' and Sir Walter Scott.

Times: Open all year, Apr-Sep, daily 9.30-6.30; Oct-Mar, Mon-Wed & Sat-Sun 9.30-4.30. Closed 25-26 Dec & 1-2 Jan. **Fee:** ✱ £3.50 (ch £1.50, concessions £2.50). Please phone or check website for further details. **Facilities:** ℗ shop 🍴

KILLIN
MAP 11 NN53

Breadalbane Folklore Centre

Falls of Dochart FK21 8XE

➲ *(on A85)*

☎ 01567 820254

e-mail: info@breadalbanefolklorecentre.com

web: www.breadalbanefolklorecentre.com

Overlooking the beautiful Falls of Dochart, the centre gives a fascinating insight into the legends of Breadalbane - Scotland's 'high country'. Learn of the magical deeds of St Fillan and hear tales of mystical giants, ancient prophesies, traditional folklore and clan history. Housed in historic St Fillans Mill which features a restored waterwheel. Tourist Information and gift shop.

Times: Open Apr-Jun, 10-5.30, daily. Jul-Aug, 10-5.30, daily. Sep-Oct, 10-5, daily. **Fee:** ✱ £2 (ch & pen £1.25, students £1.50). Family ticket £5.25. **Facilities:** ℗ (30mtrs) ♿ shop ⊗ ◼

MILNGAVIE
MAP 11 NS57

Mugdock Country Park
FREE

Craigallian Rd G62 8EL

➲ *(N of Glasgow on A81, signed)*

☎ 0141 956 6100 & 6586

e-mail: rangers@mcp.ndo.co.uk

web: www.mugdock-country-park.org.uk

This country park incorporates the remains of Mugdock and Craigend castles, set in beautiful landscapes as well as an exhibition centre, craft shops, orienteering course and many walks.

continued

Times: Open all year, daily. **Facilities:** 🅿 💷 🍽 licensed ♿ (mobility equip, audio leaflet, large print media) toilets for disabled shop garden centre ■

PORT OF MENTEITH   MAP 11 NN50

Inchmahome Priory
FK8 3RA
➲ *(4m E of Aberfoyle, off A81)*
☎ 01877 385294
web: www.historic-scotland.gov.uk

Walter Comyn founded this Augustinian house in 1238, and it became famous as the retreat of the infant Mary, Queen of Scots in 1547. The ruins of the church and cloisters are situated on an island in the Lake of Monteith.

Times: Open Apr-Sep, daily 9.30-6.30. **Fee:** ✱ £4 (ch £1.60, concessions £3). Charge includes ferry trip. Please phone or check website for further details. **Facilities:** 🅿 shop ■

STIRLING   MAP 11 NS79

Mar's Wark   `FREE`
Broad St FK8 1EE
web: www.historic-scotland.gov.uk

A remarkable Renaissance mansion built by the Earl of Mar, Regent for James VI in 1570 and later used as the town workhouse. It was never completed and now the façade can be seen.

Times: Open all reasonable times. **Facilities:** ⊗ ■

Museum of Argyll & Sutherland Highlanders
The Castle FK8 3PA
➲ *(museum in Stirling Castle)*
☎ 01786 475165
e-mail: museum@argylls.co.uk
web: www.argylls.co.uk

Situated in the King's Old Building in Stirling Castle, the museum tells the history of the Regiment from 1794 to the present day. Displays include uniforms, medals, silver, paintings, colours, pipe banners, and commentaries.

Times: Open Etr-Sep, daily 9.30-5; Sep-Etr, daily 10-4.15. **Fee:** Entry to museum free but entry fee to castle. **Facilities:** 🅿 (Castle Esplanade) 🍽 shop ⊗

The National Wallace Monument
Hillsfoot Rd, Causewayhead FK9 5LF
➲ *(from A907 [Stirling to Alloa road] follow brown tourist signs)*
☎ 01786 472140
e-mail: info@nationalwallacemonument.com
web: www.nationalwallacemonument.com

Meet Scotland's national hero, Sir William Wallace, and join his epic struggle for a free Scotland. Step into Westminster Hall and witness his trial. Climb the 220 foot tower and experience one of the finest views in Scotland. Each August there is a dramatic performance commemorating the life of Sir William Wallace.

Times: Open all year Jan-Feb & Nov-Dec, daily 10.30-4; Mar-May & Oct, daily 10-5; Jun, daily 10-6; Jul-Aug, daily 9-6; Sep, daily 9.30-5.30.

continued

Fee: ✱ £6.50 (ch £4, concessions £4.90). Family ticket £17. **Facilities:** 🅿 💷 🍽 ♿ (limited access) shop ■

Old Town Jail
Saint John St FK8 1EA
➲ *(follow signs for castle up hill, jail on left at top of Saint John's St)*
☎ 01786 450050
e-mail: info@oldtownjail.com
web: www.oldtownjail.com

Experience life in a Victorian prison, where real history performances bring the past to life. Come face to face with Stirling's notorious hangman and you may even witness an attempted jailbreak. Stunning rooftop panorama and gift shop. Multi-lingual audio tour.

Times: Open Apr-Sep, daily 9.30-6; Oct & Mar, daily 9.30-6; Nov-Feb, daily 10.30-4.30 (last admission) **Fee:** ✱ £5-£5.95 (ch £3.20-£3.80, concessions £3.80-£4.50). Family ticket £13.25-£15.70. **Facilities:** 🅿 🍽 ♿ toilets for disabled shop ⊗ ■

Stirling Castle
Upper Castle Hill FK8 1EJ
☎ 01786 450000
web: www.historic-scotland.gov.uk

Sitting on top of a 250ft rock, Stirling Castle has a strategic position on the Firth of Forth. As a result it has been the scene of many events in Scotland's history. James II was born at the castle in 1430. Mary, Queen of Scots spent some years there, and it was James IV's childhood home. Among its finest features are the splendid Renaissance palace built by James V, and the Chapel Royal, rebuilt by James VI.

Times: Open all year, Apr-Sep, daily 9.30-6; Oct-Mar, daily 9.30-5. Closed 25-26. **Fee:** ✱ £8.50 (ch £3.50, concessions £6.50). Please phone or check website for further details. **Facilities:** 🅿 (charged) 🍽 licensed ♿ toilets for disabled shop ⊗ ■

Stirling Smith Art Gallery & Museum
Dumbarton Rd FK8 2RQ
➲ *(M9 junct 10, follow Stirling Castle signs)*
☎ 01786 471917
e-mail: museum@smithartgallery.demon.co.uk
web: www.smithartgallery.demon.co.uk

This award-winning museum and gallery presents a variety of exhibitions drawing on its own rich collections and works from elsewhere. Please telephone for details of events running throughout the year.

Times: Open all year, Tue-Sat 10.30-5, Sun 2-5. Closed Mon, 25-26 Dec & 1-2 Jan. **Fee:** Small charge for special events. **Facilities:** 🅿 💷 🍽 ♿ (wheelchair lift, induction loop in theatre) toilets for disabled shop

WEST DUNBARTONSHIRE

DUMBARTON   MAP 10 NS37

Dumbarton Castle
G82 1JJ
☎ 01389 732167
web: www.historic-scotland.gov.uk

The castle, set on the 240ft Dumbarton Rock above the River Clyde, dominates the town (the capital of the Celtic kingdom of Strathclyde)

continued

and commands spectacular views. Most of what can be seen today dates from the 18th and 19th centuries, but there are a few earlier remains.

Times: Open all year, Apr-Sep, daily 9.30-6.30. Oct-Mar, Mon-Wed & Sat-Sun 9.30-4.30. Closed 25-26 Dec & 1-2 Jan. **Fee:** ✱ £3.50 (ch £1.50, concessions £2.50). Please phone or check website for further details. **Facilities:** ❷ shop ⊗ ♮

WEST LOTHIAN

LINLITHGOW   MAP 11 NS97

Blackness Castle

EH49 7AL

➲ (4m NE)

☎ 01506 834807

web: www.historic-scotland.gov.uk

This was once one of the most important fortresses in Scotland. Used as a state prison during covenanting time and in the late 19th-century as a powder magazine, it was one of four castles left fortified by the Articles of Union. Most impressive are the massive 17th-century artillery emplacements.

Times: Open all year, Apr-Sep, daily 9.30-6.30; Oct-Mar, daily 9.30-4.30. Closed Thu & Fri in winter, 25-26 Dec & 1-2 Jan. **Fee:** ✱ £3.50 (ch £1.50, concessions £2.50). Please phone or check website for further details. **Facilities:** ❷ shop ♮

House of The Binns

EH49 7NA

➲ (4m E of Linlithgow, off A904)

☎ 01506 834255

e-mail: houseofthebinns@nts.org.uk

web: www.nts.org.uk

An example of changing architectural tastes from 1612 onwards, this house reflects the transition from fortified stronghold to spacious mansion. The original three-storey building, with small windows and twin turrets, evolved into a fine crenellated house with beautiful moulded plaster ceilings - the ancestral home of the Dalyell family. There is a magnificent display of snowdrops and daffodils in spring.

Times: ✱ Open House: Jun-Sep, Sat-Mon 2-5. Parkland: Apr-Oct, daily 10-7, Nov-Mar, daily 10-4. Times may change for 2007 please telephone or check website **Facilities:** ❷ ♿ (Braille sheets) ⊗ (ex guide dogs) ⴾ

Linlithgow Palace

EH49 7AL

➲ (off M9)

☎ 01506 842896

web: www.historic-scotland.gov.uk

The magnificent ruin of a great Royal Palace, set in its own park or 'peel'. All the Stuart kings lived here, and work commissioned by James I, III, IV, and VI can be seen. The great hall and the chapel are particularly fine. James V was born here in 1512 and Mary, Queen of Scots in 1542.

Times: Open all year, Apr-Sep, daily 9.30-6.30; Oct-Mar, daily 9.30-4.30. Closed 25-26 Dec & 1-2 Jan. **Fee:** ✱ £4.50 (ch £2, concessions £3.50). Please phone or check website for details. **Facilities:** ❷ shop ⊗ ♮

LIVINGSTON   MAP 11 NT06

Almond Valley Heritage Trust   [2 for 1]

Millfield EH54 7AR

➲ (2m from M8 junct 3)

☎ 01506 414957

e-mail: info@almondvalley.co.uk

web: www.almondvalley.co.uk

A combination of fun and educational potential ideal for children, Almond Valley has a petting zoo of farm animals, an interactive museum on the shale oil industry, a narrow gauge railway, and tractor rides. Please telephone for details of events running throughout the year.

Times: Open all year, daily 10-5. Closed Dec 25-26, Jan 1-2 **Fee:** ✱ £3 (ch £2). Family (2ad+4ch) £10. **Facilities:** ❷ ⬛ 🝙 ♿ toilets for disabled shop ◧

SCOTTISH ISLANDS
ISLE OF ARRAN

BRODICK   MAP 10 NS03

Brodick Castle, Garden & Country Park

KA27 8HY

➲ (Ferry from Ardrossan-Brodick or Lochranza-Kintyre - frequent in summer, limited in winter)

☎ 01770 302202 & 302462

e-mail: brodick@nts.org.uk

web: www.nts.org.uk

The site has been fortified since Viking times, but the present castle dating from the 13th century was a stronghold of the Dukes of Hamilton. Splendid silver, fine porcelain and paintings acquired by generations of owners can be seen, including many sporting pictures and trophies. There is a magnificent woodland garden, started by the Duchess of Montrose in 1923, world famous for its rhododendrons and azaleas.

Times: ✱ Open Apr-Oct, daily 11-4.30 (closes 3.30 in Oct). Country Park: open all year, daily 9.30-sunset. Times may change for 2007 please telephone or check website **Facilities:** ❷ 🝙◧♿ (Braille, wheelchairs, motorised buggy & stairlift) toilets for disabled shop ⊗ (ex guide dogs) ⴾ

Isle of Arran Heritage Museum

Rosaburn KA27 8DP

➲ (right at Brodick Pier, approx 1m)

☎ 01770 302636

e-mail: tom.macleod@arranmuseum.co.uk

web: www.arranmuseum.co.uk

The setting is an 18th-century croft farm, including a cottage restored to its pre-1920 state and a 'smiddy' where a blacksmith worked until the late 1960s. There are also several demonstrations of horse-shoeing, sheep-shearing and weaving and spinning throughout the season - please ring for details. There is a large archaeology and geology section with archive, where help with research is available.

Times: Open Apr-Oct, daily 10.30-4.30. **Fee:** ✱ £2.50 (ch £1.25, pen £175) Family £6.50. **Facilities:** ❷ ⬛ 🝙 ♿ toilets for disabled shop ⊗ (ex guide dogs & in garden)

Scotland

Scotland

LOCHRANZA
MAP 10 NR95

Isle of Arran Distillery Visitor Centre
KA27 8HJ

⮕ *(from Brodick Ferry Terminal take coast road N for 14m. Distillery on edge of village)*

☎ 01770 830264

e-mail: visitorcentre@arranwhisky.com

web: www.arranwhisky.com

Located amidst beautiful surroundings, the distillery was built to revive the dormant traditions of Arran single malt whisky production. After a guided tour of the distillery, visitors can now taste some of the first whiskies to be ready after production began in 1995.

Times: ✱ Open daily 10-6 **Facilities:** ℗ ⅰ◉⅃ licensed & (ex working distillery, chair lift in visitor centre) toilets for disabled shop ⊗ (ex guide dogs) ⬛

ISLE OF BUTE

ROTHESAY
MAP 10 NS06

Ardencraig
FREE
PA20 9HA

⮕ *(1m off A844, S of Rothesay)*

☎ 01700 504225

e-mail: allan.macdonald@argyll-bute.co.uk

web: www.argyll-bute.gov.uk

Particular attention has been paid to improving the layout of the garden and introducing rare plants. The greenhouse and walled garden produce plants for floral displays throughout the district. A variety of fish is kept in the ornamental ponds and the aviaries have some interesting birds.

Times: ✱ Open May-Sep. **Facilities:** ℗ 🖳 & ⊗ (ex guide dogs)

Bute Museum
7 Stuart St PA20 0EP

⮕ *(on road behind castle)*

☎ 01700 505067

e-mail: lvor@butemuseum.fsnet.co.uk

Local and natural history displays, including birds, mammals and seashore items; varied collections of recent bygones, a collection of early Christian crosses, and flints and pots from various Mesolithic and Neolithic burial cairns.

Times: Open all year, Apr-Sep, Mon-Sat 10.30-4.30, Sun 2.30-4.30; Oct-Mar, Tue-Sat 2.30-4.30. Closed Sun & Mon. **Fee:** ✱ £2 (ch £1, pen £1.50) **Facilities:** ℗ (3 mins walk) (50p per hour) 🎫 & (touch table for blind, ramps) shop

Rothesay Castle
PA20 0DA

☎ 01700 502691

web: www.historic-scotland.gov.uk

The focal point of Rothesay is this 13th-century castle. It has lofty curtain walls defended by drum towers that enclose a circular courtyard.

Times: Open all year, Apr-Sep, daily 9.30-6.30; Oct-Mar, Mon-Wed & Sat-Sun 9.30-4.30. Closed 25-26 Dec & 1-2 Jan. **Fee:** ✱ £3.50 (ch £1.50, concessions £2.50). Please phone or check website for further details. **Facilities:** ℗ shop ⋒

GREAT CUMBRAE ISLAND

MILLPORT
MAP 10 NS15

Museum of the Cumbraes
FREE
Garrison Grounds KA28 0DG

⮕ *(Ferry to Millport, from Largs Cal-Mac Terminal. Bus meets each ferry)*

☎ 01475 531191

e-mail: namuseum@north-ayrshire.gov.uk

web: www.north-ayrshire.gov.uk/museums

A small museum which displays the history and life of the Cumbraes. There is also a fine collection of local photographs.

Times: Open Etr-Sep, Thu-Mon 10-1 & 2-5. **Facilities:** ℗ & shop ⊗ (ex guide dogs)

ISLE OF LEWIS

ARNOL
MAP 13 NB34

Black House Museum
PA86 9DB

⮕ *(11m NW of Stornoway on A858)*

☎ 01851 710395

web: www.historic-scotland.gov.uk

A traditional Hebridean dwelling, built without mortar and roofed with thatch on a timber framework. It has a central peat fire in the kitchen, no chimney and a byre under the same roof.

Times: Open all year, Apr-Sep, Mon-Sat 9.30-6.30; Oct-Mar, Mon-Sat 9.30-4.30. Closed 25-26 Dec & 1-2 Jan. **Fee:** ✱ £4.50 (ch £2, concessions £3.50). Please phone or check website for further details. **Facilities:** ℗ & toilets for disabled shop ⊗ ⋒

CALLANISH
MAP 13 NB23

Callanish Standing Stones
PA86 9DY

⮕ *(12m W of Stornoway off A859)*

☎ 01851 621422

web: www.historic-scotland.gov.uk

An avenue of 19 monoliths leads north from a circle of 13 stones with rows of more stones fanning out to south, east and west. Probably constructed between 3000 and 1500BC, this is a unique cruciform of megaliths.

Times: ✱ Site accessible at all times. Visitor Centre open Apr-Sep, Mon-Sat 10-7; Oct-Mar, Mon-Sat 10-4. **Facilities:** ℗ ⅰ◉⅃ & toilets for disabled shop ⋒

CARLOWAY
MAP 13 NB24

Dun Carloway Broch
FREE

⮕ *(1.5m S of Carloway on A858)*

web: www.historic-scotland.gov.uk

Brochs are late-prehistoric circular stone towers, and their origins are mysterious. One of the best examples can be seen at Dun Carloway, where the tower still stands about 30ft high.

Times: Open at all reasonable times. **Facilities:** ℗ ⋒

ISLE OF MULL

CRAIGNURE — MAP 10 NM73

Mull & West Highland Narrow Gauge Railway `2 for 1`

Craignure (old pier) Station PA65 6AY

➲ (0.25m from Craignure Ferry Terminal, just off road to Iona, by Police station)

☎ 01680 812494 (in season) or 01680 812567

e-mail: mullrail@dee-emm.co.uk

web: mullrail.co.uk

The first passenger railway on a Scottish island, opened in 1983. Both steam and diesel trains operate on the ten-and-a-quarter inch gauge line, which runs from Craignure to Torosay Castle. The 1.25 mile line offers dramatic woodland and mountain views taking in Ben Nevis, Glencoe and the Isle of Lismore.

Times: Open Etr-end Oct, 11-5 **Fee:** ✱ Return £4 (ch £3); Single £3 (ch £2). Family ticket return £12, single £8, Dogs Free.
Facilities: ❷ ⅙ (provision to carry person seated in wheelchair on trains) shop ◀

Torosay Castle & Gardens

PA65 6AY

➲ (1.5m S of Ferry Terminal at Craignure)

☎ 01680 812421

e-mail: info@torosay.com

web: www.holidaymull.org/members/torosay

The Scottish baronial architecture of this Victorian castle is complemented by the magnificent setting, and inside the house there are displays of portraits and wildlife pictures, family scrapbooks and a study of the Antarctic. The gardens include a statue walk and water garden, an avenue of Australian gum trees, and an Oriental garden. Within the grounds there is a narrow gauge steam and diesel railway.

Times: Open end Apr-Oct, daily 10.30-5. Gardens all year.
Facilities: ❷ 🖤 🎛 shop ⊗ (ex guide/hearing dogs) ◀

ORKNEY

BIRSAY — MAP 16 HY22

Earl's Palace `FREE`

KW15 1PD

➲ (on A966)

☎ 01856 721205 & 841815

web: www.historic-scotland.gov.uk

The gaunt remains of the residence of the 16th-century Earl of Orkney, constructed round a courtyard.

Times: Open at all reasonable times. **Facilities:** ⊗ ⅍

DOUNBY — MAP 16 HY22

Brough of Birsay

➲ (off A966)

☎ 01856 841815

web: www.historic-scotland.gov.uk

This ruined Romanesque church stands next to the remains of a Norse village. The nave, chancel and semicircular apse can be seen, along with claustral buildings. Crossings must be made on foot at low-water - there is no boat.

Times: Open mid Jun-Sep (tides permitting), daily 9.30-6.30.
Fee: ✱ £2.50 (ch £1, concessions £2). **Facilities:** ⅍

Click Mill `FREE`

➲ (2.5m from Dounby on B905)

☎ 01856 841815

web: www.historic-scotland.gov.uk

The last surviving horizontal water mill in Orkney, of a type well represented in Shetland and Lewis. The mill is in working condition and visitors should wear sensible footwear.

Times: Open at all reasonable times. **Facilities:** ⅍

Skara Brae

KW16 3LR

➲ (19m W of Kirkwall on B9056)

☎ 01856 841815

web: www.historic-scotland.gov.uk

Engulfed in drift sand, this remarkable group of well-preserved Stone Age dwellings is the most outstanding survivor of its kind in Britain. Stone furniture and a fireplace can be seen.

Times: Open all year, Apr-Sep, daily 9.30-6.30; Oct-Mar, daily 9.30-4.30. Closed 25-26 Dec & 1-2 Jan. **Fee:** ✱ £6.50 (ch £2.50, concessions £5). Please phone or check website for details. **Facilities:** ❷ 🍴 ⅙ toilets for disabled shop ⊗ ⅍

FINSTOWN — MAP 16 HY31

Maes Howe Chambered Cairn

➲ (9m W of Kirkwall, on A965)

☎ 01856 761606

web: www.historic-scotland.gov.uk

The masonry of Britain's finest megalithic tomb is in a remarkably good state of preservation. Dating from neolithic times, it contains Viking carvings and runes.

Times: Open all year, Apr-Sep daily 9.30-6.30; Oct-Mar, daily 9.30-4.30.

continued

Closed 25-26 Dec & 1-2 Jan. (Visits must be pre-booked). **Fee:** ✱ £4.50 (ch £2, concessions £3.50). Please phone or check website for further details. **Facilities:** ♿ 🍴 shop 🐾 🎦

Stones of Stenness Circle and Henge
➲ *(5m NE of Stromness on B9055)*
☎ 01856 841815
web: www.historic-scotland.gov.uk
Dating back to the second millennium BC, the remains of this stone circle are near the Ring of Brogar - a splendid circle of upright stones surrounded by a ditch.

Times: Open at any reasonable time. **Facilities:** ♿ 🎦

HARRAY   **MAP 16 HY31**

Corrigall Farm & Kirbuster Museum
KW17 2JR
☎ 01856 771411 & 771268
The museum consists of two Orkney farmhouses with outbuildings. Kirbuster (Birsay) has the last surviving example of a 'Firehoose' with its central hearth; Corrigall (Harray) represents an improved farmhouse and steading of the late 1800s.

Times: Open Mar-Oct, Mon-Sat 10.30-1 & 2-5, Sun 2-7. **Facilities:** ♿ 🍴 ♿ toilets for disabled shop 🐾 (ex guide dogs) 🚌

KIRKWALL   **MAP 16 HY41**

Bishop's & Earl's Palaces
KW15 1PD
➲ *(In Kirkwall on A960)*
☎ 01856 875461
web: www.historic-scotland.gov.uk
The Bishop's Palace is a hall-house of the 12th century, later much altered, with a round tower built by Bishop Reid in 1541-48. A later addition was made by the notorious Patrick Stewart, Earl of Orkney, who built the adjacent Earl's Palace between 1600 and 1607 in a splendid Renaissance style.

Times: Open Apr-Sep, daily 9.30-6.30. **Fee:** ✱ £3 (ch £1.30 concessions £2.30). Please telephone for further details or check website **Facilities:** shop 🎦

Scapa Flow Visitor Centre & Museum
Lyness, Hoy
➲ *(on A964 to Houton, ferry crossing takes 30 mins, visitors centre 2 mins from ferry terminal)*
☎ 01856 791300
e-mail: museum@orkney.gov.uk
web: www.orkneyheritage.com
Also known as the Lyness Interpretation Centre, this fascinating museum is home to a large collection of military equipment used in the defence of the Orkneys during the First and Second World Wars. There are also guns salvaged from the German ships scuppered in WWII. Visitors arrive at the island after a short boat trip from the Orkney mainland.

Times: Open all year: Mon-Fri 9-4.30 (mid May-Oct also Sat, Sun 10.30-3.30) **Facilities:** ♿ 🍽 🍴 ♿ toilets for disabled shop 🐾 (ex guide dogs) 🚌

The Orkney Museum
Broad St KW15 1DH
➲ *(town centre)*
☎ 01856 87355
e-mail: museum@orkney.gov.uk
web: www.orkneyheritage.com
One of the finest vernacular town houses in Scotland, this 16th-century building now contains a museum of Orkney history, including the islands' fascinating archaeology.

Times: Open, Oct-Mar Mon-Sat, 10.30-12.30 & 1.30-5, Apr-Sep, 10.30-5 Mon-Sat. **Facilities:** ℗ (50yds) 🍴 ♿ toilets for disabled shop 🐾 (ex guide dogs) 🚌

STROMNESS   **MAP 16 HY20**

Orkney Maritime & Natural History Museum
52 Alfred St KW16 3DF
☎ 01856 850025
The museum focuses on Orkney's broad maritime connections, including fishing, whaling, the Hudson's Bay Company, the German Fleet in Scapa Flow, and the award-winning Pilot's House extension. The Natural History Gallery is fully restored, displaying a fine collection of curios and rare and interesting exhibits.

Times: Open Apr-Sep, Mon-Sun 10-5; Oct-Mar, Mon-Sat 11-3.30. Closed Xmas, New Year & 3 wks Feb-Mar. **Fee:** ✱ £3 (ch 50p concessions £2). Family ticket £5. **Facilities:** ℗ (50yds) ♿ (stair lift and ramps) toilets for disabled shop 🐾 (ex guide dogs)

Pier Arts Centre
KW16 3AA
☎ 01856 850209
e-mail: info@pierartscentre.com
web: www.pierartscentre.com
A permanent collection of modern art and sculpture including works by Barbara Hepworth and Ben Nicholson, given to Orkney by the late Margaret Gardiner. These works are housed in a landmark 18th-century building that has served as merchants offices, a cooperage, stores and private lodgings.

Times: Open from Spring, Tue-Sat. **Facilities:** ℗ (100yds) ♿ toilets for disabled shop 🐾 (ex guide dogs) 🚌

WESTRAY   **MAP 16 HY44**

Noltland Castle
➲ *(1m W of Pierowall village)*
☎ 01856 841815
web: www.historic-scotland.gov.uk
A fine, ruined Z-plan tower, built between 1560 and 1573 but never completed. The tower is remarkable for its large number of gun loops and impressive staircase.

Times: ✱ Open 11 Jun-Sep, daily 9.30-6.30. **Facilities:** 🐾 🎦

SHETLAND

LERWICK
MAP 16 HU44

Clickimin
FREE

ZE1 0QX
⊃ *(1m SW of Lerwick on A970)*
☎ 01466 793191
web: www.historic-scotland.gov.uk

The remains of a prehistoric settlement that was fortified at the beginning of the Iron Age with a stone-built fort. The site was occupied for over 1000 years. The remains include a partially demolished broch (round tower) which still stands to a height of 17ft.

Times: Open at all reasonable times. **Facilities:** ▮

Fort Charlotte
FREE

ZE1 0JN
⊃ *(in centre of Lerwick)*
☎ 01466 793191
web: www.historic-scotland.gov.uk

A five-sided artillery fort with bastions projecting from each corner. The walls are high and massive. It was built in 1665 to protect the Sound of Bressay from the Dutch, but taken by them and burned in 1673. It was rebuilt in 1781.

Times: Open at all reasonable times. Key available locally. **Facilities:** ▮

Shetland Museum
FREE

Hay's Dock
☎ 01595 695057
e-mail: shetland.museum@sic.shetland.gov.uk
web: www.shetland-museum.gov.uk

Please note the Museum closed in 2005. It will re-open as the New Shetland Museum and Archives in January 2007.

Times: Re-launch of museum. Please telephone for details of opening times and admission prices. **Facilities:** ℗ 🖵 🍴 licensed ♿ (lift, wheelchair available) toilets for disabled shop ⊗ (ex guide dogs) ⬛

MOUSA ISLAND
MAP 16 HU42

Mousa Broch
FREE

⊃ *(accessible by boat from Sandwick)*
☎ 01466 793191
web: www.historic-scotland.gov.uk

This broch is the best-preserved example of an Iron Age drystone tower in Scotland. The tower is nearly complete and rises to a height of 40ft. The outer and inner walls both contain staircases that may be climbed to the parapet.

Times: Open at all reasonable time. **Facilities:** ▮

SCALLOWAY
MAP 16 HU33

Scalloway Castle
FREE

ZE1 0TP
⊃ *(6m from Lerwick on A970)*
☎ 01466 793191
web: www.historic-scotland.gov.uk

The ruins of a castle designed on the medieval two-step plan. The castle was actually built in 1600 by Patrick Stewart, Earl of Orkney.

continued

When the Earl, who was renowned for his cruelty, was executed in 1615, the castle fell into disuse.

Times: Open at all reasonable time. **Facilities:** ℗ ▮

SUMBURGH
MAP 16 HU30

Jarlshof Prehistoric Site

⊃ *(at Sumburgh Head, approx 22m S of Lerwick)*
☎ 01950 460112
web: www.historic-scotland.gov.uk

One of the most remarkable archaeological sites in Europe. There are remains of Bronze Age, Iron Age and Viking settlements as well as a medieval farm. There is also a 16th-century Laird's House, once the home of the Earls Robert and Patrick Stewart, and the basis of 'Jarlshof' in Sir Walter Scott's novel *The Pirate*.

Times: Open Apr-Sep, daily 9.30-6.30. **Fee:** ✱ £4 (ch £1.60, concessions £3). Please phone or check website for further details. **Facilities:** ℗ shop ▮

ISLE OF SKYE

ARMADALE
MAP 13 NG60

Armadale Castle Gardens & Museum of the Isles

IV45 8RS
⊃ *(16m S of Broadford on A851. Follow Clan Donald Centre or Armadale Castle Gardens & Museum of the Isles signs. Easily reached by Skye Bridge or the Mallaig A830 to Armdale Ferry)*
☎ 01471 844305 & 844227
e-mail: office@clandonald.com
web: www.clandonald.com

Armadale Castle and Gardens were built in 1815 as the home of Lord Macdonald. The warming effect of the Gulf Stream allows exotic trees and plants to flourish. Within the 40 acres of gardens is the Museum of the Isles, where visitors can discover the history of the Highlands.

Times: Open daily 9.30-5.30. Garden & Museum open Apr-Oct. **Fee:** £5 (concessions & Group 8+ £4). **Facilities:** ℗ 🖵 🍴 licensed ♿ (wheelchairs available) toilets for disabled shop garden centre ⊗ (ex on leads) ⬛

DUNVEGAN
MAP 13 NG24

Dunvegan Castle

IV55 8WF
⊃ *(follow A87 over Skye Bridge. Turn onto A863 at Sligachan and continue to castle)*
☎ 01470 521206
e-mail: info@dunvegancastle.com
web: www.dunvegancastle.com

This fortress stronghold set on the sea loch of Dunvegan has been the home of the Chief of Macleod for 800 years. On view are books, pictures, arms and treasured relics of the clan. A pedigree Highland Cattle fold is also an attraction, as is the boat trip to the nearby Seal Colony.

Times: ✱ Open 24 Mar-Oct, daily 10-5.30 (last entry 5). Castle & Gardens, Nov-Mar, daily 11-4 (last entry 3.30). Closed 25-26 Dec & 1-2 Jan **Facilities:** ℗ 🖵 🍴 licensed ♿ (restaurant has ramps for wheelchair access) toilets for disabled shop garden centre ⊗ (ex guide dogs & in grounds) ⬛

Scotland

Wales

Rhosilli, Gower,
Vale of Glamorgan

Wales has an amazing 1,200km (750 miles) of coastline, offering everything from sandy beaches to rocky sea-swept cliffs, home to thousands of sea birds. There are breathtaking mountains too – Snowdonia comes in at 1085m (3,560ft), making it the highest peak in Wales, but the Brecon Beacons and the Cambrians are also pretty impressive. Cardiff is a resurgent, regenerated city, with elegant Victorian and Edwardian architecture as well as a Norman castle, and throughout the country you'll find many other castles, both ruined and well-preserved, evidence of the troubled history of the Principality.

BRIDGEND

BRIDGEND   MAP 03 SS97

Newcastle   `FREE`
☎ 01656 659515
web: www.cadw.wales.gov.uk

The small castle dates back to the 12th century. It is ruined, but a rectangular tower, a richly carved Norman gateway and massive curtain walls enclosing a polygonal courtyard can still be seen.

Times: Open - accessible throughout the year. Key keeper arrangement.
Facilities: ❷ ❽ ⊕

COITY   MAP 03 SS98

Coity Castle   `FREE`
CF35 6BG
➲ (2m NE of Bridgend, off A4061)
☎ 01656 652021
web: www.cadw.wales.gov.uk

A 12th to 16th-century stronghold, with a hall, chapel and the remains of a square keep.

Times: Open all year, at all times. Key keeper arrangement.
Facilities: ℗ ❽ ⊕

CAERPHILLY

CAERPHILLY   MAP 03 ST18

Caerphilly Castle
CF8 1JL
➲ (on A469)
☎ 029 2088 3143
web: www.cadw.wales.gov.uk

The concentrically planned castle was begun in 1268 by Gilbert de Clare and completed in 1326. It is the largest in Wales, and has extensive land and water defences. A unique feature is the ruined tower - the victim of subsidence - which manages to out-lean even Pisa! The south dam platform, once a tournament-field, now displays replica medieval siege-engines.

Times: Open Apr-May & Oct, daily 9.30-5; Jun-Sep, daily 9.30-6; Nov-Mar, Mon-Sat 9.30-4, Sun 11-4. Telephone for Xmas opening times.
Fee: ✱ £3.50 (ch 5-15, concessions £3, disabled visitors and assisting companion free). Family ticket (2ad+all ch/grandch under 16) £10.00. Group rates available. Prices quoted apply until 31 Mar 2007.
Facilities: ❷ ⅋ shop ❽ ⊕ ◄

Llancaiach Fawr Manor   `2 for 1`
Gelligaer Rd, Nelson CF46 6ER
➲ (M4 junct 32, A470 to Merthyr Tydfil. Towards Ystrad Mynach A472, follow brown heritage signs)
☎ 01443 412248
e-mail: llancaiachfawr@caerphilly.gov.uk
web: www.llancaiachfawr.co.uk

Step back in time to the Civil War period at this fascinating living history museum. The year is 1645 and visitors are invited into the

continued

Manor to meet the servants of 'Colonel' Edward Prichard - from the puritanical to the gossipy. Please telephone for details of events running throughout the year.

Times: Open daily 10-5. Closed Mon, Nov-Feb and 24 Dec-1 Jan.
Fee: ✱ £4.95 (ch £3.50) concessions £3.75. Family ticket £14.
Facilities: ❷ ⅋ ❙◎❙ licensed 🍴 shop ❽ (ex guide dogs) ◄

CWMCARN   MAP 03 ST29

Cwmcarn Forest Drive
Nantcarn Rd NP11 7FA
➲ (8m N of Newport on A467, follow brown tourist signs)
☎ 01495 272001
e-mail: cwmcarn-vc@caerphilly.gov.uk
web: www.caerphilly.gov.uk/visiting

A seven-mile scenic drive with spectacular views over the Bristol Channel and surrounding countryside. Facilities include barbecues, picnic and play areas, and forest and mountain walks. There are also a bike trail and downhill trail on site. Special events are held throughout the year, please ring for details.

Times: Open Forest Drive: Mar & Oct 11-5; Apr-Aug 11-7 (11-9 wknds during Jul & Aug); Sep, 11-6; Nov 11-4 (wknds only). Visitor Centre: all year except between Xmas & New Year. **Fee:** Cars & Motorcycles £3, Minibus £6, Coaches £20. Car season ticket £15. **Facilities:** ❷ ⅋ ⅙ toilets for disabled shop ◄

CARDIFF

CARDIFF   MAP 03 ST17

Cardiff Castle
Castle St CF10 3RB
➲ (from M4, A48 & A470 follow signs to city centre)
☎ 029 2087 8100
e-mail: cardiffcastle@cardiff.gov.uk
web: www.cardiffcastle.com

Cardiff Castle is situated in the heart of the city. Contained within its mighty walls is a history spanning nearly 2000 years, dating from the coming of the Romans to the Norman Conquest. Discover spectacular interiors on your guided tour, and enjoy magnificent views of the city from the top of the 12th-century Norman keep. Regular events throughout the year include a teddy bears picnic, open air theatre, medieval and Roman re-enactments, and 1940s-style celebrations to mark the 60th anniversary of the gifting of Cardiff Castle by the 5th Marquis of Bute.

Times: Open all year, daily (ex 25-26 Dec & 1 Jan) including guided tours, Mar-Oct, 9.30-6 (last tour 5); Nov-Feb, 9.30-5.00 (last tour 4). Royal Regiment of Wales Museum closed Tue. **Fee:** ✱ Full guided tour, Norman Keep, green and military museum, £6.95 (ch £4.30, pen £5.40). Family £22.40. Norman Keep, green and military museum £3 (ch £3.20, pen £2.70). Family £11.40. **Facilities:** ℗ (200 yds) ⅋ ⅙ (access to Castle Green) toilets for disabled shop ❽ (ex in grounds & guide dogs) ◄

Dyffryn Gardens

St Nicholas CF5 6SU

⮎ *(A4232 towards Barry, rdbt take 1st exit, exit at junct with A48/A4050. At Culverhouse Cross rdbt take 4th exit A48 signed Cowbridge. Left at lights in St Nicholas village, Dyffryn on right after 1.5m)*

☎ 029 2059 3328

e-mail: kbaker@valeofglamorgan.gov.uk

web: www.dyffryngardens.org.uk

One of Wales' finest Edwardian gardens, the beautiful grounds offer an endless variety of colour and form with many small garden rooms now restored with the aid of a Heritage Lottery fund grant. Additional works are still ongoing and some areas may be subject to closure.

Times: Open Apr-Sep 10-6; Oct 10-5. Nov-Dec, 10-4 (free admission) **Fee:** ✱ £3.50 (ch & pen £2.50, disabled £2, carers free). Family ticket £7. **Facilities:** ♿ ⬛ 🚻 ♿ (wheelchairs for hire, parking, ramps) toilets for disabled shop garden centre ◀

Llandaff Cathedral

Llandaff CF5 2LA

⮎ *(W on M4 junct 29 to A48(M), then onto A48 and follow brown signs. E on M4 junct 32 onto A470 towards Cardiff, leave A48 and follow brown signs)*

☎ 029 2056 4554

e-mail: office@llandaffcathedral.org.uk

web: www.llandaffcathedral.org.uk

A medieval cathedral begun in the 12th century on the site of an early Christian place of worship. The cathedral was severely damaged during the bombing raids on Cardiff during World War II. The interior is dominated by a modernistic post-war 'Christ in Majesty' sculpture by Epstein. Please visit website for details of events running throughout the year.

Times: Open all year, daily 8-7 (Sun 7-7 & Mon 8.30-7). **Fee:** Donations expected. No group bookings on Sun or Holy Days. **Facilities:** ℗ (100yds) (parking limited) 🍴 ♿ (wheelchair available) shop ⊗ (ex guide dogs)

Millennium Stadium Tours

Millennium Stadium, Westgate St, Gate 3 CF10 1JA

⮎ *(A470 to city centre. Westgate St opposite Castle far end. Turn by Angel Hotel on corner of Westgate Street.)*

☎ 029 2082 2228

e-mail: mgibbons@wru.co.uk

web: millenniumstadium.com/tours

In the late 1990s this massive stadium was completed as part of an effort to revitalise Welsh fortunes. It replaced Cardiff Arms Park, and now hosts major music events, exhibitions, and international rugby and soccer matches. Its capacity of around 75,000 and its retractable roof make it unique in Europe. The current home of five controlling bodies; Welsh Rugby, Welsh Football, English Football Association, Football league (English) & British Speedway.

Times: Open all year Mon-Sat, 10-5; Sun 10-4 **Fee:** £5.50 (ch up to 16 £3, ch under 5 free, concessions £3.50) Party 20+ 15% discount. **Facilities:** ℗ (opposite gate 3) ♿ (lifts, escalators, disabled parking) toilets for disabled shop ⊗ (ex guide dogs) ◀

National Museum Cardiff

FREE

Cathays Park CF10 3NP

⮎ *(in Civic Centre, 5 mins walk from city centre & 20 mins walk from bus & train station)*

☎ 029 2039 7951

e-mail: post@museumwales.ac.uk

web: www.museumwales.a.uk   /

This establishment is unique amongst British museums and galleries in its range of art and science displays. 'The Evolution of Wales' exhibition takes visitors on a spectacular 4600-million year journey, tracing the world from beginning of time and the development of Wales. There are displays of Bronze Age gold, early Christian monuments, Celtic treasures, silver, coins and medals, ceramics, fossils and minerals. A significant collection of French Impressionist paintings sits alongside the work of Welsh artists, past and present in the elegant art galleries. 2007 sees the centenary of the museum.

Times: Open all year, Tue-Sun 10-5. Closed Mon (ex BHs) & 24-26 Dec. **Facilities:** ♿ (charged) ⬛ 🍴 licensed ♿ (wheelchair available, Tel 029 2057 3509 for access guide) toilets for disabled shop ⊗ (ex guide dogs) ◀

Techniquest

2 for 1

Stuart St CF10 5BW

⮎ *(A4232 to Cardiff Bay)*

☎ 029 2047 5475

e-mail: info@techniquest.org

web: www.techniquest.org

Located in the heart of the Cardiff Bay, there's always something new to explore at this exciting science discovery centre. Journey into space in the planetarium, enjoy an interactive Science Theatre Show or experience one of the 150 hands-on exhibits. Please visit website for details of events running throughout the year.

Times: Open all year, Mon-Fri 9.30-4.30; Sat-Sun & BHs 10.30-5, school hols 9.30-5. Closed Xmas. **Fee:** £6.90 (ch 5-16 & concessions £4.80). Family ticket £20 (2ad + 3ch). Friend season ticket £47. Groups 10+ **Facilities:** ℗ (50mtrs) (limited parking for disabled visitors) ⬛ 🍴 ♿ (lift, hearing loop) toilets for disabled shop ⊗ (ex guide dogs) ◀

ST FAGANS   **MAP 03 ST17**

St Fagans: National History Museum

FREE

CF5 6XB

⮎ *(4m W of Cardiff on A4232. From M4 exit at junct 33 and follow brown signs)*

☎ 029 2057 3500

e-mail: post@nmgw.ac.uk

web: www.nmgw.ac.uk

A stroll around the indoor galleries and 100 acres of beautiful grounds will give you a fascinating insight into how people in Wales have lived, worked and spent their leisure hours since Celtic times. You can see people practising the traditional means of earning a living, the animals they kept and at certain times of year, the ways in which they celebrated the seasons.

Times: Open all year daily, 10-5. Closed 24-26 Dec. **Facilities:** ♿ (charged) ⬛ 🍴 licensed ♿ (wheelchairs, motorised buggy-must pre-book) toilets for disabled shop ⊗ (ex in grounds on lead) ◀

Wales

TONGWYNLAIS   MAP 03 ST18

Castell Coch

CF4 7YS

➲ *(A470 to Tongwynlais junct, then B4262 to castle on top of hill)*

☎ 029 2081 0101

web: www.cadw.wales.gov.uk

Castell Coch is Welsh for red castle, an appropriate name for this fairy-tale building with its red sandstone walls and conical towers. The castle was originally built in the 13th century but fell into ruins, and the present castle is a late-19th-century creation. Inside, the castle is decorated in fantasy style.

Times: Open Apr-May & Oct, daily 9.30-5; Jun-Sep, daily 9.30-6; Nov-Mar, Mon-Sat 9.30-4, Sun 11-4. Telephone for Xmas opening times. During the periods 18-29 Sep 06 & 8 Jan-9 Feb 07 the monument will be closed for essential conservation works. **Fee:** ✱ £3.50 (ch 5-15, concessions £3, disabled visitors and assisting companion free). Family ticket (2ad+all ch/grandch under 16) £10.00. Group rates available. Prices quoted apply until 31 Mar 2007. **Facilities:** ♿ shop ⊗ ✦ ◼

CARMARTHENSHIRE

ABERGWILI   MAP 02 SN42

Carmarthenshire County Museum   `FREE`

SA31 2JG

➲ *(2m E of Carmarthen, just off A40, at Abergwili rdbt)*

☎ 01267 228696

e-mail: museums@carmarthenshire.gov.uk

web: www.carmarthenshire.gov.uk/

Housed in the old palace of the Bishop of St David's and set in seven acres of grounds, the museum offers a wide range of local subjects to explore, from geology and prehistory to butter making, Welsh furniture and folk art. Temporary exhibitions are held.

Times: Open all year, Mon-Sat 10-4.30. Closed Xmas-New Year **Facilities:** ♿ ◼ ♿ (lift) toilets for disabled shop ⊗ (ex guide dogs)

CARREG CENNEN CASTLE   MAP 03 SN61

Carreg Cennen Castle

SA19 6UA

➲ *(unclass road from A483 to Trapp village)*

☎ 01558 822291

web: www.cadw.wales.gov.uk

A steep path leads up to the castle, which is spectacularly sited on a limestone crag. It was first built as a stronghold of the native Welsh and then rebuilt in the late 13th century. Most remarkable among the impressive remains is a mysterious passage, cut into the side of the cliff and lit by loopholes. The farm at the site has a rare breeds centre.

Times: Open all year, Apr-Oct, daily 9.30-6.30; Nov-Mar, daily, 9.30-4. Telephone for Xmas opening times. **Fee:** ✱ £3.50 (ch 5-15, concessions £3, disabled visitors & assisting companion free). Family ticket (2ad+all ch/grandch under 16) £10. Group rates available. Prices quoted apply until 31 Mar 2007. **Facilities:** ♿ ◼ shop ⊗ ✦ ◼

DRE-FACH FELINDRE   MAP 02 SN33

National Woollen Museum   `FREE`

SA44 5UP

➲ *(16m W of Carmarthen off A484, 4m E of Newcastle Emlyn)*

☎ 01559 370929

web: www.museumwales.ac.uk

The museum is housed in the former Cambrian Mills and has a comprehensive display tracing the evolution of the industry from its beginnings to the present day. Demonstrations of the fleece to fabric process are given on 19th-century textile machinery.

Times: Open Apr-Sep, daily 10-5; Oct-Mar, Tue-Sat 10-5. Closed Xmas. **Facilities:** ♿ ◼ ♿ (wheelchair access to ground floor & ample seating) toilets for disabled shop ⊗ (ex guide dogs) ◼

DRYSLWYN   MAP 02 SN52

Dryslwyn Castle   `FREE`

➲ *(on B4279)*

☎ 029 2050 0200

web: www.cadw.wales.gov.uk

The ruined 13th-century castle was a stronghold of the native Welsh. It stands on a lofty mound, and was important in the struggles between English and Welsh. It is gradually being uncovered by excavation.

Times: Open-entrance by arrangement with Dryslwyn Farm. **Facilities:** ♿ ⊗ ✦

KIDWELLY   MAP 02 SN40

Kidwelly Castle

SA17 5BQ

➲ *(via A484)*

☎ 01554 890104

web: www.cadw.wales.gov.uk

This is an outstanding example of late 13th-century castle design, with its 'walls within walls' defensive system. There were later additions made to the building, the chapel dating from about 1400. Of particular interest are two vast circular ovens.

Times: Open Apr-May & Oct, daily 9.30-5; Jun-Sep, daily 9.30-6; Nov-Mar, Mon-Sat 9.30-4, Sun 11-4. Telephone for Xmas opening times. **Fee:** ✱ £2.90 (ch 5-15, concessions £2.50, disabled visitors & assisting companion free). Family ticket (2ad+all ch/grandch under 16) £8.30. Group rates available. Prices quoted apply until 31 Mar 2007. **Facilities:** ♿ ♿ toilets for disabled shop ⊗ ✦ ◼

Kidwelly Industrial Museum   `FREE`

Broadford SA17 4LW

➲ *(signed from Kidwelly by-pass & town, stack visible from by-pass)*

☎ 01554 891078

Two of the great industries of Wales are represented in this museum: tinplate and coal mining. The original buildings and machinery of the Kidwelly tinplate works, where tinplate was hand made, are now on display to the public. There is also an exhibition of coal mining with pit-head gear and a winding engine, while the more general history of the area is shown in a separate exhibition.

Times: Open Etr, Jun-Sep, BH wknds, Mon-Fri 10-5, Sat-Sun 12-5. Last admission 4. Other times by arrangement for parties only. **Facilities:** ♿ ◼ ♿ (ramps on entrances) toilets for disabled shop

Wales

LAUGHARNE   MAP 02 SN31

Dylan Thomas' Boat House
Dylans Walk SA33 4SD
➲ *(14m SW of Carmarthen)*
☎ 01994 427420
e-mail: dylanthomas@carmarthenshire.gov.uk
web: www.dylanthomasboathouse.com

The home of Dylan Thomas and his family during the last four turbulent and creative years of his life. The house and its surrounding estuary, town and countryside feature considerably in the poet's work, including his famous '*Under Milk Wood*'. The house contains interpretive display, original furniture, bookshop and tearoom. Please telephone for details of events running throughout the year.

Times: Open all year, May-Oct & Etr wknd, daily 10-5.30 (last admission 5); Nov-Apr, daily 10.30-3.30 (last admission 3) **Fee:** ✱ £3.50 (ch under 7 free, pen £2.75, concessions £2.50). Family and group rates available. **Facilities:** ℗ (200yds) ⬤ & (not accessible for wheelchairs) shop ⊗ (ex guide dogs) ◀

Laugharne Castle
King St SA33 4SA
➲ *(on A4066)*
☎ 01994 427906
web: www.cadw.wales.gov.uk

Newly opened to the public, picturesque Laugharne Castle stands on a low ridge overlooking the wide Taff Estuary. A medieval fortress converted into an Elizabethan mansion, it suffered a civil war siege and later became the backdrop for elaborate Victorian gardens, now recreated. Laugharne Castle has also inspired two modern writers - Richard Hughes and Dylan Thomas.

Times: Open Apr-Sep, daily 10-5. Closed at all other times. **Fee:** ✱ £2.90 (ch 5-15, concessions £2.50, disabled visitors & assisting companions free). Family ticket (2ad+all ch/grandch under 16) £8.30. Group rates available. Prices quoted apply until 31 Mar 2007. **Facilities:** ℗ (150mtrs) & toilets for disabled shop ⊗ ✿ ◀

LLANARTHNE   MAP 02 SN52

The National Botanic Garden of Wales
2 for 1
Middleton Hall SA32 8HG
➲ *(8m E of Carmarthen on A48, dedicated intersection - signed)*
☎ 01558 668768
e-mail: info@gardenofwales.org.uk
web: www.gardenofwales.org.uk

Set amongst 568 acres of Parkland in the beautiful Towy Valley in West Wales, just 7 miles from Carmarthen. The Gardens centrepiece is the Great Glasshouse, an amazing tilted glass dome with a six-metre ravine. The Mediterranean landscape enables the visitor to experience the aftermath of an Australian bush fire, pause in an olive grove or wander through Fuchsia collections from Chile. A 220mtr herbaceous board walk forms the spine of the garden and leads to the children's play area and our 360-surround screen cinema to the Old Stables Courtyard. Here the visitor can view art exhibitions, wander in the gift shop or enjoy a meal in the restaurant. Land train tours will take the visitor around the necklace of lakes, which surround the central garden.

Times: Open 30 Mar-25 Oct 10-6, 26 Oct-27 Mar 10-4.30 **Fee:** £7.50 (ch 5-16 £2.50, concessions £5.50). Family £16.50. Carer with wheelchair user/blind visitor free. **Facilities:** ℗ ⬤ ⦿ licensed 🍴 & (Braille interpretation wheelchairs/scooters shuttle svc) toilets for disabled shop garden centre ⊗ (ex assist dogs) ◀

LLANDEILO   MAP 03 SN62

Dinefwr Park
2 for 1
SA19 6RT
➲ *(off A40 Carmarthenshire, on W outskirts of Llandeilo)*
☎ 01558 823902
e-mail: dinefwr@nationaltrust.org.uk
web: www.ukindex.co.uk/nationaltrust

At the heart of Welsh history for a thousand years, the Park as we know it today took shape in the years after 1775 when the medieval castle, house, gardens, woods and deer park were integrated into one vast and breathtaking landscape. Access to Church Woods and Dinefwr Castle is through the landscaped park.

Times: Open Mar-Oct, daily (ex Tue & Wed) 11-4.30. (Last admission 30 mins before closing) **Fee:** ✱ Park only £3 (ch £1.50) Family ticket 7.50 Party 15+ £2.60 **Facilities:** ℗ (charged) ⬤ 🍴 & toilets for disabled ⊗ (ex outer park on lead) ✿ ◀

LLANELLI   MAP 02 SN50

National Wetland Centre Wales
2 for 1
Penclacwydd, Llwynhendy SA14 9SH
➲ *(3m E of Llanelli, off A484)*
☎ 01554 741087
e-mail: info.llaneli@wwt.org.uk
web: www.wwt.org.uk

A wide variety of wild birds, including oystercatchers, redshanks, curlews, little egrets and occasionally ospreys, can be seen here during the right season. The grounds are beautifully landscaped, and include CCTV transmitting pictures of wild birds on the reserve, a wetland craft area and a flock of colourful Caribbean Flamingos. There is also a Discovery Centre and outdoor activities for visitors to take part in.

continued

Wales

Wales

Facilities for the disabled include easy access on level paths, special viewing areas and wheelchair loan.

Times: Open summer 9.30-5; winter 9.30-4.30. Closed 24-25 Dec. **Fee:** ✱ £5.50 (ch £3.50, pen £4.50). Family £14.50. **Facilities:** ❷ ➍ ⍟⍟ ⛛ toilets for disabled shop ⊗ (ex guide/hearing dogs) ◀

LLANGATHEN   MAP 02 SN52

Aberglasney Gardens

SA32 8QH
➲ *(4m W of Llandeilo, follow signs from A40)*
☎ 01558 668998
e-mail: info@aberglasney.org.uk
web: www.aberglasney.org

Aberglasney is a 10-acre restoration project, containing a variety of rare and unusual plants, providing interest throughout the seasons. At its heart is a unique and fully restored Elizabethan/Jacobean cloister and parapet walk. Please telephone for details of events running throughout the year.

Times: ✱ Open all year, Apr-Oct, daily 10-6 (last entry 5); Nov-Mar, daily 10.30-4. Closed 25 Dec **Facilities:** ❷ ⍟⍟ licensed ⛛ (most areas accessible, wheelchairs available, parking) toilets for disabled shop garden centre ⊗ (ex guide dogs) ◀

LLANSTEFFAN   MAP 02 SN31

Llansteffan Castle   `FREE`

➲ *(off B4312)*
☎ 01267 241756
web: www.cadw.wales.gov.uk

The ruins of this 11th to 13th-century stronghold stand majestically on the west side of the Towy estuary.

Times: Open - access throughout the year. **Facilities:** ⊗ ⌁

PUMSAINT   MAP 03 SN64

Dolaucothi Gold Mines

SA19 8RR
➲ *(on A482, signed both directions)*
☎ 01558 650177
e-mail: dolaucothi@nationaltrust.org.uk
web: www.nationaltrust.org.uk

Here is an opportunity to spend a day exploring the gold mines and to wear a miner's helmet and lamp while touring the underground workings. The information centre and a walk along the Miners' Way disclose the secrets of 2,000 years of gold mining. This is the only place in Britain where the Romans mined gold.

Times: ✱ Open end Mar-end Oct, daily 10-5. **Facilities:** ❷ ➍ ⌗ ⛛ toilets for disabled shop ⍟⍟ ◀

CEREDIGION

ABERAERON   MAP 02 SN46

Llanerchaeron   `2 for 1`

Llanerchaeron, Ciliau Aeron SA48 8DG
➲ *(2.5m E of Aberaeron off A482)*
☎ 01545 570200
e-mail: llanerchaeron@nationaltrust.org.uk
web: www.nationaltrust.org.uk

Llanerchaeron, a few miles inland from Aberaeron on the Cardigan Bay coast, is centred round a Regency Villa designed by John Nash. The self sufficient country estate, villa, service courtyard, grounds, working organic farm and outbuildings remain virtually unaltered. The 18th century estate features; The Walled Garden and farm complex, mature woodland and ornamental lake, vast parkland and farmland containing Llanwennog sheep and Welsh Black Cattle. Produce and plants from the walled gardens are sold in the visitor building. Please telephone for details of events running throughout the year.

Times: Open late Mar-late Oct, Wed-Sun & BH Mons 11-5. (Last admission 1hr before closing). Park open all year dawn to dusk. **Fee:** ✱ £5.20 (ch £2.60). Family ticket £12.60 (2ad+2ch). Special group rates available **Facilities:** ❷ ➍ ⌗ ⛛ (ramp access to villa, wheelchair, Braille guide) toilets for disabled shop ⊗ (except guide dogs) ⍟⍟

ABERYSTWYTH   MAP 06 SN58

National Library of Wales

Penglais SY23 3BU
➲ *(Off Penglais Hill, A487 in N area of Aberystwyth)*
☎ 01970 632800
e-mail: holi@llgc.org.uk
web: www.llgc.org.uk

The largest library in Wales celebrates its hundred birthday this year, as it was established in 1907. Its collections include books, manuscripts, archival documents, maps and photographs as well as paintings, film, video and sound recordings. The library is recognised as the leading research centre for Welsh and Celtic studies, and is popular with those studying family history. Lectures, screenings and conferences throughout the year.

Times: Open on selected BHs. Please check details by telephone or on website before travelling. **Fee:** Free. Admission to reading rooms available by readers ticket, two proofs of identity required, one including address. Free admission to all exhibitions. **Facilities:** ❷ ➍ ⍟⍟ licensed ⛛ (lift) toilets for disabled shop ⊗ (ex guide dogs)

CENARTH   MAP 02 SN24

The National Coracle Centre
Cenarth Falls SA38 9JL

➲ *(on A484 between Carmarthen and Cardigan, centre of Cenarth village, beside bridge and river)*
☎ 01239 710980
e-mail: martinfowler.coraclecentre@virgin.net
web: www.coracle-centre.co.uk

Situated by the beautiful Cenarth Falls, this fascinating museum has a unique collection from all over the world, including Tibet, India, Iraq, Vietnam, and North America. Cenarth has long been a centre for coracle fishing, coracle rides are often available in village during summer holiday. Look out for the salmon leap by the flour mill.

Times: Open Etr-Oct, daily 10.30-5.30. All other times by appointment. **Fee:** ✱ £3 (ch £1, concessions £2.50). Party rates 12+. **Facilities:** ❷ 🎡 ♿ (top floor of mill inaccessible for disabled) shop ◀

EGLWYSFACH   MAP 06 SN69

RSPB Nature Reserve
Visitor Centre, Cae'r Berllan SY20 8TA

➲ *(6m S of Machynlleth on A487 in Eglwys-Fach. Signed from main road)*
☎ 01654 700222
e-mail: ynyshir@rspb.org.uk
web: www.rspb.co.uk

The mixture of different habitats is home to an abundance of birds and wildlife. The saltmarshes in winter support the only regular wintering flock of Greenland white-fronted geese in England and Wales in addition to peregrines, hen harriers and merlins. The sessile oak woodland is home to pied flycatchers, wood warblers, redstarts in the summer but woodpeckers, nut hatches, red kites, sparrow hawks and buzzards are here all year round. Otters, polecats, 30 butterfly and 15 dragonfly species are also present. Guided walks and children's activities. Please telephone for details of events running throughout the year.

Times: Open daily, 9am-9pm (or sunset if earlier). Visitor Centre: Apr-Oct 9-5 daily; Nov-Mar 10-4 (Wed-Sun) **Fee:** ✱ £3.50 (ch £1, concessions £2.50) Family £7 RSPB members free. **Facilities:** ❷ 🎡 ♿ (Can take car to viewpoint) shop ⊗ (ex guide dogs) ◀

FELINWYNT   MAP 02 SN25

Felinwynt Rainforest Centre
SA43 1RT

➲ *(from A487 Blaenannerch Airfield turning, onto B4333. Signed 6m N of Cardigan)*
☎ 01239 810882 & 810250
e-mail: dandjdevereux@btinternet.com
web: www.butterflycentre.co.uk

A chance to wander amongst free-flying exotic butterflies accompanied by the recorded wildlife sounds of the Peruvian Amazon. A waterfall, ponds and streams contribute to a humid tropical atmosphere and provide a habitat for fish and native amphibians. See the exhibition of rainforests of Peru and around the world. Free paper and crayons to borrow for children.

Times: Open daily 4 Apr-27 Oct **Fee:** ✱ £3.95 (ch 4-14 £1.95, pen £3.75) **Facilities:** ❷ 🍴 🎡 ♿ toilets for disabled shop ⊗ (ex guide dogs) ◀

STRATA FLORIDA   MAP 03 SN76

Strata Florida Abbey
SY25 6BT

➲ *(unclassified road from Pontrhydfendigaid, accessed from B4340)*
☎ 01974 831261
web: www.cadw.wales.gov.uk

Little remains of the Cistercian abbey founded in 1164, except the ruined church and cloister. Strata Florida was an important centre of learning in the Middle Ages, and it is believed that the 14th-century poet Dafyd ap Gwilym was buried here.

Times: Open Apr-Sep, Wed-Sun. Monument will be opened and unstaffed with no admission charge on Mon and Tue (except BH Mon) between Apr-Sep. The monument will be open but unstaffed at all other times. During this period the opening hours will be between 10-4 daily. **Fee:** ✱ £2.90 (ch 5-15, concessions £2.50, disabled visitors & assisting companion free). Family ticket (2ad+all ch/grandch under 16) £8.30. Group discounts available. Prices quoted apply until 31 Mar 2007. **Facilities:** ❷ ♿ shop ⊗ ♿ ◀

BETWS-Y-COED   MAP 06 SH75

Conwy Valley Railway Museum
Old Goods Yard LL24 0AL

➲ *(signed from A5 into Old Church Rd, adjacent to train station)*
☎ 01690 710568

The two large museum buildings have displays on both the narrow and standard-gauge railways of North Wales, including railway stock and other memorabilia. There are working model railway layouts, a steam-hauled miniature railway in the grounds, which cover over four acres, and a 15inch-gauge tramway to the woods. The latest addition is the quarter-size steam 'Britannia' loco that is now on display. For children there are mini-dodgems, Postman Pat, school bus and Toby Tram.

Times: Open all year daily, 10-5.30. Closed Xmas **Fee:** ✱ £1.50 (ch & pen 80p). Family ticket £4.00. Steam train ride £1.50. Tram ride £1.00. **Facilities:** ❷ 🍴 ♿ (ramps & clearances for wheelchairs) toilets for disabled shop ◀

CERRIGYDRUDION   MAP 06 SH94

Llyn Brenig Visitor Centre   [FREE]
LL21 9TT

➲ *(on B4501 between Denbigh & Cerrigydrudion)*
☎ 01490 420463
e-mail: llyn.brenig@dwrcymru.com
web: www.dwrcymru.com

The 1800-acre estate has a unique archaeological trail and round-the-lake walk of 10 miles. A hide is available and disabled anglers are catered for with a specially adapted fishing boat and an annual open day. The centre has an exhibition on archaeology, history and conservation and an audio-visual programme.

Times: Open mid Mar-Oct, daily 9-5. **Facilities:** ❷ (charged) 🍴 ♿ (boats for disabled & fishing open days) toilets for disabled shop ⊗ (ex guide dogs)

COLWYN BAY
MAP 06 SH87

Welsh Mountain Zoo
Old Highway LL28 5UY
➲ *(A55 junct 20 signed Rhos-on-Sea. Zoo signed)*
☎ 01492 532938
e-mail: info@welshmountainzoo.org
web: www.welshmountainzoo.org

Set high above Colwyn Bay with panoramic views and breath-taking scenery, this caring conservation zoo is set among beautiful gardens. Among the animals are many rare and endangered species, and there are daily shows which include Penguins Playtime, Chimp Encounter, Sealion Feeding and Birds of Prey.

Times: Open all year, Mar-Oct, daily 9.30-6; Nov-Feb, daily 9.30-5. Closed 25 Dec. **Fee:** ✱ £7.75 (ch & students £5.50, pen £6.60). Family ticket (2ad+2ch) £23.40 **Facilities:** ℗ 🍽 🐟 licensed 🍴 ঐ toilets for disabled shop ⊗ (ex car park area) 🛥

CONWY
MAP 06 SH77

Aberconwy House
LL32 8AY
➲ *(Llanerchaeron is situated 2.5m E of Aberaeron off the A482)*
☎ 01492 592246
e-mail: kenneth.grover@nationaltrust.org.uk

This house dates from the 14th century; it is the only medieval merchant's house in Conwy to have survived the centuries of turbulence, fire and pillage in this frontier town. Furnished rooms and an audio-visual presentation show daily life in the house at different periods in its history.

Times: Open 19 Mar-30 Oct, Wed-Mon 11-5. (Last admission 30 mins before closing). **Fee:** ✱ £3 Joint £3.50 Party adult £2.10 & ch £1 (ch £1.20). Family ticket £7.50. Party £6.50. **Facilities:** ℗ (100yds & 0.5m) shop ⊗ (ex guide dogs) 🛥

Conwy Castle
LL32 8AY
➲ *(via A55 or B5106)*
☎ 01492 592358
web: www.cadw.wales.gov.uk

The castle is a magnificent fortress, built 1283-7 by Edward I. There is an exhibition on castle chapels on the ground floor of the Chapel Tower. The castle forms part of the same defensive system as the extensive town walls, which are among the most complete in Europe.

Times: Open Apr-May & Oct, daily 9.30-5; Jun-Sep, daily 9.30-6; Nov-Mar, Mon-Sat 9.30-4, Sun 11-4. Telephone for Xmas opening times.
Fee: ✱ £4.50 (ch 5-15, concessions £4, disabled visitors & assisting companion free). Family ticket £14 Joint ticket for both monuments £7 (concessions £6, disabled visitors & assisting companion free) Family ticket £22. Group rates available. Prices quoted apply until 31 Mar 2007.
Facilities: ℗ ঐ toilets for disabled shop ⊗ ⊕ 🛥

Conwy Suspension Bridge
LL32 8LD
➲ *(adjacent to Conwy Castle)*
☎ 01492 573282
e-mail: kenneth.grover@nationaltrust.org.uk

Designed by Thomas Telford, one of the greatest engineers of the late 18th and early 19th century, this was the first bridge to span the river at Conwy. The bridge has been restored and the toll house furnished as it would have been a century ago.

Times: Open daily 19 Mar-Oct 10-5. **Fee:** ✱ £1 (ch 70p) Joint £3.50 Family £2.50. **Facilities:** ℗ 100 yds 🍴 ঐ (except house) 🛥

Plas Mawr
High St LL32 8DE
☎ 01492 580167
web: www.cadw.wales.gov.uk

Plas Mawr is an excellent example of an Elizabethan townhouse. Built by Robert Wynn between 1576 and 1585, the interior remains almost unaltered and displays decorated plaster ceilings and wooden screens.

Times: Open Apr-May 9:30-5 Tue-Sun; Jun-Aug 9:30-6 Tue-Sun; Sep 9.30-5 Tue-Sun; Oct 9:30-4 Tue-Sun, site closed on Mon (excl. BH), site closed completely Nov 06-Mar 07 **Fee:** ✱ £4.90 (ch 5-15, concessions £4.50, disabled visitors & assisting companion free). Family (2ad+all ch/grandch under 16) £15. Joint ticket for both monuments available £7 (ch 5-15, concessions £6, disabled visitors & assisting companion free). Family (2ad+all ch/grandch under 16) £22. **Facilities:** shop ⊕ 🛥

Smallest House
The Quay LL32 8BB
➲ *(leave A55 at Conwy sign, through town, at bottom of High St for the quay, turn left)*
☎ 01492 593484

The *Guinness Book of Records* lists this as the smallest house in Britain. Just 6ft wide by 10ft high, it is furnished in the style of a mid-Victorian Welsh cottage.

Times: Open Apr-May & Oct 10-5; Jun & Sep, 10-6, first half Jul 10-6 rest of Jul & Aug 10-9 **Fee:** £1 (ch under 16 50p, under 5 free).
Facilities: ℗ (100yds) 🍴 ঐ shop

DOLWYDDELAN
MAP 06 SH75

Dolwyddelan Castle
LL25 0EJ
➲ *(on A470 Blaenau Ffestiniog to Betws-y-Coed)*
☎ 01690 750366
web: www.cadw.wales.gov.uk

The castle is reputed to be the birthplace of Llywelyn the Great. It was captured in 1283 by Edward I, who immediately began strengthening it for his own purposes. A restored keep of around 1200, and a 13th-century curtain wall can be seen. An exhibition on the castles of the Welsh Princes is located in the keep.

Times: Open all year, Apr-Sep, Mon-Sat 10-6 & Sun 11-4; Oct-Mar, Mon-Sat 10-4, Sun 11-4. On occasions the site may be open but unstaffed with no admission charge. Phone for Xmas opening hours. **Fee:** ✱ £2.50 (ch 5-15, concessions £2, disabled visitors & assisting companion free). Family ticket (2ad+all ch/grandch under 16) £7. Group rates available. Prices quoted apply until 31 Mar 2007. **Facilities:** ℗ ⊗ ⊕ 🛥

LLANDUDNO
MAP 06 SH78

Great Orme Bronze Age Copper Mines NEW
Pyliau Rd, Great Orme LL30 2XG
⮑ *(Follow 'copper mine' signs from Llandudno Promenade)*
☎ 01492 870447
e-mail: gomines@greatorme.freeserve.co.uk
web: www.greatormemines.info

Browse in the visitor centre with a model of a Bronze Age village depicting life in Bronze Age times. Take a look at some original 4,000 year old Bronze Age artefacts and a selection of Bronze Age mining tools. After watching two short films and make your way down to the mines. Walking through tunnels mined nearly 4,000 years ago look into some of the smaller tunnels and get a feel for the conditions our prehistoric ancestors faced in their search for valuable copper ores. Excavation on the surface will continue for decades and one of the team is usually available to answer visitors questions as they walk around the site and view the prehistoric landscape being uncovered.

Times: Open Mar-Oct, daily 10-5. **Fee:** ✱ £5 (ch £3.50, students £4.50). Family ticket £15. **Facilities:** ❷ 🍽 shop 🛒

LLANDUDNO JUNCTION
MAP 06 SH77

RSPB Nature Reserve
LL31 9XZ
⮑ *(off A55, signed)*
☎ 01492 584091
e-mail: alan.davies@rspb.org.uk
web: www.rspb.org.uk

The visitor centre has a viewing area which overlooks the estuary and Conwy Castle, and there's a nature trail and four hides for viewing lapwings and shelduck amongst many others. Phone for details of events.

Times: Open all year, daily, 10-5 (or dusk whichever is earlier). Closed 25 Dec **Facilities:** ❷ 🍽 ♿ (use of wheelchair) toilets for disabled shop ⊗ (ex guide dogs) 🛒

LLANRWST
MAP 06 SH86

Gwydyr Uchaf Chapel
FREE
⮑ *(0.5m SW off B5106)*
☎ 01492 640578
web: www.cadw.wales.gov.uk

Built in the 17th century by Sir John Wynn of Gwydir Castle, the chapel is noted for its painted ceiling and wonderfully varied woodwork.

Times: Open any reasonable time. **Facilities:** ❷ ⊗ 🚗 ⟳

PENMACHNO
MAP 06 SH75

Ty Mawr Wybrnant
LL25 0HJ
⮑ *(From A5 3m S of Betws-y-Coed take B4406 to Penmachno. House is 2.5m NW of Penmachno by forest road)*
☎ 01690 760213

Situated in the beautiful, secluded Wybrnant Valley, Ty Mawr was the birthplace of Bishop William Morgan (1545-1604), the first translator

continued

of the entire Bible into Welsh. The house has been restored to its probable 16th-17th century appearance. The Wybrnant Nature Trail, a short walk, covers approximately one mile.

Times: Open 30 Mar-Sep, Thu-Sun & BH Mon 12-5; Oct, Thu, Fri & Sun 12-4. (Last admission 30 mins before closing). **Fee:** ✱ £3 (ch £1.50). Family ticket £7.50. Party 15+. **Facilities:** ❷ ⊗ (ex in grounds) 🐾

TAL-Y-CAFN
MAP 06 SH77

Bodnant Garden
LL28 5RE
⮑ *(8m S of Llandudno & Colwyn Bay off A470. Signposted from the A55 exit at junct 19)*
☎ 01492 650460
e-mail: ann.harvey@nationaltrust.org.uk
web: www.bodnantgarden.co.uk

Set above the River Conwy with beautiful views over Snowdonia, this garden is a delight. Five Italian style terraces were constructed below the house - on the lowest terrace is a canal pool with an open-air yew hedge stage and a reconstructed Pin Mill. The garden is renowned for its collections of magnolias, camellias, rhododendrons and azaleas and the famous Laburnum Arch, and the colourful displays in summer and autumn are a spectacular sight. Contact for details of open-air theatre.

Times: Open 10 Mar-4 Nov, daily 10-5 (last admission half hour before closing) **Fee:** £6.50 (ch £3.25) Party of 20+ £5.50 **Facilities:** ❷ 🍽 🏛 ♿ (ramps to gardens, wheelchairs & Braille guides) toilets for disabled shop garden centre ⊗ (ex assist dogs) 🐾 🛒

TREFRIW
MAP 06 SH76

Trefriw Woollen Mills
FREE
Main Rd LL27 0NQ
⮑ *(on B5106 in centre of Trefriw, 5m N of Betws-y-Coed)*
☎ 01492 640462
e-mail: info@t-w-m.co.uk
web: www.t-w-m.co.uk

Established in 1859, the mill is situated beside the fast-flowing Afon Crafnant, which drives two hydro-electric turbines to power the looms. All the machinery of woollen manufacture can be seen here: blending, carding, spinning, dyeing, warping and weaving. In the Weaver's Garden, there are plants traditionally used in the textile industry, mainly for dyeing. Hand-spinning demonstrations.

Times: Mill Museum open Etr-Oct, Mon-Fri 10-1 & 2-5. Weaving demonstrations & turbine house: open all year, Mon-Fri 10-1 & 2-5. Handspinning & weaver's garden Jun-Sep Tue-Thu, Jul-Aug Mon-Fri 10-5 **Facilities:** ❷ (35yds) 🍽 🏛 ♿ (access to shop, cafe, weaving & turbine house) shop ⊗ (ex assist dogs & on lead) 🛒

DENBIGHSHIRE

BODELWYDDAN
MAP 06 SJ07

Bodelwyddan Castle
LL18 5YA
⮑ *(just off A55, near St Asaph, follow brown signs)*
☎ 01745 584060
e-mail: enquiries@bodelwyddan-castle.co.uk
web: www.bodelwyddan-castle.co.uk

Bodelwyddan Castle houses over 100 portraits from the National Portrait Gallery's 19th-century collection. The portraits hang in

continued

Wales

beautifully refurbished rooms and are complemented by sculpture and period furnishings. Interactive displays show how portraits were produced and used in the Victorian era. The Castle Gallery hosts a programme of temporary exhibitions and events. The castle is set within 200 acres of woodland.

Times: ✱ Open Apr-Sep, daily 10.30-5. Oct-Apr, 10.30-4. Closed Mon & Fri
Facilities: ❷ ➌ 🏛 ⅋ (lift to first floor, Braille & audio guides) toilets for disabled shop ⊗ (ex guide dogs) ⬛

CORWEN
MAP 06 SJ04

Ewe-Phoria Sheepdog Centre
Glanrafon, Llangwm LL21 0PE
➲ *(off A5 to Llangwm, follow signs)*
☎ 01490 460369
e-mail: info@ewe-phoria.co.uk
web: www.ewe-phoria.co.uk

Ewe-Phoria is an Agri-Theatre and Sheepdog Centre that details the life and work of the shepherd on a traditional Welsh farm. The Agri-Theatre has unusual living displays of sheep with accompanying lectures on their history and breed, while outside sheepdog handlers put their dogs through their paces.

Times: ✱ Open Etr-end Oct, Tue-Fri & Sun. Closed Sat & Mon ex BHs
Fee: £4.75 (ch £3.50, concessions £4.20). **Facilities:** ❷ ➋ 🍽 licensed ⅋ toilets for disabled shop ⊗ (ex guide dogs)

Pen-Y-Bryn Farm Park
LL21 9PB
➲ *(off A5 onto B5105. 5m from Cerrigydrudion)*
☎ 01490 420244 &
e-mail: islwynhawkeye@hotmail.co.uk
web: www.pybfarmpark.co.uk

Proudly catering to all ages, Pen-y-Bryn Park has a petting zoo, falconry, and 'Solo', its very own llama.

Times: ✱ Open Etr-Sep, Tue-Sun & BHs, 10-5 **Facilities:** ❷ ➋ ⅋ toilets for disabled shop garden centre

Rug Chapel
Rug LL21 9BT
☎ 01490 412025
web: www.cadw.wales.gov.uk

Rug Chapel was built in 1637 for Colonel William Salusbury, famous Civil War defender of Denbigh Castle. A rare, little altered example of a 17th-century private chapel, it reflects the Colonel's High Church religious views. Prettily set in a wooded landscape, the chapel's modest exterior gives little hint of the interior where local artists and carvers were given a free reign, with some spectacular results.

Times: Open Apr-Sep, Wed-Sun 10-5. Access to Llangar is arranged Wed-Sun, through Custodian at Rug Chapel, telephone 01490 412025 for details. Both monuments closed Mon & Tue (ex BH wknds) between Apr-Sep & are closed at all other times. **Fee:** ✱ £3.50 (ch 5-15, concessions £3, disabled visitors & assisting companion free). Family ticket (2ad+all ch/grandch under 16) £10. Group rates available. Prices quoted apply until 31 Mar 2007. **Facilities:** ❷ ⅋ toilets for disabled shop ⊗ ⊕ ⬛

DENBIGH
MAP 06 SJ06

Denbigh Castle
➲ *(via A525, A543 & B5382)*
☎ 01745 813385
web: www.cadw.wales.gov.uk

The castle was begun by Henry de Lacy in 1282 and has an inspiring and impressive gatehouse, with a trio of towers and a superb archway, which is surmounted by a figure believed to be that of Edward I.

Times: Open Apr-Sep, 9.30-5.30. (Monument open and unstaffed with no admission charge at all other times). Telephone for Xmas opening hours.
Fee: ✱ £2.90 (ch 5-15, concessions £2.50, disabled visitors & assisting companion free). Family ticket (2ad+all ch/grandch under 16) £8.30. Group rates available. Prices quoted apply until 31 Mar 2007.
Facilities: ❷ ⅋ shop ⊗ ⊕ ⬛

LLANGOLLEN
MAP 07 SJ24

Horse Drawn Boats Centre
The Wharf, Wharf Hill LL20 8TA
➲ *(A5 onto Llangollen High St, across river bridge to T-junct. Wharf opposite)*
☎ 01978 860702 & 01691 690322
e-mail: bill@horsedrawnboats.co.uk
web: www.horsedrawnboats.co.uk

Take a horsedrawn boat trip along the beautiful Vale of Llangollen. Visit the canal museum, inside the motor museum, approx 1m along the towpath from the wharf, which illustrates the heyday of canals in Britain. The displays include working and static models, photographs, murals and slides. There is also a narrowboat trip that crosses Pontcysyllte Aqueduct, the largest navigable aqueduct in the world. Full bar on board, commentary throughout.

Times: Open: mid Mar-Etr wknds. Etr-late Oct daily, 10-5. **Fee:** ✱ Horse Drawn Boat Trip from £4.50 (ch £2.50). Family ticket £12. Narrowboat Trip £9 (ch £7). **Facilities:** Ⓟ (400yds) ➋ 🏛 ⅋ (alighting/pick-up point available) toilets for disabled shop ⬛

Llangollen Railway
Abbey Rd LL20 8SN
➲ *(Llangollen Station - off A5 at Llangollen traffic lights onto A539, cross river bridge. Station on left at T-junct. Carrog Station - from A5 at Llidiart-y-Parc take B5437, station on right downhill after crossing railway bridge)*
☎ 01978 860979 & 860951(timetable)
e-mail: office@llangollen-railway.co.uk
web: www.llangollen-railway.co.uk

Heritage Railway featuring steam and classic diesel services along the picturesque Dee Valley. The journey consists of a 15-mile roundtrip

continued

Wales

between Llangollen and Carrog. A special coach for the disabled is available on some services. Please contact for more information.

Llangollen Railway

Times: ✱ Open Station wknds, reduced services off peak, daily services Apr-Oct. Principally steam hauled, diesel trains please refer to timetable for off peak services. **Facilities:** Ⓟ (400yds) (free parking at Carrog Station) ♨ 🗞 ♿ (special coach for disabled on some trains, notice required) toilets for disabled shop (at Llangollen only) ▬

Plas Newydd

Hill St LL20 8AW
➾ *(follow brown heritage signs from A5)*
☎ 01978 861314
e-mail: rose.mcmahon@denbighshire.gov.uk

The 'Ladies of Llangollen', Lady Eleanor Butler and Sarah Ponsonby, lived here from 1780 to 1831. The original stained-glass windows, carved panels, and domestic miscellany of two lives are exhibited along with prints, pictures and letters.

Times: Open Apr-Oct, daily, 10-5. **Fee:** ✱ £3 (ch & pen £2). Family £8. **Facilities:** Ⓟ ♨ ♿ (Virtual, signed & touch tours) toilets for disabled shop ⊗ (ex guide dogs or in grounds) ▬

Valle Crucis Abbey

LL29 8DD
➾ *(on B5103, off A5 W of Llangollen)*
☎ 01978 860326
web: www.cadw.wales.gov.uk

Set in a deep, narrow valley, the abbey was founded for the Cistercians in 1201 by Madog ap Gruffydd. Substantial remains of the church can be seen, and some beautifully carved grave slabs have been found. There is a small exhibition on the Cistercian monks and the abbey.

Times: Open Apr-Sep, daily 10-5. Monument open and unstaffed with no admission charge at all other times between 10-4. Telephone for Xmas opening times. **Fee:** ✱ £2.50 (ch 5-15, concessions £2, disabled visitors & assisting companion free). Family ticket (2ad and all ch/grandch under 16) £7. Group rates available. Prices quoted apply until 31 Mar 2007. **Facilities:** Ⓟ ♿ shop ⊗ ⊕ ▬

RHUDDLAN   MAP 06 SJ07

Rhuddlan Castle

LL18 5AD
☎ 01745 590777
web: www.cadw.wales.gov.uk

The castle was begun by Edward I in 1277, on a simple 'diamond' plan with round towers linked by sections of 9ft thick curtain wall. The moat was linked to a deep-water canal, allowing Edward's ships to sail from the sea right up to the castle.

Times: Open Apr-Sep, daily 10-5. **Fee:** ✱ £2.90 (ch 5-15, concessions £2.50, disabled visitors & assisting companion free). Family ticket (2ad+all ch/grandch under 16) £8.30. Group discounts available. Prices quoted apply until 31 Mar 2007. **Facilities:** Ⓟ ♿ shop ⊗ ⊕ ▬

FLINTSHIRE

EWLOE   MAP 07 SJ36

Ewloe Castle   `FREE`

➾ *(1m NW of village on B5125)*
web: www.cadw.wales.gov.uk

Standing in Ewloe Wood are the remains of Ewloe Castle. It was a native Welsh castle, and Henry II was defeated nearby in 1157. Part of the Welsh Tower in the upper ward still stands to its original height, and there is a well in the lower ward. Remnants of walls and another tower can also be seen.

Times: Open at all times. **Facilities:** ⊗ ⊕

FLINT   MAP 07 SJ27

Flint Castle   `FREE`

CH6 5PH
➾ *(NE side of Flint)*
☎ 01352 733078
web: www.cadw.wales.gov.uk

The castle was started by Edward I in 1277 and overlooks the River Dee. It is exceptional for its great tower, or Donjon, which is separated by a moat. Other buildings would have stood in the inner bailey, of which parts of the walls and corner towers remain.

Times: Open at all times. **Facilities:** Ⓟ ⊗ ⊕

HOLYWELL   MAP 07 SJ17

Basingwerk Abbey   `FREE`

Greenfield Valley Heritage Pk, Greenfield
CH8 7GH
➾ *(just S of A458)*
☎ 01352 714172
web: www.cadw.wales.gov.uk

The abbey was founded around 1131 by Ranulf de Gernon, Earl of Chester. The first stone church dates from the beginning of the 13th century. The last abbot surrendered the house to the crown in 1536. The Abbey is close to the Heritage Park Visitor Centre and access to the Museum and Farm Complex at Greenfield Valley.

Times: Open all year, daily 9-6. **Facilities:** Ⓟ ⊙ ♿ (disabled facilities in Heritage Park) toilets for disabled shop ⊗ ⊕

Wales

Greenfield Valley Heritage Park

Greenfield Rd CH8 7GH

☎ 01352 714172

e-mail: info@greenfieldvalley.com

web: www.greenfieldvalley.com

This fascinating park covers one and a half miles of woodlands, reservoirs, ancient monuments and industrial history. Among the multitude of sights are a footpath that was once a railway line, the remnants of a number of mills relating to the copper industry, an environment centre, the shrine of St Winefride's Well, and Basingwerk Abbey.

Times: ✱ Park open all year. Museum & farm Apr-Oct, 10-4.30.
Facilities: ❷ ⬛ 📖 ♿ (ramps to enter buildings) toilets for disabled shop

GWYNEDD

BANGOR   MAP 06 SH57

Penrhyn Castle   `2 for 1`

LL57 4HN

➲ *(1m E of Bangor, off A5122 at Llandegai)*

☎ 01248 353084

e-mail: penrhyncastle@nationaltrust.org.uk

web: www.nationaltrust.org.uk

A massive 19th-century castle built on the profits of Jamaican sugar and Welsh slate, crammed with fascinating artefacts such as a one-ton slate bed made for Queen Victoria and a grand staircase that took ten years to build. Also houses a doll museum, two railway museums and one of the finest collections of Old Master paintings in Wales. Regular programme of events throughout the season.

Times: Open 25 Mar-29 Oct, daily (ex Tue) Castle 12-5. Grounds and stableblock exhibitions 11-5 (Jul & Aug 10-5.30). (Last admission 4.30). Last audio tour 4. **Fee:** ✱ All inclusive ticket: £8 (ch £7). Family ticket £20. Party 15+ £6.50 each. Grounds & stableblock only £5.40 (ch £2.70).
Facilities: ❷ ⬛ ⑩ licensed 📖 ♿ (wheelchairs & golf buggies pre bookable) toilets for disabled shop ⚘

BEDDGELERT   MAP 06 SH54

Sygun Copper Mine

LL55 4NE

➲ *(1m E of Beddgelert on A498)*

☎ 01766 890595 & 510101

e-mail: sygunmine@hotmail.com

web: www.syguncoppermine.co.uk

Spectacular audio-visual underground experience where visitors can explore the workings of this 19th-century coppermine and see the magnificent stalactite and stalagmite formations. Other activities include archery, panning for gold, metal detecting and coin making. Marvel at the fantastic coin collection from Julius Caesar to Queen

continued

Elizabeth II, and visit the Time-Line Museum with Bronze Age and Roman artefacts.

Sygun Copper Mine

Times: Open Apr-Oct, 9.30-5. Special opening 10-4, 26 Dec-1 Jan and Feb half term. **Fee:** £7.95 (ch £5.95, pen £6.95). Family £26. **Facilities:** ❷ ⬛ 📖 ♿ (wide access) toilets for disabled shop ◧

BLAENAU FFESTINIOG   MAP 06 SH74

Llechwedd Slate Caverns

LL41 3NB

➲ *(beside A470, 1m from Blaenau Ffestiniog)*

☎ 01766 830306

e-mail: quarrytours@aol.com

web: www.llechwedd-slate-caverns.co.uk

The Miners' Underground Tramway carries visitors into areas where early conditions have been recreated, while the Deep Mine is reached by an incline railway and has an unusual audio-visual presentation. Free surface attractions include several exhibitions and museums, slate mill and the Victorian village which has Victorian shops, bank, Miners Arms pub, lock-up and working smithy.

Times: ✱ Open all year, daily from 10. Last tour 5.15 (Oct-Feb 4.15). Closed 25-26 Dec & 1 Jan **Facilities:** ❷ ⬛ ⑩ licensed 📖 ♿ toilets for disabled shop ✖ (ex on surface) ◧

CAERNARFON
MAP 06 SH46

Caernarfon Castle
LL55 2AY
☎ 01286 677617
web: www.cadw.wales.gov.uk

Edward I began building the castle and extensive town walls in 1283 after defeating the last independent ruler of Wales. Completed in 1328, it has unusual polygonal towers, notably the 10-sided Eagle Tower. There is a theory that these features were copied from the walls of Constantinople, to reflect a tradition that Constantine was born nearby. Edward I's son and heir was born and presented to the Welsh people here, setting a precedent that was followed in 1969, when Prince Charles was invested as Prince of Wales.

Times: Open Apr-May & Oct, daily 9.30-5; Jun-Sep, daily 9.30-6; Nov-Mar, Mon-Sat 9.30-4, Sun 11-4. Telephone for Xmas opening times.
Fee: ✻ £4.90 (ch 5-15, concessions £4.50, disabled visitors & assisting companion free). Family ticket (2 ad & all ch/grandch under 16) £15. Group rates available. Prices quoted apply until 31 Mar 2007. **Facilities:** ❸ shop ⊗ ✢ ◼

Segontium Roman Museum

Beddgelert Rd LL55 2LN
➲ (on A4085 to Beddgelert approx 1m from Caernarfon)
☎ 01286 675625
e-mail: info@segontium.org.uk
web: www.segontium.org.uk

Segontium Roman Museum tells the story of the conquest and occupation of Wales by the Romans and displays the finds from the auxiliary fort of Segontium, one of the most famous in Britain. You can combine a visit to the museum with exploration of the site of the Roman Fort, which is in the care of Cadw: Welsh Historic Monuments. The exciting discoveries displayed at the museum vividly portray the daily life of the soldiers stationed in this remote outpost of the Roman Empire.

Times: ✻ Open all year Tue-Sun 12.30-4. Closed Mon except BH
Facilities: Ⓟ ⊗ (ex guide dogs) ◼

Welsh Highland Railway
St. Helen's Rd LL55 2YD
➲ (SW of Caernarfon Castle beside harbour. Follow brown signs)
☎ 01286 677018 & 01766 516000
e-mail: enquiries@festrail.co.uk
web: www.festrail.co.uk

A Millennium funded project to restore the old railway line from Caernarfon to Porthmadog. Experience the stunning scenery of

continued

Snowdonia National Park as the narrow gauge, steam and diesel trains travel between Caernarfon and Rhyd Ddu at the foot of Snowdon.

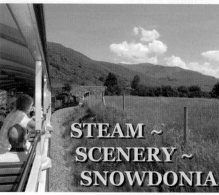

STEAM ~
SCENERY ~
SNOWDONIA

Welsh Highland Railway

Times: Open Etr-end Oct, limited service in Winter **Fee:** ✻ £16 ad return
Facilities: ❸ (charged) ▰ ⓖ (prior booking advisable) toilets for disabled shop ⊗ (ex in 3rd class) ◼

CRICCIETH
MAP 06 SH43

Criccieth Castle
LL52 0DP
➲ (off A497)
☎ 01766 522227
web: www.cadw.wales.gov.uk

The castle dates from the 13th century and was taken and destroyed by Owain Glyndwr in 1404. Evidence of a fierce fire can still be seen. The gatehouse leading to the inner ward remains impressive, and parts of the walls are well preserved.

Times: Open Apr, May & Oct, daily 10-5; Jun-Sep, daily 10-6; Nov-Mar, Fri & Sat 9.30-4, Sun 11-4 (Monument open and unstaffed with no admission charge at all other times) **Fee:** ✻ £2.90 (ch 5-15, concessions £2.40, disabled visitors & assisting companion free). Family ticket (2ad+all ch/grandch under 16) £8.20. Group rates available. Prices quoted apply until 31 Mar 2007. **Facilities:** ❸ shop ⊗ ✢ ◼

CYMER ABBEY
MAP 06 SH71

Cymer Abbey
FREE
➲ (2m NW of Dolgellau on A494)
☎ 01341 422854
web: www.cadw.wales.gov.uk

The abbey was built for the Cistercians in the 13th century. It was never very large, and does not seem to have been finished. The church is the best-preserved building, with ranges of windows and arcades still to be seen. The other buildings have been plundered for stone, but low outlines remain.

Times: Open all year, early Apr-Oct, daily 9.30-6; Nov-Mar, daily 9.30-4. Closed 24-26 Dec & 1 Jan **Facilities:** ❸ ⓖ ⊗ ✢ ◼

Wales

FAIRBOURNE MAP 06 SH61

Fairbourne Railway
Beach Rd LL38 2EX

➲ (on A493 follow signs for Fairbourne, main terminus is just past level crossing on left)

☎ 01341 250362

e-mail: enquiries@fairbourne-railway.co.uk

web: www.fairbournerailway.com

One of the most unusual of Wales's 'little trains'; built in 1890 as a horse-drawn railway to carry building materials it was later converted to steam, and now covers two-and-a-half miles. Its route passes one of the loveliest beaches in Wales, with views of the beautiful Mawddach Estuary.

Times: Open Feb half term (ex Fri) Apr-23 Sep (closed most Fri ex late Jul and all of Aug). Oct wknds & 20 Oct-28 Oct (ex Fri). **Fee:** ✱ Return £6.90 (ch £3.90, pen £5.80). Family £17.50 (2ad+3ch) **Facilities:** ℗ 30m 🍽 shop ◀

GROESLON MAP 06 SH45

Inigo Jones Slateworks
LL54 7UE

➲ (on A487, 6m S of Caernarfon towards Porthmadog)

☎ 01286 830242

e-mail: slate@inigojones.co.uk

web: www.inigojones.co.uk

Inigo Jones was established in 1861 primarily to make school writing slates. Today the company uses the same material to make architectural, monumental and craft products. A self-guided audio/video tour takes visitors round the slate workshops, and displays the various processes used in the extraction and working of Welsh slate.

Times: Open all year, daily 9-5. Closed 25-26 Dec & 1 Jan. **Fee:** ✱ £4 (ch & pen £3.50). **Facilities:** ℗ 🍽 📖 ఈ toilets for disabled shop ⊗ (ex guide dogs) ◀

HARLECH MAP 06 SH53

Harlech Castle
LL46 2YH

➲ (from A496)

☎ 01766 780552

web: www.cadw.wales.gov.uk

Harlech Castle was built in 1283-89 by Edward I, with a sheer drop to the sea on one side. Owain Glyndwr starved the castle into submission in 1404 and made it his court and campaigning base. Later, the defence of the castle in the Wars of the Roses inspired the song Men of Harlech. Today the sea has slipped away, and the castle's great walls and round towers stand above the dunes.

Times: Open Apr-May & Oct, daily 9.30-5; Jun-Sep, daily 9.30-6; Nov-Mar, Mon-Sat 9.30-4, Sun 11-4. Telephone for Xmas opening times.
Fee: ✱ £3.50 (ch 5-15, concessions £3, disabled visitors & assisting companion free). Family ticket (2ad+all ch/grandch under 16) £10. Group rates available. Prices quoted apply until 31 Mar 2007.
Facilities: ℗ (disabled spaces in car park) shop ⊗ ⊕ ◀

LLANBERIS MAP 06 SH56

Dolbadarn Castle FREE
LL55 4UD

➲ (A4086)

web: www.cadw.wales.gov.uk

Built by Llywelyn the Great in the early 13th century, this Welsh castle overlooks Llyn Padarn in the Llanberis Pass.

Times: Open any reasonable time. **Facilities:** ℗ ⊗ ⊕ ◀

Llanberis Lake Railway
Padarn Country Park LL55 4TY

➲ (off A4086 at Llanberis)

☎ 01286 870549

e-mail: info@lake-railway.co.uk

web: www.lake-railway.co.uk

Steam locomotives dating from 1889 to 1948 carry passengers on a five-mile return journey along the shore of Lake Padarn. Passengers are treated to some spectacular views of Snowdon and other mountains. The terminal station is adjacent to the Welsh Slate Museum, in the Padarn Country Park. The railway was formerly used to carry slate.

Times: ✱ Open mid Mar-late Oct, Sun-Fri, 11-4 (Sat in Jun-Aug) 10.30-4.30 in peak season. Nov-Feb, send for free timetable or check website.
Fee: ✱ £6 (ch £4). Family ticket available. Reduced rates for groups.
Facilities: ℗ (charged) 🍽 📖 ఈ (disabled carriage available) toilets for disabled shop ◀

Snowdon Mountain Railway
LL55 4TY

➲ (on A4086, Caernarfon to Capel Curig road. 7.5m from Caernarfon)

☎ 0870 4580033

e-mail: info@snowdonrailway.co.uk

web: www.snowdonrailway.co.uk

The journey of just over four-and-a-half miles takes passengers more than 3,000ft up to the summit of Snowdon; breathtaking views include, on a clear day, the Isle of Man and the Wicklow Mountains in Ireland. The round trip to the summit and back takes two and a half hours including a half hour at the summit.

Times: Open 15 Mar-5 Nov, daily from 9 (weather permitting).
Fee: Return £21 (ch £14). Early bird discount on 9am train, pre-booking only **Facilities:** ℗ (charged) 🍽 ఈ (some carriages suitable for wheelchairs - must notify) toilets for disabled shop ⊗ (ex assist dogs) ◀

Welsh Slate Museum FREE
Gilfach Ddu, Padarn Country Park LL55 4TY

➲ (0.25m off A4086. Museum within Padarn Country Park)

☎ 01286 870630

e-mail: slate@museumwales.ac.uk

web: www.museumwales.ac.uk

Set among the towering quarries at Llanberis, the Welsh Slate Museum is a living, working site located in the original workshops of Dinorwig Quarry, which once employed 15,000 men and boys. You can see the foundry, smithy, workshops and mess room which make up the old quarry, and view original machinery, much of which is still in working order.

continued

Wales

Times: Open Etr-Oct, daily 10-5; Nov-Etr, Sun-Fri 10-4.
Facilities: ❷ (charged) 🅿♿ (all parts accessible except patten loft) toilets for disabled shop ❽ (ex guide dogs) 🍴

LLANFIHANGEL-Y-PENNANT   MAP 06 SH60

Castell-y-Bere   FREE
➲ (off B4405)
☎ 029 2050 0200
web: www.cadw.wales.gov.uk

The castle was begun around 1221 by Prince Llewelyn ap Iorwerth of Gwynedd to guard the southern flank of his principality. It is typically Welsh in design with its D-shaped towers. Although a little off the beaten track, the castle lies in a spectacular setting, overshadowed by the Cader Idris range.

Times: Open all reasonable times. **Facilities:** ❽✛

LLANGYBI   MAP 06 SH44

St Cybi's Well   FREE
➲ (off B4354)
☎ 01766 810047
web: www.cadw.wales.gov.uk

Cybi was a sixth-century Cornish saint, known as a healer of the sick, and St Cybi's Well (or Ffynnon Gybi) has been famous for its curative properties through the centuries. The corbelled beehive vaulting inside the roofless stone structure is Irish in style and unique in Wales.

Times: Open at all times. **Facilities:** ♿❽✛

LLANUWCHLLYN   MAP 06 SH83

Bala Lake Railway
The Station LL23 7DD
➲ (off A494 Bala to Dolgellau road)
☎ 01678 540666
web: www.bala-lake-railway.co.uk

Steam locomotives which once worked in the slate quarries of North Wales now haul passenger coaches for four-and-a-half miles from Llanuwchllyn Station along the lake to Bala. The railway has one of the few remaining double-twist lever-locking framed GWR signal boxes, installed in 1896. Some of the coaches are open and some closed, so passengers can enjoy the beautiful views of the lake and mountains in all weathers.

Times: Open Etr-last wknd in Sep, daily. (Closed certain Mon & Fri, telephone for details). **Fee:** ✱ £7 return (pen £6.50). Family ticket (2ad+2ch) £17. **Facilities:** ❷ 🅿♿ (wheelchairs can be taken on train) shop

LLANYSTUMDWY   MAP 06 SH43

Lloyd George Museum & Highgate Victorian Cottage
LL52 0SH
➲ (on A497 between Pwllheli & Criccieth)
☎ 01766 522071
e-mail: amgueddfeydd-museums@gwynedd.gov.uk
web: www.gwynedd.gov.uk/museums

Explore the life and times of David Lloyd George in this museum. His boyhood home is recreated as it would have been when he lived

continued

there between 1864 and 1880, along with his Uncle Lloyd's shoemaking workshop.

Times: Open Etr, daily 10.30-5; Apr-May, Mon-Fri 10.30-5 (open Sat in Jun); Jul-Sep, daily 10.30-5; Oct, Mon-Fri, 11-4. Open BHs; Other times by appointment, telephone 01286 679098 for details. **Fee:** ✱ £3 (ch & pen £2). Family ticket £7. **Facilities:** ❷ 📱♿ (induction loop in audio visual theatre, shop & cottage) toilets for disabled shop ❽ (ex guide dogs) 🍴

PENARTH FAWR   MAP 06 SH43

Penarth Fawr   FREE
➲ (3.5m NE of Pwllheli off A497)
☎ 01766 810880
web: www.cadw.wales.gov.uk

The hall, buttery and screen are preserved in this house which was probably built in the 15th century.

Times: Open at all times. **Facilities:** ♿❽✛

PLAS-YN-RHIW   MAP 06 SH22

Plas-yn-Rhiw
LL53 8AB
➲ (12m from Pwllheli signed from B4413 to Aberdaron)
☎ 01758 780219
e-mail: plasynrhiw@nationaltrust.org.uk
web: www.nationaltrust.org.uk

This is a small manor house, part medieval, with Tudor and Georgian additions. The ornamental gardens have flowering trees and shrubs including sub-tropical specimens, divided by box hedges and grass paths. There is a stream and waterfall, which descends from the snowdrop wood behind.

Times: Open: Apr-29 May, Thu-Mon, 12-5. 31 May-Sep, Wed-Mon, 12-5. 1-22 Oct, Sat-Sun, 12-4. 23-29 Oct, daily, 12-4. **Fee:** ✱ £3.40 (ch £1.70). Family ticket £8.50. **Facilities:** ❷♿ (Braille guides/scented plants) toilets for disabled shop ❽ (ex assist dogs) 🚗♿🍴

PORTHMADOG   MAP 06 SH53

Ffestiniog Railway
Harbour Station LL49 9NF
➲ (SE end of town beside the harbour, on A487)
☎ 01766 516000
e-mail: enquiries@festrail.co.uk
web: www.festrail.co.uk

A narrow gauge steam railway running for 13.5 miles through Snowdonia National Park, with breathtaking views and superb scenery. Buffet service on all trains including licensed bar (in corridor carriages). Please telephone for details of special events. The company also runs the Welsh Highland Railway Caernarfon, which will eventually link up with the Ffestiniog Railway.

Times: Open daily late Mar-late Oct. Limited Winter service mid week trains Nov & early Dec. Santa specials in Dec. Open Feb half term. **Fee:** ✱ Full distance return £16 (pen £12.80). Other fares available. **Facilities:** ❷ (charged) 🅿🍴 licensed ♿ (Wheelchair ramps, trains mostly accessible) toilets for disabled shop ❽ (ex 3rd class) 🍴

PORTMEIRION
MAP 06 SH53

Portmeirion
2 for 1

LL48 6ET

➲ *(off A487 at Minffordd)*

☎ 01766 770000

e-mail: info@portmeirion-village.com

web: www.portmeirion-village.com

Welsh architect Sir Clough Williams Ellis built his fairy-tale, Italianate village on a rocky, tree-clad peninsula on the shores of Cardigan Bay. A bell-tower, castle and lighthouse mingle with a watch-tower, grottoes and cobbled squares among pastel-shaded picturesque cottages let as holiday accommodation. The 60-acre Gwyllt Gardens include miles of dense woodland paths and are famous for their fine displays of rhododendrons, azaleas, hydrangeas and sub-tropical flora. There is a mile of sandy beach and a playground for children. The village is probably best known as the major location for 1960s cult TV show, *The Prisoner*.

Times: Open all year, daily 9.30-5.30. **Fee:** ✱ £6.50 (ch £4, pen £5). **Facilities:** ♿ 💺 🍽 licensed 🍴 ♿ (w/chair available, disabled parking) toilets for disabled shop ⊗ (ex guide dogs) 🔊

TYWYN
MAP 06 SH50

Talyllyn Railway
Wharf Station LL36 9EY

➲ *(A493 Machynlleth to Dolgellau for Tywyn station, B4405 for Abergynolwyn)*

☎ 01654 710472

e-mail: enquiries@talyllyn.co.uk

web: www.talyllyn.co.uk

The oldest 27in-gauge railway in the world, built in 1865 to run from Tywyn on Cardigan Bay to Abergynolwyn slate mine some seven miles inland. The railway climbs the steep sides of the Fathew Valley and with stops on the way at Dolgoch Falls and the Nant Gwernol forest. The return trip takes 2.5 hours. All scheduled passenger trains are steam hauled.

Times: Open Sun mid Feb-Mar; Apr-early Nov & 26 Dec-1 Jan daily. Ring for timetable. **Fee:** ✱ £11Day Rover (ch accompanied £2). Intermediate fares available. **Facilities:** ♿ (charged) 💺 🍴 ♿ (prior notice useful, wheelchair ramps into carriages) toilets for disabled shop 🔊

Y FELINHELI
MAP 06 SH56

Greenwood Forest Park
2 for 1

LL56 4QN

➲ *(A55 junct 11, follow Llanberis signs onto A4244, signed from next rdbt. Located between Bangor and Caernafen)*

☎ 01248 670076

e-mail: info@greenwoodforestpark.co.uk

web: www.greenwoodforestpark.co.uk

This forest park provides a wide range of exciting activities for the whole family. Try the Great Green Run - the longest slide in Wales, shoot a real longbow, build dens in the woods and saw a log. Ride the Green Dragon, the world's first people-powered family rollercoaster. Try the Jungle Boat Adventure and explore the rainforest. There are

continued

large interactive exhibitions in the oak-framed great hall and the Forest Theatre stages events and shows during school holiday periods. The Toddlers Village is ideal for young children. New attractions include the Treetop Towers, and the Crocodile Maze.

Times: Open daily mid Mar-late Oct 10-5.30 (Sep & Oct 10-5). **Fee:** ✱ Seasonal. £5.95-£8.50 (ch £4.95-£7.75, pen £5.30-£7.50, disabled 20% discount). Family ticket (2ad+2ch) £19.50-£29. **Facilities:** ♿ 💺 🍽 ♿ (grounds mostly accessible, parking) toilets for disabled shop ⊗ (ex on leads) 🔊

ISLE OF ANGLESEY

BEAUMARIS
MAP 06 SH67

Beaumaris Castle
LL58 8AP

☎ 01248 810361

web: www.cadw.wales.gov.uk

Beaumaris was built by Edward I and took from 1295 to 1312 to complete. In later centuries it was plundered for its lead, timber and stone. Despite this it remains one of the most impressive and complete castles built by Edward I. It has a perfectly symmetrical, concentric plan, with a square inner bailey and curtain walls, round corner towers and D-shaped towers in between. There are also two great gatehouses, but these were never finished.

Times: Open Apr-May & Oct, daily 9.30-5; Jun-Sep, daily 9.30-6; Nov-Mar, Mon-Sat 9.30-4, Sun 11-4. Telephone for Xmas opening times. **Fee:** ✱ £3.50 (ch 5-15, concessions £3, disabled visitors and assisting companion free). Family ticket (2ad+all ch/grandch under 16) £10. Group rates available. Prices quoted apply until 31 Mar 2007. **Facilities:** ♿ ♿ shop ⊗ ⊕ 🔊

Museum of Childhood
1 Castle St LL58 8AP

➲ *(turn off A55 onto A545 opposite Beaumaris Castle)*

☎ 01248 712498

web: www.aboutbritain.com/museumofchildhoodmemories.htm

The museum illustrates the life and interests of children and families over 150 years. There are around 2,000 items in the museum's collection including money boxes, dolls, educational toys and games, early clockwork trains, cars and aeroplanes, push toys and cycles.

Times: Open daily 10.30-5.30, Sun 12-5. (Last admission 4.30, Sun 4). Closed Nov-2nd wk Mar **Fee:** ✱ £4 (ch £2.25, concessions £3.25). Family ticket £11. Free entry for wheelchair users. **Facilities:** ℗ (50yds) 🍴 ♿ shop ⊗ (ex guide dogs)

BRYNCELLI DDU
MAP 06 SH57

Bryn Celli Ddu Burial Chamber

➲ *(3m W of Menai Bridge off A4080)*

☎ 029 2050 0200

web: www.cadw.wales.gov.uk

Excavated in 1865, and then again in 1925-9, this is a prehistoric circular cairn covering a passage grave with a polygonal chamber.

Times: Open at all times. **Facilities:** ♿ ⊗ ⊕

BRYNSIENCYN
MAP 06 SH46

Anglesey Sea Zoo

LL61 6TQ

➲ (1st turning off Britannia Bridge onto Anglesey then follow Lobster signs along A4080 to zoo)

☎ 01248 430411

e-mail: info@angleseyseazoo.co.uk

web: www.angleseyseazoo.co.uk

Nestling by the Menai Straits, this all-weather undercover attraction contains a shipwreck bristling with conger eels, a lobster hatchery, a seahorse nursery, crashing waves and the enchanting fish forest.

Times: Open Feb half term-late Oct half term. Check website or telephone for times. **Fee:** ✱ £5.95 (ch & student £4.95, pen & UB40 £5.50). Family ticket £14.95-£21.95. Party 10+. + £1 for high season. Please telephone to confirm 2007 prices. **Facilities:** ℗ ☕ 🍴 licensed 🎪 ⅋ (2 wheelchairs available, Braile tour notes) toilets for disabled shop ⊗ (ex guide dogs) ◀

Foel Farm Park

Foel Farm LL61 6TQ

➲ (left off Britannia Bridge A55 onto A5/A4080 to Llanfairpwllgwyngyll, left on A4080 to Brynsiencyn & follow signs)

☎ 01248 430646

e-mail: foelfarm@btinternet.com

web: www.foelfarm.co.uk

Children will love this friendly farm experience, where they can meet animals big and small, and take tractor and trailer rides. The park also contains a luxury handmade chocolate business, a bistro and bar, as well as a tea room and gift shop.

Times: ✱ Open daily Mar-Oct 10.30-5.30; Also wknds Nov-Feb 10.30-4.30. Also open Feb half term. **Facilities:** ℗ ☕ 🍴 licensed 🎪 ⅋ toilets for disabled shop ⊗ (ex guide dogs) ◀

HOLYHEAD
MAP 06 SH28

RSBP Nature Reserve South Stack Cliffs

FREE

Plas Nico, South Stack LL65 1YH

➲ (A5 or A55 to Holyhead then follow brown heritage signs)

☎ 01407 764973

web: www.rspb.org.uk/reserves/southstack

South Stack Cliffs is an expanse of heathland with dramatic sea cliffs and a tremendous view. In summer breeding seabirds, including puffins, can be seen from the Information Centre at Ellins Tower where telescopes are provided and staff are on hand to help.

Times: Open: Information Centre daily, Etr-Sep, 10-5.30. Reserve open daily at all times. **Facilities:** ℗ 🎪 ⅋ toilets for disabled

LLANALLGO
MAP 06 SH58

Din Llugwy Ancient Village

FREE

➲ (0.75m NW off A5025)

web: www.cadw.wales.gov.uk

The remains of a 4th-century village can be seen here. There are two circular and seven rectangular buildings, still standing up to head height and encircled by a pentagonal stone wall some 4 to 5ft thick.

Times: Open at all times. **Facilities:** ⊗ ⊕

PLAS NEWYDD
MAP 06 SH56

Plas Newydd

LL61 6DQ

➲ (2m S of Llanfairpwll, on A4080)

☎ 01248 714795

e-mail: plasnewydd@nationaltrust.org.uk

web: www.nationaltrust.org.uk

Set amidst breathtakingly beautiful scenery and with spectacular views of Snowdonia, this elegant 18th-century house was built by James Wyatt and is an interesting mixture of Classical and Gothic. The comfortable interior, restyled in the 1930s, is famous for its association with Rex Whistler, whose largest painting is here. There is also an exhibition about his work. A military museum contains campaign relics of the 1st Marquess of Anglesey, who commanded the cavalry at the Battle of Waterloo. There is a fine spring garden and Australasian arboretum with an understorey of shrubs and wild flowers, as well as a summer terrace and, later, massed hydrangeas and autumn colour. A woodland walk gives access to a marine walk on the Menai Strait.

Times: Open Apr-Oct, Sat-Wed. House 12-5; Garden 11-5.30. (Last admission 4.30) **Fee:** £6 (ch £3). Family £15 (2ad+2ch). Parties 15+ £5.40 **Facilities:** ℗ ☕ 🎪 ⅋ (close parking, wheelchairs, garden shuttle, Braille guide) toilets for disabled shop ⊗ (ex assistance dogs) 🐾 ◀

MERTHYR TYDFIL

MERTHYR TYDFIL
MAP 03 SO00

Brecon Mountain Railway

Pant Station Dowlais CF48 2UP

➲ (follow Mountain Railway signs from A470 or A465 N of Merthyr Tydfil)

☎ 01685 722988

web: www.breconmountainrailway.co.uk

Opened in 1980, this narrow-gauge railway follows part of an old British Rail route which closed in 1964 when the iron industry in South Wales fell into decline. The present route starts at Pant Station and continues for 3.5 miles through the beautiful scenery of the Brecon Beacons National Park, as far as Taf Fechan reservoir. The train is pulled by a vintage steam locomotive and is one of the most popular railways in Wales.

Times: Opening times on application to The Brecon Mountain Railway, Pant Station, Merthyr Tydfil. **Fee:** ✱ Fares are under review, please ring for details. **Facilities:** ℗ ☕ 🍴 licensed ⅋ (adapted carriage) toilets for disabled shop ◀

Cyfarthfa Castle Museum & Art Gallery

FREE

Cyfarthfa Park CF47 8RE

➲ (off A470, N towards Brecon, follow brown heritage signs)

☎ 01685 723112

e-mail: museum@merthyr.gov.uk

web: www.museums.merthyr.gov.uk

Set in wooded parkland beside a beautiful lake, this imposing Gothic mansion now houses a superb museum and art gallery. Providing a fascinating glimpse into 3,000 years of history, the museum displays wonderful collections of fine art, social history and objects from around the world in a Regency setting.

Times: Open Apr-Sep, daily 10-5.30; Oct-Mar, Tue-Fri 10-4, Sat-Sun 12-4. Closed between Xmas & New Year **Facilities:** ℗ ☕ 🎪 ⅋ (stair lift & wheelchair available) toilets for disabled shop ⊗ (ex guide dogs)

Wales

423

MONMOUTHSHIRE

CAERWENT
MAP 03 ST49

Caerwent Roman Town
FREE

➲ *(just off A48)*

☎ 029 2050 0200

web: www.cadw.wales.gov.uk

A complete circuit of the town wall of 'Venta Silurum', together with excavated areas of houses, shops and a temple.

Times: Open - access throughout the year. **Facilities:** ⊗ ⊕

CALDICOT
MAP 03 ST48

Caldicot Castle, Museum & Countryside Park
Church Rd NP26 4HU

➲ *(M4 junct 23A onto B4245. From M48 junct 2 follow A48 & B4245. Signed from B4245)*

☎ 01291 420241

e-mail: caldicotcastle@monmouthshire.gov.uk

web: www.caldicotcastle.co.uk

Caldicot Castle's well-preserved fortifications were founded by the Normans and fully developed by the late 14th century. Restored as a family home by a wealthy Victorian, the castle offers the chance to explore medieval walls and towers in a setting of tranquil gardens and wooded country parkland, plus the opportunity to play giant chess or draughts.

Times: Open Apr-Sep, daily 11-5 **Fee:** ✱ £3.75 (ch, pen, student & disabled £2.50). Family (2ad + 3ch) £12. Party 10+. **Facilities:** ᴾ ☕ 🖼 ঈ (taped tour, level trails, induction loop, access guide) toilets for disabled shop ◀

CHEPSTOW
MAP 03 ST59

Chepstow Castle
NP6 5EZ

☎ 01291 624065

web: www.cadw.wales.gov.uk

Built by William FitzOsbern, Chepstow is the first recorded Norman stone castle. It stands in a strategic spot above the Wye. The castle was strengthened in the following centuries, but was not besieged (as far as is known) until the Civil War, when it was twice lost to the Parliamentarians. The remains of the domestic rooms and the massive gatehouse with its portcullis grooves and ancient gates are still impressive, as are the walls and towers.

Times: Open Apr-May & Oct, daily 9.30-5; Jun-Sep, daily 9.30-6; Nov-Mar, Mon-Sat 9.30-4, Sun 11-4. Telephone for Xmas opening times.
Fee: ✱ £3.50 (ch 5-15, concessions £3, disabled visitors and assisting companion free). Family ticket (2ad+all ch/grandch under 16) £10. Group rates available. Prices quoted apply until 31 Mar 2007.
Facilities: ᴾ ঈ shop ⊗ ⊕ ◀

GROSMONT
MAP 03 SO42

Grosmont Castle
FREE

➲ *(on B4347)*

☎ 01981 240301

web: www.cadw.wales.gov.uk

Grosmont is one of the 'trilateral' castles of Hubert de Burgh (see also Skenfrith and White Castle). It stands on a mound with a dry moat,

and the considerable remains of its 13th-century great hall can be seen. Three towers once guarded the curtain wall, and the western one is well preserved.

Times: Open - access throughout the year. **Facilities:** ঈ ⊗ ⊕

LLANTHONY
MAP 03 SO22

Llanthony Priory
FREE

☎ 029 2050 0200

web: www.cadw.wales.gov.uk

William de Lacey discovered the remains of a hermitage dedicated to St David. By 1108 a church had been consecrated on the site and just over a decade later the priory was complete. After the priory was brought to a state of siege in an uprising, Hugh de Lacey provided the funds for a new church, and it is this that makes the picturesque ruin seen today. Visitors can still make out the west towers, north nave arcade and south transept.

Times: Open - access throughout the year. **Facilities:** ᴾ ঈ toilets for disabled ⊗ ⊕

LLANTILIO CROSSENNY
MAP 03 SO31

Hen Gwrt
FREE

➲ *(off B4233)*

☎ 029 2050 0200

web: www.cadw.wales.gov.uk

The rectangular enclosure of the former medieval house, still surrounded by a moat.

Times: Open - access throughout the year. **Facilities:** ⊗ 🚐 ⊕

MONMOUTH
MAP 03 SO51

Nelson Museum & Local History Centre
FREE

New Market Hall, Priory St NP25 3XA

➲ *(in town centre)*

☎ 01600 710630

e-mail: nelsonmuseum@monmouthshire.gov.uk

One of the worlds major collections of Admiral Nelson-related items, including original letters, glass, china, silver, medals, books, models, prints and Nelson's fighting sword feature here. The local history displays deal with Monmouth's past as a fortress market town, and include a section on the co-founder of the Rolls Royce company, Charles Stewart Rolls, who was also a pioneer balloonist, aviator and, of course, motorist.

Times: Open all year, Mar-Oct, Mon-Sat, 11-1, 2-5, Sun, 2-5, including BH. Nov-Feb, Mon-Sat, 11-2, 2-4, Sun, 2-4. **Facilities:** ᴾ (200yds) (small daily charge) 🖼 ঈ toilets for disabled shop ⊗ (ex guide dogs) ◀

RAGLAN
MAP 03 SO40

Raglan Castle
NP5 2BT

➲ *(signed off A40)*

☎ 01291 690228

web: www.cadw.wales.gov.uk

This magnificent 15th-century castle is noted for its 'Yellow Tower of Gwent'. It was built by Sir William ap Thomas and destroyed during the Civil War, after a long siege. The ruins are still impressive however,

continued

continued

Wales

and the castle's history is illustrated in an exhibition situated in the closet tower and two rooms of the gate passage.

Times: Open Apr-May & Oct, daily 9.30-5; Jun-Sep, daily 9.30-6; Nov-Mar, Mon-Sat 9.30-4, Sun 11-4. Telephone for Xmas opening times. **Fee:** £2.90 (ch 5-15, concessions £2.50, disabled visitors & assisting companions free). Family ticket (2ad+all ch/grandch under16) £8.30. Group discounts available. Prices quoted apply until 31 Mar 2007. **Facilities:** ❷ ♿ shop ⊗ ⊕ ■

SKENFRITH   MAP 03 SO42

Skenfrith Castle   FREE
➲ *(on B4521)*
☎ 029 2050 0200
web: www.cadw.wales.gov.uk

This 13th-century castle has a round keep set inside an imposing towered curtain wall. Hubert de Burgh built it as one of three 'trilateral' castles to defend the Welsh Marches.

Times: Open - access throughout the year. Key keeper arrangement. **Facilities:** ❷ ⊗ ⊕ ♨

TINTERN PARVA   MAP 03 SO50

Tintern Abbey
NP6 6SE
➲ *(via A466)*
☎ 01291 689251
web: www.cadw.wales.gov.uk

The ruins of this Cistercian monastery church are still surprisingly intact. The monastery was established in 1131 and became increasingly wealthy well into the 15th century. During the Dissolution, the monastery was closed and most of the buildings were completely destroyed. During the 18th century many poets and artists came to see the ruins and recorded their impressions.

Times: Open Apr-May & Oct, daily 9.30-5; Jun-Sep, daily 9.30-6; Nov-Mar, Mon-Sat 9.30-4, Sun 11-4. Telephone for Xmas opening times. **Fee:** £3.50 (ch 5-15, concessions £3, disabled visitors & assisting companions free). Family ticket (2ad+all ch/grandch under 16) £10. Group rates available. Prices quoted apply until 31 Mar 2007 **Facilities:** ❷ ♿ toilets for disabled shop ⊗ ⊕ ■

WHITE CASTLE   MAP 03 SO31

White Castle
NP7 8UD
➲ *(7m NE of Abergavenny, unclass road N of B4233)*
☎ 01600 780380
web: www.cadw.wales.gov.uk

The impressive 12th to 13th-century moated stronghold was built by Hubert de Burgh to defend the Welsh Marches. Substantial remains of walls, towers and a gatehouse can be seen. This is the finest of a trio of castles, the others being at Skenfrith and Grosmont.

Times: Open Apr-Sep, Wed-Sun & BH Mon 10-5. Monument open and unstaffed on Mon & Tue between Apr-Sep. Monument open and unstaffed with no admission charge at all other times between 10-4. Telephone for Xmas opening times. **Fee:** £2.50 (ch 5-15, concessions £2, disabled visitors & assisting companion free). Family ticket (2ad+all ch/grandch under 16) £7. Group rates available. Prices quoted apply until 31 Mar 2007. **Facilities:** ❷ ♿ ⊗ ⊕ ■

NEATH PORT TALBOT

ABERDULAIS   MAP 03 SS79

Aberdulais Falls
SA10 8EU
➲ *(from M4 junct 43, take A465 signed Vale of Neath. Onto A4109, Falls next to Dulais Rock Pub)*
☎ 01639 636674
e-mail: aberdulais@nationaltrust.org.uk
web: www.ukindex.co.uk/nationaltrust

For over 300 years this famous waterfall has provided energy to drive the wheels of industry. The Turbine House allows visitors access to the top of the falls, with views of the power equipment, fish pass and displays. Please contact for details of special events.

Times: Open 2-25 Mar, Fri-Sun, 11-4. 26 Mar-2 Nov, Mon-Fri, 10-5. 31 Mar-4 Nov, Sat-Sun, 11-6. Winter opening times 12 Jan-23 Mar **Fee:** ✱ £3.20 (ch £1.60) Family ticket £8. Parties 15+ £2.40 (ch £1.20) **Facilities:** ❷ ■ ▦ ♿ (lifts for disabled to view falls) toilets for disabled shop ♨ ■

CRYNANT   MAP 03 SN70

Cefn Coed Colliery Museum   FREE
SA10 8SN
➲ *(1m S of Crynant, on A4109)*
☎ 01639 750556

The museum is on the site of a former working colliery, and tells the story of mining in the Dulais Valley. A steam-winding engine has been kept and is now operated by electricity, and there is also a simulated underground mining gallery, boilerhouse, compressor house, and exhibition area. Outdoor exhibits include a stationary colliery locomotive. Exhibitions relating to the coal mining industry are held on a regular basis.

Times: Open Apr-Oct daily, 10.30-5; Nov-Mar, groups welcome by prior arrangement. **Facilities:** ❷ shop ■

CYNONVILLE   MAP 03 SS89

South Wales Miners Museum
Afan Argoed Country Park SA13 3HG
➲ *(M4 junct 40 onto A4107, 6m NE of Port Talbot)*
☎ 01639 850564
e-mail: aandmboast@btinternetnet.com
web: www.southwalesminersmuseum.co.uk

The picturesquely placed museum gives a vivid picture of mining life, with coal faces, pit gear and miners' equipment. Guided tours of the museum on request. The country park has forest walks and picnic areas, and a visitor centre.

Times: ✱ Open all year daily, Apr-Sep 10.30-5 (Sat & Sun 10.30-6); Oct-Feb 10.30-4 (Sat & Sun 10.30-5). Closed Xmas week. **Fee:** ✱ £1.20 (ch & pen 60p). Concessionary rate for advance bookings. **Facilities:** ❷ (charged) ■ ▥ ♿ (mechanical & manual wheelchairs on request) toilets for disabled shop ⊗ (ex guide dogs) ■

Wales

NEATH   MAP 03 SS79

Gnoll Estate Country Park
SA11 3BS

➲ *(follow brown heritage signs from town centre)*

☎ 01639 635808

e-mail: e.ford@npt.gov.uk

web: www.neath-porttalbot.gov.uk

The extensively landscaped Gnoll Estate offers tranquil woodland walks, picnic areas, stunning views, children's play areas, adventure playground, 9-hole golf course, and coarse fishing. Varied programme of events and school holiday activities.

Times: Open all year - Vistor centre, daily from 10. Closed 24 Dec-2 Jan
Fee: ✱ Pitch & Putt £3.80 (ch £ 1.90) Fishing permit £4.20 (ch £2.55)
Facilities: ⓟ 💺 ⚒ (wheelchair & scooter for hire, designated parking) toilets for disabled shop ⊗ (ex guide dogs)

Neath Abbey   `FREE`
SA10 7DW

➲ *(1m W off A465)*

☎ 01639 812387

web: www.cadw.wales.gov.uk

These ruins were originally a Cistercian abbey founded in 1130 by Richard de Grainville.

Times: Open at all times. Key keeper arrangement. **Facilities:** ⓟ ⚒ ⊗ ⊹

NEWPORT

CAERLEON   MAP 03 ST39

Caerleon Roman Baths
NP6 1AE

➲ *(on B4236)*

☎ 01663 422518

web: www.cadw.wales.gov.uk

Caerleon was an important Roman military base, with accommodation for thousands of men. The foundations of barrack lines and parts of the ramparts can be seen, with remains of the cookhouse, latrines and baths. The amphitheatre nearby is one of the best examples in Britain.

Times: Open Apr-Oct, daily 9.30-5; Nov-Mar, Mon-Sat, 9.30-5, Sun 11-4. Telephone for Xmas opening times. **Fee:** ✱ £2.90 (ch 5-15, concessions £2.50, disabled visitors & assisting companion free). Family ticket (2ad+all ch/grandch under 16) £8.30. Group rates available. Prices quoted apply until 31 Mar 2007. **Facilities:** ⓟ ⚒ shop ⊗ ⊹

National Roman Legion Museum   `FREE`
High St NP18 1AE

➲ *(close to Newport, 20 min from M4, follow signs from Cardiff & Bristol)*

☎ 01633 423134

e-mail: roman@museumwales.ac.uk

web: www.museumwales.ac.uk

The museum illustrates the history of Roman Caerleon and the daily life of its garrison. On display are arms, armour and equipment, with a collection of engraved gemstones, a labyrinth mosaic and finds from the legionary base at Usk. Please telephone for details of children's holiday activities.

Times: Open all year: Mon-Sat 10-5, Sun 2-5. **Facilities:** ⓟ (100yds) ⚒ toilets for disabled shop ⊗ (ex guide dogs)

NEWPORT   MAP 03 ST38

Tredegar House & Park
NP10 8YW

➲ *(2m W of Newport, signed from A48 & M4 junct 28)*

☎ 01633 815880

e-mail: tredegar.house@newport.gov.uk

web: www.newport.gov.uk

Tredegar House is a fine example of restoration and reflects the rise and fall of the Morgan family through 5 centuries. The house and gardens are set in a 90 acre landscaped park and feature formal gardens, self guided trails, craft workshops and boating.

Times: Open Etr-late Sep, Wed-Sun 11.30-4. **Facilities:** ⓟ 💺 🎏 ⚒ (wheelchairs for loan) toilets for disabled shop ⊗ (ex guide dogs)

PEMBROKESHIRE

AMROTH   MAP 02 SN10

Colby Woodland Garden
SA67 8PP

➲ *(1.5m inland from Amroth beside Carmarthen Bay, follow brown signs from A477 Tenby-Carmarthen road, or off coast road at Amroth Castle)*

☎ 01834 811885

web: www.nationaltrust.org.uk

From early spring to the end of June the garden is a blaze of colour, from the masses of daffodils to the rich hues of rhododendrons, azaleas and bluebells. Followed by hydrangeas in shaded walks through summer to glorious shades of autumn

Times: ✱ Open 26 Mar-29 Oct, daily 10-5. **Fee:** ✱ £4 (ch £2). Family ticket £10. Group £3.40 (ch £1.70) NT members free. **Facilities:** ⓟ 💺 🎏 ⚒ (limited due to terrain) toilets for disabled shop ⊗ 🍴

CAREW   MAP 02 SN00

Carew Castle & Tidal Mill
SA70 8SL

➲ *(on A4075, just off A477 Pembroke to Kilgetty road)*

☎ 01646 651782

e-mail: enquiries@carewcastle.com

web: www.carewcastle.com

This magnificent Norman castle has royal links with Henry Tudor and was the setting for the Great Tournament of 1507. Nearby is the Carew Cross (Cadw), an impressive 13ft Celtic cross dating from the 11th century. Carew Mill is one of only four restored tidal mills in Britain, with records dating back to 1558.

Times: Open Apr-1 Nov **Fee:** ✱ £3 (concessions £2). Family ticket £8. **Facilities:** ⓟ shop ⚒

continued

Wales (vertical side tab)

CILGERRAN
MAP 02 SN14

Cilgerran Castle
SA43 2SF

⮑ (off A484 & A478)

☎ 01239 615007

web: www.cadw.wales.gov.uk

Set above a gorge of the River Teifi - famed for its coracle fishermen - Cilgerran Castle dates from the 11th to 13th centuries. It decayed gradually after the Civil War, but its great round towers and high walls give a vivid impression of its former strength.

Times: Open Apr-Sep, daily 9.30-6; Oct 9.30-5 daily; Nov-Mar, daily 9.30-4. Telephone for Xmas opening times. **Fee:** ✱ £2.90 (ch 5-15, concessions £2.50, disabled visitors & assisting companion free). Family ticket (2ad+all ch/grandch under 16) £8.30 Group rates available. Prices quoted apply until 31 Mar 2007 **Facilities:** ❹ shop ⊗ ⊹ ◼

CRYMYCH
MAP 02 SN13

Castell Henllys Fort
Pant-Glas, Meline SA41 3UT

⮑ (off A487 between Cardigan and Newport)

☎ 01239 891319

e-mail: celts@castellhenllys.com

web: www.castellhenllys.com

This Iron Age hill fort is set in the beautiful Pembrokeshire Coast National Park. Excavations began in 1981 and three roundhouses have been reconstructed, another roundhouse has been completed and is the largest on the site. Celtic roundhouses have been constructed in the original way using hazel wattle walls, oak rafters and thatched conical roofs. A forge, smithy and looms can be seen, with other attractions such as trails and a herb garden. Please telephone for details of special events.

Times: Open Apr-early Nov, daily 10-5. Last entry 4.30
Facilities: ❹ ❹ (ramp access to shop, hearing loop in shop) toilets for disabled shop ◼

FISHGUARD
MAP 02 SM93

OceanLab
The Parrog, Goodwick SA64 0DE

⮑ (A40 to Fishguard, turn at by-pass, follow signs for Stenaline ferry terminal, pass 2 garages, turn right at rdbt & follow signs to attraction)

☎ 01348 874737

e-mail: fishguardharbour-tic@pembrokeshire.gov.uk

web: www.ocean-lab.co.uk

Overlooking the Pembrokeshire coastline, OceanLab is a multifunctional centre, which aims to provide a fun-filled experience for the family. There is also a hands on ocean quest exhibition, a soft play area and a cybercafé where visitors can surf the internet. New exhibition, 'Ollie the Octopus's Garden', with hands on displays and activities.

Times: Open Apr-Oct 9.30-5, Nov-Mar 10-4. **Fee:** ✱ Telephone for details
Facilities: ❹ ❹ ◼ ❹ (lift, flat even ground, low counter) toilets for disabled shop ⊗ (ex guide dogs) ◼

LAMPHEY
MAP 02 SN00

Lamphey Bishop's Palace
SA71 5NT

⮑ (off A4139)

☎ 01646 672224

web: www.cadw.wales.gov.uk

This ruined 13th-century palace once belonged to the Bishops of St David's.

Times: Open Apr-Mar, daily 10-5 The Visitor Centre will be closed at times during the Winter, but the gate will be left open for access to the site.
Fee: ✱ £2.90 (ch 5-15, concessions £2.50, disabled visitors & assisting companion free). Family ticket (2ad+all ch/grandch under 16) £8.30. Group discounts available. Price quoted apply until 31 Mar 2007.
Facilities: ❹ ❹ toilets for disabled shop ⊗ ⊹ ◼

LLAWHADEN
MAP 02 SN01

Llawhaden Castle
FREE

⮑ (off A40, 3m NW of Narberth)

☎ 01437 541201

web: www.cadw.wales.gov.uk

The castle was first built in the 12th century to protect the possessions of the Bishops of St David's. The 13th and 14th-century remains of the bishops' hall, kitchen, bakehouse and other buildings can be seen, all surrounded by a deep moat.

Times: Open at all times. Key keeper arrangement. **Facilities:** ❹ ⊗ ⊹

NARBERTH
MAP 02 SN11

Oakwood Park
Canaston Bridge SA67 8DE

⮑ (M4 W junct 49, take A48 to Carmarthen, signed)

☎ 01834 861889

e-mail: info@oakwoodthemepark.co.uk

web: www.oakwoodthemepark.co.uk

Wales' premier theme park, featuring the world's No. 1 wooden roller coaster Megafobia, the 50m-high sky coaster Vertigo, shot n' drop tower coaster The Bounce, and Snake River Falls. For young children there is KidzWorld featuring The Wacky Factory, The Lost Kingdom, Techniquest and Playtown. In summer there are firework displays and live shows at night.

Times: ✱ Open 24 Mar-25 Sep daily from 10 (closing times vary)
Facilities: ❹ ❹ ❹ ❹ ❹ (wheelchair hire, special access to some rides) toilets for disabled shop ⊗ (ex guide dogs) ◼

NEWPORT
MAP 02 SN03

Pentre Ifan Burial Chamber
FREE

⮑ (3m SE from B4329 or A487)

☎ 029 2050 0200

web: www.cadw.wales.gov.uk

Found to be part of a vanished long barrow when excavated in 1936-37, the remains of this chamber include the capstone, three uprights and a circular forecourt.

Times: Open - access throughout the year. **Facilities:** ⊗ ⊹

Wales

PEMBROKE
MAP 02 SM90

Pembroke Castle
SA71 4LA
➲ *(W end of main street)*
☎ 01646 681510 & 684585
e-mail: info@pembrokecastle.co.uk
web: www.pembrokecastle.co.uk

This magnificent castle commands stunning views over the Milford estuary. Discover its rich medieval history, and that of Henry VII, the first Tudor king, through a variety of exhibitions. There are lively guided tours and events each Sunday in July and August. Before leaving, pop into the Brass Rubbing Centre and make your own special souvenir. To complete the day, wander round the tranquil millpond and medieval town walls, which surround other architectural gems from Tudor and Georgian times. Special Events: 1st week in Sep 'Pembroke Festival'. Please telephone for details.

Times: Open all year, daily, Apr-Sep 9.30-6; Mar & Oct 10-5; Nov-Feb, 10-4. Closed 24-26 Dec & 1 Jan. **Fee:** £3.50 (ch under 16 & pen £2.50, ch under 5 & wheelchairs users free). Family ticket £10.
Facilities: Ⓟ (100yds) ☗ 🍽 ♿ (induction loop, handrails, portable ramp) toilets for disabled shop 🍴

ST DAVID'S
MAP 02 SM72

St Davids Bishop's Palace
SA62 6PE
➲ *(on A487)*
☎ 01437 720517
web: www.cadw.wales.gov.uk

These extensive and impressive ruins are all that remain of the principal residence of the Bishops of St David's. The palace shares a quiet valley with the cathedral, which was almost certainly built on the site of a monastery founded in the 6th century by St David. The Bishop's Palace houses an exhibition: 'Lords of the Palace'.

Times: Open Apr-May & Oct, daily 9.30-5; Jun-Sep, daily 9.30-6; Nov-Mar, Mon-Sat 9.30-4, Sun 11-4. Telephone for Xmas opening times.
Fee: ✱ £2.90 (ch 5-15, concessions £2.50, disabled visitors & assisting companions free). Family ticket (2ad+all ch/grandch under16) £8.30. Group discounts available. Prices quoted apply until 31 Mar 2007.
Facilities: Ⓟ ♿ toilets for disabled shop 🍴⛲🍽

St Davids Cathedral
The Close SA62 6PE
➲ *(from Haverfordwest A487 into St Davids, pass Cross Sq, left into car park)*
☎ 01437 720202
e-mail: info@stdavidscathedral.org.uk
web: www.stdavidscathedral.org.uk

Begun 1181 on the reputed site of St David's 6th-century monastic settlement. The present building was altered during the 12th to the 14th centuries and again in the 16th. The ceilings of oak, painted wood and stone vaulting are of considerable interest.

Times: ✱ Open all year 8.30-6. **Facilities:** Ⓟ (300yds) (no coach parking) ☗ ♿ (hearing loop) toilets for disabled shop ♿ (ex guide dogs) 🍽

ST FLORENCE
MAP 02 SN00

Manor House Wildlife & Leisure Park
Ivy Tower SA70 8RJ
➲ *(on B4318 between Tenby & St Florence)*
☎ 01646 651201

The park is set in 35 acres of delightful wooded grounds and award-winning gardens. The wildlife includes exotic birds, reptiles and fish. Also here are a pets' corner, a children's playground with free rides on an astraglide slide, and roundabouts. Other attractions include a natural history museum, a go-kart track, model railway exhibition. Daily falconry displays. Telephone for details of displays and animal feeding times.

Times: ✱ Open Etr-end Sep, daily 10-6. Please telephone for late opening Jul & Aug. **Facilities:** Ⓟ ☗ ♿ toilets for disabled shop ♿ 🍽

SCOLTON
MAP 02 SM92

Scolton Visitor Centre
SA62 5QL
➲ *(5m N of Haverfordwest, on B4329)*
☎ 01437 731328 (Museum) & 731457 (Park)

Scolton Manor Museum is situated in Scolton Country Park. The early Victorian mansion, refurbished stables and the exhibition hall illustrate the history and natural history of Pembrokeshire. There are new displays in the house and stables, plus a 'Pembrokeshire Railways' exhibition. The 60-acre grounds, partly a nature reserve, have fine specimen trees and shrubs. Environmentally friendly Visitor Centre,

continued

alternative energy and woodland displays, guided walks and children's play areas.

Times: ✱ Open Museum Apr-Oct, Tue-Sun & BHs 10.30-1 & 1.30-5.30; Country Park all year, Etr-Sep 10-7, Oct-Etr 10-6. Closed 25-26 Dec.
Facilities: ❷ (charged) 💷 🎦 ♿ (disabled parking area near house) toilets for disabled shop ⊗ (ex guide dogs & in grounds)

TENBY
MAP 02 SN10

Tenby Museum & Art Gallery
Castle Hill SA70 7BP
⊃ *(near town centre above Harbour)*
☎ 01834 842809
e-mail: tenbymuseum@hotmail.com
web: www.tenbymuseum.free-online.co.uk

The museum is situated on Castle Hill. It covers the local heritage from prehistory to the present in galleries devoted to archaeology, geology, maritime history, natural history, militaria and bygones. The art galleries concentrate on local associations with an important collection of works by Augustus John, Gwen John and others.

Times: ✱ Open all year, Etr-7 Dec, daily 10-5; 8 Dec-Etr, Mon-Fri 10-5. (Last admission 4.30). **Facilities:** ❷ (10 mins walk) 🎦 ♿ (lifts, levelled floors, ramps) toilets for disabled shop ⊗ (ex guide dogs)

Tudor Merchant's House
Quay Hill SA70 7BX
⊃ *(turn left off lower end of High St, past Lifeboat PH and Caldey Shop)*
☎ 01834 842279
e-mail: alysonbush@nationaltrust.org.uk
web: www.nationaltrust.org.uk

Recalling Tenby's history as a thriving and prosperous port, the Tudor Merchant's house is a fine example of gabled 15th-century architecture. There is a good Flemish chimney and on three walls the remains of seccos can be seen. A small herb garden has been created.

Times: Open Apr-Oct, Sun-Fri, 11-5 (last admission 4.30) **Fee:** ✱ £2.50 (ch £1.20). Family £6.20. Group 15+ £2 (ch£1). NT members free.
Facilities: ❷ (500yds) (no coaches nearby) 🎦 ♿ (garden could be accessed, Braille guide, photo album) shop ⊗ (ex guide dogs) 🎋

POWYS

ABERCRAF
MAP 03 SN81

Dan-Yr-Ogof The National Showcaves Centre for Wales
SA9 1GJ
⊃ *(M4 junct 45, midway between Swansea & Brecon on A4067, follow brown tourist signs for Dan-Yr-Ogof)*
☎ 01639 730284 & 730801
e-mail: info@showcaves.co.uk
web: www.showcaves.co.uk

This award-winning attraction includes three separate caves, dinosaur park, Iron Age Farm, museum, shire horse centre and covered children's play area.

Times: Open Apr-Oct, daily from 10 (last admission 3). **Fee:** £10 (ch 4-16 £6). Group rates 15+. **Facilities:** ❷ 💷 🎦 shop ⊗ (ex assist dogs) 🛥

BERRIEW
MAP 07 SJ10

Glansevern Hall Gardens
Glansevern SY21 8AH
⊃ *(signed on A483 between Welshpool and Newtown)*
☎ 01686 640644
web: www.glansevern.co.uk

Built in the Greek Revival style for Arthur Davies Owen, who chose a romantically positioned site on the banks of the River Severn. The current owners have developed the gardens, respecting the plantings and features of the past, and added a vast collection of new and interesting species. There are many fine and unusual trees, a lakeside walk, walled garden, water gardens and a rock garden with grotto.

Times: Open May-Sep, BH Mon,Thu-Sat 12-5. Parties other dates by arrangement. **Fee:** ✱ £3.50 (pen £3, ch under 15 free). **Facilities:** ❷ 💷 🍴 licensed 🎦 ♿ (most areas accessible) toilets for disabled shop ⊗ (ex on lead)

BRECON
MAP 03 SO02

Brecknock Museum & Art Gallery `2 for 1`
Captain's Walk LD3 7DS
⊃ *(near town centre at junct of The Watton & Glamorgan St)*
☎ 01874 624121
e-mail: brecknock.museum@powys.gov.uk
web: www.powys.gov.uk/index.php?id=2114+L=0

A wealth of local history is explored at the museum, which has archaeological and historical exhibits, with sections on folk life, decorative arts and natural history. Victorian Assize Court is interpreted with life-size figures, sound and light and there is one of the finest collections of Welsh Lovespoons. The museum also runs a lively programme of Welsh contemporary art exhibitions.

Times: Open all year, Tue-Fri 10-5, Sat 10-1 & 2-5; also open Sun 12-5 Apr-Sep. Closed Good Fri, 25-26 Dec & 1 Jan. Closed Mon ex BH. **Fee:** £1 (ch & residents free, concessions 50p) **Facilities:** ❷ ♿ (limited parking, must be accompanied by able-bodied) toilets for disabled shop ⊗ (ex guide dogs) 🛥

The Royal Regiment of Wales Museum
The Barracks, The Watton LD3 7EB
⊃ *(close to town centre, well signed)*
☎ 01874 613310
e-mail: swb@rrw.org.uk
web: www.rrw.org.uk

The museum of the South Wales Borderers and Monmouthshire Regiment, which was raised in 1689 and has been awarded 23 Victoria Crosses. Amongst the collections is the Zulu War Room, devoted to the war and in particular to the events at Rorke's Drift, 1879, when 121 men fought 4,500 Zulus.

Times: Open all year wkdays 10-5, Apr-Sep Sat & BHs 10-4. See website for special Sun opening times. **Fee:** £3 (ch up to 16 free) **Facilities:** ❷ (town centre 200yds) 🎦 ♿ toilets for disabled shop ⊗ (ex guide dogs) 🛥

Wales

LLANFAIR CAEREINION   MAP 06 SJ10

Welshpool & Llanfair Light Railway

SY21 0SF

⮣ *(beside A458, Shrewsbury-Dolgellau road)*

☎ 01938 810441

e-mail: info@wllr.org.uk

web: www.wllr.org.uk

The Llanfair Railway is one of the Great Little Trains of Wales. It offers a 16-mile round trip through glorious scenery by narrrow-gauge steam train. The line is home to a collection of engines and coaches from all round the world. Please ring for details of special events.

Times: Open Etr-end Oct wknds, daily during holiday periods, phone for timetable enquiries. **Facilities:** ♿ 🅿 🖳 📶 ⓛ ♿ (three coachs adapted for wheelchairs) toilets for disabled shop ◼

MACHYNLLETH   MAP 06 SH70

Celtica

Y Plas, Aberystwyth Rd SY20 8ER

⮣ *(well signed to south of town)*

☎ 01654 702702

e-mail: celtica@celticawales.com

web: www.celticawales.com

Located in a restored mansion house, Celtica is an exciting heritage centre introducing the history and culture of the Celtic people. The sights and sounds of Celtic life are brought alive as you go on a journey portraying the Celtic spirit of the past, present and future. There's an interpretive centre dedicated to Welsh and Celtic history, a children's indoor play area, and conference rooms. Education resources are available and groups are welcome. Storytelling, lectures, music and craft events take place.

Times: ✱ Open daily 10-6. Closed Xmas, New Year & some dates in Jan. **Facilities:** ♿ 🅿 🖳 🍽 licensed 📶 ♿ (lift & ramps to public areas, induction loop) toilets for disabled shop ⊗ (ex guide dogs) ◼

Centre for Alternative Technology

SY20 9AZ

⮣ *(3m N of Machynlleth, on A487)*

☎ 01654 705950

e-mail: info@cat.org.uk

web: www.cat.org.uk

The Centre for Alternative Technology promotes practical ideas and information on sustainable technologies. The exhibition includes displays of wind, water and solar power, organic gardens, low-energy dwellings, and a unique water-powered railway which ascends a 200ft cliff from the car park. The Wave Tank and the underground 'Mole-Hole' are particularly popular with children.

Times: ✱ Open 7 Apr-Oct, daily 10-5; Nov-6 Apr, daily 10-4. **Facilities:** ♿ 🅿 🖳 ♿ (wheelchair available) shop ⊗ (ex guide dogs) ◼

King Arthur's Labyrinth

King Arthur's Labyrinth, Corris SY20 9RF

⮣ *(on A487 between Machynlleth and Dolgellau)*

☎ 01654 761584

e-mail: king.arthurs.labyrinth@corris-wales.co.uk

web: www.kingarthurslabyrinth.com

A subterranean storybook, a boat ride through the great waterfall and into the Labyrinth of tunnels and caverns carved into the ancient rocks of Wales. Tales of King Arthur and other legends are re-told as you walk through this underground setting.

Times: Open 31 Mar-4 Nov, daily, 10-5. **Fee:** ✱ £5.15 (ch £3.60, pen £4.60). **Facilities:** ♿ 🅿 🖳 📶 ♿ toilets for disabled shop ⊗ (ex guide dogs) ◼

MONTGOMERY   MAP 07 SO29

Montgomery Castle   FREE

☎ 029 2050 0200

web: www.cadw.wales.gov.uk

Initially an earth and timber structure guarding an important ford in the River Severn, Montgomery was considered a 'suitable spot for the erection of an impregnable castle' in the 1220s. Building and modifications continued until 1251-53, but the final conquest of Wales by Edward I meant the castle lost much of its role.

Times: Open all year, any reasonable time. **Facilities:** ♿ ⊗ ⊕

PRESTEIGNE   MAP 03 SO36

The Judge's Lodging

Broad St LD8 2AD

⮣ *(in town centre, off B4362, signed from A44 & A49)*

☎ 01544 260650

e-mail: info@judgeslodging.org.uk

web: www.judgeslodging.org.uk

A restored Victorian town house with integral courtroom, cells and service areas - step back into the 1860s, accompanied by an 'eavesdropping' audiotour of voices from the past. Explore the fascinating world of the Victorian judges, their servants and felonious guests at this award-winning, 'hands on', historic house.

Times: Open Mar-Oct daily, 10-5. **Fee:** ✱ £4.95 (ch £3.95, concessions £4.50). Family ticket £15. Party rates available. **Facilities:** ℗ (200mtrs) 📶 ♿ (lift, disabled pack for inaccesible items, Braille guides) shop ⊗ (ex guide dogs)

RHAYADER   MAP 06 SN96

Gilfach Nature Discovery Centre and Reserve

St Harmon LD6 5LF

⮣ *(off A470, 3m N of Rhayader)*

☎ 01597 870301 & 823298

e-mail: info@radnorshirewildlifetrust.org.uk

web: www.radnorshirewildlifetrust.org.uk

Situated in the Cambrian Mountains, Gilfach is locally unique due to its wide variety of habitats; high moorland to enclosed meadow, oak

continued

woodland to rocky upland river. The reserve therefore supports a tremendous abundance of plants and animals within a relatively small area. This richness of wildlife has adapted to living in the various habitats created over the centuries through the practice of traditional farming. Visitors can take a number of planned walks including the Nature Trail, the Monks Trod Trail, and the Oakwood Path. The Nature Discovery Centre offers the opportunity to learn about the various habitats and wildlife featuring footage from cameras in nestboxes, games and quizzes. Special Events: Childrens activities every Thursday in July and August.

Times: Open Reserve all year. Centre Apr-Jun, & Sep-Oct Fri-Mon 10-4.30; Jul-Aug daily 10-4.30 **Facilities:** ❷ ❚ 🔳 ♿ (wheelchair access path to viewpoint) toilets for disabled shop ⊗ (ex on lead)

TRETOWER   MAP 03 SO12

Tretower Court & Castle
NP8 2RF
➲ (3m NW of Crickhowell, off A479)
☎ 01874 730279
web: www.cadw.wales.gov.uk

The castle is a substantial ruin of an 11th-century motte and bailey, with a three-storey tower and 9ft-thick walls. Nearby is the Court, a 14th-century fortified manor house which has been altered and extended over the years. The two buildings show the shift from medieval castle to more domestic accommodation over the centuries.

Times: Open Mar & Oct, Tue-Sun, 10-4; Apr-Sep, Tue-Sun. The monument is closed at all other times. **Fee:** ✱ £2.90 (ch 5-15, concessions £2.50, disabled visitors & assisting companion free). Family ticket (2ad+all ch/grandch under 16) £8.30. Group rates available. Prices quoted apply until 31 Mar 2007. **Facilities:** ❷ ♿ toilets for disabled shop ⊗ ✣ ▬

WELSHPOOL   MAP 07 SJ20

Powis Castle
SY21 8RF
➲ (1m S of Welshpool, signed off A483)
☎ 01938 551920 & 551929
e-mail: powis.castle@nationaltrust.org.uk
web: www.nationaltrust.org.uk

Laid out in the Italian and French styles, the Garden retains its original lead statues, an Orangery and an aviary on the terraces. The medieval castle contains one of the finest collections of paintings and furniture in Wales and a beautiful collection of treasures from India. Please visit website for details of events running throughout the year.

Times: Open 6 Apr-29 Oct, Thu-Mon (Wed-Mon during Jul-Aug). Castle and museum 1-5, gardens, 11-6. **Fee:** ✱ Castle, Museum & Gardens £9.60 (ch under 17 £4.80). Family ticket £24. Group member £8.60. Garden only £6.60 (ch £3.30). Family £16. Group member £5.60. NT members & ch under 5 free. **Facilities:** ❷ †◉† licensed 🔳 ♿ (photos of interior, Braille guides) shop garden centre ⊗ (ex assist dogs) ▥ ▬

RHONDDA CYNON TAFF

TREHAFOD   MAP 03 ST09

Rhondda Heritage Park   🎟 2 for 1
Lewis Merthyr Colliery, Coed Cae Rd CF37 7NP
➲ (between Pontypridd & Porth, off A470, follow brown heritage signs from M4 junct 32)
☎ 01443 682036
e-mail: reception@rhonddaheritagepark.com
web: www.rhonddaheritagepark.com

Based at the Lewis Merthyr Colliery, the Heritage Park is a fascinating 'living history' attraction. You can take the Cage Ride to 'Pit Bottom' and explore the underground workings of a 1950s pit, guided by men who were miners themselves. There are children's activities, an art gallery and a museum illustrating living conditions in the Rhondda Valley. Special events throughout the year, phone for details.

Times: Open all year, daily 10-6. Closed Mon from Oct-Etr. (Last admission 4). Closed 25 Dec-early Jan. **Fee:** £5.60 (ch £4.30, pen £4.95). Family(4)ticket from £16.50, (6) £21. **Facilities:** ❷ ❚ †◉† licensed 🔳 ♿ (wheelchair available, accessible parking, lifts) toilets for disabled shop ⊗ (ex guide dogs) ▬

SWANSEA

LLANRHIDIAN   MAP 02 SS49

Weobley Castle
SA3 1HB
➲ (from B4271 or B4295)
☎ 01792 390012
web: www.cadw.wales.gov.uk

A 12th-to 14th-century fortified manor house with an exhibition on the history of Weobley and other historic sites on the Gower peninsula.

Times: Open all year daily, Mar 9:30-5, Apr-Oct 9:30-6, Nov-Mar 9:30-5 **Fee:** ✱ £2.50 (ch 5-15, concessions £2, disabled visitors & assisting companion free). Family ticket (2ad+all ch/grandch under 16) £7. Group rates available. Prices quoted apply until 31 Mar 2007.
Facilities: ❷ ♿ shop ⊗ ✣ ▬

Oxwich Castle

SA3 1NG

➲ (A4118 from Swansea)

☎ 01792 390359

web: www.cadw.wales.gov.uk

Situated on the Gower peninsula, this Tudor mansion is a striking testament in stone to the pride and ambitions of the Mansel dynasty of Welsh gentry. The E-shaped wing houses an exhibition on historical Gower and 'Chieftains and Princes of Wales'.

Times: Open Apr-Sep, daily 10-5. The monument is closed at all other times. **Fee:** ✱ £2.50 (ch 5-15, concessions £2, disabled visitors & assisting companion free). Family ticket (2ad+all ch/grandch under 16) £7. Group rates available. Prices quoted apply until 31 Mar 2007.

Facilities: ⊘ ⅙ (Radar key toilet) toilets for disabled ⊗ ⟡ ◼

Gower Heritage Centre   `2 for 1`

Y Felin Ddwr SA3 2EH

➲ (follow signs for South Gower on A4118 W from Swansea. W side of Parkmill village)

☎ 01792 371206

e-mail: info@gowerheritagecentre.co.uk

web: www.gowerheritagecentre.co.uk

Based around a 12th-century water-powered cornmill, the site also contains a number of craft workshops, two play areas, animals, a museum and a miller's cottage, all set in attractive countryside in an Area of Outstanding Natural Beauty.

Times: Open daily, Mar-Oct 10-5.30; Nov-Feb 10-4.30. Closed 25 Dec. **Fee:** ✱ £3.95 (ch under 5 free, concessions £2.80). Family ticket £12.50. **Facilities:** ⊘ ⬛ ⍓ licensed ⍓ ⅙ (ramp entrance access) toilets for disabled shop ◼

Glynn Vivain Art Gallery

Alexandra Rd SA1 5DZ

➲ (M4 junct 42 along Fabian Way A483 up Wind St. Left at train station opposite library)

☎ 01792 516900

e-mail: glynn.vivian.gallery@swansea.gov.uk

web: www.glynnviviangallery.org

A broad spectrum of visual arts form the original bequest of Richard Glynn Vivian, including old masters and an international collection of porcelain and Swansea china. The 20th century is also well represented with modern painting and sculpture by British and foreign artists, with the emphasis on Welsh artists. On-going temporary exhibitions showcase the work of contemporary artists.

Times: Open all year, Tue-Sun & BH Mon 10-5. Closed 25-26 Dec & 1 Jan. **Fee:** Donations welcome. **Facilities:** ⓟ (200 yds) ⅙ (hearing loop/audio guides) toilets for disabled shop ⊗ (ex guide & hearing dogs) ◼

Plantasia

Parc Tawe SA1 2AL

➲ (M4 junct 42, follow A483 into Swansea, follow car park signs for attraction)

☎ 01792 474555

e-mail: swansea.plantasia@swansea.gov.uk

web: www.plantasia.org

A unique, giant hot house garden located in the city centre, Plantasia houses a huge variety of unusual and exotic plants of great interest including several species that are extinct in the wild. Also visit the Butterfly House and see a variety of species fly freely and observe various stages of butterfly development.

Times: ✱ Open Tue-Sun 10-5 (BH Mons & all Mons Jun-Aug) **Facilities:** ⊘ ⬛ ⍓ ⅙ toilets for disabled shop ⊗ (ex guide dogs) ◼

Swansea Museum   `FREE`

Victoria Rd, Maritime Quarter SA1 1SN

➲ (M4 junct 42, on main road into city centre)

☎ 01792 653763

e-mail: swansea.museum@swansea.gov.uk

web: www.swanseaheritage.co.uk

This is the oldest museum in Wales, showing the history of Swansea from the earliest times until today. The museum has a Tramshed and floating boats to explore (summer only). There is a continuous programme of temporary exhibitions and events all year around.

Times: Open all year, Tue-Sun 10-5 (last admission 4.45). Closed Mon except BH Mon, 25-26 Dec & 1 Jan. **Facilities:** ⓟ (50yds) (on street) ⍓ ⅙ toilets for disabled shop ⊗ (ex guide dogs) ◼

Wales

TORFAEN

BLAENAVON   MAP 03 SO20

Big Pit National Mining Museum of Wales

NP4 9XP

➲ *(M4 junct 25/26, follow signs on A4042 & A4043 to Pontypool & Blaenavon. Signed off A465)*

☎ 01495 790311

e-mail: bigpit@nmgw.ac.uk

web: www.nmgw.ac.uk/bigpit

The Real Underground Experience! Big Pit is the UK's leading mining museum. It is a real colliery and was the place of work for hundreds of men, woman and children for over 200 years. A daily struggle to extract the precious mineral that stoked furnaces and lit household fires across the world.

Times: ✱ Open mid Feb-late Nov, daily 9.30-5, telephone to confirm
Facilities: ❶ ☕ 🍴 ♿ (underground tours by prior arrangement) toilets for disabled shop

Blaenavon Ironworks

North St

☎ 01495 792615

web: www.cadw.wales.gov.uk

The Blaenavon Ironworks were a milestone in the history of the Industrial Revolution. Constructed in 1788-99, they were the first purpose-built, multi-furnace ironworks in Wales. By 1796, Blaenavon was the second largest ironworks in Wales, eventually closing down in 1904.

Times: Open Apr-Oct, Mon-Fri 9.30-4.30, Sat 10-5, Sun 10-4.30. For details of opening outside this period, telephone Torfaen County Borough Council on 01633 648081. **Fee:** ✱ £2.50 (ch 5-16, concessions £2, disabled visitors & assisting companion free). Family ticket (2ad+all ch/grandch under 16) £7. Group discounts available. Prices quoted apply until 31 Mar 2007.
Facilities: ❶ ⊕ ❀ ⊕ ◼

CWMBRAN   MAP 03 ST29

Greenmeadow Community Farm

Greenforge Way NP44 5AJ

➲ *(M4 junct 26. Follow signs for Cwmbran then brown signs)*

☎ 01633 862202

e-mail: greenmeadow_community_farm@compuserve.com

This is one of Wales' leading tourist attractions - a community farm that was built during the 1980s on land threatened by developers. There are milking demonstrations, tractor and trailer rides, a dragon adventure play area, a farm trail, a nature trail and lots more. Please telephone for details of special events running throughout the year.

Times: Open daily Summer 10-6, Winter 10-4. Closed 23 Dec-1 Feb.
Fee: ✱ £4.50 (ch £3.50) Family (2ad+3ch) £16 **Facilities:** ❶ ☕ 🍴
♿ (tractor & trailer rides for wheelchair users) toilets for disabled shop ◼

VALE OF GLAMORGAN

BARRY   MAP 03 ST16

Welsh Hawking Centre

Weycock Rd CF62 3AA

➲ *(on A4226)*

☎ 01446 734687

There are over 200 birds of prey here, including eagles, hawks, owls, buzzards and falcons. They can be seen and photographed in the mews and some of the breeding aviaries. There are flying demonstrations at regular intervals during the day. A variety of tame, friendly animals, such as pigs, lambs and rabbits will delight younger visitors.

Times: ✱ Open late Mar-Sep, daily 10.30-5, (1hr before dusk in winter).
Facilities: ❶ ☕ 🍴 ♿ toilets for disabled shop ❀ ◼

OGMORE   MAP 03 SS87

Ogmore Castle

➲ *(2.5m SW of Bridgend, on B4524)*

☎ 01656 653435

web: www.cadw.wales.gov.uk

Standing on the River Ogmore, the west wall of this castle is 40ft high. A hooded fireplace is preserved in the 12th-century, three-storey keep and a dry moat surrounds the inner ward.

Times: Open - access throughout the year. Key keeper arrangement.
Facilities: ❶ ♿ ❀ ⊕

PENARTH   MAP 03 ST17

Cosmeston Lakes Country Park & Medieval Village

Lavernock Rd CF64 5UY

➲ *(on B4267 between Barry and Penarth)*

☎ 029 2070 1678

e-mail: NColes@valeofglamorgan.gov.uk

web: www.valeofglamorgan.gov.uk

Deserted during the plagues and famines of the 14th century, the original village was rediscovered through archaeological excavations. The buildings have been faithfully reconstructed on the excavated remains, creating a living museum of medieval village life. Special events throughout the year include re-enactments and Living History.

Times: Open all year, daily 11-5 in Summer, 11-4 in Winter. Closed 25 Dec. Country park open at all times. **Fee:** ✱ Entry to Village £3.50, (concessions £2) Family ticket £8. Entry to Country Park free. **Facilities:** ❶ ☕ 🍴 🍴
♿ (access ramps & wheelchair hire) toilets for disabled shop

ST HILARY   MAP 03 ST07

Old Beaupre Castle [FREE]

➲ *(1m SW, off A48)*

☎ 01446 773034

web: www.cadw.wales.gov.uk

This ruined manor house was rebuilt during the 16th century. Its most notable features are an Italianate gatehouse and porch. The porch is an unusual three-storeyed structure.

Times: Open - access throughout the year. Key keeper arrangement.
Facilities: Ⓟ ❀ ⊕

Wales

WREXHAM

CHIRK
MAP 07 SJ23

Chirk Castle
LL14 5AF
➲ *(8m S of Wrexham, signed off A483)*
☎ 01691 777701
e-mail: chirkcastle@nationaltrust.org.uk

Chirk Castle is one of a chain of late 13th-century Marcher castles. Its high walls and drum towers have hardly changed, but the inside shows the varied tastes of 700 years of occupation. One of the least altered parts is Adam's Tower. Many of the medieval-looking decorations were created by Pugin in the 19th century. Varied furnishings include fine tapestries. In the garden there are beautiful views that take in seven counties.

Times: Open 24 Mar-4 Nov, Wed-Sun & BH Mon, Tue-Sun in Jul-Aug, 12-5 (castle), 10-6 (gardens); Oct, Wed-Sun 12-4 (castle), 11-5 (gardens). (Last admission 30 mins before closing). **Fee:** £7.40 (ch £3.70). Family ticket £18.50. Party. Garden only £4.70 (ch £2.40) Family ticket £11.80 **Facilities:** ❷ �🍽️ licensed ⴵ (stairclimber, hearing loop, coach from car park) toilets for disabled shop ⊗ (ex guide dogs & estate walks) ⛌ 🚃

WREXHAM
MAP 07 SJ35

Erddig
LL13 0YT
➲ *(off A525, 2m S of Wrexham & A483/A5152)*
☎ 01978 355314
e-mail: erddig@ntrust.org.uk
web: www.nationaltrust.org.uk

Built in 1680, the house was enlarged and improved by a wealthy London lawyer with a passion for gilt and silver furniture. Original furnishings remain, including a magnificent state bed in Chinese silk. The house is notable for the view it gives of both 'upstairs' and 'downstairs' life. The gardens, unusually, have been changed very little since the 18th century.

Times: Open 25 Mar-1 Nov, Sat-Wed (open Good Fri), house 12-5, garden 11-6 (Jul-Aug gardens 10-6); Oct-1 Nov, Sat-Wed, house 12-4, garden 11-5. **Fee:** ✱ All inclusive tickets inc: Family rooms, below stairs, outbuildings & gardens £6 (ch £3). Party 15+. Below stairs, outbuildings & garden £4 (ch £2) Family ticket £10. National Trust members free. **Facilities:** ❷ 🍽️ licensed ⴵ (4 wheelchairs available) toilets for disabled shop garden centre ⊗ (ex guide dogs) ⛌ 🚃

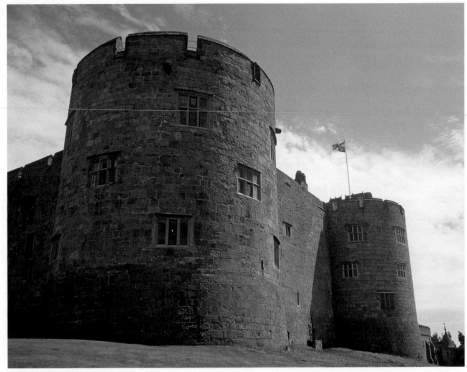

Chirk Castle, Wrexham

Northern Ireland

Carrick-a-Rede,
Co Antrim

Made up of six counties, which are part of the United Kingdom, Northern Ireland has
consistently drawn tourists, primarily for its inspiring scenery. Any visitor should try and
take in some of the Ulster Way, which makes its way through all six counties, and takes in
the Giant's Causeway, the Glens of Antrim and the granite Mountains of Mourne on its 430
mile (700km) length. One of the best loved attractions is Carrick-a-Rede Rope Bridge and
Larrybane limestone quarry. At the centre of the area is the largest lake in the British Isles,
Lough Neagh. Legend has is that the lough was created when the Irish giant, Fionn mac
Cumhaill, picked up a lump of earth to throw at a rival Scottish giant. The hole left became
Lough Neagh, while the lump became the Isle of Man.

BELFAST

BELFAST   MAP 01 D5

Belfast Zoological Gardens

Antrim Rd BT36 7PN

⮎ *(M2 junct 4 signed to Glengormley. Follow signs off rdbt to Zoo)*

☎ 028 9077 6277

e-mail: blackrhonda@belfastcity.gov.uk

web: www.belfastzoo.co.uk

The 50-acre zoo has a dramatic setting on the face of Cave Hill, enjoying spectacular views. Attractions include the award-winning primate house (gorillas and chimpanzees), penguin enclosure, free-flight aviary, African enclosure, and underwater viewing of sealions and penguins. There are also red pandas, free-ranging lemurs and a group of very rare spectacled bears. Recent additions to the collection include Barbary lions, maned wolves, and barn owls.

Times: Open all year, daily Apr-Sep 10-5; Oct-Mar 10-2.30. Closed 25 & 26 Dec. **Fee:** Summer: £7.50 (ch £4), Winter: £6.30 (ch £3.20, ch under 4, pen and disabled free) **Facilities:** ℗ ⬛ 🍴 licensed 🍴 & (free admission & reserved parking) toilets for disabled shop ⊗ (ex guide dogs) ⬛

Botanic Gardens

3 College Park, Off Botanic Ave. BT7 1LP

⮎ *(from City Hall, Bedford St then Dublin road for Botanic Avenue)*

☎ 028 9032 4902

e-mail: maxwellr@belfastcity.gov.uk

web: www.belfastcity.gov.uk

One highlight of the park is the beautiful glass-domed Victorian Palm House, built between 1839-52. This palm house pre-dates the one in Kew Gardens and is one of the earliest curved glass and iron structures in the world. Another feature is the Tropical Ravine - stand on a balcony to get a wonderful view through a steamy ravine full of exotic plants.

Times: Open Palm House Tropical Ravine: Apr-Sep 10-12, 1-5; Oct-Mar 10-12, 1-4. Sat, Sun & BHs 1-5 (Summer), 1-4 (Winter). **Fee:** ✱ Entry free. Guided tours £10 **Facilities:** ℗ (street) & toilets for disabled

Giant's Ring   FREE

⮎ *(0.75m S of Shaws Bridge)*

☎ 028 9023 5000

web: www.ehsni.gov.uk

Circular, Bronze-age enclosure nearly 200ft in diameter similar in style to Stonehenge, with a stone chambered grave in the centre and bordered by banks 20ft wide and 12ft high. Very little is known for certain about this site, except that it was used for ritual burial.

Times: Open all times. **Facilities:** ℗

Ulster Museum   FREE

National Museums of N.Ireland, Botanic Gardens BT9 5AB

⮎ *(1m S of city centre on Stranmillis road)*

☎ 028 9038 3000

e-mail: info@magni.org.uk

web: www.ulstermuseum.org.uk

The Ulster Museum is the perfect place to explore the arts, ancient and modern history, and the nature of Ireland. Art displays change

continued

regularly but always include a rich variety of Irish and international paintings, drawings and sculpture, along with ceramics, glass and costume. The history galleries tell the story of the north of Ireland from the Ice Age to the present day. The natural environment is explored in the Habitas galleries.

Times: ✱ Open all year, Mon-Fri 10-5, Sat 1-5, Sun 2-5. Closed 3 days Xmas **Facilities:** ℗ (100yds on street) ⬛ 🍴 & (lifts, loop system) toilets for disabled shop ⊗ (ex assist dogs) ⬛

W5 at Odyssey

2 Queens Quay BT3 9QQ

☎ 028 9046 7700

web: www.w5online.co.uk

W5 investigates Who? What? Where? When? Why?... and that pretty much sums up the intent behind Ireland's first purpose built discovery centre. Visitors of any age will want to get their hands on interactive science and technology displays that include the laser harp, the fog knife, microscopes, robots and computers. W5 is part of a massive Millennium Landmark Project in the heart of Belfast.

Times: ✱ Open all year Mon-Sat 10-6, Sun 12-6. Closed 25-26 Dec & 12 Jul. **Facilities:** ℗ (charged) 🍴 licensed & (hearing loop) toilets for disabled shop ⊗ (ex guide dogs) ⬛

CO ANTRIM

ANTRIM   MAP 01 D5

Antrim Round Tower   FREE

BT41 1BJ

⮎ *(N of town)*

☎ 028 9023 5000

web: www.ehsni.gov.uk

Antrim round tower stands among lawns and trees but it was once surrounded by monastic buildings. Antrim was an important early monastery, probably a 6th-century foundation, closely linked with Bangor.

Times: Open all year. **Facilities:** ℗ &

BALLYCASTLE   MAP 01 D6

Bonamargy Friary   FREE

⮎ *(E of town, at golf course)*

☎ 028 9023 5000

web: www.ehsni.gov.uk

Founded by Rory MacQuillan around 1500 and later passed on to the MacDonnells, Earls of Antrim, there are still remains of the friary gatehouse, church and cloister for visitors to see.

Times: Open all year. **Facilities:** ℗ & 🚐

BALLYLUMFORD   MAP 01 D5

Ballylumford Dolmen   FREE

⮎ *(on B90 on NW tip of Island Magee)*

☎ 028 9023 5000

web: www.ehsni.gov.uk

Incorporated in the front garden of a house in Ballylumford Road are the remains of this huge 4-5,000-year-old single-chamber Neolithic tomb, also known as the Druid's Altar.

Times: Open all year. **Facilities:** &

BALLYMENA
MAP 01 D5

Ecos Millennium Environmental Centre

Ecos Centre, Kernohams Ln, Broughshane Rd BT43 7QA
➲ *(follow signs from M2 bypass at Ballymena)*
☎ 028 2566 4400
e-mail: info@ecoscentre.com
web: www.ecoscentre.com

At the Ecos Centre visitors can enjoy a fun day out on the Ecos Island free of charge where there is a wide range of fun activities for all including electric bikes, remote control boats, toy tractors and diggers sand pit, BBQ's and picnicking facilities, duck feeding, play park and much more. The visitor centre is packed with fun with lots of information on the environment and renewable energy technologies and children's quizzes. This is all set in a 150-acre park and nature reserve where visitors can follow any of the picturesque walking trails along the riverside, and through developing woodlands.

Times: Open all year. Please phone for opening dates. Closed 24 Dec-1 Jan **Facilities:** ♿ 💺 ♿ toilets for disabled shop garden centre ⊗ (ex guide dogs) 🚢

Harryville Motte

➲ *(N bank of River Braid)*
☎ 028 9023 5000
web: www.ehsni.gov.uk

On a ridge to the south of the town, this Norman fort, with its 40ft-high motte and rectangular bailey, is one of the finest examples of Norman earthworks left in Northern Ireland.

Times: Open all year. **Facilities:** ♿ ♿ 🚌

BALLYMONEY
MAP 01 C6

Leslie Hill Open Farm

Leslie Hill BT53 6QL
➲ *(1m NW of Ballymoney on MacFin Rd)*
☎ 028 2766 6803
web: www.lesliehillopenfarm.co.uk

An 18th-century estate with a Georgian house, magnificent period farm buildings, and fine grounds with paths, lakes and trees. Attractions include an extensive collection of rare breeds, poultry, horsedrawn machinery and carriages, exhibition rooms, a museum, working forge, deer park, walled garden and an adventure playground.

Times: Open Jul-Aug, Mon-Sat 11-6, Sun 2-6; Jun, Sat-Sun & BHs 2-6; Etr-May, Sun & BHs 2-6, open all Etr wk 11-6. **Fee:** ✱ £3.50 (ch £2.50). Family ticket £10. **Facilities:** ♿ 💺 ♿ (ramps) toilets for disabled shop ⊗ (ex on lead)

BUSHMILLS
MAP 01 C6

Old Bushmills Distillery

BT57 8XH
➲ *(on Castlecatt Rd, in Bushmills Village)*
☎ 028 2073 1521
e-mail: sheelagh.croskery@diageo.com
web: www.bushmills.com

Old Bushmills was granted its licence in 1608 and is the oldest licenced whiskey distillery in the world. There's a guided tour, and

continued

afterwards you can take part in a comparative tasting session and become a whiskey expert.

Times: Open Apr-Oct, Mon-Sat 9.30-5.30, Sun 12-5.30 (last tour 4); Nov-Mar, Mon-Fri 5 tours daily, 10.30, 11.30, 1.30, 2.30 & 3.30. Sat & Sun 3 tours, 1.30, 2.30, 3.30. Closed 12 July , Good Fri pm, Xmas & New Year **Fee:** ✱ £5 (accompanied ch £2.50, concessions £4). Family ticket (2ad+2ch) £13 (ch 8 years & under cannot take tour) **Facilities:** ♿ 🍴 licensed 🍷 ♿ (audio visual theatre, shops & restaurant) toilets for disabled shop ⊗ (ex guide dogs) 🚢

CARRICK-A-REDE
MAP 01 D6

Carrick-a-rede Rope Bridge and Larrybane Visitors Centre

BT54 6LS
➲ *(E of Ballintoy on B15)*
☎ 028 2076 9839 & 2073 1582 (office)
e-mail: carrickarede@nationaltrust.org.uk
web: www.ntni.org.uk

On the North Antrim Coastal Path is one of Northern Ireland's best-loved attractions: Carrick-a-Rede Rope Bridge and the disused limestone quarry of Larrybane. The island of Carrick is known as 'the rock in the road', as it is an obstacle on the path of migrating salmon, and fishermen have taken advantage of this to net the fish here for over 300 years.

Times: ✱ Open Bridge daily (weather permitting), 12 Mar-12 June, 10-6; 13-30 Jun 10-7, Jul & Aug 10-7; Sep 10-6. (Last admission 45 mins before closing). Coastal path open all year. **Facilities:** ♿ 💺 ♿ (information centre, telescope at wheelchair height) toilets for disabled 🦽

CARRICKFERGUS
MAP 01 D5

Carrickfergus Castle

BT38 7BG
➲ *(on N shore of Belfast Lough)*
☎ 028 9335 1273
web: www.ehsni.gov.uk

Imposingly based on a rocky headland overlooking Belfast Lough, this is the best preserved and probably the most fought-over Norman castle in Ireland. Built by John de Courcy, Earl of Ulster, after 1180, it served a military purpose for more than eight centuries. Exhibits include a giant model of the castle, a short film, and a banqueting suite. The castle is often used as a venue for medieval banquets and fairs. There is a visitors' centre, shop and refreshment point.

Times: ✱ Open all year, Apr-Sep, wkdays 10-6, Sun 2-6; Oct-Mar closes at 4. **Facilities:** ♿ 💺 ♿ toilets for disabled shop ⊗

Town Walls

☎ 028 9023 5000
web: www.ehsni.gov.uk

Lord Deputy Sir Arthur Chichester enclosed Carrickfergus with stone walls from 1611 onwards and more than half the circuit is still visible, often to its full height of 4 metres to the wall walk.

Times: Visible at all times. **Facilities:** ♿ ♿

Ireland (side tab)

CHURCHTOWN

MAP 01 D5

Cranfield Church

FREE

➲ *(3.75m SW of Randalstown)*

☎ 028 9023 5000

web: www.ehsni.gov.uk

This small medieval church is situated on the shores of Lough Neagh. Beside it is a famous holy well.

Times: Open all year. **Facilities:** ℗ & 🚐

GIANT'S CAUSEWAY

MAP 01 C6

Giant's Causeway Centre

44 Causeway Rd BT57 8SU

➲ *(2m N of Bushmills on B146)*

☎ 028 2073 1855

e-mail: causewaytic@hotmail.com

web: www.northantrim.com

This dramatic rock formation is undoubtedly one of the wonders of the natural world. The Centre provides an exhibition and audio-visual show, and Ulsterbus provides a minibus service to the stones and there are guided walks, and special facilities for the disabled.

Times: ✱ Open all year, daily from 10 (closes 7 Jul & Aug). Closed 1 wk Xmas. **Facilities:** ℗ (charged) 💷 ⼱& (mini bus transport with wheelchair hoist, reserved parking) toilets for disabled shop ⊗ (ex guide dogs) 🍴

LARNE

MAP 01 D5

Olderfleet Castle

FREE

☎ 028 9023 5000

web: www.ehsni.gov.uk

A 16th-century tower house, the last surviving of three which defended Larne.

Times: Open at all times.

LISBURN

MAP 01 D5

Duneight Motte and Bailey

FREE

➲ *(2.3m S beside Ravernet River)*

☎ 028 9023 5000

web: www.ehsni.gov.uk

Impressive Anglo-Norman earthwork castle with high mound-embanked enclosure, making use of the defences of an earlier pre-Norman fort.

Times: Open all year.

Irish Linen Centre & Lisburn Museum FREE

Market Square BT28 1AG

➲ *(Signed both in and outside town centre. Follow tourist signs from M1 motorway)*

☎ 028 9266 3377

e-mail: irishlinencentre@lisburn.gov.uk

web: www.lisburncity.gov.uk

The centre tells the story of the Irish linen industry past and present. The recreation of individual factory scenes brings the past to life and a series of imaginative hands-on activities describe the linen manufacturing processes. The Museum has a range of temporary exhibitions of local interest.

continued

continued

Times: Open all year, Mon-Sat, 9.30-5. **Facilities:** ℗ (100 mtrs) (limited for disabled and coaches) 💷 & (lift, induction loop, staff trained in sign language) toilets for disabled shop ⊗ (ex guide dogs) 🍴

PORTBALLINTRAE

MAP 01 C6

Dunluce Castle

➲ *(off A2)*

☎ 028 2073 1938

web: www.ehsni.gov.uk

Extensive and picturesque ruins of a 16th-century castle perched on a rocky crag high above the sea. Stronghold of the MacQuillans and MacDonnells, who significantly altered the original stonebuilt fortress. Randal MacDonnell built a house in the centre of the castle, of which parts of the Great Hall remain, as do the towers and early 17th-century gatehouse. The castle has new displays and there is an audio-visual show. The cave below the ruins provided a secret way into and out of the castle from the sea.

Times: ✱ Open all year, Apr-Sep, wkdays 10-7, Sun 2-7; Oct-Mar, Tue-Sat 10-4, Sun 2-4. **Facilities:** ℗ & toilets for disabled shop

TEMPLEPATRICK

MAP 01 D5

Pattersons Spade Mill

751 Antrim Rd BT39 0AP

➲ *(2m SE of Templepatrick on A6)*

☎ 028 9443 3619

web: www.ntni.org.uk

This is the last surviving water-driven spade mill in Ireland. It has been completely restored by the National Trust and is now back in production.

Times: ✱ Open Mar, Sun 2-6; Apr-May, wknds, BHs, 2-6 ; Jun-Aug, daily 2-6; Sep, wknds & BHs 2-6. **Facilities:** ℗ 🍴 & (ramps, wheelchair available) toilets for disabled ⋇

Templetown Mausoleum FREE

BT39

➲ *(in Castle Upton graveyard on A6, Belfast-Antrim road)*

web: www.ntni.org.uk

Situated in the graveyard of Castle Upton, this family mausoleum is in the shape of a triumphal arch and was designed by Robert Adam.

Times: Open daily during daylight hours. **Facilities:** ℗ 🚐 ⋇

CO ARMAGH

ARMAGH

MAP 01 C5

Armagh County Museum

FREE

The Mall East BT61 9BE

➲ *(in city centre)*

☎ 028 3752 3070

e-mail: acm.um@nics.gov.uk

web: www.magni.org.uk

Housed in a 19th-century schoolhouse, this museum contains an art gallery and library, as well as a collection of local folkcrafts and natural history. Special events are planned thoughout the year.

Armagh County Museum

Times: ✱ Open all year, Mon-Fri 10-5, Sat 10-1 & 2-5. **Facilities:** ❷ 🏛 ♿ (entrance, ramp & lift for disabled) toilets for disabled shop ⊗ (ex guide dogs) 🍴

Armagh Friary

FREE

➲ *(SE edge of town)*
☎ 028 9023 5000
web: www.ehsni.gov.uk

Situated just inside the gates of the former Archbishop's Palace are the remains of the longest friary church in Ireland (163ft). The friary was established in 1263 by Archbishop O'Scanail and destroyed by Shane O'Neill in the middle of the 16th century to prevent it being garrisoned by Elizabethan soldiers.

Times: Open all year. **Facilities:** ❷ ♿

Armagh Planetarium

College Hill BT61 9DB
➲ *(on Armagh-Belfast road close to mall, city centre)*
☎ 028 3752 3689 & 4725
e-mail: info@armaghplanet.com
web: www.armaghplanet.com

The Planetarium is home to The Digital Theatre, a multi-media environment equipped with the latest technology including a virtual reality digital system. Also featured are The Galileo hall, Copernicus Hall, Tycho, Cassini and Kepler rooms and surrounding the Planetarium is the Astropark, a 25-acre 'hands on' park.

Times: Open all year, Mon-Sat 10-5, Sun 12-5. Term time closed Mon. Closed 12 Jul, 25-26 Dec & 1 Jan. **Fee:** ✱ £3.75 (ch, concessions £2.75). Family ticket £11. Exhibition area £1. **Facilities:** ❷ 🍺 ♿ (loop system in theatre lifts/ramps) toilets for disabled shop ⊗ (ex guide dogs) 🍴

Navan Centre & Fort

2 for 1

Killylea Rd BT60 4LD
➲ *(2.5m W on A28)*
☎ 028 3752 1801
e-mail: navan@armagh.gov.uk
web: www.visitarmagh.com

Navan was once known as Emain Macha, the ancient seat of kings and earliest capital of Ulster. Today it is an impressive archaeological site with its own museum and visitor centre located in a building that blends into the landscape. The Navan Centre uses audio-visuals and

continued

interactive devices to unravel history from myth. Travel into the 'Real World' of archaeology and the 'Other World' to hear the legends of the Ulster Cycle.

Times: Open Apr-Sep daily 10-5, Sun 12-5. Closed 12 Jul. Other times by arrangement for tour groups and educational visits. **Fee:** ✱ £4.50 (ch £2.75, concessions £3.50). Family ticket £11 **Facilities:** ❷ 🏛 ♿ (loop for hearing aids, parking) toilets for disabled shop ⊗ (ex guide dogs) 🍴

Palace Stables Heritage Centre

2 for 1

The Palace Demesne BT60 4EL
➲ *(off Friary Rd beside council offices)*
☎ 028 3752 1801
e-mail: stables@armagh.gov.uk
web: www.visitarmagh.com

This picturesque Georgian building, set around a cobbled courtyard, has been lovingly restored and now houses a heritage centre. The building was home to the Archbishops of the Church of Ireland from 1770 up to the 1975. A daily Georgian interpretation is provided by authentic costumed characters. The centre also features a chapel, gardens, a Victorian conservatory, the ruins of a Franciscan Friary, and an ice house.

Times: Open all year, Jul-Aug, Mon-Sat 10-5.30, Sun 1-5.30; Sep-Apr, Mon-Sat 10-5, Sun 2-5. (Last tour 1hr before closing) **Fee:** £4.50, (pen £3.50). Family £1, **Facilities:** ❷ 🍴 licensed ♿ (ramps & lift in stables) toilets for disabled shop 🍴

Saint Patrick's Trian Visitor Complex

2 for 1

40 English St BT61 7BA
➲ *(in city centre)*
☎ 028 3752 1801
e-mail: info@saintpatrickstrian.com
web: www.saintpatrickstrian.com

An exciting visitor complex in the heart of the city. Incorporating three major exhibitions - The Armagh story: traces Armagh's historic Pagan monuments through to the coming of St Patrick and Celtic Christianity to the modern day city. Patrick's Testament: takes a closer look at Ireland's patron saint through the writings found in ancient manuscript the *Book of Armagh*. The Land of Lilliput: Jonathan Swift's most famous book, *Gulliver's Travels* is narrated by a 20-foot giant.

Times: Open all year, Mon-Sat 10-5, Sun 2-5. Closed 12 Jul. **Fee:** ✱ £4.50 (ch £2.75, concessions £3.50). Family ticket £11 **Facilities:** ❷ (charged) 🍴 licensed ♿ (specially designed for disabled) toilets for disabled shop ⊗ (ex guide dogs) 🍴

CAMLOUGH   MAP 01 D5

Killevy Churches

FREE

➲ *(3m S lower eastern slopes of Slieve Gullion)*
☎ 028 9023 5000
web: www.ehsni.gov.uk

The ruins of the two churches (10th and 13th-century) stand back to back, at the foot of Slieve Gullion sharing a common wall, but with no way through from one to the other. The churches stand on the site of an important nunnery founded by St Monenna in the 5th century. A huge granite slab in the graveyard supposedly marks the founder's grave. A holy well can be reached by climbing the path north of the graveyard. The nunnery was in use until the Dissolution in 1542.

Times: Open all year. **Facilities:** ♿

Ireland

JONESBOROUGH MAP 01 D5

Kilnasaggart Inscribed Stone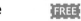
➲ *(1.25m S)*
☎ 028 9023 5000
web: www.ehsni.gov.uk
A granite pillar stone dating back to 8th century, with numerous crosses and a long Irish inscription carved on it.
Times: Open all year. **Facilities:** ℗

MOY MAP 01 C5

Argory
Derrycaw Rd BT71 6NA
➲ *(3m NE)*
☎ 028 8778 4753
e-mail: argory@nationaltrust.org.uk
web: www.ntni.org.uk
Originally the home of the McGeough family, this Regency house is situated on a hillside overlooking the Blackwater River. The house is full of period furniture and bric-a-brac. Of particular interest is the very unusual acetylene lighting, installed by the family in 1906.
Times: ✱ Grounds: Open Oct-Apr, daily 10-4; May-Sep, daily 10-7. House: Open 17 Mar 1-6; 19 Mar-May & Sep, wknds & BH/PH, 1-6; Jun-Aug, daily 1-6; Sep wknds 1-6; 1-9 Oct, wknds 1-5. **Facilities:** ❷ (charged) 💼 📱 ♿ (parking facilities, wheelchair available, Braille) toilets for disabled shop ⊗ (ex guide dogs) ♨ ➡

NEWRY MAP 01 D5

Moyry Castle
➲ *(7.5m S)*
☎ 028 9023 5000
web: www.ehsni.gov.uk
This tall, three-storey keep was built by Lord Mountjoy, Queen Elizabeth's deputy, in 1601, its purpose to secure the Gap of the North which was the main route into Ulster.
Times: Open all year

OXFORD ISLAND MAP 01 D5

Lough Neagh Discovery Centre
Oxford Island National Nature Reserve BT66 6NJ
➲ *(signed from M1 junct 10)*
☎ 028 3832 2205
e-mail: oxford.island@craigavon.gov.uk
web: www.oxfordisland.com
In a spectacular setting on the water's edge, discover natural history, wildlife, family walks and much more.
Times: Open Apr-Sep, Mon-Sat 10-6; Sun 10-7, Oct-Mar, Mon-Sun 10-5.
Fee: Free except for events **Facilities:** ❷ 💼 ♿ (grounds accessible in part, bird watching hides) toilets for disabled shop ⊗ (ex guide dogs) ➡

PORTADOWN MAP 01 D5

Ardress House
64 Ardress Rd, Annaghmore BT62 1SQ
➲ *(on B28, 5m from Moy, 5m from Portadown, 3m from M1 junct 13)*
☎ 028 3885 1236
e-mail: ardress@ntrust.org.uk
web: www.ntni.org.uk
A plain 17th-century house, transformed around 1770 by its visionary architect-owner George Ensor, who added elegant wings and superb Adamesque plasterwork. The house has a fine picture gallery on loan from the Earl of Castlestewart. The grounds are beautifully unspoilt and there is a farmyard with livestock and a display of farm implements.
Times: ✱ Open 17 Mar, 2-6; 19 Mar-25 Sep, wknds, BHs & PHs 2-6
Facilities: ❷ 📱 ♿ toilets for disabled shop ⊗ (ex guide dogs) ♨

TYNAN MAP 01 C5

Village Cross
☎ 028 9023 5000
web: www.ehsni.gov.uk
A carved High Cross, 11ft tall, which lay broken in two pieces for many years, but was skilfully mended in 1844.
Times: Open all year **Facilities:** ❷ ♿

CO DOWN

ARDGLASS MAP 01 D5

Jordan's Castle
☎ 028 9054 6552
web: www.ehsni.gov.uk
Although Ardglass is an important fishing port today, it was once the busiest seaport in Northern Ireland. Between the 14th and 15th centuries a ring of tower houses and fortified warehouses was built to protect the port. Jordan's Castle, a late 15th-century, four-storey tower house situated in the centre of town, is one of these. Besieged in the early 1600s and held for three years, the castle was bought, repaired and filled with bygones by a Belfast solicitor in the early part of the 20th century.
Times: ✱ Open Jul-Aug; Tue, Fri & Sat 10-1, Wed-Thu, 2-6. Other times on request. **Facilities:** ⊗

BALLYWALTER MAP 01 D5

Grey Abbey
➲ *(on E edge of village)*
☎ 028 9054 6552
web: www.ehsni.gov.uk
Founded in 1193 by Affreca, daughter of the King of the Isle of Man, these extensive ruins of a Cistercian abbey, sitting in lovely sheltered parkland, are among the best preserved in Northern Ireland. The chancel, with its tall lancet windows, magnificent west doorway and an effigy tomb - believed to be Affreca's - in the north wall, are particularly interesting. The abbey was burned down in 1572, and then re-used as a parish church. There are many 17th and 18th-century memorials to be seen in the church ruins, which occupy a pleasant garden setting. The abbey now has a beautiful medieval herb garden, with over 50 varieties of plants, and a visitors' centre.
Times: ✱ Open Apr-Sep; Tue-Sat 10-7, Sun 2-7; Oct-Mar, wknds, Sat 10-4, Sun 2-4. **Facilities:** ❷ ♿ toilets for disabled

CASTLEWELLAN MAP 01 D5

Drumena Cashel `FREE`
↪ (2.25m SW)
☎ 028 9023 5000
web: www.ehsni.gov.uk

There are many stone ring forts in Northern Ireland, but few so well preserved as Drumena. Dating back to early Christian times, the fort is 30m in diameter and has an 11m accessible underground stone-built passage, probably used as a refuge and for storage.

Times: Open all times **Facilities:** ℗

COMBER MAP 01 D5

WWT Castle Espie `2 for 1`
Ballydrain Rd BT23 6EA
↪ (12m SE of Belfast. A22 from Comber towards Killyleagh, 1st left into Ballydrain Rd)
☎ 028 9187 4146
e-mail: info.castleespie@wwt.org.uk
web: www.wwt.org.uk

Home to the largest collection of wildfowl in Ireland. Comfortable hides enable you to watch the splendour of migratory waders and wildfowl. Beautiful landscaped gardens, a taxidermy collection and fine paintings by wildlife artists can also be seen. Thousands of birds migrate to the reserve in winter and birdwatch mornings are held on the last Thursday of every month. The Centre's effluent is treated in a reed bed filtration system which can be seen on one walk.

Times: Open all year (ex 23-25 Dec). Nov-Feb, Mon-Fri 11-4. Sat & Sun 11-4.30. Mar-Jun, Mon-Fri 10.30-5. Sat & Sun 11-5.30. Jul-Aug, Mon-Fri 10.30-5.30. Sat & Sun 11-5.30. **Fee:** £4.80 (ch £2.95, pen £3.90). Group (12 or more people) £3.90 (ch £2.50 concession) £3.40 **Facilities:** ℗ 💺 📖 ♿ (hides have wheelchair platforms) toilets for disabled shop ⊗ (ex guide dogs) 🍴

DOWNPATRICK MAP 01 D5

Down County Museum `FREE`
The Mall, County Down, Northern Ireland
BT30 6AH
↪ (on entry to town follow brown signs to museum)
☎ 028 4461 5218
e-mail: museum@downdc.gov.uk
web: www.downcountymuseum.com

The museum is located in the restored buildings of the 18th-century county gaol. In addition to restored cells that tell the stories of some of the prisoners, there are exhibitions on the history of County Down. Plus temporary exhibits, events, tea-room and shop.

Times: Open all year, Mon-Fri 10-5, wknds 1-5 **Facilities:** ℗ (100yds) 💺 📖 ♿ (wheelchair available, handling boxes on application) toilets for disabled shop ⊗ (ex guide dogs) 🍴

Inch Abbey
↪ (0.75m NW off A7)
☎ 028 9023 5000
web: www.ehsni.gov.uk

Beautiful riverside ruins of a Cistercian abbey founded by John de Courcy around 1180. Of particular note is the tall, pointed, triple east window.

Times: ✳ Open all year Apr-Sep 10-7, Sun 2-7. Oct-Mar free access.
Facilities: ℗ ♿

Loughinisland Churches `FREE`
↪ (4m W)
☎ 028 9023 5000
web: www.ehsni.gov.uk

This remarkable group of three ancient churches stands on an island in the lough, accessible by a causeway. The middle church is the oldest, probably dating back to the 13th century, with a draw-bar hole to secure the door. The large North church was built in the 15th century, possibly to replace the middle church and continued in use until 1720. The smallest and most recent church is the South (MacCartan's) church.

Times: Open all times **Facilities:** ℗ ♿ 🚌

Mound of Down `FREE`
↪ (on Quoile Marshes, from Mount Crescent)
☎ 028 9023 5000
web: www.ehsni.gov.uk

A hill fort from the Early Christian period, conquered by Anglo-Norman troops in 1177, who then built an earthwork castle on top. This mound in the marshes, beside the River Quoile, was the first town before the present Downpatrick.

Times: Open all times **Facilities:** ℗

The St Patrick Centre `2 for 1`
St Patrick Visitor Centre, Market St BT30 6LZ
↪ (A7 from Belfast, follow brown heritage signs)
☎ 028 4461 9000
e-mail: director@saintpatrickcentre.com
web: www.saintpatrickcentre.com

This 21st-century multimedia, interactive, audio-visual feast is dedicated to the fascinating story of Ireland's Patron Saint Patrick, who brought Christianity to Ireland in the 5th century. The Centre is located beside the saint's grave, in the heart of St. Patrick's country, forty minutes from Belfast and two hours from Dublin.

Times: Open all year Oct-Mar, Mon-Sat, 10-5 & St Patricks Day 9.30-7; Apr-May & Sep, Mon-Sat 9.30-5.30, Sun 1-5.30 (morning opening on request), Jun-Aug Mon-Sat 9.30-6, Sun 10-6. (Last admission 1.5 hrs before closing). **Fee:** ✳ £4.90 (ch £2.50, concessions £3.30) family ticket (2ad+2ch) £11.70. Groups 25+, £3.25 (ch £2.20, concessions £2.65) **Facilities:** ℗ 💺 🍴 📖 ♿ (lifts & wheelchairs available) toilets for disabled shop garden centre ⊗ (ex guide dogs) 🍴

Struell Wells `FREE`
↪ (1.5m E)
☎ 028 9023 5000
web: www.ehsni.gov.uk

Pilgrims come to collect the healing waters from these holy drinking and eye wells which are fed by a swift underground stream. Nearby are the ruins of an 18th-century church, and, even more interesting, single-sex bath-houses. The men's bath-house is roofed, has an anteroom and a sunken bath, while the ladies' is smaller and roofless.

Times: Open all times **Facilities:** ℗ 🚌

Ireland

DROMARA
MAP 01 D5

Legananny Dolmen
 FREE
➲ *(4m S)*
☎ 028 9023 5000
web: www.ehsni.gov.uk

Theatrically situated on the slopes of Slieve Croob, this tripod dolmen with its three tall uprights and huge capstone is the most graceful of Northern Ireland's Stone Age monuments. There are views to the Mourne Mountains.

Times: Open at all times **Facilities:** ♿ 🚌

HILLSBOROUGH
MAP 01 D5

Hillsborough Fort
FREE
☎ 028 9268 3285
web: www.ehsni.gov.uk

On a site that dates back to early Christian times, the existing fort was built in 1650 by Colonel Arthur Hill to command a view of the road from Dublin to Carrickfergus. The building was ornamented in the 18th century. It is set in a forest park with a lake and pleasant walks.

Times: ✱ Open all year; Apr-Sep, Tue-Sat 10-7, Sun 2-7; Oct-Mar, Tue-Fri 10-4, Sat 10-4, Sun 2-4 **Facilities:** ❷ ♿

HOLYWOOD

Ulster Folk and Transport Museum
 2 for 1
Cultra BT18 0EU
➲ *(12m outside Belfast on A2, past Holywood on main rout to Bangor)*
☎ 028 9042 8428
e-mail: uftm.info@magni.org.uk
web: www.uftm.org.uk

Voted Northern Ireland's Best Visitor Attraction and Irish Museum of the Year, this attraction illustrates the way of life and traditions of Northern Ireland. The galleries of the Transport Museum display collections of horse drawn carts, cars, steam locomotives and the history of ship and aircraft building. Please telephone for details of special events running throughout the year.

Times: Open all year Mar-Jun, Mon-Fri 10-5, Sat 10-6, Sun 11-6; Jul-Sep, Mon-Sat 10-6, Sun 11-6; Oct-Feb, Mon-Fri 10-4, Sat 10-5, Sun 11-5.
Fee: Folk Museum: £7 (ch 5-16 and concessions £4, under 5 free) Family ticket (2ad + 3ch) £19. Disabled visitors free. Transport Museum: as Folk Museum. Combined ticket £6.50 (ch 5-16 and concessions £4) Family ticket £19. **Facilities:** ❷ 🍽 🏪 ♿ toilets for disabled shop ▪

KILKEEL
MAP 01 D4

Greencastle
➲ *(4m SW)*
☎ 028 9023 5000
web: www.ehsni.gov.uk

Looking very much like an English Norman castle with its massive keep, gatehouse and curtain wall, this 13th-century royal fortress stands on the shores of Carlingford Lough, with fine views of the Mourne Mountains. Greencastle has an eventful military history, it was beseiged and taken by Edward Bruce in 1316, attacked and spoiled by the Irish at least twice later in the 14th century, and maintained as a garrison for Elizabeth in the 1590s.

Times: ✱ Open Jul-Aug, Tue-Sat 10-7, Sun 2-7. **Facilities:** ❷ ♿

KILLINCHY
MAP 01 D5

Sketrick Castle
 FREE
➲ *(3m E on W tip of Sketrick Islands)*
☎ 028 9023 5000
web: www.ehsni.gov.uk

A badly ruined tall tower house, probably 15th century. The ground floor rooms include a boat bay and prison. An underground passage leads from the north-east of the bawn to a freshwater spring.

Times: Open at all times. **Facilities:** ❷ ♿

NEWCASTLE
MAP 01 D5

Dundrum Castle
FREE
➲ *(4m N)*
☎ 028 9054 6518
web: www.ehsni.gov.uk

This medieval castle, one of the finest in Ireland, was built in 1777 by John De Courcy in a strategic position overlooking Dundrum Bay, a position which offers visitors fine views over the sea and to the Mourne Mountains. The castle was captured by King John in 1210 and was badly damaged by Cromwellian troops in 1652. Still an impressive ruin, it shows a massive round keep with walls 16m high and 2m thick, surrounded by a curtain wall, and a gatehouse which dates from the 13th century.

Times: ✱ Open Apr-Sep, Tue-Sat 10-7, Sun 2-7; Oct-Mar, wknds, Sat 10-4, Sun 2-4. **Facilities:** ❷ ♿ toilets for disabled

Maghera Church
FREE
➲ *(2m NNW)*
☎ 028 9023 5000
web: www.ehsni.gov.uk

The stump of a round tower, blown down in a storm in the early 18th century, survives from the early monastery, with a ruined 13th-century church nearby.

Times: Open all year. **Facilities:** ❷ ♿

NEWTOWNARDS
MAP 01 D5

Mount Stewart House, Garden & Temple of the Winds
Greyabbey BT22 2AD
➲ *(5m SE off A20)*
☎ 028 4278 8387
e-mail: mountstewart@nationaltrust.org.uk
web: www.ntni.org.uk

On the east shore of Strangford Lough, is a fascinating house which has survived for three centuries, famous for its many illustrious owners and guests and well renowned for its magnificent gardens created by Edith Lady Londonderry, wife of the 7th Marquess. In the inspired gardens, which are now a nominated world heritage site, many rare and subtropical trees thrive. Located by the shore is the Temple of the Winds, built by James 'Athenian' Stuart in 1782 for the first Marquess.

Times: ✱ Lakeside Gardens & Walks: open all year daily 10-sunset;. Formal Gardens: Mar wknds & BHs 10-4; Apr & Oct, daily 10-6; May-Sep 10-8 (closed Nov-Feb). House: 12 Mar-end Apr wknds (including Etr) 12-6.; May, Jun & Sep, wknds 12-6, wkdays (ex Tue) 1-6; Oct, wknds 12-6 closed Nov-Feb). Temple of Winds Apr-Oct, Sun & BH, 2-5. **Facilities:** ❷ 🍽 🍽 licensed 🏪 ♿ (4 wheelchairs (2 electric) available) toilets for disabled shop 🐾 ▪

Scrabo Tower

 FREE

Scrabo Country Park, 203A Scrabo Rd BT23 4SJ

➲ *(1m W)*

☎ 028 9181 1491

web: www.ehsni.gov.uk

The 135ft high Scrabo Tower, one of Northern Ireland's best-known landmarks, dominates the landscape of North Down and is also the centre of a country park around the slopes of Scrabo Hill. The Tower provides a fascinating series of interpretative displays about the surrounding countryside and the viewing platform boasts spectacular views over Strangford Lough and Co. Down. The park provides walks through fine beech and hazel woodlands and the unique sandstone quarries display evidence of volcanic activity as well as being breeding sites for peregrine falcons.

Times: ✱ Open late Mar-mid Sep, Sat-Thu 10.30-6. **Facilities:** ❷ shop ⊗

PORTAFERRY   MAP 01 D5

Exploris Aquarium

The Rope Walk, Castle St BT22 1NZ

➲ *(A20 or A2 or A25 to Strangford Ferry Service)*

☎ 028 4272 8062

e-mail: info@ards-council.gov.uk

web: www.exploris.org.uk

Exploris Aquarium is Northern Ireland's only public aquarium and now includes a seal sanctuary. Situated in Portaferry on the shores of Strangford Lough it houses some of Europe's finest displays. The Open Sea Tank holds 250 tonnes of sea water. The complex includes a park with duck pond, picnic area, children's playground, caravan site, woodland and bowling green.

Times: ✱ Open all year, Mon-Fri 10-6, Sat 11-6, Sun 1-6. (Sep-Feb closing 1 hr earlier). **Facilities:** ❷ ▦ ⅏ (2 lifts within complex) toilets for disabled shop ⊗ (ex guide dogs) ➡

SAINTFIELD   MAP 01 D5

Rowallane Garden

BT24 7LH

➲ *(1m S of Saintfield on A7)*

☎ 028 9751 0131

e-mail: rowallane@nationaltrust.org.uk

web: www.ntni.org.uk

Beautiful and exotic 52-acre gardens, started by the Rev John Moore in 1860, containing exquisite plants from all over the world. They are particularly noted for their rhododendrons and azaleas and for the wonderful floral displays in spring and summer.

Times: ✱ Open Oct-Apr, 10-4; May-Sep, 10-8. Closed 24 Dec-1 Jan. **Facilities:** ❷ ▦ ⅏ (parking facilities, manual wheelchairs, scented plants) toilets for disabled ⅏

STRANGFORD   MAP 01 D5

Audley's Castle   FREE

➲ *(1.5m W by shore of Strangford Lough)*

☎ 028 9023 0560

web: www.ehsni.gov.uk

15th-century tower house on Strangford Lough which offers lovely views from its top floor. The internal fittings are complete.

Times: ✱ Open Apr-Sep, daily 10-7. **Facilities:** ❷ ⊗

Castle Ward

BT30 7LS

➲ *(0.5m W of Strangford on A25)*

☎ 028 4488 1204

e-mail: castleward@nationaltrust.org.uk

web: www.ntni.org.uk

The curious diversity of styles in this house is due to the fact that its owner and his wife could never agree; so classical themes and a more elaborate Gothic look were both incorporated. The servants' living quarters are reached by an underground passage. Gardens, complete with a small lake and classical summerhouse, are richly planted and especially beautiful in spring.

Times: Open Ground daily 8 May-Sep 10-4. House & Wildlife Centre; 15 Mar-Apr wknds, BH/PH 12-6; May wknds 12-6, Mon, Wed & Fri 1-6; Jun-Aug, daily noon-6 (Jun wkdays from 1); Sep-Oct wknds 12-6 **Facilities:** ❷ (charged) ▦ 🍴 ⅏ (wheelchair available, may be driven to house, Braille) toilets for disabled shop ⅏ ➡

Strangford Castle   FREE

☎ 028 9023 5000

web: www.ehsni.gov.uk

A three-storey tower house built in the 16th century, overlooking the small double harbour of Strangford.

Times: Open all reasonable times. **Facilities:** ⊗

CO FERMANAGH

BELLEEK   MAP 01 B5

Belleek Pottery

3 Main St BT93 3FY

➲ *(A46 from Enniskillen to Belleek. Pottery at entrance to village)*

☎ 028 6865 9300 & 8501

e-mail: visitorcentre@belleek.ie

web: www.belleek.ie

Known worldwide for its fine Parian china, Ireland's oldest pottery was started in 1857 by the Caldwell family. Meet the craftspeople at work whilst touring the Pottery and visit the museum, which has exhibits dating back over 140 years.

Times: Open all year, Apr-Sep Mon-Fri 9-6, Sat 10-6 & Sun 2-6; Jul & Aug Sun 11-6; Oct Mon-Fri 9-5.30. Closed wknds except Oct, Sat 10-5.30 & Sun 2-6. Also closed 1 Jan, 17 Mar & Xmas. **Fee:** ✱ Guided tours £4 (ch under 12 free, pen £2). **Facilities:** ❷ 🍴 ⅏ (2 wheelchairs) toilets for disabled shop ⊗ (ex guide dogs) ➡

CASTLE ARCHDALE BAY   MAP 01 C5

White Island Church

➲ *(in Castle Archdale Bay; ferry from marina)*

☎ 028 9023 5000

web: www.ehsni.gov.uk

Lined up on the far wall of a small, roofless 12th-century church are eight uncanny carved-stone figures. Part Christian and part pagan in appearance, their significance has been the subject of great debate. The church ruins sit on an early monastic site.

Times: ✱ Open Jul-Aug, Tue-Sat 10-7, Sun 2-7. **Facilities:** ❷ ⊗ 🚌

Ireland

DERRYGONNELLY   MAP 01 C5

Tully Castle   FREE

➲ (3m N, on W shore of Lower Lough Erne)

☎ 028 9054 6552

web: www.ehsni.gov.uk

Extensive ruins of a Scottish-style stronghouse with enclosing bawn overlooking Lough Erne. Built by Sir John Hume in the early 1600s, the castle was destroyed, and most of the occupants slaughtered, by the Maguires in the 1641 Rising. There is a replica of a 17th-century garden in the bawn.

Times: ✱ Open Jul & Aug, Wed-Sun, 10-6. **Facilities:** ❷ ⅃ ⊗

ENNISKILLEN   MAP 01 C5

Castle Coole

BT74 6JY

➲ (on A4, 1.5m from Enniskillen towards Belfast)

☎ 028 6632 2690

e-mail: castlecoole@nationaltrust.org.uk

web: www.ntni.org.uk

No expense was spared in the building of this mansion. James Wyatt was the architect, the lovely plasterwork ceilings were by Joseph Rose, and the chimneypieces the work of Richard Westmacott. Vast amounts of Portland stone were specially imported, together with an Italian expert in stonework. The house is filled with beautiful Regency furniture.

Times: ✱ Open Grounds, Oct-Mar, daily 10-4; Apr-Sep, daily 10-8. House: 12 Mar-May, wknds & PHs/BHs 12-6; Jun, Wed-Mon 1-6; Jul-Aug daily 12-6; Sep wknds 12-6; 1-9 Oct wknds 1-5 **Facilities:** ❷ ⅃ ⅃ (may be driven to house, large print guide) toilets for disabled shop ⊗ (ex in park & guide dogs) ⅃ ⊟

Enniskillen Castle

BT74 7HL

☎ 028 6632 2711

web: www.ehsni.gov.uk

Overlooking Lough Erne, this castle, a three-storey keep surrounded by massive stone-built barracks and with a turreted fairytale 17th-century water gate, now houses two museums and a heritage centre. In the castle keep is a small museum displaying Royal Enniskillen Fusiliers regimental exhibits, while the other rooms contain the Fermanagh County Museum's collection of local antiquities.

Times: ✱ Open all year Mon 2-5, Tue-Fri 10-5 (closed 1-2, Oct-Apr), Sat 2-5 May-Aug, Sun 2-5 Jul-Aug, all day BHs. **Facilities:** ❷ ⅃ shop ⊗

Florence Court

BT92 1DB

➲ (8m SW of Enniskillen via A4, then A32 to Swanlibar, well signed)

☎ 028 6634 8249

e-mail: florencecourt@nationaltrust.org.uk

web: www.ntni.org.uk

An 18th-century mansion overlooking wild and beautiful scenery towards the Mountains of Cuilcagh. The interior of the house,

continued

particularly noted for its flamboyant rococo plasterwork, was gutted by fire in 1955, but has been restored. There are pleasure grounds with an Ice House, Summer House, Water Powered Sawmill and also a walled garden.

Times: ✱ Open daily. Grounds, Oct-Mar 10-4; Apr-Sep 10-8. House: 12 Mar-May, wknds & BHs 12-6. Jun, Mon-Fri (ex Tue) 1-6, wknds 12-6; Jul-Aug, daily 12-6. Sep, wknds 12-6; 1-9 Oct, wknds 1-5

Facilities: ❷ (charged) ⅃ ⅃⊘ ⅃ ⅃ (electric wheelchair available & wheelchair path, Braille) toilets for disabled shop ⅃ ⊟

Marble Arch Caves

Marlbank Scenic Loop BT92 1EW

➲ (off A4 Enniskillen to Sligo road. Left onto A32 and follow signs)

☎ 028 6634 8855

e-mail: mac@fermanagh.gov.uk

web: www.marblearchcaves.net

One of Europe's finest cave systems, under the Mountains of Cuilcagh. Visitors are given a tour of a wonderland of stalagmites, stalactites and underground rivers and lakes, starting with a boat trip on the lower lake. The streams, which feed the caves, flow down into the mountain then emerge at Marble Arch, a 30ft detached limestone bridge. The geological, historical and economic benefits of Marble Arch Caves and Cuilcagh Mountain Park were recognised on an international scale when they were jointly awarded the title of European Geopark.

Times: Open late Mar-Sep, daily, 10-4.30; Jul & Aug 10-5. **Fee:** ✱ £7.50 (ch £4.50, concessions £6.75). Family ticket £18. Group rates available.

Facilities: ❷ ⅃ ⅃ ⅃ (induction loop in AV theatre) toilets for disabled shop ⊗ (ex guide dogs) ⊟

Monea Castle   FREE

➲ (6m NW)

☎ 028 9023 5000

web: www.ehsni.gov.uk

A fine example of a plantation castle still with much of its enclosing bawn wall intact, built around 1618. Of particular interest is the castle's stone corbelling - the Scottish method of giving additional support to turrets.

Times: Open at any reasonable time. **Facilities:** ❷ ⅃

The Sheelin Irish Lace Museum

Ballanaleck BT92 2BA

➲ (from Enniskillen take A4 onto A509. Thatched Sheelin restaurant on left after 3m, museum in restaurant car park)

☎ 028 6634 8052

e-mail: infoirishlacemuseum.com

web: www.irishlacemuseum.com

The Irish Lace Museum has the largest and most comprehensive display of antique lace anywhere in Ireland. There are around 400 exhibits, representing the five main types of Irish lace: Inishmacsaint Needlelace, Crochet, Limerick, Carrickmacross, and Youghal Needlelace. The history of the Irish lace-making industry is described, and antique items can be bought in the museum shop.

Times: ✱ Open all year Mon-Sat 10-6. **Facilities:** ❷ ⅃⅃ licensed ⅃ ⅃ (toilets for disabled in restaurant) shop ⊗ (ex guide dogs) ⊟

Ireland

LISNASKEA
MAP 01 C5

Castle Balfour
FREE

☎ 028 9023 5000
web: www.ehsni.gov.uk

Dating from 1618 and refortified in 1652, this is a T-plan house with vaulted rooms. Badly burnt in the early 1800s, this house has remained in ruins.

Times: Open at all times. **Facilities:** ℗ &

NEWTOWNBUTLER
MAP 01 C5

Crom Estate

BT92 8AP

⊃ *(3m from A34, well signed from Newtownbutler)*
☎ 028 6773 8118 & 8174
e-mail: crom@nationaltrust.org.uk
web: www.ntni.org.uk

Featuring 2,000 acres of woodland, parkland and wetland, the Crom Estate is one of Northern Ireland's most important conservation areas. Nature trails are signposted through woodlands to the ruins of the old castle, and past the old boat house and picturesque summer house. Day tickets for pike fishing and boat hire are available from the Visitor Centre.

Times: ✱ Open Grounds: 12 Mar-Jun, daily 10-6; Jul-Aug, daily 10-8; Sep, daily 10-6; Oct, wknds 12-6. Visitor centre: 15 Mar-24 Apr, wknds & BH 10-6; May-Sep, daily 10-6; 1-9 Oct, wknds 1-5. **Facilities:** ❷ (charged) 🌞 🍴 & (adapted picnic bench & holiday cottage) toilets for disabled shop 🌱 ⬛

CO LONDONDERRY

COLERAINE
MAP 01 C6

Hezlett House

107 Sea Rd, Castlerock BT51 4TW

⊃ *(5m W on Coleraine/Downhill coast road 1m from Castlerock)*
☎ 028 7084 8728
e-mail: hezletthouse@nationaltrust.org.uk
web: www.ntni.org.uk

A low, thatched cottage built around 1690 with an interesting cruck truss roof, constructed by using pairs of curved timbers to form arches and infilling around this frame with clay, rubble and other locally available materials.

Times: ✱ Open Jun-Aug, please contact for opening times 028 7084 8728 **Facilities:** ❷ & (parking) toilets for disabled ⊗ (ex in gardens on lead) 🌱

Mount Sandel
FREE

⊃ *(1.25m SSE)*
☎ 028 9023 0560
web: www.ehsni.gov.uk

This 200ft oval mound overlooking the River Bann is believed to have been fortified in the Iron Age. Nearby is the earliest known inhabited place in Ireland, where post holes and hearths of wooden dwellings, and flint implements dating back to 6650BC have been found. The fort was a stronghold of de Courcy in the late 12th century and was refortified for artillery in the 17th century.

Times: Open at all times. **Facilities:** ❷ &

DOWNHILL
MAP 01 C6

Mussenden Temple Bishop's Gate and Black Glen

Mussenden Rd BT51 4RP

⊃ *(1m W of Castlerock off A2, 6m from Coleraine)*
☎ 028 7084 8728
e-mail: downhillcastle@nationaltrust.org.uk
web: www.ntni.org.uk

Spectacularly placed on a cliff edge overlooking the Atlantic, this perfect 18th-century rotunda was modelled on the Temple of Vesta at Tivoli. Visitors entering by the Bishop's Gate can enjoy a beautiful glen walk up to the headland where the temple stands. If you enjoy open windswept walks with views that stretch over the whole of the north coast of Ireland, then you must visit Downhill.

Times: ✱ Open Grounds, all year, dawn-dusk. Temple, 12 Mar-May wknds & BH 11-6; Jun, daily, 11-6; Jul-Aug, daily, 11-7.30; Sep wknds 11-6; Oct, wknds, 11-5. **Facilities:** ❷ (charged) 🍴 & toilets for disabled 🌱

DUNGIVEN
MAP 01 C5

Banagher Church
FREE

⊃ *(2m SW)*
☎ 028 9023 5000
web: www.ehsni.gov.uk

This church was founded by St Muiredach O'Heney in 1100 and altered in later centuries. Today impressive ruins remain. The nave is the oldest part and the square-headed lintelled west door is particularly impressive. Just outside, the perfect miniature stone house, complete with pitched roof and the sculpted figures of a saint at the doorway, is believed to be the tomb of St Muiredach. The saint was said to have endowed his large family with the power of bringing good luck. All they had to do was to sprinkle whoever or whatever needed luck with sand taken from the base of the saint's tomb.

Times: Open at all times. **Facilities:** ❷ &

Dungiven Priory
FREE

⊃ *(SE of town overlooking River Roe)*
☎ 028 9023 5000
web: www.ehsni.gov.uk

Up until the 17th century Dungiven was the stronghold of the O'Cahan chiefs, and the Augustinian priory, of which extensive ruins remain, was founded by the O'Cahans around 1150. The church, which was altered many times in later centuries, contains one of Northern Ireland's finest medieval tombs. It is the tomb of Cooey na Gall O'Cahan who died in 1385. His sculpted effigy, dressed in Irish armour, lies under a stonework canopy. Below are six kilted warriors.

Times: Open Church at all times, chancel only when caretaker available. Check at house at end of lane. **Facilities:** ❷ &

Ireland

If an attraction name appears in *italics*, details have not been confirmed for 2007

445

LIMAVADY   MAP 01 C6

Rough Fort   FREE
➲ *(1m W off A2)*
☎ 028 7084 8728
e-mail: downhillcastle@nationaltrust.org.uk
web: www.ntni.org.uk

Early Christian rath picturesquely surrounded by pine and beech trees, making it a significant landscape feature. The Rough Fort is one of the best examples of an earthwork ring fort in Ireland.

Times: Open at all times. **Facilities:** 🚍 🐾

LONDONDERRY   MAP 01 C5

City Walls
☎ 028 9023 5000
web: www.ehsni.gov.uk

The finest and most complete city walls to be found in Ireland. The walls, 20-25ft high, are mounted with ancient cannon, and date back to the 17th century. The walled city is a conservation area with many fine buildings. Visitors can walk round the city ramparts - a circuit of one mile.

Times: Open all times. **Facilities:** 🅿 (charged) ♿

Tower Museum
Union Hall Place BT48 6LU
➲ *(behind city wall, facing guildhall)*
☎ 028 7137 2411
e-mail: museums@derrycity.gov.uk

This exhibition recounts the history of Londonderry from pre-historic times to the present day using real artefacts, theatrical displays and eleven audio-visual programmes showing the spread of Irish monasticism, the famous Siege of Derry and the road to the partition of Ireland.

Times: ✳ Open all year, Sep-Jun, Tue-Sat 10-5. Jul-Aug, Mon-Sat 10-5, Sun 2-5. Also open BH Mons. **Facilities:** 🅿 (300yds) ♿ toilets for disabled shop ⊗ (ex guide dogs) 🍴

MAGHERA   MAP 01 C5

Maghera Church   FREE
➲ *(E approach to the town)*
☎ 028 9023 5000
web: www.ehsni.gov.uk

Important 6th-century monastery founded by St Lurach, later a bishop's see and finally a parish church. This much-altered church has a magnificently decorated 12th-century west door. A cross-carved stone to the west of the church is supposed to be the grave of the founder.

Times: Key from Leisure Centre. **Facilities:** 🅿 ♿

MONEYMORE   MAP 01 C5

Springhill
BT45 7NQ
➲ *(1m from Moneymore on B18 to Coagh)*
☎ 028 8674 8210 & 7927
e-mail: springhill@nationaltrust.org.uk
web: www.ntni.org.uk

This pleasingly symmetrical manor house dates back to the 17th century. Today much of the family furniture, books and bric-a-brac have been retained. Outside, the laundry, stables, brewhouse, and old dovecote make interesting viewing, as does the excellent costume museum.

Times: ✳ Open 15 Mar-Jun, wknds & BH 2-6; Jul-Aug, daily 2-6; Sep, wknds only 2-6. **Facilities:** 🅿 🍽 🗐 ♿ (photograph album of 1st floor, wheelchair, scented plants) toilets for disabled shop 🐾

CO TYRONE

ARDBOE   MAP 01 C5

Ardboe Cross   FREE
➲ *(off B73)*
☎ 028 9023 5000
web: www.ehsni.gov.uk

Situated at Ardboe Point, on the western shore of Lough Neagh, is the best example of a high cross to be found in Northern Ireland. Marking the site of an ancient monastery, the cross has 22 sculpted panels, many recognisably biblical, including Adam and Eve and the Last Judgment. It stands over 18ft high and dates back to the 10th century. It is still the rallying place of the annual Lammas, but praying at the cross and washing in the lake has been replaced by traditional music-making, singing and selling of local produce. The tradition of 'cross reading' or interpreting the pictures on the cross, is an honour passed from generation to generation among the men of the village.

Times: Open at all times. **Facilities:** 🅿 ♿

BALLYGAWLEY   MAP 01 C5

U S Grant Ancestral Homestead & Visitor Centre
Dergenagh Rd BT70 1TW
➲ *(off A4, 2m on Dergenagh road, signed)*
☎ 028 8555 7133
e-mail: killymaddy@dstbc.org
web: www.dungannon.gov.uk

Ancestral homestead of Ulysses S Grant, 18th President of the United States of America. The homestead and farmyard have been restored to the style and appearance of a mid-19th-century Irish smallholding. There are many amenities including a children's play area, purpose built barbecue and picnic tables and butterfly garden.

Times: Open by appointment only **Fee:** ✳ £1.50 (ch & concessions 75p). **Facilities:** 🅿 ♿ (wide doorway to audio-visual area/entrances/exits) ⊗ (ex guide dogs)

BEAGHMORE
MAP 01 C5

Beaghmore Stone Circles and Alignments
 FREE

☎ 028 9023 5000
web: www.ehsni.gov.uk

Discovered in the 1930s, these impressive, ritualistic stones have been dated back to the early Bronze, and maybe even Neolithic Ages. There are three pairs of stone circles, one single circle, stone rows or alignments and cairns, which range in height from one to four feet. This is an area littered with historic monuments, many discovered by people cutting turf.

Times: Open at all times. **Facilities:** ❷ ও

BENBURB
MAP 01 C5

Benburb Castle
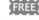 FREE

☎ 028 9023 5000
web: www.ehsni.gov.uk

The castle ruins - three towers and massive walls - are dramatically placed on a cliff-edge 120ft above the River Blackwater. The northwest tower is now restored and has dizzy cliff-edge views. The castle, built by Sir Richard Wingfield around 1615, is actually situated in the grounds of the Servite Priory. There are attractive walks down to the river.

Times: Castle grounds open at all times. Special arrangements, made in advance, necessary for access to flanker tower. **Facilities:** ❷ ও ❀

CASTLECAULFIELD
MAP 01 C5

Castle Caulfield
 FREE

☎ 028 9023 5000
web: www.ehsni.gov.uk

Sir Toby Caulfield, an Oxfordshire knight and ancestor of the Earls of Charlemont, built this manor house in 1619 on the site of an ancient fort. It was badly burnt in 1641, repaired and lived in by the Caulfield/Charlemont family until 1670. It boasts the rare distinction of having had Saint Oliver Plunkett and John Wesley preach in its grounds. Some fragments of the castle are re-used in the fine, large 17th-century parish church.

Times: Open at all times. **Facilities:** ℗ ও

COOKSTOWN
MAP 01 C5

Tullaghoge Fort
 FREE

➲ (2m S)
☎ 028 9023 5000
web: www.ehsni.gov.uk

This large hilltop earthwork, planted with trees, was once the headquarters of the O'Hagans, Chief Justices of the old kingdom of Tyrone. Between the 12th and 16th centuries the O'Neill Chiefs of Ulster were also crowned here - the King Elect was seated on a stone inauguration chair, new sandals were placed on his feet and he was then anointed and crowned. The last such ceremony was held here in the 1590s; in 1600 the stone throne was destroyed by order of Lord Mountjoy.

Times: Open at all times. **Facilities:** ❷

Wellbrook Beetling Mill
20 Wellbrook Rd, Corkhill BT80 9RY
➲ (4m W, 0.5m off A505)
☎ 028 8674 8210 & 8675 1735
e-mail: wellbrookl@nationaltrust.org.uk
web: www.ntni.org.uk

This 18th-century water-powered linen mill was used for bleaching and, until 1961, for finishing Irish linen. Beetling was the name given to the final process in linen making, when the material was beaten by 30 or so hammers (beetles) to achieve a smooth and slightly shiny finish.

Times: ✱ Open 15 Mar-Jun wknds & BHs, daily 12-6; Jul-Aug daily 12-6; Sep, wknds only 12-6. **Facilities:** ❷ ◧ ও toilets for disabled shop ⛟

DUNGANNON
MAP 01 C5

Tyrone Crystal Visitor Centre
 2 for 1

Tyrone Crystal, Killybrackey BT71 6TT
➲ (M1 junct 14/A45 to T-junct, left towards Dungannon. Attraction 2.5m on left, signed)
☎ 028 8772 5335
e-mail: annamarie@tyronecrystal.com
web: www.tyronecrystal.com

Crystal making in Tyrone is a comparatively modern enterprise, dating its beginnings from the days of Benjamin Edwards in the 1770s. Tyrone Crystal is hand-cut, and visitors can see this craft in action on guided tours of the factory. The spacious visitor centre and facilities contribute to a fascinating insight of the history and heritage of this industry.

Times: Open all year Visitor Centre Mon-Sat 9-5, Sun 1-5 (seasonal); Tour times Mon-Fri 11, 12, 2, 3. Sat tours prior booking only, no tours on BH.
Fee: £2 for tour. Visitor Centre free. **Facilities:** ❷ ⦿◧ ◧ ও (disabled parking spaces) toilets for disabled shop ❀ (ex guide dogs) ⛟

NEWTOWNSTEWART
MAP 01 C5

Harry Avery's Castle
 FREE

➲ (0.75m SW)
☎ 028 9023 5000
web: www.ehsni.gov.uk

The hilltop ruins of a Gaelic stone castle, built around the 14th century by one of the O'Neill chiefs, are the remains of the oldest surviving Irish-built castle in the north. Only the great twin towers of the gatehouse are left. A stairway enables the public to gain access to one of these.

Times: Open at all times. **Facilities:** ❀ ⛟

Are there any excellent Days Out that we have missed? Use the Readers' Report form at the back of the book to tell us about them.

OMAGH   MAP 01 C5

Ulster American Folk Park
BT78 5QY
➲ (5m NW Omagh on A5)
☎ 028 8224 3292
e-mail: info@uafp.co.uk
web: www.folkpark.com

An outdoor museum that traces the history of Ulster's links with America and the emigration of Ulster residents to the US during the 18th and 19th centuries. The 70-acre site is divided into two parts - Old World and New World. There are demonstrations of Old and New World crafts, and a visitor centre, with exhibitions and audio-visual presentations. The Centre for Emigration Studies is based here, with a research library and emigration database - please ring for details.

Times: ✴ Open all year Etr-Sep, daily 10.30-6, Sun & BH 11-6.30; Oct-Etr Mon-Fri 10.30-5. (Last admission 1hr 30mins before closing).
Facilities: ❷ 🍽️ 🍴 📖 ♿ toilets for disabled shop ⊗ (ex guide dogs) 🚩

STEWARTSTOWN   MAP 01 C5

Mountjoy Castle   FREE
Magheralamfield
➲ (3m SE, off B161)
☎ 028 9023 5000
web: www.ehsni.gov.uk

Ruins of an early 17th-century brick and stone fort, with four rectangular towers, overlooking Lough Neagh. The fort was built for Lord Deputy Mountjoy during his campaign against Hugh O'Neill, Earl of Tyrone. It was captured and re-captured by the Irish and English during the 17th century and was also used by the armies of James II and William III.

Times: Open at all times. **Facilities:** ❷

STRABANE   MAP 01 C5

Gray's Printing Press
49 Main St BT82 8AU
➲ (in centre of Strabane)
☎ 028 7188 4094
web: www.ntni.org.uk

Strabane was once an important printing and book-publishing centre, the only relic of this is a small shop in Main Street which now houses a museum illustrating the history of Strabane. The Print Museum, in a separate building, contains three 19th-century presses and shows the development of printing techniques over 150 years.

Times: ✴ Open Apr-Sep, Tue-Sat 2-5. **Facilities:** ℗ (100yds) ♿ toilets for disabled ⊗ (ex guide dogs) 🚩

19th century Beetling water-powered cloth mill, Wellbrook, Cookstown, Tyrone

Ireland

Republic of Ireland

Blarney Castle
Co Cork

If you've ever wondered why it's known as the Emerald Isle, it will become apparent as soon as you arrive. The lush countryside is amazingly green, and you're never far from water, from the craggy Atlantic -coast, the countless loughs, rivers and bogs, to the regular falls of rain, or Irish mist. County Kerry is justifiably famous for the beauty of its scenery, best explored by following the Ring of Kerry, while The Burren in County Clare offers a completely different landscape of exposed limestone and beautiful wildflowers. Visit Blarney Castle and kiss the Blarney Stone ro receive 'the gift of the gab'. Dublin is an elegant and cosmopolitan city, and certainly has more than its share of cultural wealth, having been home to many famous writers and musicians.

CO CLARE

BALLYVAUGHAN
MAP 01 B3

Aillwee Cave
2 for 1

➲ *(3m S of Ballyvaughan. Signed from Galway and Ennis)*

☎ 065 707 7036

e-mail: barbara@aillweecave.ie

web: www.aillweecave.ie

An underground network of caves beneath the world famous Burren. Guided tours take you through large caverns, over bridged chasms and alongside thunderous waterfalls. There is a craftshop, a dairy where cheese is made, a speciality food shop and a tearoom. Santa uses the cave as a workshop around Christmas time, while Easter sees a massive egg hunt in the woods. In addition, a garden shop has opened here in the last year. Special Events: Santa's Workshop, appointments necessary, Dec 2006 & 2007.

Times: Open all year from 10. Dec by appointment only. **Fee:** € 12 (ch€ 5.50 pen € 9). Family ticket € 29-€ 35 **Facilities:** ❷ ⬛ 🍴 licensed ⬛ ♿ toilets for disabled shop garden centre ⊗ (ex guide dogs) ⬛

BUNRATTY
MAP 01 B3

Bunratty Castle & Folk Park

➲ *(located 10km from Shannon Airport just off the main dual carriageway (N18) between Limerick and Ennis. Follow the tourist sign from the N18)*

☎ 061 360788

e-mail: reservations@shannondev.ie

web: www.shannonheritage.com

Magnificent Bunratty Castle was built around 1425. The restored castle contains mainly 15th and 16th century furnishings and tapestries. Within its grounds is Bunratty Folk Park where 19th-century Irish life is tellingly recreated. Rural farmhouses, a village street and Bunratty House with its formal Regency gardens are recreated and furnished, as they would have appeared at the time.

Times: Open all year (ex Good Fri and 24-25 Dec. Low season : 9.30-4.15. (Last admission 3.30) High season : 9-5:30 (Last admission 4.15) Castle closes 4pm all year round. Times subject to change. **Fee:** ✱ Castle & Folk Park € 13 (ch€ 6.50, pen € 7.50 & student € 8.95). **Facilities:** ❷ ⬛ 🍴 licensed ♿ toilets for disabled shop garden centre ⬛

KILLALOE
MAP 01 B3

Brian Boru Heritage Centre
2 for 1

➲ *(N7 via Parkway Rdbt in Limerick city via Annacotty, Lisnagry and Birdhill. Turn left at Ballina R494)*

☎ 061 360788

e-mail: reservations@shannondev.ie

web: www.shannonheritage.com

The 11th century High King of Ireland, Brian Boru one of the most influential and colourful figures in Irish history. The heritage centre reveals the story of Brian Boru through a series of colourful exhibits, graphic illustrations and inter-active audio-visual presentation.

Times: Open May-Sep daily, 10-6 **Fee:** ✱ € 3.15 (ch € 1.55) **Facilities:** ❷ ♿ shop ⬛

LISCANNOR
MAP 01 B3

Cliffs of Moher Visitors Centre

➲ *(6m NW of Lahinch)*

☎ 065 7081 565

e-mail: reservations@shannondev.ie

web: www.cliffsofmoher.ie

The Cliffs of Moher stand as a giant natural rampart against the aggressive might of the Atlantic Ocean, rising in places to 700ft, and stretch for almost 5 miles. O'Brien's Tower was built in the early 19th century as a viewing point for tourists on the highest point. A new visitors centre is set to open in early 2007, and will include a state-of-the-art interpretation area.

Times: Open Visitor Centre all year. Oct-Apr 9.30-5.30. May-Sep: 8:30-9:00pm **Fee:** O'Briens Tower € 4 (ch€ 2.50).Family € 11.98 Facilities charge per vehicle. Car € 8. Separate charge for Buses and Coaches - see website. **Facilities:** ❷ (charged) ⬛ 🍴 licensed ♿ (induction loops at reception & audio visual theatre) toilets for disabled shop ⊗ (ex guide dogs in grounds) ⬛

QUIN
MAP 01 B3

Craggaunowen The Living Past Experience
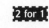

➲ *(signed from N18 Limerick to Galway road, off R462 from Cratloe and R469 from Ennis)*

☎ 061 360788

e-mail: reservations@shannondev.ie

web: www.shannonheritage.com

The project includes a reconstructed ring fort and replicas of furniture, tools and utensils. Also on display is the 'Brendan', a replica of the leather canoe used by St Brendan the Navigator in the 6th century. The boat was sailed across the Atlantic Ocean in 1976 and 1977. A Bronze Age lake dwelling is currently under construction.

Times: Open Apr-mid Oct, daily 10-6 (last admission 5). **Fee:** ✱ € 7.85 (ch € 4.75, concessions € 5.85). **Facilities:** ❷ ⬛ ♿ toilets for disabled shop ⬛

Ireland

Knappogue Castle & Walled Garden `2 for 1`
⮡ *(off N18 3m from Quin)*
☎ 061 360788
e-mail: reservations@shannondev.ie
web: www.shannonheritage.com

Built in 1467, Knappogue has a long and varied history. Occupied by Cromwell's troops in 1641 and completely restored in the mid-19th century, the castle fell into disrepair in the 1900s. In 1966 the careful restoration was completed and today the castle is famous for its medieval events. The attractive restored Victorian walled garden includes among many of its features a collection of plants from the Victorian era.

Times: Open May-mid Sep daily 9:30-5:30 **Fee:** ✱ €6.95 (ch €3.15 pen €3.10) **Facilities:** ⛄ shop 🛒

CO CORK

BLARNEY   MAP 01 B2

Blarney Castle & Rock Close
⮡ *(5m from Cork on main road towards Limerick)*
☎ 021 4385252
e-mail: info@blarneycastle.ie
web: www.blarneycastle.ie

The site of the famous Blarney Stone, known the world over for the eloquence it is said to impart to those who kiss it. The stone is in the upper tower of the castle, and, held by your feet, you must lean backwards down the inside of the battlements in order to receive the 'gift of the gab'.

Times: Open Blarney Castle & Rock Close. Mon-Fri, May & Sep 10-4, Jun-Aug 9-7. Oct-Apr 9-sundown or 6. Sun, Summer 9.30-5.30, Winter 9.30-sundown. Closed 24-25 Dec. **Fee:** ✱ Blarney Castle & Rock Close €8 (ch 8-14 €2.50, concessions €6). Family ticket (2ad+2ch) €18.00 **Facilities:** ⛄ 📷 ⛄ shop 🐾 (ex guide dogs)

CARRIGTWOHILL   MAP 01 B2
(CARRIGTOHILL)

Fota Arboretum & Gardens   `FREE`
Fota Estate
⮡ *(14km from Cork on Cobh road)*
☎ 021 4812728
e-mail: info@heritageireland.ie
web: www.heritageireland.ie

Fota Arboretum contains an extensive collection of trees and shrubs extending over an area of approx 27 acres and includes features such as an ornamental pond and Italian walled gardens. The collection includes many tender plants that could not be grown at inland locations, with many examples of exotic plants from the Southern Hemisphere.

continued

Times: Arboretum - open Apr-Oct, Mon-Sat 9-6, Sun 11-6; Nov-Mar, Mon-Sat 9-5, Sun 11-5. Walled Gardens - Apr-Oct, Mon-Fri. Selected Sun openings please ring for times and dates. **Facilities:** ⛄ (charged) ⛄ toilets for disabled.

Fota Wildlife Park
Fota Estate
⮡ *(16km E of Cork. From N25 (Cork to Waterford road) take Cobh road)*
☎ 021 4812678
e-mail: info@fotawildlife.ie
web: www.fotawildlife.ie

Established with the primary aim of conservation, Fota has more than 90 species of exotic wildlife in open, natural surroundings. Many of the animals wander freely around the park. Giraffes, zebras, ostriches, antelope, cheetahs and a wide array of waterfowl are among the species here.

Times: Open 17 Mar-Oct, daily, 10-6 (Sun 11-6) (last admission 5); Nov-17 Mar 10-4.30 (Sun 11-4.30). (Last admission 3.30). **Fee:** €11.50 (ch, concessions €7, ch under 3 free). Family day ticket €45. **Facilities:** ⛄ (charged) 🍴 📷 ⛄ (ramps where required) toilets for disabled shop 🐾 🛒

CLONAKILTY   MAP 01 B2

West Cork Model Village Railway
Inchydoney Rd
⮡ *(From Cork N71 West Cork left at junct for Inchydoney Island, signed at road junct. Village on bay side of Clonakilty)*
☎ 023 33224
e-mail: modelvillage@eircom.net
web: www.modelvillage.ie

This miniature world depicts Irish towns as they were in the 1940s, with models of the West Cork Railway and various animated scenes.

continued

The tea room is set in authentic railway carriages that overlook picturesque Clonakilty Bay. Also take a guided tour of Clonakilty and the surrounding area on the road train.

West Cork Model Village Railway

Times: ✱ Open daily Feb-Oct 11-5; Jul-Aug, 10-6. **Facilities:** ℗ 💺 🏛 ♿ toilets for disabled shop ⊗ (ex guide dogs) ◀

COBH   MAP 01 B2

The Queentown Story   `2 for 1`

Cobh Railway Station

➲ *(off N25, follow signs for Cobh. Attraction at Deepwater Quay, adjacent to train station)*

☎ 021 4813591
e-mail: info@cobhheritage.com
web: www.cobhheritage.com

A dramatic exhibition of the origins, history and legends of Cobh. Between 1848 and 1950 over 3 million Irish people were deported from Cobh on convict ships. Visitors can explore the conditions onboard these vessels and learn about the harbour's connections with the *Lusitania* and the *Titanic*.

Times: Open May-Nov, 10-6 (last admission 5). Nov-May, 10-5 (last admission 4) **Fee:** ✱ €6 (ch & student u 18 €3, pen €5) Family ticket €16.50 **Facilities:** ℗ 💺 🍴 licensed 🏛 ♿ (fully wheelchair accessible, wide access) toilets for disabled shop ⊗ (ex guide dogs) ◀

CORK   MAP 01 B2

Cork City Gaol   `2 for 1`

Convent Av, Sundays Well

➲ *(2km NW from Patrick St off Sundays Well Rd)*

☎ 021 4305022
e-mail: corkgaol@indigo.ie
web: www.corkcitygaol.com

A restored 19th-century prison building. Furnished cells, lifelike characters and sound effects combine to allow visitors to experience day-to-day life for prisoners and gaoler. There is an audio-visual presentation of the social history of Cork City. Individual sound tours are available in a number of languages. A permanent exhibition, the Radio Museum Experience, is located in the restored 1920s broadcasting studio, home to Cork's first radio station, 6CK.

continued

Unfortunately the 1st and 2nd floors are not accessible to wheelchair users.

Cork City Gaol

Times: Open all year Mar-Oct, daily 9.30-6; Nov-Feb, daily 10-5. (Last admission 1hr before closing). Closed 23-28 Dec. **Fee:** ✱ €6 (ch €3.50, concessions €5) Family ticket €18 **Facilities:** ℗ 💺 🏛 ♿ (customer care policy - individual attention) toilets for disabled shop ⊗ (ex guide dogs)

Cork Public Museum

Fitzgerald Park, Mardyke

➲ *(N of University College)*

☎ 021 4270679
e-mail: museum@corkcity.ie

Displays illustrating the history of the city are housed in this museum. The collections cover the economic, social and municipal history from the Mesolithic period onwards. There are fine collections of Cork Silver and Glass and Youghal Needlepoint Lace.

Times: ✱ Open all year, Jun-Aug Mon-Fri 11-1 & 2.15-6, Sun 3-5; Sep-May Mon-Fri 11-1 & 2.15-5, Sun 3-5. Closed Sat, BH wknds & PH **Facilities:** ℗ (100yds) shop ⊗ (ex guide dogs)

GLENGARRIFF   MAP 01 B2

Garinish Island

➲ *(1.5km boat trip from Glengarriff)*

☎ 027 63040

Ilnacullin is a small island of 37 acres known to horticulturists and lovers of trees and shrubs all around the world as an island garden of rare beauty. The gardens of Ilnacullin owe their existence to the creative partnership, some 80 years ago, of Annan Bryce, then owner of the island and Harold Peto, architect and garden designer.

Times: Open Mar & Oct, Mon-Sat, 10-4.30, Sun 1-5; Apr, Mon-Sat, 10-4.30 Sun 1-6.30; May & Sep, Mon-Sat, 10-6.30, Sun 12-6.30; Jun, Mon-Sat, 10-6.30, Sun 11-6.30, Jul & Aug, Mon-Sat 9.30-6.30, Sun 11- 6.30. Last landing 1 hour before closing. **Fee:** ✱ €3.70 (ch & students €1.30, pen €2.60) Family ticket €8.70. Group rate €2.50 each. **Facilities:** 💺 🏛 ♿ (limited access) toilets for disabled

KINSALE

MAP 01 B2

Charles Fort

Summer Cove

➲ (3km from Kinsale)

☎ 021 4772263

e-mail: charlesfort@opw.ie

web: www.heritageireland.ie

Built as part of the fortifications of the Irish coast in the late 17th century, Charles Fort was named after King Charles II. After the Battle of the Boyne in 1690, Williamite forces attacked and successfully besieged Charles Fort and the nearby James Fort, both of which held out for King James. The Fort also played a role in the Napoleonic Wars and was made a National Monument in 1973.

Times: Open mid Mar-Oct, daily 10-6; Nov-mid Mar, daily 10-5. Last admission 45 minutes before closing. **Fee:** ✱ €3.70 (ch & student €1.30 & pen €2.60). Family ticket €8.70. Group rate €2.60 each.
Facilities: ℗ 💷 🗐 ♿ (lift) toilets for disabled 🐾 (ex guide dogs)

Desmond Castle

Cork St

➲ (R600 from Cork city to Kinsale. From post office, 1st left then right, opposite Regional Museum then left and right again, castle on left)

☎ 021 4774855

e-mail: desmondcastle@opw.ie

web: www.desmondcastle.ie

Built by the Earl of Desmond around the beginning of the 16th century, this tower was originally a custom house, but has also served as an ordnance office, prison, workhouse, stable and meeting place for the Local Defence Force during World War II. In 1938 it was declared a National Monument and restored. The Castle now houses the International Museum of Wine.

Times: Open mid Apr-Oct, daily 10-6. Last admission 45 mins before closing. **Fee:** ✱ €2.90, (ch & students €1.30, pen €2.10) Family €7.40 **Facilities:** ℗ (200mtrs) (parking discs required in town) 🗐 🐾 (ex guide dogs)

MIDLETON

MAP 01 C2

Old Midleton Distillery

➲ (E end of main street on left. Well signed)

☎ 021 4613594

e-mail: bookings@omd.ie

web: www.jamesonwhiskey.com

A tour of the Old Midleton Distillery consists of a 15-minute audio/visual presentation, then a 35-minute guided tour of the Old Distillery and then back to the Jameson Bar for a whiskey tasting -

continued

mineral water is available for children. The guided tour and audio-visual aids are available in seven languages.

Old Midleton Distillery

Times: Open Nov-Feb daily, tours 11.30, 2.30 & 4. Mar-Oct daily 10-6 (last tour 5). Closed Good Fri & Xmas **Fee:** ✱ €8.50 (ch €3.50) family ticket €22 **Facilities:** ℗ 💷 🍴 licensed 🗐 ♿ toilets for disabled shop 🐾 (ex certain areas/guide dogs) 🍽

CO DONEGAL

BALLYSHANNON

MAP 01 B5

The Water Wheels

FREE

Abbey Assaroe

➲ (cross Abbey River on Rossnowlagh Rd, next turning left & follow signs)

☎ 071 9851580

Abbey Assaroe was founded by Cistercian Monks from Boyle Abbey in the late 12th century, who excelled in water engineering and canalised the river to turn water wheels for mechanical power. Two restored 12th-century mills, one is used as coffee shop and restaurant; the other houses a small museum related to the history of the Cistercians. Interesting walks in the vicinity.

Times: Open May-Oct, daily 10.30-6.30 **Facilities:** ℗ 💷 🍴 licensed 🗐 ♿ toilets for disabled shop garden centre

DONEGAL

MAP 01 B5

Donegal Castle

☎ 074 9722405

e-mail: donegalcastle@opw.ie

This restored 15th-century castle and adjoining 17th-century ruined English manor house contain exhibitions of Irish historical events. Guided tours are available.

Times: Open mid Mar-end Oct daily 10-6; Nov-6 Mar (incl) wknds, Fri, Sat, Sun 9.30-4.30 Last admission 45 mins before closing. **Fee:** ✱ €3.70 (ch & students €1.30, pen €2). Family ticket (2 adults & 3 ch) €8.50 **Facilities:** ℗ 🐾 (ex guide dogs)

Ireland

LETTERKENNY — MAP 01 C5

Glebe House & Gallery
Churchill
➲ *(signed from Letterkenny on R251)*
☎ 074 9137071
web: www.glebegallery@opw.ie

This Regency house, set in beautiful woodland gardens along the shore of Lough Gartan, was given to the nation along with his art collection by artist Derek Hill. The interior of the house is decorated with original wallpapers and textiles by William Morris.

Times: Open Easter daily 11-6.30 Closed until mid May. Mid May-Sep, Sat-Thu 11-6.30 (Closed Fri). Last tour 1 hour before closing. **Fee:** ✱ €2.90 (ch & student €1.30, pen €2). Family ticket €7. Group rate €2.10 each. **Facilities:** ❷ 💺 🗐 க் ⊗ (ex guide dogs)

Glenveagh National Park & Castle `2 for 1`
Churchill
➲ *(left off N56 onto L77)*
☎ 074 9137090 & 9137262
e-mail: talchorn@duchas.ie
web: www.heritageireland.ie

Over 40,000 acres of mountains, glens, lakes and woods. A Scottish-style castle is surrounded by one of the finest gardens in Ireland, contrasting with the rugged surroundings.

Times: Open daily, St. Patrick's Day 17 Mar-1st Sun in Nov **Fee:** Park: free, Castle €3 (ch & students €1.50, pen €2). Family ticket €7, group 20+ €2. Buses €1 &€2 **Facilities:** ❷ 💺 🍴 🗐 க் (visitor centre, gardens have paths) toilets for disabled shop

LIFFORD — MAP 01 C5

Cavanacor Historic House & Art Gallery
Ballindrait
➲ *(1.5m from town off N14 Strabane/Letterkenny road)*
☎ 074 9141143
web: www.parsons.edu/~cokane/cavanacorgallery

Built in the early 1600s and commanding a view of the Clonleigh Valley and the River Deele, Cavanacor House is the ancestral home of James Knox Polk, 11th President of the USA (1845-1849). King James II dined under the sycamore tree in front of the house in 1689. There are over 10 acres of landscaped gardens and an old-fashioned walled garden. The Art Gallery will feature exhibitions of new work by national and international artists. Please ring for details.

Times: ✱ Open Etr & Jul-Aug Tue-Sat 12-6, Sun 2-6. Art gallery open all year **Facilities:** ❷ 💺 🍴 🗐 க் shop 🍴

The Old Courthouse NEW `2 for 1`
Visitor Centre, The Diamond
☎ 091 41733
e-mail: info@liffordoldcourthouse.com
web: www.liffordoldcourthouse.com

One of Ireland's oldest courthouse and jail provides an insight into legal history and some of the terrible conditions endured by prisoners in the 18th century. Witness re-enactments of famous trials held in this historic building.

Times: Open all year, Mon-Fri, 10-5 & Sun 12.30-5 (last tour 4). Closed Sat & BHs. **Fee:** €6 (ch €3, concessions €4) **Facilities:** ℗ 100mtrs 💺 🍴 licensed shop ⊗ (ex assist dogs) 🍴

CO DUBLIN

BALBRIGGAN — MAP 01 D4

Ardgillan Castle `2 for 1`
➲ *(R127 or M1 past Dublin Airport then follow signs)*
☎ 01 8492212

A large and elegant country manor house built in 1738, set in 194 acres of parkland, overlooking the sea and coast as far as the Mourne Mountains. There is a permanent exhibition of the 17th century 'Down Survey' maps and various temporary exhibitions. Tours of the Gardens (June, July and August) begin at 3.30pm every Thursday. Guided tours of the house are conducted daily.

Times: Open all year Apr-Sep, Tue-Sun & BHs 11-6 (daily Jul-Aug); Oct-Mar, Wed-Sun & BHs 11-4.30. Closed 23 Dec-1 Jan. **Fee:** ✱ €6 (concessions €4.50) Family ticket €12.50 **Facilities:** ❷ 💺 🗐 க் toilets for disabled shop ⊗ (ex guide dogs)

DONABATE — MAP 01 D4

Newbridge House and Traditional Farm
Newbridge Demesne
➲ *(take N1 and follow signs for Donabate)*
☎ 01 8436534 & 8462184
e-mail: newbridgehouse@fingalcoco.ie

Newbridge House was designed by George Semple and built in 1737 for Charles Cobbe, Archbishop of Dublin. Set in 350 acres of parkland, the house contains many splendidly refurbished rooms featuring plasterwork, furniture and paintings. The house also features a fully restored courtyard surrounded by; a dairy, estate workers house, carpenters shop and blacksmiths forge. The grounds contain a 29 acre traditional farm with many rare breeds and children's playground.

Times: ✱ Open Apr-Sep Tue-Sat 10-5, Sun & PH 2-6; Oct-Mar Sat-Sun & PH 2-5. Parties at other times by arrangement. **Facilities:** ❷ 💺 shop ⊗ guide dogs 🍴

DUBLIN — MAP 01 D4

The Casino
off Malahide Rd, Marino
➲ *(Turn left at pedestrian lights after Dublin Five Brigade Training HQ)*
☎ 01 8331618
e-mail: casinomarino@opw.ie
web: www.heritageireland.ie

Designed in 1757 by Sir William Chambers as a pleasure house for James Caulfield, 1st Earl of Charlemont, The Casino is possibly one of the finest 18th-century neo-Classical buildings in Europe. Its name means "small house", but The Casino surprisingly contains 16 finely-decorated rooms.

Times: Open Feb & Mar, Sat & Sun 12-4; Apr Sat & Sun 12-5; May & Oct daily 10-5; Jun-Sep, daily 10-6; Nov & Dec, Sat & Sun 12-4. Last admission 45 mins before closing. **Fee:** ✱ €2.90 (ch & students €1.30, pen €2.10). Family ticket €7.40 **Facilities:** ❷ 🗐 க் ⊗ (ex guide dogs)

The Chester Beatty Library `FREE`

The Clock Tower Building, Dublin Castle
➲ *(10 mins walk from Trinity College, up Dame St towards Christ Church Cathedral)*
☎ 01 4070750
e-mail: info@cbl.ie
web: www.cbl.ie

The contents of this fascinating gallery was bequeathed to Ireland by its first honorary citizen, American mining engineer and collector, Sir Alfred Chester Beatty (1875-1968). The collection includes manuscripts, prints, icons, miniatures, and objets d'art of great importance from 2700BC to the present day. See illuminated copies of the Qur'an and the Bible, Egyptian papyrus texts, and Buddhist paintings.

Times: ✱ Open all year, May-Sep, Mon-Fri 10-5; Oct-Apr, Tue-Fri 10-5, Sat 11-5, Sun 1-5. Closed BHs. **Facilities:** Ⓟ (5mins walk) 🍽 ⭗ ♿ toilets for disabled shop ⊗ (ex guide dogs)

Christ Church Cathedral

Christchurch Place
➲ *(at top end of Dame St)*
☎ 01 6778099
e-mail: welcome@cccdub.ie
web: www.cccdub.ie

Founded in 1030, the present building dates from 1180 with a major restoration in the 1870s. The crypt is the second largest medieval crypt in Britain or Ireland. There are daily services and choral services on Sundays and during the week.

Times: Open all year, Mon-Fri 9.45-5, Sat & Sun 10-5. Closed St Stephens Day 27 Dec. **Facilities:** Ⓟ (100yds) 🗊 ♿ (for access to crypt advance notice required) shop ⊗ (ex guide dogs) 🔙

Drimnagh Castle

Long Mile Rd, Drimnagh DL12
➲ *(Dame St, left at Christchurch Cathedral into Patrick St, right into Cork St, through Dolphins Barn up to Crumlin Rd, past Halfway House. 500yds on right)*
☎ 01 4502530 & 4508927
e-mail: drimnaghcastle@eircom.net

The last surviving medieval castle in Ireland with a flooded moat, Drimnagh dates back to the 13th century and was inhabited until 1954. The Castle consists of a restored Great Hall and medieval undercroft, a tall battlement tower and lookout posts, and other separate buildings including stables, an old coach house and a folly. One of the most attractive features of Drimnagh is the garden, a formal 17th-century layout with box hedges, yews and mop heads.

Times: Open Apr-Oct, Wed & Sun 12-5; Nov-Mar, Sun 2-5. (Last tour 4). Other times by appointment. Large groups advisable to book
Facilities: Ⓟ 🗊 ♿ (limited access gravel courtyard and gardens) ⊗ (ex guide dogs)

Dublin Castle

Dame St
☎ 01 6777129

With two towers and a partial wall, this is the city's most outstanding legacy of the Middle Ages. Of interest are the Record Tower, state apartments, Church of the Most Holy Trinity and Heraldic Museum. The inauguration of the President of Ireland and related ceremonies are held in St. Patrick's Hall, an elegant state apartment.

Times: ✱ Open all year, Mon-Fri 10-5, Sat-Sun & BH 2-5. Closed 24-26 Dec & Good Fri. **Facilities:** Ⓟ ⭗ ♿ toilets for disabled

Dublin City Gallery The Hugh Lane `FREE`

Charlemont House, Parnell Square Off O'Connell St `2 for 1`
➲ *(Parnell Monument At the top of Parnell Square)*
☎ 01 2222550
e-mail: info@hughlane.ie
web: www.hughlane.ie

Situated in Charlemont House, a fine Georgian building, the gallery's collection includes one of the most extensive collections of 20th-century Irish art. A superb range of international and Irish paintings, sculpture, works on paper and stained glass is also on show. Possibly the most fascinating aspect of the gallery is Francis Bacon's Studio, a complete reconstruction of the painters studio, and a complete database of all the items in it. There are public lectures every Sunday and regular concerts (at noon on Sundays) throughout the year. 2 for 1 voucher - check Gallery for details.

Times: Open all year, Tue-Thu 10-6, Fri-Sat 10-5, Sun 11-5. Closed Mon, Good Fri & 24-25 Dec. **Facilities:** Ⓟ (100mtrs) (meter parking) 🍽 ♿ (ramp & reserved parking) toilets for disabled shop ⊗ (ex guide dogs)

Dublinia & The Viking World `2 for 1`

St Michael's Hill, Christ Church
☎ 01 6794611
e-mail: info@dublinia.ie
web: www.dublinia.ie

The story of medieval Dublin. Housed in the former Synod Hall beside Christ Church Cathedral and developed by the Medieval Trust, Dublinia recreates the period from the arrival of Strongbow and the Anglo-Normans in 1170 to the closure of the monasteries by Henry VIII in 1540.

Times: Open Apr-Sep 10-5; Oct-Mar, Mon-Sat 11-4, Sun & BH 10-4.30. Closed 23-26 Dec & 17 Mar. **Fee:** ✱ €6 (ch €3.75 concessions €5). Family ticket (2ad+3ch) €16 **Facilities:** Ⓟ (100yds) 🍽 🗊 ♿ (2 floors accessible, but bridge and tower are not) toilets for disabled shop ⊗ (ex guide dogs) 🔙

Dublin Writers Museum

18 Parnell Square
➲ *(on Parnell Sq, at North end of O'Connell St)*
☎ 01 8722077
e-mail: writers@dublintourism.ie
web: www.writersmuseum.com

The Dublin Writers Museum is housed in a restored 18th-century mansion and is a collection featuring personal items, portraits, books and letters relating to Dublin's most important literary figures, including Swift, Sheridan, Shaw, Wilde, Yeats, Joyce and Beckett. The mansion is a pleasure in itself, with sumptuous plasterwork and decorative stained windows. There is a special room dedicated to childrens' literature and a full programme of workshops, lectures and receptions.

Times: Open all year, Mon-Sat 10-5, Sun & BH 11-5; Jun-Aug, Mon-Fri 10-6. **Fee:** ✱ €6.70 (ch €4.20, concessions €5.70). Family ticket €19. Group discounts & combined ticket for related attractions available.
Facilities: Ⓟ (charged) 🍽 ⭗ licensed shop ⊗ (ex guide dogs) 🔙

Ireland

Dublin Zoo

Phoenix Park

➲ *(10mins bus ride from city centre)*

☎ 01 4748900

e-mail: info@dublinzoo.ie

web: www.dublinzoo.ie

Dublin Zoo first opened to the public in 1830, making it one of the oldest zoos in the world and has consistently been Ireland's favourite attraction. The new 'African Plains' is the biggest single development undertaken by the zoo. This 30-acre development has doubled the size of the zoo and provides spacious new areas for African species. Dublin Zoo is a modern zoo with conservation, education & study as its mission. The majority of the animals here have been born and bred in zoos and are part of global breeding programmes to ensure their continued survival.

Times: ✱ Open Mar-Oct, Mon-Sat 9.30-6, Sun 10.30-6; Nov-Feb, daily 10.30-dusk. **Facilities:** ❷ 💺 ❗️◎ licensed ⚑ (wheelchairs available) toilets for disabled shop ❸ ⬛

Guinness Storehouse

St James's Gate Brewery

➲ *(from Dame St near Trinity College keep straight, follow road around passing Christchurch on right into Thomas St. Pass main brewery gates on left. At junct of James's St & Echlin St take left turn. At top of road turn left then 1st left on to Market St - pedestrian entrance on left)*

☎ 01 4084800 & 4538364

e-mail: guinness-storehouse@guinness.com

web: www.guinness-storehouse.com

Established in 1876, the Storehouse remained crammed with hopsacks until 1957, then it was converted and is now a high-tech, 21st-century mix of an art centre, conference facility, restaurant and bar. Find out about the drink's history and then sample a glass.

Times: ✱ Open daily 9.30-5 (last admission 5). Late summer opening Jul & Aug until 8pm. **Facilities:** ❷ 💺 ◎ ❑ ⚑ toilets for disabled shop ❸ ⬛

Howth Castle Rhododendron Gardens

Howth

➲ *(9m NE of city centre, by coast road to Howth. Before Howth follow signs for Deer Park Hotel)*

☎ 01 8322624 & 8322256

e-mail: sales@deerpark.iol.ie

Overlooking the sea on the north side of Dublin Bay, the rhododendron walks command spectacular views of the Castle and Ireland's Eye. The flowers are at their best in May and June. Visitors should be aware that the gardens are in some disrepair and the paths somewhat rough and overgrown in parts.

Times: ✱ Open all year, daily 8am-dusk. Closed 25 Dec. **Facilities:** ❷ ⚑ (steep hills unsuitable, ramped entrance) toilets for disabled ❸ (ex guide dogs) ⬛

Irish Museum of Modern Art

Royal Hospital, Military Rd, Kilmainham

➲ *(3.5km from city centre, just off N7 opposite Heuston Station)*

☎ 01 6129900

e-mail: info@imma.ie

web: www.imma.ie

Housed in the Royal Hospital Kilmainham, an impressive 17th-century building, the Irish Museum of Modern Art is Ireland's leading national institution for the collection and presentation of modern and contemporary art. It presents a wide variety of art and artists' ideas in a dynamic programme of exhibitions, which regularly includes bodies of work from the museum's own collection, its award-winning Education and Community Department and the Studio and National Programmes.

Times: ✱ Open all year, Tue-Sat 10-5.30, Sun & BHs 12-5.30. Closed Mon & 24-26 Dec. **Facilities:** ❷ 💺 ❑ ⚑ toilets for disabled shop ❸ (ex guide dogs)

James Joyce Centre

35 North Great George's St

➲ *(signed from N end of O'Connell Street and Parnell Square)*

☎ 01 8788547

e-mail: marketing@jamesjoyce.ie

web: www.jamesjoyce.ie

Situated in a beautifully restored 18th-century Georgian town house, the Centre is dedicated to the promotion of a greater interest in, and understanding of, the life and works of James Joyce. After an introductory film visitors follow a self-guided tour through the house, that includes the door to No.7 Eccles Street, home of Leopold Bloom, the hero of *Ulysses*; furniture from Joyce's Paris flat, and an extensive reference library.

Times: ✱ Open all year, Mon-Sat 9.30-5, Sun & BH 12.30-5. Closed Good Fri & 24-26 Dec. **Facilities:** ❷ ❑ ⚑ toilets for disabled shop ❸ (ex guide dogs) ⬛

Kilmainham Gaol

Inchicore Rd

➲ *(3.5km from city centre)*

☎ 01 4535984

web: www.kilmainhamgaol.opw.ie

One of the largest unoccupied gaols in Europe, covering some of the most heroic and tragic events in Ireland's emergence as a modern

continued

457

nation from the 1720s. Attractions include a major exhibition detailing the political and penal history of the prison and its restoration.

Times: Open Apr-Sep, daily 9.30-6 (last admission 4.45); Oct-Mar, Mon-Sat 9.30-5.30 (last admission 4), Sun 10-6 (last admission 4.45). Access by guided tour only. **Fee:** ✱ €5.30 (ch & students €2.10, pen €3.70). Family ticket €11.50 **Facilities:** ℗ (on street) ☕ 🎁 ♿ (tours available by prior appointment) toilets for disabled ⊗

See advert on page 457

Marsh's Library

St Patrick's Close

➲ *(beside St Patrick Cathedral)*

☎ 01 4543511

e-mail: keeper@marshlibrary.ie

web: www.marshlibrary.ie

The first public library in Ireland, dating from 1701. Designed by William Robinson, the interior has been unchanged for 300 years. The collection is of approximately 25,000 volumes of 16th, 17th and early 18th century books.

Times: Open all year Mon & Wed-Fri, 10-1 & 2-5; Sat 10.30-1.
Fee: ✱ €2.50 (ch free, concessions €1.50). maybe subject to change.
Facilities: ℗ (100mtrs) 🎁 ⊗ (except guide dogs) 🚌

National Botanic Gardens

FREE

Glasnevin

➲ *(on Botanic Road, between N1 and N2)*

☎ 01 8374388 & 8377596

Ireland's premier Botanic Gardens, covers a total area of 19.5 hectares (48 acres), part of which is the natural flood plain of the River Tolka. The Gardens contain a large plant collection, which includes approximately 20,000 species and cultivated varieties. There are four ranges of glasshouses including the restored Curvilinear Range. Notable features include herbaceous borders, rose garden, rockery, alpine yard, arboretum, extensive shrub collections and wall plants.

Times: ✱ Open all year, Gardens: Summer Mon-Sat 9-6, Sun 11-6; Winter Mon-Sat 10-4.30, Sun 11-4.30. (Closed 25 Dec). Glasshouses: Summer Mon-Wed & Fri 9-5, Thu 9-3.15, Sat 9-5.45, Sun 2-5.45; Winter, Mon-Wed, Fri & Sat 10-4.15, Thu 10-3.15, Sun 2-4.15. **Facilities:** ❷ (charged) ☕ 🎁 ♿ toilets for disabled ⊗ (ex guide dogs)

National Gallery of Ireland

Merrion Square

➲ *(5 mins walk from Pearse Station)*

☎ 01 6615133

e-mail: artgall@eircom.net

web: www.nationalgallery.ie

The gallery, founded in 1854 by an Act of Parliament, houses the national collections of Irish art and European Old Masters including Caravaggio, Poussin, El Greco, Roderic O'Conor, and the Yeats'.

Times: ✱ Open all year, Mon-Sat 10-5.30 (Thu 10-8.30), Sun 2-5. Closed 24-26 Dec & Good Fri. **Facilities:** ℗ (5 mins walk) (meter parking, 2hrs max) 🍴 licensed 🎁 ♿ (Braille/audio tours, lifts, ramps, parking bay) toilets for disabled shop ⊗

National Library of Ireland

FREE

Kildare St

☎ 01 6030200

web: www.nli.ie

Founded in 1877 and based on collections from The Royal Dublin Society. The National Library holds an estimated 5 million items. There are collections of printed books, manuscripts, prints and drawings, photos, maps, newspapers, microfilms and ephemera. The library's research facilities are open to all those with genuine research needs. In addition to research facilities, services include a regular programme of exhibitions open to the public and Genealogy Service.

Times: ✱ Open all year, Mon-Wed 10-9, Thu-Fri 10-5 & Sat 10-1. Closed Sun, BHs, Good Fri & 23 Dec-2 Jan. **Facilities:** 🎁 ♿ toilets for disabled shop ⊗ (ex guide dogs) 🚌

National Photographic Archive

FREE

Meeting House Square, Temple Bar

➲ *(opposite The Gallery of Photography)*

☎ 01 6030200

e-mail: photoarchive@nli.ie

web: www.nli.ie

The National Photographic Archive, which is part of the National Library of Ireland, was opened in 1998 in an award-winning building in the Temple Bar area of Dublin. The archive holds an unrivalled collection of photographic images relating to Irish history, topography and cultural and social life. The collection is especially rich in late 19th and early 20th century topographical views and studio portraits, but also includes photographs taken during the Rebellion of 1916 and the subsequent War of Independence and Civil War, as well as other historic events.

Times: ✱ Open all year, Mon-Fri 10-5. (Closed BH's, Good Fri & 23 Dec-2 Jan). **Facilities:** 🎁 ♿ toilets for disabled shop ⊗ (ex guide dogs) ◀

Natural History Museum

FREE

Merrion St

➲ *(in city centre)*

☎ 01 6777444

e-mail: education.nmi@indigo.ie

The Natural History Museum, which is part of The National Museum of Ireland, is a zoological museum containing diverse collections of world wildlife. The Irish Room, on the ground floor, is devoted largely to Irish mammals, sea creatures and insects. It includes the extinct giant Irish deer and the skeleton of a basking shark. The World Collection, has as its centre piece, the skeleton of a 60ft whale suspended from the roof. Other displays include the Giant Panda and a Pygmy Hippopotamus.

Times: ✱ Open all year, Tue-Sat 10-5, Sun 2-5. Closed Mon, 25 Dec & Good Fri **Facilities:** ℗ (parking meters wkdays) ⊗

Newman House

University College Dublin, 86 St Stephens Green

➲ *(S side of St Stephens Green)*

☎ 01 7067422 & 4757255

Newman House consists of two superb Georgian town houses, containing some of Ireland's finest 18th-century plasterwork and decoration. As the founding home of University College Dublin in

continued

1854, the house has been associated with many famous literary and historical figures, including John Henry Newman, Gerard Manley Hopkins and James Joyce.

Times: ✱ Open Jun-Aug, Tue-Fri 12-5, Sat 2-5. Tours, Tue-Fri; 12, 2, 3 & 4; Sat 2, 3 & 4. At other times tours by prior arrangement only. **Facilities:** Ⓟ (100yds) 🍽 licensed ⊗ (ex guide dogs)

Number Twenty Nine
`2 for 1`

29 Lower Fitzwilliam St

⤷ *(on corner of Lower Fitzwilliam St & Mount Street Upper; adjacent to Merrion Square)*

☎ 01 7026165

e-mail: numbertwentynine@mail.esb.ie

Number Twenty-Nine is a lovingly restored middle class Dublin home from the late 18th and early 19th century, filled with a unique collection of original pieces, with excellent examples of Irish and international craftsmanship. Visitors are guided through the house from the basement kitchen to the attic nursery.

Times: Open all year, Tue-Sat 10-5, Sun 1-5. Closed Mon & 2 wks prior to Xmas & Good Fri. **Fee:** ✱ €4.50 (ch under 16 free) concessions €2). **Facilities:** Ⓟ (on street/meter) 🍽 🎦 shop ⊗ ◼

Phoenix Park Visitor Centre

Phoenix Park

⤷ *(4km from Dublin)*

☎ 01 677 0095

e-mail: phoenixparkvisitorcentre@opw.ie

Situated in Phoenix Park, the Visitor Centre provides an historical interpretation of the park from 3500BC, through a series of attractive displays. Part of the building is devoted to nature and there is a colourful film of Phoenix Park. The castle, probably dating from the early 17th century has been restored to its former glory.

Times: Open all year, Jan-mid Mar, Sat & Sun 10-5; mid-end Mar, daily 10-5.30; Apr-Sep, daily 10-6; Oct, daily 10-5.30; Nov & Dec, Sat & Sun 10-5. (Last admission 45 mins before closing) **Fee:** ✱ €2.90 (ch & students €1.30, pen €2). Family ticket €7.40 Group rate €2.10 each. **Facilities:** Ⓟ 🍽 🎦 ♿ toilets for disabled ⊗ (ex guide dogs)

DUN LAOGHAIRE   **MAP 01 D4**

James Joyce Tower

Joyce Tower, Sandycove

⤷ *(1m SE Dun Laoghaire by coast road to Sandycove Point or turn off main Dun Laoghaire-Dalkey road)*

☎ 01 2809265 & 8722077

e-mail: joycetower@dublintourism.ie

web: www.visitdublin.com/museums

Built by the British as a defence against a possible invasion by Napoleon, the tower has walls approximately 8ft thick and an original entrance door 13ft above the ground. The tower was once the temporary home of James Joyce, who depicted this setting in the opening scene of Ulysses. The structure is now a museum devoted to the author. Bloomsday, the day in 1904 on which all the action of *Ulysses* is set, is celebrated annually on 16th June. On this day, the museum is open from 8-6 for visits, readings from Ulysses and performances of various kinds. Edwardian costume is encouraged.

Times: Open Mar-Oct, Mon-Sat 10-1 & 2-5, Sun & BHs 2-6; Nov-Jan by arrangement. **Fee:** ✱ €6.50 (ch 3-11 €4, pen, students & ch 12-17 €5.50). Family ticket €18. Parties 20+. **Facilities:** Ⓟ (100yds) ♿ shop ⊗ (ex guide dogs) ◼

MALAHIDE   **MAP 01 D4**

Fry Model Railway

Malahide Castle Demesne

⤷ *(in grounds of Malahide Castle, 8m N of Dublin city centre, follow signs for Malahide)*

☎ 01 8463779 & 8462184

e-mail: fryrailway@dublintourism.ie

web: www.visitdublin.com

The Fry Model Railway is a rare collection of '0' gauge trains and trams, depicting the history of Irish rail transport from the first train that ran in 1834. Cyril Fry began to build his model collection in his attic, in the late 1920s. All the models are built to scale, and they are now housed in a purpose-built setting adjacent to Malahide Castle.

Times: ✱ Open Apr-Sep, Mon-Sat 10-5, Sun & PH 2-6; Parties at other times by arrangement. Closed 1-2 & on Fri. **Facilities:** Ⓟ ♿ shop ⊗ ◼

Malahide Castle

⤷ *(from Dublin city centre follow signs for Malahide, then approaching village, main entrance to castle is signed to right off main road)*

☎ 01 8462184

e-mail: malahidecastle@dublintourism.ie

web: www.malahidecastle.com

One of Ireland's oldest castles, this romantic and beautiful structure, set in 250 acres of grounds, has changed very little in 800 years. Tours offer views of Irish period furniture and historical portrait collections. Additional paintings from the National Gallery depict figures from Irish life over the last few centuries.

Times: Open Jan-Dec, Mon-Sat, 10-5. Apr-Sep, Sun & PH, 10-6. Oct-Mar, Sun & PH 11-5. **Fee:** ✱ €6.70 (ch €4.20, concessions €5.70). Family ticket €19 (2ad + 3ch u12). Group rates available. Combined tickets for related attractions available. **Facilities:** Ⓟ 🍽 🎦 shop ⊗ ◼

Talbot Botanic Gardens

Malahide Castle

⤷ *(off R107 onto Back Rd, entrance 0.25m on left, well signed)*

☎ 01 8462456

Malahide Castle has long been associated with ornamental gardening. Over seven hectares of shrubbery, and a Walled Garden of nearly two hectares are mainly the creation of Lord Milo Talbot de Malahide, whose family had lived at the estate for 800 years until his death in 1973. Lord Milo Talbot had travelled the world and brought home many exotic plants from Australia and Chile, among others. Visitors follow a path through the gardens, which gives them the best view of this impressive botanic garden.

Times: ✱ Open May-Sep 2-5. Groups by appointment only. Guided tour for general public on Wed at 2. **Facilities:** Ⓟ 🍽 licensed 🎦 ♿ shop ⊗ (ex in parkland)

SKERRIES   **MAP 01 D4**

Skerries Mills
`FREE`

⤷ *(signed off M1)*

☎ 01 8495208

e-mail: skerriesmills@indigo.ie

A collection of restored mills, including a watermill, a five-sail, and a four-sail windmill, all in working order. The site dates from the 16th century and was originally part of a monastic establishment. It came

continued

Ireland

into private ownership in 1538, and a bakery has been there since 1840. Nature lovers will enjoy the millpond, nearby wetlands and town park, of which the mills are the focal landmark.

Times: Open all year Apr-Sep, daily 10.30-5.30; 2 Jan-Mar & Oct-19 Dec, daily 10.30-4.30. Closed Good Fri **Facilities:** ⓟ 💺 🍴 licensed shop 🚫

CO GALWAY

GALWAY   MAP 01 B3

Galway Atlantaquaria
Salthill
➲ *(follow signs for Salthill. Next to Tourist Office at seafront rdbt)*
☎ 091 585100
e-mail: atlantaquaria@eircom.net
web: www.nationalaquarium.ie

Concentrating on the native Irish marine ecosystem, the Galway Atlantaquaria contains some 170 species of fish and sealife, and features both fresh and saltwater exhibits.

Times: Open Apr-Jun & Sep daily 10-5; Jul & Aug daily 10-6; Oct-Dec, & Jan-Mar Wed-Sun 10-5. Closed Mon & Tue. **Fee:** €9 (ch 3-14 €5.50, student, pen €6). Family ticket (2ad+2ch) €26, (1ad+2ch) €18. **Facilities:** ⓟ 💺 🍴 licensed ♿ toilets for disabled shop 🚫 (ex guide dogs) 🍴

Nora Barnacle House Museum
Bowling Green
➲ *(close to St Nicholas Collegiate Church, in city centre)*
☎ 091 564743
e-mail: norabarnaclehouse@eircom.net
web: www.norabarnacle.com

The smallest museum in Ireland, this tiny turn-of-century house was the home of Nora Barnacle, companion, wife and lifelong inspiration of James Joyce. It was here in 1909, sitting at the kitchen table that Joyce first met his darling's mother. Letters, photographs and other exhibits of the lives of James Joyce and Nora Barnacle make a visit here a unique experience.

Times: Open Jun-Aug, days may change during week, opening times posted on window. **Fee:** €2.50 (students €2). **Facilities:** ⓟ (100yds) (disc parking)

Royal Tara China Gift Centre
Tara Hall, Mervue
➲ *(N6 from Tourist Office. At rdbt take 2nd left & at lights turn right)*
☎ 091 705602
e-mail: mkilroy@royal-tara.com
web: www.royal-tara.com

Royal Tara China visitor centre, located minutes from Galway City Centre, operates from a 17th-century house situated on five acres.

Times: Open all year, Mon-Sat 9-5, Sun 10-5 **Facilities:** ⓟ ♿ (all facilities accessible for disabled) toilets for disabled shop 🚫 (ex guide dogs) 🍴

GORT   MAP 01 B3

Coole Park Visitor Centre NEW
Coole Nature Reserve
➲ *(3km N of Gort on N18 Limerick-Galway road, left turn signed)*
☎ 091 631804
e-mail: info@coolepark.ie
web: www.coolepark.ie

Once the home of Lady Augusta Gregory, dramatist and co-founder of the Abbey Theatre with Yeats and Martyn. Now a nature reserve, the Seven Woods celebrated by Yeats is part of a nature trail taking in woods and river to Coole lake. The restored courtyard has a visitor centre with exhibits and displays of Coole Parks history.

Times: Open Apr-May & Sep, daily, 10-5; Jun-Aug, daily, 10-6. **Fee:** ✱ €2.90 (ch & student €1.30, concessions €2.10). Family €7.40. Free admission to park. **Facilities:** ⓟ 💺 🍴 ♿ (hand rail, wide doors) toilets for disabled shop 🚫 (ex assist dogs & on lead)

Thoor Ballylee
➲ *(1km off N18 & N66)*
☎ 091 631436 & 537733

This tower house is the former home of the poet William Butler Yeats and is where he completed most of his literary works. The tower, restored to appear exactly as it was when he lived there, houses an Interpretative Centre with audio-visual presentations and displays of his work.

Times: Open 27 May-Sep Mon-Sat 9.30-5 **Fee:** ✱ €6 (concessions €5.50). Family ticket €12. Party. **Facilities:** ⓟ ♿ (audio-visual presentation) toilets for disabled shop 🚫 (ex guide dogs) 🍴

KINVARRA   MAP 01 B3

Dunguaire Castle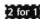
➲ *(off N18 Ennis to Galway road, through Gort. Left at Ardrahan & continue to Kinvara)*
☎ 061 360768
e-mail: reservations@shannondev.ie
web: www.shannonheritage.com

The castle has stood for hundreds of years on the site of the 7th-century stronghold of Guaire, the King of Connaught. Today the restored castle gives an insight into the lifestyle of the people who lived there from 1520 to modern times.

Times: Open May-Sep, daily 9.30-5 (last admission 4.30). Medieval banquet, Apr-Oct 5.30 & 8.45 (reservations necessary). **Fee:** ✱ €4.75 (concessions €2.95). **Facilities:** ⓟ shop 🚫 (ex guide dogs) 🍴

PORTUMNA

MAP 01 B3

Portumna Castle & Gardens

☎ 090 9741658

e-mail: portumnacastle@opw.ie

The great semi-fortified house at Portumna was built before 1618 by Richard Burke or de Burgo, 4th Earl of Clanricarde. This important Jacobean house, while influenced by Renaissance and English houses, remains distinctively Irish. It was the main seat of the de Burgo family for over 200 years, until it was gutted by fire in 1826. The ground floor of the house is now open to the public. To the north of the house is a formal, geometrically laid out garden, a feature often associated with large Jacobean mansions.

Times: Open 25 Mar-mid Apr, daily 10-5; mid Apr-Oct, daily 10-6 (Last admission 45mins before closing). **Fee:** ✱ €2.10 (ch & students €1, pen €1.10). Family ticket €5.80. Group rate €1.30 each. **Facilities:** Ⓟ 🖼 ♿ (access limited) ⊗ (ex guide dogs)

ROSSCAHILL

MAP 01 B4

Brigits Garden NEW

2 for 1

Pollagh

➲ *(signed from N59 between Moycullen & Oughterard)*

☎ 091 550905

e-mail: info@galwaygarden.com

web: www.galwaygarden.com

At the heart of Brigits Garden are four unique gardens based on symbolism of the old Celtic festivals and representing the cycle of life. Featuring Irish sculpture and crafts designed to reflect the west of Ireland landscape. 11 acres of woodland and wildflower meadows to explore with nature trail, a wind chamber, an original ring fort and the impressively large Brigits Sundial.

Times: Open mid Apr-end Sep, daily, 10-5.30. By appointment at other times. **Fee:** €6.75 (ch €4, under 5 free, concessions €5.75). Family €20. **Facilities:** Ⓟ 🖼 ♿ (w/chair accessible) toilets for disabled shop 🔳

ROUNDSTONE

MAP 01 A4

Roundstone Music, Crafts & Fashion   FREE

Craft Centre

➲ *(N59 from Galway to Clifden. After approx 50m turn left at Roundstone sign, 7m to village. Attraction at top of village)*

☎ 095 35875

e-mail: bodhran@iol.ie

web: www.bodhran.com

The Roundstone Music Craft and Fashion shop is located within the walls of an old Franciscan Monastery. Here you can see Ireland's oldest craft: the Bodhran being made, and regular talks and demonstrations are given. The 1st RiverDance stage drums were made here and are still on display in the Craftsman's Craftshop. There is an

continued

outdoor picnic area in a beautiful location alongside the bell tower by the water where the dolphins swim up to the wall in summer.

Roundstone Music, Crafts & Fashion

Times: Open Apr-Oct 9.30-6, Jul-Sep 9-7, Winter 6 days 9.30-6. **Facilities:** Ⓟ 🖼 🖼 ♿ toilets for disabled shop ⊗ (ex guide dogs)

See advert below

Ireland

CO KERRY

CASTLEISLAND   MAP 01 B2

Crag Cave   `2 for 1`

➲ *(1m N, signed off N21)*
☎ 066 7141244
e-mail: info@cragcave.com
web: www.cragcave.com

Crag Cave is one of the longest surveyed cave systems in Ireland, with a total length of 3.81km. It is a spectacular world, where pale forests of stalagmites and stalactites, thousands of years old, throw eerie shadows around vast echoing caverns complemented by dramatic sound and lighting effects. Now features new indoor and outdoor soft play areas, which are priced seperately. Tours of the caves last about 30 minutes.

Times: Open mid Mar-1 Nov, daily 10-6 (Jul-Aug until 6.30). (Last tour 30 mins before closing time). Dec-Feb, telephone for times. **Fee:** ✱ €9 (ch €5, concessions €7.50). Family ticket (2ad + 2ch) €25 (2ad + 4ch) €30 **Facilities:** ❷ 🍴 licensed 📖 licensed 📖 & (ramp to visitor centre) toilets for disabled shop ✪ (ex guide dogs) ◼

KILLARNEY   MAP 01 B2

Killarney Transport Museum

Scotts Hotel Gardens
➲ *(town centre, opposite railway station)*
☎ 064 34677

A unique collection of Irish veteran, vintage and classic cars, motorcycles, bicycles, carriages and fire engines. Exhibits include the 1907 Silver Stream, reputed to be the rarest car in the world, it was designed and built by an Irishman and he only made one!

Times: Open Apr & Oct 11-4; May & Sep 11-5; Jun, Jul & Aug 10-6 **Facilities:** ❷ &

Muckross House, Gardens & Traditional Farms

Muckross
➲ *(4m on Kenmare road)*
☎ 066 31440 & 35571
e-mail: mucros@iol.ie
web: www.muckross-house.ie

The 19th-century mansion house of the formerly private Muckross Estate. It now houses a museum of Kerry folklife. In the basement craft centre, a weaver, blacksmith and potter demonstrate their trades. The grounds include Alpine and bog gardens, rhododendrons, azaleas and a rock garden.

Times: ✱ Open all year Jul-Aug, daily 9-7; mid Mar-Jun & Sep-Oct, 9-6; Nov-16 Mar 9-5.30. **Facilities:** ❷ 🍴 licensed & toilets for disabled shop ✪ (ex guide dogs) ◼

TRALEE   MAP 01 A2

Kerry The Kingdom Museum

Ashe Memorial Hall, Denny St
➲ *(in town centre, follow signs for museum & tourist information office)*
☎ 066 7127777
e-mail: info@kerrymuseum.com
web: www.kerrymuseum.com

The museum tells the story of Kerry (and Ireland) from the Stone Age to the present day. Archaeological treasures are displayed in the Museum Gallery, while a stroll through the Medieval Experience reveals the streets of Tralee as they were in 1450, with all the sights, sounds and smells of a bustling community. Discover what people wore, what they ate and where they lived, and find out why the Earls of Desmond, who founded the town, also destroyed it.

Times: ✱ Open Jan-Mar, Tue-Fri 10-4.30; Apr-May, Tue-Sat 9.30-5.30; Jun-Aug, daily 9.30-5.30; Sep-Dec, Tue-Sat 9.30-5; BH wknds Sun & Mon 10-5. **Facilities:** ❷ (charged) 🖳 & (special time car through Medieval Experience) toilets for disabled shop ✪ (ex guide dogs) ◼

VALENCIA ISLAND   MAP 01 A2

The Skellig Experience   `2 for 1`

➲ *(Ring of Kerry road, signed after Cahersiveen then Valentia bridge, or ferry from Rena Rd Point)*
☎ 066 9476306
e-mail: info@skelligexperience.com
web: www.skelligexperience.com

The Skellig Rocks are renowned for their scenery, sea bird colonies, lighthouses, Early Christian monastic architecture and rich underwater life. The two islands - Skellig Michael and Small Skellig - stand like fairytale castles in the Atlantic Ocean, rising to 218 metres and their steep cliffs plunging 50 metres below the sea. The Heritage Centre, (on Valentia Island, reached from the mainland via a bridge), tells the story of the Skellig Islands in an exciting multimedia exhibition. Cruises around Valentia Habour are also available.

Times: Open May-Jun 10-6; Jul-Aug 10-7; Sep 10-6. Mar, Apr, Oct, Nov 10-5 **Fee:** €5 (ch €3, concessions €4). Family ticket €14. **Facilities:** ❷ 🖳 📖 & toilets for disabled shop ✪ (ex guide dogs) ◼

CO KILDARE

CELBRIDGE   MAP 01 D4

Castletown

➲ *(13m from Dublin, follow signs to Celbridge from N4)*
☎ 01 628 8252
e-mail: castletown@opw.ie
web: www.heritageireland.ie

Ireland's largest and finest Palladian country house, begun c1722 by William Conolly, Speaker of the Irish House of Commons. The state rooms include the 'Pompeian' Long Gallery with its Venetian chandeliers, green silk drawing room and magnificent staircase hall with Lafranchini plasterwork. There is a fine collection of 18th-century Irish furniture and paintings.

Times: Open Etr Sun-Sep, Mon-Fri 10-6, Sat, Sun & BH 1-6; Oct, Mon-Fri 10-5, Sun & BH 1-5 **Fee:** €3.70 (ch & students €1.30, pen €2.60). Family ticket €8.70. Pre-booked groups 10+ €2.50. **Facilities:** ❷ 🖳 📖 & (restricted access for disabled visitors) toilets for disabled ✪ (ex guide dogs)

Ireland

KILDARE
MAP 01 C3

Irish National Stud & Japanese Gardens St Fiachra's Garden

Irish National Stud, Tully

➲ *(off N7, junct 11 then R415 towards Nurney & Kildare. Attraction well signed from rdbt)*

☎ 045 521617

e-mail: stud@irish-national-stud.ie

web: www.irish-national-stud.ie

Situated in the grounds of the Irish National Stud, the gardens were established by Lord Wavertree between 1906 and 1910, and symbolise 'The Life of Man' in a Japanese-style landscape. You can also visit the Horse Museum which includes the skeleton of Arkle, an Irish racehorse that won a number of major races in the 1960s. The Commemorative Millennium Garden of St Fiachra has 4 acres of woodland and lakeside walks and features a Waterford Crystal garden and monastic cells of limestone.

Times: ✱ Open 12 Feb-1 Nov, daily 9.30-6 (last admission 5).
Facilities: ❷ 🍽 licensed 🚻 ♿ (all parts of stud accessible, only small part of gardens) toilets for disabled shop 🛒

CO KILKENNY

KILKENNY
MAP 01 C3

Kilkenny Castle

☎ 056 772 1450

Situated in a beautiful 50-acre park, the castle dates from 1172. The first stone castle was built 20 years later by William Marshall, Earl of Pembroke. It was home of the very powerful Butler family, Earls and Dukes of Ormonde from 1391 to 1935. Due to major restoration works, the central block now includes a library, drawing room, and bedrooms decorated in 1830s splendour, as well as the beautiful Long Gallery.

Times: Open all year, Apr-May, daily 10.30-5; Jun-Aug, daily 9.30-7; Sep, daily 10-6.30; Oct-Mar, daily 10.30-12.45 & 2-5. (Last tour 45mins before closing). Closed Xmas & Good Fri. **Fee:** ✱ €5.30 (ch & students €2.10). Family ticket €11.50. Group rate €3.70 each. **Facilities:** ℗ (local authority restrictions) 🍽 🚻 ♿ (toilet close by) shop 🐾 (ex guide dogs)

CO LIMERICK

FOYNES
MAP 01 B3

Foynes Flying Boat Museum

➲ *(on N69 in Foynes)*

☎ 069 65416

e-mail: famm@eircom.net

web: www.flyingboatmuseum.com

The museum recalls the era of the flying boats during the 1930s and early 1940s when Foynes was an important airport for air traffic between the United States and Europe. There is a comprehensive range of exhibits, graphic illustrations and a 1940s style cinema featuring a 17-minute film - all original footage from the 30s and 40s. Where Irish coffee was first invented by chef, Joe Sheridan, in 1942.

Times: ✱ Open Mar-Oct, daily 10-6. (Last admission 5.15)
Facilities: ❷ 🍽 ♿ toilets for disabled shop 🐾 (ex guide dogs) 🛒

HOLYCROSS
MAP 01 C3

Lough Gur Stone Age Centre
2 for 1

Bruff Rd

➲ *(17km S of Limerick, off R512 towards Kilmallock)*

☎ 061 360788

e-mail: reservations@shannondev.ie

web: www.shannonheritage.com

Lough Gur introduces visitors to the habitat of Neolithic Man on one of Ireland's most important archaeological sites. The visitor centre interprets the history of the area which dates back to 3000BC.

Times: Open May-mid Sep, daily 10-6 (last admission 5.30) **Fee:** ✱ €4.75 (concessions €2.95). **Facilities:** ❷ ♿ toilets for disabled shop 🐾 (ex guide dogs) 🛒

KILCORNAN
MAP 01 B3

Celtic Park & Gardens

➲ *(N69 Limerick to Tralee road)*

☎ 061 394243

Located on an original Celtic settlement in one of the most important Cromwellian plantations in the south-west of Ireland. As you walk through the park there's plenty to see, including a church built in 1250, a Mass rock, dolmen, a stone circle, lake dwellings, cooking site, Celtic tomb and a fine example of a ring fort. The gardens contain over 1,000 roses, flowering shrubs, a rockery, herbaceous borders, shrubbery, large pool and colonnades.

Times: ✱ Open mid Mar-Oct, daily 9.30-6. **Facilities:** ❷ 🍽 shop

LIMERICK
MAP 01 B3

The Hunt Museum
2 for 1

The Custom House, Rutland St

➲ *(a short walk from Arthur's Quay)*

☎ 061 312833

e-mail: info@huntmuseum.com

web: www.huntmuseum.com

On show at the Hunt Museum is one of Ireland's finest private collections of art and antiquities. Reflecting Ireland's Celtic past as well as masterworks by da Vinci and Renoir. Set in an 18th-century Custom House beside the broad majestic Shannon.

continued

Ireland

Times: Open all year Mon-Sat 10-5, Sun 2-5. **Fee:** ✱ €7.20 (ch €3.50, concessions €5.80). Family ticket €16.50. **Facilities:** ℗ (50mtrs) (parking discs for street parking) ▆ ⑩ licensed ⑪ ♿ toilets for disabled shop ⊗ (ex guide dogs) ◢

King John's Castle [2 for 1]
Nicholas St
➲ *(on Kings Island in city)*
☎ 061 360788
e-mail: reservations@shannondev.ie
web: www.shannonheritage.com

The Castle was built between 1200 and 1210 and was repaired and extended many times in the following centuries. The interpretative centre at the Castle has been completely redesigned and now contains an imaginative historical exhibition. The courtyard and the Castle display some of the trades and traditions of the 16th century.

Times: Open all year Mar, Apr, & Oct daily 9.30-5 (last admission 4); May-Sep 9.30-5.30 (last admission 4.30); Nov-Feb 10-4.30 (last admission 3.30). Closed Good Fri & 24-26 Dec. **Fee:** ✱ €8.35 (ch€4.95, concessions €6.25). **Facilities:** ℗ ♿ (lifts and ramps) toilets for disabled shop ⊗ (ex guide dogs) ◢

CO LONGFORD

KEENAGH   MAP 01 C4

Corlea Trackway Visitor Centre [FREE]
➲ *(off R397, 3km from village, 15km from Longford)*
☎ 043 22386
e-mail: ctrackwayvisitorcentre@opw.ie

The centre interprets an Iron Age bog road which was built in the year 148BC across the boglands close to the River Shannon. The oak road is the largest of its kind to have been uncovered in Europe and was excavated over the years by Professor Barry Raferty of University College Dublin. Inside the building, an 18-metre stretch of preserved road is on permanent display in a specially designed hall with humidifiers to prevent the ancient wood from cracking in the heat.

Times: Open Apr-Sep, daily 10-6 **Facilities:** ℗ ▆ ♿ toilets for disabled ⊗ (ex guide dogs)

CO MAYO

BALLYCASTLE   MAP 01 B5

Céide Fields
➲ *(5m W of Ballycastle on R314)*
☎ 096 43325
e-mail: ceidefields@opw.ie
web: www.heritageireland.ie

Beneath the wild boglands of North Mayo lies Céide Fields, the most extensive Stone-age monument in the world; field systems, dwelling areas and megalithic tombs of 5,000 years ago. In addition, the wild flora of the bog is of international importance and is bounded by some of the most spectacular rock formations and cliffs in Ireland.

Times: Open 25 Feb-15 Oct, 10-6. Advance bookings only. Last tour 1 hr. before closing time. **Fee:** ✱ €3.70 (ch & students €1.30, pen €2.60). Family ticket €8.70. Group rate €2.50 each. **Facilities:** ℗ ▆ ⑪ ♿ (parking) toilets for disabled ⊗ (ex guide dogs)

CO MONAGHAN

INNISKEEN   MAP 01 C4

Patrick Kavanagh Rural & Literary Resource Centre
Candlefort
➲ *(from Dublin take N2, exit at Carrickmacross, left along R178 to Essexford. Left at Kelly's pub for Inniskeen)*
☎ 042 937 8560
e-mail: infoatpkc@eircom.net
web: www.patrickkavanaghcountry.com

Birthplace of Patrick Kavanagh, one of Ireland's foremost 20th-century poets. The village grew around the ancient monastery of St Daig MacCairill, founded by 562, and its strong, 10th-century round tower still stands. The centre, housed in the former parish church, chronicles the ancient history of the region and its role in developing Kavanagh's work.

Times: Open all year, Tue-Fri 11-5, Sat 2-5. Jun-Sep Sun, 2-5. Closed Oct-May, wknds & BHs Dec-16 Mar. **Fee:** ✱ €5 (ch €12 - free when accompanied by an adult, concessions €3). Kavanagh trail guide map available €0.65. Kavanagh Country Tours - a guided tour with live performances lasting 90 mins, advance booking essential €7.50 including admission to centre. **Facilities:** ℗ ▆ ♿ toilets for disabled shop ◢

MONAGHAN   MAP 01 C5

Monaghan County Museum [FREE]
1-2 Hill St
➲ *(near town centre, opposite market house exhibition galleries)*
☎ 047 82928
e-mail: comuseum@monghancoco.ie
web: www.monaghan.ie

This is an award-winning museum of local archaeology, history, arts and crafts. Throughout the year various special exhibitions take place. Please telephone for details.

Times: ✱ Open Sep-May, Tue-Fri 10-1 & 2-5 Sat 11-1 & 2-5. Jun-Aug, Mon-Fri 11-5, Thu 11-7, Sat 11-1 & 2-5. **Facilities:** ℗ (near town centre) (restricted on-street parking) ⑪ ♿ ⊗ (ex guide dogs)

CO OFFALY

BIRR   MAP 01 C3

Birr Castle Demesne [2 for 1]
➲ *(in town sq take exit beside Bank of Ireland and bear right. Turn left, entrance on right, car park on left)*
☎ 057 9120 336
e-mail: mail@birrcastle.com
web: www.birrcastle.com

A large landscaped park with a lake, rivers and waterfalls, with important plant collections including magnolias, maples, limes and oaks. The Demesne is particularly colourful in the spring and autumn, and is noted for its formal gardens, containing the tallest box hedges in the world. It is also home to the Great Birr Telescope, built in 1844,

continued

and Ireland's Historic Science Centre, a series of galleries focusing on Ireland's scientific past.

Times: Open all year, Mar-Oct 9-6, Nov-Mar 10-5 **Fee:** ✱ €8.50 (ch €4.50, concessions €6.50). Family ticket (2ad+2ch) €24. **Facilities:** ❷ 💺 ♿ toilets for disabled shop ◼

CO ROSCOMMON

BOYLE   MAP 01 B4

King House Interpretive Galleries & Museum   `2 for 1`
☎ 071 9663242
e-mail: kinghouse@roscommoncoco.ie
web: www.kinghouse.ie

King House is a magnificently restored Georgian mansion built around 1730 by Sir Henry King, whose family were one of the most powerful and wealthy in Ireland. After its first life as a home, King House became a military barracks to the famous Connaught Rangers from 1788-1922. In more recent years it has also been a barracks for the National Irish Army. Today visitors can explore and delve into its history with interactive presentations on: Gaelic Ireland, the lives of the King family, the architecture and restoration of the building and its military history.

Times: Open Apr-Sep, daily 10-6 (last admission 5). Pre-booked groups welcome all year round, telephone for details. **Fee:** €7 (ch €4, concessions €5). Family ticket €18. Party rates available **Facilities:** ❷ 🍴 licensed 🗐 ♿ (lift to all areas, ramps, wide doors, parking) toilets for disabled shop ❀ (ex guide dogs)

STROKESTOWN   MAP 01 C4

Strokestown Park House Garden & Famine Museum   `2 for 1`
Strokestown Park
➲ (23km from Longford on N5)
☎ 071 9633013
e-mail: info@strokestownpark.ie
web: www.strokestownpark.ie

A fine example of an early 18th-century gentleman farmer's country estate. Built in Palladian style the house reflects perfectly the confidence of the newly emergent ruling class. The pleasure garden has also been restored, and the Famine Museum, located in the stable yard, commemorates the Great Irish Famine of the 1840s.

Times: Open 17 Mar-Oct, daily. **Fee:** ✱ €13 (ch €6, concessions €11.50). Family ticket €28.50. Group 20+ €10.50 each **Facilities:** ❷ 🍴 licensed 🗐 ♿ toilets for disabled shop garden centre ❀ (ex guide dogs & in grounds) ◼

We endeavour to be as accurate as possible, but changes to times and other information can occur after the guide has gone to press.

CO TIPPERARY

CASHEL   MAP 01 C3

Brú Ború Heritage Centre
➲ (below Rock of Cashel in town)
☎ 062 61122
e-mail: bruboru@comhaltas.com
web: www.comhaltas.com

At the foot of the Rock of Cashel, a 4th-century stone fort, this Heritage Centre is dedicated to the study and celebration of native Irish music, song, dance, story telling, theatre and Celtic studies. There's a Folk Theatre where three performances are held daily in the summer, and in the evening, banquets evoke the Court of Brian Ború, 11th-century High King of Ireland with songs, poems and sagas. Promoted by Comhaltas Ceoltóiríéireann. There is also a Subterranean, "Sounds of History", experience.

Times: Open Jan-May & Oct-Dec, Mon-Fri 9-5; Jun-Sep Tue-Sat 9-11, Sun-Mon 9-5. **Fee:** ✱ Admission to centre free. Night show €18. Exhibition, 'Sounds of History' €5. Dinner Show/Option €48. **Facilities:** ❷ (charged) 💺 🍴 licensed ♿ (wheelchair bay in theatre) toilets for disabled shop ❀ (ex guide dogs) ◼

CO WATERFORD

LISMORE   MAP 01 C2

Lismore Castle Gardens & Art Gallery   `2 for 1`
➲ (on N72 near town centre)
☎ 058 54424
e-mail: lismoreestates@eircom.net
web: www.lismorecastle.com

Lismore Castle is the Irish home of the Duke of Devonshire. The beautifully situated walled and woodland gardens contain a fine collection of camellias, magnolias and other shrubs and a remarkable Yew Walk. Several pieces of contemporary sculpture have been installed in the garden. The West Wing has been converted into a contemporary art space and is planned to host art exhibitions from around the world.

Times: Open 15 Apr-1 Oct, daily 1.45-4.45. Open at 11 during Jun-Aug. **Fee:** ✱ €6 (ch under 16: €3, party 20+ €2.50). Party 20+ €5.50. **Facilities:** ❷ 🗐 ♿ (some of grounds are accessible)

WATERFORD

MAP 01 C2

Waterford Crystal Visitor Centre

➲ *(on N25, 1m from city centre)*

☎ 051 73311

web: www.waterfordvisitorcentre.com

There are factory tours to see mastercraftsmen mouth-blow and hand-cut this famous crystal. You can talk to the master engravers and see the crystal being sculpted. In the gallery there is the finest display of Waterford Crystal in the world.

Times: ✱ Tours of factory: Apr-Oct, daily 8.30-4, gallery daily 8.30-6; Nov-Feb, Mon-Fri 9-3.15, gallery 9-5. **Facilities:** ♿ ⬛ ⬛ & (special tours on request) toilets for disabled shop ⊗ ⬛

CO WEXFORD

FERRYCARRIG

MAP 01 D3

Irish National Heritage Park

2 for 1

➲ *(3m from Wexford, on N11)*

☎ 053 912 0733

e-mail: info@inhp.com

web: www.inhp.com

Sixteen historical sites set in a magnificent 35-acre mature forest explaining Ireland's history from the Stone and Bronze Ages, through the Celtic period and concluding with the Vikings and Normans. Among the exhibits are a reconstructed Mesolithic camp, a Viking boatyard with two full size ships and a Norman motte and bailey. Please visit website for details of events running throughout the year.

Times: Open daily: Oct-Apr, 9.30-5.30. Apr-Oct, 9.30-6.30. **Fee:** €7.50 (concessions €6). Family (2 ad & upto 3 ch) €19. Group rates available on request. **Facilities:** ♿ ⬛ ⬛ licensed ⬛ & toilets for disabled shop ⊗ (ex guide dogs) ⬛

NEW ROSS

MAP 01 C3

Dunbrody Abbey Visitors Centre

Dunbrody Abbey, Campile

➲ *(10m from New Ross at base of Hook Peninsular)*

☎ 051 88603

e-mail: patrickbelfast@aol.com

web: www.dunbrodyabbey.com

The visitor centre is based around the Abbey itself and Dunbrody Castle. There is an intriguing yew hedge maze with 1,550 yew trees and a museum. In addition there is a golf pitch-and-putt course, a local craft centre and Dunbrody Abbey Cookery School.

Times: Open May-Sep 10-6. **Fee:** Abbey €2, Family ticket €5. Maze/Golf €4, (ch €2). Family €10. **Facilities:** ♿ ⬛ ⬛ ⬛ & shop garden centre

John F Kennedy Arboretum

➲ *(12km S of New Ross, off R733)*

☎ 051 388171

e-mail: jfkarboretum@opn.ie

The Arboretum covers 623 acres across the hill of Slievecoiltia which overlooks the Kennedy ancestral home at Dunganstown. There are 4,500 types of trees and shrubs representing the temperate regions of the world, and laid out in botanical sequence. There's a lake and a visitor centre.

Times: Open all year daily, May-Aug 10-8; Apr & Sep 10-6.30; Oct-Mar 10-5. (Last admission 45 mins before closing). Closed Good Fri & 25 Dec. **Fee:** ✱ €2.90 (ch & student €1.30, pen €2.10). Family ticket €7.40 Heritage cards €21 (pen €16, ch & student €8) Family €55. **Facilities:** ♿ ⬛ & toilets for disabled shop

WEXFORD

MAP 01 D3

Johnstown Castle Gardens

Johnstown Castle

➲ *(4m SW of town, signed off N25)*

☎ 053 42888

e-mail: aosullivan@johnstown.teagase.ie

The 19th-century mansion is closed to the public but visitors can explore the 50 acres of grounds containing over 200 different varieties of trees and shrubs, ornamental lakes with wildfowl, and walled gardens and hothouses. The ruins of Rathlannon Castle, a medieval tower house, can also be seen.

Times: ✱ Open all year, daily 9-5.30. Closed 25 Dec. **Facilities:** ♿ ⬛ ⬛ & toilets for disabled

The Irish Agricultural Museum

Johnstown Castle Old Farmyard

➲ *(4m SW of town, signed off N25)*

☎ 053 42888

e-mail: aosullivan@johnstown.teagasc.ie

web: www.research.teagasc.ie/johnstown

This museum has displays on rural transport, farming and the activities of the farmyard and farmhouse; and includes a large exhibition on the history of the potato and the Great Famine (1845-49). Large scale replicas of different workshops, including a blacksmith, cooper and basket worker, and include displays on dairying, cycling, and sugar-beet harvesting and a collection of Irish country furniture. New permanent exhibitions on gardening and the Ferguson System.

Times: ✱ Open all year, Jun-Aug Mon-Fri 9-5 & Sat-Sun 11-5; Apr-May & Sep-14 Nov Mon-Fri 9-12.30 & 1.30-5, Sat-Sun 2-5; 15 Nov-Mar Mon-Fri 9-12.30 & 1.30-5. Closed 25 Dec-2 Jan. **Facilities:** ♿ (charged) ⬛ & toilets for disabled shop

Wexford Wildfowl Reserve　　FREE
North Slob
➲ *(8km NE from Wexford)*
☎ 053 23129
e-mail: info@heritageireland.ie

The reserve is of international importance for Greenland white-fronted geese, Brent geese, Bewick's swans and wigeon. The reserve is a superb place for birdwatching and there are hides and a tower hide available as well as a visitor centre.

Times: Open all year daily, 9-5. Other hours by arrangement with the warden. Closed 25 Dec. Reserve may be closed temporarily for management operations - Notice on Gate. **Facilities:** ❷ ⛭ toilets for disabled ⊗ (ex guide dogs)

CO WICKLOW

ENNISKERRY　　　　　　　　**MAP 01 D4**

Powerscourt Gardens Exhibition
Powerscourt Estate
➲ *(take N11 S, after 12m take exit left to Bray S, Enniskerry. Left at rdbt, over flyover, rejoin N11 N. Take 1st left for Enniskerry Village entrance 600m)*
☎ 01 2046000
web: www.powerscourt.ie

In the foothills of the Wicklow Mountains, these gardens were begun by Richard Wingfield in the 1740s, and are a blend of formal plantings, sweeping terraces, statuary and ornamental lakes together with secret hollows, rambling walks and walled gardens. The gardens cover a massive 20 hectares and contain more than two hundred varieties of tree and shrub. The house itself incorporates an exhibition which traces the history of the estate, and tells the story of the disastrous fire of 1974 which gutted the house. The grounds also contain Powerscourt Waterfall, Irelands highest at 398ft.

Times: Open Gardens & House Exhibition daily 9.30-5.30 (Gardens close at dusk in winter). Waterfall open daily, May-Aug 9.30-7, Mar-Oct, 10.30-5.30, Nov-Feb, 10.30-4. Closed 2 weeks before Christmas. **Fee:** Gardens & House Exhibition €9 (ch under 16 €5 ch under 5 free, students€7.50). Gardens only €7.50 (ch under 16 €4.50 ch under 5 free, students €6.50). Waterfall €5 (ch under 16 €3.50 ch under 2 free, students €4.50).
Facilities: ❷ ⬛ ⛴ licensed ▤ ⛭ (lift to first floor, 2 wheelchairs available) toilets for disabled shop garden centre ◀

KILQUADE　　　　　　　　**MAP 01 D3**

National Garden Exhibitions Centre
Calumet Nurseries
➲ *(7m S of Bray - turn off N11 at Kilpedder)*
☎ 01 281 9890
e-mail: calumet@clubi.ie
web: www.clubi.ie/calumet

There are 20 different gardens designed by some of Ireland's leading landscapers and designers. There are lectures during the year and guided tours during summer. Ring for details and a calendar of events. The exhibitions are constantly changing and enjoy a high standard of maintenance. All plants are clearly labelled.

Times: Open all year Mon-Sat 9-5.30; Sun 1-5.30. (Closed 24 Dec-1st Mon in Jan) **Facilities:** ❷ ⬛ ▤ ⛭ shop garden centre ⊗ (ex guide dogs) ◀

RATHDRUM　　　　　　　　**MAP 01 D3**

Avondale House & Forest Park　　2 for 1
➲ *(S of Dublin on N11. At Rathnew on R752 to Glenealy and Rathdrum)*
☎ 0404 46111
e-mail: costelloe_j@coillte.ie
web: www.coillte.ie

It was here in 1846 that one of the greatest political leaders of modern Irish history, Charles Stewart Parnell, was born. Parnell spent much of his time at Avondale until his death in October 1891. The house is set in a magnificent forest park with miles of forest trails, plus a children's play area, deer pen, orienteering courses and picnic areas.

Times: Open House 17 Mar-Oct, 11-6. Closed Mon (Mar, Apr, Sep & Oct). (Last admission 5). **Fee:** House €6 (pen €5.50). Family ticket (2ad+3ch) €16. Parking; car €5. **Facilities:** ❷ (charged) ⛴ licensed ⛭ (car park & one forest trail accessible) ⊗ (ex on lead) ◀

Ireland

County Maps

The county map shown here will help you identify the counties within each country. You can look up each county in the guide using the county names at the top of each page. To find towns featured in the guide use the atlas and the index.

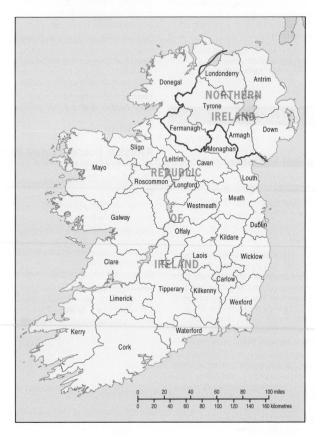

England

1 Bedfordshire
2 Berkshire
3 Bristol
4 Buckinghamshire
5 Cambridgeshire
6 Greater Manchester
7 Herefordshire
8 Hertfordshire
9 Leicestershire
10 Northamptonshire
11 Nottinghamshire
12 Rutland
13 Staffordshire
14 Warwickshire
15 West Midlands
16 Worcestershire

Scotland

17 City of Glasgow
18 Clackmannanshire
19 East Ayrshire
20 East Dunbartonshire
21 East Renfrewshire
22 Perth & Kinross
23 Renfrewshire
24 South Lanarkshire
25 West Dunbartonshire

Wales

26 Blaenau Gwent
27 Bridgend
28 Caerphilly
29 Denbighshire
30 Flintshire
31 Merthyr Tydfil
32 Monmouthshire
33 Neath Port Talbot
34 Newport
35 Rhondda Cynon Taff
36 Torfaen
37 Vale of Glamorgan
38 Wrexham

Western
Isles

Orkney Islands

Shetland Islands

Highland

Moray

Aberdeenshire

Aberdeen City

SCOTLAND

Angus

Argyll
& Bute

Perth &
Kinross

Dundee City

Stirling

Fife

East
Lothian

Argyll
& Bute

Stirling

18

22

Fife

North
Ayrshire

Inverclyde

25

20

Falkirk

City of
Edinburgh

23

17

North
Lanarkshire

West
Lothian

Midlothian

19

24

North
Ayrshire

21

South Lanarkshire

Scottish
Borders

South
Ayrshire

19

Scottish
Borders

Dumfries &
Galloway

Northumberland

Tyne & Wear

Isle
of Man

Cumbria

Durham

North
Yorkshire

Lancashire

East Riding
of Yorkshire

Isle of
Anglesey

Merseyside

West
Yorkshire

6

Conwy

30

Cheshire

South
Yorkshire

Derbyshire

Lincolnshire

Gwynedd

29

38

11

13

ENGLAND

Shropshire

9

12

Norfolk

WALES

15

Ceredigion

Powys

16

14

10

5

Suffolk

Pembrokeshire

7

1

Carmarthenshire

Gloucestershire

4

8

Essex

Swansea

3

Oxfordshire

2

Greater
London

33

31

26

32

Wiltshire

Surrey

Kent

35

36

Somerset

Hampshire

27

28

34

Cardiff

West
Sussex

East
Sussex

37

Devon

Dorset

Isle of
Wight

Cornwall

Isles of
Scilly

Guernsey

Jersey

0   20   40   60   80   100 miles

0   20 40 60 80 100 120 140 160 kilometres

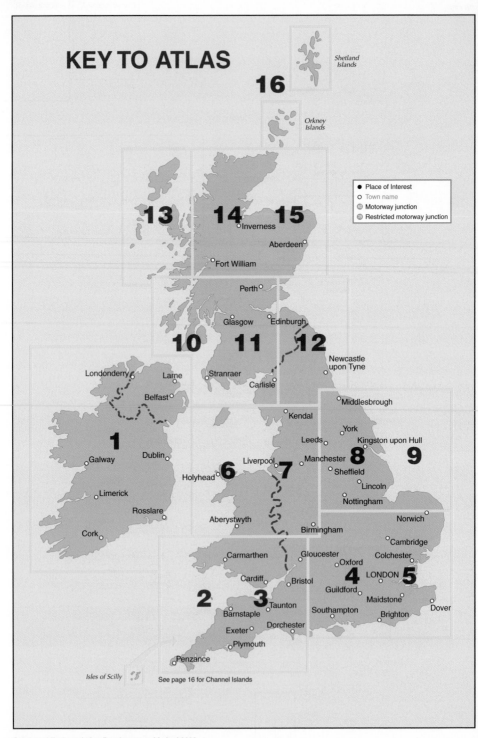

KEY TO ATLAS

16 Shetland Islands

Orkney Islands

- ● Place of Interest
- ○ Town name
- ⓜ Motorway junction
- ⓡ Restricted motorway junction

13   **14**   **15**
Inverness

Aberdeen

Fort William

Perth

10   **11**   **12**

Glasgow   Edinburgh

Newcastle upon Tyne

Londonderry   Larne   Stranraer
Carlisle

Belfast   Kendal
Middlesbrough

York

1   Leeds   Kingston upon Hull

Galway   Dublin   Liverpool   Manchester   **8**   **9**
6   **7**   Sheffield
Holyhead   Lincoln

Limerick   Nottingham

Rosslare   Norwich
Aberystwyth
Cork   Birmingham   Cambridge

Carmarthen   Gloucester   Colchester
Oxford
2   **3**   Cardiff   Bristol   **4** LONDON **5**
Guildford
Taunton   Maidstone   Dover
Barnstaple   Southampton   Brighton
Exeter   Dorchester
Plymouth

Penzance

Isles of Scilly   See page 16 for Channel Islands

© Automobile Association Developments Limited 2006

2

●	Place of Interest
○	Town name
BLAE G	Blaenau Gwent
BRDGND	Bridgend
CAERPH	Caerphilly
MYR TD	Merthyr Tydfil
NEWPT	Newport
RHONDD	Rhondda Cynon Taff
TORFN	Torfaen
V GLAM	Vale of Glamorgan

Aberaeron

CER

Felinwynt

A487 A486

Cardigan Lampeter

Cilgerran Cenarth

Newport

Strumble Head

Fishguard Crymych Dre-Fach Felindre

A487 A484 A485 SM

St David's PEMBROKESHIRE CARMARTH

Ramsey Island Scolton Abergwili Llang Dryslwy

A478

St Brides Bay Llawhaden Carmarthen Llanarthne

Haverfordwest A40 St Clears A48

A4076 Narberth Laugharne Llansteffan

Skomer Island A477 A484 A476

Milford Haven Carew Amroth Kidwelly

Skokholm Island St Florence

Pembroke Lamphey Tenby Llanelli

Caldey Carmarthen Llanrhidian

Island Bay

Oxwich Pa

SW

Goonhavern St Austell

A3058

Probus A390

Truro Pentewan

Redruth A393 A39 A3078 Gorran

Zennor St Ives Pool Trelissick Garden

Chysauster Ancient Village Godolphin St Mawes

Pendeen Cross Wendron Falmouth

Sancreed Marazion Mawnan Smith

A30 Penzance Helston Gweek

Land's End

Mount's Bay A3083

Lizard Lizard Point

Lundy

Ilfracombe **SS** C M

A361 Arlin

Barnstaple

Hartland Point Clovelly Bideford Great Torrin

A39

A388 A386

Bude A3072

A3079 Okehamp

A388 A30

Tintagel Launceston

Land's End **SW** A395 Lydford

Camelford

Isles of Scilly Trevose Head Padstow CORNWALL

St Mary's A39 Bodmin

Moor Morwellham Tavisto

Wadebridge A390

Tredinnick Bodmin Calstock Yelv

Newquay Lanhydrock A38 Dobwalls Buckland Abbey

Trerice A392 Liskeard

A30 Restormel PLYMOUTH Plyn

A3075 A387

Fowey Looe Torpoint

A30 **SX**

A390

SEE INSET

Dodman Point

For continuation pages refer to numbered arrows

For continuation pages refer to numbered arrows

6

Point of Ayre

Ravenglass

Ballaugh
Isle of Man
Peel
Ramsey
Maughold Head
ISLE
OF
MAN
Laxey
DOUGLAS
Cregneish
Ballasalla
Castletown
Port
St Mary

SC

*Irish
Sea*

Carmel Head

Great
Ormes
Head

Llandudno

Holyhead
Llanallgo
Anglesey
Colwyn
Bay
Rhudd
Holy Island
Beaumaris
Bryncelli
Ddu
Conwy
Llandudno
Junction
Bodelwy
ISLE OF
ANGLESEY
Brynsiencyn
Bangor
Plas Newydd
Y Felinheli
Tal-y-Cafn
Den
Caernarfon
Llanberis
Trefriw
Llanrwst

Caernarfon
Bay

Groeslon
SH
Dolwyddelan
Betws-y-Coed
CONWY
DENBI
Rut
Beddgelert
Penmachno
A5
Cerrigydrudion
Corw
Llangybi
Blaenau
Ffestiniog
Llanystumdwy
Porthmadog
Lleyn Peninsula
Penarth
Fawr
Criccieth
Portmeirion
Bala
Harlech
Llanuwchllyn
Plas-yn- Rhiw
GWYNEDD
Bardsey
Island
Cymer Abbey
Fairbourne
Dolgellau
Llanfihangel-y-pennant
Llan
Caere
Tywyn
Machynlleth
POWYS
Newtow
Cardigan Bay
Eglwysfach

SN
Aberystwyth

CEREDIGION
Rhayader

	Place of Interest
○	Town name
FLINTS	Flintshire
WEST MIDS	West Midlands

0   10   20 miles
0   10   20   30 kilometres

For continuation pages refer to numbered arrows

10

Place of Interest
○ Town name
C EDIN City of Edinburgh
C GLAS City of Glasgow
CLACKS Clackmannanshire
W DUNS West Dunbartonshire
E DUNS East Dunbartonshire
E RENS East Renfrewshire
INVER Inverclyde
N LANS North Lanarkshire
RENS Renfrewshire

0   10   20 miles
0 10 20   30 kilometres

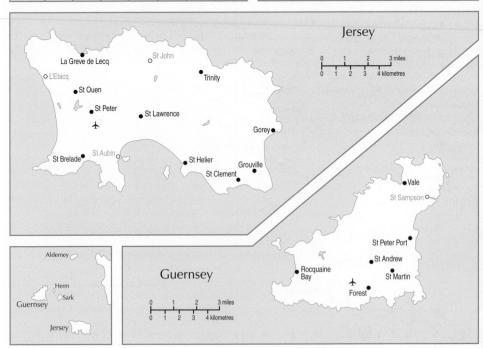

16

Place of Interest
Town name

HY

Westray
Westray
Rousay
Sanday
Birsay
Mainland
Dounby
Harray
Finstown
Kirkwall
Stromness
Shapinsay
Eday
Stronsay
Hoy
ND
South Ronaldsay
Orkney Islands

HP
Unst
Yell
Fetlar
Whalsay
Mainland
Lerwick
Scalloway
Bressay
HU
Mousa Island
Sumburgh
Shetland Islands

Jersey

La Greve de Lecq
St John
L'Etacq
Trinity
St Ouen
St Peter
St Lawrence
Gorey
St Brelade
St Aubin
St Helier
Grouville
St Clement

Vale
St Sampson

St Peter Port
St Andrew
Rocquaine Bay
St Martin
Forest

Alderney
Herm
Guernsey
Sark
Jersey

Guernsey

Index of Days Out

Index

Index

Index

Index

Index

Index

Index

The Automobile Association wishes to thank the following picture library, and photographers for their assistance in the preparation of this book:

Purestock/Alamy Front cover. All remaining pictures are held in the Association's own photo library (AA World Travel Library) with contributions from the following photographers:1 AA/M Jourdan; 2r AA/J Beazley; 3tr AA/M Jourdan; 3bl AA/E Meacher; 3bc AA/D Corrance; 3br AA/I Burgum; 4tl AA/S Day; 5tr AA/M Jourdan; 5cl AA/T Souter; 7 AA/M Birkitt; 10b AA/ M Birkitt; 11 AA/W Voysey; 16 AA/T Souter; 19b AA/S Day; 20 AA/M Birkitt; 25 AA/M Birkitt; 30b AA/M Birkitt; 31 AA/C Jones; 38 AA/C Jones; 48 AA/M Birkitt; 58 AA/J Beazley; 66 AA/C Jones; 79b AA/C Jones; 80 AA/R Ireland; 88 AA/J Beazley; 92b AA/C Lees; 93 AA/M Birkitt; 98 AA/H Palmer; 106b AA/S Day; 107 A/S Beer; 113 AA/W Voysey; 127 AA/H Williams; 130 AA/M Birkitt; 134b AA/C Jones; 135 AA/D Noble; 147b AA/J Miller; 148 AA/V Greaves; 153 AA/A Tryner; 157b AA/T Woodcock; 158 AA/M Birkitt; 162b AA/D Forss; 163 AA/J McMillan; 187 AA/S Day; 192 AA/A Perkins; 203 AA/M Birkitt; 206 AA/C Lees; 211 AA/P Baker; 215b AA/M Birkitt; 216 AA; 223b AA/M Short; 224 AA/M Birkitt; 225b AA/M Birkitt; 226 AA/A Perkins; 231 AA/R Moss; 240 AA/A Tryner; 246 AA/T Mackie; 252 AA/D Forss; 256 AA/W Voysey; 257 AA; 265 AA/J Miller; 271b AA/P Brown; 272 AA/C Lees; 275b AA; 276 AA/F Stephenson; 282 AA/H Palmer; 283 AA; 289b AA/P Baker; 290 AA/S McBride; 295 AA/E Meacher; 302b AA/C Jones; 303 AA/K Doran; 307b AA/H Palmer; 308 AA/D Tarn; 312 AA; 326 AA/T Woodcock; 328b AA; 329 AA/L Whitwam; 336 AA/W Voysey; 338b AA/W Voysey; 339 AA/S Abraham; 342 AA/S Abraham; 343 AA; 346/7 AA/S Day; 406/7 AA/H Williams; 434b AA/I Burgum; 435 AA/G Munday; 448b AA/M Diggin; 449 AA/S McBride.

Every effort has been made to trace the copyright holders, and we apolgise in advance for any accidental errors. We would be happy to apply the corrections in the following edition of this publication.

Please send this form to:
Lifestyle Guides,
The Automobile Association
14th Floor
Fanum House
Basingstoke RG21 4EA

Readers' Report form

or fax: 01256 493907
or e-mail: lifestyleguides@theAA.com

Please use this form to recommend any visitor attraction you have been to, whether it is in the guide or not currently listed. Feedback from readers helps us to keep our guide accurate and up to date. Please note, however, that if you have a complaint to make during a visit, we strongly recommend that you discuss the matter with the establishment management there and then so that they have a chance to put things right before your visit is spoilt. The AA does not undertake to arbitrate between you and the attraction's management, or to obtain compensation or engage in correspondence.

Date:

Your name (block capitals)

Your address (block capitals)

....

....

....

e-mail address: ....

Comments (please include the name & address of the attraction)

....

....

....

....

....

....

....

....

(please attach a separate sheet if necessary)

PTO

Have you bought this guide before? YES NO

Have you bought any other Days Out guides recently? If yes, which ones?

....

....

Why did you buy this guide? (circle all that apply)

family holiday short break school holidays special occasion

other...

How often do you have a Day Out? (circle one choice)

more than once a month   once a month   once in 2-3 months

once in six months   once a year   less than once a year

Please answer these questions to help us make improvements to the guide:

Which of these factors are most important when choosing a Day Out?

Price   Location   Previous experience   Recommendation   Type of attraction

Other (please state):...

Do you use the location atlas?   YES NO

Which elements of the guide do you find the most useful when choosing somewhere to visit?

Description   Photo   Advertisement

Can you suggest any improvements to the guide?

....

....

....

....

....

Days Out Guide 2007

Please send this form to:
Lifestyle Guides,
The Automobile Association
14th Floor
Fanum House
Basingstoke RG21 4EA

Readers' Report form

or fax: 01256 493907
or e-mail: lifestyleguides@theAA.com

Please use this form to recommend any visitor attraction you have been to, whether it is in the guide or not currently listed. Feedback from readers helps us to keep our guide accurate and up to date. Please note, however, that if you have a complaint to make during a visit, we strongly recommend that you discuss the matter with the establishment management there and then so that they have a chance to put things right before your visit is spoilt. The AA does not undertake to arbitrate between you and the attraction's management, or to obtain compensation or engage in correspondence.

Date:

Your name (block capitals)

Your address (block capitals)

....

....

....

e-mail address: ....

Comments (please include the name & address of the attraction)

....

....

....

....

....

....

....

....

(please attach a separate sheet if necessary)

PTO

Have you bought this guide before? YES NO

Have you bought any other Days Out guides recently? If yes, which ones?

....

....

Why did you buy this guide? (circle all that apply)

family holiday short break school holidays special occasion

other..

How often do you have a Day Out? (circle one choice)

more than once a month   once a month   once in 2-3 months

once in six months   once a year   less than once a year

Please answer these questions to help us make improvements to the guide:

Which of these factors are most important when choosing a Day Out?

Price   Location   Previous experience   Recommendation   Type of attraction

Other (please state):..

Do you use the location atlas?   YES NO

Which elements of the guide do you find the most useful when choosing somewhere to visit?

Description   Photo   Advertisement

Can you suggest any improvements to the guide?

....

....

....

....

....

Please send this form to:
Lifestyle Guides,
The Automobile Association
14th Floor
Fanum House
Basingstoke RG21 4EA

or fax: 01256 493907
or e-mail: lifestyleguides@theAA.com

Readers' Report form

Please use this form to recommend any visitor attraction you have been to, whether it is in the guide or not currently listed. Feedback from readers helps us to keep our guide accurate and up to date. Please note, however, that if you have a complaint to make during a visit, we strongly recommend that you discuss the matter with the establishment management there and then so that they have a chance to put things right before your visit is spoilt. The AA does not undertake to arbitrate between you and the attraction's management, or to obtain compensation or engage in correspondence.

Date:

Your name (block capitals)

Your address (block capitals)

....

....

....

e-mail address: ....

Comments (please include the name & address of the attraction)

....

....

....

....

....

....

....

....

(please attach a separate sheet if necessary)

PTO

Have you bought this guide before? YES NO

Have you bought any other Days Out guides recently? If yes, which ones?

....

....

Why did you buy this guide? (circle all that apply)

family holiday short break school holidays special occasion

other..

How often do you have a Day Out? (circle one choice)

more than once a month   once a month   once in 2-3 months

once in six months   once a year   less than once a year

Please answer these questions to help us make improvements to the guide:

Which of these factors are most important when choosing a Day Out?

Price   Location   Previous experience   Recommendation   Type of attraction

Other (please state):..

Do you use the location atlas? YES NO

Which elements of the guide do you find the most useful when choosing somewhere to visit?

Description   Photo   Advertisement

Can you suggest any improvements to the guide?

....

....

....

....

....

Terms: This voucher is valid at any venue specified as accepting vouchers within the AA 'The Days Out Guide 2007'. This voucher admits one adult or child free when presented at the time of purchase of one fully priced adult ticket. Valid until 31 Oct 2007. Subject to availability at the venue when presented. Photocopies will <u>not</u> be accepted.

 Lifestyle Guides

Terms: This voucher is valid at any venue specified as accepting vouchers within the AA 'The Days Out Guide 2007'. This voucher admits one adult or child free when presented at the time of purchase of one fully priced adult ticket. Valid until 31 Oct 2007. Subject to availability at the venue when presented. Photocopies will <u>not</u> be accepted.

Lifestyle Guides

Terms: This voucher is valid at any venue specified as accepting vouchers within the AA 'The Days Out Guide 2007'. This voucher admits one adult or child free when presented at the time of purchase of one fully priced adult ticket. Valid until 31 Oct 2007. Subject to availability at the venue when presented. Photocopies will <u>not</u> be accepted.

 Lifestyle Guides

Terms: This voucher is valid at any venue specified as accepting vouchers within the AA 'The Days Out Guide 2007'. This voucher admits one adult or child free when presented at the time of purchase of one fully priced adult ticket. Valid until 31 Oct 2007. Subject to availability at the venue when presented. Photocopies will <u>not</u> be accepted.

Lifestyle Guides

Terms: This voucher is valid at any venue specified as accepting vouchers within the AA 'The Days Out Guide 2007'. This voucher admits one adult or child free when presented at the time of purchase of one fully priced adult ticket. Valid until 31 Oct 2007. Subject to availability at the venue when presented. Photocopies will <u>not</u> be accepted.

 Lifestyle Guides

Terms: This voucher is valid at any venue specified as accepting vouchers within the AA 'The Days Out Guide 2007'. This voucher admits one adult or child free when presented at the time of purchase of one fully priced adult ticket. Valid until 31 Oct 2007. Subject to availability at the venue when presented. Photocopies will <u>not</u> be accepted.

 Lifestyle Guides

Terms: This voucher is valid at any venue specified as accepting vouchers within the AA 'The Days Out Guide 2007'. This voucher admits one adult or child free when presented at the time of purchase of one fully priced adult ticket. Valid until 31 Oct 2007. Subject to availability at the venue when presented. Photocopies will <u>not</u> be accepted.

Lifestyle Guides

Terms: This voucher is valid at any venue specified as accepting vouchers within the AA 'The Days Out Guide 2007'. This voucher admits one adult or child free when presented at the time of purchase of one fully priced adult ticket. Valid until 31 Oct 2007. Subject to availability at the venue when presented. Photocopies will <u>not</u> be accepted.

Lifestyle Guides

Terms: This voucher is valid at any venue specified as accepting vouchers within the AA 'The Days Out Guide 2007'. This voucher admits one adult or child free when presented at the time of purchase of one fully priced adult ticket. Valid until 31 Oct 2007. Subject to availability at the venue when presented. Photocopies will <u>not</u> be accepted.

 Lifestyle Guides

Terms: This voucher is valid at any venue specified as accepting vouchers within the AA 'The Days Out Guide 2007'. This voucher admits one adult or child free when presented at the time of purchase of one fully priced adult ticket. Valid until 31 Oct 2007. Subject to availability at the venue when presented. Photocopies will <u>not</u> be accepted.

 Lifestyle Guides

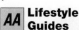 **Lifestyle Guides**

AA Lifestyle Guides

Conditions: Only one voucher per person or party accepted. No change given. This voucher is valid during the published opening times for the establishments concerned, and will not be valid after 31 Oct 2007. This voucher cannot be used in conjunction with any other discount voucher or special offer. Redeemable cash value .01p. No cash alternative available.

AA Lifestyle Guides

Conditions: Only one voucher per person or party accepted. No change given. This voucher is valid during the published opening times for the establishments concerned, and will not be valid after 31 Oct 2007. This voucher cannot be used in conjunction with any other discount voucher or special offer. Redeemable cash value .01p. No cash alternative available.

AA Lifestyle Guides

Conditions: Only one voucher per person or party accepted. No change given. This voucher is valid during the published opening times for the establishments concerned, and will not be valid after 31 Oct 2007. This voucher cannot be used in conjunction with any other discount voucher or special offer. Redeemable cash value .01p. No cash alternative available.

AA Lifestyle Guides

Conditions: Only one voucher per person or party accepted. No change given. This voucher is valid during the published opening times for the establishments concerned, and will not be valid after 31 Oct 2007. This voucher cannot be used in conjunction with any other discount voucher or special offer. Redeemable cash value .01p. No cash alternative available.

AA Lifestyle Guides

Conditions: Only one voucher per person or party accepted. No change given. This voucher is valid during the published opening times for the establishments concerned, and will not be valid after 31 Oct 2007. This voucher cannot be used in conjunction with any other discount voucher or special offer. Redeemable cash value .01p. No cash alternative available.

AA Lifestyle Guides

Conditions: Only one voucher per person or party accepted. No change given. This voucher is valid during the published opening times for the establishments concerned, and will not be valid after 31 Oct 2007. This voucher cannot be used in conjunction with any other discount voucher or special offer. Redeemable cash value .01p. No cash alternative available.

AA Lifestyle Guides

Conditions: Only one voucher per person or party accepted. No change given. This voucher is valid during the published opening times for the establishments concerned, and will not be valid after 31 Oct 2007. This voucher cannot be used in conjunction with any other discount voucher or special offer. Redeemable cash value .01p. No cash alternative available.

AA Lifestyle Guides

Conditions: Only one voucher per person or party accepted. No change given. This voucher is valid during the published opening times for the establishments concerned, and will not be valid after 31 Oct 2007. This voucher cannot be used in conjunction with any other discount voucher or special offer. Redeemable cash value .01p. No cash alternative available.

AA Lifestyle Guides

Conditions: Only one voucher per person or party accepted. No change given. This voucher is valid during the published opening times for the establishments concerned, and will not be valid after 31 Oct 2007. This voucher cannot be used in conjunction with any other discount voucher or special offer. Redeemable cash value .01p. No cash alternative available.

AA Lifestyle Guides

Conditions: Only one voucher per person or party accepted. No change given. This voucher is valid during the published opening times for the establishments concerned, and will not be valid after 31 Oct 2007. This voucher cannot be used in conjunction with any other discount voucher or special offer. Redeemable cash value .01p. No cash alternative available.